S0-AXZ-035

HANDBOOK OF
SOCIAL
GERONTOLOGY

HANDBOOK OF
SOCIAL
GERONTOLOGY

SOCIETAL ASPECTS OF AGING

EDITED BY

Clark Tibbitts

THE UNIVERSITY OF CHICAGO PRESS
CHICAGO & LONDON

Library of Congress Catalog Card Number: 60-5469

THE UNIVERSITY OF CHICAGO PRESS, CHICAGO & LONDON
The University of Toronto Press, Toronto 5, Canada

Foreword

The Gerontological Society, Inc., like other scientific organizations, brings together research investigators who have knowledge of the growing edges of their sciences and an awareness of the emerging needs of their fields. It was just such a circumstance that led the Society in 1955 to establish a committee to consider the pressing question of how to increase the number of university and college teachers equipped to train others in the psychological and social aspects of aging. Initial consideration of the problem by the committee made it evident that far more would be required to accomplish this end than merely convening a representative group of educators to propagandize the need and affirm their intentions to give more instructional emphasis to individual and societal components of aging. The newness and unorganized state of knowledge about psychosocial aging, the breadth of the subject matter to be covered, and the difficulties of introducing a new field of study and inquiry into the established academic structure were problems clearly requiring a comprehensive and creative approach and the investment of the thinking of scholars from a number of disciplines. Accordingly, with the assistance of a grant from the National Institute of Mental Health,[1] the committee convened a working conference of distinguished students of aging in Palm Beach, Florida, in July, 1956, to explore methods and make plans for meeting the need for training of scientific and professional personnel in social gerontology.

[1] Grant No. 3M-9114.

At this conference a multiuniversity training project in social gerontology was designed, an executive committee was selected, the director of the project was named, and plans for an Inter-University Council in Social Gerontology representing the sixteen participating universities were drawn up. Subsequently, grants in support of the project were made by the National Institutes of Health[2] to the University of Michigan, Institute for Human Adjustment, Division of Gerontology, which established the Inter-University Training Institute in Social Gerontology in January, 1957, to administer the program.

Thus began what was destined to be the arduous twin tasks of developing and shaping a new scientific field of social gerontology, the subject matter for which was almost momentarily unfolding, and then of introducing the newcomer to the scientific and academic communities. To accomplish these ends, two major lines of action were undertaken. The first, and basic to the field of social gerontology as a proper area of education and research, was the collection, organization, and publication of existing scientific knowledge in the psychological and social aspects of aging to provide comprehensive reference works for use by educators in the training of students for teaching, service, and research in aging. The second was to provide through summer institutes intensive postgraduate training for established univer-

[2] National Institute of Mental Health Grant No. 3M-9118, and National Heart Institute Grant No. HTS-5205.

sity and college faculty members in the psychological and social sciences and allied fields. By these means, the Inter-University Council mobilized the most distinguished and sophisticated scholars in aging to delineate the field of social gerontology, to develop teaching tools, and to offer instruction to a total of seventy-five faculty members selected for their interest in and potential for advancing in the field.

It was originally intended that a single handbook of psychosocial gerontology would be prepared. In structuring the field of aging, however, it became evident that somewhat different foci were required to provide the emphasis and perspectives which would make the technical summaries equally useful to those concerned with individual aging and those involved with the nature of social aging and its impacts on the individual and society. Thus two comprehensive reference works have been produced to enable maximum use of the materials.

One of the two, *Handbook of Aging and the Individual: Psychological and Biological Aspects,* was done under the able editorship of James E. Birren, whose position as chief of the Section on Aging of the National Institute of Mental Health made him the natural choice of the Inter-University Council to undertake the creative task of bringing about an orderly conceptualization of the field of human aging and of giving oversight to the preparation of the technical summaries of pertinent research. In these tasks he has given a brilliant account of himself.

This volume, *Handbook of Social Gerontology: Societal Aspects of Aging,* is the second of the companion books. The Council considered none other than Clark Tibbitts for its editor because of his long apprenticeship on the national scene as pioneer in social gerontology and because it was he who first glimpsed its potentials for providing a rational approach to aging as a positive force in American life. In

1954 he introduced the term "social gerontology" into the literature when he used it in a review of the newly published *Older People* by Ruth Albrecht and Robert J. Havighurst. The *Handbook* is testimony of the depth and definitiveness of his encyclopedic knowledge of aging and of his skill in organizing it into a meaningful whole. Under his effective direction the outstanding authorities who contributed to the book offer a dynamic view of the emerging field of social gerontology.

Believing that social gerontology in the United States could be better understood if seen against a background of other cultural groups that had experienced the phenomenon of aging at an earlier date, the Council planned for a third book which would offer a review of major trends and developments in aging in several countries of western Europe and Great Britain. The book, *Aging in Western Societies: A Survey of Social Gerontology,* was prepared under the editorship of Professor Ernest W. Burgess. There could have been no more fortuitous circumstance than to have had Dr. Burgess available to undertake this assignment. Having achieved one of the most distinguished scientific careers in the United States prior to his retirement as professor and chairman of the Department of Sociology at the University of Chicago, he brought to the project a perspective and sensitivity refined by years of study, research, and experience. Thus he was able to give meaning to the social scene as observed in the various countries and to offer guidance to the contributors in relating these data to current trends in the United States.

As director of the Inter-University Training Project in Social Gerontology, I want to express my thanks not only to the editors of the three books but also to the sixty or more contributors to the volumes. To the members of the Executive Committee and the Inter-University Council, I am indebted for their continued support, dedication, and long hours of work which made possible the achievement of the objectives of the project. The sixteen universities sponsoring the project have been well represented and can take pride in the contribution which their co-operative effort has made to scientific thinking and to the advancement of the understanding and welfare of the older people of our country.

WILMA DONAHUE

ANN ARBOR, MICHIGAN
January 14, 1960

INTER-UNIVERSITY TRAINING INSTITUTE IN SOCIAL GERONTOLOGY

Director: WILMA DONAHUE
University of Michigan

Assistant Project Director: HAROLD L. ORBACH
University of Michigan

EXECUTIVE COMMITTEE

JOHN E. ANDERSON
University of Minnesota
JAMES E. BIRREN
National Institute of Mental Health
ERNEST W. BURGESS
University of Chicago
EWALD W. BUSSE, M.D.
Duke University
ROBERT J. HAVIGHURST
University of Chicago

WOODROW W. MORRIS
State University of Iowa
CLARK TIBBITTS
United States Department of Health, Education, and Welfare
IRVING L. WEBBER
University of Florida
RICHARD C. WILCOCK
University of Illinois

INTER-UNIVERSITY COUNCIL

JOHN S. ALLEN
University of Florida
JOHN E. ANDERSON
University of Minnesota
HARRY W. BRAUN
University of Pittsburgh
JOSEPH H. BRITTON
Pennsylvania State University
MARION E. BUNCH
Washington University (St. Louis)
FEDELE F. FAURI
University of Michigan
ROBBEN W. FLEMING
University of Illinois
EUGENE A. FRIEDMANN
University of Wisconsin

HERBERT C. HUNSAKER
Purdue University
HAROLD E. JONES
University of California
DONALD P. KENT
University of Connecticut
RAYMOND G. KUHLEN
Syracuse University
WOODROW W. MORRIS
State University of Iowa
BERNICE L. NEUGARTEN
University of Chicago
LLOYD SAVILLE
Duke University
GORDON F. STREIB
Cornell University

Preface

This *Handbook* represents a first attempt to identify and structure a new field of research and learning—social gerontology. The rapid developments over the past few years which led to the Inter-University Training Institute in Social Gerontology and to the preparation of this and the companion handbooks are the result of two parallel and somewhat interrelated forces. One of these forces has been the progress of research itself. Students working in a number of fields became aware, more or less simultaneously, of age or time as a variable to be reckoned with in the study of organisms and their performance. This led, in turn, to interest in the life-cycle of organisms and of human individuals and to the scientific study of aging itself.

The parallel force was the sudden and explosive increase in the number and proportion of older people in the populations of all highly developed countries. In the United States the population 65 years of age and over increased twofold in proportion and fourfold in number during the first half of the century. These increases were accompanied by a vast complex of technological and socioeconomic changes which came with equal rapidity and over the same time period. The two factors of population and technological and socioeconomic change operating together resulted in separating large numbers of older people from the social roles traditionally assigned to adults and in raising them almost at once to the status of a problem group. Thus individual and population aging have become major phenomena in American life over the past 20–30 years and have come to represent a whole new area of national interest and concern.

Social gerontology is a part of the broader field of gerontology which is concerned with biological and physiological aging in all animal and plant species and with the psychological and sociocultural aspects of aging in man and societies. Social gerontology separates out (1) the phenomena of aging which are related to man as a member of the social group and of society and (2) those phenomena which are relevant to aging in the nature and function of the social system or society itself.

From the point of view of aging in the individual, social gerontology deals with the changes in the circumstances, status, roles, and position which come with age, with the influence of age-related biological and psychological factors on the individual's performance and behavior in society, and with his personal and social adjustment to the events and processes of aging. Societally, the study of aging is concerned with changes in the age composition and structure of populations, with the elements in the value system and institutional patterns which have a bearing on the status and roles of older people, with the effects of these factors and of technological and social change on older people, and, reciprocally, with the influence of older people on the values, institutions, and organization of society.

The appearance and the rapid rise of social gerontology are reflections of the fact that aging is, in the last analysis and broadly speaking, a societal matter. Aging, as we are coming to know it today, is introducing a new dimension to both individual and societal life in all advanced civilizations. For the first time in history, virtually all men and women in such societies are being freed from the necessity of devoting their entire lifetimes to the tasks of making a living. The great majority of people are now living beyond the period of procreation and nurture of children and are able to enjoy increasing amounts of leisure in the second half of life, culminating in a lengthening period of total retirement from their work careers.

In a real sense, the onset of old age is being pushed backward, and extended periods of middle age and later maturity are being introduced into the human life-cycle. The implications both for the individual and for society are enormous. The outlook for both can be positive or negative, depending, in considerable part, upon the adjustments we make in our personal and social value systems and in the conditions and opportunities of living.

Much will depend, too, of course, upon the knowledge of aging that we are able to achieve through research and upon its dissemination through teaching and learning. Toward the attainment of these ends, the present volume aims to provide a comprehensive view of the field, to identify its many facets, and to suggest how they may be integrated into a whole. Each of the contributors was requested to provide a conceptual framework for the topic assigned to him, to review the major though by no means all of the research that had been done, and to point out the directions which future research might most usefully take. The *Handbook* is thus a collection of nineteen essays and critical reviews, each dealing with a separate topic and thus, *in toto*, reflecting the broad scope and ramifications of the field.

The *Handbook* is addressed primarily to research workers, teachers, and graduate students for use as a text and as a guide

to research. It does not deal with problems, policies, and programs as such. Nevertheless, it does identify and throw considerable light on many practical matters, for problems and the ways in which they are approached are part of the subject matter of all social science and, hence, of social gerontology. Accordingly, it may be assumed that policy-makers, administrators, program developers, and professional workers will find much of value in the chapters related to their fields of interest.

The *Handbook* is organized into three parts. Part I deals with the basis and theory of the societal aspects of aging, beginning with an introductory chapter which undertakes to trace the origins of social gerontology and to provide a framework for the book as a whole. This is followed by a chapter which sets forth the principal, relevant demographic changes of the past half-century and projects some of them into the future. A benchmark chapter describing approaches to aging in more or less static preindustrial societies sets the stage for two more which seek to identify the changes characteristic of the transition from low-energy to high-energy societies and to suggest how the transition may affect and may be affected by increasing numbers of older persons.

Part II, entitled "The Impact of Aging on Individual Activities and Social Roles," deals with the effects of biological and psychological aging, of changes in health and income status, and of technological and sociocultural influences on the position, roles, and behavior of middle-aged and older people. Considerable attention is given to the basically important changing values and functions of work and leisure, with reference to social status and to personal and social adjustment.

Part III, "Aging and the Reorganization of Society," serves a number of purposes. It suggests how technological and social change is affecting nine major societal or organizational complexes with reference to aging, suggests numerous questions for study with reference to how these changing institutions may be affecting the environment of older people, and identifies the ways in which institutions and organizations may be modifying their structures and activities in response to population aging and to the efforts of older people to meet their changing needs.

Many minds and hands have necessarily gone into the preparation of this *Handbook of Social Gerontology,* and the editor is grateful to all of them for their contributions and their co-operation in bringing it to fruition. First recognition is due Dr. Wilma Donahue, chairman of the University of Michigan's Division of Gerontology, for providing the initial stimulus for the total project and for serving as its over-all continuing director. Special credit is due to the chapter contributors, several of whom were pioneering new fields and all of whom worked hard to organize their material within the framework of social gerontology, to collect the scores of pieces of widely scattered literatures, and to winnow and incorporate the comments of those who reviewed the chapters in draft, all the time maintaining objectivity in the handling of their subjects, many of which have been prejudged in the value system.

The members of an editorial board— Dr. Ernest W. Burgess, Dean John W. McConnell, and Professor Leo W. Simmons—shared willingly of their time and wisdom at various stages of the project. They are not to be held responsible, of course, for what happened to their ideas and suggestions after they had been interpreted by the editor and translated into his own approach to the field.

Particular acknowledgment is made also to the many other individuals who read and commented on the chapters; to Mr. Harold L. Orbach and Mrs. Dorothy Coons, of the Division of Gerontology at the University of Michigan, and Mr. George D. Coons for accepting responsibility for much of the editing, the proofreading, and the preparation of the Index; and to Mr. John B. Goetz and his staff at the University of Chicago Press for their understanding and efficient handling of the processes involved in converting the book from manuscript into a finished volume. Finally, I wish to thank the United States Department of Health, Education, and Welfare for permitting me to accept the editorship of the *Handbook* as an avocational activity. Naturally, the opinions expressed by the editor are his own and do not necessarily represent those of the Department.

C. T.

Contributors

LEONARD Z. BREEN, PH.D.
Associate Professor and Co-ordinator of Research in Gerontology, Department of Sociology, Purdue University, Lafayette, Indiana

EUGENE A. CONFREY, M.A.
Public Health Adviser, Division of Public Health Methods, Public Health Service, United States Department of Health, Education, and Welfare, Washington, D.C.

FRED COTTRELL, PH.D.
Chairman, Department of Sociology and Professor of Government, Miami University, Oxford, Ohio

WILMA DONAHUE, PH.D.
Chairman, Division of Gerontology, Institute for Human Adjustment, University of Michigan, Ann Arbor, Michigan

EUGENE A. FRIEDMANN, PH.D.
Assistant Professor of Sociology, Department of Economics, Sociology, Anthropology, and Social Work, University Extension Division, University of Wisconsin, Madison, Wisconsin

MARCUS S. GOLDSTEIN, PH.D.
Public Health Research Analyst, Division of Public Health Methods, Public Health Service, United States Department of Health, Education, and Welfare, Washington, D.C.

MARGARET S. GORDON, PH.D.
Associate Director, Institute of Industrial Relations, University of California, Berkeley, California

MAX KAPLAN, PH.D.
Director, The Arts Center, School of Fine and Applied Arts, Boston University, Boston, Massachusetts

JOHN W. McCONNELL, PH.D.
Dean, New York State School of Industrial and Labor Relations, Cornell University, Ithaca, New York

PAUL B. MAVES, PH.D.
Professor of Religious Education, Drew University Theological School, Madison, New Jersey

HAROLD L. ORBACH, B.S.
Assistant Director, Social Gerontology Project, Division of Gerontology, Institute for Human Adjustment, University of Michigan, Ann Arbor, Michigan

OTTO POLLAK, PH.D.
Professor, Department of Sociology, Wharton School of Finance and Commerce, University of Pennsylvania, Philadelphia, Pennsylvania

ARNOLD M. ROSE, PH.D.
Professor, Department of Sociology, University of Minnesota, Minneapolis, Minnesota

GEORGE ROSEN, M.D., PH.D.
Professor of Health Education, School of Public Health and Administrative Medicine, Columbia University, New York, New York

HENRY D. SHELDON, PH.D.

Chief, Demographic Statistics Branch, Population Division, Bureau of the Census, United States Department of Commerce, Washington, D.C.

LEO W. SIMMONS, PH.D.

Professor of Education, Executive Officer, Institute for Research and Service in Nursing Education, Teachers College, Columbia University, New York, New York

FRED SLAVICK, PH.D.

Associate Professor, New York State School of Industrial and Labor Relations, Cornell University, Ithaca, New York

GORDON F. STREIB, PH.D.

Professor, Department of Sociology and Anthropology, Cornell University, Ithaca, New York

WAYNE E. THOMPSON, PH.D.

Assistant Professor, Department of Sociology and Anthropology, Cornell University, Ithaca, New York

CLARK TIBBITTS, SC.D. (HON.)

Special Staff on Aging, United States Department of Health, Education, and Welfare, Washington, D.C.

WALTER K. VIVRETT, M.INARCH.

Associate Professor of Architecture and Planning, Institute of Technology, University of Minnesota, Minneapolis, Minnesota

RICHARD H. WILLIAMS, PH.D.

Sociologist and Acting Director, Professional Services Branch, National Institute of Mental Health, Bethesda, Maryland

SEYMOUR L. WOLFBEIN, PH.D.

Deputy Assistant Secretary, United States Department of Labor, Washington, D.C.

Contents

PART ONE

The Basis and Theory of Societal Aging

PART TWO

The Impact of Aging on Individual Activities and Social Roles

PART THREE

Aging and the Reorganization of Society

PART ONE

The Basis and Theory of Societal Aging

The Bird and the

I

Origin, Scope, and Fields of Social Gerontology

CLARK TIBBITTS

I. ORIGINS OF SOCIAL GERONTOLOGY

A. Forerunners of Interest

The field of social gerontology is finally emerging out of well over 3000 years of recorded effort to extend the length of life and to enhance the circumstances of living in the later years. Two interests are said long to have dominated a good deal of human thought and striving: one is the desire to change lead into gold, and the other is to discover an elixir of youth. There are many today who insist that, if we could achieve these two results, we should rather promptly resolve all the serious problems of aging.

Evidence of efforts among primitive peoples to prolong life and preserve vigor in old age is found in magic and rituals, in reservation of special foods to the old, in feeding breast milk and blood of slain gladiators to the elderly, in various devices for warming old bodies, and in lightening the tasks assigned to the older members of the group. Later on, as empirical medicine developed, the range of medical and surgical treatments was extended, and scientific speculation began as to the nature and causes of aging and natural death.

With reference to psychological aging, some of the ancients, Cicero (1951), for example, made reasonably astute observations regarding the characteristics, potentialities, and limitations of older persons and undertook to describe the good life in retirement. Anthropologists, explorers, and missionaries reported observations on the roles and position of old people in preliterate societies and on societal accommodations to their presence (Simmons, 1945). In general, it would seem that early, stable, agrarian economics were quite well adapted to making use of the assets and residual capacities of the middle-aged and aged, with the result that the relatively few who survived into these years were accommodated without much difficulty and, often, with some advantage—at least as long as they remained functional.

The length of life was gradually extended over a period of several millenniums, though hardly as a consequence of the measures devised in these early cultures. The increase down to pre-modern times seems more likely to have been related to the increase in the supply and variety of food and to the adoption of less violent ways of living. The accommodations worked out between primitive men and their societies appear to have improved for some older people with the gradual advance of civilization, so that the aged in our own agricultural era are said to have been better off than those of any other period, before or since (Smith, 1950; Simmons, 1952). That this was not uniformly true, however, is witnessed by the passage of the Elizabethan poor laws, by the establishment of almshouses here and abroad for those detached from family and kinship groups, and by the extent of pauperism revealed through Booth's (1894) survey of the aged in England. The development of transportation, the rise of cities, the increasing differentiation of economic functions, and rising technology were interfering with the ability of some of the aged to shape the pattern of life to meet their needs, and they began to become a rising concern to themselves and to society.

Interest in aging has developed rapidly within the present generation and has provided an increasingly favorable climate for research, if not, indeed, an insistence upon it. Pollak (1948) has suggested that the principal underlying factors have been the greater visibility of the aged due to their increasing numbers and to their growing detachment from the household and the work force, our value system with its stress on individual well-being, and the progress of research itself. Certainly, the advances of science and technology leading to a rapid increase in the numbers of older persons and their accumulation in urban industrial areas, the accelerated growth in average life-expectancy, and at least relatively earlier completion of traditional adult roles without provision of adequate substitutes have greatly altered the proportion of older people and their position in society and served to focus attention upon them. A good many studies of social and economic aspects of aging were made during the 1920's, 1930's, and early 1940's, but these were almost entirely in the nature of inventories, surveys, and observational researches designed to aid in the immediate solution of practical problems. No doubt they did serve, however, to call attention to the need for more basic, systematic, verifiable knowledge.

B. Evolution of Scientific Interest in Aging

Systematic approaches to the study of aging are of relatively recent origin, beginning with research on biological and psychological aspects, followed by studies of behavioral and social science phenomena.

BIOLOGICAL RESEARCH

While the eighteenth and nineteenth centuries gave rise to a considerable body of literature on the subject (Comfort, 1956), biological research on aging per se appeared initially as a by-product of other studies and has developed only within the past generation or two. Thus, in the words of MacNider (1945), the first real "contributions [to scientific knowledge] came about not primarily as previously planned studies on aging, but as the life of plants and animals was in the process of investigation, . . . factors of change with age insinuated themselves for detailed consideration. They forced the investigator to take an excursion into one of the many bypaths which develop during research and which if their significance is realized may led to plateaus affording broad vision of problems that await solution of greater worthwhileness than the meticulous problem which prompted the original investigation" (pp. 166–67). And Lansing (1959) states that "disciplined analysis . . . of the phenomena involved in the process of growing old, of the differences that exist between the young and the old, and of the mechanisms associated with natural death began with the opening of the twentieth century" (p. 119).

The advance has been most rapid since the late 1930's, when those biological scientists interested in time-related changes in living cells, tissues, and physiological mechanisms gave impetus to the development of a gerontological science through the formation of mutual interest groups. In 1939 "a group of British scientists and professors of various branches of medicine decided to form an International Club for Research on Aging and, as a start, to establish the British Branch" (Korenchevsky, 1950, p. 7). Korenchevsky was dispatched to the United States later that year to inspire the formation of a similar club in the "colonies." The publication of Cowdry's *Problems of Ageing* in 1939 foretold that Korenchevsky was destined to find fertile ground among biologists in the United States, and, indeed, later that year the American Research Club on Aging was organized under the aegis of the Josiah

Macy, Jr., Foundation (1955). The founding of the Gerontological Society, Inc., in 1945 and the increasing availability of funds have further stimulated research among those interested in the biologics of aging.

PSYCHOLOGICAL STUDIES

The evolution of psychological research on aging appears to have been much the same. Thus Oscar Kaplan (1946) states that, although "interest in the psychological aspects of aging goes back at least several thousand years, . . . it is only within the last decades that comparative studies of adult age groups have put such interest on a scientific basis. Young human adults have been exhaustively scrutinized since the very inception of psychological science, but older individuals have failed to arouse curiosity on an equal scale" (p. 370). (It might be observed that older adults even now are much less readily available as subjects to the psychologist.)

"A few scattered papers on later maturity appeared during the first thirty years of the present century, and in 1922 G. Stanley Hall published a book on senescence which was intended as a companion volume to an earlier work on adolescence. The Stanford Later Maturity Research Project, conducted by Miles and his associates in the early thirties, was the first systematic attempt to investigate the subject" (Kaplan, 1946, p. 370). Miles (1939) summarized the results of his research and of other studies in Cowdry's (1939) first edition, but it was not until 1946 that the American Psychological Association set up a Division of Later Maturity and Old Age. Progress has come rapidly over the past decade. Research is proceeding in many directions, as may be seen in the companion volume, *Handbook of Aging and the Individual: Psychological and Biological Aspects* (Birren, 1959).

SOCIAL SCIENCE RESEARCH

Research on aging in the social sciences seems to have sprung from several developments which occurred within a relatively short span of time under the impetus of the factors earlier mentioned. Older people did become visible very rapidly, doubling in number between 1900 and 1930 and again between 1930 and 1950. The sheer increase in numbers compelled attention to the rising problems of financial dependency, employment, and housing and living arrangements and to the alarming increase in the prevalence of long-term illness and disability. The findings of the surveys which resulted led, naturally, to efforts to find causative factors. Thus studies began to appear on work performance in relation to age; on the interrelationship of age, economic dependency, and health; and on the age factor in mental illness. As the need for societal action became clearer, interest arose in the demographic aspects of aging, in the capacity of the economy to support an aging population, and in the extension of governmental functions into the welfare field. While there is some parallel with the origins of biological and psychological research on aging, social research appears to have been more purposively and more specifically focused on the aged per se.

In 1946 Lawrence Frank reflected this development in the lead article in the first issue of the *Journal of Gerontology*, in which he enumerated a large number of social and economic problems needing study. Frank went on to point out that, in the last analysis, aging is a problem of social science. He was, however, unable to report the existence of any significant amount of social research or any attempt to outline or systematize the field, as he indicated the biologists were doing.

Yet there were other forces at work. During the 1930's Leo W. Simmons had done a doctoral dissertation on the aged in primitive societies. His monumental book, *The Role of the Aged in Primitive Society*, appeared in 1945 and set the stage for evaluating the effects on the aged of the transition from agrarian to industrial cultures. In 1940 Landis completed his pioneering study, "Attitudes and Adjustments of Aged Rural People in Iowa," and others began to report studies of personal adjustment of older persons, primarily in institutions.

In 1943, Dr. E. W. Burgess, serving as chairman of the Social Science Research Council's Committee on Social Adjustment, secured the establishment of a Committee on Social Adjustment in Old Age. This committee published a research planning report (Pollak, 1948) which called attention to the need for research in individual adjustment to aging and retirement; old age and the family; aging, employment, and income maintenance; and aging in relation to other institutions.

From this point forward, there has been considerable development of research and training facilities. The University of Chicago began to direct graduate students toward research on aging, Burgess and Havighurst and their associates initiated their studies of personal and social adjustment in old age (Cavan *et al.*, 1949), and the Committee on Human Development gave specific focus to the periods of later maturity. In 1948 the University of Michigan began its studies and its long series of conferences devoted to dissemination of emerging knowledge and definition of new problems for study (Tibbitts, 1949; Donahue, 1960*a*). The pattern was quickly adopted by the University of Florida (Smith, 1951), the State University of Iowa, Duke University, and the University of Connecticut, all of which established institutes or councils of gerontology during the fifties. In 1950 the University of California obtained a major grant for studies in economic and political aspects of aging as well as in the physiological and psychological aspects (Steiner and Dorfman, 1957).

Eight sections of the first National Conference on Aging, held in 1950, were devoted to social, economic, and related aspects of aging, and all urged the need for research (U.S. Federal Security Agency, 1951). In 1952, membership in the Gerontological Society was differentiated through the creation of a Division of Psychology and Social Science. And in 1956 the Inter-University Training Institute in Social Gerontology was formed and given support by the National Institutes of Health (Donahue, 1960*b*). The same year witnessed the formation of an interdisciplinary Committee on Social Science Research within the International Association of Gerontology, following the initiation of a series of triennial international research seminars (Tibbitts, 1959).

The sections which follow will undertake to identify the principal areas of research interest and the content and organization of the field of social gerontology.

II. Aging and the Individual

Aging is usually thought of in terms of changes occurring in the individual. Up to the present time most of the attention of research workers and of practitioners has been focused on the aging of the organism and on alterations in the circumstances of older people. More recently there has been a rising interest in personality changes and adjustment in response to the underlying processes and to the situational changes. The present section will set forth some of the basic considerations regarding the individual aspects of aging.

A. Aging as a Process

Aging of the human individual is now regarded as a process or series of changes taking place over a major portion of the life-span. From one point of view the aging process may be said to cover the entire life-span. The early years, however, are characterized almost entirely by growth of the organism and by enlargement, differentiation, and refinement of capacities. The middle and later years are often characterized by the terms "involution" or "senescence," which imply decline, decrement, or loss of function. For the purpose of delineating the field, students are now generally agreed that gerontology should be concerned with the period which follows the attainment of maximum growth and function. While this is a convenient position to take, aging is a multidimensional process, and it is not easy to determine when these changes in direction occur.

B. Four Aspects of Aging

For our present purpose, current knowledge of aging in the individual may be organized in four categories of varying degrees of discreteness and overlap. These may be called the "biological," the "psychological," the "sociological" or "situational," and the "sociopsychological" or "behavioral."[1]

BIOLOGICAL AGING

Biologists regard the normal aging process as a complex of progressive changes in cellular composition and capacity for growth; in tissue structure and function; in the speed, strength, and endurance of the neuromuscular system; and in the reduction in the capacity to integrate organ systems (Shock, 1951). Parallel to these changes and no doubt related to them is an increasing prevalence of long-term, chronic disease arising from cumulated insults to the organism (Carlson and Stieglitz, 1952). The results of a multiplicity of factors are seen in the slowing-down in performance, the decline in energy reserve, and a variety of cosmetic and structural changes. The extent to which the changes are natural or pathologic is not known, and there are several theories of aging as a biologic process (Lansing, 1959).

PSYCHOLOGICAL AGING

Psychological aging is being studied in terms of changes in the central nervous system, in sensory and perceptual capacities, and in ability to organize and utilize information (Anderson, 1956). The litera-

[1] For another discussion of the levels of aging see J. E. Birren, "Principles of Research on Aging," in *Handbook of Aging and the Individual: Psychological and Biological Aspects,* chap. i.

ture is becoming fairly rich with studies of intellective and motor performance, including changes in learning, memory, creativity, speed of input and output, skills, and performance of work. Attention is being given to external influences, such as cultural expectations and environmental factors. Most of the changes in these areas are currently thought to be normal aging processes or functions of such processes. There is evidence, however, that maturation of some capacities may extend into middle adulthood and that declines are highly differential and usually very gradual.

Psychologists are concerned also with changes in personality and with the external behavior of the aging individual which are discussed in the fourth category below.

SITUATIONAL CHANGES WITH AGE

The third category of age changes in the individual are those which have to do with his changing circumstances or situation as a member of the family, community, and society. These may be called the "sociological," "socioeconomic," or "situational" changes. They include completion of parental role; social attitudes and behavior toward the aging or aging individual; retirement from work and reduced income; restricted mobility induced by disease, disability, or loss of energy; need for special living arrangements; and loss of spouse.

The alterations may occur abruptly, as is usually the case with retirement, or slowly, as with decline in energy reserve and as children gradually orient themselves toward the community. Departure of children and cessation of paid employment result in larger and larger amounts of free time, which may be partially offset by the slowing-down of physical and psychological processes but which nevertheless call for intensification of residual roles or development of new ones. In the sociological area the changes are clearly not related to age except as a limiting factor, nor are the changes all declines, as will be suggested later on.

A fourth aspect of aging is concerned with the meaning to the individual of the changes previously discussed and with the internal and external adjustments he makes to them. Interest lies, on the one hand, in his inner reactions with regard to such matters as changing self-image, feelings, efforts to maintain ego balance, maintenance or loss of mental well-being, and tolerance of stress. On the other side, social psychologists and social gerontologists are studying changing status and roles through successive phases of the life-cycle; relationship to family, work, and others; and organization of behavior in terms of content and expansion or constriction of life-space. The behavioral aspects of aging will be developed more fully in Section IV below.

C. Characteristics of the Aging Process

Three aspects of aging appear to stand out quite clearly on the basis of present knowledge. One is that aging seems to be a developmental process, embodying elements of growth as well as decline throughout most of the life-span. Second, continued research makes it increasingly apparent that there is a good deal of interrelationship among the several facets of the aging process. And, third, there is an enormous amount of variation in time of onset of the various changes and circumstances within each individual and among individuals.

Biological gerontology has almost universally defined aging in terms of declines and losses. Lansing (1951), for example, says that aging is "a process of unfavorable, progressive change, usually correlated with the passage of time, becoming apparent after maturity, and terminating in-

variably in death of the individual." Linden (1955) has noted a "widespread tendency among people to regard progress through life as an uphill development from infancy to some vague plateau or prime called middle life, followed by a general decline." He then goes on to say that "this point of view fails to take account of the fact that different qualities and faculties of the human organism have different rates of achieving prime, and that, throughout most of life's course—for every faculty that has reached its zenith of achievement there is another that has yet to reach its developmental goal."

Linden was referring primarily to psychological and behavioral aging, and there is some research in support of his view. Thus Miles (1939) states that, while psychophysiological capacities may show decrements with age, such traits as interpretation and imagination unrestricted by speed may decline very little over the life-span. Wechsler (1955) calls attention to possible improvements in sagacity and in performance of adult roles. More recently Peck (1956) has suggested that "the ability to interpret perceptions farsightedly, foresee complex consequences, and make wise decisions . . . may require more lived-through experience than the years of youth permit" (p. 42). And Dennis (1956) has found very little decline in the productivity of creative workers between the ages of 30 and 70, a point confirmed but not emphasized by Lehman (1953) in his classic studies. None of this is to say, of course, that decline does not come eventually, though certainly there are individuals who continue at high functional levels until death.

The potential for growth in middle age and even later is clearer with respect to situational changes. Thus free time resulting from the tapering-off or completion of parental and work roles may lead to the establishment of new and more socially oriented goals (Linden and Courtney, 1953; Peck, 1956) and to expansion of interests and life-space. Interestingly, Valaoras (1958) reflects this point of view when he says that a population with "a sizable proportion of the persons surviving beyond their 65th birthday preserves mental and physical abilities which add immeasurably to the intellectual and material wealth of the community" (p. 82).

INTERRELATIONSHIPS AMONG THE FACETS OF AGING

Although there is considerable independence among certain aspects of aging, other aspects at different levels are clearly interrelated. Thus marked loss of energy and capacity for endurance obviously place limitations on certain types of activity. Physical deterioration may be hastened or retarded by the way an individual lives, by economic status, and by how he reacts to situational changes. Health status may improve or decline in retirement (Thompson and Streib, 1958).

Psychologists are well aware, of course, that the attitudes a society expresses toward older people and the roles it assigns to them may be factors in continuance of intellectual performance, motivation, and interest in learning. Expectations regarding older people may result in maintenance of mental health or in onset of mental illness and functional senility (Weinberg, 1959). Similarly, a decline in sensory capacities and in the ability to organize stimuli may lead to efforts that shut out stimuli and to withdrawal from certain types of situations (Donahue, 1959).

Thus it becomes essential to view individual aging as a multidimensional process and for many research problems to correlate the observations and approaches of two or more disciplines.

VARIATIONS IN ONSET

The parallel facts that the onset of changes varies greatly within a single individual and also among individuals do not need to be labored. Changes in motor, manipulative, and verbal abilities are differential as to degree, onset, and among individuals. Disability, age of retirement from work, cosmetic changes, and many other events occur at varying points within and among individuals. Havighurst (1958) has pointed out that social competence may extend well beyond physiological decline. Variations among individuals occur on the basis of both the nature and severity of the declines and the demands or stresses imposed by changes in life-situations.

D. Stages in the Later Life-Cycle

It has been observed that the onset of aging is variable and that the process includes both gains and losses occurring simultaneously. While aging is largely a gradual process with relatively few abrupt changes, there are certain stages within which there is considerable homogeneity, and there may be considerable value in identifying them.

It has been customary to assume that old age sets in somewhere during the seventh decade of life, and, until recently, much of the research and the majority of action programs have focused on the period beginning at or near age 65. It is now recognized, however, that the real turning point in adult life comes much earlier. On the basis of present knowledge, it seems possible to identify three stages of advanced adulthood: middle age, later maturity, and old age.

MIDDLE AGE

Young adulthood may be characterized as the period in which growth in the size and functional capacity of the organism are completed, when the basic psychological capacities are at the peak of development, when the individual is setting his goals for adult life, forming his family, launching his career, and establishing himself in the community. The ensuing years are spent largely in family and work activities, with the majority of leisure time devoted to maintenance of the home and family-oriented social activities.

A number of changes take place at the end of the fourth or during the fifth decade of life which appear to mark the beginning of a new stage. Physiologically, most people become aware of declining energy with an increasing recognition of the need to look to mental activity as the source of ego rewards (Peck, 1956). Curves of the prevalence of chronic illness and of changes in visual and auditory acuity show inflection points during the fifth decade. Women commonly pass through the menopausal period.

Many people seem to experience a sense of having achieved the goals set earlier in life or at least of having reached a plateau in their careers. Most seem to develop an awareness of time and come to the first realization that life does have length and will eventually terminate.

Children become increasingly independent in adolescence, and by age 50 one-half of all parents have witnessed the departure of the last child from the home. A considerable number of women return to the work force, though they, along with others who become unemployed, may experience difficulty in finding employment because they are thought to be too old. Women who are not gainfully employed may find that they have a good deal of time on their hands but no clearly defined societal expectations as to how they shall use it. It has been said that this period of life may give rise to considerable restlessness, with a conscious or unconscious need to develop new goals (Lindbergh, 1955).

At any rate, middle age is coming to be rather sharply defined as a stage of adulthood marked by a considerable number of events and changes, some of which are changes in direction, when there seems to be opportunity for either expansion or contraction of life-space, and when it is recognized that the aging process has set in.

LATER MATURITY

Middle age may be said to last until progress along a number of gradients, together with a cluster of new events, gives identification to the next phase, which may be termed "later maturity." Between ages 60 and 70 most individuals become aware of a marked diminution of energy reserve, are fully aware of sensory losses, and have experienced the onset of some long-term, chronic health condition, any or all of which may become a limiting factor on their behavior. The shortness of life becomes more compelling, and it is difficult to remain future oriented (Weinberg, 1959). Retirement comes to most workers and with it reduction of income. Personal contacts may be broken through retirement, children moving away from the community, and death of spouse and friends. By the middle sixties the majority of married women have become widows.

The losses which occur to many during later maturity clearly exceed the gains. For others, however, complete freedom from parental responsibilities and work removes constraints and gives the individual greater opportunity for choice of action and role than he has known at any earlier stage of life. For many, health and psychological capacities are maintained, and the individual is able to draw upon and integrate a lifetime of experience in developing the interests, friendships, and activities which appeal to him. There are, indeed, individuals who report the retirement period as the most satisfying of their lives (Hart, 1957).

OLD AGE

The final period of life is old age, though it does not come to all. Physiologically, old age may be said to have arrived when general decline or debilitating disease have resulted in extreme frailty, disablement, or invalidism. Psychologically, the mental processes have slowed down, and the individual turns to self-contemplation, retrospection, and concern over the meaning of life. There is distinct awareness of old age and the approach of death. Activity becomes greatly constricted, and there is increased voluntary withdrawal and abandonment of independent living. Little is known about the positive aspects of old age, though it is suspected that there is a good deal of isolation, loneliness, boredom, and mental pathology.

E. Résumé

Aging in the individual may be characterized as gradual change and movement through a number of stages marked by various events associated with age as a limiting factor. Biological, psychological, situational, and behavioral factors are present and interrelated in complex forms. In a generalized way, growth may be said to continue as long as gains are exceeding losses; maturity is reached and maintained when gains and losses are roughly equal; senescence sets in when losses exceed gains. Variations within and among individuals are so great that categories or stages identified in chronological-age terms must always be rough and of limited usefulness. The effective turning point of maturity or onset of aging occurs somewhere near middle life. Thus most of the chapters in the present *Handbook* consider the period of middle age beginning, for statistical purposes, at age 45, and later maturity beginning at the conventional breakpoint of age 65.

III. Societal Aspects of Aging

The preceding section dealt with aging as a phenomenon of the individual organism and personality. Aging may also be examined as a societal phenomenon, and, as in the case of individual aging, studies may be undertaken from a number of points of view. There is interest, first, in how any society organizes and behaves with reference to its older people; second, in how a rapidly changing society, such as ours, affects and is affected by its older population; and, third, in aging as a phenomenon of society itself. The present section seeks to identify these three approaches as leads to further understanding of both the societal aspects of aging per se and the role of society with reference to the aging and adjustment of the individual.

A. The Nature of Society

A society is an aggregation of individuals organized to meet individual and collective needs. A society functions within an environment which includes a physical base and the equipment and tools of its material culture. The process of living together gives rise to a culture with values as to what is good and bad for the individual and for the society, with patterned or expected ways of behaving which define the functions and positions of members of the society, and with organizations created to carry out specific purposes. The culture becomes a part of the environment which shapes and controls the individual through the actions of members and groups in the society. Similarly, the actions of individuals and groups may operate either to preserve the culture or to change it better to satisfy their needs. And such changes are often extended to the material culture and even to the basic physical environment.

It may be quite readily conjectured that the desire to extend the length of life, the presence of older individuals with special needs, and changes in the number and proportion of older people may well influence both the culture and the behavior of the various elements within a society. So, too, changes in any aspect of the environment, including the culture, may affect the status or position of the older persons within society. Thus most aspects of societal behavior and organization may be assumed to have relevance to the study of aging.

B. Aging as a Cultural Phenomenon

All societies of record contain or have contained older people. Accordingly, all societies have been concerned with the size of the older population, with the places of older people in the social structure, and with the influences older people exerted on the structure and institutions of society such as the family, the economy, and the social and political organization. Thus societies may be studied with reference to how they accommodate their older populations, to the values they assign to age and to older people, and to the expectations and positions defined for older persons.

The classical work of Simmons (1945) reports on the observations and researches he and a good many others have made of aging in preliterate societies. Saville (1959) has suggested that it would be useful to study the place and methods of care of the aged in earlier stages of our own society. And, currently, considerable interest is being shown in comparative studies of aging among the highly developed countries of Europe, North America, and the Pacific (International Association of Gerontology, 1957; Tibbitts, 1959). One of the volumes sponsored by the Inter-University Training Institute in Social Gerontology, *Aging in Western Societies,* is devoted to cross-national comparisons of approaches to aging in western Europe and the United States (Burgess, 1960).

Similarly, surveys and research within the United States have led to recognition of differences in both individual and societal responses to aging among various subcultural groups and hence to the need for considering such variables as urban or rural origin or residence, ethnic background, socioeconomic class, and religious preference.

C. Aging in Changing Societies

When studies of societal aspects of aging are undertaken in most modern societies, new dimensions are introduced as a result of changes in the size and structure of the populations involved and by the vast and continuing complex of technological and social changes characteristic of the present day. Change has long been characteristic of many human societies, of course, and has probably always influenced the position of older people and measures to provide for them. Thus it became necessary for both aged persons and relevant aspects of the social structure to accommodate to the appearance of cities, the development of the market, and changing uses of land.[2]

Over the past century or so, change has occurred much more rapidly and is having more and wider implications.

POPULATION CHANGES

One of the fundamental and the most readily measurable changes has been that of the increase in the size of the older population and the shift, within the population of all highly developed societies, in the proportion of older people. These changes have come about in response to a complex variety of factors, including the natural increase of the population, differential declines in fertility and mortality rates, immigration, growing capacity of the economy to sustain a larger population, improved nutrition and control of the sanitary environment, prevention of infectious disease, and better control and treatment of all disease.[3] The sudden growth in the older population was cited earlier as a principal factor in the rise of social gerontology. It is reflected in most programs of social action and is an important variable in most studies of the societal aspects of aging.

TECHNOLOGICAL AND SOCIAL CHANGE

Parallel to the growth of the older population, and deriving in part from the same matrix of scientific discovery and invention, has been the phenomenal expansion in the use of power and machines in the production of goods and services. The last 100 years have seen a tenfold increase in the per capita output of energy, which, in turn, has resulted in more than quadrupling per capita output while, at the same time, shortening the hours of work, transferring many household activities to the community (Ogburn and Tibbitts, 1933), and introducing the practice of retirement. Combined with increased life-expectancy

[2] See below, chap. iv, "The Technological and Societal Basis of Aging."

[3] In chap. ii, "The Changing Demographic Profile," Sheldon assesses the relative contributions of the three major constellations of factors.

and with extended work-life expectancy of younger workers,[4] these changes have had their greatest impact on middle-aged and older persons, giving them vast amounts of unconstrained time and eventually virtually complete freedom from parental and work responsibilities.

Concomitant with the changes in longevity and in the economy, there have been equally dramatic changes in urbanization, in transition from independent-worker status to that of employee, in the dissolution of the kinship system and rise of individualism, in the proliferation of books as repositories of knowledge, in the spread of education, and in the speed of change itself.

All these factors have combined greatly to alter the position of the older person in society, his activities, family relationships, housing needs, sources of financial support, etc. The environment of the aging individual has become a dynamic one, indeed. People no longer age in a static society in which status could be foretold but in an environment which is itself changing and uncertain. Thus technological and cultural change are relevant to the subject matter of social gerontology.

D. Societal Aging

The discussion thus far has dealt with the manner in which a society organizes at any one time to accommodate its older people and with the changes in modern cultures which are affecting the position of older people and forcing societies to alter their approaches to a wide variety of problems. It remains to be considered that societies themselves may age. Attention is again drawn to demographic changes, on the one hand, and to sociocultural changes, on the other, though, in fact, they are not entirely separable phenomena.

POPULATION AGING

The population of the United States has been thought to have become older or to

4 See below, chap. x.

have aged very rapidly since the turn of the century. In some respects this has been the case, but population aging may be measured in a variety of ways, and the conclusions reached are, to some extent, dependent upon the particular measure employed. Thus the average age of the United States population did increase from 1900 onward, but more recently it has been declining, as a result, largely, of the rising fertility rate. So, also, and for the same reason, the increase in the proportion of older people, which took place between 1900 and 1950, seems all but to have leveled off during the past decade. There continues to be, however, a net annual increase of more than 300,000 persons 65 and over.

The changes which this country has experienced appear to parallel those associated with the evolution from undeveloped to highly developed economies, wherever such evolution has taken place. Valaoras (1958) has noted that in preindustrial societies roughly 40 per cent of the population is under the age of 15, from 2 to 4 per cent 65 and over, and the majority—nearly 60 per cent—in the so-called productive period, 15–64. With the transition to a high level of scientific development and industrialization, the proportion under age 15 years tends to drop to around 25–30 per cent, while that 65 and over rises to approximately 10 per cent, the proportion in the middle range remaining fairly stable. Valaoras suggests that this phenomenon may better be described as "maturation" than as "aging."

In the United States the age periods commonly employed are under 20, 20–64, and 65 and over. The ratio of the combined proportions in the younger and older ages to those in the 20–64 period times 100 is often cited as the "dependency ratio" and regarded as a rough index of the number of dependents per 100 productive members of the population. The dependency ratio has declined markedly in the United States since 1890 and now appears to be stabilizing at from 75 to 80.

Valaoras (1958) has drawn attention to yet another index—one which seeks to describe the character or quality of the dependent population. He suggests that a number of implications result from variations in an index of population aging computed as the ratio of older persons to younger persons times 100. This ratio (using the groups 65 and over and under 21) has risen from 9 in 1900 to 23 in the United States today, much as it has in other developed societies.

In summary, older people are becoming more numerous both absolutely and in relation to other age groups but, taken in combination with younger people, are not, over the long run, increasing the size of the dependent population.

AGING OF SOCIETIES

Within the present context it seems relevant to suggest that there may be phenomena of aging of institutions and of total societies which will someday come within the purview of social gerontology. Are there, for example, institutional and societal analogies to maturation and decline in the life-cycle of the individual organism? The question has also been raised as to the possible effect of increasing numbers and proportions of older people on societal development. Will such increases impose an economic burden which will arrest the upward trend in leisure and the quality of living for the total population? Concern has also been expressed that the loss of energy and vitality which accompany old age, together with rigidities and exacerbated need for security which are alleged concomitants of aging, may lead older persons to resist the social changes which appear to be necessary adjustments to scientific and technological development or desirable responses to new ideologies. Social progress could be retarded, according to this line of thinking. Others have argued that an increasing proportion of socially motivated older people with time at their disposal may devote their energies to leading the way toward the solutions of major social problems and toward a society which offers its members still greater freedom for personal development and fulfilment. Such questions would seem to have a number of compelling facets, but, for the most part, they remain to be formalized.

IV. THE FIELDS OF SOCIAL GERONTOLOGY

The foregoing discussion makes it readily apparent that social gerontology is a many-faceted and complex field of study. The two preceding sections have served to identify the two broad aspects of the field, namely, aging as a phenomenon of the individual organism and person and as a phenomenon of society itself. In the present section an attempt is made to develop a further refinement of the evolving subject matter within these two basic areas. The suggested organization is necessarily tentative and will be further refined as more research is done and as new concepts emerge.

It is obvious, of course, that the division between even the gross categories of societal and individual aging is often one of the focus of the investigator or of the particular problem under study, for, as in any field of human behavior, the elements involved are mutually interacting and interdependent. To suggest one example, the practice of chronological-age typing, responsibility for which is shared by older people, becomes part of the environment to which the aging individual is required to adjust. And his efforts at adjustment may, in turn, result in changes in the system of social relationships in the society. Thus it may be said that the individual is adjusting to an environment which he has helped to create and which he is also helping to modify, and it is essential to consider both aspects if the process is to be understood. Nevertheless, the analytic categorization of phenomena which is suggested appears to be necessary if we are to achieve a systematic organization of the field.

A. The Demography of Aging

One aspect of social gerontology focuses on the size, distribution, and composition of the population, with particular reference to those in the older age groups. It has already been indicated that it is essential to know how many older people there are, the proportion they constitute of the total population, whether they are increasing or decreasing, and the factors involved in such changes. Mobility, migration patterns, and distribution geographically and by size of place are significant in themselves and with reference to many specific problems.

In a generalized way data on population composition make possible descriptions of a population and interpopulation comparisons, provide an inventory of human resources of a society, describe variables essential for analyzing demographic processes such as morbidity and mortality, and are important conditions affecting formation and change of social structure (Hawley, 1959).

The most common variables employed in the study of aging are age, sex, race, marital and family status, income, labor-force status and occupation, education, health status, and living arrangements. All of these are significant with reference to such matters as housing, pension programs, health facilities and services, expenditure patterns, governmental functions, opportunities for recreation, education, and religious observance, employment and retirement policies, and assignment of postretirement roles.

Increasing attention is being given to the collection and publication of detailed population data by federal agencies, states, and communities.

B. Behavior and Personality

Four levels of aging of the individual were identified in Section II. Not all the subject matter implied there belongs to the field of social gerontology. The line between social gerontology and the biological and psychophysiological aspects, however, will always be a fuzzy one because of the complex interrelationships involved. In a strict sense, social gerontology might be said to begin when the particular phase of the aging process which is under scrutiny is affected by one or more factors which relate to the behavior or status of the individual as a member of society. Thus the metabolic processes or nutritional status may be influenced by the goals an older person has set for himself or by his reaction to forced retirement or social isolation. More realistically, however, the study of individual aging may be said to fall into the category of social gerontology when some aspect of the aging process or some situational change associated with age influences the attitudes, thinking, or behavior of the individual or his position in society.

PERSONALITY AND PERSONAL ADJUSTMENT

If this is a tenable statement, then one area of social gerontology as it relates to individual aging is concerned with the meaning of biological, psychological, and situational changes to the individual and with the manner in which he responds to and undertakes to integrate them in an effort to maintain a sense of well-being and freedom from anxiety and emotional stress (Kuhlen, 1956). Among the more important variables and problems being investigated are changes and factors in motivation, changing image or images of the self, reactions to both interior and exterior stimuli and ability to cope with the complexities of living, flexibility and expansion versus rigidity and constriction, changes in interests, goals, and sources of satisfaction, attitudes toward life, and aberrational behavior and pathological reactions in the form of mental illness. These are among the topics dealt with in the *Handbook on Aging and the Individual: Psychological and Biological Aspects* (Birren, 1959).

SOCIAL BEHAVIOR

A parallel area of investigation deals with the effects of aging and the environment of the older individual on his social behavior. How does he modify his behavior with reference to psychobiological and situational changes? What change takes place in the individual's position in society as certain roles are completed? What roles are maintained, intensified, or abandoned? What new roles may be adopted? What changes occur in range and types of social contacts and participation in groups and organizations? What relationships are developed with children after they set up their own families? What substitutes are found for the activities connected with work after retirement takes place? What uses are made of leisure? What are the activity patterns of the disabled? Are new living arrangements sought and, if so, at what stage of later life and by what types of individuals? What measures, if any, are taken in anticipation of the changes and events associated with age? And with what results? What types of individuals take initiative in finding new interests and roles? How do all these reactions vary among individuals with different occupational, ethnic, educational, and religious backgrounds? These are illustrative of the kinds of questions which students of the behavioral aspects of social gerontology are translating into research tasks.

MEASURE OF ADJUSTMENT

This field of social gerontology is interested, also, in discovering methods of measuring the extent to which individuals are successful in adapting or adjusting to their changing characters and circumstances. Efforts of this nature presuppose the development of valid concepts of adjustment, both in terms of the individual's own feeling about whether or not his needs are being adequately met and in terms of his overt responses or external behavior.

C. Cultural and Environmental Aspects of Aging

Individual and group behavior are determined not only by the capacities and predispositions of the individuals within a society but also and perhaps to a greater extent by the environment in which they live. The components of the environment were identified in an earlier section where it was indicated, too, that certain aspects of it, such as the culture, are susceptible to modification by the members of the society to which it is host. Social gerontology is, therefore, concerned with the influence of the total environment on the aging individual and, conversely, with the impact older people have on the material culture and on the system of ideas, values, and patterned ways of behavior.

ROLE OF THE CULTURE IN AGING

It was suggested in Section A, above, that the number and proportion of older people in a population are functions of a complex of environmental and cultural factors which call for continuing study. Similarly, middle age and old age are, in part, functions of the way in which society defines age itself, and the position of older people in society is determined largely by the roles society assigns to them. Age-grading and the definition of expectations based on chronological age are well established in our society (Cottrell, 1942; Parsons, 1942). To a considerable extent, they represent a survival of expectations and role assignments worked out in primitive societies on the basis of observed changes in the individual, declining energy, and accumulation of experience and knowledge and with reference to activities essential to group survival (Wissler, 1939). Study is needed of the nature of age-grading, of relative values assigned to youth and age, of changes in roles available to older people, of the increasing numbers available for old age roles, and of the relationship among concepts of aging, actual capacities, and the nature of the tasks assigned to older people (Havighurst, 1958).

The place of work in all cultures is one of the major factors in the environment of older people. Its values have been determined by the need to survive, by consumption levels and aspirations, by ideas as to its essential goodness, and by the opportunities it affords for prestige, social participation, and other satisfactions (Friedmann and Havighurst, 1954). Recent changes in the length of life and in the economy are reducing the hours of work and freeing most older people from it altogether. Long-established values and habits with reference to work tend to become abstracted from work itself, and their tendency to outlast the work requirements of the economy, together with society's lag in providing alternative role expectations and adequate pensions, leaves the retired person in an ambiguous situation and creates some of his most difficult problems of adjustment.

Similar problems are created by the completion of parental responsibilities in middle age which appears to deprive many women of their principal time-consuming and status-giving activity. This relative absence of defined roles and status positions for older people becomes one of the principal elements in their environment.

Another cultural value which may have attained its greatest strength while the present generation of older people was growing up was the emphasis placed on individual or personal responsibility for one's own welfare. Success and economic independence or failure and want were held to be largely the outcomes of one's own industry, initiative, alertness, frugality, etc. This concept of individual responsibility placed many older people in a difficult position when their status shifted to that of wage-earners in a society increasingly characterized by large-scale associations, corporations, labor unions, and bureaucratic government. There often appeared little the individual could do on his own to maintain income, position, and status as he was overtaken by the frailties of physiological and psychological aging (Williams, 1959).

These examples are merely illustrative of the cultural and environmental circumstances within which the individual is required to adapt to the changes which occur in the organism and in his mental capacities. They suggest many research problems for sociology, social psychology, and social gerontology.

IMPACT OF OLDER PEOPLE ON THE VALUE SYSTEM

The other side of the picture is equally provocative. The culture changes constantly, and part of the change is in response to pressures exerted by or on behalf of older people. One of the more dramatic changes occurring at the present time is with reference to concepts of work and leisure. Leisure and the ways in which it is used appear to be becoming ends in themselves and no longer merely recuperative interludes in the work cycle. And, correlatively, much of the value of work appears to be shifting to that of a means. While changes in values such as these may have been set into motion by larger forces, they are clearly receiving impetus from people in middle age and later maturity with thousands of uncommitted hours to fill.

In a similar way some of the values attached to individual responsibility appear to be breaking down in favor of others attached to financial security and the right of the individual to a sense of personal worth and a share in the rising output of the economy in retirement. Thus the large-scale collective programs for financial security and the appearance of hundreds of new state and community facilities and services for older people are manifestations of cultural values which are emerging in response to the presence and changing circumstances of older people.

Still another example may be found in the changing concepts of family responsibility. While there is still much insistence upon the obligation of adult children to support aged parents and care for them during their declining years, higher values are also being attached to the exercise of parental responsibility for young children and to independence and autonomy on the part of older people. These, too, are resulting in the creation of new patterns of behavior and new institutions for both the middle and the older generations.

Here too, then, is another field rich in opportunity for analysis along with subcultural and cross-cultural comparisons.

D. Aging and Social Organization

Society is built up of patterned relationships, groups, and organizations of its member agents which transmit cultural values, customs, and ideas; assign roles, status positions, and behavioral norms; define and enforce sanctions; and provide vehicles through which its members strive to satisfy their desire, carry out their assigned functions, and adjust to life-situations. It is through the social organization and the opportunity it affords for social interaction that society influences and determines the position and welfare of its members, including those in middle and later adulthood—by means of such devices as the expression of attitudes and expectancies regarding behavior, employment, and retirement policies and practices and the facilities and services it provides for maintenance of income, medical care, recreation, and so on. And it is through their own behavior and interaction within groups and organizations that older people, in turn, influence the behavior and structure of society.

SOCIETAL INFLUENCES ON OLDER ADULTS

Enough has been said already about age-grading, changing patterns of work, shifts in the life-cycle of the family, methods of providing economic security, and role expectations or their lack to suggest how the society and its organization may affect aging and older people. It remains to be considered how older people respond, in the aggregate, and what effect their presence has on social organizations.

SOCIETAL BEHAVIOR OF OLDER PEOPLE

The ways in which older adults behave as groups or aggregates will necessitate a good deal of continuing study because much of the present situation is new and because it will continue to evolve and change. One of the inherent questions is whether age in itself will become a unifying principle leading to the development of a society of middle-aged and older persons with groups and a structure of its own within the framework of the larger society. Will people at different stages of adulthood seek identity or particular status as pressure groups?

Organizations of older people have already come into existence. Under what circumstances are they organized? From where does the stimulus come? What kind of leadership is involved, and where does it come from? What are the nature and purposes of the organization? What types of objectives can be achieved? Will the organizations be recognized by society? What place(s), if any, will they occupy in the social structure?

Closely related to such questions is the much-debated one of segregation versus integration of older people. Are there activities and relationships which older people prefer to enjoy within peer groups? For what purposes will older people wish to be integrated with other age groups? To what extent and at what stages will older adults seek grouped or institutional living arrangements, such as retirement hotels, residence clubs, proximate housing, and villages? Within the area of family relationships, will a new form of extended family develop, based on affection, voluntary mutual assistance, and observance of rituals? What new reference groups will appear to provide friendships and social contact if intergenerational alienation continues?

With regard to the utilization of free time what activities will come to have meaning for older adults? In this connection, what is the pertinence of the action of society in extending or withholding recognition for free-time pursuits? What contributions can and will older people make to community life? Will society encourage and call upon them for voluntary services? How much initiative will older people take and how much activity will be dependent upon expectations developed by society? These are among the questions which are beginning to receive the attention of sociologists and of others in related disciplines.

IMPACT ON EXISTING ORGANIZATIONS
AND STRUCTURE

There are already many manifestations of the effects of older people on the pattern of social organization and institutions. Some of the changes in economic and political institutions are identified in the two sections following. Similarly, many religious groups and voluntary organizations, such as professional societies, service groups, labor unions, and community agencies, are developing special activities for their own members. Some have added aging as a service field, supporting or setting up programs in the community. Among the questions raised for study are: Will it be possible for these organizations to develop programs which will hold young, middle-aged, and older adults within the same organization? Will the positions offered older people be honorific, or will they be such as to give meaning through actual content? What relationship will develop between organizations with new programs for older persons and established community agencies? What effect will programs for older people have on the traditional structure and policies of community funds and councils? Will professional organizations succeed in fostering actual interchange of ideas and knowledge among representatives of several disciplines? Many national organizations and community agencies are now revaluating themselves with reference to such questions.

Some new agencies are being created, notably the sponsored club for older people and the activity center offering a variety of free-time pursuits. Will these succeed, since they tend to separate older people into identifiable groups apart from young adults? If so, at what stage of life may they expect older adults to affiliate with them? To what extent will their programs meet such needs as maintenance of physical and mental health, desire for social contacts and close friendships, and status-giving activity? Will they become vehicles for maintaining or expanding life-space and contribution to community life?

The increasing number of aged people has greatly expanded the need for housing for the frail and socially isolated, for the mentally ill, and for the long-term sick. Mental hospitals are growing in number and size; geriatric centers, hospitals, and nursing homes are proliferating; and homes for the aged are increasing in number and capacity. What will be the eventual effect on the community structure of health services and on requirements for trained personnel? Will the tendency toward housing well and sick older people together continue, and, if so, what will be the effects on concepts of old age and on the physical and mental health of the aged? What changes will take place in the patterns of distribution of older people in the community? What are the futures and emerging community relationships of villages and hotels for the retired? Of grouped housing with built-in recreation and health centers? Here and abroad there are now many new health, rehabilitation, and housing developments which may be regarded as experimental from the point of view of the researcher.

E. Aging and the Economy

One of the major areas of research and action in social gerontology lies in the broad, two-way relationship between aging and the methods of creating, using, and distributing income. The problems are numerous and involve consideration of characteristics and behavior of individuals, cultural values, political and social action, and economic factors per se. Some of the more compelling questions are discussed under several headings.

EFFECTS OF ECONOMIC CHANGE ON
AGING AND AGED PEOPLE

It was suggested in an earlier section that changes in methods of production and distribution have been one of the major factors in altering the status and roles of middle-aged and older adults in all economies and particularly in the highly developed ones. Increased use of machines and inanimate energy and the organization for their use have affected the nature of work and the extent of work-force participation for older men and women, the bases for and the length of retirement, income needs, methods of achieving financial security in retirement, and the responsibilities of younger adults for the support and care of aged relatives. All these represent problems or groups of problems about which much needs to be known.

WORK-FORCE PARTICIPATION

The matter of employment or work-force participation of middle-aged and older persons raises questions of total life and work-life expectancy, social attitudes toward work and retirement, individual meanings and values attached to work, performance and employability of older workers, retirement practices and criteria, relationships between pension systems and employment opportunities and retirement policies, participation of women in paid employment, effects of changing health status, automation and obsolescence of skills, trainability of adults at various ages, worker mobility, and measures to assist older workers in finding employment and in giving satisfactory performance on the job. All these and many other questions are receiving attention, and all represent prime subjects for research (Corson and McConnell, 1956; Steiner and Dorfman, 1957).

INCOME NEEDS

The rising number of old people with longer periods of retirement has focused a good deal of attention on their income needs and on the adequacy of current receipts. While various estimates of income are available (Epstein, 1959), there is very little information about budgetary needs and patterns of expenditure. Research is needed which will relate income and spending to roles and status, social integration and participation, maintenance of activity levels, changing health status, and individual preferences as to living arrangements and housing.

INCOME-MAINTENANCE PROGRAMS

One of the revolutionary changes brought about by population aging and the changing status of older people has been in the methods of providing income for the retirement years. Public and private old age insurance and pension systems have grown phenomenally over the past century and are posing many questions for research. One of the moot questions is what, from the point of view of the individual and of society, should be the relative roles of compulsory savings programs, quasi-voluntary systems such as individual life insurance, and purely personal savings? What are the effects of public programs on other forms of savings? How much will employed persons set aside for retirement? What are the relative merits of providing income in kind, as with subsidized medical care and recreation, as against cash payments to cover all needs? Can the insurance principle be extended to cover medical payments and housing in retirement without damaging the quality of services or destroying important values? How much of the national income can be used, or is the population willing to use, for payment of services to older people? What, precisely, is the problem of maintaining the purchasing power of retirement income, and how can it best be achieved? This is one of the areas in which research on foreign programs and practices would be useful to the United States.

PENSION RESERVES AND THEIR USES

The wide spread of old age insurance and pension programs has resulted in an accumulation of more than $70 billion in reserves, beyond those held by life insurance companies, trust funds, and other accumulations of individuals (McConnell, 1958). Economists are concerned with the manner in which these funds are used, their possible effects on stimulating or retarding production and on inflation and deflation, and whether or not they should be used for self-liquidating projects, such as housing and medical facilities, for older people (Corson and McConnell, 1956; McConnell, 1958). There is also interest in the extent to which retirement systems and payments contribute to the stabilization of the economy and of employment and the extent to which payments should be made out of current income.

LONG-TIME CAPACITY OF THE ECONOMY

Finally, there is much concern and need for research on the long-range capacity of the economy to support a rising older population in longer retirement and at levels consistent with their needs. Involved are questions of future work-life expectancy and retirement practices, availability of funds for capital investment, continuance of past and current trends in output, availability of natural resources, and the amount of income deemed adequate by retired persons and by others whose levels of living would be affected.

F. Aging, Government, and Politics

The presence of a growing population of older people with unmet needs is bound to affect the government and political life of society, and this has clearly been the case in our own. While there has been, thus far, little research activity in the field of aging on the part of political scientists, problems are being identified, and it may be anticipated that interest will develop. At least four research areas may be identified at the present time.

POLITICAL BEHAVIOR OF OLDER PEOPLE

One area revolves around the political activity and voting behavior of individuals at different stages of life. Is there a life-cycle of interest in government, politics, and voting, as Linden and Courtney (1953) have suggested? Are there differences in the kinds of measures young, middle-aged, and older people support? Does behavior remain constant or change toward liberalism or conservatism with age? What are the positions and roles of older people in political parties? Do politics and government service offer new roles for those in middle age or later maturity?

POLITICAL PRESSURE GROUPS

A special case in the field of political behavior has to do with the formation, structure, and activities of pressure groups working for candidates and legislation designed to serve the interests of their older members. There are examples of groups which have had considerable success, and there are continuing efforts to set up new ones. It would seem useful to know whether or not older people are likely to take on characteristics of active minority groups (Barron, 1953), what factors make for or against the organization of pressure groups, the methods of organizing and maintaining membership, and the kinds of objectives which are likely to be sought.

GOVERNMENTAL FUNCTIONS

The functions of government have both influenced and been influenced by the aged. The long-time erosion of household functions in favor of community agencies, including government, has deprived older people of a number of traditional family roles. Simultaneously, government has intervened to protect the position of older people and to make financial security, health and welfare services, housing, education, and recreation available to them. Questions arise as to how much responsibility government will be asked to assume. What factors determine the participation of government in programs for older people? What is the effect of governmental activity on the programs of other institutions and agencies? Do programs develop more rapidly under governmental or other auspices? Under what auspices do programs become institutionalized and less responsive to new ideas and new knowledge? What is the effect of government activity on individual initiative and assumption of responsibility for working out his own solutions to his changing needs?

GOVERNMENT ORGANIZATION

Finally, a number of questions may be raised with reference to aging on the structure of government itself. All levels of government have now assumed some responsibility for the welfare of older persons. Questions have arisen as to whether new agencies should be created or the functions of existing agencies expanded; as to the optimum division of responsibility among the several levels of government; and as to the effectiveness of various methods of sharing responsibility, such as by means of grant programs, professional consultation services, conferences, and in-service training programs.

The federal government and most states have set up official co-ordinating councils or commissions on aging. These should be studied with reference to their functions, their place in government structure with special reference to their relationships to other governmental units serving older people, and in terms of their composition in relation to the kinds and effectiveness of the objectives they seek to achieve.

In this section an attempt has been made to identify and suggest an organization of the subject matter of an emerging field of scientific inquiry having to do with the aging of people and with associated sociocultural phenomena. A recent paragraph written by Professor Ernest W. Burgess (1958), who gave the new field much of its initial and continuing impetus, provides a clear and succinct summary.

Social Gerontology is a new field of research and teaching which is not directly concerned with the biological aspects of aging but concentrates rather upon its economic, social psychological, sociological, and political aspects. Its object of research is not individual organisms but people as population aggregates, as members of society and its component groups, and as the creators and the carriers of culture. Specifically social gerontology studies the status and roles of older persons, their cultural patterns, social organization, and collective behavior as they are affected by and as they affect social change [p. 1].

V. SOCIAL GERONTOLOGY AS A FIELD OF RESEARCH AND TRAINING

A. Emergence of the Field

The foregoing analysis makes it evident that social gerontology is emerging as an organized field of knowledge concerned with the behavioral aspects of aging in the individual, with aging as a societal phenomenon, and with the interrelationships between the two. While the field is developing rapidly, there are some who question that it will ever be recognized as a separate discipline. Although this question will have to be decided in the future, social gerontology, even at present, seems to have characteristics which point toward separate identification.

First of all, as with the field of child growth and development, it deals with phenomena of a particular phase of the lifecycle—middle age and beyond—and with the societal phenomena related thereto. As the field is explored, it becomes increasingly apparent that a large body of knowledge will be embraced and that many problems are sufficiently peculiar to later life to warrant specific focus and separate consideration.

The second factor is that many of the problems it sets for study cannot be investigated within the framework of a single, established discipline. Thus, while changes in perception may be studied largely within the framework of physiological psychology, any complete understanding of age changes in personality necessarily involves consideration of biological and psychological factors, cultural expectations, and the nature of the family and work cycle. New problems, such as the manner in which the increasing older population influences governmental functions, law, and the distribution of the national income require consideration of the characteristics of older people as well as the capacity of the economy and the nature of the social value system. Thus it seems altogether likely that much of the gerontological research of the future will be done by students who have a working background in two or more of the older disciplines.

Third, methodological problems involved in such matters as determination of factors related to motivation in learning, measurement of role changes and personal adjustment, determination of adequacy of income, and the nature of limitations imposed by chronic illness and disability suggest that new research techniques will have to be invented in order to gain understanding of some of the central research problems in the field.

None of this is to gainsay, of course, the need for development of such areas as the psychology of aging, the sociology of aging, or of aging in its political and economic aspects. There are, indeed, numerous scientific problems of aging in these fields which can and will be studied within the framework of established theory and by means of the extension of familiar approaches.

Current trends and evolving conceptualizations do seem to point, however, to the continued development of social gerontology as an identifiable field. In considerable measure, it will be eclectic, as is the case with certain other specialized fields, but much of the subject matter will be developed out of its own approaches. Controversy over the matter seems largely beside the point as long as there are researchers and teachers working in the field and as long as they find facilities, support, and methods of communication. The demand for the knowledge they are able to produce will continue to grow.

B. Applied Social Gerontology

The development of knowledge and principles with regard to almost any aspect of aging will have immediate practical application. Indeed, in social gerontology the need for sound bases for social action may be said to have demanded the appearance of the field itself. Most professional fields concerned with human and social welfare are feeling the impact of the growing older population, and most of them are recognizing the special characteristics and needs of older people. Hence the field of applied social gerontology is developing parallel with the basic field itself. Principles for social action are being formulated in such fields as public health, public administration, social welfare, adult education, recreation, and institutional administration. There is also a marked rise of interest in evaluative studies of programs and services.

C. Personnel and Training

GROWING NEED FOR TRAINED PERSONNEL

The emergence of social gerontology and the rapid growth of facilities, programs, and services for older people are having a major impact on the requirements for trained personnel and on the curriculums of universities and professional schools. It is becoming increasingly clear that both research and teaching have need for individuals with advanced training in social gerontology and in aging within the older disciplines. Needs for specially trained personnel to work with older people are being defined (Aldridge, 1955; Harlan, 1959), and it is well known that there are acute shortages in all fields. There is beginning recognition of the importance of understanding the salient behavioral and societal aspects of aging by all individuals and all citizens and hence of the need for college and secondary-school teachers equipped to offer courses or units in aging.

There is also growing evidence of interest on the part of individuals in obtaining training in one or more aspects of gerontology. Major centers of activity in aging receive a good many inquiries from individuals wishing to obtain specific information or generalized training for work in the field. Applicants for fellowships in the Inter-University Council's training institutes in social gerontology were from four to six times as numerous as the places available.

TRAINING OPPORTUNITIES

An increasing number of educational centers are responding to the one or more of the needs defined above. At the time of this writing, not fewer than fifty colleges, universities, and professional schools are offering credit courses or seminars in one or more aspects of social gerontology. Currently, the majority of the offerings are in psychology and sociology, with some in economics and a growing number in schools of public health, social work, and education. Many schools are giving short courses, in-service training, and a variety of educational opportunities for persons seeking personal guidance. There is also an observable trend toward incorporating material on aging in textbooks and in courses such as population, family, growth and development, learning, and mental testing.

The institutes of gerontology, mentioned in Section I, B, above, have broadened their programs to include research, seminars, in-service training, conferences, and consultation, and some are now offering core courses in gerontology. Graduate students may now specialize in aging at the University of Chicago, at the State University of Iowa, and in psychological aspects of aging at Washington University. It seems likely that advanced degrees in social gerontology may be offered within the relatively near future.

THE QUESTION OF SPECIALIZATION

This discussion leads to the question of the extent to which specialization in social gerontology is desirable, a matter which is receiving considerable attention. There are some who foresee the need for social gerontologists broadly trained in behavioral and societal aging to direct institutes, stimulate and co-ordinate multidimensional research, organize curriculums, and offer core courses. Others hold that most aspects of the field are so complex in themselves that no one

individual can acquire sufficient breadth of understanding to be effective in interdisciplinary research or teaching. Notwithstanding, there are some professional persons who are extending their competence beyond the field of original training in order to work in the field of aging.

There is even more insistence on the need for generalists in the applied aspects of social gerontology. An increasing number of occupations are appearing which call for a broad knowledge of individual and societal aspects of aging. These include administrators of government programs, co-ordinators of planning and action programs in states and communities, administrators of homes for the aged and other congregate living facilities, and specialists on aging in voluntary organizations.

D. Financial Support

Recent years have brought an increasing amount of support for both research and training in social gerontology. The National Institutes of Health of the United States Department of Health, Education, and Welfare (1959) are supporting the majority of the work at the present time, but other federal agencies, such as the Veterans Administration and the Office of Vocational Rehabilitation (Federal Council on Aging, 1959), are also heavily involved. A number of foundations, notably those of Ford, Kellogg, and Rockefeller, following the lead of the Josiah Macy, Jr., Foundation, have made sizable grants in the field. The interest of the Congress is demonstrated through its appropriations for research and training and in the White House Conference on Aging Act (Public Law 85-908), which is designed to further the scientific aspects of the field as well as to promote action programs.

REFERENCES

ALDRIDGE, G. J. 1955. Training for work with older people. *In* WILMA DONAHUE (ed.), Education for later maturity, pp. 299–311. New York: William Morrow & Co.

ANDERSON, J. E. 1956. Summary and interpretation. *In* J. E. ANDERSON (ed.), Psychological aspects of aging, pp. 267–89. Washington, D.C.: American Psychological Association.

BARRON, M. L. 1953. Minority characteristics of the aged in American society. J. Gerontol., **8**, 477–82.

BIRREN, J. E. (ed.). 1959. Handbook of aging and the individual: psychological and biological aspects. Chicago: University of Chicago Press.

BOOTH, C. 1894. The aged poor in England and Wales. London: Macmillan & Co.

BURGESS, E. W. 1958. Preface. J. Social Issues, **14**, 1–2.

—— (ed.). 1960. Aging in Western societies: a survey of social gerontology. Chicago: University of Chicago Press.

CARLSON, A. J., and STIEGLITZ, E. J. 1952. Physiological changes in aging. Ann. Am. Acad. Political & Social Sc., **279**, 18–31.

CAVAN, RUTH S., BURGESS, E. W., HAVIGHURST, R. J., and GOLDHAMER, H. 1949. Personal adjustment in old age. Chicago: Science Research Associates.

CICERO. 1951. On old age. *In* M. HADAS (ed.), The basic works of Cicero. New York: Modern Library.

COMFORT, A. 1956. The biology of senescence. London: Routledge & Kegan Paul.

CORSON, J. J., and McCONNELL, J. W. 1956. Economic needs of older people. New York: Twentieth Century Fund.

COTTRELL, L. S., JR. 1942. The adjustment of the individual to his age and sex roles. Am. Sociological Rev., **7**, 617–20.

COWDRY, E. V. (ed.). 1939. Problems of ageing. Baltimore: Williams & Wilkins Co. 2d ed., 1942. (The 3d ed. appeared as Cowdry's problems of ageing, ed. A. I. LANSING, 1952.)

DENNIS, W. 1956. The use of biographical materials in psychological research on aging. *In* J. E. ANDERSON (ed.), Psychological aspects of aging, pp. 191–94. Washington: American Psychological Association.

DONAHUE, WILMA. 1959. Mental health of the aged. *In* Proceedings of the Louisiana Conference on Aging, pp. 1–6. Baton Rouge: Louisiana State University.

——. 1960a. Gerontology at the University of Michigan. Geriatrics, Vol. **15**. (In press.)

——. 1960b. Professional training in social gerontology. *Ibid.* (In press.)

EPSTEIN, LENORE A. 1959. Money income of aged persons: a 10-year review, 1948 to 1958. Social Security Bull., **22** (June), 3–11.

FEDERAL COUNCIL ON AGING. 1959. Programs and resources for older people. Report to the President. Washington, D.C.: Government Printing Office.

FRANK, L. K. 1946. Gerontology. J. Gerontol., **1**, 1–12.

FRIEDMANN, E. A., and HAVIGHURST, R. J. 1954. The meaning of work and retirement. Chicago: University of Chicago Press.

HALL, G. S. 1922. Senescence: the last half of life. New York: Appleton & Co.

HARLAN, W. H. 1959. The training of the professional educator in social gerontology. Adult Education, **9**, 67–74.

HART, G. R. 1957. Retirement, a new outlook for the individual. New York: Harcourt, Brace & Co.

HAVIGHURST, R. J. 1958. The sociological meaning of aging. Geriatrics, **13**, 43–50.

HAWLEY, A. H. 1959. Population composition. *In* P. M. HAUSER and O. D. DUNCAN (eds.), The study of population, pp. 361–82. Chicago: University of Chicago Press.

INTERNATIONAL ASSOCIATION OF GERONTOLOGY, SOCIAL SCIENCE RESEARCH COMMITTEE. 1957. The need for cross-national surveys of old age. Ann Arbor: University of Michigan, Division of Gerontology.

JOSIAH MACY, JR., FOUNDATION. 1955. The Josiah Macy, Jr., Foundation, 1930–1955. New York: The Foundation.

KAPLAN, O. J. 1946. The psychology of maturity. *In* P. L. HARRIMAN (ed.), The encyclopedia of psychology, pp. 370–78. New York: Philosophical Library.

KORENCHEVSKY, V. 1950. The problem of aging, and the ways and means of achieving the rapid progress of gerontological research. *In* The social and biological challenge of our aging population, pp. 7–24. New York: Columbia University Press.

KUHLEN, R. G. 1956. Changing personal adjustment during the adult years. *In* J. E. ANDERSON (ed.), Psychological aspects of aging, pp. 21–29. Washington, D.C.: American Psychological Association.

LANDIS, J. T. 1940. Attitudes and adjustments of aged rural people in Iowa. (Unpublished Ph.D. dissertation, Louisiana State University.)

LANSING, A. I. 1951. Some physiological aspects of aging. Physiol. Rev., **31**, 274–84.

——. 1959. General biology of senescence. *In* J. E. BIRREN (ed.), Handbook of aging and the individual: psychological and logical aspects, pp. 119–34. Chicago: University of Chicago Press.

LEHMAN, H. C. 1953. Age and achievement. Princeton, N.J.: Princeton University Press (for the American Philosophical Society).

LINDBERGH, ANNE MORROW. 1955. Gift from the sea. New York: Pantheon Books.

LINDEN, M. E. 1955. Later maturity. *In* O. S. ENGLISH and G. H. J. PEARSON (eds.), Emotional problems of living: avoiding the neurotic pattern, pp. 437–63. New York: W. W. Norton & Co.

LINDEN, M. E., and COURTNEY, D. C. 1953. The human life cycle and its interruptions: a psychologic hypothesis. Studies in gerontologic human relations. Am. J. Psychiat., 109, 906–15.

McCONNELL, J. W. 1958. The impact of aging on the economy. J. Gerontol., Vol. 13, Suppl. 2, pp. 43–48.

MacNIDER, W. deB. 1945. Age, change, and the adapted life. Biological Symposia, 11, 165–76.

MILES, W. R. 1939. Psychological aspects of aging. *In* E. V. COWDRY (ed.), Problems of ageing, pp. 535–71. Baltimore: William & Wilkins Co.

OGBURN, W. F., and TIBBITTS, C. 1933. The family and its functions. *In* PRESIDENT'S RESEARCH COMMITTEE ON SOCIAL TRENDS, Recent social trends in the United States, pp. 661–708. New York: McGraw-Hill Book Co.

PARSONS, T. 1942. Age and sex in the social structure of the United States. Am. Sociological Rev., 7, 604–16.

PECK, R. 1956. Psychological developments in the second half of life. *In* J. E. ANDERSON (ed.), Psychological aspects of aging, pp. 42–53. Washington, D.C.: American Psychological Association.

POLLAK, O. 1948. Social adjustment in old age. New York: Social Science Research Council.

SAVILLE, L. 1959. Changing costs in the public care of the aged. J. Gerontol., 14, 349–54.

SHOCK, N. W. 1951. Biology of aging. *In* T. L. SMITH (ed.), Problems of America's aging population, pp. 37–46. Gainesville: University of Florida Press.

SIMMONS, L. W. 1945. The role of the aged in primitive society. New Haven, Conn.: Yale University Press.

———. 1952. Social participation of the aged in different cultures. Ann. Am. Acad. Political & Social Sc., 279, 43–51.

SMITH, T. L. 1950. The aged in rural society. *In* M. DERBER, (ed.), The aged in industrial society, pp. 40–53. Champaign, Ill.: Industrial Relations Research Assn.

——— (ed.). 1951. Problems of America's aging population. Gainesville: University of Florida Press.

STEINER, P. O., and DORFMAN, R. 1957. The economic status of the aged. Berkeley: University of California Press.

THOMPSON, W. E., and STREIB, G. F. 1958. Situational determinants: health and economic deprivation in retirement. J. Social Issues, 14, No. 2, 18–34.

TIBBITTS, C. (ed.). 1949. Living through the older years. Ann Arbor: University of Michigan Press.

——— (ed.). 1959. Aging and social health in the United States and Europe. Ann Arbor: University of Michigan, Division of Gerontology.

UNITED STATES DEPARTMENT OF HEALTH, EDUCATION, AND WELFARE. 1959. Aging, a review of research and training grants supported by the National Institutes of Health. Washington, D.C.: Government Printing Office.

UNITED STATES FEDERAL SECURITY AGENCY. 1951. Man and his years. Raleigh, N.C.: Health Publications Institute.

VALAORAS, V. G. 1958. Young and aged populations. Ann. Am. Acad. Political & Social Sc., 361, 69–83.

WECHSLER, D. 1955. The measurement and evaluation of intelligence of older persons. *In* Old age in the modern world, pp. 275–78. Edinburgh: E. & S. Livingstone.

WEINBERG, J. 1959. Aging of groups. *In* VETERANS ADMINISTRATION, VA prospectus research in aging, pp. 107–16. Washington, D.C.: Government Printing Office.

WILLIAMS, R. H. 1959. The changing matrix of American culture and problems of aging. *In* C. TIBBITTS (ed.), Aging and social health in the United States and Europe, pp. 156–66. Ann Arbor: University of Michigan, Division of Gerontology.

WISSLER, C. 1939. Human cultural levels. *In* E. V. COWDRY (ed.), Problems of ageing, pp. 83–99. Baltimore: Williams & Wilkins Co.

II

The Changing Demographic Profile

HENRY D. SHELDON

I. INTRODUCTION

A. *Age and Demography*

Demography, narrowly defined, is the study of the factors—fertility, mortality, and migration—which determine the changing composition of human populations and their growth or decline. All but the most superficial demographic analysis is, of necessity, made in the context of the age structure of the population under consideration. Fertility and mortality rates show typical patterns of variation with age, and the effects of given levels of fertility or mortality can be worked out only in the context of the age structure of the population. Similarly, migrants at the time of migration show a typical age distribution, and the assessment of the effects of migration needs to be made within this frame of reference.

Conversely, the age structure of a population at any given time reflects past trends in fertility, mortality, and migration. If the older population is defined as the population 60–89 years old, then its size reflects the number of births in an appropriate earlier 30-year period as reduced by the shifting mortality schedule in intervening years. This number of births, in turn, reflects the number of women of childbearing age in this earlier period and the level of their fertility. The number of women in this earlier period reflects the number of births in a still earlier period and the intervening mortality rates—and

so on, *ad infinitum.* This process, in actuality, is of course further complicated by patterns of immigration and emigration and the fertility and mortality levels of migrants in the intervening years.

It is proposed, in this chapter, to examine the changes in the age structure of the population of the United States in the past 50 years with particular reference to the growth in the number and proportion of middle-aged and older persons and to attempt some evaluation of the relative contributions of past trends in fertility, mortality, and immigration to this growth. This analysis, in turn, becomes a kind of crystal ball in which to look for possible future trends in age structure to the end of this century. Finally, some examination is made of the geographic distribution of the older and middle-aged population within various types of areas within the country— urban and rural areas, suburban and urban areas, states, and counties.

B. *Contexts in Which Middle and Old Age May Be Defined*

Conventionally, and most simply, old age is defined in terms of chronological age. Once this has been done, however, and studies are made to determine the unique and typical characteristics of older persons —physiological, psychological, social, and economic—it becomes apparent that, although the incidence of conditions thought to be associated with old age is, in reality,

high, the correlation is by no means perfect. While conditions such as heart disease
and cancer, usually associated with later
years, are found to occur with greater frequency in the older ages, they are also
found among younger persons and do
not begin at a given age. Similarly, physiological changes associated with old age
are found to occur before old age in terms
of chronology is reached, and, furthermore,
there are wide individual differences in the
chronological age of the physiologically
aged. If difficulty in obtaining employment
is a symptom of economic old age, then the
experience of the state employment services suggests that aging begins in the forties rather than at age 65. Likewise, the
period in the family cycle in which children
have grown up and left the parental home
is one which might be designated as old
age, but the inception of this period is variable with respect to chronological age.
Findings of this character suggest the possibility of redefining the older population
in terms of physiological, psychological, or
socioeconomic age rather than chronological age. There seems little to be gained by
such a procedure, however. The specialized
types of age are in the last analysis inferred from correlations with chronological age (mental age, for example, is the
chronological age of the average performer
on intelligence tests), and chronological
age is the type of age on which independent observers from different fields can most
readily agree.

It is, nevertheless, important to recognize that there is rarely a one-to-one correspondence between characteristics of older persons and chronological age, and
therefore the most fruitful approach is to
examine the incidence of these characteristics as they vary with chronological age
and to avoid drawing sharp lines between
the aged and the non-aged in terms of a
fixed chronological age. This generalization
applies not only to the fixing of a lower
limit for the older population or the middle-aged population but to the treatment
of them as homogeneous groups. For ex-

ample, within the population 65 years old
and over there are marked gradients with
increasing age in such characteristics as
labor-force participation, income, sex composition, and living arrangements.

C. Middle and Old Age in Statistical Terms

If, however, these populations are to be
studied in terms of statistics, it is necessary to make some kind of arbitrary definitions. In theory, of course, it is possible
to examine the whole range of age with respect to any given characteristic and describe its variation with age. Such a procedure, however, extends greatly the range
of analysis and becomes, in a sense, a study
of the correlates of age structure rather
than of the older or middle-aged population as such. Here the attempt is to focus
attention primarily on the middle and upper end of the age distribution and, at the
same time, give to the lower ranges of the
age distribution such consideration as adds
depth to the analysis.

For the present purposes the older population is defined in terms of persons 60
years old and over in some contexts and in
terms of persons 65 years old and over in
others. The lower limit of 65 years is sanctioned by tradition and by legislation relating to retirement, although recent social
security legislation has breached this uniformity. A lower limit of age 60, on the
other hand, mitigates to some extent the
bias in the reporting of age in census statistics.[1] Middle age is given the lower lim-

---

[1] An examination of census age statistics indicates clear evidence of bias in age reporting. Sex
ratios and survival rates derived from census age
statistics appear irrational when they are compared with expected values derived from life-
tables. The existence of the same type of bias is
revealed by a comparison of the ages reported in
the census with those reported in a reinterview such
as the Post Enumeration Survey of 1950, or by a
check against independent records such as birth
certificates. Unfortunately, although studies of
these types reveal the existence of bias, they are
by no means in complete agreement as to its character. In recent censuses, however, it appears that

it of 45 years, with an upper limit of 59, or
64, years, depending upon the lower limit
assigned to the older population in any
given context. Generally speaking, the
choice of one level or the other has been
dictated primarily by convenience, and, in
any event, instances are rare in which general conclusions drawn from statistics relating to one age level are not equally applicable to the other.

II. Past Trends in Age Structure

A. General

AGING IN HUMAN POPULATIONS

As indicated in the preceding discussion,
there are problems in defining a middle-
aged or older person. When the concept of
aging is applied to human populations,

there has been an overstatement of the number
of persons 65 and over and an understatement of
the number of persons in the 10-year interval immediately below 65. Thus, if the population 55–
64 at one census is brought forward by the use of
appropriate survival rates, with appropriate adjustments for immigration and the like, the expected number of persons 65–74 at the next census is appreciably lower than the enumerated number. This discrepancy has sometimes been called
the "social security" bias, on the assumption that
a considerable number of persons, once they have
arrived within striking distance of age 65, claim
the age in order to receive benefits. Representatives of the Social Security Administration, however, point out that the discrepancy may be an
understatement of age in the earlier census rather
than an overstatement at the later one. They indicate that appreciable numbers of persons come
into the system at ages which have been understated in order to maintain or obtain employment.
When, however, their true age becomes 65, there
is an established procedure by which they can
prove their true age and become eligible for retirement, and many persons make use of this procedure. A detailed discussion of the age biases implied by a comparison of the 1950 population
expected from 1940 and the enumerated population of 1950 appears in U.S. Bureau of the Census
(1954), "Estimates of the Population of the United
States and of the Components of Change, by Age,
Color, and Sex: 1940 to 1950." A more general discussion of the difficulties with census age statistics
and an estimated correction of the 1950 figures are
presented in Coale (1955).

these problems become more involved. The
implication is certainly that aging populations are those whose average age is increasing and in which the proportion at the
upper end of the age distribution is increasing in relation to that at the lower end
of the distribution.

Valaoras (1950) has formalized this latter definition in terms of an index of aging,
which he defines as the ratio of the population 60 years old and over to the population under 15 years old times 100. With
an index of this type it is possible to establish empirical standards and on this
basis to define "young" and "old" populations. The data presented in Table 1 show

TABLE 1*

INDEX OF AGING FOR SELECTED COUNTRIES
AND CENSUS DATES

(Population in Thousands)

Country and Census Date	Population under 15 Years	Population 60 Years and Over	Index of Aging†
Thailand, 1947.....	7,375	732	9.9
Formosa, 1950......	3,129	317	10.1
Brazil, 1950........	21,695	2,205	10.2
Puerto Rico, 1950‡..	955	135	14.1
Ceylon, 1946.......	2,478	360	14.5
India, 1951.........	133,621	20,190	15.1
Egypt, 1947........	7,198	1,137	15.8
Japan, 1950........	29,459	6,417	21.8
United States, 1850‡	9,636	959	10.0
Great Britain, 1851..	7,383	1,528	20.7
Sweden, 1850.......	1,145	272	23.8
Canada, 1951.......	4,242	1,591	37.5
New Zealand, 1951..	517	251	48.5
Australia, 1947.....	1,899	926	48.8
Norway, 1950......	800	453	56.6
Germany, 1950§....	11,237	6,575	58.5
Switzerland, 1950...	1,111	662	59.6
Austria, 1951.......	1,587	1,083	68.2
France, 1950.......	9,098	6,983	76.8
United States, 1950.	40,483	18,329	45.3
Sweden, 1950.......	1,648	1,055	64.0
Great Britain, 1951..	10,981	7,665	69.8

* Source: United Nations, Department of Economic and
Social Affairs, *The Aging of Populations and Its Economic and
Social Implications* ("Population Studies," No. 26 [New York:
United Nations, 1956]).

† Ratio of population 60 and over to population under 15.

‡ Based on data from Bureau of Census reports.

§ The Federal Republic, excluding West Berlin.

contrasts of this type for selected countries. These countries were, of course, selected to illustrate the contrast, and there are many countries which fall between these extremes. The data presented, however, do serve to illustrate the empirical extremes of "young" and "old" populations in terms of those areas for which age data are available.

GEOGRAPHIC AND HISTORICAL CONTRASTS

It will be noted that, generally speaking, the countries with "young" populations are "underdeveloped" countries, whereas the countries with "older" populations are the industrialized countries of western Europe and their offshoots in other parts of the world. It is also apparent that a century ago typical "developed" countries had indexes of aging of about the same level as those of the underdeveloped countries of today.

These same generalizations are illustrated by the age pyramids presented in Chart I. These pyramids, which show the percentage distribution of the population by sex and in 15-year intervals to the age group 60 years old and over, display for the typically "young" populations the pyramidal form which usually has been associated with "normal" populations. This "normality" is based on the implicit assumption that the normal population is increasing, or at least holding its own, and that the amount of migration is limited and thus has little effect on the age distribution. Under these conditions the largest number of persons will be found in the youngest age group, and, with the increasing attrition from mortality with age, each succeeding age group will be smaller, until the vanishing point is reached.

The pyramids for the "older" population tend toward a rectangular shape, with only a minimum contraction of the age groups as age increases. (To be sure, if the age group 60 and over were subdivided into appropriate intervals, these figures would have a peak at the top; but it is note-worthy that in the "younger" populations this is achieved without subdivision.) It is this latter type of age structure which may be said to describe human populations which have grown old. Here, again, the age pyramids for Sweden, Great Britain, and the United States in or around 1850 resemble those of "young" populations, so that the transition in age structure from 1850 to 1950 provides an empirical illustration of aging populations.

DEMOGRAPHIC TRANSITION AND AGING

The aging of the populations of the United States and the countries of western Europe has been associated with the process which has been described variously as the demographic revolution or transition. This process may be defined loosely in terms of the unprecedented declines in mortality and fertility which occurred during the nineteenth and twentieth centuries in those areas. Demographers are by no means in agreement as to the details of the process—as to whether the decline in death rates preceded the decline in birth rates, as to whether the industrial revolution and rising levels of living initiated these changes, or as to whether this historical experience is applicable as an interpretative device in the analysis of current and future trends related particularly to underdeveloped countries. In spite of these differences of opinion, however, there is general agreement that such declines in fertility and mortality did occur and that there was a concomitant aging of the populations involved.

AGING OF THE POPULATION OF THE UNITED STATES

The population of the United States has been an aging population during the entire period for which relevant statistics have been recorded. The median age of white males was 15.9 years in 1790; by 1850 it had increased to 19.5 years; by 1900, to 23.8 years; and, by 1950, to 30.4 years. In 1830, 4.0 per cent of the total white popu-

CHART I

Population of Selected Countries, by Age and Sex

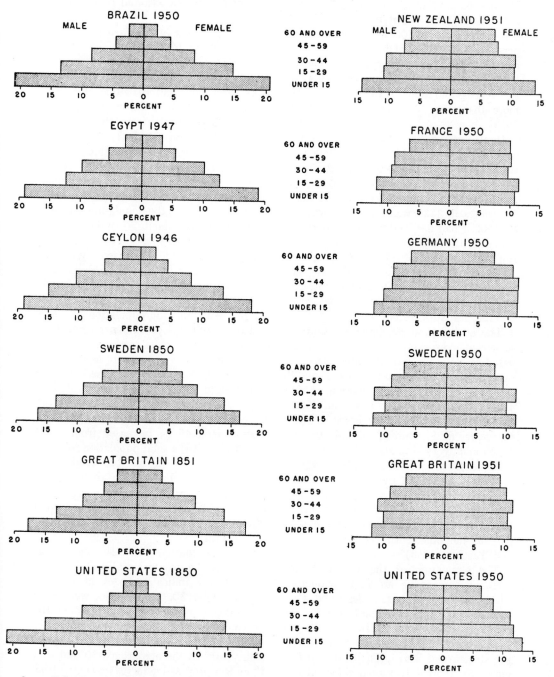

Source: United Nations, Department of Economic and Social Affairs, *The Aging of Populations and Its Economic and Social Implications* ("Population Studies," No. 26 [New York: United Nations, 1956]).

lation was 60 years of age and over, and by 1950 this percentage had increased to 12.6. Persons 65 and over constituted 2.6 per cent of the total population in 1850 but 8.1 per cent in 1950. The proportion of persons 45–64 years of age about doubled in the 1850–1950 century. They constituted a little less than 10 per cent (9.8) of the total population in 1850 and a little more than 20 (20.3) in 1950 (Sheldon, 1958).

It also seems clear that fertility rates, until the decade 1940–50, have fallen in the United States since early in the nineteenth century. Thompson and Whelpton (1933) estimate that the crude birth rate for whites in 1820 was about 53, whereas by 1900 it had declined to 30. Similar estimates for the total population indicate corresponding figures of 55 and 32 (Sheldon, 1958). In 1940 the crude birth rate, adjusted for underregistration of births, was 19.4; in 1950, 24.1 (U.S. National Office of Vital Statistics, 1954a).

The evidence on declining mortality is somewhat more sketchy. Various estimates based on data for several states place the expectation of life around 1850 at about 40 years (Kennedy, 1853; Meech, 1898; Jaffe and Lourie, 1942; Jacobson, 1957). By 1900 this figure had increased to about 49 years (U.S. Bureau of the Census, 1921) and by 1950 to about 68 years (U.S. National Office of Vital Statistics, 1954b). It is clear, then, that there has also been a decline in mortality in the United States, although there is some element of uncertainty with respect to trends in the early part of the nineteenth century (Taeuber and Taeuber, 1958).

The population of the United States, then, appears to be an aging population within the general context described. Over the last century or more both fertility and mortality have declined. In 1850 its age structure was not dissimilar to the current age structure of Brazil, Thailand, and Formosa. By 1950 it had aged sufficiently to place it in the same class with, but at a slightly lower level than, the populations of France, Great Britain, Sweden, Austria, Switzerland, Germany, and Norway and of Australia and New Zealand (Table 1).

B. Trends in Age Structure
1900–1950

THE TOTAL POPULATION

Between 1900 and 1950 the total population of the United States increased by nearly 100 per cent—from about 76 million to 151 million (Table 2). In the same period, however, the population 65 and over increased by nearly 300 per cent—from 3.1 to 12.3 million—and the population 60 and over by about 274 per cent. During these years the population aged 45–64 increased by about 20 million, an increase of almost 194 per cent, and the population aged 45–59 increased by almost 185 per cent, or by almost 16 million.

In percentage terms the population 65 years old and over increased from 4.1 to 8.1 per cent, and the population 60 years and over from 6.4 to 12.2 per cent. Thus the proportion of older persons, defined either as persons 65 and over or 60 and over, nearly doubled in the 50-year period under consideration. Though it did not double, the proportion of middle-aged persons did increase between 1900 and 1950. The population aged 45–64 increased from about 14 per cent of the total population to about 20 per cent, and the persons aged 45–59 increased from about 11 to about 16 per cent. The figures, then, indicate the degree to which the population of the United States "aged" in the first half of the twentieth century.

An examination of the percentage changes in the proportion at each five-year age interval indicates losses in the age groups under 30. These losses were most heavily concentrated in the age groups 10–14 and 15–19 and reflect the relatively small number of births during the depression years. In the age groups 30 and over there is a progressive increase ranging from 4.1 per cent for the age group 30–34 to 100 per cent or more for the groups 75 and over. Generally, then, in terms of proportions there was a contraction at the ages under 30, and a progressive expansion at the ages above 30.

NATIVITY, COLOR, AND SEX

All the major components of the population of the United States shared in the increase in the proportion of older persons. The foreign-born population, both white and non-white, showed a greater increase in the proportion of persons 60 and over than the corresponding respective elements in the native population (Table 3). The

increase in both the native and the foreign-born population was greater among whites than among non-whites.

In both the white and the non-white components of the foreign-born population the increase in the proportion of older men exceeded the increase in the proportion of older women. In the native population, however, the increase in the percentage of older women was greater than that of older men for both whites and non-whites. Thus, in the total native population of 1900, the number of women 65 years old and over exceeded the number of men in

TABLE 2*

POPULATION OF THE UNITED STATES, BY AGE AND SEX, 1950 AND 1900†

(In Thousands)

AGE (IN YEARS)	TOTAL					MALE		FEMALE	
	No.		Percentage Distribution			1950	1900	1950	1900
	1950	1900	1950	1900	Per Cent Change, 1900–1950				
All ages......	150,697	75,995	100.0	100.0	....	74,833	38,816	75,864	37,178
Under 5..........	16,164	9,195	10.7	12.1	− 11.6	8,236	4,649	7,927	4,546
5– 9............	13,200	8,898	8.8	11.7	− 24.8	6,715	4,494	6,485	4,404
10–14..........	11,119	8,102	7.4	10.7	− 30.8	5,660	4,097	5,459	4,005
15–19..........	10,617	7,576	7.0	10.0	− 30.0	5,311	3,763	5,305	3,813
20–24..........	11,482	7,355	7.6	9.7	− 21.6	5,606	3,637	5,876	3,718
25–29..........	12,242	6,547	8.1	8.6	− 5.8	5,972	3,334	6,270	3,212
30–34..........	11,517	5,571	7.6	7.3	+ 4.1	5,625	2,911	5,892	2,660
35–39..........	11,246	4,978	7.5	6.6	+ 13.6	5,518	2,625	5,729	2,352
40–44..........	10,204	4,258	6.8	5.6	+ 21.4	5,070	2,263	5,134	1,995
45–49..........	9,070	3,464	6.0	4.6	+ 30.4	4,526	1,844	4,544	1,620
50–54..........	8,272	2,951	5.5	3.9	+ 41.0	4,129	1,570	4,144	1,381
55–59..........	7,235	2,217	4.8	2.9	+ 65.5	3,630	1,149	3,605	1,068
60–64..........	6,059	1,796	4.0	2.4	+ 66.7	3,038	920	3,022	876
65–69..........	5,003	1,306	3.3	1.7	+ 94.7	2,425	670	2,578	636
70–74..........	3,412	886	2.3	1.2	+ 91.7	1,629	451	1,783	435
75–79..........	2,152	521	1.4	0.7	+100.0	1,002	262	1,151	259
80–84..........	1,125	252	0.7	0.3	+133.3	505	123	620	129
85 and over.......	577	123	0.4	0.2	+100.0	237	54	340	68
45 and over.......	42,907	13,515	28.5	17.8	+ 60.1	21,120	7,043	21,787	6,474
45–59..........	24,578	8,631	16.3	11.4	+ 43.0	12,285	4,563	12,293	4,068
60 and over.....	18,329	4,884	12.2	6.4	+ 90.6	8,835	2,481	9,494	2,404
45–64..........	30,637	10,427	20.3	13.7	+ 48.2	15,323	5,483	15,314	4,945
65 and over.....	12,270	3,088	8.1	4.1	+ 97.6	5,797	1,560	6,473	1,528

* Source: H. D. Sheldon, *The Older Population of the United States* (New York: John Wiley & Sons, 1958), Appendix Table A-2.
† Figures independently rounded to nearest thousand; hence sum of parts may differ slightly from total shown. Figures for 1900 adjusted for age not reported.

the same age group by about 7000, but by 1950 this difference had increased to about 700,000 (Sheldon, 1958).

In most general terms, the trends in the size of the older native population reflect the trends in the number of births in the appropriate periods prior to 1900 and 1950, and those in the foreign-born population reflect trends in the number of immigrants in analogous periods.

C. Factors in the Increase in Number of Older Persons

The age structure of a native population is the end product of the progressive attrition of mortality from successive cohorts of births. The maximum size of a cohort is the number of births in a given time period—a year, 5 years, or any fixed period. As time passes, the cohort grows older and, as the result of mortality, becomes smaller. Its size at any time in this process, however, is in part a function of its initial size, and therefore the initial number of births is always a factor in determining its size at any age. Since a native population is made up of a succession of cohorts, a knowledge of their initial sizes (i.e., the number of births in appropriate earlier periods) provides a considerable in-

TABLE 3*

PERCENTAGE OF TOTAL POPULATION 60 AND 65 YEARS AND OVER, BY
NATIVITY, COLOR, AND SEX, 1950 AND 1900

NATIVITY AND COLOR	BOTH SEXES		MALE		FEMALE	
	1950	1900	1950	1900	1950	1900
60 Years and Over						
Total.........	12.2	6.4	11.8	6.4	12.5	6.5
Native...........	10.2	5.1	9.6	5.1	10.7	5.2
Foreign-born.......	39.1	14.6	39.9	14.0	38.2	15.2
White..........	12.6	6.6	12.2	6.6	13.0	6.7
Native...........	10.4	5.2	9.8	5.1	11.0	5.3
Foreign-born.......	39.6	14.7	40.6	14.2	38.6	15.3
Non-white.......	8.3	4.9	8.4	5.0	8.2	4.7
Native...........	8.1	4.9	8.1	5.0	8.1	4.7
Foreign-born.......	18.8	5.3	19.4	5.1	17.8	6.5
65 Years and Over						
Total.........	8.1	4.1	7.7	4.0	8.5	4.1
Native...........	6.8	3.2	6.3	3.2	7.3	3.3
Foreign-born.......	26.2	9.2	26.0	8.8	26.3	9.7
White..........	8.4	4.2	8.0	4.2	8.9	4.3
Native...........	7.0	3.3	6.4	3.2	7.5	3.4
Foreign-born.......	26.6	9.3	26.5	9.0	26.6	9.7
Non-white.......	5.7	3.0	5.7	3.0	5.7	3.0
Native...........	5.6	3.0	5.5	3.1	5.6	3.0
Foreign-born.......	11.2	2.1	11.5	1.9	10.8	4.2

* Source: H. D. Sheldon, *The Older Population of the United States* (New York: John Wiley & Sons, 1958), Appendix Tables A-2, A-3, and A-4.

sight into the age structure of such a population at any given time.

BIRTHS

Thus native children under 5 years of age in 1950 were the survivors of births in the period 1945–50, and children under 5 in 1900 were the survivors of births in the period 1895–1900. Similarly, the general dimensions of the population 60–89 years old in 1950 were set by the number of births in the period 1860–90; those of the corresponding 1900 population, by the number of births between 1810 and 1840. Both sets of births were, of course, subject to mortality over a considerable period of time, but the relationship between the number of survivors at the two censuses still reflects, to a considerable degree, the

initial relationship between the two sets of births.

The relationship is illustrated in the upper set of age pyramids presented in Chart II. The pyramids are designed to show both the estimated number of births from which a given age group has survived and the number of survivors in the age group at the indicated date. Thus the entire bar represents the total number of births in the designated time period, the center blank portion the survivors in the given age group, and the shaded portion the losses from mortality. For example, the estimated number of births in the period 1840–55 was about 16 million. Of these births, about 6 million persons survived to the ages 45–59 in 1900; and the loss from mortality was approximately 10 million, or

CHART II

BIRTHS PRIOR TO CENSUS DATE, BY PERIOD OF BIRTH AND SURVIVORS AT CENSUS DATE (NATIVE POPULATION), BY AGE, FOR THE UNITED STATES, 1900 AND 1950

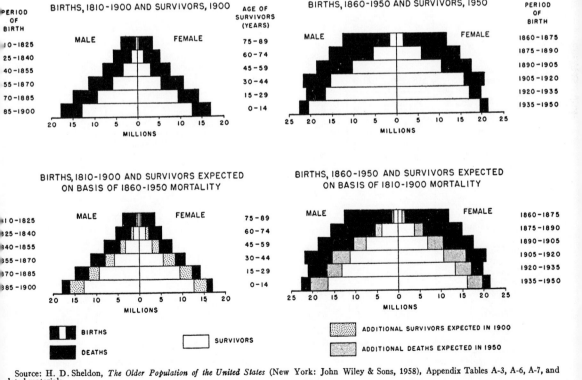

Source: H. D. Sheldon, *The Older Population of the United States* (New York: John Wiley & Sons, 1958), Appendix Tables A-3, A-6, A-7, and related materials.

about 60 per cent (Table 4).[2] In short, the outer margins of the pyramids represent the age structure as it would have been had the population of the United States lived

[2] For a description of the methods by which these estimates were developed and their limitations see Sheldon (1958, Appendix A, pp. 137–46). The materials presented here represent some elaboration of the original estimates materials. In dealing with the relationship between period of birth and age of the native population, this population has been arbitrarily cut off at age 90 for convenience in calculation and presentation. In 1950, native persons 90 and over constituted about 0.1 per cent of the total native population.

in a "Brave New World" in which no one died until the end of their eighty-ninth year, and the inner pyramid represents the age structure of the actual surviving population in the real world.

A comparison of the two sets of data indicates that, even after mortality has taken its toll, there is still a considerable similarity between the birth and the population pyramids. The age pyramid for 1900 has essentially the triangular form from which the term "pyramid" derives. It is generally assumed that this triangular form reflects,

TABLE 4*

ESTIMATED BIRTHS, BY PERIOD OF OCCURRENCE, AND SURVIVING NATIVE POPULATION
UNDER 90 YEARS, BY AGE, FOR THE UNITED STATES, 1950 AND 1900†

(In Thousands)

PERIOD OF BIRTH	BIRTHS		CENSUS DATE AND AGE (IN YEARS) AT CENSUS DATE	SURVIVORS (NATIVE POPULATION)		IMPLIED SURVIVAL RATE	EXPECTED SURVIVORS, FROM 100,000 BIRTHS PER ANNUM IN EACH PERIOD‡	
	No.	Per Cent		No.	Per Cent		No.	Per Cent
			1950					
1860–1950.....	218,350	100.0	Total, under 90..	140,161	100.0	....	5,308	100.0
1935–50........	44,087	20.2	Under 15.........	40,283	28.7	0.9137	1,371	25.8
1920–35........	40,707	18.6	15–29............	33,644	24.0	.8265	1,240	23.4
1905–20........	42,441	19.4	30–44............	31,250	22.3	.7363	1,104	20.8
1890–1905......	36,231	16.6	45–59............	20,844	14.9	.5753	863	16.3
1875–90........	30,624	14.0	60–74............	11,247	8.0	.3672	551	10.4
1860–75........	24,259	11.1	75–89............	2,893	2.1	0.1193	179	3.4
1860–90........	54,884	25.1	60–89............	14,140	10.1	....	730	13.8
			1900					
1810–1900.....	120,213	100.0	Total, under 90..	65,627	100.0	....	3,952	100.0
1885–1900......	34,797	28.9	Under 15.........	25,680	39.1	0.7380	1,107	28.0
1870–85........	29,128	24.2	15–29............	18,860	28.7	.6475	971	24.6
1855–70........	22,022	18.3	30–44............	11,427	17.4	.5189	778	19.7
1840–55........	15,803	13.1	45–59............	6,308	9.6	.3992	599	15.2
1825–40........	10,998	9.1	60–74............	2,741	4.2	.2492	374	9.5
1810–25........	7,464	6.2	75–89............	611	0.9	0.0819	123	3.1
1810–40........	18,463	15.4	60–89............	3,352	5.1	....	497	12.6

* Source: H. D. Sheldon, *The Older Population of the United States* (New York: John Wiley & Sons, 1958), Appendix Tables A-3 A-6, A-7, and related materials.
† Figures independently rounded to nearest thousand; hence sum of parts may differ slightly from totals shown. Population figures for 1900 adjusted for age not reported.
‡ Sum of survivors computed independently for each sex.

in the main, the increasing attrition of mortality as age increases, and this, of course, is true. It is worthy of note, however, that the same general form was attained purely in terms of births in the 1900 population as the result of the rapid growth of population in the preceding 90 years.

The 1950 birth pyramid, in contrast to that of 1900, shows a less rapid contraction in the length of the bars as age increases. In 1950 there were about 35 native persons 60–89 for every 100 native persons under 15, whereas in 1900 there were only about 13 such persons. In 1950, similarly, there were almost 52 native persons 45–59 for every 100 native persons under 15, whereas in 1900 there were only about 25 (derived from Table 4). This difference reflects the much less rapid increase in the number of births within the period 1860–1950 than in the period 1810–1900. For example, as the 1950 pyramid shows, there were fewer births in the period 1920–35 than in the period 1905–20.

Of course, the decline in mortality between the two periods also affected this difference. If, however, the implied survival ratios for the period 1810–1900 are applied to the births in the period 1860–1950, a hypothetical age distribution for 1950 is obtained on the assumption of no decline in mortality. In this age distribution there are about 30 persons 60–89 for every 100 persons under 15 years old and about 44 persons aged 45–59 for every 100 such persons. Thus the difference between 1900 and 1950 attributable to differences in the number of births is less than that observed in the actual population but still relatively large.

DECLINING MORTALITY

The simplest and most popular explanation of the increase in our older population is that of declining mortality; that is, the expectation of life has increased, people are living longer, and thus there are more older people.

It is perfectly clear that the initial premise is correct. The expectation of life at birth at about the middle of the nineteenth century has been variously estimated at about 40 years. The United States life-tables of 1900, based on data from the twelve registration states of that time, indicate a figure of 49.2 years. By 1950, this figure, calculated on the basis of data for the entire country, was 68.1 years (Table 5).

The inference that the increase in life-expectation means that people are living longer needs examination. The increase means that there has been an increase in the number of man-years lived by a cohort of births, but these years have been gained largely at the younger ages, particularly by the reduction of infant mortality. As figures in Table 5 indicate, the gain in expectation of life at the older ages has not been large. The increase in life-expectation does mean, however, that more persons have survived to attain the upper ages. Under the mortality conditions of 1950, for the total population, about 76 per cent of a cohort of births would survive to age 60, whereas, under the mortality conditions of 1900, the comparable figure would be 48 (U.S. Bureau of the Census, 1921; U.S. National Office of Vital Statistics, 1954b).

Although life-tables permit precise statements of the implications of mortality schedules for age structure at given points in time, they are not ordinarily in a form which provides measures which can be applied to births spread over a period of time. For example, the life-table of 1900 is applicable to an analysis of the births in the 90-year period prior to 1900 only on the assumption that the mortality schedule observed in 1900 obtained throughout the entire period, and obviously it did not. For this reason, but with a considerable loss of precision, recourse is had here to the survival rates implied by the estimates of births prior to 1900 and 1950 and the survivors in the native population observed in the censuses of these dates.

These rates, presented in Table 4, give some indication of the decline in mortality between the two periods of time under consideration. Thus it appears that about 55 per cent of the births between 1810 and 1900 survived to 1900, whereas about 64 per cent of the births between 1860 and 1950 survived to 1950. For the population 60–89 the corresponding percentages for 1900 and 1950 were 18 and 26 per cent, respectively; for the population 45–59, about 40 and 58 per cent, respectively.

As indicated in the discussion of the effects of births on age structure, these survival rates provide a basis for estimating the relative contributions of birth trends and declining mortality to the changes in age structure between 1900 and 1950. The lower set of age pyramids on Chart II yields a general impression as to the effects of the difference in survival rates. The pyramid for 1900 indicates the age structure of the surviving population on the basis of 1950 survival rates; the crosshatched area, the gain in survivors as the result of the higher survival rates. The 1950 pyramid indicates the results of assuming the 1900 survival rates for the births prior to 1950. Here the inner pyramid represents the surviving population on the basis of 1900 rates, and the crosshatched area shows the loss in survivors resulting from the lower survival rates. These two cross-

TABLE 5*

EXPECTATION OF LIFE AT SELECTED AGES, BY COLOR AND SEX
1949–51 AND 1900–1902

YEAR AND SEX	AT AGE						
	At Birth	20	40	60	65	70	75
Total							
1949–51...........	68.1	51.2	32.8	17.0	13.8	10.9	8.4
1900–1902†.........	49.2	42.8	28.3	14.8	11.9	9.3	7.1
White							
Male:							
1949–51..........	66.3	49.5	31.2	15.8	12.8	10.1	7.8
1900–1902†.......	48.2	42.2	27.7	14.4	11.5	9.0	6.8
Female:							
1949–51..........	72.0	54.6	35.6	18.6	15.0	11.7	8.9
1900–1902†.......	51.1	43.8	29.2	15.2	12.2	9.6	7.3
Non-White							
Male:							
1949–51..........	58.9	43.7	27.3	14.9	12.8	10.7	8.8
1900–1902†.......	32.5	35.1	23.1	12.6	10.4	8.3	6.6
Female:							
1949–51..........	62.7	46.8	29.8	17.0	14.5	12.3	10.2
1900–1902†.......	35.0	36.9	24.4	13.6	11.4	9.6	7.9

* Source: U.S. Bureau of the Census, *United States Life Tables: 1890, 1901, and 1900–1910* (Washington, D.C.: Government Printing Office, 1921); U.S. National Office of Vital Statistics, *United States Life Tables, 1949–1951* ("Vital Statistics—Special Reports," Vol. **41**, No. 1 [Washington, D.C.: Government Printing Office, 1954]).

† Based on data from original Death Registration States. Figures for non-whites cover only Negroes, who in 1900 comprised more than 95 per cent of the total non-white population in the registration area.

hatched margins, then, suggest the relative magnitude of the differences in age structure resulting from declining mortality.

Actually, the native population 60–89 years increased by about 320 per cent between 1900 and 1950; the population 45–59, by about 185 per cent. If the number of births had been equal in each of the 15-year periods under consideration, these percentages would have been slightly less than 50. Evidently, the contribution of declining mortality accounts for only a minor part of the 1900–1950 change.

sketchy, and thus any attempt to trace in detail this relationship is, of necessity, a kind of arithmetic fantasy.

The data presented in Table 6 indicate that in a 40–70-year period prior to 1950 (1880–1910), nearly 18 million immigrants entered the country, whereas in the corresponding period prior to 1900 (1830–60) the number of immigrants was about 5 million. Assuming that the foreign-born population 60–89 in 1950 was largely derived from immigration in the period 1880–1910, and the corresponding population in

TABLE 6*

IMMIGRATION IN 70-YEAR PERIOD PRIOR TO CENSUS DATE AND AGE OF THE FOREIGN-BORN POPULATION AT CENSUS, 1950 AND 1900

IMMIGRATION PRIOR TO CENSUS DATE AND AGE (IN YEARS) OF FOREIGN-BORN AT CENSUS	1950		1900	
	No. (Thousands)	Per Cent	No. (Thousands)	Per Cent
Immigration in 70-year period prior to census date:				
Total, 70.	29,136	100	18,972	100
0–40.	11,406	39	14,061	74
40–70.	17,730	61	4,911	26
Foreign-born population by age:				
Total, all ages.	10,422	100	10,341	100
Under 60.	6,348	61	8,836	85
60 and over.	4,074	39	1,506	15

* Source: H. D. Sheldon, *The Older Population of the United States* (New York: John Wiley & Sons, 1958), Appendix Tables A-4 and A-5.

IMMIGRATION

As the age structure of the native population reflects past trends in births, so the age structure of the foreign-born population reflects past trends in immigration. An analysis of this relationship is somewhat more complicated than the analysis of births and age structure, because the relationship between date of birth and age is fixed, but the relationship between date of immigration and age is variable; that is, everybody is born at age zero, but immigrants enter the country at various ages. Moreover, the statistical information on the age of immigrants to the United States for the period 1810–1950 is extremely

1900 from immigration in the period 1830–60, it follows that the increase in the older foreign-born population between 1900 and 1950 is, in large part, a function of variation in the volume of immigration in the appropriate earlier periods. This assumption is obviously extremely rough but, in view of the large differences involved, not too wide of the mark.

The effect of emigration, like that of mortality, is to remove individuals from a population as it ages and thus ultimately to reduce the number of older persons. Since, however, statistics on emigration have been collected only since 1908, it is not possible to assess the role of emigration in the increase in the older population between 1900 and 1950. The life-tables for foreign-born white males and females for 1901 and 1910 suggest a decline in mortality rates among the foreign-born similar to that observed in the native population which contributed to the growth of the older population. The erratic variations, however, in the trends in both emigration and immigration during the period under

a basis for such an estimate. The upper-left-hand cell in this table presents figures for the total native population and the native population 60–89 years as observed in 1950. The second cell in the second row presents corresponding figures for 1900. The total difference in the number of persons 60–89 was about 10.8 million.

The second cell in the first row indicates what the population 60–89 would

TABLE 7*

NATIVE POPULATION UNDER 90 YEARS AND 60–89 YEARS OBSERVED
1950 AND 1900, AND EXPECTED ON BASIS OF A REVERSAL
OF SURVIVAL RATES

(In Thousands)

ASSUMPTION AS TO BIRTHS IN 90-YEAR PERIOD PRIOR TO CENSUS DATE	MORTALITY ASSUMPTIONS		DIFFERENCE
	Survival Rates 1860–1950	Survival Rates 1810–1900	
Birth distribution, 1860–1950:			
Total under 90.........	140,161	104,995	....
No. 60–89............	14,140	9,618	4,523
Percentage 60–89......	10.1	9.2	0.9
Birth distribution, 1810–1900:			
Total under 90.........	86,105	65,627	....
No. 60–89............	4,930	3,352	1,578
Percentage 60–89......	5.7	5.1	0.6
Difference:			
No. 60–89............	9,210	6,266	2,944
Percentage 60–89......	4.4	4.1	0.3

* Source: H. D. Sheldon, *The Older Population of the United States* (New York: John Wiley & Sons, 1958), Appendix Tables A-3, A-6, A-7, A-8, and related materials. The present table is an elaboration of Table A-8; the figures are derived from a more detailed set of age-specific survival rates and as a result are not in complete agreement with those presented in Table A-8.

consideration and the lack of adequate data make it impractical to analyze the effects of both emigration and mortality.

RELATIVE CONTRIBUTIONS

The preceding discussion suggests that each of the factors—number of births in appropriate earlier periods, declining mortality, and immigration—contributed to the increase in the older population between 1900 and 1950. It is perhaps of some interest to estimate the relative contribution of each factor.

The figures presented in Table 7 suggest

have been in 1950 if the survival rates for the appropriate period prior to 1900 had obtained in the appropriate period prior to 1950, that is, if there had been no decline in mortality. Thus the difference of about 6.3 million between the figure in this cell for persons 60–89 in 1950 (9.6 million) and the corresponding figure observed in 1900 (3.4 million) represents the increase solely attributable to the increase in the number of births between the periods 1810–40 and 1860–90, since mortality has been assumed to be the same for both periods.

The first cell in the second row indicates what the population 60–89 would have been in 1900 if the survival rates for the appropriate births had been at the 1950 level rather than at the observed level. The difference of about 1.6 million between this figure (4.9 million) and that observed in 1900 (3.4 million) represents the sole contribution of declining mortality, since the number of births in both cases was the same.

It will be noted that effects of differences in the number of births and in survival rates have been evaluated by holding first one and then the other factor constant at the 1900 level. That is, the questions asked were: (1) What would the increase in older population due to the increase in the number of births have been, if mortality had remained at the 1900 level? (2) What would the increase in older population due to declining mortality have been if the number of births prior to 1900 obtained in both periods? It will also be noted that the sum of the increases attributed to births and mortality (7.8 million) falls short by about 2.9 million of accounting for the observed increase of 10.8 million.

The problem could, of course, be approached in a complementary way in which the reference point is 1950 rather than 1900. The questions here are: (1) What would be the contribution of births at 1950 mortality levels? (2) What would be the contribution of declining mortality at the 1860–90 level of births? In this case the sum of the estimated contributions (13.7) is more than the observed increase. The excess here (2.9 million) is, however, equal to the shortage which develops when 1900 levels are used as a base for comparison. This number represents the interaction of the change in the number of births with the change in the survival rates. A given increase in survival rates will produce a greater increase in expected population when applied to a large number of births rather than to a small number, or, conversely, an increase in the number of births will produce a greater increase in expected population at a high survival-rate level than at a low survival-rate level.

If the problem is viewed from the perspective of 1900, that is, defined as the determination of the effects of the increase in births if there was no improvement in mortality between the two periods, and the determination of the effect of improved mortality if there had been no increase in the number of births, then the amount of population change attributable to the interaction factor is positive. If, however, the point of departure is 1950, then this factor becomes negative.

TABLE 8*

INCREASE IN THE POPULATION 60–89 YEARS 1900–1950, BY COMPONENTS OF INCREASE

Components of Increase	No. (Thousands)	Per Cent
Total increase.........	13,331	100.0
In native population.......	10,788	80.9
From increase in number of births.............	6,266	47.0
From decrease in mortality	1,578	11.8
From increase in births and decrease in mortality................	2,944	22.1
In foreign-born population..	2,543	19.1

* Source: Table 7 and H. D. Sheldon, *The Older Population of the United States* (New York: John Wiley & Sons, 1958), Appendix Tables A-2, A-3, and A-4.

Viewing the problem from the perspective of 1900, then, data on the relative contributions of births, declining mortality, and immigration are summarized in Table 8. The figures indicate that, of the increase of over 13 million in the total population 60–89 between 1900 and 1950, about 6.3 million, or 47 per cent, can be attributed to differences in the number of births in appropriate periods prior to the two censuses; about 1.6 million, or about 12 per cent, to the decline in mortality per se; about 2.9 million, or 22 per cent, to the interaction of the increase in the number of births with declining mortality; and about 2.5 million, or nearly 20 per cent, to immigration. The increase attributed to immigration is simply the increase in the number of foreign-born 60–89 between 1900 and 1950 and thus includes the contribution of declining mortality among the foreign-born.

D. Factors in the Increase in Proportion of Older Persons

The relation of trends in mortality, fertility, and migration to the *proportion* of older persons is somewhat different from the relation of these factors to the *number* of older persons. In explaining changes in the proportion of older persons, it is necessary to know not only the impact of the above factors on the size of the older population but also their impact on the remainder of the population, since the proportion of older persons is really a matter of the relation between the rate of change in each part of the population. Thus, for example, an increase in survival rates will surely increase the number of older persons; but, if it applies uniformly throughout the whole age distribution, the proportion of older persons will not be increased. In short, it is necessary to determine the effects of the factors throughout the entire age distribution and then to examine the results for the older population in relation to the balance.

BIRTHS AND FERTILITY

The proportion of older persons in a native population reflects the distribution by periods of birth of all the births prior to the year under consideration. Thus the number of births in a period 60–90 years prior to the given date, expressed as a percentage of the births in the total 90-year period, gives some indication as to the percentage 60 and over at the given date. In these terms births in the period 1810–40 constituted 15.4 per cent of the births in the period 1810–1900, whereas births between 1860 and 1890 constituted 25.1 per cent of all the births in the 90-year period prior to 1950 (Table 4). It is reasonable to infer, therefore, that the distribution by

period of birth made a contribution to the increase in the proportion of older persons between 1900 and 1950.

The difference between the percentage distribution of births prior to 1900 and 1950 reflects, generally speaking, the decline in the rate of increase in the number of births during the nineteenth century and the first half of this century. Decade by decade the number increased, but the percentage gains from decade to decade decreased, until the decades 1920–30 and 1930–40, when the decreasing rate of increase became an actual decrease, as the number of births in each of these decades was less than the number in the decade 1910–20.

Thus, in the period 1810–1900, the rate of increase in births was greater, and the number of births in the first 30 years of the period was relatively small, compared with the number in the last 60 years. In the period 1860–1950 the rate of increase was less, particularly in the last 60 years, and therefore the births in the first 30 years were a considerably larger proportion of the total.

The declining rate of increase in the number of births generally reflected the decline in fertility, that is, the decline in the number of children produced per woman, measured in terms of fertility ratios, crude or age-specific birth rates, or more refined measures such as gross and net fertility rates. With the exception of the depression decades, child production per woman was high enough to insure that one generation of women more than replaced themselves in the next generation, but the number of births per woman declined.

The trend in the number of births was, however, not entirely a matter of declining fertility—it was also a matter of the number of women producing children. Purely in terms of fertility, this accounts for the so-called geometric rate of population change. Given a level of fertility which insures that one generation of women will more than reproduce themselves in the next generation, then the number of child-producers in this next generation is larger, and so on *ad infinitum*. Conversely, if they fail to reproduce themselves in the next generation, the number of child-producers has decreased, and this generation will, in turn, produce fewer childbearers in the subsequent generation.

Other factors also contribute to the number of women producing children. Declines in mortality at the ages below and during the childbearing ages have the net effect of increasing the number of childbearing women. In the same way, immigration contributes to the number of childbearing

centage points to the percentage of the projected 1960 population 60 and over. Assuming no migration in both projections, the percentage 60 and over was 15.3 on the basis of observed (declining) fertility and mortality and 10.5 on the basis of no decline in fertility. Similar projections of the white population (Table 9) for the period 1890–1950 indicate a corresponding difference of 2.5 percentage points. Under the assumption of no migration, observed fertility ratios result in a percentage 60 and over of 11.6 in 1950, whereas the fertility ratios of 1900 (reflecting fertility

TABLE 9*

PERCENTAGE 60 YEARS AND OVER IN PROJECTIONS OF THE 1890 WHITE TO 1950 UNDER VARIOUS ASSUMPTIONS

Assumptions	Percentage 60 and Over, 1950
Total white population, observed 1950	12.6
Total white population assuming no migration, 1890–1950:	
Observed fertility ratios and survival rate	11.6
1900 fertility ratio and observed survival rates	9.1
1890–1900 survival rates and observed fertility ratio	11.4
Fertility ratios for native white women and observed survival rates	13.2
Foreign-born white population assuming no migration, 1890–1950:	
Fertility ratios for foreign-born white women and observed survival rates	4.6

* Source: Computed from data presented in U.S. Bureau of the Census, *1950 Census of Population*, Vol. **2**: *Characteristics of the Population*, Part I, "U.S. Summary," Table 39 (Washington, D.C.: Government Printing Office, 1952–53); Vol. **4**: *Special Reports*, Part III, Chapter A, "Nativity and Parentage," Tables 3 and 4 (Washington, D.C.: Government Printing Office, 1953); and *United States Life Tables: 1890, 1901, and 1900–1910* (Washington, D.C.: Government Printing Office, 1921).

women. Both of these factors have served to mitigate to some extent the decline in fertility in the period under consideration.

One approach to the evaluation of the effects of declining fertility on age structure is in terms of population projections under various fertility assumptions. Valaoras (1950), for example, has projected the total population of the United States in 1900–1960 on the assumption of no migration, observed survival rates, and observed fertility rates and has then repeated the projection assuming no decline in fertility. The results of the projections, as revised in the United Nations report, *The Aging of Populations and Its Economic and Social Implications* (1956), indicate that declining fertility contributed about 5 per-

in the decade 1890–1900) give a corresponding figure of 9.1. It seems reasonable to suppose, then, that declining fertility has made an appreciable contribution to the increase in the proportion of older persons.

DECLINING MORTALITY

As in the case of the number of births, the effects of declining mortality on the proportion of older population depend on the balance between the gain in the population 60 and over (or whatever age group is defined as the older population) and the gain in the remainder of the population. Clearly, declining mortality has made an appreciable contribution to the population under 60 and has thus to some degree canceled the contribution to the population 60 and over as far as the proportion of older persons is concerned.

Coale (1957) has argued cogently that, in general, the two gains tend to cancel out each other. He demonstrates that a flat percentage increase in survival rates throughout the entire age range would in no way alter an age structure—there would be more people, but the percentage age distribution would remain the same. He then points out that mortality data from most sources suggest that the net effect of gains in mortality as far as the older population is concerned is that of a uniform increase.

Elsewhere, Coale (1956) points out that the gains in infant mortality have had, from the point of view of age structure, the effect of reducing the effects of declining fertility by adding to the supply of childbearing women. Thus only when improvements in mortality at the ages above the childbearing period outweigh those below this period will mortality make an appreciable contribution to the proportion of older persons.

Reviewing the situation in the United States in this context, some pertinent evidence is as follows: the stationary life-table population of 1900 shows a percentage 60 and over of 14.4, whereas that of 1950 shows a corresponding percentage of 19.0; and it is contrasts of this type which give rise to the assumption that declining mortality has contributed to the increase in the proportion of older persons. It is already indicated, however, that evidence from life-tables is so abstract as to be somewhat misleading as an adequate explanation of actual historical trends.

The age distributions, based on the survival rates implied by the data on births and survivors and presented in Table 4, indicate an increase of about 1 percentage point in the per cent 60 and over between 1900 and 1950—from 12.6 to 13.8 per cent. These figures are, however, limited in interpreting the actual changes in the proportion 60 and over, since they are based on the assumption of equal annual complements of births in the periods prior to 1900 and 1950.

The effects of improved mortality are also implied in population projections. Among Valaoras' projections of the 1900 population to 1960 is one based on observed fertility but one assuming no improvement in mortality throughout the entire period of the projection. The revised figures (United Nations, 1956) suggest that the decline in mortality contributed an increase of about 0.4 percentage point (15.3 versus 14.9 per cent). Similar projections for the white population from 1890 to 1950 (Table 9) suggest a difference of about the same magnitude (11.6 versus 11.4 per cent).

It appears, then, that the contribution of mortality to the increase in the proportion of older persons is variable, depending on the context in which measurement is attempted. Its contribution, however, appears less than that of declining fertility.

IMMIGRATION

If the effects of immigration are defined purely in terms of the foreign-born population, it is clear that immigration has increased the proportion of older persons. In the period prior to 1900, immigration was heavily concentrated in the late part of the period, whereas in the period prior to 1950 it was concentrated in the early part of the period, with the result that persons 60 and over increased from 14.6 of the foreign-born population in 1900 to 39.1 per cent in 1950 (Table 3). If the contribution of this increase to the increase in the percentage 60 and over in the total population is calculated by computing a weighted average of the percentage 60 and over in the native population and in a foreign-born population of the same size as observed in 1950 but with the 1900 percentage 60 and over, the contribution would appear to be about 1.7 percentage points.

If, however, the effects of immigration are defined in terms of the foreign-born and their contribution in childbearing women and their descendants, the picture is by no means clear. Valaoras' projections as revised (United Nations, 1956) indicate that, in 1945, the percentage 60 and over in the population projections assuming no migration was about 1 percentage point *higher* than the percentage in the actual population. On the other hand, a similar projection of the white population from 1890 to 1950 showed the population projected in the absence of migration to have a percentage 60 and over (11.6), about 1 percentage point *lower* than the actual population (Table 9).

These results are not necessarily contradictory. The projection of the white population for 1940 showed a percentage 60 and over identical with that of the actual white population and higher percentages for 1930 and 1920. Some insight into the cycle of age structure of a foreign-born population and its descendants is provided by a projection of the foreign-born white population of 1890, assuming no further migration, observed fertility ratios for foreign-born women, and life-table survival rates (Table 9). In 1890 the percentage 60 and over (12.7) was higher than that of the total white population. The percentage for the foreign-born and their children increased decade by decade as the group aged, reaching a peak of about 14 in 1920 and then dropping to a low of about 5 in 1950. By this time, a large part of the initial population had aged and died, and the result of the high fertility of foreign-born women was clearly apparent. These results are somewhat exaggerated, because in the latter part of the period a fair proportion of the births were to the daughters of the initial population, whose fertility level was a good deal lower than that of their mothers.

There is some element of analogy between this 1890 population and the total foreign-born population. The really heavy immigration to this country occurred in the decade 1900–1910 and was supplemented in the period between the end of World War I and the passage of restrictive legislation in 1924. Thereafter, the volume of immigration remained at a relatively low level. In a very general sense, then, with a lag of several decades, the total foreign-born population, like that of 1890, is dying out; but its descendants are increasing on a large scale. The analogy, of course, breaks down in terms of the actual figures, since, if 1950 represented a peak for the total foreign-born population similar to that of 1930 for the foreign-born population of 1890, then the 1930 and 1920 percentages for the population projected without migration should have been lower rather than higher than those in the actual population. The conclusion indicated seems to be agnostic. Time variations in the volume of immigration are so erratic that the data do not lend themselves to the support of simple generalizations as to the effects of immigration on age structure.

There is one other facet of the effects of immigration on age structure. It has been pointed out that immigration contributes to the supply of childbearing women and thus increases the number of births. It has also been indicated that the fertility of foreign-born women is high. It is conceivable, then, that immigration not only increases the number of childbearing women but also raises the level of fertility and thus further increases the number of births and retards aging. A further projection of the white population of 1890, using fertility ratios for native white women rather than for all white women, tends to support this hypothesis. If there had been no migration between 1890 and 1950, and if the fertility level had been that of the native population, the percentage 60 and over in 1950 would have been 13.2 rather than the observed 12.6 (Table 9).

RELATIVE CONTRIBUTIONS

The evidence reviewed would seem to indicate that declining fertility has made a substantial contribution to the increase in the proportion of older persons, that of declining mortality a rather modest one, and that of immigration a variable one. On balance, it would seem that an analysis of the relative contributions of the three factors, in a fashion similar to the analysis of their contributions to the number of older persons, provides a convenient summary statement which has the advantage of systematic presentation and draws conclusions which are reasonably sound (Tables 7 and 8).

If the contribution of the distribution of births prior to each period is measured against the mortality level of 1900, and the

TABLE 10*

PERCENTAGE-POINT INCREASE IN PROPORTION OF POPULATION 60–89 YEARS OLD, 1900–1950 BY COMPONENTS OF INCREASE

Components of Increase	Percentage-Point Increase	Per Cent
Total increase.........	5.7	100.0
In native population........	5.0	87.7
From increase in number of births...............	4.1	71.9
From decrease in mortality.	0.6	10.5
From increase in births and decrease in mortality....	0.3	5.3
In foreign-born population...	0.7	12.3

* Source: Table 7 and H. D. Sheldon, *The Older Population of the United States* (New York: John Wiley & Sons, 1958), Appendix Tables A-2, A-3, and A-4.

contribution of declining mortality against the distribution of births prior to 1900, then, of the total percentage-point difference in the percentage 60 and over between 1900 and 1950 (5.7 percentage points), about 4.1 percentage points, or 72 per cent of the total difference, is attributable to the difference in the distribution of births; 0.6 percentage point, or 10 per cent, to declining mortality; 0.3 percentage point, or about 5 per cent, to the interaction of these two factors, and about 0.7 percentage point, or 12 per cent of the total difference, to immigration (Table 10). The contribution of immigration is represented by the percentage-point increase in the percentage-point difference between the total and the native population from 1900 to 1950.

If, as the evidence suggests, the major part of the increase in the proportion of older persons is a matter of declining fertility, then the process of the aging of the population is, as Kiser (1950) indicates, a matter of the population of reproductive age contributing progressively fewer children to the lower age levels and thus becoming, along with the population above the reproductive ages, a larger proportion of the total. He illustrates this process by referring to a percentage age pyramid—any decline in the length of the bars at the base of the pyramid means that automatically the length of the remaining bars increases. Thus, as fertility declined successively from generation to generation, the length of the bars at the base showed a relative decline, and there was a corresponding relative increase in the succeeding bars for the older ages. Thus, in a very general sense, the percentage of older persons bears a complementary relationship to the birth rate.

III. POSSIBLE FUTURE TRENDS

The future growth of the older population is a matter of concern to those interested in the problems of aging, but it is also a matter of conjecture. Such current conjectures, to be sure, are reasonably sophisticated and rounded out with a great deal of technical skill, but nevertheless they remain conjectures. That is to say, considerable progress has been made in the technique of population projections, but the projections still rest on assumptions as to future trends in fertility and mortality; in predicting these, the demographer has had no more success than the economist in anticipating future trends in the stock market, the political scientist in foretelling the future course of international events, or the meteorologist in forecasting the weather.[3]

Given, however, the situation in which estimates of the future size and age structure of our population are required, it

[3] For a discussion of the accuracy of population projections see Shryock (1954) and Hajnal (1955).

seems reasonable to suppose that informed guesses which exploit past and current knowledge and which are developed systematically provide the best available answers. Short-range projections, in which a considerable proportion of the projected population is derived from projected mortality for the population alive at the beginning of the projection period, narrow the margin of error, since it is more nearly confined to that involved in projecting mortality. It is also conceivable that recent developments in the study of cohort fertility may make it possible to stabilize, to some degree, projections of fertility in much the same way.

All this is to say that, although population projections are useful in indicating something as to the size and age structure of the population at future dates, it is a mistake to assume that any of them provide definitive answers.

A. Increase in the Number of Older and Middle-aged Persons

A good deal of the literature on aging appears to take for granted that the rapid growth of the older population in the first half of the twentieth century will continue unabated throughout the remaining half. However, the indications are that, although the older population will continue to increase, it will increase at a somewhat less rapid rate. Persons becoming 60–69 in the decade 1940–50 were the survivors of births in the decade 1880–90. In the subsequent decades, the relative increase in the number of births declined until, for the decades 1920–30 and 1930–40, the numbers of births were less than in the decade 1910–20. It seems reasonable to suppose that the growth of the older population will follow a similar course.

In 1955, it is estimated, there were approximately 21 million persons 60 and over in the continental United States (U.S. Bureau of the Census, 1957), and more than 200,000 in the offshore areas—Alaska, Hawaii, Puerto Rico, etc. (U.S. Bureau of the Census, 1952–53). Since, with the ex-

ception of future immigrants, the population from which the population 60 and over in the year 2000 will come was already in the population of 1955 (persons 15 years old and over), this number (about 116 million) provides an upper limit below which the population 60 and over in the year 2000 will fall. If it is assumed that past mortality experience, which suggests that few human beings live beyond the age of 90, is a sure guide to the general character of mortality within the next several decades, then this limit can be reduced to the population 15–44 years in 1955 (about 69 million), the population from which persons 60–89 in the year 2000 will survive.

From this point on, it becomes a matter of making explicit assumptions as to future trends in age-specific death rates. A recent set of illustrative projections has been prepared by the Division of the Actuary of the Social Security Administration under two mortality assumptions.[4] The low assumption specifies that an expectation of life at birth for females was 78.87 years

[4] Since these projections have been developed in connection with the operational needs of the social security system, they are of necessity long-range projections and work out the implications of a reasonably wide variety of combinations of fertility and mortality assumptions. As a result they present a wide and illuminating range of possibilities in the future trends in the number and proportion of older persons.

Projections prepared by the Bureau of the Census have in recent years been short-term projections on the theory that they are less subject to the error in projecting future fertility and, therefore, are of more use to the consumers of census statistics. The most recent projections (U.S. Bureau of the Census, 1958) extend only to 1980 and, for that year, show figures for the older population not essentially different from those of the Social Security Administration.

While these projections were made in consultation with the Bureau of the Census, they are based on a population different from that of the Bureau's estimate. The Bureau of the Census population is that of the continental United States and armed forces overseas, while that of the Division of the Actuary includes also Alaska, Hawaii, Puerto Rico, the Canal Zone, the Virgin Islands, certain civilians overseas, and an allowance for net census underreporting (Greville, 1957).

in the year 2000, an increase of 11.1 per cent from the 1949–51 life-tables; for males, an increase from 65.47 to 73.97 years, an increase of 13.0 per cent. It is based on an optimistic view of results of advances in medicine between 1953 and the years to 2000. This view was applied individually to various cause-of-death groups, percentage declines were determined, and the result was totaled to obtain age-sex-specific rates for all causes combined.

The high mortality assumption still allows for some gain in life-expectation at birth—about 5 per cent for males and 6 per cent for females. Here the view taken was somewhat less expansive, particularly with reference to the reduction of death rates for the diseases typical of old age (Greville, 1957).

The assumption with respect to immigration specified that the survivors of net migration would amount to 1.2 million in the period 1955–60 and to 1.0 million in each quinquennial period thereafter (Greville, 1957). This assumption illustrates the central problem of population projections. Currently, there is little reason to believe that there will be significant changes in immigration legislation, and, thus, present levels of immigration appear to be the most natural choice. It is not inconceivable, however, that within the next 10 or 15 years the whole picture may have changed and the assumed level of immigration radically altered. This possibility can be recognized, but there is no rational basis for predicting the date, the extent, or the direction of the change.

Under the low mortality assumption of the projections under consideration, the population 60 and over in the year 2000 would be about 45.9 million; under the high assumption, 39.5—a difference of from 6 to 7 million (Greville, 1957). According to these projections, then, the population 60 and over in the year 2000 might be from two to two and a half times as large as it was in 1950, whereas this population in

1950 was nearly four times as large as it had been in 1900. Use of the different assumptions does not make such a difference in the projections for the 45–59 group. Under the low mortality assumption the population 45–59 in the year 2000 would be 50.2 million; under the high assumption, 48.8 million—a difference of only about 1.4 million.

It is of some interest to note, however, that among the population projections extending to the year 2000 which have been made in the last 20 years the projected number of the age group 65 and over has steadily increased. In 1934 it was estimated at 19.3 million, whereas in the current projections of the Social Security Administration (Greville, 1957) it has jumped to a range of from 29.5 to 35.2 million.

B. *Change in the Proportion of Middle-aged and Older Persons*

If there are difficulties in projecting the number of older persons, they are relatively minor compared to projecting the total population, which is the base for determining the proportion under discussion. Immediately, the demographer is confronted with the problem of making assumptions regarding the future course of fertility, which has a greater impact than mortality on the determination of the total projected population under consideration and which, if we take past experience as a guide, is less predictable.

The major projections prepared by the Social Security Administration are based on "high" and "low" fertility assumptions. In the low assumption the age specific fertility rates represent for the period from 1955 to 1975 an interpolation decreasing from the 1950–53 level to a level of about that observed in the early 1940's. Rates for the period from 1970 to 1975 again represent a downward interpolation to a 2005–10 level, at which rates producing a gross reproduction rate of 1 are postulated; that is, if all females survived to the end of the childbearing period, they would, on the average, have one female child.

Under these assumptions the percentage of the population 60 and over would be about 17, assuming low mortality, and about 15, assuming high mortality; and the proportion of the population 45–59 would be about 18 per cent under both mortality assumptions.

In the high-fertility series, rates for 1955–60 are assumed to be 105 per cent of the 1954–55 level; those for 1970–75, to be at about the 1950–53 level; and those of 2005–10, at about the level of the early 1940's. Rates for the intervening 5-year periods were obtained by interpolation. Under this assumption the low-mortality assumption gives a percentage 60 and over in the year 2000 of 13.4; the high-mortality assumption, a percentage of 11.9— slightly under the level of 1950. In this series the percentage of the population 45–59 would be almost 15 under both mortality assumptions.

Under the "very high" fertility assumption, which assumes roughly the unabated continuance of 1954–55 fertility levels, and which results in the year 2050 in a total population of more than a billion, the percentages 60 and over in 2000 would be 11.8 and 10.5, respectively, under the "low"- and "high"-mortality assumptions. In this very high fertility series the percentage of the population aged 45–59 would be 12.9 under both mortality assumptions (Greville, 1957). As Greville indicates, it is very unlikely that the results of this projection will eventuate. This seems to be an eminently reasonable conclusion, but it illustrates the dilemma faced in making projections. A population of more than a billion in 2050 is so fantastically large that no rational human being can accept it as a possibility; therefore, fertility rates must decline between the present and that date.

The results of these various projections suggest that it is not unreasonable to assume that between 1955 and 2000 the rate of growth of the older population will not differ greatly from that of the total population. If both mortality and fertility rates are low, the older population will increase at a somewhat more rapid rate; if they are somewhat higher, it will increase at about the same or at a slightly lower rate.

C. Changes in the Age-Sex Composition

In addition to the sheer size of the older population and its relation to the total population, several other aspects of the changing age structure have considerable relevance to the problems of aging: sex differences in mortality produce sizable excesses in the number of women at the upper ages; employment problems relate not only to the age group 65 and over but also to the age group 45–64; and, finally, interest attaches to the relation between the size of the "dependent" and "productive" age groups. Data relating to these subjects are presented in Table 11.

During the course of this century it appears that the number of women will have increased at a considerably more rapid rate than the number of men. In 1900 the number of men 65 and over exceeded the number of women of the same age by about 34,000, or, in terms of the sex ratio, there were about 102 men for about 100 women. The larger number of men was in part, of course, the result of the relatively high immigration of the period, in which men predominated. By 1950, however, women 65 and over outnumbered men of the same age by about 650,000, and the sex ratio had dropped to 90. In terms of either low or high fertility or mortality the projections indicate for the year 2000 an excess of women of at least 4.7 million and a sex ratio of at most 76 (Table 11).

The percentage of the population 65 and over rose from about 4.0 to 7.9 between 1900 and 1950. The projections suggest that by 2000 it might range between 9 and 13 per cent. From 1900 to 1950 the age group 45–64 as a proportion of the total population increased from about 14 to about 20 per cent. In 2000, under high-mortality and high-fertility conditions, this percentage would be 17.7, but 22.4 under low assumptions. The age group 20–44 showed little change between 1900 and 1950, and the projections suggest a continuation of this trend.

The ratio of persons in the "dependent" ages (under 20 and 65 and over) to persons in the "productive" ages (20–64 years) dropped sharply from 1900 to 1950. This net result was effected by an increase in the ratio for persons 65 and over, which was more than compensated for by a substantial drop in the ratio for persons under

TABLE 11*

TRENDS IN AGE STRUCTURE, 1900–2000†

(In Thousands)

SUBJECT	1900	1950	2000 (PROJECTIONS)	
			"High" Fertility and Mortality	"Low" Fertility and Mortality
Population, 65 and over	3,124	12,308	29,490	35,198
Male	1,579	5,827	12,008	15,209
Female	1,545	6,481	17,482	19,989
Excess of females over males	−34	654	5,474	4,780
Sex ratio	1,022	899	687	761
Percentage distribution by age:				
Total	100.0	100.0	100.0	100.0
Under 20	44.4	34.5	37.0	30.0
20–44	37.9	37.5	36.4	34.7
45–64	13.7	20.1	17.7	22.4
65 and over	4.0	7.9	8.9	12.9
Percentage of persons 20–64 years old:				
Under 20	86.1	60.0	68.5	52.6
65 and over	7.8	13.8	16.4	22.7
Under 20 plus 65 and over	93.9	73.8	84.9	75.3

* Source: T. N. E. Greville, *Illustrative United States Population Projections* ("Actuarial Study," No. 46 [Washington, D.C.: U.S. Department of Health, Education, and Welfare, Social Security Administration, Division of the Actuary, 1957]), derived from Tables 8, 10-I, 10-IV, 11-I, 11-IV, 12 and 13.

† Figures are for the United States and its offshore areas and therefore will not agree exactly with census figures for continental United States.

20. The projections suggest that the over-all ratio may have increased by the year 2000—a small increase under the low assumptions and a larger increase under the high assumptions. In general, changes in the total ratio have been more affected by relative change in the number of persons under 20, simply because they have constituted the larger portion of the total for the dependent ages. At fertility levels under which a population was not reproducing itself the older population would carry a greater weight in this ratio.

As indicated in the note to Table 11, the figures used in this analysis purport to cover the population of the United States and its offshore areas and thus, for 1900 and 1950, differ slightly from the census figures for the continental United States. This, of course, would also be true in connection with projections which cover only the continental United States. It is extremely doubtful, however, that projections of this type would lead to conclusions materially different from those drawn from Table 11.

Generally speaking, an examination of the projected populations leads to no startling conclusion as to changes in age structure in the remainder of this century. The older population will increase in size but, the indications are, at about the same or only a slightly higher rate than the total population. The projections do not suggest startling changes in the relative size of the age group 45–64 or in the dependency ratios. The clearest indication of the intensification of an already-acute problem is the sharp increase in the number of older women relative to the number of older men.

IV. GEOGRAPHIC DIFFERENCES

A. Introduction

The concentration of older persons varies considerably among the component areas of the United States. In 1950 the proportion of the population 60 and over in the state with the highest percentage was about twice that of the state with the lowest percentage (Table 15). Among counties, the percentage 65 and over ranged from less than 1.0 to about 20 per cent. Among standard metropolitan areas the range was less striking—from about 4 to 12 per cent.

In addition to the variation among specific political areas, there was also variation among general types of areas. The percentage of older persons in the rural-farm population tended to be lower than the percentages in the urban and rural-non-farm populations. Among cities and towns the highest proportions of older persons tended to occur in small villages, and the concentration of older persons tended to be higher in central cities than in new suburban areas (Sheldon, 1958).

It is proposed here to examine some of these differences and the circumstances under which they have arisen.

B. Urban-Rural Differences

Since in the past there have been appreciable differences in the urban and rural way of life and since the role of older persons in these situations has been assumed to be similarly different, some interest attaches to differences in the concentration of older persons in the urban, the rural-non-farm, and the rural-farm populations.

AT THE NATIONAL LEVEL

Between the Census of 1920, when the urban-rural classification under consideration was established, and that of 1940, the highest percentages 65 and over were found in the rural–non-farm population, and the percentages for the urban and rural-farm populations were not essentially different. The over-all differences between the urban and rural proportions of older persons were not large—at no time did the maximum difference between lowest and highest exceed 1.7 percentage points (Table 12).

In 1950, according to the "old" rural-urban definition, that is, the one used between 1920 and 1940, the percentage 65 and over for the urban population was higher than that for the rural–non-farm

population. According to the "new" urban-rural definition, however, the rural–non-farm population had the highest percentage.

The explanation of this difference lies in the heterogeneous character of the rural–non-farm population and in the character of the change in definition. Under the old definition, disregarding special rules affecting only a minor segment of the total pop-

TABLE 12*

PERSONS 45–64 YEARS AND 65 YEARS AND OVER AS PERCENTAGE OF TOTAL POPULATION, BY URBAN AND RURAL RESIDENCE, 1950

Age and Year	United States	Urban	Rural Non-Farm	Rural Farm
	Persons 45–64 Years Old			
New definition, 1950.	20.3	21.4	17.6	19.4
Old urban definition:				
1950.	20.3	21.8	17.5	19.4
1940.	19.8	21.2	17.8	18.3
1930.	17.4	18.1	16.8	16.4
1920.	16.1	17.0	15.9	14.7
	Persons 65 Years and Over			
New definition, 1950.	8.1	8.1	8.6	7.6
Old urban definition:				
1950.	8.1	8.3	8.0	7.6
1940.	6.8	6.8	7.3	6.6
1930.	5.4	5.1	6.6	5.1
1920.	4.7	4.3	6.0	4.4

* Source: U.S. Bureau of the Census, *1950 Census of Population*, Vol. **2**: *Characteristics of the Population*, Part I, "U.S. Summary" (Washington, D.C.: Government Printing Office, 1952–53), Table 38, and *1940 Census of Population*, Vol. **2**: *Characteristics of the Population*, Part I, "U.S. Summary" (Washington, D.C.: Government Printing Office, 1953), Tables 7 and 9.

ulation, the urban population was defined as the population of incorporated places of 2500 inhabitants or more, and the remainder of the population was rural. The rural population was in turn split into the population living on farms (the rural-farm population) and the residue (the rural–non-farm population).

In this latter category there were three rather discrete but not separately identified segments: the population of small villages, the population in open country not living on farms, and the population living in unincorporated areas on the outskirts of urban places. The village population contained a high percentage of older persons; the other two elements had relatively low percentages.

During the decade 1940–50 the rapid growth of suburban population, which in its earlier stages is a young population, increased the weight of this element in the rural–non-farm population sufficiently to retard the increase in the proportion of older persons in this segment of the population. Whereas, under the old definition, the urban and rural-farm percentage increased by 1.5 and 1.0 percentage points, respectively, the increase for the rural–non-farm population was only 0.7 percentage point.

The change to the new urban-rural definition in 1950 involved the shift of persons living in unincorporated territory on the outskirts of cities of 50,000 or more from the rural to the urban category. This shift involved a population of approximately 7 million, in which the proportion aged 65 and over was about 5 per cent (Sheldon, 1958). This change was sufficient to restore the rural–non-farm population as the segment of the population with the highest concentration of older persons.

In contrast to the older population, persons in the middle years—45–64—showed the highest concentration in the urban population, and, with the exception of 1930, the lowest concentration in the rural–non-farm population. Their relative distribution was not appreciably affected by the 1950 change in the urban-rural definition. As in the case of the older population, the differences in the proportion of middle-aged persons and the type-of-residence categories were not large.

AMONG THE STATES

The general pattern in the proportion of older persons by urban-rural residence according to the new urban definition in 1950 did not occur consistently among the states. The national pattern did occur in a considerable number of states in the Middle West, but in the South Atlantic Division the percentage 65 and over was highest in the rural-farm population; in the Mountain and Pacific divisions the typical state had the highest proportion of older persons in urban areas (Sheldon, 1958). This situation suggests that there is nothing inevitable about the pattern at the national level and that in the individual states the ranking of the three segments of the population with respect to the proportion of older persons arises in response to peculiar local conditions.

C. Differences by Size of Place

AT THE NATIONAL LEVEL

In general terms, there appears to be a negative relationship between size of place and the proportion of the population at the upper age levels. Thus, with the exception of the largest size class of urbanized areas, which comprises New York, Chicago, and Los Angeles, there was a steady increase in the percentage 65 and over from urbanized areas of 1–3 million to incorporated places of less than 1000. The population outside the places identified in the census (roughly the open country) had a lower proportion of persons 65 and over than places of any size class, and the largest urbanized areas fell in the middle range of the size class continuum (Table 13).

These data clearly support the generalization that the village component of the rural–non-farm population contains a high concentration of older persons and that in the open-country component the concentration is low. This element contains the major proportion of the rural-farm population but also a large non-farm population, and the difference in the proportion of older persons is low (Sheldon, 1958).

Again, in contrast to the pattern for the older population, there is a general positive relationship between size of place and the proportion of the population which is middle-aged. This positive relationship holds for all places, both in and outside urbanized areas, except for the incorporated places of less than 1000, where a relatively high percentage (45–64) is found. As in the case of the older population, the lowest percentage is in the open country.

BY REGIONS

Although the pattern by regions is somewhat variable, and not all regional distributions conform exactly to that observed at the national level, the pattern is generally the same. The percentage 65 and over is lowest in the open-country segment of the population and highest in small villages, and, with some exceptions, this percentage increases as size of place declines. A part of the irregularity arises from the fact that, in the larger size classes in some regions, the class is represented by a very small number of cases. In the West, for example, the difference between urbanized areas of 3 million or more and 1–3 million is the difference between the Los Angeles and the San Francisco–Oakland Urbanized Areas (Sheldon, 1958).

TABLE 13*

PERSONS 45–60 YEARS AND PERSONS 65 YEARS AND OVER AS PERCENTAGE OF
TOTAL POPULATION, BY SIZE OF PLACE AND REGION, 1950

Age and Size of Place	United States	North-east	North Central	South	West
	Percentage 45-64 Years				
All areas............................	20.2	22.3	21.4	17.4	20.1
In urbanized areas:					
Areas of 3,000,000 or more..............	23.6	24.0	23.3	....	22.5
Areas of 1,000,000–3,000,000..............	21.9	21.9	23.0	20.0	21.6
Areas of 250,000–1,000,000..............	21.2	22.9	22.3	19.3	21.7
Areas of less than 250,000...............	20.5	22.6	21.0	18.6	19.1
Outside urbanized areas:					
Places of 25,000 or more..................	20.1	22.2	21.1	18.0	19.9
Places of 10,000–25,000..................	19.7	22.1	20.7	17.7	19.0
Places of 2500–10,000	19.3	21.4	20.7	17.6	18.1
Places of 1000–2500.....................	19.3	20.6	20.7	17.6	18.8
Incorporated places of less than 1000......	20.7	20.8	21.7	19.4	19.1
Other rural territory....................	17.8	19.7	19.9	15.9	18.4
	Percentage 65 Years and Over				
All areas............................	8.1	8.8	8.9	6.9	8.2
In urbanized areas:					
Areas of 3,000,000 or more..............	7.9	7.7	7.3	....	9.1
Areas of 1,000,000–3,000,000..............	7.6	8.6	6.7	6.4	8.2
Areas of 250,000–1,000,000..............	7.8	8.7	8.3	6.5	9.2
Areas of less than 250,000...............	8.0	9.2	8.5	6.5	8.4
Outside urbanized areas:					
Places of 25,000 or more..................	8.5	10.3	9.2	6.7	8.5
Places of 10,000–25,000..................	8.8	9.9	10.2	7.1	8.3
Places of 2500–10,000....................	9.2	10.3	11.4	7.5	8.0
Places of 1000–2500.....................	10.3	10.5	12.9	8.3	8.5
Incorporated places of less than 1000......	13.5	12.0	15.7	11.3	9.6
Other rural territory....................	7.4	9.0	8.1	6.6	6.6

* Source: U.S. Bureau of the Census, *1950 Census of Population*, Vol. 4: *Special Reports*, Part V, Chapter A, "Characteristics by Size of Place," Tables 1 and 6.

D. Urban-Suburban Differences

INTRODUCTION

As noted in the discussion of urban-rural differences in the proportion of older persons in 1950, the population of thickly settled unincorporated territories adjacent to cities of 50,000 or more—roughly the suburban population—had a low percentage 65 and over. If this population may be defined as the suburban population, then it

TABLE 14*

PERCENTAGE 65 YEARS AND OVER IN SUBURBS, CLASSIFIED BY PERIOD IN WHICH 50 PER CENT OR MORE OF TOTAL DWELLING UNITS WERE BUILT, FOR SELECTED URBANIZED AREAS, 1950

Component of Urbanized Area and Age of Suburb	New York-Northeastern New Jersey	Chicago	Los Angeles
Total urbanized area	7.6	7.3	9.1
Central cities..........	7.6	7.6	9.6
Suburbs†...............	8.0	6.6	9.8
50 per cent or more of dwelling units built:			
1940–50............	5.1	3.8	5.9
1930–50............	6.1	5.5	10.3
1920–50............	8.0	6.6	13.5
Before 1920........	8.5	8.5	.....
Remainder of area......	6.2	5.2	6.7

* Source: H. D. Sheldon, *The Older Population of the United States* (New York: John Wiley & Sons, 1958), Appendix Table B-8.

    † Places of 2500 or more in urban fringe.

appears that the population of suburbs is a younger population than that of the central cities which they surround.

Another approach to the definition of suburban population is in terms of the urban fringe which, in addition to the territory just described, includes incorporated places adjacent to the central cities of 50,000 or more. Here, for all urbanized areas, the percentage 65 and over was 8.2 for central cities but 7.1 for the urban fringe. In urbanized areas of 3 million or more the corresponding percentages were 8.0 and 7.7, and the difference tended to

increase as the size of the urbanized area decreased (Sheldon, 1958). The differences generally, however, were small compared to the difference between central cities and unincorporated territory. This observation suggests that, in the aggregate, the age level for the incorporated place in the urban fringe is higher than that for the unincorporated territory, although there may be considerable variability in age structure from suburb to suburb.

"OLD" AND "NEW" SUBURBS

An examination of the data on this point from the 1950 Census suggested that some variability did exist and that there appeared to be a positive relationship between the age of the suburb and the age of its population. For example, in Park Forest, Illinois, a suburb of Chicago which was "mass produced" in the decade 1940–50, the percentage 65 and over was 0.8 as compared with 7.6 for the city of Chicago itself. On the other hand, for Forest Park, another suburb—first recognized in the 1880 Census with a population of 923—the percentage 65 and over in 1950 was 10.6 (Sheldon, 1958).

In order to provide a more systematic observation on this issue, an index of the age of suburbs was developed from housing statistics on the year in which dwelling units were built. The suburbs (defined as incorporated places of 2500 or more) in the urban fringe of the New York–Northeastern New Jersey, the Chicago, and the Los Angeles Urbanized Areas were classified by this index, and the percentage 65 and over in each class was computed. The results of this procedure are presented in Table 14.

These results indicate that in each of the urbanized areas there is a gradient in the direction expected. The proportion of older persons is relatively low in "new" suburbs and increases as "age" of suburb increases. The range among the suburbs spans the proportion for the central city in each area. In the New York–Northeastern New Jersey Area and in the Los Angeles Area the aggregate percentage 65 and over in the suburbs was higher than that of the central city, but it was lower in the Chicago Area. The percentages for the remainder of the urban fringe were low but not so low as the "newest" suburbs.

The differences by "age" class, however, were not large; they were fittingly greatest in the Los Angeles Area. There was also a considerable amount of overlap between the members of the classes. If this analysis had been made in terms of smaller, more homogeneous areas, such as census tracts, the relationship might conceivably have been more dramatic. An examination of the relationship between median year built and percentage 65 and over in the Los Angeles tracted area indicates a reasonably high positive relationship between the two variables, not only in the entire area, but in the city itself and in larger suburbs such as Pasadena and Long Beach.

IN-MIGRATION AND SUBURBAN AGE STRUCTURE

A rough hypothesis which would serve to interpret the data on urban and suburban age structure might be something as follows: The population of central cities is constantly supplemented by the in-migration of young adults who, in the course of time, marry and have families. At this point many of them move and settle down in subdivisions adjacent to the central city. A "new" suburb, then, is an area in which such settlement has been made within the last one or two decades—such as, for example, Park Forest. If it can be assumed further that a majority of these families remain in the areas throughout their lifetime, then, as time passes, the area becomes an "old" suburb, and the population becomes an "old" population.

The assumption that all families that move to the suburbs remain there permanently is untenable in any categorical sense, but the data seem to suggest that the net effect of aging and migration op-erating over time produces an age structure consistent with the hypothesis.

Some limited examination of the role of migration in this context is enlightening. The total population expected in 1950 on the basis of the 1930 population and no migration was calculated for the suburbs of the Los Angeles Urbanized Area. As befitting this area, there was no evidence of net out-migration in any suburb—in every case the observed 1950 population was greater than that expected in the absence of migration. It was then possible to compare the observed percentage 65 and over with that expected and obtain a measure in terms of percentage point change of the effects of in-migration. In 25 out of the 34 suburbs examined, it appeared that in-migration had the expected effect of reducing the percentage 65 and over below expectation. Arcadia is perhaps the outstanding example. The percentage 65 and over in 1930 was 8.7. The percentage expected in 1950 was 15.2, but the observed percentage was 9.4; thus net in-migration in the period 1930–50 served to keep the proportion of older population at an approximately constant level through the two decades (Sheldon, 1958).

On the other hand, in a minority of the suburbs examined, net in-migration appears to have raised the percentage of older persons above expectation. Thus in Pasadena net in-migration appears to have raised the percentage 65 and over by 1.0 percentage point in the two decades; in Covina, by 2.0 percentage points. These findings suggest that the effects of in-migration are not necessarily uniform, and the possibility that in the case of suburbs of this type it is selective with respect to age. In other words, certain communities are especially attractive to older persons.

E. State Differences

Among the states in 1950 the percentage 60 and over ranged from 15.4 in New Hampshire to 7.5 in New Mexico (Table 15). Superficially, it might be expected

TABLE 15*

PERCENTAGE 60 YEARS AND OVER, OBSERVED AND EXPECTED, 1950, AND MIGRATION RATES, BY LIFE-EXPECTATION AND FERTILITY RATIO, FOR STATES

FERTILITY RATIO: UNDER 36‡

Expectation of Life, 1930†	State	Percentage 60 and Over — Observed	Percentage 60 and Over — Expected‖	Migration Rate§ 1890–1920	Migration Rate§ 1920–50
62 and over	Ore.	13.2	14.9	62	40
58–61	N.H.	15.4	13.5	5	−2
58–61	Mass.	14.7	15.0	28	−2
58–61	Conn.	13.4	13.9	31	11
58–61	R.I.	13.3	14.4	26	2
58–61	Ill.	13.3	13.9	15	5
58–61	N.Y.	13.1	15.7	26	12
58–61	Calif.	12.7	17.0	102	96
58–61	N.J.	12.6	13.9	38	15
58–61	D.C.	10.8	21.9	65	49

FERTILITY RATIO: 36–41‡

Expectation of Life, 1930†	State	Percentage 60 and Over — Observed	Percentage 60 and Over — Expected‖	Migration Rate§ 1890–1920	Migration Rate§ 1920–50
62 and over	Iowa	15.0	12.9	−8	−14
62 and over	Kan.	14.7	12.7	−10	−15
62 and over	Wis.	13.5	11.5	5	−3
62 and over	Wash.	13.3	14.5	98	30
58–61	Mo.	14.9	12.9	−9	−7
58–61	Vt.	14.7	11.8	−6	−14
58–61	Me.	14.4	12.0	1	−8
58–61	Ind.	13.4	12.7		2
58–61	Ohio	13.3	11.9	16	4
58–61	Pa.	12.8	11.9	9	9
58–61	Del.	12.3	12.6	3	9
58–61	Mich.	11.2	11.9	21	15
54–57	Colo.	12.8	12.5	38	1
54–57	Nev.	10.7	13.8	43	45
54–57	Md.	10.5	11.9	3	15

FERTILITY RATIO: 42–47‡

Expectation of Life, 1930†	State	Percentage 60 and Over — Observed	Percentage 60 and Over — Expected‖	Migration Rate§ 1890–1920	Migration Rate§ 1920–50
62 and over	Neb.	14.5	12.2	−14	−21
62 and over	Minn.	13.5	11.5	13	−7
58–61	Mont.	13.3	10.8	88	−19
58–61	Ky.	11.5	8.5	−15	−17
58–61	Tenn.	10.4	8.6	−14	−7
58–61	Wyo.	9.9	10.2	60	2
54–57	Fla.	12.5	9.2	33	65
54–57	Tex.	9.9	8.5	9	4
54–57	La.	9.6	7.7	−3	−5
54–57	Va.	9.6	8.0	−8	−2

FERTILITY RATIO: 48 AND OVER‡

Expectation of Life, 1930†	State	Percentage 60 and Over — Observed	Percentage 60 and Over — Expected‖	Migration Rate§ 1890–1920	Migration Rate§ 1920–50
62 and over	S.D.	12.8	9.9	10	−26
62 and over	Okla.	12.5	8.9	116	−24
62 and over	N.D.	11.6	8.4	32	−32
62 and over	Idaho	11.2	8.9	77	−9
58–61	Ark.	11.3	7.2	−10	−25
58–61	W.Va.	10.2	7.7	4	−14
58–61	Utah	9.3	7.5	9	7
54–57	Miss.	10.0	6.5	−14	−20
54–57	Ala.	9.4	6.9	−8	−16
54–57	Ga.	9.3	7.2	−7	−18
54–57	N.C.	8.3	6.5	9	−7
Under 54	Ariz.	9.1	9.1	127	35
Under 54	S.C.	8.0	5.6	−13	−20
Under 54	N.M.	7.5	7.0	16	1

* Source: H. D. Sheldon, *The Older Population of the United States* (New York: John Wiley & Sons, 1958), Appendix Tables B-1 to B-5.

† Weighted mean of sex-color groups. State values for the non-white population estimated by applying the ratio of non-white to white values at the national level to the observed state values for the white population.

‡ Mean ratio, children under 5 years per 100 women 15–49 years old, 1900–1950.

§ Aggregate net migration of population 10 years old and over for indicated three-decade periods expressed as a percentage of expected population at end of period, that is, the difference between the observed (or actual) population and the aggregate net migration.

‖ Percentage 60 and over expected on the assumption of no migration between 1890 and 1950.

that states with low fertility and mortality would have high proportions of older persons in their populations. In a general way, this relationship appears to hold, particularly for carefully selected states; thus the percentages 60 and over in Arizona, New Mexico, and South Carolina are relatively low, and those in Iowa, Kansas, and Massachusetts are relatively high. If, however, the attempt is made to account for all states in this framework, by no means do all of them fall neatly into place. This lack of expected correspondence between age structure and fertility and mortality levels can be attributed to the effects of migration, which has materially altered the age structure of many states from expectation on the basis of a knowledge of trends in fertility and mortality.

The materials presented in Table 15 provide a basis for some examination of the separate effects of past trends in migration, fertility, and mortality. In this table there are sixteen fertility-mortality level categories into which the state may be classified—four categories based on the mean fertility ratio, 1900–1950, cross-classified by four categories based on life-expectation in 1930. There were three of the major cells into which no states fell; that is, there were no states in the lowest life-expectation class except at the highest fertility level.

Within each major cell, figures are presented for each state on the observed percentage 60 and over in 1950, the expected percentage 60 and over assuming no migration between 1890 and 1950, and net in-migration rates for the periods 1890–1920 and 1920–50. A comparison, then, of the observed and expected percentages gives some indication of the effects of migration, and an examination of the expected percentages gives a somewhat clearer picture of the effects of trends in mortality and fertility uncomplicated by migration (Sheldon, 1958).

MIGRATION

The comparison of the expected and observed percentages 60 and over indicates not only the effects of the initial migration but also the effects of natural increase among members of the migrant population. Thus in a state with a consistent pattern of in-migration the difference indicates the impact of the initial migrants plus their descendants, and in a state with a consistent pattern of out-migration it indicates the impact of the loss of the initial migrants plus their potential descendants. In these terms the effects of migration on age structure among the states appear to be as follows.

States with consistent in-migration: 1890–1950.—In general, in-migration appears to have lowered the percentage 60 and over in states for which there was a consistent pattern of in-migration during the six decades between 1890 and 1950. The Pacific Coast states of Oregon, Washington, and California are notable examples. On the Eastern Seaboard, in those states in which a reasonably high proportion of the in-migrants were immigrants from abroad—Massachusetts, Rhode Island, Connecticut, New York, and New Jersey—there still appeared to be some reduction of the percentage 60 and over as the result of in-migration.

States with consistent out-migration: 1890–1950.—These states showed appreciable gains in the proportion of older persons as the result of out-migration. Thus, in the middle western states such as Iowa, Kansas, Missouri, and Nebraska, which were among the states with the highest observed percentages 60 and over in 1950, the expected percentages were, on the average, about 2 percentage points lower than the observed percentages. Likewise, at the other end of the fertility-mortality scale, in states such as Mississippi, Alabama, Georgia, and North Carolina, out-migration appeared to have raised appreciably the proportion of older persons.

In-migration and out-migration: 1890–1950.—In a number of states such as Montana, the Dakotas, Oklahoma, and Idaho, there was relatively heavy in-migration between 1890 and 1920 but extensive out-migration between 1920 and 1950.

This pattern appears to have increased the observed percentage above expectation by appreciable amounts.

California and Florida.—The growth of the older population in both of these states has frequently been discussed in the context of the migration of older persons. The present analysis would seem to indicate that Florida is a genuine case of the in-migration of older persons but that California is not.

According to the present estimates, the population of California in 1950, if there had been no migration since 1890, would have been about 1.5 million rather than 10.5 million and the percentage 60 and over would have been about 17 rather than 12. In 1950 there were perhaps about a million in-migrants 60 years old and over in California. Estimates of net migration indicate that about 25 per cent of these persons had entered California during the decade 1940–50 at ages which would make them 60 and over in 1950.

In Florida, in contrast, the estimates indicate that the heavy in-migration into Florida had the net effect of raising the percentage 60 and over by about 3 percentage points. To be sure, without the in-migration the total population would have been substantially smaller, but the percentage would have been lower. Of the in-migrants 60 and over in Florida in 1950, about 100,000, or 45 per cent, had come into Florida in the previous decade (Sheldon, 1958).

The case of Florida illustrates the fact that no universal generalization can be made about the effects of migration. The generalization that in-migration depresses the growth of the percentage of older persons and that out-migration accelerates it is based primarily on the assumption that migrants are heavily concentrated in the young adult ages. Data on net migration for states (Lee *et al.*, 1957) tend to support this assumption generally, but in the case of Florida the age level is appreciably higher. It is possible, then, that a sufficient proportion of the in-migrants to Florida

enter the state at ages above the reproductive period and therefore do not contribute enough children to the population to counterbalance their own aging.

FERTILITY

An examination of the expected percentage 60 and over among the several fertility classes suggests a general decline in the proportion of older persons as the fertility ratios increased (Table 15). A perfect correlation is not to be expected here because fertility classification is relatively crude, as is the method of projection, and, since it extends only over a 60-year period, it is affected by anomalies in the age and sex distributions of the 1890 population.

MORTALITY

There appears to be even less relationship between mortality levels and the proportion of older persons. In the two higher fertility classes there is a suggestion of a decline in the proportion of older persons as the expectation of life declines.

A comparison of New Mexico and North Dakota is of interest in this connection. New Mexico had one of the lowest life-expectations at birth and North Dakota one of the highest. The mean fertility ratio in both states was the same. In terms of the observed percentages 60 and over the proportion for North Dakota exceeded that for New Mexico by 4.1 percentage points. In terms of the expected population this difference dropped to 1.4. If the survival rates for New Mexico are applied to North Dakota, the percentage 60 and over decreases by 0.8 percentage point, and, if the North Dakota rates are applied to New Mexico, the percentage rises by a like amount (Sheldon, 1958). This difference is of about the same level of magnitude as that obtained at the national level in using projections to isolate the effects of mortality.

F. County Differences

In 1950, of the 3103 counties or county equivalents in the United States, there were 45 in which the percentage 65 and over was 15 or greater. This percentage appears to be a sort of average upper limit, since, of the 45, in only 16 was the percentage 65 and over greater than 15, and for a majority of the counties in this latter group the percentage was 16 (Table 16).

In some of the counties the explanation of the high proportion of older persons is specific and obvious. For example, St. Pe-

percentage 65 and over drops from 16.1 to 11.5 (U.S. Bureau of the Census, 1952–53, 1953).

Of the remaining 14 counties, all but 3 were located in Missouri. Missouri was one of the states in which out-migration materially increased the percentage 60 and over, and it is possible that the counties in question illustrate this process at the county level. The counties with 15 per cent

TABLE 16*

CHARACTERISTICS OF COUNTIES WITH 16 PER CENT OR MORE OF POPULATION 65 YEARS OR OVER, 1950

State and County	Percentage 65 and Over	Total Population	Per Cent Change, 1940–50	Per Cent Rural	Institutional Population
Florida:					
Osceola........	21.6	11,406	12.7	35.9	32
Pinellas........	18.8	159,249	73.4	13.5	1,239
Iowa:					
Van Buren.....	16.0	11,007	− 8.7	100.0	63
Missouri:					
Caldwell.......	17.3	9,929	−14.6	100.0	10
Cedar.........	16.1	10,663	− 8.8	75.4	23
Clinton........	16.7	11,726	−11.6	70.6	35
De Kalb.......	16.6	8,047	−17.5	98.5	23
Grundy........	16.1	13,220	−15.9	53.4	17
Macon.........	16.9	18,332	−14.3	77.4	255
Monroe........	16.2	11,314	−14.3	100.0	36
Montgomery....	16.8	11,555	− 7.1	100.0	31
Schuyler.......	17.5	5,760	−13.1	100.0	10
Scotland.......	16.2	7,332	−14.3	100.0	21
Shelby.........	19.3	9,730	−13.3	100.0	53
Nevada:					
Esmeralda......	17.1	614	−60.5	100.0	3
New York:					
Seneca.........	16.1	29,253	13.7	62.2	3,992

* Source: U.S. Bureau of the Census, *1950 Census of Population*, Vol. 2: *Characteristics of the Population* (Washington, D.C.: Government Printing Office, 1952–53), Parts 10, 15, 25, 28, and 32, Tables 12 and 42.

tersburg is located in Pinellas County, Florida, and here it would seem unequivocal that the heavy concentration of older persons is the direct result of in-migration. Seneca County, New York, is a relatively small county for New York State, and Willard State Hospital is located in it. The population of this hospital for mental disease (slightly less than 4000) is heavily weighted with older persons, and thus the high percentage is explained by the presence of the institution in the area. If the institutional population is removed, the

or more of the population 65 and over were again heavily concentrated in Missouri, with appreciable numbers in Iowa and Kansas, neighboring states in which the same phenomena were observed.

Thirteen of these 16 counties lost population between 1940 and 1950, and, in turn, in all but 3 of these the decline was greater than 10 per cent. In the United States as a whole 708 counties, or about 23 per cent, had losses of this magnitude (U.S. Bureau of the Census, 1952–53). The counties in question, then, are not unique in losing population, but it is reasonable to suppose that the counties with high proportions of older persons are likely to be found among those with declining population.

In 1950 the median size of counties in the United States was 19,837. All the 13 counties which lost population fell below this level, but they obviously were not uniquely small counties. In 1950, 36 per cent of the population of the country as a whole was rural. Among the counties in question the percentage was considerably higher. An examination of the data on places or villages in these counties indicated that the proportion of older population was higher in the villages than in the counties as a whole (U.S. Bureau of the Census, 1952–53). Thus they were essentially rural counties but still clearly displayed the differences by size of place observed at the national level.

Thus, with the exception of those counties where unique and specifiable situations accounted for the high percentage 65 and over, the counties with the greatest proportion of their population 65 and over are small, predominantly rural counties in which population is decreasing. What distinguishes these counties from other counties of the same description is not clear. It seems not improbable, however, that the difference lies in the past history of out-migration.

G. Implications of Area Differences

A high concentration of older population in an area is one descriptive facet of the population of the area and may well be a basis for inferences as to the character of the population of the area. A state with a high proportion of older persons may be one in which there has been a long history of out-migration, such as Missouri, or a history of specialized in-migration, such as Florida. A census tract with a high proportion of older persons may be one of relatively old housing and genteel decay, or a high concentration of the elderly in a small rural town may be the basis for develop-ing a reasonably adequate description of the social structure of the town.

This reasoning, however, is not necessarily reversible. Neither all nor most of the older population of the country lives in states from which there has been out-migration over a number of decades. Similarly, among the census tracts of a city, only a relatively small proportion of the older population lives in tracts in which the proportion of older persons is high— the great majority of them live in tracts in which the proportion of older persons is about that of the area as a whole. It follows, then, that the characteristics of areas in which the proportions of older persons are high rarely are descriptive of the conditions under which the modal group of older persons live.

REFERENCES

COALE, A. J. 1955. The population of the United States in 1950 classified by age, sex, and color—a revision of census figures. J. Am. Stat. A., **50**, 16–54.

———. 1956. The effects of changes in mortality and fertility on age composition. Milbank Mem. Fund Quart., **34**, 79–114.

———. 1957. How the age distribution of a human population is determined. Cold Spring Harbor Symposia on Quantitative Biology, **22**, 83–89.

GREVILLE, T. N. E. 1957. Illustrative United States population projections. ("Actuarial Study," No. 46.) Washington, D.C.: U.S. Department of Health, Education, and Welfare, Social Security Administration, Division of the Actuary.

HAJNAL, J. 1955. The prospects for population forecasts. J. Am. Stat. A., **50**, 309–22.

JACOBSON, P. H. 1957. An estimate of the expectation of life in the United States in 1850. Milbank Mem. Fund Quart., **35**, 197–201.

JAFFE, A. J., and LOURIE, W. I., JR. 1942. An abridged life table for the white population of the United States in 1830. Human Biol., **14**, 352–71.

KENNEDY, J. C. G. 1853. The Seventh Census: report of the Superintendent of the Census for December 1, 1852. Washington, D.C.: Government Printing Office.

KISER, C. V. 1950. The demographic background of our aging population. *In* The social and biological challenge of our aging population: proceedings of the Eastern States Health Education Conference, March 31–April 1, 1949, pp. 44–66. New York: Columbia University Press.

LEE, E. S., MILLER, A. R., BRAINERD, C. P., and EASTERLIN, R. A. 1957. Population redistribution and economic growth: United States, 1870–1950, Vol. 1: Methodological considerations and reference tables. Philadelphia: American Philosophical Society.

MEECH, L. W. 1898. System and tables of life insurance. New York: Spectator Co.

SHELDON, H. D. 1958. The older population of the United States. New York: John Wiley & Sons.

SHRYOCK, H. S. 1954. Accuracy of population projections for the United States. Estadistica, J. Inter. Am. Stat. Inst., 12, 578–98.

TAEUBER, C., and TAEUBER, IRENE B. 1958. The changing population of the United States. New York: John Wiley & Sons.

THOMPSON, W. S., and WHELPTON, P. K. 1933. Population trends in the United States. New York: McGraw-Hill Book Co.

UNITED NATIONS. 1956. DEPARTMENT OF ECONOMIC AND SOCIAL AFFAIRS. The aging of populations and its economic and social implications. ("Population Studies," No. 26.) New York: United Nations.

U.S. BUREAU OF THE CENSUS. 1921. United States life tables: 1890, 1901, and 1900–1901. Washington, D.C.: Government Printing Office.

———. 1952–53. 1950 census of population, Vol. 2: Characteristics of the population. Washington, D.C.: Government Printing Office.

———. 1953. 1950 census of population, Vol. 4: Special reports, Part II, Chapter C, Institutional population. Washington, D.C.: Government Printing Office.

———. 1954. Current population reports: population estimates. (Series P-25, No. 98.) Washington, D.C.: The Bureau.

———. 1957. Current population reports: population estimates. (Series P-25, No. 170.) Washington, D.C.: The Bureau.

———. 1958. Current population reports: population estimates. (Series P-25, No. 187.) Washington, D.C.: The Bureau.

U.S. NATIONAL OFFICE OF VITAL STATISTICS. 1954a. Vital statistics of the United States: 1950, Vol. 1: Analysis and summary tables with supplemental tables for Alaska, Hawaii, Puerto Rico, and Virgin Islands. Washington, D.C.: Government Printing Office.

———. 1954b. United States life tables, 1949–1951. Vital Statistics—Special Reports, Vol. 41, No. 1. Washington, D.C.: Government Printing Office.

VALAORAS, V. G. 1950. Patterns of aging of human populations. *In* The social and biological challenge of our aging population: proceedings of the Eastern States Health Education Conference, March 31–April 1, 1949, pp. 67–85. New York: Columbia University Press.

III

Aging in Preindustrial Societies

LEO W. SIMMONS

I. GENERAL CONSIDERATIONS

Studies of aging in different societies involve such general questions as these: What are the chances that a person may have, in a given time and place, to live beyond his "prime" and how far? How does aging in people differ from aging in animals, and how wide are the contrasts in the experience of old age for men and women in primitive, historical, and contemporary times? At what point in aging does change of status in an individual's relations with others become a serious matter in personal adjustments? What have been the common interests or universal goals of old people everywhere, and are there any standard ways of achieving these goals? What can be learned from the study of the place and role of old people in primitive and agrarian cultures that may provide background and shed light on the problems of aging in our present highly industrialized society?

In order to appraise the position of the aged in any society, certain information must be gathered as a sort of base line and of a more detailed nature. It is necessary, for instance, to know the customarily accepted criteria of old age, and these vary greatly even when reliable birth records are kept. Reliable estimates are needed on the incidence of aged men and women in the population. These should include occupational and professional groupings of the old, their marital status, the reputed causes and rates of death, and the extent of de-

pendency and decrepitude. It is important to know the nature and severity of the physical environment, the relative scarcity or abundance of food, the permanency of residence, the prevailing types of economic enterprise, the system of political control, and the form of family organization. The current magical and religious beliefs and practices may be very relevant in terms of opportunities for the aged to participate in group activities and also for the treatment that they receive.

Attempts should be made to note cases of extreme longevity and significant physical or psychological factors associated with it, such as absence of gray hair, pronounced preservation of teeth or eyesight, excessive sexual interests and capacity, outstanding endurance, exceptional mental abilities, and major individual achievements late in life.

Further inquiry relates to the popular conceptualizations of old age: the conventional stereotypes of senescence, how aging is assessed, and how abrupt or formalized the transitions from middle to old age are. What are the stock explanations of aging—mythical, philosophical, or realistic? What are its popular symbols and synonyms, both praiseworthy and derogatory? What are the cultural idealizations of old age, and what guides are offered for achievement of them?

If the aged are regarded as dangerous or useless, if they are neglected, abused, abandoned, or killed, what are the culturally approved justifications for such treatment, and to what extent do old people themselves acquiesce in or resist it?

Since the aged hold an advantage in length of life, accumulated experience and skills, and often in knowledge and wisdom, what use is made of these acquirements in prolonged activities, in interpersonal relationships, in the exercises of political influence, and in other functions that serve to intrench elders in positions of power and security? It is of particular importance to note the position and role of old people in family life, their opportunities for remarriage to younger mates, the authority they possess in family affairs, and the recognized claims that they may make upon children and other relatives.

Other prerogatives of the aged that require examination include questions as to whether they are subject to pronounced fear, respect, or obedience on the part of younger people; what exemptions from social obligations are accorded them as their rights; and what social privileges they may enjoy which are prohibited to others? Are they lionized in heroic roles accorded to them in legends and mythologies? Equally important are customary restraints imposed upon them on account of age. These include the right of employment or tenure of office, restrictions on the exercise of property rights, penalties imposed upon them for alleged witchcraft or sorcery, restraints on religious or ceremonial functions, or prohibitions on attempts at self-destruction. In short, what rights and privileges are denied to persons because of their age?

Studies of the role of the aged in preindustrial societies should provide information also on prevailing attitudes toward death and the manner of release in senescence as well as any posthumous benefits bestowed upon them. Is death in old age regarded as a natural event? Should anything be done to hasten or delay it? Are there honorable and dishonorable ways of departure? Are exceptional prerogatives and power attributed to the last acts or words of aged people? Are the aged accorded special mortuary rites? Are they promoted to higher positions in the hereafter, and are they believed to be able to revisit and bestow rewards or punishment upon survivors who fail to pay them homage?

Any summary answers to such questions on aging in world-wide perspective require qualifications that take into account special differences characteristic of particular groups of people. A notable contrast that cuts across "time, tribe, and place" in man's experience with age is the positive or negative attitude that he takes toward it. To illustrate extremes here, old age may be viewed as a problem that plagues man or as a challenge that confronts him. Whole societies of people, in accord with their customs and sentiments, may manifest pronounced negative or positive appraisals of old age; or individuals in the same society may face it as a dire curse or anticipate it as a rare blessing. An example of the former is Cato the Elder, who is reported to have said, "For my part, I prefer to be an old man for a somewhat shorter time than to be an old man before my time" (Brigham, 1934). He saw the problem side, which is, of course, always there. One Joseph Choate of our own times concludes that people may be happiest in their seventies and eighties; his advice is: "Hurry up and get there." He sees the challenge which may also exist (Corson and McConnell, 1956).

It is easy to generalize on this attitudinal contrast with respect to aging in primitive and historical perspective. For example, old age may be regarded as beginning relatively early or late in life and to last a long or short time. Its appearance may be resented and disparaged or welcomed and treasured. Some peoples actually try to "hurry up" with aging, while others deny and postpone it to ridiculous degrees. When it comes, it may be regarded as an idle and useless period or as an active and fruitful one. The added years may bring promotions in position and prestige or demotions and degradations. For some peoples it is expected to drag itself out in dull tedium and, for others, to pass all too swiftly with its rich harvest of experience. Even the end of an old person's existence may be viewed by himself and his friends in such extremes of negative and positive terms and also be remembered by his survivors as the best or worst event in his long life.

Added to the contrasting attitudes toward, and assessments of, aging are equally wide variations in the patterns of adjustment that different peoples have made to the experience. It would seem, indeed, that every possible plan for a successful old age has been tried out sometime and somewhere in the world in mankind's attempts to enrich and round off the last years of life. It is our purpose in this chapter to examine and summarize a fair sampling of these "experimental endeavors" by varied human societies to come to terms with the inevitabilities of old age.

II. Aging as a Human Achievement

Nature in the raw has never been very kind to old age in any species. The cycle of life begins and ends under conditions of dependency; but in the end stages of dependency there are, apparently, no "instincts" or inborn propensities which impel the offspring to sustain the ancestor or that match or compare at all with the biologically determined "parental drives." It is not common to find animals providing for their parents and grandparents.

Everywhere the human cycle also begins with the dependency of the young on those who are older, and, unless it is cut off early, it ends with dependency of the old on those who are younger. Now, while it is generally recognized that the inborn patterns of response in man are less specific and far more modifiable than in the "lower animals," we do find human beings all over the world either neglecting or taking care of their dependent ancestors. What, then, is the chief difference in old age dependency

in man as compared with other forms of life?

In substance, the difference is this. While the offspring of man *can be* as indifferent to the dependency needs of his ancestors as any of the lower animals, and perhaps even more cruel, he *can also* learn, be taught, inspired, or impelled to respect, succor, and sustain his grandparents. Moreover, in man these patterns of intergenerational responsibility can be "handed down" to succeeding generations. This very unique phenomenon in the human species is called the capacity to create, inculcate, and transmit through socializing processes a heritage of culture that accumulates, changes, and is, thereby, continually adaptive over time. The fact that man is a culture-building and a culture-bearing animal has made it possible for him to have an old age that is vastly different from that of any other species and that may vary as greatly among his own kind.

Security for old age is distinctly a human-culture achievement. The "taming" and the use of fire are simple examples of how man's material culture can serve and comfort the aged. When fire was finally brought under control, used as a protection against climate, a defense against wild animals, applied to the manufacture of implements and the preparation of food, and made a stabilizing factor in family life—with its warm hearth and cozy corner—a new day had dawned for the elders. Indeed, the advantages of fire were soon so closely associated with the frailties of age that, when the necessity arose to abandon an old and enfeebled relative—a not uncommon circumstance—it became a widespread practice, a highly cherished rite, and a parting favor to leave with him or her a supply of food, a flame, and some fuel.

There are equally important examples of prolonged securities for the aged in the development of social relations, such as rules obligating the young to respect, heed, and provide for the old in many and varied forms. Property rights, special privileges tabooed to others, and prerogatives within the family are outstanding types of social expedients for elders. But whether or how well any of these gains have been realized depends greatly on the existing culture of the time and place and on the organization of the society involved.

A rich and ripe old age is not guaranteed by nature for anybody. Success with the last of life is a distinct achievement, and it constitutes a two-way relationship. On the one hand, the environment must permit it, and the culture must provide for and sustain it. On the other hand, the aging person must fit in and fulfil his functions within the social setting. Thus a good old age must be active and gamy to as near the end as possible. The chief means of security and success in aging are by expedient adjustments to other persons and to the social system within which they live. In other words, anyone's power and security in old age must rest primarily upon his or her social prerogatives—upon such duties, rights, and privileges as may be established in the mores of the time and place. To put the matter somewhat bluntly, a satisfactory old age depends primarily upon the amount of persuasion or coercion that may be exerted upon the young and strong to serve and pay homage to the needs and interests of the old and physically feeble.

It is noteworthy that in some societies such deference to, and solicitude for, the aged has seemed to fall squarely in line with the needs and self-interests of the young. In such cases the doting youth could have said of his services to an elder, truthfully and without pathos, "Grandfather, this helps me more than it does you." In other societies with different cultures youth does not see such a connection. Why? The answer lies largely either in the culture or in the behavior of the elder.

Here is an important general principle to consider: Whenever society through its culture has created and sustained a mutually supportive relationship between its youth and its elders, old age security has had its firmest foundation. In contrast, the severest hazard of the aged and infirm

has been to find themselves unnecessary to, and cut off from, the interests of the young and able-bodied upon whom they have had to rely. One could speculate that the time may come when youth can manage very well without the aged; but whatever widens the gap between the two will, more than likely, be at the expense of the latter, especially in the extremities of their dotage. On the side of the old, there is no substitute for the ties that bind youth and age in common interests.

III. Interests of the Aged

Among many peoples in primitive and historical settings, we have looked for two things: (1) The persistent and recurrent interests of aging persons: What are their needs or what do they appear to want out of the last of life, irrespective of where they live and when? (2) The major solutions that different societies have made to the problems of aging: What have various peoples done about the needs of the aged? What solutions appear most fundamental, widespread, and similar?

It has turned out, as I see it, that the basic interests of old people have been more uniform than the ways and means for the fulfilment of these needs. It has helped, also, to distinguish roughly between what may be regarded as the primary interests and the secondary ones. Here again the primary goals appear to be more nearly "universal," while the secondary interests are more flexible and adaptive to different societies. Perhaps it would be helpful to regard these latter as "instrumental goals" that contribute to the achievement of the primary ones. The learning of skills or the acquirement of property rights, in contrast to the exercise of prestige and power, are examples of secondary as compared with primary interests.

A careful survey over a long period of time of seventy-one different peoples, distributed world wide (Simmons, 1945), has disclosed recurring and apparently primary interests of aging persons that can be summed up fairly well in a fivefold way:

1. To live as long as possible, or at least until life's satisfactions no longer compensate for its privations, or until the advantages of death seem to outweight the burdens of life. With few exceptions, life is, indeed, still precious to the old.
2. To get more rest, or, better stated, to get some release from the necessity of wearisome exertion at humdrum tasks and to have protection from too great exposure to physical hazards—opportunities, in short, to safeguard and preserve the waning physical energies. Old people have to hoard their diminished resources.
3. To safeguard or even strengthen any prerogatives acquired in mid-life such as skills, possessions, rights, authority, and prestige. The aged want to hold on to whatever they have. Thus seniority rights are zealously guarded.
4. To remain active participants in the affairs of life in either operational or supervisory roles, any sharing in group interests being preferred to idleness and indifference. "Something to do and nothing to be done" is perhaps the main idea.
5. Finally, to withdraw from life when necessity requires it, as timely, honorably, and comfortably as possible and with maximal prospects for an attractive hereafter.

These five interests—longer life, rest, prerogatives, participation, and an easy and honorable release—can be summed up under the two words "influence" and "security" if they are used with broad connotations.

Thus the goals of aging for human beings are substantially socially and culturally oriented, involving accumulated attitudes and obligations on the part of group members toward the dependent aged and corresponding attitudes and efforts on the part of the aged to maintain their place in the group and to insure their support and care. The three major types of societies and cultures that differ most from our present industrial era are the so-called primitive societies, the historical agrarian economies of the Western world, and certain oriental civilizations, such as China, India, and Ja-

pan. This essay deals mainly with the experience of aging in primitive and Western agrarian cultures, and, for purpose of contrast with our present industrial society, more attention is paid to the primitive backgrounds. It is among primitive peoples that the widest range of differences may be found in attitudes toward, and adaptations made to, the problems and opportunities for aging.

There are further important reasons for special consideration of aging in primitive societies: Relatively few aged persons survived, and they apparently played more significant parts in the affairs of the groups than do very old people in our times. Shifts in the sex balance showed wide fluctuations in the later years; customary adaptations of individuals to aging provided striking contrasts from tribe to tribe; and persons were not infrequently faced with sharp alternatives between conventional adaptations and the dangers of elimination. The more crucial adjustments to aging had to be made *while* the individual was aging and not *before* its serious onset. Moreover, entrance into the "status of the aged" for primitive peoples was gradual and with transition less abrupt and specific than in our time. For instance, there was rarely ever a calendar with a delineated year in which one became "old." Another substantial difference in aging in primitive and civilized times is that death generally came earlier for helpless old age than in civilized societies with modern facilities and techniques for keeping bodies alive. Moreover, the cultural norms provided for very wide extremes in terms of the neglect and abandonment of old people, on the one hand, or, on the other, for their succor, support, and even glorification in death. Perhaps the most significant range of contrast to be observed in the adjustments to aging from very primitive to highly industrialized societies is that in the former the "terms" or conditions for aging were imbedded in the cultural developments as by-products of broad societal interests, while in the latter the trend has been toward a breakdown of the traditional types of adaptations to aging and the growth of planned and legislated forms of old age security as specific objectives and through the instrumentality of group-action programs. Such *planned* social provisions for the aged in primitive societies were extremely rare. The social provisions for the aged were more nearly "automatic" and traditional in form.

IV. Distribution of the Aged

The farther back we go into primitive and rudimentary forms of human association, the fewer old people are to be found, and, quite generally, old age is attributed to these persons at an earlier chronological date than in advanced societies. It is reported, for example, that the Arawak of British Guiana, under native conditions, seldom attained more than 50 years. "Between the thirtieth and fortieth years, in the case of men, and even earlier in the case of women, the rest of the body, except the stomach, shrinks, and fat disappears, the skin hangs in hideous folds" (Im Thurn, 1883). Length of life for the Adamanese of West Burma rarely exceeded 60 years (Portman, 1895), and Arunta women of Australia were regarded as fortunate to reach 50, displaying a "stage of ugliness that baffles description" (Spencer and Gillen, 1927). Among the Bontoc Igorot in the Philippines (Jenks, 1905) a woman reached "her prime" at 23; at 30 she was "getting old," before 45 she was "old," and by 50, if she was so fortunate to live that long, she had become a "mass of wrinkles from foot to forehead." "Probably not more than one or two in a hundred lived to be 70."

Among the Bushmen in South Africa (Bleek, 1928) old people were rare. "The women die off at about 50 or 60; the men wear better. . . . Almost every Bushman presented to me as being exceptionally old proved on investigation to be 20 or 30 years younger than that supposed." The Creek of North America (Adair, 1775) were called lucky if they lived to see gray hair

on the heads of their children. Both sexes of Labrador Eskimo (Hutton, 1912) were "worn out" before 70, and a great-grandmother was a rarity. Seventy or 80 was rare for the Chukchi of Siberia (Bogoraz, 1904), and 65 was "very old" for the Polar Eskimo (Steensby, 1910). For the Point Barrow Eskimo (Murdock, 1892) it was "exceedingly difficult to form an estimate of the age to which these people lived. Men and women who appear to be 60 or over are rare." According to Ray (1885), they "very rarely" attained a great age, and "the majority by far die under the age of 40 years, and a man of 60 becomes very decrepit."

The statistical data generally are inadequate to form definite conclusions concerning the time of onset for old age or the prevalence of old people in primitive societies. As to when in life old age begins, the simplest and safest rule is to consider a person "old" whenever he has become so regarded and treated by his contemporaries. Few reliable enumerations are available that report the proportion of the population for a given age category. For example, a census of the Bontoc Igorot, secured from a Spanish manuscript in 1884 (Jenks, 1905), indicated that 4.5 per cent of the men and 5.9 per cent of the women were above 50. Rivers reported (1906) a census of the Toda of India that showed 4.7 per cent of the men and 5.3 per cent of the women above 50. A census of the Omaha in America for 1884 (Fletcher and La Flesche, 1907) showed 7.2 per cent of the men and 8.2 per cent of the women above 55. Most of the scattered reports, however, are based in part upon rough estimates of age. From a wide survey of the sources it seems safe to assume that in most primitive societies the number of persons 65 or over has very rarely been more than one to three per hundred of the population and possibly with a slightly higher proportion of women than men except in the most rudimentary social organizations.

This provides a sharp contrast with the prevalence of old people in our contemporary, Western, industrialized civilization, where the proportion of aged men above 65 reaches one in eleven of the population, or even better, and the proportion of women of the same age category reaches one in nine or better, with predictions of further increases for both men and women. But even now, in terms of world population, the aged are not of great statistical significance. As late as 1948 in India only 2.2 per cent of the population was 65 years of age and over. In Mexico they comprised only 2.9 per cent, in Brazil 2.5 per cent, and in the United States at the turn of the century only 4.1 per cent (Smith, 1950).

Although there have been fewer old people in primitive societies than in our civilized times, some persons apparently lived to about as great age then as now. Samples culled from many sources include references to men among the Abipone in South America (Dobritzhofer, 1822) who reached "almost a hundred years," and certain Araucanians (Smith, 1855), also in South America, whose lives "span a century." In North America there are reported cases of Chippewa Indians of 95 (Densmore, 1929), of Hopi men and women "nearly 100" (Simmons, 1945), and of Iroquois men of 103 (Seaver, 1860). The Chin in Burma are reported to reach great age (Carey and Tuck, 1896), and Todas in India are called "centenarians" (Thurston, 1909). A chief among the Kazak in South Russia is reported to have lived to 111 (Hedin, 1889). Tregear (1904) mentions Maori in New Zealand who were "over 100" and reports one man who saw his descendants of the sixth generation. While such noteworthy, and perhaps somewhat exaggerated, examples of longevity are to be found in primitive societies and can be duplicated widely, they must be regarded as exceptions to the general pattern of a relatively limited span of life and a rather early onset of old age.

It appears to be a fact, however, that human societies, in contrast to animal groups, succeeded, even in early times and primitive conditions, in solving the problem of insuring a very long and perhaps fruitful old age for at least a few of its members. Moreover, as we shall see, in certain rather primitive societies the aging years came to be regarded as the best part of life. Probably nowhere, for instance, has old age been viewed in a more favorable light or accorded greater homage than among the Palaung in North Burma, where the privilege of a long life was attributed to virtuous behavior in a previous existence. The old people had "happy lives" among the Palaung (Milne, 1924). No one dared to step upon their shadow lest harm befall him. The stool of a father was periodically anointed after his death, and the dutiful son often prayed: "Thou art gone, my father, but I still respect these things that belong to thee. Give me long life and health, O my father." It was such a privilege and honor to be old among the Palaung that, as soon as the girl married, she was eager to appear older than her age. "The older a person becomes, the greater is the respect that is paid her. The young women are expected to do a great deal of hard work along with the girls, such as bringing wood and water to the village before any festival; so married women are a little inclined to make out that they are older than they really are, in order that they may evade the extra work."

V. Emerging Security in Food-sharing

In retrospect it is plain that advancing age has been barely possible, and quite intolerable, without a sustaining social order and that old age security has depended upon reciprocal relationships between generations. It is desirable, therefore, to examine these relationships within the broadest possible range of social and cultural differences and to note, as clearly as possible, what effects they have had on old people.

Accumulations of data now make it possible to survey extremes in social developments from very early and primitive groups to our own present agrarian and industrial societies. Although we have much more information on primitive and contemporary cultures than is available for the wide mid-span of history, this gap may be bridged for our purpose with some material from agrarian and handicraft economies of the Middle Ages and from those still surviving in backward rural regions.

Some generalizations are suggested even before detailed comparisons are made. It is clear, for instance, that many of the social rights and roles for the aged that emerged early and became firmly rooted in primitive societies later reached their fullest development within farm and handicraft economies.

In their adjustments to the physical and social environments within primitive backgrounds, old people generally gained in influence and security with the gradual establishment of permanent residence, the achievement of a stable food supply, the rise of herding, the cultivation of the soil, and the increase of closely knit family relationships. Their functions and securities were further enhanced by the growth of magical and religious beliefs and practices and by the accumulation of knowledge and technical skills. But, with the evolution and elaboration of social systems, a gain at one point was often counterbalanced by a loss at another. It will be instructive, therefore, to follow through some of the growing prerogatives of age within the shifting currents of primitive, historical, and contemporary societies.

An early instance of emerging rights of the aged was some special assurance of food. With advancing age, food becomes a matter of increasing concern. Its provision at frequent intervals, in suitable form, and in proper amounts (sometimes a bite at a time and under supervision) depends more and more upon the efforts of others who are in a position to provide or withhold it. As life goes on, a stage is reached at which the aged require no less than the choicest morsels and the gentlest care. As far back as we can go in human associations, the hands of the aged have reached out for food when they could do little else—and they have not been entirely ignored or always filled.

Some rules and conventions for food-sharing have been found among the most primitive peoples, often with special favors for the old and feeble. Examples of food-sharing customs are reported from widely dispersed areas. The Labrador Eskimo share food with those in misfortune (Hawkes, 1916), and there was "always someone to give a little food or an old garment" to widows and other persons in need. Similar practices are reported among the Point Barrow (Murdock, 1892) and the Polar Eskimo (Rasmussen, 1908). The Lapp (Scheffer, 1674) "freely received and entertained" poor and helpless persons in their huts and "afterwards conducted them with their reindeer to another place."

The Norsemen cared for their poor and aged under the rules of hospitality:

While chatting at one of the houses an old man entered dressed in a suit of new clothes and wearing a high hat, and was bidden to take a seat; when, upon inquiry, it was whispered in my ear that he was a pauper. . . . Each person who has to be supported has to prove beforehand before the board of elders that he is too old and infirm to work, then he goes and remains six days on every farm. It was surprising to see how kindly they were treated—in many cases like visitors—having better food than the daily use for the family, and a good bed; so they go from one farm to another. They are well cared for, for it would be a great disgrace if the report should spread that farmer So-and-So was hardhearted to the poor [Du Chaillu, 1888].

Similar reports have come from the Yukaghir in Siberia (Jochelson, 1926) and also from the Chukchi (Bogoraz, 1904). Of the Siberian Yakuts in an equally harsh climate, it was said that "care of the poor and unfortunate has always been regarded as an obligation of the sib." According to Sieroshevski (1901), they would not believe him when he told them of rich and populous cities in which poor people sometimes starved to death. "They asked why anyone should die when he could go and eat with his neighbors."

Food-sharing with the aged and helpless was a common practice among the American Indians, including the Omaha (Dorsey, 1884), the Crow (Curtis, 1909; Lowie, 1913), the Kwakiutl (Curtis, 1915), and the Chippewa (Densmore, 1929). The Iroquois showed great hospitality in food-sharing (Morgan, 1901). "Upon the operation of such a simple and universal law of hospitality, hunger and destitution were entirely unknown among them." Every Creek Indian belonged to a particular clan, with village groups scattered over a wide area. In any of these, and among persons who were total strangers to him, he had the right of food and lodging as long as he chose to stay. Aged men often spent their last days going from house to house among members of their own clan. Bossu observed (quoted by Swanton, 1928): "I have often noted that when they returned from the chase the chiefs took great care, before dividing the food, to set aside the share for the old men." Among the Hopi no aged person needed to fear starvation as long as his many relatives had food to spare and he was able to go to their houses to eat. But the very aged and decrepit who could no longer walk or feed themselves were sometimes neglected and died alone (Simmons, 1945).

In South America, Africa, the South Pacific, and other areas of the world the story of food-sharing with the aged and helpless by primitive peoples and as a conventional practice can be pieced together, but the strength and the pattern of the custom vary widely (Simmons, 1945).

Among a sample of the somewhat higher "ancient civilizations" the practice became better structured and more uniformly regulated. The ancient Hebrew made certain provisions for the unfortunate in their code of laws.

When thou cuttist down thine harvest in the fields, and hast forgot a shief in the field, thou shalt not go again to fetch it; it shall be for the stranger, for the fatherless, and for the widow; that the Lord thy God may bless thee in the work of thy hands. When thou beatest thine olive tree, thou shalt not go over the boughs again; it shall be for the stranger, for the fatherless, and for the widow. When thou gatherest the grapes of the vineyard, thou shalt not glean it afterwards; it shalt be for the stranger, the fatherless, and the widow [Deut. 24:17 (A.R.V.)].

Aged Incas were supplied with food and clothing from the public storehouse:

There was no such thing as poverty and destitution, for the infirm or incapable were cared for by their neighbors according to the law, a regular order in tilling the soil being observed. First the land assigned to the Sun was cultivated (for religious purposes); second, those of widows, orphans, sick or aged, or persons otherwise unable to work, as also the land of absent soldiers. After the land of the poor and distressed had been attended to—and only then—the people worked their own lots, neighbors assisting each other. The people also paid another sort of tribute, which was to make clothes, shoes, and arms for the soldiers and the poor who could not work for themselves owing to age or infirmity [Markham, 1869].

According to Enock (1912), their laws decreed that the poor, the blind, the lame, the aged, and the infirm who could not till their own lands so as to clothe and feed themselves should receive sustenance from the public stores.

Aztec dependents were also provided for at public expense. When their leader, Athuitzotl, about A.D. 1500, received tribute sent by the provinces, he would call the people together and distribute clothes and provisions among those in need. Moteuczoma II established an asylum for citizens who, having served the country either in public office or in the army, might be of limited means (Biart, 1892). A portion of the numerous contributions, augmented by the spoils of war and by presents from governors of provinces and from feudatories, went "to help widows, orphans, invalids, and old men." A counselor in the coronation address advised a new ruler in the following terms: "Look to what you do; take into account the conditions of the orphans, the widows, the old men and women who can no longer work, because they are the plumage, eyebrows, the eye-lashes of the former ruler" (Biart, 1892; Saville, 1929).

A social expedient of some special advantage to the aged has been food taboos. Indiscriminate eating was recognized as dangerous everywhere. Who would know better the proper things to eat by different categories of persons than those who have lived long? Many food taboos deprived the young and able-bodied of delicate morsels and favored the aged. Long lists of special foods were forbidden to children, young and middle-aged men, and childbearing women. Countless examples of such food prohibitions can be gathered. Among the Polar Eskimo, eggs, entrails, lungs, and livers and such small animals as seals, hares, and ptarmigan grouse were regarded as safest and preferred for hunters who had captured at least one of every animal that is hunted and for women who had given birth to more than five children (Rasmussen, 1908).

Aged Omaha advised the young to leave alone the choice morsels that were customarily returned in borrowed kettles (Fletcher and La Flesche, 1907). "If you eat what is brought home in the kettle your arrows will twist when you shoot. . . . The youth who thinks first of himself and forgets the old will never prosper, nothing will go straight for him." Young men who unjointed bones to eat the marrow were warned by old men, "You must not do that; if you do, you will sprain your ankle." Neither could a young man drink the broth: "If he does his ankles will rattle and his joints become loose." When the marrow fat was tried out and the youth desired some of it with his meat, the old men would say, "If you eat of the marrowfat you will become quick tempered, your heart will become soft, and you will turn your back on your enemy." A cautious Crow turned over the entrails and the marrow bones to

the aged (Lowie, 1915). Larks among the Pomo were said to be eaten safely only by the old people. Loeb (1926) adds that the young were warned against worms and caterpillars, but they might sip the water in which the worms were stewed—for the aged. It was said of the Witoto that only the aged could eat the flesh of enemies (Farabee, 1922). Old Aztec men (Bunzel, 1940) were permitted to drink stimulants, prohibited to others, in order to "warm the cooling blood of their age." Many food taboos favored the aged among the Lango (Driberg, 1923). Old people claimed the heads of goats in the ceremonial slayings after a battle. Women were not allowed to eat chicken or the flesh of goats until after the birth of a third child, and only those too old to bear could eat mutton. Tobacco could be smoked only by old men, since it was said to be injurious to women, hunters, warriors, and suitors in love-making. Young men among the Fan (Trilles, 1912; Frazer, 1927) were not supposed to eat tortoise, being told that it would slow them down in running. "But the old men ate tortoise freely." The brains, the lungs, and the soft parts of other animals also went to them. Ostrich eggs were eaten chiefly by the aged Bushmen in South Africa (Bleek, 1928), and it was believed that women who had not become mothers and children would fail to mature if they ate steenbock. For the Hottentot, a sheep struck down by lightning was very dangerous to all but the aged (Hoernle, 1918). Among the Xosa only the very young and the very old could eat certain ducks, domestic fowl, birds' eggs, and porcupines or drink fresh milk without danger. Kidney meat was thought to make men sterile; thus the phrase "kidney-eater" signified an old man who no longer cared about sterility (Shooter, 1857; Kidd, 1904). At an Akamba circumcision ceremony it was the exclusive right of the oldest men to drink honey beer (Dundas, 1913; Lindblom, 1916).

The Chukchi of Siberia claimed that the milk of the reindeer caused impotence in men and flabby breasts in women; but the aged could drink it safely (Bogoraz, 1904). Hutton (1921) writes of the Sema Naga in India: "Besides prohibited flesh, food ordinarily good may become prohibited for some special reason. Thus if a spoon breaks with which the cooked rice is being taken from the pot, males may not eat of the rice (except the very old and practically bed-ridden)." If this prohibition were not observed and the eater were at any time to run, he would get a pain of violent and appalling severity "as though a piece of bamboo spoon were piercing his vitals." Food taboos that could be safely disregarded by the aged and children among these people included flying squirrels, because the eaters might beget idiotic children; the huluk ape, lest the eater bear children crying "hualu, hualu, hualu" like this ape; the otter, since hair on the head would become hard, dry, and difficult to shave; the muskrat, to avoid a horrible smell; and the fork-tails, who induce a timid and fearful disposition in the offspring of the eater. The hornbill was believed to cause coughing and choking in the young, the dung crow turned the hair white, the house martin or swallow caused dysentery, and goats' meat made young women too passionate.

While examples of culturally patterned food-sharing and food-taboo privileges favorable to the aged can be found freely among preliterate peoples, any generalizations should be based on statistical analysis which takes into account negative as well as positive evidence. A summary of data on 71 tribes that had been selected for detailed study showed "no information" on 38 tribes with favors accorded to aged men and 41 for aged women. But in only one tribe was definite negative data reported (Simmons, 1945).

In summary (Simmons, 1945) people everywhere in primitive societies became progressively dependent upon others for their food after the onset of old age. The assurance of food from a group or communal source was not entirely lacking in the simplest known societies. In fact, it appears that customs of food-sharing with the aged have been strongest on a conventional basis in the very harsh and difficult environments, where the food supply has been less constant, and where types of economic activities have been less well developed, as among the gatherers of food, fishers, and hunters. With advance to herding and agriculture, and the development of cultural traits characteristic of "higher" civilization, such as grain supplies, property, trade, debt relations, and slavery, support of the aged through communal sharing of food appears to have declined in importance or to have taken on features more characteristic of "organized group support." In the analysis of food-taboo privileges favorable to the aged, trends could not be clearly traced or correlated with economic developments. It would appear that these privileges have also occurred as adaptations within limited phases of social development and that they, too, eventually gave way to other and more adequate forms of social security in old age.

VI. Activities, Skills, and Rights as Related to the Economic System

By all odds, the most basic and widespread form of continuing participation for aging persons in preindustrial societies has been to assist others with economic enterprises and household chores—essentially simple and routine work with the hands. Indeed, the *hands* of the aged, as adaptive and surviving organs of participation, grow in significance along with the years. Everywhere the old people have been found helping out with the lighter tasks: on the trail, in the field, at the camp site, in the shop, in the "office," and in the household and at almost any jobs they could find to do. By these activities they retained a sense of place and performance in the groups and gained thereby a little more consideration.

The case is neatly presented in a report by James Moffat, the missionary, quoting an old Hottentot woman whom he found abandoned in a desert:

Yes, my own children, three sons and two daughters, are gone to yonder blue mountain and have left me here to die. . . . I am very old, you see, and am not able to serve them. When they kill game, I am too feeble to help with carrying home the flesh. I am not able to gather wood and make a fire, and I cannot carry their children on my back as I used to do [Dowd, 1907, quoting Moffat].

Opportunities for auxiliary tasks, although available everywhere to a degree, have varied from place to place and have been conditioned by such factors as climate, permanency of residence, constancy of the food supply, and especially by the economic practices of the particular group. A general survey of tribes has seemed to indicate that such opportunities are less prevalent in the simple societies characterized by collecting, hunting, and fishing; more opportunities are usually found among herders and cultivators of the soil. For lack of space only a few examples are cited.

Among the Polar Eskimo (Rasmussen, 1908) old people, the infirm, and cripples went every summer to the cliffs to help cache the winter's reserve of bird meat. Old women too feeble to travel stayed indoors, attended to household chores, repaired garments, tanned leather—chewing it to make it soft—and shredded with their very worn teeth the sinew of dried caribou and narwhal. Old Chippewa women winnowed rice, made fish nets, tanned hides, and supervised the storing of fish and the work of the young girls (Densmore, 1928). While the Chippewa family slept with their feet toward the coals, an old man kept watch, smoked, and fed fuel to the fire. During the day he carved ladles and pipe stems (Densmore, 1929). The aged Andamanese, a very primitive tribe, supervised the moving of camps, and both old men and women made baskets and cared for children and the sick while stronger persons searched for food. They also super-

vised and assisted the young men in canoe-making (Brown, 1922).

According to Inca laws, elderly persons unfit for work should serve as scarecrows to frighten birds and rodents from the fields (Sumner, 1907). "Occupation was found for all from the child four years old to the aged matron not too infirm to hold a distaff. No one, at least none but the decrepit and sick, was allowed to eat the bread of idleness" (Prescott, 1847).

A final illustrative case may be chosen from the Hopi in northeastern Arizona, a herding and farming people. Old men tend their flocks until feeble and nearly blind. When they can no longer follow the herd, they work on in their fields and orchards, frequently lying down on the ground to rest. They also make shorter and shorter trips to gather herbs, roots, and fuel. When unable to go to the fields any longer, they sit in the house or kiva where they card and spin, knit, weave blankets, carve wood, or make sandals. Some continue to spin when they are blind or unable to walk, and it is a common saying that "an old man can spin to the end of his life." Cornshelling is woman's work, but men will do it, especially in their dotage. Old women will cultivate their garden patches until very feeble and "carry wood and water as long as they are able to move their legs." They prepare milling stones, weave baskets and plaques out of rabbit weed, make pots and bowls from clay, grind corn, darn old clothes, care for children, and guard the house; and, when there is nothing else to do, they will sit out in the sun and watch the drying fruit. The old frequently express the desire to "keep on working" until they die. One observer notes:

Retirement is impossible at any age. One cannot in Hopi society pile up credit which will support one, nor can one save material on which to live long. Some of the "rich" may have enough corn to last for four or five years, but that is always to be treated as a reserve store, never as something which in the future will provide leisure. The aged who have sons and daughters who could provide for them continue to work as long as they are able to do anything whatsoever [Simmons, field notes for 1938].

It appears clear that in primitive societies the aged had their fullest opportunity for prolonged and useful physical employment among the sedentary cultivators of the soil. Here they could shift so gradually to lighter and lighter tasks that they rarely ever lacked for "something to do," seldom suffered from abrupt retirement, and usually turned their hands to useful efforts until very near the end of life.

From all reports, the agrarian and handicraft economies of the Middle Ages afforded for aging persons similar and even greater shares of useful employment. Indeed, simple agriculture and home crafts have insured for individuals with even modest residues of energy and skill considerable security against the fear of enforced idleness. In this connection it is interesting to note the recent comment of a missionary from a backwoods region in the Blue Ridge Mountains (Bruere, 1914): "There isn't any old age problem here; we aren't modern enough to have one."

Self-employment or ancillary services in agrarian systems probably have provided the most secure and continuous occupational status that society at large has yet afforded for the majority of its aged. According to Smith (1950), "One could probably demonstrate beyond all possibility of reasonable doubt that the relative position of the aged reaches its maximum in the most highly developed rural civilizations. This is to say that when the rural mode of existence rules supreme, the lot of the aged is probably far superior to what it is in pre-rural (primitive) groups, on the one hand, or in the more highly industrialized civilizations, on the other." It is true, however, that the recent and more advanced developments in agriculture mark for the aged a critical middle zone between old rural and modern industrial life. In contemporary, large-scale, mechanized farming the vast majority of workers have become wage employees and are subject to almost as great occupational hazards as the men and women who work in the great industries.

Opportunities to keep on working at essential but light tasks are obvious psychological and social assets in old age; but such labors which continue far into senescence may insure little more than bare subsistence, if that, and quite often become very burdensome. Complete release from enforced labor may sometimes prove more rewarding than repeated demotions into lower levels of drudgery. Compromise tasks, while lighter than previous work, often involve threats to prestige, as in the case of a dignified old warrior confined to "woman's work" in the house. The physical efforts in the late stages of one's dotage prove to be little more than toeholds on security.

There are certain activities, however, in which the aged have participated to much greater advantage. They have often retained directive roles in labor through the accumulation of experience and familiarity with special skills. In most primitive societies, in fact, the aged commonly possess degrees of expertness that have enabled them to be leaders, if not monopolists, in certain specialized functions. Not infrequently they have been skilled in the arts and crafts, such as pottery, basketry, housebuilding, boat construction, metalwork, and the manufacture of clothes, tools, weapons, and other implements. Furthermore, they have been in great demand as initiators of complicated techniques and procedures; and they quite generally have filled the roles of magician, healer, shaman, and priest—activities to be described later on.

A surprising specialization of old people has been that of "beauty experts," usually with ritualistic implications. In many instances they have been in charge of operations made on the body to enhance its charm, to signify adult status, or to protect against evil spirits.

Midwifery is a specialty that has been

associated almost universally with older women. Although aged men generally have treated sick women and prescribed remedies for pregnant ones, they rarely assisted in childbirth. They more often had a prominent part in naming children and in the performance of rites believed to safeguard their welfare. Such expert skills and practices doubtless provided old people with social advantages, for those who influence and assist their associates in the major crises of life do not go without reward.

The knowledge and experience of the aged also qualified them to be leaders or directors in games, songs, dances, and various other forms of entertainment. The rules for games were stored in their memories, the songs often came first to their lips, and the dances were under their guidance. Above all, they functioned as leaders of festivals and ceremonies whenever ritual was important.

Another popular and very common function of the aged was storytelling, an activity that served a threefold purpose of entertainment, instruction, and moral admonition. Anyone who enjoys modern facilities for such benefits can hardly appreciate the enviable position of old men and women in preliterate societies who possessed an ample supply of traditional techniques, legends, tales, songs, and rituals. The able and renowned were in great demand and could profit thereby.

In summary, it may be concluded that an important means of participation and security for old people when they became too feeble to forage for themselves was active association with others and assistance in their interests and enterprises. They could and did engage in secondary economic functions in field, camp, shop, and household. They concentrated on the lighter tasks or utilized their experience and skills in production, entertainment, specialties related to health and life, and rituals and ceremonies. Although such opportunities differed for men and women, and in different cultures, they were basic adjustments in securities for both sexes in old age.

But in our complex civilization, with its modern facilities and where the range and number of specialties are so vastly magnified, the aged really find few opportunities to compete successfully with more youthful experts. In fact, except for a few highly gifted persons, the organization and professionalization of the specialties have reached such high development, and the training of youth in these arts and skills is accomplished so early in life, that a capable young person may reasonably expect to overtake or surpass a parent or grandparent long before he himself begins to age.

Probably never before in the history of man have the skills of the aged become so effectively shelved by the trained aptitudes of youth. Unless the aged are very gifted, their chances now for prolonged participation, except as a pastime, are better in the esoteric or "fringe" activities or specialties, where competition is light, than in the services and skills that are in common demand. Relatively few old people are regarded as indispensable any more because of their specialized capabilities. And perhaps it is chiefly this fact that calls for and justifies in our culture the use of the modern hobby interests, which provide at best a kind of playful participation.

One of the most important areas for prolonged and effective participation is in the acquirement and exercise of property rights. Long life affords opportunity to establish such claims in close accord with the cultural codes, and these intrenched rights can be used like long arms to reach out and hold on to a continued share in the affairs of life. In many primitive societies the effects of these prerogatives are felt long after death has claimed their possessors, as, for example, in the last testaments respecting the disposition of property.

Property rights have been perhaps the most flexible, impersonal, and effective means of influencing others with a minimum of physical effort. When such rights are firmly fixed in a society, they generally enable the long-lived to accumulate and store up credits against the harder days ahead. With a backlog of such claims, he is in a position to share in affairs and influence others long after he is too feeble to accomplish much on his own initiative. It is almost a certainty that, wherever these rights are well developed in society, there is a marked difference between growing old with and without property. Indeed, few contrasts are more pronounced in their effects upon sociological aging. The person who controlled property was able to get, and to give, more out of life and to do it much longer.

Whenever such prerogatives were firmly intrenched in primitive cultures, they have supplemented, and sometimes supplanted, communal forms of food-sharing and support. Perhaps the simplest and most universal form of property rights shared by the aged has been the exchange of gifts and the receipt of fees for services rendered or in the fulfilment of obligations made. Such transactions in one or another form can be found practically everywhere. They require only brief illustration here.

Old women among Labrador Eskimo (Turner, 1894) received food for the care of men's boots and other services. Chippewa men (Densmore, 1929) "purchased" knowledge of medical herbs from the old "doctors." The Crow (Lowie, 1917) surrendered their marital rights to older men in exchange for "medicine," and a feast was a suitable reward to an aged storyteller. Navaho natives (Reichard, 1928) bartered with old men for knowledge of magic songs, charms, names, etc.; and young men trained in magic were required to give their aged teachers large gifts, sometimes equal to half their earnings. Some old men "made a good living" by the performance of healing rites. Aged Hopi received substantial "gifts" for treating diseases and for almost any other service they could render; and they held on to their property rights into very old

age, exchanging them bit by bit for care and support in their "helpless stage." Old women owned the houses in which they lived, household equipment, objects they had made with their own hands, and, not infrequently, fruit trees, garden patches, and small herbs. Where the aged Hopi had property, they got better care in their old age and even in death, for relatives who buried them received extra shares of the personal possessions (Simmons, field notes, 1938). In the 71 tribes under survey no instance of negative information was found in the literature with respect to the exchange of gifts as an asset to aging (Simmons, 1945).

A more pertinent question, however, is the extent of property rights shared by the aged in various social systems. Even in the simpler societies, characterized by food-gathering, hunting, and fishing, some important property rights existed and were utilized by the aged. Among herders property rights were generally much more pronounced. Keane (1885) and Leem (1908) report, for instance, the custom of the Laplanders to bury their wealth, especially "money," so cautiously that their heirs could not recover it. If, at the hour of death, the father did not choose to reveal the secret hiding place, the heirs simply lost it.

Old men among the Chukchi received great consideration, especially in the reindeer-breeding section of the tribe, because the herd belonged to the father as long as he lived:

In many camps in various parts of the territory of the Chukchee, I have met very old men, perhaps of seventy or eighty. . . . Some of these old men were almost in their dotage; still they had retained possession of the herd and the general direction of life in their camps. For instance in a camp on the Oloi River, a man named Kauno, who had great-grandnephews ten years old, owned two large herds and decided himself the most important question of the seasonal migration of the Chukchee, that of choosing the place of abode for the summer time. Though enfeebled by age, he still made the April trip to the Wolverine River every spring for barter with the maritime traders from the Arctic villages, who came there at that time, bringing maritime products and American wares. Kauno's own housemates told me that the old man had grown childish and often purchased things of little use in their life. Instead of sugar he took bottled molasses, because it was red and pleased his eye; he bought table knives instead of hunting knives, because they were brighter, etc. This was told, however, with broad grins and without any visible signs of protest. "Foolish One," they added quite good-humoredly, "What is to be done? He is an old man." And I am quite sure that Kauno kept the direction of his house till his natural end [Bogoraz, 1904].

In the survey of data from primitive tribes, two outstanding generalizations can be reported. First, sex differences have been striking; aged men and women have not shared alike in opportunities to acquire control of property, and apparently the same social factors have not operated uniformly to favor both. Second, the opportunities to acquire and exercise property rights by either sex in old age have been quite variable and conditioned by both environmental and cultural factors. How much security an aged person might achieve through property rights has been determined largely by circumstances beyond personal control, and these factors seem to show an orderly development when viewed upon a broad cultural background.

Aged women have had some advantage over men in property rights among collectors, hunters, and fishers, although the difference appears less in the latter. Among farmers, and especially herders, aged men had advantages over women. Old men also seem to have had the advantage where property rights have existed in land, in durable objects other than land, where techniques for mining and smelting of metals have developed, where slavery existed, where "money" was used as a standard medium of exchange, where debt relations were recognized, where trade in place of barter had become a common practice,

and under a patriarchal system of family organization (Simmons, 1945).

It is obvious, however, that even in primitive societies such findings merely show trends and do not indicate that the possession of property by the aged has been determined primarily by any single or small number of these cultural factors. Innumerable social forces, closely interrelated and interdependent, have worked together. "In their adjustments the mores move forward in rank, not in file, though that rank may not be without its irregularities. . . . Property, law, rights, government, classes, marriage, religion—are all born together and linked together. They all march together for the sake of expediency and under the strain of consistency" (Sumner and Keller, 1927).

It seems clear, then, that property rights as a means of influence and security for the aged had a very simple beginning and have increased in importance with the growth of more complex social systems and advanced cultures. Of course, whenever the existing property of a society becomes concentrated into the hands of a very small proportion of the population, and without adequate means of redistribution, its effectiveness as a means of participation for the majority of old people is greatly diminished. If concentration of property ownership is carried too far, large numbers of old people will become very dependent in an otherwise rich society.

VII. Government and the Aged

We have stressed that old people must depend largely upon others for the fulfilment of their interests and that the deference which they receive from younger persons is crucial to their success. Surveys of the activities of the aged have shown that some consideration is obtainable from them by assistance at lighter tasks that are useful to others. Such menial efforts are rarely as rewarding, however, as the utilization of wisdom, skill, and tact in interpersonal relations. Thus deference to the aged depends more upon the exercise of their wits than of their work; and fruitful fields for such talents have been found in political, civil, and judicial affairs.

The office of chieftainship and/or membership in official councils, regulative organizations, clubs, and secret societies have afforded old people, especially men, positions of usefulness and prestige in which established prerogatives, ripe experience, and special knowledge often could more than compensate for physical handicaps or waning vitality. Not infrequently age itself has been regarded as a primary requisite for such functions; but more often those who showed exceptional ability or who had achieved positions of importance and power through long and active lives retained it into their late old age.

It seems well established that the basic institutions and agencies of political regulation and social control have existed in rudimentary form in simple cultures and developed gradually with advancing economic organizations, reaching in primitive societies their greatest strength and complexity among herders and tillers of the soil (Sumner and Keller, 1927; Simmons, 1945). From this it could be expected that among herders and farmers the aged might be able to derive their greatest opportunities of a civil and political character.

The chieftainship has been a key position, existing to some degree almost universally in primitive societies, and it has not infrequently been occupied by aged persons. A few examples will suffice.

Although the Polar Eskimo possessed no organized political power, aged magicians were the recognized headmen and leaders (Rasmussen, 1921). Among the Haida (Harrison, 1925) a leader, once elected, always retained the honorable title of chief "until he died." Many references are made to aged chiefs among the Kwakiutl (Boas, 1895), the Chippewa (Kohl, 1860), the Crow (Curtis, 1909), and the Omaha (Dorsey, 1884); according to Loeb (1926), a Pomo chief was usually a man well past

his prime. A native offered an instructive account of the place aged men held in the political life of the Pomo:

My uncle Jose was a chief; my grandfather was also a chief . . . over 80 years of age; I was 19. . . . It never entered my mind that they had decided to resign their post and make me chief. . . . Well, one time my grandfather told me to stay in the next Sunday. . . . He said that he would need me. . . . I began to get uneasy. . . . I noticed that my uncle was going in and out and talking to the people outside, so I guessed that they were preparing a feast. . . . Then my grandfather told my uncle, "All right, go and tell the people to get ready." Then he said to me, "Son, I am getting old. I have taken care of our people for a long time; I have always tried to do good and to do what is right; I have kept away from quarrels and have made peace. I have gone around among our people and told them good words. . . . Now I am an old man and your uncle is old. . . . We have decided to give you our post."

Aged chiefs generally ruled in Samoa (Mead, 1928), and a native of 27 complained of his awkward position:

I have been a chief only four years, and look, my hair is gray, although Samoan gray hair comes very slowly, not in youth as it comes to a white man. But always, I must act as if I were old. I must walk gravely and with a measured step. I may not dance except on solemn occasions, neither may I play games with the young men. Old men of sixty are my companions, and watch my every word, lest I make a mistake. Thirty-one people live in my household. For them I must plan, I must find them food and clothing and settle their disputes, arrange their marriages. There is no one in my whole family who dares to scold me or even address me familiarly by my first name. And the old men shake their heads and agree that it is unseemly for one to be a chief so young.

One of the most powerful Araucanian chiefs (Smith, 1855; Featherman, 1890) was a "corpulent, thick-set old gentleman, with a big head and a pleasant good-natured face," and another chief "between 90 and 100 years of age" had eight wives, much property, and was called "The Grass of Heaven." The aged Araucanian rulers appointed their successors. An old chief among the Arawak (Brett, 1868) was described as infirm but influential. It was said of the Jivaro (Karsten, 1923; Up de Graff, 1923) that a person who qualified for the office of chief should be "elderly and experienced," and a chief was always called "the old one." Bogoraz (1904) relates how on his earliest visits to the camps of the Chukchi, those who came to meet him would say, "Let us take you to the oldest man. First talk to him."

Such cases, easily found in primitive societies, show that old men commonly occupied the office of headman or chieftain. They generally exercised authority in very late age and not infrequently had the right to select their successors. Of 71 tribes under survey (Simmons, 1945), old men were reported as chiefs in 56; in 8 more it was implied that they could hold office; while in no tribe was it stated that chiefs were regularly deposed on account of their age. The record was different for aged women, however. In only 2 tribes was it reported that they held positions equivalent to chiefs; and in 7 more it was implied that they might hold such offices.

If tenure of office had involved chiefs only, the subject would not be very significant in a study of old age. But usually they have been associated with rulers, aged councilmen, and advisers who exercised considerable influence. The fact that the use of the term "elder" has commonly implied leader, headman, or councilman suggests the important role of the aged in government. In fact, there have been societies in which age alone has qualified men for membership in government councils, but active participation has usually depended, also, on other qualifications.

Probably in no place on earth have aged men exercised greater authority than in Australia. The Dieri (Howitt, 1904) offer a good example of what was called "The Great Council." Their assembly consisted of all fully initiated men, but within it was a Great Council composed of all men of advanced age or those eminent because of some physical or mental superiority combined with their years.

The younger men looked forward for years to the time when having been presented at the great Mindari ceremony, they will be permitted to appear, and ultimately to speak, at the council of men. . . . The younger the man, the less he would have to say. Indeed, I never knew a young man who had been lately admitted to the rights of manhood presume to say anything or to take any part in the discussion.

Closely associated with eldership and council influence has been the arbitration of disputes and the "administration of justice." In fact, very often the office of ruler and judge, the authority of scepter and bench, could not be distinguished. Such roles of old people in reaching decisions involving crimes and in settling disputes—as guardians of the status quo— have been so prevalent that it seems useless to cite instances.

The aged, especially men, have also been frequently associated with secret societies and were thereby able to increase their influence through well-guarded information and elaborate, sometimes very severe, initiatory rites. The monopoly of secret knowledge and the manipulation of the *rites de passage* from youth into adulthood provided very convenient and effective instrumentalities for instruction, discipline, and domination of young upstarts who might challenge the authority of their elders.

The attainment of such positions of power and influence in the political and civil affairs of preliterate societies has been dependent, however, upon at least three factors: individual ability and initiative, sex, and a favorable combination of social and cultural conditions. In relatively rare instances does age alone qualify one for such positions of responsibility, and in most instances a state of senescence could be reached where the incumbent of office ceased active participation, retaining little more than symbolic powers. Old men have been overwhelmingly favored over aged

women in important political and civil
offices in most societies, although elderly
women have often performed prominent
functions in initiatory rites. With advancing economy, greater complexity and integration of social organization, and increases in societal stability, the aged tended
to exercise more functions, and the old men
gained considerably in civil and political
activities.

VIII. THE AGED IN THE FAMILY

In primitive and agrarian societies another way old people have found power
and exercised their rights to good effects
has been in family relationships. Within
the bonds of kith and kin the obligations
of youth to age are spelled out in greatest
detail and are so nearly universal that they
cut across many cultural differences and
transcend several historical periods. But
this does not imply that they are infallible
or unchangeable. Not infrequently the aged
have used such ties to very great advantage, finding in them opportunities for participation and shared prerogatives that
reach far into senility and sometimes past
it into the last rites and testaments. But,
wherever the social forms of family life
have become unfavorable to aging, these
securities have soon collapsed.

One very obvious way in which some
old people have gained advantages in the
family has been to marry younger mates,
especially by men in primitive societies
where the practice has been widespread.
And, where old women have been unable
to marry younger mates, they have often
encouraged their husbands to take young
wives in order to lighten their own labors
and perhaps to enhance their position within the family.

Examples of the union of youth and age
are plentiful. A report of the Omaha custom is matter of fact:

Looking at the duties and customs of the
tribe, it seems that the question of domestic
labor had a great deal to do with the practice

of polygamy. "I must take another wife. My
old wife is not strong enough now to do all the
work alone," was a remark made not as offering
an excuse for taking another wife, but as stating a condition that must be met and remedied
in the only way that custom permitted [Fletch-
er and La Flesche, 1907].

The practice has been common not only
among American tribes, both north and
south, but also in Africa, where often a
man's wealth was measured by the number
of his wives and their vigor and youthfulness. There a native remarked: "To own
one wife is as big a risk as to own only one
belt for palm climbing. If it breaks, you
are done for" (Claridge, 1922).

Holden (1871) described rather poeti-
cally the proud position of an aged Xosa
or Kafir:

The man is then supported in Kafir pomp and
plenty; he can eat, drink, and be merry, bask
in the sun, sing, and dance at pleasure, spear
bucks, plot mischief, or make bargains for his
daughters; to care and toil he can say farewell,
and go on to the end of life. As age advances
he takes another young wife or concubine, and
then another, to keep up eternal youth, for he is
never supposed to grow old as long as he can
obtain a youthful bride; she by proxy imparts
her freshness to his withered frame and throws
her bloom over his withered brow.

In a Chukchi family in Siberia (Bogoraz, 1904), the first wife was generally
much older and had several children when
a second wife was obtained. Then she became the mistress of the household while
the younger woman was treated like a maid.
"The first wife sits with her husband in
the warm sleeping room, while the second
works outside in the cold . . . prepares the
food, and serves it." Cases have occurred
where "the first wife insisted that her husband marry a younger and more able-
bodied woman."

Milne (1924) wrote of a Palaung couple:

In a village near Namshan I met a civil and
most obliging head-man and his wife. I asked
the wife if she had many sweethearts as a girl.
She smiled and said, "yes," adding, "when they

came to sit with me in the evenings, I never listened for any other footsteps but his." Here she nodded her head to her old husband, saying, "I cared only for him." The husband smiled and said, "When I went to sit with the other girls the time seemed long, but it went as quickly as a chew of betel-nut when I was with her."

Mrs. Milne added: "Their children being all dead, the old lady persuaded her husband to take another wife, and he agreed, stipulating that she choose the young lady. This was done, and they appeared to be a happy family. The young woman did all the housework."

When such reports from widely dispersed tribes were brought together for analysis, it appeared that old men have had far greater opportunities to marry young mates than have aged women, but the success or failure of either seemed conditioned by cultural factors. Old men tended to find greater opportunities in patriarchal societies and perhaps among herders. With general cultural advances the practice appeared to have persisted longer in favor of men than of women, but it had tended to decline for both (Simmons, 1945).

A relationship of tender interest in the family has been the close association of the old with the very young. Frequently they have been left together while the able-bodied of both sexes sallied forth to obtain the family fare. The old people protected and instructed the children, who, in turn, served them as "eyes, ears, hands, and feet." In a sense the aged thus turned back toward another childhood, finding therein useful occupation and a projective association for the lengthening years.

More important for the interests of the aged than marriage to young spouses or their relationships with small children, however, has been the possession of rank and authority within the family circle. The authority of parents over their children has prevailed in the most rudimentary as well as the more complex societies. Other vested interests have affected a wide circle of relatives—in-laws, siblings, nephews, nieces,

grandchildren, and others who come within the orbit of the kinship system. Such family prerogatives for the aged vary greatly, and no classification of particular rights can be offered here. Most of the data drawn from societies with matrilineal descent indictated that in such tribes aged men *and* women have usually been able to realize considerable authority and prestige through family and kinship ties and that the women appeared to hold about as high prestige as the men, perhaps a little higher. In patrilineal societies the aged men were found able to realize a great deal of power, much more indeed than in matrilineal groups; but it was questioned whether old women enjoyed equal rights. Many striking cases could be cited of the extreme authority of aged fathers over their wives and descendants.

The Aino of Japan provide a good example from a primitive society (Bishop, 1881; Batchelor, 1927). The father possessed great authority. He could divorce his wives or disinherit his children. Even when old and blind, he was entirely supported by his children "and received until his dying day filial reverence and obedience." Aged women did not exert such influence, nor did they fare as well (Landor, 1893). Left to the mercy of their sons and daughters, they were often regarded as worthless creatures. A vivid example of this was portrayed in the instance of a feeble old woman who was found crouched in the dark corner of a hut. Landor relates:

As I got closer I discovered a mass of white hair and two claws, almost like thin human feet with long hooked nails. A few fish bones were scattered on the ground and a lot of filth was massed together in that corner. . . . I could hear someone breathing under that mass of white hair, but I could not make out the shape of a human body. I touched the hair, I pulled it, and with a groan, two thin bony arms suddenly stretched out and clasped my hand. . . . Her limbs were merely skin and bones, and her long hair and long nails gave her a ghastly appearance. . . . Nature could not have afflicted more evils on that wretched creature. She was nearly blind, deaf, dumb; she was apparently suffering from rheumatism, which had doubled up her body and stiffened her bony arms and legs; and moreover, she showed many symptoms of leprosy. . . . She was neither ill-treated, nor taken care of by the village or by her son, who lived in the same hut; but she was regarded as a worthless object and treated accordingly. A fish was occasionally flung to her.

The position of the patriarch in Roman society illustrates perhaps the ultimate expression of the authority of an old man in his family. As Cicero put it:

Appius being, beside his extreme old age, also blind, ruled and kept in awe his four tall sons, five daughters, his family, and household (which was great), and extended the patronage of his suppliant clients. For he had his mind bent like a bow, and never shrunk from his years, neither suffered he old age to have the victory over him. He reserved and kept his authority over all them that were under his charge, and his family was ready at his beck and commandment; his servants feared him, his children honored and revered him, and all men entirely loved him. In his household the customs of his noble pedigree and ancestors, and the discipline of his country, took place effectually. For herein is old age honest and honorable, in defending and maintaining itself, in retaining and keeping its authority, in saving itself free from bondage and servitude, and in exercising rule and authority over them that are under his charge, even until the last hours of death [Cicero, 1928].

It has been such family structures, with their intrenched "power rights of parents" that were backed up by social and cultural sanctions, which have characterized many of the more complex primitive and agrarian societies. These cultures and family systems also flourished in the Middle Ages, in China, in Japan, in ancient Greece, and in Rome; and they survive to some degree in isolated rural areas today, remnants of a way of life now largely vanished.

Describing the patriarchal family of the nineteenth century, Dell (1930) wrote: "The old parents, finding ample means of subsistence in the nature of their locality, are able to gather around them four generations of their own blood. The father of the family, whose power is justified by his long experience, possessed the necessary ascendency to hold both youth and ripe age in submission to the Decalogue and to customs." Thus was built up over a long past a solid concept of children's responsibility to their parents. Intergenerational responsibility was the keynote of the family, and it embraced all age groups, the waxing and the waning alike. Such a family system guaranteed probably the greatest sense of security that aging persons have yet known.

IX. The Use of Knowledge, Magic, and Religion

In primitive societies and among preliterate agrarian peoples well up into historical times an aged man or woman had a distinct advantage in experience, knowledge, and wisdom. Without written records, or with poor access to them, when what was known had to be retained by memory, old people were repositories of valuable information and were in favored positions to make good judgments. The possessors of such qualifications were in great demand for imparting general knowledge, interpreting strange and mysterious phenomena, deciding between "right and wrong," diagnosing personal ailments, and providing comfort and guidance to the distraught and bereaved. Seers, magicians, medicine men, and priests were very frequently old people. They served as mediators between man and the great unknown, the imaginary environment which was believed to be peopled with unfriendly spirits as well as benevolent gods. When faced with common perplexities and personal crises of every kind, our forebears generally turned to the "old wise ones" for help and counsel; and the aging individual with enough experience, insight, and gumption to suggest or do something, or even make it appear that something could be done in the hour of human need, had a rare opportunity to feel useful and to be rewarded. There are unlimited examples of the treasured roles of the aged as custodians of folk wisdom and mediators between the people and the crises in their lives.

The old seemed particularly qualified for the practice of shamanism. They had the longest experience and the most knowledge; sometimes, even, it was believed that parts of their bodies had acquired supernatural power. Not infrequently they claimed to be in communication with the dead and other spirits and also with the gods. They had strange and mysterious remedies for breaking taboos, treating disease, foretelling the future, and driving out evil spirits. Sometimes they boasted; more often they were accused of possessing powers of sorcery and witchcraft. Being so near the end of their lives, they would soon become spirits themselves, perhaps powerful ones who might be able to punish those who had neglected or offended them.

Moreover, to preliterate peoples the problems most frequently treated by magic appeared not to be manageable by purely practical means but called for the more subtle and esoteric methods possessed by the old wise ones. It was not, for example, strength of brawn alone that won in battle or staved off bad luck, captivated the maiden's heart, or healed the dreaded disease. It was not a common skill that removed poisoned or magic arrows, brought the rain or sunshine, divined omens, "fixed" the enemy, subdued evil spirits, and placated angry gods. It was a special power, mysterious and most potent in the hands of old men and women who had survived all these dangers and who could exercise this power in the light of their sanctity, wisdom, and experience. Not all magicians were old, to be sure, but superannuation and the supernatural were very commonly and closely linked.

For the aged in many areas in the world the "call to magic" was well-nigh irresistible, especially since their services were urgently sought after. Thus the old person who could work "miracles," or even appear to do so, could find plenty of younger and stronger individuals both able and willing to do his bidding, in order to secure his aid in situations in which they felt helpless. Here the aged possessed a further advantage, for, with their superior knowledge, should a charm or a bit of magic miscarry, they were in a position to explain away their mistakes. Any knowledgeable and wise old shaman could confidently affirm in the face of mishap that, had it not been for this or that additional factor, for which he was not at all responsible, the "medicine" would have worked; or, better still, except for his timely intervention something much worse would have happened. The luck element thus could become for these old people a useful ally.

Let us cite just one example of the claims of occult power attributed to the aged. Certain old men among the Polar Eskimo (Rasmussen, 1908) were reputedly able to raise storms, produce calms, call up or drive off birds and seals, steal men's souls out of their bodies, and cripple anyone for life. They could fly up to heaven or dive down to the bottom of the sea, remove their skins like dirty garments, and put them on again. Old women could make "soul flights" to the realm of the dead in order to save the lives of very sick persons. All these mighty works were said to be wrought by magic words. It was held that

the combination of words had been dreamt by old men, and afterwards acquired magic power in their mouths. . . . Old men die now-a-days before their tongues acquire power. But the traditional formulae still pass from mouth to mouth. Old men are not eager to teach them, and the young ones know nothing of them; it is as they grow older that they ask to learn them, and then the teacher regards himself as the giver of a great gift . . . the best that an old man can give to a young one.

The aged have also found many opportunities to use their experience and talents in more formalized religious and ceremonial roles. They have served as keepers of shrines, temples, and sacred paraphernalia, as officers of the priesthood, and as leaders in the performance of rites associated with prayers, sacrifices, feast days, dedications, annual or historic celebrations, and the initiations of important and hazardous enterprises such as wars or migrations. They have also been prominent in ceremonies linked with the critical periods in the lifecycle—birth, puberty, marriage, and death, including the mortuary rites. In fact, very few of the great and critical occasions of life have not been presided over and supervised by some aged man or woman. Although there has often been an overlapping of shamanism and priestly functions, a general difference can be recognized. While shamanism has been extremely widespread among preliterate peoples, complex ceremonial functions and the development of organized priesthoods have been more characteristic of sedentary groups and relatively advanced herding and agricultural societies.

X. Respect for the Aged

In brief, the evidence indicates that, when conditions and conventions call for respect for old people, they generally get it; when these factors change, they may lose it. But prestige for aging is a complex matter involving many aspects of a culture. The problem is further complicated by the fact that certain kinds of treatment of the aged may be considered as marks either of esteem or of abuse depending upon social interpretations and local standards of propriety. In any study of attitudes toward the aging, consideration must be paid to the customary meaning attributed to the treatment that they receive.

One may state with confidence that all primitive and agrarian societies have accorded some considerable respect to old people—often remarkable deference—at least until they have reached such "overage" that they are obviously powerless and incompetent. Under close analysis, respect for old age has been, as a rule, accorded to persons on the basis of some special assets possessed by them. They may receive some consideration because of their usefulness in the performance of economic, camp, or household chores. They may be regarded highly for their skill in crafts, games, dances, songs, storytelling, and the care of small children. They may be respected and heeded because of their control of property rights and the exercise of family prerogatives. They may be accorded great homage for their extensive knowledge, seasoned experience, good judgment, gifts in magic, and functions in religious rites and practices. It is important to note the extent of general respect received by them and the range of existing avenues that afford for them "access to homage."

Some social systems provide many "paths to prestige" for old people, while in others the opportunities are much fewer. It should be recalled, also, that sex differences have been significant. In general, a favorable cultural milieu for aged men has existed within a patriarchal type of family organization, where herding and agriculture have been the chief means of subsistence; where residence has been more or less permanent, the food supply constant, and the political system well regulated; and when property rights in land, crops, herds, goods, and even women are deeply intrenched. Aged women, on the other hand, have seemed to gain relatively more prestige in simpler societies characterized by collection, hunting, and fishing, particularly under matriarchal forms of family organization. Their position also has appeared to be higher among farmers than herders. Old men have been able to achieve considerable prestige, even under circumstances normally conducive to elevating the rights of women; but aged women have been at distinct disadvantage where cultural factors are weighted in favor of old men. Wherever women have been respected in old age, men are rarely without honor, but prestige for aged men has been no assurance of a similar status for women.

XI. Death

The closing scene in the drama of aging is, of course, death. By departing honorably and heroically, one may get a final opportunity to inspire respect and sometimes even to be worshiped by one's survivors. It is pertinent, therefore, to survey the various means by which some societies have provided or deprived old people of achieving such a last full measure of prestige.

In many primitive and early agrarian societies death generally came quite abruptly. Hardships of climate, shortages in food, accidents, and the hazards of disease and warfare forced weaker members to succumb. Moreover, death took children, youths, and persons in their prime more frequently than the old, for relatively few got to be old. Thus death was more commonly associated with youth than with age, and life was more often snuffed out suddenly than left to flicker and fade by degrees. As a consequence, the deaths of old people, especially those prominent for their sanctity and esoteric wisdom and powers, took on special significance.

Necessity forced the rather drastic deaths of a few helplessly aged persons in certain societies, and opportunities arose in others for gaining added prestige by the timeliness and manner of one's death and through the development of customs and procedures that prescribed appropriate, respectable, and even honorific ways of dying. Not infrequently the manner and the means of an old person's death became both for himself and his contemporaries more significant than the fact of death itself. Nevertheless, while a dignified, and even glorified, death for the aged became possible in some societies, and even obligatory in others, such instances remained relatively exceptional and required a favorable combination of both personal qualities and cultural circumstances. In the great majority of instances, and over a wide range of cultures, death occurred in old age as a sad and trying experience, particularly when long delayed.

Actual neglect or even abandonment of the helpless old was rather common and not necessarily disrespectful. Of 39 tribes on which definite information could be obtained, neglect and abandonment were customary in 18 (Simmons, 1945). Such practices were well known among the North American Indians, particularly nomadic tribes; but they can also be found in certain sedentary agricultural groups. Even the Hopi, who placed such a high premium on old age, made a distinction between the useful period of life and the "helpless stage"; and, when the latter state was reached by anyone, he or she was apt to be neglected, and sometimes even "helped to die" (Simmons, 1945). The Omaha hesitated to leave their aged alone on the prairie, fearing punishment from their god (Wakanda); but the very feeble were customarily left at a camp site provided with shelter, food, water, and a fire (Dorsey, 1884). It was considered even better treatment to leave them a growing cornfield or a cache of dried meat, promising to return within a month or so.

The very old among the Arawaks in South America were "stowed away in small corners of the house, neglected, left to themselves" (Roth, 1924). Whiffen (1915) said of the Witoto: "Old people are not killed but they are left to die. . . . Cassava may be thrown to them occasionally, or it may be forgotten." Because of their great fear of the ghost, the Abipone (Dobritzhofer, 1822) abandoned the house in which any person was believed to be dying.

In northern Europe the Lapp, when moving camp, felt obliged to abandon their sick and very old:

To carry the sick and disabled persons such a long journey is impossible, and so there is no choice but that he or she, whoever it may be, perhaps one's own father or mother, must be left behind, provided with food, in some miserable hut on the mountain, with the alternative of following later or else of dying entirely alone. . . . But a father or mother does not think this being left alone on the mountain a sign of cruelty or ingratitude on the part of their children. It is a sad necessity and a fate that perhaps had befallen their parents before them [Friis, 1888].

The available data, although sketchy, leave little doubt that neglect and abandonment were fairly frequent means of eliminating old and enfeebled persons. To move on and leave behind permanently helpless people has been the simplest, and perhaps the most humane, method of dealing with an inescapable necessity. The practice has probably existed at some time in the past history of every group. On the whole, such treatment has tended to be discarded under more favorable circumstances; but when associated with fear of the dead, and when established through wont and custom, it has often survived long after conditions which once required it have changed.

Some societies, as noted above, have provided more honorable, though abrupt and violent, forms of death for their old folks. Not infrequently relatives and friends have regarded these acts as deeds of mercy, and the aged have sometimes welcomed and even demanded such a death as their right.

Hawkes (1916) has reported that the Labrador Eskimo were treated with great respect, but he states that "this does not prevent them, however, from putting the old folks out of the way, when life becomes a burden to them, but the act is usually done in accordance with the wish of the persons concerned and is thought to be proof of devotion." These people believed there were special heavenly compensations for dying violent deaths. They would be transported higher up, in the vicinity of the Aurora Borealis, and spend their time there "playing football with a walrus head" in company with other courageous spirits.

Among the Samoans, to cite just one other instance (see Simmons, 1945, for many examples), the aged were once buried alive (Turner, 1894). It was even considered a disgrace to the family of an aged chief if he were not so honored.

When an old man felt sick and infirm, and thought he was dying, he deliberately told his children and friends to get ready and bury him. They yielded to his wishes, dug a round deep pit, wound a number of fine mats around his body, and lowered down the poor old man into his grave in a sitting posture. Live pigs were then brought, and tied, each with a separate cord, one end of the cord to the pig and the other end to the arm of the old man. The cords were cut in the middle, leaving the one half hanging at the arm of the old man, and the pigs were taken to be killed and baked for the burial feast. The old man, however, was supposed still to take the pigs with him to the world of spirits. The greater the chief, the more numerous the pigs, and the more numerous the pigs the better the reception. . . . His grave was filled up, and his dying groans drowned amid the weeping and wailing of the living.

Studies show that the killing of old people, often dramatically, and either enforced or voluntary, has been prevalent among many peoples. But the custom has been by no means uniform over wide areas of the world—unless it be in the extreme north—and it is improbable that the majority of the aged in any society have been able to achieve greater prestige by such a death. The killing under any circumstances, derogatory or honorific, was reported as an accepted practice in less than one-third of the tribes covered in a special investigation (Simmons, 1945).

It would appear in broad perspective that the abandonment, exposure, or killing of the aged have occurred more often from dire necessity than from personal whims; the hardness of primitive life, not the hardness of the primitive heart, was the basic reason.

Furthermore, the gaining of sympathy and prestige by old people by means of such deaths has depended largely upon a combination of physical necessity and a willingness on the part of the old to die courageously. Only in about half the tribes in which the aged were killed was special respect or honor indicated. Thus maximum opportunities for old people to gain glory by dramatic deaths were relatively rare and seemed to require a certain combination of circumstances and courage. Environmental conditions should make it a necessity; cultural beliefs about life, death, gods, and the hereafter should justify the deed and cushion the blow; established precedents should prescribe the manner of dying and delegate the proper agents to perform the execution. An audience, and possibly a celebration, should attend the ceremony. Finally, the aged candidate should possess sufficient force of character to accept the hard challenge courageously; and the act should not be put off too long, until senility had set in.

XII. Discussion

From here on I will list a few simple lessons that I have learned about aging—five, in fact.

First, aging has become a complex and challenging proposition to face personally. Let me illustrate this lesson with the mention of two common mistakes. The first mistake is to try to compare and to choose between old age and youth. We cannot do that. The choice, really, is between aging and dying. We have had our youth, some of us at any rate. Now, for us, it is age or else. The second mistake is to regard aging primarily as a time of resting, however much we think we like resting. "Old age for rest" is only a half-truth at best. The efforts and the strategy of life had better go on, refined and intensified to be sure.

My second lesson in broad perspective is that aging can be good or bad. When it is good, it generally is more of an achievement than a gift. A person, of course, must get to be old before he can make it good, and most human beings have never been able to get there.

Here was a great surprise to me in my studies of aging. Societies solved the problems of a successful old age for a few long before they could assure any old age at all for the many. For a long time, in a few spots on earth, one has been able to say realistically, "The happiest years of life are in old age." Now civilization has made the aging period for most of us something less than the best of life. All this ties in with the social determinants of when we become old, on what terms, and how long we are permitted to last. A secret of success for most people facing old age is to find for themselves places in society in which they can age with participation and fulfilment and to keep on participating tactfully and strategically up to as near the end as possible. Aging must be gamy to the end to be very good.

The third lesson is that a stage is reached in aging everywhere in which social assessments of the condition are uniformly dismal.

Among all peoples a point is reached in aging at which any further usefulness appears to be over, and the incumbent is regarded as a living liability. "Senility" may be a suitable label for this. Other terms among primitive peoples are the "over-aged," the "useless stage," the "sleeping period," the "age-grade of the dying," and the "already dead." Then, without actual death, the prospects are gloomy. There is no question about this generalized social decision; the differences lie in the point at which it is reached. All societies differentiate between old age and this final pathetic plight. Some do something positive about it. Others wait for nature to do it or perhaps assist nature in doing it.

The big point for us is that, in primitive societies and, indeed, in all societies until modern civilization, this over-age period has not been very significant. Few persons reached this stage; they did not last long in it. Some were dispatched with varying degrees of dignity and prestige.

The helpless and hopeless period takes on paramount importance, however, in our own civilized times. We are so successful in keeping very old people alive that we do not know what to do with them. Added to this is the recognized fact that the useless period is largely socially and culturally determined and that it may be moved up or put off in years. The social fates are most unfortunate, of course, when so many old people are made to feel useless relatively early in life and to find the twilight years empty, lonely, and long-lasting. More and more of life with less and less in it is not a happy prospect. Thus can civilization create more problems for aging than it has yet solved. Death is really the only ultimate solution. Whether life can be good to the last drop or not really depends on when and how we drop.

Our fourth lesson is that there is a pattern of participation for the aged that becomes relatively fixed in stable societies but suffers disruption with rapid social change. We know that stable societies provide a structured framework for participation, with status and roles that are defined, sex typed, aptitude rated, and age graded. If the pattern stays fixed over many generations, the aging get a lifetime to fit in and intrench themselves.

Here is one way to express the general principle: In the long and steady strides of the social order, the aging get themselves fixed and favored in positions, power, and performance. They have what we call seniority rights. But, when social conditions become unstable and the rate of change reaches a galloping pace, the aged are riding for an early fall, and the more youthful associates take their seats in the saddles. Change is the crux of the problem of aging as well as its challenge.

The fifth and last lesson is that the modern challenge is to explore and experiment anew with aging. We have more aged persons than the world has ever known: fifteen million in the United States 65 years old or more and twenty-six million anticipated by A.D. 2000. And these people are already born! Old age is beginning earlier with more untapped and unused resources than in earlier times. The old tried and tested patterns of participation and security have been disrupted, and they are passing away.

XIII. SUMMARY

The world has never before witnessed such a high proportion of people living on what has been called borrowed time. The problems are greater for us than they were for our forefathers or for our primitive forebears. We are emotionally confused and cannot decide how long to stay young or when to get old. Most of us are really younger or older than we think, and we do not know what to do about it.

In broad historical background there is much more agreement on what old people want than there is consensus on how to get it. Five wishes seem to be shared by aging people everywhere: to live as long as possible; to hoard waning energies; to keep on sharing in the affairs of life; to safeguard any seniority rights; and to have an easy and honorable release from life if possible. How to get these wishes fulfilled in later life has differed greatly around the world and still does.

We are now accustomed to hearing much about the problems and little about the opportunities of aging—and after all our efforts to attain it! It should be kept freshly in mind that the prospect of so many of us reaching old age is in itself a remarkable achievement that constitutes more of a challenge than a curse. Let us not forget, therefore, that our society, and our country, can and probably will accept it as such and create, before long, a brave new climate in which to grow old. It is very probable that within our highly complex civilization there lie all around us untapped potentialities for aging that may be explored to our advantage. Herein lies an old frontier that invites new pioneering.

Perhaps the most important single conclusion that has come out of the past so far is that the basic qualities of successful aging rests, after all, upon the capacities and the opportunities of individuals to fit well into the social framework of their own times and in ways that insure prolonged but not overlong influence and security. Herein lies, perchance, the Holy Grail for aging.

REFERENCES

ADAIR, J. 1775. The history of the American Indians. London: E. C. Dilly.

BATCHELOR, J. 1927. Ainu life and lore. Tokyo: Kyobunkwan.

BIART, L. 1892. The Aztec. Chicago: A. C. McClurg.

BISHOP, ISABELLA L. (BIRD). 1881. Unbeaten tracks in Japan. New York: G. P. Putnam's Sons.

BLEEK, DOROTHEA F. 1928. The Naron: a Bushman tribe of the Central Kala-hari. Cambridge: Cambridge University Press.

BOAS, F. 1895. Social organization and the secret societies of the Kwakiutl Indians. *In* U.S. NATIONAL MUSEUM, Annual report, **50**, 311–738. Washington: The Museum.

BOGORAZ, W. 1904. The Chukchee. Memoirs of the American Museum of Natural History, Vol. **11**. New York: G. E. Stechert.

BRETT, W. H. 1868. The Indian tribes of New Guiana: their conditions and habits. London: Bell & Daldy.

BRIGHAM, J. 1934. The youth of old age. Boston: Marshall Jones Co.

BROWN, A. R. 1922. The Andaman Islanders. Cambridge: Cambridge University Press.

BRUERE, MARTHA B. 1914. Growing old together. Good Housekeeping, **58**, 86–92.

BUNZEL, RUTH L. 1940. The role of alcoholism in two Central American cultures. Psychiatry, **3**, 361–87.

CAREY, B. S., and TUCK, N. H. 1896. The Chin Hills, Vol. **1**. Rangoon: Superintendent, Government Printing.

CICERO. 1928. De senectute, De amicitia, De divinatione. Trans. W. A. FALCONER. London: W. Heinemann.

CLARIDGE, G. C. 1922. Wild bush tribes of tropical Africa. London: Seeley Service.

CORSON, J. J., and McCONNELL, J. W. 1956. Economic needs of older people. New York: Twentieth Century Fund.

CURTIS, E. S. 1909. The North American Indians, Vol. **4**. Cambridge, Mass.: Harvard University Press.

———. 1915. The North American Indians, Vol. **10**. Norwood, Mass.: Plimpton Press.

DELL, F. 1930. Love in the machine age. New York: Farrar & Rinehart.

DENSMORE, FRANCES. 1928. Uses of plants by the Chippewa Indians. *In* U.S. BUREAU OF AMERICAN ETHNOLOGY, 44th annual report, 1926–27, pp. 275–397. Washington, D.C.: Government Printing Office.

———. 1929. Chippewa customs. (U.S. Bureau of American Ethnology, Bull. 86.) Washington, D.C.: Government Printing Office.

DOBRITZHOFER, M. 1822. An account of the Abipones, an equestrian people of Paraguay. London: J. Murray.

DORSEY, J. O. 1884. Omaha sociology. *In* U.S. BUREAU OF AMERICAN ETHNOLOGY, 3d annual report, 1881–82, pp. 205–370. Washington, D.C.: Government Printing Office.

DOWD, J. 1907a. The Negro races, Vol. **1**. New York: Macmillan Co.

———. 1907b. The Negro races, Vol. **2**. New York: Walter Neale.

DRIBERG, J. H. 1923. The Lango. London: T. F. Unwin.

DU CHAILLU, P. B. 1888. The land of the midnight sun. London: J. Murray.

DUNDAS, C. 1913. History of Kitui. J. (Roy.) Anthropol. Inst. Great Britain & Ireland, **43**, 480–549.

ENOCK, C. R. 1912. Peru. London: T. F. Unwin.

FARABEE, W. C. 1922. Indian tribes of eastern Peru. (Archeological and Ethnological Papers of the Peabody Museum, Harvard University, Vol. **10**.) Cambridge, Mass.: The Museum.

FEATHERMAN, A. 1890. Social history of the races of mankind, Vol. **3**. London: Kegan Paul, Trend & Trubner.

FLETCHER, ALICE C., and LA FLESCHE, F. 1907. The Omaha. *In* U.S. BUREAU OF AMERICAN ETHNOLOGY, 27th annual report, 1905–6, pp. 15–672. Washington, D.C.: Government Printing Office.

FRAZER, J. G. 1927. The golden bough: a study in magic and religion. Abridged ed. New York: Macmillan Co.

FRIIS, J. A. 1888. Lajla: a tale of Finmark. London: G. P. Putnam's Sons.

HARRISON, C. 1925. Ancient warriors of the North Pacific. London: H. F. & G. Witherby.

HAWKES, E. W. 1916. The Labrador Eskimo. (Canada, Department of Mines, Memoir 91.) Ottawa: Government Printing Bureau.

HEDIN, S. A. 1889. Through Asia, Vol. **1**. London: Harper & Bros.

HOERNLE, AGNES W. 1918. Certain rites of transition and the conception of Inau among the Hottentots. *In* O. BATES (ed.), Harvard African studies, **2**, 65–69. Cambridge, Mass.: African Department of Peabody Museum.

HOLDEN, W. C. 1871. The past and future of the Kaffir races. London: The Author.

HOWITT, A. W. 1904. Native tribes of southeast Australia. London: Macmillan & Co.

HUTTON, J. H. 1921. The Sema Nagas. London: Macmillan & Co.

HUTTON, S. K. 1912. Among the Eskimos of Labrador. Philadelphia: J. B. Lippincott Co.

IM THURN, E. F. 1883. Among the Indians of Guiana. London: Kegan Paul, Trench & Trubner.

JENKS, A. E. 1905. The Bontoc Igorot. (Ethnological Survey Publications, Vol. 1.) Manila: Bureau of Public Print.

JOCHELSON, V. 1926. The Yukaghir and the Yukaghirized Tungas. (Memoirs of the American Museum of Natural History, Vol. 13.) New York: G. E. Stechert.

KARSTEN, R. 1923. Blood revenge: war and victory feasts among the Jibaro Indians of eastern Ecuador. (U.S. Bureau of American Ethnology, Bull. 79.) Washington, D.C.: Government Printing Office.

KEANE, A. H. 1885. The Lapps: their origin, ethnical affinities, physical and mental characteristics, usages, present status and future prospects. J. (Roy.) Anthropol. Inst. Great Britain & Ireland, 15, 23.

KIDD, D. 1904. The essential Kaffir. London: A. & C. Black.

KOHL, J. G. 1860. Kitchi-Gami. London: Chapman & Hall.

LANDOR, A. H. S. 1893. Alone with the hairy Ainu. London: J. Murray.

LEEM, K. 1808. An account of the Laplanders of Finmark, their language, manners, and religion. *In* J. PINKERTON (ed.), A collection of voyages, 1, 376–490. London: Longman, Hurst, Rees & Orme.

LINDBLOM, G. 1916. The Akamba. Uppsala: K. W. Appelbergs.

LOEB, E. M. 1926. Pomo folkways. *In* University of California Publications in American Archeology and Ethnology, 19, 149–409. Berkeley: University of California Press.

LOWIE, R. H. 1913. Societies of the Crow, Hidatsa, and Mandan Indians. *In* Anthropological papers of the American Museum of Natural History, 11, 145–358. New York: The Trustees.

———. 1915. The sun dance of the Crow Indians. *Ibid.*, 16, 1–50.

———. 1917. Notes on the social organization and custom of the Mandan, Hidatsa, and Crow Indians. *Ibid.*, 21, 1–99.

MARKHAM, C. R. 1869. Royal commentaries of the Incas. London: Hakluyt Society.

MEAD, MARGARET. 1928. Coming of age in Samoa. New York: William Morrow & Co.

MILNE, LESLIE. 1924. The home of an eastern clan. Oxford: Clarendon Press.

MORGAN, L. H. 1901. League of the Ho-De-No-Sau-Nee or Iroquois. New York: Dodd, Mead & Co.

MURDOCK, J. 1892. Ethnological results of the Point Barrow expedition. *In* U.S. BUREAU OF AMERICAN ETHNOLOGY, 9th annual report, 1887–88, pp. xlii–xliii. Washington, D.C.: Government Printing Office.

PORTMAN, M. V. 1895. Notes on the Andamanese. J. (Roy.) Anthropol. Inst. Great Britain & Ireland, 25, 361–71.

PRESCOTT, W. H. 1847. History of the conquest of Peru. Paris: Baudry's European Library

RASMUSSEN, K. 1908. The people of the Polar North. London: Kegan Paul, Trench & Trubner.

———. 1921. Greenland by the Polar Sea. London: W. Heinemann.

RAY, P. H. 1885. Report of the International Polar Expedition to Point Barrow, Alaska. Washington, D.C.: Government Printing Office.

REICHARD, GLADYS A. 1928. Social life of the Navajo Indians. (Columbia University Contributions to Anthropology. Vol. 7.) New York: Columbia University Press.

RIVERS, W. H. R. 1906. The Todas. London: Macmillan & Co.

ROTH, W. E. 1924. An introductory study of the arts, crafts, and customs of the Guiana Indians. *In* U.S. BUREAU OF AMERICAN ETHNOLOGY, 38th annual report, 1916–17, pp. 23–745. Washington, D.C.: Government Printing Office.

SAVILLE, M. H. 1929. Tizoc, great lord of the Aztecs, 1480–1486. (Contributions from the Museum of the American Indian, Vol. 7, No. 4.) New York: The Museum.

SCHEFFER, J. 1674. The history of Lapland. Oxford: G. West & A. Curtein.

SEAVER, J. E. 1860. Life of Mary Jemison. New York: C. M. Saxton, Barker.

SHOOTER, J. 1857. The Kaffirs of Natal and the Zulu country. London: E. Stanford.

SIEROSHEVSKI, W. 1896. The Yakut. St. Petersburg.

———. 1901. The Yakuts. Abridged and trans. W. G. SUMNER. J. (Roy.) Anthropol. Inst. Great Britain & Ireland, 31, 65–110.

SIMMONS, L. W. 1945. The role of the aged in primitive society. New Haven, Conn.: Yale University Press.

SMITH, E. R. 1855. The Araucanians. New York: Harper & Bros.

SMITH, T. L. 1950. The aged in rural society. *In* M. DERBER (ed.), The aged and society, pp. 40–53. Champaign, Ill.: Industrial Relations Research Association.

SPENCER, B., and GILLEN, F. J. 1927. The Arunta, Vol. 1. London: Macmillan & Co.

STEENSBY, H. P. 1910. Contributions to the ethnology and anthropo-geography of the Polar Eskimo. Meddelelser om Grønland (Copenhagen), **34**, 253–405.

SUMNER, W. G. 1907. Folkways: a study of the sociological importance of usages, manners, customs, mores, and morals. Boston: Ginn & Co.

SUMNER, W. G., and KELLER, A. G. 1927. The science of society. New Haven, Conn.: Yale University Press.

SWANTON, J. R. 1928. Religious beliefs and medical practices of the Creek Indians. *In* U.S. BUREAU OF AMERICAN ETHNOLOGY, 42d annual report, 1924–25, pp. 463–72. Washington, D.C.: Government Printing Office.

THURSTON, E. 1909. Castes and tribes of southern India, Vol. 7. Madras: Government Press.

TREGEAR, E. 1904. The Maori race. Wanganui, N.Z.: A. D. Willis.

TRILLES, R. P. H. 1912. Le Totemisme chez les fans. Münster: Ashendorff.

TURNER, L. M. 1894. Ethnology of the Ugava District, Hudson Bay Territory. *In* U.S. BUREAU OF AMERICAN ETHNOLOGY, 11th annual report, 1889–90, pp. 159–350. Washington, D.C.: Government Printing Office.

UP DE GRAFF, F. W. 1923. Head-hunters of the Amazon. London: H. Jenkins.

WHIFFEN, T. 1915. The northwest Amazons. London: Constable.

IV

The Technological and Societal Basis of Aging

FRED COTTRELL

There is probably nothing on which social scientists agree more completely than upon the thesis that, to a very great extent, social change is tied up with technological change. Throughout this *Handbook* there will be continuous reference to the way modern technology has modified the position of the aged, so in a sense all the chapters will refer to the product of interaction between technology and the condition of older people. This chapter will therefore be devoted largely to general theory, while the empirical evidence in its support or contradiction will be found in many of the other chapters.

I. TECHNOLOGIC CHANGE AND SOCIETY

VARIOUS TYPOLOGIES

The relationship between technology and other aspects of society has been the subject of a great deal of speculation and has produced a number of theories, at least one of which, Marxism, has led to revolutionary consequences. There has also been accumulated a great deal of empirical data about the way specific technological changes have resulted in specific alterations in other elements of specific societies (Allen *et al.*, 1957). Most of the theories explain to some degree the observed events for which they are supposed to account. But none is so well established that postulates derived from the theory can be shown to be very useful in predicting what *will* occur in any society into which a given technology is introduced.

This does not mean that these theories have not been useful or effective. In fact, it is often because they anticipate that certain social changes *will* result from technological changes that innovators have introduced new techniques (Barnett, 1953). Decisions to industrialize a society flow from the belief that this will contribute to the achievement of the goals held by the decision-makers. Both capitalist and communistic economists agree that increased productivity, whether measured in terms of price or some physical unit, is to a great degree the result of using new technology. Their disagreement lies in a different estimate of the social conditions under which that technology is likely most rapidly and at least cost to be introduced. Nor is there agreement as to what other changes are likely to result when technology *is* changed. It therefore remains an unfortunate fact that changes in technology still have a great many consequences which are unforeseen and perhaps unforeseeable by those who make the decisions which result in technological change.

The best that can be said in behalf of existing theory is that it has permitted potential innovators to examine some putative consequences of their acts which pure empiricism would necessarily have neglected. The potential value of well-developed theory which *would* permit accurate assessment and prediction of the major consequences of technological change is enormous. As a single example, much of the future clearly depends upon the way we use and control the technology implementing atomic energy. For this reason every effort at developing theory which is at all promising should be vigorously tested until its potentiality is demonstrated. In the meantime, we must make do with such theory as offers us here the best explanation we know about.

It is obvious that technology has had much to do with the present condition of older people. Medical technology is responsible for much of the increased longevity which accounts, in part, for the presence of so many older people among us, as shown in chapter ii. Similarly, developments in nutrition have led to increased longevity. The substitution of engine power for muscle power has altered both directly and indirectly the fate of the aged. Most of these developments will be dealt with in other chapters which handle the specific changes and the specific biological and psychological results which flow from them. We will not attempt to deal with these here. Our concern is rather with the massive sociological changes which have accompanied technological changes and have also given rise to new social positions for those in the later years of life. To deal effectively with these, we will have to specialize in the general and build categories into which a tremendous number of separate events can be meaningfully classified.

The authors of the *Handbook* have in effect made two categories of societies, based on technological differences, in assigning to Professor Simmons, in the chapter preceding this one, the task of showing what the fate of the aged was in pre-industrial societies. Thus they imply that industrial societies make up one category or type, while all societies which existed before any society was industrialized, and all societies which are not as yet industrialized, make up the other. The line separating them was not drawn for us, however, nor are we given a hint as to the way it was or should be drawn. Since here we have the task of showing how technology affects all kinds of societies, we shall have to show clearly where the line separating various types is to be drawn, so that, when we get hold of the evidence about a particular people, practicing given techniques, we will know whether to classify them in this category or that one. We could do this, as many have done, by assigning to England the origin of the "industrial revolution" and classifying all countries on the basis of whether they have reached the stage of development which was supposed to have been reached in England at the time of this event. Obviously, this assumes that every society which industrializes will go through the stages England went through, which may be true; but, if we are to characterize these stages, we will have to know just *what* in England's history was essentially due to the technology used and what related to other aspects of English history.

More recently other typologies have come into use. The one which is probably most widespread among American sociologists is that developed by Ogburn (1923) in his work *Social Change*. He distinguished between material and non-material culture and held that it is the geometric accumulation of the former which is the cause of technological change. The prestige which this theory holds evidences its usefulness. But there has not been a great deal of empirical research stemming from it, nor has there developed a body of critical literature demonstrating the limitations of the theory which become apparent under careful scrutiny. This lack of interest in a well-substantiated theory concerning the interrelationships among technological and other aspects of societies has deep roots in American culture and is a subject which itself could well occupy all the space at our disposal here, so we will have reluctantly to abandon its further pursuit.

The anthropologists who have concentrated on earlier cultures have made more progress in developing and utilizing a typology. Whether or not their models will serve well to illuminate the modern scene is at least doubtful. As Simmons shows, it is useful to discriminate between the social practices and organizations of herders, food-gatherers, and cultivators. He says, for example, that "self-employment or ancillary services in agrarian systems probably have provided the most secure and continuous occupational status that society at large has yet afforded for the majority of its aged" (chap. iii, p. 74). For comparison, nomadic herders and food-gatherers sometimes have had to go so far as to abandon their aged when survival of younger members demanded it. The results of using this kind of classification are thus shown by Simmons to be of great value in showing some of the social likenesses which are to be found where particular types of technology are used. It also demonstrates that the value systems and the institutions of a society are not completely independent of technological, geographic, and biological facts.

In a recent work, Steward (1955) has modified to some degree the classifications of those anthropologists upon whose work Simmons relied most heavily. Instead of classifying cultures in terms of the way sustenance is secured (e.g., by food-gathering, herding, cultivation, etc.), he emphasizes the amount and kinds of energy which can be secured by the techniques which are employed and the way this fact modifies what can be done and what is likely to occur. Steward also revives the use of the evolutionary model but emphasizes its multilinear character. He considers energy flow to be one of the elements which influences whether or not events will be repeated. Though his theory differs somewhat from that of Simmons and the students upon whom Simmons relies, it seems, on inspection, to fit equally well or better than empirical evidence which is presented in support of the other theories. It has for us the additional value that it can be quantified fairly accurately. Thus, if a new classification of evidence is made concerning the relationships of technology to society, certain figures as to the energy used to do certain things can be worked out for each of the societies to be categorized. If once this has been done, it should become clear that there *is* a direct variation of some social phenomena when the flow of energy is al-

tered; we will have quantified our data and made them susceptible to the use of mathematical and other forms of logic which we otherwise could not use.

It was as a consequence of getting data into this form not only for pre-industrial societies but for all societies that the theory expounded by Cottrell (1953) was worked out. The model used, stripped to its skeleton is, like that of Steward, a multilinear version of evolution. It attempts to show that the survival of patterns of relationships depends in part upon their ability to secure and direct the flow of energy. Chances for survival of any pattern are enhanced if the pattern results in increased flow, and they decline if it impeded that flow. The energy flowing through a particular system can serve through feedback to increase the capacity of that system so that it will secure and channel more energy. So, to use a simple example, a plant, using the energy stored in root or seed, puts out a leaf, which through photosynthesis converts the energy of the sun and the inorganic products of the soil flowing through the leaf into materials which are then built into new roots, stems, and more leaves, which in turn are able to convert more solar energy, and so on, until the limits of the system of which the leaf is a part are reached. Or, to cite another example, food brought overseas by wind-powered ships from a place where there is no shipbuilding timber can be eaten by men in places where there is timber but no food, to build more ships which can deliver more food. The social structure required to permit this kind of relationship among men is just as necessary as are the physical techniques or the materials used. The kind of social structure which permits a particular kind of energy flow to take place is strengthened by feedback from that flow. On the other hand, competing social structures which prevent such a flow are at a disadvantage—a disadvantage which may be very great or quite insignificant but is nonetheless real and worthy of investigation.

The illustrations we have just given are of course not significant as evidence. They are cited only to permit the reader to get a glimpse of the way this basic conception of the way energy exerts an influence upon society is here used. In elaborating the scheme, and providing limited evidence of its usefulness, each of the major sources of energy used by man, such as food and feed, water, wind, coal, petroleum, gas, and nuclear fuel, is studied. This shows how the scientific and technological facts which determine *how* energy from a source used by man sets limits upon and encourages or discourages his use of it for various purposes. Investigated also are means for discovering how much of the energy produced from a given source must be fed back into the system to keep it going and to enlarge it. Thus the amount of "surplus energy" (energy brought under man's control in excess of that previously under his control which was expended to secure it) can be calculated. One of the fundamental theses developed is that it is around the disposal of newly available surplus energy, and around decisions as to whether or not to do what is required to increase the amount of surplus energy available, that much of the conflict in present-day society occurs. As relates to this chapter this thesis would hold that changes in the amount and kinds of energy used in our society constitute one of the most significant factors which have altered the status and role of middle-aged and older people.

Using this model, it is possible to classify societies in terms of the number of units of energy available daily or annually for each member of the population. An arbitrary figure may be set, marking off classes of societies in such terms, and societies distributed into those categories. Continued study of the results so secured may give evidence that societies might most usefully be divided into two or three or five or ten or more categories. But at the moment, and for our purposes here, we have simply divided them into two categories, "low-energy societies" (those in which energy is secured almost entirely from plants and animals, including of course man himself) and "high-energy societies" (those which

make use of other sources). As a means of roughly dividing them, a point is set at about 5 horsepower-hours per day per person. Those below that figure are "low-energy" and those above are "high-energy" societies. The reason for making the choice of this figure is that in the limited research done so far we have not found a society utilizing only muscle power which reached anywhere near this figure, while societies using extensive trade through wind-driven ships, such as Rome and Greece and England (before about 1750), apparently did reach somewhere around this figure. Since we regard societies like these latter three as the prototypes of "high-energy" society, we set the lowest figure at a point which would include them.

II. The Energy Base of Low-Energy Society

The recent development of energy from nuclear fusion and fission has led to a rash of speculation about a brave new world in which most work will be done without human effort. But the energy of the sun, which has always been used by men, is enormous even when compared with that which man can conceivably control through harnessing the atom. It is *not* the absence of a *source* of abundant energy in nature which limits man's use of it. This limit is rather to be found in the process by which that energy can be converted for the purposes to which man seeks to put it.

In low-energy societies this process starts with photosynthesis by plants and ends when man eats those plants to produce mechanical or other forms of energy through his own body or utilizes energy made available to him through the consumption of plants by other animals. Most men in the history of the world, and perhaps even today, live in societies which fall into this category, although almost all men now have access to at least some small use of energy from other sources. Thus all societies, since they all grew up under these conditions, will show some common characteristics which derive from the limits so imposed on them. They may also exhibit other characteristics in which they do not resemble each other. For some purposes the differences between societies sharing the same kind of energy base are far more significant than their likenesses. For other purposes it is the likenesses which matter. If our categorization is useful, it is to be found in dealing with and accounting for the likenesses.

Among the patterns which all low-energy societies will share are those which result from the characteristics of plant life. A given plant can synthesize only a given percentage of the sunlight which falls upon it —no matter how fertile the soil, how abundant the water, how carefully protected from weeds and plant pests it may be. Therefore the people who use it can get only a maximum of so much from that plant. If they are short of land, afflicted by pests, have limited water, and so on, they may not be able to cultivate as many plants as they otherwise could; therefore, they have even less energy available. But, even with abundant land, and without the other handicaps, they, using the energy of their bodies, can cultivate only so much, and the plants will only produce so much. Then, if men want to use the energy of the plant in the form of mechanical energy, they must either eat it or feed it to an animal. The average man can convert only a small amount of food energy into muscle energy per day. The total is only about what an average horse can do in 40 minutes, less than enough each day to keep a 100-watt light bulb burning for 8 hours. So whatever he gets done in work, travel, or play must not in total require more energy than that.

These facts have many social consequences. One of the most significant is that low-energy societies carry on most of their activities in relatively small groups occupying relatively small areas. Until recently, many of their people lived and died without ever leaving the village in which they were born or ever hearing a strange voice or an idea introduced by a stranger. The institutions which such people maintain are those that will serve *their* needs, and these relate intimately to their own survival and that of their immediate relatives and neighbors. They also must assure the continuity of the culture through which the society will be reproduced.

One means of assuring this arises from the fact that all local institutions interact in the same personalities. What is good as defined at work is also good at home, at play, and in worship. The separation of values into such categories as political, economic, religious, and familial is rare. A man's religion supports the family, and the family his religion. There is religious meaning to economic activity, and a portion of what he produces is certain to be devoted to the maintenance of his religion. Most of what is outside the village community and the kinship group is equally foreign and frequently taboo. There is too little energy for many in the group to waste it on extended travel or transport to and from distant places. Such contacts with different people as may take place are likely to be rigorously formalized so as to insulate against change, else they become the source of conflict. Within such limited systems, very extended division of labor, either territorial or functional, is impossible. Most people have to labor at producing food and fiber. Too much labor is required in the cultivation or gathering of food to permit men to spend the time or to reward them for learning difficult and expensive specialties which can be used seldom and only by a few. This reinforces the effects of special limitation for members of a society who not only live close to each other but do pretty much the same things; and, therefore, the consequences of their acts are likely to be pretty much the same as those encountered by their neighbors.

There are few cities, for there is little surplus energy which can be removed from the control of those who produce it without so impoverishing them as to reduce their ability to continue to produce. Thus the bulk of the population remains rural, and the difference between those who live in the cities and those who live on the land is perpetuated so long as the cities survive. Population tends to multiply in the river valleys where surplus energy from food is greater and cheap water transportation can be added to the energy from food.

All these limits affect the kind of communication and social control it is possible to use. Written documents are difficult to reproduce without some form of energy other than man; so spoken language carries the burden of maintaining day-to-day coordination as well as perpetuating the generation. Much social control depends upon tradition spread through the verbal teaching of the elders. We could continue to elaborate the likenesses of low-energy societies, but it would be redundant for our purposes here. Let us rather look at the consequence of these conditions as they affect the character of the institutions to be found in low-energy society.

III. INSTITUTIONS IN LOW-ENERGY SOCIETY

A. The Family

Perhaps the foremost fact to be noted is the great significance of the family. In most low-energy societies life is relatively short, so that obligation between parents and offspring and the reverse does not often extend to the members of more than two generations. But, in the few cases where grandparents and great-grandparents do survive, their position in the society is usually well fixed, and there is no doubt as to what their roles are or where they stand status wise (see chap. xiii).

In most of these societies the extended family is characteristic. That is, they recognize obligations and rights among a much greater proportion of those who are "related by blood," one to another, than do the people of the United States generally. In fact, it is only in urban-industrial societies, using very large quantities of energy per capita, that so much emphasis is placed, as it is in America, upon the relation of wife and husband and their children. It is easy to see that, where resources are scarce and productivity limited, the extended family will add greatly to the chances for survival (at least among food cultivators) as compared with the small conjugal family. The flexibility with which the extended family can meet special demands for peak-load energy, such as is required at planting or harvest time, helps greatly to assure the complete use of the resources available. On the other hand, the small family may be unable to use its land or tools effectively because of temporary labor shortage. Similarly, in meeting the catastrophe which comes when a father or mother is made non-productive by accident, illness, or death, the extended family is a superior form. It also provides for a division of labor between the age and sex categories that is more efficient. So, for example, grandmothers and the children can carry on household tasks while the stronger young women do field work; or grandfathers can teach the young boys while their sons are carrying on the more arduous arts. Among low-energy societies, these advantages do not accrue to the small conjugal family.

Let us look for a moment, then, at some of the functions carried on by the family in low-energy societies, keeping in mind that we will later review them to see how they relate to the place of the aged. In the extended family the decisions concerning the birth of children do not rest alone on the husband and wife. It may well be, in some societies, that no girl will be accepted into her husband's family until she has borne a child or even a male child. Later, unless she produces her share of the offspring, she is not considered to be a good wife and will suffer the consequences. Unless a man has sons, he may be denied a share in the lands held by his family, since his daughters have no such claim and will be forced to marry into another family; or the reverse may be true, and rights to use land or other property may descend only through daughters. On the other hand, where long experience has taught that the land will produce only a given amount of food, excess children may be unwanted. The survival of a new baby may here be assured only by starving others now living.

Thus the group may require abortion or infanticide or may adopt taboos in relation to sexual intercourse which effectively control the birth rate. We do not wish to go further into this, generalizing on the kinds of controls and their extent; we want only to point out that in the extended family the control over the birth rate lies at a point different from that in the conjugal small family system. The decision-makers are not the same in the two systems, nor are the results to them of limiting births or permitting unlimited births the same.

In the conjugal family there are, to the parents, many predictable consequents of childlessness. These extend from such facts as the extinction of a property-inheriting direct family line to being deprived of the affections of children and inability to provide for one's own emergencies and catastrophes. On the other hand, in an extended family the inheritance of property by one's own children may not be thought of as being particularly significant, and a man may receive affection and care from nieces and nephews much like that shared in the small family only between parents and children. Thus, to the husband and wife, the consequences of bearing children may be quite different in the two systems.

Romantic marriage, widely prevalent where "individualism" is considered to be the ultimate test of social well-being, encourages a relation in which those who decide whether or not to beget and rear children are expected to make the judgment largely in terms of the effect this decision will have on them personally. But the effects of the birth rate extend to a great many people who are thus put in a position where they are unable to influence the choice being made. The aged are probably the most significantly affected group of all these, and in recent times they have probably become the most numerous.

In low-energy society the family carries on the greater part of the economic activities performed there. Among the cultivators of food the labor force generally consists of the members of the family physically capable of engaging in production, though often there are also work groups made up from the members of different families. Since the division of labor between the sexes is largely based on the fact that a man is physically not capable of doing some of the things necessary in the reproduction and the early feeding of infants, women do what is not incompatible with their role as biological mothers. There is a great variety of roles which are played by men in one society and by women in another, but some things women cannot do if they are to reproduce and suckle the young child. Therefore, food preparation and as much of its production as is compatible with woman's necessary role are likely to be carried on by women. Activities demanding heavier musculature are carried on by men. Here, again, what we are emphasizing is that decisions as to what is to be produced, by whom, where, when, and how, are made within the family and kept at least minimally compatible with the primary function of the family. This fact has important implications for aging and the aged.

Within its capabilities the family also provides the means to assure the care of the sick and injured and to maintain the health of its members. As we have seen, most available economic resources are in the hands of those who have a concern for the well-being of the family. It is usually also true that the obligation to care for family members who are unable to care for themselves is fixed in the cultures, so even if the members of a particular family do not personally care about what happens to one of them, they are constrained to look out for him because of the sanctions which will be imposed upon them by the rest of the community if they do not do so.

The family also serves to pass on to its members much of the culture which they receive. In the process, of course, the values which are necessary to the survival of the society are created. The most significant of these—the sacred or religious elements—usually include values necessary to the preservation of the family itself. Like other elements of the sacred, "Honor thy father and thy mother" is not merely a slogan to be repeated on auspicious occasions but a directive, the violation of which may have dire consequences, including sometimes banishment, torture, or death. Sometimes the wrath of the gods falls on those who fail to respect their elders.

The family in this case, and very frequently where supernatural sanction is not often used to secure compliance with mundane obligations, may exercise physical coercion. The head of the family may be held accountable for the behavior of any of its members, but he is, in turn, legitimately entitled to punish them physically and to deprive them of privileges.

In consequence of all these facts and many which we cannot elaborate here, the family is in a position to dictate many of the roles which an individual may play and the status which is attached to them and hence to him. The conception that he has any being apart from the family may be completely absent; but, even where there is recognition of the person apart from the role, the range of autonomous behavior is greatly circumscribed. From birth to death the individual retains his identity in the family, which is itself immortal. The idea that at some time in his life he would cease to be associated with his children and their children may be as much or more difficult to conceive or to accept as is cannibalism or incest. This again has very significant consequences for the elders, which we will examine as we consider the aged in the total environment of low-energy society.

B. Religion and the Church

Among people in low-energy societies that which is sacred tends to be served by special persons designated to carry on the functions necessary to preserve and implement it. In some cases the head of a family may himself be so designated, and "ancestor worship," which sanctifies family ways and makes saints out of real or mythical forebears, prevails. In many more, there is a kind of priesthood which functions among the membership of a number of families. It is their task to assure that the

sacred elements of the culture are passed on unchanged to the next generation. They must also sanction acts prescribed or proscribed. Much of what is sacred behavior takes place in or through the family, and the structure which maintains the sacred is very likely to be devoted to a great extent to the preservation of family life. Thus "the church," as we in the West call it, supports a morality which glorifies and sanctifies the human family, and the family in turn teaches children, when they are very young, the necessity to respect and honor the church.

In some low-energy societies the church has itself become an economic system which competes with other forms. Very often this competing economic system is devoted to the care of those who are not cared for through failure to function of another economic system such as the family. Care of the unattached sick, the blind, the mentally ill and retarded, the epileptic, crippled, and the aged has frequently been maintained out of surplus energy derived from the land by childless servants of the church. So long as agriculture remained the prime source of energy, and the converters used consisted primarily of human beings, an institution such as this was well fitted to compete with or supplement the family or the manor. Old technology and the social structure capable of serving it were sanctioned through time. Sacred ways and technologically competent ways were not necessarily antithetic.

C. Government

As contrasted with the very great significance of family and religious values, low-energy society makes much less use of government than does that using more energy. We here designate government as the institution which performs a complex or cluster of functions centered around or dependent upon the legitimate use of physical coercion. Many low-energy societies assign the roles required to carry on such functions to the members of the family and the religious institution, and there is no secular state at all. But many others, particularly those which developed out of irrigated agriculture, developed an institution in which the power to coerce was monopolized. That is to say, they might permit the church or the family to coerce its own membership but denied them the right to coerce others. At the same time the agents of the state became legitimately entitled to coerce within limits both church and family members.

Where the governmental institution emerged, as separated from the family and church, it performed only limited functions. It was not expected that it would operate as a complete social system. Apart from its police function to control the behavior of certain types of deviants, the most common activity was that of making war or providing for the common defense. Whether the police function resulted from the necessity to create a means to control large amounts of energy to be used in conquest or its repulsion, or whether military potential resulted from the aggregation of force necessary for "internal" policing, the fact that such an aggregation *was* created and maintained is crucial for understanding the functions of government. We do not, here, have the time to dwell on the various theories of the way the state originated. We want merely to point out that the power legitimately to exercise force in a particular manner is related to the whole moral system of the society and, hence, to its total social structure.

Political power, to be legitimate, rests fundamentally upon what children learn in the family, the church, the neighborhood, and other "character-forming" experiences. In low-energy society neither the family nor the church was willing or able to abdicate all its functions in favor of an omnicompetent state. Rulers were thus confined in the functions they controlled to those which did not have the effect of disrupting or destroying the substructure upon which the society rested. Such of them as disregarded this necessity were able only to destroy the society; they could not build a self-perpetuating total state. No state in

low-energy society could seize absolute power, though it might well seize almost all the surplus energy produced in that society —and some of them did and do. Apart from the police and military functions of the state, what, then, are the functions it commonly performs in low-energy society?

A very common one is that of protecting "property." The amount and kinds of things which may be classed as such vary tremendously among societies. As we shall see later, a great deal of what is classed this way today did not exist in low-energy society; thus the state could have no power over it. On the other hand, for example, property in slaves, fairly common in low-energy society, is rare in high-energy society.

In low-energy society there was frequently no idea at all of the personal possession of land as such. A particular territory was recognized as "belonging" to a tribe, clan, or other social entity. A particular area was conceived to be that on which a particular family was expected to make its living or from which it was entitled to take natural products. Even sections of the sea might be claimed in this way. But there was no thought that this right could be alienated or permanently transmitted to another person not sharing the role in which the property was attached as a prerogative. The state protected a common right of a group, a family, a continuously existing entity, not that of an individual. So, to select an example from our own system, a particular President of the United States is not expected to be able to sell the White House or dispose of its furnishings by giving them to his favorites or deeding them to members of his family. Our present concept of property "owned" by a corporation, like Harvard University, corresponds more nearly to the idea of ownership of land in most low-energy societies than does the idea of property which one individual can dispose of as he sees fit.

In low-energy society, where land is basic to the production of energy, the power of the state to transfer title to land is usually limited; and the irresponsible exercise of this power is very likely to rob the state of its legitimacy. The power of the state is thus quite small as compared with that which it might have where other competing energy systems exist to provide a different basis for power than that which lies in the hands of the food cultivators.

Very often in low-energy society there is little resort to the state to resolve personal disputes or to secure redress for injury. Morality may well require the individual to seek to deal with problems of this kind or find their solution through resort to the family head or the priest. The formation and dissolution of marriages may be considered to be matters of no concern to the state, even though they are of great concern to the church; and the sanction of family feuds may be the basis for solving family disputes. Thus many decisions about family obligations lie outside the competence of secular governors.

On the other hand, where sacred elements of the culture call for physical coercion, the state may be required to enforce the sanctity of the marriage or to permit family members to violate its monopoly on the use of coercion by resort to the "unwritten law." In this case the state is more the servant of the family than its master. Similarly, the secular state may be required to protect the prerogatives of the priest, on pain of having its claims to legitimacy reduced or destroyed. The norms are thus set, not through political machinery such as legislature or a bureaucracy, but through social processes in which heads of families and the priesthood play the dominant roles. These are likely to be the elders.

In such low-energy societies as have developed spatially extensive political systems, and in particular in irrigated areas, the state also protects communication. To keep the flow of water at the proper level, in the proper place and time, requires constant accurate communication. Similarly, the mobilization of force for military and police purposes requires that the governor's messages are conveyed accurately and swiftly. A communication network necessary to perform a function, like the control over the water of a river, may be utilized to extend the military power of a centralized government. This, for example, was certainly one element of the rise of such government in China. But here, again, we must recognize that government was controlling only one very limited type of communication among people, most of whose thoughts were transmitted locally and verbally, so that control over communication was distinctly limited.

Similarly, in areas subject to periodic crop failure, the existence of a central agency which has the power to seize surpluses produced in good years and hold them for lean ones may contribute to survival sufficiently to compensate for the cost of maintaining governmental services. But here, again, it must be recalled that these surpluses are created by people in local, family-community-type economic systems who are likely to resist passively, if not actively, unless they accept the legitimacy of the state in this activity. In the few cities possible to low-energy society, the state occasionally has also been expected to carry on services like the provision of sewers, canals, roads, and aqueducts; but these functions pertain to the limited commercial or industrial areas much more than to agricultural places.

Only extremely rarely is "government" expected to provide for the welfare functions so common to it in high-energy society. On occasion a tribal leader might attempt to alleviate temporarily the condition of a village or family hit by catastrophe. Some particular form of dependency may be considered to be related to the sacred in such a way that special care is given to those suffering from it. On the whole, however, responsibility for the care of the ill, the injured, the blind or deformed, the mentally diseased or deficient, and the aged falls upon the family or, in feudal society, upon the manor, with an occasional share devolving upon institutionalized religion. It is from such societies as this that much of our present culture stems; it is not surprising that it has been difficult for people reared in this culture to accept government as legitimately carrying on these functions.

D. The Market

Of all the institutions which characterize America today, none is more ubiquitous than the market. But, on the other hand, in low-energy society the role of the "free market" is extremely circumscribed. As we have seen, the great bulk of economic activity took place under the control of the family and community, with an assist from organized religion and limited participation by government. The idea that the economic activities of men are separable from their familial, religious, and moral or political consequences was unthinkable under these circumstances. The disadvantage of trading where there was to be no regard for the consequences of economic production and consumption other than those felt by the trader at the moment when he made a trade was quite apparent. Until recently there was no system of production which made use of the market, which was also so much more physically productive than that carried on in traditional ways that it could compensate for these quite apparent liabilities. Thus, such trade as was permitted at all was usually confined to a very limited area and to goods not necessary for the preservation of the sacred culture. Recently, some of the proponents of business civilization have attempted to show that the "natural" form of society is one in which all man's values are put on the auction block to be ordered on the basis of his economic desires as implemented by his wealth. Such a view will not bear more than a moment's scrutiny in the light of man's history. The widespread importance of the market as an institution and of market mentality is very recent and relatively rare in the history of the peoples of the world, though it has always played much larger and more significant functions in the urban region of low-energy society than in the food-producing regions outside the city. It was not often that the aged found themselves entirely dependent on the market for life's necessities.

There are a good many other elements of low-energy society that affected the role of the aged. It is not our purpose here to show more than the barest outlines of its institutional character, in the most general of terms. We do it so that we may see more clearly the position of the aged in the societies from which the American people came and in such portions of American society as retained the way of life dependent upon the exploitation of energy initially converted by plants. So now let us look at the position of the aged in light of what we have learned.

IV. Position of the Aged in Low-Energy Society

A. Control over Family and Population

As we pointed out, it was the extended family which determined the birth rate. This put the aged in a strategic location to influence it. Every man who lives long enough will grow old. As he looks at the contemporary condition of the aged, he contemplates his own future. The addition of another child to the family has, to grandfather, much the same meaning as it has for father, who will be grandfather tomorrow. If a man begets too many children, there will not be sufficient food to nourish all of them and provide also for him. If too few, there will be no one to care for him in his old age. It does not require excessive rationality to observe this relationship; and, where the particular individual is thoughtless, the culture is likely to carry sanctions against his deviancy from what is considered moral in this respect. Control over birth may be ineffective because the vagaries of life are such as to provide no clear guide as to what the number of children should be; epidemic disease, for example, may occur so irregularly that no system of planning can assure the "proper" number of births to maintain the "proper" numbers. Similarly, the very early death of most people may make it desirable that every possible child be born. But, for the most part, low-energy societies have had societal controls which served to preserve a balance between births and deaths well inside those which would have resulted from complete dependency upon starvation and disease to bring about that balance. Thus, it was usually not necessary purposefully to limit the lives of the aged.

It is not true that people in every one of the cultures which contributed to the American civilization had an equally high regard for the aged or gave them the dominant voice in the determination of the birth rate. But, in most of them, the voice of the elders, expressed in the culture and transmitted by them to the children, was likely to be listened to much more attentively than it is in America today.

B. Control of Economic and Social Roles

The influence of the aged in this, as well as many other respects, was greatly enhanced by the control they exercised over economic activities. Family life has been so idealized in recent years in the West that its exploitive character is often neglected. If we see it clearly, however, we may realize how fully one age or sex group may exploit another where the family is absolutely necessary to individual well-being and survival. Men do not live long in low-energy society; thus the concept "aged" should be used carefully. But the head of the family was frequently the oldest surviving member of the group. He had much to do with the assignment of tasks and the reward to be secured for performance, although he was, of course, greatly circumscribed in his control by tradition and custom. But, as anyone who has ever worked knows, there are a myriad of ways by which a work supervisor, regardless of what rules he is supposed to work under, can favor one worker over another. The wishes of the old man were often influential when he exercised economic control, and his favor was particularly sought after where

the culture permitted him to determine who would inherit goods, position, or power. Similarly, the old woman could determine a good many of the consequences which would flow from the acts of the younger ones; and, where the sexual division of labor limited women to very few roles, almost all of them centered on child-bearing and care, the rule of the old woman might be even more absolute than that of the old man. Care of the aged was among the first of the obligations laid on family members. The strong were required to care for the weak, the ill, and the unfavored; and, since the aged often were in a position to decide whether they or some other dependent should be favored, they occupied here, too, a strategic position.

His frequent right, as family head, to ordain physical punishment to members of the group gave the elder an effective means to secure his own well-being. It did not apparently occur to the young Isaac that he should resist when his aging father, Abraham, decided he should be offered as a sacrifice to Jehovah. The Jews were not atypical in their attitude that the old man's word was law, no matter how harsh his edict might seem to his offspring. Their position could be duplicated in many low-energy societies.

But power did not stop with the exercise of coercion; it could be extended through supernatural sanction too. Violation of taboo, as it related to the position of the aged, might mean eternal damnation as well as mundane punishment. Secure in his ability to wield this weapon, the old man could envisage his physical decline without fear that it meant loss of power.

He then controlled tremendous resources, not the least of which was that of assigning within limits role and status to individual members of the society and thus forming a personality and a social structure which would inevitably assure that he would not become a non-entity by loss of function and control. He could see to it that what the child learned would produce an image of the aged, such that it would require destruction of his whole personality to extirpate it or even change it much. The variations in societal behavior which threatened his position in each generation were dropped out when cultural transmission took place, unless there was some compelling reason why succeeding generations should repeat them; but the idealized image of the aged was transmitted over and over again. Where a particular family head was absent, or unable or unwilling to insist upon his prerogatives, both state and church often insisted upon them. Judges, both secular and sacred, were most often themselves elders. A man too weak to demand of his children the honor due him might be despised or even punished. The offspring who failed to give respect due the aged were even more likely to feel the pressure of the organized state or church. In the administration of governmental services, too, it was often the aged who played the dominant roles. The picture of old men sending young ones to their death in war has not faded even in modern times. The tests of battle, however, did put a limit on the capacity of the old to rule in military society or during wars. Most of the fighting has to be done by younger men, and the recurrent rise of the corporal to seize the marshal's baton is good evidence that where low-energy society exploited young men too harshly it might be altered or destroyed by them.

The use of forced levies to build roads, aqueducts, or canals also had the effect of weakening communal, family, and religious controls over the young. Where extensive public works were developed, these forces were likely to constitute a check on family and community dominance. This was particularly true where the right to cultivate the land descended to only one of the sons, the others being left to attach themselves to the economic system in some other role than that of husbandman. Frequently, they joined an army which had to be paid for "protection." No matter what the economic system, it is rare that the young males are starved for long, though they may be otherwise greatly underprivileged.

V. Influence of Low-Energy System Cultures on the United States

The United States, like all other modern states, was built up by people whose culture was derived from low-energy systems. A great many of its institutions can be understood only by tracing the origin of its present characteristics back to situations much like those of which we have been speaking. The Polish family might differ greatly from that of the English, the German from the Italian, the Japanese from the Chinese; but all shared in greater or less degree the characteristics which were necessary to the culture, social structure, and the values of these people while they depended upon plants for their energy.

As Simmons has indicated, there was no difference among pre-industrial societies which is as great in degree as the differences which separate them from industrial societies. Whether we trace a particular aspect of our cultural heritage back to the Continent or to Pre-Columbian America, we find elements which reflect the nature of low-energy society.

The basic religions of the United States emphasize the primary values developed in the family. They idealize family relationships and regard the Deity as being one whose characteristics symbolize the father figure. All make sacred some forms of family living. All taboo some kinds of relationships which might in fact better serve high-energy technology than does the inherited sacred structure. The conditions of life encountered in pre-industrial societies have had much to do with creating the matrix of institutions, morals, and religion which make up a large part of present-day American culture.

VI. Some Elements of High-Energy Technology

As we have indicated, we are here separating those societies which make use of less than 5 horsepower-hours of energy per person per day from those which use more. Obviously, any technology has many attributes besides its ability to channel energy. A typology based on those elements may in some cases serve better than that which we use here. Students of our economic system have paid considerable attention to the advantages of scale and those of subdivision of labor. Both, of course, contribute to the effectiveness with which energy is used. It is possible to produce a great deal more, using the same amount of energy, if men are highly trained in a specialty and co-ordinated by a specialist in management, than if each man has to do many things at some of which he is likely not to be so competent as in others. It is possible so to specialize, however, only if there is a relatively large demand for identical goods from the same source. Hence large-scale production, standardized consumption, and specialization go hand in hand. These social attributes may characterize some operations even in low-energy society, but the costs of transportation by muscle power prevent widespread trade and thus limit the size of the market. Low-cost transport is thus needed to make gains from specialization and scale possible. Such transport depends upon the use of energy not secured by way of plants as converters. Thus, while neither specialization nor scale owe their gains directly to a new form of energy, they indirectly depend on its use. Of course it is also true that many societies have existed in which there was available far more energy than could be used, given the social organization and other elements of the society operating there. Gains made only as a result of superior technique and organization often result in increased use of energy so that it serves rather as an index of their effectiveness than as a cause in itself. Our emphasis upon energy is, however, directed at another element of the system, that is, the dynamic effect of surplus energy.

The major source of surplus energy used in the world until around 1750 was that secured from plants. Since these plants have fixed limits on the amount of energy they can convert, and since until very recently it was not possible deliberately to alter them much, surplus energy was al-

ways small and relatively constant. The use of the steam engine to capture surplus energy stored in fossil fuels made it possible to increase energy from these sources at a rate totally disproportionate to that which man had previously experienced. The addition of the internal-combustion engine and the electrical generator made surplus from coal, gas, petroleum, and, now, the atom available for thousands of purposes. The outcome, of course, is seen in the proliferation of machines to convert energy from these sources, together with gross changes in the necessary social organization, in the growth, size, location of population, and in values.

TABLE 1*

GROWTH OF HORSEPOWER-HOURS OF ENERGY PRODUCED AND OF POPULATION IN THE UNITED STATES, 1850–1950

Year	Horse-power-Hours (In Billions)	Population (In Millions)	Horsepower-Hours (Per Person)
1850.........	10	23.2	440
1900.........	78	76.0	1,030
1950.........	675	150.7	4,470

* Source: C. Tibbitts, "Aging as a Modern Social Achievement," in C. Tibbitts and Wilma Donahue (eds.), *Aging in Today's Society* (Englewood Cliffs, N.J.: Prentice-Hall, Inc., 1960).

In Table 1, Tibbitts (1960) has set forth the changes which have taken place in the amount of energy used in the United States. He has also demonstrated how this increase in energy has been accompanied by a change in the source of energy and in the converter through which it was put to use (Table 2).

More recent figures show that the energy output per person is still climbing though perhaps at a less accelerated rate than previously. Obviously, too, the percentage of energy derived from human beings is beginning to approach so small a figure that even tremendous increases in the energy used will not reduce it much.

Also of outstanding importance is the increased length of our working years. As Wolfbein and Slavick show in chapter x, remaining life-expectancy for males at age 20 has increased from 42.2 in 1900 and a work life of 39.4 in that year to a life-expectancy of 69.5 years in 1955 and a work life of 43.0 years. The productive years available to society from each person born into it are thus on the average greater than was formerly the case. We might also deal at length with the way variance in the demographic profile has accompanied increased use of energy. But it would be extremely difficult if not impossible to indicate the degree to which these changes are dependent upon technological as distinguished from other changes. This is likewise true with regard to such alterations as the amount of urbanization and indus-

TABLE 2*

PERCENTAGE DISTRIBUTION OF SOURCES OF
ENERGY USED IN PRODUCING GOODS
AND SERVICES, 1850–1950

Year	All Sources	Human	Animal	Inanimate
1850......	100	13	52	35
1900......	100	5	22	73
1950......	100	1	1	98

* Source: C. Tibbitts, "Aging as a Modern Social Achievement," in C. Tibbitts and Wilma Donahue (eds.), *Aging in Today's Society* (Englewood Cliffs, N.J.: Prentice-Hall, Inc., 1960).

trialization taking place, each of which is shown in subsequent chapters to have very significantly altered the meaning of aging in the modern world. Here we can only take up broadly the consequences of change as they are related to the use of new fuels and their converters.

The first social consequence in the use of high-energy technology in point of time and perhaps also in terms of significance was the destruction of the integrity of the village community as the basic unit of cultures based primarily upon agriculture. Outstanding in this process was the divorce of consumption and production patterns from the land on which they take place. It will be recalled that, where cultivated plants furnished the bulk of energy surpluses, there was necessarily some accommodation at the local level between those who con-

sume and those who produce. Wind power operating on the sailing ship permitted goods produced at points quite remote from one another to be exchanged. The social codes under which production took place were therefore not related to those under which consumption of those goods took place in the intimate manner which had characterized production and consumption in low-energy society. This terminated the automatic character of a great deal of social adjustment. The processes of time alone could not certainly be relied upon to produce reciprocal adjustments. Those in control of transportation by ship could redirect the flow of goods as their self-interest dictated. This interest was rarely equated with that of the consumers or the producers, so that, when changed conditions might have righted an imbalance, the trader was able to respond to them in a way quite unlike that which was possible to a producer rooted through soil to the local situation. For example, he could introduce into a market food produced by slave labor and with it support the growth of cities which would have stopped growing had they depended upon local produce. He could continue this process so that the local food-raiser was reduced to penury, but the moral outcry of the farmer went unheard in the market places of the city. City-reared soldiers fed with cheap or free slave-produced food could be depended upon to put down any rebellion among the tillers of the soil. The gradual destruction of the local husbandry, the erosion of land, and the destruction of the old social organization might go unnoted by those fed from ships. While the use of the price system to mediate the relationship between producer and consumer thus stripped both acts of much of the moral significance they once had, it still remained true that the moral consequences of both production and consumption constituted an integral part of the social system of any society. We will later note in greater detail what some of these consequences were. We here want only to emphasize that it was the fact that the new techniques could use great quantities of free surplus energy which led to a great part of the changed character of economic acts. Those who adopted these techniques gained in economic power. They simultaneously gained political and military power. Those who refused to permit the kind of trade which made possible the use of increased surplus thus became more and vulnerable before those wielding the power of new technology.

As we have indicated, low-energy society rested on a land base composed for the most part of village communities or of small groups moving about in quite narrowly limited geographic areas. High-energy technology undermines this kind of unit.

Low-energy societies which are based on muscles as prime movers cannot escape the limitation imposed on them by the necessity to use land for the production of food and feed. But, when they shift to the use of, say, petroleum products and means to convert them into work, the nature of the limits change, and so does the kind of production which is least costly and most productive. The human is much more often paid in proportion to the time it takes to do a job than in proportion to the energy expended upon it. When human energy was the basic source of energy, however, there was little opportunity to increase the energy used without simultaneously increasing the time taken. This is where the new fuels became so important. Those who produce petroleum products make available for man's use thousands of times the energy which is used to produce them. Thus a farmer can, by increasing the energy he uses, greatly speed up the operations he performs; but, since the surplus energy from petroleum is produced at so little human time cost, the time gained by using it is greatly in excess of that spent in producing the surplus energy. As a matter of fact, in the United States we have reached the point where more calories are expended in the production of some crops than can be secured from those crops. It is apparent that those who control production in agriculture find it increasingly advantageous to use techniques requiring more and more

energy from petroleum and other cheap sources, substituting it for time payments to human beings. Since a man driving a tractor can cultivate or harvest a much larger area in a given time than one can who drives a draft animal or uses hand power, many fewer people are needed in the old cultivated areas. They must, if they are to use the new techniques effectively, migrate to places where they too can have access to fuel-produced power. So the village community which is the backbone of low-energy society is threatened both by the decline in its effectiveness to serve agriculture and by the development of the market. In its place there arises a new kind of rural life which is often served almost as poorly by the old institutions as is the urban industrial complex into which so large a part of the population is drawn by the character of the technology it serves (Nelson, 1954).

It would not be possible in this short space to delve into all the relationships between changing technology, changing values, and other ecological factors which give rise to and affect the character of urban life. We here point only to the part that the modern metropolitan community could not exist without the power grid, steam and internal-combustion engines, and the fuels which serve them. And one other thing is certain: there is no high-energy society in which cities are not growing. An ordering of societies in terms of their energy consumption places them in almost the same position as does ordering them in terms of their urbanization. The city and high-energy technology go hand in hand. But city life is not well served by the institutions which developed in low-energy society.

The new technology also required a complete change in the nature of the division of labor. Age and sex grading remain universal forms of social structure which have very important consequences for the aged. But the assignment of roles and statuses in terms of those functions that are required by new techniques are of perhaps equal consequence. The body of science and technology which is in use has grown to such enormous proportions that no man can know more than a tiny fraction of it. Effectively to use it, some new kinds of social organization are required. The knowledge once possessed only by the elders is not enough. In many cases it is, in fact, obsolete, and its possession is a hindrance rather than a help.

To co-ordinate the activities of a great many people, each a specialist in terms of his knowledge and skills, requires more than the family or similar kinship organization can provide. A science and an art of management are needed and new institutions to serve them. The concern of management for efficient use of resources replaces the concern of the traditionalist for the preservation of the old social structure, at whatever cost in terms of efficiency. Members of functional groups, exercising power and influence as such, place demands upon the system in which values associated with the preservation of the family, the community, and the state are sometimes subordinated to those of the union, the corporation, or the profession. Since in many cases these organizations serve as the nexus through which most of the major values of the individual are secured to him, values which enhance the power and primacy of that organization gain for him ascendancy over those necessary for the preservation of older forms of organization. The fractionization of morality is thus in some degree a direct result of technology itself, and in others it derives from the emergence of new forms of social organization which grow up to serve technology.

New means of communication have also appeared. Through the mass media it is possible for outsiders acting at a distance successfully to compete in the promotion of values with those who rely for their success upon face-to-face communication in primary groups. Since it was the monopoly upon child-rearing which gave the family in the local community so strategic a place in low-energy society, the destruction of that monopoly by the establishment of other institutional controls carries with it a threat to all family-and-community-cen-tered value hierarchies. The development of new educational and promotional organizations has been affected to an as yet unknown degree by modern technology, but the arts of mass communication have been much more frequently put at the service of the market, the corporation, and the state than the family or the community. Reliance upon the family to transmit the culture has declined as the character of the culture has made such reliance an impossibility. To an increasing degree education has become a function of government and of specialized research and information agencies. While it remains true that a great reliance is still placed on the family to provide the primary-group values upon which so much of the rest of the social structure depends, the family is not capable of providing the technical information or the specialized morality necessary to the performance of the modern roles of the individual. Technology has thus served at almost every turn to weaken and destroy the patterns familiar to low-energy society.

What must happen, then, as high-energy technology develops is a reconsideration of the values and the institutions of the society into which it is spreading or within which it is evolving. Every value which affected choice in the old system will be re-examined in the light of its costs in the new one. Every institution will be under strain, losing or gaining in its capacity to perform functions for the members of the society in which it is operating. In this welter of change the position of the aged will be altered along with that of every other category of persons.

We may see more clearly just how the aged are affected by noting the specific changes which occur among institutions by seeing what the status of the aged is in these institutions and thus discovering how the status of the aged is altered by these changes. We may also note how the shift from community relations in rural society to those found to exist in urban society also has given rise to alterations in the life-chances of the older person. Other chapters will in turn show how the shift in these relations has altered the attitudes and values of the people undergoing change.

VII. Changing Position of Institutions in High-Energy Society

A. Decline of the Extended Family's Power and Functions

As we have already indicated, much of the old structure depended for its effectiveness upon the fact that men in a local community commonly shared many of the same tasks, faced the same conditions, and fared the same way under given local conditions. But, because the use of high-energy technology calls for extremes of specialization, the extended family is a very poor device to provide effective social structure (Ogburn and Nimkoff, 1955). The division of labor between the sexes and age groups may, in a given specialty, be necessarily quite different from that which results from the formation and production of family life. The family cannot produce the specialists needed. The skills are transmitted outside the family. Specialized knowledge must be acquired elsewhere. Industrial discipline may require morals quite different from those that could be made compatible with the requirements for family stability. Rarely is the family large enough to consume the total output of a production unit or to use high-energy technology effectively in production. For example, efforts to utilize only the members of a single family to conduct such co-ordinated activities as are carried on by the New York Central, Standard Oil, or United States Steel must obviously fail. With the failure of the family to serve technology goes loss of its ability to assign role and determine status. With it, also, goes the ability effectively to transmit control over the economic means to living through social inheritance under family control. The old man thus loses a great deal of his power. His prerogatives decline in numbers and significance. He is no longer the teacher; he cannot initiate youth into the mysteries of effective knowledge and skill under conditions which will assure that, at the same time, youth will be required to absorb and effectively adopt codes which protect the weakening aged from the energy of the young. In fact, the very skills and knowledge upon which he depended to assure his control may become obsolescent and thus impose a handicap upon the pious youngster who heeds the old man's advice or respects his position.

In place of the extended family appears the small conjugal system based primarily on the marital relationship. This type of group can much more easily meet the demands for rapid mobility, both spatial and social, which are imposed by changing technology, than can the extended family which served low-energy society so well. The old man no longer selects his daughters-in-law; nor can a mother, through influencing a choice of groom, assure her future position. In fact, it is difficult to convince the young that the family has any legitimate function after the children have selected mates of their own. It is difficult to impose on them a sense of obligation to their elders. Claims established by the state, the corporation, the union, and particularly by their own children take priority. Those priorities are respected by the parents, who can expect to enter no effective protests when, in the interest of "getting ahead," their children enter employment far from their parent's place of residence in a world whose codes are bound to alienate them from their parents.

As we have observed, the exploitation of high-energy technology requires this redistribution of population at an ever increasing rate. The proportion of the populace residing outside the metropolitan areas continuously declines, and the emergence of new population centers follows from the invention of new means of production, new materials, and new weapons, vehicles, machines, and other industrial products. So the assertion of old rights in the name of piety, and the demonstration that effective personal living depends upon family unity, the persistence of family ties, and the maintenance of childhood friendships, is met by the conflicting demands of the state, the corporation, and the market—demands implemented by the flow of energy from sources which the extended family cannot effectively control. With the decline of the extended family goes a loss of control by the aged over the birth rate. The young adult is free to choose how many children he will have, solely on the basis of the values which he holds at the moment. He may be without the experience to understand how an increase in his children will rob him of his ability to aid his parents or even provide for his old age. He may be unmoved by the fact that, in enlarging his family, he renders housing inadequate, capital insufficient, and the number of hospitals, roads, and other collective services incapable of serving his own and future generations. Whatever influences him during those few years that he is begetting children is alone considered to be of significance. It is no longer in the hands of the aged to affect the factor, which probably, more than any single thing, will affect them.

As already indicated, in place of face-to-face communication, there is mass communication or specialized publics, each learning elements of life not shared with others. Neither permits the development through interaction of an effective common code. The persistence of ideal images of the aged, once assured, now becomes extremely doubtful. In the market place of ideologies such symbols as carry the father image of the past compete with those new symbols dreamed up by the businessmen and the proponents of power politics.

Secularized knowledge is required for the effective use of modern technology. It conflicts at a myriad of points with the sacred. To assure technological competence, even the church is required to teach this body of knowledge which undermines its own authority. Continuous "reinterpretation" of the gospel creates schisms and throws doubt on the validity of the whole theology. With the undermining of supernatural authority, the old man is deprived of another means to assure his position. There is no longer a bastion to protect him against the superior energy and knowledge of his young competitor.

The decline in the size of the group which can claim the services of its stronger and wiser members for the protection of the weaker, sick, or otherwise ineffective members means that the family can no longer assure its members against such disasters. It also means that the position of the old man in the family gives him no strategic advantage over others who are unable successfully to compete in the struggle for life. The great emphasis upon youth, which a rapidly changing society like ours is apt to adopt, is accompanied by increasing concern over all the unfortunate young as against the declining aged. Public education of the young is justified by the contribution they may yet make. Worry over the young deviant is multiplied by the years of damage he may yet inflict upon society. The dramatization of the young victim of polio or palsy is much easier than it is presenting an appealing picture of the problems of the aged. Aid to dependent children fits the pattern of responsibility to one's children which is generated in the conjugal family. The reciprocal claims of parents on their children are in this context often considered by parents themselves to border on the immoral. Since the claims of all the dependent are no longer mediated by the elders in a family system, the decision-makers today are less likely to see, understand, and respect the needs of the aged.

The necessity to set up special institutions to teach secular knowledge and technological skills has given the state a tremendous advantage over the family and local community in the transmission of culture. In fact, it has permitted the creation for the first time of a system in which the young may systematically be taught to despise the ways of their forebears. The United States is a nation composed of immigrants and of their offspring. Many of them came bearing cultures which were not only in conflict with each other but almost always poorly suited to provide for living in a country continually advancing to new frontiers, both geographic and technological. To "Americanize" the child almost always meant, and frequently means, that family ways are "old-fashioned" or "old country." In either case they were such that, if the child attempted to persist in them at school, he was likely to be ridiculed by the teacher and most often by his peers as well. Rapid changes in technology and in science have made it dangerous for the youngster to depend upon his parent for help in school. In part, this results from advancing the frontiers of substantive knowledge, and part of it derives from the development of new techniques of teaching which the parents neither understand nor approve. When the new methods are combined with the traditional means known to parents, the result is confusing to the child who wants to know the "right" way to solve his problems.

B. The Church

The aged can no longer rest secure in the belief that other institutions will reinforce their authority. They can, in fact, be almost certain of at least some conflict with other authorities which may serve to weaken not only their own power but also that of all other agencies so that the child may become alienated from all legitimate control. This great increase in secular knowledge not only reduces the role and authority of the aged in the family but also reduces the power and the authority of the priesthood. Of all the agencies creating moral behavior, the church probably has demonstrated more continuous care for the aged than any other, except the family itself (see chap. xix). But its capacity to do so is weakened by the fact that, while it can verbally sanctify the love of the aged and glorify their care, the decisions as to what physical goods shall be used in their behalf no longer can be made primarily among the elders of the church, for it can no longer supply the necessary goods from its own economic resources. Beginning with the revolutions which accompanied the kinds of trading which the widespread use of the sailing ship made possible and profitable, the position of the Western church as an economic system was progressively

undermined. Most of its lands were taken from it or rendered relatively less economically productive than they had previously been. So the religious agencies, too, have lost much of their capacity to serve those for whom the family is unable or unwilling to care. Stripped of its wealth-getting activities, the Western church is relatively less well able to provide for the aged pious than in earlier times. Thus neither of the institutions which once provided a fairly powerful position, from which the aged could promote and administer to their own needs, can any longer be depended upon adequately to do so.

C. Legal Institutions

Nor do the aged fare much better when they rely upon the dictates of ancient law administered by the elders. One of the early means through which adjustment was made to trade and industrial production was the substitution of private contract for public law. Under it "free men," in return for a place in the new economic system, were permitted to barter away most of the protections built into the old by agreeing to forego what the law had previously guaranteed to them. The courts were then required, in most instances, to enforce contractual obligations even though this might have the effect of making many other parts of the old social system inoperable. The employer was absolved from legal responsibilities toward his aging employee by terminating the contract. It is now clear that it is not possible this easily to dissolve the social obligations which a breadwinner or a citizen is expected to meet. Yet the courts recognized no legal obligations establishing the rights of the individual to such economic resources as would permit him to do what morals and law required him to do. Thus the aged were barred from asking, in the name of an old system of law, what changing social institutions denied them.

Moreover, it is not only in terms of this substitution of contract for status that the legal position of the aged has been altered. With the rise of high-energy technology there have emerged new forms of social control almost, if not quite, as effective and pervasive as the common or civil law. Administrative law and industrial jurisprudence grow out of the special requirement of high-energy technology and the bureaucracy which is required to serve it. Professional codes and union rules provide a whole range of effective controls which lie outside the bounds of what is dealt with by legislatures and courts. Occasionally, these codes are modified, or the sphere they are permitted to rule is reduced by statute. Again the courts, operating on the basis that they exceed the limits permitted by the Constitution, reduce the sphere within which these controls operate. For the most part, however, they are allowed to function with only the barest kind of interference because the rules in question have grown up in very special situations. A high degree of technological competence is required to understand and interpret them—a kind of competence seldom shared by the old men who occupy the bench and know only the traditional forms of law. Sometimes the elders, among those who participate actively in the evolution of these specialized codes, are able to use them to reassure a position for themselves. Union seniority provisions represent a case in point. But far more frequently the changing demands of the situation make technological competence an absolute necessity and functional efficiency of greater moment than the preservation of inherited social structure. They thus deny any great influence to those who may be interested in the preservation of social structure and of human values not immediately pertaining to the problems confronting the administrative decision-makers.

D. Increasing Functions of the Market

As we have already indicated, the use of price-measured value stripped from its connection with other kinds of value is not widespread in the history of man. It was the introduction of new technology which served to upset the way goods and services were exchanged in low-energy societies and permitted them to be offered freely in the market place. We need, perhaps, to look for a moment or two at the reasons why this took place before proceeding to show what has been its significance to institutional development.

We have already pointed out how, in low-energy society, most of man's activity tends to be centered around a very limited geographic site. Here, the costs of goods and services can fairly easily be ascertained. The number of bushels a husbandman produces and the number of man-days which go into their production often remain relatively constant even over generations. Similarly, almost everyone knows the number of sheep required to provide the wool, for, say a coat, the number of days the spinner must spin, the time it takes the weaver to weave it, and the difficulty of learning and performing the necessary skills. Over time, since all goods and services depend upon the same energy sources, and all use man as a common converter, a system of rewards and deprivations gets worked out which is adequate to secure, generation after generation, the behavior necessary to produce and distribute the goods and services which a people utilize. This system may be quite exploitive of one set of people and reward another quite "unfairly," as compared with what some egalitarian or other moral principle would dictate. It may, for example, provide rewards primarily on the basis of assigned status, with little attention being given to "productivity" as measured some other way. The point is not that this stable arrangement conforms to some universal principle of justice or of technical efficiency but that it becomes capable of survival because it is part of what successively induces generations of people to do what they must do to make the system work.

Once any such system gets working, it is difficult to alter it. The culture, the social structure, and the value system serve to assure that each class of persons necessary for production will be taught to carry on its necessary activities. They will also learn that variation from their assigned roles will be considered to be immoral and may result in severe punishment, including in extreme cases even eternal damnation. The "just price" promoted in medieval Europe is only one example of this kind of system. In low-energy society generally, then, goods and services are produced in a social matrix which largely establishes their rate of exchange. Often the economic function is intimately connected with another; thus, for example, families may agree to an interchange of goods at a rate fixed through the intermarriage of their members. This arrangement will, in many cases, continue until that marriage is dissolved. It is easy to see that this kind of relationship is much easier to maintain when the limits under which production takes place are permanent and do not fluctuate widely from time to time. There is, then, little opportunity continuously to alter physical productivity in any particular direction so that, say, the weaver is able to produce more and more cloth in a given time.

The introduction of a new source of energy changes this relationship. As noted earlier with the use of the wind-driven ship, it was possible to bring goods from afar, produced there in some kind of stable system which made their exchange value low, to other points in which it was higher. From there in turn the ship could move goods with low exchange value to other points where they would bring a higher return.

What must be remembered is that the exchange value of goods in low-energy society was based only in part on physical productivity. Thus, a trader might, in exchanging goods between two societies, be taking advantage of the fact that the role and status system of one society differed from another in the rewards it offered—a given productive agent. For example, the weaver in one society, because he was the head of the family, might be rewarded more highly for a day's work than was the spinner, who in that society might be an unmarried sister of the breadwinner or of his wife. She, having fewer social responsibilities and lower status, could expect only less for her day's

work. In another society perhaps the situation would be different, and the obligations and the rewards of the spinner would be as great as, or greater than, those of the weaver. An exchange which permitted the trader, and perhaps the consumer, to benefit from lower exchange value of goods produced by one kind of worker in each of these systems would have the effect of upsetting both systems without necessarily producing an increase in their physical productivity. The trader could encourage such an exchange and seek the support of such consumers as were more concerned about the exchange value of cloth than other values which were sacrificed to permit trade. But the original producers who suffered from this kind of exchange would similarly seek support from all those who looked with suspicion or fear upon alteration of the sacred ways or who discovered the ramifications which resulted from, say, depriving the weaver of the means adequately to play his expected role as breadwinner.

The introduction of trade, then, might greatly upset the whole system of statuses and roles upon which the operation of a society rested. Those who wished to preserve their sacred system could be expected to react to prevent trade, and since, in the circumstance cited above, the trading system produced no real increase in the goods and services available, expansion of trade might be limited or even stopped altogether.

On the other hand, the introduction of the ship, permitting trade at a distance, sometimes resulted in real, persistent gains in physical output by some groups in the economy. So, for example, it permitted more wool to be grown in areas where wool, because of climate and soil, could be produced more abundantly than food and exchanged with those living in an area where the reverse was true. Thus both food and wool became more abundant among the trading partners. While this kind of shift in land use and in the roles which producers were required to play might also have disastrous consequences to the previous system, the rewards offered for compliance with the demands of technology were sufficiently high, for example, to turn many British corn fields into sheep runs. This real increase in physical production could be used to encourage or force enlargement of exchange based on price. Thus the introduction of the new energy source, which required in turn the enlargement of the market, also affected the way the family or other institutions operated. If to preserve its old ways one society prevented trade, they also prevented the use of the ship and the surplus energy it could provide them. It was often subsequently overrun by a neighboring one which, complying with the demands of technology, had made it possible to support a bigger population, accumulate more wealth, or otherwise increase its power. The range of the market was then further extended, and gains which arose from specialization of labor and from larger-scale production were added to those arising originally from ecological differences.

It was often not possible to find culturally sanctioned exchange relationships extending between people who did not share the same culture. Under these circumstances a system of free markets developed rapidly, money became a common denominator of values, and price served to reflect the alternatives which different societies permitted among their members.

With the use of the price system, goods could be secured on the basis of their desirability as objects without reference to the conditions under which they were produced. Exchange value in the market, measured in price terms, thus replaced the values sanctioned by the community, its culture, and its social structure.

But, in the market, values which could not be dealt with in price terms were frequently made subordinate to price considerations. Of course, where this new ordering of values was sufficiently disturbing, there was reaction which in its turn limited the use of pricing. But in the West there was no turning back. Price-measured values rose higher and higher in the hierarchy of values.

With the price system established to carry on some kinds of exchange, the op-

portunity to add other energy sources was expanded. To supplement the energy of the weaver and spinner, the British added that of falling water and eventually coal. The skills and the social organization required to supply an increasing demand for cloth were supported by many groups which could benefit by this physically more effective production system. The prestige and power of those associated with trade, shipbuilding, and textiles were raised. It is not necessary here to show how British industry designed to serve trade expanded from this base, so that eventually most of the energy used was coming not from plants, wind, or water power but from coal. Nor can we explore the way other nations, who borrowed British technology and set it down in their own society, modified the British model.

The point of particular interest to us is the theory which developed around British experience, for it is that theory which had so much to do with the way institutions have developed in the United States. As we saw, in British experience it was through the use of the price system that trade was expanded, and it was through trade via the sailing ship that a new source of energy was added to those generally used in low-energy society. Given British conditions, the physical gains in productivity were inseparable from the particular kind of social structure which facilitates trade. Thus the use of the price system and the gains in productivity which resulted from substituting coal for plants as a source of energy were inextricably tied together. British theorists could not see how an industrial system could emerge or be sustained without the free market, by which they had themselves escaped the barriers to economic productivity established by low-energy societies. They thus held that the only way great gains in physical productivity might be made was through permitting the market and the values and social structure which it supports and which support it to take precedence over such other values and structure as would interfere with it. Government, for example, could create nothing, and, if it were to be effective, it could interfere only with a system which would in the long run assign every person to the role he should take and provide him the "proper" reward for his productivity. On the other hand, since "you can't interfere with the law of supply and demand," government itself would eventually be forced to recognize the claims of the market; there was no reason, therefore, for it to intervene at all.

This was their verbal position; but a study of British history will reveal that the trader was himself continually using political and military power to expand the area in which he was to be free to operate. The British Empire was not created merely by allowing British salesmen to peddle the cheaper products of British industry to an eager world. The power of government was constantly being used to prevent those who were opposed to the spread of trade and the disturbances in their value system which it brought with it from interfering. Freedom of the seas meant that British traders could go where they pleased, but, so long as Britannia ruled the waves, there was no such guaranty to other traders. In fact, then, it is apparent that it was, perhaps, as much because of the *political power* of the trader and the industrialist who was allied with him that Britain became the workshop of the world as because of the *price system* which they also used to achieve this position. It will be recalled by those who know British history that "Free Trade," as a doctrine, appeared only after British industry had become so physically productive that it need no longer interpose political and military barriers to protect it against other systems.

Be that as it may, the doctrine that price-measured values are dominant among those shared by men became an article of faith among American businessmen, and, insofar as the territory of the United States itself was concerned, this doctrine was implemented by means which prevented the various states from interfering with interstate commerce. While undermining the social structure of low-energy society, businessmen led the movement which reduced the capacity of the states to protect their citizens against the ravages of disorganization which accompanied the dominant use of high-energy technology served by the free market.

VIII. POSITION OF THE AGED IN THE FREE MARKET

We cannot explore this thesis further, but it has been developed sufficiently far that we can now examine the position in which it put the aged. We have seen that the family and religious institutions were stripped of many of their most important functions through their inability to direct and control the new forms of technology. How, then, do the aged fare in the free market?

The first aspect to be noted is that the market tends to penalize those who permit values other than those measured in the market place to interfere with its operation. If the purpose of those in the market is to secure for themselves the greatest price-measured value, they will seldom find that this result is secured by taking first into account the integrity of the family, the advantage to the state, or gains to the church. Thus, for example, the banker who is permitted only to measure in monetary terms the consequences of his handling of the bank's money may not refuse to collect from the widow or foreclose the mortgage on the orphan's heritage. To do so would be to violate his obligation to those who expect that their money will be secure and earn all that it is possible to collect. This kind of situation is one which the defenders of a pure price system have some difficulties with. They waver between attempting to justify the collection of all that the market will bear by showing that "in the long run" this is certain to produce the best of all possible economic worlds, and, on the other hand, denying that the price system in action is in fact so heartless as it is made to appear. It is clear, however, that if managers permit other considerations than price to prevail in the market, they violate the propositions upon which the proponents of the free market base their case.

This case rests on the assumption that no other kind of value judgment is as fair or as economically sound as that secured by freely offering goods for exchange in the market. So nothing justified the interposition of any other kind of value judgment.

This point was not made with the idea of invading the field of economic theory. It was designed to show that, by the logic of the market, there is no place for consideration of many of the values by which the aged were in the past able to buttress their competitive position against others. The use of the labor market puts a penalty on aging, as will be shown over and over in this volume. It does so because, in market terms, the aged are frequently not worth as much as younger men. Many people suffer in aging a decline in the abilities which the market is willing to use. It is often easier to train the young than to retrain the old. The young have yet more years of top productivity remaining to them. On the average, they have more physical stamina and greater agility and dexterity. They are not burdened with internalized standards of production which have been made obsolete by the use of power-driven machinery. Where these things count, and often they do count in determining price-measured productivity, the market penalizes the employer who hires or continues to employ the aged. The market is also ruthless in selecting for extinction the firms which are not, in terms of the values measured in the market, as efficient as their competitors. Thus the savings of the aging proprietor may go down the drain with the chances for future employment of his older employees. Where a business does not fail, its securities may greatly decline in value, so that aging investors become the victim of the market-measured inefficiency of the firm in which they have invested their savings.

There is no place in the market for the unemployable aged, widowed, disabled, or mentally incompetent. But the market itself is frequently responsible for having destroyed the economic capacity of some other agency, like the family, to care for those whose services have no price-measured value.

In the market the young unencumbered worker and others with few social responsibilities receive a reward based on their market-measured productivity. So, too, do those with many social obligations. In effect, then, the irresponsible are given higher rewards than those who carry on more socially desirable activities. The market treats human labor as if it were like any other commodity to be bought and sold. But the worker who accommodates himself to the system of rewards and punishments which the market establishes frequently must become immoral or dysfunctional in terms of other roles he plays. The investor finds that technological obsolescence threatens the security of his investment as competitors, unburdened by plant and machinery adapted to an earlier method of production, are able to offer goods at a price which he cannot meet and simultaneously pay for outmoded equipment and obsolescent man power.

Thus for all the flexibility which the market permits, it has distinct handicaps as a means to organize economic activity. Each type of person affected by these adverse effects has tried to assure its own position. Investors and managers were the first to be able to do this.

IX. DEVELOPMENT OF THE CORPORATION AND ITS EFFECT ON THE POSITION OF THE AGED

Early captains of industry found in the corporation an institution which was able to provide a new framework in which the new technology could be operated successfully but which at the same time extended much greater security to the investor than he could secure in the market. Government was called upon to create this legal person. In addition, it provided patents, trade marks, tariffs, and subsidies which the corporate manager was able to use in such a way that he could escape many of the dangers of free competition in the market place. Thus those of the aged who were protected by this new economic institution found themselves more secure. But those who remained in the free market faced new insecurities. The free market spreads the danger of loss among all those involved in a transaction. But the corporation which protects its investors and managers simultaneously throws an additional burden upon others who are left to keep the necessary balance between supply and demand in the market. Aging farmers, workers, and small proprietors thus gained little security through the rise of the corporation and the administered price system which has developed to serve it.

Until quite recently corporate managers regarded the protection of their stockholders and maximization of gains to stockholders and managers as their sole concern, and most still make all judgments with an eye to the largest profit that can safely be made. They continued to use the market mechanism to determine the value of the services of "outsiders" even though they had to develop a different means to evaluate the services of corporate "insiders." For this reason the corporation was no better a means than the market itself to serve the needs of unorganized and unprotected workers, small businessmen, and "unemployables," among whom, of course, there were numerous older people.

So far, then, the emergence of high-energy technology had been accompanied by weakening of the elements of the social structure upon which the aged had in the past relied to secure their ends. The new emphasis upon the market and other economic institutions, while it made the system more technically competent to provide an increased flow of goods, provided no certain way by which the aged could claim a share of that increase or even to guarantee to them the economic goods and services which they were able to enjoy in low-energy society. As we have indicated, they were not alone in this respect. Unorganized workers of all ages found themselves in the same condition, as did small farmers, the

widowed and orphaned, the sick, injured, and otherwise handicapped. Under these circumstances we should expect that they would all simultaneously be seeking means through which their well-being could more certainly be secured.

The history of the United States bears witness to the variety of movements that were spawned in this situation. There is not room here for more than a passing glance at the way the different needs of various sets of people gave rise to specific movements. There have, however, been a host of such experiments. Many, such as the Amish, for example, sought to re-create the closed community based on self-subsistent agriculture. They were willing to forego the gains to be made by adopting technological change in order to preserve traditional values and institutions. Others, accepting the new technology, sought to channel its gains differently from what would have been done by the operations of the free market or those administered-price systems which were favored by managers and investors. The trade unions and the farmers set out to gain for themselves what semimonopolistic trade was delivering to other groups. Very commonly, the farmers made use of their votes in the legislature to direct the state in such a way as to benefit them.

Their action took the form of establishing private title to land at very low cost, providing credit at a rate far below what was ordained by the money market, the creation of scientific and technological research, the results of which were distributed freely to farmers, and, more recently, direct controls designed to give the farmer "parity" with industrial groups. The institutions thus developed did not provide any particular gain to the aged as such and, in fact, in many cases may have served to deprive them of some benefits they might otherwise have reaped.

The same has generally been true of other new organizations such as the trade unions. While seniority provisions have helped to assure positions to older members of some craft unions, it has also happened particularly in the industrial unions that the agreements made have required the early retirement of capable older workers to make way for younger union men.

During the great depression many of these disadvantaged groups were combined in support of the New Deal. It was only then that older people as such got favored treatment. In part this probably stemmed from their growing potential political power. In part it represented the effort of other age groups to take over the roles of their elders without at the same time violating basic moral values. In part it stemmed from the recognition of the justice of the claim put in by those in the later years of their lives. Various chapters in this *Handbook* discuss the development of, and the consequences arising from, the new institutions. The degree to which the changes relate to technological as distinguished from other factors may be inferred by the reader.

X. CURRENT STATUS OF THE AGED

There are, however, a few generalizations about the position of the aged in the community which we might beneficially note here. There is a general decline in the power position of the aged. Studies indicate that growing patterns of retirement dealt with in chapter xi result in the forced abdication of the holder of even very powerful positions in the hierarchy of management. As Rose indicates in chapter xviii, there is a decline in participation of those over 54 years of age in voluntary organizations. A lower percentage of those over 54 vote than in the 10-year cohort just younger than they. There are a few elective offices to which a man once elected is likely to be continually re-elected so long as he chooses to run, and in these older people predominate. However, the functions of the organizations controlled by those in the later years are declining in significance, and the power they wield is correspondingly less.

Activities in which there has been an increased participation by the elders greater than their proportional increase in the population are of less public and more personal concern, like recreation and activities connected with physical health and its maintenance. But there is not much evidence that this increased participation by older people in these activities has been accompanied by growing power over them. There are few communities in which either the health or recreation facilities and activities are designed primarily to serve the needs of older people. What is done is as likely to be done for them as by them.

Research to discover what are the changes in the public image of the aged is not currently conclusive. As Williams shows in chapter ix, the people of the United States do not generally share the prevalent European attitude that old people should be let alone to enjoy life as they see fit. This is not the image the aged have of themselves, nor is it that which others hold. Further research may show how increased leisure time and other fruits of increased productivity are being distributed to the various age groups and the way this is likely to affect the changing image of the elders.

In the meantime conflicting efforts to create an image are being undertaken. On the one hand, there is the effort to portray the latter years of life as the "golden years"; on the other are groups showing the same period of life to be one full of deprivation and unnecessary anxiety. Those who would succeed in gaining public support for subsidies with which to relieve the condition of older people must present a picture showing how dire is the need for these subsidies. Since the effort must be directed at the entire age category, differences in the condition of various sets of aging people are disregarded. This is, of course, most true in the pursuit of social legislation. Where specific groups suffering from specific ailments or handicaps are involved, the differences may be emphasized. However, *were* the private agencies which seek to teach people to anticipate the later years rather than to dread them *to be* successful in portraying the image they pursue, public support for those presumably now living well and happily would undoubtedly fall off. So efforts to create one image reflecting one status are at least in part offset by efforts to demonstrate the existence of another. The changing statuses and roles to which the elders are being assigned and the effects of these changes are to be discussed more fully by Williams in chapter ix. The general economic position now occupied is discussed by McConnell in chapter xiv, and the specific effects of social legislation and other means to assure the well being of those past the prime of life is delineated by Gordon in chapter viii. In chapter xvii Cottrell shows how changing technology has altered the politics of aging.

In fact, it is probably apparent that no chapter fails to deal with some direct or derivative consequence of changing technology. The degree to which change is attributable to technology is in some cases quite manifest. In others technology seems to be only remotely related to what is going on. While it would be interesting to tease out the strands of the complexes which lead back to technology, it would in many cases be almost useless to do so because the ability to change other factors more manifestly and immediately connected with what is happening provides more strategic and efficient means to achieve desired goals.

On the other hand, many "reform" movements, particularly those which are in fact reactionary, are doomed from the start by reason of the fact that they do not take into account recalcitrant technological facts. Often they would interfere with or prevent the adoption of technological changes manifestly beneficial to other age groups and often to some sets of older people themselves. Those who would benefit take action designed to permit them to make the desired technological changes, and the conflict which results is far more frequently resolved by making technological changes beneficial to others than to the aged. Thus those who seek to alter the condition of

older people need carefully to scrutinize the way the changes they propose will affect technology. By studying intimately the outcome of various proposals for action in some terms not colored by values themselves (such as energy, which was proposed here), it may be possible to avoid commitment to programs proscribed by their technological effects. Often there are a number of paths leading to the same goal. If those ways, precluded by their technological effects, are abandoned in favor of other means which do not bear this handicap, the ends sought will more certainly be achieved and at less cost. For this reason, an examination of the technological origins and consequences of various social movements may well be worth more careful attention than has previously been given them. In any case it is apparent that the discovery of technological components of a social system is of more than historical interest. It is one of the basic foundations of any effective action program.

REFERENCES

ALLEN, F. R., HART, H., MILLER, D. C., OGBURN, W. F., and NIMKOFF, M. F. 1957. Technology and social change. New York: Appleton-Century-Crofts.

BARNETT, H. G. 1953. Innovation. New York: McGraw-Hill Book Co.

COTTRELL, F. 1953. Energy and society. New York: McGraw-Hill Book Co.

OGBURN, W. F. 1923. Social change. New York: Viking Press.

OGBURN, W. F., and NIMKOFF, M. F. 1955. Technology and the changing family. Boston: Houghton Mifflin Co.

NELSON, L. 1954. American farm life. Cambridge, Mass.: Harvard University Press.

STEWARD, J. H. 1955. Theory of culture change. Urbana: University of Illinois Press.

TIBBITTS, C. 1960. Aging as a modern social achievement. *In* C. TIBBITTS and WILMA DONAHUE (eds.), Aging in today's society. Englewood Cliffs, N.J.: Prentice-Hall, Inc.

V

The Impact of Aging on the Social Structure

EUGENE A. FRIEDMANN

I. AGE AND THE SOCIAL STRUCTURE

A. The Reckoning of Age

Aging is a statement of change. As biological aging refers to changes in the functioning of the human organism through time, so social aging refers to changes in individual role performance through time. The inevitability of aging is the inevitability of change itself. But, in the context of a social system, the determination of age is conditioned by the rate and manner in which a society decrees these changes ought to take place.

Age, as reckoned by society, is a statement of *behavioral expectations* at given points in the life-span. These expectations relate less to the individual's ability to undertake a task than they do to society's definition of appropriate behavior for him as a member of a particular age group. Thus the 10-year-old is expected to master long division, while the 9-year-old is not; the 21-year-old is permitted the full rights of citizenship, while the 20-year-old is not; the 35-year-old couple is considered suitable for the adopting of a child, while the 40-year-old couple is not; and the 65-year-old is considered able to perform adequately at a job, while the 66-year-old is not. For the individual the awareness of age expectations becomes an important basis for his own self-perception; for the society age-group expectations form a basis for the allocation of social roles (Eisenstadt, 1956).

Age groups represent a *categorical assessment* of individual abilities to perform. Participation in an age group affects a whole range of role behaviors for the individual. Yet entry into or separation from an age group is usually arbitrarily decided on the basis of his observed or expected ability to perform in but one or two of his age-determined roles. Thus even in primitive societies, where the individual is known to the entire group, the boy's successful completion of the limited range of tasks represented in puberty rites (usually tests of his ability to perform in the adult work role) automatically grants him full adult status in the family, religious, political, and other structures of his society without the necessity of tests of competence in these areas (Linton, 1936). In modern society, where the individual participates in many groups and his performance capacities are only imperfectly known in each, age-group assignments based upon the convention of chronological age have supplanted even the limited considerations of individual differences found in simpler societies.

B. Significance of Age Categories in Industrial Society

Categorizations by age and sex are the bases for differentiation of roles in all known societies (Sorokin, 1927). Eisenstadt (1956), in his discussion of the significance of age groupings, states that from the point of view of the individual they represent a system of role expectations which define behavioral norms in the occupational, po-

120

litical, and other structures of his society. From the point of view of the society, they perform an "integrative function" to the extent that they lend continuity through the recruitment and training of younger persons in the major institutional roles to which they will succeed.

He also distinguishes between *age-heterogeneous* and *age-homogeneous* age groupings. The first is typical of societies in which the kinship system is the basic unit of the division of labor; social interaction is between members of different age grades within the kinship system, tending toward a progressive and continuous development of the youth toward the full social status of the adult. The second is characteristic of societies, such as modern industrial societies, in which the kinship system is not the basic unit for the division of labor and does not represent the structure in which the individual attains full social status; in this case, the solidarity of the age-heterogeneous group is broken, and patterns of interaction tend to be segmented in terms of common or homogeneous age associations. There is, further, a corresponding decrease in continuities between age groups and an increase in difficulties of transition to the next highest age grouping. However, his analysis, insofar as it treats age groupings in industrial societies, is limited to a discussion of the discontinuities which exist between adult and youth age groupings. It does not develop the significance, if any, of age distinctions within the adult age range; nor does it identify the old age group in industrial societies.

In pre-industrial societies, age categorizations represent the major criteria for the assignment of roles and for the determination of status as well (Bernardi, 1952; Prins, 1953; Flornoy, 1958; Warner, 1958). As social systems become more complex, additional criteria for the differentiation of roles emerge. Factors such as class, caste, income, occupation, religion, ethnicity, family position, and others may also become determinants of role assignment.

Industrial societies have tended to emphasize factors other than age for the as-signment of roles, particularly in the adult years. The increasing differentiation of social roles which accompanies industrialization is associated with a diversification of assignment procedures (Barber, 1957). Further, the increasing degree of social mobility which has accompanied industrialization has tended to diminish the importance of ascribed statuses such as that conferred by age (Eisenstadt, 1956).

Observers of contemporary American social structure (Parsons, 1942; Davis and Moore, 1945) have noted that, although age categorizations are useful in distinguishing the roles of the adult from those of the child, they are not of themselves primary determinants of role assignments within the adult ranges. They also indicate that, where age distinctions do occur, they are "interwoven with other structural elements" (Parsons, 1942), usually acting to confer seniority in established adult roles rather than to define distinct roles for various stages of adulthood (Davis and Moore, 1945). Warner (1957) regards age stratification in industrial society as a "major subtype of rank, rudimentary and nonspecialized to be distinguished from all specialized and developed forms."

C. Aging of Industrial Societies

The development of high-energy technologies which have been associated with the rise of industrialization (Cottrell, 1955) has led to increasing complexity of social organization and a change in significance of age-determined social roles. Coincidental with the shifting bases of participation of age groups in high-energy societies has been a major change in age composition of these populations. Declining fertility, associated with advanced stages of industrialization, has led to an increase in proportion of aged in these societies (Valaoras, 1950; Sauvy, 1954).

An examination of the age structures of current populations shows a variation in the percentages of persons 65 years and over ranging from a minimum of 1.5 per cent in Togoland and the Gold Coast to a maximum of 11.8 per cent in France. If we define as relatively aged those countries with 7 per cent or more of their population in the age group 65 and over, we find that nineteen countries comprising about one-fifth of the world's population can be so classified (Table 1). All these countries are identified with Western culture. Most of them are characterized by relatively low birth and death rates and by high standards of living. And, with the significant omission of the U.S.S.R., this list represents the overwhelming bulk of the world's present industrial capacity.

For those countries which now have relatively aged population structures, the rapid increase of the population 65 and over has been a recent phenomenon. In 1850 only one country—France—had as much as 6 per cent of its population in the age group 65 and over. In 1900 only three countries of the world—France, Sweden, and Nor-way—had as much as 7 per cent of the population in this age group. For the remaining European countries on this list, the 1900–1930 interval was the period of most rapid population aging. And for the United States and other non-European countries of the list the period of most rapid increase of the older population group did not begin until after 1930, as shown in Table 2.

For the United States population aging has been a twentieth-century phenomenon. This increase in numbers from 3 million in 1900 to 12 million in 1950 to approximately 15 million in 1958 represents a doubling of size at approximately 25-year intervals, a rate of growth unmatched by our population as a whole since the time of the American Revolution (Taeuber and Taeuber, 1958). The increase in proportion from 4 per cent to a present 9 per cent of our population represents a rate of in-

TABLE 1*

COUNTRIES WITH 7 PER CENT OR MORE OF THEIR POPULATIONS IN
THE AGE GROUP 65 YEARS AND OVER

Year	Country	Per Cent of Population 65 and Over	Total Population (In Thousands)
1951	Australia	8.02	8,431.3
1951	Austria	10.13	6,905.7
1950	Belgium	11.05	8,639.4
1951	Canada	7.75	14,009.5
1947	Czechoslovakia	7.58	12,146.6
1950	Denmark	9.11	4,281.1
1950	France	11.79	41,943.0
1950	Germany: Federal Republic	9.28	47,695.7
1946	Germany: U.S.S.R. Zone	9.98	17,313.7
1951	Great Britain	10.83	48,840.9
1950	Iceland	7.52	143.6
1951	Ireland	10.69	2,960.6
1950	Italy	8.06	46,279.4
1951	Netherlands	7.86	10,264.5
1951	New Zealand (excl. Maoris)	9.58	1,822.4
1950	Norway	9.64	3,278.3
1950	Spain	7.23	27,961.3
1950	Sweden	10.32	7,043.9
1950	Switzerland	9.57	4,814.5
1950	United States of America	8.18	150,696.0
Total			465,471.5

* Source: United Nations, Department of Economic and Social Affairs, *The Aging of Populations and Its Economic and Social Implications* ("Population Studies," No. 26 [New York: United Nations, 1956]).

crease unmatched by that of any other age grouping during this period (Table 3).

The population explosion of the 65-and-over age group has occurred within a relatively brief time span as population changes are reckoned. The demographic forces which triggered it—the aging of the immigrant group of the 1890–1920 period and the declining birth rate of the 1900–1940 period—are now dissipating themselves, and our rate of aging is being slowed (Sheldon, 1958). The current proportion of 9 per cent for this age group is expected to level off at about 10 per cent by 1975 and is not expected appreciably to exceed this percentage for the remainder of the century (Taeuber, 1957). Thus the aging of our population which has occurred at an unprecedented rate within the span of a half-century is now approaching a stabilization point.[1]

D. Significance of Age Categories in United States Social Structure

To the extent that age is a determinant of role, it may (a) qualify the individual

[1] A more detailed analysis of population trends and forecasts appears in chap. ii.

TABLE 2*

INCREASE IN PERCENTAGE OF POPULATION 65 YEARS AND OVER
FOR SELECTED COUNTRIES, 1900–1950

COUNTRY	PER CENT OF TOTAL POPULATION			PER CENT INCREASE		
	1900	1930	1950	1900–1930	1930–50	1900–1950
United States....	4.07	5.41	8.14	32.1	50.4	100.0
France..........	8.20	9.35	11.80	14.0	26.2	43.9
Germany........	4.88	7.36	9.27	48.5	25.9	87.9
Great Britain....	4.69	7.40	10.83	57.5	46.3	130.9
Sweden..........	8.37	9.20	10.31	9.8	12.6	24.2
New Zealand.....	4.06	6.56	9.57	61.5	45.8	135.7

* Source: United Nations, Department of Social and Economic Affairs, *The Aging of Populations and Its Economic and Social Implications* ("Population Studies," No. 26 [New York: United Nations, 1956]).

TABLE 3*

CHANGING PROPORTION OF AGE GROUPS IN THE POPULATION
OF THE UNITED STATES, 1900–1950

AGE	PER CENT DISTRIBUTION			PER CENT CHANGE
	1900	1930	1950	1900–1950
Under 10..........	23.8	19.6	19.5	−18.1
10–19.............	20.7	19.2	14.4	−30.4
20–34.............	25.6	24.3	23.4	− 8.6
35–44.............	12.1	14.0	14.3	17.3
45–54.............	8.4	10.6	11.5	38.1
55–64.............	5.3	6.9	8.8	66.0
65 and over........	4.1	5.4	8.1	97.8
20–64.............	49.4	55.8	58.0	17.4
Under 20..........	44.5	38.8	33.9	−23.8

* Source: Calculated from data in C. Taeuber and Irene B. Taeuber, *The Changing Population of the United States* (New York: John Wiley & Sons, 1958), and U.S. Bureau of the Census, *Historical Statistics of the United States, 1789–1945* (Washington, D.C.: Government Printing Office, 1949).

for participation in social structures; (*b*) exclude him from participation; or (*c*) act as a limiting factor where other variables become the determinants of participation. Even a partial listing of some of our most obvious age categorizations would reveal that age determinations affect the following social structures:

1. *Educational structures*. These exhibit elaborate age-grading systems represented by "pre-school" school, kindergartens, elementary schools, secondary schools, colleges and graduate levels, postgraduate training, and the recently developed area of pre-retirement education.
2. *Economic structures*. Age factors regulate:
   a) Participation in the labor force—child labor laws, fixed-age retirement practices, age discrimination in hiring practices.
   b) Position in the labor force—minimum and maximum age practices associated with specific statuses within an industrial organization (e.g., considerations of appropriate age for stock boys, department heads, chairmen of the board, etc.).
   c) Income-tax concessions—the double exemption for persons 65 and over.
   d) Beneficiary rights—age-related pensions, annuity, and public assistance rights.
   e) Voluntary associations of businessmen— e.g., membership in the Junior Chamber of Commerce, as compared with membership in the Chamber of Commerce.
3. *Political structures*. Age factors are among the determinants of the right to vote and to hold political office; organizations such as the Young Republicans indicate an age grading in political party participation.
4. *Religious structures*. We find age-related confirmation rites and church boards of "elders," perhaps vestigial in character but widespread practices nevertheless.
5. *Legal structures*. Age is a factor in defining contractual rights, in guardianships, and in distinctions between juvenile and criminal codes governing similar forms of deviant behavior. There is also an extensive age grading of penal and remedial institutions.
6. *Recreational structures*. These exhibit age-graded activities and services second only to the educational structure in their elaborateness and specificity.
7. *Miscellaneous rights and duties*. Age, for example, is a factor in the right to purchase alcohol and cigarettes, in the licensing of motor-vehicle and airplane operators, in the censorship of movies, in the drafting of men for the armed service, etc.

The listing is not complete, however, if it is restricted to the more formalized age distinctions to be found in contemporary American society. Evidences of age-related behavioral expectations are abundant in our folkways as well. The accepted etiquette of social usages prescribes deference of the young to the old in the manner of address, in the relationships with in-laws, and in the extending of many minor courtesies (Post, 1955). The joking relationships of our society prescribe the types of jokes and stories that may be told within age groupings and those which may be told across age groupings. The content of our humor stresses as ludicrous conduct which is not consistent with the behavior expectations for our major age groups. Conversely, we find that our society has reserved specific types of accolades for the honored retiring employee, the elder or "dean" in various occupations and professions, the couple that has completed fifty years of marriage, and others who are appropriately terminating their age-related social roles.

II. Impact of Aging upon Our Social Structure

A. Impact of Aging upon the Economy

RELATION BETWEEN LABOR-FORCE AGING AND PRODUCTIVITY

The impact of a changing age composition upon productivity is difficult to measure simply because our concepts of contribution to the labor force and to total productivity are not adequate measures of the social utility of individuals or of population groups. First, if we consider rate of labor-force participation as a measure of an age group's contribution to the economy, we are computing the contributions of older and most experienced workers at the same rate as that of the youngest apprentices. Second, labor-force and productivity data do not reflect individual contributions to the work of the home, family, community, and society for which no pay is received. And, third, this type of data completely ignores the historic contributions made by the leisure classes to government, art, literature, philosophy, and science.

The analysis of the economic consequences of population aging is usually made in terms of its implications for the changing relationship between measures of production and total population. These can be measured indirectly by comparing the changes in labor-force productivity which

creasing from 23.7 to 35.7 per cent. It may be argued that productivity might have increased even more rapidly with a younger work force. There is some evidence as to age differences in productivity which indicates a gradual reduction in speed of performance with age (e.g., Shock, 1955); but there are also indications that older workers are preferred in jobs which require experience and judgment (e.g., Peterson, 1955). While the evidence is still far from conclusive, it would be difficult to support the contention that the aging of the labor

TABLE 4*

POPULATION GROWTH, LABOR-FORCE AGING, AND PRODUCTIVITY CHANGE
FOR THE UNITED STATES, 1900–1950

Year	Population (In Thousands)	Productivity (National Income in Cents per Man-Hour in 1950 Prices)	Per Cent of Labor Force Aged 45 or Over	Index of Manufacturing Production	Gross National Product in 1950 Prices (In Billions)
1900................	75,995	75.5	23.7	100	$ 94.4†
1930................	122,775	106.9	30.3	311	143.6
1940................	134,669	131.5	31.2	429	183.4
1950................	151,132	193.5	35.7	627	286.8
Per cent change, 1900–1950..............	97.4	156.3	50.6	627.0	184.7‡

* Source: J. F. Dewhurst and Associates, *America's Needs and Resources* (New York: Twentieth Century Fund, 1955); U.S. Bureau of the Census, *Historical Statistics of the United States, 1789–1945* (Washington, D.C.: Government Printing Office, 1949).
† In 1909 prices.
‡ Per cent change, 1909–50.

occur during a period of labor-force aging. In the United States the 1900–1950 interval saw our manufacturing production increase at more than three times the rate of our population growth, and our gross national product increase at more than double the rate of population growth (Table 4). This was the period of unprecedented industrial development for the United States. Having but recently begun the process of industrialization at the start of the period, we emerged as the world's leading industrial producer at its end.

Labor-force efficiency, as measured by man-hour productivity, tripled in this period. And, significantly, these increases were occurring with a labor force whose proportion of members 45 years and over was in-

force has adversely affected our productivity. Certainly, the spectacular rise in our national output and standard of living during our period of rapid labor-force aging would cast doubt upon it.

CHANGING PROPORTION OF "NON-PRO-
DUCERS" IN THE ECONOMY

Although there is no evidence to indicate that labor-force aging adversely affected our productivity in the 1900–1950 interval, the separation of the male worker 65 and over from the labor force which occurred did increase the proportion of non-productive members of this group. The question then arises as to the effect which the addition of large numbers of older persons had upon the proportion of the non-productive population which the productive segment must support.

If we arbitrarily consider the 20–64 age group as the potentially productive segment of our society, we find that the proportion of our population in this age group actually increased from 49.4 to 58.0 per cent in the 1900–1950 interval despite a sizable increase in proportion of the age group 65 and over (Table 2). Conversely, the proportion of "non-producers" decreased from 50.6 to 42.0 per cent in this interval.

If we examine the impact of an aging population upon the size of the labor force, we find that the labor force increased from 37.4 to 41.3 per cent of our population between 1900 and 1950; conversely, our proportion of "non-workers" declined from 62.6 to 58.7 per cent, despite a sharp increase in the numbers and proportion of older workers removed from the labor force during the interval.

EFFECT OF AGING UPON THE ECONOMY'S ABILITY TO MAINTAIN ITS MEMBERS

Although our measures are crude and definitions loose, several conclusions can be offered regarding the impact of aging upon our society's ability to maintain and improve its levels of productivity and standard of living:

1. The period of most rapid growth in our older population (1900–1950) has coincided with our period of most rapid rise in productivity and standard of living.
2. The aging of our labor force has not adversely affected our productivity to any demonstrable degree.
3. The increasing flow of older people into the non-worker group during this period did not increase the total proportion of non-workers in our population.
4. The doubling in proportion of our population 65 and over has not decreased the proportion of our population in the productive age ranges of 20–64.

The seeming paradox of an increase in proportion of aged persons occurring simultaneously with a decrease in the per cent of our non-working or non-productive population can, of course, be explained by the sharp decrease in proportion of the pre-adult group. The dependency ratio of workers to non-workers in a society is altered principally by changes in the proportion of young persons; changes in the proportion of aged persons affect it but slightly. Actually the same factors—the decrease in fertility associated with advanced stages of industrialization—are responsible for both a decline in the proportion of young and an increase in the proportion of aged. The proportion of dependents is not increased under these conditions; it is reduced somewhat, and its age composition changed. Further, the vast increase in productivity which occurs with these age changes greatly improves a society's ability to support its non-productive members.

THE ECONOMIC POSITION OF THE AGED

The industrial bounty of the twentieth-century United States and our success in eliminating want and in achieving the world's highest standard of living are basic to our concept of ourselves as a nation and the image we present to other nations. The extent to which we have reduced poverty in this century is described by Wilensky and Lebaux:

> That the percentage of poverty-stricken people has dropped in recent decades is indisputable. Hazel Kyrk estimates that in 1901 at least 40 percent of the families of wage-earners and clerical workers were trying to live on a "less than adequate" income. She judges "less than adequate" for that year to be less than $700 for a two-child family. During the depression of the 1930's, this group had perhaps contracted to the "one-third of the nation" Franklin D. Roosevelt found "ill-housed, ill-clothed, ill-fed." By 1950, taking account of price changes, Kyrk's 1901 standard could be maintained by an average-size urban, wage-earner's family of 3.4 persons for $1,700—a level below which less than 10 percent of such families lived. This ignores, of course, our vastly changed ideas of what "adequate" is, but it does show roughly that the objective conditions of the poor have improved [1958, pp. 104–5].

Yet the economic gains of the twentieth century have not been shared by all groups. Steiner and Dorfman (1957), in a special census survey of income status of the aged, found that, in 1952, 45 per cent of couples 65 and over had incomes below a "standard" budget level—which they defined as annual incomes ranging from $1825 for urban couples living alone to a low of $1025 for farm couples living with children. These figures offer a striking contrast to the statement of general reduction in poverty since 1900 cited above. That the aged had failed to achieve a proportionate share of our industrial success by the early 1950's is further evidenced by such facts as the following:

1. In 1952 the median income of aged couples was only 38 per cent of that for all spending units in the same year.
2. In 1953 one older person in every five was dependent upon public assistance for support.
3. In 1954 one out of every three low-income (i.e., under $2000) families in the United States was headed by a person over 65 years of age.

Although some conclusions can be drawn about their present position, their relative economic status during this century is more difficult to determine. Direct historical comparisons cannot be made because the data are inadequate. Money income data for the aged today do not fully reflect standard of living; and money-income data for the aged at the turn of the century would have relatively little meaning even if they could be obtained.

Despite the difficulties of comparison, estimates of their economic status earlier in the century both here and in England indicate that the aged have occupied a depressed economic status throughout the 1900–1950 period. Gillin (1937) states that, in Great Britain at the beginning of the century, "it was estimated that . . . out of 1,000 men living at the age of 20, 500 would be living at the age of 65, two-fifths of whom would become paupers." Estimates of old age dependency in the United States early in the century, for which even meager data were available, range from 24 per cent (Squier,

1912) to 33 per cent (Epstein, 1928). These define dependency in terms of receipt of public and private charity and do not indicate the percentage dependent upon their families for support. Epstein (1928) reports an opinion, circulated among insurance companies and banks of this period, that, "of 100 young men starting life at 25, 36 will die before reaching 65; of the 64 living at the age of 65, one will be wealthy, four will be well-to-do, five will be just able to get along and the remaining 54 will be dependent upon children or upon charity."

It would seem that the present economic status of the aged does not represent a retreat from a more favored position earlier in the century. Rather it indicates a failure to keep pace with an over-all advance from the conditions of poverty which have characterized the earlier stages of industrialization of Western nations.

B. Impact of Aging upon the Labor Force

INDUSTRIALIZATION AND THE OLDER WORKER

The introduction of modern systems of industrial production and the growth of corporate forms of organization which accompanied them created a new industrial milieu for the older worker (Moore, 1950). He was confronted with changing expectations of role performance which found him at a competitive disadvantage with younger men and by newly developing age-determined systems of labor-force removal. A new concept—"superannuation"—was to exclude the older person from the labor market. These changes were marked by:

1. *The dilution of industrial skills.*—The simplification and segmentation of tasks minimized the importance of craft skills and experience by which the older worker formerly had been able to maintain a favored position in the craft system.
2. *The introduction of new concepts of industrial efficiency.*—Output in the new system was determined by the effectiveness with which individuals performing a standardized task could maintain the *pace* of the productive system; declining speed particularly put

the older worker at a competitive disadvantage with the younger man.

3. *Changing requirements for supervisory positions.*—Successful movement from production to supervisory roles was based upon ability to lead a work "team" and deal with its problems of social organization rather than upon mechanical skill alone; this deprived the older worker of the automatic gains in status which came to him with increased skill under the craft system; it also put him at a competitive disadvantage with rising younger men who had mastered the new ground rules for the organization of industrial production.

4. *Obsolescence of skills.*—As techniques changed, new skills had to be learned; preference was given to younger workers for instruction in new skills.

5. *The growth of fixed age retirement practices.*—The growth in size and complexity of industrial enterprises and the development of a professional managerial group, interposed in the traditional owner-employee relationship, has resulted in a substitution of impersonal age-based employee separation procedures for the individual determinations of retirement age characteristic of the small-owner–operated plant.

6. *The growth of industrial pension systems.*— The corporate life-span exceeds that of any single group of owners, and its obligations do not cease with their death; considerations of continuing industrial efficiency which led to the development of fixed-age retirement practices also led to the creation of industrial pension systems as compensation for separation. In the logic of corporate survival it could be justified as a device which avoided a "serious impact upon the morale of their continuing work force" [Brown, 1950].

LABOR-FORCE PARTICIPATION BY THE OLDER WORKER

The concept of industrial superannuation and fixed-aged retirement practices extended beyond the ranks of the factory production worker up into the clerical and administrative staffs of our modern corporations and into our governmental and educational institutions as well. But the amount of public discussion of the merits of these practices in recent years has led to a distorted view of the extent to which our productive system has been able to accommodate the older worker. Although the proportion of older males in the labor force has declined from 64.9[2] per cent in 1900 to 45 per cent in 1950, the actual proportion of the labor force composed of older workers has risen from 3.9 to 4.9 per cent in this interval.[3] Thus the proportionate gain of 26 per cent in the older worker's share of the labor force would negate any conclusion that the shift from an agricultural to an industrial society has decreased employment opportunities for the older person. We might reasonably assume that a pre-industrial economy would also have difficulty absorbing at appropriate levels the members of any group whose numbers had expanded as rapidly as those of the aged within a span of 50 years.

While the labor force was accommodating proportionately more workers over 65 in 1950 than in 1900, the occupational distribution of the older male differed sharply from his younger counterpart. Approximately 50 per cent of this group were to be found in agricultural and service industries, as compared with a total of 31 per cent for the male labor force as a whole (Table 5). Forty per cent of the age group 65 and over were dependent upon self-employment as contrasted with 16 per cent of the labor force under 65 (U.S. Federal Security Agency, 1952).

Occupations characterized either by self-employment or by small enterprises, of course, are not likely to require retirement at a fixed age. On the other hand, as of 1950, these occupations were not yet included under Old-Age and Survivors Insurance, nor were they likely to have other pension provisions to enable the person to retire.

[2] Woytinsky (1953) regards this figure as too high. It includes farm heads who were listed as gainful workers in the 1900 Census even though they were not working in the field. They would not be included in the labor force under current definitions.

[3] Chapter x gives more detailed data with regard to labor-force participation.

PATTERNS OF LABOR-FORCE SEPARATION

The question of causation in labor-force removal is often difficult to determine.[4] The forces which push a worker out are usually more readily identified than the factors which pull or attract him out. The depression of the 1930's saw the growth of aged-based retirement practices. The impact of an aging labor force in a declining economy led to pressures for their removal from younger workers seeking to maintain a supply of employment openings and promo-

[4] For another discussion of reasons for retirement see chap. xi.

tional opportunities and from employers fearing loss of labor-force efficiency. Industries characterized by large corporations and the new concepts of industrial efficiency as well as by unionized work forces were the ones which adopted fixed-age retirement practices. Table 5 indicates that the separation rate for the older worker was as high as 80 per cent in mining, transportation, and the utilities and 68 per cent in manufacturing. This contrasts with a separation rate of 32 per cent in agriculture. The industries which have a high separation rate for older workers are also the ones whose members were eligible for OASI re-

TABLE 5*

EMPLOYMENT DISTRIBUTION AND RATES OF LABOR-FORCE SEPARATION FOR
MEN AGED 55–64 AND 65 AND OVER, 1950

TYPE OF EMPLOYMENT	PERCENTAGE DISTRIBUTION			LABOR-FORCE SEPARATION RATE†
	All Men	55–64	65 and Over	
Major occupation group................	100	100	100	42.8
Professional, technical, and kindred workers..................................	7.4	6.2	6.0	39.7
Farmers and farm managers............	10.7	15.3	25.0	70.0
Managers, officials, and proprietors, except farm.........................	10.8	12.8	12.9	43.1
Clerical and kindred workers...........	6.5	5.6	4.2	32.3
Sales workers........................	6.2	5.6	5.5	42.3
Craftsmen, foremen, and kindred workers.	18.3	20.1	9.7	29.7
Operatives and kindred workers........	20.0	14.7	14.0	26.1
Private household workers............	0.2	0.3	0.4	53.3
Service workers, except private household	5.6	7.4	10.0	58.4
Farm laborers, except unpaid and foremen	3.5	2.9	3.5	52.6
Farm laborers, unpaid family workers...	1.5	0.3	1.1	60.0
Laborers, except farm and mine........	8.0	7.9	6.6	35.5
Occupation not reported...............	11.7	0.9	1.8	....
Major industry:				
Agriculture..........................	16.2	19.0	30.1	32.1
Mining..............................	2.3	2.4	1.1	81.3
Construction........................	8.4	8.5	7.3	63.0
Manufacturing.......................	26.2	23.3	12.3	68.2
Transportation, communication, and other utilities.............................	8.8	9.8	4.7	79.5
Wholesale and retail trade.............	17.2	14.8	13.8	60.0
Service industries....................	14.7	15.9	19.3	59.1
All other industries...................	5.0	5.1	4.2	64.7
Industry not reported.................	1.2	1.2	2.0	....
Total employed (in thousands)........	40,317	5,229	2,239	....

* Source: Calculated from data presented by J. J. Corson and J. W. McConnell, *Economic Needs of Older People* (New York: Twentieth Century Fund, 1956), p. 51.

† The "Labor-Force Separation Rate" is the reciprocal of the ratio of men in the 65 and over group to those in the 55–64 age group for each occupational and industrial category. Since different cohorts are used, it is not a true attrition rate but only a rough approximation of the actual separation rate.

tirement benefits in 1950 and in which industrial pension systems first developed.

The resistance of the older worker to
these separation procedures was most pronounced during the 1940's. The depression
years had substantially reduced the personal financial reserve needed to see them
through retirement. The industrial system,
although providing proportionately more
jobs for older workers, did not keep up with
the demand for employment by this group.
And the new retirement-income provisions
of government and industry during this
period failed to provide adequately for the
needs of newly retiring workers.

INSTITUTIONALIZATION OF RETIREMENT

The impact upon the industrial system
of the rapid increase in older workers, thus
far traced, has been:

a) The expansion of the proportionate share
of the older worker's share of the labor force.
b) A concentration of older workers in agriculture and other industries characterized by
self-employment or by enterprise of relatively small size.
c) The separation of the older worker from
large-scale corporate or governmental enterprises, through the development of fixed-age
retirement practices.
d) The development of both public and private
retirement income provisions in both public
and private forms.
e) A *lag* in the industrial system's ability to
cope with the increase either through the
creation of a sufficient number of work roles
or through the development of pension provisions adequate to meet the needs of retired workers.

To this list we can add one more factor:

f) The acceptance of retirement as a role expectation for older workers.

Although compulsory retirement procedures were instituted for the convenience
of industry, often contrary to the wishes of
the affected workers, they have had the
ultimate effect of establishing retirement
itself as an appropriate and expected role
transition for the older worker. The initial
resistances to it were based upon the work-

er's financial inability to retire, upon his
reluctance to separate himself from a major
status and satisfaction-defining activity of
our work-oriented society (Friedmann and
Havighurst, 1954), and possibly upon the
type of resistances which are elicited by
any major social innovation in its early
stages. Recent studies (Corson and Mc-
Connell, 1956; Streib and Thompson,
1957) have shown a much higher level of
acceptance of retirement by the older worker himself than was true a decade ago.
Steiner and Dorfman (1957) found that
only 13 per cent of the retired males in
1952 were forced out by formal retirement
systems.[5] And there is even evidence to
indicate that among our largest group of
self-employed—the farmer—retirement is
beginning to be defined as a career expectation (Sewell *et al.*, 1933). It would seem
that, as we develop an economic base for
retirement and as the leisure of retirement
becomes defined as a rightful reward for
a lifetime of work, we are institutionalizing
a new age role for our society. The forces
which push the older worker out of the
labor force, dramatized through public discussion, now have to be measured against
the forces which are attracting the worker
into this newly defined age role.

C. Impact of Aging upon the Family

INCLUSION OF THE AGED IN MULTI-
GENERATIONAL HOUSEHOLDS

Evidence on household size for early
America and even for our pre-industrial
progenitors in medieval Britain do not indicate that the large household of the extended kinship family was the prevailing
mode during either of these periods. Population estimates for late-fourteenth-cen-
tury Britain put average household size at

---

[5] This figure is considerably lower than previous
estimates reported in the literature. However, it
represents the only available estimate based upon
a representative cross-section of the retired. Earlier
studies dealt with industrial workers or else workers covered by Social Security—groups in which
compulsory retirement practices are overrepre-
sented.

3.45[6] (Russell, 1948). Nor was there an appreciable variation between the small villages and the urban areas. The aged parents tended to remain in their own households, separate from the children, and in a great many cases even the widow had the cottage of her husband turned over to her rather than join the household of her children. For the villager "the chances that families would pile under one roof did not seem too great. Houses were poor and not difficult to construct. All dwelt usually in villages where there was a reasonable degree of protection even though life was rough and subject to careless treatment" (Russell, 1948).

Estimates for Colonial America similarly fail to indicate the predominance of the extended kinship household. The enumeration of "masters" of families for the city of New York in 1703 lists a total of 818 families with an average household size of 4.5 for the white population (U.S. Bureau of the Census, 1909). Further evidence as to distribution indicates that, of the 55 white males over 60 in the population (3.3 per cent of the white male population), 31 (56 per cent) lived in families with children under 16 (how many of these were three-generation families is not indicated), 13 (24 per cent) lived alone or with their mates, and the remaining 11 (20 per cent) lived in households with persons between the ages of 16 and 60. Thus at least 40 per cent of the aged were not living in three-generation households, and further evidence showed that only 4 per cent of all the family units could be considered three-generational.

Other eighteenth-century evidences, although not so complete as the data above, would indicate an average household of about four persons for the white colonists, if servants are excluded from the count.[7]

[6] Based upon poll-tax returns of 1377.

[7] If we included non-whites residing in the household in our 4.5-person family for New York City in 1703, as cited above (as would have been done in 1790–1890 Census estimates), we would have increased the median family size to 5.4 persons.

Nineteenth-century evidence, such as that of the New York State Census of 1865, indicated that only 2.8 per cent of the families contained three generations[8]—and this would include households whose oldest member is less than 60 or 65.

Census data for the 1790–1950 interval indicate a reduction of median household size from 5.7 persons in 1790 to 5.6 in 1850 to 4.7 in 1900 to 3.5 in 1950. However, the census definition of household and family prior to 1900 included household servants and slaves in the total. Further, a steady decline in median age of marriage which occurred between 1890 and 1950 (and presumably a decline in the age at which children left home) would also be a factor in accounting for the decrease in family size since the turn of the century.

Thus we lack evidence that the three-generation or the extended kinship family was ever a prevailing or even a common family form in this country. And, although evidence is inadequate, we do not know whether a majority of the aged were ever cared for in this manner in our country's history. Certainly, the amount of mobility which has characterized American life—not just with the onset of industrialization and urbanization but from early in our history with the opportunity for sons to break from the parental household and establish their own households on the frontier— would act to deter the development of a three-generation family system.

CHANGING FAMILY FUNCTIONS OF THE AGED

The partial transference of many traditional family functions to outside agencies (Ogburn and Tibbitts, 1933)—for example, productive, protective, economic, recreational, educational—has greatly altered the role expectations for individual family members during the past 100 years. From the point of view of the older person the loss of some of the former tasks of the

[8] Families were enumerated in terms of both children and grandchildren in the household.

elder, such as instruction of the young or supervision of household crafts, may have diminished their utility and thus weakened the bond with the younger generation. But the significance of the apparent loss of function by the grandparent should not be overstated, in view of the relatively few family units which historically have included the grandparent in their households.

The major functional changes which are responsible for the dislocation of the aged in contemporary society involve the *parent* rather than the grandparent. If we accept the two-generation family as the appropriate focus for our analysis, we find that

fore the completion of the child-rearing period, now can look forward to surviving for an average of 14 years *beyond* the termination of the child-rearing period. And, from the point of view of the individual parent, the male has seen his survival expectation rise from 7 years beyond the termination of the child-rearing period in 1890 to 21 years in 1950, and the woman's expectation has increased from 12 to almost 30 years in the same interval. The magnitude of this change can be appreciated if we consider that the post–child-rearing period for today's older couple is approximately two-thirds as long as the child-rear-

TABLE 6*

MEDIAN AGE OF HUSBAND AND WIFE AT SELECTED STAGES OF THE LIFE-CYCLE
OF THE FAMILY, UNITED STATES, 1950, 1940, AND 1890

STAGE OF THE LIFE-CYCLE OF THE FAMILY	MEDIAN AGE OF HUSBAND			MEDIAN AGE OF WIFE		
	1950	1940	1890	1950	1940	1890
A. First marriage..............	22.8	24.3	26.1	20.1	21.5	22.0
B. Birth of last child...........	28.8	29.9	36.0	26.1	27.1	31.9
C. Marriage of last child.......	50.3	52.8	59.4	47.6	50.0	55.3
D. Death of one spouse†........	64.1	63.6	57.4	61.4	60.9	53.3
E. Death of other spouse‡......	71.6	69.7	66.4	77.2	73.5	67.7

* Source: Paul C. Glick, "The Life Cycle of the Family," *Marriage and Family Living*, **18** (February, 1955), 4.
† Husband and wife survive jointly from marriage to specified age.
‡ Husband (wife) survives separately from marriage to specified age.

functional changes have affected the duration rather than the nature of the older parents' family roles.

Thus child-rearing, which has not diminished in importance as a family function, is now terminated at an earlier age than before.[9] Glick (1955) in his analysis of the changing family cycle has shown that the median age at which child-rearing is completed (i.e., the age at which the last child is married) has fallen from 59.4 years in 1890 to 50.3 years in 1950 for the male and from 55.3 to 47.6 years for the female in the same interval (Table 6). Further, the parental couple which in 1890 had the expectation of being disrupted by the death of one partner approximately 2 years *be-*

[9] Family and family functions are discussed in chap. xiii.

ing period itself; and, for the individual, the male will spend approximately as much time and the female will spend 37 per cent more time in the post–child-rearing period as in the period of performance of their major family function.

The married male of the last part of the nineteenth century was more likely to find his family role at age 60 defined in terms of his function as parent and husband than as grandparent. And it was also likely that his life-span would not appreciably exceed the duration of his parental role. His 1950 counterpart, however, found a 14-year span of time confronting him at the conclusion of his child-rearing functions, during which his role as husband continues. Thus a new period has emerged in the family cycle, one for which we have no historical precedent.

CHANGING ABILITY OF THE FAMILY TO MAINTAIN ITS AGED

The special census survey of 1952 provided us with the first national data of the family relation of households in which aged persons resided (Steiner and Dorfman, 1957). Their evidence indicates that 32.6 per cent of the population over 65 was residing in households containing two or more generations.[10] If we project this proportion, we find that 4.2 million persons, or 2.6 per cent of our population, for the year 1952 were both over 65 and living in households with their children. If we compare this with the estimated 2.9 per cent total over 65 in our population in 1850, and if we consider that not all these persons were living in households, it is highly probable that the *present American family system includes a greater proportion of aged persons in households consisting of two or more interdependent generations than did the family system of 1850.* The year 1850 has been selected as the date which immediately precedes our major period of urbanization and industrialization.

To summarize our discussion of the impact of the increasing number of aged upon the family structure, we can now attempt to state some conclusions:

1. It is unlikely that the three-generation extended kinship family structure was ever the predominant form of living arrangement for the aged in the United States.
2. There is no evidence to indicate that contemporary urban, industrial society is providing proportionately fewer roles for the aged in multigenerational family units than did its pre-industrial forebears.
3. The significant functional changes which have affected the family position of the aged have been those which have acted to limit the *duration* of their major adult-role functions of parent and income-producer.

[10] Their data were presented in terms of economic units. This figure converts their data into a proportion of the total number of individuals represented. Havighurst and Albrecht (1953) in their study of the aged in a small midwestern community report that 32 per cent of the persons over 65 were living in households containing two or more generations.

III. THE INTEGRATION OF THE AGED IN OUR SOCIETY

We have no evidence to justify the conclusion that the present dislocation of the aged has occurred because our changing family and work structures have reduced the number of roles available to them. They seem to be providing opportunities for participation for a somewhat greater proportion of older persons than did their pre-industrial counterparts. But the magnitude and suddenness of the explosion in our aged population have created a surplus of aged for the proportion of roles which have previously been allotted to them. And we have witnessed our society's inability to close the gap by expanding the proportion of role opportunities, either in its traditional structures or through the creation of new ones, in the relatively brief span of time during which our population aging has occurred.

Now that their rate of growth is being slowed to a more orderly pace, we might expect that the next decade will see the beginnings of the integration of this new group of aged in American society. If we accept the proposition that our economy can now support a larger proportion of older persons than ever before, the integration of the aged in our social structures will depend upon our definitions of the manner in which they ought to be maintained and the types of participation which are available to them rather than upon the society's ability to maintain them.

A. Changing Definitions of Obligations toward the Aged

THE CONFLICT BETWEEN GENERATIONS

The custom by which a man as he grew older made over his land to a son and heir, whereupon the heir took a wife, and not before, is not limited to medieval England. It was and is common in parts of Europe where descent of peasant holdings to one son was the rule. . . .

The time when the change is made is an anxious one. Not only is the father displaced in the management of the holding, but the man who displaces him is his son. He is hard put to it to keep himself from interfering with what the new manager determines to do, especially when the latter is one who has hitherto been subject to him in all the business of life. Furthermore, a new woman is brought into the house: the son's wife displaces his mother in the kitchen and at the head of the women's work. The old couple continue to live with their son, but they move into the room which in the traditional farm house is reserved for the old folk, the room called in Ireland the "west room." In time they become used to their new position and adopt new attitudes but there is always a period of transition. In reconstructing any ancient society, our knowledge of what happens today must give flesh and blood to the dry bones of records: in medieval England, sentiments and behavior like those of modern Irish countrymen must have accompanied the retirement of the father and the marriage of the son. The court rolls tell us nothing about these matters, except sometimes to admit that discords might arise between the new husbandman and the old so that they would not wish to dwell together in one house [Homans, 1941, pp. 157–58].

The myth of the idyllic existence of the aged secure in their positions as members of extended kinship families in pre-industrial society has done much to obscure the genesis of our present value definitions as to the maintenance of the aged in our present social structures. The patriarchal family system in which the authority of the head is based upon his control of the family land and wealth has frequently seen the hostility of the young toward the old in their struggle to enfranchise themselves as independent members of adult society (Malinowski, 1927). The position of the aged in such societies has been based upon their ability to maintain their position by retaining their economic controls to the end or to obtain satisfactory support agreements with their children if they turned over the family property during their lifespan. The King Lear legend as told and retold in medieval English literature was a statement of the consequences of the relinquishment of power to undeserving youth.

The stability of these patriarchal systems depended upon a working relationship which compromised the rights of the old with the aspirations of the young. The type

of balance achieved between generations undoubtedly varied widely with time and place, depending upon the manner in which the authority of the elders was used and the alternatives to their rule which existed for the young. Thus the dominance of the elders which characterized the rise of Puritanism in England during the first half of the seventeenth century was challenged in the last half of the century during the Restoration's reaction against Puritan values.[11]

Colonial America was to receive its share of patriarchs in the model of the early Puritan (Morgan, 1944) or Amish (Kollmorgen, 1940) settler. But it also received, and probably in larger number, the rebellious youth breaking from the control of the extended family. Perhaps they were younger sons without hope of obtaining the land necessary to marriage and the establishment of an independent household, perhaps they were the designated heirs unwilling to wait for the land to be turned over to them, or perhaps they just wanted to seek their own fortune in the newly developing commercial life of the cities of England and in her colonies.

MIGRATION AND THE ABANDONMENT OF THE AGED

You went to make money and you forgot that you left your parents; may God and your own children care for you as you for us [Handlin, 1952, p. 230].

[11] This remarkable degree of vehemence of their protest against the aged is indicated in Mignon's (1947) analysis of Restoration drama. She notes that, while the aged in Elizabethan drama were subjects both for satire and for sympathetic portrayal, the 1660–1700 period of the Restoration was crowded with comedies portraying the conflict between youth and old age in which the young "Airily superior for four acts . . . always triumph in the fifth." She notes that "the traditional hostility towards 'crabbed age' reached in these comedies the point of violence. The defiant sons and daughters voice their rebellion with a new frankness." She considers this period of revolt "a postwar reaction against a constricting morality and a social standard which no longer carried force. The relaxing of the social conscience under Charles II brought with it the denial of an outmoded code and the ridiculing of its champions."

It would seem that the patriarchal family system had achieved only a tenuous sort of stability at the close of the Middle Ages. It was most fully developed when the young had no alternative; it tended to disintegrate when they did. Primogeniture encouraged the migration of the young, leaving the aged dependent upon one child for support. The oldest son who remained was dependent upon the decision of his father to retire—a wait which often carried him into middle age before he could assume the position of household head (Handlin, 1952). The opening-up of new forms of economic opportunity in commerce, the expanding merchant marine, and—in the seventeenth century—the peopling of new lands made it possible now for even the eldest son to leave the parental household. Industrialization when it arrived was not a precipitating cause but rather one more contributing cause in the process of isolation of generations which had begun at least a century before the industrial revolution.

In America the existence of free land on the frontier during Colonial days and in the nineteenth century established the expectation of independent households for generations even in a rural setting. Calhoun (1917–19) states: "The pioneer environment created a specific economic situation that tended to emancipate childhood and youth. . . . Where parents stretched their prerogatives or tried to retain jurisdiction past the majority of the boy, estrangement was likely to ensue." He further notes that sons frequently left the parental home to establish their own households, leaving their fathers the difficult task of running their farms in their old age without the help of their sons.

The great waves of migration of the late nineteenth and early twentieth centuries drew from the rural areas of central, southern, and eastern Europe. The sudden increase in the survival rate of the young, coupled with a subdivision of existing farms to the point where they could no longer support an extended family, made out-migration of the young adult almost mandatory. The mores of the patriarchal family system were for the first time interpreted to include the obligation of the child to support the parents when separated from his household. But the forces of the new industrial society which reduced the family pattern to the conjugal unit among those who migrated also tended to sever the bonds with the aged parent in Europe.

The unity of the extended family system, where it was found, was based upon the existence of a common household reinforced by the consensus of a community. The separation of generations in space—be it the English youth migrating to the colonies, the pioneer's son setting up his own farm in a neighboring state, or the European peasant crossing to the factories of the American city—disrupted the traditional patterns of family support for the aged. The attempt to redefine the obligations of child to parent so as to span the distance between Europe and America—or even between Ohio and Indiana in the nineteenth century—was a phenomenon unique to the development of the American family and apparently not to be found in earlier family systems.

OBLIGATION TO MAINTAIN THE AGED

Here will be found a never-failing asylum for the friendless orphans and the bereft widows, the distribution of labor and the improvements in machinery happily combining to call into profitable employment the tender services of those who have just sprung from the cradle, as well as those who are tottering to the grave, thus training up the little innocents to early and wholesome habits of honest industry, and smoothing the wrinkled front of decrepitude with the smiles of competency and protection [Calhoun, 1918, 2, 173].

While, historically, the maintenance of the aged has been primarily a family responsibility, the failure of families to do so has always been backstopped by some broader social assumption of responsibility. In feudal Europe, both the lord of the manor and monastery assumed responsibility for aiding the destitute aged. In the cities the craft guild also served as a social insurance system for its members. The breakup of the manor system during Tudor England saw the growth of unemployment in the cities and the rise of begging. Despite the stern measures which were taken to repress begging, an exception was made during the reign of Edward VI—the indigent aged were given a license to beg as the state's contribution to their maintenance.

The Elizabethan Poor Law of 1601 represented a statement of public obligation for the support of the aged and disabled indigent through the establishment of public almshouses or through relief furnished to them in their own homes. It was to become the model for the New England poor laws and eventually set the pattern for most of our states. It was characterized by the almshouse, with its collection of petty thieves and unfortunates of all sorts, and the boarding-out system, in which the aged were auctioned off to the family who made the lowest bid for their care. The care of the indigent aged was early recognized as a community responsibility, but the manner in which the care was given defined their indigency as a mark of personal failure and unworthiness.

The predominant consideration in our early systems of public support for the aged seems to have been that of minimum cost (Gagliardo, 1949; Clarke, 1957). Where possible, the aged were left in their own houses, living alone or possibly dependent upon an indentured servant for care. The indigent aged were also assigned as servants in community homes. Nor were our ancestors reluctant to condone a bit of exploitation of the aged, as our earliest sweatshops—the textile mills—were recommended for their employment (Calhoun, 1917, Vol. 1). The grim history of Western society's patterns of maintenance for its aged also received a few new modifications in industrial America as our dumping grounds for the unwanted—the "skid rows," "hobo jungles," and insane asylums—began to receive increasing numbers of older people abandoned by family and community.

The growing productivity of our industrial economy in the twentieth century has greatly altered our ability to support groups excluded from productive functions and has been accompanied by a redefinition of the manner in which such groups *ought* to be supported. The industrial promise of the early part of the century saw the concept of the subsistence wage of classical economics replaced by the notion of the "fair" wage (as defined by the rising labor unions or implicit in Ford's original $5.00 day) which enabled the individual to share in the fruits of an expanding economy. The rejection of the subsistence wage as the appropriate level of living by the worker was accompanied by a protest against the marginal existence of those separated from the work force. The monumental documentation by the Webbs (1909) and by Booth (1894) of the dimensions of poverty in England at the turn of the century had its impact upon social thought in America. The disproportionate share of poverty among the aged noted in their studies was confirmed for the United States by the work of Epstein (1928) during the 1920's. The mounting pressures for social welfare reforms were directed toward the replacement of the traditional poorhouse with institutions more compatible with the needs of specific categories of dependents and, in the case of the aged, with the provision of pensions by the state or by industry.

From the point of view of the changing position of the older person in our society these pressures had the effect of defining him as a social "problem." Whether the extent of poverty was greater among the aged of the early part of the twentieth century than it was in earlier centuries is difficult to determine. But the significant fact was society's growing conviction that the aged represented an economically "depressed" group—their position was below that which society felt it *ought* to be. And in the language of social welfare a new status—indigent aged—was being created, based upon the individual's age as well as upon his ability to maintain himself.

Society's attempt to provide for its newly recognized group of indigent aged in the

1900–1934 era was divided between a re-affirmation of the individual's duty to provide for his old age and experimentation with new forms of public and private pension systems.[12] The industrial pension which in its nineteenth-century origins was informal and discretionary with the employer became institutionalized in industry and by 1929 covered four million employees. Although most of these pensions compelled retirement at age 65, they usually contained no contractual liability on the part of the employer, and payments could be altered or even discontinued at will (Corson and McConnell, 1956). The same period saw the states move into the old age assistance field. Abraham Epstein, working first with the Fraternal Order of the Eagles and in 1927 organizing the American Association for Old-Age Assistance, did much to promote the idea of state responsibility for its aged. By 1934, thirty states were conducting some form of public assistance program, eighteen state programs having been enacted in the thirties. But in only ten states were the systems state-wide, and in most qualification was difficult and benefits were small (Gagliardo, 1949; Clarke, 1957).

A significant but, as yet, poorly documented aspect of the 1920's was the assumption of philanthropic responsibilities by the middle class. This decade saw the rise of our large fraternal societies, businessmen's clubs, and a proliferation of women's groups of all sorts—many of which were to adopt philanthropic or social "betterment" undertakings as part of their organizational aims. The conviction of the era that poverty was remedial had added to it the belief that collective action on the part of private voluntary organizations was a means of accomplishment. From the point of view of the aged this meant that the economic safeguards for old age need not depend solely upon their own ability to save or upon the occasional grant of a large donor (e.g., Carnegie's grant of

12 Chapter viii describes the solution of the development of programs of economic security for the aged.

$10,000,000 in 1905 to provide retirement pensions for college professors) but that additional safeguards could be gained through the collective action of their own groups. The twenties saw the beginnings of widows and orphans provisions by fraternal orders and the beginnings of the work which led to the establishment of homes for the aged by the Moose, Elks, and Odd Fellows and by labor unions and church groups as well.

The economic holocaust of the thirties put to severe test the ability of individuals to provide for their own old age and found the weakest points in the funding of the then existing pension plans. The Civil Service Retirement System was the only major pension plan to emerge unscathed. Most of the private-employer plans were discontinued, and many of the mutual plans, such as those established by unions, were bankrupted (Corson and McConnell, 1956). The states similarly found that they were unable to provide for the rapidly increasing numbers of dependent aged. The combination of family inability to support the aged, the state's inability to backstop the family, a mounting demand for separation of the aged from the labor force to make room for the younger worker, and a changing value system which demanded that the federal government assume a share of the responsibility for the maintenance of the aged were all instrumental in the passage of the Social Security Act of 1935.

The forties saw only a partial recovery from the depression years as far as the aged were concerned. Many who had lost their jobs found new employment difficult to obtain despite the expansion of the economy. Further, the savings which they may have set aside for their old age had been seriously depleted, and many of them had lost their homes. Old-Age and Survivors Insurance was still in its infancy, covering a relatively small proportion of aged and providing them with only meager retirement benefits. The dependency status represented by old age assistance characterizes the aged during this period. The year 1943 saw a peak of 23.4 per cent of our nation's aged drawing old age assistance benefits, while only 3.4 per cent were receiving income from the retirement insurance provisions of Old-Age and Survivors Insurance (Table 7).

The forties also witnessed the acceptance of the new status designation of "indigent aged" or "dependent aged" for the old person in our society. The discrepancy between their level of living and the standards we had come to consider appropriate for our society became dramatically apparent. Particularly in the cities, where the

baux (1958) as a shift away from the society's assumption of "residual" functions (i.e., those of temporary assistance in crises situations), where the structures of the family and the market are unable to make provision for individuals. This traditional concept of social welfare was replaced by the assumption of what the authors term "institutional functions," which "provide a broader, more permanent framework of services designed to aid individuals and groups to attain satisfying standards of life and health." Undoubtedly, the aging of our

TABLE 7*

OLD AGE ASSISTANCE RECIPIENTS AND OLD-AGE AND SURVIVORS INSURANCE AGED BENEFICIARIES PER 1000 AGED POPULATION, JUNE, 1940–57

YEAR	RATE PER 1000 AGED POPULATION		YEAR	RATE PER 1000 AGED POPULATION	
	OAA†	OASI‡		OAA†	OASI‡
1940	217	7	1949	218	149
1941	233	23	1950	226	170
1942	234	34	1951	215	235
1943	219	41	1952	203	260
1944	205	50	1953	194	314
1945	194	62	1954	187	358
1946	194	87	1955	179	415
1947	202	106	1956	173	454
1948	205	126	1957	168	527

* Source: U.S. Bureau of Public Assistance, *Trend Report* (Washington, D.C.: The Bureau, 1957).
† Excludes OAA recipients under 65 years.
‡ Excludes beneficiaries residing in foreign countries.

visibility of the indigent older person living in relative isolation was high, did the problem seem most acute. The problem was given further significance by the population forecasts of the period, based on the assumption of a declining fertility rate, which put the estimate of our proportion of aged in the 1970's at 12 per cent and expecting an ultimate leveling-off point at 14–16 per cent.

The identification of a group of dependents as "aged" extended our concept of "maintenance" from that of providing economic assistance to that of meeting the needs of a specific age group over a broad range of their social participation. This change in concept of social welfare has been characterized by Wilensky and Le-

population has been partly responsible for this shift in view, as the group of aged have been the recipients of the largest share of all public assistance granted in this country since the 1930's and have been the subject for many of the welfare innovations under the new concept.

The forties, too, saw the development of a variety of new services designed to maintain the dependent aged. The problem of chronic illness coupled with the inability of the family and the conventional hospital facilities to provide them with adequate nursing care led to the development of new institutions in the form of proprietary and non-profit nursing homes as well as the use of county homes for nursing care. The ecology of the life-cycle in recent times, not too well understood, apparently saw the aged residing in homes too large for them to maintain in areas which were suffering from the blight which comes with age in American cities, or else it saw them drift into rooming-house and dilapidated apartment-house areas of the city. The public housing projects of the decade made no provision for including the aged in their supply of low-cost housing, and some of their regulations effectively precluded them. The problem was approached by the development of institutional housing in the form of public and private "homes for the aged." The isolation of urban aged from their usual companions and forms of participation led to the attempt to provide new activities and patterns of voluntary association for them.

However, the identification of the dependent aged and the developing of a network of services for them which occurred during the 1940's had the effect of identifying old age itself rather than dependency as the problem of the old. *It further posited dependency, disability, and isolation as the normal expectation for the aged in our society.* Perhaps symbolic of public attitude toward old age in the decade was recognition by the Bureau of Internal Revenue of the economic hardships of the aged by granting them a double tax exemption, thus defining old age itself as a disability comparable to blindness.

The decade of the 1950's witnessed the beginning of the shift away from a dependent status for the aged. A progressive improvement in their economic position accompanied by and, in part, resulting from a growing awareness of their political potential provides a basis for the emergence of a new status for them.

Two events at the turn of the decade were to lay a new foundation for financial security in old age. The first was the Supreme Court's decision in the Inland Steel case of 1949 (69 Sup. Ct. 887), which established pensions as a bargainable issue under the Taft-Hartley Act. This led to pension settlements in auto, steel, and some other industries in which the company was to pay a maximum of $100 a month *less*

the amount paid by Social Security to the retired worker. Second, as these settlements were being reached, the 1950 Congress made sweeping changes in the Social Security Act, sharply raising the level of benefits paid under it and extending its coverage. Although Social Security had been supported and its extension recommended in the platforms of both major political parties since 1944, no effective action had been taken on improving its coverage since 1939.

In the 1950–58 interval Social Security coverage has been steadily extended from three-fourths to well over nine-tenths of the labor force, industrial pensions coverage has expanded from less than one-fifth of the labor force in 1950 to over a fourth today—with predictions for a steady rise coverage. Following these changes we have seen the proportion of persons dependent upon old age assistance drop from 22.6 per cent in 1950 to 16.8 per cent in 1957, and we have seen the proportion of aged covered by OASI rise from 17.0 in 1950 to 52.7 per cent in 1957 (Table 7). If we add to this the fact that the percentage of homeownership is increasing among the aged and the fact that tomorrow's retiree will have had a period of 18 years of relatively full employment in which to acquire additional reserves for retirement, we can trace the shift in economic position of the aged from that of dependency during the thirties, forties, and early fifties to one characterized by relative financial independence within the next decade.

The improving economic position of the aged is also being buttressed by increasing commitment of our political structures to maintaining and continuing the improvement (see chap. xvii). The Townsend movements and similar political action groups of the thirties developed our first national awareness of the political potential of the aged. However, it presented them as a conflict group whose interests were contrary to and threatening to those of our society as a whole. The marked improvement in their political position in the fifties was more subtle and went largely unnoticed. They were an unorganized group and therefore not a prominent factor in the political scene. But, as they were unorganized, they were also uncommitted to either party, and the fact by the middle of the decade the numbers of persons over 65 exceeded the number of voting members of organized labor (by way of illustration) could not have gone unnoticed. Bipartisan support of Social Security, begun in 1950, continued through the decade. In each of the even-numbered years from 1950 on, Congress made improvements in Social Security legislation as well as passed other bills of benefit to the aged. It is also significant that in 1957 "practically every inaugural message by a governor to his legislature included an important section on aging" (Council of State Governments, 1955). Our national concern for the aged has played a prominent part in the defining of society's obligation to the individual and in the development of the institutional structures and values which we now regard as characteristics of a "welfare" state.

B. *Emerging Participation Patterns for the Aged*

The transition from low- to high-energy technologies is accompanied by changes in institutional structures defining participation by the aged, as shown in chapter iv. The increasing specialization of function in high-energy technologies tend to throw into sharp focus changes in specific role-performance expectations which occur in the later years. The shortening of the period of performance of major adult functions which characterize high-energy societies has further acted to change the patterns of participation of the aged from limited involvement to that of separation from adult functions. Thus in pre-industrial and in early industrial societies work and family responsibilities tended to continue to the end of life. Old age implied physical incapacity which limited the person's abilities to perform his major adult functions. However, the foreshortening of the work and family cycles, combined with a gradual extension of the life-span, which have oc-

curred in high-energy societies have established a late period of life during which the historic bases for social participation by the adult have vanished without the requisite of physical incapacity.

Advanced industrial societies such as the United States have tended toward a *redefinition* of old age as a period of *separation* from, rather than limited *participation* in, major adult functions (Tibbitts, 1958). To this extent a new age category has been created distinct from any age-related seniority classifications within the adult period itself, a category which is without a historical parallel.

The relative separation of this age group from interaction with younger groups gives them some of the characteristics of an *age-homogeneous* grouping as defined by Eisenstadt (1956) and applied by him to the analysis of the position of the adolescent in our society. The focus of participation is within the age group rather than across age groupings. Participation in the younger age group is not, therefore, fully preparatory for the transition to the older age group, and the aged have not been assigned roles or functions integrated within the structure of the broader social system.

Thus the rapid aging of our own population structure has been compounded by the increased scope of the new definition of old age as well as by an increase in the number of persons in the later years of life.

The problems of maintenance of the increasing numbers of aged are being met in part through the increased assumption of responsibility by the state for providing minimal levels of support and by the increasing provision for retirement which our rising levels of productivity allow to the individual and to his employer. There is now the promise that the dependency status which characterized the aged through most of our history may be substantially eliminated during the decades ahead. The possibility exists that this period may be defined as a potentially high-status form of reward for the latter part of life. But the impact of future generations of aged upon their social structure will depend upon the patterns of participation and reciprocities which are defined for them. As to these we can only speculate.

1. *Family participation.*—Increasing mobility, which in the past has tended to isolate generations, is now serving to increase contacts and strengthen ties between generations now separated in space. Increasing ability to travel as well as increasing use of long-distance telephone and other means of long-distance interpersonal communication are resulting in a greater rate of interaction between generations separated by several thousand miles than would have been true of generations separated by only a hundred miles a century ago. The persistence of primary-group identifications by individuals or generations separated by space has been noted by Faris (1932). The ties which link these generations have been reported by Sussman (1953) and Streib (1958) to be voluntary ones of affection, economic assistance, counsel, and personal services.[13] Thus the model of the companionate family as described by Burgess and Locke (1945) seems to be developing an extended-family modification—that of separate households for generations, relative financial independence of each, with the bonds uniting them being those of affection and voluntary assistance.

2. *Community participation.*—The ecological determinants of participation by the aged are not too well understood. The last few decades have seen an apparent concentration of urban aged in the older residential areas in the central sections of the city, of rural aged in the rural village, and the growth of retirement communities in such states as Florida, California, and Arizona. Cowgill's (1957) analysis of changes in the concentration of aged in the central areas of thirty-nine American cities between 1940 and 1950 showed that, although the percentage of aged in these areas continued to increase, this was due more to the out-migration of the younger population than to the growth rate of the aged themselves. He found that the numerical increase in aged was greatest outside the central areas.

[13] See chap. xiii for a research report on this topic.

The apparent concentration of aged in these central areas, however, has strongly influenced our pattern of community services to them. As a dependent group of relatively high visibility in areas which had come to be defined as "problem areas," the social welfare concepts of the 1930's and 1940's were most readily interpreted in terms of this group. The pattern of Golden Age clubs, community centers, sheltered workshops, public housing, and other services for the aged were by virtue of their location if not by their ideology directed toward the dependent urban aged in these areas of greatest deterioration. The reversal of the trend toward concentration of the aged in central areas coupled with a projected decline in their dependency status will require a re-examination of our patterns of services. To the extent that the American urban community represents a network of services, it has evolved primarily in terms of the needs and interests of the young and middle-aged adults and their children. They have not been adapted to servicing recreational, transportation, economic, housing, and health needs of the population group whose family and work careers have terminated. To the extent that specialized services for the aged have been localized, they have failed to reach the bulk of the urban aged. And to the extent that they have been directed toward a particular group of dependent urban aged isolated from family and community participation —who were forced to look to social agencies for economic support, health care, and the opportunities for the most elementary forms of recreational and social participation—they fail to elicit the participation of the emerging group of self-sufficient aged, related to a family structure, able to contribute in purchasing power, knowledge, and skill to the various civic and economic structures of urban life.

The trend of the rural farm aged to the village will undoubtedly be accelerated by the extension of OASI to the farmer. Cowles (1954) has indicated that the farm aged tend to retire to the village if they are not forced to work the farm as a means of livelihood. Little research has been done on the impact of this increasing migration of aged upon the village and town and upon the developing of a pattern of services to meet their needs within the more limited resources of the small community.

The development of the retirement community in the milder climates of the United States represents a type of homogeneous age-structured communal organization that is perhaps unprecedented in the history of the human community. The attraction of these communities for the upper-income aged (Manley, 1954) could see their development increasing rapidly during the coming decades if there is a continued improvement in the economic position of the aged. The impact of the aged upon these communities has been seen in the development of a pattern of institutions and services focused almost entirely upon their needs (Harlan, 1954). If we contrast this community with the urban community, we can establish a continuum using these types as poles. The urban community represents a maximum potential for the development of an age-heterogeneous structure incorporating the aged. The extent to which the aged are incorporated into a community with a balanced age structure will be dependent upon the ability of the community to service the aged, the specific uses the community can make of the contributions to community life which the aged are capable of rendering, and the barriers to their participation which exist. The extent to which the aged prefer withdrawal into an age-homogeneous retirement community structure will depend upon their ability to afford this alternative, the adequacy with which the urban community is able to meet their needs, and the extent to which they prefer and society defines as appropriate the segregated participation of the retirement community or integrated participation in a city or town with a balanced age structure.

WORK AND LEISURE PARTICIPATION

The separation of the aged from participation in the work, family, and community structures of America has been accompanied by the development of a set of norms which define as appropriate segregated patterns of participation for them. Thus migration to a retirement community is regarded as desirable for those who can afford it, retirement to the village with its concentration of older people is sought by the farmer, and public opinion still regards as appropriate withdrawal to an old people's home once the major adult roles have terminated (although this evaluation is not apparently shared by older people themselves). Even in the city, where the maximum potential for integrated participation by the aged exists, participation norms have been defined in terms of the segregated forms of participation which had been devised for the indigent and physically disabled aged served by welfare agencies in the central areas of the city.

The consequences of the growing segregation of the aged in American society are difficult to forecast. The establishment of separate communities for the aged, or enclaves within the urban community, require a duplication of community facilities and services which may prove to be as economically unfeasible as attempts to provide "separate but equal" facilities for other groups in our society. But the cost to our society of segregation of the aged must also be reckoned in terms of potential services lost as well as additional facilities required. Thus the separation of the aged from the work function may deprive the industrial system of needed skills in an age of automation which again may put a premium on the judgment and experience of the older worker valued in an earlier craft age (Friedmann, 1958). The withdrawal of financially self-sufficient aged from the community may constitute a net economic loss if the gains from their purchasing power, taxes, and reduced school costs are balanced against the costs of special services which they require.[14] The value of the potential contributions of this new leisure class in the performing of non-work (i.e., non-paid) functions essential in the conduct of political and civic affairs may be

[14] The impact of the aged on the economy is discussed in chap. xiv.

lost to the community and society if this group is excluded from participation in activities relating to the ends of the over-all social structure. Havighurst (1957) has noted that there is little reduction in social competence between the ages of 40 and 70 in roles other than that of worker and spouse. But he has also noted (Havighurst, 1958) that our society cannot utilize the skills of the new leisure class unless it reduces emphasis upon work as "the major avenue to social competence" and gives more weight to the values of competencies in the performance of family, friendship, citizenship, and other leisure roles. In our emerging leisure structures the aged represent a pilot group for the study of the coming impact of leisure upon our society. As the only major leisure class we possess at this moment, they may represent the leisure innovators for America, establishing patterns and precedents to be followed by other adult age groups.[15]

REFERENCES

BARBER, B. 1957. Social stratification. New York: Harcourt, Brace & Co.

BERNARDI, B. 1952. The age system of the Nilo-Hamitic peoples. Africa, **22**, 316–33.

BOOTH, C. 1894. The aged poor in England and Wales. London: Macmillan & Co.

BROWN, J. D. 1950. The role of industry in relation of the older worker. *In* M. DERBER (ed.), The aged and society, pp. 65–74. Champaign, Ill.: Industrial Relations Research Association.

BURGESS, E. W., and LOCKE, H. J. 1945. The family. New York: American Book Co.

CALHOUN, A. W. 1917–19. Social history of the American family from Colonial times to the present. Cleveland: Arthur H. Clark Co.

CLARKE, HELEN I. 1957. Social legislation. 2d ed. New York: Appleton-Century-Crofts Co.

CORSON, J. J., and McCONNELL, J. W. 1956. Economic needs of older persons. New York: Twentieth Century Fund.

COTTRELL, F. 1955. Energy and society. New York: McGraw-Hill Book Co.

COUNCIL OF STATE GOVERNMENTS. 1955. The states and their older citizens. Chicago: The Council.

COWGILL, D. O. 1957. Trends in the ecology of the aged in American cities, 1940–1950. J. Gerontol., **12**, 75–80.

COWLES, MAY. 1954. Meeting housing needs of older people. Am. J. Sociology, **59**, 324–31.

DAVIS, K., and MOORE, W. E. 1945. Some principles of stratification. Am. Sociological Rev., **10**, 242–49.

EISENSTADT, S. N. 1956. From generation to generation. Glencoe, Ill.: Free Press.

EPSTEIN, A. 1928. The challenge of the aged. New York: Vanguard Press.

FARIS, E. 1932. Primary group: essence and accident. Am. J. Sociology, **38**, 41–50.

FLORNOY, B. 1958. The world of the Inca. Garden City, N.Y.: Doubleday Anchor Books.

FRIEDMANN, E. A. 1958. The work of leisure. *In* WILMA DONAHUE, W. W. HUNTER, DOROTHY H. COONS, and HELEN K. MAURICE (eds.), Free time: challenge to later maturity, pp. 119–31. Ann Arbor: University of Michigan Press.

FRIEDMANN, E. A., and HAVIGHURST, R. J. 1954. The meaning of work and retirement. Chicago: University of Chicago Press.

GAGLIARDO, D. 1949. American social insurance. New York: Harper & Bros.

GILLIN, J. L. 1937. Poverty and dependency. New York: D. Appleton–Century Co.

GLICK, P. C. 1955. The life cycle of the family. Marriage & Family Living, **17**, 3–9.

HANDLIN, O. 1952. The uprooted. Boston: Little, Brown & Co.

HARLAN, W. H. 1954. Community adaptation to the presence of aged persons: St. Petersburg, Florida. Am. J. Sociology, **59**, 332–39.

HAVIGHURST, R. J. 1957. The social competence of middle aged people. Genet. Psychol. Monogr., **56**, 297–373.

———. 1958. Sociologic meaning of aging. Geriatrics, **13**, 43–50.

HAVIGHURST, R. J., and ALBRECHT, RUTH. 1953. Older people. New York: Longmans, Green & Co.

HOMANS, G. C. 1941. English villagers of the thirteenth century. Cambridge, Mass.: Harvard University Press.

KOLLMORGEN, W. M. 1940. The Old Amish of Lancaster County, Pennsylvania. *In* U.S. BUREAU OF AGRICULTURE ECONOMICS, Culture of a contemporary rural community. ("Rural Life Studies.") Washington, D.C.: The Bureau.

LINTON, R. 1936. The study of man. New York: D. Appleton–Century Co.

[15] Chapter xii deals with older people and the uses of leisure.

MALINOWSKI, B. 1927. Sex and repression in savage society. New York: Harcourt, Brace & Co.

MANLEY, C. R., JR. 1954. The migration of older people. Am. J. Sociology, **59**, 324–31.

MIGNON, ELISABETH. 1947. Crabbed age and youth. Durham, N.C.: Duke University Press.

MOORE, W. E. 1950. The aged in industrial societies. *In* M. DERBER (ed.), The aged and society, pp. 24–29. Champaign, Ill.: Industrial Relations Association.

MORGAN, E. S. 1944. The Puritan family. Boston: Trustees of the [Boston] Public Library.

OGBURN, W. F., and TIBBITTS, C. 1933. The family and its functions. *In* Recent social trends in the United States, **1**, 661–708. New York: McGraw-Hill Book Co.

PARSONS, T. 1942. Age and sex in the social structure of the United States. Am. Sociological Rev., **7**, 604–16.

PETERSON, R. L. 1955. Older workers and their job effectiveness. Geriatrics, **10**, 34–38.

POST, EMILY. 1955. Etiquette: the blue book of social usage. New York: Funk & Wagnalls Co.

PRINS, A. H. J. 1953. East African age-class systems. Groningen: J. B. Walters.

RUSSELL, J. C. 1948. British medieval population. Albuquerque: University of New Mexico Press.

SAUVY, A. 1954. Le Vieillessment des populations et l'allongement de la vie. Population, **9**, 675–82.

SEWELL, W. H., RAMSEY, C. E., and DUCOFF, L. J. 1953. Farmers' conceptions and plans for economic security in old age. (Agric. Exp. Sta. Research Bull. No. 182.) Madison: University of Wisconsin Agricultural Experiment Station.

SHELDON, H. D. 1958. The older population of the United States. New York: John Wiley & Sons.

SHOCK, N. W. 1955. Skill and employment. Pub. Health Rep., **70**, 851–54.

SOROKIN, P. 1927. Social mobility. New York: Harper & Bros.

SQUIER, L. W. 1912. Old age dependency in the United States. New York: Macmillan Co.

STEINER, P. O., and DORFMAN, R. 1957. The economic status of the aged. Berkeley: University of California Press.

STREIB, G. F. 1958. Family patterns in retirement. J. Social Issues, **14**, No. 2, 46–60.

STREIB, G. F., and THOMPSON, W. E. 1957. Personal and social adjustment in retirement. *In* WILMA DONAHUE and C. TIBBITTS (eds.), The new frontiers of aging. Ann Arbor: University of Michigan Press.

SUSSMAN, M. B. 1953. The help pattern in the middle class family. Am. Sociological Rev., **18**, 22–25.

TAEUBER, C. 1957. Population changes to 1975. Ann. Am. Acad. Political & Social Sc., **313**, 25–31.

TAEUBER, C., and TAEUBER, IRENE B. 1958. The changing population of the United States. New York: John Wiley & Sons.

TIBBITTS, C. 1958. Aging as a modern social achievement. *In* WILMA DONAHUE, W. W. HUNTER, DOROTHY H. COONS, and HELEN K. MAURICE (eds.), Free time: challenge to later maturity, pp. 17–28. Ann Arbor: University of Michigan Press.

U.S. BUREAU OF THE CENSUS. 1909. A century of population growth. Washington, D.C.: Government Printing Office.

———. 1949. Historical statistics of the United States, 1789–1945. Washington, D.C.: Government Printing Office.

U.S. BUREAU OF PUBLIC ASSISTANCE. 1957. Trend report. Washington, D.C.: The Bureau.

U.S. FEDERAL SECURITY AGENCY. 1952. Fact book on aging. Washington, D.C.: Government Printing Office.

VALAORAS, V. G. 1950. Patterns of aging of human populations. *In* The social and biological challenge of our aging population: Proceedings of the Eastern States Health Education Conference, March 31–April 1, 1949, pp. 67–85. New York: Columbia University Press.

WARNER, W. L. 1957. The study of social stratification. *In* J. B. GITTLER (ed.), Review of sociology: analysis of a decade, pp. 221–58. New York: John Wiley & Sons.

———. 1958. A black civilization. Rev. ed. New York: Harper & Bros.

WEBB, S., and WEBB, BEATRICE. 1909. Minority report. London: Longmans.

WILENSKY, H., and LEBAUX, C. 1958. Industrial society and social welfare. New York: Russell Sage Foundation.

WOYTINSKY, W. S., and ASSOCIATES. 1953. Employment and wages in the United States. New York: Twentieth Century Fund.

VI

The Aging Individual

LEONARD Z. BREEN

I. THE BASIS OF AGING

All human beings grow through a series of interrelated and interdependent age-related life-stages. Successively, we are infant, child, adolescent, adult, middle-aged, and aged. For any one individual these various age-designated periods may occur at points in the chronological span of his life which are quite different from those of other persons. For instance, the onset of the period of life which is known as "middle-aged" may vary by as much as 20 years, depending upon the culture, designator, or criteria employed as well as upon the sort of person being so designated. Not only may the stages of life themselves be somewhat nebulous in terms of the time periods which they are each supposed to cover but an individual's perception of one's self as fitting into any given stage at a particular time will also vary. Human beings have long wished for themselves the gift, as Robert Burns said, "to see oursels as others see us." Each person does have self-conceptions developed through the machinery of patterned social intercourse. These self-concepts follow from the not-always-conscious consideration of how the individual believes others see him. Sometimes the perception of views held by others are askew, and one's concept of the self is thereby distorted. The person may, as one result of such an error, find himself somewhat surprised at the response of others when reacting to a specific situation. The self-

styled living-room comic may be quite abashed one day to find that his companions have been laughing at rather than with him. In this sense, then, one's life-stages are perceived in response to the clues assembled in social situations. It is said of some youngsters that they act "grown-up," and there are older persons who are said to be in their "second childhood." The stages, for any one individual, may be more or less discernible and more or less accurately taken on as a critical element in one's concept of the self.

The transitional phases of change from stage to stage are even more amorphous, with probably less personal awareness of the process of modification than of the specific stages themselves. The separate and specific stages are somewhat fuzzy, but certainly the time when one begins to "fade out" of one stage and emerge in the next is even more difficult to identify. Thus, rather than recognize with certainty the time periods of stage transition, it is more likely that the individual will be generally aware of the stage in which he finds himself (or is placed by others) at any designated time in his life.

The clarity, then, with which one perceives a particular stage of life varies considerably from person to person, as does the acceptance of and adjustment to the situations and definitions attaching thereto. The functional response that an individual makes following upon such perception is, by most persons, relatively rational

145

and, for the most part, conscious. The human responds to a situation in terms of his own judgment of the nature, meaning, and significance of that situation; he is a wilful, interpreting, responding animal. In his interpretations and responses are to be found a highly refined, organized, and internalized life-history. The individual began life as an entity produced out of biological functions and prepared to act in a socialized world by virtue of an intricately balanced and highly organized biological mechanism. In the socialization process a personality was formed; a psyche flowered and was organized. This psyche was tested and strengthened in the social situations confronting the developing individual. Throughout life the process continues. Each life-stage calls into play new understandings, new definitions, new social groups, and new tests of one's psychological organization; new responses are formed for old situations, and old responses are reshaped to fit new conditions.

One of the channels through which such stages are developed, recognized, interpreted, and felt in their influence upon behavior is the process of "growing older." As one proceeds through consecutive age periods, new sets of social expectations appear and new response patterns are developed for them. Clearly, these expectations and their satisfactions are parts of the interrelated processes of life-change.

II. Aging as a Dependent Variable

Until relatively recently, aging was seen simply as a procession of years. The individual's rate of change, measured in terms of physical, mental, or social functions, was related to chronological age in virtually all discussions of aging. "Senescence" was a common descriptive term used to identify a specific age-related stage of life. Beeson's paper, in 1920, on intelligence was reflective of the general approach to research on aging. He studied "twenty subjects" (ten men and ten women) to find at what chronological age certain changes in the

"mental processes" took place. As in the case of many researches now current, Beeson saw age as an independent variable, accurately measured by years lived, to which other indexes might be related.

During the mid-1930's, Lorge (1935), in apparent recognition of this problem, separated his subjects into two groups, one younger (age 20–25) and one older (over age 40). He thus sought to define broad age groups by use of which other significant differences might be detected. Somewhat later, Parsons (1942) suggested the possibility of investigating aging as a function of social judgment and societal classification. He noted the two chief times when there is a clear example of such social judgment: (1) isolation of the parental couple after the children have left home and (2) abrupt retirement as a part of the occupational structure, leaving the older man cut off from participation in most important interests.

At present, most research continues to identify the aged as persons from specific chronological age groups, despite the frequent protestations that aging is not measured by chronological years alone. Clearly, researchers have not yet learned to implement their protests. Equally clearly, aging is now coming to be studied as a partly dependent variable, changing with respect to other broad categories of change operative in our society, rather than as an independent variable changing only with the number of years lived.

Such definition of aging as a partly dependent variable implies certain specific kinds of researches. If aging is at least in part dependent upon social and cultural forces, then the measurement of aging will become a function of the researcher's judgment of researchable areas. The danger, obviously, is that of tautological research. As in other fields, if we state the criteria by which we shall research aging as a field, then our findings must be reflective of our criteria. If aging cannot be demonstrated to have independent phenomenological existence, the personal judgments of individual researchers concerning the definition of that which they study—here aging—must structure the research design. That for which they seek is often found. The hypotheses frequently, in effect, become self-fulfilling. One of the basic requirements for continued research in aging, therefore, must be a more adequate description of the studied phenomenon than the general word "aging."

For this writer, aging is a process of change; it is not a state of being. It is dynamic. Aging is not adjustment, physical structure, or social dissatisfaction. It is itself a process without inherent qualities of goodness or badness. This statement of events, this continuous change, is that which we in general may understand as "aging."

III. The Definitions of Age and Aging

Aging has been variously defined and used by researchers from different disciplines—a fact which has complicated the interdisciplinary approach to and understanding of collected data (for an elaboration of the problems see Breen, 1957). A commonly noted statement in the literature concerning the nature of aging is that it "begins with conception (or birth) and terminates only with death." Yet, while many writers take this position of understanding aging as a growth process, in implementing research other definitions are employed—occasionally explicitly, often implicitly. What, then, are these definitions? Is old age recognized as that period of life when the appliances for which we have lifetime guaranties begin to wear out? Or, more seriously, like beauty, does it lie in the eye of the beholder? To the child of 7, the adolescent is old. To the adolescent, his parents' generation in their forties is old. To the 45-year-old parent, the octogenarian is the old one. A man may be as old as he feels, as he looks, as he acts, as his arteries, or, perhaps, as his friends think him to be.

In general, aging is seen in one of two ways: as an orderly and regular process of change or as an irregular but continuous process. The first position is characterized by many who argue, with Cameron (1945), that aging is

a gradually accelerating decline in the speed and precision of motor performances, of perception, and of learning and immediate recall. Sensory acuity eventually suffers in all spheres. Neural and humoral coordinations, muscular and secretory responses are apt to show some decrement in efficiency. The somatic musculature begins to fatigue more easily and to recover more slowly after exertion. Tonic and phasic action becomes less steady and less well coordinated [p. 144].

On the other hand, aging is seen as irregular, as a period of "subtle variations."

It is not a simple slope which everyone slides down at the same speed. It is a flight of irregular stairs, down which some journey more quickly than others. Progress may be hastened or retarded by many factors, such as heredity, environment, disease, emotion, or past habits [Howell, 1953, p. 45].

Most current writers would no doubt agree with Tibbitts and Sheldon (1952) that the aging process involves "numerous interrelated elements, biological, psychological, and sociological in nature. Aging per se is so complicated with disease processes on the one hand and with the restrictions of culturally assigned roles on the other that it is difficult as yet to describe or measure it with any degree of confidence" (p. 7). In general, definitions of age and aging which may be found in the literature can be classified under three rubrics: (1) as a natural process of change; (2) as a pathological system; or (3) as a process or condition evoked by response to one's social environment. The following review illustrates these three positions.

A. Aging as Natural Process

Aging is often defined as a process of change which is continuous. "The differentiation and maturation of cellular material and its involution and senescence constitute the continuously changing biological sub-structure of the aging organism. . . . [It is characterized] by environmental stress to which the aging individual is exposed" (Donahue, 1952, p. 115). Shock (1951b) suggests that "all living matter changes with time in both structure and function, and the changes which follow a general trend constitute aging" (p. 1). Aging is not a natural process of decline alone; there is also implied the element of growth. Thus "growth, development and maturation are just as much consequences of the occult processes of aging as are the atrophies and the degenerations of senility" (Stieglitz, 1954, p. 3).

B. Aging as Pathology

A view of aging which is now losing pop-ularity has to do with the process as a pathological condition. Were this condition not present, a human being might conceiv-ably live on endlessly. One of the better-known statements of this position is that of Bogomolets (1946), who proposed a "phys-iochemical theory" of aging and proposed that "the ability to lengthen life is first of all not to shorten it." Aging, to him, was a disease, susceptible of control. Clearly, if one could control certain of the biological functions, one need not "catch" old age, since "aging is a chronic disease and its cause a combination of bad habits" (Ras-mus, 1926, p. 224). One of the specific ways one might deal with this chronic dis-ease is proposed by Rasmus: "Aging is not so much a matter of years as of defective circulation . . . ; that which maintains good circulation conserves youth" (p. 13). More recently, Korenchevsky (1950) re-iterated this position, noting that "at pres-ent, aging is a pathological condition, a kind of disease."

Among physiologists and biologists, this view is now giving way to positions which try to account for pathological findings as functions of a disease which may or may not be related to the aging process itself. Despite Alfred Cohn's (1940) admonition

that "aging is either disease or not dis-ease," Howell (1949) wonders "whether old age has any diseases of its own . . . [al-though] the reaction of the aged to disease is not the same as that of the young." It has further been suggested by some phys-iologists that perhaps one way to account for the reactions of older persons to disease has to do with impaired homeostasis. Per-haps, says Shock (1945), "most of the phenomena of aging can be attributed to a progressive loss in the homeostatic capaci-ties of the organism" (p. 53). Others have proposed varying means for understanding and detecting the aging process via exam-inations of the skin, teeth, muscle system, etc. (see Lansing, 1954).

C. Aging as a Sociological Phenomenon

Superimposed upon the natural physio-logical processes of change which accom-pany increasing years for an individual is his conditioned response to the social envi-ronment. Perhaps an individual is only as old as he feels, but how he feels is in large part a function of how the society about him expects him to feel and act. The social judgments concerning the nature of old age, and older persons, are constantly passed in such a manner as to define for the individual the society's expectations of his behavior. Operationally, then, old age may begin "at that point in an individual's life when he ceases to perform all those du-ties, and enjoy all those rights, which were his during mature adulthood, when he be-gins to take on a new system of rights and duties" (Hutchinson, 1955, p. 1).

The time or point of life at which old age and the new system of rights and duties be-gin is in part determined by the social judgments concerning old age and the re-sponse of the individual to such judgments. One group of writers thinks that there is a transition point between middle and old age which is measured not by chronological age but by "a given degree of deviation from adulthood. . . . Old age commences when a person is no longer able to maintain some stated proportion of the achievements of the average adult in his culture" (Cavan *et al.,* 1949, p. 8).

Most writers in the field of aging who have taken account of the social environment have dwelt upon the negative aspects of aging, as have those cited above. Old age, they hold, is a period of social withdrawal, either voluntary or imposed, and of social deprivation. Others have been concerned with the position of the older person with respect to some productive unit. "Old age is a period when losses affect the social status of the person more seriously than do similar losses earlier in life—loss of one's partner, if married, of one's family . . . loss of job" (Randall, 1950, p. 36).

For the most part, sociologists have taken the position that aging is as aging does. Aging must be studied, interpreted, and understood in terms of the behavior characteristics of persons designated by the society as aged. If persons of a given chronological age (say, 65 or older) are designated "old" and the society acts toward them in a special way as if they were "old" (i.e., through programs of compulsory retirement or specification of an age at which one becomes eligible for Social Security payments), then we must know if such age does in fact generate differential behavior. How do "old people" walk, talk, and act? Are their attitudes and personalities different from other groups as a result of their being designated by the society as being "old" or by their having survived a specified number of years?

Each successive period of life calls into play the normative judgments related to that period as determined by the society in its interactions. The individual who is a part of that society behaves as he does within the confines of the social norms. In this sense, then, the norms are not statistical means computed on the basis of measures of observed behavior. They are rather the expectations of behavior for each of the members of the society which has erected the norms whether or not most persons in the society actually behave as specified. The expectations are of many kinds, defining characteristics of social intercourse and personal behavior. Thus, just as children are expected to "be seen and not heard," so also are the aged parents residing with their grown children. Persons in our society are graded by age (Parsons, 1942), and behavior characteristics are denoted for each of the several age grades. Such expectations are reinforced by various media of expression (e.g., the popular song with the line "Nobody loves you when you're old and gray—there'll be some changes made"). Youth is associated with vigor; old age, with reflection. Young persons are expected to "sow wild oats" and be "young in heart"; their symbols are the "crew cut" and the speeding automobile. The aged are supposed to be reserved, quiet, and dignified; their symbols are the hoary brow and the rocking chair. All through life we are cautioned by others to abide by the expectations of society. The child is told by his parents to "be good" and then goes through life dragging admonitions along. Persons do respond to the social norms, and in such manner behavior is effected and the social amenities and patterns of conduct maintained.

D. Résumé

Clearly, evidence is inconclusive as to the nature of aging or of an acceptable (to most researchers) definition of either the state or the process. The problems have been succinctly stated by Friedenwald (1939):

Are these changes [of aging] brought about by the unavoidable processes inherent in the mere existence of . . . tissues over a prolonged period of time; are these changes . . . produced by the prolonged and cumulative effects of subclinical insults inflicted by the imperfect environment in which we live, or finally, are they the evidence of disease processes which happen to occur most frequently in the aged, but which are themselves not directly related to the passage of time? These questions are for the most part unanswerable on the basis of the present data and may, indeed, be essentially unanswerable [p. 501].

Friedenwald's concern also covers questions which might be similarly posed concerning aging as a function of social interaction. Aging research, to be properly reported, must begin with the researcher's statement of definition and frame of reference. If the research is to be capable of replication by others (if only through thought processes), his point of departure must be known. Until there is a generally accepted definition of the nature of aging, understanding the implication of a piece of research will hinge upon careful reporting.

IV. The Aging Individual: The Findings of Research

Much research has been carried out which helps us better to understand the aging individual. Unfortunately, to report on such research, we too must employ certain chronological definitions of "old age" and "aging" to permit us to weave together the fabric composed of many research threads. In general, the term "aged" is understood by most writers to mean "65 years or over." This definition can be assumed unless there is a clear statement to the contrary. For want of a better classification scheme, the findings summarized below will, in general, be reported within the framework of the major approaches to aging: biology, physiology, psychology, and sociology.

A. Biological and Physiological Changes with Age

Despite the suggestions by Stieglitz, Shock, and others to the effect that aging is a process of change implying growth in certain respects as well as decline in others, physiologists and biologists virtually universally look upon aging as a period of decline. Their research documents this position by studies of "senescence," "atrophy," "tissue susceptibility," and "involu-

tion." Such studies of biological change have been highly specialized, most likely in response not only to the researcher's own interests but also to the significant position advanced by Shock (1951a), who noted that "all our studies have shown that with increasing age individuals become less similar" (p. 354).

Within such a framework there can be no general answer to the question, "When is a man old?" The more significant question becomes, "Old with respect to what?" The "what" can be one of many things—organic, structural, or sensory changes. Clearly, changes do appear—what their significance is, we do not yet know. The researchers are varied, each contributing something to our knowledge about aging. Biological research too often fails to report an organizing theory. Without a theoretical framework, one wonders how the researches can be best utilized to cast light upon the aging process. Given a focus of research to answer the question, "Old with respect to what?" the further clarification becomes especially significant—"Within the framework of what theoretical system?" At present, the reported findings, some of which are cited below, are interesting and enlightening but of unknown long-range significance.

Kowalewski (1950) shows a diminution of the 17-ketosteroids in the urine, with increasing age for both males and females; Miller *et al.* (1952) find that the glomerular filtration rate and the tubular resorptive capacity for glucose show a linear decrease with age; Tirman and Hamilton (1952) find significant differences by age for changing dimensions of the thorax. Research on the skin shows a decrease in the amount of elastic tissues (Ma and Cowdry, 1950), while the average width of the collagen fibrils increases with age (Banfield, 1955). Pulse rate (Howell, 1948) and cardiac output (Brandfonbrenner *et al.*, 1955) both decrease with age, with a reduction in the latter estimated at about 1 per cent per year. Average systolic blood pressure increases significantly with age, while the average diastolic blood pressure shows little variation after the sixth decade; frequency of systolic hypertension increases sharply with age, while incidence of diastolic hypertension remains fairly constant after age 70 (Russek *et al.*, 1946). Vitamin serum level has been found to decrease with advancing age (Chow *et al.*, 1956). Each of the cited researches, which are characteristic of reported findings, takes note of physical changes related to increasing number of years lived. We do not know, however, if, when studying the human, such reports show measures of the aging process or only present evidence of two sets of data varying in the same direction, both related to a third factor as yet unidentified.

In addition to studies of specific biological functions, there has grown up a large body of literature on sensory changes with age. Variation by age and by sex in the performance of the senses is frequently described. Males experience greater hearing loss in the high tones than do females, and impairment in hearing at a conversational level proceeds more rapidly for men than women, although for both there is a progressive decrease in hearing ability with age (Beasley, 1938). Similar variations are to be found in the research recorded for each of the other senses.

Research on changes in vision has been reported extensively, and similar results have been obtained. There is increasingly poor dark adaptation with age and lowering of the light threshold (Birren, 1948). Although Tiffin (1942) reported the deterioration of color-discrimination efficiency with increasing age, other researchers have since raised questions concerning his findings. Boice *et al.* (1948), with carefully controlled experiments in 1948, reported no evidence of such deterioration. While there is no general agreement on the relationship between color-blindness and age, researchers do agree that, with increasing age, general vision acuity decreases; ability of the eye to respond to variations in light and to discriminate accurately in "flicker-fusion" tests also decreases (Feree *et al.*, 1935; Erlick and Landis, 1952; Coppinger, 1955; and Kornzweig, 1956). Changes in visual functions with age have been studied more extensively than have any of the other senses; the literature in this field is extensive and wide-ranging. A good review of the early pertinent literature has been made by Brozek (1951).

The standard work on the relationship between physical strength and age is that of Fisher and Birren (1947). By use of a hand dynamometer, they showed a maximum hand strength in the middle twenties, with a continuous decline thereafter. The writers are cautious in their interpretation of the results, pointing out that, while part of the change is obviously related to physiological conditions, much of it may also be attributed to changes in environment. In many occupations older persons may find themselves in positions which are relatively more sedentary, thus making for some loss of strength through disuse.

As the flicker-fusion test for eye responses has become classical, so has the finger-reaction-time test for the evaluation of motor skills. Early reports suggested the possibility that reaction time for older persons might, for a significant portion of the population, be faster than for younger persons owing to the importance of the experience factor (Miles, 1931). More recent research has shown that reaction time and reaction-time variation both increase regularly with age (Obrist, 1953).

Along with physiological changes which take place for older persons is a change which is often used as a visual index of aging—namely, the cosmetic changes. If "a man is as old as he looks," then indeed we have yet to do the definitive research on aging. In many surveys of older persons, responses to questions about aging are characterized by concern with changing physical appearance. Cosmetic changes are obviously functions of variations in physiological condition with advancing age and probably produce more extreme social adjustments than most other biological changes. Certainly, more money is spent in an effort to thwart or to delay such changes than is true for any other physical function.

All the above-noted time-related changes affect the ability of the individual to relate to other persons. As the bodily functions become altered, as a person begins to "look" older, there is an increasing likelihood of withdrawal from the larger society. To the extent that these changes are defined as measures of deterioration and decline, the probability of the individual literally retiring from the social groups of which he is a part will be enhanced. His psychological adjustment will be effected, and he will further support society's judgment of the relationship between increasing chronological age and degeneration.

B. Psychological Changes with Age

In general, research on age-related psychological changes has followed four paths: investigation of mental disorders, psychomotor changes, personality changes, and intellectual changes in the later years. The researches reported in the literature tend to fall into two general categories: the organic approach and the functional approach. Among the former are to be found the reports on brain-function and brain-damage tests, with the results of such tests being related to social behavior. Among the latter are to be found the behavioristic reports.

A key to much of the literature on the psychology of aging is the conception of senility, a diagnosis which is made for many older disoriented persons without a reasonable attempt to ascertain the real illness. It is because of a generally accepted notion that senility is a disease which accompanies aging that so many older persons envision this as "normal." The fear (and often an expectation) of becoming senile is frequently found among older people.

There are those, like the classical writers Henderson and Gillespie (1951), who take the position that senility is a period of life which "may be stated to occur from sixty-five years onwards" and is a period in which "the machine is becoming worn out both physically and mentally [and] the individual . . . is unable to keep pace with changing conditions and events." Rosonoff (1949) thinks of senility in behavioristic terms—to him it is a form of "progressive mental and physical deterioration" the cause of which is unknown and which terminates fatally "within a few years from the time of onset." Senile dementia, Rosonoff notes, has sex as one important etiological factor, the rate for females estimated as almost twice that for males; it is clearly a psychosis, is progressive, and its prognosis is "wholly unfavorable." A more recent work clearly identifies senility as a psychosis for which there is not yet any adequate curative treatment. The authors state:

The insidious personality deterioration found in the senile psychotic results from diffuse, widespread organic damage occurring within the brain structure. . . . Medical science as yet is unable to offer any clear and fundamental understanding of the senile process in this type of psychosis. It is generally part of an over-all pattern in the direction of atrophic changes of senility occuring throughout the body. . . . Why such changes appear at an earlier age in certain individuals while other people show only a minimum of these changes even at very advanced ages is not understood [English and Finch, 1954, p. 495].

Senile patients experience a deterioration of all personality functions over a period of years. Usually such persons are placed in mental hospitals where they receive no active therapy, becoming merely vegetative, waiting for death to take them. Contrary to the statement above by Rosonoff to the effect that death usually comes in "a few years" from the time of onset of the disease, such persons may languish in a mental hospital for from 15 to 25 years. They are a major burden on the facilities and resources of the society. More effort is now being expended upon this widespread problem in an effort to lessen the burden upon the hospitals and to make more useful these now almost totally wasted lives.

Tests of older persons have shown that they undergo significant changes in the psychomotor functions such as reaction time, vision, hearing, and strength. Persons over age 65 react slower (when responding to a buzzer by lifting their finger from a telegraph key) than do persons under that age and show greater variability in reaction time (Obrist, 1953). Visual acuity undergoes a change with age, decreasing gradually during the years to age 45 and more rapidly beyond (Tiffin, 1949; Kleemeier, 1952). There is a decline in the sensitivity of the dark-adapted eye with age; older persons are less well able to see under conditions of low illumination than are younger persons (Birren *et al.*, 1948). McFarland (1953) finds similar changes in visual acuity by age in his studies of airline pilots, but he believes that these changes "are not, on the whole, very marked."

While the ability to hear low tones (128 cycles per second) does not decline very much, the ability to hear high tones (4096 cps) does decrease with age (Bunch, 1929; Kleemeier, 1955). Changes in hearing ability vary considerably among individuals, but, as is the case with many of these measures, the absence of systematically collected longitudinal data makes interpretation difficult. We need to know not only how older people and younger people differ today but also how a cohort of persons would change if followed for a period of years. In measures of strength, Fisher and Birren (1947) find that data collected over a period of 120 years show that "the development of muscular strength [throughout one's life] follows a systematic trend with an increase in strength up to the late twenties and a decline, usually at an increasing rate, from that time on."

When all the psychomotor functions combine in carrying out complex activities, changes in such performance also appear by age. An interesting aspect of such change is that, while total performance of the complex activity may not vary by age, the method by which this is accomplished may itself show an age variation. Thus an older individual may compensate for specific decreased functions by increased effort (see, e.g., Welford, 1950, pp. 120–22). It is clear that increased training and continued exercise of a skill will delay its decline, but Kleemeier (1954) points out that, even here, older persons will slow down somewhat on repetitive tasks. This is so because the aging individual must continually "marshal all possible sensory data in task performance" and may thereby perform similar tasks as younger persons but at the cost of increased effort. What the increased effort is, and what the "cost" might be, we are as yet unable to say with assurance. Answers to this question wait upon further research.

In recent years a substantial literature has accumulated on the personality of older persons and on personality changes with age. There are, however, important problems of interpretation of such reports. The tests upon which the reports are based are most often measures of specific segmentalized personality traits or characteristics—they are not indicators of personality organization or adaptiveness. Earlier writings about the personality of older persons spoke of their "conservativism," "resistance to change," or "rigidity." We still find reference to their being "set in their ways." Heglin (1956) examined these characteristics experimentally by use of tests designed to evaluate a "problem-solving set." He found older persons to be more set in their problem-solving than either middle-aged or younger persons. After training, the middle-aged group showed least set, while the older group improved least. Although there was considerable variation among the groups, the differences between them was significant.

Lorge (1936) found a group of older persons to be "more stable" in their habits, ideas, and other tendencies than a matched group of younger persons. Three years later, he found the social attitudes of older persons still more stable than younger persons (Lorge, 1939). Lorge concluded that the greater reliability and consistency of social attitudes of older adults suggest the development of a generalized frame of reference which becomes stereotyped for the older person. This is then used by older individuals to direct their reactions in isolated new experiences. Some social psychologists (especially those who follow George Herbert Mead) suggest that this position needs review and re-examination. They hold that the individual reacts to stimuli not only on the basis of a predetermined frame of reference but also in terms of the meaning of the stimulus to the individual within the framework of the situation confronting him. Recently, Lorge and Helfant (1953) pointed out that there was no statistically significant relationship between age and attitude toward three sociopolitical attitudes (toward Russia, international relations, and war) for a group of 328 adults ranging in age from 36 to 64. "A person's age," they concluded, "in and of itself, is of no value in estimating sociopolitical verbal attitudes."

Following upon a study comparing a group of younger prisoners with 172 incoming prisoners age 60 or over at a federal penitentiary, Corsini and Fassett (1952) conclude that the results unequivocally demonstrate (*a*) that intelligence does not decrease from early to late maturity; (*b*) that the results of speed, vision, and hearing tests remain relatively constant; (*c*) that verbal tests show an increasing score with age; and (*d*) that tests involving speed, vision, or close attention show decreasing scores with age. The sample was that of a very special population, thus limiting the general applicability of the findings. In the Kansas City study of aging, 475 persons age 60 or over were scored on the Wechsler Adult Intelligence Scale. For these persons until age 70, the decline in verbal abilities was relatively small and was only somewhat larger for performance. Beyond age 70 the decline in both verbal and performance scores is more rapid (Doppelt and Wallace, 1955). Such results have been reported for the last 30 years by many researchers. Unfortunately, the samples tested have been highly selected and relatively small. Further, these are measures of test intelligence, the results and interpretation of which will be dependent upon the test employed and the researcher's conception of intelligence. Much has been written concerning the nature of such tests. Questions have been raised not so much about their reliability (the measurement of logical consistency) as about their validity (whether they measure what it is assumed they measure). The validation of such tests is, at best, difficult, and all too many researchers have retreated by saying that the test merely "measures what it measures"— a position which, while accurate, is not the least helpful in the development of a theory of aging and of its relationship to personality and intellectual changes.

C. The Sociology of Aging

As in other age periods throughout life, older people continue some old-established relationships, discontinue some, and form new ones. As with other persons, the age of the individual will, to some extent at least, affect these relationships. The view of the individual held by the society of which he is a part will be conditioned by his age and by the society's conception of persons of similar age. Age grading is one way our society makes judgments about individuals as members of groups about which the society holds opinions. Two articles which appeared in the same issue of the *American Sociological Review* detailed the kinds of judgments passed by many societies about age and sex categories of persons. Linton (1942) stated that age grading seems to be common to most societies, although there is great variation as to ages, number of grades, rewards, significance, and other factors. Parsons (1942) then added that, in the United States, age grading does not involve formal categorization but rather is interwoven with other structural elements. An example of such interwoven relationship is that of abrupt retirement as part of the occupational structure, leaving the older individual cut off from participation in most important interest areas. While the focus of attention is on the act of retirement, such act often takes place solely because of the chronological age of the individual involved. As our society responds to persons in terms graded by age, other social manifestations of grading appear. The older person, as part of the larger society, shares in the social judgment, thereby affecting his own self-conception.

As one ages in our society, he does so by passing through a series of life-stages which, while they vary from person to person and by ethnicity, class, and region, have a significant effect upon the social and self-conception of the individual. These sequential stages are organized about and recognized by traumatic events in the history of an individual, profoundly altering the direction and adjustment of his life.

Life-stages have been variously defined and interpreted by many writers. Perhaps illustrative of the significant and separable positions are those of Sanford, Linden, and Tibbitts. In 1902 Sanford set out to investigate the "course of mental development" from the first beginnings of the mind at or before birth to the final failure of the mind at the end of life. To examine the "life course," he set up a series of periods based upon chronological age. These seven periods were (1) babyhood (birth to 2 or 3 years); (2) childhood (from 2 or 3 to 12 or 13); (3) youth (from 12 or 13 to 25); (4) young manhood (from 25 to 40); (5) middle age (from 40 to 55 or 60); (6) elderly (from 55 or 60 to 70); and (7) aged (70 and beyond). The first four periods were listed as those of growth. Beginning with the fifth period, Sanford saw regular decline, and, by the seventh period,

he spoke only of incapacities and degeneration.

Linden and Courtney (1955) use the concept of psychic maturity to identify the significant "stages of maturation" which are measured as "the resultant of two vectors: selfish (instinct-gratifying) drives and culture-directed (protective and altruistic) drives." The stages they identify are infancy, adolescence, early adult, middle adult, and late adult. Each of these stages is to be understood as a theoretical identification in terms of "increments of psychosocial orientation."

Following upon the observation that there are two principal functions from which men derive status, namely, perpetuation of the species and maintenance of the economy, Tibbitts (1954) took note of the fact that important modifications of behavior appear upon completion of these functions. The first function is completed between age 45 and 55, when children leave home to establish their own families; the second function comes to a close in the sixties, when compulsory retirement policies become operative or because of illness.

Tuckman and Lorge (1954) interviewed 1032 persons of all ages (79 were under 20 and 19 were over 80 years of age), asking them to select one of three choices based upon whether they considered themselves "young, middle aged, or old." Under age 30, the respondents all classified themselves as young. From age 30 to 60, increasingly larger numbers classified themselves as middle-aged. Starting at age 60, a small proportion described themselves as old, but even at ages past 80, when 53 per cent of the group called themselves old, 11 per cent continued describing themselves as young. Self-classification, they concluded, is a function of the self-concept, an important reference factor in the process being the "acceptance of, and stereotyping of, the cultural attitudes toward aging."

Many authors in the field of human development speak of the whole of life as a continuum, devoid of "stages," yet each deals with the "human development tasks" in terms of rather specific life-stages, such as "infancy," "youth," "adulthood," "middle age," and "old age" (see, e.g., Havighurst and Albrecht, 1953; Pressey and Kuhlen, 1957). Such classification schemes have developed out of a need for systematizing the description of periods of life with common characteristics. While there is considerable variation among individuals in the same age period, there is a tendency toward homogeneity. If these periods can be delineated in behavioristic terms, the analysis of their significance will do much to help us better understand the interrelatedness of age grades, self-conception, role, and conduct.

Much has been written concerning the older person in the family, and such writings have often represented the sentimental approach to the "problem" of older people in the family. Other publications, based upon findings of research on the family, tell us more about the nature of the older person. Gardner (1948), in reporting on a study of 193 "aged" persons living with relatives, found that the dominance relationships between children and their aged parents produced frustrating conflicts mainly centered around "the older person's interference in family affairs and personal habits." This oversimplified view of the family setting reveals little either of the nature of aging or of the aging individual in an interdependent relationship with his kin. That interpersonal relationships are in part affected by ethnicity and religion was shown by Dinkel (1944) in his study of 1324 young persons who responded to questions on supporting aged parents and on "giving aged parents a home." Catholics more than Protestants, and rural persons more than urban, believe in responsibility of children for their aged parents.

In a study by Fried and Stern (1948), some individuals reported that enforced retirement because of illness in the later years actually improved the relationship between mates by providing gratification to the protecting partner and satisfactorily providing the afflicted with a reason for retirement. Further, some individuals reported an improved relationship with their spouse for several reasons: better sexual adjustment as a result of the decreased demands in the later years, death of a parent-in-law who was excessively dominant, or the maturation of children, thus permitting the mother to return to work. Less satisfactory relationships in some cases were reported due to few common interests at the beginning of marriage leading to further growing apart, sexual discord, and growing incompatibility with advanced years.

A two-article sequence by Ruth Albrecht (1953, 1954) reported on an investigation of the 700 persons aged 65 or over in a small (7000) midwestern town. These persons were studied in terms of (a) their relationships with their children and (b) their relationships with their parents. Some 550 of these persons had living children toward whom most of the parents related with "independence and responsibility" (85 per cent), while the rest related with dependence, distance, or neglect (15 per cent). Of this same group of older persons, 18 per cent had no close contact with their parents, 71 per cent had no parents requiring care or else had parents taken care of by others, and 11 per cent discharged "their responsibilities" toward their parents. The views of either children or parents are further complicated when all three generations reside together. While such households are often not long lived because of the age of the oldest generation, in the period of time they are in existence they can create many hazardous situations. The elders find it difficult to relinquish power to the children, while the middle generation finds itself most often in conflict because of the varying pressures. As a result, only half of the more than 1000 families interviewed in one study thought it was good for the aged parents to be brought into an existing two-generation household.

In the 249 three-generation families interviewed, "most" such households were created when the mother of the wife moved in (Koller, 1954). The re-entry of the aged parent into the family, but with reversed responsibilities, may create a situation in which the younger generation interprets this as the devaluation of the elders. As this symbol of authority is devalued, the traditions are flouted. As the child watches such treatment of the grandparent by the parent, he will absorb this pattern toward the elder and may repeat it with his own parents (Linden, 1956).

In many respects the aged show characteristics of a minority group. They are subject to categorical discrimination, they have relatively high visibility, and, in many parts of our society, they constitute a functioning subgroup. Stereotypes are held about the group, and individuals are judged thereby. Prejudice is not uncommon, especially in industry, where persons over age 40 are discriminated against in employment practices. Thus the ingredients necessary to the development of minority-group status are present for the aged. The characteristics commonly attributed to minority groups as a result of such categorization may be expected to develop among older persons. The wide literature on minority-group behavior clearly would be applicable to the aged also. A survey of 94 employment agencies in New York found that the agencies believed the older job-seeker was "his own worst enemy," destroying his job opportunities by such alleged personality deviations as "talking too much, being too hard to please, being too set in his ways, and lacking poise and grooming" (Barron, 1953).

The conception of the aged as a minority group is reinforced by the practice of segregation of older persons. Homes for the aged, public housing projects, medical institutions, recreation centers, and communities which are devoted to the exclusive use of the retired have been increasing in number and size in recent years. Retire-

ment "villages" have been sponsored by philanthropic organizations, unions, church groups, and others. Even established communities which are now known as "retirement centers" have become inundated by older migrants seeking identification and spatial contiguity with "the clan." St. Petersburg, Florida, has developed such a reputation. One-third of the increase in population of that city in recent years is attributable to persons age 65 or over, so that now over 22 per cent of its population is in that age group (Harlan, 1954). A continuation of social judgments which influence, develop, and implement such conceptions of the aged in communities will undoubtedly further establish the aged as more clearly a minority group in the sociological as well as the political sense.

One result of the development of minority-group status for the aged is likely to have an important political impact upon our society. Minority status has always led groups to greater solidarity based upon mutual interdependence for emotional and social support. To the extent that any group is set apart from the larger society for special consideration and treatment, a collective group concern has developed. Minorities have often expressed common concerns in unified action. The aged, too, may function as a minority group by expressing mutual needs through concerted political action. As the social norms connected with aging are articulated by the larger society, they are implemented by older persons. As there is identified a special aged subgroup of our society, minority status becomes more likely and more meaningful.

D. Résumé

The above consists of an overview of some of the research which has recently taken place in the several disciplines concerned with aging. Each of the disciplines has begun with a theoretical frame of reference (not always explicit) which has somewhat narrowly channeled research on older persons. To be sure, this is the way in which man has always been studied—viewed by the several disciplines separately, each of them telling us something more about the nature of man and of his social and cultural product and milieu. In this sense, then, the aged have been seen by economists as a needy group competing for scarce goods. Political scientists view them as a potential political instrument which, if coalesced (as was almost done under the Townsend Plan, for instance), could conceivably constitute a potent political force. Anthropologists have pictured them as the carriers of the culture and rituals of their societies. Biologists have seen them as complex organisms in a non-reversible process of deterioration. Sociologists have conceived of them in terms of their social adjustment, adaptation, and interaction leading to special social conceptions and minority-group status. Psychologists have examined the aged as complex organisms reacting to individual and social stimuli in such a way as to produce behavior patterns of a special kind.

Each of these disciplines has contributed much to our understanding of the aged as a group. Aging as a process, however, is characterized by sequential interrelated and interdependent human changes. A matter of pressing concern and present need is the development of a set of consistent theoretical formulations to permit interdisciplinary research to make a greater contribution to our better understanding of the aged. If aging is economic, biologic, psychologic, and social—all at once—as many profess and believe, then interdisciplinary research should be encouraged to demonstrate such fact. This would provide us with a theoretical structure from which clearly testable hypotheses could be formulated and examined and analysis and interpretation enhanced. Lip service is often given to the notion of interdisciplinary research, but little implementation has taken place.

V. Crisis Periods in the Later Years

Throughout life, one assumes roles which functionally are characteristic of the position of the individual in his society at any given life-stage. Such roles are the substance of the life-stages and reflect the social judgments of the larger society within which the individual lives and acts. Ofttimes, individual judgments concerning social roles are rather strong, as those by Vollmer (1937) that "grandmothers exert an extraordinarily pernicious influence on their grandchildren" and by Strauss (1943) that "the presence of grandparents in the home has caused delinquency in a considerable number of instances" show.

In general, the changing role activities of older persons involve decreased physical activity and social responsibility. As the individual ages, he assumes new roles in areas appropriate to the later years, such as the role of grandparent. There is increased leisure time and church activity and less occupational activity. That there is a relationship between role activity and personality (and adjustment) is shown by Albrecht (1951). In a study of a group of persons aged 65 or over, she found that the 11 per cent who rated low on a role-activity scale were also rated low in adjustment and that the 35 per cent who rated high were alert and had "youthful" personality patterns. In reviewing role changes with age, Havighurst (1954) lists homemaking and church activities as the roles which become intensified. Those which are reduced are the roles of parent, spouse, employee, sexual partner, club member, and leader. Certain roles *may* become intensified, such as citizen, friend, kin, or neighbor. The most important new role is that of grandparent, though others may be developed, depending upon one's "role flexibility," which is conditioned by the variety of roles during early life and by retirement preparation. To the extent that the individual is able to maintain "role flexibility," social adjustment and personal satisfaction and happiness are enhanced. The flexible person finds an easier adjustment to the inevitable changes which occur with age.

As one advances in age, crisis periods appear. Children grow up, get married, and leave home to become independent. Grandchildren are born; women experience the menopause. Lifelong friends begin to pass away, retirement comes for men, the spouse may die, income is suddenly decreased, or chronic illnesses may threaten. While men retire occupationally, their wives often do not, and they find themselves in a new social status removed from occupational ties and with reduced incomes (Cavan, 1952). Many adjustments need to be made following the death of a spouse. With some 55 per cent of the women over 65 widowed, the problem is a common one for the older female—which may account for the discussion of the grandmother as a disturbing influence, as noted above. Many older persons, left alone and with a home, move in with their children—a situation productive of much tension (see, e.g., Cavan, 1953).

Gravatt (1952) has taken note of the reported changes in behavior accompanying passage through crisis periods, but he suggests that there is a continuity to personality adjustment within the family despite the major changes of middle and later life which demand changes in behavior patterns. Such continuity would lead one to the general conclusion that the nature of behavior in the later years will clearly be a function of behavior in the earlier years. The proposition that the older individual who is well adjusted is the same person who was well adjusted throughout his life is not uncommon. Adjustment after retirement, however, may depend upon earlier maladjustment. On the other hand, the poorly adjusted person who hated his job may find real satisfaction in not having to work after retirement, thus making an excellent adjustment in his later years.

VI. SUMMARY

Aging is a process of change. When seen biologically, this change is one which for the most part takes place continuously throughout life in a fairly regular manner. Socially and psychologically, however, the aging individual experiences many periods of significant change, adaptation, and adjustment in the later years. Such changes and adjustments are a function of the social conceptions of aging held by both the society and the individual himself. There is clearly an interdependence between such judgments. One's self-concept is conditioned by what his group thinks of him—among the aged, no less so. To be sure, the self-concept is also conditioned by the individual's physical condition. The larger society, too, builds its picture of the aged upon physiological data and upon psychological considerations. Aging, then, is an interdependent process, the understanding of which hinges upon an understanding of the contributions made by each of the disciplines interested in aging and the aged. One needs to understand the whole of man's life—the career and the potential. When aging becomes the focus of attention, we must recognize it for what it is—the selection for research of one of the stages in life from among many. Linden and Courtney (1955) have said it succinctly:

An individual at any time in his life is the aggregate and interaction of many functions, some in development, some at peak, and some in decline. Any approach toward comprehending the nature of man that uses for measurement a single function, or even a group of functions, such as sensory acuity, motor response, intelligence, vocabulary, etc., succeeds in describing merely a dissected part of a totality [p. 358].

The synthesis of researches must be made to get the broad view. Sociological research helps us better to know the nature of the older person and the process by which that nature was generated, but we must go beyond this to know the man as well as the process. The physiological human machine is conceived, born, and reared; it ages and deteriorates—but within a context which permits differential change in its many parts. Thus, while one part of the mechanism is declining in function, another improves. This variation in the parts of the mechanism is demonstrated by the research recited above. The body, the psyche, and the social and economic being are truly one—one man—and, as such, age together but at varying rates. As one part is born, so are the others —as one dies, so do the rest. Thus we must study man as a whole being in the process of maturation—each man differentiated from his society yet a product and part of it.

The aging individual is, in effect, a responsive and responding nexus for social and sociological judgments. He plays a series of roles, in part determined by age, set out for him by society which has formulated certain expectations of behavior on the part of the aged. These roles are played with varying degrees of success and cognition. Each generation learns from its elders and thus continues the patterns with nuances which identify it as its own. At present, patterns of social isolation and rejection have developed in our society, reinforced by the reaction of the aged to such conceptions. Increased disorders and institutionalization can likely be expected as a result.

With increasing public education concerning the nature of the aged and of aging as a process of change rather than merely a state of being, it is likely that greater acceptance of older people will become possible, with concomitant reversal of social judgments and, hence, self-conceptions. This sort of change may eventually lead to the integration of aging individuals into the social fabric, where they can make greater contributions to society, lessen the social burden, and reduce society's frustrations and guilt. Not only will the larger society be thus benefited but the aging individual will himself be better able to understand the process and product of personal change in a social context.

REFERENCES

ALBRECHT, RUTH. 1951. Social roles in the prevention of senility. J. Gerontol., **6**, 380–86.

———. 1953. Relationships of older people with their own parents. Marriage & Family Living, **15**, 296–98.

———. 1954. Relationships of older parents with their children. *Ibid.*, **16**, 32–35.

BANFIELD, W. G. 1955. Width and length of collagen fibrils during the development of human skin. J. Gerontol., **10**, 13–17.

BARRON, M. L. 1953. Minority group characteristics of the aged in American society. J. Gerontol., **8**, 477–81.

BEASLEY, W. C. 1938. Generalized age and sex trends in hearing loss. (National Health Survey, Preliminary Report, Hearing Study Series, Bull. 7.) Washington, D.C.: The Survey.

BEESON, M. F. 1920. Intelligence at senescence. J. Appl. Psychol., **4**, 219–34.

BIRREN, J. E. 1948. The relation of dark adaptation with age. Am. Psychol., **3**, 308.

BIRREN, J. E., BICK, M. W., and FOX, C. 1948. Age changes in the light threshold of the dark adapted eye. J. Gerontol., **3**, 267–71.

BIRREN, J. E., BICK, M. W., and YIENGST, M. 1950. The relation of structural changes of the eye and vitamin A to elevation of the light threshold in later life. J. Exper. Psychol., **40**, 260–66.

BOGOMOLETS, A. A. 1946. The prolongation of life. New York: Duell, Sloan & Pearce.

BOICE, M. J., LINKER, M. A., and PATERSON, D. G. 1948. Color vision and age. Am. J. Psychol., **61**, 520–26.

BRANDFONBRENNER, M., LANDOWNE, M., and SHOCK, N. W. 1955. Changes in cardiac output with age. Circulation, **12**, 557–66.

BREEN, L. Z. 1957. Some problems of research in the field of aging. Sociology & Social Research, **41**, 412–16.

BROZEK, J. 1951. Changes in sensory, motor, and intellectual functions with age. Geriatrics, **6**, 221–26.

BUNCH, C. C. 1929. Age variation in auditory acuity. Arch. Otolaryng., **9**, 625–36.

CAMERON, N. 1945. Neuroses of later maturity. *In* O. J. KAPLAN (ed.), Mental disorders in later life, pp. 201–43. Stanford, Calif.: Stanford University Press.

CAVAN, RUTH S. 1952. Adjustment problems of the older woman. Marriage & Family Living, **14**, 16–18.

———. 1953. The American family. New York: Thomas Y. Crowell Co.

CAVAN, RUTH S., BURGESS, E. W. HAVIGHURST, R. J., and GOLDHAMER, H. 1949. Personal adjustment in old age. Chicago: Science Research Associates.

CHOW, B. F., WOOD, RUTH, HORONICK, A., and OKUDA, K. 1956. Agewise variation of vitamin B_{12} serum levels. J. Gerontol., **11**, 142–46.

COHN, A. E. 1940. Old age and aging from the point of view of the cardiovascular system. Am. J. Orthopsychiat., **10**, 43–55.

COPPINGER, N. W. 1955. The relationship between critical flicker frequency and chronologic age for varying levels of stimulus brightness. J. Gerontol., **10**, 48–52.

CORSINI, R. J., and FASSETT, K. K. 1952. Wechsler-Bellvue age patterns for a prison population. J. Gerontol., **7**, 477. (Abstract.)

DINKEL, R. M. 1944. Attitudes of children toward supporting aged parents. Am. Sociological Rev., **9**, 370–79.

DONAHUE, WILMA. 1952. Education's role in maintaining the individual's status. Ann. Am. Acad. Political & Social Sc., **279**, 115–25.

DOPPELT, J. E., and WALLACE, W. L. 1955. The performance of older people on the Wechsler Adult Intelligence Scale. Am. Psychol., **10**, 338.

ENGLISH, O. S., and FINCH, S. M. 1954. Introduction to psychiatry. New York: W. W. Norton & Co.

ERLICK, D., and LANDIS, C. 1952. The effect of intensity, light-dark ratio, and age on the flicker-fusion threshold. Am. J. Psychol., **65**, 375–88.

FEREE, C. E., RAND, G., and LEWIS, E. F. 1935. Age as an important factor in the amount of light needed by the eye. Arch. Ophth., **13**, 212–26.

FISHER, M. B., and BIRREN, J. E. 1947. Age and strength. J. Appl. Psychol., **31**, 490–97.

FRIED, EDRITA G., and STERN, K. 1948. The situation of the aged within the family. Am. J. Orthopsychiat., **18**, 31–54.

FRIEDENWALD, J. S. 1939. The eye. *In* E. V. COWDRY (ed.), Problems of aging, pp. 501–22. Baltimore: Williams & Wilkins Co.

GARDNER, L. P. 1948. Attitudes and activities of the middle aged and aged. Am. Psychol., **3**, 306–8.

GRAVATT, A. E. 1952. Family relations in middle and old age: a review. J. Gerontol., **7**, 197–200.

HARLAN, W. H. 1954. Community adaptation to the presence of aged persons: St. Petersburg, Florida. Am. J. Sociology, **59**, 332–39.

HAVIGHURST, R. J. 1954. Flexibility and the social roles of the retired. Am. J. Sociology, **59**, 309–11.

HAVIGHURST, R. J., and ALBRECHT, RUTH. 1953. Older people. New York: Longmans, Green & Co.

HEGLIN, H. J. 1956. Problem solving set in different age groups. J. Gerontol., **11**, 310–16.

HENDERSON, D., and GILLESPIE, R. D. 1951. A text-book of psychiatry. 7th ed. London: Oxford University Press.

HOWELL, T. H. 1948. The pulse rate in old age. J. Gerontol., **3**, 272–75.

———. 1949. Old age. Geriatrics, **4**, 281–92.

———. 1953. Our advancing years. London: Phoenix House.

HUTCHINSON, B. 1955. Old people in a modern Australian community. Melbourne: Melbourne University Press.

KLEEMEIER, R. W. 1952. The relationship between Orth-Rater tests of acuity and color vision in a senescent group. J. Appl. Psychol., **36**, 114–16.

———. 1954. Age changes in psychomotor capacity and productivity. J. Business of the University of Chicago, **27**, 146–55.

———. 1955. Second annual report of the Moosehaven Research Laboratory, Orange Park, Florida. Orange Park, Fla.: Moosehaven Research Laboratory.

KOLLER, M. R. 1954. Studies of three generation households. Marriage & Family Living, **16**, 205–6.

KORENCHEVSKY, V. 1950. The problem of aging and the ways and means for achieving the rapid progress of gerontological research. *In* Social and biological challenge of our aging population, pp. 7–24. New York: Columbia University Press.

KORNZWEIG, A. L. 1956. Physiological effects of age on the visual process. Psychol. Abstracts, Vol. **30**, No. 331.

KOWALEWSKI, K. 1950. Urinary neutral-17 ketosteroids in the aged. J. Gerontol., **5**, 221–26.

LANSING, A. I. (ed.). 1952. Cowdry's problems of aging. 3d ed. Baltimore: Williams & Wilkins Co.

LINDEN, M. E. 1956. The older person in the family. Social Casework, **37**, 75–81.

LINDEN, M. E., and COURTNEY, D. C. 1955. The human life cycle and its interruptions—a psychologic hypothesis. *In* A. M. ROSE (ed.), Mental health and mental disorder, pp. 358–76. New York: W. W. Norton & Co.

LINTON, R. 1942. Age and sex categories. Am. Sociological Rev., **7**, 589–603.

LORGE, I. 1935. Confusion as an aspect of the learning of older adults. Psychol. Bull., **32**, 559.

———. 1936. Attitude stability in older adults. *Ibid.*, **33**, 759.

———. 1939. The Thurstone attitude scales. II. J. Social Psychol., **10**, 199–208.

LORGE, I., and HELFANT, K. 1953. The independence of chronological age and sociopolitical attitudes. J. Abnorm. & Social Psychol., **48**, 598.

MA, C. K., and COWDRY, E. V. 1950. Aging of elastic tissue in human skin. J. Gerontol., **5**, 203–10.

McFARLAND, R. A. 1953. Human factors in air transportation. New York: McGraw-Hill Book Co.

MILES, W. R. 1931. Correlation of reaction and coordination speed with age in adults. Am. J. Psychol., **43**, 377–91.

MILLER, J. H., McDONALD, R. K., and SHOCK, N. W. 1952. Age changes in the maximal rate of renal tubular reabsorption of glucose. J. Gerontol., **7**, 196–200.

OBRIST, W. D. 1953. Simple auditory reaction time in aged adults. J. Psychol., **35**, 259–66.

PARSONS, T. 1942. Age and sex in the social structure of the United States. Am. Sociological Rev., **7**, 604–16.

PRESSEY, S. L., and KUHLEN, R. G. 1957. Psychological development through the life span. New York: Harper & Bros.

RANDALL, OLLIE A. 1950. Living arrangements to meet the needs of older people. *In* WILMA DONAHUE and C. TIBBITTS (eds.), Planning the older years, pp. 31–59. Ann Arbor: University of Michigan Press.

RASMUS, C. 1926. Outwitting middle age. New York: Century Co.

ROSONOFF, A. J. 1949. Manual of psychiatry and mental hygiene. 7th ed. New York: John Wiley & Sons.

RUSSEK, H. I., RATH, M. M., MILLER, I., and ZOHMAN, B. L. 1946. The influence of age on blood pressure. Am. Heart J., **32**, 468–79.

SANFORD, E. C. 1902. Mental growth and decay. Am. J. Psychol., **13**, 426–49.

SHOCK, N. W. 1945. Physiological aspects of mental disorders in later life. *In* O. J. KAPLAN (ed.), Mental disorders in later life, pp. 47–97. Stanford, Calif.: Stanford University Press.

———. 1951*a*. The age problem in research workers: physiological viewpoint. Scientific Monthly, **72**, 345–52.

———. 1951*b*. Trends in gerontology. 2d ed. Stanford, Calif.: Stanford University Press.

STIEGLITZ, E. J. 1954. Foundations of geriatric medicine. *In* E. J. STIEGLITZ (ed.), Geriatric medicine, pp. 3–26. Philadelphia: J. B. Lippincott Co.

STRAUSS, C. A. 1943. Grandma made Johnny delinquent. J. Orthopsychiat., **13**, 343–46.

TIBBITTS, C. 1954. A sociological view of aging. Proc. Am. Philosophical Soc., **98**, 144–48.

TIBBITTS, C., and SHELDON, H. D. 1952. A philosophy of aging. Ann. Am. Acad. Political & Social Sc., **279**, 1–10.

TIFFIN, J. 1942. Industrial psychology. New York: Prentice-Hall, Inc.

———. 1949. Industrial psychology. 3d ed. New York: Prentice-Hall, Inc.

TIRMAN, W. S., and HAMILTON, J. B. 1952. Aging in apparently normal men. J. Gerontol., **7**, 384–97.

TUCKMAN, J., and LORGE, I. 1954. Classification of the self as young, middle aged, or old. Geriatrics, **9**, 534–36.

VOLLMER, H. 1937. The grandmother: a problem in child rearing. J. Orthopsychiat., **7**, 378–82.

WELFORD, A. 1950. Skill and age. London: Oxford University Press.

PART TWO

*The Impact of Aging on Individual Activities
and Social Roles*

VII

The Health Status of Aging People

EUGENE A. CONFREY AND MARCUS S. GOLDSTEIN

Health is a central factor in every aspect of the older person's life. It cuts across every social, occupational, and economic line. It affects every proposal for improving the lot of older people in family life, employment, recreation, and participation in community affairs [Burney, 1956, p. 1168].

This chapter describes the health status of people in middle and later years of life in the United States. The chapter is divided into five sections: (I) "The Meaning of Health"; (II) "The Measurement of Health"; (III) "Health Status"; (IV) "Health Promotion"; and (V) "Discussion." In the first of these, health is considered as a concept, especially as it pertains to the middle and later years of life. The second section, on measurement, is concerned with the reasons for assessing health, the various criteria of health and illness, the sources of statistical information, and the definition of some basic terms and indexes. Most of the health data presented will be found in Section III, which consists of a review, first, in terms of general health status; second, in terms of specific types of illness and causes of death; and, third, in terms of the socioeconomic factors that are interrelated with health and sickness in the older ages. Some of the implications of the data as they relate to the promotion of health among older adults are presented in Section IV, which is then followed by an over-all discussion in Section V.

I. THE MEANING OF HEALTH

The complexity of the "health" of a person or of a population is suggested by the constitution of the World Health Organization (1946), in which the following definition is proposed: "Health is a state of complete physical, mental and social well-being and not merely the absence of disease or infirmity" (p. 1268).

Several parts of the definition have a bearing on efforts to measure the health status of older persons. First, since "health" is not a simple property but rather a composite state, it is clear that our present quantitative descriptions of the health of *groups* of people (i.e., statistical data on population characteristics) represent only some aspects of health as reflected in certain arbitrarily chosen indexes. Further, our information about the health of populations—such as the millions of persons in the United States age 45 and over—is mainly an inference derived from observations about sickness, although health can be considered more than "the absence of disease or infirmity." Moreover, the word "complete" in the WHO definition suggests that perfect health is an ideal postulate. The concept of health encompasses a range of meaning from death to "complete" or optimum health. Hence, instead of thinking of health and sickness in absolute terms, as an "either-or" relationship, it may be more useful to interpret health in terms of a graduated scale.

When assessing health status in later years, one is evaluating not only a situation as of age 60 or age 70 but the product of heredity and early environment as well. All the elements of health—such as nutrition, exercise, sanitation, dental care, mental stimulation—have come into play before the appearance of health changes in old age. It is equally true, of course, that new elements enter the health situation in later life, few without recognizable effect on a person's total physical and mental health. Some of these are aspects of biological aging itself, such as decreased speed, strength, and dexterity. Others are of a social nature, such as the often abrupt role change from employment to retirement, marital state to widowhood, and position as head of a family to that of a member of a family.

Nevertheless, in the realm of health and sickness, the gerontological problem is one that ought to be viewed in the perspective of several ages, not merely "65 years and over." This is demonstrated by the significance of medical care and health practices during childhood, young adulthood, and middle age. It is further illustrated in terms of a community's resources for health, its physicians, dentists, nurses, hospitals, clinics, rehabilitation centers—virtually all of which serve both young and old.

II. THE MEASUREMENT OF HEALTH

The enjoyment of the highest attainable standard of health is one of the fundamental rights of every human being without distinction of race, religion, political belief, economic or social condition [World Health Organization, 1946, p. 1268].

When a society recognizes health as a value, or as a means to other values, it must then address itself to the task of assessing health, that is, of determining to what degree its people experience good health. That the health of a nation will influence its economic, social, and military security has long been recognized. In re-

cent years a less familiar corollary has come to assume more importance, namely, that the health of a population is no better than the aggregate health of segments of that population. The import of this becomes clear when we consider how our population is aging, that is, the proportionate increase in the number of older people, and the impact that widespread disease or disability among older adults will have on the nation's vitality.

The physician evaluates health in order to maintain or improve the health and well-being of his patient. Similarly, those who assess the health of the population, or of groups in the population, do so in order to identify and understand health problems, such as sickness and its impact on society, in terms of which prevention, medical care, and rehabilitation programs can be planned. With respect to older adults, measurement of health status can serve various purposes, for example, to clarify the need for additional professional services such as rehabilitation, for additional facilities such as outpatient clinics and nursing homes, for medical and health personnel, and for medical insurance coverage. The data presented in this chapter were selected with a view toward indicating the over-all dimensions of the problem of health in middle and later years and its effect on society.

A. Criteria of Health and Illness

The familiar criteria of a population's health are life-expectancy (at birth and at later ages), other expressions of mortality experience, and morbidity. As is well known, the United States ranks high among the countries of the world in average life-expectancy at birth (Health Information Foundation, 1956). This has been achieved mainly by the reduction of infant mortality and of deaths from such diseases as diphtheria, tuberculosis, typhoid fever, pneumonia, and other communicable diseases. Mortality rates in the later years of life, however, have not been reduced correspondingly. In fact, Dublin and Spiegelman (1952) have shown that, in the ages above middle life, the death rates for males in the United States are considerably higher than those of Italy, France, or Ireland.

There is something paradoxical, of course, in interpreting life-expectancy at birth, or death rates, as criteria of the health of the aged. Increased longevity may have raised more health problems than it resolved. Certainly, the gerontological goal is not merely added years of life but additional years of well-being. Nevertheless, age-specific mortality rates are one indication of the state of health of a population and often emphasize the need for health programs (as in home-accident prevention, early diagnosis and treatment of neoplastic conditions, etc.).

Most difficult of all to measure is the third criterion of health, namely, morbidity or illness, beginning with

asymptomatic disease, e.g., the undetected case of diabetes, which causes no symptoms and has not become manifest in any way. Next comes illness of which the person is aware but which does not affect his behavior; he does not change his usual activities nor does he seek medical attention because of it, e.g., a mild intestinal upset. Further along the range occurs illness which . . . may cause the person affected to seek medical attention, perhaps including hospitalization . . . or . . . may cause varying degrees of interference with usual activities. . . . Finally, at the other extreme, are illnesses which terminate in death [California Department of Public Health, 1958, p. 8].

"Morbidity," as the World Health Organization (1957) reminds us, "is far less definite than mortality, and represents a dynamic rather than a static phenomenon" (p. xxxv). This suggests one reason why the various countries of the world have collected less information on the illnesses of their people than on the causes of death.

B. Sources of Health Statistics in the United States

In the United States we have considerably less knowledge of the health of our middle-aged and elderly population than we have of other demographic characteristics. Mortality data are derived from information recorded on death certificates and reported to the National Office of Vital Statistics by state offices (U.S. National Office of Vital Statistics, 1954). Our information about mortality experience is relatively complete, although many recording and reporting problems in this field still remain.

For many years, however, morbidity data have been at best fragmentary. The major sources of morbidity data in the United States include the following:

(1) the notifiable disease reporting system, by means of which cases of certain infectious diseases (e.g., scarlet fever, streptococcal sore throat, acute poliomyelitis) are reported to the Public Health Service by the State departments of health; (2) insurance and prepaid medical care plans; (3) tax-financed public assistance and medical care plans, such as programs to aid the blind, general public assistance programs, and the medical service programs of the armed services, the Veterans Administration, etc.; (4) hospital and clinic admission and discharge records; (5) absenteeism records and records of routine physical examinations in industry and in school; (6) Selective Service examination records; (7) case-finding programs, such as mass chest X-ray screening; (8) the Census Bureau's Current Population Survey; and (9) local morbidity surveys [U.S. National Committe on Vital and Health Statistics, 1953, p. 14].[1]

As emphasized by the United States National Committee on Vital and Health Statistics, each of these sources has its limitations as well as its merits. For instance, the diseases reported under the notifiable system represent only a small part of the total illness experienced by the general population; insurance and prepaid medical care plans are limited by a selection factor in their coverage and frequently exclude cer-

[1] For additional items on the sources of morbidity data see Collins (1951) ; Health Information Foundation (1958c) ; and U.S. Public Health Service (1957b).

tain types of illness as well as persons above a specified age; tax-financed public assistance and medical care plans are limited to special groups in the population and are thus not representative of the total population; and data from hospital and clinic records are limited to illness attended in a medical treatment facility.

When one seeks information about the health *needs* of the general population (as contrasted, for example, with the actual utilization of services and facilities), one of the primary sources is the morbidity survey involving household interviews with a representative number of families. These families—healthy and ill alike—provide a population base in terms of which morbidity can be expressed as a rate.

The first morbidity survey of national scope was the 1935–36 National Health Survey conducted by the Public Health Service (1951). Since then, there have been additional studies, which, although confined to specific areas, have contributed to the field of the measurement of illness. Among these are the Baltimore Eastern Health District Study (Collins *et al.*, 1950), the California Health Survey (California Department of Public Health, 1958), the study by the Committee for the Special Research Project of the Health Insurance Plan of Greater New York (1957), surveys conducted by the Commission on Chronic Illness (1956, 1957*a*, 1957*b*), the survey by United Community Services of Metropolitan Boston (Rosenfeld *et al.*, 1957), and other studies which are cited in this chapter.

In July, 1957, a new National Health Survey, sponsored by the Public Health Service, went into continuing operation. Under this program comprehensive statistics on health and illness are being compiled for the general population (U.S. National Health Survey, 1958*a*). Since many of the tabulations from this survey will include a distribution by age, the program should prove to be a valuable instrument in appraising the health needs of our older population. Data from the National Health Survey relevant to our subject, published at the time of this writing, are included in the chapter.

It should be mentioned that most of the data quoted are derived from cross-sectional surveys of the population. There have been very few longitudinal studies— in which repeated observations are made of the *same* group of persons over a period of years—conducted in the United States because of the time and expense involved. As researchers in the social sciences are aware, the basic utility of the longitudinal study is that it provides data which show the effects of changes among the group studied. Two studies using the longitudinal approach are cited in this chapter, the studies in Hagerstown, Maryland (Turner, 1952), and the survey in the Eastern Health District of Baltimore (Collins *et al.*, 1950).

Thus various sources of morbidity data are used in this chapter to illustrate the health status of older adults in the United States, some of which are of national coverage, others of which are derived from community studies. In some cases we have presented composite tables which comprise data from several community surveys in different parts of the country. The usual purpose of such composite tables is to illustrate trends and patterns rather than to compare actual magnitudes of illness experience.

Since so much of the data quoted herein are derived from household interviews and thus represent what a member of a family has reported to a lay interviewer, an additional word is required about this type of survey. It is recognized that what the household respondent can report most readily is the social effect of disease, injury, or impairment on himself or on his family, as well as the illness he is experiencing (i.e., how he feels). The former type of information is valuable in determining the impact of illness, for example, the utilization of professional services and the effect on normal activities of life, on family stability, and on financial resources. Moreover, for many of the diseases that cause illness, the household interview is probably a reliable means of collecting information.

For some diseases, however, particularly many of the chronic diseases of later life, household reports tend to understate prevalence—especially so in the case of those diseases that may be undiagnosed or asymptomatic (e.g., general arteriosclerosis). To approximate the true prevalence of such diseases, it may be necessary to subject a sample of the population to a careful clinical examination, including diagnostic and laboratory tests. Few such clinical surveys have been attempted, chiefly because of the expense involved, although the resultant data would have applications in prevention and control programs. Under the current National Health Survey program, a sample of persons interviewed in the household survey will be asked to take a diagnostic examination (U.S. National Health Survey, 1958a).

Later we shall consider further the relationship of the clinical survey to the household survey. For the present, the principal point is that the available statistics represent mainly illness (i.e., subjective feeling or manifest symptoms of sickness), and do not purport to present an enumeration of underlying pathological changes (Woolsey and Nisselson, 1956; Krueger, 1957).

C. Terms and Indexes

Several of the basic terms of health statistics have familiar and reasonably well-established meanings, such as the two measures used to delineate the amount of illness, namely, prevalence and incidence. Prevalence of illness is commonly considered as the number of affected persons in a specified population *at a particular time*, for example, a single day. Thus the prevalence of tuberculosis might be expressed as a rate representing the number of cases existing (prevailing) at last count per 100,000 persons in the population studied. Incidence is the number of *new* cases with onset *during a prescribed period*, for example, a year.

Other terms, including several with particular application to the health problems of older persons, admit of a variety of interpretations. "Chronic illness" is illustrative: "Depending on the definitions used and the study cited, we find that between '4 million' and '28 million' people are 'chronically ill'" (Treloar and Chill, 1957, p. 34). The Commission on Chronic Illness has defined the term as comprising

all impairments or deviations from normal which have *one or more* of the following characteristics: Are permanent; Leave residual disability; Are caused by nonreversible pathological alteration; Require special training of the patient for rehabilitation; May be expected to require a long period of supervision, observation, or care [Conference on Preventive Aspects of Chronic Disease, 1952, p. 14]. [Italics ours.]

In accord with the objectives of a specific health survey, many such terms are defined rigorously. But definitions do vary among surveys, and the manner of definition will determine the meaning of the resultant data.

"Disabling" illness is generally used in the sense of an illness or impairment causing inability to work or take part in usual activities for a specified period of time. The magnitude of case rates obtained in a survey will depend upon the definition of disabling illness, that is, the number of consecutive days of disability used as the lower limit in defining a disabling illness.

III. Health Status

A. General Health Status

When one assesses informally the health of our population as a whole, the first impression is that the nation compares favorably with other countries of corresponding socioeconomic status. High average life-expectancy rates, for example, imply that our people have attained a reasonably high degree of health. When the assessment of health status is in terms of surveys of illness, particularly among persons in middle age or older, a less favorable pattern begins to emerge—a pattern that is reflected in the statistics on disabling illness.

PREVALENCE OF DISABLING ILLNESS

The sociological significance of disabling illness as an index of health is that such

chronic cases) are shown separately. This chart, of course, reflects only a sample of one population, but it does suggest several trends that are of interest to gerontological health. For instance, in the Eastern Health District there was apparently a noticeable increase in the prevalence rate of disabling illness among adults in their late thirties and early forties, following a decline in rates throughout young adulthood. From about age 45 on, the rates increased steadily throughout the fifties and sixties (58 and 79 per 1000 [Table 1]).

TABLE 1*

PREVALENCE OF DISABLING ILLNESS IN SURVEYED POPULATIONS OF THE
UNITED STATES AND CANADA, BY SELECTED AGE GROUPS

(Number of Persons per 1000 Population Disabled on Day of, or Day Preceding, Interview)

SURVEYED POPULATION AND YEAR OF SURVEY	AGE				
	All Ages	45–54	55–64	65–74	75 and Over
Eastern Health District of Baltimore, 1938–43....	36.6	30.3	58.1	78.9	164.9
United States, February, 1949—September, 1950..	41.9†	54.0	93.8	....	....
Canadian Sickness Survey, 1950–51.............	29.0	45.0		70.0	
Commission on Chronic Illness, Baltimore, 1952–56	29.2	........|........		78.2	
Boston Metropolitan Area, 1956................	30.1	49.1		104.4	

* Source: After S. D. Collins, F. Ruth Phillips, and Dorothy S. Oliver, "Age Incidence of Specific Causes of Illness Found in Monthly Canvasses of Families—Sample of the Eastern Health District of Baltimore, 1938–1943," *Public Health Reports*, 66 (1951), 1230; T. D. Woolsey, *Estimates of Disabling Illness Prevalence in the United States: Based on the Current Population Survey of February 1949 and September 1950* (Public Health Service Pub. 181 [Washington, D.C.: Government Printing Office, 1952]), p. 2; Dominion Bureau of Statistics and the Department of National Health and Welfare, *Canadian Sickness Survey, 1950–51*, No. 7: *Incidence and Prevalence of Illness, National Estimates* (Ottawa: Edmond Cloutier, Queen's Printer . . . , April 1955), p. 14; Commission on Chronic Illness, *Chronic Illness in the United States*, Vol. IV: *Chronic Illness in a Large City—the Baltimore Study* (Cambridge, Mass.: Harvard University Press, 1957), p. 271; and L. S. Rosenfeld, S. Donabedian, and J. Katz, *Medical Care Needs and Services in the Boston Metropolitan Area* (Boston: United Community Services of Metropolitan Boston, 1957), p. 45.

† Includes only ages 14–64.

illness limits to some degree participation in normal activities. Table 1 shows the results of some recent surveys of disabling illness among several populations. Although the rates may not be comparable for various reasons, the pattern of increase of disabling illness with age is indicated.

The rates from the Eastern Health District Survey[2] are plotted in Figure 1 for additional age intervals (all cases), and the components of this total (acute and

[2] In this survey the same households were visited monthly over a period of 5 years, thus providing an unusually valid picture of the volume of illness in a population.

Then, during the years above 75, a sharp increase occurred (to 165 per 1000 persons). It will be interesting to compare these results with data from surveys now in process, since two implications are at issue: first, that the gerontological health problem must continue to be carefully related to the middle years and, second, that "65 and over" may be too broad as an age category, since there appears to be a substantial contrast between the ages 65–74 and 75 and over.

Figure 1 also indicates that the prevalence of acute illness tended to level off at about age 20. Acute illness is not, of course,

uncommon among elderly persons, and such episodes are often of longer duration as age advances. It is the prominence of chronic illness in the later years, however, that Figure 1 particularly illustrates, increasing gradually in the forties and sharply thereafter. Throughout the middle and later years of life, chronic diseases and impairments are the principal challenge to health programs.[3]

INCIDENCE OF CHRONIC DISEASE AND IMPAIRMENT

The complex of disorders that are termed "chronic" may be viewed from incidence rates which show changes with age in the experience of a given population. Among the few longitudinal studies conducted is one of a sample of the Hagerstown, Maryland, population, surveyed in 1923 and again in 1943. The results of this study have been published in various articles (Turner, 1952), including one by Ciocco and Lawrence (1952), from which Figure

[3] In Figure 1, note that, at the ages 50 and above, the rates of acute illness are consistently *less* than the rates of chronic illness. One would not expect the rates of chronic illness to exceed those of acute disorders, since the latter include common colds, minor injuries, etc. The explanation here lies in the type of index represented, namely, a one-day prevalence. On any *single* day the major portion of disabling illness in the population, especially among persons in middle and later life, is likely to be due to chronic diseases, since these tend to be of long duration. Over a fairly *long interval,* cases of acute illness, usually of short duration, tend to occur much more frequently than episodes of chronic illness, except in very old age.

Thus the following rates from the Eastern Health District, covering a 1-year interval, illustrate the above principle:

ANNUAL FREQUENCY OF DISABLING CASES PER 1000 POPULATION*
(Disabling for 1 or More Days)

	AGE				
	All Ages	45–54	55–64	65–74	75 and Over
Acute.......	575	372	383	329	233
Chronic......	76	122	191	222	298

* Source: Collins *et al.* (1951a), p. 1230.

2 is taken. In their analysis the authors estimate the chances that a person, well at a specified age, will experience chronic disease or a major impairment within 5 years.

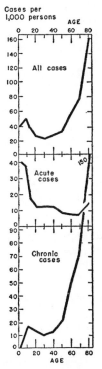

Fig. 1.—Prevalence of disabling illness, by age group, Eastern Health District of Baltimore, 1938–43. (After Collins *et al.,* 1951a.)

The curve indicates that the rate of occurrence of new cases of chronic diseases and major impairments increases relatively slowly to 35 persons per 1,000 at age 25. Under age 25, these rates may be considered as roughly the equivalent of 5–7 persons per 1,000 annually. As seen from the graph, the curve increases for persons in the next 20 years of age to about 100 persons per 1,000 at age 45. From this point on, the rate is accelerated. A person fortunate enough to have escaped chronic illness until he is 75 years old stands about a 50-50 chance of being free of chronic disease or major impairment if he lives to be 80 [Ciocco and Lawrence, 1952, p. 34].

These statistics may also be viewed in terms of the probable need for medical treatment:

Of every 1,000 persons who are well at age 45, approximately 100 will require, during the next 5 years, medical attention for the onset of a chronic disease or major impairment. Some of these 100 will then have to have periodic medical treatment, and a few of them will need almost constant medical care of some type until they die. Nearly 25 per cent of the persons well at age 60 will develop within the ensuing 5 years a chronic ailment for which they probably will seek or need medical treatment, and, in many cases, will continue to require care throughout their remaining lifetime. The percentage increases to about 40 at age 70, 57 at age 80, and 90 at age 90, although with advancing age the absolute number of persons subject to the risk of developing a chronic disease decreases in accordance with the age composition of the population [Ciocco and Lawrence, 1952, pp. 34–35].

From data such as these on prevalence and incidence, it is evident that the later years bring increased amounts of disabling and chronic illness. This fact was documented by the first National Health Survey, nearly a quarter of a century ago, and it is being reinforced by the data from the current National Health Survey (U.S. Public Health Service, 1951; Perrott *et al.*, 1952; U.S. National Health Survey, 1958*d*).

The impact of chronic illness on the health of older adults is further demonstrated by the statistics on duration, which are presented in the section that follows.

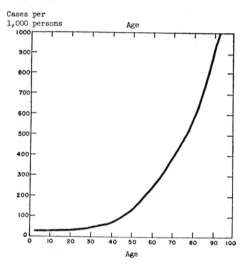

Fig. 2.—Incidence of chronic diseases and major impairments at 5-year age intervals, Hagerstown, Maryland, Survey, 1923 and 1943. (After Ciocco and Lawrence, 1952.)

TABLE 2*

DURATION OF DISABLING ILLNESS IN SELECTED POPULATIONS
FOR SPECIFIED AGE GROUPS

(Days of Disability per Person per Year)

POPULATION AND DIAGNOSIS CATEGORY	AGE				
	All Ages	45–54	55–64	65–74	75 and Over
U.S. National Health Survey, 1957–58					
All cases	20.0	25.4		47.3	
California Health Survey, 1954–55					
All cases	23.9	30.2		65.3	
Acute only	3.7	1.3		1.1	
Chronic only	13.6	21.9		49.3	
Both acute and chronic conditions	6.7	7.0		14.9	
Eastern Health District of Baltimore, 1938–43					
All cases	15.9	17.3	29.9	41.3	71.9
Acute	5.9	4.5	5.3	5.6	6.0
Chronic	10.0	12.8	24.6	35.7	65.9

* Source: After U.S. National Health Survey, *Health Statistics from . . . Survey; Selected Survey Topics, United States, July 1957—June 1958* (Series B-5, Public Health Service Pub. 584-B5 [Washington, D.C.: Government Printing Office, 1958]), p. 6, Fig. 2; p. 9, Table 3; and unpublished data from the Survey; California Department of Public Health, California Health Survey, *Health in California* (Sacramento, Calif.: Documents Section, California State Printing Office [1958]), p. 87, Table 8; and S. D. Collins, F. Ruth Phillips, and Dorothy S. Oliver, "Age Incidence of Specific Causes of Illness Found in Monthly Canvasses of Families—Sample of the Eastern Health District of Baltimore, 1938–1943," *Public Health Reports,* 66 (1951), 1230.

DURATION OF ILLNESS

In the middle and later years of life the duration of disabling illness is notably higher than in the population at large, as data from the three health surveys quoted in Table 2 show. For instance, persons in the ages 45–64 experienced 25 days of restricted activity due to illness per year in 1957–58, according to the National Health Survey findings. At ages 65 and over, nearly 50 days of restricted activity per person per year were reported. In the data from the Eastern Health District study, also shown in Table 2, it can be seen that the average duration of illness at age 65–74 (41 days) is much closer to that at age 55–64 (30 days) than to the average at age 75 and over (72 days).

What are the components of this increase in days of disabling illness among the aging? Figure 3, based on the Eastern Health District study, throws some light on the question. The index "disabled days per person" refers to the average number of days disabled for all persons in the age intervals shown, that is, persons who experienced disabling illness as well as those who did not. The index "disabled days per case" refers to sick people only, that is, the average duration of cases of disabling illness.

Regarding the *acute* conditions, it will be seen that there is a definite increase in duration per *case* from about 10 days per year in the forties to about 20–25 days per year in the late seventies, probably due to declining recuperative powers in the older years. As previously indicated, however, the prevalence of acute conditions is generally lower among older persons than among the young. These two circumstances (increase in duration and decrease in prevalence), in combination, result in the average number of days per *person* of disability from *acute* conditions remaining relatively constant in the later years (Table 2 and Fig. 3).

Thus the chronic conditions emerge as the principal contributor to the pattern of increase with age in the days of disability

per person shown in Table 2. This increase is a function of the markedly higher prevalence rates (Fig. 1) and incidence rates (Fig. 2) of chronic conditions and the extremely long duration per *case* of chronic illness in the advanced years. In the Eastern Health District study, average duration of chronic cases ranged from 100 to 200 days in the ages above 40 (Fig. 3).[4]

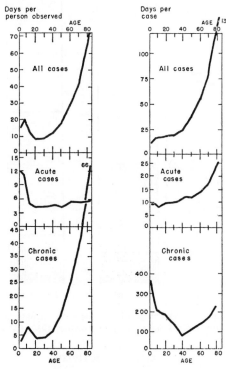

Fig. 3.—Days of disability per year from illness disabling for 1 or more days, by age group, Eastern Health District, Baltimore, 1938–43. (Note differences in scales.) (After Collins *et al.*, 1951a.)

Part of the explanation of these lengthy average durations in later life can be found in number of older persons who experience long-term disabling illness. Prevalence of disabling illness of more than 3 months' duration was estimated to be about 3 per cent at ages 45–54 and 7 per cent at ages 55–64 in the population of the United States around 1950 (Woolsey, 1952). Com-

---

[4] Average duration rates of chronic illness in childhood are even greater than in old age (Fig. 3).

parable data for the later ages, on a national scale, are not presently available. However, in the Baltimore study of 1954, 6 per cent of those 65–74 years and 14 per cent of those 75 and over had experienced disabling illness of more than 3 months' duration within a 12-month period (Commission on Chronic Illness, 1957*b*).

other words, about three of every four persons above age 64 have at least one chronic condition.

Figure 4 also indicates, however, that the health status of older men and women in the United States is not nearly so unfavorable as the statistics on "chronic conditions" first suggest. In the age interval

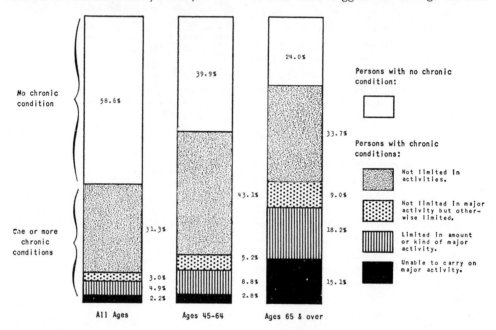

Fig. 4.—Percentage of persons with chronic conditions and limitation of activity, by specified age groups, United States, July–September, 1957. (After U.S. National Health Survey, 1958*d*.)

LIMITATION OF ACTIVITY AND MOBILITY

Until recently, relatively few statistics have been available on the degree of activity limitation among older persons who are ill, yet this measure of severity may well change our perspective on health in the later years. Consider, for example, some of the findings from the new National Health Survey, as shown in Figure 4. In accord with the data previously cited, it is seen that the percentage of persons who report that they have "one or more chronic conditions" increases with age. At ages 45–64, 60 per cent report such conditions; at ages 65 and above, the percentage is 76. In

45–64, about 40 per cent report no chronic condition, and an additional 43 per cent (all of whom have chronic conditions) state that they are not limited in their activities. Thus over 83 per cent of persons age 45–64 report either no chronic condition or no limitation of activity. As one would expect, at the ages 65 and above there is an increase in limitation of activity; nevertheless, nearly 58 per cent are without chronic condition or limitation.

Limitation of mobility provides another index of the effect of "chronic conditions" on the lives of older persons. Although there is a marked increase of such limitation at the older ages, as Table 3 shows, a substantial percentage of older persons ei-

TABLE 3*

PERCENTAGE DISTRIBUTION OF PERSONS BY LIMITATION OF MOBILITY
OWING TO CHRONIC CONDITIONS, UNITED STATES, AUGUST, 1957

Limitation of Mobility	All Ages	Ages 45–64	Ages 65 and Over
All persons............................	100.0	100.0	100.0
With no chronic condition...............	58.6	39.9	24.0
With one or more chronic conditions......	41.4	60.1	76.0
Not limited in mobility...............	38.1	55.7	55.4
With trouble getting around alone......	1.9	2.7	11.5
Unable to get around alone............	0.6	0.6	4.1
Confined to house....................	0.8	1.1	4.9

* Source: After U.S. National Health Survey, *Health Statistics from . . . Survey: Preliminary Report on Disability, United States, July–September 1957* (Series B-4, Public Health Service Pub. 584-B4 [Washington, D.C.: Government Printing Office, 1958]), p. 22, Table 17.

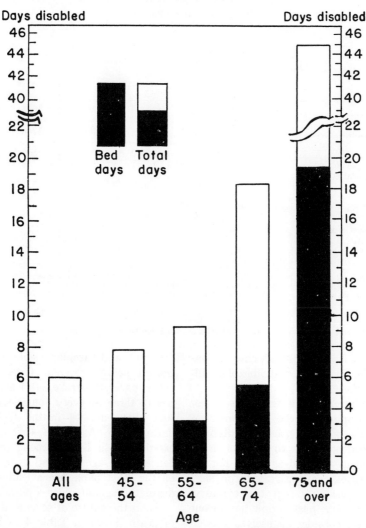

FIG. 5.—Average number of days of disability due to chronic conditions during 12 months preceding interview, per person interviewed, by all ages and selected age groups, Baltimore, 1954. (After Commission on Chronic Illness, 1957*b*.)

ther have no chronic condition or their mobility is not limited by the chronic conditions they experience (79.4 per cent of persons age 65 and over). Moreover, although the average duration of disabling illness increases with age (as shown in the preceding section), it is worth noting that even at the ages 65 and above the major portion of illness duration is spent in ambulation and not in bed. Such was found

B. *Specific Causes of Illness and Death*

SELECTED DIAGNOSES

From consideration of general health status, as indicated by such broad measures as prevalence rates of chronic or disabling illness, we turn to the specific causes of sickness and death among older adults.

Diseases of heart, malignant neoplasms

TABLE 4*

FIVE LEADING CAUSES OF DEATH FOR SPECIFIED AGE GROUPS
CONTINENTAL UNITED STATES, 1955

(Deaths per 100,000 Population)

CAUSE OF DEATH	AGE				
	All Ages	45–54	55–64	65–74	75 and Over
All causes.............................	925.1	752.8	1736.5	3954.5	10,472.2
Leading five causes......................	688.3	578.5	1400.8	3268.0	8,798.3
Diseases of heart........................	355.8	273.2	741.8	1804.3	4,928.9
Malignant neoplasms....................	145.6	173.7	393.8	738.3	1,200.2
Vascular lesions affecting central nervous system...	105.4	56.0	163.9	525.1	1,782.8
All accidents............................	56.5	51.9	64.6	105.3	347.6
Influenza and pneumonia, except pneumonia of newborn...........................	26.9†	‡	‡	‡	‡
General arteriosclerosis..................	‡	‡	‡	‡	528.8
Diabetes mellitus........................	‡	‡	37.4	95.1	‡
Cirrhosis of liver.......................	‡	22.7	‡	‡	‡

* Source: Computed from U.S. National Office of Vital Statistics, "Mortality from Selected Causes, by Age, Race, and Sex: United States, 1955," *Vital Statistics—Special Reports*, **46**, No. 5 (1957), 122–39, Table 1; and U.S. Bureau of the Census, "Estimates of the Population of the United States, by Age, Color, and Sex: July 1, 1950 to 1955," *Current Population Reports: Population Estimates*, Series P-25, No. 121 (1955), p. 6.

† The fifth leading cause of death for "all ages" is actually "certain diseases of early infancy." As this cause relates only to the one specified age group, the disease category next in rank is used.

‡ The specified cause of death was not among the leading five causes for the age interval cited.

to be the case for persons with chronic conditions (Fig. 5) and for all disabling illness as well (see Fig. 11, p. 189).

This interpretation of the data is not intended to minimize the seriousness of chronic illness in old age, for that problem is a very real one. The above data, however, remind us that old age need not be, and often is not, coextensive with physical and mental disability. On the contrary, millions of persons past middle age in our present society consider themselves to be in reasonably good health and to have no serious limitations in their normal activities.

(cancer), and vascular lesions affecting the central nervous system (cerebral hemorrhage, paralytic stroke, etc.) accounted for nearly three of every four deaths of persons above age 44 in the United States during 1955. As Table 4 shows, general arteriosclerosis is not among the first five causes until ages 75 and over. Accidents, on the other hand, are a leading cause of death throughout older adulthood.

From the nature of several of the causes of death shown in Table 4, it is apparent that some of the deaths that occur in middle life or later—some deaths from heart diseases, cancer, vascular lesions, etc.— were not preventable in view of our limited scientific knowledge about many of the degenerative diseases. In this connection, mortality data give further emphasis to the need for continuing medical research that will provide additional means of preventing the inception of disease and retarding its progression. On the other hand, many of the premature deaths from disease might have been averted had appropriate preventive measures been followed. For example, incipient cancer sometimes develops slowly in the aged, allowing considerable time for diagnosis and treatment. A recent proj-

ect "demonstrated that at least five years elapse between the appearance of a preinvasive localized tumor and the development of invasive cancer of the uterine cervix" (Burney, 1957, p. 441). Obesity, often controllable by appropriate nutritional habits, is commonly recognized as contributing to fatal cases of some heart diseases.

Very little information is available that provides detailed data by age on the specific causes of illness in a representative population. There are the results of several local surveys, such as the recent survey in New York City (Committee for the Special

TABLE 5*

DIAGNOSES WITH THE TWELVE HIGHEST ANNUAL RATES† OF DISABLING ILLNESS‡ PER 1000 POPULATION FOR SPECIFIED AGE GROUPS, WHITE FAMILIES CANVASSED PERIODICALLY IN FIVE HOUSEHOLD SURVEYS§

DIAGNOSIS	AGE				
	All Ages	45–54	55–64	65–74	75 and Over
All diagnoses‖	612.0	480.4	567.5	683.7	869.2
Influenza and pneumonia	82.1	74.8	75.4	77.3	86.3
Influenza	74.4	69.9	69.4	75.1	64.5
Pneumonia	7.7	4.9	6.0	2.2	21.8
Coryza, cold, sore throat	80.6	46.7	49.4	41.9	48.4
Bronchitis	51.1	39.0	53.2	48.8	57.8
All accidents	39.1	41.4	47.1	48.1	57.8
Arthritis and chronic rheumatism	8.5	17.0	26.5	35.9	57.8
Functional digestive disturbances	26.7	19.4	24.6	31.8	37.9
Tonsilitis and peritonsillar abscess	17.8	8.7	#	#	#
Diarrhea and enteritis	16.8	13.0	12.9	20.0	#
Diseases of heart	10.3	15.3	35.5	75.1	118.5
Headache	5.6	9.7	#	#	#
Neuritis and neuralgia	4.7	8.9	12.7	#	#
Hypertension and arteriosclerosis	4.2	#	16.5	34.0	63.5
Cerebral hemorrhage, embolism, and thrombosis	2.0	#	#	21.8	38.9
Cholecystitis and biliary calculus	4.1	7.8	11.5	#	#
Backache and other ill defined	1.3	#	#	20.0	49.3
Nephritis, all forms	2.4	#	7.9	16.6	31.3
Malignant neoplasm	2.0	#	#	#	26.5
Person-years of observed population	80,768	8358	4795	2703	1055

* Source: After S. D. Collins, Katharine S. Trantham, and Josephine L. Lehmann, *Sickness Experience in Selected Areas of the United States* (Public Health Service Pub. 390 [Washington, D.C.: Government Printing Office, 1955], Appendix Table 2, pp. 87–91, with supplemental data from Dr. S. D. Collins.

† Case rates include sole, primary, and contributory causes of illness. Recurring attacks of chronic disease within the period of observation are counted along with the original attack or illness. Thus the rates represent the number of attacks of chronic disease in the same sense as attacks of acute disease.

‡ Disabling for 1 or more days.

§ The five surveys, conducted between 1928 and 1943, were: Baltimore, Md.; Syracuse, N.Y.; Cattaraugus County, N.Y. Committee on the Cost of Medical Care (two surveys).

‖ Includes diagnoses listed and all other diagnoses reported in the surveys.

The specified diagnosis was not among the leading twelve for the age interval cited.

Research Project in the Health Insurance Plan of Greater New York, 1957), but these results are not tabulated by fine age intervals. To provide such data, we have selected for illustration the findings of five household surveys conducted between 1928 and 1943, representing more than 80,000 man-years of observation. The rates shown in Table 5 are annual rates and thus cover an interval of such length that the acute diseases appear with considerable frequency.[5] As in the younger years, persons above

[5] See n. 3 above.

age 44 were affected to a large degree by the acute respiratory disorders (influenza, pneumonia, common cold, bronchitis, etc.). Although many such episodes of illness are minor, in the aggregate they cause considerable disabling illness in the population. Accidents, as Table 5 shows, are still a problem in the years 45 and above. What Table 5 particularly highlights, however, is the increasing importance, with age, of such illnesses as arthritis and chronic rheumatism, diseases of heart (ranked second in the ages 65–74, first in the ages 75 and

TABLE 6*

Ten Diagnoses with the Greatest Number of Days of Disability per Year per 1000 Persons in Specified Age Groups—Three Household Surveys†

DIAGNOSIS	AGE			
	All Ages	45–54	55–64	65 and Over
All diagnoses:				
Non-institutional cases	11,101	11,725	17,269	32,506
Institutional and non-institutional cases	12,276	12,758	19,290	33,091
Heart diseases:				
Non-institutional	1,070	986	2,671	8,818
Institutional	24	7	‡	324
Accidents	765	856	1,087	1,256
Mental and neurological disease:§				
Non-institutional	730	1,088	877	‡
Institutional	741	569	1,479	137
Arthritis and rheumatism	680	2,011	1,037	3,838
Influenza	559	549	‡	‡
Bronchitis	539	426	642	‡
Rheumatic fever	374	‡	678	‡
Tuberculosis, all forms:				
Non-institutional	312	‡	666	1,320
Institutional	235	196	30	‡
Hypertension and arteriosclerosis	305	‡	1,202	2,070
Nephritis, all forms	294	‡	1,138	2,444
Diabetes mellitus	‡	631	815	855
Ulcer of stomach	‡	620	‡	‡
Malignant neoplasm	‡	400	‡	1,592
General infectious diseases‖	‡	395	‡	‡
Vascular lesions affecting central nervous system	‡	‡	‡	1,699
Diseases of organs of locomotion#	‡	‡	‡	1,498
Person-years of observed population	37,988	4,700	3,181	2,656

* Source: Collated data of three household surveys—Syracuse, N.Y., 1930–31; Cattaraugus County, N.Y., 1929–32; and Eastern Health District of Baltimore, Md., 1938–43—made available by Dr. S. D. Collins, Division of Public Health Methods, Public Health Service.

† Survey visits made at intervals of 1–3 months.

‡ The specified diagnosis was not among the leading ten for the age interval cited.

§ Other than neuritis and neuralgia, neurasthenia, nervousness, and psychoneurosis.

‖ Other than tuberculosis.

Other than lumbago and arthritis.

above), and hypertension and arteriosclerosis (ranked third in the ages 75 and above). The survey conducted in New York City in 1952 revealed that during an 8-week period conditions such as arthritis and rheumatism and hypertension were reported most frequently for ages 45–64; in the ages 65 and above, arthritis and rheumatism ranked first, hypertension second, and heart disease third (Committee for the

64), heart disease caused the most disability in terms of annual days, followed by mental and neurological diseases, hypertension and arteriosclerosis, and nephritis. Heart disease was by far the leading cause of disability in the ages 65 and above, followed by arthritis and rheumatism, nephritis, hypertension and arteriosclerosis, etc. Similarly, in the recent California Health Survey, many such chronic conditions—

TABLE 7*

PERCENTAGE OF PERSONS INJURED PER YEAR, BY CLASS OF ACCIDENT, SEX, AND AGE, UNITED STATES, JULY, 1957—JUNE, 1958†

(Injuries Involved 1 or More Days of Restricted Activity or Medical Attendance)

AGE	CLASS OF ACCIDENT				
	All Classes	Motor Vehicle	Work	Home	Other
Male					
All ages..............	33.1	3.5	8.0	11.0	10.5
45–64.................	24.9	4.1	10.6	3.8	6.4
65 and over...........	16.8	1.9	3.4	10.0	1.4
Female					
All ages..............	22.9	2.1	1.8	11.7	7.3
45–64.................	24.1	2.2	3.9	10.7	7.3
65 and over...........	31.9	2.2	0.7	23.9	5.2

* Source: After U.S. National Health Survey, *Health Statistics from . . . Survey; Selected Survey Topics, United States, July 1957—June 1958* (Series B-5, Public Health Service Pub. 584–B5 [Washington, D.C.: Government Printing Office, 1958]), p. 24, Table 18, and unpublished data from the Survey.

† Data are based on household interviews beginning July 1, 1957, and continuing through June 30, 1958. This period included the Asian influenza epidemic, during which many cases of vaccination reactions (which are classified as injuries and are included in the class of accident category "Other") were reported.

Special Research Project in the Health Insurance Plan of Greater New York, 1957, p. 92).

Table 6 shows another aspect of chronic illnesses in later life, namely, their effect in terms of days of disability. Of the surveyed populations between the ages of 45 and 54, the greatest number of annual days of disability was reported for arthritis and rheumatism (2011 days per 1000 persons per year), followed by mental and neurological diseases, heart diseases, and accidents, respectively. In the next age interval (55–

various forms of heart disease, arthritis and rheumatism, hypertension without heart involvement, and diseases of the central nervous system affecting motion—were reported as the leading causes of days of disability (California Department of Public Health, 1958). From one point of time to another, and among various populations, changes occur in the magnitudes of rates and in the rank order of specific conditions. The general relationships remain relatively stable, however.

ACCIDENTS

Injuries occur more frequently among the young than among persons in the middle and later years of life, yet the toll from accidents—especially accidents in the home—continues at a serious rate throughout older adulthood. According to estimates of the National Health Survey, between July, 1957, and June, 1958, some 33 per cent of males and 23 per cent of females (all ages) in the United States suffered an injury due to an accident involving one or more days of restricted activity or medical attendance (Table 7). Among men, the rates in the ages above 44 declined from 25 per cent (45–64 years) to 17 per cent (65 years and over). Women exhibited an opposite trend, with the respective proportions increasing from 24 to 32 per cent. This difference between the sexes is largely the result of the much higher rate of injuries in the home among older women, as Table 7 shows. At age 65 and over, accidents in the home were the major cause of injuries among both men and women.

The duration of disability due to accidents, as indicated in Table 8 (U.S. National Health Survey, 1958c), also shows the pattern of a higher rate in old age, particularly among the females.

Fatal accidents increase sharply in later life, from 52 per 100,000 at ages 45–54 to 348 per 100,000 at ages 75 and over (Table 4). In the year shown in Table 4 (1955), more than 26,000 persons age 65 and over died as a result of accidents (U.S. National Office of Vital Statistics, 1957c). Figure 6 illustrates, by sex and cause of injury, the rates of death resulting from accidents. The increasing role of falls as a cause of accidental death in later life is significant, particularly in comparison with the morbidity data cited in Table 7, which emphasized the frequency among older persons of accidents in the home. The rate of death from motor-vehicle accidents also increases among men and women above age 45. Increasingly the pedestrian is the victim of such fatal accidents. At ages 45–54,

for example, 19 per cent of total motor-vehicle fatalities among males involved a traffic accident to a pedestrian; in old age (75 and over), the corresponding percentage is 54 (U.S. National Office of Vital Statistics, 1957b). In sum, impaired motor function, poor vision, and other infirmities usually associated with increasing old age, probably make the older person more prone to accidents, particularly home accidents involving falls, many of which are fatal.

MENTAL ILLNESS

One of the problems associated with estimates of the extent of "mental illness" in the United States is that of defining the term. Mental illness signifies a wide range of emotional reactions, including the mild, transient disturbance involving little incapacitation, as well as the totally disabling psychosis that requires long-term custodial care. Diseases of the senium (cerebral arteriosclerosis, senile psychosis, etc.) are among the more important serious disorders affecting older adults, although the conditions that manifest themselves during middle age (e.g., involutional psychoses, alcoholism, and certain psychoneurotic symptoms) are also significant in their effect on society.

Statistical information about mental illness is derived from two principal sources: reports of admission of patients to mental hospitals and allied facilities and community surveys of the problem among persons in the general population. Admission data are valuable, but, like other hospital statistics, they reflect only the cases selected for inpatient care. Unfortunately, there have been few community surveys of mental illness among the general population, undoubtedly because of the difficulty of identifying and measuring these complex characteristics of human personality on the basis of a single household or clinical interview. Three widely quoted surveys are those of the Eastern Health District of Baltimore (1936), Williamson County, Tennessee (1935–38) (Felix and Kramer,

1953), and the more recent survey in Baltimore (1953–55) by the Commission on Chronic Illness (1957b). From these sources, many of the estimates of national prevalence are derived, for example, the estimate that 16 million persons have some form of mental illness (National Health Education Committee, 1957).

Regardless of the limitations of such estimates, it is evident that mental illness constitutes a problem of large dimensions, and one in which many older adults are involved. Since 1903 there has been a significant increase in the hospitalization of

patients in mental facilities in the United States (150,000 resident patients in 1903, or 1.9 per 1000 population; 577,000 patients in 1950, or 3.8 per 1000 population)

TABLE 8

DAYS OF RESTRICTED ACTIVITY OWING TO ACCIDENTS, PER PERSON PER YEAR

SEX	AGE		
	All Ages	45–64	65 and Over
Both sexes.......	2.6	3.6	6.9
Male............	2.7	4.0	5.5
Female.........	2.4	3.2	8.1

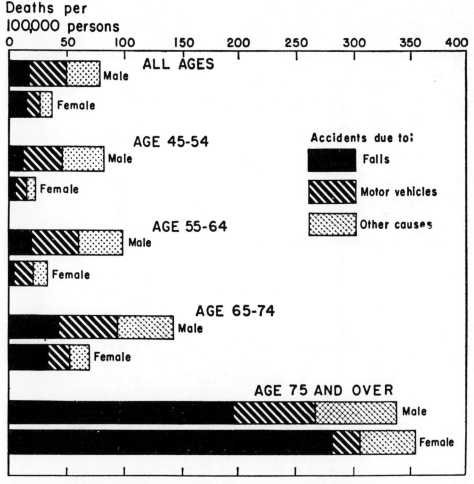

FIG. 6.—Deaths from accidents by cause of injury, and by specified age groups and sex, continental United States, 1955. (After U.S. National Office of Vital Statistics, 1957b, and U.S. Bureau of the Census, 1955a.)

(Felix and Kramer, 1953). Moreover, in recent years, more and more older persons have been admitted to mental hospitals, with the result that nearly four of every ten persons admitted is 60 years of age or older (National Health Education Committee, 1957), and the largest group of first admissions (27 per cent) represents patients with diseases of the senium (Felix and Kramer, 1953).

Figure 7 provides an indication of the types of condition for which patients are admitted to mental hospitals at various ages. Schizophrenia and the manic-depressive psychoses are prominent in young adulthood, involutional, syphilitic, and alcoholic psychoses in the middle years, and mental diseases of the senium during older adulthood (Kramer, 1956). Although persons with disorders of senility represent the largest segment of total admissions and exhibit the highest admission rates by age, such patients constitute only 12 per cent of the resident population of mental hospitals, as compared, for example, with schizophrenia patients, who constitute 46 per cent of the resident population (Kramer, 1956). Patients with schizophrenia are usually admitted in youth and have a long duration of stay in the hospital, averaging 10.5 years (Kramer, 1956). Many senile patients die soon after admission (70 per cent die in the hospital); their average duration of stay is 2.4 years (National Health Education Committee, 1957).

What is responsible for the fourfold increase since 1903 in the number of patients in mental hospitals and the twofold in-

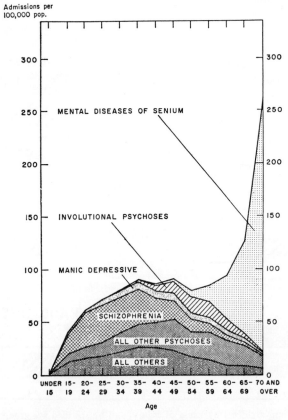

Fig. 7.—Age-specific rates of first admissions, by selected diagnoses, to state hospitals for mental disease, civilian population, United States, 1950. (After Kramer, 1956.)

crease in the ratio of patients to population? Several factors have been suggested, including the possibility of a real increase in the incidence of mental illness, the aging of the population, greater awareness of the problems of mental illness, and the constant increase in availability of hospital space (Felix and Kramer, 1953).

The confinement in our mental hospitals of about 200,000 persons age 60 years and over (U.S. Bureau of the Census, 1953) raises serious questions for social gerontology. Among the reasons for the increase in admissions of elderly people to mental hospitals, this factor is often cited: "the change in family organization, housing conditions, and concepts of family responsibility that make children more willing to solve the problem of dealing with senile parents by placing them in psychiatric hospitals" (Felix, 1951, p. 27).[6]

A recent study in Syracuse, New York, suggests additional sociological factors that may influence the hospitalization of older adults. In that city the socioeconomic environment was analyzed of patients admitted to mental hospitals because of cerebral arteriosclerosis or senile psychosis. There were indications that the high admission rate area of the city had, on the average, "the highest proportion of widowed and divorced, multiple dwelling structures, tenant occupancy, one-person households, and persons seeking work or unable to work" (New York State Department of Mental Hygiene, 1958, p. 82).

What proportion of "senile" patients in mental hospitals might be cared for elsewhere in the communities? Estimates of this figure vary widely; one study in California indicated that more than half of the

patients age 60 and over in state mental hospitals might receive care outside the mental hospitals if other accommodations were available (Commission on Chronic Illness, 1956). In 1954 a Philadelphia Mental Health Survey Committee sent a questionnaire to officials in charge of mental hospital programs in 47 states as well as to 33 psychiatrists in the mental hospital field. Sixteen of 50 respondents indicated that between 10 and 75 per cent of patients admitted to mental hospitals presumably with senile psychoses or psychosis with cerebral arteriosclerosis were not psychotic (Philadelphia Mental Health Survey Committee, 1954).

Hospital data certainly help to define important aspects of the problem of mental illness in the United States—in terms of any humanitarian criterion, the cost of medical care, requirements for facilities, requirements for professional staff and services, and so on. However, it should be remembered that a very small percentage of adults are patients in mental hospitals at any one time, specifically, about 1 per cent of all persons age 45 and over (U.S. Bureau of the Census, 1952, 1953). Information about the mental health of adults who are not in institutions, who live in the communities, is scant.[7] Some estimates of the prevalence of mental illness seem quite high, for example, the estimate that 50 per cent of all general practitioners' patients have some form of mental illness (Council of State Governments, 1950); such estimates undoubtedly would require careful analysis of terms before interpretation. Nonetheless, it is generally agreed that for many persons older adulthood brings periods of increased environmental stress at climacteric, at retirement, at the loss of a spouse, and at the time of other events whose effects may be traumatic.

What can be done to cure or alleviate

[6] It is still too early to assess fully the effects of the introduction of tranquilizing drugs on hospital admission rates, length of stay, or rates of discharge from mental hospitals. Preliminary reports, however, from mental hospitals in various states indicate that the rates of discharge may be increasing, concomitant with the increased use of tranquilizing drugs (National Health Education Committee, 1957). This effect will require further study (Kramer, 1956).

[7] In December, 1956, the Joint Commission on Mental Illness and Health reported a plan to conduct a "nationwide sample survey of mental health" (Joint Commission on Mental Illness and Health, 1957, Appendix J, p. 1).

the mental disorders of older adulthood? How can good mental health be maintained in old age? Many cases with diseases of the senium "have an organic basis and will follow a continued and inevitable downhill course" (Felix, 1951, p. 41). Yet mental illness classified as senile dementia or arteriosclerotic brain disease is often not confirmed by post mortem examination of the brain (Busse, 1957). Rather, such conditions may be, and often are, induced by a complex of chronic poor physical health, enforced idleness, reduced income, lack of social outlets (social obsolescence), and other emotional, psychological, and envi-

TABLE 9*

	AGE				
	All Ages	45–54	55–64	65–74	75 and Over
Per cent of persons edentulous........	13	22	36	56	65

* Source: U.S. National Health Survey, *Health Statistics from . . . Survey: Preliminary Report on Volume of Dental Care, United States, July–September, 1957* (Series B-2, Public Health Service Pub. 584-B2 [Washington, D.C.: Government Printing Office, 1958]), p. 7.

ronmental stresses peculiar to older people in our culture (Felix, 1951; Cameron, 1956; Stieglitz, 1956; Donahue, 1957; Streib and Thompson, 1957). There is evidence to support the claim that, given appropriate treatment and relief from major environmental stress, many aged patients can be restored to a state of mental health normal for their age (Felix, 1951; Rothschild, 1956).

Basic needs for maintaining good mental health in older persons have been cited by the director of the National Institute of Mental Health, Dr. R. H. Felix (1951):

One of the basic needs is health . . . maintaining the sound body that is so important in maintaining the sound mind [pp. 28–29].

Another basic need for the aged is for economic security [p. 31].

The third fundamental need of the aged is for useful activity. . . . Probably the most satisfactory activity is gainful employment . . . [p. 32].

. . . need for a home. This means not only the physical need for a shelter but also the need for a place of one's own which is familiar and secure . . . [p. 37].

The last basic need of the aged . . . is independence and self respect [p. 39].

From the point of view of mental health, the central problem is to give older people a sense of participation and continued purpose in life [p. 43].

DENTAL DISEASE

It is commonly recognized that the retention of sound teeth and healthy supporting tissue is conducive to proper mastication, to the enjoyment of food, and to good health in general. Yet the statistical evidence leads inevitably to the conclusion that many persons—those of middle age as well as the elderly—are not enjoying optimum health because of dental deficiencies.

One index of the degree of dental health is the DMF rate, which indicates the number of decayed, missing, or filled teeth out of a full complement of 32 teeth. Various studies (Hollander and Dunning, 1939; Pelton *et al.*, 1954; Commission on Chronic Illness, 1957*b*) may be cited showing the cumulative effect of dental morbidity as age advances, the DMF rate increasing from about 16 between the ages of 25 and 34 to about 26 in the ages 65 and over.

Another index of dental morbidity is the number of edentulous persons, that is, those who have lost all their permanent teeth, regardless of whether or not they have dentures. In August, 1957, it was estimated that there were 21.6 million edentulous persons in the United States, or 13 per cent of the entire population; the percentage increases with age, as shown in Table 9.

What are the causes for this loss of teeth? Certainly, dental caries (decay) is a major cause at various ages. Yet most of the preventive measures that will reduce the incidence of caries among adults must be applied during the early and formative years of life, such as the use of fluorides and the restriction of carbohydrate intake (Commission on Chronic Illness, 1957*a*). In the middle and later years of life, however, it is not so much caries as it is periodontal disease that is responsible for teeth loss.

This disease, commonly called pyorrhea, often originates as gingivitis. . . . Good oral hygiene practices and removal of agents impinging on gingival tissues figure prominently in the primary prevention of this disease in its early stages. Early recognition and prompt treatment is essential in the control of periodontal disease. Control measures include removal of calculus and surgical eradication of pockets [Commission on Chronic Illness, 1957*a*, p. 238].

Among other important oral diseases is cancer. It has been estimated that 10 per cent of the cancer in men and 2 per cent in women occur in the oral cavity (Commission on Chronic Illness, 1957*a*). Dentists, as has been pointed out, who treat 60 or 80 million persons each year, are in an opportune position to detect oral cancer as well as non-dental chronic disorders (diabetes, leukemia, etc.) and other diseases that have oral manifestations.

Dental health has a particular significance in the physical and emotional well-being of older adults, not only for those who are otherwise well, but for those in need of rehabilitation because of a chronic illness. A dental disease may interfere with the rehabilitation of such patients. Unless infection is removed from the mouth and masticatory function is restored, the patient is not fully rehabilitated (Commission on Chronic Illness, 1957*a*). Moreover, there are undoubtedly many elderly persons whose health, comfort, and general outlook would be vastly improved if they were provided with properly fitting dentures.

C. Differentials in Health Status

Some of the health and illness characteristics of populations at different ages have been indicated in the foregoing discussion, primary emphasis having been given to the age variable. Within an aging population, of course, not all component groups display a similar pattern of health or illness. There are identifiable differences in morbidity and mortality experience for components grouped by sex, race, income, occupation, education, marital status, and so on, which suggest biosocial factors associated with health. The effect of widowhood on mental illness in old age, the relationship of compulsory retirement to physical health, the association of specific attitudes and emotional stability in the later years of life—these are illustrative of the factors which probably exert significant influence on the health of older adults. Instead of approaching health from a single axis—namely, the association of age and illness—the more we succeed in identifying the mode and extent of these socioeconomic influences, the clearer our understanding of the entire gerontological health complex should be.

As students of the behavioral sciences are aware, however, the compiled information on the relationships of health and socioeconomic factors is still comparatively meager. A review of the literature provides ample testimony that the unanswered questions exceed by far the definitive data. Moreover, what often appears at first to be a characteristic accounting for a difference in health, such as the racial composition or marital status of a subgroup of an aging population, may actually mask other factors responsible for the difference (e.g., income or education). In order to determine the influence on health of one characteristic of a population, it is necessary to hold constant other factors. Since investigations of this type often require large samples and are complex and expensive, relatively few have been conducted.

In this section some of the differentials

in morbidity and mortality experience of our aging population are indicated. It must be remembered, however, that generalizations based on one factor alone can be fallacious, since they emphasize a characteristic of a group (e.g., rates of specific illness among adult men) while ignoring distinctions within the group (e.g., differences in rates according to occupation). Although the various statistical measures are useful in identifying tendencies of the group as such, the hasty inference of a property inextricably associated with a group is hazardous. As the reader will appreciate, the discovery of a gross differential in health status among older adults should signify not the end of analysis but the beginning of more definitive studies. Health and socioeconomic factors are probably interrelated in enormously complex ways, which research has just begun to untangle.

SEX

Since the end of the nineteenth century, death rates for females have declined more steeply than for males. This trend in the middle and later years of life is indicated in Figure 8. Thus, at ages 45–64, the total female rate was 10 per cent less than that of males in 1900 and 82 per cent less in 1955; at age 65 and over, the female rate was 6 per cent lower than that of the male rate in 1900 and 31 per cent lower in 1955. One of the effects of this mortality differential between the sexes has been the large increase in the number of widows in the population.[8]

Among the specific conditions that contribute to this marked mortality differential between adult men and women are fatal injuries (see Fig. 6), cancer, ulcer of the stomach and duodenum, and the cardio-

[8] See Sec. III below.

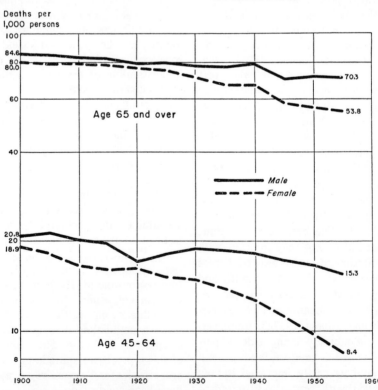

Deaths per 1,000 persons

FIG. 8.—Annual death rates at 5-year intervals, for males and females at ages 45–64 and 65 and over, United States, 1900–1955. (After U.S. National Office of Vital Statistics, 1956a, 1956c, 1957e.)

vascular-renal disorders. The only major disease with a higher age-adjusted mortality rate for women than men is diabetes mellitus (U.S. National Office of Vital Statistics, 1957d).

With respect to cancer, both incidence and mortality show a similar pattern of higher rates among males than among females in the later years of life (Figs. 9 and 10). As Dorn and Cutler (1955) point out, about half the persons diagnosed as having cancer are between 50 and 70 years of age. The modal or most frequent age is between 60 and 65 years. The mortality rate for all ages from cancer is 15 per cent higher for males than for females. The following explanation has been cited:

The relative frequency of the parts of the body affected by cancer differs considerably between the two sexes. A larger percentage of malignant neoplasms among males originate in organs and tissues where early diagnosis is difficult and existing therapy is not very effective [Dorn and Cutler, 1955, pp. 11–12].

Cases per
100,000 persons

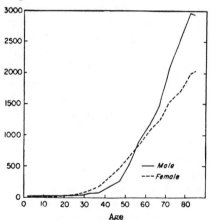

FIG. 9.—Cancer incidence rates by age and sex, United States, ten urban areas, 1947. (After U.S. National Cancer Institute, 1958.)

One of the most remarkable differences in the mortality experience of middle-aged men and women pertains to the cardiovascular-renal diseases. For such diseases, Moriyama *et al.* (1958) have recently

shown that the death rates among white males aged 35–64 years increased or remained relatively high between the years 1920 and 1955, while the corresponding rates for white females have been declining markedly. In 1955, for example, the mortality rate from major cardiovascular-renal diseases among white males aged 55–64 years was 1263.5 per 100,000, as contrasted

Deaths per
100,000 pop.

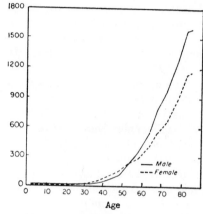

FIG. 10.—Death rates for cancer (all sites) by age and sex, United States, 1954. (After U.S. National Cancer Institute, 1958.)

with a rate of 550.8 per 100,000 for white females of corresponding ages. This difference between the sexes is attributed to an increment in male death rates for arteriosclerotic heart disease.

A number of expert consultants, asked to present their views on the increase of coronary disease among middle-aged men, offered several possible explanations, among them the suggestions that men are tending toward more sedentary modes of life, that obesity may have become more common among males, and that their occupational situations tended to be associated with ever greater psychological stress. There is less obesity among women, it was suggested, and, by virtue of smaller families and mechanical aids, they have been liberated from exhausting household drudgery. Moreover, women, in contrast to men, now find it more possible to slow down at the ages of 40–60 years, with their children grown (Moriyama *et al.*, 1958). Very little is known about the influence of such factors as these.

Recognizing that, on the average, women live longer than men, we inquire into the differences in patterns of illness of men and women. On the basis of mortality data, one might assume a priori that there is more illness among adult men than adult women, but surveys do not bear this out. When surveys have collected information covering an extended period of time, such as a year, proportionately more women than men have reported illness (Collins *et al.*, 1955).

For example, incidence surveys have repeatedly indicated excess female morbidity in the years 45 and over (Collins *et al.*, 1951*b;* Dominion Bureau of Statistics and Department of National Health and Welfare, 1955; California Department of Public Health, 1958). Since such surveys include new cases occurring over an extended interval, the acute diseases are reported with greater frequency. It has been suggested that women experience more illness of an episodic nature than men. Besides the higher rates of injuries among older women (see Table 7), other major illnesses reported in incidence surveys as occurring more frequently in adult women are arthritis and rheumatism, the cardiovascular diseases (certain heart diseases, hypertension), and the previously mentioned neoplastic disorders (Collins *et al.*, 1951*b;* Collins *et al.*, 1955; California Department of Public Health, 1958).

In terms of annual number of days of restricted activity and bed disability, the National Health Survey figures for the fiscal year 1958 show higher averages for women than men (Fig. 11), markedly so in the middle years of life. Yet, according to preliminary estimates from the National Health Survey of persons aged 65 and over with chronic conditions, 27 per cent of the males, in contrast to 15 per cent of the females, were unable to carry on their major activity[9] (computed from U.S. National Health Survey, 1958*d*, Table 14).

RACE

In 1955 the non-white population of the United States[10] totaled an estimated 17,848,000, or 11 per cent of the total population. At this time, some 5.4 per cent of the non-white group was aged 65 and over, compared with 8.9 per cent of the white population (U.S. Bureau of the Census, 1957). The percentage of elderly persons among the non-whites is increasing, along with improvement in their life-expectancy rates. In 1900, for example, the difference in life-expectancy at birth between the white and non-white populations was nearly 15 years on the average. In 1955 life-expectancy at birth was about 6.1 years more for white males than for non-white males and 7.7 years more for white females than for non-white females. At age 65, however, life-expectancy was virtually the same in the two groups (U.S. National Office of Vital Statistics, 1957*a*).

For every 1000 persons, the excess of deaths of non-whites over whites was 10.2 at the turn of the century, 8.6 in 1925, 4.3 in 1950, and 3.4 in 1955 (U.S. National Office of Vital Statistics, 1957*e*). Associated with the decline in excess mortality among non-whites has been a shift in the principal causes of excess mortality in the non-white group. Communicable diseases in 1914 accounted for nearly half of the total excess non-white mortality. As a consequence of the decline in such diseases among both racial groups, diseases of the cardiovascular-renal system are now a much more important part of the total

[9] To analyze in detail the effect of illness in later life on availability for work, one should classify the sexes by labor-force participation, occupational group, attitudes toward employment, and other variables besides limitation of activity or mobility. This has been done in a small methodological study in Hagerstown (Lawrence, 1958), but the sample is too small to generalize from the findings.

[10] Including armed forces overseas.

excess non-white mortality pattern (Health Information Foundation, 1958*b*).

Higher rates of disabling illness among non-whites have been recognized for some years, but recent morbidity data by race are less than definitive on this point. Based upon sample surveys in 1949 and 1950, the prevalence of disabling illness in the civilian United States population aged 14–64 years was estimated for non-whites as 5.8 per cent and for whites as 4.0 per cent. The differential between whites and non-whites increased with age and was particularly marked between white and non-white females (Woolsey, 1952). Data from the first (1935–36) National Health Survey similarly indicated a higher prevalence of disabling illness among non-whites (Holland and Perrott, 1938).

Several recent morbidity surveys, however, have produced results different from earlier findings. Statistics from the 1954–55 California Health Survey show higher rates of illness for white persons than for Negroes, although the rates are not adjusted by age (California Department of Public Health, 1958). According to the Baltimore City morbidity survey of 1953–55, the percentage of persons disabled one or more days during the 4 weeks preceding the interview was greater among whites than non-whites at all age intervals through 45–54 and was about the same in both groups in the older ages (Commission on Chronic Illness, 1957*b*). The number of days disabled per person was somewhat higher among the non-whites after ages 45–54, although there was no significant

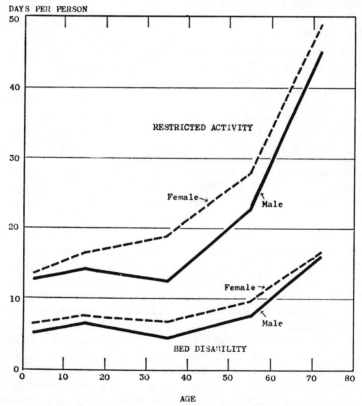

Fig. 11.—Days of restricted activity and bed disability per person per year, by sex and age, United States, July, 1957—June, 1958. (After U.S. National Health Survey, 1958*e*, and unpublished data from Survey.)

difference between the two groups in the proportion reporting a disability of more than 3 months due to a chronic condition.

What are the implications of these diverse morbidity findings? Apart from the fact that more conclusive data are needed, there is again the suggestion that gross differentials (e.g., differences in illness rates by sex, race, etc.) mask other factors which may account for the differences. In one study, when racial morbidity data were adjusted for age and standard of living, differences in level of illness between whites and non-whites were diminished considerably (Holland and Perrott, 1938). Environmental factors, such as education, income, occupation, and housing, undoubtedly play a dominant role in the differences in health status between non-whites and whites in our population. Examples of these factors have been cited by the Health Information Foundation:

In 1957 white men and women 25 and over had completed an average of 10.7 and 11.3 school years, respectively, while among nonwhites the comparable figures were 7.3 and 8.1. A similar trend prevails for income: The median for nonwhite families in 1955 was $2,549, only 55 per cent as high as that for whites ($4,605). . . . And the proportion of persons living in overcrowded nonfarm dwellings was four times as high among nonwhites as among whites in 1950; the proportion of nonwhites in dilapidated nonfarm dwellings was five times as high [1958*b*, p. 2].

As proportionately more of the non-white group is given an opportunity to improve its socioeconomic status, the differences in mortality and health status between non-whites and whites should decrease even farther. As the president of the Health Information Foundation has pointed out, when ill-health forces an ethnic group into a dependent position, the public must bear a good deal of the cost, but, when the health of a less-privileged group is improved, "corresponding advances are often stimulated in other social and economic areas" (Health Information Foundation, 1958*b*, p. 6).

MARITAL STATUS

Among adult men and women, changes in health status are felt by various classes of the population—married, single, widowed, and divorced—though not, apparently, to the same degree in all classes.

Of course illness in maturity, especially prolonged illness, not only incapacitates the person afflicted but has far-reaching effects on other members of the family. For an elderly married person, the illness of a spouse may have a serious impact on physical and psychological strength as well as on personal financial resources. However, the husband or wife of a disabled older adult often provides a source of emotional support in such crises.

For the unmarried person this type of personal assistance may be unavailable. The single man or woman of advanced years, living alone and dependent on his or her own resources, is in a precarious situation when sudden illness or impairment strikes. The widower may experience a lowering of nutritional standards and personal care. For the surviving man, the loss of a long-time companion and source of affection may bring periods of loneliness and depression, followed by loss of physical vigor.

In terms of the total gerontological health problem, the increasing number of unmarried adult women in the population constitutes a major factor. From age 45 on, the group "unmarried women" comprises mainly widows (ages 45–64, 62 per cent of unmarried women are widows; at 65 years and over, 86 per cent) (U.S. Bureau of the Census, 1958*a*). The greater longevity of women, combined with the tendency of men to marry women younger than themselves, has resulted in an increase in the number and the proportion of widows. If the pattern of higher prevalence of disabling illness among unmarried women (Fig. 12) continues into the advanced ages, it is clear that illness among unmarried women (widows, primarily) may represent a large part of the total problem of illness in later life. Widowed, separated, and divorced women also experience a greater number of days of disability per person and a higher frequency and duration of hospitalization than their married contemporaries (Rosenfeld *et al.*, 1952, 1957; California Department of Public Health, 1958).

Mortality rates among older married men and women are generally lower than the rates for single, widowed, and divorced persons, as Table 10 shows. This, again, may indicate a differential in health according to marital status in the older ages. Unless our society can improve its measures to cope with the social problems related to divorce and widowhood, the physical and emotional disabilities that accompany the unmarried state will increase with the increase of the population aged 65 and over.

ECONOMIC STATUS

There is considerable evidence pointing to the association between economic status and health (Sydenstricker, 1933; Perrott, 1936; Goldstein, 1954; Commission on Chronic Illness, 1957b). The National Health Survey of 1935–36 indicated this relationship by showing, for example, that for all persons age 65 and over, the number

of days disabled per person during the year was 36.1 for all income groups, as contrasted with 58.8 for persons on relief (Britten *et al.*, 1940). A recent study of 577 apparently healthy subjects over age 50 found a high correlation between the condition of teeth and economic status: an edentulous condition occurred among 51 per cent of persons in the low economic group, compared with 37 per cent in the middle and 4 per cent in the high economic groups, a circumstance possibly explained

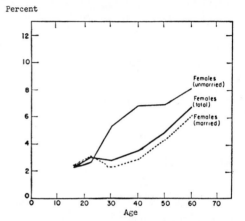

Fig. 12.—Percentage of surveyed, civilian population with a disabling illness or condition, by age, sex, and marital status, continental United States, February, 1949, and September, 1950, surveys combined. (After Woolsey, 1952.)

TABLE 10*

MORTALITY IN RELATION TO MARITAL STATUS IN MIDDLE AND LATER LIFE BY SEX, UNITED STATES, 1950

(Deaths per 1000 Population)

MARITAL STATUS	MALE			FEMALE		
	45–54	55–64	65 and Over	45–54	55–64	65 and Over
Total.........	10.6	23.4	73.5	6.3	13.7	58.8
Married...........	9.3	20.6	59.5	5.7	12.2	39.3
Single............	14.7	32.2	93.1	6.9	14.8	67.8
Widowed.........	20.1	36.7	105.0	9.3	16.9	69.7
Divorced.........	26.5	50.6	85.5	10.0	17.9	99.6

* Source: After U.S. National Office of Vital Statistics, "Mortality from Selected Causes by Marital Status, United States, 1949–51," *Vital Statistics—Special Reports*, 39, No. 7 (1956) 306–7, Table 1; and U.S. Bureau of the Census, "Marital Status and Family Status, April 1954," *Current Population Reports: Population Characteristics* (Series P-20, No. 56 [Washington, D.C.: Government Printing Office, 1955]), p. 6, Table 1.

"by both poor diet and inadequate dental care in the low economic group" (Chope and Breslow, 1956, p. 65).

One of the problems of measuring the association between economic status and health is that of separating the effects of age on health status from the effects of low income. In the report of the 1953–55 survey in Baltimore, a comparison was made of the prevalence of chronic diseases according to income, with the rates presented both on unadjusted and on age-adjusted bases (Table 11). On the basis of unadjusted rates, prevalence is seen to be

Health Survey, a yearly *family* income of less than $2000 was reported by 12 per cent of the total population studied, compared with 43 per cent of those aged 65 and over (California Department of Public Health, 1958). In the United States as a whole in 1955, 66 per cent of the men and 91 per cent of the women aged 65 and over (omitting those persons without any income) had a total money income of less than $2000 a year. Furthermore, some 38 per cent of the former and 74 per cent of the latter had an income of less than $1000 (U.S. Bureau of the Census, 1956).

TABLE 11*

PREVALENCE OF ALL CHRONIC DISEASES, BY ANNUAL FAMILY
INCOME (UNADJUSTED AND AGE ADJUSTED)
BALTIMORE, 1953–55

INCOME	NO. OF DISEASES (UNWEIGHTED)	RATE PER 1000 PERSONS (BASED ON WEIGHTED NO. OF DISEASES)	
		Unadjusted	Age Adjusted
All incomes†	1892	1566.5	1566.5
Under $2000	475	1985.6	1806.9
$2000–$3999	533	1501.9	1592.0
$4000–$5999	412	1460.3	1518.7
$6000 and over	214	1462.7	1418.8

* Source: After Commission on Chronic Illness, *Chronic Illness in the United States*, Vol. IV: *Chronic Illness in a Large City—the Baltimore Study* (Cambridge, Mass.: Harvard University Press, 1957), p. 53, Table 7.
† Includes cases for whom income was unknown.

highest in the low-income group and lower (but similar) in the other groups. When the age differential is taken into account, a pattern of increasing chronic illness with decreasing income is demonstrated.

There may well be a question whether poor health is a cause rather than an effect of low income, especially in the case of chronic diseases with disabilities of long duration (Commission on Chronic Illness, 1957*b*). There is little doubt, however, that low economic status often has a bearing on the adequacy of housing, nutrition, opportunity for education, and other factors related to health. In this connection it might be noted that, in the California

One can recognize in these circumstances a leading gerontological problem. It has been shown that older people tend to experience more disabling illness and episodes of longer duration than the population at large. At a time when income is declining (see chap. viii), the older person's expenditures for medical care are increasing. For example, the average medical care costs of a person 65 or over approximate $104 per year, as compared with $66 per capita for all ages (Anderson and Feldman, 1956). One study indicated that the average cost of an acute illness requiring hospital care for persons aged 65 and over was about $436, or some 57 per cent higher than the average for the population at large (Goldstein and Spector, 1958). As age increases, proportionately more of the older person's total consumer expenditures are allocated for medical care (see chap. xv). Moreover, the elderly person is far less likely to have some form of health insurance. While 63.6 per cent of the civilian population had hospital insurance in 1956, only 36.5 per cent of the aged had such insurance (Brewster, 1958). The percentage of older persons covered by health insurance will undoubtedly increase with time, but many obstacles remain, such as the practice of cancellation of individual policies by commercial companies, the problem of conversion from a group to an individual policy, higher premiums and reduced benefits, etc.[11]

In summary, not only are older people least able to afford health care at a time in life when the need is greatest, but those with the least financial resources are most subject to the illness of later life.

OCCUPATION AND RETIREMENT

Like economic status, the relationship between occupation and health is often reciprocal in nature, with each factor affecting the other. In the younger years, health is clearly a consideration in the choice of, and selection for, various types of employment. In later life, as certain physical capacities wane and the frequency and duration of illness tend to increase, the influence of health on occupation assumes additional importance.

The question of the precise effect of illness on the older worker's productivity is beyond the scope of this chapter, but two indexes of efficiency deserve mention, namely, absenteeism and accidental injury rates of older employees. Since illness is a major cause of absenteeism among employed persons and since the rate of

[11] By early 1959 a number of health insurance plans had made progress in extending coverage to older persons (U.S. Department of Health, Education, and Welfare, 1959).

illness increases in later life, one might expect to find progressively more total absenteeism as workers grow older. On the contrary, in "a survey of the records of almost 18,000 employees in over 100 companies, it was found that the absentee rate decreased consistently as age increased" (Rosen, 1957, p. 1). Findings from other studies comparing job performance by age, however, suggest the absence of any pattern by age and "refute current ideas that there are striking differences between age groups as to regularity of attendance at work" (U.S. Bureau of Labor Statistics, 1957a, p. 26).

The rate of occupational injuries decreases between the ages of 45 and 64 and age 65 and over, as previously shown (Table 7). Since the duration of illness episodes increases in later life, however, it is not surprising that the rate of *prolonged* absence due to illness is higher at the older ages (Research Council for Economic Security, 1957).

With respect to the influence of specific occupation on health, it is evident that life-expectancy, illness, and mortality rates vary among persons of different occupations. However, there is often a problem of determining whether a measurable influence on health is a direct or indirect effect of the occupation, since other socioeconomic factors are involved. Some occupations are patently hazardous. Others are associated with low income and a standard of living not conducive to proper nutrition, suitable housing, or desirable health practices. In Figure 13 the disabling illness experience of persons in selected occupations is shown, as indicated by household surveys in February, 1949, and September, 1950. This chart illustrates the importance of differentiating by activity or occupation when describing the prevalence of disabling illness among men or women. There are obvious differences in the rates of morbidity between unemployed and employed men and between employed women and those unemployed or keeping house.

For the older years (65 and over), relatively little detailed published material is available correlating occupation and illness. This circumstance is regrettable, particularly since 57 per cent of men aged 65–69 and 40 per cent of men aged 70–74 are still in the labor force at these ages. In fact, nearly 20 per cent of men 75 and

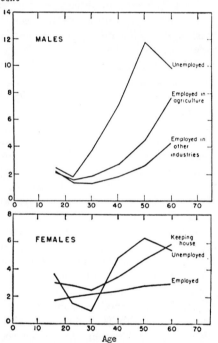

Percent

Fig. 13.—Percentage of surveyed, civilian population with a disabling illness or condition, by sex and age for certain employment status categories, continental United States, February, 1949, and September, 1950, surveys combined. (From Woolsey, 1952.)

over are in the labor force (Corson and McConnell, 1956). However, the trend in the last 50 years has been for the percentage of older persons in the labor force to decrease (U.S. Bureau of Labor Statistics, 1957b).

The percentage of persons who remain in the labor force after reaching age 65 varies with different occupations, manual workers tending to leave the labor force, and non-manual workers tending to re-

main. Retirement is due in most cases either to a decline in the health or fitness of the worker or to the widespread pattern in industry and government of compulsory retirement at or about age 65. Most men aged 65 and over who are not in the labor force report that they are not well enough to work. However, the percentage not well enough to work varies markedly by occupation; for example, of the professional and technical workers, less than half consider themselves not well enough to work; for farm laborers, the corresponding percentage is 74; for other laborers, 85 (see chap. viii below).

To what extent does retirement from work affect health? Myers (1954a, 1954b), reviewing data on longevity in relation to retirement, has shown that death rates for voluntarily retired workers, during the first year or two of retirement, are considerably higher than those of all males in the corresponding ages. Myers attributes this finding to the tendency of those in poor health to retire as soon as they can under voluntary provisions in retirement plans. When retirement is compulsory, mortality rates are about the same as actuarially expected, probably because many healthy workers are among this retired group.

Two recent studies provide evidence that retirement either does not materially affect health status or is even beneficial thereto. A study of mortality and morbidity of retired men in a large Canadian communications industry, covering a period of nearly 50 years, disclosed that some 77 per cent showed either no change or an improvement in health on the basis of evaluation of medical and personal histories before and after retirement (Tyhurst *et al.*, 1957). Similar results were found by Thompson and Streib (1957) in a longitudinal study of 1260 males aged 68–70. The hypothesis that retirement necessarily leads to a decline in health was found untenable on the basis of changes in health among persons who retired, as compared with those who continued in gainful employment. A higher incidence of poor health was found among persons who were retired than among the employed, but this was interpreted "in terms of poor health leading to retirement and not the reverse." Moreover, in some instances, health actually tended to improve during retirement. The authors conclude:

Our data do *not* necessarily refute the notion that a radical withdrawal from sustaining activities results in a decline in health. In fact, there is a suggestion of support for this hypothesis in the fact that a decline in health occurs in somewhat larger proportion among the reluctant retirees as compared with the willing retirees. And it is among the reluctant retirees that one would expect retirement more often to be experienced as an activity vacuum. But even here no markedly disproportionate decline occurs, and we conclude that retirement as a social process does not generally have an ill effect on health, most probably because retirement for most people does not represent an irremediable loss of sustaining activities [Thompson and Streib, 1957].

The event of retirement undoubtedly affects the health of people in various ways. For some persons retirement marks a transfer from a usual occupation to other meaningful activities. For others the event signifies an abrupt withdrawal from sustaining interests. What one's physical and emotional health status in retirement will be would seem to depend on many factors besides retirement per se. The medical history prior to the event as well as the emotional makeup of the individual are obviously involved. Some persons have the capacity to confront an unfamiliar situation with equanimity; others react with anxiety. Moreover, it seems unlikely that a person on reaching retirement age will suddenly develop the ability to use his leisure in a more satisfying manner than he has succeeded in doing previously. Psychological as well as financial preparation before retirement is surely important, as are the opportunities to pursue the interests one considers meaningful. A mean-

ingful activity for one elderly person may be a passive role as a spectator of society; satisfaction may come to another only after he has made a personal contribution to society—a product, a service—and his contribution has been recognized and appreciated. Opportunities for such activities and the attitudes and demeanor of relatives and friends are probably highly significant influences on health after retirement.

OTHER FACTORS

In addition to the above biological and socioenvironmental factors that affect health in later years—race, sex, marital status, economic status, occupation, and retirement—other factors have been described as influencing health and illness, among them heredity, education, place of residence, exposure to ionizing radiation, air pollution, etc.

A hereditary influence has been suggested for such chronic diseases as blindness, deafness, diabetes mellitus, cardiovascular conditions, hypertrophic arthritis, tuberculosis, and neoplasms. Assessment of the genetic influence in the occurrence of chronic diseases is difficult, however, particularly the diseases where the primary etiology represents a complex interplay of genetic and environmental factors. Little is known about the precise mechanism of this interplay (Commission on Chronic Illness, 1957a).

There is some evidence, derived from household surveys, that disability and education are inversely related. In a recent Boston study "a marked inverse relationship" was found "between annual days of disability and years of education of the head of the household" (Rosenfeld *et al.*, 1957, p. 51). It is common knowledge that levels of education and income are positively correlated, and, as pointed out previously, there tends to be an inverse relationship between income level and prevalence of disabling illness. Undoubtedly, education per se is conducive to an awareness of the value of early and good medical care and to an appreciation of preventive measures and other health practices.

Differences in mortality and morbidity by place of residence have been reported, although the health status of any community is probably more a reflection of its population than its geographic location, climate, and similar characteristics. The health of a community usually differs from that of another to the extent that the population varies in age and sex distribution, ethnic composition (affecting customs relating to health maintenance), economic and occupational characteristics, and the "stage to which public health practices and medical and hospital facilities have been developed" (Dublin *et al.*, 1949, pp. 69–70). Differences in health between city and rural residents, as well as regional differentials, have noticeably decreased in recent years (Health Information Foundation, 1958*a*).

IV. Health Promotion

From the foregoing statistics it is evident that chronic disease is the basic health problem in later years. To reduce the impact of such morbidity on older adults will require an intensification of prevention, medical care, and rehabilitation.

A distinction is usually made between two types of "prevention":

Primary prevention means averting the occurrence of disease. . . . Secondary prevention means halting the progression of a disease from its early unrecognized stage to a more severe one and preventing complications or sequelae of disease [Commission on Chronic Illness, 1957*a*, p. 16].

Primary prevention brings to mind such measures as immunization and environmental sanitation and is usually associated with control of the acute communicable diseases, with air- and water-pollution programs, occupational health, and similar activities. Clearly, this aspect of preventive medicine is applicable to all ages and ex-

tends from maternal and child health programs to geriatrics. As medical authorities emphasize, the significant relationship of primary prevention during childhood and youth to health in later years is that prevention of acute diseases and injuries can reduce the chronic sequelae. Examples of this relationship are well known: inoculation and paralytic poliomyelitis, fluoridation and dental caries, etc. (Commission on Chronic Illness, 1957*a*).

In view of the number of serious disorders to which medical science is still unable to apply primary prevention—arteriosclerosis, degenerative joint disease, diabetes mellitus, essential or primary hypertension, multiple sclerosis, primary glaucoma, rheumatoid arthritis, etc. (Commission on Chronic Illness, 1957*a*), the place of secondary prevention in health programs is evident. In connection with prevention—primary and secondary—the illness data cited suggests the importance to gerontological health of personal health practices, that is, measures to avert or reduce disease that are in large part the responsibility of the individual and often depend solely on his initiative. Illustrative are home-accident prevention, proper nutritional habits, avoidance of fatigue, suitable exercise and recreation, periodic health examination, and other practices recommended by medical authorities as means of health conservation (Bortz, 1957*b*; Holle, 1957; Johnson, 1957; Klumpp, 1957; Pollack, 1957; White, 1957).

A. Periodic Health Examination

With respect to periodic health examinations, the Commission on Chronic Illness (1957*a*) has recently emphasized that all persons "should have a careful health examination, including selected laboratory tests at appropriate intervals" (p. 29). The scope and frequency of such examinations will vary with age, sex, location, occupation, and other socioeconomic factors. When a man or woman is beyond middle life, however, the importance of periodic examination becomes even more critical than in youth. Accordingly, Mountin (1951) and others have recommended for persons in these ages a physical checkup annually, or at least every few years. It was recently urged by the medical profession that all persons past middle age be reminded by their birthdays that another complete physical examination is called for (Johnson, 1957).

As one views the practice of periodic health examination in its sociogerontological dimensions, it is apparent that there are many obstacles to implementing a large-scale examination program, a fact fully recognized by those who stress the importance of such examinations. One obstacle is the increment of medical resources —personnel and facilities—that would be required to provide even a majority of Americans with annual examinations. Physicians, kept busy caring for the sick and injured, have little time for examining seemingly healthy persons. Apart from the question of medical resources, however, the fact remains that the American public, except for a small minority, has not adopted the practice of regular physical checkups voluntarily. In part this is attributable to the expense of such examinations, involving as they do costly tests and other procedures. Even when this is not a significant factor, however, those who have the opportunity and the resources for a health examination often decline (Commission on Chronic Illness, 1957a). The reasons for this attitude of apathy are far from clear. Some statistics suggest that people avoid physical examination because they fear the discovery of serious disease (Commission on Chronic Illness, 1957a). It has also been suggested that when neither physical pain nor incapacity is present health care is often neglected in favor of other goods and services (Weeks et al., 1958).

A primary objective in the periodic health examination program is to detect early signs of disease or other abnormalities in order to institute prompt corrective measures. This presupposes not only a comprehensive examination but a careful history, appropriate laboratory procedures, and health counseling and follow-up (Commission on Chronic Illness, 1957a). Those who question the advisability of recommending periodic examinations en masse do not of course deny that prevention and early treatment of diseases are highly important objectives. Instead their position is this: in view of the limited number of medical personnel available, the yield from such examinations—that is, the number of morbid conditions discovered—does not justify the huge expenditure of time, skill, and money required.

Many comparative studies will be required before the utility of health examinations can be fully evaluated. Meanwhile, however, the results of a number of studies tend to support those who urge health examinations as a fruitful means of reducing the burden of chronic illness. For example, Dr. Norbert J. Roberts recently reviewed the results of a dozen studies in which a total of 16,715 persons were given health examinations. Only 13.8 per cent of these examinees were found "entirely healthy." In 37.1 per cent of the examinees significant new disease was discovered (Roberts, 1958). Baker et al. (1956) conducted 7147 examinations between 1948 and 1955 and made more than 7000 disease diagnoses at Greenbrier Clinic. As further indication of the value of periodic examination for the early detection of disease, Franco (1956) has reported the findings from a 1949–55 study of 707 male employees of Consolidated Edison Company of New York: 35 per cent of those examined were made aware of conditions for the first time (more than half of these conditions were asymptomatic); 20 per cent of the noted conditions were entirely corrected; and 33 per cent improved by treatment. (The merits and limitations of the periodic examination are discussed in a recent article by Roberts [1959].)

Since the feasibility of implementing periodic examination programs on a wide scale is so questionable at present, many authorities have recommended a program of limited screening for most of the United States population (e.g., blood specimens for syphilis, diabetes; hearing and vision tests; blood-pressure readings, etc.) and a meticulous examination for selected individuals (Mountin, 1951; Commission on Chronic Illness, 1957a). There is no disagreement among medical authorities as to the advisability of closer medical supervision in later life.

B. Accidents

Besides periodic examination, a second personal health practice of importance to health in the later years of life is the prevention of accidents in the home. The number of deaths resulting from falls, especially at the ages 65–74 and 75 and over, as well as the prevalence rates and disability rates of accidents in these years, are indicative of the significance of injury as a health problem in maturity. Considerable educational material for the general public has been published on this aspect of preventing premature death and disability, for example, the booklet entitled *The Older Person in the Home,* which lists simple precautions (U.S. Public Health Service, 1957a).

C. Nutrition

Among the aged, poor nutrition has been found to affect adversely mental and physical vigor of those otherwise well, to add to the hazards of disease, to retard convalescence, and to dull all activity (Monroe, 1951; Spies, 1958). In cases of heart disease, malnutrition may make the difference between compensation and failure of the heart (Priest, 1957). Many confusional states of mind among the aged in mental institutions have disappeared after initiation of a good diet with supplements (Gruenberg, 1957). There can be little doubt that proper nutrition is conducive to prevention of illness, yet many old people manifest poor nutritional habits and malnutrition to some degree (Monroe, 1951; Bortz, 1957a; Commission on Chronic Illness, 1957a). According to the above authorities, common causes of poor nutrition among old people include: (1) inadequate income (a good protein diet needed by the aged is relatively expensive, often beyond the income of old people); (2) living alone (preparation of cooked meals by the older person for himself or herself only is often considered too much bother); (3) loss of teeth or poorly fitting dentures which interfere with proper mastication of food or avoidance of needed foods; (4) limited energy and capacity for shopping; and (5) long-standing faulty habits and beliefs about foods and nutrition.

Faulty nutrition may also adversely affect health in middle age. Earlier it was mentioned that death rates in middle and later life appear to be higher in the United States than in many other countries. This circumstance, according to Dublin and Spiegelman (1952), is probably the result of "prosperity and abundance" in the United States, a large number of our people "literally eating themselves to death," since overweight in midlife, common in the United States, is associated with higher than average mortality. Dublin and Spiegelman also mention that a generally better level of medical care in the United States may result in a larger proportion of persons with organic disease surviving into middle and later life, with consequent higher mortality rates due to such diseases at this time.

D. Exercise

As Whittenberger (1956) has pointed out, much could be done to preserve function of faculties and organs in the elderly by maintenance of high levels of mental and physical activity. It has been found, for example, that the vascular tissues are in better condition in those who exercise, or whose occupation involves considerable physical activity, than in the sedentary (Bortz, 1957a), a matter of special relevance in view of the high prevalence of vascular diseases in the later years. Even individuals with cardiac impairment are advised to avoid a completely sedentary life, except when the impairment is extreme (Priest, 1957). It is well known that, the more a diabetic person exercises, the less the amount of supportive insulin is required. Physical activity, therefore—provided overexertion and strain are avoided—is indicated as another personal health practice important in the promotion of good health.

E. Economic Status

Finally, in this discussion of the promotion of health among older adults, we should like to call attention to the persistent suggestion in the data that the socioeconomic factors must be taken into account in any attempt to improve health in the later years. Economic status is a factor that is clearly important to health conservation in later life. While the older person's need for suitable clothing, adequate housing, and proper food continues, his need for medical care, drugs, and periodic examinations often increases. Apart from the financial demands that episodes of illness bring, as well as the costs of periodic medical examination, there is the need of elderly persons for eyeglasses, properly fitting dentures, foot treatment, and other medical necessities. Although adequate income is a prerequisite to health maintenance, future research into this subject of health and economic status will probably confirm that the problem is not one of income alone but involves many attitudinal factors, habits, education, and so on.

V. Discussion

Several observations suggested by the foregoing review of health in later years of life have implications for social gerontology.

1. *The "aging" of the population has increased the amount of illness in our society.*

It has long been evident that the amount of disabling illness, especially chronic illness, increases in the middle and later years of life. This circumstance becomes a matter of more social concern with the increase in the number and proportion of older people in the population. Thus, even assuming that rates of illness remain at present levels, by 1975 persons aged 65 and over who are limited by chronic conditions or unable to carry on their major activity will number about 7.3 million—as compared with 4.8 million in 1957—solely as a consequence of the expected greater old age population.[12]

Apart from projections of the situation that may obtain 20 years hence, there is sufficient evidence in the statistics quoted in this chapter to identify gerontological health as one of the serious social problems today. There are the conditions that presently cause millions of days of disability among older persons: arthritis and rheumatism, mental and neurological disease, heart diseases, hypertension and arteriosclerosis, nephritis, and other disorders.

Furthermore, some aspects of the problem which the data seem to represent as minimal—such as the 6 per cent of those 65–74 years with a long-term disabling illness—amount to considerable impairment and loss of potential contribution to society, aside from personal suffering and discomfort. Hundreds of thousands of older people are involved, not only those afflicted but their families as well. A chronically ill person may require of the family extraordinary amounts of time, attention, and financial resources, often beyond the capacity of the family.

[12] Estimates based on data from the U.S. National Health Survey (1958d) and applied to population projections (U.S. Bureau of the Census, 1958b).

2. *More chronic illness in the population necessitates a corresponding increase in, and better utilization of, health resources.*

Since chronic illness often calls for an array of health services—diagnostic clinics, long-term hospital care, restorative services, nursing-home care, social work, home care—community programs to regain and maintain adult health are complex and expensive endeavors. Thus the increasing amount of disability that has accompanied the aging of the population challenges the capacity of many components of society to meet these unprecedented needs with suitable personnel, facilities, and financial resources.

In recent years much attention has been devoted not only to increasing the supply of health resources but also to improving the utilization of existing resources. Yet in only a few communities is there an adequate supply of such ancillary personnel as homemakers, therapists, dieticians, etc., to provide, for example, care for the aged person at home. Community facilities for the early diagnosis of disease among adults, or for applying the rehabilitation techniques now available, are often inadequate. Too seldom is there adequate control of the quality of nursing-home care and medical supervision of nursing-home patients. Most communities are in need of better integration and co-ordination of the health services available.

These subjects, discussed in chapter xv, are mentioned here because the health status of any population group depends in large measure on the quality of health resources in a community as well as on the effective demand for such services.

3. *Although the aged experience more chronic illness than the young, the data indicate that the health status of most older adults is reasonably good.*

Statistics that show an increase with age in the frequency of chronic and disabling conditions do not imply an identification of old age with infirmity. One should keep in mind these facts:

a) The terms "disabling" and "chronic" are broad and should be used with caution. The concept "disabling" includes the less as well as the more serious types of illness —those that indispose for a day, as well as those that cause long-term disability. A chronic disease may involve only infrequent or brief episodes of illness rather than continuing incapacitation, as the term may connote.

b) When the illness of older adults is considered in terms of interference with normal activities, in terms of roles in society, most older persons report that they are not seriously limited in activity or mobility.

c) A large part of the aggregate restricted activity among the aged is contributed by a minority of older persons with long-duration disability.

d) Morbidity statistics suggest a marked difference between the average health status of persons aged 65–74 and that of persons aged 75 and over. In fact, the average health status of persons age 65–74 may be much closer to that of persons age 55–64. Much more evidence will have to be assembled on this point, but such data as are available cast doubt on the suitability of "65 and over" as a class denoting members with closely similar health characteristics.

In view of the emphasis on the poorer health status of the old, as compared with the young, we perhaps need to be reminded that millions of persons past middle age consider themselves to be in reasonably good health and capable of performing useful tasks in our society. Modern medicine and public health practice, as well as a generally high standard of living, are contributing much to maintain and extend the period of physical and mental vigor well beyond age 65 for large numbers of people. Moreover, for those older persons who do become ill, there are increasing advances in surgical techniques, medical diagnosis, and drug and other types of therapy, all of which contribute to recovery or rehabilitation.

One question that seems to challenge any optimistic interpretation of the health status of the aging is this: Is it not true that large numbers of older people who in a household interview report that they are free from disabling illness actually may have chronic conditions that would be discovered upon clinical examination? In other words, do not household reports tend to understate the "true" prevalence of the undiagnosed and asymptomatic chronic diseases? The recent survey in Baltimore, for instance, indicated that many older adults interviewed considered themselves relatively well, but, when a subsample of this population was clinically evaluated, "substantial chronic conditions" were found among 66 per cent of those aged 35–64 and 85 per cent among those 65 and over. Such conditions were described as ones that might limit or interfere with activity in the future or require care (Commission on Chronic Illness, 1957*b*).

Without questioning, of course, the importance of medical examinations and laboratory tests as indexes of physical fitness, or denying their essentiality in prevention, care, and rehabilitation, it should be pointed out the information reported by the respondent in a household interview—how he feels, whether he has been disabled by illness—remains a highly significant index of his "health status," particularly the effect of illness on his role in society. Accordingly, it is questionable whether clinical results should be thought of as contradicting survey data, since in some respects these two methods of assessing health status are designed to answer different questions.

Because of the importance of the discovery of incipient chronic disease, however, particularly in the middle years of life, all efforts conducive to such discovery (e.g., periodic examinations) should be encouraged.

4. *To reduce disability among the aged, health maintenance should begin early in life, and good personal health practices should be cultivated.*

As suggested in the preceding propositions, a primary task is, first, to reduce the amount of disability in the population and, second, to maintain and improve the state of health among as many older people as possible. To attain this objective will require health programs of a scope described in chapter xv. It will further require an appreciation of two facts emphasized in this chapter: the significance of health maintenance in the early years of life and the importance of personal health habits and practices.

One of the principal reasons for providing data on health status in the middle years rather than confining the analysis to age 65 and over has been to show how the incidence of disabling and chronic illness begins to increase noticeably during this earlier period of life. As medical authorities have emphasized, the appropriate time for preventive geriatrics, for exerting efforts to prevent or reduce much of the invalidism of old age, is 20 or more years before the onset of senescence (Shock, 1950).

Improvement in the health status of older adults would seem to depend not only on the family physician and better health and welfare programs in the community but also on the degree of success achieved by the individual, or by the family, in improving the personal health practices mentioned in Section IV above.

5. *The health of the aging is a social as well as a biological phenomenon.*

As pointed out at the beginning of this chapter, health is not a simple property but a composite state comprising physical, mental, emotional, and social aspects. To what degree does the health of an older person depend on his surroundings, on the adequacy of his life-situation? There is already evidence of this relationship, for example, the interdependence of health and social welfare. Such factors as financial security and suitable housing are clearly important.

But there is another factor that deserves emphasis in the control of illness in later life, namely, what Dr. R. H. Felix calls "a sense of participation and continued purpose in life." It probably comprises many elements—useful activity, companionship, self-respect, and other conditions pertinent to psychological security. The relevancy of this factor is suggested by the comparatively high rate of admission to mental hospitals of persons who live alone, are widowed or divorced, or are seeking work. It is further suggested by the high rates of disabling illness among unemployed persons and unmarried women and by the high rates of mortality among unmarried persons. Particularly for the elderly retired person, a sense of purpose and of continuing participation in life is essential.

6. *More definitive research is needed on the health of the aging, including the interrelationships of health and socioeconomic factors.*

The results of medical research, such as laboratory investigations of the etiology of cancer and of circulatory disorders, will probably have in the future a marked influence on the health of older persons. It is conjectural, however, whether all the physical ailments associated with aging can be controlled in the near future, if ever. One consequence of this research, nevertheless, is likely to be a further increase in average life-expectancy, with additional millions of men and women surviving into advanced years. The critical question will remain: Shall the additional years be healthful in the broad sense of the term "health"?

Efforts toward making the added years of life healthy will necessitate not only more intensive research in the biology and chemistry of disease but also more extensive study of the impact on health of socioeconomic factors (e.g., occupation, marital status, economic position, social attitudes). Longitudinal studies should be particularly fruitful.

Thus improvement of health of the aging may depend in no small measure on clarification of such questions as: What are the supporting factors that enable so many aged persons with chronic conditions to pursue their normal activities? What is the significance of non-manifest, asymptomatic chronic diseases in the elderly? Why is the arteriosclerotic heart disease death rate for men so much higher than that of women? What are the motivational factors in periodic health examinations? In the development of good personal health habits? Is there a long-term trend of increase in the rate of serious disability in the adult population, and, if so, what are the causes? What can be done in our society to assure a "sense of participation and purpose in life" among older people?

REFERENCES

ANDERSON, O. W., and FELDMAN, J. J. 1956. Family medical costs and voluntary health insurance: a nationwide survey. London: Blakiston Division, McGraw-Hill Book Co.

BAKER, J. P., BALLOU, H. C., MORHOUS, E. J., CRUMPACKER, E. L., and BRAY, S. P. 1956. The effectiveness of periodical medical evaluation. Indust. Med., **25**, 248–50.

BORTZ, E. L. 1957a. The vitality of the vascular system. Geriatrics, **12**, 275–83.

———. 1957b. Stress and exhaustion. Second of series of papers on various aspects of aging. J.A.M.A., **164**, 2059–60.

BREWSTER, AGNES W. 1958. I. Health insurance coverage by age and sex, September 1956. (Research and Statistics Note No. 13.) Washington, D.C.: Social Security Administration, Division of Program Research. (Offset.)

BRITTEN, R. H., COLLINS, S. D., and FITZ-GERALD, J. S. 1940. The National Health Survey: some general findings as to disease, accidents, and impairments in urban areas. Pub. Health Rep., **65**, 444–70.

BURNEY, L. E. 1956. Programs for the aged. Pub. Health Rep., **71**, 1168–69.

———. 1957. Health problems of the aging: a challenge to preventive medicine. J.A.M.A., **165**, 440–43.

BUSSE, E. W. 1957. Mental health in advanced maturity. *In* WILMA DONAHUE and C. TIBBITTS (eds.), The new frontiers of aging, pp. 143–51. Ann Arbor: University of Michigan Press.

CALIFORNIA DEPARTMENT OF PUBLIC HEALTH. 1958. California Health Survey. Health in California. Sacramento: Documents Section, California State Printing Office.

CAMERON, N. 1956. Neuroses of later maturity. *In* O. J. KAPLAN (ed.), Mental disorders in later life, pp. 201–43. 2d ed. Stanford, Calif.: Stanford University Press.

CHOPE, H. D., and BRESLOW, L. 1956. Nutritional status of the aging. Am. J. Pub. Health, **46**, 61–67.

CIOCCO, A., and LAWRENCE, P. S. 1952. Illness among older people in Hagerstown, Maryland. *In* Illness and health services in an aging population: four papers . . . second International Gerontological Congress, St. Louis, Missouri, . . . 1951, pp. 26–37. (Public Health Service Pub. 170.) Washington, D.C.: Government Printing Office.

COLLINS, S. D. 1951. Sickness surveys. *In* H. EMERSON (ed.), Administrative medicine, pp. 511–35. New York: Thomas Nelson & Sons.

COLLINS, S. D., PHILLIPS, F. RUTH, and OLIVER, DOROTHY S. 1950. Specific causes of illness found in monthly canvasses of families—sample of the Eastern Health District of Baltimore, 1938–43. Pub. Health. Rep., **65**, 1235–64.

———. 1951*a*. Age incidence of specific causes of illness found in monthly canvasses of families—sample of the Eastern Health District of Baltimore, 1938–43. *Ibid.*, **66**, 1227–45.

———. 1951*b*. Disabling illness from specific causes among males and females of various ages—sample of white families canvassed at monthly intervals in the Eastern Health District of Baltimore, 1938–43. *Ibid.*, pp. 1649–71.

COLLINS, S. D., TRANTHAM, KATHARINE S., and LEHMANN, JOSEPHINE L. 1955. Sickness experience in selected areas of the United States. (Public Health Service Pub. 390.) Washington, D.C.: Government Printing Office.

COMMISSION ON CHRONIC ILLNESS. 1956. Chronic illness in the United States, Vol. **2**: Care of the long-term patient. Cambridge, Mass.: Harvard University Press.

———. 1957*a*. Chronic illness in the United States, Vol. **1**: Prevention of chronic illness. Cambridge, Mass.: Harvard University Press.

———. 1957*b*. Chronic illness in the United States, Vol. **4**: Chronic illness in a large city—the Baltimore study. Cambridge, Mass.: Harvard University Press.

COMMITTEE FOR THE SPECIAL RESEARCH PROJECT IN THE HEALTH INSURANCE PLAN OF GREATER NEW YORK. 1957. Health and medical care in New York City: a report by the Committee. . . . Cambridge, Mass.: Harvard University Press.

CONFERENCE [ON] PREVENTIVE ASPECTS OF CHRONIC DISEASE. 1952. Proceedings, Conference [in] 1951, Chicago, Illinois, sponsored by the Commission on Chronic Illness, National Health Council, and the Public Health Service. Baltimore: The Commission.

CORSON, J. J., and McCONNELL, J. W. 1956. Economic needs of older people. New York: Twentieth Century Fund.

COUNCIL OF STATE GOVERNMENTS. 1950. The mental health programs of the forty-eight states: a report to the Governors' Conference. Chicago: The Council.

DOMINION BUREAU OF STATISTICS AND THE DEPARTMENT OF NATIONAL HEALTH AND WELFARE. 1955. Canadian sickness survey 1950–51, No. 7: Incidence and prevalence of illness, national estimates. Ottawa: Edmond Cloutier, Queen's Printer.

DONAHUE, WILMA. 1957. Emerging principles and concepts: a summary. *In* WILMA DONAHUE and C. TIBBITTS (eds.), The new frontiers of aging, pp. 198–206. Ann Arbor: University of Michigan Press.

DORN, H. F., and CUTLER, S. J. 1955. Morbidity from cancer in the United States, Part I: Variation in incidence by age, sex, race, marital status, and geographic region. (Public Health Service Pub. 418.) Washington, D.C.: Government Printing Office.

DUBLIN, L. I., LOTKA, A. J., and SPIEGELMAN, M. 1949. Length of life: a study of the life table. Rev. ed. New York: Ronald Press Co.

DUBLIN, L. I., and SPIEGELMAN, M. 1952. Factors in the higher mortality of our older age groups. Am. J. Pub. Health, **42**, 422–29.

FELIX, R. H. 1951. Mental health in an aging population. *In* WILMA DONAHUE and C. TIBBITTS (eds.), Growing in the older years, pp. 23–44. Ann Arbor: University of Michigan Press.

FELIX, R. H., and KRAMER, M. 1953. Extent of the problem of mental disorders. Ann. Am. Acad. Political & Social Sc., **286**, 5–14.

FRANCO, S. C. 1956. The early detection of disease by periodic examination. Indust. Med., **25**, 251–57.

GOLDSTEIN, M. S. 1954. Longevity and health

status of whites and nonwhites in the United States. J. Nat. M.A., **46**, 83–104.

GOLDSTEIN, M. S., and SPECTOR, M. I. 1958. Cost of hospitalized acute illness in old age. (Unpublished manuscript in files, Division of Public Health Methods, Public Health Service.)

GRUENBERG, E. M. 1957. Application of control methods to mental illness. Am. J. Pub. Health, **47**, 944–52.

HEALTH INFORMATION FOUNDATION. 1956. Increasing life expectancy at birth. Progress in Health Services, Vol. **5**, No. 4. New York: The Foundation.

———. 1958a. Improvements in urban health. Progress in Health Services, Vol. **7**, No. 1. New York: The Foundation.

———. 1958b. The health of the nonwhite population. Progress in Health Services, Vol. **7**, No. 4. New York: The Foundation.

———. 1958c. An inventory of social and economic research in health. 7th ed. New York: The Foundation.

HOLLAND, DOROTHY F., and PERROTT, G. ST.J. 1938. Health of the Negro. Part I. Disabling illness among Negroes and low-income white families in New York City—a report of a sickness survey in the spring of 1933. Milbank Mem. Fund. Quart., **16**, 5–38.

HOLLANDER, F., and DUNNING, J. M. 1939. A study by age and sex of the incidence of dental caries in over 12,000 persons. J. Dent. Res., **18**, 43–60.

HOLLE, H. A. 1957. Health maintenance for the oldster. Fourth of series of papers on various aspects of aging. J.A.M.A., **165**, 164–66.

JOHNSON, W. M. 1957. The oldster and his doctor. First of a series of papers on various aspects of aging. J.A.M.A., **164**, 1928–31.

JOINT COMMISSION ON MENTAL ILLNESS AND HEALTH. 1957. First annual report of the Joint Commission . . . year 1956. Cambridge, Mass.: The Commission.

KLUMPP, T. G. 1957. Control of fatigue in older persons. J.A.M.A., **165**, 605–7.

KRAMER, M. 1956. Facts needed to assess public health and social problems in the widespread use of the tranquilizing drugs. (Public Health Service Pub. 486.) Washington, D.C.: Government Printing Office.

KRUEGER, D. E. 1957. Measurement of prevalence of chronic disease by household interviews and clinical evaluations. Am. J. Pub. Health, **47**, 953–60.

LAWRENCE, P. S. 1958. Availability for work: chronic disease and limitation of activity.

(Public Health Service Pub. 556.) Washington, D.C.: Government Printing Office.

MONROE, R. T. 1951. Diseases in old age: a clinical and pathological study of 7941 individuals over 61 years of age. Cambridge, Mass.: Harvard University Press.

MORIYAMA, I. M., WOOLSEY, T. D., and STAMLER, J. 1958. Observations on possible factors responsible for the sex and race trends in cardiovascular-renal mortality in the United States. J. Chronic Dis., **7**, 401–12.

MOUNTIN, J. W. 1951. Community health services for older people. *In* WILMA DONAHUE and C. TIBBITTS (eds.), Growing in the older years, pp. 71–83. Ann Arbor: University of Michigan Press.

MYERS, R. J. 1954a. Mortality after retirement. Social Security Bull., **17**, No. 6 (June), 3–7.

———. 1954b. Factors in interpreting mortality after retirement. J. Am. Statistical A., **49**, 499–509.

NATIONAL HEALTH EDUCATION COMMITTEE (comp.). 1957. Facts on the major killing and crippling diseases in the United States today. New York: The Committee.

NEW YORK STATE DEPARTMENT OF MENTAL HYGIENE, MENTAL HEALTH RESEARCH UNIT. 1958. Technical report. . . . Albany, N.Y.: State Department of Mental Hygiene.

PELTON, W. J., PENNELL, E. H., and DRUZINA, A. 1954. Tooth morbidity experience of adults. J. Am. Dent. A., **49**, 439–45.

PERROTT, G. ST.J. 1936. The state of the nation's health. Ann. Am. Acad. Political & Social Sc., **188**, 131–43.

PERROTT, G. ST.J., GOLDSTEIN, M. S., and COLLINS, S. D. 1952. Health status and health requirements of an aging population. *In* Illness and health services in an aging population: four papers . . . second International Gerontological Congress, St. Louis, Missouri, . . . 1951, pp. 1–25. (Public Health Service Pub. 170.) Washington, D.C.: Government Printing Office.

PHILADELPHIA MENTAL HEALTH SURVEY COMMITTEE. 1954. Old age and mental disease. Supplemental report of the . . . Committee, appointed by Honorable John S. Fine to make a study of the mental health needs of the Philadelphia area. Philadelphia: The Committee.

POLLACK, H. 1957. Nutritional problems in the aging and aged. (Fifth of series of papers on various aspects of aging.) J.A.M.A., **165**, 257–58.

PRIEST, W. S. 1957. Anticipation and management of cardiac decompensation. Geriatrics, 12, 290–96.

RESEARCH COUNCIL FOR ECONOMIC SECURITY. 1957. Prolonged illness absenteeism: summary report. Study of prolonged absences due to nonoccupational disabilities among employed persons in private nonagricultural industries in the United States, 1953–1956. Chicago: The Council.

ROBERTS, N. J. 1958. The periodic evaluation of health. Indust. Med., 27, 153–58.

———. 1959. The values and limitations of periodic health examinations. J. Chronic Dis., 9, 95–116.

ROSEN, J. C. 1957. Utilizing older workers in small industry. ("Management Aids for Small Manufacturers," No. 81.) Washington, D.C.: Small Business Administration. (Offset.)

ROSENFELD, L. S., DONABEDIAN, S., and KATZ, J. 1957. Medical care needs and services in the Boston Metropolitan Area. Boston: United Community Services of Metropolitan Boston.

ROSENFELD, L. S., MOTT, F. D., and TAYLOR, M. G. 1952. Health services for the aging in Saskatchewan. *In* Illness and health services in an aging population: four papers . . . second International Gerontological Congress, St. Louis, Missouri, . . . 1951, pp. 51–68. (Public Health Service Pub. 170.) Washington, D.C.: Government Printing Office.

ROTHSCHILD, D. 1956. Senile psychoses and psychoses with cerebral arteriosclerosis. *In* O. J. KAPLAN (ed.), Mental disorders in later life, pp. 289–331. 2d ed. Stanford, Calif.: Stanford University Press.

SHOCK, N. W. 1950. Broadening horizons in gerontology. *In* WILMA DONAHUE and C. TIBBITTS (eds.), Planning the older years, pp. 9–30. Ann Arbor: University of Michigan Press.

SPIES, T. D. 1958. Some recent advances in nutrition. J.A.M.A., 167, 675–90.

STIEGLITZ, E. J. 1956. Orientation of the problems. *In* O. J. KAPLAN (ed.), Mental disorders in later life, pp. 476–96. 2d ed. Stanford, Calif.: Stanford University Press.

STREIB, G. F., and THOMPSON, W. E. 1957. Personal and social adjustment in retirement. *In* WILMA DONAHUE and C. TIBBITTS (eds.), The new frontiers of aging, pp. 180–97. Ann Arbor: University of Michigan Press.

SYDENSTRICKER, E. 1933. Health and environment. New York: McGraw-Hill Book Co.

THOMPSON, W. E., and STREIB, G. F. 1957. Re-

tirement and health. Paper presented at the annual meeting of the Gerontological Society, Cleveland.

TRELOAR, A. E., and CHILL, D. 1957. Sense or jabberwocky? Hospitals, 31, No. 12, 34–36, 114.

TURNER, VIOLET B. 1952. Hagerstown health studies: an annotated bibliography. (Public Health Service Pub. 148.) Washington D.C.: Government Printing Office.

TYHURST, J. S., SALK, L., and KENNEDY, MIRIAM. 1957. Mortality, morbidity and retirement. Am. J. Pub. Health, 47, 1434–44.

U.S. BUREAU OF THE CENSUS. 1952. United States Census of Population, 1950, Vol. 2: Characteristics of the population, Part 1, U.S. summary, Chapter B. Washington, D.C.: Government Printing Office.

———. 1953. United States Census of Population, 1950, Vol. 4: Special reports, Part 2, Chapter C, Institutional population. Washington, D.C.: Government Printing Office.

———. 1955a. Estimates of the population of the United States, by age, color, race, and sex, July 1, 1950 to 1955. Current Population Reports: Population Estimates. (Series P-25, No. 121.) Washington, D.C.: Government Printing Office.

———. 1955b. Marital status and family status, April 1954. Current Population Reports: Population Characteristics. (Series P-20, No. 56.) Washington, D.C.: Government Printing Office.

———. 1956. Income of persons in the United States, 1955. Current Population Reports: Consumer Income. (Series P-60, No. 23.) Washington, D.C.: Government Printing Office.

———. 1957. Estimates of the population of the United States, by age, color, and sex, July 1, 1955 to 1957. Current Population Reports: Population Estimates. (Series P-25, No. 170.) Washington, D.C.: Government Printing Office.

———. 1958a. Marital status, economic status, and family status, March 1957. Current Population Reports: Population Characteristics. (Series P-20, No. 81.) Washington, D.C.: Government Printing Office.

———. 1958b. Illustrative projections of the population of the United States, by age and sex 1960 to 1980. Current Population Reports: Population Estimates. (Series P-25, No. 187.) Washington, D.C.: Government Printing Office.

U.S. BUREAU OF LABOR STATISTICS. 1957a.

Comparative job performance by age: large plants in the men's footwear and household furniture industries. (Bull. 1223.) Washington, D.C.: Government Printing Office.

U.S. BUREAU OF LABOR STATISTICS. 1957b. Employment and economic status of older men and women. (Bull. 1213.) Washington, D.C.: Government Printing Office.

U.S. DEPARTMENT OF HEALTH, EDUCATION, AND WELFARE. 1959. Hospitalization insurance for OASDI beneficiaries. Report submitted to the U.S. House of Representatives, Committee on Ways and Means, by the Secretary of Health, Education, and Welfare. Committee Print. Washington, D.C.: Government Printing Office.

U.S. NATIONAL CANCER INSTITUTE. 1958. The extent of cancer illness in the United States. (Public Health Service Pub. 547.) Washington, D.C.: Government Printing Office.

U.S. NATIONAL COMMITTEE ON VITAL AND HEALTH STATISTICS. 1953. Proposal for collection of data on illness and impairments, United States: a report of the Subcommittee on National Morbidity Survey. (Public Health Service Pub. 333.) Washington, D.C.: Government Printing Office.

U.S. NATIONAL HEALTH SURVEY. 1958a. Origin and program of the U.S. National Health Survey. (Series A-1.) (Public Health Service Pub. 584-A1.) Washington, D.C.: Government Printing Office.

———. 1958b. Health statistics from . . . Survey: Preliminary report on volume of dental care, United States, July–September 1957. (Series B-2.) (Public Health Service Pub. 584-B2.) Washington, D.C.: Government Printing Office.

———. 1958c. Health statistics from . . . Survey: Preliminary report on number of persons injured, July–December 1957. (Series B-3.) (Public Health Service Pub. 584-B3.) Washington, D.C.: Government Printing Office.

———. 1958d. Health statistics from . . . Survey: Preliminary report on disability, United States, July–September 1957. (Series B-4.) (Public Health Service Pub. 584-B4.) Washington, D.C.: Government Printing Office.

———. 1958e. Health statistics from . . . Survey: Selected Survey Topics, United States, July 1957—June 1958. (Series B-5.) (Public Health Service Pub. 584-B5.) Washington, D.C.: Government Printing Office.

U.S. NATIONAL OFFICE OF VITAL STATISTICS. 1954. History and organization of the vital statistics system. *In* Vital statistics of the United States, 1950, Vol. 1: Analysis and summary tables . . . pp. 1–19. Washington, D.C.: Government Printing Office.

———. 1956a. Mortality in the age group 45 to 64 years: United States, 1900–1950. Vital Statistics—Special Reports, Vol. 45, No. 6. Washington, D.C.: Government Printing Office.

———. 1956b. Mortality from selected causes by marital status, United States, 1949–51. Vital Statistics—Special Reports, Vol. 39, No. 7. Washington, D.C.: Government Printing Office.

———. 1956c. Mortality in the age group 65 years and over, United States, 1900–1950. Vital Statistics—Special Reports, Vol. 45, No. 7. Washington, D.C.: Government Printing Office.

———. 1957a. Abridged life tables: United States, 1955. Vital Statistics—Special Reports, Vol. 46, No. 9. Washington, D.C.: Government Printing Office.

———. 1957b. Accident fatalities, United States and each state, 1955. Vital Statistics—Special Reports, Vol. 46, No. 10. Washington, D.C.: Government Printing Office.

———. 1957c. Mortality from selected causes, by age, race, and sex: United States, 1955. Vital Statistics—Special Reports, Vol. 46, No. 5. Washington, D.C.: Government Printing Office.

———. 1957d. Summary of vital statistics: United States, 1955. Vital Statistics—Special Reports, Vol. 46, No. 19. Washington, D.C.: Government Printing Office.

———. 1957e. Vital statistics of the United States, 1955, Vol. 1: Introduction . . . ; Vol. 2: Mortality data. Washington, D.C.: Government Printing Office.

U.S. PUBLIC HEALTH SERVICE. 1951. The National Health Survey, 1935–36, Part 1: Scope and method; Part 2: Annotated bibliography. (Public Health Service Pub. 85.) Washington, D.C.: Government Printing Office.

———. 1957a. The older person in the home: some suggestions for health and happiness in the 3-generation family. (Public Health Service Pub. 542.) Washington, D.C.: Government Printing Office.

———. 1957b. Sources of morbidity data, listing No. 5, 1957. (Public Health Service Pub. 565.) Washington, D.C.: Government Printing Office.

WEEKS, H. A., DAVIS, MARJORIE B., and FREE-

MAN, H. E. [1958.] Apathy of families toward medical care: an exploratory study. New York: New York University, Department of Sociology. (Offset.)

WHITE, P. D. 1957. The role of exercise in the aging. Third of series of papers on various aspects of aging. J.A.M.A., **165**, 70–71.

WHITTENBERGER, J. L. 1956. The nature of the response to stress with aging. Bull. New York Acad. Med., **32**, 329–36.

WOOLSEY, T. D. 1952. Estimates of disabling illness prevalence in the United States. Based on the Current Population Survey of February 1949 and September 1950. (Public Health Service Pub. 181.) Washington, D.C.: Government Printing Office.

WOOLSEY, T. D., and NISSELSON, H. 1956. Some problems in the statistical measurement of chronic disease. Reprinted from a collection, Improving the quality of statistical surveys: papers contributed as a memorial to Samuel Weiss, sponsored by the Washington Statistical Society in Collaboration with the American Statistical Association, pp. 75–87. Washington, D.C.: Public Health Service, Division of Public Health Methods.

WORLD HEALTH ORGANIZATION. 1946. Constitution of the World Health Organization. Pub. Health Rep., **61**, 1268–77.

———. 1957. International classification of diseases: manual of the International Statistical Classification of Diseases, Injuries, and Causes of Death, Vol. **1**. (1955. Rev. ed.) Geneva: World Health Organization.

AUTHORS' NOTE.—Since the statistical material for the first printing was compiled, more recent data on the health status of older persons have been published by several sources, among them the National Health Survey Program of the United States Public Health Service. See, for example, *Health Statistics from the U.S. National Health Survey* (Series B and Series C-4 [Washington, D.C.: Government Printing Office]).

VIII

Aging and Income Security[1]

MARGARET S. GORDON

I. INTRODUCTION

A. The Problem of Poverty among the Aged

During the last two decades the United States has made substantial progress toward the development of a comprehensive system of economic security for older persons. Yet poverty among the aged remains one of our most persistent and difficult economic and social problems. As recently as 1957, slightly more than a sixth of all persons aged 65 or over in the United States had no income, and about three-fifths had incomes of less than $1000 a year (U.S. Bureau of the Census, 1958a).

Unlike the situation that formerly prevailed, aged families and individuals now represent a large proportion of low-income groups. As one writer has put it, the lowest-income groups today "are composed, to a large extent, of 'broken' families, aged persons, and others who live on fixed incomes or who are unable to take full advantage of the increased employment opportunities" (Miller, 1951, p. 218). Prolonged illness and disability are also important factors in explaining low-income status. It scarcely needs to be added that dur-

ing economic recessions the families of unemployed workers constitute a larger proportion of the lowest-income groups than in periods of relatively full employment.

THE IMPACT OF URBANIZATION AND INDUSTRIALIZATION

It has sometimes been implied that the problem of poverty among the aged is largely a result of industrialization. This is not altogether true. It would be more accurate to say that, under conditions of industrialization, poverty in old age tends to become a major social problem, whereas in agrarian societies the problem is usually handled through the extended family structure or through a feudal social structure.

The forces responsible for this development have been demographic, economic, and social. The long-run decline in both death rates and birth rates has resulted in a rising proportion of elderly persons in the population, although the relatively high birth rates that have prevailed since the early 1940's have resulted in a slowing-down of this trend.[2] The changes in technology and in the occupational structure of the labor force brought on by industrialization have tended to place older people at a disadvantage in competing for available jobs, to bring on relatively earlier retirement from the labor force, and to render the transition from full-time work to

[1] This chapter has benefited greatly from the many constructive suggestions and critical comments of those who read an earlier draft. Particular mention should be made of Dorothy McCamman, Herman M. and Anne R. Somers, and Peter O. Steiner.

[For the second printing of this volume data on the 1960 amendments are included on page 260.]

[2] For more extensive discussion of these developments see chaps. ii, iv, and xiv.

208

retirement a more disrupting and more abrupt process for the average worker. Finally, the increase in geographical mobility and the process of urbanization that have accompanied industrialization have tended to weaken family ties and to change the attitudes of adult sons and daughters toward the support of elderly parents.

It must be recognized, in this connection, that even before the industrial revolution the rapidly growing urban communities of England and continental Europe were encountering the problem of poverty and devising methods of dealing with it and that the aged represented an important sector of the poor. Nor was the problem of poverty among the aged unknown in the ancient world. In an important sense, the emergence of the social problem of poverty among the aged has been associated with urbanization rather than with industrialization per se, although the two developments have clearly been closely associated.

CHANGES IN THE ECONOMIC STATUS OF THE AGED

In what ways has the economic status of the aged changed in recent decades? Unfortunately, this question cannot be answered with any degree of precision, since adequate income data have not been collected until comparatively recent years.

Between 1948 and 1957 the money incomes of elderly persons rose appreciably, although their incomes in the latter year still tended to be far below those of persons in the age groups from 20 to 64. According to the Current Population Survey of the Bureau of the Census, the median income of men aged 65 and over increased from $998 in 1948 to $1421 in 1957, or 42 per cent (see Table 1).[3] Although this was a substantial increase, it was somewhat smaller than the 54 per cent increase in median income of all men during the same period. The medians apply only to men

[3] Data on the distribution of income for persons aged 65 and over are presented in chap. xiv, Table 10.

with income, but the data also show that the proportion of elderly men reporting *some* income increased from 89 per cent in 1948 to 95 per cent in 1957.

The incomes of women rose substantially less than those of men during this period, but incomes of elderly women increased, percentagewise, considerably more than did those of all women. The median income of women aged 65 and over rose from $589 to $741, or about 26 per cent, as compared with an increase of only 19 per cent for all women with income. There was an appreciable increase, also, in the proportion of aged women reporting some income—from about 49 per cent in 1948 to 72 per cent in 1957.

These changes in the money-income position of elderly men and women reflect in considerable part, as we shall see at a later point, a marked rise in the proportion receiving old age and survivors insurance during this period, as well as a substantial increase in benefit levels under the program. Aged persons also benefited to some extent from the rise in wage levels that occurred between the two dates, but not so much as persons in younger age groups with higher rates of labor-force participation. In fact, the proportion of aged men in the labor force declined almost steadily during this period—from 46.8 per cent in 1948 to 37.5 per cent in 1957—while the proportion of elderly women in the labor force rose only slightly—from 9.1 per cent in the earlier year to 10.5 per cent in the later year (U.S. Bureau of the Census, 1949, 1958b).

Family income data present a somewhat less favorable picture of the relative change in the money-income status of the aged during this period. The median income of families with heads aged 65 or over rose from $1907 in 1948 to $2490 in 1957, or 31 per cent, as compared with a 56 per cent increase for all families (U.S. Bureau of the Census, 1950, 1958a). Aged unrelated individuals (persons not living with any relatives) experienced an increase of

32 per cent in median income between the two years, whereas the median income of all unrelated individuals rose 50 per cent. Many factors are responsible for this differing picture presented by family and individual income data, but there is one that is particularly deserving of mention, since it probably reflects a significant long-run trend. The proportion of elderly people who are maintaining their own households is apparently rising as the income status of elderly persons improves. Census data indicate that the proportion of elderly men and women who were classified as household heads or wives of heads rose between 1947 and 1953, while the proportion clas-

sified as "other relatives of head" declined (U.S. Bureau of the Census, 1948, 1953). Since these changes are probably occurring chiefly among those with relatively low incomes, they would tend to depress the rise in income for aged family heads and unrelated individuals.

Thus far we have been considering only changes in *money* incomes of the aged. Between 1948 and 1957 the BLS consumer price index rose 17 per cent (U.S. Bureau of Labor Statistics, 1958). This was substantially less than the percentage increase in income of either elderly individuals or families with aged heads during the same period, suggesting that the real income po-

TABLE 1*

MEDIAN INCOME OF PERSONS 14 YEARS OF AGE AND OVER WITH INCOME, AND PERCENTAGE
WITH INCOME, BY AGE AND SEX, UNITED STATES, 1948 AND 1957

YEAR AND INCOME STATUS	AGE							
	All Ages	14–19	20–24	25–34	35–44	45–54	55–64	65 and Over
	Men							
1948:								
Total no.	52,681	6,027	5,518	11,050	9,969	8,366	6,547	5,205
Per cent with income	89.9	44.2	91.2	97.5	98.5	97.8	95.6	89.1
Median income	$2,396	$ 449	$1,849	$2,724	$3,046	$2,828	$2,412	$ 998
1957:								
Total no.	57,583	7,074	4,587	11,154	11,264	9,680	7,166	6,658
Per cent with income	91.8	51.6	94.2	98.4	98.7	98.1	97.2	95.2
Median income	$3,684	$ 411	$2,377	$4,372	$4,745	$4,494	$3,681	$1,421
1948–57 (percentage change):								
Per cent with income	+ 2.1	+16.7	+ 3.3	+ 0.9	+ 0.2	+ 0.3	+ 1.7	+ 6.8
Median income	+53.8	− 8.5	+28.6	+60.5	+55.8	+58.9	+52.6	+42.4
	Women							
1948:								
Total no.	55,592	6,338	5,930	11,932	10,436	8,590	6,594	5,772
Per cent with income	40.9	32.9	50.8	38.9	41.2	39.3	37.2	49.4
Median income	$1,009	$ 479	$1,319	$1,349	$1,333	$1,310	$ 857	$ 589
1957:								
Total no.	62,219	7,376	5,373	11,839	11,916	10,094	7,709	7,912
Per cent with income	52.6	42.8	61.3	45.6	49.4	52.9	51.3	71.8
Median income	$1,199	$ 388	$1,638	$1,717	$1,784	$1,818	$1,342	$ 741
1948–57 (percentage change):								
Per cent with income	+28.6	+30.1	+20.7	+17.2	+19.9	+34.6	+37.9	+45.3
Median income	+18.8	−19.0	+24.2	+27.3	+33.8	+38.7	+56.6	+25.8

* Source: U.S. Bureau of the Census, *Current Population Reports: Consumer Income*, Series P-60, No. 6, February 14, 1950, and Series P-60, No. 30, December, 1958.

sition of the aged improved considerably. At a later point we shall consider some of the complications involved in any attempt at careful appraisal of the real income status of the aged.

Long-term analysis of changes in the income status of the aged is much more difficult, since adequate income data are not available. Beginning with a study conducted in Massachusetts in 1910, there were a large number of special surveys of the problem of old age dependency in the first few decades of the present century, but the methods used differed so widely that the results are, for the most part, not at all comparable (Massachusetts, 1910, 1914, 1916, 1925; Pennsylvania, 1919, 1925, 1926; New York, 1930; Connecticut, 1932). Some of the British social surveys, such as those conducted by Rowntree (1902, 1941) and Rowntree and Lavers (1951) in York, lend themselves to long-term comparison more readily than American studies, but it is hazardous to draw conclusions about changes in the income status of the aged even from these studies, since they shed no light on the incomes of elderly persons who were not family heads. As Rowntree himself pointed out, an elderly impoverished individual in England at the beginning of this century had to choose between living with relatives or going to the workhouse. Even so, taking into account evidence drawn from a number of British and American studies, it is probably safe to conclude that (1) the proportion of families and individuals living in acute poverty has diminished greatly since the beginning of this century in the Western industrialized nations; (2) the proportion of aged individuals living in acute poverty has also probably diminished but not as much; and (3) aged individuals and families headed by an aged person have come to represent a substantially larger percentage of the lowest-income groups. This latter development, however, reflects in part a rise in the proportion of aged persons in the population and a great-

er tendency for them to maintain their own households, as well as the impact of rising wage levels on the incomes of younger adults. To the extent that there has been a shift in sources of support of older people, it has been largely a shift from adult sons and daughters to society as a whole. There is little evidence that individual saving for old age has ever represented an important source of support for the great bulk of aged persons.

B. The Life-Cycle in Income, Spending, and Saving

INCOME OF PERSONS

The income status of the aged cannot be adequately interpreted without an analysis of the life-cycle in income, spending, and saving. An individual's income typically does not increase right up to the age of retirement but tends to rise from youth to some point in middle age and then to level off or decline.

Census income data indicate that median income is highest in the 35–44 age bracket for men and that age variations in male income increased between 1948 and 1956 (Fig. 1). This reflected the tendency for the median incomes of men in the age brackets from 25 to 54 to increase, percentagewise, considerably more than those of either younger or older men. However, men aged 65 or over experienced a substantial increase in median income, whereas youths aged 14–19, at the other end of the age scale, experienced an actual decline, probably reflecting a rise in the proportion of youthful workers who were engaged in part-time work (Bancroft, 1958).

The median incomes of women vary less with age than do those of men, partly because women in most age brackets are more likely to work part time or intermittently (Reder, 1954). But age variations in income have increased for women as well as for men in recent years, and there has been an interesting shift in the pattern of age variation, with women in the

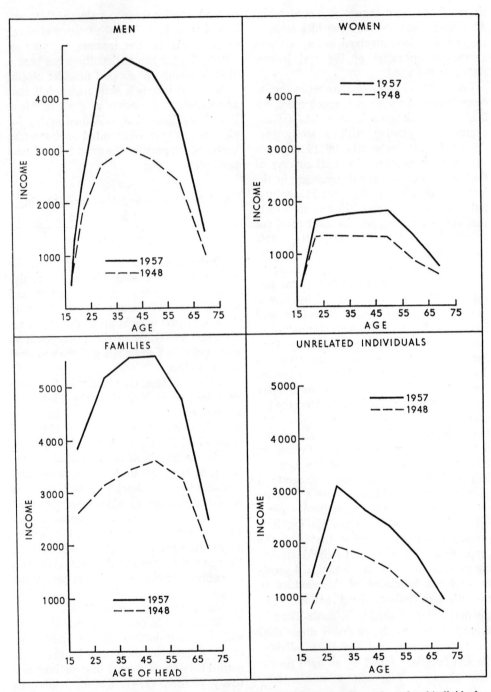

Fig. 1.—Median income by age, for men and women with income, families and unrelated individuals, United States, 1948 and 1957. (After U.S. Bureau of the Census, 1950, 1958a.)

age brackets from 35 to 64 gaining ground in relation to other age groups. These changes clearly reflect chiefly the marked increase that has been occurring in the proportion of women in these age brackets who are in the labor force.

Age variations in income partly reflect the fact that older people tend to have had less education than younger people, and income at all ages varies with education (Miller, 1955). Differences in the occupational distribution of workers in the various age groups, as well as differences in the life-cycle of earnings by occupation, also affect age variations in income, although the influences of education and occupation tend to be closely related. In addition, there is evidence of a considerable amount of downward occupational mobility in the later years of working life (Steiner and Dorfman, 1957).

An extremely important factor affecting age variations in income is the fact that the proportion of workers who are steadily employed on a full-time basis varies with age (see chap. x). Middle-aged males are more likely to be in the labor force, less likely to be unemployed, and less likely to be engaged in part-time work than either younger or older men (Fig. 2). However, the proportion of unemployed men who are out of work 15 weeks or longer tends to rise steadily with advancing age, reflecting the difficulty older men experience in finding re-employment.

Among women, it is those aged 20–24 who are most likely to be in the labor force and least likely to be engaged in part-time work. The proportion in the labor force rises to a second peak at ages 45–54 and drops off in the older age brackets. But the percentage of women who are unemployed falls off steadily with advancing age (probably reflecting some tendency for older women who fail to find employment to drop out or remain out of the labor force), while the percentage of women who are out

of work 15 weeks or longer *rises* steadily with age, as in the case of men.

INCOME OF FAMILIES

Median family income reaches its maximum point when the family head is aged 45–54. There has been a tendency for age variations in family income to increase in recent years, as in the case of personal income (see Fig. 1). The cross-sectional data that we have been examining thus far, however, do not tell us how the income of particular families or individuals changes over time. They simply tell us how income varies with age at a particular time. Since the long-run trend of income and wage levels has been predominantly upward, it is probable that most individuals and families reach their peak incomes somewhat later in life than the cross-sectional data indicate (Woytinsky, 1943).

For this reason the data collected in the Survey of Consumer Finances on the changes in income experienced by spending units during the preceding year are of special interest (Fig. 3). In both 1950 and 1955—years when income levels were rising—the great majority of spending units with heads in the 18–24 age bracket experienced an increase in income, but the proportion of spending units with rising incomes fell off steadily with advancing age of the head. From ages 45 to 54 on, a majority of spending units experienced either no substantial change in income or a decline. Although the proportion experiencing a decline tended to rise with advancing age, it represented a minority at all ages. These data suggest that there is a distinct tendency toward leveling-off in the income of spending units with heads aged 45 or more but that the majority do not experience an actual decline, at least in years of rising income levels. The fact that an abrupt drop in income typically occurs at the time of retirement is obscured in data combining all spending units headed by persons aged 65 or over.

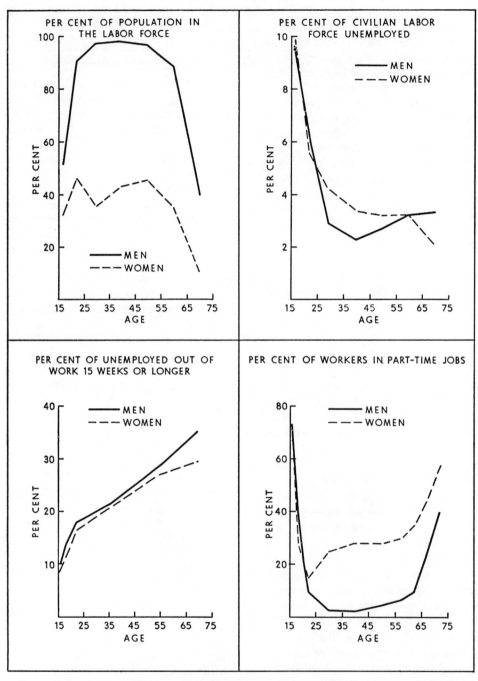

Fɪɢ. 2.—Labor-force participation, unemployment rates, duration of unemployment, and proportion of part-time workers, by age and sex, United States, 1956. (After U.S. Bureau of the Census, 1957a.)

214

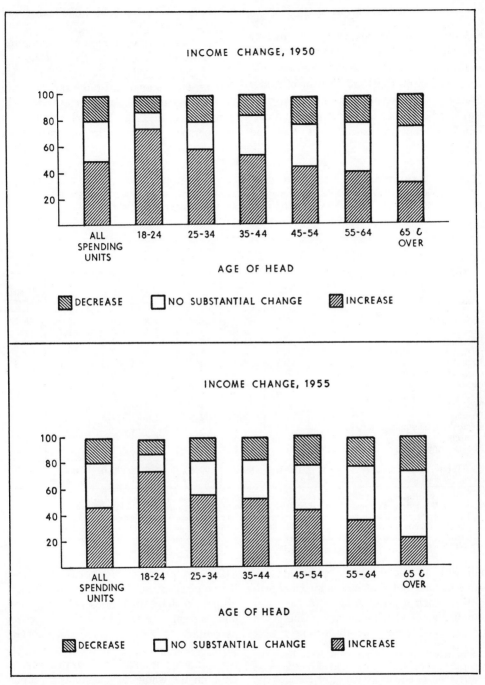

Fig. 3.—Percentage distribution of spending units by change in income from previous year and age of head, United States, 1950 and 1955. (After U.S. Board of Governors of the Federal Reserve System, 1951a, 1956.)

FAMILY EXPENDITURES

Family expenditures vary with income and family size.[4] The most complete data available on family consumption expenditures, based on the 1950 Bureau of Labor Statistics Survey of Consumer Expenditures, indicate that family income and current consumption expenditures rise and

maximum (Wharton School of Finance and Commerce, 1957).

The distribution of family consumption expenditures changes appreciably as the age of the family head changes. These variations can be analyzed most satisfactorily if family size and income class are held constant, as in Table 2, which relates to a two-person family with an income of

TABLE 2*

FAMILY EXPENDITURES FOR MAJOR GROUPS OF GOODS AND SERVICES PURCHASED FOR CURRENT
CONSUMPTION, TWO-PERSON FAMILIES WITH INCOME FROM $1000 TO $2000, BY
AGE OF FAMILY HEAD, URBAN UNITED STATES, 1950

(Percentage Distribution)

MAJOR GROUPS OF GOODS AND SERVICES	ALL FAMILIES	AGE OF FAMILY HEAD						
		Under 25	25–34	35–44	45–54	55–64	65–74	75 and Over
Food and beverages........	35.9	34.8	33.2	36.4	33.8	35.6	38.1	36.7
Tobacco.................	2.0	2.7	2.2	1.9	2.6	2.2	1.6	1.3
Housing†.................	14.8	16.0	15.8	13.4	14.6	13.3	14.7	18.4
Fuel, light, and refrigeration.	6.9	1.8	3.8	5.4	5.5	7.2	8.2	9.7
Household operation‡......	4.5	2.5	3.3	4.3	4.2	4.5	5.0	5.3
Furnishings and equipment..	5.3	8.1	7.1	5.9	4.0	5.7	4.8	4.6
Clothing and clothing services	7.6	11.6	10.8	12.6	8.1	6.7	6.2	5.0
Transportation§...........	8.8	9.0	11.1	7.3	11.9	10.7	6.2	5.8
Medical care..............	6.6	6.6	4.5	4.9	6.2	7.1	7.4	7.5
Personal care.............	2.3	2.6	2.9	2.9	2.4	2.3	2.0	1.7
Recreation, reading, and education.................	3.3	4.1	4.3	3.8	3.6	3.3	3.2	2.0
Miscellaneous............	1.9	0.2	0.8	1.0	2.9	1.4	2.6	1.9
Total................	99.9	100.0	99.8	99.8	99.8	100.0	100.0	99.9

* Source: Wharton School of Finance and Commerce, *Study of Consumer Expenditures, Incomes and Savings*, Vol. XVIII (tabulated by the U.S. Bureau of Labor Statistics) (Philadelphia: University of Pennsylvania, 1957), Tables 2-2 and 8-2.

† Includes rent, repairs, taxes, insurance and interest payments, and miscellaneous housing expenses.

‡ Includes laundry sent out, wages to domestic servants, telephone costs, and miscellaneous household expenses.

§ Includes net purchase price of automobiles, financing charges, costs of operating automobile, bus fares, and miscellaneous transportation expenses.

fall with advancing age in somewhat the same manner but that consumption expenditures reach a peak at ages 35–45, when family size is at a maximum, rather than at ages 45–55, when family income is at a

[4] In recent years several economists have developed theories of the consumption function that are relevant to an understanding of the life-cycle in the relationship (Duesenberry, 1952; Modigliani and Brumberg, 1954; Friedman, 1957), but, since these theories have been tested empirically only to a very limited extent, we shall not attempt to discuss them here.

$1000–$2000, chosen for analysis because it is typical in the aged population. Expenditures for food, fuel, household operation, and medical care tend to represent a rising percentage of total consumption expenditures, while spending on tobacco, furnishings and equipment, and transportation tend, on the whole, to decline as a proportion of the total with advancing age of the family head. Largely because families with young heads are predominantly renters, housing expenditures represent a relatively large proportion of total expenditures at first but decline in comparative importance with increasing homeownership. In the older age brackets, however, they tend to increase as a proportion of the total, reflecting the fact that homeownership drops off somewhat (see Table 2). Although elderly couples spend a larger proportion of their incomes on food than do younger couples in the same income class, the actual amounts spent by the elderly couples

head of the spending unit until about age 65, when it falls off substantially (Table 3). But the proportion saving 10 per cent or more of income rises to a plateau in middle age and declines after age 65. Furthermore, the proportion dissaving 10 per cent or more of income is appreciably higher among spending units with heads aged 65 or more than among younger spending units.

Since many individual spending units

TABLE 3*

INCOME SAVED OR DISSAVED BY AGE OF HEAD OF SPENDING UNIT
UNITED STATES, 1950

AGE OF HEAD†	ALL CASES		INCOME SAVERS			ZERO SAVERS	INCOME DISSAVERS		
	No.	Per Cent	Positive Savers‡	Percentage of Income Saved			Nega-tive Savers	Percentage of Income Dissaved	
				10 and Over	1–9			1–9	10 and Over
All spending units .	3415	100	61	37	24	7	32	12	20
18–24............	269	100	60	29	31	6	34	17	17
25–34............	711	100	61	38	23	3	36	15	21
35–44............	781	100	65	40	25	4	31	14	17
45–54............	659	100	63	42	21	6	31	10	21
55–64............	540	100	66	40	26	6	28	9	19
65 or over.......	434	100	46	26	20	19	35	8	27

* Source: U.S. Board of Governors of the Federal Reserve System, "1951 Survey of Consumer Finances," Part IV: "Distribution of Consumer Saving in 1950," *Federal Reserve Bulletin*, Vol. 37 (September, 1951).

† Data for individual age-of-head groups exclude spending units for which age of head was not ascertained and thus add to less than 3415 cases.

‡ Positive savers are spending units with money incomes in excess of expenditures, and negative savers (dissavers) are spending units with expenditures in excess of money incomes.

are smaller. To some extent, because their incomes are lower, elderly couples are forced to allocate larger proportions of their incomes to necessities.

FAMILY SAVING

At all stages of the life-cycle there are families and individuals that save substantial amounts and others that do not save at all or spend more than their incomes, drawing on assets or increasing their indebtedness (dissaving). The proportion of positive savers among spending units does not change markedly with advancing age of the

experience appreciable fluctuations from year to year in income and family needs, data relating to asset holdings and indebtedness are needed to provide an adequate picture of the extent to which spending units succeed in saving for old age. These data, as shown in Table 4, indicate that amounts of financial assets held by spending units tend to increase steadily with advancing age of the head up to about age 65, after which they drop off. Similarly, the proportion owning homes increases sharply prior to age 35, but it falls off somewhat after age 65. The great majority of spending units own some life insurance in all age groups through the 55–64 age bracket, but here again the percentage falls off sharply for the 65 and over group. Data on average amounts held by age are not available, but the average amount of life insurance owned per American family in 1957 was $8300 (Institute of Life Insurance, 1958). However, average amounts held varied sharply with income, and the amounts held by low-income families would tend to be much smaller than this.

II. BUDGETS FOR ELDERLY PERSONS AND COUPLES

A. Total Consumption Needs

Unfortunately, there have been few studies of the consumption needs of aged couples or individuals, and such nation-wide studies as have been undertaken are out of date. A budget study published by the Social Security Administration in 1948, presenting a budget for an elderly couple liv-

TABLE 4*

PERCENTAGE FINANCIAL ASSETS, HOMEOWNERSHIP, AND DEBT STATUS OF
SPENDING UNITS BY AGE OF HEAD, UNITED STATES, EARLY 1957

AGE OF HEAD†	TOTAL FINANCIAL ASSETS‡									PER CENT OWNING LIFE INSURANCE POLICY	PER CENT OWNING HOME	PER CENT WITH SOME DEBT	
	All Cases		Zero	$1–$499	$500–$1999	$2000–$9999	$10,000 and Over	Not Ascertained				Some Debt	Mortgage Debt Only
	No.	Per Cent											
All spending units.	3041	100	24	30	21	17	7	1		79	54	67	8
18–24	271	100	29	48	19	4	§	§		69	9	63	1
25–34	600	100	22	41	22	14	1	§		88	40	83	6
35–44	686	100	21	34	23	16	4	2		86	62	83	12
45–54	586	100	22	23	24	20	10	1		85	67	69	9
55–64	433	100	20	19	20	26	13	2		81	74	51	10
65 and over	420	100	31	14	18	24	11	2		56	64	30	5

* Source: U.S. Board of Governors of the Federal Reserve System, "1957 Survey of Consumer Finances, Housing and Durable Goods,"*Federal Reserve Bulletin,* **43** (June, 1957), 639, and "The Financial Position of Consumers," *ibid.,* August, 1957, pp. 895, 898, and 901.

† Data for individual age-of-head groups exclude spending units for which age of head was not ascertained and thus add to less than 3041 cases.

‡ Financial assets include U.S. government savings bonds, checking accounts, savings accounts in banks, postal savings, and shares in savings and loan associations and credit unions; marketable U.S. government bonds; corporate, state and local government bonds; and corporate stocks.

§ No cases reported or less than one-half of 1 per cent.

The data suggest that most spending units approach old age owning a home, a moderate amount of life insurance, and financial assets of less than $2000. The difficulty is that these holdings are clearly not enough to support an extended period of retirement. As Ewan Clague (1954) has pointed out, "To buy from an insurance company a modest annuity of say $75 a month beginning with age 65 requires for a man an accumulation of about $11,900, and for a woman, since women live longer than men, about $13,900" (p. 22).

ing alone in an urban area, provides the basis for most recent estimates of living costs for elderly couples and individuals (U.S. Social Security Administration, 1948). Steiner and Dorfman (1957), in their study of the economic status of the aged, utilized this budget, and other data based on earlier federal government studies of family expenditures, to develop estimates of the cost of living of various sectors of the aged population in 1951 (Table 5). Their estimates were developed at three levels, as follows:

1. The "standard" budget, which is the budget published by the Social Security Administration in 1948, adjusted for changes in the cost of living to 1951, represents "a modest but adequate level of living." It is "intended to include those goods and services that are necessary for a healthful, self-respecting mode of living that allows normal participation in the life of the community in accordance with current American standards" (U.S. Social Security Administration, 1948, p. 7).

2. The "cash equivalent standard" budget makes appropriate adjustments for the reduction in cash requirements attributable to homeownership and to the consumption of homegrown food by farm families.

3. The "subsistence" budget is intended to represent a critically low level of income and is arbitrarily defined as 70 per cent of the cash-equivalent standard budget.

The Welfare and Health Council of New York City (1955) developed a budget standard for elderly families and individuals in the city in 1954 that corresponds to the level of the elderly couple's budget of the Social Security Administration but incorporates recent information on consumer needs and practices. The total cost of goods and services for an elderly couple living alone in the city was estimated at $2137 if the head and his wife were both retired. Estimates for non-married elderly persons living alone ranged from about $2000, after taxes, for an employed man or woman to about $1500 for a woman not working or seeking work.

B. Consumption Needs for Particular Goods and Services

In developing the Social Security Administration's budget for an elderly couple, allowances for the various categories in the budget were largely determined on the basis of records of yearly expenditures obtained by the Bureau of Labor Statistics from families of the type represented

TABLE 5*

ANNUAL BUDGETS FOR AGED COUPLES AND UNRELATED INDIVIDUALS, LIVING
ALONE OR WITH NON-RELATIVES, UNITED STATES URBAN AND RURAL

(In 1951 Dollars)

TYPE OF BUDGET AND FAMILY STATUS	URBAN				RURAL NON-FARM†		RURAL FARM†	
	All Urban Areas	Population of Area			High	Low	High	Low
		1,000,000 and Over	250,000– 999,000	Under 250,000				
"Standard" budget:‡								
Couples......................	$1832	$1900	$1852	$1782	$1396	$1117	$1243	$ 931
Unrelated males..............	1121	1140	1112	1070	840	673	749	560
Unrelated females............	1064	1083	1056	1016	798	638	711	532
Cash equivalent standard budget:‡								
Couples......................	1731	1767	1723	1657	1258	1005	745	559
Unrelated males..............	980	998	973	937	714	572	448	336
Unrelated females............	931	948	923	889	678	542	426	319
"Subsistence" budget:‡								
Couples......................	1212	1237	1206	1160	881	704	522	391
Unrelated males..............	686	699	681	656	500	400	314	235
Unrelated females............	652	664	646	622	475	379	298	223

* Source: P. O. Steiner and R. Dorfman, *The Economic Status of the Aged* (Berkeley: University of California Press, 1957), pp. 204–6.

† Because of the inadequacy of the data available for estimating costs of living in rural non-farm and rural farm areas, high and low estimates were developed to give an indication of the range within which the estimates might be expected to fall for those areas.

‡ See text for description of these budgets.

in the budget (U.S. Social Security Administration, 1948). In the case of food and housing, however, scientific nutritional and housing standards were utilized to determine the total dollar amounts allotted. The food budget takes account of the fact that elderly people, largely because of their reduced physical activity, need fewer calories per day than younger persons. The housing budget assumes that the couple is living alone in a two- or three-room rented apartment, conforming to specific standards relating to structure, sanitation, heating and lighting, character of the neighborhood, and availability of community facilities.

The relative costs of the various items entering into the elderly couple's budget have changed appreciably since it was constructed. Increases in various major categories of the BLS Consumer Price Index from the 1947–49 base period to 1957 ranged from 7 per cent for apparel to 38 per cent for medical care (U.S. Bureau of Labor Statistics, 1958). In response to these differential price increases, elderly couples and individuals may well have changed their spending patterns substantially. The Welfare and Health Council (1955) budget for an elderly couple in New York City allows for the effects of these changes up to 1954, but we need up-to-date budgets for various categories of elderly families and individuals in communities of varying size.

III. The Income Status of the Aged

The mere fact that the aged represent a large proportion of low-income groups does not in itself prove that their incomes are seriously inadequate. The critical problem in appraising the adequacy of the incomes of the aged is to determine what percentage of aged couples and individuals have incomes that fall below those required for carefully defined levels of living.

The Steiner-Dorfman (1957) study, which was based on a nation-wide survey of persons aged 65 and over conducted by the Bureau of the Census in 1952, attempted this type of appraisal, and we shall summarize its findings at some length. Government surveys of old age and survivors insurance beneficiaries in 1951 and in 1957 and of old age assistance recipients in 1953 also provided a wealth of information about large sectors of the aged population (U.S. Bureau of Old-Age and Survivors Insurance, 1953, 1954, 1958; Epler, 1954; Hawkins, 1956, 1957a, 1957b; Hanmer, 1957; Kaplan, 1957). If allowance is made for the differences in the dates of the surveys and in the characteristics of the samples, the findings of these large-scale studies tend to be consistent with one another.

A. Variations in Income within the Aged Population

LABOR-FORCE STATUS AND OCCUPATION

From middle age onward, there is a persistent tendency for the proportion of persons in the labor force to decline with advancing age. Thus, within the population of those aged 65 and over, the older an individual is, the less likely he or she is to be in the labor force. Furthermore, even among those with some degree of attachment to the labor force, the proportion engaged in part-time work rises with advancing age, as we have seen (Fig. 2). These factors are of basic importance in explaining variations in income within the aged population.

A striking indication of the influence of labor-force status on the incomes of aged men is provided by the Bureau of the Census income data for 1957. Although the median income of all men aged 65 and over was $1421 in that year, those who were year-round full-time workers (about a fifth of the total) had a median income of $3427 (U.S. Bureau of the Census, 1958a).

What is less generally recognized is that the occupation in which a male worker has been engaged during his working life has an important influence on whether he is likely to be in the labor force after age 65. The Steiner-Dorfman (1957) study showed that, when men aged 65 or more were classified by longest occupation—the occupation with which the individual had been identified for the longest time during his working career—those who had been engaged in non-manual work were more likely, on the whole, to be in the labor force than those who had been in manual occu-

and clerical categories reported that they had retired because of ill-health.

These relationships have a pervasive influence on the inequality of income within the aged population. As a broad generalization, we may say that, at least among the men, the occupation groups with the highest earning potential prior to age 65 are also those with the greatest capacity to go on working after age 65.

Among aged women, the situation is

TABLE 6*

PERCENTAGE LABOR-FORCE STATUS OF MEN AGED 65 AND OVER, BY
LONGEST OCCUPATION GROUP, UNITED STATES, APRIL, 1952

LONGEST OCCUPA-TION GROUP	TOTAL 65 AND OVER		IN LABOR FORCE	NOT IN LABOR FORCE				
	Percentage Distribution	All Men		Total	Not Well Enough To Work	Well and Interested	Well and Not Interested	Reason Not Ascertained
Professional and technical........	6	100	67	33	15	5	12	2
Farmers and farm managers.......	26	100	43	57	46	2	8	1
Non-farm managers and proprietors..	8	100	53	47	29	5	12	2
Clerical..........	4	100	31	69	45	6	19	0
Sales............	4	100	49	51	33	5	12	0
Craftsmen.......	19	100	33	67	53	5	7	2
Operatives.......	13	100	36	64	55	3	6	1
Services.........	5	100	37	63	55	7	1	0
Farm labor........	4	100	35	65	48	6	8	3
Other labor.......	7	100	31	69	59	3	7	0
Not available.....	4	100	....	....	....	....	....	....
All groups....	100	100	41	59	45	4	8	2

* Source: P. O. Steiner and R. Dorfman, *The Economic Status of the Aged* (Berkeley: University of California Press, 1957), p. 41.

pations (Table 6). Within the non-manual group there were marked variations in the proportion in the labor force, ranging from two-thirds of the professional workers to only about three-tenths of the clerical workers, whereas there was comparatively little variation between manual groups in this respect. Careful analysis indicated that these differences were chiefly attributable to variations in the proportion of men who felt well enough to work in the various occupation groups. Furthermore, the majority of retired men in all occupation groups except the professional, managerial,

somewhat different. The proportion with any work experience after age 50 was too small to permit a detailed analysis of the relationship of occupation to labor-force status, income, and health. The obstacles to labor-force participation of elderly women appear to be the lack of recent work experience and, particularly for those over 70, ill-health or lack of physical strength.

SEX AND MARITAL STATUS

Some of the factors already discussed affect variations in income by sex and marital status. Since the income status of an elderly married woman depends in most cases on that of her husband, Steiner and Dorfman classified aged men and women into three types of "economic units"— couples, unrelated males, and unrelated females.

Partly because the life-expectancy of women exceeds that of men and partly because men tend to marry younger women who are likely to survive them, unrelated females—widows, single women, and divorcees—constituted a large proportion, 43.1 per cent, of the aged economic units

In part, these income differences reflect differences in the age composition of the marital-sex groups. Within the aged population unrelated males and unrelated females tend to be older than married men and women, since, the older an individual is, the more likely he is to be widowed. Furthermore, not only is there a tendency for the proportion in the labor force to decline with advancing age but married men of all ages are more likely to be in the labor force than single, widowed, or divorced men.

TABLE 7*

LIVING ARRANGEMENTS OF AGED ECONOMIC UNITS, UNITED STATES, APRIL, 1952

(Median Incomes Refer to Calendar Year 1951)

| | TYPE OF UNIT | | | | | | | |
| FAMILY STATUS | Couples | | Unrelated Males | | Unrelated Females | | All Units | |
	Per Cent	Median Income	Per Cent	Median Income	Per Cent	Median Income	Per Cent	Median Income
Not living with relatives....	69.1	$1455	50.8	$736	40.8	$557	53.5	$894
Head, no children over 21 present.................	4.5	1417†	6.8	813†	4.3	654†	4.9	867
Head, children present.....	22.6	1280	11.0	732†	15.9	221	17.6	691
Parent of head............	3.3	536†	19.7	352	29.4	0	17.6	48
Other relative of head......	0.5	....	11.6	500†	9.5	136	6.5	274
Total................	100.0	$1387	100.0	$662	100.0	$273	100.0	$682

* Source: P. O. Steiner and R. Dorfman, *The Economic Status of the Aged* (Berkeley: University of California Press, 1957), p. 22.
† Small sample.

in 1952. Furthermore, these women, with a median income of $273, tended to have by far the lowest incomes of the three types of economic units (Steiner and Dorfman, 1957).

Unrelated males represented less than a fifth of the aged economic units and had a median income of $662. Aged couples constituted nearly four-tenths of the aged economic units and were relatively favorably situated with respect to income, with a median of $1387. (They included all couples in which the husband was at least 65 years of age, even though the wife may have been younger.)

LIVING ARRANGEMENTS

Although more than half of all aged economic units were not living with relatives in April, 1952, the proportion varied from 40 per cent for unrelated females to 70 per cent for couples (Table 7). Those who were not living with relatives and those who were family heads without children present tended to have significantly higher incomes than those who were designated as family heads but were living with adult children. Distinctly lower than these groups in income status were the aged couples and individuals who were parents of the family head. The data suggest that inadequacy of income is an important factor in the decisions of aged persons to live with adult children or other relatives.

B. Income Adequacy and Dependency within the Aged Population

INCOME ADEQUACY IN 1951

In 1951 a surprisingly large proportion of the aged population had receipts which not only were below the standard budget but were also below the subsistence budget.[5] Receipts were defined to include (1)

How were those with inadequate receipts managing to get along? The presumption would be that a substantial proportion were dependent on non-monetary assistance from children or relatives. Although this was apparently true of the distinct majority of unrelated females with inadequate receipts and of roughly half of the unrelated males, only a minority of the couples with inadequate receipts appeared to be dependent on non-monetary support from others (Steiner and Dorfman, 1957). Furthermore, a majority of those who were living independently below budget levels

TABLE 8*

AGED ECONOMIC UNITS WITH TOTAL RECEIPTS BELOW
BUDGET LEVELS, UNITED STATES, 1951

	TYPE OF BUDGET†					
TYPE OF UNIT	Subsistence		Cash-Equivalent Standard		Total Standard	
	No. below (000)	Per Cent below	No. below (000)	Per Cent below	No. below (000)	Per Cent below
Couples.................	1000–1150	27–31	1475–1650	39–44	1675–1875	45–50
Unrelated males..........	600–660	33–36	850–900	47–50	950–1050	52–58
Unrelated females........	2125–2275	50–54	2750–2900	65–69	3000–3175	71–75

* Source: P. O. Steiner and R. Dorfman, *The Economic Status of the Aged* (Berkeley: University of California Press, 1957), p. 80.
† Percentages are based on sample data; numbers are estimates of total population based upon the sample and are rounded to the nearest 25,000 persons.

income from all sources, public and private; (2) occasional cash gifts; (3) lump-sum receipts (such as insurance payments or inheritances); and (4) the use of savings or assets to meet living expenses (dissaving).

On the basis of everything that has been said thus far, it is not surprising that couples fared the best of the aged economic units, followed by unrelated males, and that unrelated females occupied the least favorable position (Table 8). But, even among the aged couples, more than a quarter had receipts below the subsistence budget and 44 per cent had receipts below the upper level of the cash-equivalent standard budget.

[5] See p. 219 above.

were not receiving monetary assistance, either from relatives or from public old age assistance or relief programs. Nevertheless, a sizable proportion of all the aged economic units were not self-supporting, that is, receiving either monetary assistance or non-monetary support. All in all, 26 per cent of the couples, 46 per cent of the unrelated males, and 63 per cent of the unrelated females were not self-supporting (Steiner and Dorfman, 1957).

SOURCES OF RECEIPTS

There were striking differences in the sources of receipts of the three types of aged economic units in 1951 (Table 9). If only major sources are counted (those amounting to at least $200 a year), the proportion receiving earnings as a principal source ranged from 42 per cent for couples to only 8 per cent for unrelated females. On the other hand, couples were the least likely of the three types of units to be dependent principally on public assistance. Pensions were more likely to constitute a principal source for unrelated males and for couples than for unrelated females, while unrelated females were somewhat more likely than the other two types of units to be living principally on asset income. Finally, about a third of the unrelated females had no source of receipts amounting to as much as $200, as compared with less than a fifth of the unrelated males and only about a tenth of the couples.

Among the various principal sources of receipts, earnings tended to be substantial-ly higher in average amount than other types of income. They were markedly higher than either pensions or assistance. Where asset income or dissaving constituted a principal source, they fell between earnings and pensions in average amount.

Thus the relatively superior economic position of aged couples reflected both the fact that they were far more likely to have earnings as a principal source of receipts and the fact that earnings tended to be substantially higher in amount than the various types of retirement income.

For all aged economic units combined (not shown in the table), earnings represented more than half of the aggregate value of receipts in 1951. Pensions represented less than a fifth of the total; asset income about an eighth; and public assistance and dissaving represented about 9

TABLE 9*

SOURCES OF RECEIPTS OF AGED ECONOMIC UNITS, UNITED STATES, 1951

SOURCE OF RECEIPTS	TYPE OF UNIT								
	Couples			Unrelated Males			Unrelated Females		
	Per Cent Received as Principal Major Source†	Mean Amount‡	Per Cent of Aggregate Value	Per Cent Received as Principal Major Source†	Mean Amount‡	Per Cent of Aggregate Value	Per Cent Received as Principal Major Source†	Mean Amount‡	Per Cent of Aggregate Value
Earnings.........	42.1	$3225	63.9	22.8	$2082	52.0	7.8	$1593	18.0
Asset income.....	8.6	2265	9.4	6.2	1543	9.2	12.0	1216	26.5
Dissaving........	4.4	1894	5.6	5.8	1157	6.6	7.0	1176	14.9
Pensions§.......	22.6	1532	16.0	25.8	909	21.0	14.6	724	19.6
Public assistance..	12.0	923	4.9	19.3	538	10.8	23.4	561	19.5
Contributions.....	0.5	‖	0.2	0.4	‖	0.4	1.1	‖	1.6
Miscellaneous.....	0.7	‖	#	1.1	‖	#	2.1	‖	#
None............	9.1	....	....	18.6	....	....	32.1	....	....
Total........	100.0	....	100.0	100.0	....	100.0	100.0	....	100.0
Total amount (in millions).....	....	....	$8392	....	....	$2252	....	....	$2936

* Source: P. O. Steiner and R. Dorfman, *The Economic Status of the Aged* (Berkeley: University of California Press, 1957), pp. 96, 97, and 99.

† Receipts from any source are included as a major source if they amount to at least $200 per annum; a "principal major" source is the largest major source of receipts for a couple or individual.

‡ In computing the mean, only those aged economic units receiving the designated type of receipt as a principal major source are included.

§ Pensions include public or private retirement benefits.

‖ Sample too small for computation of mean.

Not available.

and 8 per cent, respectively. But, again, there were marked differences in the distributions for the various types of units.

RECENT CHANGES IN SOURCES OF INCOME

There is considerable evidence that both the money and the real income status of the aged have improved since the Steiner-Dorfman study was conducted. Only an up-to-date study of the same type, however, would provide the basis for an adequate appraisal of the current income status of the aged population as a whole.

The most marked change that has occurred in recent years has been a shift in the relative importance of various sources of money income for aged persons. As Table 10 indicates, the proportion receiving old age and survivors insurance rose sharply between 1948 and 1958.[6] This resulted in part from liberalization of coverage and eligibility provisions and in part from the fact that, as the program has matured, a larger proportion of those reaching the age of retirement are eligible for benefits. There

[6] For data on sources of income for men and women separately in 1956 see chap. xiv, Table 9.

TABLE 10*

ESTIMATED NUMBERS OF PERSONS AGED 65 OR OVER RECEIVING MONEY INCOME FROM SPECIFIED SOURCES,† UNITED STATES, JUNE, 1948, AND JUNE, 1958

SOURCE OF MONEY INCOME‡	No. (000's)		PERCENTAGE CHANGE	PERCENTAGE DISTRIBUTION	
	1948	1958	1948–58	1948	1958
Total, aged 65 or over...............	11,540	15,190	+ 32	100.0	100.0
Employment.........................	3,830	3,950	+ 3	33.2	26.0
Earners...........................	2,930	3,070	+ 5	25.4	20.2
Earners' wives not themselves employed.........................	900	880	− 2	7.8	5.8
Social insurance and related programs§..	2,330	10,360	+345	20.2	68.2
Old age, survivors, and disability insurance......................	1,460	8,840	+505	12.7	58.2
Railroad retirement insurance........	300	580	+ 93	2.6	3.8
Government employees' retirement program......................	300	750	+150	2.6	4.9
Veterans' compensation and pension programs.......................	350	1,160	+231	3.0	7.6
Public assistance‖.................	2,400	2,520	+ 5	20.8	16.6
No money income or income solely from other sources...................	3,400	1,500	− 66	29.4	9.9
Income from more than one of specified sources.......................	420	3,140	+648	3.6	20.7
Employment and social insurance or assistance.....................	270	2,500	+826	2.3	16.5
Social insurance and public assistance.	150	640	+327	1.3	4.2

* Source: Lenore A. Epstein, "Money Income of Aged Persons: A 10-Year Review, 1948 to 1958," *Social Security Bulletin*, 22 (June, 1957), 3–11.

† 1958 data for the continental United States, Alaska, Hawaii, Puerto Rico, and the Virgin Islands; 1948 data for the continental United States. Persons with incomes from sources specified may also have received money income from other sources, such as interest, dividends, private pensions or annuities, or cash contributions from relatives.

‡ The sum of the persons shown under the four categories exceeds the number in the population by the estimated number with income from more than one of the three main sources. The estimates of persons with income from more than one source, developed from survey data, are subject to sampling variability (which may be relatively large for the smaller estimates) and to such errors as may result from attempts to adjust for developments since the sample surveys were conducted.

§ Persons with income from more than one of the programs listed are counted only once. Unemployment insurance, workmen's compensation, and temporary disability insurance programs also provide income for some aged persons, but information is lacking as to the numbers.

‖ Old age assistance recipients and persons aged 65 and over receiving aid to the blind or to the permanently and totally disabled; includes a small number receiving vendor payments for medical care but no direct cash payment.

were also substantial increases in the proportions receiving benefits from other government programs, as well as from private pension plans, although data relating to income from private pensions are not shown in the table. In addition, the proportion of persons receiving income from both employment and social insurance or assistance and from both social insurance and public assistance increased during this period. Meanwhile, there were a moderate decline in the proportion receiving old age assistance and a sharp decline in the percentage with no money income or income solely from sources not covered by the table.

At the same time the number receiving earnings has not kept pace with the rise in the aged population and represented a smaller proportion of the total in 1958 than in 1948. This reflects the decline that has been taking place in the rate of labor-force participation of aged men.

RECENT INCOME STATUS OF OASI BENEFICIARIES

For OASI beneficiaries, who now represent a majority of the aged population, data on the proportions and amounts of income received from specified sources are available from the 1957 *National Survey of Old-Age and Survivors Insurance Beneficiaries*. The median annual income of aged beneficiaries from all sources was substantially higher than in the similar survey which had been conducted in 1951—ranging from $882 for aged widows to $2249

TABLE 11*

MONEY INCOME OF AGED BENEFICIARIES FROM SPECIFIED SOURCE, BY BENEFICIARY GROUP
NATIONAL SURVEY OF OLD-AGE AND SURVIVORS INSURANCE BENEFICIARIES, 1957

SOURCE OF MONEY INCOME	MARRIED COUPLES		SINGLE RETIRED WORKERS		AGED WIDOWS	
	Per Cent with Income from Specified Source	Median Amount from Specified Source	Per Cent with Income from Specified Source	Median Amount from Specified Source	Per Cent with Income from Specified Source	Median Amount from Specified Source
Total income:						
Including OASI benefits........	100	$2249	100	$1140	100	$ 882
Other than OASI benefits........	91	1237	82	639	75	525
Independent retirement income:						
Including OASI benefits........	100	1580	100	828	100	722
Other than OASI benefits†......	68	595	56	335	57	303
Income from assets..	60	180	45	102	52	149
Employer or union pensions.......	25	835	15	657	2	638‡
Veterans' compensation and pensions..........	6	1074	6	995‡	6	794‡
Earnings...........	38	989	32	594	14	406
Public assistance....	7	670	14	487	12	465‡
Contributions from relatives outside household......	5	299‡	8	213	11	314‡

* Source: U.S. Bureau of Old-Age and Survivors Insurance, *National Survey of Old-Age and Survivors Insurance Beneficiaries, 1957: Highlights from Preliminary Tabulations—Income* (Washington: The Bureau, 1958), Tables 200–209.

† Includes employer, union, and veterans' pensions; rents, interest, dividends, and annuities; and income from trust funds and from other reasonably permanent sources.

‡ Median computed on small base and therefore subject to large sampling variation.

for elderly married couples (Table 11).[7] If we consider independent retirement income alone, however, the median amounts were substantially lower—ranging from $722 for the widows to $1580 for the couples.

Earnings clearly represented the most significant source of "other money income." Nearly four-tenths of the couples, a third of the single retired workers, and a seventh of the aged widows had income from earnings, and the median amounts received were large enough to represent an appreciable source of supplementary income. Pensions represented a significant source of other income for 25 per cent of the couples and for 15 per cent of the single retired workers, but for very few of the widows. Relatively few of the couples received income from public assistance or relatives' contributions, but more than a fifth of the single retired workers and aged widows received some income from one or both of these sources. Veterans' compensation or pensions were important for a small proportion of aged beneficiaries, while asset income was received by a substantial proportion but was typically small in amount.

Although OASI beneficiaries now represent well over half of the aged population, recent data on the incomes of the other important sectors of the aged population would be needed to provide a complete picture. In general, we should expect the incomes of full-time workers to be appreciably higher, and those of persons relying primarily on old age assistance payments to be considerably lower, than those of OASI beneficiaries.

IV. SOCIAL POLICIES TOWARD THE SUPPORT OF AGED PERSONS

A. Sources of Support in the Middle Ages

The aging medieval serf was protected from destitution by the lord of the manor,

[7] Comparative data for 1951 are not presented, since the categories used in the 1951 survey are not precisely comparable.

who provided him with subsistence in kind. But other medieval institutions also played a role in the relief of poverty among the aged and among the poor in general (de Schweinitz, 1943). One of these was the medieval guild, which emphasized co-operative self-help and brotherhood, developing mutual benefit programs for the aid of its needy members, and carrying out charitable works for the poor of the towns. Another was the private charitable foundation or bequest, which provided funds for almshouses and other institutions. More important than either of these was the church, which was a major channel of poor relief. And, finally, there was the ancient institution of begging, which was looked on with a greater degree of social approval in the Middle Ages than in more modern times.

The forces that brought about the breakdown of feudalism and the growth of large urban communities also led to the growth of a working class that was unattached to the land and dependent in many cases on casual, irregular, intermittent, or seasonal employment. The increase in beggary and destitution which accompanied these changes outstripped the capacity of private channels of relief and gradually led to the introduction of an organized system of public relief.

B. The Development of Poor Relief in England

It is to England that we must look primarily for the antecedents of many features of our state and local public assistance and relief laws, since the relief policies of the American Colonies were modeled after the poor laws of Elizabethan England. Although the history of the English poor laws is usually traced from the enactment of the Statute of Labourers in 1350 (de Schweinitz, 1943; Clarke, 1957), it was not until 1572, in the reign of Elizabeth, that the principle of taxation for the relief of the poor was established. The provisions of earlier laws were codified in the famous Poor Law of 1601, often referred to as "43

Elizabeth," which provided the framework for poor relief in England for three centuries. Its features may be summarized as follows (de Schweinitz, 1943; Friedlander, 1955; Leyendecker, 1955; Clarke, 1957):

1. Government responsibility for the care of the poor who could not be supported by their relatives was recognized. The administrative units were parishes; officials responsible for dispensing relief were the "overseers of the poor."

2. The justices of the peace and other local officials were authorized to tax every inhabitant of the parish and every occupier of lands to provide the funds for relief.

3. The law distinguished three classes of poor people: (*a*) *the able-bodied poor*—who could be compelled to work or, if employment could not be found, to serve in a workhouse or in a house of correction; (*b*) *the impotent poor*— the sick, the old, the blind, the demented, and mothers with young children—who were to be placed in an almshouse or to be given assistance ("outdoor relief") in their own homes; and (*c*) *dependent children*—orphans, foundlings, and children whose parents had deserted them or were too poor to support them—who could be placed in foster-homes or indentured to householders who would teach them a trade and provide them with subsistence.

4. A person could not be registered as in need of charity if his relatives were able to support him. This "principle of relatives' responsibility" dates from 1597.

5. Although anticipated in earlier legislation, the principle that each parish was responsible only for its "own" poor was reinforced in the Law of Settlement of 1662, which provided that any newcomer to a parish, renting property valued at less than ten pounds a year, could be sent back, within 40 days of his arrival, to the place in which he had last been legally settled.

Volumes have been written about the administration and effects of the poor laws. Suffice it to say here that the spirit of their administration was restrictive and punitive, the relief granted was meager, paupers were frequently shipped from parish to parish like so many pieces of baggage, and conditions in the workhouses and almshouses were such that commitment to them was regarded as a fate to be forestalled at all

costs. The whole system was based on the underlying assumption that the poverty of the "able-bodied poor" was attributable to indolence or dissipation and could be prevented by forcing "paupers" to work.

Toward the end of the nineteenth century, as the work of social scientists and social reformers led to a more enlightened view of the causes of poverty in a modern industrial society, public criticism of the poor laws became widespread, culminating in the famous majority and minority reports of the Royal Commission on the Poor Laws and Relief of Distress, issued in 1909 (Great Britain, 1909). Though the minority, led by Beatrice Webb, failed to carry the day in its advocacy of the abolition of the poor law and the development of specialized social services for the victims of economic distress, its views ultimately prevailed. Meanwhile, Britain had taken a first feeble step toward the development of a modern social security system with the enactment of the Old Age Pensions Act of 1908. It was not until 1948, however, with the passage of the National Assistance Act, that the last vestiges of the poor laws were eliminated (Webb and Webb, 1910; Stockman, 1957).

C. The Growth of Modern Systems of Social Security

The first modern social insurance measure, a compulsory health insurance law, was enacted in Germany in 1883. The German government followed with the passage of a workmen's compensation act in 1884 and a law providing for invalidity, old age, and death benefits in 1889. From Germany, social insurance spread to other European countries and to a few countries in other parts of the world. By 1935, when the American Social Security Act was passed, twenty-three countries had compulsory health insurance laws, twenty had old age insurance systems, and ten had compulsory unemployment insurance programs (Epstein, 1936; and U.S. Committee on Economic Security, 1937). In addition, certain countries had non-contributory old age pension programs, and some had subsidized voluntary health insurance systems. Since World War II the number of countries with social security systems has increased substantially, and there has been a marked trend toward broader coverage and more generous provisions. We shall summarize the features of foreign old age security programs in a later section.

V. AMERICAN OLD AGE SECURITY PROGRAMS

Before the Great Depression of the 1930's, there was widespread opposition to social insurance in the United States, in large part on the ground that such programs would discourage thrift and self-reliance. About the middle of the nineteenth century, some of the states had begun to establish separate institutions for the mentally ill, and in some cases special institutional arrangements were made for needy children and aged persons, the blind, the deaf, and the mentally retarded (Merriam, 1953). Public health measures were also initiated at about this time. There followed the settlement-house movement, the spread of compulsory public education, and, around the turn of the century, the drive for workmen's compensation legislation. About the beginning of the present century, also, there was evidence of growing concern over the economic plight of the aged. During the 1890's some of the trade unions established homes for their aged members and soon after began to develop retirement benefit plans. Even earlier, a number of large companies, led by the American Express Company and the railroads, began to establish pension plans for their employees.

In the second decade of this century some of the states began to establish old age assistance programs. By the end of 1928, however, despite attempts to achieve the enactment of old age assistance laws in a substantial number of states, only six states and one territory had such laws in effect (U.S. Committee on Economic Security, 1937). Although the earlier laws

were of the optional type, California, in 1929, was the first state to enact a law which made the establishment of old age assistance programs mandatory upon the counties and provided for state financial assistance to the localities. From that time on, the agitation for state legislation increased, and by 1934 laws were in effect in twenty-eight states and in Alaska and Hawaii. Although most of these laws were of the California type, many of them had long residence requirements and other restrictive conditions, and the amount of aid actually provided was very limited (Merriam, 1953).

Meanwhile, mounting unemployment had placed an impossible burden on local relief agencies, and the federal government had taken a series of emergency steps to cope with the relief problem. In June, 1934, President Roosevelt appointed a Committee on Economic Security, headed by Secretary of Labor Frances Perkins, to draw up recommendations for a social security program of a more permanent nature. The final report of this committee, which was transmitted to Congress the following January, became, with certain modifications, the basis of the Social Security Act of 1935, which provided for (1) a federal program of old age insurance; (2) a federal-state program of public assistance to the needy aged, the blind, and dependent children; and (3) a federal unemployment insurance tax program designed to induce the states to enact their own unemployment insurance laws.[8]

A. Old-Age and Survivors Insurance

The old age insurance program was originally intended to provide monthly benefits to retired aged workers and lump-sum death benefits (U.S. Committee on Economic Security, 1937). The Old-Age, Survivors, and Disability Insurance program, as we know it today, is considerably broader in scope as well as in coverage. It is

[8] It also included provisions for grants to states for maternal and child welfare.

designed to provide protection for the worker and his family when the earnings on which they have depended are cut off by his retirement or death or by permanent and total disability. The President pointed out in his social security message of January, 1954, that the "system is not intended as a substitute for private savings, pension plans, and insurance protection. It is, rather, intended as the foundation upon which these other forms of protection can be soundly built" (Christgau, 1955, p. 12).

The system is entirely a responsibility of the federal government, in contrast with other social insurance programs (workmen's compensation and unemployment insurance) in which the states play a major role. Benefits are payable as a matter of right to eligible individuals; they do not have to submit to a means test, as under public assistance programs. Although benefit levels are related to a worker's previous earnings in covered employment, the relationship is not one of strict proportionality. Under the benefit formula, low-income workers receive a larger fraction of their previous earnings than do workers with higher incomes. The maximum and minimum provisions reinforce this tendency. In addition, the provisions for dependents' benefits introduce the element of family need as an important criterion. Funds are built up through tax contributions which are shared equally by employers and employees; the employer is subject to a payroll tax and the employee to a withholding tax on his earnings.

The details of the program can best be examined through a description of provisions currently in effect, with some reference to the more significant changes that have been adopted since 1935 (U.S. Committee on Economic Security, 1937; U.S. Congress, 1957*b*, 1958; U.S. Social Security Administration, 1957*b*).

COVERAGE PROVISIONS

At present the OASDI program covers more than nine out of every ten employed workers. Although originally applicable only to employees in private non-agricultural employment (with certain exceptions), successive amendments have extended coverage to a number of groups that were at first excluded. The act excludes employment of newsboys under 18, certain types of family employment, agricultural and domestic workers who are not regularly employed, and self-employed workers with very low earnings. Ministers and members of religious orders may elect coverage as self-employed, whether they are actually self-employed or are employed by a non-profit institution. All self-employed professional people are covered except self-employed doctors. Federal employees and railroad workers, for whom there are special retirement systems, are covered only in special circumstances. Most employees of state and local governments may be covered by special agreement even if they are under a state or local government retirement system. Elective coverage is also possible for employees of non-profit institutions.

GROUPS ELIGIBLE FOR BENEFITS

OASDI now provides benefits to the following classes of individuals:

1. Retired male workers aged 65 or more and retired female workers aged 62 or more (women who retire before age 65 receive actuarially reduced benefits).

2. Totally and permanently disabled workers aged 50–64, after a 6-month waiting period.

3. Wives of eligible retired or disabled workers if they are aged 62 or more (actuarially reduced benefits are paid to those claiming benefits before age 65).

4. Dependent husbands of eligible disabled or retired workers if the husband is aged 65 or more.

5. Widows aged 62 or more, and widowers aged 65 or more if they have been dependent on a deceased worker.

6. Children of an eligible deceased, retired, or disabled worker who are under age 18 or have been permanently and totally disabled since before age 18.

7. Mothers of eligible children regardless of the mother's age.

8. Dependent parents of a deceased worker (if the mother is aged 62 or more and the father 65 or more).

In addition, a lump-sum payment is made on the death of a deceased worker to his widow, if she was living in the same household with him or had paid his burial expenses. Otherwise, the payment may be made to an individual who can show that he has paid the funeral costs.

In general, no individual can receive more than one type of monthly payment, but only the largest for which he is eligible. For example, a widow may not receive both a widow's benefit and a retired female worker's benefit.

OTHER ELIGIBILITY CONDITIONS

In addition to the age and other eligibility conditions discussed above, benefits may be received only if the primary beneficiary, the person whose earnings in covered employment have built up rights to benefits, has achieved insured status. An individual may be "fully insured" or "currently insured." In general, fully insured status provides rights to both retirement and survivorship benefits, while currently insured status provides them only for certain types of survivorship benefits.

Insured status is based on quarters of coverage. An individual who is paid $50 or more of non-farm wages in a calendar quarter is credited with a quarter of coverage. A farm laborer is credited with a quarter of coverage for each $100 of annual wages, while an individual with creditable self-employment income in a year (in general, $400 or more) is entitled to four quarters of coverage.

To be fully insured, an individual must, at the time of retirement or death, fulfil one of three alternative requirements: (1) have forty quarters of coverage; (2) have at least six quarters of coverage, including at least one quarter (acquired at any time after 1936) for every two quarters elapsing after 1950 (or age 21 if later); or (3) have quarters of coverage after 1954 at least equal to the number of quarters between 1955 and the quarter in which he reaches retirement age or dies. The second and third alternatives were designed to "blanket in" persons who were newly covered under the 1950 or 1954 amendments. Currently insured status requires six quarters of coverage within the thirteen quarters preceding death or entitlement to old age benefits.

In addition, a person claiming retirement benefits must satisfy the so-called retirement test. Originally, the old age insurance system was designed to provide annuities only for elderly persons who were for all practical purposes completely retired. Under the impact of the depression experience, the view was widely held that elderly persons should be encouraged to retire to make way for younger job-seekers who were having difficulty finding employment. From 1950 on the retirement test was progressively liberalized under the influence of tighter labor market conditions and a growing concern over employment opportunities for elderly persons (Cohen, 1957*b*). Since January, 1955, an individual claiming retirement benefits has been permitted to earn up to $1200 a year without loss of benefits. If he earns more than $1200 a year, 1 month's benefit is suspended for each $80 (or fraction thereof) by which his earnings exceed the $1200. This means that, when the worker earns more than $2080 a year, his entire year's benefits *could* be withheld. However, no benefit will be withheld for any month in which he does not do substantial work in self-employment or earn wages over $100. This latter amount was $80 until the 1958 amendments went into effect.

It should be noted that there is no absolute ceiling on the amount an individual may earn while drawing benefits, *provided* his earnings are distributed over the year in a sufficiently irregular manner. This gives an advantage to the self-employed, who are more likely than the average wage-earner to be in a position to distribute their reported net earnings over the year in such a way as to minimize the number of months in which benefits will be withheld.

Persons aged 72 or more may receive benefits regardless of the amount of their earnings, on the theory that some elderly persons might go on working more or less indefinitely and never receive any benefit from their years of contributions in the absence of such a provision. It should be noted, also, that benefits paid to dependents of a retired worker under age 72

mary insurance amount is based on the worker's average monthly wage in covered employment. In computing the average monthly wage, the starting date is usually December 21, 1950, or the last day of the year in which he reached age 21, whichever results in the higher primary insurance amount. Certain periods of low or non-existent earnings may be eliminated ("dropped-out") from the computation, as follows: (1) the 5 years of lowest earnings for persons with six quarters of coverage after June 30, 1953, or becoming eligible

TABLE 12*

BENEFIT FORMULAS UNDER THE SOCIAL SECURITY ACT
AND ITS AMENDMENTS, 1935–54

Year of Legislation	Monthly Benefit for Retired Worker	Period over Which Average Monthly Wage Is Computed
1935.......	$\frac{1}{2}\%$ of first $3000 of cumulative wage credits $+ \frac{1}{12}\%$ of next $42,000 + \frac{1}{24}\%$ of next $84,000	Not applicable
1939.......	40% of first $50 of average monthly wage $+$ 10% of next $200, all increased by 1% for each year of coverage	Entire period of potential coverage under system after 1950†
1950.......	50% of first $100 of average monthly wage $+$ 15% of next $200	Entire period of potential coverage under system after 1950†
1952.......	55% of first $100 of average monthly wage $+$ 15% of next $200	Entire period of potential coverage under system after 1950†
1954.......	55% of first $110 of average monthly wage $+$ 20% of next $240	Entire period of potential coverage under system after 1950, excluding periods of extended disability and 4 or 5 years of lowest earnings†

* Source: R. J. Myers, "Old-Age and Survivors Insurance: History of the Benefit Formula," *Social Security Bulletin*, 18 (May, 1955), 13.

† For those who did not have 6 quarters of coverage after 1950, a conversion table was used.

will be reduced if his earnings exceed the permissible amount. Furthermore, an eligible wife or child of a retired or disabled worker who earns more than the amounts mentioned above will lose benefits, as will widows and children of deceased or disabled workers and dependent parents of deceased workers.

BENEFIT FORMULAS

When an eligible insured worker reaches age 65, he is entitled to a monthly benefit for life called the *primary insurance amount*. All other benefits are expressed as a percentage of this amount. The pri-

after August, 1954, and (2) periods of total disability of at least 6 months' duration.

In all computations annual earnings of any individual over and above the amount subject to tax under the old age insurance system are disregarded. Although the maximum annual amount taxed was originally $3000, it was raised to $3600 under the 1950 amendments, to $4200 under the 1954 amendments, and to $4800 under the 1958 amendments. These increases apply, however, only to annual earnings after the effective date of the change.

The changes in the benefit formula from 1935 to 1954 are shown in Table 12. The minimum old age benefit rose from $10 under the 1935 act to $30 under the 1954 amendments, while the maximum benefit rose from $85 to $108.50 (Cohen, 1957a). The 1958 amendments, effective January 1, 1959, increased benefit amounts by about 7 per cent. The increases applied to all beneficiaries—those currently on the rolls as well as those who would come on in the future. The new benefit amounts are determined from a conversion table. The minimum primary insurance amount is $33 and the maximum is $127. However, the maximum applies only to those with an average monthly wage of $400 and thus will be attainable only by persons coming on the rolls in the future whose average monthly wage is based on earnings after the end of 1958, when the new ceiling of $4800 on annual taxable earnings became effective.

An eligible wife or dependent husband receives half the primary benefit amount, while a widow, dependent widower, or dependent parent receives three-fourths. A single eligible child receives three-fourths. If there is more than one eligible child, each receives a half, and an additional fourth is divided among the children. The lump-sum death payment is three times the primary benefit but not more than $255.

Thus the amount which may be received by an elderly couple varies from $49.50 to $190.50 if both are aged 65 or more at the time of claiming benefits. If the wife is aged 62–64 when benefits are claimed, the amounts are slightly less. The maximum family benefit is $254.

FINANCING

The general objective of the financing provisions of the old age and survivors insurance program is that the system shall be self-supporting. It has been anticipated from the start that the cost of the program would gradually rise as the proportion of elderly people in the population and the percentage eligible for benefits increased

(U.S. Social Security Administration, 1953b). The original Social Security Act provided for a schedule of tax rates that would be increased from 1 per cent of taxable wages on both employer and employee in 1937 to 3 per cent in 1949. The rates were set in such a way that contributions would exceed benefits paid out for some years. In other words, the financing plans contemplated the accumulation of a sizable fund which, together with accrued interest, would be available to meet rising benefit payments in later years. The objective was to ease the burden of rising costs on future generations. As many experts (e.g., Burns, 1956) have shown, however, this can be accomplished only if the amounts saved by the current generation of taxpayers are invested in such a way as to increase future productivity, since the goods and services consumed by non-producers in any given year must, with certain qualifications, come out of current output in that year.

As a result of rising employment and wage levels, contributions during the decade of the 1940's were much higher than had been anticipated, and the tax rates were not raised in accordance with the original schedule. In 1950, when benefits were raised, the entire financing program was reviewed, and a new schedule of rates was established. These rates have been changed several times since 1950.

At present (1960), employer and employee each pay 3 per cent on the first $4800 of the employee's wage. A self-employed person pays $4\frac{1}{2}$ per cent on the first $4800 of his net earnings. The tax rates include $\frac{1}{4}$ per cent each on employer and employee that is earmarked to finance disability benefits. The rate applicable to employers and employees is scheduled to rise gradually to $4\frac{1}{2}$ per cent in 1969, while that on the self-employed will rise to $6\frac{3}{4}$ per cent.

BENEFITS PAID UNDER THE PROGRAM

In judging the adequacy of old age and survivors insurance benefits, it is important to take account of the fact that very few aged beneficiaries qualify for the maximum benefits. At the end of 1956, when maximum primary benefits were $108.50, average monthly benefits paid to aged male beneficiaries were $68.20, while a fourth of these aged men were receiving less than $50 a month. Only 2 per cent were receiving $105 a month or more. Elderly female beneficiaries were receiving average payments of $43.20 a month (U.S. Social Security Administration, 1958b).

The low average monthly payments reflect the fact that changes in benefit provisions have lagged behind increases in wage levels, while some aged beneficiaries are receiving benefits based on part-time or intermittent earnings. Furthermore, the increases in maximum taxable earnings from 1950 to 1958, and the related increases in maximum benefits, applied, as we have seen, only to earnings after the effective date of the change.

If these average monthly payments are considered in relation to the budgetary requirements of elderly couples and individuals discussed earlier in the chapter, it is difficult to escape the conclusion that the average aged beneficiary is usually not in a position to be self-supporting unless he has access to an appreciable amount of other money income in addition to his OASDI benefits. The 1957 *National Survey of Old-Age and Survivors Insurance Beneficiaries* indicated that about a fourth of all aged widows and somewhat smaller proportions of couples and single retired workers received no income from other sources. Half of the aged widows received less than $271 from other sources, half of the single retired workers less than $469, and half of the couples less than $1105 (U.S. Bureau of Old-Age and Survivors Insurance, 1958).[9] The relative importance of the various sources of other income has been indicated earlier (see Table 12). It

[9] These amounts differ from the medians shown in Table 12, which apply only to those persons or couples who *had* "other money income."

is pertinent to recall here that earnings represented the most significant source of other income, while pensions also played a role of considerable importance. The relative significance of earnings helps to explain the keen interest displayed in proposals affecting the retirement test.

DISPUTED ISSUES

The data presented in the preceding section strongly suggest that, despite the many liberalizing amendments enacted from 1950 to 1958, the benefits made available under the old age and survivors insurance program do not provide an adequate income for a substantial proportion of aged beneficiaries. The chief problem is one that is common to nearly all social security programs—that of maintaining adequate benefits in the face of long-term inflationary pressures. The difficulty is exacerbated in a long-term program, such as OASDI, which relates benefits to average lifetime earnings and pays them, in many cases, throughout a lengthy period of retirement.

Innumerable proposals have been made for changes in the program, some of which would fundamentally alter the character of our old age insurance system (Corson and McConnell, 1956). More likely to receive serious consideration in the future are a variety of suggestions that have been made for improving the existing system while retaining its basic characteristics (Burns, 1956; Corson and McConnell, 1956; Somers and Somers, 1957; Witte, 1958).

To meet the problem of built-in rigidity, it has sometimes been proposed that a benefit formula be adopted under which benefits would be automatically adjusted for changes in the cost of living. As we shall see at a later point, a number of European countries have adopted such a policy, while several have adopted complex formulas which relate benefits to current levels of earnings but retain the link to past-earnings records. Another proposal designed to meet the problem of long-term inflation would involve computing the average monthly wage on the basis of the five or ten consecutive years of highest earnings rather than on the basis of all years in covered employment less permissible drop-out periods. It has also been argued that the ceiling on annual taxable earnings should be removed entirely or automatically adjusted so that total annual earnings of the great majority of wage-earners are covered, in accordance with the original intention of the law.

In recent years the rapidly rising costs of medical care, the relative importance of these costs in the budgetary requirements of the aged, and the comparatively high costs of private health insurance coverage for elderly people have given rise to increasing concern. Heated controversy has been aroused over the Forand bill, first introduced in Congress in August, 1957, and reintroduced in February, 1959, which would modify the OASDI program through various liberalizing amendments and through providing insurance against the costs of hospital, nursing-home, and surgical service for elderly insured persons and their dependents (U.S. Congress, 1957a, 1959).

Other proposals aimed at providing more adequate protection include: (1) varying benefits in accordance with years of service; (2) raising benefits for wives and for widows without dependents and/or lowering the eligibility age for such women; (3) extending coverage to groups now excluded; and (4) broadening the scope of disability benefits. There has also been discussion of a number of proposals for modifying the retirement test and raising or lowering the age at which retired workers become eligible for benefits. Each of these proposals requires careful consideration on its merits and with due attention to its impact on the costs of the program. Although discussion of all the issues involved cannot be attempted here, we shall refer to some of them in a concluding section.

B. Disability Benefits

For many years critics of the old age and survivors insurance program pointed out that one of its greatest weaknesses was its failure to provide any protection for the worker who was forced out of the labor force because of disability prior to age 65. In contrast, many European old age insurance systems had been accompanied by "invalidity" insurance programs from the beginning.

To be sure, protection for those with work-connected disabilities was provided in this country under workmen's compensation laws, for service-connected and non-service-connected veterans' disabilities under the veterans' and Armed Forces programs, for the blind under the program of aid to the blind, and for other special groups. In addition, four states enacted temporary disability insurance laws in the 1940's. But all these provisions left many individuals with permanent or prolonged disabilities unprotected by any public program.

The first major step taken by the federal government to meet this problem was the inauguration, under the Social Security Amendments of 1950, of a program of grants-in-aid to help the states finance public assistance payments to needy individuals who were permanently and totally disabled (Cohen, 1957b; Cohen and Myers, 1950). Then, in 1954, the old age and survivors insurance provisions were amended to permit the so-called "disability freeze," under which periods of total disability of at least 6 months' duration were excluded in determining insured status and average monthly wage, provided the disabled worker was currently insured and had at least twenty quarters of coverage in the forty quarters ending with the quarter in which he was disabled. Fully insured status is now required for the freeze.

Under the 1956 amendments, Congress went a step further and inaugurated a program of benefits for the permanently and totally disabled under the old age and survivors insurance system. This program was liberalized in certain respects under the 1958 amendments. As we have already indicated, those eligible for disability benefits are (1) permanently and totally disabled workers aged 50–64; (2) dependent adult disabled children of eligible retired, disabled, or deceased workers if the children became totally disabled before reaching age 18; and (3) mothers having such children in their care. In the case of those aged 50 or over, benefits cannot be paid until after a waiting period of 6 months. The disabled person aged 50–64 must be fully insured and must have had at least twenty quarters of coverage in the forty-quarter period ending with the quarter in which the disability begins. The monthly benefits are equal to the primary insurance amount to which the person would be entitled at age 65. The beneficiary receives payments up to age 65 (so long as he continues to be disabled), at which time he qualifies for retirement benefits. Under the 1958 amendments these disability benefits are not reduced by the amount of any other federal disability benefit or workmen's compensation benefit.

The 1958 amendments also provided for the payment of benefits to wives, dependent husbands, and children of disabled workers aged 50–64 under the same eligibility conditions as those prevailing for dependents of old age insurance beneficiaries.

The chief problem in administering this program is that of determining whether a person is permanently and totally disabled. For purposes of these provisions, disability is defined as "inability to engage in any substantial gainful activity by reason of any medically determined physical or mental impairment which can be expected to result in death or to be of long-continued and indefinite duration" (U.S. Congress, 1957*b*). The determination of disability is made by state agencies but is subject to review by the Secretary of Health, Education, and Welfare. Vocational rehabilitation is considered an important adjunct to the administration of both the disability

freeze and disability cash benefits, and applicants are referred to state rehabilitation agencies (Schottland, 1956).

The number of applications under the program has been considerably larger than was anticipated. By the end of September, 1957, more than 900,000 initial applications for the disability freeze or disability benefits had been filed. The great majority were applications for disability benefits by persons aged 50–64. Among the cases on which final determinations had been made, approximately 55 per cent had been allowed periods of disability. Most of these persons were disabled by chronic diseases rather than by crippling injuries. Approximately a fourth had heart ailments or diseases of the blood vessels, while another fourth had diseases of the nervous system or impaired sight or hearing. An eighth were suffering from mental disorders. The distribution of ailments among the applicants who were rejected was similar, but most of these cases were not considered severe enough to prevent the applicant from engaging in gainful work (Hess, 1957).

C. Old Age Assistance

The planners of the Social Security Act recognized that a comprehensive social security program would require both social insurance and public assistance. There would always be some needy persons in various categories who would not qualify for insurance benefits. The old age insurance program, in particular, would be slow to mature, and, even when a stage was reached at which most retired persons would be eligible for benefits, there would be some who would not qualify or who would require supplementary assistance to meet their special needs.

FEDERAL PROVISIONS

The old age assistance provisions of the Social Security Act established a federal program of grants-in-aid to the states to enable them to provide more adequately for the needy aged. The act requires that a state program for old age assistance must cover all political subdivisions in the state, even though the program may be administered by local governmental units (U.S. Congress, 1957*b*). The state must participate financially in the program, and a single state agency must either administer the program itself or supervise the local governmental units administering it. An opportunity for a fair hearing before the state agency must be granted to any individual whose claim for old age assistance is denied or is not acted on with reasonable promptness. The state must provide for the selection and retention of personnel administering the program through a merit system. The act provides for safeguards against the disclosure of information about assistance recipients for purposes other than the administration of the program, although a 1951 amendment (to the revenue act of that year) permits public inspection of the lists of recipients for other than political or commercial purposes.

Assistance is granted only in case of need, and the state agency must take into consideration any other income and resources of an applicant for old age assistance. If the plan includes payments to individuals in private or public institutions, the state must establish and maintain standards for such institutions.

For the purpose of modifying some of the highly restrictive provisions common under earlier state old age assistance programs, the federal act also stipulates that the age requirement may not be more than 65 years, the residence requirement may not exceed 5 out of the preceding 9 years and 1 year immediately preceding the date of application, and the citizenship requirement may not exclude any citizen of the United States.

The act also provides for a formula limiting the amount of federal financial participation but leaves the states responsible for determining how much assistance will be given. Under the 1958 amendments the federal government's contribution represents a certain proportion of the first $65 of the average monthly payment made by the state. The formula provides for a federal contribution of 80 per cent of the first $30 of the average monthly pension plus a variable percentage of the remainder. For states whose per capita income is equal to or above the national average, the federal government contributes 50 per cent of the remainder; in the case of those states with per capita incomes below the national average, the federal government's contribution is from 50 to 65 per cent of the remainder, varying inversely with the ratio of state to national per capita income. In other words, the states with the lowest per capita incomes receive somewhat larger proportions than those with higher income levels. In the case of Puerto Rico, the Virgin Islands, and Guam, the federal government's contribution is simply one-half of the first $35 of the average monthly payment.

The 1958 amendments are the most recent of a series of changes representing a substantial liberalization of the original formula, which provided for a federal contribution of half of the first $30 (U.S. Committee on Economic Security, 1937). The federal government also contributes half of the administrative expenses and half of any payments made to vendors of medical care up to $6 per old age assistance recipient.

QUALIFYING CONDITIONS UNDER STATE ACTS

Within the limits imposed by federal requirements, state laws vary widely as to qualifying conditions and average monthly payments. Practically all the states set 65 as the minimum age at which old age assistance may be obtained (U.S. Bureau of Public Assistance, 1957; Windhauser and Blaetus, 1958).[10] More than two-thirds have no provision relating to citizenship, while the majority of the remaining states

[10] In discussing the provisions of state laws, we shall, for the sake of simplicity, refer to all jurisdictions having old age assistance programs as states, even though Puerto Rico, the Virgin Islands, and the District of Columbia are included.

require an applicant to be either a citizen or a long-term resident of the United States —in most cases a resident for at least 25 years, though a few states require fewer years. So far as residency in the state is concerned, slightly more than half of the states require only 1 year, while the majority of the remainder require 5 out of the preceding 9 years and at least 1 year immediately preceding the application for assistance. Nearly all the states have statutory provisions setting limits on the amount of property an eligible individual may own. These property limits vary a good deal and cannot be readily summarized, but a somewhat typical provision is Alabama's, which permits ownership of a home with a net value of no more than $5000 and other property not exceeding $1000 in value (U.S. Bureau of Public Assistance, 1957). An applicant who disposes of property in order to qualify for assistance is ineligible under practically all the state laws.

The state laws vary widely in their provisions relating to relatives' responsibility (Epler, 1954). Approximately two-thirds of the states impose some type of financial obligation on specified relatives, principally children, but the laws differ greatly. A few of the laws specifically provide that an applicant cannot be regarded as being in need if he has certain relatives who are able to support him, but in most states aid is not actually withheld when relatives found able to contribute fail to do so. A frequent practice is to extend aid on a temporary basis pending an agreement of the legally responsible relatives to provide support or, if necessary, a court order (Bond et al., 1954).

Until the late 1940's conflicting trends were apparent in these provisions, with some states tightening their regulations and others relaxing them, but more recently the changes have tended to strengthen the provisions. In addition, state agencies have sought to develop more specific and equitable methods of determining ability of children to support their aged parents.

One final type of provision needs to be mentioned. Nearly three-fourths of the states provide for reimbursement from the recipient's estate for aid granted (Bond et al., 1954). The majority of these states secure the state's claim by taking a lien on the property, while the remaining states merely hold a creditor's claim against the estate. The provisions differ considerably. In most of the states liens are imposed only on real property, and in some of them property below a certain minimum value is exempt.

MONTHLY PAYMENTS IN THE VARIOUS STATES

In principle, the monthly payments made to old age assistance recipients are related to individual need, but in practice there is a tendency to relate the payments to assumed *average* need (Bond et al., 1954). A large majority of the states use the so-called budget-deficit method, under which the payment is equal to the difference between the individual's income from other sources and his total requirements as measured by the state's standards. In the determination of budgetary needs the Social Security Administration requires the states to establish minimum standards which must be applied uniformly throughout the state.

An alternative principle used in some states is the "flat-grant-minus" method, under which a statutory or administrative provision specifies an amount regarded as necessary to meet basic needs, and the individual's income in cash and kind is deducted from the established amount. Actually, no state follows this method strictly, since an individual's income from other sources is not deducted from the flat amount *regardless* of need. Rather, the flat amount tends to be regarded as the minimum monthly amount that should be available to every recipient from all sources (Bond et al., 1954).

Thirty-six states imposed a statutory or administrative maximum on the size of monthly payments in 1957 (U.S. Bureau of Public Assistance, 1957). Maximums for individual payments to persons without special needs ranged from $30 in Mississippi to approximately $100 in several states, but more than half of the states fell within a group in which the maximum payment varied from $50 to $75 a month. In Illinois and Utah the administrative agency could adjust the maximum upward or downward with changes in the cost of living, while, in Colorado, the legal maximum

the states. Nearly all the eleven states with averages below $50 a month were in the South, while there were twenty-nine states that fell in the group with averages between $50 and $80.

It is important to recognize that the financial burden of old age assistance payments is not necessarily greatest in those states with high average monthly payments. In fact, there is some tendency for the reverse to be true. Some of the highly indus-

TABLE 13*

AVERAGE MONTHLY PAYMENTS TO OLD AGE ASSISTANCE
RECIPIENTS, BY STATES, MARCH, 1959

State	Average Payment	State	Average Payment	State	Average Payment
All states†	$64.34	Kentucky	$43.41	North Dakota	$84.39
		Louisiana	66.16	Ohio	65.72
Alabama	$43.56	Maine	63.60	Oklahoma	76.51
Alaska	60.09	Maryland	56.92	Oregon	82.14
Arizona	57.24	Massachusetts	98.03	Pennsylvania	67.61
Arkansas	48.34	Michigan	70.49	Rhode Island	73.90
California	83.94	Minnesota	84.99	South Carolina	38.07
Colorado	94.26	Mississippi	29.19	South Dakota	57.45
Connecticut	108.41	Missouri	55.79	Tennessee	43.40
Delaware	49.11	Montana	63.16	Texas	52.07
Florida	53.13	Nebraska	68.29	Utah	66.56
Georgia	47.64	Nevada	67.30	Vermont	56.53
Hawaii	57.85	New Hampshire	70.71	Virginia	40.76
Idaho	63.70	New Jersey	87.43	Washington	88.51
Illinois	69.38	New Mexico	62.24	West Virginia	33.36
Indiana	59.21	New York	101.15	Wisconsin	79.84
Iowa	70.00	North Carolina	39.93	Wyoming	70.75
Kansas	76.52				

* Source: *Social Security Bulletin,* **22** (June, 1959), 38.

† Average includes payments in the District of Columbia ($64.00), Puerto Rico ($8.16), and the Virgin Islands ($23.30).

of $100 could be increased on the basis of a rise in the cost of living. In most of the states with a maximum individual payment an eligible spouse would also have been entitled to receive the maximum individual amount, but in some states the amount allowed for a spouse was less than the primary amount.

In March, 1959, average monthly payments to old age assistance recipients, including special payments for medical care, varied from $29.19 in Mississippi to $108.41 in Connecticut, as shown in Table 13. Puerto Rico and the Virgin Islands had average payments well below any of

trialized states, such as New York and Connecticut, with relatively generous old age assistance programs, have comparatively few old age assistance recipients, largely because a substantial proportion of their aged residents qualify for OASDI and/or other retirement benefits. In these states, amounts expended on old age assistance per inhabitant tend to be low. On the other hand, some of the southern states, where average monthly payments are low, rank above average in amounts expended per inhabitant (including federal contributions), because substantial proportions of their aged residents lack other means of support. At the same time, we must recognize that some of the states with high average monthly payments, such as Colorado and California, rank high in amounts expended per inhabitant because of a combination of factors, such as comparatively generous maximum grants and allowances for special needs, relatively low labor-force-participation rates of elderly men, and only moderately high proportions of OASDI beneficiaries.

Finally, it should be noted that the trend in average monthly old age assistance payments for the nation as a whole has been sharply upward—from $15.04 in April, 1936 (Roney, 1955), to $64.34 in March, 1959. If price levels continue their predominantly upward movement, this trend is likely to continue.

PAYMENTS FOR MEDICAL CARE AND OTHER SPECIAL NEEDS

The majority of states recognize, in addition to the basic items needed by practically all recipients, "specific needs" arising because of individual circumstances. The most common and important of these needs is that for medical care. However, the states vary greatly in the extent to which they provide for the costs of needed medical care and in their methods of paying for it. Under the 1956 amendments to the Social Security Act, the federal government participates on a fifty-fifty basis in medical care expenditures up to a maximum of $6 a month. This legislation has led to a number of changes in state laws to enable the states to take advantage of the federal matching grants (Windhauser and Blaetus, 1958).

CONTROVERSIAL ISSUES IN OLD AGE ASSISTANCE

Although the number and proportion of elderly persons receiving old age assistance payments has declined somewhat in recent years, the decline is taking place slowly, and it may be anticipated that there will always be some needy elderly persons who will require assistance. Meanwhile, there is much controversy over certain aspects of the program, particularly in those states with strong and active old age pressure groups.

Disputed issues range all the way from the amounts of aid provided to details of administrative practices and procedures. Probably the two problems of greatest concern to experts are the wide variations from state to state in average monthly payments and the difficulties arising as a result of relatives' responsibility clauses.

With respect to neither of these issues is the answer clear cut or easy. Since the amounts of aid granted are intended to vary with individual need, and since there are wide variations from state to state in such relevant factors as the urban-rural distribution of recipients and the amounts of income received from other sources, some differences in average monthly payments would be expected even if state standards were uniform. The new federal formula adopted under the 1958 amendments, which provides a basis for slightly higher proportional payments to states with relatively low per capita incomes, represents a step toward meeting the need for greater uniformity, although it should be noted that states with maximum grants well below $65 a month will not be in a position to take full advantage of the new formula unless they raise their maximums.

Relatives' responsibility requirements are defended on the grounds that taxpayers should not be burdened with the support of those who have financially capable relatives and that elimination of the requirements would serve further to weaken family ties. Many people argue, however, that, because of the difficulties involved in enforcing these requirements, the saving to the taxpayer is actually very little and that the requirements, far from strengthening family ties, aggravate family tensions in those situations in which adult children are reluctant to assume any financial responsibility for their parents (Leyendecker, 1955; Burns, 1956). A middle position is taken by those who think the requirements should be retained but rarely invoked, on the ground that their existence does tend to encourage the preservation of attitudes of mutual responsibility within the family.

D. Other Governmental Programs

In addition to OASDI and OAA, there are a number of government retirement programs affecting particular groups. These will be considered very briefly.

THE RAILROAD RETIREMENT PROGRAM

The railroad retirement system, although somewhat similar to OASDI, is substantially more generous. Monthly benefits are paid to retired workers at age 65 or over after 10 years of railroad service or at ages 60–64 after 30 years of service. For men who receive benefits before age 65, however, the monthly amount is reduced. Wives or dependent husbands who are aged 65 or over receive 50 per cent of the full retirement annuity up to the maximum allowable under OASDI (U.S. Social Security Administration, 1957a). If there is a dependent child under 18, the wife receives benefits regardless of age. The act also contains a provision which guarantees that in no case will an employee's protection be less than it would have been if his railroad service had been covered by OASDI. Furthermore, if an employee is ineligible for railroad retirement benefits because he has had less than 10 years of railroad service when he dies or retires, his credits are transferred to OASDI, and he is entitled to social security benefits based on his combined railroad service and any service covered by the OASDI program.

Survivor benefits include lump-sum payments and monthly payments to widows (or dependent widowers) aged 60 or over or with a dependent child under 18. Children of deceased workers who are under age 18 also receive benefits.

Disability annuities are paid to workers who are permanently disabled for any regular gainful employment if they have had 10 years of covered railroad service. A worker who is currently connected with the railroad industry and is permanently disabled for his regular occupation (but not necessarily for other work) may receive an annuity at age 60 with 10 years of covered railroad service, or prior to age 60 if he has had 20 years of covered service.

Benefit amounts depend on a worker's past earnings and length of railroad service. The benefit formula is complex, but a long-service worker will typically receive more than a worker with comparable earnings under OASDI. The average monthly benefit in August, 1956, was $102.32 (U.S. Congress, 1957c). Benefits of retired workers and their dependents are not reduced because of income from any other source, unless the worker renders compensated service to any railroad employer or his last employer before the annuity accrued.

Partly because the railroad retirement system is more mature than OASDI (counting years of service before 1937), partly because the average age of railroad workers is comparatively high, and partly because of the more generous benefit structure, tax rates are relatively high under the program, with employers and employees each contributing $6\frac{1}{4}$ per cent of earnings up to $4200 a year.

FEDERAL GOVERNMENT EMPLOYEES

Most civilian employees of the federal government are covered by the civil service retirement system, which was established in 1920. In addition, there are special programs for certain groups, such as foreign-service officers.

The civil service retirement system provides annuities to qualified employees who retire because of age or disability, to the widows and minor children of deceased employees, and, in certain circumstances to the survivors of annuitants. Wives of retired employees are not entitled to benefits.

As under the railroad retirement program, benefit amounts depend on earnings and length of service. Retirement is compulsory at age 70 if the individual has had 15 years or more of service. Optional retirement with full benefits is permitted at age 62 after 5 years of service or at age 60 after 30 years of service. Employees may also retire and receive reduced benefits at age 55 after 30 years of service. Benefits are not reduced because of any other income unless the annuitant becomes re-employed in the federal service, in which case the annuity is deducted from his salary.

In general, benefits are relatively generous for career employees but inadequate for those with less than, say, 15 years of service (Corson and McConnell, 1956). The average monthly benefit for a retired worker in 1956 was $175 (U.S. Congress, 1957c). In all cases the maximum annuity is 80 per cent of the highest average salary earned during any 5 consecutive years, but the annuity can be increased above this amount by voluntary contributions. Employees contribute $6\frac{1}{2}$ per cent of their basic pay, while each federal agency pays an equivalent amount into the retirement fund for its employees.

STATE AND LOCAL GOVERNMENT EMPLOYEES

Retirement systems for certain groups of state and local government employees were established very early. At present it is estimated that almost three-fourths of the employees of state and local governments are covered by general or special state and local government retirement systems.

These systems vary greatly in the generosity of their provisions. Three types may be distinguished, in order of liberality —those for policemen and firemen, those for teachers, and programs for all other employees (Corson and McConnell, 1956; Turnbull *et al.*, 1957). Nearly all the plans are contributory, and most of them provide for retirement because of disability as well as in old age. Qualifying conditions

and amounts of benefits differ greatly. Typically, an employee must have had a considerable period of service to qualify or receive a substantial annuity, but, in general, the benefits are less liberal than those received by federal civil servants. Except for the systems for policemen and firemen, most of the programs make only limited provision for survivors. Ordinarily, survivors' benefits take the form of a refund of contributions or of continuing payments to the survivors of an annuitant who has chosen to take a reduced benefit for himself as long as he lives (U.S. Social Security Administration, 1957b).

As we have seen, the Social Security Act permits a state to enter into a voluntary agreement with the federal government to provide coverage under OASDI for groups of state or local government employees. Where a state or local retirement program exists, a majority of its members must favor OASDI coverage in a secret referendum before it can be effected. By the end of 1957, more than three million state and local government employees had been covered under the federal system. Well over half of these were also members of state or local systems. According to a survey conducted in 1952, the significance of old age and survivors coverage was especially apparent in some of the states that had provided virtually no protection ten years earlier (McCamman, 1953).

VETERANS' BENEFITS

Ever since the American Revolution, the government has assumed some measure of responsibility for the economic security of veterans. Historically, disability benefits and old age pensions have been the most common types of aid provided, but there have also been cash bonuses, medical and hospital care, and other types of benefits.

The case for a special pension program for aged veterans has been weakened by the expansion of coverage under OASDI, so that from now on the great majority of veterans reaching retirement age will be eligible for old age and survivors insurance. At present, a "service" pension is provided for veterans of the Spanish-American War and earlier wars. Veterans of World War I, World War II, and the Korean War are entitled to (1) compensation for service-connected disabilities or (2) to pensions awarded to those with non-service-connected disabilities (March, 1956; President's Commission on Veteran's Pensions, 1956).

Service-connected disabilities are rated in accordance with extent of impairment of earning power, and monetary compensation rates range from $17 a month for a 10 per cent rating to $181 for total disability, plus dependents' allowance up to $91 monthly for those disabled 50 per cent or more. These are the rates for wartime disabilities; peacetime disabilities are compensated at 80 per cent of these rates.

In the case of non-service-connected disabilities, the veteran receives a pension if he is totally and permanently disabled, is unemployable, and his income is not more than $1400 a year if single or $2700 if he is married or has dependent children. At age 65, however, a 10 per cent disability is regarded as total. On this basis it has been estimated that half the veterans of the recent wars would be eligible for a pension at age 65 (President's Commission on Veterans' Pensions, 1956). For a permanent and total disability that is not service-connected, the pension is $66.15 a month, but after 10 years, or age 65, the pension is raised to $78.75.

Continuation of these policies would mean substantially expanded expenditures for pensions when the average World War I veteran reaches age 65 (in 1959) and very heavy expenditures when the large number of World War II and Korean War veterans reach age 65. A presidential commission headed by General of the Army Omar N. Bradley, reporting in 1956, recommended retention of the veterans' pension program, but with a number of changes that would result in "practical coordination of benefits under the old-age and survivors insurance and Veterans Administration programs that would avoid duplication when old-age and survivors insurance reaches reasonable maturity" (President's Commission on Veterans' Pensions, p. 18).

ARMED SERVICES PROGRAMS

Retirement programs for members of the armed services are financed by annual congressional appropriations and are non-contributory. The programs of the various branches of the services differ somewhat, but, in general, a serviceman may retire after 20 years of service (with the consent of his branch) and receive a monthly income for life. Benefits are related to his highest base pay and his years of service. If the serviceman dies after he leaves the service, survivors' benefits depend on his status as a veteran. If he dies while on active duty, his family receives a lump sum equal to 6 months' pay plus the burial benefits and service-connected death compensation available to families of veterans.

Members of the armed services on active duty have also been covered by OASDI since January 1, 1957. Those in service after 1956 receive credit for service from 1951 on even if it is used for purposes of other retirement benefits paid by the armed services or the Veterans Administration. World War II veterans and those in service thereafter are, with certain restrictions, given wage credits of $160 for each month of active military service through December, 1956.

E. Private Pension Plans and Other Employee Benefit Plans

The rapid growth of private employee benefit plans has been one of the most significant and striking developments of the period since 1940. To a considerable extent, the more recent plans have been developed under collective bargaining, largely in response to union pressure, in contrast with earlier employee benefit plans, which were frequently adopted on the employer's initiative. At the end of 1957, hospitalization and life insurance were the most common types of protection provided, covering some 37–38 million employees in each case, but large numbers of workers were also covered under plans providing for surgical or other medical expenses, accidental death benefits, temporary disability benefits, or retirement benefits (Skolnik and Zisman, 1959). The more recently developed supplemental unemployment benefit plans covered only about 2 million workers.

Although we shall be concerned primarily with private pension plans, it is important to recognize that group life insurance plans also contribute to the economic security of older persons, and, at a later point, we shall discuss the coverage of retired workers under health and welfare plans.

THE GROWTH OF PRIVATE PENSION PLANS

The first industrial pension plan in this country was established by the American Express Company in 1875 (Zisman, 1957). Although other employers followed suit, the movement developed slowly and was chiefly confined to large companies. Enactment of the Social Security Act stimulated a good many employers to adopt plans which provided for supplementation of OASI benefits, but it was not until World War II that the real upsurge of private pension plan coverage got under way, spurred on by government wage-stabilization policies which permitted the granting of "fringe benefits" in lieu of wage increases and by tax policies which permitted an employer to treat contributions to an approved pension plan as a business expense. The ruling of the National Labor Relations Board in 1948 that pensions were a proper subject for collective bargaining touched off a third expansionary stage, which is still under way.

At the end of 1957 it was estimated that 17.7 million persons were covered by private pension or deferred profit-sharing plans (Skolnik and Zisman, 1959). They represented only about 36 per cent of all wage earners and salary workers, however, and were concentrated to a considerable extent in relatively large firms and in manufacturing or finance and insurance companies. A study made in New York State, for example, indicated that the proportion of workers covered by pension plans rose from 14.1 per cent for establishments with less than 20 workers to 88.6 per cent for establishments with 2500 or more (New York, 1955).

MAJOR FEATURES OF PLANS

Although the majority of pension plans adopted prior to 1930 were non-contributory, those established during the 1930's were usually contributory. Then, in the 1940's, the pendulum tended to swing in the other direction, and, especially since 1949, most new plans have been non-contributory, while some of the older plans have been shifted to a non-contributory basis (Civic, 1956).

Most early pension plans were on a pay-as-you-go basis, but the majority are now funded, that is, provide for the accumulation of reserves to meet future benefit payments. At the end of 1956 approximately 4.5 million workers were covered by plans funded with insurance companies, while about 8.4 million were covered by trusteed plans—those that were funded under corporate, multiemployer, or union auspices. Approximately 1.1 million workers were under pay-as-you-go plans (Holland, 1957).

In at least one frequently cited survey of pension plans, a useful distinction has been made between "pattern" plans—those adopted by certain international unions and negotiated, with only minor variations, with individual companies or groups of companies—and "conventional" plans—all other plans, including practically every plan dating from the years before 1950. The study was based on 240 plans (covering 4 million workers) in effect in 1953–55, including some 55 pattern plans and 185 conventional plans (Bankers Trust Company, 1956). Pattern plans, it was found, were generally non-contributory and, except in the steel and rubber industries, provided for flat benefit amounts which varied with years of service but not with rates of earnings. Conventional plans usually provided benefits which varied both with years of service and with earnings rates. Almost half of the conventional plans were contributory, but the larger plans tended to be non-contributory. It has been estimated that about 27 per cent of all employees covered are under pattern plans, while the remainder are under conventional plans (Holland, 1957).

ELIGIBILITY PROVISIONS

Eligibility requirements are of two main types: (1) those relating to participation in the plan and (2) those relating to benefit eligibility. Pattern plans usually have requirements of the second type only, calling for the completion of 10–15 years of service in order to qualify for benefits. There has been a trend toward reducing the number of years of service required for benefit eligibility. The conventional plans tend to have similar provisions but, in addition, usually require the completion of a certain number of years of service, ranging from less than 1 to 5 years, before an employee may participate in the plan. Many plans also have maximum age requirements, typically limiting eligibility to those under age 65. The majority of plans have no minimum age requirement, but, in those that do, a frequent stipulation is that an employee must have attained age 25 or age 30 before participating in the plan (Zisman, 1957). The trend is in the direction of liberalizing these requirements.

RETIREMENT AGE

Under most pension plans the normal retirement age (i.e., the earliest age at which an employee may retire with full benefits) is 65. Some of the conventional plans used to set a lower normal retirement age for women (60, or sometimes 55), but this practice seems to be disappearing.

Retirement is not necessarily automatic at the normal retirement age, however. The automatic or compulsory retirement age is the age at which an employee must retire unless special consent is obtained from the employer, and in a good many plans the automatic retirement age is higher than the normal retirement age.[11] The Bankers Trust Company found that 35 per cent of the pattern plans included in its study set 68 as the automatic retirement age, while 33 per cent had no automatic age, and in 27 per cent of the plans the automatic and normal retirement ages were the same (age 65). There appeared to be a trend away from establishing any automatic retirement age in these plans.

Under three-fourths of the conventional plans, however, 65 was both the normal and the automatic retirement age, and there was no clear-cut trend in the direction of raising or eliminating the automatic retirement age. Another distinction between pattern and conventional plans is that under the pattern plans deferred retirement is more likely to result in increased benefits.

Optional early retirement with actuarially reduced benefits is frequently permitted, from age 55 or age 60, but usually only if the employee has completed a specified period of service (commonly 10 or 15 years) and under a number of plans only with the consent of the employer. The great majority of pattern plans and nearly half of the conventional plans also permit early retirement because of disability—usually specified as total and permanent disability. Disability benefits are frequently not pay-

[11] In a recent study conducted by the Bureau of Labor Statistics, a distinction was made between compulsory retirement provisions, in which the employee must retire unless the employer gives him special permission to continue working, and automatic retirement provisions, which irrevocably ban employment beyond a specified age (Kolodrubetz, 1958). Most studies, however, have not made this distinction, although some plans provide for compulsory retirement at, say, age 65 and automatic retirement at a somewhat later age (see chap. xi).

able unless the employee has served a certain number of years (usually 15 or more). Some of the plans also have a minimum age requirement for these benefits (generally 50). There has been a trend toward liberalizing early retirement provisions and toward including provisions for early retirement because of disability in an increasing proportion of the pattern plans (Bankers Trust Company, 1956).

BENEFIT FORMULAS

Benefit formulas in private pension plans vary widely. As already indicated, pattern plans usually provide for a flat amount per month per year of service, regardless of rate of earnings, and there has been a trend toward eliminating any provision for deducting social security benefits from the amount provided under the private plan (Bankers Trust Company, 1956).

Under conventional plans the most common type of benefit formula provides for benefits amounting to a certain percentage of average earnings during the employee's entire credited period of service for each year of service. A frequent formula in plans adopted in the early 1950's, for example, was 1 per cent per year of service on the first $3000 of average annual earnings and 2 per cent on the excess of earnings above $3000 (U.S. Social Security Administration, 1956).

In recent years, however, under the impact of rising price and wage levels, there has been a tendency to shift to formulas under which retirement benefits are related to average compensation in the last 5 or 10 years of service. An example of this type of formula might be $1\frac{1}{2}$ per cent of average annual compensation in the 5 years preceding retirement for each year of service. The Bankers Trust Company study (1956) found that 38 per cent of the conventional plans studied provided benefits based in whole or in part on compensation in an employee's final years of service and that the proportion of plans including such formulas was rising. There is growing interest,

also, in plans providing for variable annuities and in escalator plans which adjust annuities for changes in the cost of living (Kolodrubetz, 1958).[12]

Under the conventional plans, also, there appears to have been a trend away from integration with social security benefits, but a substantial proportion still provide for it, usually through one of the following methods: (1) deduction of all or part of social security benefits from the benefits provided under the plan; (2) exclusion of taxable earnings (now defined under OASDI as annual earnings under $4800) from the private pension plan; or (3) use of a graduated percentage formula which results in a larger pension on non-taxable than on taxable earnings (Civic, 1956; Turnbull *et al.*, 1957).

Private pension plans make no provision for dependents' benefits and rarely provide specifically for survivorship benefits, in contrast with private plans in a number of European countries, which do make some provision for survivors' benefits (U.S. Social Security Administration, 1953a). Under most conventional plans in this country, however, the employee may elect to receive one of several types of annuities under which reduced benefits are paid during his lifetime, and a residual amount is paid to his widow or another beneficiary after his death.

On the basis of information compiled in 1956 relating to thirteen of the larger plans, employees with 30 years of service and level monthly wages of $350 would have received monthly pensions varying from $50 to $146. The data suggest, not only that amounts payable vary widely, but also that even for 30-year service workers they would rarely be adequate (except for those with high salaries) in the absence of OASDI benefits. However, virtually all workers now retiring who are eligible for private pensions are also eligible for OASDI, and the combined amounts are

[12] For further discussion of variable annuities see chap. xiv.

probably adequate in most instances for workers who have had steady earnings and lengthy service.

VESTING PROVISIONS

Under contributory pension plans an employee who leaves his job before retirement is always entitled to his accumulated contributions, sometimes in a lump sum but more often as a right to receive whatever pension has accrued when he reaches retirement age. If he may also leave his job without forfeiting his employer's contributions, he is said to have acquired "vested" rights. Under non-contributory plans, an employee who terminates his employment prior to retirement forfeits his pension rights unless there are vesting provisions or early-retirement provisions. Although an early-retirement provision with specified minimum age and service requirements is equivalent to a vesting provision with the same age and service requirements, in practice early retirement frequently requires the employer's consent, and special vesting provisions are often more liberal as to age and service requirements than early-retirement provisions.

Labor economists have argued that pension plans which do not provide for vesting discourage labor mobility (Kerr, 1949; Palmer, 1954; Clague, 1956). Furthermore, workers who are permanently laid off for any reason may lose all their pension rights. Hence there has been a great deal of interest in vesting provisions.

Although many early conventional plans, and practically all of the early pattern plans, did not provide for vesting, there has been a trend toward inserting and liberalizing vesting provisions. Twenty-seven per cent of the pattern plans studied by the Bankers Trust Company included special vesting provisions, while about half of the conventional plans included such provisions.

If vesting provisions alone are analyzed, the majority of the plans covered by the Bankers Trust Company study that included vesting provisions had a combination of age and service requirements for vesting, but a large minority had service requirements only.[13] The most common age requirement was 50 years, but considerable numbers of plans specified age 40, 45, or 55. Service requirements most frequently stipulated 10 years of service, but a large number of plans specified 15 years, while smaller numbers of plans specified 5 or fewer years, or, at the other end of the scale, 20 or more years. In most cases, full vesting was provided, but a significant minority of plans called for partial vesting, with full vesting rights to accrue gradually with additional years of service or in a series of steps.

In recent years a number of multiemployer pension plans have been negotiated, usually covering the members of a single union in a particular geographical area and in many cases providing that an employee will retain all accrued pension credits if he shifts from one employer to another *within* the plan. Examples of such plans are those of the Distributing, Processing, and Office Workers in the New York area, the International Longshoremen's and Warehousemen's Union on the Pacific Coast, and the Western Conference of Teamsters.

STRENGTHS AND WEAKNESSES OF PRIVATE PENSION PLANS

Most observers are agreed that private pension plans provide a valuable supplement to OASDI for those workers who are covered. Union pressure for private pension plans, moreover, has probably influenced employers to offer less resistance to liberalization of the OASDI program. But there is no doubt (1) that it is the worker in the strong union and the large company

---

[13] The Bankers Trust Company report lumped vesting and early-retirement provisions in its analysis of vesting provisions, but, for reasons indicated in the text, this procedure does not provide a clear picture of vesting provisions. However, the report furnishes details of the individual plans, which permits separate analysis of vesting provisions.

who has chiefly benefited from the expansion of private pension plans, (2) that employers have frequently cited pension costs or benefit eligibility provisions of pension plans as one reason for not hiring older workers, and (3) that firms with pension plans are much more likely to have compulsory retirement policies than firms without such plans. Whether and to what extent pension plans have actually impeded voluntary labor mobility is a more debatable point (Ross, 1958).[14]

F. Other Social Policies Affecting the Economic Position of the Aged

INCOME-TAX PROVISIONS

Tax exemptions are widely used as instruments of governmental policy to assist elderly persons in living on reduced income. A number of state governments provide for special tax exemptions of one kind or another for the elderly. Under federal government legislation, elderly persons benefit from a number of special provisions affecting their income-tax liability. An individual who has reached the age of 65 is not required to file a federal income tax return unless he has a gross annual income of $1200 (rather than the usual $600). Furthermore, many forms of retirement income are wholly or partially exempt from taxation. Old age and survivors insurance benefits, old age assistance payments, railroad retirement benefits, and veterans' benefits are wholly exempt and need not be included in reported gross income. But annuities resulting entirely from employers' contributions (under non-contributory pension plans) must be included in gross reported income (U.S. Internal Revenue Service, 1957). On other types of annuities the recipient receives annual exclusions which, in effect, are equal to his investment in the annuity prorated over his life-expectancy.

[14] Recently there has been growing recognition of the fact that pension costs are not necessarily higher for older workers (see chap. xiv).

Since 1954, moreover, a tax credit of 20 per cent is permitted on up to $1200 of certain types of retirement income for persons who have earned at least $600 in any 10 years preceding the taxable year and for widows whose husbands had such earnings before death. There is also a special provision applying to deductions for medical expenses for persons aged 65 and over. Although other taxpayers may deduct only those medical and dental expenses which exceed 3 per cent of their adjusted gross income, the 3 per cent limitation is not applicable to those aged 65 and over. However, for all taxpayers these deductions are subject to maximum limitations and to special limitations on the amounts spent for medicine and drugs.

HOUSING POLICY

Although the housing problems of the aged are discussed in detail in chapter xvi, an analysis of economic security programs for older persons would not be complete without some mention of efforts which have been made to provide subsidized housing or, in other ways, to assist older persons in meeting their special housing needs.

Governmental housing policy in relation to older persons is in its infancy in this country in comparison with the situation in certain European countries (particularly England and the Scandinavian countries) which have been developing housing policies to meet the needs of various categories of elderly persons for many years. Certain unions, churches, and other organizations in this country have maintained homes for their elderly or retired members for some years, and charitable homes for the needy aged have been maintained by community chest organizations in a number of communities. Under the impetus of the federal provisions of the old age assistance program, moreover, there has been some improvement in the standards maintained by nursing homes and other institutions providing sheltered care for old age assistance recipients. The need for such accommodations may be expected to expand in view of the rising proportion, within the total aged population, of those aged 75 and over, who are most likely to need institutional care.

There has been a growing interest, however, in the housing needs of the non-institutional aged population (Donahue, 1954). The National Housing Act was amended in 1950 to provide for aid to non-profit, co-operative housing organizations in financing co-operative housing projects for older people, while the Housing Act of 1956 included several provisions relating to housing for the aged (U.S. Congress, 1957c). Prior to 1956, low-rent public housing units had been available only for families, but the new act permits a single person aged 65 or over to qualify for public housing if he meets the other eligibility requirements. It further provides that public housing authorities may (1) assist the construction of new housing or the remodeling of existing housing in order to provide accommodation for elderly families; (2) extend preference to elderly families with respect to housing units suitable to their needs; (3) waive the requirement that they must come from unsafe, unsanitary, or overcrowded dwellings; and (4) incur a cost of up to $2250 per room for public housing units specifically designed for elderly families, in contrast with $1750 per room for regular units.

The 1956 act also amended FHA requirements to permit the payment of a down payment by an individual or corporation other than the mortgagor when the mortgagor was 60 years of age or older. This permits an elderly person to borrow the down payment, subject to regulations of the FHA commissioner. In addition, more liberal financing requirements were adopted in connection with the construction or rehabilitation of rental housing specifically designed for elderly families if the mortgagor is a qualified non-profit organization.

HEALTH AND MEDICAL CARE

Vitally affecting the economic status of older persons are their special needs for medical care.[15] The California Health Survey indicated that those 65 years of age and over experienced nearly three times as many days of disability in a year, on the average, as the general population and were twice as likely to be suffering from chronic conditions (California, 1957). The average annual cost of private medical care for persons 65 years of age and over in 1952–53 was $102, compared with $65 a year for the general population, according to a nation-wide survey (Anderson and Feldman, 1956).

Even in those cases in which the income of an elderly person is adequate to cover annual costs of this magnitude, it will rarely suffice to meet the above-average costs of a period of unusually extended illness, which frequently requires extensive dissaving or assistance from relatives. Hence the question of health insurance coverage for the aged is critical. A nation-wide survey by the Bureau of the Census in September, 1956, indicated that only 36.5 per cent of all persons aged 65 or over had health insurance as compared with 63.6 per cent of the population as a whole (U.S. Social Security Administration, 1958a). However, the health insurance owned by aged persons applies for the most part, as does that owned by the general population, only to hospitalization and surgical procedures.

This relative absence of health insurance protection for elderly persons reflects the fact that many of those who have been retired for some time were never covered by the health and welfare plans which have become so prevalent in industry and also the fact that many of these plans do not cover retired workers. A National Industrial Conference Board study, published in 1955, though indicating a significant development in the direction of covering re-

[15] A more detailed discussion of this problem is presented in chaps. vii and xv.

tired workers, showed that in only 40 per cent of the 327 companies studied were retired workers eligible for hospital benefits and in only 37 per cent were they eligible for surgical benefits (Brower, 1955). Furthermore, the amount of protection was decreased for retired workers in nearly half of those plans that did provide continued eligibility for benefits.

A retired worker may in some cases continue to be covered on an individual basis under Blue Cross and Blue Shield plans, but the rates for individual coverage are comparatively high, and the majority of these plans limit non-group enrolment to persons under 65. Some insurance companies also sell individual policies to older persons, but the rates tend to rise quite sharply with age, and there are other disadvantages, including the fact that many policies are cancelable (Turnbull *et al.,* 1957).

In recent years there has been a marked rise in public concern over the problem of more adequate health protection for older persons. The new federal program of grants-in-aid for medical expenses for old age assistance recipients will aid those coming under that program, although its implementation at the state level is being opposed by doctors in some of the states. Earlier we have referred to the controversy that has been generated over the Forand bill, which would provide hospital and surgical insurance for elderly persons and their dependents under OASDI. Perhaps partly in response to the pressures for government programs, some of the private insurance companies have recently begun to make health insurance available for elderly persons at more moderate rates and on a "guaranteed renewable" basis.

VI. Contrasting Features of Foreign Old Age Security Programs

A. *Insurance and Assistance Programs*

By 1958, fifty-seven countries, in addition to the United States, had a govern-

ment old age security program (Gerig, 1958). About forty-five of the programs were of a social insurance character, but there were six countries (Canada, Denmark, Finland, New Zealand, Norway, and Sweden), in which a pension was available to every resident above a specified age, without conditions as to past contributions or employment. In addition, there were three countries (Australia, Iceland, and South Africa) in which pensions were provided only on an income-test or means-test basis and several other countries in which the only form of public protection against long-term risks was a government-operated provident or compulsory saving fund or (in Nationalist China) a program providing lump-sum payments.

Most of the foreign programs provided for survivors' benefits, while about a fourth of the countries had a supplemental assistance program providing for payments to needy aged persons, invalids, or survivors. In Ireland, old age payments were available on an assistance basis only, but there was an insurance program for disabled persons and survivors.

B. *Characteristics of Insurance Programs*

COVERAGE

Throughout Europe, old age security plans tend to cover all wage-earners and salaried employees, although a few countries also cover the self-employed. Some European countries exclude agricultural workers and/or domestic workers. In Britain, the Netherlands, the Scandinavian countries, and Switzerland, coverage is not limited to employed persons but covers all adult residents or resident citizens, with certain exceptions, under pensionable age.

Under the more recently adopted plans in South America, the Middle East, and Asia, coverage tends to be somewhat less broad, frequently excluding agricultural workers, who constitute a large proportion of the employed population in many of these countries. On the other hand, the old age pension programs in Australia, Egypt, New Zealand, and South Africa call for payments to aged residents or citizens, in some cases on the basis of an income test, as we have already indicated.

QUALIFYING CONDITIONS

The normal pensionable age for men is 65 in approximately half of the foreign programs and 60 in about a third. In a few countries it is as low as 50 or 55 or as high as 67 or 70. The countries with low normal pensionable ages are chiefly non-European relatively underdeveloped countries with comparatively high death rates. Many of the programs also provide that men engaged in mining or other unhealthful occupations may receive normal pension benefits 5 years (in some cases 10 years) earlier than those in other occupations. The most common pensionable age for women is 60, but about a fourth of the countries set age 65, about a third age 55 or age 50, and a few age 67 or 70. A number of programs permit reduced benefits at an earlier age, while some permit retirement with full benefits at earlier ages if contributions have been paid over a sufficiently long period.

Most of the old age insurance programs in foreign countries require a specified period in covered employment as a condition of eligibility for benefits. There is wide variation in the length of the required period, however, ranging from 5 years or less in some countries to 30 years for normal retirement benefits in France and in Uruguay. A few countries require a shorter period for women, while in some cases the required periods vary in length according to broad occupational categories. A number of countries, particularly in Europe, provide credit for specified periods of non-employment (e.g., periods of unemployment or illness).

Retirement is not always a condition for the receipt of benefits under foreign old age insurance systems. Some countries—Albania, Greece, and Rumania, for exam-ple—do not require retirement as a condition for receiving benefits. The Soviet Union formerly belonged to this group of countries, but, under a new pension law which recently became effective, a retirement test was imposed (International Labour Office, 1958*b*). Certain other countries—Austria, except for casual work, Costa Rica, the Dominican Republic, Greece, Nicaragua, Portugal, and Uruguay—specifically require retirement. Many countries, however, have no specific provision relating to retirement but use a benefit formula with an annual increment feature which would result in increased benefits for those postponing retirement beyond the normal age. About a dozen countries have specific provisions providing increased benefits for those who postpone retirement. Great Britain, for example, increases benefits by 1*s.* 6*d.* per week for every 25 contributions paid for weeks of employment between pensionable age (65 for men and 60 for women) and 5 years later. Persons receiving retirement pensions in this 5-year age bracket may earn up to 50*s.* a week without incurring any reduction in benefits. From age 70 on for men, and age 65 for women, retirement is not a condition for the receipt of benefits (Great Britain, 1946; International Labour Office, 1957*a*, 1957*b*, 1958*a*).

BENEFIT FORMULAS

The benefit formulas under foreign old age insurance systems resemble, in most cases, the type of formula used in our conventional private pension and civil service retirement plans—benefit amounts represent a certain percentage of earnings for each year of service. In response to inflationary pressures, many countries have adopted *ad hoc* increases in benefits since World War II. More recently, however, there has been growing interest in more fundamental changes under which benefit levels would be automatically adjusted for changes in the cost of living or the wage level, and, in some cases, entire benefit structures would be brought into line with recent earnings levels (Myers, 1958).

The most far-reaching innovation of this type is embodied in the amendments adopted by the West German government early in 1957 (Farman, 1957; International Labour Office, 1957c; Myers, 1958). Under the new benefit formula, the unadjusted monthly benefit amount equals 1.5 per cent of the individual's earnings for each year of coverage. This amount is then adjusted so that it bears the same relationship to the general wage level in the 3 years preceding the individual's retirement that his total covered earnings bore to national average earnings during his period of coverage. If, for example, an individual was employed for 40 years with earnings at the national average, his monthly benefit would amount to 60 per cent of the national average wage level in the 3 years before his retirement. If his earnings had been above or below the national average, his benefit would be proportionately higher or lower. The new formula applies to all those retiring after the effective date of the amendments, while those currently on the rolls received an adjustment which would bring their benefits into line with the new method of computation.

A somewhat different approach to the problem of rising earnings levels has been adopted under several new or revised laws enacted recently in eastern Europe. Benefits are related to an individual's final earnings but not to total lifetime earnings, except that those with particularly long periods of coverage get slightly higher benefits. Under the new Russian law, for example, monthly benefits are based on the average monthly wage in the last 12 months before retirement or, if the applicant chooses, on the average wage in any 5 consecutive years out of the last 10 years of work. Benefits range from 100 per cent of the base wage for those with average monthly earnings under 350 rubles to 50 per cent for those with over 1000 rubles. A supplement of 10 per cent of the pension is granted to persons with unusually long earnings records, while the provisions are somewhat more generous for those who have been engaged in underground or unhealthy work (International Social Security Association, 1958). Laws recently enacted in Czechoslovakia and Poland have somewhat similar provisions (Erben, 1957; International Labour Office, 1958c).

The countries with universal pension systems, together with Israel, the Netherlands, Spain, and the United Kingdom, provide for flat monthly benefits. In general, the aim has been to provide the aged with a minimum level of subsistence and to rely on individual saving, private pension plans, and, in some countries, government-sponsored supplementary pension programs to provide additional protection. Historically, old age pensions in most of these countries have been granted on the basis of an income test, but in some cases the income test has been eliminated or retained only for supplementary pensions. The problem of adjusting the flat benefit amounts for changes in the cost of living has been approached in a variety of ways.

In Great Britain the regular contributory pension has been raised several times in the postwar period. In 1958 it amounted to 50s. for an individual and to 80s. for an elderly couple (International Labour Office, 1958a). The British Labour party (1957), however, has recently issued a policy statement announcing support for a drastically revised scheme under which the present flat benefits would be supplemented by national "superannuation" benefits which would be wage-related and computed on the basis of a formula similar to the one recently adopted in West Germany. Private pension plans would be integrated with the new system, so that a worker might be covered by a private pension scheme as an alternative to the national superannuation program, but the private plans would have to be brought into line with the national system and would have to permit transferability of pension rights for all workers shifting jobs.

In the Scandinavian countries the

amount of the flat benefit varies by size of community and in most cases is automatically adjusted for changes in the cost of living. In a recent referendum held in Sweden, the voters expressed preference for a system under which the basic pension would take the form of a flat benefit, while a new employer-financed supplementary pension would be added, with benefits computed on the basis of a formula on the West German model (International Labour Office, 1958*b*).

FINANCING PROVISIONS

Although the majority of foreign old age insurance systems provide for payroll and withholding taxes on employer and employee, as does our system, most of them also call for a sizable government contribution. Not infrequently the law provides that the government contribution shall be adjusted to take care of any deficit.

Here again, however, the provisions in some of the British Commonwealth and Scandinavian countries deviate from the general pattern, calling for earmarked income taxes. Denmark, for example, has a special national pension tax amounting to 1 per cent of each taxpayer's total income. Canada provides for a 2 per cent individual income tax (up to a maximum of $60 a year) that is earmarked for the program, plus a 2 per cent corporate income tax and a 2 per cent manufacturer's sales tax, also earmarked, with the sales tax constituting the government's contribution. The British financing system provides for flat weekly contributions from insured persons (including non-employed insured persons), employers, and the government rather than the more usual wage-related contributions.

INVALIDITY INSURANCE

Almost every foreign country with an old age insurance program also has an invalidity insurance program that is closely associated with it. The majority, moreover, have compulsory health insurance systems.

The invalidity insurance systems differ from the American program of disability benefits in that they usually apply to all adults who have been covered for a minimum period (generally much less than that required for old age benefits) and are payable in cases of severe partial as well as permanent and total disability. Benefit amounts are sometimes defined as a specific percentage of average earnings or recent earnings, sometimes are computed on the same basis as old age benefits, and sometimes vary with the severity of the disability.

VII. CONCLUSIONS

Clearly, we have made substantial progress in the last two decades toward the goal of eliminating destitution in old age. Although it is still true that an appreciable proportion of elderly persons, particularly among the women, are without any money income, the proportion is declining and will continue to decline as more and more elderly people become eligible for retirement and survivors' benefits.

The goal of providing an *adequate* income for older persons, however, is reached with greater difficulty. We may look forward to a continued rise in real national income and to a probable leveling-off in the proportion of older people in the population, which will facilitate providing a more adequate level of real income for retired persons. But the long-run inflationary trend, which most economists expect to continue, is likely to mean a continued decline in the real purchasing power of accumulated savings and to necessitate difficult decisions as to how often, and by what methods, we are prepared to adjust retirement benefits to keep pace with the rising level of consumer prices.

A. Benefit Adequacy and the Problem of Inflation

The problem of maintaining adequate benefits under old age security programs in the face of inflationary pressures is, as we have suggested earlier, particularly complex, especially if benefits are related to past earnings. As Wilbur Cohen (1957*a*) has pointed out, tying the level of OASDI benefits to changes in the Consumer Price Index would represent only a partial solution. It would imply that current benefit levels are adequate and that their adequacy can be maintained in the future simply by making adjustments for changes in the consumer price level. But our discussion of budgetary requirements suggests, as a rough approximation, that an elderly couple or individual living in an urban area would require monthly benefits somewhere in the neighborhood of the current maximums to maintain an adequate level of living in the absence of other sources of income. Yet the great majority of OASDI beneficiaries are, as we have seen, receiving benefits which are far below the current maximums, based as they are in many cases on earnings received when wages were well below current levels. To shift the entire benefit structure to a reasonable relationship with current wage levels, as has been done in West Germany, would greatly increase the current cost of the program and probably call for special financing provisions for a transitional period. Yet, in reckoning the actual net cost of such a step, it would be important to bear in mind the probability of certain offsetting savings, such as a decline in old age assistance payments to persons concurrently receiving grossly inadequate OASDI benefits.

There are other alternative methods of revising benefit levels that might be considered, such as liberalizing the provisions for drop-out periods in reckoning past earnings or going over to a formula under which benefits would be related to the 5 or 10 consecutive years of highest individual earnings. The pros and cons of these alternative methods cannot be fully discussed here, but it is important to bear in mind that any proposal for a change in the benefit formula requires consideration of whether it shall apply only to persons qualifying for benefits in the future or to all

persons currently receiving benefits as well. Furthermore, even a formula which relates benefits to earnings in the last few years before retirement does not, in the absence of other provisions, protect beneficiaries from inflation occurring during the course of their retirement. In addition, there is the important related issue as to whether the ceiling on taxable earnings under the program should be automatically adjusted so as to cover total earnings of the great majority of covered workers.

B. Equity and the Problem of Multiple Programs

Problems of adequacy and equity cannot be neatly separated in appraising social security programs, since interrelated questions of adequacy and equity enter into all decisions with respect to the benefit and contribution structure under every program. Nevertheless, our complex American system of public old age security programs for various groups and at various governmental levels, together with numerous private programs, poses more difficult problems of equity than are likely to be encountered in an appraisal of the somewhat more unified foreign programs.

Now that the vast majority of workers are covered by OASDI or some other federal or state government retirement program, it can be argued that nearly everyone has an opportunity for basic protection under a government program, while a rising proportion have an opportunity for supplementary protection under a private pension plan or some other public program. Yet this broad argument glosses over the glaringly sharp contrasts in the extent of protection attainable by individuals in various situations.

At one extreme are the aged individuals who have never qualified for OASDI and live in states with unusually low monthly OAA payments or those who barely qualify for minimal OASDI benefits. At the other extreme—leaving out of consideration elderly persons with ample private assets—

are those fortunate individuals who can qualify for benefits under each of three or four retirement programs. In between are large numbers who may at one time have been covered by both OASDI and a second retirement program, public or private, but who shifted jobs either voluntarily or involuntarily before serving long enough to be eligible for benefits under the second program.

Although we are undoubtedly committed to a complex system of multiple programs for the indefinite future, some of the inequities could be removed through closer integration of certain programs with OASDI, as recommended by the Bradley Commission in the case of veterans' pensions. On the whole, however, the most effective way of meeting the problem of inequity is to improve the basic protection offered under OASDI.

C. The Need for a Preventive Approach

In the long run the goal of economic security for older people must be sought, not merely through income-security measures for the aged, but also through greater emphasis on the preventive approach in attacking the sources of economic distress in old age. Adoption of the preventive approach implies directing attention at the *social and economic adjustments associated with aging* rather than at the *social and economic problems of old age*. It implies analyzing the sources of economic distress in old age in relation to their antecedents in an individual's earlier career.

If widowhood, illness, and obsolescence of skills are the major sources of economic distress in old age, as Steiner and Dorfman (1957) have cogently argued, we are provided with a set of clues as to where to direct at least part of our attention in developing a preventive approach.

Widows constitute the largest single group (by sex and marital status) in the aged population, and this will become even more true in the future. They are also the most seriously impoverished group. As a

result of the rapid rise in the labor-force-participation rate of married women—particularly those aged 35–65—the elderly widows of the future will be much more likely to be eligible for retirement benefits on their own, both public and private, than the aged widows of today and will thus be likely to receive substantially higher amounts than if they were dependent solely on survivors' benefits. Should this trend be encouraged? Should we seek to expand retraining facilities for married women with rusty skills who want to re-enter the labor force after their children are in school? Should employers modify hiring policies that discriminate against the older women? Whatever one's views as to the impact of this trend on the sanctity of the home, its implications for the income security of the aged are obvious.

The antecedents of illness in old age also require attention, not merely from the growing number of doctors who are turning their attention to geriatrics, but also from social scientists, who need to analyze the relationships between labor-force status, occupation, income, and health, particularly in the later years of working life. We have seen that persons who have been engaged in certain occupations are more likely to be in good health in old age than those who have been in other occupations. But we know relatively little about the factors lying behind this relationship. Is it the physical strain of certain types of manual jobs, or the relative absence of regular physical check-ups, or other factors which lie behind the less satisfactory physical condition of elderly men who have been engaged in manual work? Only research directed toward these problems will provide the answers.

And what about the problem of obsolescence of skills, that is, the case in which a man's skills are no longer adapted to labor-market requirements? The preventive approach would emphasize educational policies which equip a young man or woman to meet the shifting skill requirements of a world of rapid technological change throughout his or her working career. In an age of automation, a skilled manual worker may find that a thorough grounding in mathematics holds up better in the long run than intricate knowledge of a particular piece of electronic equipment. The preventive approach would also emphasize the desirability of varied job experience rather than exclusive dependence on a particular skill.

The preventive approach to the problem of old age security would also give explicit recognition to the interdependence of all social security programs. The individual who has received adequate unemployment insurance benefits during periods of unemployment is likely to approach retirement with more assets, including at least a mortgage-free house, than one who has experienced serious loss of income through unemployment. The disabled person who has received disability benefits is also likely to approach old age in a better financial position and may, indeed, have been assisted back to work through access to vocational rehabilitation. Thus, though we may not swing over to Britain's "cradle-to-grave" approach to social security, we need to take more explicit account of the impact of each program on all the others and, specifically, on the social and economic adjustments associated with aging.

D. Implications of Certain Labor-Force Trends

Long-run changes in the age, sex, and occupational distribution of the labor force have important implications for the problem of old age security in future decades. We have already referred to the rising proportion of mature married women in the labor force, which will improve the economic position of future generations of elderly wives and widows. On the other hand, the declining labor-force-participation rate of elderly men has had, and probably will continue to have, a deleterious effect on the income status of the aged. This trend has recently been aided and abetted by the rapid growth of private pension plans with their compulsory retirement features. It can be combated through efforts directed toward more flexible retirement provisions and toward improving employment opportunities for elderly men, particularly in part-time jobs.

Another labor-force trend which is likely to have the effect of improving the income status of future generations of older persons is the gradual shift of the occupational structure away from manual jobs, particularly of the heavy, unskilled variety, and toward professional and other white-collar jobs. This means a shift, in general, not only toward higher-income occupations, with steadier employment conditions, but also toward those occupations which appear to be associated with better health and a greater capacity to go on working in old age.

REFERENCES

ANDERSON, O. W., and FELDMAN, J. J. 1956. Family medical health insurance: a nationwide survey. New York: McGraw-Hill Book Co.

BANCROFT, GERTRUDE. 1958. The American labor force: its growth and changing composition. New York: John Wiley & Sons.

BANKERS TRUST COMPANY. 1956. A study of industrial retirement plans. New York: Bankers Trust Co.

BOND, F. A., BABER, R. E., VIEG, J. A., PERRY, L. B., SCAFF, A. H., and LEE, L. J., JR. 1954. Our needy aged: a California study of a national problem. New York: Henry Holt & Co.

BRITISH LABOUR PARTY. 1957. National superannuation: Labour's policy for security in old age. London: Labour Party.

BROWER, F. BEATRICE. 1955. Insurance for retired employees. Management Rec., **17**, 104–8.

BURNS, EVELINE M. 1956. Social security and public policy. New York: McGraw-Hill Book Co.

CALIFORNIA. STATE. 1957. DEPARTMENT OF PUBLIC HEALTH. Health in California. Berkeley: California State Printing Office.

CHRISTGAU, V. 1955. Old-age and survivors insurance after twenty years. Social Security Bull., **18** (August), 12–17.

CIVIC, MIRIAM. 1956. Income and resources of older people. ("Studies in Business Economics," No. 52.) New York: National Industrial Conference Board.

CLAGUE, E. 1954. Do American workers save for retirement? *In* G. B. HURFF (ed.), Economic problems of retirement, pp. 9–27. Gainesville: University of Florida Press.

———. 1956. Long-term trends in quit rates. Employment & Earnings, **3** (December), 7–9.

CLARKE, HELEN I. 1957. Social legislation. New York: Appleton-Century-Crofts Co.

COHEN, W. J. 1957a. Income adequacy and pension planning in the United States of America. Bull. Internat. Social Security A., **10**, 483–509.

———. 1957b. Retirement policies under social security. Berkeley: University of California Press.

COHEN, W. J., and MYERS, R. J. 1950. Social security amendments of 1950: a summary and legislative history. Social Security Bull., **13** (October), 3–14.

CONNECTICUT. STATE. 1932. COMMISSION TO INVESTIGATE THE SUBJECT OF OLD AGE PENSIONS. Report on old age relief. Hartford: Published by the State.

CORSON, J. J., and McCONNELL, J. W. 1956. Economic needs of older people. New York: Twentieth Century Fund.

DE SCHWEINITZ, K. 1943. England's road to social security: from the Statute of Laborers in 1349 to the Beveridge Report of 1942. Philadelphia: University of Pennsylvania Press.

DONAHUE, WILMA (ed.). 1954. Housing the aging. Ann Arbor: University of Michigan Press.

DUESENBERRY, J. S. 1952. Income, saving, and the theory of consumer behavior. Cambridge, Mass.: Harvard University Press.

EPLER, ELIZABETH. 1954. Old-age assistance: plan provisions on children's responsibility for parents. Social Security Bull., **17** (April), 3–12.

EPSTEIN, A. 1936. Insecurity: a challenge to America. New York: Random House.

EPSTEIN, LENORE A. 1959. Money income of aged persons: a 10-year review, 1948 to 1958. Social Security Bull., **22** (June), 3–11.

ERBEN, B. 1957. Social security in the Czechoslovak Republic: V. Social Security. Bull. Internat. Social Security A., **10**, 192–201.

FARMAN, C. H. 1957. World trends in social

security benefits, 1955–57. Social Security Bull., **20** (August), 3–14.

FRIEDLANDER, W. A. 1955. Introduction to social welfare. New York: Prentice-Hall, Inc.

FRIEDMAN, M. 1957. A theory of the consumption function. Princeton, N.J.: Princeton University Press.

GERIG, D. 1958. Foreign social security programs in 1958. Social Security Bull., **21** (November), 3–11.

GREAT BRITAIN. 1946. National Insurance Act, 1946. 9 & 10 Geo. 6, chap. 67.

———. 1909. ROYAL COMMISSION ON THE POOR LAWS AND RELIEF OF DISTRESS. Report. Ca. 4499.

HANMER, F. J. 1957. Recipients of old-age assistance: personal and social characteristics. Social Security Bull., **20** (April), 3–13.

HAWKINS, C. E. 1956. Recipients of old-age assistance: income and resources. Social Security Bull., **19** (April), 3–6, 27.

———. 1957a. Recipients of old-age assistance: their requirements. *Ibid.*, **20** (February), 3–8, 27.

———. 1957b. Recipients of old-age assistance: their housing arrangements. *Ibid.* (September), pp. 9–12, 16.

HESS, A. E. 1957. Old-age, survivors, and disability insurance: early problems and operations of the disability provisions. Social Security Bull., **20** (December), 11–21.

HOLLAND, D. M. 1957. The pension climate. *In* E. STEIN (ed.), Proceedings of Tenth Annual Conference on Labor, pp. 1–39. New York: Matthew Bender & Co.

INSTITUTE OF LIFE INSURANCE. 1958. Life insurance fact book. New York: The Institute.

INTERNATIONAL LABOUR OFFICE. 1957a. Social security changes in Great Britain. Industry & Labour, **17**, 35–36.

———. 1957b. Recent social insurance legislation in Great Britain. *Ibid.*, **18**, 396–97.

———. 1957c. Reform of pension schemes in the Federal Republic of Germany. *Ibid.*, pp. 235–42.

———. 1958a. Increases in war pensions, national insurance benefits and national assistance in Great Britain. *Ibid.*, **19**, 107–11.

———. 1958b. Referendum on pension reforms in Sweden. *Ibid.*, pp. 223–36.

———. 1958c. Pensions insurance in Poland. *Ibid.*, **20**, 276–81.

INTERNATIONAL SOCIAL SECURITY ASSOCIATION. 1958. The new state pension law in the U.S.S.R. Bull. Internat. Social Security A., **11**, 220–30.

KAPLAN, S. 1957. Old-age assistance: children's contributions to aged parents. Social Security Bull., **20** (June), 3–8.

KERR, C. 1949. Social and economic implications of private pension plans. Commercial & Financial Chronicle, **170** (December 1), 21, 26.

KOLODRUBETZ, W. W. 1958. Characteristics of pension plans. Monthly Labor Rev., **81**, 845–53.

LEYENDECKER, H. M. 1955. Problems and policies in public assistance. New York: Harper & Bros.

McCAMMAN, DOROTHY. 1953. Retirement protection for state and local employees: ten years of growth. Social Security Bull., **16** (May), 3–10, 24.

MARCH, M. S. 1956. President's Commission on Veteran's Pensions: recommendations. Social Security Bull., **19** (August), 12–18, 32.

MASSACHUSETTS. STATE. 1910. COMMITTEE ON OLD AGE PENSION, ANNUITIES AND INSURANCE. Report. Boston: Wright & Potter.

———. 1914. COMMISSION ON PENSIONS. Report, March 16, 1914. Boston: Wright & Potter.

———. 1916. Report of a special inquiry relative to aged and dependent persons in Massachusetts, 1915. Boston: Wright & Potter.

———. 1925. COMMISSION ON PENSIONS. Report on old-age pensions, November 1925. Boston: Wright & Potter.

MERRIAM, IDA C. 1953. Social welfare programs in the United States. Social Security Bull., **16** (February), 3–12.

MILLER, H. P. 1951. Factors related to recent changes in income in the United States. Rev. Economics & Statistics, **31**, 214–18.

———. 1955. Income of the American people. New York: John Wiley & Sons.

MODIGLIANI, F., and BRUMBERG, R. E. 1954. Utility analysis and the consumption function: an interpretation of cross section data. *In* K. KURIHARA (ed.), The post-Keynesian economics. New Brunswick, N.J.: Rutgers University Press.

MYERS, R. J. 1955. Old-Age and Survivors Insurance: history of the benefit formula. Social Security Bull., **18** (May), 13–17.

———. 1958. International trends in social security. Bull. Internat. Social Security A., **11**, 41–51.

NEW YORK. STATE. 1930. COMMISSION ON OLD AGE SECURITY. Old age security report, February 17, 1930. Albany, N.Y.: J. B. Lyon.

———. 1955. DEPARTMENT OF LABOR. Health and welfare benefits in New York State, June 1954. (Division of Research and Statistics Pub. B-83.) Albany, N.Y.: The Department.

PALMER, GLADYS L. 1954. Social values in labor mobility. *In* E. W. BAKKE (ed.), Labor mobility and economic opportunity. Cambridge, Mass.: Technology Press.

PENNSYLVANIA. STATE. 1919. COMMISSION ON OLD AGE PENSIONS. Report, March 1919. Harrisburg: J. L. L. Kuhn.

———. 1925. COMMISSION ON OLD AGE ASSISTANCE. Report, January 1925. Harrisburg: The Commission.

———. 1926. OLD AGE PENSION COMMISSION. The problem of old age pensions in industry, 1926. Harrisburg: The Commission.

PRESIDENT'S COMMISSION ON VETERANS' PENSIONS. 1956. Veterans' benefits in the United States: findings and recommendations, Vol. **3**. Washington, D.C.: Government Printing Office.

REDER, M. W. 1954. Age and income. Am. Economic Rev., **44**, 661–70.

RONEY, J. L. 1955. Twenty years of public assistance. Social Security Bull., **18** (August), 17–23.

ROSS, A. M. 1958. Do we have a new industrial feudalism? Am. Economic Rev., **48**, 903–20.

ROWNTREE, B. S. 1902. Poverty: a study of town life. London: Macmillan & Co.

———. 1941. Poverty and progress: a second social survey of York. London: Longmans, Green & Co.

ROWNTREE, B. S., and LAVERS, G. R. 1951. Poverty and the welfare state. London: Longmans, Green & Co.

SCHOTTLAND, C. I. 1956. Social security amendments of 1956: a summary and legislative history. Social Security Bull., **19** (September), 3–15, 31.

SKOLNIK, A. M., and ZISMAN, J. 1959. Growth in employee-benefit plans, 1954–57. Social Security Bull., **22** (March), 4–14.

SOMERS, H. M., and SOMERS, ANNE R. 1957. Unemployment insurance and workmen's compensation. Proc. 9th Ann. Meeting Industrial Relations Research A., pp. 120–44.

STEINER, P. O., and DORFMAN, R. 1957. The economic status of the aged. Berkeley: University of California Press.

STOCKMAN, H. W. 1957. History and development of social security in Great Britain. Bull. Internat. Social Security A., **10**, 3–71.

TURNBULL, J. G., WILLIAMS, C. A., JR., and

CHEIT, E. F. 1957. Economic and social security. New York: Ronald Press Co.

U.S. BOARD OF GOVERNORS OF THE FEDERAL RESERVE SYSTEM. 1951a. 1951 Survey of consumer finances, Part III: Distribution of consumer income in 1950. Federal Reserve Bull., **37**, 920–37.

———. 1951b. 1951 Survey of consumer finances, Part IV: Distribution of consumer saving in 1950. *Ibid.*, **37**, 1061–78.

———. 1956. 1956 Survey of consumer finances: the financial position of consumers. *Ibid.*, **42**, 559–72.

———. 1957a. 1957 survey of consumer finances: housing and durable goods. *Ibid.*, **43**, 628–45.

———. 1957b. 1957 survey of consumer finances: the financial position of consumers. *Ibid.*, **43**, 878–901.

———. 1958. 1958 survey of consumer finances: the financial position of consumers. *Ibid.*, **44**, 1027–57.

U.S. BUREAU OF THE CENSUS. 1948. Characteristics of single, married, widowed, and divorced persons in 1947. Current Population Reports: Population Characteristics. (Series P-20, No. 10.) Washington, D.C.: Government Printing Office.

———. 1949. Annual report on the labor force, 1948. Current Population Reports: Labor Force. (Series P-50, No. 13.) Washington, D.C.: Government Printing Office.

———. 1950. Income of families and persons in the United States, 1948. Current Population Reports: Consumer Income. (Series P-60, No. 6.) Washington, D.C.: Government Printing Office.

———. 1953. Marital status, year of marriage, and household relationship, April 1953. Current Population Reports: Population Characteristics. (Series P-20, No. 50.) Washington, D.C.: Government Printing Office.

———. 1957a. Annual report on the labor force, 1956. Current Population Reports: Labor Force. (Series P-50, No. 72.) Washington, D.C.: Government Printing Office.

———. 1957b. Work experience of the population in 1956. Current Population Reports: Labor Force. (Series P-50, No. 77.) Washington, D.C.: Government Printing Office.

———. 1958a. Income of families and persons in the United States, 1957. Current Population Reports: Consumer Income. (Series P-60, No. 30.) Washington, D.C.: Government Printing Office.

———. 1958b. Annual report on the labor force,

1957. Current Population Reports: Labor Force. (Series P-50, No. 85.) Washington, D.C.: Government Printing Office.

U.S. BUREAU OF LABOR STATISTICS. 1958. Consumer and wholesale prices. Month. Labor Rev., **81**, 949.

U.S. BUREAU OF OLD-AGE AND SURVIVORS INSURANCE. 1953. Selected findings of the national survey of Old-Age and Survivors Insurance beneficiaries, 1951. Washington, D.C.: The Bureau.

———. 1954. More selected findings of the national survey of Old-Age and Survivors Insurance beneficiaries, 1951. Washington, D.C.: The Bureau.

———. 1958. National survey of Old-Age and Survivors Insurance beneficiaries, 1957: highlights from the preliminary tabulations —income. Washington, D.C.: The Bureau.

U.S. BUREAU OF PUBLIC ASSISTANCE. 1957. Characteristics of state public assistance plans under the Social Security Act. (Public Assistance Report 33.) Washington, D.C.: The Bureau.

U.S. COMMITTEE ON ECONOMIC SECURITY. 1937. Social Security in America: the factual background of the Social Security Act as summarized from staff reports to the Committee on Economic Security. Washington, D.C: Government Printing Office.

U.S. CONGRESS. 1957a. HOUSE OF REPRESENTATIVES. H.R. 9467 (85th Cong., 1st sess.), introduced by Mr. Forand. Washington, D.C.: Government Printing Office.

———. 1957b. SENATE. Compilation of the social security laws: including the Social Security Act as amended, and related enactments through December 31, 1956. (S. Doc. 156 [84th Cong., 2d sess.].) Washington, D.C.: Government Printing Office.

———. 1957c. SENATE. COMMITTEE ON LABOR AND PUBLIC WELFARE. Studies of the aged and aging: summary of federal legislation relating to older persons. Washington, D.C.: Government Printing Office.

———. 1958. Public Law 85-840. (85th Cong., H.R. 13549.) Washington, D.C.: Government Printing Office.

———. 1959. HOUSE OF REPRESENTATIVES. H.R. 4700 (86th Cong., 1st sess.), introduced by Mr. Forand. Washington, D.C.: Government Printing Office.

U.S. INTERNAL REVENUE SERVICE. 1957. Your income tax forms: 1957. Washington, D.C : Government Printing Office.

U.S. SOCIAL SECURITY ADMINISTRATION. 1948. A budget for an elderly couple. Social Security Bull., **11** (February), 4–12.

———. 1953a. Private pension plans in six countries. *Ibid.*, **16** (August), 10–17.

———. 1953b. Social security financing. (Division of Research & Statistics, Bureau Rept. 17.) Washington, D.C.: The Administration.

———. 1956. Analysis of 157 group annuity plans amended in 1950–54. Washington, D.C.: The Administration.

———. 1957a. 1956 amendments to the Railroad Retirement Act. Social Security Bull., **20** (May), 18–21.

———. 1957b. Social security in the United States. Washington, D.C.: Government Printing Office.

———. 1958a. Health insurance coverage by age and sex, September 1956. Washington, D.C.: The Administration.

———. 1958b. Social security bulletin: annual statistical supplement, 1956. Washington, D.C.: The Administration.

WEBB, S., and WEBB, BEATRICE. 1910. English poor law policy. London: Longmans, Green & Co.

WELFARE AND HEALTH COUNCIL OF NEW YORK CITY. RESEARCH DEPARTMENT. 1955. A family budget standard for the use of social and health agencies in New York City. New York: The Council.

WHARTON SCHOOL OF FINANCE AND COMMERCE. 1957. Study of consumer expenditures, incomes, and savings, Vol. **18**. (Tabulated by the U.S. Bureau of Labor Statistics.) Philadelphia: University of Pennsylvania.

WINDHAUSER, MARGUERITE, and BLAETUS, G. J. 1958. State public assistance legislation, 1957. Social Security Bull., **21** (January), 3–7, 23–24.

WITTE, E. E. 1958. The future of social security. *In* J. STIEBER (ed.), U.S. industrial relations: the next twenty years, pp. 137–66. East Lansing: Michigan State University Press.

WOYTINSKY, W. S. 1943. Income cycle in the life of families and individuals. Social Security Bull., **6** (June), 8–17.

ZISMAN, J. 1957. Private employee benefit plans today. Social Security Bull., **20** (January), 8–21.

1960 AMENDMENTS

Under the 1960 amendments to the Social Security Act, a number of significant changes were made in provisions discussed in the present chapter. The changes in OASDI provisions included: (1) extending disability insurance benefits to eligible workers under age 50; (2) liberalizing the retirement test by reducing the amount of benefits withheld on earnings above $1200 a year; (3) liberalizing the requirements for fully insured status by calling for only one quarter of coverage for every three quarters between the end of 1950 and the year in which the worker becomes disabled, reaches retirement age, or dies (but not less than six quarters or more than forty quarters are required); (4) increasing benefits for each child of a deceased worker to three-quarters of the primary benefit amount (subject to the maximum on benefits payable to a family); and (5) certain other minor changes.

In addition, there were several other important changes in the Social Security Act which affected the public assistance program. These included: (1) liberalizing the provisions relating to federal sharing in medical-care expenditures for old age assistance recipients and (2) establishing a new program of grants-in-aid to states for medical assistance to aged persons (MAA) who are not recipients of old age assistance but who have insufficient resources to meet necessary medical expenses. The MAA program was adopted by Congress after efforts to secure passage of legislation of the Forand type had failed.

Other important developments were the adoption of significant amendments to the veterans' pension program in 1959 and the publication by the Bureau of Labor Statistics, in November, 1960, of a revised elderly couple's budget, indicating annual 1959 costs in twenty large cities ranging from $2641 in Houston to $3366 in Chicago.

IX

Changing Status, Roles, and Relationships[1]

RICHARD H. WILLIAMS

I. A CONCEPTUAL FRAMEWORK

A. The Theory of Action

THE IMPORTANCE OF THEORY

The present chapter is written from the point of view of the theory of action as developed by Talcott Parsons and others (Parsons, 1949, 1951; Parsons and Shils, 1951; Parsons et al., 1953; Parsons and Bales, 1955). Theory is a body of logically interrelated concepts and propositions which facilitates the entire process of scientific investigation, from exploratory descriptions of a field and the early formulation of research questions through the development and testing of specific hypotheses. As we are using the term, "theory" does not refer exclusively to a body of law-type statements with substantive content or, in other words, to empirically testable or tested hypotheses. The development of an empirically tested body of interrelated propositions is, of course, the goal of all scientific endeavor. However, theory has an active role to play throughout all aspects of scientific work.

Following the excellent suggestions of Robert K. Merton (1945), some of the principal functions of theory can be indicated as follows: (1) it guides the selection of facts in terms of their pertinence; (2) it provides a framework for coherent organization and arrangement of facts and thereby increases the scope of significance of facts; (3) it provides a cumulative element in scientific endeavor because it points the way to additions to a *system* of interrelated propositions; (4) it increases the fruitfulness of findings, including their fruitfulness for practical application; (5) it provides better grounds for making predictions; (6) it increases precision by requiring that concepts and propositions be sufficiently precise to be determinant or testable; and (7) it reveals gaps in knowledge and hence serves as a guide for future research. In general, theory serves as an extremely important control in all scientific activities. It reduces the chance of bias and error in both observation and interpretation by explicit attention to the assumptions, postulates, and hypotheses and by explicit codification of what is being done.

Research relating to changing status, roles, and relationships associated with the aging process is in a very early and formative stage. Explicit attention to theory is of particular importance under these circumstances and can serve to obviate wastage of the very scarce resources of scientific manpower which are available in this field.

GENERAL CHARACTERISTICS OF THE THEORY OF ACTION

All theories are necessarily abstract in the sense of selecting aspects of total con-

[1] Acknowledgment is gratefully made for the able assistance of Dr. James H. Fox, sociologist in the Professional Services Branch, National Institute of Mental Health, who searched and analyzed much of the available literature.

261

crete situations which are presumed to be systematically related. The theory of action selects those aspects of behavior which are meaningfully oriented to the behavior of others. It is concerned with behavior insofar as it is to a significant degree influenced by or systematically controlled by such orientation to others. It is primarily concerned with human behavior. The extent to which action, as here defined, occurs in other animals is a moot question, the answer to which probably depends on whether other animals develop significant symbols, a self, and are capable of taking the attitudes of others in the classical sense defined by G. H. Mead (1934). This theoretical approach by no means maintains that all the variance in human behavior is to be accounted for in terms of action. Genetic factors, biological changes with age, and other types of environmental influences play an important part in determining the course of behavior of individuals and groups. It does, however, postulate that meaningful orientation to others occurs in systematic ways, called "social systems," which do account for a significant proportion of the variance in actual human behavior.

The theory of action is concerned with social systems of various scales, including very large-scale groups such as whole societies, intermediate-scale groups such as industries or hospitals, small-scale groups such as families, and still smaller scale systems such as *individual personalities* as organized systems of action. Some of the characteristic terms in the theory, which indicate its element, are "means and ends," "norms," "rules and regulations," "attitudes," "sentiments and values," "expectations," "aspirations," "self-images," and "images of others." All these terms are "subjective" in the sense of referring to the points of view of subjects and their relations to others. The characteristic instruments used to get data of this type are direct interviewing, indirect interviewing through questionnaires, certain types of

tests, notably projective tests, and direct observation of behavior, from which its action components can sometimes be inferred. The "meaningful orientation," which is postulated about action, is not confined to cognitive orientation or knowing something about the situation. It also includes teleological or instrumental orientation, that is, doing something about or intervening in the situation, and affective orientation or the feelings and emotions which actors have. Although the theory of action is much concerned with the role of values in human behavior, it attempts to remain entirely free of value judgments which would bias either the observation of facts or the interpretation of the observations made.

RELEVANCE OF THE THEORY OF ACTION TO PROBLEMS OF AGING

It is hoped that this chapter will indicate, or at least strongly suggest, that the theory of action is highly relevant and pertinent to an understanding of problems of aging. As the author has pointed out elsewhere, there is a considerable body of evidence that aging has grown to have a problematical status in American society (Williams, 1959). As Simmons (1957) has stated, "Every human being has either to die or grow older, and, in this dilemma, the social and cultural factors have been extremely important." One of the keys to an understanding of social and cultural change is the range of common human problems and events, such as suffering, shame, aging, or death, which are given relatively "problematical" as contrasted with "self-evident" meanings (Williams, 1940, 1942). One of the important conditions of action today, which relates to the increase in the problematical status of aging, is the well-known fact that there are proportionately and absolutely more older people than there have been in the past in our society. Changes in our technological and economic systems (which are discussed elsewhere in this volume and which are essentially subsystems of action) also account for part of the problem. However, fully to understand it, it is to be presumed that we should take a careful look at what happens to the actor, or social self, as people age in our society and at what the institutional and cultural factors are which link these happenings together systematically. As this chapter will attempt to indicate, when we are concerned with changing status, roles, and relationships, we are dealing with the essential core of the social system. Relatively little research has been done in this area. The research which has been done either has made direct use of the theory of action, in one form or another, or is amenable to interpretation, and hopefully some clarification, within this conceptual framework.

B. Social Control and Social Motivation

As the author has indicated elsewhere, the theory of action, at its core, is concerned with two closely related problems:

It is concerned with the genesis and development of social personality, and the tendency of actors to conform to meaningful patterns of behavior. In earlier versions, it tended to look at the problem in terms of the postulates that social systems are "real" and that they have their own requirements, and that man, at least, could not do without them. It tended to think of conformity largely in terms of a constraint to conform, emanating from society as a set of conditions external to the individual. As this theory has evolved, it has tended to be concerned with the intimate processes of personality development from earliest infancy on, and to regard the major elements of the social system as being built into the structure of personality. In fact, the "individual versus society" has, essentially, ceased to be a theoretical issue. Put in slightly different terms, problems of social "motivation" and of social "control" acquired a common theoretical base.

It is concerned with the genesis and development of deviant behavior. The systematic development of this aspect of the theory is much more recent, but it promises to be most fruitful. . . . Parsons (1951, pp. 255 ff.) for example, has proposed a fundamental paradigm of the genesis and development of deviant behavior in terms of "cumulative motivation to deviance" through inter-action of complementary ambivalences. He has given a systematic statement both of the sources of needs disposing the actor toward alienation and withdrawal, in relation to underlying needs of security, and of the sources of more "aggressive" deviance, in relation to underlying needs for adequacy. And he has established a fundamental link between these concepts and concepts pertaining to the requirements of larger social systems. For example, the alienative or withdrawing tendencies are the most directly dangerous to the stability of a social system, since they attack the most fundamental requirement of socialization (p. 264). Furthermore, this theory throws much light on the nature and sources of strain in the basic processes of socialization, and on processes of adjustment to strain (pp. 248 ff.) [Williams, 1957, p. 622].

This general approach, to date, has primarily been used in relation to studies of the development of social personality in the early years of life. However, this same perspective should prove particularly fruitful in relation to other stages in the life-cycle, particularly stages involving a crisis of transition—for example, between youth and adulthood and between adulthood and old age. Does the aging process, under certain specifiable circumstances, involve a "cumulative motivation to deviance" and result in alienation, withdrawal, or aggressive rebellion against the values and modes of conduct generally shared and considered to be acceptable in a community? What are the stresses and strains put on the personality of the aging individual and on the social systems within which he lives? What are the sources and processes of adjustment to these stresses and strains? Will an analysis along these lines really account for the fact that aging has become defined as a major social problem, or, upon examination of the evidence, will we have to conclude that the degree of attention to the *problem* of aging is a societal symptom of underlying *tensions* which are only indirectly, and perhaps remotely, related to aging itself? Again, research has certainly not proceeded far enough to give even approximate answers to questions of this type. But these questions are worth raising, and this general perspective can give direction to our research efforts in the field.

C. The Framework of Social Positions

It is characteristic of action within social systems to be institutionalized. Institutions are normative patterns consisting of rules, regulations, and general moral codes which control and motivate action in its pursuit of immediate ends or goals in such a way that it will conform with, and contribute to the realization of, the more ultimate ends or values shared by the participants in the system. Institutions provide and maintain the major structure within which action takes place. Institutions need to be understood not only on the level of manifest functions, goal-directed activity of a specific sort, and formal organizations but also, and in many ways more importantly, on the level of latent functions, expressional activities, and informal organization.

An essential aspect of institutionalized action, both formal and informal, is a framework of social positions. Persons are "positioned" or placed in relation potentially to all other persons in the same system of action, and the positions themselves form a pattern or framework. Its general function, like the general function of all aspects of social structure, is to create a certain minimum of stability and predictability within the multiple, ongoing activities which compose the system. The extent of its significance can be formulated in the following proposition: No social system can survive (maintain its relative equilibrium) unless the persons who compose it can be institutionally placed ("positioned") in relation to one another.

The frequency with which the question, "*Who* is he?" is asked and the frequency with which it is left without a satisfactory answer are among the most important indexes of the degree of integration of social systems. The depth to which this aspect of general social structure tends to be worked into social personality, and, consequently, the extent to which it tends to be emotionally anchored, may be seen by the intensity of moral indignation generally associated with such judgments as "So-and-so does not know his place," or, for example, "He does not behave the way an *old* man should." Initiation and investiture ceremonies serve to publicize the fact that a person has changed position and also to reaffirm the importance of the position he is to occupy.

The terms "role" and "status" are frequently used in research on the social and the social-psychological aspects of the aging process. The early definition of these terms by Ralph Linton has had a marked influence on their use. Linton (1936) defined status as a "position in a particular pattern," and he stated that "a role represents the dynamic aspects of a status. The individual is socially assigned to a status and occupies it with relation to other statuses. When he puts the rights and duties which constitute the status into effect, he is performing a role. Role and status are quite inseparable, and the distinction between them is of only academic interest. There are no roles without statuses or statuses without roles" (pp. 113–14). Roles involve several related *tasks*. They define the mode of participation of the actor in a social system as a *system*.

The author has found it convenient to introduce certain modifications and distinctions into this terminology which, it is believed, are empirically relevant when studying a variety of problems including the process of aging. We shall use the term "position" in much the sense that Linton used the term "status" and then distinguish three major elements in positions: (1) role, or the functional content of the position—what persons do—the framework conceived as an interdependent system of "jobs"; (2) status, or the moral (in the broadest sense) evaluation of the position

—amount of prestige and esteem attached to it—the framework conceived as a system of social stratification; and (3) social power (authority when institutionalized), or the amount of influence carried by the position—the framework conceived as a distributive system of power relations. Cutting across all three aspects of the framework of social positions are the codes of conduct, attitudes, sentiments, and, especially, expectations associated with positions. Without relatively stable expectations about the conduct of persons who must interact in an organized course of action, and hence without relative conformity to institutionally defined positions, a social system becomes badly disorganized. Similarly, when an individual person finds himself in an ill-defined position or a position which puts conflicting demands on him, it may be presumed that he will be thereby under greater stress and suffer a considerable amount of frustration and anxiety.

AGE, SEX, AND SOCIAL CLASSES—GENERALIZED FRAMEWORKS OF POSITION

All organizations or groups, both primary (such as the family) or secondary (such as a large-scale association), have their frameworks of social position. In addition, the culture of a community, or of a whole society, establishes some more generalized frameworks within which people are placed. The most important, or at least the most commonly found, of these frameworks pertain to age, sex, and social class. In meeting someone for the first time, it would be extremely difficult, if not impossible, to relate adequately to him unless one knows how old the person is, what is the person's sex, and from what general stratum of society he comes. There are certain very general respects in which we treat all persons simply as human beings, but prolonged or detailed interaction would certainly founder without some awareness of these three variables. The degree of importance of age-grading as a general framework for placing people varies considerably from one society and its culture to another. Its degree of importance in our own society is a moot question, about which there has been very little research and somewhat conflicting evidence. Its importance during the school ages can scarcely be denied. There appears to be a somewhat variable period from the late teens to the early twenties, depending very largely upon the educational channels followed and levels achieved, which marks the transition from youth to adulthood. In some segments of our society at least, there appear to be important positional differences between persons in early adulthood, up to the age of about 45, and middle adulthood, from 45 to the mid-sixties. Old age is also a somewhat variable positional line in our society, although the age of 65 has taken on special significance largely because of many retirement practices.

Differentiation of position by sex is also of variable importance from one society to another. Relatively speaking, it was probably more important in the United States of 100 years ago than it is at the present time. However, its importance has by no means disappeared, and, as will be brought out later in the chapter, the relatively large accumulation of women in the later age groups in our society is a fact of considerable social importance.

In addition to the particular statuses a person occupies within specific patterns of social stratification, people tend also to occupy a generalized status, which we shall refer to by the term "station." Class stratification is essentially an ensemble of persons occupying the same station. It has general effects, of varying degrees of intensity, depending upon the rigidity of the structure, on one's life-opportunities, the kinds of people with whom one can associate, and the kinds of roles which one can play. Class stratification relates to the personality as a whole and, also, in all societies, bears a very close relation to the family as a primary group. There is a strong tendency for all members of a given family to be in the *same* social class. Where the system of class stratification is very rigid, as in the case of caste systems, endogamous rules of marriage, within one's station, are adhered to rigidly. Where the class system is somewhat looser, and where there is considerable vertical mobility from class to class, these rules are not so strict, but there is still a tendency for at least the members of the immediate, conjugal family to be classed together. In fact, the size of the effective family structure—for example, whether it includes three generations or collateral kin—tends to vary inversely with the amount of social mobility. As will be indicated later, this feature of modern society has its important effects on the aging process. Social classes are generally not organized groups, especially where the open class system prevails. Families and cliques of families act as organizational units within the class structure.

Accurately to analyze the pattern of class stratification in a given community requires an intimate and detailed knowledge of styles of life, of patterns of social relationship, and of who interacts with whom under what circumstances. A few studies of this kind have been done, such as Warner's classic study of "Yankee City" (Warner and Lunt, 1941) and Richard Coleman's (1958) painstaking analysis of social classes in Kansas City in connection with the University of Chicago's Study of Adult Life. However, in most studies of aging, various readily obtainable indexes of "socioeconomic status" are used. These indexes do turn out to relate significantly to a number of variations in the population, and they correspond reasonably well with some of the major determinants of class station. Among certain upper-class groups, cliques of families may be the prime determinants of class positions, but more generally such characteristics as income, occupation, place of residence, and amount of education determine one's general position in the class structure, and they, in turn, are used in building the indexes.

SOME DYNAMIC ASPECTS OF THE FRAMEWORK

A formal descriptive statement of the framework of social positions in any social system is always a useful first step. However, one wants also to know what people are doing in these positions, what moves they make within them from one position to another, and, in short, what the major motivational and control patterns are. The motivational elements of needs, expectations, and aspirations vary tremendously in their actual content. On a basic analytical level it is useful to think of four categories of needs:

1. *Wealth.*—Insofar as scarcities of means exist, actors must acquire a minimum of command over them. All actions, however trivial, have an element of real cost, that is, the sacrifice of certain ends, values, or satisfactions in order to accomplish others.

2. *Power.*—Among the means at the actor's disposal and the ends which he seeks will be things which others can give him. Hence to act implies the need for a basic minimum of influence over other persons. Various types of influence may be used, such as enlightenment or fraud, exchange or coercion, persuasion or conversion. Of these various means, fraud and coercion are directly dangerous to and disruptive of the social system, and conversion is a potentially dangerous form of influence in that it tends to result in too rapid a change in value systems to permit stability of the institutional structure. Hence these forms of influence tend to be hedged about with a variety of social controls.

3. *Success recognition.*—Social action and social personality (the "self" or the "ego") arise and develop in a basic context of self-other relationships. To act at all, the actor needs to realize or accomplish a basic minimum of his ends and values (i.e., his action must have a minimum of "effectiveness"), and such accomplishment is made meaningful by recognition by others.

4. *Emotional satisfaction.*—Actors need a basic minimum of hedonic satisfaction, moral satisfaction, affective response of others, and emotional security. Particularly to avoid a blocked or "neurotic" action system, the actor needs a basic minimum of such emotional satisfaction.

A crucial question about the aging process is the extent to which it involves shifts in social position and, particularly, the extent to which such shifts in turn change the actor's ability to satisfy these basic needs. As we shall see in subsequent sections of the chapter, there are segments of the aging population in our society which are seriously affected in relation to all four types of needs at once. They have lost their ability to command scarce means (through loss of income, property, savings, etc.), they are not able to influence anyone, they have lost any sense of accomplishment and recognition, and they lead an emotionally empty life. Such persons truly sink into a position of "anomie" or normless, listless confusion. Apparently, many of them end up in mental hospitals or various homes for the aged. But we need to know a good deal more about the extent to which such shifts occur in the general population and, especially, about the factors which produce these shifts.

D. The Social Life-Space as a Matrix of Social Relationships

THE SOCIAL LIFE-SPACE AS A CONCEPTUAL TOOL FOR EMPIRICAL RESEARCH

The social sciences have done relatively little research and have evolved relatively little by way of a systematic conceptual scheme for describing and evaluating the social life of a particular person. The term "social system" is generally referred to groupings of persons with identifiable, although sometimes changing, membership. But, for many purposes, it may prove extremely valuable to analyze the social system with a particular person as the point of departure, as has been pointed out by

Williams and Loeb (1956). It does seem possible, and desirable, to develop a conceptual framework which will allow for generalizations comparing individual patterns of social relations. In order to develop such a framework, one starts with the individual and works out to his broader social relations rather than starting with society and working toward the individual. Social workers, vocational rehabilitation counselors, some psychiatrists, and others work practically in this way, from the "case" to *his* social world. Investigation of the individual's social life-space, or the system in which *he* lives day by day, appears to be a particularly fruitful approach to problems of aging.

Further investigation is needed to define the dimensions of the social life-space and then to explore these dimensions empirically as variables in the aging process. An important step in this direction has been taken in the Kansas City studies, to which reference will be made later. For the moment we tentatively propose the following dimensions:

I. Structure
  A. Number of persons and frequency of interactions or "transactions"—what are the "affiliate points"?
  B. Intensity of relations (degree of intimacy and emotional involvement)
  C. Social position in relation to others
    1. Roles played
    2. Statuses occupied
    3. Amount of authority exercised and protected rights enjoyed

II. Dynamics of functioning within this structure
  A. Communication—degree of realism, resonance, etc., within "conversations" with others
  B. Dynamic relations between the person's self-image, his ideal self (what a person of his age and situation should be), his conception of what others expect of him, and the actual expectations of others
  C. The demands stemming from the "affiliate points," family relations, bosses, doctors, etc., in the person's social life-space

D. The amount of energies of others required to maintain a person as a "going concern" and, conversely, the degree of autonomy of the person in the satisfaction of his basic needs

As the author has pointed out elsewhere (1957, p. 624), one of the most important analytical tools for this type of analysis

is to be found in the concept of differentiation, which Parsons (1955) indicates is a *"reorganization of the system"* which disturbs whatever approximation to a stable state may have existed before it began. Reorganization creates a series of crises and discontinuities in the socialization process. We may presume that personality development at any point of time may affect ways in which these crises have been met. Intensive case studies of posthospital experience by Ozzie Simmons and his co-workers at the Harvard School of Public Health suggest that patients tend to regress in the sense of returning to, and coping with, a less differentiated social system than they had prior to hospitalization. During hospitalization, what happens to regressed patients who are surrounded by a highly differentiated system, the bases for which are not clear to the actors themselves? There is great promise in further exploration along these lines both for an understanding of action systems in general, and for the development of guidelines concerning the optical dimensions of action systems in relation to specific social problems. There is need for theoretical refinement of the dimensions of the social systems of individual actors, so that major points of vulnerability and the significance of the actor's moves within the system can be better understood.

A significant question to ask concerning the aging process has to do with the extent to which it involves a "de-differentiation" and possibly "regression" in the above defined sense, a matter which we will consider again later in relation to the study by Quinn *et al.* (1957).

In relation to all these suggested analyses the applied or operational question becomes, essentially, "What is an appropriate or healthy pattern of social life for an individual of given age, sex, social class and physical health status?" What is the available social life-space, and how much of the available does the individual person actually utilize? The concept of "successful" aging, and related concepts of healthy or pathogenic factors, may be approached both analytically and empirically. Analytically, successful aging would mean that a person is able to maintain an optimal position within his social life-space in relation to his psychological and biological capacities. Some balance is maintained between inner resources and the immediate social system surrounding the person. Shifts in either aspect of this balance can produce stress. There is a continuum from "success" to "failure" in the way such stresses are met. We can presume from our general knowledge of social and cultural systems that successful aging, as abstractly defined, can have a variety of empirical contents. There will probably be significant variations in this respect by subgroups, perhaps particularly by social classes and by careers and career clusters. We can also expect some margin of idiosyncratic variation. Hence we should not establish specific criteria of success, in terms of its content, a priori.

In order to probe more deeply into problems of this kind, both on basic and on applied levels, we need to introduce another theoretical concept.

THE CONCEPT OF "COMPLEXITY" IN RELATION TO PERSONALITY THEORY AND TO SOCIAL LIFE-SPACE

A number of questions have been asked recently concerning the ways in which personality responds emotionally to a variety of life-situations and the ways in which these responses change with age. Weinberg (1956) suggests that, "since the aging process curtails one's capacity to deal with the multitude of stimuli that clamor for attention in our complex society, the organism begins to exclude them from awareness." Frenkel-Brunswik (1949) has developed the concept of "intolerance for ambiguity" as an emotional and perceptual variable. This variable probably has a significant relation to the process and problems of aging, and recent but as yet unpublished research which Frenkel-Brunswik initiated, and to which reference will be made later, bears directly on this point. Kuhlen (1956) has presented some evidence that "beyond a relatively young age there are progressive losses in self-concept and increasing insecurity and susceptibility to threat, hence an increasing need to protect and conserve against losses, a need that often evidences itself in negative defensiveness and thus can prove self-limiting and handicapping."

William E. Henry, of the University of Chicago, who has been very closely associated with research in Kansas City to which reference will be made later, has drawn much of this thinking together and has proposed the concept of "affective complexity" as a major investigatory axis for the study of adult personality. In his own words:

It is proposed that the inner aspects of adjustment and the reactions to stress in the adult be studied from the point of view of the *range and variety of emotional adaptations made by adults at any age period.* Specifically, it is proposed that the concept of *affective complexity* function as a central one to this investigation. To no small extent, this concept itself will require much analysis and definition. However, it is possible at this point to suggest some of the logic of its use and to indicate its seeming appropriateness to the task of describing normal adult personality, of relating personality to external situations and to judgments of successful aging.

Affective complexity may be seen as an attribute of the person characterized by both the inner resources and sensitivity which would serve to make him aware of and able to accept emotionally the experiential complexities of life. . . . The relationships between affective complexity, seen as an attribute of the inner adjustment of the individual, and the overt behavior or experiential complexity of the individual, is by no means clear at this point. The relationship between this inner adjustment and external events should constitute a major task

of research. . . . It seems probable that the continuum of affective complexity will be such that the upper and bottom ranges will counter-indicate successful outer adjustment [Henry, 1956, pp. 35–36].

As Henry points out, there is considerable doubt that affective complexity can be treated as a single variable. It may be more profitable to study it in terms of the "range and variety of emotional adaptations made by adults at different ages." He has also proposed that

a *second major investigatory axis* by which adult personality may be explored might well be the *perceptions of available roles in the individual social life space.* It may be suggested that these *role perceptions* constitute a major definition of the world of action possible for the individual and at the same time a definition of the nature and amount of external influences acting upon him and in terms of which he must act in implementing his own goals. The term "act" is here intended to include the category "feeling" since it is clear that these external events also assist to define what "feeling" the individual should attribute to an event or expect other persons to attribute to him [p. 37].

A similar concept of complexity can be applied to the social life-space itself. Again, considerable research will be necessary, some of which is currently being done in Kansas City, to define the major dimensions of complexity of the life-space or social systems of individual actors. Certainly, this concept will be closely related to, if not almost identical with, the concept of differentiation as discussed earlier. Certainly, the life-spaces of some persons contain more people, more demands, and hence greater potential for conflict and stress than do others. Changes in the various aspects of social position with age may well be expected to involve changes in the complexity of life-space. A crucial issue, and a fruitful line of analysis, in relation to "success" in the aging process is the way in which different personalities cope with changes in the complexity, or degree of differentiation, in their social life-space. Similarly, it is useful to probe into the degree of congruence between the structure of personality and the structure of the social system within which the person operates. Difficulties may well arise if a person with a high degree of affective complexity *moves* into a life-space of relatively simple structure and, conversely, if a person with a low degree of affective complexity is forced to cope with a complex structure in his life-space.

E. Summary

This section of the chapter has attempted to indicate a general theoretical frame of reference which, it is proposed, is useful in the analysis of some of the problems associated with the process of aging. It should be able to throw some light on why and how aging has become relatively *problematical* in our contemporary society. It does not pretend to analyze all aspects of the many problems of aging, but it does purport to deal with what may well turn out to be some quite central ones.

Relatively little research on aging has been done explicitly with this frame, or similar frames, of reference. In the following section we shall present a brief résumé of some of the evidence which bears on the general questions we are raising. We shall not deal with this evidence extensively, because much of it is also presented in other chapters of this volume. The major questions are: What are the major factors associated with changing social position in the later years? What is their dynamics (or how do they operate systematically)? What is their bearing on the development of social *problems?* How do they relate to "success" or its lack in coping with these problems?

II. The Empirical Evidence

A. Some Evidence from Non-literate Societies

Leo Simmons (1945, 1948, 1952) has provided some very useful material, which is quite pertinent to the general questions raised in this chapter, by making a careful study of attitudes, beliefs, and practices regarding aging and the aged among some 71 different peoples, many of them non-literate or pre-industrial. His data indicate that aging tends to be viewed either as a dismal and hopeless problem or as a hopeful challenge, without much room for neutrality of attitude. Hence changing positions with age tend to be somewhat problematical in all societies. He also indicates that the ways in which peoples cope with the problems of aging vary significantly, which, in itself, is good evidence that aging is a social process, socially determined. It can be viewed as fruitfully in these terms as it can in terms of biological changes or changes in mental abilities. Fortunately, Simmons has summarized much of this material in chapter iii of the present volume. A few specific points will be made here, however, because they provide particularly apt illustrations of the point of view developed in the preceding sections.

The Tai tribes of the Yunnan-Burma frontier as described by T'ien Ju-k'ang (1949) illustrate a case where age-grading forms a central and pivotal part of the entire framework of social positions and is symbolized in the major rituals. The Tai are Buddhist in their religious orientation. Buddhism in general has a very long-term orientation to values, which involves a conception of several successive existences. Such an orientation produces a high degree of respect for age, which has been typical of most oriental people. In the case of the Tai, however, the role of age in the total social structure is particularly clear.

As T'ien puts it:

Pai is the comprehensive name given to the series of religious activities which express the peoples' belief in Buddha. In this particular region there are six Pai cults of which the Great Pai is the most important. The Great Pai, in its essentials, consists of the exhibition of certain articles which the householder offers in the village Buddhist temple. The ceremony extends over at least three days. During this period a great many other activities take place as well, for instance, dancing, singing, feasting, and processions [p. 46].

In all Pai ceremonies younger people perform various services for older people, and it is the elders of the community who play the leading role in the ceremonies.

This differentiation of task according to age is very marked, and means that in one sense Pai performances may be regarded as the occasions on which individuals make public their transition from one period of their life history to another. The Tai people lay particular stress on the significance of age, and in the course of their lives all Tai men and women pass through four distinct periods [p. 47].

These four periods correspond essentially to childhood, youth, marriage and adult family life, and old age. However, transitions from one stage to the next in this sequence must be achieved and ceremonially recognized; it does not come about automatically.

The social age of a Tai person is certainly not determined by actual physical age; in the first period we find many girls of eighteen who still wear long trousers, while in the third period there are many girls of sixteen. . . . Furthermore, there are great numbers of people who spend their whole lives in a particular group, never finding the opportunity of being promoted from it. . . . Again those people who cannot afford to perform the Great Pai, can never reach the fourth stage [pp. 49–50].

If one does succeed in passing through the four stages of social age, he becomes a highly respected person, regardless of his wealth or political power. "No individual, however wealthy or politically powerful, can compete in the peoples' estimation with an old man who spent all he had to perform the Great Pai twelve times and had nothing left to live on. Only to such a person do the local people give their respect, and only such a one do they attempt to imitate" (p. 50).

Thus in this society the social process of aging and changes of social position with age symbolize the ultimate values of the culture and provide the structure which determines the generalized characteristics of one's role, status, and authority. To have "aged" successfully, means to have achieved the highest goal of passing into the fourth period of social ages through performance of the Great Pai ceremonial.

The system of age-grading in Japan, as described by Norbeck (1953), is a good illustration of a culture in a transition. There is considerable evidence that age-grading did have a central place in Japanese social structure, at least in rural areas, and this situation obtains in a few isolated places in Japan today. One does find vestiges of age-grading practices. For example, there are

many indications of the recognition of old age as placing one in a distinct age and status category. The traditional age of retirement from active work in Japan is sixty-one—although few persons of present-day Japan actually retire from active labor until they are well into their sixties. Traditionally, one is allowed to wear the brightly colored clothing of childhood after reaching the age of sixty-one, and parties are still given in honor of parents and grandparents who reach this age [p. 381].

It is especially interesting to find ceremonial recognition of the *crisis* of transition from adulthood to old age. "The sixtieth year is one of several years of life commonly believed in both rural and urban Japan to be calamitous years (*yakudoshi*) for the individual. Ritual is often observed by all members of the household at the beginning of a *yakudoshi* of one of its members to avert misfortune. Observances at the end of the sixtieth year (beginning of the sixty-first year) ceremonially mark the termination of a period of danger and entry into a new and felicitous period" (p. 381). Traditionally, older people were given special privileges, essentially dispensations, in their modes of conduct. "A grandfather or grandmother may use with impunity terms of speech, including obscenities, considered improper for younger persons. Although these practices are now rapidly vanishing, the privileged behavior of the aged is still strongly evident in isolated rural communities, where older women may at parties do lewd dances and make sexual jokes, behavior inacceptable if indulged in by young women" (p. 381). This situation may well be a symbolic expression of basic changes in modes of orientation to action, from instrumental to expressive, which accompany the aging process in many societies, perhaps including our own, as suggested by some of the analyses of the Kansas City data to be referred to below.

The Eskimo of Greenland, as described by Mirsky (1937), illustrate a society in which the cultural values revolve around adult instrumental roles of hunting, fishing, and providing clothing and shelter. The position of old people—and people are generally considered old in their fifties—is anomalous, and sometimes essentially *anomic* in the technical sociological sense. Among some of the Eskimo a man is considered dead when he is too old to hunt, and he will be ceremonially walled up and left to die. Among other tribes, such as the Amnassalik of the east coast of Greenland, this practice is not found, but a person who becomes moribund will be thrown in the sea to avoid the necessity of handling his dead body, or a son-in-law may tell his mother-in-law that she is too old to be of use in the world, and she will thereupon throw herself in the sea to commit suicide. The actual treatment afforded a particular person in his old age is an individual matter, without group sanctions, and varies from case to case. The rest of the social structures are relatively simple ones. There is no political unity or organized leadership and social stratification is at an absolute minimum. "They have no complicated relationship system nor any set of kinship attitudes that defines by its terms the rights and obligations obtaining among its members" (p. 61). Children are rushed into adulthood as early as possible, and this is the major social position in life within which people concentrate on the arduous instrumental role of providing food, clothing, and shelter.

Simmons (1946) has made a generalization from his material that "throughout human history the family has been the safest haven for the aged. Its ties are the most intimate and long lasting, and on them the old rely with greatest success. When other supports crumble and disappear, old people cling to kith and kin even more closely; and the astute among them not infrequently manipulate such bonds to great personal advantage. Indeed, many persons are able to find in family relations opportunities for effective participation well on into senility, and even to exploit some rights which outlast life itself, for the last wishes of aged parents are not likely ignored by their offspring" (p. 74). Although this chapter is not primarily concerned with the role of the family in relation to aging, the subject of another chapter in this volume, it is important to consider the effects on social positions of older people of the changing structure and functions of the family.

These illustrations should suffice to indicate that the social process of aging, in the sense of changing social positions with age and moves within the framework of social positions, varies significantly from one society to another. These variations are systematically related to the total social structure and indeed sometimes have a crucial place within this structure.

B. Some General Sources of Evidence

FACTS ABOUT LONGEVITY AND THE NEW LIFE-CYCLE

The general facts about longevity changes in the life-cycle in recent years have become widely known, and their details are well analyzed in other chapters of this volume. For present purposes they may be reduced to two major propositions.

The life-span has shown no marked increase. Although more people are reaching ages about 65, after the age of 65 there has been relatively little increase in life-expectancy (U.S. Federal Security Agency, 1952, p. 20). For example, at age 60, from 1900 to 1950 only 2 years of life have been added, and, by 75, hardly more than

1 year (Connecticut, 1954, p. 36). Essentially, this means that no fundamental changes have occurred which increase the number of years for which the human organism can live under optimal conditions. More specifically, it means that marked reductions in infant mortality and in epidemic and contagious diseases have greatly increased life-expectancy from birth and through the middle years of life, whereas relatively little progress has been made with the degenerative diseases which affect people primarily in their later years. If some major medical breaks do occur in relation to degenerative processes, either in their "normal" or in their "pathological" form, this picture could change significantly.

The number and proportion of individuals 65 and over have been increasing steadily since 1900. This increase has been particularly marked in recent years. For example, the number of persons 65 and over practically doubled between 1930 and 1950 from 6,630,000 to 12,270,000 (Steiner and Dorfman, 1957). This increase is expected to continue, and it is anticipated that the number of older people will reach 24,500,000 by 1980, approximately double the 1950 population 65 and over (U.S. Bureau of the Census, 1958). However, as Steiner and Dorfman point out, if one assumes the relatively high rates of fertility of recent years, the *proportion* of older people will not increase but will stabilize at around 9 or 10 per cent by 1975 (p. 12).

Thus there are significantly more older people, both absolutely and proportionately, than there were 50 or even 20 years ago, and we can expect still more in absolute numbers, if perhaps not proportionately, in the future. However, as the author pointed out elsewhere, although these profound demographic shifts have certainly been a necessary condition of the problem of aging as we face it today, they are by no means a sufficient reason to explain why they are felt to be so problematical (Williams, 1959). Why should large numbers of older

people in the society constitute a problem in any sense? One might conceivably regard this phenomenon as signifying a great triumph of modern medicine and let it go at that.

FACTS ABOUT SEX RATIOS AND MARITAL STATUS

Sex and marital status are general variables of considerable importance and relevance to the framework of social position. Fortunately, the basic demographic facts are available, on a nation-wide basis, through the work of the Bureau of the Census.

Until 1940 the sexes were about equally represented in the population 65 and over. From 1940 to the present the female population 65 and over has increased more rapidly than the male, until in 1950 females represented 52 per cent of this population. There are estimates of 58 per cent females by 1975 and 60 per cent by the end of the century (Steiner and Dorfman, 1957). Furthermore, there are significant numbers of women who reach the age of 75, about a third of older women in 1950, and it is estimated that by the end of the century 45 per cent of the women 65 years of age and older will be 75 or older. The immigration pattern in the late nineteenth and early twentieth centuries increased the number of males in the entire adult population. This factor is no longer operative, and the marked increases in the number of women in the age group 65 and over is due to differential mortality in this age group.

Table 1 gives a general picture of the distribution of marital status in the population 65 years and older from 1900 to 1950. It can be seen that the proportions married have remained rather constant. The other statuses have varied, with an increase in the proportions single in each sex, a decrease in the proportions widowed (females to a greater extent than the males), and some increase in the proportions divorced in each sex. About the same percentage of men and women are single in this age group, but there are significant differences between the statuses of married and widowed; more than half of the females 65 and over are widows, whereas only about one-fourth of the males are widowers. The grouping of these data according to married and not married (including single, widowed, and divorced) describes this situation in an even more striking way. The proportion of males and

females married has been fairly constant since 1900, with only about a third of the males in the not-married status and two-thirds of the females. Table 2 indicates the percentage of females in each marital status in this age group over the period 1900–1950.

When the data are grouped in this way, the effect of the greater increase of the older female population can be seen. For example, whereas the proportion of females

TABLE 1*

PERCENTAGE DISTRIBUTION OF MARITAL STATUS OF MALES AND
FEMALES AGED 65 AND OVER, 1900–1950

MARITAL STATUS	1900		1910		1920		1930		1940		1950	
	Male	Female	Male	Female	Male	Female	Male	Female	Male	Female	Male	Female
Married........	67.1	34.2	65.6	35.0	64.7	33.9	63.6	34.7	63.8	34.3	65.7	35.7
Total not married	32.6	65.6	34.0	64.8	34.9	65.9	36.1	65.2	36.2	65.6	34.3	64.3
Single........	5.7	6.0	6.2	6.3	7.3	7.1	8.4	8.1	9.8	9.3	8.4	8.9
Widowed.....	26.4	59.3	27.1	58.1	26.9	58.4	26.6	56.6	25.1	55.6	24.1	54.3
Divorced.....	0.5	0.3	0.7	0.4	0.7	0.4	1.1	0.5	1.3	0.7	1.8	1.1
Unknown.......	0.3	0.2	0.4	0.2	0.3	0.2	0.2	0.2	......	......	......	......
Total.......	100.0	100.0	100.0	100.0	99.9	100.0	99.9	100.1	100.0	99.9	100.0	100.0
No. of individuals (in thousands).	1555	1525	1986	1964	2483	2450	3325	3310	4405	4613	5734	6522

* Source: U.S. Bureau of the Census, *Seventeenth Census . . . Population* (Washington, D.C.: Government Printing Office, 1952) Vol. **2**, Part I, Table 102, pp. 179–80.

TABLE 2*

PERCENTAGE FEMALE IN EACH MARITAL STATUS, PERSONS AGED 65 AND OVER, 1900–1950
(In Thousands)

MARITAL STATUS	1900		1910		1920		1930		1940		1950	
	Total Both Sexes	Per Cent Female	Total Both Sexes	Per Cent Female	Total Both Sexes	Per Cent Female	Total Both Sexes	Per Cent Female	Total Both Sexes	Per Cent Female	Total Both Sexes	Per Cent Female
Single..........	180	50	247	50	355	49	548	49	863	50	1,060	55
Married........	1565	33	1991	35	2437	34	3264	35	4395	34	6,093	38
Widowed.......	1316	69	1680	68	2100	68	2753	68	3670	70	4,921	72
Divorced.......	11	36	20	35	28	36	55	33	91	33	182	41
Unknown.......	8	......	12	......	13	......	13	......	......	......	......	......
Total.......	3080	......	3950	......	4933	......	6633	......	9019	......	12,256	......

* Source: U.S. Bureau of the Census, *Seventeenth Census . . . Population* (Washington, D.C.: Government Printing Office, 1952), Vol. **2**, Part I, Table 102, pp. 179–80.

who are widowed actually declined very slightly between 1940 and 1950, as indicated in Table 1, the proportion of widowed who are females increased during this period by 2 per cent, and by about 3 per cent of what it had been over the 50-year period. In fact, the proportion of females in each category remained quite constant from 1900 to 1940, and then the proportion of females in each category has increased since 1940. Since about two-thirds of the females over the age of 65 are not married (Table 1), and, since the number of females in this age group is increasing rapidly, and more rapidly than men, we can expect increasingly large numbers of females in the not-married category in the coming years.

The general significance of these facts has been recognized by several students in this field. For example, Cavan (1949) states that, "because of widowhood, we find more women than men without homes of their own, living in institutions, or with their children" (p. 61). Pollak (1948), in his challenging monograph, raised some very interesting questions. For example, he wondered about the very elderly widow, the woman who becomes a widow at 75 after 50 years of married life—are her adjustment problems similar to younger widows? There are interesting problems of role shifts which are required when widows move into an adult family. One study of a group of ministers' widows has probed into the living arrangements and the concerns of this selected group within the population of the widows. Forty-four per cent of them were living alone, 13 per cent with children, and 13 per cent with other relatives. Furthermore, if given the choice, many of these widows (43 per cent) would prefer to live alone; 20 per cent would like to live with another widow, and 19 per cent would like to live with their children. Ideologically, they are overwhelmingly (97 per cent) opposed to living in the household of their married children (Hibbard and Lee, 1954). However, in a study of

three-generation families in two rural communities in Pennsylvania, only about six out of ten first-generation respondents indicated that they preferred to be in their own homes alone (Smith *et al.*, 1958). This somewhat smaller proportion who desires to live independently may be a reflection of the rather well-defined roles for older persons in a rural-familistic setting. In the study by the Connecticut Commission on the Potentials of Aging, only 3 per cent of the men between the ages of 55 and 64 expected to live with their children, whereas 14 per cent of the men between 65 and 74 actually do live with their children. The authors hypothesize that the death of spouse accounts for the difference between expectation and actuality.

The demographic evidence presented in this section should be borne in mind in relation to all the succeeding sections, because it forms a very important background for understanding the total picture of the social positions of older people.

FACTS ABOUT HEALTH AND DISEASE

One of the most important conditions of action affecting the social positions and movement within the life-space of older people is their state of health. Again, for this section as well as for the following sections on retirement and economic resources, the basic facts are well analyzed in other sections of this volume, and only a few sample facts will be given here to suggest their relevance to the major questions raised in this chapter.

The 1957–58 National Health Survey indicated that the disability rate, as measured by "days of restricted activity" of those 65 and over is slightly less than three times that of the general population (U.S. National Health Survey, 1958). When only chronic conditions are considered, the rate is about four times that of the total population (U.S. National Health Survey, 1958). Chronic diseases are the leading causes of death in this age group.

Fry (1957) has given an interesting picture of what a private practice in England of 315 patients looks like from the point of view of the care and treatment of older patients. In this practice, patients 70 and over represented almost 6 per cent of the practice population but accounted for 10 per cent of the total volume of work. He found that hospital and nursing homes played a small part in the care of this type of group—only 8.5 per cent of these elderly patients were hospitalized during the year preceding the study, and most of them were in hospitals for less than 3 months. The degree of disability in this type of practice seems to be relatively mild. The moderately and severely disabled represented a minority and 65 per cent of those 70–79, and 59 per cent of those 80 and over were not sufficiently disabled to create interference with their daily routine. He found that the five most common diseases, in this practice are: cardiovascular disorders, rheumatic conditions, and diseases of the respiratory tract, the digestive tract, and the central nervous system.

These very broad facts suggest that there are two major types of health problems and situations among the elderly. On the one hand, there are significant numbers of chronically disabled, most of whom have to be cared for in specialized residential settings, and whose position in the social structure and whose life-space are overwhelmingly affected by this situation. On the other hand, there are elderly patients served by private practitioners who require a somewhat higher proportion of the time of the medical profession but whose disability is not severe and whose social position in life-space *need not* be markedly affected by their health status. It is suggested that the material in chapters vii and xv of this volume be considered from this point of view.

It has been suspected that psychosomatic and neurotic factors play an important part in the disorders of the elderly and that there are sex differences in this regard. Cavan (1949) reports that women feel less satisfied with their health than men—they report more physical handicaps, more illness, more nervous neurotic symptoms, and more accidents. Busse and his colleagues at Duke University (Busse *et al.*, 1954; Busse, 1956) have been studying this problem for a number of years. He has stated that

guilt as an important psychodynamic force is infrequently seen in our subjects living in the community. It appears that old people become involved in very little guilt-producing behavior. The older person is no longer living in a highly competitive situation which mobilizes hostile, aggressive impulses that end in self-condemnation. However, the change in the manner of living, that is the lack of competition with others appears to foster the development of inferiority feelings which form the basis of depressive episodes. The aged cannot counteract inferiority feelings by demonstrating his superiority through competition. The source of these feelings is primarily an inability to fulfill needs and drives, and the doubts which develop when the older person is reminded of the decreasing efficiency of his bodily function. Older people who have methods of reducing their inferiority feelings and can maintain supplies to their self-esteem can usually avoid depressive periods [1954, p. 901].

Cavan and her associates (1949) have indicated that "the societal pattern fails to define clearly what the role of the old person is with reference to other age groups or within the old group. This failure is especially marked in the case of the old man, whose role was previously closely related to his employment and his position as chief wage earner in the family. For the old married woman, the shift in role is less marked. In fact, such a shift may never be necessary if she is able to maintain her position as manager of her house" (p. 23). Material from the Kansas City studies, to be referred to below, throws additional light on this problem.

There are, however, some puzzling features about the data reported by Cavan and her co-workers. For example, the women in a special study they report generally exhibited more nervous and neurotic symptoms, felt less satisfaction with their health, were less happy, felt less useful, and reported less zest for living than did the men. The women in this study were younger than the men, which should serve to raise their adjustment attitude scores, yet their scores, on the average, were lower than or identical with the men. They do indicate that the percentages of the study group and of the total population that are married and that are widowed are very similar. This would mean that the female group has many more widowed persons than the male group. However, they also indicate that, "although for both men and women, the mean attitude score is highest for those who are married and living with the spouse and lowest for those who are separated or divorced, the differences are slight" (p. 193). The differences are even smaller between the married females and the widowed females. Of course these differences refer to total attitude score and not specifically to neurotic symptoms or happiness.

There is need for a controlled comparison between married and widowed females to test the hypothesis that older married females exhibit fewer indexes of a neurotic or psychosomatic nature, or other indexes of personal disorganization, than do comparable widowed females. This hypothesis could be related to the general thesis of easier acceptance of old age by married females because the role shift, if there is a role shift, is less traumatic. There is also need for refinement of such concepts related to personal disorganization as "adjustment," "morale," "anomie" and the like. This aspect of the problem is being explored tentatively in the Kansas City studies, to be referred to below.

More specifically, Busse and his group (1956) have found that depression, hypochondria, restlessness and wandering, and irritability and hostility are found frequently in their sample. They have formulated a number of suggestions for the treatment of these disorders. In each case these methods prominently involve restructuring of the patient's activities so that he has a meaningful position within a meaningful social life-space.

Disturbances of this kind can and do lead to hospitalization if treatment is not given adequately and in time. Disorders of this type, plus the more severe senile psychoses, have increased to a point where the number of older patients entering mental hospitals has become a major public health problem. According to data assembled by Dr. Morton Kramer (1957), chief of the Biometrics Branch of the National Institute of Mental Health, first-admission rates for persons 65 and over have increased from 157 per 100,000 in 1933 to 205 per 100,000 in 1950, an increase of 31 per cent. In addition, these hospitals are burdened with the accumulated corps of patients who have grown old in the institution. There are, however, wide variations in rates of first admissions to mental hospitals of persons over 65 by state. Furthermore, there are variations by smaller units, such as county. Gruenberg and Kaufman (1956) have stated that the rate per 100,000 of first admissions over 65 for Essex County, New York, is 142, whereas in Duchess County it is 466. We do not really know the reasons for these variations. Certainly, some of them are reflections in part of the formal policies practiced in different areas and of the availability of alternative resources such as nursing homes. It may be guessed, however, that most of the variance can be accounted for by factors in the social system. This would certainly be the case on the probably correct assumption that these differences in rates reflect social practices and not true incidence rates of mental disorders in the populations as a whole.

There has been considerable controversy of late as to whether the mental hospital is the most appropriate place for the treatment, management, and rehabilitation of older persons with mental and emotional disturbances. Many people feel that a variety of problems of older people are being dumped improperly on the mental hospitals, whereas others believe that older people who are admitted to mental hospitals could not properly be treated elsewhere, as has been indicated by Kolb (1956). To arrive at an adequate answer to a question of this type will require detailed analysis of the personal social systems (social positions within a life-space) from which the elderly patients come and also of the type of social system provided by the hospital. Unfortunately, mental hospitals have tended to produce "hospitalitis" or institutionally conditioned invalidism for significant numbers of older patients. This means that the older patient finds himself in a "box" or a "bind" which makes it extremely difficult for him to achieve a position and function within an alternative social system.

The National Institute of Mental Health has recently sponsored an intensive study of first admissions to mental hospitals to be undertaken at the Langley-Porter Neuropsychiatric Institute in San Francisco. Particular attention will be paid to factors in the social life-space and its relation to personality development, which precipitated the illness, and to similar factors as they are affected by hospitalization. It may be guessed that a major source of this problem lies in the fact that, under present practices, becoming a patient in a mental hospital is one of the most radical changes in social position possible and, once made, is difficult to reverse. The work done by Linden (1953) at Norristown State Hospital in Pennsylvania suggests that reversal can be effected. Hopefully, current studies in this field will make it possible to change both the methods of treatment and the attitudes toward treatment so that the change will be at once less traumatic and more reversible.

FACTS ABOUT LABOR-FORCE PARTICIPATION AND RETIREMENT

It has been widely held that retirement constitutes a major *problem* for older people on the seemingly plausible grounds that occupational roles play a very central part in our total framework of social positions and that loss of this role constitutes a traumatic shifting of position, at least for most males. There has been much concern about compulsory retirement practices, on the grounds that people are being forced into this traumatic shift of position without regard to their individual capacities, interests, and needs. However, several recent studies—by Steiner and Dorfman (1957) in California, a nation-wide study directed by Streib and Thompson (1955) of Cornell, studies by Havighurst and Friedmann (1954) and Tuckman and Lorge (1953), and a study by the Connecticut Commission on the Potentials of Aging (1954)—have cast some doubt on this type of formulation. The evidence seems to indicate that most men retire voluntarily and that most of the voluntary retirements are due to poor health. There are occupational variations in this respect. Of those who retire voluntarily, "blue-collar" workers are most likely to retire for reasons of health. As one moves up the occupational ladder, the desire to retire diminishes. More than half of the compulsory retirants in the Cornell Study had favorable pre-retirement attitudes (Cornell University, 1956). This study also indicates that most people readjust readily and successfully to retirement as such. The major problems associated with retirement seem to be economic deprivation and poor health. However, the evidence strongly indicates that poor health is not caused by retirement; rather, those in poor health are most likely to retire. Tuckman and Lorge, as well as Streib and Thompson, have presented some evidence to indicate that retirement may actually lead to an improvement in health. Some men certainly want to continue or do continue to work beyond the age of 65. The Connecticut Commission report indicates economic need as the most important reason for continuing work. Again there are occupational differences. Both the Connecticut Commission Study and the data presented by Havighurst and Friedmann indicate that, as one moves up the occupational ladder, the extra-economic meanings of work become more important. The Connecticut Commission Study (1954) has found that

problems that have confronted men 65–74 years of age are quite similar to the adjustments that the younger group [55–64] of men expected to face. A significantly larger proportion of the men 65–74 have a health problem than was expected by the younger group. . . . Over one-third of the men 65–74 years of age mentioned health as one of their problems and nearly a fifth were concerned over their incomes. Only a few men suggested that loneliness and the use of leisure time presented a problem to them [pp. 88–89].

The relationships among labor-force participation, age, sex, and health were also explored by Lawrence (1958) in Hagerstown, Maryland. Only 7 per cent of the males in the age group 45–64 were not in the labor force; most of these (90.5 per cent) were suffering from a current chronic illness. Contrariwise, 40 per cent of the males in the 65-and-over age group were not in the labor force; slightly more than half (57.4 per cent) of this group were suffering from a chronic illness. However, participation in the labor force of those men suffering no illness was practically the same for both age groups: 73.4 per cent for the younger group and 73.2 per cent for the older. This similarity, as the author points out, is probably the result of the older employed group being a select one.

Among women, 36 per cent of the younger age group (45–64) were in the labor force, as were 18 per cent of the older. Of those women not in the labor force, 57.6 per cent of the younger group reported no current chronic illness; in the older group the percentage was 42.9 (Lawrence, 1958).

There are marked differences by sex in relation to participation in the labor force. Steiner and Dorfman (1957), working with national data, found that 58 per cent of the men age 65 or more were not in the labor force and that 42 per cent were. Six out of seven of the older men were either in the labor force or not well enough to work, according to their own subjective estimates. (When more stringent criteria of "able to work" were used, it was found to apply to just one-third of the percentage that considered themselves "not well enough to work.") These figures are even more striking when it is remembered that half of the men 65 and over are 70 and nearly a third are over 75. By contrast, only 9 per cent of the women were in the labor force at the time of their survey in 1952, and only 38 per cent had had any gainful employment in the 15 or more years since they were 50. As they put it, "out of every 100 older women only 38 had worked since they were fifty. Of the 38 who had worked, 22 did not regard themselves as well enough to work. Nine of 16 who were well enough to work were in the labor force, 5 of the remaining 7 were not interested in even part-time employment and, with allowance for rounding, only one expressed interest in obtaining full- or part-time employment" (pp. 60–61).

Thus it would appear that retirement as such cannot be considered as the single major variable, involving a dramatic shift in social position within the life-space and traumatic problems of adjustment. Rather it is one element in a complex of factors involved in successful or unsuccessful aging. Among them, the conditional factors of health and economic resources appear to be quite important. There are probably equally important factors related to the available life-space and alternatives to the position of full-time employment. A man who retires in poor health with few if any economic resources, no family, and few if any friends is certainly in an anomic position. It appears, however, that such people constitute a small, although significant, minority in the older population.

FACTS ABOUT ECONOMIC RESOURCES OF THE ELDERLY

One of the most thorough studies of the economic resources of the elderly has been made by Steiner and Dorfman (1957).

They indicate that significant numbers and percentages of the aged they studied have receipts below the "subsistence" budget— 25 per cent of the couples, 33 per cent of the unrelated males, and 50 per cent of the unrelated females. The problem of inadequate receipts is a dominant feature of the situation and is only slightly mitigated by non-monetary sources of support. Dependency is a major problem. There are significant variations in the numbers who are self-supporting in relation to their status as couples, unrelated males, or unrelated females. Twenty-six per cent of the couples, 46 per cent of the unrelated males, and 63 per cent of the unrelated females are not self-supporting. Self-support here was defined as not having received old age assistance, relief, or more than $200 in contributions. This generally poor economic position of the aged is not greatly mitigated by assets. Thirty-three per cent of the unrelated females, 38 per cent of the unrelated males, and 58 per cent of couples had some liquid assets, but the size of the available cushions against economic shock seem frequently to be inadequate.

Thus, in general, older people seem to be notably disadvantaged in terms of wealth or in their command over scarce means. This, in turn, places restrictions on the type of social systems in which they can participate. However, it must be remembered that this problem tends to be cumulative with others and to be acutely concentrated in certain groups. When it is combined with poor health, loss of power, prestige, and recognition through loss of employment, and loss of emotional response through death of a spouse and friends, the problem can indeed become acute.

C. The Evidence from a Study in a Large Metropolitan Area

NATURE OF THE STUDY

A major study of people over 60 living in the Kips Bay–Yorkville area of New York City has been completed by Kutner and his associates (1956). It was concerned with the social and cultural factors which are related to adjustment in aging, the kinds of people who successfully adjust themselves, and the kinds of programs which might be designed to serve the need of older people. A major concern of the study revolved around the concept of morale, which they defined as "a continuum of responses to life and living problems that reflect the presence or absence of satisfaction, optimism, and expanding life perspective" (p. 48). A morale scale was constructed, and the responses were divided into three groups of approximately equal size representing high-, medium-, and low-morale scores.

THE GENERAL PICTURE OF MORALE

It was found that morale, as measured by this scale, declines gradually and systematically over the years. The most marked decline seems to occur in the period from 65 to 69. There are some interesting sex differences in this respect. The morale of women declined gradually with increasing age. Among men, however, there is a much sharper decline in morale between the ages of 65 and 69 and then a mild upturn in the 70–74-year-old group. Also among women a more even distribution was found between the high, medium, and low scorers in the later years, whereas among men in the seventh and eighth decades morale tended to be either high or low, with comparatively few in the medium group.

FACTORS ASSOCIATED WITH MORALE

A significant relationship was found between morale and socioeconomic status, low status being associated with low morale, and vice versa. The data also suggest an interesting relation among socioeconomic status, health, and morale. Among the high status group, poor health failed substantially to affect morale, whereas, among low-status groups, poor health has a profound negative effect on morale. Thus those in the low-status group with poor health are very low in morale, whereas those in the high-status group tend to be high in morale in spite of poor health. Those in the low-status group who are in good health have about the same index of morale as those in the high-status group who are in poor health.

There is also a relationship between marital status and morale, with married people having higher indexes than single people, and the widowed occupying an intermediate position. Again, however, it is important to see the interdependence of various factors. People of high socioeconomic status who are married tend to have the highest indexes of morale, low-status single men form the statistical group with the lowest index of morale, whereas high-status married men form a statistical group with a high morale index. Among widows, the length of widowhood seems to be of some significance. Those who have been widowed less than 10 years have lower morale than those who have lived widowed for a longer period.

These data suggest a more marked negative relation between retirement and morale than was indicated in the studies referred to above. The employed had the highest morale rating within each socioeconomic status group. However, it is important to note that the decline in morale within the low-status group is significantly greater than in the high-status group. Similarly, they found significant differences in morale between widows and married housewives. The loss of a meaningful role in a meaningful context among the widowed housewives appeared to be sufficiently serious to affect their scores on the instrument used. Single employed people maintain a relatively high level of morale, whereas single retired people have a low level. Conversely, married working women have a relatively low level of morale.

Their evidence also indicates that economic resources do not operate as single variables but derive their significance and effects in combination with other factors. As they put it:

How one derives his income seems to be more importantly related to one's level of morale than *what* the income is itself. . . . A person who is working but receiving less than $25 per week has a morale rating similar to that of a person who is retired but receiving a higher income. It is also quite clear that as earnings or income increase, morale rises. However, . . . while the extent of this rise is great among the employed group . . . it is only moderate among the retired group [Kutner *et al.*, 1956, pp. 77–78].

Similarly, their findings indicate that the influence of retirement itself is dependent upon its context. They state that, "summarizing these and related findings, a negative evaluation of retirement is found among those: (1) whose self-image (reflecting feelings of deprivation) is also negative; (2) who are relatively isolated socially; (3) who tended to dislike the idea of retirement in the first place; and (4) who had to give up their jobs because of poor health" (pp. 88–89).

They also developed an instrument to assess positive or negative self-images. The group was rated by this instrument and divided into two nearly equal groups, one labeled "negative" and the other "positive." The findings with the use of this instrument closely paralleled the findings in terms of the morale scale.

Two other variables which are frequently alleged to be closely related to morale and adjustment were analyzed—activity (particularly in the sense of activities provided by recreation and other special programs) and social isolation. Their data lend only partial and highly qualified support to the widely held assumption that "the busy older person is the happy individual" (p. 121). They also suggest that activity used simply to fill "free time" is less likely to produce good adjustment than is gainful activity. A social isolation index was developed in terms of which a little over half of the sample was classed

as having a quite limited range to their
network of relations and hence as being
relatively isolated. Again, the most striking
aspect of their findings is that social isolation does not operate as an independent
variable and that its effects are dependent
upon the total context of the situation. The
findings in this regard are particularly
pertinent to the general argument of the
present chapter and are quoted in summary as follows:

1. Residential isolation and social isolation are
   not necessarily coincident.
2. As might be expected, social isolation increases with advancing age, with a sharp decrease in social relationships occurring past
   the age of seventy-five.
3. Social isolation is significantly more marked
   among low socio-economic status persons
   than among those of high status, and isolation has a depressing effect on morale among
   low status individuals. The relatively high
   level of morale among the high status groups
   is maintained regardless of the extent of
   social isolation.
4. Ethnic group variations in social isolation
   reflect cultural differences with respect to
   in-family ties. . . .
5. The supposition is not confirmed that social
   isolation, with its increased opportunity and
   time for self-observation and introspection,
   may result in an exaggerated concern with
   one's health status. In fact, when health is
   good, social isolates express less concern
   about health than do nonisolates.
6. Among nonisolates in poor health, self estimates of health are inflated and conform
   least to an objective health status rating. . . .
7. Although it might be expected that frequent
   social relationships with children, relatives,
   and friends would be conducive to good adjustment, we do not find this generally to be
   the case. Among the low status group, frequency of visiting with family and associates
   was found to have no relationship to morale.
   Among those of high status, increased proportions of persons having *low* morale was
   found to accompany frequent visiting with
   children and relations. This was not true of
   frequent contacts with friends [pp. 121–22].

They close this analysis with the caution
that it should be recognized that some

older individuals may prefer the state
which is operationally defined in this study
as "isolation" (i.e., defined in terms of the
range or volume of relations within the
life-space). Some recent theoretical developments in the Kansas City studies, concerning the concept of morale and the
modes of orientation to action, throw further light on these findings, as will be indicated below.

D. The Evidence from a Self-survey

GENERAL CHARACTERISTICS OF THE STUDY

A very interesting approach to several
of the questions raised in this chapter was
made by Hunter and Maurice (1953) by
means of a community self-survey of older
people in Grand Rapids, Michigan. A sample of 151 people 65 years of age and
older was drawn, 60 males and 91 females.
The study was concerned with the health
and physical status of older people, their
work, financial security, living quarters,
social relationships, family and living arrangements, leisure-time activities, religion
and attitudes toward the community. Older
people were involved in the construction
of the interview guide and were used as
interviewers. Hence every effort was made
to determine the range of problems, as
well as satisfactions, of older people *from
the point of view* of the subjects themselves. It is interesting to note that the
questions and answers are couched in terms
which lend themselves readily to the frame
of reference of action theory proposed in
this chapter.

HEALTH AND PHYSICAL STATUS

Questions were designed to determine
how older people *perceive* their health and
physical status and what they believe the
effects of the status are on the social roles
which they can play. Eight out of ten of
the respondents reported one or more ailments. Fifty-six per cent of them indicated
a skeletal-muscular condition, and 44 per

cent reported circulatory disability. These conditions do tend to limit participation in social systems. About 47 per cent of the females who reported one or more ailments indicated nervousness, while only 17 per cent of the males did so. If shifts in social position with age are more traumatic for males, and if the unemployed or retired male has less certainty or clarity of role, one might expect more "nervousness" among males. However, these variables are not so simply related. The *reporting* of "nervousness" by males is so negatively evaluated in the culture that males tend to display appropriate behavior in this respect even though they may be in a relatively *anomic* position.

Ecological mobility is certainly one important condition affecting the structure of the social life-space. It was found that 81.5 per cent of the total sample could go almost any place unassisted; 16.6 per cent were confined to home or yard. Only six-tenths of 1 per cent were confined to bed or chair. It would appear that the great majority of older people who are not in specialized residential treatment centers have a range of potential mobility which would not drastically affect the structure of the social systems in which they can participate. On the other hand, almost one-fifth of them are effectively confined to their homes and cannot, therefore, participate fully in the social life beyond its confines and become significantly dependent upon the extent to which the rest of their social system really comes to their door. In the total sample, 46 per cent indicated that they had to give up at least one of their activities because of their health or physical condition; 52 per cent did not have to give up any (for the other 2 per cent there were no data). Of those who reported ailments, 55 per cent had to give up one or more activities, and 42 per cent were not so required. The authors comment that "nearly all the older people mentioned the fact that it was necessary to adjust their activities to lessened physical strength and vigor. . . . At the

same time, most of them appeared to accept this adjustment as a natural concomitant of aging" (p. 13).

Some important differences were found by sex: "*a*) More women than men reported ailments. *b*) More women than men were confined to their homes, or to beds or chairs. *c*) More women than men reported the necessity to limit their activities. *d*) Women gave themselves a poorer health rating than did men" (p. 16). The qualification should be made that the women in this sample were older than the men. This fact probably accounts for only a small part of the difference. There were also more widows than widowers, as one would expect from the demographic data presented earlier. Women faced somewhat more serious economic problems and generally had more *problems* associated with their positions in life.

WORK

Approximately half of the men and one-fifth of the women were working for pay, either full time or part time. The men tended to be in full-time employment and the women in part-time employment. Of those who were working, the men overwhelmingly indicated that they preferred working to doing nothing, whereas the women had a stronger tendency to indicate that they were working because they needed money. Two-thirds of the older people who were not working indicated they did not want to work. Thus, in general, it would appear that the great majority of this sample were satisfied with their positions in relation to the world of work, and only a small minority wished to change their status from employed to retired, or vice versa, and most who so wished were women.

Retirement, in this study, was given a narrower definition than working or not working and was defined as separation from regular work at one's usual occupation. After excluding 48 housewives who had never been employed, it was determined that 67 per cent were retired. Fifty-eight per cent of them had retired between the ages of 60 and 69. The prevalent reason given for retirement by the men was the fact that they had reached a defined age limit, while for women the most common reason was health or physical condition, including, in some cases, the poor health of a family member. Of those who had retired, about 39 per cent claimed that they had no major problem since retirement. Financial problems were mentioned by 18.8 per cent. Approximately 18 per cent of the males said that their major problem was finding something useful to do—this was a problem for only 6.4 per cent of the women. Apparently, the women felt that doing housework was doing something useful. In this regard about 55 per cent of women did all their housework, 36.3 per cent did some of it, and only 7.7 per cent did no housework.

FINANCIAL SECURITY

Approximately 60.9 per cent of the sample had less than $1500 cash income during 1952. For Detroit, Michigan, which is probably reasonably comparable, it had been estimated that a budget of $1818 was required for an elderly couple. Forty-seven per cent of the women received less than $1000, whereas one-third of the men were in this category. Similarly, wages represented the principal source of income for about four out of ten men, whereas Old-Age and Survivors Insurance was mentioned most frequently by women as the major source of income. A still more striking difference appears in terms of marital status. "Married older people derived the larger share of their income from wages. In contrast . . . widowed and single people received the largest proportion of their income from Old Age and Survivors Insurance and Old Age Assistance grants" (p. 27).

It has long been established that *relative deprivation* is an important factor in morale and adjustment and, above a certain minimum level, is probably a more potent factor than the intrinsic character-

istics of the deprivation itself. This study reported that "approximately two out of every three subjects reported that their 1952 income was less than it had been in 1942. Women reported less income to a greater extent than did the men. It was evident from what older people said in this connection that reduced income and decreased purchasing power of the dollar produce a difficult situation to overcome" (p. 28). As far as adequacy of income was concerned, about two-thirds of the respondents said that they had just enough with which to get along, nearly 15 per cent could not make ends meet, and slightly more than 15 per cent had more than was needed. Married and single people were more likely to have more income than was needed than were the widowed; conversely, the widowed were more likely to report an inadequate income. Again, one of the interesting features of this study is that it went on to probe the *consequences for action* of the changed conditions reported.

Each individual with less income in 1952 than in 1942, on an average reported three types of adjustments to decreased income. Nearly two-thirds of the group spent less on clothing; over half stopped saving; one-fourth entertained friends less and spent less on food. Women had a greater tendency than did the men to make adjustments to less income by entertaining friends less often, by moving to less expensive quarters, by giving up insurance, by giving up church and club attendance, and by depending more on children. Men, on the other hand, tended more than did the women to adjust by giving up a car (probably true that men were more likely to be car owners) [p. 30].

SOCIAL RELATIONSHIPS

In response to a question as to whether the respondent had friends in the vicinity, only 2 of the 151 subjects said that they did not. Having at least some friends is such a deeply rooted cultural value that, even though life-space may become highly constricted, it is not reported in these terms. About three-fourths of the sample said that they had close friends in the sense of people with whom they could talk over almost anything. The majority, 6 out of 10, reported that they saw their friends frequently, and about 4 out of 10 indicated that they saw them sometimes or not at all. When it was reported that friends were seen infrequently or not at all, physical limitations were the most frequent reason given. Women were in this category more frequently than men. There were small but significant minorities who said that they had lost interest in friends or that their friends did not come to see them anymore. There was a still smaller minority whose friends had died or who felt that they could no longer see their friends because they did not have the means to entertain them or because their homes had become too shabby. In general, the widowed had fewer friends and tended to see their friends less often than did older couples.

Thus one gets a general picture of constriction in the life-space with age, but the constriction is unevenly distributed in the older population and varies significantly with such factors as health, employment, income, and marital status.

FAMILY AND LIVING ARRANGEMENTS

This sample, too, revealed a greater proportion of widowhood among women than among men. In the age group 65–74 the largest proportion of men lived with their spouses, whereas the largest proportion of women lived alone. Women in this same age group had a greater tendency to live with their children or relatives than did the men. A somewhat different picture obtains in the age group 75 and older. The largest proportion of men in this age group lived with their children, whereas the largest proportion of women in this age group still fall into the category of living alone. The most dissatisfaction with present living arrangements was expressed by those who were living alone. But it was also noted that 13.3 per cent of those who were dissatisfied were living with their children. However, the great majority of this sample, 85 per cent, expressed satisfaction with their present living arrangements.

LEISURE-TIME ACTIVITY

The pattern of use of leisure time and participation in "activities" also show considerable variation, particularly in relation to health and to marital status. People in relatively poor health reported more "leisure" time than did people in good health, and men reported somewhat more than did women. In general, one does not get a picture of emptiness of time, since only 11 per cent reported that they did not know what to do with their leisure time, 60 per cent said that they managed to keep adequately busy, and more than 25 per cent had more things to do than time in which to do them.

III. Some Evidence from Current Studies

A. Description and Identification of the Studies

A series of studies is currently under way, with varying degrees of completeness, all of which are concerned ultimately with the difficult problem of delineating the major variables which differentiate between successful, or mentally healthy, aging and unsuccessful aging, with geriatric mental illness as its extreme.

THE KANSAS CITY STUDY OF ADULT LIFE

A study of a sample of men and women between the ages of 40 and 70, representative of the population in this age range of Greater Kansas City, has been undertaken by the University of Chicago's Committee on Human Development. A modified probability sample was drawn which was then stratified by socioeconomic status. Four parallel samples were established, with 240 people in each, containing equal numbers of men and women of the four social class groups, and with an age distribution which is approximately that found in the Kansas

City population. It is recognized that re-fusals and failures to complete assigned in-terviews biased the sample to some extent, especially in the direction of more stable residents, to the exclusion of people living in institutions, hotels, and rooming houses and of people who refused to co-operate with a study of this kind. A single detailed interview was had with each person in each of the four samples. Some questions were asked of the total sample of 1000, and, in addition, special questions were asked in each of the four parallel samples, with an emphasis on one of four areas—social role, age grade, mobility, and personality. Hav-ighurst (1957) has published the data from the social role study, and Neugarten, in collaboration with associates in the study, has published some aspects of the data from the age grade and personality studies (Neugarten and Gutmann, 1956, 1958; Neugarten and Garron, 1957; Neugarten and Peterson, 1957). Other aspects of this study are currently being prepared for pub-lication.

THE KANSAS CITY STUDY OF PSYCHOLOGI-CAL AND SOCIOLOGICAL FACTORS IN SUCCESSFUL AGING

The cross-sectional study referred to above is being followed by a more inten-sive study of a panel over a period of time. The panel consists of approximately 120 respondents who will be interviewed four or five times over a 5-year period. The ma-jor instrument used in this study is an in-tensive focused interview. It is sometimes accompanied with modifications of the Thematic Apperception Test and other in-struments as they seem appropriate. The age range in the panel is from 50 to 70. It was thought that this age period would en-compass some of the major crises of transi-tion which accompany the aging process, such as children leaving home, widowhood, and retirement. Purposive samples are also being drawn for special studies and include a group of people in their eighties. One paper is in publication, and others are in preparation (Cumming *et al.*, 1958).

THE STUDY OF SOCIAL AND PSYCHOLOGI-CAL PROBLEMS OF AGING AT THE UNIVERSITY OF CALIFORNIA

The late Else Frenkel-Brunswik had di-rected a study of social and psychological problems of aging in California. The study group was composed of 87 male, white, non-supervisory workers in industry and trades in the San Francisco metropolitan area. Forty-two members of the group were retired, and 45 were not yet retired at the time of the study. They ranged in age from 55 to 84. The median age of the retired group was 70.5; of the non-retired group, 63, Eighty per cent of the group were mar-ried and currently living with spouse. The subjects were volunteers, and this factor of course must be borne in mind in relation to sampling problems and generalizability of the findings. In particular, it means that all members of the group were in sufficient-ly good health to come in for extensive and intensive interviewing. A rich body of data was gathered on each subject, which re-quired from 9 to 16 hours of interviewing. This study is currently being completed by members of the original team, under the di-rection of Dr. Suzanne Reichard.

A MULTIDISCIPLINARY STUDY AT THE NATIONAL INSTITUTES OF HEALTH

An intensive multidisciplinary study of a group of retired men has been undertaken at the National Institutes of Health, with primary but not exclusive emphasis on mental health. Many assessments have been made—medical, psychological, and social. The results of this work have not yet been published, but two papers have been presented dealing with its social-psy-chological aspects (Quinn *et al.*, 1957; Yarrow and Quinn, 1957).

A STUDY OF GERIATRIC MENTAL ILLNESS AT THE LANGLEY-PORTER NEURO-PSYCHIATRIC INSTITUTE

As indicated earlier, an intensive study has just begun at the Langley-Porter Neuropsychiatric Institute of factors related to the development of mental disorders in the later years. The subjects will be first admissions to a mental hospital of people over the age of 60. Medical and psychiatric assessments will be made. The primary focus of the study is on the social life-space and personality factors which are associated with the development and course of the disorder. Comparison groups will be sought who have similar difficulties but who do not become hospitalized for mental illness. This project is expected to complement the Kansas City Study of a "normal" population, further to delineate the problem of "successful" aging, and to provide knowledge on which to base improved programs for the care, treatment, and rehabilitation of patients in this age group.

B. Morale, Success, and Types of Aging

Several approaches have been taken to the crucial problem of morale, or success, in relation to aging in the studies referred to above, each of which has had an important contribution to make, and all of which together are beginning to add up to some understanding of various types of adjustment and reaction to the aging process.

ROLE PERFORMANCE

Havighurst (1957), using data from the Kansas City Study of Adult Life, has been primarily concerned with the competence with which people of various ages perform their social roles. General definitions of common social roles, and the expectations associated with them, were sought, and rating scales were devised on this basis. "The rating scales for role performance then consist of the *culture-wide* definitions of success and failure in these roles, and omit the particular variance on the general themes which are characteristic of one or another sub-group" (p. 305). For this purpose reliance was placed on the "spokesmen of American values—the social philosophers and ethical leaders." Hence the criteria for

the various points on the scale tend to reflect middle-class values and behavior. Particular attention was paid to the amount of energy which a person invests in a particular role. "Thus the meaning of competence in the performance of social role, in this study, includes the level of overt performance, judged against common American standards combined with attitudes toward the role as disclosed in an interview" (p. 308). In addition to the specific ratings on role performance in each of the role areas, assessments were made of a number of factors assumed possibly to be related to role performance: socioeconomic status, amount of education, attitude, adjustment, an S score (a composite score derived from the attitude and adjustment scores rated equally), manifest complexity (a rating of complexity of a person's past and present experience), and motivation. Havighurst's data indicate that "performance, as measured by the scales devised for this study, is better in the roles of Worker, Parent, Spouse, Homemaker than it is in the roles of Citizen, Churchmember, Friend, and Association Member. It is also evident that performance is closely related to socioeconomic status in most role areas, but not to age" (p. 317). Havighurst himself believes that there is no middle-class bias in the scales used.

Some support for this view is found in the social class difference and Attitude score. The Attitude score is a kind of self-rating on one's satisfaction with one's work, family, home, friends, associations, health, and economic security. The fact that this score tends to decrease with decreasing socio-economic status is some evidence for the view that lower status people generally regard themselves as less successful in meeting their own expectations of themselves than higher status people do [p. 318].

Havighurst draws an important distinction among first-, second-, and third-order roles in terms of degrees of internalization of role expectations.

The first order roles are those which have been most thoroughly internalized and therefore are most adequately filled. These are the roles of Parent, Spouse, Homemaker and Worker. Second order roles are less deeply internalized, but they have enough reward value to be filled fairly well. These are the roles of Friend and User of Leisure Time. Third order roles are not deeply internalized and have no great reward value for most people; consequently they are generally poorly performed. These are the roles of Citizen and Club and Association Member [p. 320].

Perhaps the most striking findings are that differences in role performances by age are very small within this 40–70-year range, although there is a consistent downward trend of scores with age, with the exception of roles of parent, spouse, and church member. However, it should be noted that retired people were not given a score in the worker role, so that average scores in the 61–70 group were not affected by retirement.

One of the most interesting methodological developments was the use of a cluster analysis. "Through a study of the intercorrelations of role performances in the several role areas it was found that there are two clusters of roles. One, called the *Family Centered Cluster,* consisted of Parent-Spouse-Homemaker; while the other consisted of Friend–Citizen–Association Member–Leisure. Thus we might speak of two general factors in role performance" (p. 342). In addition, it was possible to describe a series of profiles or patterns of role performance. Twenty-seven such patterns were differentiated, each one of which represents a "way of life" shared by a number of people. These patterns were then grouped into five major clusters, two of which are designated as family centered, one characteristic of the middle class, and one of the "common man."

The five large families of role-pattern are closely related to social class positions, so that one can speak of middle class patterns, common man or lower middle-upper lower class patterns, and lower-class patterns. These patterns of role performance are minimally related to age and sex. That is, there are very few patterns which are characteristically feminine or masculine,

and very few that are more characteristic of people in their sixties than in their forties. . . . From the pattern analysis one may conclude that a person's pattern of role performance or "life style" is established in early middle age— by the forties—and tends to persist into the sixties at least [pp. 342–43].

Thus this study gives a picture of the period from 40 to 70 as essentially a plateau in relation to the competence with which people perform social roles, with a slight decline toward the later years. Havighurst suggests the following general interpretation:

Thus there is a persistence of *function* in spite of a declining structural (biological) base for function. Function declines less rapidly than structure. This leads to the general proposition that, in human beings in the latter part of the life cycle, *function resists structural decline.* Or, to put it in a different way, *function becomes partly independent of structure.* . . . This distinction between function and structure might also be stated as a distinction between *social* function and *biological* function. It is the *biological functioning* of the body that falls off more rapidly than its *social functioning* [pp. 345–46].

He also found that the dispersion, or standard deviation, of role performance scores increased slightly with age, and he suggests that this points toward a relatively permissive attitude toward people in late middle age in our society.

ROLE PERCEPTIONS AND EXPECTATIONS

Neugarten and Gutmann (1957) have found a marked and significant shift with age in the perceptions of key roles in the family by the use of a TAT-type picture depicting a young man, a young woman, an old man, and an old woman. With increasing age the old man is viewed as becoming less authoritative, increasingly submissive, and playing a generally less dominant role than the old woman. Age is the factor which accounts significantly for variation in the data, while factors of sex and social status did not approach statistical significance. There was also a common change in ego qualities for both men and women with age; the personality appears to become more constricted, more detached from the mastery of affairs, and less in control impulse life.

The nature of the shift in the positions of the old man and old woman, with age, appears to be as follows:

As he moves from a dominant to a submissive posture, the Old Man is seen by younger respondents as struggling with issues of assertion, guilt, nurturance and affiliation. The resulting conflicts he attempts to solve in terms of complex role patterns, role patterns which embody these disparate elements. In later years he is seen as one who has reached the solution mainly through relinquishing the assertive role element (usually to the older woman) and who has abandoned significant attempts at manipulating the environment. Rather than actually altering the environment he alters himself; he conforms, rather than dealing with people and events, he only organizes through "thought" the conceptual traces of the environment, as they intrude on his inner world. . . . The Old Woman is seen modally by younger respondents as one who does not play a decisive controlling part in the family affairs. Women in their forties and early fifties typically see her as a kind of shrew, one who doesn't dominate the course of events in the family, but rather makes a nuisance of herself there. Either she is kept in line by a wise controlling husband, or, if she dominates her husband, her children effectually oppose her and gain their autonomy despite her protest. In both these cases younger women are assuring us that, while the mother is being difficult, outer forces insure that she isn't really hurting anyone, or getting away with anything. Younger men see her most frequently as either an emotional, fluttery "little woman" type, a good complement to her wise, strong, husband; or they see her as an essentially benign, nurturant, somewhat controlling mother, whose control depends on the fact that her gratified family want her to have it. Older respondents rarely see the older woman as submissive; almost always assigning her to some category of dominance. For both men and women respondents, her dominance is rarely benign; good results do not proceed from it. Typical of this

period is to see the Old Woman as an embodiment of the "id": all primal wrath and narcissistic impulse, or, as a tentative superego armed with the energies of the "id"—a superego figure who rigidly defines and harshly enforces the moral law. Thus, for the Old Woman, with increasing age of respondent, submission gives way to dominance, and perception of an environment which controls and limits the Old Woman's expressivity gives way to perception of a familial environment dominated by the Old Woman [pp. 6–8].

They recognize that these patterns may appear to be overdrawn and stereotypic. However, they feel that the fact that "the same personality components are described time and again, far beyond chance expectation, to the same stimulus figures, we can only deduce that the role patterns and changes reported here reflect the social and cultural reality" (p. 8). (This material has subsequently been published in revised and expanded form [Neugarten and Gutmann, 1958].)

PERSONALITY TYPES

Just as there are different patterns of role performance, so there are probably significantly different personality types in relation to adjustment to aging. Factors of this order must be taken into consideration in attempting to answer the question of why some people are able to make the shifts of position with age successfully and others are not.

In the University of California Study, referred to above, a cluster analysis, based on 115 separate ratings of each subject, has resulted in the definition of five types of personality in relation to adjustment to aging. Three of these types show a relatively high degree of adjustment, and two of them show a low degree of adjustment—the middle group was left out of this analysis. High 1 is labeled as a "mature" type. It presents a well-integrated ego structure, genuine and realistic self-appraisal, respect for the opposite sex, especially to the wife, and considerable trustingness. High 2 can be labeled the "rocking-chair" type and is characterized by a high degree of passivity. High 3 can be labeled "counterphobic" and is characterized by a dislike of dependency and the development of numerous psychological defenses against dependency. Low 1 can be termed "extra-punitive," taking things out on the world around them, and Low 2 "intra-punitive," characterized by a high degree of depression.

In general, adjustment to aging is found to have high positive correlations with sublimation, ego strength, adjustment to work, mild ego-integrated aggression, a realistic optimism, self-perception of being successful, freedom from anxiety, positive affect toward wife, and genuine acceptance of aging. There are high negative correlations with the schizoid mechanism of withdrawal, with overt depression, and with pessimism. Thus, as might be expected, but should never be overlooked, adjustment to aging is positively related to variables indicative of *general* adjustment and negatively related to variables indicative of maladaptive or pathological patterns. In this study appropriate statistical precautions were taken to demonstrate that the rating of adjustment to aging was evaluated independently of over-all personality adjustment, so that the relations between these two aspects of adjustment is not an artifact. Furthermore, the above classification indicates that there are different personality clusters and different degrees of maturity which can all be related to adjustment to aging.

FURTHER EVIDENCE ABOUT RETIREMENT

As indicated above, in the California study about half of the subjects were retired and half were not. Evidence will be available concerning changes in patterns of activity and the structure of social life space in relation both to retirement and to age (with, of course, a good deal of overlap between these two categories), some of which can be tentatively indicated here.

The only significant difference with age in relation to leisure-time activities was found in relation to participation in sports. There were marked shifts in degree of involvement in various activities with age and with retirement. The older and the retired group invest more energies in useful maintenance activities, such as house repairs, and also in productive manual activities. Thus in this study group, which, it must be remembered, was a group of voluntary subjects well enough to participate in the study, there is a general picture of sustained activities.

There is a marked increase, both with age and with retirement, in preoccupation with problems of economic security, which in turn has an impact on the general social and political outlook.

One of the most striking findings in this study thus far is considerable evidence for a higher degree of adjustment of the older and the retired group than for the younger and not yet retired. It is, of course, an interesting theoretical question as to whether the differences found reflect lifelong differences between these age groups or changes with age. In most instances, at least, it seems more plausible to attribute the difference to changes with age. The older and retired group seem generally more content with their lot in life. There was less discrepancy between their life-goals and their actual social position. There was considerable shift in sources of satisfaction from instrumental to affective social roles. The older and retired group expressed more satisfaction with the secondary aspects of work and less dissatisfaction with the work situation and with work itself. There seems to be a general shift in goals and a process of coming to terms with one's life-situation. There is a curtailment of modifiability of position as one gets older and perhaps a process of coming to terms with current role commitments. The older and retired groups perceive their earlier lives as more satisfying than did the younger, not yet retired. The disappointments of life were outweighed by satisfactions, and disappointments seem to have lost their potency in retrospect with the retired group. This group also presents a more benign picture of its early family milieu. As indicated above, 80 per cent of the entire group were married and living with their spouse. The older and retired groups had more equalitarian relations with their wives, more realistic evaluation of them, and less evidence of neurotic entanglement. In this group, health, as perceived and reported by the respondents, did not decline with age or with retirement. The older group had in general more realistic attitudes about health. The younger and not-yet-retired group made more use of active health regimes and seemed to be more concerned about health. Again it appears that the crisis of transition had abated in the older and retired group, and there was greater acceptance of the realities of their situation. They did realistically report an increase in fatigue and physical weakness.

A REDEFINITION OF MORALE AND SUCCESSFUL AGING

The Kansas City Study of Psychological and Sociological Aspects of Successful Aging, currently in progress, has made some important contributions to the theoretical formulations of these problems and has tested these formulations empirically on a limited basis to find significant differences with age.

Particular use has been made of two of Talcott Parsons' pattern variables—diffuse-specific and affective-neutral. When these two sets of variables are combined, they yield four styles of interaction: the diffuse-affective, the diffuse-neutral (which is quite rare), the specific-affective, and the specific-neutral. A diffuse relationship encompasses a relatively large range of interactions, and the burden of proof is on a person in such a relationship who would exclude something from it. A specific relation is more limited in range, the burden of proof being on the person who would add something to the relationship, and it is one which has no sequelae. Affective and neu-

tral refer to the amount of emotional involvement and expression. There is suggestive evidence that aging involves some retreat from diffuse-affective relations, especially in instrumental contexts and a tendency for specific-affective relations to become predominant. In groups above 60, and particularly in the very old groups of 80 and above, affective or emotionally charged relationships become burdensome unless they are primarily specific, and, similarly, diffuse relationships cannot be tolerated unless they are primarily neutral. This seems to parallel a general process which the Kansas City group has labeled "disengagement" from the norms and requirements of society. The very old people differ significantly from those between 50 and 70 in the degree of freedom from care or concern about various norms in answering questions. For example, when asked, "What is the most important thing in life to you just now?" several of the quite old people replied, "Eating." The respondents in the younger age group invariably would mention more normatively controlled and expected activities such as work and family. Thus there appear to be orderly ways for people to withdraw from roles of society and to reduce their engagement with life. This finding, if substantiated, will have important implications for programs of action. There has been a strong tendency to accept the view that the problems of aging are best attacked by extending the ideals of involvement and reciprocal obligation and a high level of activity. As Cumming and Udell (1957) put it, "We say that the grandmother wants to feel wanted, to feel that she is part of the decision making family unit, and so on. We are suggesting that she does not want to feel wanted at the price of being needed; maybe she would really like a sports car, and when her coordination fails her, a television set, and in the last confines, when her vision fails her, good meals and a comfortable place to nap until the end comes."

Considerations of this order have led, in

turn, to a searching attempt to determine what "success in aging" or "morale" really means. The problem is a particularly interesting one in terms of the types of data obtained in the Kansas City Study, which has used three principal instruments of observation: relatively structured interviews of an extensive type, relatively unstructured intensive interviews, and protocols from six of the Thematic Apperception Test cards. As Cumming *et al.* (1958) point out, there is a major problem in uniting the evidence from these sources, "since the categories of analysis are not the same for each technique. For example, if a respondent says in an interview that he feels successful, but his projective test shows that he has deep conflicts regarding certain undesirable impulses which he is managing to handle by means of a system of defense mechanisms, how do we equate these two evaluations, . . . and how are we to translate all this into terms of 'success' or 'failure,' high or low 'morale'?" The first step in an attempt to solve this type of problem was to utilize scales developed by others in the same general field. Kutner's (1956) morale scale and Srole's (1956) "anomia" scale were used for this purpose. The two scales appeared upon inspection to be a good deal alike. Srole's items deal primarily in generalities about the state of society, whereas Kutner's deal with the subjective state of personal morale. It was found possible to scale Kutner's and Srole's items separately and together. "We ended with a seven-item scale, containing four of Kutner's seven items and three of Srole's five, and having a reproducibility of 90.7 per cent. *At this point then, we define morale, for our purposes, as the intervening variable between the social nexus and the individual act of total failure, or suicide; and we declared this variable to be the logical correlate of what we meant by success in aging"* (Cumming *et al.*, 1958). On the other hand, some of the empirical findings in Kansas City were strongly suggestive that the Srole-Kutner scale was indeed measuring something but not necessarily "morale." One of the most highly skilled intensive interviewers had interviewed a small panel within the larger panel and had the impression of discrepancy between the scores of these panel members on the Kutner-Srole scale and the interviewers' own impression of the respondent's "morale." Upon further examination of the scale, it appeared that it contains a number of general statements about the state of the world and the individual's relationship to the world, and thus is tapping a cultural, or ideological dimension. The element which appears to run through all the items is a tendency toward a positive or optimistic world view, as against a negative or misanthropic one. We suspected that we were getting responses that expressed two sets of norms. First, the respondents were telling us about the nature of the world as they see it; and overlaid upon that set of norms was another—namely, their norms about what it is appropriate to say to the University of Chicago interviewer. Although this normative complex might bear a relationship to personal morale, it could not by itself be thought of as morale, or for that matter as anomia [Cumming *et al.*, 1958].

It was further found that the scores on the Kutner-Srole scale correlated well with socioeconomic class and with quantity of interaction. The ideology of the respondent is a function of class and interaction rates. This scale was then called the "Alienation Scale," and attention was then turned to a more direct attack on the meaning of personal morale itself. An interesting feature of this scale is that it groups "happy well-adjusted" but self-alienated people together with the depressed and involuntarily alienated.

The intensive interviewer then ranked ten of the panel members who had been most intensively interviewed according to her judgment of relative morale. "We assumed, in other words, that *whatever* morale is, it is possible to recognize it through the myriad complicated symbolic communications of the interview and to gauge its extent, or levels." These rankings turned out to have no relationship with scores on the Alienation Scale (a correlation of — .2). There was also no correlation between this ranking and class or interaction rates.

The next, and in many ways the most interesting, step was an interview of the intensive interviewer by a skilled psychiatrist, who is also well versed in the social sciences, in an attempt to discover the subjective basis for the morale rankings which the interviewer had made. There appears to have been a complex of five elements involved in the ranking:

1. Sheer energy or vitality as contrasted with listlessness or apathy.
2. Respondent's ability to form a relationship in the interview situation—a matter not of the kind of relationship but of its degree.
3. "Motility" or the ability of the individual to change both his means and, if necessary, his goals.
4. "Fortitude" or a level of resolution that allows the individual to accept responsibility for his own behavior without excessively blaming either himself or others.
5. Goodness of fit between the respondent's goals and his ability to achieve them—particular attention being given to interactional or relational goals and rewards.

In connection with the last of these elements, Parsons' fourfold classification of relational rewards has been used, which, briefly, yields a classification of "approval-seekers," "response-seekers," "esteem-seekers," and "total acceptance-seekers." These four types can be related to the pattern variables referred to above.

The approval-seeker is specific and neutral in his orientation to interaction; the response-seeker is specific and affective; the esteem-seeker is diffuse and neutral; the acceptance-seeker, diffuse and affective. The "goodness of fit" contained in the Dean morale ranking, then, refers, where interaction is concerned, to the fit between the respondent's *preferred interaction style* and the *interaction style his present life situation most consistently demands of him.* Thus, a person who characteristically seeks esteem or affection, but who works for a job where the institutionalized reward is approval, would be considered to have a bad fit [Cumming *et al.,* 1958].

The major difference between this approach to morale and that involved in the Kutner-Srole scale is that it is relatively content-free and does not include ideological orientations.

Another member of the team has made an independent estimate of morale. Without knowledge of the respondent's identity, he selected ten questions from the structured interviews and then ranked the ten respondents on the basis of his understanding of this meaning of morale. "The correlation of his rank scores with the Dean ranking is .8, which is at the .01 level of significance even for so small a number as ten" (Cumming *et al.,* 1958). Also his scores were unrelated to the Alienation Scale (Kutner-Srole). These operations will be continued in a variety of ways and through them it is hoped to "pin down an estimate of success and morale which has a reasonable *inner* validity, as well as external predictive value. In this way, we hope to enhance the meaning of our variables, even though answering the metaphysical question as to the *real* nature of morale and successful aging is beyond our scope. We will *not,* in short, end by knowing what morale *really is;* but we *will* know what order of measuring instrument most accurately assesses it" (Cumming *et al.,* 1958). The combined instrument, or Alienation Scale, seems basically to be a good index of conformity versus alienation.

It is interesting that Yarrow, Quinn, and others at the National Institute of Mental Health, working quite independently from the Kansas City group, have been developing similar concepts of "personal social structure." They have focused particularly on losses or constrictions in the social life-space of their subjects and, tentatively, are finding significant relations between loss of structure and such things as "de-differentiations" in the organization of daily life and complexity of goals and the inability to use or to enjoy time. They also found that the amount of loss has to be judged in terms of what is left. Tentatively, it would appear that these variables are significantly related to various aspects of physiological functioning and mental health (Quinn *et al.,* 1957; Yarrow and Quinn, 1957).

Thus detailed analyses of the structure of social life-space and of styles of living within life-spaces seem to be promising lines of research which should give some answers to the general question of what is successful aging and how people achieve successful aging.

GENERAL TYPES OF AGING

Early in the course of the first of the Kansas City studies, David Riesman (1954) proposed a threefold typology of the aging process, which still serves a useful purpose in drawing together the various dimensions of successful aging and morale as discussed above. The autonomous types carry their own preservative and remain creative throughout the shifts and changes which go on about them. Probably relatively few people fall into this category. A much larger category can be described as the "adjusted type." They "have no such resources within them but are the beneficiaries of the cultural preservative (derived from work, power, position, and so on) which sustains them, although only so long as the cultural conditions remain stable and protective" (p. 379). A third group is labeled the "anomic" and has neither of these sources of preservation so that decay sets in with aging. "If responsibility accompanies maturity for the autonomous and takes the place of maturity for the adjusted, the anomic find their way to neither. Like the person who is afraid to overshoot the green when he drives from the tee (or, more probably, gives up acting as if he wanted to make the green at all), they start out in life with aims that will not carry them through a career. And they do not succeed in boarding an institutional escalator that will define for them what it is to have a career" (p. 383). Such people constitute a small but socially important minority of older people.

IV. SUMMARY

The theory of action is particularly well suited to explore the problems of changing status, roles, and relationships with age. What moves in the framework of social po-sition are associated with aging, how much stress is created by these moves, and to what extent or under what circumstances do they involve a cumulative tendency to deviance are among the significant questions it poses about the aging process. How does the structure of the individual's social life-space alter with age, and how does he cope with these changes? That these factors are important in the total process of aging and are not wholly dependent on biological changes with age is strongly suggested by comparative evidence from different societies.

Although there has been no increase in life-span, the number and proportion of individuals 65 and over have increased steadily since 1900. The increasingly large numbers of females over 65 in the not-married category must be borne in mind in studying the social positions of older persons. Also there are significant numbers of older people whose health is sufficiently poor to affect the size and structure of the social life-space in which they can operate. But there are also significant numbers, and probably much larger numbers, where these effects are minimal. Among health problems, mental health assumes a particularly important place, and it, in turn, is significantly related to the types of social positions people occupy.

Retirement cannot be considered as a single major variable which necessarily involves a *traumatic* shift in social position. Its problems must be understood in a context involving health, economic security (in which the aged appear to be particularly disadvantaged), and available social life-space. The study by Kutner and his associates in the metropolitan setting of New York City gives further evidence of the constellation of factors involving health, retirement, socioeconomic status, marital status, family relations, morale (as defined in their scale), self-image, amount of activity, and social isolation. The retirement studies conducted at Cornell and the material presented in the self-survey in a smaller community in Michigan give a similar picture. A general tendency toward constriction of the life-space in later years is seen but with significant variations that are related to these other factors.

Several approaches undertaken recently have been designed to add greater precision to the understanding of morale and "successful" aging. Havighurst has approached the problem in terms of social competence, as measured by ratings of performance in various categories of roles. Little variation is found in these terms in the 40–70 age groups. However, there are significant differences in styles of life which, in turn, involve different styles of aging and which vary, especially by class position. Neugarten and Gutmann, on the other hand, find significant changes in the images, perceptions, and expectations of age and sex roles with age. Also both the Kansas City and the University of California studies are beginning to find systematic differences in social personality associated with different types of adjustment to aging. Some people are able to make the transition and shifts in position in "mature" ways, and others are not. Important steps have been taken in the assessment of personal morale.

Certain personality types have inherent difficulties with aging. If they also have poor health, economic insecurity, and a poor fit between their preferred interaction styles and the structure of the life-space in which they are living, they will have low morale and be unsuccessful in aging. These factors tend to cluster and to be cumulative in their effects. This creates the truly anomic group with a cumulative tendency to deviance, especially in the direction of withdrawal and dependency. In general, the evidence seems to indicate that persons characterized by this type of aging constitute a small but important minority group. The importance of a concern with this group goes beyond purely humanitarian considerations with this group itself, because they absorb a disproportionate amount of the energies of others and probably have a negative influence on the mental health of those who must deal with

them. Programs for care, treatment, and rehabilitation of this group already show some promise, but much research remains to be done, along the general lines indicated in this chapter, before we know the true extent of the problem and develop better guidelines for its management.

REFERENCES

BUSSE, E. W. 1956. Treatment of the non-hospitalized emotionally disturbed elderly person. Geriatrics, **11**, 173–79.

BUSSE, E. W., BARNES, R. H., SILVERMAN, A. S., SHY, G. M., THALER, M., and FROST, L. J. 1954. Studies of the process of aging: factors that influenced the psyche of elderly persons. Am. J. Psychiat., **110**, 897–903.

CAVAN, RUTH S., BURGESS, E. W., HAVIGHURST, R. S., and GOLDHAMER, H. 1949. Personal adjustment in old age. Chicago: Science Research Associates.

COLEMAN, R. 1958. The social structure of Kansas City. Chicago: University of Chicago, Committee on Human Development. (Mimeographed.)

CONNECTICUT. STATE. COMMISSION ON THE POTENTIALS OF THE AGING. 1954. Report of the Connecticut Commission on the Potentials of the Aging. Hartford, Conn.: The Commission.

CORNELL UNIVERSITY. DEPARTMENT OF SOCIOLOGY AND ANTHROPOLOGY. 1953. The study of occupational retirement, first progress report. Ithaca, N.Y.: The Department. (Mimeographed.)

———. 1954. The study of occupational retirement, second progress report. Ithaca, N.Y.: The Department. (Mimeographed.)

———. 1956. Study of occupational retirement newsletter. Ithaca, N.Y.: The Department.

CUMMING, ELAINE, DEAN, LOIS, and NEWELL, D. 1958. What is morale? A case study in validity. (Paper read at the annual meeting of the Society for Applied Anthropology, Syracuse.) Human Organization (in press).

CUMMING, ELAINE, and UDELL, BESS. 1957. Interaction styles during the life cycle. (Paper read at the annual meeting of the American Sociological Society, Washington, D.C.)

FRENKEL-BRUNSWIK, ELSE. 1949. Intolerance of ambiguity as an emotional and perceptual personality variable. J. Personality, **18**, 108–43.

FRIEDMANN, E. A., and HAVIGHURST, R. J.

1954. The meaning of work and retirement. Chicago: University of Chicago Press.

FRY, J. C. 1957. Care of the elderly in general practice. Brit. Med. J., **2**, 666–69.

GRUENBERG, E. M., and KAUFMAN, M. R. 1956. Mental health. *In* Charter for the aging. Albany, N.Y.: Governor's Conference on Problems of the Aging.

HAVIGHURST, R. J. 1957. The social competence of middle-aged people. Genet. Psychol. Monogr., **56**, 297–375.

HENRY, W. E. 1956. Affective complexity and role perceptions: some suggestions for a conceptual framework for the study of adult personality. *In* J. E. ANDERSON (ed.), Psychological aspects of aging, pp. 30–41. Washington, D.C.: American Psychological Association.

HIBBARD, D. L., and LEE, J. P. 1954. Presbyterian ministers and their widows in retirement. J. Gerontol., **9**, 46–55.

HUNTER, W. W., and MAURICE, HELEN. 1953. Older people tell their story. Ann Arbor, Mich.: University of Michigan, Division of Gerontology.

KOLB, L. 1956. The mental hospitalization of the aged—is it being overdone? Am. J. Psychiat., **112**, 627–36.

KRAMER, M. 1957. Problems of research on the population dynamics and therapeutic effectiveness of mental hospitals. *In* M. GREENBLATT, D. LEVINSON, and R. H. WILLIAMS (eds.), The patient and the mental hospital, pp. 145–69. Glencoe, Ill.: Free Press.

KUHLEN, R. G. 1956. Changing personal adjustment during the adult years. *In* J. E. ANDERSON (ed.), Psychological aspects of aging, pp. 21–29. Washington, D.C.: American Psychological Association.

KUTNER, B., FANSHEL, D., TOGO, ALICE M., and LANGNER, T. S. 1956. Five hundred over sixty: a community survey on aging. New York: Russell Sage Foundation.

LAWRENCE, P. S. 1958. Availability for work: chronic disease and limitation of activity. (Public Health Monogr. No. 51.) Washington, D.C.: Government Printing Office.

LINDEN, M. E. 1953. Group psychotherapy with institutionalized senile women: study in gerontologic human relations. Internat. J. Group Psychotherapy, **3**, 150–70.

LINTON, R. 1936. The study of man. New York: Appleton-Century Co.

MEAD, G. H. 1934. Mind, self, and society. Chicago: University of Chicago Press.

MERTON, R. K. 1945. Sociological theory. Am. J. Sociology, **50**, 462–74.

MIRSKY, JEANNETTE. 1937. The Eskimo of Greenland. *In* MARGARET MEAD (ed.), Cooperation and competition among primitive peoples. New York: McGraw-Hill Book Co.

NEUGARTEN, BERNICE L., and GARRON, D. C. 1957. The attitudes of middle-aged persons toward growing older. (Paper read at the annual meeting of the Gerontological Society, Cleveland.)

NEUGARTEN, BERNICE L., and GUTMANN, D. 1956. A study of age changes in adult sex roles. (Paper read at the annual meeting of the Gerontological Society, Chicago.)

———. 1958. Age-sex role images and personality in old age: a thematic apperception study. Psychol. Monogr. No. 470.

NEUGARTEN, BERNICE L., and PETERSON, W. 1957. A study of the American age-grade system. (Paper read at the Fourth Congress of the International Assoc. of Gerontology, Merano, Italy.)

NORBECK, E. 1953. Age-grading in Japan. Am. Anthropologist, **55**, 373–84.

PARSONS, T. 1949. Essays in sociological theory, pure and applied. Glencoe, Ill.: Free Press.

———. 1951. The social system. Glencoe, Ill.: Free Press.

PARSONS, T., and BALES, R. F. 1955. Family, socialization, and interaction process. Glencoe, Ill.: Free Press.

PARSONS, T., BALES, R. F., and SHILS, E. A. 1953. Working papers in the theory of action. Glencoe, Ill.: Free Press.

PARSONS, T., and SHILS, E. A. (eds.). 1951. Toward a general theory of action. Cambridge, Mass.: Harvard University Press.

POLLAK, O. 1948. Social adjustment in old age. New York: Social Science Research Council.

QUINN, OLIVE W., YARROW, MARIAN R., and YOUMANS, E. G. 1957. Relationships between behavioral and physiological functioning in the healthy aged. (Paper read at the annual meeting of the American Sociological Society, Washington, D.C.)

RIESMAN, D. 1954. Some clinical and cultural aspects of aging. Am. J. Sociology, **59**, 379–83.

SIMMONS, L. W. 1945. The role of the aged in primitive society. New Haven, Conn.: Yale University Press.

———. 1946. Attitudes toward aging and the aged; primitive societies. J. Gerontol., **1**, 72–95.

————. 1948. Old age security in other societies. Geriatrics, **3**, 237–44.

————. 1952. Social participation of the aged in different cultures. Ann. Am. Acad. Political & Social Sc., **279**, 43–51.

————. 1957. An anthropologist views old age. Pub. Health Rep., **72**, 290–94.

SMITH, W. M., JR., BRITTON, J. H., and BRITTON, JEAN O. 1958. Relationships within three-generation families. (Res. Publ. 155.) University Park: Pennsylvania State University, College of Home Economics.

SROLE, L. 1956. Social integration and certain corollaries. Am. Sociological Rev., **21**, 709–16.

STEINER, P. O., and DORFMAN, R. 1957. The economic status of the aged. Berkeley: University of California Press.

STREIB, G. F. 1956. Morale of the retired. Social Problems, **3**, 270–76.

————. 1958. Research on retirement: a report on the Cornell longitudinal study. *In* Proceedings of seminars, 1957–1958, pp. 67–87. Durham, N.C.: Duke University Council on Gerontology.

STREIB, G. F., and THOMPSON, W. E. 1955. Personal and social adjustment in retirement. *In* WILMA DONAHUE and C. TIBBITTS (eds.), The new frontiers of aging, pp. 180–97. Ann Arbor: University of Michigan Press.

————. 1957. Value orientations and interpersonal relations. (Paper read at the annual meeting of the American Sociological Society, Washington, D.C.)

THOMPSON, W. E., and STREIB, G. F. 1957. Retirement and health. (Paper read at the annual meeting of the Gerontological Society, Cleveland.)

T'IEN JU-K'ANG. 1949. Pai cults and social age in the Tai tribes of the Yunnan-Burma frontier. Am. Anthropologist, **51**, 46–57.

TUCKMAN, J., and LORGE, I. 1953. Retirement and the industrial worker. New York: Columbia University, Teachers College, Bureau of Publications.

U.S. BUREAU OF THE CENSUS. 1952. U.S. Census of population, 1950, Vol. **2**: Characteristics of the population. Washington, D.C.: Government Printing Office.

————. 1958. Illustrative projections of the population of the United States, by age and sex 1960 to 1980. (Series P-25, No. 187.) Washington, D.C.: The Bureau.

U.S. FEDERAL SECURITY AGENCY. COMMITTEE ON AGING AND GERIATRICS. 1952. Fact book on aging. Washington, D.C.: Government Printing Office.

U.S. NATIONAL HEALTH SURVEY. 1958. Health statistics: preliminary report on disability, United States, July–September 1957. (Ser. B-4, Pub. Health Service Pub. No. 584-B4.) Washington, D.C.: Government Printing Office.

WARNER, W. L., and LUNT, P. S. 1941. The social life of a modern community. New Haven, Conn.: Yale University Press.

WEINBERG, J. 1956. Personal and social adjustment. *In* J. E. ANDERSON (ed.), Psychological aspects of aging, pp. 17–20. Washington, D.C.: American Psychological Association.

WILLIAMS, R. H. 1940. Method of understanding as applied to the problem of suffering. J. Abnorm. & Social Psychol., **35**, 367–85.

————. 1942. Scheler's contributions to the sociology of affective action with special attention to the problem of shame. Philos. & Phenom. Res., **2**, 348–58.

————. 1957. Implications for theory. *In* M. GREENBLATT, D. LEVINSON, and R. H. WILLIAMS (eds.), The patient and the mental hospital, pp. 620–32. Glencoe, Ill.: Free Press.

————. 1959. The changing matrix of American culture and problems of aging. *In* C. TIBBITTS (ed.), Aging and social health in the United States and Europe, pp. 156–66. Ann Arbor: University of Michigan, Division of Gerontology.

WILLIAMS, R. H., and LOEB, M. B. 1956. The adult social life space and successful aging. (Paper read at the annual meeting of the Gerontological Society, Chicago.)

YARROW, MARIAN R., and QUINN, OLIVE W. 1957. Social psychological aspects of aging. (Paper read at the annual meeting of the Midwest Psychological Association, Chicago.)

X

The Evolving Work-Life Pattern

FRED SLAVICK AND SEYMOUR L. WOLFBEIN

I. INTRODUCTION

The working life of an individual represents, in a basic and overridingly important way, the long prologue to the drama of the older years which are the concern of the gerontologist. How long a person works, what he does on the job, how much he earns, his attitudes and satisfactions in his work—these and many other aspects of a person's working life have a decisive influence on how he fares in the later years. By the same token, the extent and kind of preparation for retirement he can experience, the financial reserves and income he can count on, what he does with his leisure time—these and many other aspects of his older age have their roots back in the individual's working past.

The relationship between work life and the older years is also underscored when we shift our focus from the individual to the societal group. How a given population cohort or a given generation positions itself in terms of labor-market participation —to what extent it is exposed to work experience, how it succeeds in obtaining skill development, what unemployment it is subject to—all will have a primary impact later on in terms of the magnitude and kinds of problems posed by an older population.

It is the purpose of this chapter (1) to develop the broad historical background of the evolution of work life in the United States; (2) to examine the forces influencing the past, current, and future labor-force participation of older persons; and (3) to present some considerations regarding choices open to the individual and some of the factors extending and limiting choice.

II. TRENDS IN WORK-LIFE EXPECTANCY

The major points to be made on the historical background of working life in this country can be gained from the brief set of figures in Table 1. As we all know, life-expectancy has increased significantly. A baby boy born today has a life-expectancy of over 18 years more than one born at the turn of the century; a baby girl has a life-expectancy of over 22 years more than one born at the turn of the century. For such a comparatively short period of time, the increases recorded are enormous.

In terms of work life there was an equally important set of developments during the last 50-odd years. Significantly enough, these extra years of added life were distributed almost equally between more years in the labor force and more years outside the labor force by both men and women. Thus, of the 18 years' increase in total life-expectancy among the men, about 10 years were added to their working lives and about 8 to their years spent outside the labor force—as young people getting more education and training and as older people with more years in retirement. Similarly, of the 22 years' increase in total life-expectancy among the women, about 12 years were added to their span of working

298

lives and about 10 years to those outside the labor force, spent in more education and training, marriage and motherhood, and retirement (Wolfbein, 1957a).

This neat balance of expenditure of our increasing life-expectancy has obviously had a number of very important consequences from the point of view we are examining in this paper. In the first place, it has meant that an increasing number of

the labor force between his eighteenth and nineteenth year; at the turn of the century more than one of every five boys 10–15 years of age was already a worker. This trend, of course, has been of critical importance in positioning our labor force to execute the tremendous increases and changes in our economy which took place in the last 50 years.

Now, with this additional expenditure

TABLE 1*

EXPECTANCY OF LIFE AND WORKING LIFE AT BIRTH IN
THE UNITED STATES, 1900–1955

YEAR	MEN			WOMEN		
	Life-Expectancy	Work-Life Expectancy	Years outside Labor Force	Life-Expectancy	Work-Life Expectancy	Years outside Labor Force
1900.......	48.2	32.1	16.1	50.7	6.3	44.4
1940.......	61.2	38.3	22.9	65.9	12.1	53.8
1950.......	65.5	41.9	23.6	71.0	15.2	55.8
1955.......	66.5	42.0	24.5	72.9	18.2	54.7

* Source: S. Wolfbein, *The Length of Working Life* (Washington, D.C.: U.S. Bureau of Labor Statistics, 1957).

persons are spending an increasing number of years in retirement. For example:

Years

Under 1900 Conditions:
A man of 20 had a life-expectancy of.. 42.2
And a work-life expectancy of....... 39.4

Thus his outlook was for a period of retirement of................... 2.8

Years

Under 1955 Conditions:
A man of 20 had a life-expectancy of.. 49.5
And a work-life expectancy of....... 43.0

Thus his outlook was for a period of retirement of................... 6.5

The reader will see that these developments have meant a doubling of the average number of years spent in retirement by men.

At the same time we should not ignore a significant development at the other end of the age scale—the increasing time spent by young persons in getting education and training. Currently, the average American male makes his first full-time entry into

of time in both the younger and the older years, the question has frequently been posed: "Doesn't this mean that we have a smaller and smaller proportion of our population supporting a bigger and bigger pro-

TABLE 2

NUMBER OF WORKERS PER 100 POPULATION
1900–1957

Year	No. of Workers per 100 Population	Year	No. of Workers per 100 Population
1900.......	36.4	1940......	40.5
1920.......	38.1	1950.......	39.9
1930.......	38.6	1957.......	41.3

portion of non-productive people?" Aside from the question of using a term like "non-productive," which really is not very fair or even realistic (housewives, for example, are not counted as part of the labor force), the answer to the question is in the negative (Table 2).

Actually, we have increased the proportion of "productive" people in this country despite the trends we have described. The reasons are quite complex, and we cannot go into a detailed explanation at this point. But the major reason is the fact that labor-market participation by adult and older women has increased so substantially that it has counterbalanced the significant declines among the younger persons and the older men. More detail on this point will be found in the next section.

There is one other factor which lends a great deal of weight to what we have just described. Not only have labor-market participation rates changed over the past half-century in such a way as to increase slightly the proportion of the total population

TABLE 3

MAN-HOURS OF WORK, 1900–1955

Year of Birth	Men	Women
1900	3,211,943	628,619
1940	3,825,580	1,214,481
1950	4,191,202	1,523,118
1955	4,204,794	1,819,496

in active economic status but those in the labor force put in many, many more years of productive life today than was possible at the turn of the century. In other words, the manpower potential of our population has increased enormously. A group of 100,000 persons born alive in the United States would produce the number of man-years of work shown in Table 3 during their lifetime. Thus a group of 100,000 males born and experiencing the mortality and labor-force conditions existing today will put in about a million more man-years of work during their lifetimes than their counterparts operating under 1900 conditions—an increase of almost one-third. A comparable group of females today is expected to triple the performance of its 1900 counterparts.

All these developments, of course, are of substantial and significant importance to the gerontologist. They have meant that

more and more people enter retirement from the vantage point of a much greater and longer exposure to economic activity, and this has enabled us to "afford" greater and greater numbers of people in retirement. These developments, therefore, involve a number of factors of consequence to the older individual's adjustment in his later years.

It was noted earlier that, while the length of working life has increased, the actual participation in the labor force of older males has been decreasing not only in recent years but throughout the decades since the turn of the century. The impact of this trend upon the labor-force participation of the entire population has been lessened by the substantially increased participation of women (Table 4). Yet the decreased labor-force participation of older males is a development of great relevance to the problems of an aging society.

Their employment status and work role for many individuals are crucial elements affecting their personal adjustment to old age. While the degree of importance of work in its relation to personal adjustment varies among older individuals, there is little doubt that for many persons continued participation in the labor force is a psychological as well as an economic necessity. Moreover, it is clear that the degree of labor-force participation among older individuals has an important bearing on the volume of goods and services available to meet not only their own material needs and wants but also those of the entire population.

The social, psychological, and economic significance of work to the older individual is discussed by other writers in this *Handbook*.[1] Whether the continuation of past trends in the labor-force participation of the aged will, on balance, be desirable or undesirable for the individual and society is a moot point which will not be discussed here. However, whether continuation or re-

[1] See particularly chap. xi, "Retirement: The Emerging Social Pattern."

versal of these trends is deemed to be in the best individual and social interest, a trend in either direction is of the utmost significance to gerontologists. It is, therefore, of importance that the forces influencing past, current, and future labor-force participation of older individuals be understood so that society can act to encourage those trends which it ultimately believes to be in the best interests of the individual and the nation.

in 1940 after a decade of depression. The labor-force participation rate of males 45–64 has remained relatively stable, increasing slightly for those in the age group 45–54 and decreasing slightly for those aged 55–64.

The reasons for the historical decline of the labor-force participation of males 65 and over are far from clear. It would appear that a number of relatively well-known developments ought to account for

TABLE 4*

LABOR-FORCE PARTICIPATION RATES BY AGE AND SEX, 1900–1958

Age (In Years)	1900	1920	1940	1944	1950	1955	1958
Both sexes..	55.0	55.8	55.9	63.1	58.3	58.7	58.5
Male..........	87.7	85.9	83.9	89.8	84.4	83.6	82.1
14–19........	63.6	52.6	44.2	70.0	53.2	49.5	47.4
20–24........	91.7	91.0	96.1	98.5	89.0	90.8	89.5
25–34	96.3	97.2	98.1	99.0	96.2	97.7	97.3
35–44			98.5	99.0	97.6	98.4	98.0
45–54	93.3	93.8	95.5	97.1	95.8	96.4	96.3
55–64			87.2	92.1	87.0	88.3	87.8
65 and over...	68.3	60.1	45.0	52.2	45.8	40.6	35.6
Female........	20.4	24.1	28.2	36.8	33.1	34.8	36.0
14–19........	26.8	28.4	23.3	42.0	31.5	29.9	29.1
20–24........	32.1	38.1	49.5	55.0	46.1	46.0	46.4
25–34	18.1	22.4	35.2	39.0	34.0	34.9	35.6
35–44			28.8	40.5	39.1	41.6	43.4
45–54	14.1	17.1	24.3	35.8	38.0	43.8	47.9
55–64			18.7	25.4	27.0	32.5	35.2
65 and over...	9.1	8.0	7.4	9.8	9.7	10.6	10.3

* Source: Data for 1900–1955 adapted from D. J. Bogue, *The Population of the United States* (Glencoe, Ill.: Free Press, 1959), p. 426. Data for 1958 from U.S. Bureau of the Census, *Annual Report on the Labor Force—1958* ("Current Population Reports," Series P-50, No. 89 [Washington, D.C.: Government Printing Office, June, 1959]), pp. 4, 19.

III. THE CHANGING LABOR-FORCE PARTICIPATION OF OLDER MEN

At the peak of World War II one of every two males 65 years of age and over was a worker. This wartime rate was significantly in excess of that in 1940 and represented a temporary reversal of a long-run downward trend (see Table 4). With the conclusion of World War II the downward trend was resumed and even accentuated. In 1958 a little over one in three males 65 and over was in the labor force, a figure substantially below the low point reached

the decrease. Thus it would be expected that the decreased employment activity of older males could be explained by (1) the declining importance of agriculture, where the labor-force participation of the aged has been higher than in manufacturing and commerce; (2) the increasing availability of the financial means to retire in the form of Old-Age, Survivors, and Disability Insurance and private pension plans; (3) the increasing use by employers of hiring-age limits and compulsory retirement policies; and (4) technological changes resulting in jobs requiring less skill but greater physical stamina. When examined carefully, however, the relation of these factors to the magnitude and persistence of the historical trend noted above is not obvious.

A. Shift from Agricultural to Non-agricultural Employment

Historically, the labor-force participation rate among older males in agriculture

croft, 1958). Given the differences in labor-force participation among the two groups, the relative decline in agricultural employment should be a major factor explaining the over-all decline in labor-force participation of the aged. Closer scrutiny, however, indicates that this may be of less importance than it first appears.

While the data on gross participation rates indicate that these are higher for farm than non-farm males 65 and over,

TABLE 5*

LABOR FORCE AS PERCENTAGE OF POPULATION, MALES, RURAL
AND URBAN, UNSTANDARDIZED BY AGE

Age Group	1890	1900	1910	1920	1930	1940	1950
				Rural			
10–13.........	20.1	19.6	13.1	9.1	6.1	....	....
14–19.........	55.7	60.3	54.2	49.4	45.5	39.2	45.1
20–24.........	90.7	90.9	89.8	89.3	90.5	88.8	88.5
25–44.........	98.1	95.5	95.7	96.1	97.4	94.2	93.0
45–64.........	95.9	93.1	93.1	93.4	94.6	88.8	86.7
65 and over....	76.5	70.4	60.9	61.6	62.2	46.4	44.1
				Urban			
10–13.........	12.4	14.1	3.0	1.8	0.5	....	....
14–19.........	60.0	62.6	59.0	56.5	36.7	29.8	35.5
20–24.........	94.0	93.0	92.4	92.4	89.5	87.4	79.6
25–44.........	96.7	97.1	97.4	97.9	97.5	95.5	92.8
45–64.........	93.8	93.6	94.1	94.1	93.7	88.7	88.4
65 and over.....	66.6	63.1	54.0	58.1	54.2	37.0	40.0

* Source: Adapted from C. Long, *The Labor Force under Changing Income and Employment* (Princeton, N.J.: Princeton University Press, 1958), Appendix Table A-3. Long's figures are based on data from the decennial census. Bogue's figures on labor-force participation cited in Table 4 are based in part on the decennial census and in part on the monthly sample surveys of the Bureau of the Census and reported in the "Current Population Reports." Data from the latter tend to yield higher rates of participation. The trends indicated by both sets of data, however, are similar.

has been higher than among those in non-agricultural employment (Table 5). Since the nineteenth century, there has been a continuing decrease in agricultural employment relative to non-agricultural employment. Thus between 1820 and the end of World War II the proportion of the labor force engaged in farming fell from 72 per cent to 14 per cent (Woytinsky and Associates, 1953). Between 1900 and 1950 the proportion of the working population engaged in agriculture fell from approximately 40 per cent to 10 per cent (Ban-

the fact that there has been significant migration of retired males from farm to non-farm areas obscures the real differences between the rates of labor-force participation of the two groups. Sheldon (1958) has estimated the net migration from farms among older persons between 1940 and 1950 as follows:

45–54 years..............	307,446
55–64 years..............	291,174
65–74 years..............	273,219
75–84 years..............	139,364
85 years and over........	17,430

Sheldon points out that, when a retired farmer moves to a non-farm area, he is lost from both the numerator and the denominator of the fraction from which the participation ratio is computed. On the other hand, in the case of the retired urban worker remaining in the urban area, he remains in the denominator but is lost from the numerator of the fraction. Thus the individual appears in the figure for total males 65 and over in urban areas but not in the urban labor force. Therefore, there is likely to be an overstatement of the participation rate of aged farmers relative to the rates for aged individuals in urban areas.

Sheldon's (1958) analysis indicates that the out-migration of retired farmers very likely narrows but does not eliminate the differences in the labor-force participation rates of the two groups. This means, however, that the impact of the declining employment trend in agriculture on the over-all participation rate of the aged is less than that which would follow from the observed (gross) differences between farm and non-farm participation rates.

Other factors indicate that the decline in agricultural employment needs further study before its significance as an explanation for the declining labor-force participation of the aged can be assessed. Clarence Long (1958), for example, notes that the participation rates for *both* the farm and the non-farm aged declined over the period 1890–1950 and that the rate of decline among aged farmers has actually been greater than among those 65 and over in non-farm areas.

Despite the above observations, it is probably correct that the participation of farmers 65 and over is greater than that of non-farmers, even though the degree of divergence between the rates may be unclear. Operation of a farm permits an individual, with the aid of his family or hired help, to maintain a marginal attachment to the labor force. This may be the case even though he is afflicted with a disability or experiences a general decline in strength

which in an urban environment would require his complete withdrawal from gainful employment. The aged farmer who continues to lend a hand with odd jobs or to operate his farm on a part-time basis is likely to indicate to a census enumerator that he is still at work. Thus, as individuals have shifted from agricultural to non-agricultural employment over time, this has at least operated in the direction of reducing the over-all rate of labor-force participation among older workers.

The shift from farm to non-farm employment appears irreversible, given the continuing mechanization and increasing productivity in agriculture. The Bureau of Agricultural Economics estimated in 1948 that by 1975 the number of farm workers needed would be reduced by 15–20 per cent (cited in Woytinsky and Associates, 1953). Therefore, whatever the relative importance of the shift from agricultural to non-agricultural employment in operating to reduce the labor-force participation of the aged, this factor is likely to operate in the same direction in future years.

B. Growth of Public and Private Retirement Plans

In 1940 benefits under Old-Age and Survivors Insurance became payable, and in the years since 1950, coverage, eligibility requirements, and benefits under this program have been liberalized periodically. A few state programs providing financial assistance to the aged on a needs basis were begun in the 1920's, and more were begun during the early years of the depression. These were later extended and liberalized as a result of federal participation under the old age assistance provisions of the Social Security Act. As in the case of Old-Age and Survivors Insurance, payments under old age assistance have been gradually increased over time. In addition to these public programs, there has been a steady growth since World War II of private pension plans financed by employers and unions. Between 1930 and the end of 1957 coverage under private pension plans and deferred profit-sharing plans increased from 2.7 million to 17.7 million employees, and the number of beneficiaries rose from 100,000 to 1,250,000. In addition, there has been a continuous liberalization of benefits (Skolnik and Zisman, 1959). These as well as other sources of income for the aged are discussed in detail in other chapters of this *Handbook*.

While the benefits provided by the programs noted above have, by and large, not been sufficient to meet the income needs of the aged,[2] their existence and growth might well be a major factor explaining the increasing propensity of older workers to leave the labor force. It is logical to assume that, for workers desiring the greater leisure of retirement or for whom physical factors have made continued employment difficult, the benefits available under these programs could make the difference between remaining in or leaving the labor force. Yet, as Long (1958) points out, aged workers left the labor force in large numbers during the years between 1890 and 1940, when these programs were nonexistent or insignificant.

The absence of these large-scale public and private welfare programs during the period between 1890 and World War II does not rule out the postwar growth of these programs as an explanation for the downward trend after the war. Forces other than public and private pension plans were obviously at work between 1890 and 1940, and these may or may not be operating currently. Until these can be explained, however, it is difficult to look with confidence to the postwar growth of pension plans as a satisfactory explanation of recent trends.

In 1951 a study of the incomes of Old-Age and Survivors Insurance beneficiaries indicated that the median money income of single male beneficiaries from all sources, including OASI and private pension plans, was $786; for married male beneficiaries whose wives were entitled to benefits, the median income from all sources was $1387.

[2] See chap. viii, "Aging and Income Security."

When OASI benefits were excluded from money-income totals, the median for single beneficiaries was $300, and for married beneficiaries it was $532 (Stecker, 1953). A similar survey made in 1957 showed that the median income from all sources for single male beneficiaries had risen to $1170; for married male beneficiaries, it had risen to $2186. When OASI benefits were excluded from 1957 money incomes, it was found that the median for single male beneficiaries was $427; for married beneficiaries the figure was $898 (Anonymous, 1958). The 1957 figures for retirement incomes, however, do not take into account increases in the cost of living since 1951.

The data on total retirement incomes cited above include amounts which the beneficiaries had earned in employment, despite the fact that they were drawing OASI benefits. In 1957, 38.2 per cent of the married male beneficiaries had earnings (median $1032), and 29 per cent of the single male beneficiaries had earned income (median $588). The respective 1951 figures for married and single male beneficiaries were 20.9 per cent (median $420) and 21.2 per cent (median $300). More nearly descriptive of the incomes of individuals who are actually retired and out of the labor force are the data yielded by the 1951 and 1957 surveys for "independent retirement income." This is defined by the Bureau of Old-Age and Survivors Insurance as including, in addition to OASI benefits, employer and veterans' pensions, rents, interest, dividends, annuity and trust-fund income, and other independent income which beneficiaries could reasonably expect to continue in future years in approximately the same amounts as in the survey year. Earnings represent the principal source of income excluded from this category. The median "independent retirement incomes" of single and married male beneficiaries in 1951 and 1957 were as shown in the tabulation on page 305.

Data are not available showing the distribution of income when combined OASI and private employer benefits are excluded, but it is clear from the figures cited earlier that OASI represents a major portion of the income of retired individuals. It is also clear that the incomes from OASI, employer pensions, and gainful employment increased between the two years. On the other hand, it is far from clear whether the *magnitude* of the increases in retirement income or the *absolute levels* of retirement incomes were such as to induce significant numbers of individuals to leave the labor force. Is the prospect of living at these income levels likely to provide an incentive to retire from gainful employment in view of the significantly greater income available from full-time work? Studies by the Bureau of the Census in 1957 indicated that the annual incomes of individuals 65 and over who were year-round wage-earners were two and one half to three times as great as those for all aged persons (Epstein, 1959).

It has been pointed out that public and private pension benefits, when added to other retirement income, do not appear to yield total retirement incomes which make retirement financially attractive. It is possible, however, that when such retirement incomes are considered in relation to the net worth and liquid assets held by aged individuals retirement might seem considerably more feasible financially. It will be recalled that the labor-force participation of women between the ages of 45 and 64 has been increasing. This may have resulted in increased savings being available to supplement family savings when both husband and wife reached their mid-sixties.

The 1951 and 1957 surveys of OASI beneficiaries discussed above also included a study of the assets and net worth of these beneficiaries. Net worth represented the difference between the value of assets and the value of liabilities. Assets included liquid and non-liquid items, with the bulk of the latter being in the form of owned homes (Epstein, 1955; Anonymous, 1959). The 1951 survey revealed that for married couples headed by a male beneficiary the median net worth was $5889. In the 1957

survey the median figure was $8786, or an increase of $2897. In 1951 the median figure for liquid assets held by aged retired couples receiving OASI was $492. Approximately 70 per cent of the couples had liquid assets of less than $2000, with 32.4 per cent of these having no liquid assets. In 1957 the median figure was $1271. The number of beneficiary couples with liquid assets of less than $2000 had fallen to 56.9 per cent, of which 27.6 per cent had none.

While both net worth and liquid assets increased during the postwar years, there is still room for debate as to whether either the increases or the absolute sizes were sufficient to make retirement financially attractive, given the levels of retirement income noted earlier. Perhaps all that can be said is that for older males whose pre-

SINGLE		MARRIED (WIFE ENTITLED)	
1951	1957	1951	1957
$581	$898	$1054	$1697

vious income and assets placed them on the margin of indifference as concerns whether or not to remain in the labor force, the marginal increase in income resulting from public and private pensions may have induced them to cease gainful employment or give up the search for work.

It is highly probable that benefits under public and private pension plans will continue to increase in future years. Whatever their significance in recent years, pension benefits are likely to become more important as a determinant of labor-force participation as they raise total retirement incomes further and further above subsistence levels. In addition, pensions are likely to assume added importance as a determinant of labor-force participation should the nation experience a prolonged depression such as that of the 1930's. Long (1958) has shown that during the 1930's there was a direct relationship between the level of unemployment and the decreased labor-force participation of older males. During these years the number of individuals covered under public and private pension plans was far smaller than at present. Extended periods of unemployment in themselves are likely to be so discouraging as to provide strong motivation for the aged to leave the labor force. If, in addition, pensions are available to make exit from the labor force more economically palatable, the incentive to continue the search for work will be reduced even further.

C. Discrimination in Hiring on the Basis of Age

During recent years there has been growing recognition of and concern with the use of maximum hiring-age limits by employers. Discrimination in hiring because of age, however, is not a new phenomenon. Long (1958) points out that in 1900 the commissioner of labor statistics in New York, in testimony before the United States Industrial Commission, noted that "we find in the free employment office conducted by the state that for a female who admits she is 45 years of age, it is very difficult to get employment; and if a man admits an age much over 50 he also finds it very difficult" (p. 170).

Studies by Barkin in New York State in 1930, and nationally by the National Association of Manufacturers at approximately the same time, indicated that from 25 to 40 per cent of the firms surveyed employed age limits in their hiring policies (cited in Abrams, 1952).

While there is convincing evidence that discrimination in hiring because of age was widespread prior to World War II, the subject was not studied as widely or intensively as it has been during the postwar years. It is, therefore, difficult to judge whether discrimination has *increased* over time so as to be a significant factor in explaining the decreasing labor-force participation of the aged. Abrams (1952) notes that in 1949 the National Association of Manufacturers and the United States

Chamber of Commerce conducted a joint nation-wide survey of 277 firms similar to that conducted by the National Association of Manufacturers two decades earlier. In the earlier survey it was found that 28 per cent of the firms had age barriers, while in the later survey the figure was 26 per cent. The difficulties and complexities of assessing the importance of age discrimination in influencing labor-force participation over time are perhaps illustrated by the fact that, despite widespread discrimination against older women (see Table 6), their rates of participation have been increasing. It is apparent that discrimination is but one element in a complex of factors which are relevant.

Whether or not discrimination has increased over the last five decades, studies during the post–World War II period make it clear that discrimination because of age currently constitutes a major barrier for the aged seeking employment. In 1948 a state-wide survey of 172 companies carried out by the New York State Joint Legislative Committee on Problems of the Aging disclosed that 39 per cent of these firms imposed age limits in hiring (Abrams, 1952).

During the spring of 1950 the Bureau of Employment Security of the United States Department of Labor, with the cooperation of the local employment service offices in Columbus, Ohio; Houston, Texas; Lancaster, Pennsylvania; Los Angeles, California; and New York, New York, examined over 13,000 job openings on file in the four local offices with a view to analyzing the pattern of hiring specifications as they related to age. This study found widespread formal and informal discriminatory hiring policies based on age. In Columbus, for example, 72 per cent of the 3952 job orders contained age restrictions, and in Houston the figure was 52 per cent of 5295 openings. Of the 511 job orders on file in Lancaster, 60 per cent contained age barriers, while 25 per cent of the 3504 job openings in the New York City office contained specific age limits. It is significant to note that at the time of the survey (spring, 1950) the labor markets in Houston and Lancaster were relatively tight, with unemployment estimated at between 3 and 5 per cent of the labor force (U.S. Bureau of Employment Security, 1951).

In another effort to ascertain the extent of age limits in hiring, the Bureau of Employment Security in April, 1956, surveyed some 21,386 openings filed with the public employment offices of seven cities. The seven cities were Worcester, Massachusetts; Philadelphia, Pennsylvania; Miami, Florida; Detroit, Michigan; St. Paul–Min-

companied by an age preference (U.S. Bureau of Employment Security, 1956a).

Upper-age limits were found most frequently in job orders for clerical, sales, professional and managerial, and unskilled jobs. Approximately two-thirds of the openings in each of these four categories had some upper-age limit. The job openings for skilled and semiskilled occupations had upper-age limits least often, with somewhat less than half (47 per cent) of the orders for these types of jobs having such limits. There were some differences between males and females as concerns the

TABLE 6*

PERCENTAGE OF JOB ORDERS FOR MALES AND FEMALES SPECIFYING
MAXIMUM AGE LIMITS BY OCCUPATION, SEVEN CITIES, APRIL, 1956

	PERCENTAGE OF JOB OPENINGS SPECIFYING UPPER-AGE LIMITS					
OCCUPATION	Under Age 35		Under Age 45		Under Age 55	
	Male	Female	Male	Female	Male	Female
Clerical.................	44	33	59	56	68	67
Sales....................	30	14	50	32	64	54
Professional and managerial	28	22	44	50	55	53
Unskilled...............	23	35	47	54	60	61
Semiskilled.............	23	5	45	17	58	21
Skilled.................	9	3	15	10	28	31
Service.................	7	10	30	38	47	48

* Source: U.S. Bureau of Employment Security, *Counseling and Placement Services for Older Workers* (Bull. No. E152 [Washington, D.C.: Government Printing Office, 1956]), pp. 31–32.

neapolis, Minnesota; Los Angeles, California; and Seattle, Washington. Of the job openings on file in the seven cities, 52 per cent specified age limits under 55, 41 per cent under 45, and 20 per cent specified 35 as the upper age limit. In five of the seven cities the percentage of job orders specifying age limits ranged from 51 per cent (Seattle) to 79 per cent (Philadelphia). In the sixth city, Los Angeles, 34.5 per cent of the job orders carried upper-age limits. In Worcester, Massachusetts, the seventh city, 23.5 per cent of the job openings specified "preferred" ages. Massachusetts has a law outlawing discrimination, but apparently job orders are permitted to be ac-

age specifications in job orders. The principal differences in the age limits between orders for males and females were in the sales occupations, which were more restrictive for males. Semiskilled occupations were also more restrictive for males, while service occupations were more restrictive for females. Table 6 summarizes the percentage of job orders for males and females specifying maximum hiring-age limits by occupation.

When analyzed by industry, it was found that finance, insurance, and real estate had the most restrictive age limits, followed by transportation, communications, and public utilities; wholesale and retail trade; durable manufacturing; non-durable manufacturing; government; construction; and service industries. It was also found that the larger industrial establishments specified age limits with greater frequency than did smaller establishments.

The impact of such age restrictions on the ability of older workers to obtain jobs is reflected in the fact that, in a sample of job applicants in the seven cities studied, workers 45 years of age and over constituted 40 per cent of the job-seekers but obtained only 22 per cent of the jobs filled by employers. When those 45 and over were broken down into specific 10-year age groups, it was found that there was a growing disparity between the percentage of job-seekers and those hired by age group as the job-seekers increased in age. Thus 15.7 per cent of the job-seekers were in the age group 45–64, while 13.7 per cent of those hired were from workers in this age group. Individuals 65 and over were 10.2 per cent of all job-seekers, but only 1.9 per cent of the total hired were from individuals 65 and over (U.S. Bureau of Employment Security, 1956*b*).

Given the amount of discrimination in hiring against older workers revealed by the pre- and postwar studies, there is little doubt that it has been an important factor in the propensity of older workers to leave the labor force. Sheldon (1958) has summarized the relationship of job discrimination to retirement as follows:

The existence of labor force turnover means that, although some people spend most of their working lives on a single job or sequence of jobs, many others hold a succession of jobs; that is, they lose or give up current work and find other work. In this process age discrimination implies that jobs are more easily lost, and new jobs progressively more difficult to obtain, as age increases. Although age discrimination may begin to operate in the early 40's, the process is long and drawn out. New jobs may be more difficult to find in the early 40's, but in the long run they are found, and it is only in the late 50's or early 60's that attrition from the labor force becomes appreciable. . . .

From the point of view of the individual seeking employment, the process is a matter of progressively increasing odds; at some point the situation seems hopeless and retirement follows [pp. 51–52].

Discrimination takes on particular significance when other factors are operating to increase labor turnover. Thus problems for the employment of older workers which may be posed by technological change, recessions, relocation of industry, compulsory retirement policies, and declines in the aggregate demand for specific products are intensified by the existence of discrimination. In addition, efforts to rehabilitate older workers physically and vocationally are nullified. The combination of displacement resulting from the above factors plus the difficulty of finding re-employment because of discrimination provide strong reasons for older workers to leave the labor market.

With the increasing recognition of discrimination in hiring on the basis of age have come intensive public and private efforts to combat it. There is currently, however, little quantitative or qualitative information with which to measure the effectiveness of these efforts or to predict the future course of discrimination. Employers give a variety of reasons for instituting hiring-age limits. These include the belief that older workers cannot maintain production standards or meet physical requirements, that they are inflexible and difficult to train, that they are excessively absent from work, and that they increase pension costs (U.S. Bureau of Employment Security, 1956*a*).

The United States Department of Labor has carried out studies of the relative productivity of older workers, of specific employer experience with older workers, and of the impact of older workers on pension costs (U.S. Bureau of Employment Security, 1956*a*, 1956*b*, 1956*c*, 1959; U.S. Bureau of Labor Statistics, 1956*b*, 1956*c*, 1956*d*). These studies represent concrete efforts by the federal government to assess the realism and consequences of the above reasons for not hiring older workers. The findings of these studies cast serious doubt upon the *general* validity of many of the above employer beliefs, and the federal government and state employment offices have attempted to disseminate these findings in the form of technical monographs, non-technical brochures, and public speeches and through the daily informal contacts with community employers.

In the seven cities studied a special effort was made to determine the extent to which more intensive and extensive counseling and placement efforts on behalf of older workers would help them overcome the special difficulties they face in securing employment (U.S. Bureau of Employment Security, 1956a). Some 7361 older job applicants at the local employment offices in the seven cities were divided into two groups: (1) a control group consisting of 3764 individuals who were given the employment services normally offered to applicants in the local employment offices and (2) an experimental group of 3597 individuals who were offered special services in the form of more intensive interviewing, individual and group counseling, aptitude tests, and other special services. In addition, increased efforts were made to solicit and develop job openings for these individuals. The two groups were similar in terms of their major personal, social, and economic characteristics. Of the 3597 in the experimental group to whom the special services were offered, 70 per cent accepted the services, and 30 per cent were not given the services because they were not interested in or were unavailable for them. The special services were carried out during a period of 3 months ending April 30, 1956, and the results were determined on the basis of follow-up questionnaires to individuals in both the control and the experimental groups.

It was found that 43.3 per cent of the applicants in the control group obtained employment during the 3-month period, compared to 48.4 per cent in the experimental group for whom specialized services

were provided. In six of the seven cities a larger proportion of individuals in the experimental group obtained employment than in the control group. In five of these six cities the differences ranged from 8 per cent to 15 per cent. The Bureau of Employment Security and local offices felt these differences were significant and have undertaken efforts to provide many of these additional services to older workers in local offices throughout the country.

During the past decade the states have become increasingly concerned with problems of the aged, and by 1958 some thirty states had set up commissions, committees, or other state-wide groups to consider and publicize problems of the aging, including employment problems and discrimination in hiring. By the end of 1958, six states (Colorado, Louisiana, Rhode Island, Pennsylvania, Massachusetts, and New York) had enacted legislation prohibiting discrimination in employment because of age. Opinion is divided concerning the actual effectiveness of legislation as a means of reducing discrimination (Ruskowski, 1957). Experience with legislation outlawing discrimination because of race, creed, and color indicates that the principal value of this type of legislation is likely to be the result of educational efforts by the staffs of the administering agencies and from mediation efforts to secure voluntary compliance rather than from the compulsory and punitive provisions of these laws. A practical method of measuring the effectiveness of anti-discrimination legislation, however, has not yet been devised, and its actual impact remains largely speculative.

In addition to the efforts of federal, state, and local governments to reduce discrimination in hiring because of age, private organizations such as the American Public Welfare Association, the National Committee on the Aging, the various philanthropic foundations, numerous service organizations, trade associations, and trade unions have become increasingly concerned with the problem of discrimination in hiring policies and have steadily increased both their research and their publicity efforts aimed at reducing age barriers.

Whether the public and private efforts to reduce discrimination noted above will be successful remains to be seen. Long-held views concerning the supposed disadvantages of employing certain groups in the population (whether these be the aged, members of the minority groups, females, or others) are not easily relinquished, even in the face of contrary evidence. Valuable as research, education, and public relations efforts may be, it is likely that the existence of full employment and tight labor markets over long periods of time will be more potent "educational tools" in inducing employers to test for themselves the validity of their assumptions concerning older workers.

D. Compulsory Retirement Practices

With the growth of private pension plans there has developed a growing interest in the propensity of industry to retire individuals compulsorily solely because of attainment of a specified chronological age. The extent of compulsory retirement provisions is indicated by a number of surveys of retirement practices carried out during the last 10 years. A 1955 study by the National Industrial Conference Board found that, of 327 companies surveyed, 158 covering over 66 per cent of the employees had mandatory retirement policies at specified ages (Brower, 1955). The United States Department of Labor in 1957–58 found that, of 100 collectively bargained pension plans studied covering 3.3 million employees, somewhat over one-half included compulsory retirement provisions (Kolodrubetz, 1958). Other surveys have confirmed the widespread inclusion of compulsory retirement provisions in pension plans (Hewitt and Associates, 1952; Bankers Trust Co., 1956).

A study of the reasons for retirement among Old-Age and Survivors Insurance beneficiaries in 1951 indicated that approximately 11 per cent of all males had retired following loss of a job because of compulsory retirement (Stecker, 1955). Steiner and Dorfman (1957), in analyzing the reasons for retirement among older workers, found that 13 per cent of the retired males interviewed gave compulsory retirement as the reason for their retirement.

It is not known to what extent compulsory retirement existed in American industry prior to the widespread adoption of formal pension plans in the late 1940's. That advanced age was an important factor causing termination of older workers during periods of recession and major technological change is generally recognized. Yet, in the absence of formal pension plans, it is likely that health, skill, and general competence were given somewhat more weight than under the more rigidly enforced compulsory retirement policies of the present day, when chronological age is the only relevant criterion.

With 11–13 per cent of the aged retiring because of compulsory retirement practices, it would appear that this factor was not as yet a major force causing individuals to leave the labor market. It must be recognized, however, that the number of employees at or near the compulsory retirement age when the pension plans were instituted was small compared to the number of younger employees covered by such plans. As these plans "mature," more and more individuals will reach age 65 under retirement policies based solely on chronological age. Thus, even if the percentage of plans with compulsory retirement provisions does not increase, a growing number of individuals will be separated from employment for this reason. If the percentage of employees covered by compulsory retirement systems does not decrease, or if the difficulties encountered by older workers in obtaining new employment do not decrease, compulsory retirement will become a major reason for exit from the labor force in future years.

One of the principal reasons firms utilize compulsory retirement is the difficulty of administering selective retirement on an individual basis. This difficulty stems in part from the absence of objective criteria upon which to base decisions concerning individual employees. In addition, many companies believe compulsory retirement is necessary in order to keep open the lines of promotion (Baker, 1952; Brower, 1955). Thus the ability of industry to develop objective criteria for retirement and the extent to which they expand sufficiently to promote younger employees while continuing to employ older workers are two of the more important variables which will influence future retirement practices. A third factor of importance will be the rate at which company pension benefits are increased, either unilaterally or as a result of collective bargaining. Pension costs increase as benefits are liberalized, and the growing costs may induce firms to re-examine policies which compel the retirement (and payment of benefits) of individuals still capable of meeting production standards.

E. Technological Change and Automation

A possible explanation for the decreased labor-force participation of aged males may lie in the impact of technological changes on skills and on the physical requirements of work. Such changes may make long-held skills obsolete and compel the older worker to seek new employment in competition with younger stronger employees who are more adaptable to the new techniques. Being at a disadvantage in competition with younger, stronger workers, and facing discriminatory hiring policies, older workers may gradually withdraw from the labor market after discouraging efforts to find employment.

This hypothesis was examined by Long (1958) and by Sheldon (1958), but neither was able to uncover supporting evidence. Long, for example, examined the annual percentage reduction in labor requirements per unit of output in a dozen manufacturing industries between the years 1889 and 1939. He compared these changes with the changes in the ratio of men aged 45 and older to all men in the chief occupations allied to these industries between 1910 and 1940. Although his analysis revealed some growth in the ratio of elderly workers to all workers, and some labor-saving in all industries, there appeared to be no relationship between these changes. Long also found that exit of elderly workers from the labor force was smaller in the United States than in Britain and Germany, despite the fact that technological progress in the latter two countries proceeded at slower rates.

Whether technological change will continue to have little effect on the labor-force participation of the aged in the future cannot be answered with much, if any, confidence, in view of the current and future technological developments somewhat loosely lumped together under the term "automation." Baldwin and Shultz (1955) have defined automation as follows:

1. The linking together of conventionally separate manufacturing operations into lines of continuous production through which the product moves "untouched by human hands." This first development, which depends primarily on mechanical engineering for its adoption, we shall refer to simply as "integration," a term already in wide use in the metal-working industries. It is also called "Detroit Automation" in honor of the industry in which it got its start. "Continuous automatic production" is another and perhaps more descriptive term being used.

2. The use of "feed-back" control devices or servomechanisms which allow individual operations to be performed without any necessity for human control. With feed-back, there is always some built-in automatic device for comparing the way in which work is actually being done with the way in which it is supposed to be done and for then making, automatically, any adjustments in the work-process that may be necessary. This second development we shall refer to simply as "feed-back" technology; it is dependent primarily not on mechanical but on electrical engineering knowledge and techniques.

3. The development of general and special

purpose computing machines capable of recording and storing information (usually in the form of numbers) and of performing both simple and complex mathematical operations on such information. We shall refer to this aspect of automation as "computer technology," a technology that rests primarily on new developments in electrical engineering [pp. 115–16].

The phenomenon of automation has serious implications for *all* age groups in the labor force. Most significant among these is the possible effect of automation on the level of employment. The most general variable determining both the short- and the long-run impact of automation on employment is the level of aggregate demand. In addition, however, the effect of automation on the marketability of currently held skills and the facility with which new skills can be acquired are of importance in determining the extent to which automation results in unemployment. These ramifications of automation are particularly important for older workers in that they may either intensify or reduce the difficulties they already face in the labor market.

The probable consequences of automation on employment have been hotly debated by all sectors of the economy, with opinions ranging from extreme optimism to extreme pessimism. By and large, however, most discussions have been of a speculative and theoretical nature, tending in part to mirror the hopes and fears of those most affected. A few excellent empirical studies of the nature and employment effects of automation have been made, and these provide some insight into the consequences of automation in the context of specific firms. Because the individual firm has been the focus of attention thus far, and because automatic equipment has been adopted in only a relatively small sector of American industry, current discussions can at best indicate the possible rather than the probable ramifications for older workers.

That the new automatic equipment significantly reduces the required amount of human labor input per unit of output or,

conversely, increases greatly the amount of output per man-hour worked can be taken for granted. This is the reason the new technology is introduced in the first place. Whether or not the new technology results in unemployment will depend on (1) whether the demand for the products or services produced by the new technology expands sufficiently to absorb the increased quantity of output which the same number of employees can produce with the more efficient capital equipment; (2) the extent to which the introduction of new equipment leads to the development of *new* products by the automated firms or other firms; (3) the extent to which the increased productivity resulting from automation results in an expansion of the demand for products of other industries so that their growth can absorb those originally displaced by the automatic equipment; and (4) the adaptability and trainability of the displaced workers for automated jobs or for older type jobs or occupations which are different from those which they formerly pursued.

The limited studies of firms which have introduced automation to at least some degree presents a fairly optimistic picture concerning the employment of individuals in those firms. The majority of the case studies indicate that thus far unemployment resulting directly from the introduction of automation has been minimal, with the employees displaced being absorbed by expansion in other departments of the automated plants or through the non-replacement of individuals lost through normal attrition (U.S. Congress, 1955; U.S. Bureau of Labor Statistics, 1956a, 1957; Bright, 1958). As has been pointed out by several writers, however, examination of the short-run employment effects of automation through case studies of individual firms is not sufficient for an analysis of the problem. It is essential that the employment effects for the industry as a whole (of which the automated firm is a part) and of complementary or related industries be examined. Killingsworth (1959) has noted that, while displacement in the automating firm may not be significant, unless demand for the product is expanding, the increased output of the automated firm may be at the expense of non-automated firms in the industry, reducing the level of employment in the latter.

Stern (1959) points out that significant displacement may occur when automation results in greater vertical integration of the productive process. This can result in a decrease in employment in firms which formerly were engaged in the production of products for the automating firm. Thus he found that, prior to the time the Ford Motor Company automated its stamping plants, it purchased about one-third of its body parts from the Murray Body Company. The increased productive capacity resulting from the automated stamping plants permitted Ford itself to produce all its needed body parts and to cancel its contracts with the Murray Body Company. This resulted in the layoff of some 5000 employees of the latter firm. This layoff occurred in the summer of 1954 shortly before the beginning of the 1955 model year. Despite the fact that the model year 1955 was a prosperous one for the automobile industry, a 10 per cent sample survey of the Murray Body workers disclosed that one year after the plant had closed only 71 per cent of the men had gained re-employment. Fifty per cent of the employees had exhausted their unemployment insurance benefits before finding employment, with older workers, women, and Negroes experiencing the greatest difficulties in finding re-employment.

Before examining more closely the possible effects of automation upon the employment prospects of older workers, it is important to take note of the impact of automation on the structure of employment generally and on the skill requirements of the labor force. Both of these factors have great relevance to the future employment problems of older workers.

Since World War II, the proportion of production workers in manufacturing employment has decreased relative to that of non-production workers. Killingsworth (1959) points out that, from 1947 to 1957, employment of production workers in manufacturing increased by only 1 per cent. During the period 1955–57 there was an absolute decrease in the number of production workers in manufacturing, while output increased by 3 per cent. Killingsworth believes that automation is "unquestionably a contributing factor to the shrinkage of production worker jobs in manufacturing" (p. 27). Stern (1959) cites the petroleum industry as an example of this. During the period 1946–56 the total operating capacity of the petroleum industry increased from 5.3 to 8.4 million barrels of crude oil per day. Yet, during this period, the mix of non-production to production workers shifted sharply toward non-production workers, total employment increased slightly, and the total number of production workers decreased by 10,000. Moreover, during this same 10-year period the number of refineries decreased from 361 to 294.

One of the most comprehensive analyses to date of the impact of automation on the individual firm and its labor force is that by Bright (1958). This study involved the following thirteen types of firms: the engine plant of a major automobile producer, a bakery, a small integrated oil refinery, a manufacturer of oil seals, a rubber-products firm, the commercial fertilizer plant of a major chemical company, a feed and grain mill, a coal mine, two plating plants, a manufacturer of automobile instruments, an electrical parts manufacturer, and a manufacturer of automobile engines. After examining the influence of automation upon skill requirements in these firms, Bright concluded that, with minor exceptions, the skill levels directly involved in production with automated equipment were generally reduced. Labor skills indirectly involved in the automated processes were also generally less, although the exceptions here were of greater importance. Such exception included certain types of setup work (such as computer or numerically controlled machine-tool programming work), machine design and building skills, and some classes of maintenance work, especially among electricians. Bright also found that the training of employees for work with automated equipment generally posed no special problems and was accomplished with relative ease.

Evidence cited by Killingsworth from a McGraw-Hill study of metalworking firms tends to confirm Bright's findings. Thus, of the firms having experience with automation, 43 per cent reported that the new operations required less skill of machine operators, and 30 per cent indicated that no changes in skills were involved. Only 27 per cent of the firms reported that machine operators required more skill on the new automated equipment than on the old machines (cited by Killingsworth, from the *American Machinist,* October 21, 1957).

Findings from the investigations thus far concerning the impact of automation on the work force may be summarized as follows: (1) the displacement of employees in the firms which automated did not appear to be significant, at least in the short run; (2) the displacement of employees is of much greater significance when the industry as a whole (or related industries) is considered; (3) the ratio of production workers to non-production workers has been decreasing and is likely to continue to decrease as automation increases; (4) with certain exceptions, the skill requirements and physical stamina of the work force are not likely to increase and, if anything, to decrease; and (5) retraining needs are not likely to be of major proportions for the individual firm or the individual employees.

Recognizing the tentative nature of the above generalizations and the limited investigations upon which they are based, what do they imply for the long-run labor-force participation of the aged?

The ability of automating firms to absorb the manpower excess resulting from the increasing productivity of the new capital equipment indicates that, for those older workers in the plants which are actually doing the automating, the future does not appear discouraging. There is little reason to believe that there will be any lessening in the ability of seniority provisions to protect older workers against the unemployment dangers arising from technological change. If company-wide and plant-wide seniority provisions are extended, the protection will be enhanced. The findings that, by and large, automation does not result in higher skill requirements or involve radical retraining should be encouraging to older workers. Moreover, assuming that the older assembly-line operations require greater physical stamina than do maintenance, supervisory work, and "machine-watching" occupations, the relative growth and importance of the latter should work in favor of older employees.

The principal danger which older workers face as a result of automation stems from the possible adverse employment effects on non-automating firms in the same industry or on non-automating firms producing complementary or supplementary products. Theoretically, the increased productivity in the automating firms and the resulting lower cost per unit of output should either increase the market for that product, lead to an expansion of the market for other products, or result in the creation of demand for new products. This should provide employment opportunities for employees displaced from the automating and non-automating firms. In fact, however, resource reallocation does not operate with the speed or smoothness postulated by a simple model of the free market-price mechanism. Inflexible prices and personal and institutional barriers to the mobility of labor and capital, at best, slow down the process, resulting in serious time lags before adjustments take place. At worst, the reallocations do not take place at all because of these barriers.

Where the reallocation of resources involves a change of employer or change of industry by older workers, the personal and institutional barriers inhibiting the necessary movement are serious. Discrimination in the hiring of older workers has already been discussed. Stern (1959) points out that, in the case of the Murray Body workers laid off as a result of the automation of the Ford stamping plants, it took the average employee 3 months to find a new job, but it took twice this length of time for the average worker 45 years of age and over to find new employment. It has already been noted that prolonged periods of unemployment tend to discourage older workers to the extent of inducing them to leave the labor force. Adding to the difficulties of older workers is the fact that reallocation of resources in response to automation may require the geographical movement of employees. Older workers faced with the prospect of uprooting themselves and moving to strange communities in order to find employment are likely to choose retirement as an alternative, particularly if benefits under public and private pension plans continue to increase and if discrimination against older workers in hiring persists. The reluctance of older workers to move from areas such as the coal and railroad areas of Pennsylvania and Kentucky and the textile regions of New England, which have long been suffering from chronic structural unemployment, does not lead one to expect large-scale migration of older workers displaced as a direct or indirect result of automation.

IV. DISABILITY AND LABOR-FORCE PARTICIPATION

Disability as it relates to employability is a difficult concept with which to come to grips. An individual may be disabled in the sense of experiencing the deterioration or breakdown of a given physical or mental process or the impairment or loss of a vital organ or body member. The extent to which such physical or mental disability reduces or destroys his employability, however, depends on the physical or mental requirements of specific jobs and on the impact of the disability on his motivation to work. Moreover, the motivation of a disabled individual to work is affected by his ability to find suitable work and the nature and amount of the demand for his services.

The employment during World War II of individuals who during the depression of the 1930's would have been considered (and would have considered themselves) unemployable indicates the ambiguities inherent in the concept of disability as it relates to employability. The literature on vocational rehabilitation is filled with examples of individuals who literally have "one foot in the grave" but are more or less gainfully employed. Despite these difficulties of definition, it is apparent from the findings of several national surveys that during the early 1950's disability constituted the major reason for retirement among males 65 years of age and over.

In a study of males 65 and over based on a "follow-up" survey of a subsample of males from the *Current Population Survey,* Steiner and Dorfman (1957) found that 60 per cent of those not in the labor force had retired because of poor health. Another study by the Bureau of Old-Age and Survivors Insurance found that 41.5 per cent of the males 65 and over who were OASI beneficiaries in 1951 had retired because they were "unable to work" (Stecker, 1955). In the BOASI study, individuals who retired because they were "unable to work" included those who had "quit because of sickness or accident, or because they were tired or thought their work was too hard for them, or that they were too old to continue working." The definition of "unable to work" used in the BOASI survey is roughly comparable to the definition of poor health used by Steiner and Dorfman.

The BOASI study found that only 3.9 per cent of the retired males retired voluntarily while in good health. Approximately 11 per cent retired because of compulsory retirement systems, 21 per cent because their jobs had been discontinued, 4 per cent had quit their jobs to seek other work, and 12 per cent had lost or quit their jobs for a variety of other reasons. An additional 7 per cent were retired by employers because they considered the aged employees unable to work. Steiner and Dorfman found that, among aged males not in the labor force, 13 per cent had retired because of compulsory retirement policies, 7 per cent were retired involuntarily because of age, 4 per cent retired because of layoffs, 2 per cent retired voluntarily because of family decisions, and 14 per cent retired for other voluntary or involuntary reasons.

While disability constituted the major reason for retirement in the early 1950's, it is difficult to determine the extent to which the historical decline in the labor-force participation of those 65 years of age and over is due to this factor. If the long-run decline is to be attributed to disability, it must be shown that the individuals who were 65 and over in the 1950's were less employable physically than those the same age in earlier years. This is a subject which has not been explored in any detail. Both Sheldon (1958) and Long (1958) doubt that this hypothesis is correct, but neither of these writers presented data with which it might be tested. However, in view of the significance of disability as a cause of retirement revealed by the studies noted above, it would appear that any significant upward trend in the labor-force participation among the aged in the future will depend on the efforts made to increase the employability of disabled older workers. This depends on the work of medical and other natural scientists, vocational educators, job counselors, and those responsible for determination and execution of hiring policies in commercial and industrial enterprises. The process in which the co-operative efforts of these individuals are combined to increase the employability of disabled individuals is called "vocational rehabilitation." We turn then to an examination of past, current, and future programs in this field.

V. VOCATIONAL REHABILITATION

Vocational rehabilitation seeks to provide to disabled or handicapped individuals services required to restore them to productive employment. These include physical restoration, vocational counseling, training and retraining, personal adjustment counseling, and assistance in finding suitable employment. Public programs for vocational rehabilitation of the handicapped in the United States had their beginnings in the second decade of the twentieth century when a number of states established vocational training for the disabled. Beginning in 1920 the federal government undertook to aid the states in their programs by providing them with small grants-in-aid on a temporary basis. With the passage of the Social Security Act of 1935, provision was made for permanent federal financial participation in state programs. Between 1920 and 1943 the federal-state programs for vocational rehabilitation were extremely limited in the amount of funds available, in terms of the number of individuals rehabilitated, and in the services provided. Vocational rehabilitation services consisted primarily of counseling, vocational training, the provision of prosthetic appliances, and placement services. The legislation providing for federal grants did not permit the expenditure of funds for physical restoration or for rehabilitating individuals suffering from mental and emotional disturbances. Nor could federal moneys be used to provide maintenance income for individuals undergoing rehabilitation.

The federal-state programs were strengthened in 1943 with the passage of Public Law 113, which increased federal grants-in-aid and authorized expenditure of federal funds for corrective medical services and rehabilitation of those suffering from mental disabilities. While the 1943 legislation resulted in significant improvement in both the services provided and the number of individuals serviced, by the end of fiscal 1953 the annual number of individuals rehabilitated had reached only 61,308 (U.S. Department of Health, Education, and Welfare, 1953). While in absolute terms this represented important progress, in relative terms the surface was only being scratched. It was estimated in 1950, for example, that from 1.5 million to 2 million persons were substantially disabled and in need of rehabilitation services, with an additional 250,000 becoming disabled each year (U.S. Congress, 1950).

In an effort to strengthen the program, Congress in 1954 passed Public Law 565 amending the vocational rehabilitation legislation to provide for federal financial participation in the training of doctors, nurses, rehabilitation counselors, physical and occupational therapists, social workers, and other types of specialists. A new three-way grant system was established for the purposes of increasing basic vocational rehabilitation services, extension and improvement of services, and development of special projects in research, training, and demonstration. Additional legislation in the form of the Medical Facilities Survey and Construction Act (Public Law 482) was passed in 1954, permitting the expenditures of federal funds to assist in the construction of rehabilitation facilities.

This brief summary of the development of public programs in the field of vocational rehabilitation is not meant to imply a lack of interest and activity by private institutions and groups. Paralleling the expansion of public programs has been highly significant activity by private institutions such as the Liberty Mutual Insurance Company, the American Federation of the Physically Handicapped, the United Mine Workers Welfare and Retirement Fund, numerous medical schools, Goodwill Industries, Inc., and numerous others. These private institutions in co-operation with public programs have made major contributions not only in the direct rehabilitation of individuals but also in research and training (Somers and Somers, 1954).

Since enactment of the 1954 legislation, the number of individuals serviced has increased slightly but steadily each year, and the scope and nature of the services provided have expanded. In addition, there has been a steady accumulation of scientific knowledge relating to rehabilitation and an increase in the availability of facilities and trained personnel. During the fiscal year 1958, 74,314 handicapped persons were prepared for employment and placed on jobs. This 1958 total represented the largest annual number of rehabilitees since the beginning of the public programs. An additional 18,584 disabled individuals were prepared for employment during 1958 but had not yet been placed on jobs at the end of the fiscal year (U.S. Department of Health, Education, and Welfare, 1958). While not large in terms of total rehabilitation needs, the 1958 figure does represent significant progress when it is noted that, during the first 15 years of the federal-state rehabilitation program, the average number of individuals rehabilitated annually was 5000 (Somers and Somers).

Since World War II the federal Office of Vocational Rehabilitation and the state agencies have been increasing their efforts on behalf of older disabled workers. This is reflected in the increasing proportion of the rehabilitees each year who are in the older age groups. Thus, for example, of the total number of individuals rehabilitated in 1958, 31 per cent were over 45 years of age compared to 18 per cent of the total in 1945 (U.S. Office of Vocational Rehabilitation, 1958). Table 7 indicates the distribution by age and sex of older workers rehabilitated during the fiscal years 1954–58.

Table 8 provides detailed information concerning a number of characteristics of the 21,086 individuals 45 years of age and over rehabilitated during 1957. It will be noted that, of the individuals aged 45–64, 12,927, or 65.3 per cent, were unemployed at the time of acceptance for vocational rehabilitation. The figures for those 65 and over were 740, or 57.5 per cent. Of the 45–64-year-old individuals who were rehabilitated, 2933, or 14.8 per cent, were on relief at the time they were accepted. Of those 65 and over, 169, or 13.2 per cent, were in a similar position at the time of undertaking vocational rehabilitation. It is also of significance to note that, during the first year following their rehabilitation, those aged 45–64 earned a total of

those 45 years of age and over. In 1954 the Social Security Act was amended to provide for a "freeze" of the wage records of individuals who were permanently and totally disabled so that their disabilities would not operate to reduce their retirement benefits. In 1956 the Act was further amended to provide benefits to individuals at age 50 or later who were permanently and totally disabled. Under the disability freeze and disability benefit provisions, in-

TABLE 7*

AGE AND SEX OF PERSONS REHABILITATED BY THE STATE VOCATIONAL
REHABILITATION AGENCIES IN FISCAL YEARS 1954–58

AGE AT ACCEPTANCE AND SEX	REHABILITATED IN FISCAL YEAR				
	1958	1957	1956	1955	1954
Total:					
All ages..........	74,317	70,940	65,640	57,981	55,825
45 and over.......	22,787	21,086	17,751	15,286	14,312
45–54..........	14,279	13,110	11,314	9,929	9,143
55–64..........	7,130	6,689	5,449	4,503	4,294
65 and over.....	1,378	1,287	988	854	875
Male:					
All ages..........	47,031	45,951	42,740	36,671	35,272
45 and over.......	15,347	14,505	12,519	10,607	10,097
45–54..........	9,467	8,863	7,877	6,805	6,288
55–64..........	4,974	4,782	3,935	3,176	3,125
65 and over.....	906	860	707	626	684
Female:					
All ages..........	27,286	24,989	22,900	21,310	20,553
45 and over.......	7,440	6,581	5,232	4,679	4,215
45–54..........	4,812	4,247	3,437	3,124	2,855
55–64..........	2,156	1,907	1,514	1,327	1,169
65 and over.....	472	427	281	228	191

* Source: Data provided the authors by the Office of Vocational Rehabilitation, Division of Statistics and Studies, October, 1959.

$33,847,500 compared to $6,822,000 before vocational rehabilitation, an increase of 396 per cent. Those 65 and over who were rehabilitated earned $1,410,000 compared to $448,000 earned during the year before rehabilitation, an increase of 215 per cent.

It is true that the number of older workers rehabilitated is small in comparison to the total who need and could benefit from such services. A number of factors indicate, however, that the future is likely to see a significant increase in the number of individuals rehabilitated, particularly

dividuals applying to have their records frozen, or applying for benefits, are assessed by the state vocational rehabilitation agencies or other agencies for their rehabilitation potential. By 1958, forty-seven states and territories had working agreements with the Bureau of Old-Age and Survivors Insurance for administration of the freeze and benefit provisions and had made 278,000 initial disability determinations. This compared to 155,000 disability determinations in 1957. The state agencies in 1958 screened more than 360,000 individuals for rehabilitation potential com-

TABLE 8*

CHARACTERISTICS OF 21,086 INDIVIDUALS 45 YEARS OF AGE AND OVER
REHABILITATED DURING FISCAL YEAR 1957

45–64 Years of Age	Characteristic	65 Years of Age and Over
19,799 27.9%	WERE REHABILITATED DURING FISCAL YEAR 1957 OF 70,940 PERSONS REHABILITATED	1,287 1.8%
	General Characteristics†	
13,645 or 68.9%	Men	860 or 66.8%
14,576 or 79.9%	White	957 or 80.0%
2,329 or 11.8%	Never married	124 or 9.6%
7	Years—average (median) schooling	
	Age at Acceptance (Years)	
7,321 or 37.0%—45–49		884 or 68.7%—65–69
5,798 or 29.3%—50–54		303 or 23.5%—70–74
4,325 or 21.8%—55–59		73 or 5.7%—75–79
2,364 or 11.9%—60–64		27 or 2.1%—80 and over
52 years	Median age at acceptance	66 years
	Age at Disablement (Years)†	
632 or 3.2%	Congenital	17 or 1.3%
1,147 or 5.8%	Under 15	50 or 3.9%
1,147 or 5.8%	15–24	50 or 3.9%
1,582 or 8.0%	25–34	58 or 4.5%
4,331 or 22.0%	35–44	74 or 5.8%
10,871 or 55.2%	45 and over	1,029 or 80.6%
89 —	Not reported	9 —
Not available	Median age at disablement	52 years
	Time on rolls† Months referral to acceptance:	
3 months	Median	3 months
4 months	Mean	3 months
	Months acceptance to closure:	
8 months	Median	6 months
11 months	Mean	9 months
	Employment and Economic Status at Acceptance†	
12,927 or 65.3%	Unemployed	740 or 57.5%
(100 or 0.5%)	(Never worked)	(7 or 0.5%)
6,490 or 32.9%	Major support—families	244 or 19.0%
2,933 or 14.8%	Major support—public relief	169 or 13.2%
1,686 or 8.5%	Major support—insurance payments	274 or 21.3%
12,648 or 64.0%	Had dependents	717 or 55.8%
12,594 or 63.6%	Married	757 or 58.9%
	Services Provided In addition to guidance, counseling, and placement:	
2,239 or 11.3%	Training	81 or 6.3%
1,593 or 8.0%	Training and physical restoration	88 or 6.9%
(2,185 or 14.2%)	(Vocational training)	(74 or 5.7%)
11,689 or 59.1%	Physical restoration	978 or 75.8%
431 or 2.2%	Other services	11 or 0.9%
3,847 or 19.4%	Guidance, counseling, and placement only	129 or 10.1%

* Source: Adapted from U.S. Office of Vocational Rehabilitation, *Persons 45 Years of Age and Over Rehabilitated in Fiscal 1957 —Facts in Brief* ("Rehabilitation Service Series," No. 450, Supplement 9 [Washington, D.C., 1958]). (Mimeographed.)
† Cases for whom data were not reported on a particular item were excluded from the total in calculating percentages and other statistics.

TABLE 8—*Continued*

45–64 Years of Age	Characteristic	65 Years of Age and Over
	Vocational Training†	
2,815 or 14.2%	Business colleges	74 or 5.7%
483 or 17.2%	Private trade schools	4 or 5.4%
432 or 15.3%	Public vocational schools	1 or 1.4%
229 or 8.1%	Sheltered workshops	0 —
411 or 14.6%	Colleges or universities	24 or 32.4%
109 or 3.9%	Business establishments	0 —
424 or 15.1%	Tutors	4 or 5.4%
403 or 14.3%	Correspondence schools	26 or 35.1%
119 or 4.2%	Other	0 —
205 or 7.3%		15 or 20.3%
	Jobs after Rehabilitation†	
4,724 or 23.9%	Service	354 or 27.3%
2,688 or 13.6%	Agricultural and kindred	208 or 16.2%
2,766 or 14.0%	Semiskilled	113 or 8.8%
2,223 or 11.2%	Skilled	127 or 9.9%
2,667 or 13.5%	Clerical, sales, and kindred	113 or 8.8%
2,376 or 12.0%	Family workers and homemakers	241 or 18.8%
1,061 or 5.3%	Professional, semiprofessional, and managerial	83 or 6.5%
1,293 or 6.5%	Unskilled	48 or 3.7%
(3,417 or 17.2%)	(Self-employed)	(323 or 25.1%)
1 —	Not reported jobs	0 —
	Estimated Annual Earnings at Closure†	
3,758 or 19.0%	Farmers or family workers	379 or 29.4%
16,041 or 81.0%	Persons receiving earnings	908 or 70.6%
	Estimated Annual Earnings the First Year	
$33,842,500	*After rehabilitation*	$1,410,300
$ 6,822,400	*Before rehabilitation*	$ 448,000
(396%)	(Increase)	(215%)

pared to 154,000 in 1957 and had accepted over 42,000 for further consideration for rehabilitation compared to 19,000 in 1957. The median age of those referred to the state vocational rehabilitation agencies for disability determination in 1958 was 58.1 years (U.S. Department of Health, Education, and Welfare, 1958).

Another factor likely to increase the scope of vocational rehabilitation services generally, and for older workers in particular, is the continuing increase in research and demonstration projects aimed at discovering and applying new and improved methods for restoring the disabled. During 1958 some eighty-one research and demonstration projects were approved, a number of which are of direct relevance to older workers. Table 9 summarizes ten projects initiated between 1956 and 1959 which are of special importance to older workers. In addition, a vast amount of re-

search in the general field of chronic diseases is under way, the findings of which are likely to be of significance to vocational rehabilitation efforts in the future.

Since passage of the 1954 vocational rehabilitation and related legislation, important steps have been taken to increase rehabilitation facilities, resources, and personnel. Thus, during the fiscal years 1956 through 1958, eighty-two rehabilitation facility projects were approved for construction under the Medical Facilities Survey and Construction Act at a cost of over $60.4 million. In addition, federal aid to rehabilitation centers under Public Law 565 was granted to rehabilitation facilities specializing in service to the mentally and emotionally ill, blind, epileptic, homebound disabled, cerebral palsied, and others. One hundred and seventy-seven teaching grants to colleges, universities, and other institutions were made in 1958 to enable them to

TABLE 9*

SUMMARY OF TEN RESEARCH AND DEMONSTRATION PROJECTS OF SPECIAL INTEREST TO
OLDER WORKERS FOR WHICH GRANTS WERE APPROVED BY THE OFFICE
OF VOCATIONAL REHABILITATION, 1956–59

Organization	Federal Fiscal Year Initiated	Estimated Duration of Project	Purpose
Highland View Hospital, 3901 Ireland Drive, Cleveland 22, Ohio. Dr. Mieczyslaw Peszczynski, project director	1956	5 years	To demonstrate that rehabilitation is possible for long-term hospital patients disabled by severe chronic diseases, utilizing a testing and training program of work activities within the hospital
Montefiore Hospital, 210th Street and Bainbridge Avenue, New York 67, N.Y. Dr. George M. Warner, project director	1956	5 years	To demonstrate the economic and psychological benefits of vocational rehabilitation for permanently shut-in chronically ill persons whose disabilities limit them to part-time homework
Illinois Public Aid Commission, 160 North La Salle Street, Chicago, Ill. Mrs. Elizabeth Breckinridge, project director	1956	5 years	To determine and demonstrate the extent to which disabled persons confined to public and private nursing homes can be returned to employment or to community life
Our Lady of Fatima Hospital, 200 High Service Avenue, North Providence, R.I. Dr. Robert E. Carroll, project director	1956	3 years	To determine and demonstrate the services needed for the most effective vocational rehabilitation of chronically ill and disabled workers 45 years of age and older, particularly those who have applied for OASI disability benefits
University of Michigan, Ann Arbor, Michigan. Wilma Donahue, Ph.D., project director	1957	3 years	To determine the nature and extent of medical and other vocational rehabilitation services needed by the disabled, 45 years of age and older, living in county medical and convalescent facilities, and to demonstrate techniques for their rehabilitation
Federation Guidance and Employment Service, 42 East 41st Street, New York 17, N.Y. Roland Baxt, project director	1958	3 years	To demonstrate, through specialized counseling and work-adjustment training, the feasibility of vocational rehabilitation for disabled workers 60 years of age and over
Hospital Research and Educational Trust, 840 Lake Shore Drive, Chicago 11, Ill. Dr. Howard A. Rusk, project director	1958	5 years	To develop a simplified method for determining the rehabilitation potential of long-term hospital patients and the feasibility of meeting their medical and rehabilitation needs by transfer to domiciliary care of the Homestead type
Community Service Society of New York, 105 East 22d Street, New York 10, N.Y. Aline F. LeMet, R.N., M.A., project director	1959	4 years	To develop and evaluate a program of comprehensive care for older disabled individuals who have received rehabilitation services and have returned to the community
Hadley Memorial Hospital, 201 East Seventh Street, Hays, Kan. Dr. H. Alden Flanders, project director	1959		Work evaluation of older disabled persons (over 50)
University of North Dakota, Medical Center Rehabilitation Unit, Grand Forks, N.D. Miss Frances D. Landon, project director	1959		Work evaluation of older disabled persons (over 50)

* Source: Adapted from U.S. Office of Vocational Rehabilitation, *Research and Demonstration Projects* ("Rehabilitation Service Series," No. 378, Supplement 8 [Washington, D.C., July, 1959]). (Mimeographed.)

expand their instructional resources in the fields of medicine, nursing, occupational and physical therapy, prosthetics education, rehabilitation counseling, social work, speech and hearing, and other fields closely related to rehabilitation. In addition, traineeship grants to educational institutions made scholarship assistance available

TABLE 10*

PROPORTION OF EMPLOYEES IN MAJOR OCCU-PATION GROUPS WHO ARE 45 YEARS OF AGE AND OVER BY SEX, 1947 AND 1959

| MAJOR OCCUPATION GROUP | PERCENTAGE 45 YEARS OF AGE AND OVER | | | |
| | Men | | Women | |
	April, 1947	April, 1959	April, 1947	April, 1959
Total.........	38	40	28	40
Non-agriculture.....	36	38	27	40
Professional and semiprofessional.	34	31	29	43
Proprietors and managers.......	48	52	54	62
Clerical and sales..	32	34	19	32
Skilled...........	40	42	31	45
Semiskilled.......	26	32	26	38
Unskilled.........	33	36	35	45
Service..........	51	45	†	†
Agriculture........	45	49	45	48
Farmers.........	56	64	65	73
Farm laborers.....	18	23	37	44

* Source: U.S. Bureau of the Census. Unpublished data.
† Combined with unskilled.

to over 950 full-time students enrolled in basic or advanced training programs in the professional fields contributing to rehabilitation. The impact of these developments is seen in the fact that in 1958 the number of persons referred to rehabilitation centers was over three times greater than in 1955, and the amounts spent in rehabilitation facilities by vocational rehabilitation agencies was over two and a half times that of 1955 (U.S. Department of Health, Edu-

cation, and Welfare, 1958). These activities should bear fruit in the years to come.

A major factor inhibiting the expansion of vocational rehabilitation services continues to be a major shortage of trained rehabilitation personnel. The need for additional occupational therapists has been estimated at 8000; for additional physical therapists at 5800; and for rehabilitation counselors at 4000 (U.S. Congress, 1957).

There is considerable reason to believe that the shortages of personnel and facilities will gradually be reduced and that the growth in these will be accompanied by continuing advances of knowledge in the area of physical medicine and in the means of applying such knowledge. With the growing interest and concern with problems of aging there is likely to be a step-up of efforts to increase rehabilitation services to the aged. Of greater significance for the long-run prospects of increasing the labor-force participation of the aged, moreover, will be the impact of rehabilitation on the disabled in the younger age groups. The extent to which the productive abilities of those *below* age 45 are restored will have a major impact on the employability of these individuals when they reach their fifties and sixties.

VI. SOME COMMENTS ON THE LABOR-FORCE PARTICIPATION OF OLDER FEMALES

The trend in the labor-force participation of older females has been different from that of older men (see Table 4). For females in the age groups 45–54 and 55–64 the rate increased gradually from 14.1 per cent in 1900 to 47.9 per cent (for those 45–54) and 35.2 per cent (for those 55–64) in 1958. The proportion of females 65 and over in the labor force increased slightly from 9.1 per cent in 1900 to 10.3 per cent in 1958. The increase for the latter group, while slight, stands in sharp contrast to the significant decline in the rate for males 65 and over during this period. Today, the older woman (45 and over) accounts for a significant proportion of female employment across the occupational structure of the United States (Table 10). About two out of every five women employed in this country are in that age group, in contrast to only 28 per cent in 1947. The two-out-of-five ratio prevails in almost every major job field except clerical and sales, where younger women engaged as typists, stenographers, etc., pull the average down. Gains by older women have been particularly noteworthy in some of the major growth areas of the economy. For example, the proportion of older women in the female professional labor force is half again as high today as it was a dozen years ago; a similar gain was recorded for older women in skilled jobs.

The upward trend in labor-force participation among older females appears to be part of the long-range upward trend among all females of working age, although for those below age 20 the increase has been slight. A number of factors account for the increased labor-force participation of women over time. The number of females over the age of 14 has increased relative to the population as a whole. Long (1958) has shown that the increase of working-age females relative to other groups in the population has meant that relatively fewer females over age 14 have been needed to perform household duties or care for children. As a result a larger percentage of the females over age 14 are "available for work" (i.e., "available" in the sense of not having to maintain a household or care for children). Long estimated that between 1890 and 1950 the number of "available" females age 14 and over per 1000 females aged 14 and over increased from 213 to 319. In addition, the time required to perform the duties of maintaining a household has decreased with the growth of laborsaving household appliances and the increased ability and propensity to purchase food, clothing, and services which were formerly produced or performed by the homemaker. While it is difficult to measure the extent to which these latter factors have decreased the time required

in performing household duties, it is clear that they operate in the direction of reducing the amount of time which the housewife or single woman living at home must spend in performing the household tasks normally performed by women.

Not only has the quantity of potential women employees increased but their quality has also very likely improved as a result of their completing a growing number of years of formal education.

The increasing availability of women has been accompanied by expanding opportunities for them in the clerical and professional occupations (i.e., clerks, bookkeepers, typists, telephone operators, teachers, nurses, etc.). At the same time there has been a migration of females from rural to urban areas where historically their participation in the labor force has been greater. In addition, the gradual reduction in hours has increased the feasibility of employment among women (Long, 1958).

Labor-force participation among females is greatest during the ages 20–24 (i.e., prior to or during the early years of marriage) and between 45 and 54, when the pressures of rearing children and caring for a household have subsided. After age 54 there is a continuous decrease with advancing age.

Sheldon (1958) points out that, since the labor-force participation of women has been increasing over time, it follows that those who are currently in the age group 55 and over were young at a time when the propensity of women to enter the labor force was lower than at present. In addition, since most women currently reaching the older age group are married or recently widowed, their rates of labor-force participation will be low due to the fact that in years past the propensity of married women to work was still lower than that of single women. This should mean that, as women who are currently in the age groups 20–45 reach the older age groups, their rates of participation are likely to be higher than the rates of those in similar age groups at the present time.

As was the case with older men, disability constitutes the major reason for declining labor-force participation with age. The surveys of the Bureau of Old-Age and Survivors Insurance (Stecker, 1955) and by Steiner and Dorfman (1957) indicated that, among women with previous labor-force experience, approximately 47 per cent retired for reasons of health. Compulsory retirement policies and other reasons for involuntary retirement appear to affect the labor-force participation rate to about the same extent as in the case of older men.

VII. FUTURE TRENDS AND NEEDS

The older workers' experience during the recent past has been a function of a complex of social, economic, and demographic forces; of considerable public and private action; and, not the least, of the record the older worker has been able to make for himself.

Against this background, then, what of the immediate future? The work-life trends of the older person behave very much like most other social and economic forces in the United States. They are apparently subject to long-term evolutionary development; but, in any given short-term period, they can either be magnified or decelerated (e.g., by war or severe depression).

In looking ahead, the social scientist uses a continuation of the major evolutionary contours of the force he is investigating, tempers them by a knowledge of a number of foreseeable events in the comparative short run (e.g., in the demographic profile of the country and/or time period he is dealing with), but recognizes that current events can exaggerate or minimize his conclusions.

The staff of the Department of Labor has recently completed a systematic investigation of this kind into the outlook for our manpower situation (U.S. Department of Labor, 1957). Working with long-term trends and a knowledge of current and immediate future population trends and assuming no war or severe depression, we have estimated manpower demand and supply for the 10-year period 1955–65. The results are extremely important for those assessing work life in general and are particularly significant for those interested in how the older worker may be expected to fare.

1. Barring catastrophic developments, such as war or severe economic downturn, we expect an increase of about 10 million in the labor force of the United States (from roughly 70 to 80 million between 1955 and 1965).

2. Where will this additional labor supply come from? Some $4\frac{1}{2}$ million are expected to be young persons 14–24 years of age; $\frac{1}{2}$ million are expected to be in the age group 25–44; and 5 million are expected to be 45 years of age and older. And half of this total increase will be represented by women.

The composition of this expected labor supply tells a pretty obvious but extremely important story. The increase among the young is very significant—but it has to be tempered by the fact that a large proportion of them will be part-time workers. Many will be attending school at the same time, continuing the trend toward a higher and higher proportion graduating from high school and going on to college.

The increase among the 25–44 age group is very small, indeed, especially when we remember that they represent a prime working age where career development normally takes place. Part of the reason for the small expected increase is obvious: Men in this age cohort are always in the labor force, and the only increase we can expect from them over a period of time is generated by an increase in their population. Significantly enough, however, the outlook is actually for a decline in one of the constituent groups—persons 25–34 years of age. This is the group who in 1965 will represent the births of the 1930's, and many children were not born during that depression decade. As a result, there will be an expected decline of almost 2 million in the population of that age group between 1955 and 1965 and a drop of almost 1 million in the number of workers of those ages during the same period of time. All this adds up to the fact that persons 45 years of age and over are going to be the major suppliers of labor for the additional jobs in prospect in the United States under continuing high levels of economic activity in the immediate years ahead.

The reader of this chapter will recognize that these prospects for 1965 are very much in line with historical and postwar trends in this country and do not represent some sudden resurgence of the older worker. As a matter of fact, the labor-supply composition for 1965 is actually based on continuation of the secular trend toward declining worker rates for older men, calling for a drop of fully 5 percentage points in their labor-market participation between 1955 and 1965. What makes the position of the older worker so important in our economy of the next decade is:

1. A significant increase in their very numbers. Nine million of the 18 million population increase during this period will be represented by persons 45 years of age and over.

2. A substantial increase in adult women workers.

3. And, perhaps most importantly of all, the strategic position of the older person on the population curve, whose unique conformation is generated by the high birth rates of the past decade and the very low birth rates of the 1930's.

VIII. INDIVIDUAL CHOICE

In a free and democratic society one of the hallmarks of progress is the extent to which an individual can exercise choice—in his choice of an educational career, a work career, a place to live, a place to work, the distribution of his income, the expenditure of his leisure time, etc. Throughout a lifetime literally hundreds of these important choices are made, and, to the population in general and the practitioners in the related disciplines in particular, it is of compelling importance that these choices be made in such a manner as (a) to make maximum utilization of the individual's aptitudes, talents, interests, motivations, and aspirations and (b) to serve, at the same time and in a compatible way, to further the standard of living and national security of the society.

Broadly speaking, these developments have characterized the United States throughout this century. The gross national product per capita in constant dollars has about tripled since the turn of the century —a technical way of saying that the goods and services available for every man, woman, and child, or our standard of living, has grown enormously. We have been able to achieve these goals with only a very small increase in the proportion of the population in the labor force—all of them working many fewer hours today than even a generation or so ago. At the same time, as we already have indicated, the number and proportion of young people able to exercise the fundamental choice of pursuing an education beyond grade school has advanced tremendously, matched in almost similar magnitude by the opportunities for some years of retirement.

These achievements can be traced to a wide variety of factors, paramount among which is the series of technological advances which resulted in the great productivity increases we have witnessed in the last 50 years. But it is difficult to see how these factors would have operated without the manpower potential of our population at least approximately keeping pace with the other factors of growth.

What these developments have made possible is the endowment of our society with the maneuverability, the flexibility, and the capacity to afford the kind of choices we have mentioned. For an extreme contrast note the situation in a primitive society where the manpower potential and productivity are low. Labor-force activity (to use our modern terms) is extremely high, with very little in the way of education and training of the young and very little place for the old, to say nothing of "retired" persons. All are needed in the battle for subsistence. As the civilization or society progresses, we can begin to afford more in terms of later entry into the work force, more women able to remain out of labor force for marriage and child-bearing and rearing, and more retirement from work activity in the older years. Apparently, we have come a long way along this road. Thus the social gerontologist may usefully measure the progress of older populations in many, if not all, aspects by the degree to which they can exercise the maximum amount of choice in their relationships to their social and economic milieu.

Choice, of course, is by no means a fixed or stable phenomenon in any society. Rather, it changes significantly over time—both in the qualitative sense (in terms of its acceptance and support in a given milieu) and in the quantitative sense (in terms of the degrees of freedom and provision for its exercise available to the individual).

Thus, in the short run, the degrees and kinds of choices available vary significantly with the level of economic activity. In a depression, we may tend to get restrictive; in very high levels of economic activity, the profusion of choice may actually get to be a problem in terms of pressures and needs exercised by an economy in want of manpower. This ebb and flow in opportunities for choice, of course, not only affects opportunities in relation to the work place but also interacts with other social and economic phenomena (e.g., note the rules during the 1930's in some states restricting and even prohibiting the employment of married women as teachers).

Over the long run, many factors also operate to change the degree and kinds of choices available. In this country we have already noted how changes in the length and pattern of life and working life had a critical impact. Contrast, too, the kinds and varieties of choices available in the

United States as an agrarian society several generations ago and in today's industrial society, or the changes generated by such institutional forces as legislation (Old-Age and Survivors Insurance) or collective bargaining (private pension plans).

As we have pointed out, however, it is fair to say that for a long time now the opportunities for choice-making, the spectrum of choices available, and the provision of resources for helping the individual in this process have all increased substantially and significantly in this country. This, of course, is not to say that all these variables have become limitless or infinite in their application. To the extent that limitations on employment by age and sex prevail, for example, choices are restricted; an industrial society brings its own restrictions as a way of life; and even the operation of more advanced mechanisms (e.g., pension plans) may generate such problems as mandatory retirement at fixed chronological ages (Wolfbein, 1957b).

Although we are focusing here on the problems of the older person in relation to his conditions of work and their ramifications, we might also at this point suggest that the dimension of choice as we have outlined it here may very well serve as an important part of the framework for consideration of allied problems in the gerontological field. Thus, is not the current issue of mandatory versus permissive retirement, in part at least, one of maximizing the individual's freedom of choice in this important phase of decision-making in his lifetime?

When we talk about the major concern with economic security of the older person, are we not emphasizing in a very important manner the provision of resources for the aged so that they can exercise some of the choices we consider so important to them? For example, the problem of work versus retirement very often gets to be quite a theoretical exercise in the absence of the basic economic means to even consider such a choice in the first place.

The same, of course, applies to education, recreation, etc. In a fundamental sense, the critical factors of physical health and mental health also become an integral part of this picture, if only because the provision of institutional resources which generate declines in mortality and morbidity are a *sine qua non* for making the choices and reaching the goals we set up for achievement.

If we accept the primary importance of choice, we underline in a very critical way the specific roles of education, guidance, and counseling as institutional forces in maximizing its effectiveness. We emphasize these because, among the various facets of this very broad problem, it may point to an approach toward a unified operating context into which we can fit the older person.

For many years most of our resources were put into the guidance and counseling process in the secondary-school systems of the United States, where some of the more overt choices in regard to an educational and work career had to be made. In more recent years much effort has been expended in developing resources in guidance and counseling in the elementary schools, because of the recognition of the almost obvious but very vital fact that many of the problems exposed in the secondary schools had their roots back in the early years.

It has been done, too, because of the perhaps equally obvious but very vital fact that mental and psychological, as well as physical, growth is a developmental process—a continuum—over the lifetime of a person and that this growth and experience and learning do not come as discrete episodes attendant on achieving some chronological age or grade in school.

Following the logic of this development, exactly the same factors apply to the experience and learning and adjustments and readjustments that occur after high school or college—whether it be in the need to change a job when young, the need for education and guidance in retraining and skill development of an older person, or the need for preretirement counseling or for help when already retired. Here, again, it is difficult to view these as discrete episodes, and the person who deals with the adult making a job change, or the older person in quest of advice on preparing for retirement, or the geriatrician dealing with chronic illness of the elderly finds many roots of the problem back in the early years.

For those of us in this general area, then —whether it be in government, business, or school situations—counseling, guidance, testing, placement, and provision of occupational information for the adult and elderly becomes a part of the unified and general and developmental process over a lifetime, aiding the individual in the many situations of choice available to him in a society which permits and affords to an increasing extent these very processes of choice—again with the two-pronged aim of the maximum development of the person in accord with the maximum development of the standard of living and national security.

In this chapter we have presented an overview of some of the major evolutionary forces affecting working life and labor-force participation in this country, a picture of more recent developments during the last dozen years, and a look at what may be in store in the immediate years ahead.

We have then placed major stress on the fundamental concept of the genetic or developmental approach to our problems and have selected the matter of choice for a principal role in that approach. This has been done because the overriding trends of the past half-century and more, both in the expectation of life and in working life, may have brought us to the point where such considerations are socially and economically feasible—and because they are apparently based on sound psychological principles.

In ending this paper, we return full circle to this basic idea, as follows:

It is fair to say that perhaps the real crux of the historical development in the

United States and in many other countries in the gerontological field stems from the changing role and status of the older person in a new social and economic milieu, generated by the transition from an agrarian to industrial society, the tremendous medical advances we have achieved, etc.

A primary goal, therefore, is providing the older person (working or retired) with a meaningful independent status in this transition and beyond. Our theme and theirs is that this should be done in a developmental manner, integrated with what develops in the younger years, especially in terms of what occurs in a person's role in relation to the work place.

REFERENCES

ABRAMS, A. J. 1952. Barriers to the employment of older workers. Ann. Am. Acad. Political & Social Sc., **279**, 62–71.

ANONYMOUS. 1958. Income of Old-Age and Survivors Insurance beneficiaries: highlights from preliminary data, 1957 survey. Social Security Bull., **21** (August), 17–23.

———. 1959. Assets and net worth of Old-Age and Survivors Insurance beneficiaries: highlights from preliminary data, 1957 survey. *Ibid.*, **22** (January), 3–6.

BAKER, HELEN. 1952. Retirement procedures under compulsory and flexible retirement policies. Princeton, N.J.: Industrial Relations Section, Princeton University.

BALDWIN, G. B., and SHULTZ, G. P. 1955. Automation: a new dimension to old problems. *In* Proceedings of Seventh Annual Meeting of Industrial Relations Research Association, December 28–30, 1954. Madison: The Association.

BANCROFT, GERTRUDE. 1958. The American labor force: its growth and changing composition. New York: John Wiley & Sons.

BANKERS TRUST COMPANY. 1956. A study of industrial retirement plans. New York: The Company.

BOGUE, D. J. 1959. The population of the United States. Glencoe, Ill.: Free Press.

BRIGHT, J. R. 1958. Automation and management. Boston: Graduate School of Business Administration, Harvard University.

BROWER, F. BEATRICE. 1955. Retirement of employees: policies—procedures—practices. ("Studies in Personnel Policy," No. 148.)

New York: National Industrial Conference Board.

EPSTEIN, LENORE A. 1955. Economic resources of persons aged 65 and over. Social Security Bull. **18** (June), 3–19.

———. 1959. Money income of aged persons: a 10-year review, 1948 to 1958. *Ibid.*, **22** (June), 3–11.

HEWITT, EDWIN SHIELDS, AND ASSOCIATES. 1952. Company practices regarding older workers and retirement. Libertyville, Ill.: Edwin Shields Hewitt & Associates.

KILLINGSWORTH, C. C. 1959. Automation in manufacturing. *In* Proceedings of Eleventh Annual Meeting of Industrial Relations Research Association, December 28–29, 1958. Madison: The Association.

KOLODRUBETZ, W. W. 1958. Characteristics of pension plans—an analysis of the principal provisions of 100 selected pension plans under collective bargaining, winter, 1957–58. Month. Labor Rev., **81**, 845–53.

LONG, C. 1958. The labor force under changing income and employment. Princeton, N.J.: Princeton University Press.

RUSKOWSKI, J. 1957. The Massachusetts law against age discrimination in employment. *In* Brightening the senior years. Albany: New York State Joint Legislative Committee on Problems of the Aging.

SHELDON, H. D. 1958. The older population of the United States. New York: John Wiley & Sons.

SKOLNIK, A. M., and ZISMAN, J. 1959. Growth in employee-benefit plans, 1954–1957. Social Security Bull., **22** (March), 4–14.

SOMERS, H. M., and SOMERS, ANNE R. 1954. Workmen's compensation. New York: John Wiley & Sons.

STECKER, MARGARET L. 1953. Old-Age and Survivors Insurance beneficiaries: income in 1951. Social Security Bull., **16** (June), 3–9.

———. 1955. Why do beneficiaries retire? Who among them return to work? *Ibid.*, **18** (May), 3–12, 35–36.

STEINER, P. O., and DORFMAN, R. 1957. The economic status of the aged. Berkeley: University of California Press.

STERN, J. 1959. Fact, fallacy, and fantasy of automation. *In* Proceedings of Eleventh Annual Meeting of Industrial Relations Research Association, December 28–29, 1958. Madison: The Association.

U.S. BUREAU OF THE CENSUS. 1958. Annual report on the labor force—1958. Current Population Reports: Labor Force. (Series

P-50, No. 89.) Washington, D.C.: Government Printing Office.

U.S. BUREAU OF EMPLOYMENT SECURITY. 1951. Older workers seek jobs. Washington, D.C.: Government Printing Office.

———. 1956a. Counseling and placement services for older workers. (Bull. No. E152.) Washington, D.C.: Government Printing Office.

———. 1956b. Older worker adjustment to labor market practices. (Bull. No. R151.) Washington, D.C.: Government Printing Office.

———. 1956c. Pension costs in relation to the hiring of older workers. (Bull. No. E150.) Washington, D.C.: Government Printing Office.

———. 1959. Employing older workers. (Bull. No. R179.) Washington, D.C.: Government Printing Office.

U.S. BUREAU OF LABOR STATISTICS. 1956a. A case study of a large mechanized bakery. ("Studies of Automatic Technology," Report No. 109.) Washington, D.C.: Government Printing Office.

———. 1956b. Job performance and age. (Bull. No. 1203.) Washington, D.C.: Government Printing Office.

———. 1956c. Older workers under collective bargaining, Part I: Hiring—retention—job termination. (Bull. No. 1199-1.) Washington, D.C.: Government Printing Office.

———. 1956d. Older workers under collective bargaining, Part II: Health and insurance plans—pension plans. (Bull. No. 1199-2.) Washington, D.C.: Government Printing Office.

———. 1957. A case study of a modernized petroleum refinery. ("Studies of Automatic Technology," Report No. 120.) Washington, D.C.: Government Printing Office.

U.S. CONGRESS. 1950. SENATE. COMMITTEE ON LABOR AND PUBLIC WELFARE. Vocational rehabilitation of the physically handicapped.

Hearings before subcommittee. (81st Cong., 2d sess.) Washington, D.C.: Government Printing Office.

———. 1955. JOINT COMMITTEE ON THE ECONOMIC REPORT. SUBCOMMITTEE ON ECONOMIC STABILIZATION. Automation and technological change. Hearings before the subcommittee. (84th Cong., 1st sess.) Washington, D.C.: Government Printing Office.

———. 1957. HOUSE OF REPRESENTATIVES. COMMITTEE ON EDUCATION AND LABOR. Welfare of the physically handicapped. Hearings before subcommittee. (85th Cong., 1st sess.) Washington, D.C.: Government Printing Office.

U.S. DEPARTMENT OF HEALTH, EDUCATION, AND WELFARE. 1953. Annual report. Washington, D.C.: Government Printing Office.

———. 1958. Annual report. Washington, D.C.: Government Printing Office.

U.S. DEPARTMENT OF LABOR. 1957. Our manpower future, 1955–65. Washington, D.C.: Government Printing Office.

U.S. OFFICE OF VOCATIONAL REHABILITATION. 1958. Persons 45 years of age and over rehabilitated in fiscal 1957—facts in brief. ("Rehabilitation Service Series," No. 450, Supplement 9.) Washington, D.C.: Office of Vocational Rehabilitation. (Mimeographed.)

———. 1959. Research and demonstration projects. ("Rehabilitation Service Series," No. 378, Supplement 8.) Washington, D.C.: Office of Vocational Rehabilitation. (Mimeographed.)

WOLFBEIN, S. L. 1957a. The length of working life. Washington, D.C.: Bureau of Labor Statistics.

———. 1957b. Employment outlook for older workers. In WILMA DONAHUE and C. TIBBITTS (eds.), The new frontiers of aging. Ann Arbor: University of Michigan Press.

WOYTINSKY, W. S., and ASSOCIATES. 1953. Employment and wages in the United States. New York: Twentieth Century Fund.

XI

Retirement: The Emerging Social Pattern

WILMA DONAHUE, HAROLD L. ORBACH, AND OTTO POLLAK

I. WHAT IS RETIREMENT? AN OVERVIEW

A. The Problem of Definition

Although retirement has come to occupy a place of central concern in contemporary Western society and is the subject of recurring popular and scientific discussion, there has been a certain degree of vagueness and lack of clarity as to its meaning. In everyday usage, retirement generally refers to separation from paid employment which has had the character of an occupation or a career over a period of time, and most gerontological considerations of the issues involved in retirement seem to have taken this as their point of departure.

While this is technically an adequate delineation of a break in the individual's work life, it emphasizes only the change in a formal economic relationship which may or may not be of a permanent nature. Thus it includes many categories of persons who are actually only in the process of changing from one occupational line to another. A prime example of this is the professional military man who may be "retiring from the service" in middle age and planning a new career based on the income floor his service pension provides. The changed character of our military manpower has provided a larger number of men and now women in this category than ever before in our nation's history. Likewise, the professional athlete (e.g., boxer or baseball, basketball, or football player)

also may "retire," in some cases with a pension, at a very young age, in terms of the over-all labor force, owing to the special conditions of his occupation. In fact, these individuals are only making job changes which have been anticipated almost from the commencement of their careers.

In the case of women a definition of this type is of limited value. What of the married woman whose family tasks have been completed and who does not engage in remunerative employment? Although she may continue to function as the manager of a household for herself and her spouse, is she not, if her spouse is retired, also a retired person? In recent years further complexities have been introduced by the increased participation of women in the labor force and by the tendency among married women to drift in and out of the labor market depending upon the state of their family's growth and finances. There also has been the suggestion that the married woman with children effectively retires when the last of her offspring leaves home to begin independent living, at which point her career as a mother comes to an end.

From another point of view, it has been argued that self-definition of the individual can serve as a criterion of retirement. Regardless of age or other aspects of social roles, a retired person would be one who so defines himself. The problems attendant on this type of subjective criterion, however, raise more issues than are solved, since, on the one hand, persons effectively retired may refuse or decline to accept this role for themselves; and, on the other hand, many persons considering themselves retired may actually be only temporarily in this role. The evaluation of one's self as retired is best seen as one of the important aspects of the retirement role and one of the problems of adjustment to retirement of those who find themselves unwillingly in this position.

The basic deficiency of these definitions, approaching retirement in terms of some linkage with the formal act of leaving a career or an occupation or by self-definition, is that they do not provide a perspective broad enough to deal with the range and variety of social patterns encompassed by retirement as an emerging form of social life in the industrial societies of the twentieth century. While the departure from a lifelong career may serve as the basic operational indicator of retirement, defining retirement raises problems of the dynamics of social and institutional roles and relationships and requires an underlying theoretical framework in which these issues can be located and treated. We shall define retirement in a manner which allows us to place it in the broad conceptual framework of role theory. This will give us a perspective capable of accommodating questions of the historical dynamics of the role at the societal level and the specific cultural and social situations in which the individual enacts the role. For it is only in the context of these two mutually interrelated foci of the phenomena of retirement that we can develop a systematic understanding of its character.

B. Retirement as a Role and Status Change

Retirement heralds a far-reaching change in a person's social role as a functioning member of society and, as such, carries with it consequential implications of changes in status. This is dramatically underscored when one recognizes that the emerging pattern of social life which we designate as retirement represents the development in modern society of a new and distinct role available universally for ever larger numbers of persons which has virtually no precedence in existing or previous forms of social organization.

Retirement is the creation of an economically non-productive role in modern societies which are capable of supporting large numbers of persons whose labor is not essential to the functioning of the economic order. As a process, retirement is the prescribed transition from the position of an economically active person to the position of an economically non-active person in accordance with the norms through which society defines this change.

At present this transition is still one that is partially open to choice on the part of the individual person to the extent that he is not automatically forced into this position, as, for example, the child is forced into the position of student at approximately the age of 5 years. There is a degree of freedom in opting the role which the individual can exercise. The extent of this freedom of choice, and the whole issue of future policy with regard to the continuation, expansion, or restriction of this freedom, is one of the major current topics with regard to the practical considerations concerning retirement policy.

Since in general terms the retirement role is considered to be one developed for the benefit of the individual (although we shall see in Section III of this chapter that there is divergence in the value orientations underlying this view), safeguarding him from the hazards of old age, such freedom of choice would appear as a natural corollary. However, in practice, retirement policies more often are the consequence of institutional interest and needs, as in the case of corporate replacement of executives or industrial retirement of workers. In the United States, while there are fixed ages for the commencement of retirement under the federal social security system, one is not forced to retire at these ages, or at any given age for that matter. One is, however, required to support throughout the working life (for most persons) the financing of this retirement and insurance system.[1] After a given age, one receives the benefits whether working or not.

Practically speaking, the defined retirement systems of constituent units of other institutional orders—especially the economic one—merge with the federal system to restrict this freedom of choice to a great degree. Thus industrial organizations and local and state governmental agencies have generally fixed age limits for working life. The confluence of the federal and other retirement systems in effect produces a situation which makes it difficult in most cases, and impossible in some, for the older person over the generally defined retirement age to continue full-time employment. This varies tremendously with the occupational category of the individual, especially between professional and nonprofessional occupations, and with the character of the specific job. Even where the individual continues working after the general retirement age, he does so under conditions which frequently place him at a disadvantage to other employees with regard to matters such as type of employment, job security, wage scales, and fringe benefits. All this serves to emphasize the changed status he carries as a result of being of retireable age. He is, strictly speaking, no longer a part of the regularly defined occupational ranking and positional hierarchy. His eligibility for the role of a retired person has put him in a new system of positions.

C. The Perspective of Role Theory

We have spoken of retirement as a new social role which involves major changes in a person's position and status in society. A framework for understanding retirement on both the level of society and that of the person is available through the broad perspective of role theory deriving from the

[1] See chaps. viii and xiv.

work of George Herbert Mead (1934) and Ralph Linton (1936). The concepts of social self and social role have become cornerstones of contemporary sociological and social psychological theory and have given rise to the development of an associated set of conceptual distinctions underlying much contemporary research.

ROLE, POSITION, AND STATUS

Objectively, a role is constituted by a collection of patterned sequences of behavior which form a meaningful unit and consequently usually can be given symbolic identification through a name (e.g., the role of a doctor, father, worker, leader, teacher, retiree, honest man, liar, etc.). Normatively, a role is characterized by a set of rules or norms of behavior which are deemed appropriate to the particular position in the social order or in interpersonal relations which its name signifies in the case of social roles, or the idealized category it refers to in the case of "valuational" roles, such as honest man or liar. This normative structure provides the accepted behavioral expectancies for the role. Thus a person is identified as having a given role *to enact* in terms of a position he *occupies* in social life. Associated with different positions are elements of prestige, honor, and the like which are designated by the concept of status. Each person normally has many roles to enact as a consequence of the various positions he occupies in the different institutional aspects of a social structure. He may be father, doctor, community leader, etc., emphasizing the fact that any person has multiple roles which taken together constitute the basis of the social behavior which uniquely identifies his social being. As Mead (1934) has shown, it is on the basis of the social relations entered into through the performance of the individual's various roles that the fundamental aspects of the person's social self are derived. One's attitudes, one's sources of meanings and values, and one's total personal integration depend on the social sources of behavioral acts and expectations. It is here, that, subjectively, the enactment of a role represents a personal interpretation and unique integration of normative and behavioral elements.

Within the total arena of social behavior, certain areas stand out as primary. A number of roles are of fundamental importance in determining the type of personal and social integration achieved. The institutional orders which supply these roles depend on the type of society of which one is a member.[2] In our own society the economic and family orders are generally predominant. This means that work or occupational and family relations will be the major foci around which many of the other subsidiary roles will revolve. A person's over-all social position and status are dependent in large measure on the nature of one's occupation, the income opportunities occupation provides, and the general standing of the social strata with which one's family is associated.

REFERENCE GROUP

On the more immediate level the particular occupational and social alignments of the person provide the direct group sources of personal and social identifications and values. This has been systematically analyzed in terms of the concept of reference-group behavior. The person evaluates his own self and others from the standpoint of the common meanings and values and the derived behavioral expectations of the relevant social groups, categories, or institutions with which he identifies or compares himself or to which he may aspire. He uses his perception and understanding of their normative structure as a basis for judgment of himself and others whether he actually holds these norms or not. While some of these involve judgments based on values limited to action immediately relevant to the areas of social functioning the groups or categories are associated with, others involve perspectives

[2] See chap. iv.

on the whole of social life. This latter type of social outlook has historically been applied to an entire society under the terms "Weltanschauung," "ethos," or "spirit of the age," implying an organized global perspective of meanings and values.[3]

THE ROLE-SET

Merton (1957a, 1957b) has introduced another dimension to the analysis of social roles, the concept of the role-set. He points out that, in normative terms, any given role is actually a composite of sets of normative and behavioral rules and expectations which he designates as the "role-set." This calls attention to the fact that a given role is characterized by a series of potentially varying interpretations of the appropriate role behavior from the differing perspectives and behavioral sources of expectations of the others in the functional situations wherein the role is performed. Thus the holder of a given position has one conception of his role based on his own perspective, while his superiors and subordinates, his colleagues and audiences, his friends and his family, etc., may have quite different conceptions of the same role. Merton discusses the important implications for an understanding of the dynamics and functioning of a given role that various conditions of agreement and divergence, specificity and ambiguity, of role conception among the members of the role-set may have. One point of particular importance is the contribution of the reference group composed of the position-hold-

[3] The preceding discussion of role theory and reference-group behavior, while diverging in some respects, has borrowed freely from the analysis of these topics to be found in Turner (1956); the reader is referred also to Kelley (1952), Merton (1957b, pp. 225–386), and Shibutani (1955) for more detailed analysis of the developing theoretical perspectives of role theory and reference-group behavior. An extensive bibliography of the literature can be found in Sarbin (1954), whose analysis differs in that he eschews the social-psychological integration of self and role, regarding the self as an underlying psychological entity which acts out roles.

ers themselves to a mutually reinforceable definition of their roles. In occupational terms the professional organization or work category represents a basic reference group which provides a definition of the role for the occupants of the position.

THE RETIREMENT ROLE

This is of fundamental importance for an understanding of the problem of retirement, for the retirement role-set is one which is beset with divergence and ambiguity of conception. Studies of the meaning of retirement have shown the widely varying conceptions held concerning the nature of retirement (Friedmann and Havighurst, 1954; Taietz *et al.*, 1956). Indeed, one might well say that the fundamental social-psychological problem of the retirement role is the lack of clarity and the ambiguity which currently characterize it.

There is, however, nothing startling about this situation. While one moves more or less clearly through the various stages of social life from childhood through adolescence and into maturity, there are for each of these age stages fairly clear social roles and behavioral expectations which society and its various institutional orders have developed, including transitional roles. Societies have evolved well-defined ceremonial situations formally to mark many such major role transitions, for example, the well-known *rites de passage* most extensively described by anthropologists such as Margaret Mead (1928) in dealing with primitive societies. There are more or less clear familial, kinship, and parental roles, educational, occupational, and professional roles, political, civic, and religious roles, etc., which are the result of developed and continuous institutional orders functioning as part of the social structure of society. Consequently, for many of these roles, the transition is gradual and preparation quite extensive both formally and informally through a series of *role gradations* which ease and modify the need for sharp role changes. We have what has been spoken of

as *anticipatory socialization* for the role to be, largely through informal antecedent preparation (Merton, 1957*b*). Thus the family prepares the child for school and work, and school prepares the child for work, and both simultaneously prepare the child in general adult social behavior.

As social change has modified the nature and character of many of the institutional orders, adaptations, modifications, and replacements of the relevant roles have occurred, not without far-reaching changes in the nature and importance of many of them as well as in their clarity and precision.[4]

Retirement, however, represents more than a change in an aspect of social life. It is a new form of social life, distinct from previous patterns of old age, which has not yet achieved any specific institutional integration. Past societies have had numbers of aged people, but these were not *retired persons*. They remained integrated in traditional institutional orders through work and kinship roles and relationships. In contemporary society, too, it is only in the last few decades that we could begin to speak of the retired as constituting a new category of persons. It has only been in this period of time that the conditions requisite for the emergence of this group of persons have matured. The resulting impact of their presence in society has created awareness of the retired as a distinct social category. Consequently, they have not had any institutionalized reference groups or clearly defined role categories with which they could identify themselves and their position in society and thus expect to have sources of role expectations. These remain to be created out of the social potentialities in society. There is, therefore, a lack of group or institutional foundations of anticipatory socialization for the retirement role. This has led to the development of programs of preparation for retirement on an extensive

[4] See chaps. iv, v, and ix for general analyses of the problems of social change and chaps. x, xii, xiii, xvii, xviii, and xix for treatments of specific areas.

organized basis. Furthermore, with the general cultural rejection of old age and the association of retirement and old age as an unpleasant situation, there has been, in effect, a large measure of rejection of socialization for an unwanted new role, much as one would decline preparing to die and avoid anticipating it.

This helps to explain the resulting lack of consensus among the retired and those anticipating retirement on the nature of the retirement role (Friedmann and Havighurst, 1954; Taietz *et al.*, 1956). Their views are an amalgam of the diverse, heterogeneous groups represented in their social life and the projections of the values and expectations derived in past contexts which, unfortunately in too many instances, are not adequate to the changed conditions of today's society. Traditional family and kinship roles and values have been greatly altered as the conditions appropriate to them have changed in accordance with the requirements of industrial society (W. E. Moore, 1951). As Cottrell points out in chapter xvii, it is only quite recently that the development of a corps of professionals, officials, and bureaucrats devoted to the problems of aging and the aged has provided the beginnings of some institutional concern with and, thus, source of role definition for the retired. Among the retired themselves, no parallel organization has yet reached the stages comparable to those existing for other groups such as agriculture, labor, or business, although groups like the Townsend Movement of the thirties had a limited period of success in attempting such a function, and a number of associations of retired persons are currently in nascent stages of development.

Lacking basic reference groups composed of holders of the position of retiree, only very limited aspects of role definition can be expected from official institutional sources such as the Social Security Administration and other governmental agencies. At the same time the impact of this new role on society has not yet reached the stage where an over-all social consensus has arisen which would make possible the development of a meaningful and socially functional role consistent with the individual's and society's needs and values.

ROLE AMBIGUITY AND ADJUSTMENT TO RETIREMENT

There have been numerous statements of the view that the fundamental problem of the aged derives from the lack of a positive creative role in society after retirement, leaving them in a peculiarly functionless position (Havighurst, 1952; Parsons, 1954; Tibbitts, 1954). W. E. Moore (1951) has expressed this view most aptly:

Perhaps the fundamental problem of the aged in industrial societies is that they have no definite place in the social structure. That is, there are no regular, institutionally sanctioned responsibilities for their care and social participation which square with both traditional values and the requirements of an industrial system [p. 330].

In turn, the problems of adjustment to aging and retirement have been centrally linked to the provision of clearly defined status-giving social roles for the retired in which they can find a replacement for the activities and interests of the earlier years (Cavan *et al.*, 1949; Albrecht, 1951; Parsons, 1954; Havighurst, 1954; Tibbitts, 1954; Willie, 1954; Orbach and Shaw, 1957).

This issue is cogently dealt with in the general theory of role change propounded by Rose (1954):

When a person moves out of a given social role into another, and the society fails to provide a full and clear-cut set of meanings and values for the guidance of behavior in the second role as in the first, the person will experience a relative loss of contact with meanings and values. . . . This experience is temporary if the individual succeeds in carving out a new role for himself which has as complete a specification of meanings and values as his earlier role [p. 23].

Rose specifies three such situations in American society—retirement, the passage from "young woman" to "old maid" for an unmarried woman, and the leaving of home of the last of her children for a married woman. The essential difference between retirement and the other two situations is that the latter do not have the full implication of passage into a state of redundancy which retirement carries. The "old maid" may no longer be clear about potential marital status, but occupation and other functions are not effectively proscribed from her; similarly, the mother whose children have left home also has the option of occupational career or other positions. But the retiree's position is unique in that he is in effect entering a period of prescribed economically non-essential activity. There is no escaping the resulting implication that he is being "put on the shelf." While leisure and peaceful enjoyment of a state of non-work may be possible values to the working person in an idealized picture, they still are not socially recognized virtues in our contemporary society, and Americans seem uniquely unable to conceive leisure in a positive fashion (witness the popular expression "killing time"). Certainly, leisure and cultural life have not reached the stage in America where persons engaged full time in leisure can find a suitable, socially approved status-giving role to replace the sense of meaningfulness and functionality associated with preretirement life activities.[5]

D. The Challenge of Retirement

This, then, is the challenge of retirement for contemporary society: to successfully create and clearly define a meaningful social role for the retired which will provide the individual with a sense of function and value and to integrate this role into the fabric of our industrial civilization.

The function of social-gerontological research on retirement can be seen as that of exploring the arena in which this process is taking place today and providing a foun-

[5] See chap. xii for a discussion of the functions of leisure.

dation of scientific knowledge for approaching the issues and problems which arise. This means an understanding of the conditions which have brought about this new phenomenon and make it possible, the value orientations underlying society's approach to retirement, the content of existing social attitudes toward retirement, the characteristics of the process of adjustment to retirement, and the trends discernible in the social life and activities of today's retirees.

Research in retirement has reached the stage where the older stereotypes and myths of retirement are giving way to systematic scientific study of its realities. The purpose of this chapter is to describe and review the results of this growing body of knowledge.

II. What Makes Retirement Possible? The Societal Background

A. Retirement and Industrial Society

Retirement is a phenomenon of modern industrial society. Previous socioeconomic systems in man's history have had varying numbers of older people, but none has ever had the number or proportion of aged that obtains in the industrialized societies of the present day. More important, the older people of previous societies were not retired persons; there was no retirement role (Simmons, 1945).[6]

The older person continued as a member of society in accordance with some function he was still able to perform or was allowed to perform. He was the direct responsibility of family, kin, or community, and the measures for his support were a consequence of his position in these institutional arrangements. For example, if the Eskimo grandmother could no longer even chew the boots of the family, she would be abandoned or walled up in an igloo to await death. The medieval serf, on the other hand, could expect his family to support him so long as he lived in consequence of

[6] See chap. iii.

the fact that the legal right to the use of the family's land was through an agreement in his name. More recently, the agrarian family head controlled his support through the ownership and legal power over the use of his property.[7] But the industrial wage-earner or salaried worker has no such functional economic means of continued support when his working life is at an end. The consequence of loss of institutional control of the means available for support is that the person then becomes dependent on such forms of benevolence as are available. Nothing more dramatically symbolizes the passage into a state of dependency through the loss of control over the means of support than the pathetic figure of Shakespeare's King Lear after he "retired" his throne. The aged person possessed no legally institutionalized *right* to continued support as a person per se unless he continued to perform some socially defined required function. The rise of retirement as an institutionalized form of social life has altered this.

The background of retirement as a phenomenon of our times involves, of necessity, an understanding of the complex economic, social, and political characteristics which distinguish contemporary industrial society from previous systems of social organization. For it is as a result of the interrelationship of these broad aspects of modern life that retirement has emerged, beginning about three-quarters of a century ago and reaching maturity only in the last two decades. Cottrell (chap. iv) and Friedmann (chap. v) have dealt with the fundamental changes in technology and social organization which have characterized modern industrial society. Sheldon (chap. ii) has discussed the altered demographic picture which has accompanied these changes. Let us examine how these have contributed the basis for the emergence of the phenomenon of retirement.

[7] See chap. v, however, for a discussion of the problems of generational conflict in such systems.

B. The Contributions of Technology and Demographic Change

DEVELOPMENT OF INDUSTRIAL TECHNOLOGY

Modern technology has made it feasible for society to support ever greater numbers of persons through the enormous increases in the productive capacity of industrial economies. While minimum subsistence characterized the past, the continuous expansion and growth of productivity through the high-energy technology of the present has created a situation of abundance in modern industrial society. Not only have the industrialized nations been able to support larger populations; they have been able also to provide a consistent raising of the standards of life at the same time and still produce surpluses of food and goods.

Tables 1 and 2 in chapter iv detail the vast increases in total energy and per capita energy production which have taken place in the United States in the 100 years from 1850 to 1950 as machines have replaced human and animal sources of energy in our industrial technology. They show that total energy has increased sixty-seven-fold in this period, while population has increased sixfold, giving a more than tenfold increase in per capita energy production. This has been marked by a rise in machine sources of energy from 35 to 98 per cent of all sources of energy and a reduction of human and animal sources from 13 and 52 per cent, respectively, to 1 per cent each.

Translating this into the monetary terms of gross national product (Table 1), we have had a more than sixfold increase in total gross national product and an almost threefold increase in per capita gross national product in the period from 1900 to 1957. Projections to 1970 indicate marked further rises based on increasing productivity. Table 2 summarizes the annual rates of growth of gross national product, personal expenditure per capita, and gross national product per man-hour of labor and projects future trends. The predicted improvement in annual rates of growth of these economic indicators means that we have the basis for important further improvements in the level of living.

We see, then, that the ability of society to support economically non-productive segments of the population has increased immensely with the growth of modern industrial technology and shows every indication of continuing to do so (Dewhurst and Associates, 1955; Galbraith, 1958; Rockefeller Brothers Fund, 1958).

The extent of this ability of high-energy

TABLE 1*

GROSS NATIONAL PRODUCT AND
GROSS NATIONAL PRODUCT
PER CAPITA, 1900–1970

(In 1958 Prices)

Year	Gross National Product (In Billions)[†]	Gross National Product per Capita[†]
1900	$ 72	$ 947
1920	141	1326
1940	228	1696
1950	352	2322
1957	451	2634
1970	790	3700

* Source: National Planning Association, *National Economic Projections, 1962–1965, 1970* (Washington, D.C.: The Association, 1959), p. 3 and Table 12, p. 143.
† 1900–1957, actual; 1970, projected judgment within high and low ranges.

society to support its population can be further appreciated when one views the changing nature of the labor force that has accompanied this rising prosperity.[8] Fewer persons are today engaged in producing food and goods and more in servicing what is produced. About 5 or 6 years ago the United States reached a historical marking point when the number of workers engaged in service activities for the first time exceeded the number engaged in actual production of goods. The other advanced industrial nations have exhibited the same trend in the composition of their labor forces.

The current state of our productive abil-

ity has led one contemporary economist to argue that we have reached a state of "affluence," so that the prime problem is no longer a sufficient volume of food and goods but the question of the type and quality of goods and services which should be provided because of their socially useful value rather than their economically calculated worth (Galbraith, 1958). Indeed, the major problem that has faced the industrial societies of the West in the last 60 years has been that of providing a sufficient consumption of the food and goods produced to assure a continuing source of employment for the entire working population. Thus technology has both made possible the support of a retired population and has generated pressures for the creation of such a population as a means of alleviating the problem of employment.

DEMOGRAPHIC REVOLUTION IN INDUSTRIAL SOCIETY

Behind modern technology's achievements is the scientific mode of thought with its organized rationality in approaching questions dealing with all spheres of human life and knowledge, a feature which Max Weber expressed as the "disenchantment of the world," the progressive extension of scientific ways of thought and action. The joint application of science and modern technology to the fields of disease, health, and standard of living has been responsible for a demographic revolution in the character of the populations of industrial societies. First, the control of epidemic disease and of the environment has made possible a lengthening of the life-span. This, however, has not been the major implication of scientific medicine. More significant is the fact that the number of persons who can attain a full life-span has been vastly increased through the reduction of mortality, especially in the earlier years of life.[9] This has meant a huge increase in the size of populations and has resulted in the avail-

[8] See chap. x.

[9] See chap. ii.

ability of more persons for longer periods of productive labor. With the changes in technology and productivity—now being dramatically accentuated by automation—the results have been fewer average hours of work per week, more average number of years in the labor force as a producer, and more years available for life in retirement after work (Wolfbein, 1959).[10]

Second, the continuing effects of this demographic revolution have provided further conditions conducive to the emergence of retirement in the context of the nature of the economy. As the immediate effect of

significant part of the composition of the population (Valaoras, 1958; Hauser and Vargas, 1960).[11]

This historical effect of reduced mortality in industrial societies has been accentuated by equally significant reductions in fertility resulting in a dramatic decline in the ratio of young dependent persons—defined as those under 20—to persons in the productive ages—those between 20 and 64. Thus, at the same time that medical and public health factors have given rise to an increasing number and proportion of adult and older persons, there has also been a

TABLE 2*

ANNUAL RATES OF GROWTH OF SELECTED ECONOMIC INDICATORS
1900–1970

(In 1958 Prices)

ECONOMIC INDICATOR	ANNUAL RATES OF GROWTH†			
	1900–1957	1949–57	1955–57 Average to 1965	1955–57 Average to 1970
Gross national product............	3.2	3.7	4.0	4.2
Personal expenditure per capita ...	1.4	1.8	2.4	2.6
Gross national product per man-hour	2.3	3.2	3.3	3.4

* Source: National Planning Association, *National Economic Projections, 1962–1965, 1970* (Washington, D.C.: The Association, 1959), p. 3.
† Projected rates based on judgment within high and low ranges.

decreased mortality is an increase in the number of those who live through childhood into the adult years and to old age, the structural effect is a resultant change in the proportions of young, adult, and aged persons in the population, the latter two gaining at the expense of the first. This phenomenon of changing age composition has been found to be closely correlated to the onset of industrialism and urbanism (especially in the period from 1850 to 1950) and has given rise to the demographic concept of the aging of populations (Valaoras, 1950, 1958; W. E. Moore, 1951; United Nations, 1956). It is only in industrial societies that the proportion of the aged, taken as those over 65, becomes a

striking decline in the proportion of younger persons, the net effect being an over-all decrease in the total ratio of dependent persons to those of working ages. The decrease between 1850 and 1950 was almost one-third, and since 1900 has been about one-fifth (W. E. Moore, 1951; Hauser and Shanas, 1952).[12] It is important in this context to note that the social cost of maintaining older persons is less than that of supporting dependent younger persons (Valaoras, 1958). Even taking the ratio of working persons to non-working persons at all ages and, thus, including non-employed women in the productive years in a class with non-working dependents, this decre-

[10] See chap. x.

[11] See chap. ii, Table 1.

[12] See chap. ii, Table 11; chap. v, Table 3.

ment in the dependent population was characteristic of the United States through 1950.[13]

Thus one factor in the ability of industrial societies to support retired older persons has been the decline in the total proportion of dependent persons of all ages. While the future status of this characteristic is a function of trends in fertility and mortality, projections of this ratio for the United States indicate that it will probably tend to increase slightly in the next half-century, as it has done in the past decade, but even so it will remain far below the ratios which existed 50 years ago.[14]

The interplay of technological and demographic factors, then, has not only made retirement possible as a practical matter but has, in fact, been an important element promoting the emergence of retirement in industrial societies.

C. Contribution of Changes in Social and Political Organization as a Consequence of Industrial Technology

As Cottrell (chap. iv) and Friedmann (chap. v) have pointed out, the rise of modern industrial technology has had far-reaching changes in the social organization of society. The fabric of social and institutional life has been greatly altered in response to the changing features of economy and industrial organization. It is important to recognize the part these changes have played in making possible the emergence of retirement.

RISE OF THE NATIONAL STATE

First, it must be recognized that the very nature of industrial production demands a rationally organized systematization of work and the economic market. The size and scale of modern technology inherently lead toward a more orderly control of all the factors involved in the total system of production, just as the machine system itself introduces this feature to the actual process of manufacture. Standardization, rationalization, and bureaucratic organization of the economic market are concomitants of industrial society. But the effects of industrialism do not stop at the market, for, in the process of rationalizing the market, the same processes take root in society.[15] Along with the rise of industrialism we have witnessed the rise of the national state as the dominant political form of societal organization, the governmental counterpart to the new forms of economic organization. It is with the organizational extension of social and political control by the national state that industrial society has come to maturity. The two are coextensive in modern history.

Without the effective organization of social and political life and its extension throughout the totality of society by the modern national state, neither the potentialities of modern technology nor those of public health and medical science could be realized. For it is only through this form of social organization that society can effectively integrate, utilize, and co-ordinate to the fullest advantage the complex character of industrial technology.

Likewise, it is only under the auspices of this form of social organization that the ability of modern industrial methods to support a large number of dependent older persons is capable of actuality. The realization of the potentialities in modern industrial society to support a segment of its population in retirement life requires a means of marshaling and pooling the necessary resources of the total society. No other institution than the national state has the requisite legitimate basis and apparatus to fill this function. It is no accident, then, that the beginnings of modern retirement should occur in the creation of general civil service pensions in England in 1810, followed by Germany in 1873, or that the beginnings of a general civil service retirement in the United States should lag until 1920, after most other advanced

[13] See chap. xiv, Table 4.

[14] See chap. ii, Table 11.

[15] See chap. xvii.

industrial societies had such programs, when one considers the relative role and status of the national government in these countries.

GROWTH OF NEW SOCIAL AND INSTITUTIONAL RELATIONSHIPS

Just as important as the ability of the national state to fulfil these functions in the practical sense is the changed relationship between the individual person and the more traditional institutional bonds of family, kin, and local community brought about by the rise of industrial society. As Cottrell (chaps. iv and xvii) points out, the disruption of traditional institutional functions of the family and local community has meant the creation of a new relationship between the individual and the national state. The state has assumed the maintenance and further development of functions once taken care of by other institutions now unable to fulfil them.

The rise to dominant form of the wage system of economic exchange as a consequence of the altered relation between man and the technological apparatus employed to support life meant the end of the traditional economic functions of the family. Likewise, the creation of mass industrial society spelled the death knell to the ability of the local community or the religious institution to perform its traditional roles of welfare and charity. At the same time the breakdown of the prime position of integral functioning roles in economic life, heralded by the division of labor into rational parts akin to the structure of the machine, provided the final step in the individualization of the person as a single component in the economic and social system. This profoundly altered the basis of the person's relation to society, emphasizing as never before the individual's rights and responsibilities as a distinct entity apart from the larger units of family, kin, or class. The requirements of industrial society transformed the traditional basis of social life (W. E. Moore, 1951).The decline of the family as an economic unit of production and the growth

of mobility and migration in the labor market, accompanied first by urbanization and now sub-urbanization and by individualization of dwelling units, transformed the underlying nature of family and kinship relationships, epitomized by Burgess and Locke's (1953) formulation, *The Family: From Institution to Companionship.* Thus the impact of economic individualism on family and kin relationships weakened the institutionally based and legitimized normative and moral claims of the individual for economic and social support from kinship units and set in motion the development of new relationships under the new conditions of social life created by industrialism.[16]

It is only in such a system of relationships that the individual person per se can come to have an institutionalized right to receive support from society apart from the particular function he serves, since all persons are equally, following Durkheim's conceptualization, organically interdependent parts of the total social system. It is, thus, toward the total system that we turn to deal with problems in its functioning which involve the society as a whole. Retirement, clearly a problem which faces society as a totality, could emerge only on a national level in consequence of a new legitimate institutional relationship between the individual citizen and the national state.

D. The Magnitude of Retirement Today

DEVELOPMENT OF RETIREMENT PROVISIONS

Before the introduction at the end of the thirties of the federal Social Security System, with its program of Old-Age and Survivors Insurance, retirement was almost non-existent as an institutionalized form of life for the great bulk of older persons in the United States. This was true despite the fact that, as early as 1900, almost one-third of all men 65 and over were no longer

[16] See chap. xiii for a discussion of contemporary patterns of family relationships.

in the labor force and thus could be considered "retired."[17] Except for the federal Civil Service Retirement System and other public employee pension schemes of states and local communities, the recently enacted Railroad Retirement System, and a small number of private pension schemes covering a relatively minor segment of the working population, no retirement provisions were in force for the mass of the labor force.

In 1926 a study of 370 existing pension schemes revealed a total of 3,300,000 workers covered and between 90,000 and 100,000 pensioners actually receiving benefits (Epstein, 1926). Most of these were non-contractual schemes and depended on the employer's initiative. Supplementing these, of the total of a hundred national and international labor unions in the United States in 1930, twelve had pension plans with a total of more than 13,000 pensioners. The ensuing depression wiped out some of these and made others financially shaky (Rubinow, 1933). These plans can be viewed against a non-agricultural labor force of 38.4 million in 1930.

In effect, therefore, only public welfare and private charity were available for the older person unable to work who had no available financial resources or sources of support, and public welfare was in its infancy. Outside the county almshouse or poor farm, there were no effective assistance programs for old age on the state level before 1928. In that year an estimated 1000 persons over 70 in the United States were recipients of state "old age pensions." This figure rose to 100,000 in 1932, of whom over half were in New York State. Three states (New York, Massachusetts, and California) accounted for almost 84 per cent of the total (Rubinow, 1933).

It is essential in this context to distinguish *retirement provisions* from *welfare assistance*. When one leaves the pure context of income maintenance for the older person, a fundamental difference in social role and status accrues between recipients

17 See chap. x, Table 4.

of "pensions" meted out in the form of welfare under conditions of proved destitution and recipients of retirement benefits or retirement pensions which accrue as *rights* of all members of a class defined as retired persons. This is crucial in differentiating the emergence of retirement as an institutionalized form of social life from an extension of traditional welfare or charity. It matters not what the precise definition or requirement of retirement is—by age, by labor-force participation, or by physical condition—the significant element is that it is retirement that is being defined as a social position and not financial dependency in old age. This is what distinguishes Old-Age and Survivors Insurance benefits from old age assistance and the various early state "pension" systems in the United States. European pension schemes, on the other hand, generally developed as true pensions in that they were universal to a defined category of pensioners and not conditional on financial need.

MATURATION OF THE INSTITUTIONAL
BASIS OF RETIREMENT LIFE

The population background of retirement shows that in 1900 there were 3.1 million persons 65 and over in the United States constituting 4.0 per cent of the total population. By 1930 the corresponding figures were 9.0 million and 5.3 per cent; in 1950 they were 12.3 million and 7.9 per cent; and by the end of 1958 they were 15.4 million and 8.7 per cent (Greville, 1957; U.S. Bureau of the Census, 1959). Estimates for the future indicate that by 1970 the population 65 and over will be in the neighborhood of 20 million and between 9.5 and 10 per cent of the total population, depending on differing assumptions of fertility and mortality in the coming years (Greville, 1957).

Thus both the absolute numbers of the aging and their proportion have shown remarkable increases in the last 60 years. Projections for the near future indicate the persistence of this new demographic characteristic, although there seems reason to conclude that we have reached a point where future increases in number will be of lesser magnitude and where changes in the proportion of older persons will be relatively small.[18]

Against the background of these demographic facts, the trends in the development of the retirement role are of equal magnitude. The increases in life-expectancy have meant a greater number of years available for retirement life, and the trend toward earlier retirement ages has heightened this phenomenon.[19] However, before

[18] See chap. ii. [19] See chap. x.

1940 only a privileged few could meaningfully look forward to a life in retirement which did not mean becoming dependent on family, kin, or friends, seeking public assistance, or turning to private charity. For the vast majority retirement was a dreaded period signifying the end of social usefulness in society whether because of sickness, infirmity, or inability to maintain employment.

At the end of 1934 it is estimated that about half of all persons 65 and over were mainly or wholly dependent on relatives or friends for support (Epstein *et al.*, 1955).

TABLE 3*

PERSONS 65 YEARS OLD AND OVER RECEIVING MONEY INCOME FROM SPECIFIED SOURCES
1948, 1950, 1956, AND 1958†

SOURCE OF INCOME	NO. OF PERSONS (IN MILLIONS)				PER CENT DISTRIBUTION			
	1948	1950	1956	1958	1948	1950	1956	1958
Total‡	11.5	12.5	14.8	15.4	100.0	100.0	100.0	100.0
1. Employment	3.8	3.8	4.1	3.7	33.2	30.8	27.7	23.9
Wage-earners	2.9	2.9	3.2	2.8	25.4	23.6	21.5	18.3
Non-working wives of wage-earners	0.9	0.9	0.9	0.9	7.8	7.2	6.2	5.7
2. Social insurance and related programs§	2.3	3.6	8.2	10.8	20.2	28.5	55.9	70.4
Old-Age, Survivors, and Disability Insurance	1.5	2.6	7.0	9.2	12.7	20.7	47.3	60.0
Railroad retirement insurance	0.3	0.4	0.5	0.6	2.6	3.0	3.5	3.8
Government employees' retirement programs	0.3	0.4	0.6	0.8	2.6	3.0	4.4	5.1
Veterans' compensation and pension programs	0.3	0.4	0.9	1.2	3.0	3.1	6.2	8.1
3. Public assistance‖	2.4	2.8	2.6	2.5	20.8	22.5	17.4	16.3
4. No money income or income solely from other sources	3.4	3.1	2.4	1.6	29.4	25.2	16.4	10.5
5. Income from more than one of specified sources	0.4	0.9	2.6	3.2	3.6	7.0	17.4	21.1
Employment and social insurance or assistance	0.3	0.5	2.0	#	2.3	4.3	13.5	#
Social insurance and public assistance	0.1	0.3	0.6	#	1.3	2.7	3.8	#

* Sources: U.S. Bureau of the Census, *Statistical Abstract of the United States, 1959* (Washington, D.C.: Government Printing Office, 1959), p. 271; Lenore A. Epstein, "Money Income of Aged Persons: A 10-Year Review, 1948–1958," *Social Security Bulletin*, 22 (June, 1959), 4, Table 2.

† As of June for 1948; December for 1950, 1956, and 1958; partly estimated. Includes Alaska, Hawaii, Puerto Rico, and Virgin Islands for 1956 and 1958. Data for 1958 are preliminary.

‡ Total population 65 and over is less than sum of the first four major classifications by the number in the fifth; persons with more than one major source of income were counted under each appropriate classification and then classified separately. Persons with income from sources specified may also have income from other sources (e.g., private pensions or interest, dividends, and other returns on investment).

§ Persons with income from more than one program counted only once. In addition, unemployment insurance, workmen's compensation, and temporary disability insurance provided income for an unknown number; overlap with other programs cannot be estimated. Includes the estimated number of male beneficiaries' wives not in direct receipt of benefits.

‖ Old age assistance recipients and persons aged 65 and over receiving aid to the blind and aid to the permanently and totally disabled. Includes a small number of persons receiving vendor payments for medical care but no direct cash payment.

Not available.

While old age assistance began to relieve the burden on individuals shortly thereafter, it was not until 1940 that the retirement provisions of Old-Age and Survivors Insurance became operative. By the end of 1940 an estimated 600,000 older persons in the United States, approximately 7 per cent of those 65 and over, were receiving various forms of social insurance retirement benefits, of whom about 100,000 were Old-Age and Survivors Insurance recipi-

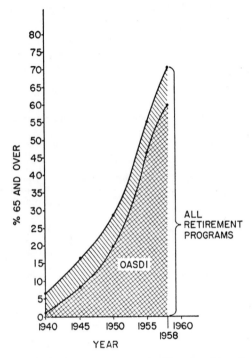

FIG. 1.—Percentage persons 65 years old and over receiving retirement income from OASDI and related programs, 1940–58. (After Table 3 and various reports of the U.S. Social Security Administration.)

ents. Between 1940 and 1945 there was a steady growth in the institutional basis of retirement life, so that at the end of 1945 there was a total of 1.7 million aged persons, or 17 per cent of those 65 and over, receiving retirement benefits, with 800,000 recipients of OASI. From 1948 on there was a dramatic leap in the growth of retirement recipients. The extent of this development of retirement life can be gauged from the figures in Table 3, which show

the tremendous changes in the number and more significantly the proportion of older persons living under retirement provisions as Old-Age and Survivors Insurance came to maturity following the almost complete universalization which took place in the 1950's (Cohen, 1959).

These figures show that in a period of 10 years, from 1948 to 1958, the number of persons 65 and over receiving income from retirement benefits has grown from 2.3 million to 10.8 million, or from 20.2 per cent to 70.4 per cent of those 65 and over. Of these, the greatest number (amounting to 85 per cent) are beneficiaries of the current federal Old-Age, Survivors, and Disability Insurance system.

In the 18-year period from 1940 to 1958, then, we have witnessed the establishment of an institutional basis of retirement life as the number of older persons receiving retirement income has grown from 600,000 to 10.8 million or from 7 per cent to 70 per cent of those 65 and over. In this process OASDI grew from a base of 100,000 persons, or 1 per cent, to 9.2 million, or 60 per cent, of the aged population to assume the position of the basic economic institutional foundation of the social phenomenon of retirement (see Fig. 1). It should be noted that it was not until 1951 that the number of aged persons receiving income from OASDI retirement provisions exceeded the number receiving public assistance. And it was not until 1953 that OASDI assumed its role as the primary source of income for persons 65 and over (Anonymous, 1953). Finally, it was in 1954 that we reached the historical point where a majority of the aged were receiving income from all the various retirement benefit sources, and it was in 1957 that a majority were recipients of OASDI benefits.

DECLINE OF EMPLOYMENT OF THE AGED

While there has come to be a considerable degree of overlapping in sources of income, the one of real interest is that between employment and receipt of retirement benefits. Here the basic fact is that, despite the large rise in the total number of persons 65 and over in the period from 1948 to 1958, the number using income from employment has slightly declined in absolute terms from 3.8 to 3.7 million while decreasing more than one-fourth in proportion. Furthermore, according to Epstein (1959), "of the 3.7 million [in 1958] who had earnings or were non-working wives of earners, it is estimated that almost 2.5 million were receiving social insurance benefits and therefore did not rely primarily on earnings for their livelihood" (p. 3).

The differential between men and women is an important facet of this picture (Table 4). As our aged population is increasingly a female one—witness the increase in the proportion of women in the 65-and-over population from 52.3 to 54.4 per cent in the 10-year period 1948–59—the over-all importance of employment declines slightly

TABLE 4*

ESTIMATED NUMBER OF PERSONS AGED 65 AND OVER RECEIVING MONEY INCOME
FROM SPECIFIED SOURCES, BY SEX, JUNE, 1948, AND JUNE, 1958†

SOURCE OF MONEY INCOME‡	NUMBER (IN THOUSANDS)				PERCENTAGE DISTRIBUTION			
	Men		Women		Men		Women	
	1948	1958	1948	1958	1948	1958	1948	1958
1. Population aged 65 and over, total	5500	6930	6040	8260	100.0	100.0	100.0	100.0
2. Employment	2410	2310	1420	1640	43.8	33.3	23.5	19.9
Wage-earners	2410	2310	520	760	43.8	33.3	8.6	9.2
Non-working wives of wage-earners	......	......	900	880	......	......	14.9	10.7
3. Social insurance and related programs§	1290	5220	1040	5140	23.4	75.3	17.2	62.2
Old-Age, Survivors, and Disability Insurance	830	4440	630	4400	15.1	64.1	10.4	53.3
Railroad retirement program	180	300	120	280	3.3	4.3	2.0	3.4
Government employees' retirement programs	160	400	140	350	2.9	5.8	2.3	4.2
Veterans' compensation and pensions	170	660	180	500	3.1	9.5	3.0	6.1
4. Public assistance‖	1060	960	1340	1560	19.3	13.9	22.2	18.9
5. No money income or income solely from other sources	1040	120	2360	1380	18.9	1.7	39.1	16.7
6. Income from more than one of sources in lines 2–4	300	1680	120	1460	5.4	24.2	2.0	17.7
OASDI and employment# Other programs and employment#	210	{990 380}	60	{910 220}	3.8	{14.3 5.5}	1.0	{11.0 2.7}
Old age assistance and OASDI Other assistance and OASDI or related programs	90	{300 10}	60	{310 20}	1.6	{4.3 0.1}	1.0	{3.8 0.2}

* Source: Lenore A. Epstein, "Money Income of Aged Persons: A 10-Year Review, 1948–1958," *Social Security Bulletin,* 22 (June, 1959), 4, Table 2.

† Data for 1958 for the continental United States, Alaska, Hawaii, Puerto Rico, and the Virgin Islands; data for 1948 for the continental United States. Persons with income from sources specified may also have received money income from other sources, such as interest, dividends, private pensions or annuities, or cash contributions from relatives.

‡ Because persons frequently have income from more than one of the sources specified, the sum of persons shown on lines 2–5 exceeds the total number in the population (line 1). The estimates of persons with income from more than one source are developed from survey data and are therefore subject to sampling and reporting errors, as well as the error inherent in projecting survey findings to additional population groups and different dates—errors that are relatively more significant in the case of small estimates.

§ Persons with income from more than one of the programs listed are counted only once. Unemployment insurance, workmen's compensation, and temporary disability insurance programs also provided income for an unknown number. Estimates of women beneficiaries under the railroad program (1948) and government employees' retirement and veterans' programs (1948 and 1958) include the estimated number of beneficiaries' wives not in direct receipt of benefits.

‖ Old age assistance recipients and persons aged 65 and over receiving aid to the blind or to the permanently and totally disabled; includes a small number receiving vendor payments for medical care but no direct cash payment.

Excludes a small number with income from employment and OASDI and another insurance or related program; the figures on line 3 have already been adjusted for overlap among the insurance and related programs.

because of the lower labor-force participation of women. The predominance of women in the retirement population has created special problems in a system where retirement benefits are linked to employment life and where women derive benefits basically as wives or survivors of workers at reduced benefit levels (Cohen, 1957).[20] The effect can be seen in the differential changes between men and women in sources of income shown in Table 4. In the 10-year period between 1948 and 1958 covered, both the number and the proportion of men 65 and over receiving income from public assistance, or having no money income, or deriving income solely from sources other than employment, retirement benefits, or public assistance, declined, the latter especially sharply. This occurred in the face of an increase of over 25 per cent in the total number of men 65 and over. In the case of women the number receiving public assistance rose, although the proportion of both of the above categories declined, but the amount of decline was much smaller than in the case of men.

PLACE OF PRIVATE PENSIONS

In 1958, private pension plans were providing only 1¼ million persons with income. Of these, it is estimated that 80 per cent were also Old-Age, Survivors, and Disability Insurance beneficiaries. This can be compared with a total of 400,000 receiving private pensions in 1948 who were much less likely to be also Old-Age and Survivors Insurance beneficiaries (Epstein, 1959). While the growth of private pension schemes, highlighted by the union-management plans, has been an important development in the postwar years,[21] they have remained subsidiary to the federal program as supplementary means of improving the economic status of the retired. Their future remains a subject of great importance in

the development of more adequate retirement income,[22] and the significance of their role in moving toward a more suitable retirement system for society as a whole is a currently evolving issue (Holland, 1959).

THE FUTURE PICTURE

Estimates for the future indicate that, by 1970, 74.4 per cent of those 65 and over will be receiving Old-Age, Survivors, and Disability Insurance benefits, so that we might conservatively estimate that 80 per cent of all persons 65 and over will be receiving retirement income of one form or another (U.S. Social Security Administration, 1959). It is this group of approximately 16 million persons which will constitute the basic retirement population of 1970, and nothing can better convey the dimensions of the emergence of retirement and its social magnitude than the growth of this social position from a bare handful at the beginnings of the 1940's.

E. Résumé

In summary, industrial society has given birth to retirement through the following:

1. The creation of a state of technology based on the scientific approach to knowledge which has shattered and continues to shatter prior conceptions of the potentialities for the production of the food and goods necessary for the sustenance and improvement of the conditions of life. One part of this has been the development, since Pasteur's germ theory of disease, of a scientific approach to the control and prevention of illness which has all but eliminated the existence of epidemic pestilence.

2. The development and extension of political and social order through powerful national states. This in itself is a corollary of the growth of rational methods of economic life inherent in industrialization, which have been able through modern tech-

[20] See chap. xiv.

[21] See chap. xiv.

[22] See chap. viii.

nology and communication to exercise an ever increasing degree of purposeful control of man's natural and social environment over a vast area of the earth.

3. A unique demographic revolution in man's history which has witnessed the growth of human population in the last 100 years in a measure unheard of in all previous time. This, as industrial societies have matured, has ushered in the phenomenon of the aging of the population.

4. The reorganization of man's economic and social life as a consequence of the new system of production and consumption into a distinctly new set of social roles based on an altered relation between man and the tools he works with and in consequence the manner and form in which he reaps the rewards of his labor. The industrial system of economic life with its rational division of labor, separation of the laborer from control of the instruments of production, and wage system of economic exchange have altered the older systems of social relationships which were built upon the existing state of economy and profoundly changed the structure of the institutional arrangements in man's life.

While the first and third of these aspects of modern society are the most basic and dramatic of the underlying factors making possible the emergence of retirement, the second and fourth are structurally the key to its appearance. Without the rational organization of social life represented by the development of powerful centralized governments, the potentialities inherent in modern technology and science could not have been exercised, nor could their benefits have been pooled to assure a means of supporting the vast populations that have arisen.

It is only in consequence of these changed relationships, too, that we can comprehend the value orientations which underlie the specific forms of retirement systems and retirement policies that have arisen and continue to develop and the controversies which they have engendered.

III. SOCIETAL VALUE ORIENTATIONS AND RETIREMENT POLICIES AND ATTITUDES

A. The Question of Underlying Values and Social Philosophy

PRACTICAL CONTEXT OF RETIREMENT-POLICY ISSUES

The discussion of retirement attitudes and the consideration of retirement policies in the United States have generally taken place in the context of the "giveness" of the empirical data. The entire process has been marked by a reflection of the essentially pragmatic approach which has characterized our development of social security. Although the historical literature makes it abundantly clear that the pioneers and innovators of retirement proposals were not unaware of underlying value orientations and social philosophies, practical considerations of a political and economic nature have dominated the environment in which positive action has occurred. The result has been that basic questions of values and philosophy have for the most part been submerged and reduced to a series of specific policy issues, quite in keeping with the traditional pragmatism found in American life. It has also been pointed out that this has been generally true to a certain degree in retirement programs in other nations, where questions of values and philosophy were often more a matter of debate than actual guideposts (Twentieth Century Fund, 1937). This did not, however, in the United States prevent the intrusion of value questions in the resolution of many of the policy questions, just as philosophical orientations marked the pre-legislative stage of debate.[23]

The adoption of the Social Security Act of 1935 came at a time when the United

[23] Excellent summaries of these policy issues and discussions of the way in which value orientations did intrude at various stages of their resolution can be found in Corson and McConnell (1956) and Cohen (1957, 1959). Douglas (1936) also discusses the manner in which tactical questions overrode basic issues of values and philosophy.

States found itself in the midst of one of the direst economic and social straits in its history. The problems of the great depression of the thirties had come to dominate the life of our nation, and in the forefront of these was unemployment. At the same time there was a great interest and concern over old age security, partially a consequence of the spectacular national rise of the Townsend Movement in the summer of 1934 (Douglas, 1936; Witte, 1955).

Traditional American values opposing any government action or interference in the economic or social system embodied in the notion of laissez faire, and the strong separation of federal and state powers under the banner of state rights, had hitherto prevented any substantial action by the national government in the area of social welfare. Under the impact of the depression, however, the breakthrough came, not easily by any means, or completely, as the history of the court battles of the thirties makes evident. Each act of the government was taken separately and, in typical pragmatic fashion, judged separately. The expansion of the concept of the general welfare powers of the federal government achieved no positive philosophical development. Instead, what occurred was the cracking of the wall resisting any action. The effect on the development of retirement was a failure to create a generalized value orientation, a fact which, we shall see, has affected the development of social attitudes toward retirement.

POLICY BACKGROUND OF OASDI

Commentators of the present often discuss the retirement system of OASDI as though it had been consciously evolved and expressly designed to fit in with traditional American values such as individualism, encouragement of self-reliance, thrift, and earning what one receives in place of getting a "handout" or charity (Larson, 1955). In point of fact, as detailed in contemporary accounts (Douglas, 1936) or recent recollections (Witte, 1955), the specific form of the unique self-supporting contributory system of OASDI had its roots in a number of practical considerations present in the depression. Its character conflicted with the views of the leaders of the American movement for old age pensions as well as with the views of organized labor (Rubinow, 1934).

OASDI was originally evolved, in the words of Witte (1955), "as a program that would help keep the financial burden of providing necessary economic support for the increasing number of old people within manageable limits" (p. 14). In other words, the system began as a means of lessening the potential burden which old age assistance costs would incur for the federal and state governments. In order to avoid direct federal contributions, the contribution rates of employees and employers were set higher than originally proposed but kept low enough so that they would not be too much of a burden in the period of depression. Large groups of workers and the self-employed were excluded because of the administrative complexities that were foreseen and their resultant high costs (Douglas, 1936; Witte, 1955). A similar concern for nationalizing the unequal costs of welfare to local communities underlay the original German contributory pension system enacted under Bismarck (Grant, 1939). The limitations of the role of OASDI are most clearly seen by the original extent of its coverage, and early commentators were quick to point out the problems of operating two systems, OASDI and Old Age Assistance, which represented different philosophies of dealing with the problem of economic security for the aged (Twentieth Century Fund, 1937). On the one hand, old age assistance continued the separation of federal and state powers and provided welfare assistance based on need. Thus poor-law connotations remained, since state laws generally provided for enforced contributions by the family when judged available, requiring proof of family as well as individual indigence. On the other hand, OASDI established a fully federal system which bypassed the states and established retirement benefits based on institutionalized right irrespective of need.

Having established a system organized on social insurance principles, a practical provision was inserted which has provided a continued source of controversy—the retirement test.[24] The purposes of the retirement test were to relieve the costs of the program in its early stages by excluding those who, while otherwise eligible for benefits, still held jobs and to provide a stimulus for opening up work opportunities for younger workers through inducements for older workers to retire. The latter could not be entirely meaningful while so large a proportion of the labor force remained uncovered by OASDI. This key provision of OASDI has been an important issue in the development of institutionalized retirement, since it controverts the basic insurance principle by denying what are otherwise seen as entitled rights at a given age. It has no fundamental philosophical connection to retirement policy other than monetary cost, since at age 72 it is removed. Accordingly, it has been criticized from its inception (Douglas, 1936) and has been progressively modified in a direction which suggests its eventual removal. Arguments for and against such provisions in retirement systems have always been presented in the context of a given labor-market situation (Wilson and Mackay, 1941), the purpose being either to expand work opportunities for younger workers or to keep older workers employed for longer periods.

The major point to be drawn from this discussion is the underscoring of the pragmatic, economics-orientated approach which has dominated the legislative enactments, giving rise to an institutional system that has come to assume such importance in our society today. In its wake there has been little basic philosophical recasting of the fundamental social values involved. And, in consequence, there has been continuing lack of clarity as to the basic social meaning of retirement as an institutional form

[24] See chap. viii.

of social life and failure to cast policy issues into consistent value positions. The result is a confounding of values on many specific questions, such as compulsory retirement, and a lack of a positive societal orientation toward retirement which would serve as a basic source of attitudes to those entering retirement life, replacing older, traditional attitudes geared to the "metaphysical drive to work" evolving out of the Protestant ethic (Williams, 1951).

For retirement does involve basic value orientations or value positions of a societal and individual nature which cannot be ignored if a consistent role and position for the retired is to be created and which should be taken into consideration in the discussion and formulation of retirement policies.

B. Societal Value Orientations toward Retirement Life

TRADITIONAL AMERICAN VALUES

Before 1935 a number of specific value elements in American life supported by the prosperity of the twenties had effectively combined to produce a basic philosophical orientation opposed to social welfare of the sort necessary to establish a system of institutionalized retirement. Laissez faire, state rights, individualism, the pioneer vision of unlimited opportunity, the Protestant ethic of success through work—all combined in an era of material wealth to oppose the intervention of government in the field of human welfare. Against this strong traditional value orientation, views asserting the social character of modern society and proclaiming the social responsibility of man made little headway. Retirement pension schemes of a social nature were opposed as socialistic and un-American, as were social welfare programs in general. The emphasis was on voluntary and private action, and such private pensions as were instituted were linked to the individual employer's own concern for his limited family of employees and the effects on his own enterprise. There was no generalized social concern (Corson and Mc-Connell, 1956). A good example of this kind of view can be found expressed by the report of the National Industrial Conference Board (1925), wherein it is suggested that governmental action to provide pensions for old age would result in administration fraught with "waste, extravagance, and corruption" and argued that "such an extension of state activity is to be avoided, if possible, and combated, if necessary, as socialist and mischievous."

That such views could continue to be expressed with conviction even during the depths of the depression was an indication of the ideological gulf that had grown between the United States and the other advanced industrial nations of the world. Their greater historical experience with limited private pensions, state-encouraged and state-subsidized voluntary societies' funds, and even voluntary governmental pension systems had led them to state systems of old age and retirement benefits (Twentieth Century Fund, 1937; Grant, 1939; Wilson and Mackay, 1941; de Schweinitz, 1947). We need but contrast the words of President Herbert Hoover to the effect that "out of savings individuals must provide for their own security" with the views of Winston Churchill (1909) almost a quarter of a century earlier:

I do not agree with those who say that every man must look after himself, and that the intervention by the State in such matters as I have referred to will be fatal to his self-reliance, his foresight, and his thrift. . . . If terror be an incentive to thrift, surely the penalties of the system which we have abandoned ought to have stimulated thrift as much as anything could have been stimulated in this world. The mass of the laboring poor have known that unless they made provision for their old age betimes they would perish miserably in the workhouse. Yet they have made no such provision . . . for they have never been able to make such provision. . . . It is a great mistake to suppose that thrift is caused only by fear; it springs from hope as well as fear; where there is no hope, be sure there will be no thrift [pp. 208–10].

THE EXPERIENCE OF GERMANY

Two decades earlier, Bismarck in Germany had come to similar conclusions. There a unique set of conditions combined to produce the first national system of institutionalized retirement, following earlier experiments in individual industries and with voluntary programs (Grant, 1939). Epstein (1938) cites Rubinow's explanation of Germany's pre-eminence as based on three closely connected factors: first, the distinction of Germany's being the country of greatest industrial growth in the second half of the nineteenth century on the Continent; second, the German conception of the state as developed by German philosophy which rejected the doctrine of laissez faire; and, third, the rapid development of the labor movement under various shadings of socialist banners with its program of social reform. Nowhere are the reasons for adoption of the retirement insurance program more clearly stated than in Bismarck's own messages to the Reichstag. He clearly delineates the changed nature of social life under the impetus of industrialism and the wage-labor system; he explicitly defines the role of the national state as a positive force acting to protect and enhance the rights and position of the laboring classes so as to gain their loyalty and support; he openly proposes the reforms as a means of state preservation and promotion of internal peace and welfare in addition to the repressive measures previously taken against the revolutionary aspects of the workers' movements; and, finally, he clearly espouses the notion of retirement benefits as an earned social right of the citizen of labor on a par with the already accepted right of the soldier to a pension as a matter of social reward due for service to society.

The workers' real complaint results from the insecurity of their livelihood; they cannot be certain that they will always be employed; they cannot be certain that they will always enjoy good health and they know that one day they will be old and unable to work . . . and society does not really recognize any obligation towards them apart from the common Poor Law provisions, however loyally and industrially any particular worker may have worked in the past.

. . . These classes must through direct and noticeable advantages bestowed upon them by legislation be brought to look upon the State as not merely an institution invented for the protection of the more well-to-do classes of society, but one that also serves their interests and needs by securing for them direct and tangible advantages through legislative measures. . . .

Greater care than has hitherto been exercised by the State for its needy citizens is not only a humanitarian and Christian duty of which all State institutions should be conscious, it is also a task of State preservation, the aim of which is to foster amongst those classes of society that are without property and at the same time the most numerous and the least informed, the view that the State is not only a necessary but also a beneficent institution. . . .

The remedy of social ills cannot be exclusively achieved through the repression of Social Democratic excesses but must at the same time envisage constructive measures for the improvement of the worker's welfare. We regard it as Our Imperial duty again to charge the Reichstag with this task and we should review with greater satisfaction the successes with which God has visibly blessed Our reign if We could one day be certain to have left to Our Fatherland new and permanent guarantees for its internal peace and to those in need that greater security and more generous assistance to which they are entitled [Braun, 1956, pp. 74–76].

The State must take the matter into its own hands, not as alms giving but as the right that men have to be taken care of when, from no fault of their own, they have become unfit for work. Why should regular soldiers and officials have old age pensions, and not the soldier of labour? This thing will make its own way: it has a future [Wilson and Mackay, 1941, p. 14].

SOCIAL RESPONSIBILITY AND SOCIAL JUSTICE CONCEPTS

Bismarck's projection of the role of the national state and his reference to the "soldiers of labor" serve to introduce the underlying frame of reference for societal value orientations toward retirement life. Fundamentally, the basic question is that which forms the basis for all social action by society as a whole for the maintenance and promotion of the general welfare: the responsibility of society for the welfare of all its members, both individually and collectively. This raises the problem of determining how such responsibility is best effected, and it is here that the role of the state and the nature of the relationship between the individual and the state come to the foreground.

These issues were raised in modern form almost from the beginnings of the industrial revolution in the middle of the eighteenth century, although there were earlier sources in seventeenth century England (Wilson and Mackay, 1941). In the classic study of the beginnings of intellectual ferment on social issues by Halévy (1955), however, there appears but one reference to a proposal for retirement among all the various social reform schemes. This was the suggestion of Tom Paine, as early as 1796, that society should provide annual pensions for all its members over the age of 50 in recognition of the contribution of their lifetime's labor to the material basis of social progress and the future wealth of society.

The basic themes of social *justice* and social *responsibility* became the twin cornerstones of the various nineteenth-century radical, reform, and revolutionary social movements which eventuated in the development of modern systems of social security. But the differing sources of values in justice or responsibility motivating these movements have given rise to differing bases of orientations upon which the systems are constructed. These, in turn, have given rise to varying interpretations of the nature and purpose of these systems.

We can roughly classify the value orientations underlying retirement systems into a polar typology of "positive" and "negative" orientations with the realization that many systems actually exhibit a mixed or eclectic combination of values. The orientations are "positive" or "negative" primarily in terms of the degree to which they view state action as a positive instrument of societal policy for the benefit of the individual, providing both security and opportunity for the individual's development of his own potentialities. Closely linked to this is the question of whether this action is seen as based upon a legitimate claim of the individual on society in consequence of the contributions of a lifetime of productive labor (i.e., social justice). Variations of a "positive" orientation can occur along the lines of whether society or the individual is the primary object of consideration; for example, contrast Bismarck's emphasis on state preservation with the Scandinavian emphasis of the individual as presented below. Examples of the contrast between positive and negative orientations may be seen in the following statements:

The hazards of life with which Social Security deals result in intensely human problems involving individuals. Yet we should understand that the interest of society as a whole in dealing with these problems is not primarily in the individual as a person, but rather in protecting society itself against the consequences which would otherwise flow from these individual tragedies. The test of the measure of social action needed in a particular situation is not basically the same test as the individual might apply but what is necessary to achieve the protection of society as a whole [Lincoln, 1952, p. 19].

All of these have a common aim: to *build* better, healthier, and stronger human beings. . . . Bear ye one another's burdens . . . [Tegner, 1956, pp. 13–14].

. . . The underlying conviction is that society should be so organized as to ensure to any member a reasonable measure of security and well-being [Nelson, 1953, p. 7].

The first statement is a view by a former chairman of the board of the Metropolitan Life Insurance Company on the American system; the latter two are statements on the Swedish and Danish systems of social security. The way in which these underlying orientations result in differing approaches to the issues of retirement policy has been clearly put by Shenfield (1957):

Are pensions to be regarded as a way of discharging a community responsibility to those unable to maintain themselves in the same way that support is organized for other disabled persons, or are they a reward for a lifetime of effort, a kind of deferred pay to which everyone should be entitled after a named period of work attendance and contributions? If the latter, then pension schemes should create a right to retirement for all workers on a pension which is adequate to meet their basic needs, while they enjoy their well-earned rest. Those who choose voluntarily to continue to work should gain, either by receiving pension and wages, or by a deferred larger pension ultimately drawn, in recognition of the surrender of leisure which might otherwise have been enjoyed. The notion of creating a "right" to a pension at a certain age is emphasized by the device of insurance as a method of financing old age [pp. 103–4].

What Shenfield is stressing is the distinction between an approach to retirement which still maintains an element of welfare assistance in its orientation and one which has substituted a clearly institutionalized right as its basic orientation. But, as she points out, old age as a disabling condition, preventing continued employment, is fundamentally different from other social insurance in that it is in no way unexpected but something foreseeable; and, to a certain extent, retirement is a matter of voluntary choice.

RETIREMENT AS AN INSTITUTIONALIZED SOCIAL RIGHT

If retirement systems are organized on an insurance basis, or if the philosophy underlying them involves the notion of a social reward, then they should tend to provide a reasonable measure of income for a standard level of living in contrast to assistance which basically provides a minimum subsistence level. In fact, the Swedish and German systems have moved in this direction. Achinger (1959) cites the official pronouncement of the German Federal Republic (West Germany): "A pension is no longer a grant-in-aid towards a person's subsistence, but will in future ensure maintenance of the living standard acquired" (p. 26).

In the United States, on the other hand, although our system has a dual character of insurance plus assistance (Schottland, 1959), it has steadily moved in the direction of a single universal insurance system. Nevertheless, the underlying orientation has remained officially one of providing "basic subsistence" rather than filling the total need (Folsom, 1955). However, it has been suggested that the implications of the trends involved in the growth of private pension systems to close this gap between subsistence and total need may result in a re-evaluation along the lines of the Swedish, German, and, more recently, the British systems (Holland, 1959). The question of the extent to which society is willing to underwrite the costs of a retirement system is a matter basically of social priorities, as Corson and McConnell (1956) have pointed out. But Abel-Smith (1959) has argued that this requires a clear understanding of what is actually involved in the social cost, which may often be clouded by social values and attitudes. What we have tried to show is that fundamental to the entire question of social values and priorities is the underlying value orientation regarding the nature of retirement.[25]

In this light, the long-range development of our retirement system will undoubtedly tend more and more to assume entirely the character of a government function as it moves in the direction of providing an adequate economic basis for the years in retirement, a direction which is evident today. How long this will take depends upon the politics of aging as well as trends in the field of private pensions.

Under present laws in the United States, private pension plans are indirectly subsidized by the government and, thus, the general public through the allowance of tax deductions for employer's contributions to such funds. Witte (1951) points out that, in the most extreme case, up to 85 per cent of the cost of industrial pensions would come from the federal government in the form of tax losses, while in the more normal case about half of the cost is so derived. The effect at present is a situation whereby employees of large companies organized in strong unions are in a more favorable position to derive adequate retirement benefits at the expense of the general public. Just as the recent Swedish system of universal work-related pensions has moved to correct this source of inequity while raising pensions to an adequate level, it has been stated that the long-range goal of organized labor in the United States is an eventual elimination of private plans in favor of a single comprehensive compulsory government system financed by employer and employee contributions with government support and supervision, an expanded version of OASDI (Henson, 1951). An approach like this can be seen to represent the culmination of the "positive" orientation toward the nature of retirement.

[25] Thus, for example, the systems of the Soviet Union and the eastern European countries following it have, in *theory*, centralized the notion of retirement as social reward not only by providing for a maintenance of retirement income based on lifetime earnings which themselves are supposed to reflect social effort but also by providing differential requirements of the number of years of work required and differing percentages of lifetime earnings in retirement pensions. These differences are based on the hazardous nature of the work performed and the greater personal risk and, thus, the social contribution undertaken (U.S. Social Security Administration, 1958).

Along the same lines, Cohen (1957) reports the action of the European regional conference of the International Labour Organization in 1955, which attempted to formulate principles to guide countries in developing more flexible arrangements for retirement. The first point stated that "legislation should provide for every worker who has completed a full working-life to be able to retire and rest with adequate pension"; the third point spoke of the provision of lower ages of retirement for those engaged in more arduous and hazardous occupations.

C. The Relation of Value Orientations to Policy Questions and Social Attitudes

ECONOMIC POLICIES AND SOCIAL ATTITUDES

Although the economic aspect of retirement life is only one part of the over-all question, it has been emphasized, because in the money economies of the industrial world value orientations are directly linked to and expressed in terms of policy priorities in the economic sphere. Retirement in the modern world could hardly become a valued social role without a legitimately defined basis of economic independence and self-respect for the individual. Indeed, a basic research question involves discovering to what extent the fuller development of institutionalized rights and adequate benefits of an economic nature contribute to the general growth of the status of the retirement role and positive social attitudes toward retirement. It has long been taken for granted that an adequate economic foundation for retirement life is the prerequisite of the development of other social aspects.

Furthermore, one of the basic viewpoints underlying the whole range of American social security programs has been that of the "wage-loss" offset concept. According to this view, the insurance basis of different social security programs, including retirement, is founded on a theory of partially offsetting the wage loss which the individual and his dependents may suffer through conditions beyond their control. The costs of these programs are shared on a social basis through various procedures, all of which ultimately are passed on to society at large through taxes or the cost of goods and services. This essentially parallels Shenfield's (1957) notion of community responsibility. But a tendency has developed for some of these benefits, especially evident in the case of old age insurance, to be regarded as institutionalized social rights. This is understandable when we realize that the insurance basis of the OASDI system provides a source of values conflicting with the pure wage-loss notion. More directly, the contemplated use and function of the OASDI to stimulate retirement to relieve employment pressures suggest a much broader social policy than that entailed by the wage-loss insurance.

If pure wage-loss principles governed the system, voluntary retirement for reasons other than health should not be recognized, and it is difficult to see how self-employed persons could be meaningfully included. Obviously, here is a situation where lack of clarity on basic value orientations toward retirement have led to situations of potential conflict concerning social policy. Except for the general approval of the federal retirement system as a broad institutionalization of social rights involving some elements of social reward, the universalization of the 1950's would have met with great opposition, since it involves changes from the original strict insurance basis to a more general social principle (Cohen, 1957).

THE BLANKETING-IN QUESTION

The universalization of the 1950's extended the original principle of compulsory retirement insurance for those who needed it because of the conditions of their employment position to all the productive sectors of society save one—the self-employed physician. In universalizing OASDI, retirement rights were in effect socialized. The presumption was not that all the newly covered categories needed retirement insurance but that they were entitled to the same rights and privileges as those already covered by OASDI. One consequence of the procedures taken for universalization was that large numbers of self-employed persons were allowed to join the system for a token period of coverage and then retire with full benefits. Few let this opportunity pass unheeded, and especially in the case of the farmer a tremendous instrument for change in retirement attitudes was presented (Sewell *et al.*, 1953; Galloway,

1955). Although technically this action represented conformance with the insurance principle, in effect it can be seen as amounting to a form of social justice. The principled rationale held that a new system requires some inequity at the start if it is to begin at full levels of benefit, and there was not a great deal of opposition.

However, proposals suggesting the blanketing-in to OASDI of those aged persons who for one reason or another missed coming under coverage because of the nature of the original laws or their age meet resistance offered in terms of maintaining the insurance principle (Larson, 1955). Obviously, if social policy wished to, it could find some legitimate basis for extending the insurance principle to these people, even if done *ex post facto*, without destroying the basic principles of the system. The major problem would rather seem to be a question of values relating to the amount and means of meeting the costs, political attitudes, and organizational considerations involved in basically eliminating the old age assistance program. One important consideration is that this action would be regressive in terms of tax burden in relation to income, since it would replace a system financed to a large extent by taxes on total income and wealth by one in which the costs would be borne equally by all insured earners on a limited amount of income (Corson and McConnell, 1956). This is another area in which research into values and practical considerations would yield important information concerning social attitudes.

COVERAGE OF PHYSICIANS

Another interesting situation involves the coverage of self-employed physicians, at present our only important occupational category not covered by social insurance. The operation of value orientations here is quite involved. On the one hand, the official spokesmen of the American Medical Association reject coverage on the grounds of not wanting this unnecessary form of governmental interference. On the other

hand, individual doctors argue that the physicians should not be denied the right to join if they wish. But, more uniquely, another view argues that it is the *duty* of the physicians to be covered because they are not, as a generally high-level income group, carrying their share of the social responsibility involved in the partial redistribution that occurs in favor of lower-income groups under OASDI (Larson, 1955, 1959).

D. The Issue of a Fixed Retirement Age

COMPULSORY AND FLEXIBLE RETIREMENT

The single most important issue in retirement policy today is the question of compulsory retirement at a fixed age. There has been widespread comparison of the relative merits of systems of fixed or involuntary retirement at a given age versus systems of flexible retirement or lack of a fixed age for retirement. Probably no other topic has occasioned more discussion and controversy in recent years or received as much attention (Brower, 1951; Johnson, 1951; Cochrane, 1952; Burns, 1954; Corson and McConnell, 1956; Mathiasen, 1957).

Flexible retirement refers to. the general idea of individualization of retirement policy and includes programs which range from simple proposals to allow employment beyond the normal retirement age on criteria of fitness to suggestions involving the reordering and readjusting of jobs and work situations to meet the need and capacities of the older worker.

Burns (1954) has summarized the major lines of argument which have developed in support of compulsory or fixed-age retirement, on the one hand, and various forms of flexible retirement, on the other:

The Case for Compulsory Retirement:

1. It permits an orderly separation and transition from employment to retirement when declining health and productivity make it timely and appropriate.

2. It provides a practical administrative procedure that is objective, impersonal, and impartial and which avoids charges of discrimination, favoritism, and bias.
3. It maintains open channels of promotion, insures more upward mobility, and strengthens incentive of younger persons as well as helps make a more efficient, effective, and adaptive organization.
4. It encourages the individual to plan and prepare for his own retirement, and it makes it necessary for the organization to make plans for adequate reserves and replacements for those who have retired.

The Case against Compulsory Retirement:

1. The majority of employees and executives resist retirement while they are still able and willing to work.
2. The sharp reduction in income and the downward adjustment in living standards occasioned by retirement create undue hardship and resentment.
3. Compulsory retirement tends to disregard important individual differences in capacity as well as differences in job requirements. It ignores the productive potential of people and deprives them of the social and occupational significance which accrues from work.
4. The argument that compulsory retirement is a convenient and practical administrative procedure for separating older employees and for maintaining channels and opportunities for promotion of younger employees overlooks the effective alternatives of flexible retirement and the advantages of selective employment and utilization of older persons.
5. Compulsory retirement is costly and wasteful for the company, the individual, and the economy [p. 138].

Burns's summary tends to emphasize the more objective aspects and minimize the subjective appeals and conflicts of values that have permeated the discussions, especially in the semipopular literature.

However, despite the raising of important conflicts of social values in the discussions, little attempt has been made to view this issue in terms of basic value orientations concerning the nature of retirement on a societal level. Further, dramatic portrayals of the problems of the employee

forced to retire when he is willing and able to continue working have sometimes been overdrawn and taken out of the broader social context.

To put the question of compulsory retirement in perspective, let us first examine the reasons given for retirement and those for continuing to work by older persons and then consider the social context of attitudes toward work and retirement.

REASONS FOR RETIRING

Numerous recent studies in the United States and England have dealt with the reasons why men retire. Almost universally, conditions of health and declining physical capacity have been reported as the major reasons (Ministry of Pensions and National Insurance, 1954; Stecker, 1955; Anderson and Cowan, 1956; Richardson, 1956; Steiner and Dorfman, 1957; Townsend, 1957). One study of an "elite" group of pensioners (Corson and McConnell, 1956) found involuntary retirement by reason of company policy to be the major reason for retirement (56 per cent), with health second, but the authors did not consider this group to be representative of all retired workers. This study did find, however, in agreement with Steiner and Dorfman's (1957) national sample of aged households, that retirement because of health reasons was related to socioeconomic status.

The lower the occupational status or income level, the more chance there was that the individual was forced to retire because of health or reported himself as not well enough to work; conversely, the higher the occupational status or income level, the greater the number who were retired because of formal retirement systems (see Table 5).

Steiner and Dorfman found that 60 per cent of their total sample retired for reasons of health, 76 per cent for all voluntary reasons including health, and only 13 per cent because of fixed-age retirement plans (see Table 6). Similarly, a study of the reasons for retirement among fifteen thousand OASDI beneficiaries in 1951 indicated that approximately 11 per cent of males had retired because of fixed-age limits, while 48 per cent had retired or were retired because of health and physical condition. A slightly higher proportion of women (50 per cent) retired because of health reasons, while only 6 per cent were involuntarily retired because of pension age (Stecker, 1955).

While the number being retired under

are unwilling to retire (Crook and Heinstein, 1958; Thompson and Streib, 1958) or that they are all in good enough health to continue working. Corson and McConnell (1956) note that the potential number of workers among the retired has tended to be exaggerated by those advancing proposals to create employment opportunities for retired workers. They point out that most older persons who wish to work are still working; that, among those not employed, over one-third are physically un-

TABLE 5*

REASONS FOR RETIREMENT FOR MALES 65 AND OVER, BY LONGEST
OCCUPATION GROUP, APRIL, 1952

Longest Occupation Group	Per Cent in Labor Force	Per Cent Voluntary Retired	Per Cent Involuntary Retired	Health Reasons as Percentage of Total Retired	Formal Retirement Systems as Percentage of Total Retired
Professional and technical......	67	21	13	21	12
Farmers and farm managers....	43	50	7	65	3
Managers and proprietors......	53	38	10	47	8
Clerical.....................	31	43	26	38	29
Sales.......................	49	35	16	55	21
Craftsmen, foremen, etc........	33	45	22	53	24
Operatives..................	36	50	14	65	12
Service, except household.......	35	46	18	56	19
Farm labor..................	35	60	5	69	2
Labor, except farm and mine...	31	52	17	57	12
Total...................	41	46	14	57	13

* Source: P. O. Steiner and R. Dorfman, *The Economic Status of the Aged* (Berkeley: University of California Press, 1957), p. 58, Table 4.9.

fixed-age retirement systems has undoubtedly increased due to the growth of industrial pensions and the association noted between pension systems and coverage under fixed-age retirement systems (Corson and McConnell, 1956; Mathiasen, 1957), the actual effects of these plans on currently retiring workers is a subject of needed research. As the workers now covered reach pensionable ages, there seems little doubt that past growth of fixed-age practices will lead to greater retirement of this type, unless other factors intervene.

However, it should not be assumed that all persons retired under fixed-age plans

able to work; and, finally, that the experience of periods of high economic incentive in recent years does not show any appreciable number of older persons seeking employment.

REASONS FOR CONTINUING TO WORK

Studies of why older persons prefer to continue working past retirement age have emphasized the interrelation of attitudes toward work and retirement as they affect the individual's general position in society. While economic considerations have been of prime importance in many cases, especially on the lower occupational levels, social and psychological factors have also loomed very large, and differences have been noted among various occupational groups (Thomas and Osborne, 1947; Tuckman and Lorge, 1953; Friedmann and Havighurst, 1954; Ministry of Pensions and National Insurance, 1954; Crook and Heinstein, 1958).

TABLE 6*

LABOR-FORCE STATUS AND REASONS FOR RETIREMENT, MEN 65 AND OVER APRIL, 1952

Status	Per Cent of All Older Men	Per Cent of Older Men Not in the Labor Force
In the labor force	41	. . . .
Never compelled to retire .	36	. . . .
Returned after compulsory retirement	1	. . . .
Not available	4	. . . .
Not in the labor force	59	100
Involuntary retirement	13	24
Retirement system	7	13
Age	1	2
Layoff	2	4
Other	3	5
Voluntary reasons	42	76
Health	33	60
Age	3	5
Family decision	1	2
Other	5	9
Reason not available	4	. . . .

* Source: P. O. Steiner and R. Dorfman, *The Economic Status of the Aged* (Berkeley: University of California Press, 1957), p. 50, Table 4.7.

In general, higher-status occupational groups, such as professionals and skilled craftsmen, lay relatively more stress on reasons relating to the intrinsic nature of their work—interest, creativity, feeling of pride and accomplishment—while lower-status occupational groups, such as manual laborers and factory workers, stress reasons extrinsic to the nature of the work—the need for having something useful to do, a way of ordering and structuring their time, a means of keeping active, and the social contacts and position which their jobs afford them. Within given occupation-

al categories differences relating to the specific type of work have been noted (Friedmann and Havighurst, 1954).

It should not be forgotten, however, that in the search for social and psychological factors there may be an unwitting tendency to gloss over the centrality of economic considerations, both in the direct sense of monetary income needed for subsistence and the consequences which a radical loss of income have on the ability to maintain general social status through the acquisition of the purchaseable status symbols which help define the individual's position in society. Harlan's (1954) study of coalminers revealed the extent to which many persons in this lower-status occupation are forced to continue working beyond retirement age primarily because of the inadequacy of retirement income. A study by the Life Extension Foundation (1956) of 1546 retired persons, most of whom were retired under compulsory retirement systems, revealed that, while 32 per cent of those with incomes under $5000 a year wanted to return to their former jobs, only 8 per cent of those with incomes over $5000 a year expressed a similar desire.

NEGATIVE CHARACTER OF REASONS FOR WORKING AND RETIRING

These studies have shown that to a great extent both reasons for retiring and reasons for continuing to work are of a negative character. Retirement because of health is often viewed as a release from an unpleasant situation, not a passage into a pleasant one. Similarly, continuing to work is often the result of a desire to avoid passing into what is viewed as a more unpleasant position rather than a positive attachment to one's work (Tuckman and Lorge, 1953; Friedmann and Havighurst, 1954).

For example, the study of garmentworkers by Tuckman and Lorge (1953) contained three samples of older persons: one group of workers still on the job ($n = 204$), one group of workers who had applied for retirement (n = 216), and one group of retired workers (n = 240). In the applicant group 50 per cent of the men and 52 per cent of the women were looking forward to retirement; in the retired group 50 per cent of the men and 67 per cent of the women liked retirement; and in the working group 59 per cent of the men and 74 per cent of the women were looking forward to retirement or would like to retire if financially able. However, when we look at the reasons for their attitudes (Table

active employment, which is an increasing strain on their physical and psychological resources" (p. 22).

CHANGING ATTITUDES AND ORIENTATION TOWARD WORK, LEISURE, AND RETIREMENT

While further clearly focused and detailed research on the reactions of specific occupational groups to retirement and its prospects is needed to develop a more sat-

TABLE 7*

REASONS FOR ATTITUDE TOWARD RETIREMENT—JOB, APPLICANT, AND RETIRED GROUPS—BY SEX AND ATTITUDE

(Percentage Distribution)

Sex and Attitude	Per Cent of Group in Attitude Category			Poor Health, Old Age			Still Able to Work			Would Rather Work But Not Able			Desire to Rest—Worked Long Enough			Financial Reasons			No Way to Pass the Time			Other		
	J	A	R	J	A	R	J	A	R	J	A	R	J	A	R	J	A	R	J	A	R	J	A	R
Male:																								
1. Looking forward to it; like it	43	50	50	35	58	42	0	0	0	0	0	0	60	32	47	0	0	0	0	0	0	5	9	10
2. Would retire if financially able	16	†	†	43	†	†	0	†	†	0	†	†	25	†	†	25	†	†	0	†	†	8	†	†
3. Not looking forward to it; dislike it	36	41	50	0	4	16	56	33	0	0	6	44	0	0	0	21	25	15	19	23	16	3	9	8
4. Undecided	5	9	‡	0	17	†	0	11	†	0	0	†	0	11	†	0	33	†	50	17	†	50	11	†
Female:																								
1. Looking forward to it; like it	58	72	67	39	62	50	0	0	0	0	0	0	50	38	44	0	0	0	0	0	0	0	11	6
2. Would retire if financially able	16	†	†	0	†	†	0	†	†	0	†	†	40	†	†	60	†	†	0	†	†	0	†	†
3. Not looking forward to it; dislike it	34	39	48	0	25	25	12	75	†	0	0	†	0	0	50	75	0	12	12	0	0	0	0	12
4. Undecided	4	9	‡	0	†	†	0	†	†	†	100	†	0	†	†	0	†	†	0	†	†	0	†	†

* Source: J. Tuckman and I. Lorge, *Retirement and the Industrial Worker: Prospect and Reality* (New York: Columbia University, Bureau of Publications, Teachers College, 1953), pp. 21 and 23, Tables 14 and 15.

† No cases in the category.

‡ Less than 0.5 per cent.

7), their negative character is quite apparent among all the groups.

Fear of financial problems and what to do with one's time loom large for those not looking forward to or desiring retirement, while poor health and a desire to rest dominate the reasons of those anticipating or liking retirement or desiring retirement if financially able. Tuckman and Lorge (1953) comment on the relatively small number of respondents viewing retirement in a positive manner: "For the majority of respondents, looking forward to retirement or liking retirement means that they are fortunate, with the availability of a union pension, in being able to withdraw from

isfactory understanding of the precise relations between the character of work and attitudes toward work and retirement, recent studies of the meaning of work and attitudes toward work in American society have probed the question of the orientations underlying these attitudes (Weiss and Morse, 1955; Riesman, 1956, 1958; Dubin, 1958; Weiss and Kahn, 1959a, 1959b).

Common to all these investigations has been an attempt to determine to what extent the traditional concept of the Protestant ethic—the preoccupation with work as a central life-interest and end in itself—was still applicable to contemporary American culture. Williams (1951) notes the changing emphasis from work as a "value incorporated in the ego ideal of the representative personality types of the culture . . . [approaching] the intensity of a true matter of conscience" (p. 396) to patterns of achievement and success in which work is only a means to the end and, thus, has been devalued.

The findings of these recent studies have all been uniformly in the same direction: work has lost its function as a central life-interest, but it has not been replaced as a means for achieving self-identification and placement in the social structure; the function of work has shifted from that of an end to a means, and its value is now instrumental rather than intrinsic. Riesman (1958) notes that having work is not an active presence but that the absence of work is an active absence. It is not work that matters but having a job.

Dubin (1958) found that only 10 per cent of his sample of industrial workers perceived the work place as a source of important primary social relationships and that only 24 per cent were job oriented in their life-interests. The series of studies by Weiss and Morse (1955) and Weiss and Kahn (1959a, 1959b) discovered that, although most men defined work as "something one would not do unless one had to" and viewed work as an externally imposed task or duty which was not enjoyed, 80 per cent of them indicated that they would continue working even though they were financially independent and did not have to work to earn a living. Although more men in the middle-class occupations found a sense of meaning and personal achievement in work and affirmed the desire to continue working (86 per cent) even if economically independent, the overwhelming majority of men in working-class occupations (76 per cent) also affirmed a desire to continue working even if economically independent. But it is basically the role of a working person, having a job identification, that they want to continue, not the specific work they may presently have. "Not work-

ing simply does not provide the basis for a viable life for most respondents. . . . Most men would take any job to escape the status of being without a job" (Weiss and Kahn, 1959b).

The job is a means and not an end, and herein lies the significance of these changing attitudes toward work. They carry a potential for changes in attitudes toward leisure and retirement—attitudes which directly grow out of the orientation toward work—and suggest that future generations may be more inclined to a positive approach toward life in retirement. Just as changes in orientations about the nature of retirement as an institution on the societal level have occurred, so changes in the individual's orientation toward retirement life may follow in the wake of the changing character of modern society. Shenfield (1957) directly asks:

Will future generations, accustomed to shorter hours of work and wider opportunities for the use of leisure, want a continued employment as a means of occupation and interest in their later years? If in our present organization of industry many workers do not derive much satisfaction from their work, and it is largely divorced from other aspects of their social life, it seems unlikely that many, given adequate pension provisions, will want to continue in employment beyond conventional retirement ages [p. 60].

The current generation of Americans appear to have developed a new attitude toward leisure as a value, although this seems to have occurred as an outcome of treating leisure as another commodity which is produced and consumed, as a means rather than as an end (Galbraith, 1958; Riesman, 1958). Americans are engrossed in working for the symbols and commodities of leisure, even though this means working harder in order to obtain them and having less time in which to use them (Swados, 1958). The economic and social basis for the enjoyment and utilization of leisure is being created, and, however much one may question the forms leisure is taking, the acceptance of leisure as a value nevertheless signifies a new orientation in the making. The extent of this change is seen by the fact that it is now even making headway among the most work-imbued segment of the population, the executives (Heckscher and De Grazia, 1959).

The arena of attitudes toward work and leisure is a crucial one in determining the extent to which a new orientation toward life in retirement is developing, one which can radically reverse the negative approach of the current generation approaching retirement and those already in retirement.[26]

If the maturing generation of today is showing a greater concern for security, for the opportunity for a more meaningful and extensive home life, and for the availability of leisure, as is so often argued, this may result in retirement becoming a sought-after release from the instrumental chores of work. Riesman (1956) finds such greater concern with security and leisure in the present generation of college students, and Heckscher and De Grazia (1959) discover today's executives desirous of more leisure and extensive retirement but not doing very much about achieving these desires. They suggest that, while these attitudes may not affect the habits of the present generation of executives, it seems likely that they will change the habits of their children.

It is difficult to ignore the growing emphasis on security which has been so characteristic of the past decade; and, although research measuring and analyzing the dimensions and significance of this phenomena is seriously lacking, its existence cannot be denied. The prominence of this theme in the appeals of employers to prospective employees has been matched in a contemporary cartoon: A young boy, cap in hand, stands before the imposing desk of a personnel officer, his eyes barely reaching over the surface of the desk. The caption reads: "I don't care about the opportunities for promotion. Just tell me what your retirement provisions are!"

If the various themes of security expressed in the popular literature and drawn to their extension in this cartoon are any accurate indication of a real change in orientation toward the potentialities of life in retirement, then many of the social and psychological problems of retirement today may be specific to what is our first generation of retirees and may be the result of a system of societal and individual value orientations molded in an age which had not yet known and could not know the realities of an era of institutionalized retirement. The concern over security in retirement began as a concern for the protection of the wage-earner when health and age no longer made it possible for him to continue earning a living. From this conception of retirement as protection from the hazards of old age in an industrial society has grown a positive conception of retirement as a period of potential enjoyment and creative experience which accrues as a social reward for a lifetime of labor. In this context we can meaningfully examine the present character of retirement policies.

CHARACTER OF RETIREMENT POLICIES TODAY

The extent of compulsory retirement.— It was pointed out in Section I, B, that there is a certain degree of individual freedom of choice to enter into retirement at present in consequence of the fact that the federal system of retirement benefits does not compel retirement at any given age but merely sets an age standard which acts as a lower limit for the receipt of retirement benefits. However, the practical effect of this lower limit has been quite another matter, since it has been commonly adopted as a standard age which private and public employers have used to enforce retirement upon their employees. This is in part a consequence of the fact that it has become general practice to structure private pensions as supplementary to OASDI as the basic retirement system, and OASDI's minimum age becomes the actuarial starting point in constructing these plans. We

[26] See chap. xii.

might, therefore, expect a trend toward lower retirement ages for women, reflecting the adoption with reduced benefits of age 62 (as a compromise for the originally suggested age of 60) as the minimum age of receipt of OASDI payments for women. Excluding this trend to lower ages of retirement for women, age 65 has thus come to represent a value-defined boundary between work and retirement.

The source of compulsory retirement practices derives from employer policy in the replacement of personnel. Compulsory retirement practices existed before the introduction of the federal system of OASDI and did not (as is still the case) necessarily entail any provision of a pension on the part of the employer. This was especially true for industrial wage-earners as opposed to public employees and salaried officials and executives in industry. Compulsory retirement can be viewed in part as a consequence of the bureaucratization of industry, business, and government. With the growth of systematic rationalized procedures, general policy rather than individual decision becomes the rule, and, just as machinery is routinely depreciated and replaced because of age and availability of more efficient and productive replacements, so is the older worker. While this may seem to be a blunt and harsh portrayal of the situation, it should not be forgotten to what extent this did characterize the early stages of industrial policy before the advent of unions and forms of public intervention in the social order and to what extent the vestiges of the social-Darwinist philosophy of the nineteenth century still remain alive today, albeit clothed in restraining garments of social responsibility. Modern industrial policy has seen the growth of employer recognition of responsibility beyond the work life for the employee which, beginning as a humanitarian impulse on the part of individual employers, in part a consequence of the moral force that a long and continuing economic relationship has tended to have in society, has grown under the prodding of organized labor and social regulation through government and public opinion.

Another source of the growth of compulsory retirement can be traced to the experience of the depression of the 1930's, when social policy seemed to come to a consensus which regarded the older worker as marginal and expendable in terms of the greater social claims to employment of those with families. This can be seen in the continued actions to lower the age of OASDI eligibility to 60 up to the beginnings of World War II in the expectation that this would facilitate the retirement of older workers. The changing conditions of the labor market as a consequence of wartime conditions halted this trend, and the continued era of economic prosperity since then has, until the present, acted as a barrier to such moves, although the recession of 1957–58 again awakened such tendencies.

It is difficult to estimate the full extent of compulsory retirement practices in effect today, since information on such practices is basically derived from samples of private pension plans, which today cover 26 per cent of the civilian labor force (Holland, 1959). These omit the vast majority of workers (over two-thirds of the labor force) who are not covered either by private or by public pension plans. But the widespread practice of age discrimination in the employment of older workers[27] would suggest that some form of age standard for "retiring" employees is commonly utilized. This is an area in which extensive research, especially in the practices of small establishments, is required. The findings of studies of reasons for retirement (Stecker, 1955; Steiner and Dorfman, 1957) yield rather low proportions (11 per cent and 13 per cent) of persons retiring because of fixed-age limits, but these reflect populations retired before the large-scale growth of private pension plans in the last decade in which fixed-age limits were quite prominent (Bankers Trust Co., 1956).

[27] See chap. x.

Studies of private pension plans in 1952, 1954, and 1958 found that approximately 60–68 per cent of the company plans sampled carried involuntary retirement provisions (U.S. Bureau of Labor Statistics, 1953; Brower, 1955; Levin, 1959).

The 1952 and 1958 studies were carried out by the Bureau of Labor Statistics and covered provisions in pension systems negotiated under collective bargaining between unions and employers. Comparing the two studies, Levin (1959) commented

contrary situations. To clarify this problem, we shall here speak of "involuntary" or "compulsory" retirement as the general form signifying the imposition of retirement upon the individual whether he desires it or not according to a fixed-age standard. Within this category we will distinguish (1) non-automatic retirement as enforcing retirement, subject, however, to the consent of the employer or some designated group allowing the continued employment of employees unwilling to retire

TABLE 8*

TYPES OF RETIREMENT PROVISIONS AND PRACTICES IN PRIVATE
PENSION SYSTEMS, 1954 AND 1958, BY PLANS AND
EMPLOYEES COVERED

(Percentage Distribution)

TYPE OF PROVISION OR PRACTICE	BROWER, 1954		BUREAU OF LABOR STATISTICS, 1958	
	Companies ($n=327$)	Employees ($n=4.1$ Million)	Plans ($n=300$)	Employees ($n=4.9$ Million)
No involuntary fixed-age retirement...	25†	10†	40	45
Involuntary (compulsory)...	67†	83†	60	55
Automatic retirement....	48	67	23	19
Non-automatic retirement	19	16	37	36

* Sources: Adapted from F. Beatrice Brower, *Retirement of Employees—Policies—Procedures—Practices* ("Studies in Personnel Policy," No. 148 [New York: National Industrial Conference Board, 1955]), Table 5; and H. L. Levin, "Involuntary Retirement Procedures," *Monthly Labor Review*, 82 (1959), 857, Table 2.

† Eight per cent of the companies have a combination of both involuntary and non-involuntary policies for different categories of workers; these cover 7 per cent of the employees.

that "it would appear that no significant change in the prevalence of involuntary provisions had occurred" (p. 857). Brower's study focused on actual company practices regardless of plan provisions. In her sample non-union companies comprised 29 per cent of the total, while the pension plans of the other companies were not necessarily developed by union-management negotiation.

A distinction has generally been drawn between types of compulsory retirement practices. Unfortunately, terminology has not been standardized so that different authors may use the same terms to apply to

at the normal retirement age (this means that the non-automatic retirement age is the age at which the employee loses the privilege of deciding whether he should retire, which he has the right to do, or continuing to work), and (2) "automatic retirement" as implying a clearly set end to employment with no expectation possible of continuation; the automatic retirement age is thus the age at which retirement is mandatory.

In these terms a comparison between the 1954 and 1958 studies reveals important differences which are more striking when one considers the number of employees involved (Table 8). The 1954 study reports only 25 per cent of the companies having 10 per cent of the total number of employees covered with non-involuntary practices, while the 1958 study reports 40 per cent of the plans having 45 per cent of the covered employees with such provisions. Furthermore, while the 1954 study reports 48 per cent of the companies having 67 per cent of the covered employees with automatic retirement practices, the 1958 study reports only 23 per cent of the plans having 19 per cent of the covered employees with these provisions.

While there may be a slight exaggeration of the differences due to different terminological definitions and method of reporting between Brower and the BLS study, they are basically comparable in categories. The 8 per cent mixed policies in Brower's study would not offset the over-all picture, and the fact that practices tend to be more flexible than provisions would lead one to expect greater rather than smaller differences in the results. These differences are undoubtedly a reflection of the general opposition of unions to compulsory, and especially automatic, retirement and indicate that, where they are a significant factor, union influences have reduced the extent of compulsory retirement practices.

Corroboration of this influence is provided by the Bankers Trust Company (1956) study of pension provisions. This investigation separated union-negotiated retirement systems from typical employer-sponsored systems by distinguishing between "pattern plans," which represent the typical non-contributory union-negotiated retirement systems of the 1950's, and "conventional plans," which represent the more traditional employer-sponsored contributory systems. Between 1950–52 and 1953–55, the proportion of "pattern plans" with no involuntary fixed-age provisions rose from 22 to 33 per cent, while the proportion of new "conventional plans" of this type were only 4 and 6 per cent of the total, respectively.

This change is significant when it is rec-

ognized that acceptance of compulsory features marked a good number of union-negotiated retirement systems in the 1950's following the establishment by the Supreme Court in the Inland Steel Case in 1949 of the principle that private pension systems are subject to negotiation by collective bargaining under the Taft-Hartley Act (Bankers Trust Co., 1956). Careful inspection of the breakdown of compulsory and non-compulsory systems by industry in the 1958 BLS study (Levin, 1959) reveals that union plans divide sharply along the lines of industry groups, with fifteen of the twenty-nine industry groups having a dominance of compulsory plans and ten having a dominance of non-compulsory plans. Since five of the fifteen industries with compulsory provisions represent 68 per cent of the employees under these provisions and four of the ten industries with non-compulsory provisions represent 74 per cent of covered employees, drastic alterations in this picture could occur through a few key changes.

Another important facet of the compulsory retirement picture relates to the size of company and the type of industry involved. Pension plans in general are found more often in large companies than in small firms. A New York State Department of Labor (1957) study found that, while 89 per cent of establishments with 2500 or more employees had pension plans, the figure was only 14 per cent among establishments having under 20 employees. This factor is not unrelated to unionization, which is more prevalent in large companies, but Brower (1955) found differences in types of retirement policies with size of firm in her sample of largely non-union companies, the larger firms tending to have more compulsory practices.

Pension coverage also varies greatly with the type of industry, another feature obviously related to the prevalence of unionization or threat of unionization—compare the steel or coal industry with service or domestic workers as extreme contrasts. There is a need for careful research into the relative importance and interdependence of size of company, type of industry or occupation, and extent of unionization as mutually related factors involved in retirement practices. This is especially clear when we note that pension experts express the opinion that we have reached the peak of growth in private pension systems, with the most favorable and likely situations already having been tapped (Holland, 1959).

Who determines retirement policy?— Prior to the entrance of the federal government into the retirement picture, retirement policy in the United States was almost exclusively determined by the employer. Although government influence through OASDI is indirect, it has greatly affected the determination of retirement policy in all major areas. Age limits have tended to fall in line with OASDI's minimum age (Bankers Trust Co., 1956). This has meant a general lowering of eligible ages for retirement. Economic characteristics of retirement provisions have been geared to OASDI benefit levels as a base line, and other provisions involving financial remuneration have followed suit (Brower, 1955; Bankers Trust Co., 1956). The view of OASDI benefits as a right earned by monetary contributions and a lifetime of labor has influenced the growing tendency to view private pensions also as a right to which employees are entitled whether as a form of deferred income—the general attitude of unions today—or as a form of social reward based on moral right and moral responsibility of industry.

The afore-mentioned establishment in 1949 of the principle that private pensions were subject to collective bargaining brought unions directly into the policy determination picture, where their previous influence was indirect, although not negligible on this account (Corson and McConnell, 1956). Since then they have shared with employers the major aspects of direct policy determination.

Government at all levels has determined policy directly only for public employees, and here, too, federal policy has provided the lead for state and local action. It is noteworthy, thus, that the federal government has moved in the direction of greater flexibility in the retirement provisions governing public employees (Cohen, 1957).

The importance and growth of retirement as a societal institution lead inevitably to the issue of more direct governmental determination of retirement policy—especially as regards the issue of compulsory retirement. So far, this aspect of the problem seems to have been bypassed in the discussions of this issue as emphasis has been mainly at those directly involved in determining policy (i.e., employers and unions). But, just as agitation for legal action preventing discrimination in employment for older workers has grown and has led to the adoption of a number of state laws of this type, it is apparent that similar action could extend to legal determination of retirement policy. While state laws preventing age discrimination in employment are directed mainly at the 45–64 age group and specifically exclude application to pension systems, there is no reason why they could not be so extended, although it would appear that an issue of this sort would be more clearly a province of federal action.

In this area, action could take any one of a number of lines. Raising or lowering the eligibility age for OASDI influences retirement policies as well as practices. This type of action is, of course, an actually existing form. Or a national age or work-capability policy could be set to govern certain types of work (e.g., the recent decision by the Civil Aeronautics Board forcing commercial airline pilots to stop flying at age 60) or to govern all categories of work and thus to assume direction of the age structure of the labor force as a matter of national policy. This would mean that action along these lines would become part of the apparatus of national policy in dealing with the general welfare and would be capable of modification in response to changing conditions of technology, economic circumstances, and social attitudes.

The acceptance of retirement policies.— There can be little doubt that retirement as such has won general social acceptance as a form of life, however hesitant and ambivalent individuals may be about actually entering into retirement and however difficult the problems of adjustment to retirement are (see Sec. VI).

Undoubtedly, in addition to personal interest, the institutionalization of retirement has acted to develop an orientation favorable to retirement as a matter of social policy and practice. The growth of belief in retirement as a matter of right leads to the expectation that this right will be capable of being exercised and not only when the individual is physically unable to continue working. The question then arises as to the extent that individuals will be willing to forego a certain degree of freedom of choice in this area without suffering serious deprivation *if such is considered necessary* in the social interest. In other words, in addition to personal interest, to what extent can and do value orientations concerning the nature of retirement and its place in the total welfare of society play a role in helping form the basis for accepting retirement policies?

Answering this question is no easy task and requires more extensive and directed research than has been carried out up to the present. In the first place, there exists the problem of determining to what extent changes in present policy would result in actual changes in work participation and attitudes toward working, questions which themselves involve some evaluation of how changes in technology, economic organization, and social structure as well as length of life and state of physical health of the population will modify the character and place of work and the orientation to work in society.

Some answers are forthcoming from recent research. Baker (1952) concludes from her study of five companies that, "with adequate annuities and consistent application, compulsory retirement at 65 is accepted without complaint. . . . The com-

mon opinion is that adequate pensions plus counseling will continue to assure employee acceptance of compulsory retirement" (p. 22). The relationship between acceptance of retirement and size of retirement income revealed in the Life Extension Foundation (1956) study has been noted previously. Sheldon (1958) reports that estimates of the number of non-employed men 65 and over able and willing to work in the early 1950's ranged between 8 and 16 per cent in various local samples. He places the national figure at somewhat more than 10 per cent of the total not in the labor force, but he notes that this estimate is based on the peak 1945 wartime participation rates of older persons as representing their maximum employment potential. The implication is clear that changing attitudes and needs governing the labor market make this figure an overestimation of the realities of the later 1950's.

A survey by the National Committee on the Aging (Haines, 1959) found that in a group of forty-seven companies about one-half of the men aged 64 desired to continue working. In the companies with fixed-age retirement policies 60 per cent did not wish to continue working, while in the companies without a fixed-age policy 60 per cent wished to continue. The basic reason for desiring to continue at work was reported to be financial; nevertheless, the implication is that the presence of compulsory provisions affects the worker's attitude toward retirement. However, this requires corroboration by more scientifically designed study before it can be accepted as more than a suggestion.

On the other hand, only about two-thirds to three-fourths of those wishing to continue working in this study are acceptable to management for further employment. This leaves a total of about 33–38 per cent both available and acceptable to management for continued work, and this is just about the percentage of men over 65 who are currently in the labor force (35.6 per cent in 1958).[28] There seems to be little

[28] See chap. x, Table 4.

implication that any major changes in the opportunities for work for those over normal retirement ages will result from liberalizing present compulsory practices unless employers also adjust their criteria of acceptability of older workers and revise the conditions of work or unless changes in economic and social policy result in changed individual attitudes toward retirement. Thus in France, too, Naville (1959) argues that changing retirement provisions to allow freedom of retirement choice would not perceptibly influence the distribution of ages of retirement.

The study of Crook and Heinstein (1958) of worker's attitudes in two areas of California found that, while only one-fourth of the older workers "really wanted to retire . . . a much larger number appeared to accept the policy of compulsory retirement at a fixed-age as right and proper. The majority of men did not even seem to feel that the worker himself should necessarily play any part at all in deciding when he should retire" (pp. 78–90).

When asked to choose the age at which persons should be retired, 47 per cent of all men and 35 per cent of all women accepted the idea of fixed-age retirement without qualification, and an additional 15 and 26 per cent, respectively, accepted the principle but with some contingency attached. The younger group of workers (under 50) suggested a median age around 60, while the older groups of workers (50 and over) suggested a median age of 65. This study consistently found older workers taking a more cautious and negative attitude to retirement than younger workers and suggested this as due to the fact that "the prospect of retirement grows less attractive the more imminent it becomes" (Crook and Heinstein, 1958, p. 49).

Thus workers over age 60 were less likely to favor compulsory fixed-age retirement than workers between the ages of 50 and 59 and suggested higher ages for retirement. One interesting finding was the fact that workers only 5–10 years from the normal retirement age of 65 had attitudes more in common with younger workers under 50 than with those over 60; the explanation offered is that they may regard retirement as still a long way off and thus retain attitudes originally held as members of a younger age group. It is hypothesized that younger workers view retirement practices as providing opportunities for their advancement and thus are favorably disposed to them on this account. That younger workers are certainly not unaware of this general problem is illustrated by a newsphoto which appeared nationally in early 1958 showing a group of unemployed younger steelworkers picketing a steelworks near Pittsburgh with placards reading: "We fought for your right to retire, why don't you?"

A final unique aspect of this investigation was an attempt to gauge the type of interests considered by the workers in expressing opinions about a fixed retirement age. While their findings did not support the hypothesis advanced that workers who appeared to favor a fixed retirement were willing to subordinate their personal interests to those of the company and society, it is of note that 19 per cent of the men and 11 per cent of the women mentioned society's interest in some fashion, while 26 per cent of the men and 27 per cent of the women mentioned the company's interest. However, 57 per cent of the men and 65 per cent of the women based their views on the interest of the worker only, and the worker's interest was mentioned in some form in 80 per cent of the men's and 82 per cent of the women's replies. It is of importance, nevertheless, that as many as one-sixth to one-fourth "definitely subordinated personal considerations" (Crook and Heinstein, 1958, p. 53).

The hypothesis of attitude changes toward retirement with age and of growing recognition of social interest deserve further study and consideration under both cross-sectional and longitudinal methods with representative populations to determine whether present attitude structures will change under newer retirement systems and changing economic and social conditions so that the actual age effects may be more precisely gauged.

While we cannot deal with the question of early retirement because this subject has not received sufficient study to justify any conclusions about actual practices, it should be noted that between 70 and 92 per cent of private retirement plans studied have such provisions without restrictions of health or disability (Brower, 1955; Bankers Trust Co., 1956). Almost 23 per cent of the respondents in the Life Extension Foundation (1956) study retired before normal pension ages; less than 14 per cent did so in the Cleveland study by Special Services (Anonymous, 1952), while a study of recent civil service retirees found 59 per cent retiring early (U.S. Executive Office of the President, 1954). One future gauge of attitudes toward retirement could be provided by attention to the tendencies in this area.

This leads to consideration of the question of age standards for retirement. While the selection of age 65 as the normal age of retirement was not a matter of scientific determination as far as can be known, it has become a general standard which has developed many rationalizations behind it. It should, however, be obvious that, although once a given age standard is adopted it is exceedingly difficult to raise but simple to lower it, the determination of "age" of retirement itself is almost exclusively a value question, little related at present to questions of individual needs so much as to societal needs and requirements.

E. Conclusion: Retirement and Societal Value Orientations

Naville (1959) has argued that the "scale of actual ages of retirement results from an equilibrium of employment offers, work capacities, and incomes," to which we should add: "and the value orientations and associated attitudes toward work, leisure, and retirement present in society and the individual." Possibly no other area of

research in retirement has been so neglected as the study of operative value orientations, their role in the shaping of retirement policy, and their effect on the attitudes of individuals toward work and retirement.

In England (Shenfield, 1957) and in France (Daric, 1948; Naville, 1959) evidence of the development of strong positive orientations toward retirement has come through both the expression of concern and direct action when suggestions for raising the age of retirement have been put forth. The institutionalization of retirement under conditions of somewhat different work attitudes has led to a much more extensive acceptance of the rights and privileges of retirement than has been true in the United States insofar as can be determined.

Increasingly in the future, as retirement systems mature in the 1960's and a new era in the position of retirement life in society commences, the question of value orientations and social attitudes toward retirement will come to the forefront of debate now that so many of the basic practical problems have been dealt with. If scientific research is to play a role in helping to meet the demands of this coming situation, it will be necessary to pay greater attention and interest to questions of values and their role in policy than has hitherto been the case.

IV. SOCIAL ATTITUDES TOWARD RETIREMENT

A. Management and Labor

GENERAL ATTITUDE TOWARD RETIREMENT

Management and labor both have come generally to view retirement in a positive fashion, although for differing reasons based on somewhat conflicting values. The result has been a difference in approach toward the types of retirement policies and programs each favors.

From a narrow management point of view retirement represents an extension of general principles of business organization involving the rational organization of the work force according to abilities, experience, and potentials of efficiency and harmonious functioning. This means that older, obsolescent, and less efficient workers must be replaced by younger, newly skilled, and more efficient workers in general. However, employee morale and general public image must be maintained at a high level to insure efficient functioning and provide a continuous source of new recruitment of labor. This creates a framework of value dilemmas for management which must be resolved on a highly specific basis for any given organization. Older employees must be replaced to insure vitality and creativity in business organization and maintain morale and loyalty of younger employees, but all employees must be assured of security and impartiality of treatment to maintain identification of interests and attachment to the company. Retirement systems must be financially in the companies' interests in terms both of short-run economic returns to investors and of long-run competitive position. While part of this is easily calculable in monetary terms, other aspects involve the calculation of the monetary worth of value elements and psychological factors. Consequently, the choice between compulsory and non-compulsory fixed-age systems for any given firm requires estimation of a large number of specific factors many of which are peculiarly unique to a given industry and the size or type of organization. Generally, managements have favored automatic fixed-age systems of compulsory retirement, although these have been more "flexible" in operation than in provision (Baker, 1952; Brower, 1955; Bankers Trust Co., 1956).

Organized labor, on the other hand, has generally approached the issue of retirement in terms of the protection of the interest of the individual worker. In the first place, retirement and disability provisions have been a consistent part of labor's drive for greater economic security for the wage-earner exposed to the conditions of modern industrial employment, from the demand for workmen's compensation to the current demands for a guaranteed annual wage. Thus, like management, economic considerations have loomed large in labor's attitudes toward retirement and have presented a source of potential conflict over the distribution of the fruits of industrial production.

One of the basic devices of labor for economic security has been the principle of seniority which conflicts with management's principles of efficiency and replacement. The resolution of this issue has been generally a compromise between the demands of both sides. Since forced retirement negates the protection of seniority, labor has historically opposed fixed-age compulsory retirement as a device which evades the seniority rights of the worker and has tended to view this as another area in which the worker's economic security must be protected (Solenberger, 1951; Barkin, 1952; Bers, 1957).

This means that labor's opposition to compulsory forms of retirement has been due not to rejection of the principle of fixed-age retirement per se but to opposition to employer imposition of the conditions of retirement under circumstances which result in involuntary economic deprivation of the worker. Therefore, it is not surprising that, "as retirement incomes have risen, so has union acceptance of automatic retirement schemes" (Bers, 1957, p. 83); and expression of union attitudes have clearly reinforced the willingness of labor to accept compulsory retirement systems under conditions approved and sanctioned by union members (Henson, 1951; Bers, 1957). This means restriction of management's right to unilateral decision on the criteria of continued employment for older workers which many managements have been reluctant to accept.

One consequence of this position has been that unions tend implicitly and explicitly to support a relatively high economic burden for support of the aged by society (Henson, 1951; Bers, 1957), an attitude which management has been historically more disposed to oppose and view with concern, especially insofar as it involves government intervention into the economic market place (National Industrial Conference Board, 1925; Corson and McConnell, 1956). Part of this has been due to differences between management and labor's conception of retirement income as a matter of business expediency, social responsibility, or social right, as indicated in the preceding section of this chapter.

Much antagonism has been aroused as a consequence of this issue. Hochman (1950) bitterly attacked management's imposition of forced retirement as motivated solely by economic considerations and cited the appeals of insurance firms which compared the older worker with obsolescent machinery. It is hard to deny this financial motivation, and its importance has been recognized to the extent that current appeals for flexible retirement prominently feature the large savings in pension costs that can accrue as the result of selective maintenance of qualified older workers past normal retirement ages.

IMPACT OF ECONOMIC AND SOCIAL CIRCUMSTANCES ON UNION AND MANAGEMENT ATTITUDES

Both management and union attitudes have changed under the impact of changing economic circumstances, and there is no reason to assume that they will not continue to do so. When conditions of prosperity and a tight labor market create demands for more workers, retirement practices have tended to be more flexible; as conditions of business downturns and surplus labor appear, practices have tended to be more rigid. Under these circumstances the attitudes of unions, especially, have been subject to cross-pressures among the demands of older workers and of younger workers and the attitude of union leaders, who tend to view the general state of the health of their own given industry and the degree of control by the union over the

labor supply of the industry as crucial variables (Bers, 1957).

Bers notes that the actual experiences of the unions in his study do not permit any conclusion that union attitudes have been shaped to any appreciable degree by consideration of the general social interest but have been strongly motivated by the interest of the specific organizational nexus of union, workers, and industry. Within this area he notes a certain degree of social responsibility which seems to be an outgrowth of the general notion of solidarity underlying union organization in general, and he cites the importance of pension systems to the continued growth and maintenance of worker identification and solidarity with the union.

ROLE AND GENERATIONAL CONFLICTS

Finally, it should be noted that in the case both of management and of the union we have a situation in which the control of retirement procedures is in the hands of persons who themselves will have to face retirement in the future; employees have to force upon other employees situations which they may be ambivalent about facing in their own future. Since in most cases these decisions for older men are put into practice and supported by younger men, feelings of hostility and guilt are likely to be aroused by this constellation of generational separation, an emotionally more difficult situation than much of the professional literature suggests.

B. The Spouse

It is interesting to note that scientific concern with social attitudes toward retirement has been, by and large, confined to the attitudes of *management* and *labor* but has disregarded the attitudes of wives. We have worried endlessly about the motives and feelings of those from whom retirement separates the employee and have paid scant if any attention to the motives and feelings of those with whom it brings him into the closest and all-embracing association (Cavan, 1953; Streib, 1958).[29] What the employer loses or gives up, the spouse receives or has to accept. It is astonishing how little attention has been paid to the fact that most American marriages during the working life of the provider are evening and week-end propositions. The separation of shop or office from the home has made most families nuclei of matriarchal organizations in our at least ideally equalitarian society. This ascendancy of woman to the virtual position of household head has not been the product of usurpation as much as the consequence of default. Over the last half-century husbands in increasing numbers have left the home for most of the day, and frequently migration into the suburbs has prolonged their absence to the extent of roughly 2 extra hours over and beyond their working time. Left without the resources of their presence for decision-making, American women have had to assume this role and, catered to by an economic organization bent on distribution, have found it in many instances to their liking. That this position of power in the domestic sphere should have provided an outlet for whatever negative feelings the marital experience may have engendered in them is probable. Similarly, this daily absence from the home except over the week ends may have enabled many husbands to adjust to marital relationships which under conditions of closer contact they might have found explosive or intolerable. At any rate, their loss of status in the home may have eluded them during their working life, where occupational success or contact with female work associates in subordinate positions might have helped them to divert their perception from status developments in the home.

Research and preparation for retirement, therefore, are beginning to pay attention to the attitudes of wives toward retirement of their husbands and to the effects of retirement upon family life (Hall, 1953; Tuckman and Lorge, 1953; Townsend,

[29] See chap. xiii.

1957; Streib, 1958). These studies show that for both lower- and upper-status groups husbands may feel closer to their wives as they grow older, and after retirement this relationship may be enhanced. Wives are aware that adjustments of their marriage which are based on the reduction of frictions due to the absence of husbands are going to become precarious. A significant proportion of women do not want their husbands to retire because they feel that there will be more housework to do, that their daily routine will be disrupted, that they do not want their husbands home all day, and that they will have to live on a lower income (Tuckman and Lorge, 1953; Townsend, 1957). Higher-status wives feel that they will lose social prestige and personal relationships (Hall, 1953). Among wives who say that they look forward to their husbands' retirement, Tuckman and Lorge (1953) found that these wives had an attitude of accomplished reality rather than a positive way of looking at retirement. Few wives, except perhaps those in the upper class (Kutner *et al.*, 1956), view their husbands' retirement as providing a time when they can enjoy life more together with their husbands.

Women are apprehensive of having a member in the household in 24-hour presence who has no established pattern for use of his waking hours at home. They are unwilling to include their husbands more than nominally in decision-making regarding the minutiae of living which formerly they handled themselves. Neugarten (1956), using a projective technique, showed the emergence of the authoritarian position of middle-aged and older women in the family constellation. The husband appeared to regress to a weak position which interfered with his asserting himself in the domestic scene. Likewise, Townsend (1957) found the role of the retired man in the working-class English family to be a segregated one, as his wife continued the pattern of working-class family structure: the wife's associations are with her female kin and daughters, the husband's with his male cronies and with women relatives through his mother at her own home. The home is a form of matriarchate, and the husbands were left without financial, domestic, or family role and found few or no substitutes for their worker roles. The situations of the retired husbands among American garmentworkers (Tuckman and Lorge, 1953) were similar. The men had little domestic responsibility and spent their time in passive undirected ways. Several other studies in England (Young, 1954; Collins and Haggett, 1955; Fox and Collins, 1956; Young and Wilmott, 1957; Drinkwater, 1959) confirm these findings by showing "Mum" to be the focal point and authoritative figure in the extended family group. Higher-status groups, as represented by Hall's executives (1953) and E. H. Moore's college professors (1951), fare somewhat better, because they are frequently able to pursue the same kinds of activities followed before retirement or have financial resources to make possible the development of new interests. In either case, the wife is relieved of some of the responsibility for assisting her husband to adjust in his retirement.

In this connection one has to consider that the normal life-cycle of a woman has provided her in most instances with two or three retirement experiences by the time her husband is facing his first one.

In our society many women have left employment for child-rearing and thus have become familiar with essential elements of the retirement experience in early adulthood. They have given up earning and income and have "retired" to other activities. When their children grow up and leave the parental home, women experience another retirement from an essential function and have to make adjustments to the cessation of the maternal role (August, 1956; Frank, 1956; Duvall, 1957; Havighurst, 1957; Neugarten and Peterson, 1959) and to select other roles and developmental tasks appropriate to their age grade and social class. For this they are likely to be prepared by the staggered experience of temporary but increasing separations from their children which our methods of child-rearing have forced upon American mothers. And, in the physiological sphere, the menopause has taught them the inevitability of retirement from the meaningful experiences of child-rearing. The husband who has to make an adjustment to retirement, therefore, should find in his spouse a person who has experienced, in varied and, to him, partly inaccessible ways, the problem of retirement which he faces for the first time. But the extent to which the retirement-experienced wife is inclined to aid her husband in his adjustment has not been reported.

In essence, retirement in our society makes marriage a 24-hour proposition for the first time. Family research as well as retirement research will have to focus on this concomitant to retirement if one of the greatest potential resources in retirement adjustment is to be understood and to be brought within the orbit of preparation for retirement (Burgess, 1952; Pollak, 1956).

C. The Children

It is part of our rural heritage to feel that adult sons and daughters are responsible for the support of their aging parents, if the latter are without adequate means of support. This is still a legal concept and referred to frequently in the practice of public assistance agencies. Our overwhelming urbanization, however, and the drainage which for better or worse our standard of living inflicts upon most incomes have changed our concepts of filial responsibility (McGill, 1955). Although social security and private pensions are expected to supply support for persons in retirement, continuous inflation makes these resources almost always less adequate than they were intended to be. In consequence adult children are likely to view the retirement of their father, and in increasing instances now also that of their mother, with some apprehension. Tradition-bound feelings of obligation are slow to disappear, particularly when substitute providers prove to be inadequate (W. E. Moore, 1951).[30]

Besides these purely economic implications which retirement is likely to have for the children of an individual, there are also implications of changes in domicile which may be more far-reaching and emotionally much more burdensome than purely financial assistance. Ours is a mobile population. Adult sons and daughters almost routinely leave the home of their parents and frequently move not only into a house or apartment of their own but actually to another community. Such spatial mobility depreciates the hold of family groups and family solidarity (Young and Wilmott, 1957; Drinkwater, 1959). How many of such geographical separations are arranged in order to relieve emotional tensions existing between parents and children is open to conjecture. That such motivations may be operative, however, can hardly be doubted. When retirement makes parents mobile, such arrangements may be put in jeopardy, and children who have tried to put distance between themselves and their parents may view retirement of their father or mother on that account with a measure of uneasiness.

Ultimately, however, the greatest threat to adult sons and daughters who want an independent existence is the wish of some retired parents, especially if ill or very frail, to take up their abode in the household of their children. This is an arrangement which is fraught with difficulties (Fried and Stern, 1948; Koller, 1954; Smith *et al.*, 1958).

Except for certain ethnic groups which represent small minorities and moreover undergo rapid Americanization, our population has come to consider the two-generation family as normal (Bossard, 1953). An aged parent in the home of an adult son or daughter is likely to be considered as a problem member. City apartments as well as modern houses reflect the expectation of occupancy only by a parental couple and their children, so that in many instances

[30] See chap. xiii.

actual crowding would result if another adult joined the household.

Another factor which complicates such arrangements is the widespread social mobility which is likely to separate parents from their adult sons and daughters in manners of living, beliefs, and types of friends. American parents have so consistently pushed their children above their own social strata that attempts at joined living arrangements are likely to fail on that account alone. This is not to say that family solidarity is necessarily lessened by social mobility of children. Although vertical social mobility of children has been reported (Dinkel, 1944; Williams, 1951) to be an agent in preventing a high development of institutionalized esteem for the aged, according to Streib's (1958) findings parents accept the upward mobility of their children and do not feel a lack of respect from them as a result of the change in social status. The retired families in Streib's study placed somewhat less importance on occupational achievement of their children than did employed families, but they, too, recognized "the importance of the achievement norms in the American occupational and stratification systems and they do not consider that adherence to them automatically impairs family relationships" (p. 50).

Over and beyond these overt reasons which may lead adult sons and daughters to view with apprehension parental retirement are deeper psychological and often unconscious factors which also come into play and are often felt if not fully understood by the persons involved. Many persons have gone through childhood without ever having outgrown dependency strivings and without having reached that degree of maturity which alone would enable them to meet the dependency needs of others. There are many people who for those very reasons cannot meet the needs of their spouses and their children. There are still more who have not reached the degree of development which would enable them to meet the needs of their parents. In relation to them they have not only inability to give but still the desire to receive. To have this desire, which may long have been dormant, stimulated by the presence of the parent in their own home and simultaneously to be under social and interpersonal pressure to reverse the relationship is something which such persons find not only impossible but deeply disturbing (Feldman, 1957). Resentment, open show of hostility, and final and overt refusal to accept the role reversal may be the result of such situations.

But even emotionally mature persons may find it difficult to meet adequately the role and status reversal between child and parent which the retirement of the latter brings about. One of the most universal human feelings in interpersonal relationships is ambivalence. And of all human relationships the one likely to create the greatest amount of ambivalence is the parent-child relationship. Child-rearing is a difficult experience both for parent and for child. The demands of physical child care on the mother and of social responsibility for the adequate development of the child on both parents and the very necessity of sharing one's abode with a dependent, unsocialized, or at least a not fully socialized individual are trying under the best of circumstances. On the other side, no child can grow up without encountering restriction and frustration from his parents no matter how loving and giving they may be. In consequence there must be ambivalence on both sides. Its negative expression is kept more or less in check by the power of parental status and the fulfilment of the parental role. When this status and role relationship, however, is reversed, the expression of the negative component of the ambivalence is likely to be stimulated on both sides. And not only is there stimulation; the actual situation offers a wealth of opportunities for acting-out. In our work- and income-conscious society retirement is status loss par excellence. The person whose familial and social power acted as a check on the expression of negative emotion is now vulnerable. He is in need

of assistance; he is a member of the household but no longer the household head. Few children can so master their old resentments that they would not utilize this reversal of the parent-child situation for a belated emotional revenge. And parents who are no longer under the self-protection of having to be giving and superior can express their own negative emotions by being demanding, reproachful, and inconsiderate.

It need not surprise us, therefore, that popular as well as scientific writings recount repeatedly the difficulties which occur when retired parents become financially dependent on or even join the households of their adult sons and daughters. On cultural as well as on psychological grounds these role and status reversals between parents and children are among the most troublesome aspects of retirement (Kardiner, 1937; Rabinovitz, 1949; Pollak, 1956).

At the same time that there are stress-producing situations in the relationships of children and their older parents, there is considerable familism among them, and assistance from family is usually available in the older generation, especially in times of illness or impoverishment. Streib (1958) studied the assistance patterns of families in retirement. There was a high degree of reciprocity of assistance between children and their parents in times of illness, with financial help and business advice as the second and third categories in which assistance was exchanged. A comparison of low- and high-income groups showed that the percentage of parents receiving gifts, financial aid, or business advice from their children was, as was to be expected, greater for those in the low-income groups. It is also of interest to note that most parents considered the maintenance of affectional and social ties of greater importance than financial assistance, although a larger percentage of retired parents as compared with those still working considered financial obligations to be more important for children to consider. The Townsend (1957) studies likewise emphasize the great amount of social interaction, help in kind, and financial aid which characterized the working-class group he studied.

While the studies reported make clear some of the emerging norms of intergenerational relationships and underscore the modifications dependent upon the changes in social, economic, occupational, and health status concomitant to old age and retirement, much more research is needed to determine normative patterns of retired families and of social attitudes toward them. The developmental tasks of the wife and husband need to be measured and related to the factors associated with adjustment in the post-working years. Studies and formulations such as those of Havighurst, Streib, Duvall, and others will need to be extended, and many new variables will need to be tested. Students of the family life-cycle have almost a fifth of the average life-span for which they have as yet established only the barest outlines of social expectancies and effective roles.

V. ATTITUDES AND EXPECTATIONS OF THE INDIVIDUAL

In interviews with retired people one sometimes hears statements like the following: "One morning I woke up and found I was retired," or "On Tuesday I still was working until 7:30 P.M., and the next morning I woke up and had nothing to do." Such statements are matched by the occasional observations of personnel officers that people do not want to think of their retirement and do not respond to invitations to come in for preretirement counseling. Apparently, the closer workers approach retirement, the more they repress the thought of retirement and then are faced with an abruptness of experience which is largely of their own making (Crook and Heinstein, 1958). Since repression is a defense against unpleasantness, it can safely be assumed that people who repress thoughts of retirement are afraid of it and expect from it essentially nothing but a deterioration of their circumstances (Fried, 1949).

The extent to which older workers reject the notion of retirement and reasons for their attitudes have been investigated in a number of studies using various occupational and geographical groups. E. H. Moore (1951) found that 41 per cent of the college professors he questioned looked forward with satisfaction to retirement; the other 59 per cent were indifferent or negative in their feelings. It has been suggested that industrial workers who have less satisfying jobs might welcome retirement more than workers in the higher-level occupations. Results are not entirely consistent, but it appears that the industrial workers look with little if any more favor upon retirement than do workers of higher occupational status. Tuckman and Lorge (1953) found that a little less than 50 per cent of the garmentworkers in their study who were still working claimed that they were looking forward to retirement. And, the authors observe, this favorable attitude is more indicative of the workers' recognition that they are no longer able to work than it is of a positive acceptance of retirement. In the San Francisco and Los Angeles areas, where a study was made of 846 industrial workers, Crook and Heinstein (1958) reported that only one out of four of the older men expressed any active interest in retiring and expected to do so voluntarily. Comparisons of the attitudes toward retirement among managerial, supervisory/professional, and manual workers employed by an oil company showed the manual workers to have a slightly less favorable attitude toward retirement than that of the other two groups (Burgess *et al.*, 1958). Retirement is also looked on with considerable disfavor by both rural and urban dwellers. Taietz *et al.* (1956) in a study of 127 persons living in rural New York showed that, of those operating farms, only 19 per cent claimed to be looking forward to retirement; the other 81 per cent disliked the notion of retirement. A somewhat higher proportion, 36 per cent, of non-farmers living in the rural area were anticipating retirement favorably. In the urban (New York City) population studied by Kutner *et al.* (1956), 34 per cent reported looking forward to retirement, while the remainder disliked the idea or were noncommittal about their feelings.

Although the populations studied in the various investigations have been small and non-representative, results are consistent in showing that, regardless of occupational level and location, no more than one-quarter to one-half of older workers approach retirement in pleasurable anticipation of the experience. Some of those who hold favorable attitudes view retirement with an anticipation of wish fulfilment and happiness which approaches a mere projection of their fantasies. Unrealistic as their expectations may be, they indicate two things. First of all, they permit the conclusion that the person's pre-retirement life has left him dissatisfied in essential areas of his need structure. Second, they suggest that this person is willing to think about his retirement and therefore is accessible to efforts intended to aid him in planning.

Perhaps one of the most realistic attitudes which an individual can have toward retirement in our culture is concern about the restriction in income which it almost invariably brings about (Hall, 1953; Crook and Heinstein, 1958). Opportunities to replace a job lost by involuntary retirement are relatively few and unlikely to bring sufficient pay to make up for the income loss. An exception to this rule seems to exist mainly for people of highly specialized knowledge or skill. In a field study of successful retirement experiences Pollak (1957) came across two instances in which persons with experience and knowledge approaching monopoly were forced into retirement at 65 and were very quickly hired as consultants by competitors of their original employers. By and large, however, a whole set of circumstances work against the income maintenance of the retired person (Steiner and Dorfman, 1957). The relentless onslaught of ever new products supported by high-pressure advertising and the

lure of instalment buying leave little income for saving in the low- and medium-income groups. The maintenance and improvement of the defense establishment of the country and the increasing demand for civilian services to be rendered by the federal, state, and local governments have finally produced a tax burden which makes substantial savings difficult even for persons with far-above-average incomes.

The destructive impact of inflation (Corson and McConnell, 1956) on financial security in old age has been mentioned in another context but has to be mentioned here also. It is doubly ravaging for the retired because no power of continued service stands behind the receipt of a pension, an annuity, or even social security, although the adjustment of the latter to inflation is somewhat protected by the voting power of our older population (McGill, 1955).

While all these factors which make numerical and real income maintenance in retirement unlikely are well known, another factor affecting the income satisfaction of the retired is generally overlooked. In our culture growth is considered a normal state of affairs. Retirement income, however, is likely to be numerically stable. This, quite apart from the initial income reduction and the actual loss of purchasing power, represents a source of discomfort. No appreciable increase can be looked forward to, and from that alone an American is likely to infer that things are somehow out of order. Inflation (if not an appreciation of the psychological implications of the stable income) is causing modifications and new experiments in pension insurance. The public pension benefits are being revised upward from time to time. It has been suggested that the Old-Age, Survivors, and Disability Insurance be pegged to the cost-of-living index.[31] Private pensions have occasionally been increased where marked hardship has resulted from very low pension levels. The variable annuity, first proposed in 1952 by the Teachers Insurance

[31] See chap. x.

and Annuity Association of America, is a new concept of insurance applicable to an individual equity-type plan to combat the threat of inflation (Greenough, 1951; Equity Annuity Life Insurance Co., 1956). To date, no pension system has been devised which provides for pension or annuity increments as the years of the pensioner advance and need for medical and personal services increases and bespeaks such an arrangement.

The loss of work, therefore, has far-reaching and realistic implications for the retired. The economic deterioration, however, by no means exhausts the consequences of losing one's job (Friedmann and Havighurst, 1954; Anderson, 1958). For men, at least, earning a living is an essential and, before retirement, the only acceptable mode of life. It is the basis of status in the eyes of their family and associates as well as in their own. It has furnished them in many instances with a basis for marital adjustment and has provided them with reference groups which they have come to consider as an anchor of their identity. Not only they but also other people are likely to think of them in terms of their jobs. And, with retirement, this identity somehow becomes a background characteristic rather than a reality. There is a world of difference between a mechanic and a retired mechanic, a minister and a retired minister, etc.

The job also determines a large number of a person's extrafamilial associations and thus provides its holder with potential human resources for the satisfaction of needs not met within his family. Frequently, it provides some kind of power experience in an organizational structure. On the other hand, where the job position places the person in a relationship of subordination, there is usually the feeling of strength which comes from being one of many in a similar position.

Most important, perhaps, a job determines a way of spending the major part of one's time. The attention and thought re-quired by the job are frequently ego supportive and protect the individual against an undue measure of self-concern. It is possible, of course, that a specific job content creates anxiety and counteracts the forces of repression, but in such instances it is unlikely that the job will be kept until retirement age. Physiologically, the demands of getting to and from the job as well as the demands of being on it force the individual to use his physical and psychological functions and thus resist the tendency to atrophy which increases with advancing years (Tuckman and Lorge, 1953; Pollak, 1956). It need not surprise us, therefore, that many people show ambivalence, if not pronounced resistance, toward retirement.

That this resistance, as we have already seen, is not universal and not the only attitude toward retirement, however, is due to a number of cultural developments which have perhaps not received enough attention in many scientific discussions of the retirement problem. In this country the recent decades have witnessed a wider and wider acceptance of the medical value system, which puts health and its maintenance over occupational performance. Retirement for reasons of health—and ultimately, if not immediately, every retirement tends to be that—becomes, therefore, an acceptable social role. The influence of regular medical checkups, which are becoming more and more part of our mores, creates in this respect probably a greater amount of preparedness than is sometimes realized by researchers. Furthermore, fun and enjoyment of leisure are being increasingly accepted among the ranks of social virtues in our culture not only for children but also for the aged. The retirement states of California, Arizona, and Florida have institutionalized these new social virtues in playgrounds for the elderly, in retirement communities, and in the subtle establishment of an atmosphere of respectability for leisure which represents a strange contrast to our Puritan heritage. Although it is exceedingly difficult for many to make the shift from the work morality for adult life to the fun morality for retirement, a certain lure is produced by this cultural development which makes the approach of retirement at least not entirely bleak. In fact, Friedmann (1958) suggests that the worker reaching retirement age during the current decade "is the transitional man; the man who is aware of the problem of enforced retirement . . . but he is also the man who has had some opportunity to prepare for retirement, to look ahead to it as a way of life which can be planned for" (pp. 124–25). Looking ahead to the decade of 1967–77, Friedmann expects the opportunity for retirement leisure to have a positive attraction. Retirement income will then afford a fairly adequate level of living; continued employment will be sought for its non-economic values. Retirement will have renewed approval, and retired people will be sought after by the community.

Finally, the increase of hierarchical organization in most work settings in our culture implies by its very nature a great number of disappointments in the expectation of advancement. Many employees must observe how others of equal age or younger outdistance them in earnings and position. Worse than that, they must continue in the same settings because of the pronounced resistance of many employers to hiring older persons. In such instances retirement attains an aspect of liberation from situations which are reminders of inadequacy or injustice and thus holds out a promise of comfort which should not be underestimated. In this context it might be appropriate to mention that in the governmental bureaucracies of Europe the expectation of retirement with a pension is one of the greatest attractions of this type of employment. The growing bureaucratization of our business organization suggests that, when pensions become more adequate to a continued decent standard of living, we may expect a tendency toward the development of similar attitudes on the part of the individual.

VI. Adjustment to Retirement

Retirement, whether it comes voluntarily, whether as a result of illness or declining capacity, or whether in response to management policy, confronts the mind and body with the problem of adjustment which change invariably implies. Retirement brings two sets of consequences. On the one hand, it offers freedom from one's long-time career activity, often routine and confining in nature, relief from the stresses of the job, and opportunity to develop new interests and activities, with room for a wider range of choices than the individual has enjoyed at any earlier point in his life. On the other hand, retirement generally results in loss of routine with regard to utilization of one's waking hours, reduction of income, reduced challenge to one's physiological performance potential, loss of status as a contributor to the economy, and broken contacts with customary associates (Friedmann and Havighurst, 1954).

These two sets of consequences present problems and ambiguities in a culture which has not yet clearly established the nature and expectancies of retirement. Some of the positive consequences may be negative in their effect, as indicated in the preceding paragraph. Thus, we find that abrupt retirement may produce a shock effect on the physiology and personality organization of the individual. This effect may be less and the adjustment may be easier if retirement has been gradual or if the individual has taken anticipatory measures. In either event, the revolutionary change from work to non-work status in a person's life pattern presents a major challenge to his inner resources.

A. Adjustment to Old Age

Ours is a culture in which attainment and maintenance of personal happiness are recognized social values and criteria of personal adequacy (Ichheiser, 1949). We want people to achieve happiness in ways which are at once personally satisfying and socially acceptable. In consequence a great deal of research interest has been devoted to an exploration of factors associated with successful and unsuccessful adjustment in old age. Moreover, if the quality of adjustment is to be evaluated, operational criteria for good and bad adjustment must be identified. The first major studies of adjustment in old age were those of Morgan (1937) and Landis (1942). These were followed by a series of important studies by Burgess and his associates at the University of Chicago, designed to determine the principal factors positively corresponding with good adjustment in old age. Using the scale "Your Activities and Attitudes" (Cavan *et al.*, 1949), they found the factors to be satisfactory health, being married and having good family relations and friendships, participation in leisure time and other activities, membership in at least one organization, lack of discriminatory or other unhappy experience of more than episodical character, a self-concept of being middle-aged rather than elderly, a feeling of permanent security, a social status equal to that held previously, plans for the future, participation in religious activities, and a belief in life after death (Burgess, 1950). A number of other studies, using the Chicago scale with various populations, has corroborated, with slight variation, the findings of the original Burgess, Cavan, and Havighurst studies (Shanas, 1950; Albrecht, 1951; Britton and Britton, 1951; Schmidt, 1951; Britton, 1953; Havighurst and Albrecht, 1953; Morrison and Kristjanson, 1958). Kutner *et al.* (1956), employing a scale of morale, and Phillips (1957), using a scale of fantasy escape from non-rewarding roles, identified essentially the same set of factors as positively related to personal adjustment in later maturity, except that Kutner found the significance of the factors varied among subcultural groups. Thus a variable posi-

tively related to adjustment for one socio-economic group might be negatively related for another. Kuhlen (1959) has given an excellent critique of these studies and of the validity of the instruments used in measuring adjustment. In general, he points out that, because of the lack of external criteria of good or poor adjustment, original misconceptions of those designing the instruments are likely to go uncorrected. However, he concludes that data on factors related to adjustment are becoming sufficiently extensive to provide a source of hypotheses for further research.

Much of the research interest, beyond establishing the characteristics of the well-adjusted old person, has been centered around the phenomenon of retirement, its effects upon the individual, and the determinants of good and poor adjustment after separation from work (Barron, 1954).

B. The Process of Adjustment

Ideally, the process of adjustment to retirement should be continuous over the life-span. If it is true that the child is father to the man, a man's retirement experience may be predetermined so early that any suggestions of having the adjustment process start with the onset of retirement or a few years earlier may seem irrevocably too little and too late. Such a conclusion, however, would presuppose that adjustment to retirement requires a basic personality change. If adjustment to retirement is viewed only as a synchronization of a man's specific need and attitude pattern with the opportunities left and opened up for him after retirement, it becomes perfectly feasible to visualize the process as beginning at a time when the individual becomes aware of the approach to his retirement. Awareness is increasingly brought about by planned management action which is intended to counteract the tendency of many employees to repress any thoughts of retirement as long as they possibly can. Methods intended to put the conscious adjustment process into motion are not yet standardized. Some companies write letters at regular intervals and distribute literature pertaining to retirement problems. Others subscribe to commercial preretirement programs whose services range from sending printed minutes to the employee at stated intervals to counseling directly with the individual worker (Hall, 1953). Still others arrange lecture series in which experts talk to employees approaching retirement age on such topics as finances, health, family relationships, and recreation (Boyle, 1952, 1953; Robson, 1952; Donahue, 1953; Tennessee Valley Authority, 1957). Others again have such employees visited sometime before the retirement date by a personnel officer who discusses their plans (Anonymous, 1951, 1953, 1957a; Hewitt and Associates, 1952; Laird, 1954).

After retirement a considerable number of persons go through a transitional period which probably includes several successive phases. Havighurst (1955) describes three. The first period immediately following separation from work has sometimes a project character. People take a long-wished-for trip, they go on an extended hunting tour, they fix up the house, or they dissolve their household and move to a retirement community. Whatever the specific content is, it lacks the promise of continuity, and this constitutes a situation which probably engenders frustration and anxiety. Kutner and his associates (1956) found in a small sample of retirees that only 19 per cent of the recently retired men achieved a high morale rating. He concludes that "for men the years immediately following the loss of traditional role of breadwinner are a period of considerable stress" (p. 88). In a study of preretirement anticipation, Thompson (1958) found that in every case those who anticipated their retirement in a positive fashion were the less likely to have taken more than 3 months to become used to retirement. Holding an accurate preconception of retirement for which the retiree makes plans facilitates the speed with which adjustment to the non-working status is made. But, among those who do not have an accurate notion of the nature of retirement life, those without plans are more likely than those with plans to take less time to get used to retirement. Thompson describes the situation as follows: "In a sense, having plans, but an inaccurate view of retirement, may create a double problem of adjustment: not only must the retiree cope with the inevitable problems of changed status, but also he must cope with the disappointment of thwarted plans and must adjust his own thinking and planning in terms of reality as he finds it" (p. 39).

The second phase of the retirement process, as noted by Havighurst, is characterized by restlessness and seeking out roles and setting new levels of aspiration compatible with the assigned roles and status of retirees in our society. The reports of companies which have kept in post-retirement touch with their employees indicate that, on an average, these first two phases of retirement adjustment are accomplished within a period of from 6 to 12 months. In a special survey of a cross-section of a group of 483 retired men in Cleveland (Anonymous, 1952) who had been retired from 1 to 5 years, 56 per cent reported that by the end of 6 months they were used to being retired; 68 per cent achieved this level of adaptation by the end of the first year.

After the initial crisis of separation from the labor force, which is of varying lengths and intensity, there follows in most instances a period of stability in adjustment to retirement which may be highly successful. During this period the retiree carries out the roles he has selected for himself or those that are left open to him. Havighurst (1960) lists the roles available beyond growing family and work life to be those of citizen, association member, church member, friend, user of leisure time, and student. These roles, though the list is smaller in number than for younger age groups, are not different from those enjoyed by younger persons, although the status they afford and the methods used in fulfilling them may be somewhat modified for the aged. According to the criteria used by Havighurst (1957), social role competency does not diminish with age. The retiree establishes a new pattern of spending the day, finds new patterns of domestic interaction, makes new contacts, and cuts expenditures to size. It is in this period of later maturity that the individual may have a second flowering and find satisfaction in new avenues of self-fulfilment (Tibbitts, 1958). According to Linden (1958), "Many people upon entering the mature years are excited by the new set of experiences and are stimulated by the challenge. [In response] such individuals go forward in life then enlarging egos, increasing the scope of their feelings and activities so that they are able to encompass many aspects of living" (p. 86).

But it must be recognized that the process of retirement is probably never quite finished, because there may be a long succession of crises which will require a long series of difficult adjustments (Webber, 1958). In the course of time the new patterns are threatened again by disease and bereavement. Again new adjustments have to be found, and it is in this last period that the presence of a philosophy of life which enables the individual to see his losses in a wider perspective is essential to positive adjustment.

C. Impact of Retirement upon Health

A popular theme for the last 10 years has been that of the injustice of administrative retirement when applied to workers able, willing, and wanting to work. The generally accepted stereotype of the effect of retirement, especially if it is abrupt and based on chronological age, described the impact in negative terms of emotional shock resulting in such consequences as breakdown in health, mental illness, or possibly death. Professional and lay people alike held this view. Results of careful in-

vestigations, carried out over the last decade, however, fail to provide support for this prevailing opinion (Parron and Associates, 1953).

Tuckman and Lorge (1953) interviewed 660 older members of the International Ladies' Garment Workers' Union in New York City and compared three groups— those still working, those still employed but already having applied for retirement, and the retired. The retired were asked to compare their health before and after retirement with reference to a three-point scale: same as before, better than before, worse than before. Almost half (48 per cent) reported that their health was better after retirement; a third said it was the same; and only one-sixth reported it was worse. Streib and Thompson (1957), in a longitudinal in-plant study of occupational retirement, likewise failed to find that retirement leads to poor health. The retired and the non-retired in their sample of over a thousand males did not differ significantly in the proportion whose health improved, worsened, or remained the same when interviewed again 12–18 months following the initial assessment.

In order to test the retirement-impact hypothesis, Emerson (1959) studied 124 men drawn from the doctors' lists at the Executive Council of a large city in England. The men were all interviewed a week prior to their sixty-fifth birthdays and again after intervals of 6 and 12 months. The four indexes used to measure the effects of retirement were (1) physical health, (2) mental health, (3) activities and social contacts, and (4) general attitudes. In addition to a general interview, the Heron Personality Inventory, the Cornell Index, and a personal diary were the instruments used to compare the reactions of those men who continued to work with those who were in one category or another of retirement. The data from all these measures failed to support the retirement-impact hypothesis, because retirement was found to have no effect on physical or mental health, although some tensions were apparent in the period immediately following retirement. Adjustments and adaptations in behavioral and attitudinal patterns took place rapidly, and a passive pattern of living was soon established. Significance of the findings of this small study are enhanced by the fact they corroborate findings of other investigations.

Some evidence has been offered that indicates retirement may actually have a beneficial effect on health and longevity. In a study of the shifts in health among those who retired during a 2-year period and those who continued working throughout the same period, Thompson and Streib (1958) found that the retirees and the gainfully employed are about equally likely to shift in their self-ratings but that the retirees are more likely to improve in health, while the gainfully employed are more likely to decline.[32] Another study which provides evidence that retirement may lead to an improvement in health is that of Tyhurst and his colleagues (1957). Evaluation of medical and personal histories taken before and after retirement of a large sample of pensioners of a large communications industry showed on an average either no change or improvement in health after retirement. A study of the mortality data of all pensioners (898) from the company between 1917 and 1954 revealed no increase in death rate ensuing upon retirement. There was also no significant difference in death rates between groups retiring at different ages, except that the death rates in the later years following retirement are higher for those who worked to a later age. The authors conclude:

All the results obtained from the various methods of study lead us to conclude that retirement in the industrial population under study does not hasten death, nor does it lead to the deterioration of health. On the contrary, we have given some evidence to show that mortality is lower in the period immediately following retirement than it is later on, regard-

[32] See chap. vii.

less of the age of retirement. There is also some indication that people retiring at a younger age have lower mortality rates in the later years than do people who retire at an older age. With regard to health, we see evidence that there is an improvement in health status rather than a decline for the majority of people studied [p. 1444].

A study of mortality tables (Myers, 1954a, 1954b) shows that death rates for males who retire voluntarily are higher immediately after retirement than they are for the same age group in the male population generally but that death rates for workers retired compulsorily are in agreement with actuarial expectancy. The voluntarily retired group is probably padded with a disproportionate number of men in poor health, while the compulsorily retired group probably includes a disproportionate number of healthy workers.

The association between retirement and mortality has also been explored by McMahan and Ford (1955) by studying survival rates of two samples of Army and Air Force officers who spent any time in retirement during a 23-year period. They failed to find lowered survival rates during the first 5-year period of retirement in comparison with comparable age groups in two subsequent 5-year periods of retirement. In a further study, McMahan (1958) reported on the analysis of mortality rates for two other population groups and again did not find support for the hypothesis that survival rates are consistently lower for the initial period of three consecutive 5-year retirement periods.

It appears, then, from these several studies that, contrary to common opinion, retirement does not generally result in rapid physical and mental decline and early death. Earlier retirement actually may conserve health and extend life. These findings do not gainsay the fact that adjustment in retirement is a major problem requiring investigation to isolate the important and interrelated variables associated with it. A number of studies have already been undertaken to establish the part played by such factors as personality dynamics, attitudes toward work and retirement, age and occupational status at the time of retirement, anticipatory socialization, economic status, health, etc.

D. Factors Associated with Adjustment in Retirement

Retirement has come to large numbers of persons only within a recent period so that not enough time has elapsed for large-scale investigations of its consequences to be completed and reported. There are, however, a number of studies of various occupational groups and one large longitudinal study—the Cornell Study of Occupational Retirement—which are yielding data useful to understanding the nature of the retirement process and to defining the factors from which predictions relating to probable adjustment in retirement may eventually be made. Admittedly, most of the populations used, as pointed out by the investigators themselves, permit only limited generalization because of the small number of subjects or because of their non-representativeness of the total working population in the United States (Shanas, 1958). Nevertheless, the consistency of results from one study to another argues for considerable validity of some of the findings.

PERSONALITY AS A FACTOR IN
RETIREMENT ADJUSTMENT

The emotional meaning of retirement to any given individual will be largely dependent upon his personality dynamics. Recently, Johnson (1958) described a depressive retirement syndrome which he encounters in clinical practice and which appears among persons who are emotionally equipped only for work. The syndrome differs from involutional melancholia in several ways, chief of which are the absence of guilt and self-accusatory attitudes and its more clear association with the age of retirement. Johnson analyzes the process as follows:

Retirement accents a defect already going on. Persons with retirement symptoms have usually functioned in work as passive recipients of implied approval, acceptance, and appreciation. . . . Much of the clinical picture in these individuals is explained by a single bit of psychopathology: inability to cathect human objects unambivalently. Work lends itself to an expenditure of energy in a relatively safe, impersonal orientation. When the worker stops . . . he feels pressure from society to invest more emotionally in other human beings . . . but his capacity to derive satisfaction from these relationships is limited, and the emotional needs continue. As a result, the compromise formations (presenting symptoms) . . . arise [p. 318].

The accuracy of Johnson's formulation and the frequency with which the retirement syndrome appears among the retired populations are subjects which bear further study.

A frame of reference which utilizes a typology that includes cultural as well as clinical considerations has been proposed by Riesman (1954). He identifies three major groups: (1) the autonomous, who are persons bearing within themselves psychological sources of self-renewal, with the consequence that they are relatively immune to cultural changes or to the meanings of their physical aging; (2) the adjusted, who lack the inner resources for self-renewal "but are the beneficiaries of a cultural preservative (derived from work, power, position, and so on) which sustains them" as long as the cultural conditions remain stable and protective; and (3) the anomic, who lack inner resources and are not equipped to make use of the cultural preservatives. For each of these kinds of individuals, retirement presents a different problem. The autonomous, immune from cultural change, merely calls on his own creativeness to continue in a "productive orientation"; the adjusted, dependent upon cultural supports, attempts to maintain the appearance of functionality even though he is faced with an inner sterility which makes it impossible for him to create really new roles for himself to substitute for work; the anomic, lacking both inner and outer support, simply deteriorates as his vital physiological processes diminish in efficiency.

Peck (1956) has proposed a developmental conceptualization as a basis for explaining the behavioral correlates of the changes which take place during the second half of life. He explains that "it is not how people 'adjust' to those attributes which decline, but how they transcend their animal limitations—how they develop new, different uniquely human powers, to the fullest extent—which may mark the truly developmental aspects of the years beyond 35" (p. 42).

Using Erikson's (1950) developmental theory as a basis, Peck suggests a series of stages of adaptation for the middle and later years. Pertinent to retirement adjustment is the stage of ego differentiation as contrasted with work-role preoccupation. Persons who have developed a high degree of ego differentiation may be expected to make a successful adaptation to old age because they will have established a variety of valued activities and self-attributes; thus they have available a number of alternatives to work which may be pursued with satisfaction and a sense of worthwhileness.

When Peck's theoretical construct is applied to members of different social classes, it becomes apparent that those from the lower socioeconomic levels as compared to those from the upper socioeconomic groups have less opportunity and, perhaps, ability to develop ego differentiations widely or to practice those achieved. Thus studies which measure social participation show that the members of the higher social class tend to have higher participation rates and engage in a greater variety of activities. Age does not change these trends, although retirement does tend to reduce participation of all groups (Albrecht, 1951; Taietz

and Larson, 1956; Orbach and Shaw 1957).

MEANING OF WORK AND ADJUSTMENT TO RETIREMENT

In a society which places prime value on the worker role, retirement to a non-worker role is generally to be interpreted as a movement to a lesser position, with consequent lowering of status in the societal hierarchy. Thus it is assumed that relatively few, by free choice, will elect this change and that the circumstances which force the downward mobility—health, administrative retirement, age, etc.—will contribute to the non-adjustment of the individual. As already pointed out, there is a good deal of resistance to retirement by most older persons. Farmers, professional workers and other self-employed persons, and the majority of wage-earners resist retirement as long as their health remains good and the job continues to have meaning and rewards (Fried, 1949; Shanas and Havighurst, 1953; Friedmann and Havighurst, 1954; Myers, 1954*a*; Tibbitts, 1954; Taietz *et al.*, 1956; Crook and Heinstein, 1958; Moore, 1959).

On the other hand, when the job has been unrewarding, when it has become too demanding physically or mentally, when it involves stressful relationships with colleagues, or when it has other strong negative qualities, retirement may come to have a relatively high positive value (Tuckman and Lorge, 1953). As a matter of fact, Michelon (1954) found this inverse correlation between a person's adjustment to his job and his adjustment to retirement when he made a study of a small sample of residents of a Florida trailer park. When the meaning of work to the individual had been positive, the transition to retirement was more difficult than when work meanings were negative or neutral. Fried (1949), on the contrary, in a study of the case histories of seventy-five persons between 50 and 80 years of age chosen from among three socioeconomic classes, found that

it is the unsuccessful person who has not been able to achieve his ambition and the person who whole or half-heartedly subscribes to the contention that old people belong on a shelf who clings most tenaciously to active working life. . . . Persons in the first category are motivated by a strong wish to demonstrate that they can yet achieve success and similarly those in the second category want to disprove the theory of decline in the old which injures their self-esteem. By contrast those who are convinced of their value both as individuals and as older persons experience their task as completed and find retirement more easily acceptable [p. 148].

Both the Michelon and the Fried studies included too few cases to be significant beyond indicating that the demands made by a job and occupational success are factors deserving further investigation.

Studies of the meaning of work (Friedmann and Havighurst, 1954) have identified the several functions of work and their attendant meanings. It is assumed that, if substitute means of supplying these positive factors associated with the worker role can be found in retirement, the retiree will be better able to adjust to his changed social circumstances. In practice, however, the relationship is not simply achieved, because, as Webber (1958) points out, "the role of producer or worker has positive meaning within the context of society and . . . the occupant of the role tends to receive social approval. By contrast the activities of the retired person have meaning within the limited personal framework rather than within the societal one" (p. 131). Lacking social approval, the retiree's own perception of his worth is impaired, and the hoped-for substitute satisfactions are not forthcoming. Thus Kutner and associates (1956) found among their Kips Bay–Yorkville population that only activities that were socially meaningful contributed to the morale of the individual. If the activities did not provide status, achievement, and recognition, they contributed lit-

tle to the individual's adjustment. Fried (1949) found for her lower-class subjects not only that activities must be considered to be useful but also that, unless they brought monetary rewards, they were felt to be culturally unacceptable. It should be added, however, that Friedmann and Havighurst (1954) found some workers in all occupational categories studied who were unable to replace in retirement the life-meanings and satisfactions they found in their work but who still found retirement a pleasant experience. Further studies will, no doubt, make clear some of the attendant factors associated with the ability to adapt satisfactorily to the loss of meaningful work roles and those related to the "hard core of workers for whom there can be no adequate substitute for the job" (Friedmann and Havighurst, 1954, p. 186). Bower (1954) found that among a small sample of salespersons "who valued their work highly there was a marked similarity in personality in that they talked readily, vividly, and at length, and experienced the feeling that nothing outside their work life could offer the rewards and satisfactions they found in their jobs" (pp. 129–30). No such similarity of personality appeared among those who placed lowest value on their work.

PRERETIREMENT ATTITUDES AND ADJUSTMENT IN RETIREMENT

A number of studies here have been concerned with how anticipatory attitudes toward retirement might be related to adjustment in retirement. If looking forward to retirement preconditions satisfaction with it, efforts at anticipatory socialization by establishing realistic expectancies of the experience should result in better adjustment. Fried (1949) studied case histories of twenty-four retired workers from various occupational groups and reported that serious illness and depression occurred more frequently among those who had no advance warning that they were to be retired than among those who had been prepared to retire at a certain age. Notably, however, 35 per cent of those who were unprepared reported satisfaction with retirement. Fifty-one per cent of the prepared were likewise satisfied. The findings of Tuckman and Lorge (1953) indicate that there was a tendency for the garment-workers who found retirement to their liking to have prepared for it to a greater extent than did those who did not like retirement.

Kutner *et al.* (1956) asked the retirees in their study population to evaluate their retirement experience as better than they expected, worse than expected, and about as expected; the retirees were also requested to indicate their recalled anticipation of retirement with reference to whether they had looked forward to it, had disliked the notion, or were noncommittal or qualified in their feelings. The findings show that approximately as many (29 per cent) found retirement better than expected as found it worse (31 per cent) than expected. Favorable expectations were reported most frequently (51 per cent) by those who assessed retirement as better than expected, and negative anticipation was reported most frequently (66 per cent) by those who found retirement worse than anticipated. With reference to the extent retirement expectations influence adjustment, it was found that, of those who had looked forward to retirement, 82 per cent found it better than or the same as expected, while, of those who disliked the idea of retirement, 85 per cent found it worse than or as they had expected it to be.

A study of the workers in the Cornell Study of Occupational Retirement who had retired by the time of a third follow-up was made by Thompson (1958) to relate differences in adjustment as indexed *after* retirement to differences in anticipation which were indexed *before* retirement occurred. Independent variables used were attitude toward retirement before the event occurred, preconception of what retirement would be like, and plans for retirement; dependent variables were length of time it took to adjust to the retirement status, difficulty in keeping busy, and dissatisfaction with retirement. "The findings suggest that in every instance the two most important factors are an accurate preconception of retirement and a favorable pre-retirement attitude toward retirement" (p. 43). Planning for retirement was of less importance to good adjustment in the post-working period, but, as Thompson points out, it may be that planning has an indirect influence through helping the worker develop a favorable anticipatory attitude toward retirement.

HEALTH AND ADJUSTMENT IN RETIREMENT

Although there is evidence to show that retirement does not lead to decline in health (see above), the health of retirees is on an average poorer than it is for those of the same age who are still employed (Kutner *et al.*, 1956; Thompson and Streib, 1958). The prevalence of ill-health among retirees thus makes the question of its relationship to adjustment in retirement of prime importance. The health status of the retired industrial workers studied by Tuckman and Lorge (1953) was found to be associated with their attitude toward retirement. Of the men who reported their health to be better after retirement, 60 per cent indicated that they liked retirement, compared with 43 per cent who reported no change and 34 per cent who reported poorer health.

In a study of morale of a nation-wide sample of males, Streib (1956) reported that health (self-evaluated), low socioeconomic status, and work status tend to act independently and to create a cumulative effect on adjustment as measured by morale. A person who was retired but who had good health and high socioeconomic status was more likely to have high morale than a person who was still employed but who lacked either good health or high income (Table 9).

In a further study Thompson and Streib (1958) concluded that health (self-evaluated) was not related to adjustment in retirement. Table 10 shows that approximately the same proportions of those in good health and of those in poor health report dissatisfaction with retirement. These authors offer the following explanation of this lack of relationship between health and adjustment in retirement:

Inasmuch as the pattern is one of poor health leading to retirement and not the reverse, we are describing a situation in which retirement with its less taxing demands has the positive value of making a given state of health more adequate. . . . Under these circumstances, it is hardly surprising that retirement specifically should be equally attractive to those who are in good or in poor health [p. 32].

The picture is a more complicated one when health and economic deprivation, on the one hand, are related to measures of adjustment to retirement, on the other. The

TABLE 9*

MORALE BY WORK STATUS, HEALTH, AND
SOCIOECONOMIC STATUS OF 897 MALES

Work Status	Health	Socio-economic Status	Per Cent with High Morale
Retired.........	Poor	Low	29
Retired.........	Poor	High	29
Employed.......	Poor	Low	31
Retired.........	Good	Low	33
Employed.......	Poor	High	51
Employed.......	Good	Low	61
Retired.........	Good	High	63
Employed.......	Good	High	75

* Source: G. F. Streib, "Morale of the Retired," *Social Problems,* **3** (1956), 275, Table 6.

person who is encumbered by both poor health and economic deprivation is more likely to be poorly adjusted in general.

These studies of Thompson and Streib indicate the importance of studying these factors as independent but interrelated aspects. It is probable that the other studies enumerated previously which found a relationship between health and personal ad-

justment in old age would, if the data were to be treated similarly, show the same type of independence and interrelatedness as found by the Cornell researchers.

In the Cleveland survey of retired men (Anonymous, 1952), 61 per cent of those who had a positive attitude toward retirement judged their health to be better after

TABLE 10*

HEALTH STATUS AND ADJUSTMENT OF
477 MALES IN RETIREMENT

Indexes of Satisfaction with Retirement	Per Cent in Good Health	Per Cent in Poor Health
Finding not working difficult...	29	27
"Dissatisfied with retirement"...	26	29
Looking for work.............	29	28

* Source: Adapted from W. E. Thompson and G. F. Streib, "Situational Determinants: Health and Economic Deprivation in Retirement," *Journal of Social Issues,* **14**, No. 2 (1958), 31.

retiring, and only 17 per cent considered themselves healthier before retirement. On the other hand, among those who had a negative attitude about retiring, 5 per cent said that they were healthier since retirement than before, but 30 per cent claimed to be in less good health than before retiring. In the Thompson-Streib (1958) study it was found that, among those whose preretirement attitude was favorable and whose economic status was not deemed deprived, 15 per cent or fewer expressed dissatisfaction; but, among those whose preretirement attitude was unfavorable and who were economically deprived, 54 per cent expressed dissatisfaction.

ECONOMIC CIRCUMSTANCES
AND ADJUSTMENT

For obvious reasons, economic security is, along with health, one of the principal variables studied in reference to adjustment in retirement and to old age. Tuckman and Lorge (1953) noted that a significant number of their older workers liked the idea of retirement and would have retired if they had been financially able to do so. Most of the studies already mentioned have reported a positive relationship between economic security and good adjustment to old age. On the other hand, Havighurst and Albrecht (1953) found in their "Prairie City" study that there was only a slight tendency for those in the lower socioeconomic status to have lower adjustment scores. They concluded that "poor old people have about as good a chance of adjustment as wealthy people." Morrison and Kristjanson (1958) analyzed the personal adjustment of residents in a South Dakota community and found that only the extremes of the income categories conform to the expected pattern of a positive relationship between level of income and personal adjustment. Hall (1953) reported that there were instances in which retired executives who viewed their financial preparation as inadequate felt that this inadequacy was the chief factor which brought unhappiness in retirement. But an equal number of retirees were getting along well in retirement who had about the same proportion of their former salaries as did the unhappy retirees. Individual differences in values and attitudes may be a determining factor when income is above that needed for the primary needs.

The multivariate technique applied by Thompson and Streib (1958) to the retired members of the Cornell study group reveals the interrelationship of economic deprivation with other determinants of adjustment to retirement.

Beginning with the assumption that a drop in income creates a problem only when it is not matched by a retrenchment in wants, the investigators, using self-evaluation of economic means, compared changes in economic deprivation reported in 1952 and 1954 and 1954 and 1956. During the first period about a third became more deprived; during the second period this number had decreased to less than a fourth. Thompson and Streib (1958) propose the following explanation:

By the second year of retirement, the initial "shock" of a radically reduced income has been overcome and the adjustment which is made includes a re-evaluation of economic means as they pertain to the new way of life. In effect, as an index of success in making an adjustment to the retired status, this finding suggests the possibility that the adaptability of retirees may have been underestimated, that a high proportion of retirees are possessed of sufficient "role flexibility" so that adjusting to greatly reduced income is possible [p. 27].

Other outcomes of the study show that whether retirement was voluntary or compulsory made no difference with reference to the self-evaluation of changes in economic means but that having a negative pre-retirement attitude toward retirement makes it more difficult to become reoriented in terms of lower income. When income was held constant, only 8 per cent of willing retirees with high incomes reported income deprivation, but 29 per cent of reluctant retirees with high incomes felt that they were so deprived. When economic deprivation is studied in relation to measures of adjustment, a positive relation appears. The economically deprived are very much more likely than the non-deprived to find not working difficult, to be dissatisfied with retirement, and to be looking for work. Further, the person who is in poor health and considers himself economically deprived is more likely to be dissatisfied with life, dejected, and without hope than if he lacks only one of the situational determinants of health and economic sufficiency.

The studies of adjustment in retirement are valuable from an actuarial point of view and furnish some useful guides for the design of a model of mental health in retirement. From the viewpoint of preparation for retirement, however, they need implementation in the area of meaning to the persons involved. What does it mean to a person to have a hobby? What does it mean to belong to an organization? What does it mean to participate in religious activities? Some people engage in a hobby to kill time. For others it is an experience of creativity. Some belong to organizations because they have not the courage to drop their membership. Others do so because the purpose of the organization matters to them. Some go to church on Sundays in order to avoid public censure, while others go for a spiritual experience.

And, even more important, how durable are some of the factors associated with good adjustment according to these correlational studies? Is good health likely to last? How long can a self-concept of being middle-aged rather than elderly be maintained? Can self-deception, however euphoric its effect, ever be considered as good adjustment? For such reasons some writers have occasionally designated a philosophy of life or an integration of one's life-experience as the essential basis of mental health in aging. Unfortunately, content descriptions of such philosophies of life are largely lacking in the professional literature. What seems to be postulated here is not retention of characteristics of youthfulness, be they physiological, mental, or social. It is rather a frame of reference for one's own existence in which the disappearance of youthfulness can be experienced with equanimity or even with affirmation. The operation of principles of good continuation and closure rather than of the principle of similarity with preceding phases of the life-cycle seems to be called for in a philosophy of life which would be sustaining man in the advanced phases of his existence. The absence of case material in this respect, however, is not surprising. Clinical studies are geared to and preoccupied with pathology. Persons burdened by emotional discomforts present themselves to the clinician. The research material comes to him. The healthy and adjusted do not come to clinics or welfare agencies. They would have to be sought out, and, for this, clinicians up to now have had neither time nor calling. It seems highly indicated, therefore, to turn research and case-study interest to cases of positive adjustment in retirement and to study its process as well as its content.

VII. THE CONTENT OF POSITIVE ADJUSTMENT TO RETIREMENT

As indicated above, disturbingly little case material is as yet available on which to base propositions regarding the nature of positive experiences in retirement. The modest beginning which Pollak (1957) was able to make in this respect suggests, however, that there exist two categories of retirement experiences which in the opinion of the retired person himself and in the opinion of his associates can be classified as positive. The first category comprises cases in which an individual is able to satisfy interests centered in himself and in the present. He has found a way to occupy himself with the pursuit of need satisfactions which are meaningful to him in the light of his life-experiences. Man's need patterns are monotonous and often remain at least partially unsatisfied. In that sense almost every person's life at the verge of retirement represents a fragment which demands completion either through continuation of essential interests or through a catching-up with one's own wishes. The past life of a person may have brought him satisfaction in the pursuit of work, service to others, or recreational pursuits. In all three areas continuation can occur after retirement, although continuation of work in such instances is frequently limited to people with rare skills or with such a devotion to their work that they are willing to take considerable diminution of status in order to maintain contact with a specific field of activities. Much more auspicious are the chances of those who have found before their retirement a service concern or a recreational activity which represents to them an essential expression of their existence. Where the interests of a person are so distributed, retirement actually creates opportunities for further concentration and far greater enjoyment. Often, however, it seems to be not the activity as such which provides the adjustment promoting gratification but a specific emotional meaning which is connected with it. Work may be a

way to please one's wife, service a way to
please a parent or a way to honor the memory of a husband long departed, gardening
a way to satisfy competitive striving.
Wherever a retirement activity seemed to
lead to positive adjustment, a special emotional meaning was attached to the activity, and that meaning was frequently related to interpersonal experiences in the
life-history of the individual.

In some ways catching up with one's own
wishes is a more dramatic form of gaining
positive experiences in retirement than continuation of meaningful interests which
had been pursued before retirement. Holding a job and making a living often are
exacting assignments which prevent an individual from doing what he really wants
to do. To people so caught in the trap of
daily demands retirement can be the first
and last opportunity of wish fulfilment or
at least of wish pursuit. Among the cases
which came to the attention of Pollak,
there were instances in which the employment experience itself had engendered
wishes for another type of work, and retirement had furnished the opportunity for its
pursuit. This new type of work was usually related to the type of work performed
before retirement, but it presented a version more congenial to the need pattern of
the individual. In other cases people caught
up with wishes which they had conceived
long before they had entered gainful employment. There were, for instance, three
persons who found fulfilment and gratification in finally doing what their fathers had
done, one by going into the real estate
business, another into newspaper work, and
the third into painting. This type of retirement conduct throws an interesting
light on the power of ambivalence toward
parental figures. That people frequently
express negative feelings toward their fathers by refusing to follow them in their
occupation or profession is well known.
That some seem to have a need to express
the positive side of the ambivalence by
managing in retirement a belated identifi-

cation in activity or conduct may furnish
important leads toward guiding people to
meaningful experiences in that stage of
life.

The reversal of the motivation just described also made its appearance in the
group of cases studied by Pollak. There
were people who managed to gain meaningful retirement experiences by turning
negative feelings toward relatives into socially acceptable retirement conduct. Apparently, leisure in retirement can be more
enjoyed by some, if by so doing they settle
old emotional scores with puritanical fathers. And some gain the impetus to civic
efforts from their negative feelings toward
relatives who have accepted a life of leisure.

A specific meaning of retirement conduct, however, does not seem to be enough
to create a positive experience. Apparently,
it has to be associated with three other factors in order to do that. It seems to require the persistence of appropriate capacities commensurate with the demands
of the interest pursued, a measure of social
acceptance if not recognition, and harmony
with the marriage partner over its pursuit.
The need for appropriate capacities is perhaps most convincingly demonstrated in
those instances in which the purpose and
meaning of inactivity in retirement is the
preservation of health. As long as the organism responds to rest with a sensation of
well-being or recuperation, the inactivity
can be a very positive experience to the retired person. When the organism fails to
respond, rest, however meaningful, fails to
provide the positive experience which it
was intended to create. Social approval,
apparently, is a greater need in retirement
than it is before. Persons with much time
ahead may be able to take comfort in the
expectation that the future will bring them
the recognition which presently they lack;
older persons have no such refuge. At any
rate, Pollak found no instance in which
pursuit of an interest, however meaningful,
satisfied a retired person when social rec-

ognition was not forthcoming. People who had taken up painting wanted to see their pictures admired. People who had taken up weaving found enjoyment in this activity only if they could sell their rugs.

Finally, no instance of successful retirement came to Pollak's attention in which the retirement conduct interfered with the gratification of the need pattern of the spouse. The increased importance of the marriage relationship in this phase of life makes harmony with the spouse apparently a *conditio sine qua non* of positive adjustment. In this respect a pitfall seems frequently to lie in the inclination of many men to choose a retirement activity which requires a change in domicile, thus uprooting the wife at a time when she needs stability more than ever. This seems to apply less to migrations to retirement states such as Florida and California than to changes from urban to rural settings. Disregard of the needs of the marriage partner in retirement planning is dangerous on two counts. It interferes, first, with the gratification potential of the one interpersonal relationship which is likely to be intensified by retirement and thus with the performance of the only social role which gains importance in that stage of life. And, second, it exposes the retired person to the hostility reactions of his spouse at a time when his defense potential composed of status and the fortress of shop or office has been materially reduced.

The second category of cases in which retirement brought positive experiences to the individuals involved was characterized by a completely different outlook on life. Instead of centering their perception upon themselves, the retired individuals composing this category focused their concern upon a larger whole in the context of which they viewed themselves only as a small part—small but not insignificant. Into this group belonged, first of all, truly religious individuals who found in retirement a liberation from secular demands which had interfered with their need to spend time in worship or preparation for the hereafter in which they believed. These people found in their worship, in their service activities, and in some instances even in their diseases and sufferings, the part which had been assigned to them in the plan of the Creator and found in this part significance and fulfilment. There were also people, however, who attained a similar orientation apparently without the aid of an organized framework of religious beliefs. Strong concern with the well-being of others or with the growth of an idea also seemed to furnish a framework of perception in which individual discomforts became relatively insignificant and in which retirement did not have the implication of loss but the implication of the task of finding and helping a successor. An orientation which subordinated the self to concern with the continuation and growth of something larger seemed to hold tremendous adjustment-promoting power, particularly under conditions in which the four-factor constellation of the individual gratification outlined above was threatened or already impaired.

VIII. Preparation for Retirement

A. The Trend toward Retirement Preparation

The dominant time orientation of our culture is future-directed. Americans mortgage their present for the future, invest in their children, anticipate that the years will bring bigger and better things. The clearly distinguishable roles of early adulthood and middle age are seen as the means by which these anticipated goals are to be achieved. As retirement begins to figure as part of the future, a gap in the institutional structure becomes apparent. Missing are the established roles for older people correlative with those of the earlier decades of life. If the retiree wants something other than what Burgess has referred to as the "roleless role" of the retired, it is, as Thompson (1958) observes, incumbent upon the retiree to create the new roles for himself. Management, unions, and employees, recognizing this hiatus in the role structure, are coming more and more to accept preparation for retirement as a function of personnel work, unionism, and individual planning. Perrow (1957), reporting on a nation-wide survey of company practices, states that, in 1952, 50 per cent of the companies in the sample claimed that they offered some type of counseling; by 1954 the proportion had increased to 65 per cent.

It has been suggested that the motives behind industry's acceptance of the proposition that it should help employees prepare for retirement are mixed and may include, in addition to a humanitarian sense of obligation to long-standing employees (Boyle, 1952; Perrow, 1957; Thompson, 1958), a desire to encourage superannuated personnel to retire (Douglas, 1955), a fear of government intervention if too many retirees are unhappy in retirement and become vocal about it (Boyle, 1952), and a belief that dissatisfied retirees will affect public relations adversely. Unions, likewise, may have complex reasons for taking leadership in the preparation of their members for the transition to a non-working status (Odell, 1959). It is of interest to note in this respect that the worker is usually allowed to retain his union membership and frequently his voting privileges after retirement. In fact, unions make the point that, while industry retires the worker, the union never superannuates him. In addition to the motivation provided by this type of competition between unions and management to serve as the cushioners of the workers' transition to retirement, the unions are feeling direct pressure from the retirees themselves. Having become accustomed to union intervention in situations which their members cannot solve for themselves, it is natural that the retirees should turn to the unions with their difficult retirement problems. This has made the unions aware of the special needs of their members for better preparation for the post-working period.

B. Extent and Nature of Employee's Plans for Retirement

The extent and nature of preparation which the worker undertakes for himself will determine in large part the responsibility which management and union have in preparing workers for their separation from the labor force. In general, most studies have shown that the majority of workers have given very little precise thought to post-retirement planning. This failure to consider the future may be the result of unwillingness to recognize age, or it may reflect the lack of a social model of retirement life which can be used by the worker to fashion his plans.

Economic preparation, underscored by social security, is common enough today, but beyond this point other kinds of preparation are at best but vaguely recognized by most. Perhaps, as has been suggested (Moore, 1959; Tibbitts, 1960), the failure to take definitive steps to get ready for the post-working period of life results from the fact that few have yet accepted retirement as a period of life which can be filled with venturesomeness and new experience. Or perhaps, as Havighurst (1954) contends, the problem is that most Americans are not ready to apply the principle of equivalence of work and play, and they have too little accomplishment in the leisure arts to make retirement attractive.

But, whatever the explanation, the failure to prepare for retirement is a characteristic found for all occupational levels. Executives (Hall, 1953), college professors (E. H. Moore, 1951), industrial workers (Tuckman and Lorge, 1953; Crook and Heinstein, 1958), and farm operators and other rural workers (Taietz *et al.*, 1956) are alike in that at least less than half make plans for the retirement period of their lives. Table 11 summarizes the data from a number of studies, none of which would be considered sufficiently representative alone to give valid results, but which, when combined, give consistent evidence that retirement planning is yet to become a universal institution of our society. Perhaps the imminence of the retirement crisis is the best motivator for planning. Only in the group of garmentworkers awaiting retirement did so large a proportion as one-half claim to have made post-retirement plans. The proportion of older workers who are vague and indefinite about their plans has generally been found to be about the same as for younger workers many years from retirement (Crook and Heinstein, 1958). It has also been suggested that workers in occupations

TABLE 11*

PERCENTAGE OF OLDER MALE WORKERS WHO HAVE MADE RETIREMENT PLANS

OCCUPATION	HAVE MADE PLANS	
	Yes	No
Active farm operators..............	7	93
Active non-farm operators.........	26	74
Garmentworkers:		
Employed.....................	32	68
Applicants for retirement........	51	49
Retired......................	36	64
Industrial workers—unskilled and skilled.......................	24	63†
National sample workers‡.........	40	60
Cleveland survey§...............	24	76

* Sources: For active and non-active farm workers, P. Taietz, G. F. Streib, and M. L. Barron, *Adjustment to Retirement in Rural New York State* (Ithaca, N.Y.: Cornell University Agricultural Experiment Station, 1956), p. 36; for garmentworkers, J. Tuckman and I. Lorge, *Retirement and the Industrial Worker: Prospect and Reality* (New York: Columbia University, Bureau of Publications, Teachers College, 1953); for industrial workers, G. H. Crook and M. Heinstein, *The Older Worker in Industry* (Berkeley: University of California, Institute of Industrial Relations, 1958), p. 36; for the national sample, W. E. Thompson, "Pre-retirement Anticipation and Adjustment in Retirement," *Journal of Social Issues*, **14** (1958), 34–45; for the Cleveland survey, Anonymous, *They Tell about Retirement* (Cleveland: Special Surveys, 1952).

† The other 13 per cent gave qualified answers.

‡ Includes industrial workers, professionals, clerical, management; self-employed and farm workers are not included.

§ Includes 483 male annuitants from all occupational levels except top executives from six companies.

where retirement is an expected event will be more likely to make plans for it. Taietz and his associates (1956) accept the difference in the proportion of their active farm operators as compared to other active workers living in the rural area as supporting this hypothesis (Table 11).

The plans for utilizing the leisure of re-

tirement are rather lacking in imagination and seldom exceed one or two ideas per person (Tuckman and Lorge, 1953). In Table 12 the plans of industrial workers, ranging from highly skilled to the unskilled in a variety of occupations, are presented. Among the garmentworkers, resting, visiting, and recreational activities account for

TABLE 12*

CONTENT OF PLANS FOR UTILIZING RETIREMENT LEISURE, MALES

RETIREMENT PLANS	WEST COAST INDUSTRIAL OLDER WORKERS (PER CENT)	NEW YORK CITY GARMENTWORKERS (PER CENT)	
		Retirement Applicants	Retired Workers
Retirement activities†..	22	10	5
Travel................	16	6	3
Self-employed (farm or business)............	34	....	....
Employed by others....	3	5	5
Care of family and home	6	2	3
Resting and other vague activities............	13	66	51
Visiting and recreation..	....	20	7
Other................	....	2	1
No thought of how to use time................	....	14	32

* Sources: G. H. Crook and M. Heinstein, *The Older Worker in Industry* (Berkeley: University of California, Institute of Industrial Relations, 1958), p. 36; J. Tuckman and I. Lorge, *Retirement and the Industrial Worker: Prospect and Reality* (New York: Columbia University, Bureau of Publications, Teachers College, 1953), p. 47.

† Retirement activities include hobbies, educational classes, gardening, voluntary community service, etc.

most of their plans. The industrial workers studied on the West Coast have somewhat more specificity in their plans, in part because many of them are looking forward to some further employment after leaving their regular jobs. A somewhat larger proportion (57 per cent) of the skilled men expect to get other jobs, while a larger proportion (59 per cent) of the semiskilled or unskilled plan to use their time in the miscellany of hobbies and travel.

C. Evaluation of Retirement Preparation

Preparation for retirement is as yet, however, a fairly untested social effort. Programs sponsored by companies, unions, commercial firms, and universities have been reported (Donahue, 1950, 1951,

1952*b;* Mack, 1954; Wyner, 1954; Anonymous, 1957*b;* Hunter, 1957; Odell, 1959; Segal, 1959; Shultz, 1959); problems that retired persons will have to face have been identified (Burns, 1954; Tibbitts, 1954; Smith, 1956); and "How To" books (Boynton, 1952; Kaighn, 1954; Buckley, 1956) have appeared. Evaluation of the effectiveness of these various efforts has employed the simple criteria of the extent of the subjects' participation, their approval (or disapproval) of specific programs, their attitudes toward retirement before and following instruction, the change in the amount of their knowledge about retirement, and the effect of participation on the amount of planning the workers do for their retirement.

All the evaluative studies (Noetzel, 1952; Robson, 1952; Donahue, 1953; Hunter, 1956; Shultz, 1959) are in essential agreement with reference to the response of preretirees to participation in the program. The workers claim that fears of growing old and of retirement are materially reduced, that a positive attitude toward retirement is established, and that discussion has stimulated the drawing-up of concrete plans and the taking of some initial steps toward realizing these plans. They agree also in rating discussion of health, finances, and where to live above those dealing with less tangible factors such as use of free time.

Although there can be little doubt from these reports that preparation for retirement is considered by the workers to have value, Barron (1956) believes that planning for retirement is a middle-class concept and that industrial workers cannot be expected to find meaning in the middle-class free-time activities such as hobbies, travel, club sociability, etc. More definitive evaluations are obviously needed to establish a body of knowledge indicating the differential effectiveness of variations in existing programs for different social economic groups. Agreement on the specific direction which preparatory effort should follow has not been reached because retirement has not yet had time to develop a system of conduct norms for the various classes of the retired or their associates; thus there is no set of established directions or expectancies. We find ourselves in a period of individual and social experimentation within the social values dominant in our culture and within the boundaries of the physiological and psychological processes concomitant with aging.

D. Principles of Effective Retirement Preparation

Within these limitations the following principles seem to be generally indorsed as essentials of effective preparation for retirement and are to be found as parts of most preretirement training programs (Donahue, 1952*a*, 1953; Robson, 1952; Delaney, 1953; Mack, 1954; Tennessee Valley Authority, 1957).

Health should be safeguarded through periodic medical checkups and appropriate changes in a person's habits and activities (Tupper and Beckett, 1958–59). To take care of one's health has become a social virtue, and, where retirement seems to be required for medical reasons, it acquires *ipso facto* social merit and corresponding approval.

ROLE FLEXIBILITY

There seems to be agreement also that an individual's definition of his own worth should not be dependent solely on his work. Here the American ideal of the well-rounded personality which dominates so strongly our education of the young makes itself felt again. A person should develop before retirement a sufficiently affirmative attitude toward social roles other than the work role and toward aspects of his own personality other than financial comfort and independence so as to fortify himself against the future loss of his work role and the resulting reduction of income. Preparation for retirement thus requires "ego differentiation versus work-role preoccupation" (Peck, 1956, pp. 46–47). Havighurst

(1954) discusses the changes in role required of workers when they retire and emphasizes the individual's need for role flexibility, and he believes that "probably the best assurance of role flexibility in later years is a reasonably successful experience in a variety of roles during the middle years, the emphasis being on *reasonably* and *variety,* for outstanding success in certain roles in middle age sometimes makes for rigidity" (p. 311).

On the assumption that deliberate cultivation of role flexibility at middle age may stimulate growth and diversification of goals which will be bulwarks against the deprivations of old age, Tibbitts and Donahue (1957) developed a study-discussion program *Aging in the Modern World*,[33] designed to help individuals assess basic needs, capacities, outlooks, interests, and conceptions of self and to identify experiences which might further the growth and development of personality and lead to new useful and creative roles. According to Anderson (1958), "in order to build an effective program at older age levels, we must build it as a new product, even though it is based on past interests and activities" (p. 41).

ACTIVITY

Retirement years should be spent actively and, if possible, constructively. Here we have a cultural preference for a specific mode of conduct extended to a period of life where activity is likely to meet social and physiological interference. Contemplation is not yet considered a social virtue (it might be questioned whether persons growing old in a culture devoted largely to sports and other outgoing experiences are prepared anyway to develop an interest in contemplation of the passing scene), and, if people cannot work any more, we expect at least that they should play. In consequence, preparation for retirement should imply the cultivation of a hobby. From

[33] Revised and published under the title *Aging in Today's Society* (New York: Prentice-Hall, Inc., 1960).

results of studies such as those of Hebb (1955) and of Heron (1957), which show the detrimental effects of inactivity and lack of stimulation from the environment, further impetus is being given to the notion that the individual should continue to be active in retirement. Anderson (1959) points out that activity is characteristic of the living system at all ages and, therefore, that use and activity are beneficial, while non-activity and non-use in the long run result in deterioration.

SOCIAL PARTICIPATION

Human contacts should be maintained. Since work contacts are likely to be lost, contacts in formal associations and informal friendships should be cultivated. Family relationships might also be included under this general principle but seldom are, presumably because it is assumed that the nuclear family of industrial society offers few interrelationship opportunities between generations. There is a tendency, also, to view older persons as family members in negative terms and as problems (Beard, 1949; Burgess, 1957). Yet a number of studies indicate that, in spite of the conjugal form of today's modal family in the United States, companionate family ties are quite strong and offer a rich source of affectional relationships for both younger and older generation.[34] Even considering variations between social classes and ethnic groups, the family tends to persist as the mainstay of the elderly and to furnish them companionship, affection, and personal service (Townsend, 1957; Shanas, 1959).

GRADUAL TRANSITION

There seems to be a great deal of agreement that transition from work to retirement should be gradual if possible, but more important it should be realistically anticipated. Although there are good reasons given for gradual retirement such as those of offering the worker opportunity to prepare for retirement by practicing it in

[34] See chap. xiii.

increasing amounts, thus providing a form of role gradation, and to conserve diminishing energies, the notion that gradual retirement is superior to abrupt retirement is still to be substantiated by research. Hoyt (1954), in a study of residents of a Florida trailer park, reports that self-employed persons retiring gradually are less likely to report difficulty in retirement than those retiring abruptly. For the non-self-employed, however, he found no reliable tendency for the abruptly retired to report less difficulty than those who retired gradually. In a study of retirement in rural New York State (Taietz *et al.*, 1956), no clear-cut relationship showed between adjustment to retirement and type of retirement, although the percentage differences were greater for those criteria in which the gradual retirants were in more difficulty. The belief in the desirability of gradual retirement apparently stems from observing the practices of self-employed professional men who pace their retirement to their gradually declining energies.

Actually most workers are retired suddenly rather than gradually but not as a result of compulsory retirement practices. Only approximately one worker in ten or twelve is retired because of reaching a mandatory age (Stecker, 1955; Sheldon, 1958); most of the others retire because of health (the largest single cause) or because employment circumstances, such as transfer of a firm, reduction in personnel, etc., cause their jobs to disappear. Thus, for nearly three-quarters or more of workers, the chance for gradual retirement is not available. It is possible that the process of gradual retirement may give rise to maladjustments because the procedure places the worker in the equivocal position of being neither a fully accepted worker nor a fully accepted retiree. Lewin (1939) and Barker and associates (1953) have made clear the negative consequences of an ambiguity in roles, and Kuhlen (1959) has applied the concept to the status of the person approaching retirement. Kuhlen believes that, while a strong case may be made for flexible retirement, "the ambiguity, the uncertainty as to actual retirement date, will likely generate anxiety; and the threat to self-concept may be great, especially if one is retired while one's colleague is viewed as 'worth' another year or two" (p. 863). Hart (1957) has given penetrating insight into the personal experience of diminishing authority and status with approaching retirement. The inherent ambivalences may give rise to frustrations and emotional behavior which will color the post-retirement period. Further, it is not now known whether forcing a worker to retire gradually will be looked upon as any less of an externally imposed role than full retirement at a stated aged. The process of retirement is one which requires much further investigation, and effective preparation for the retirement experience must wait on a more comprehensive investigation of its psychological and sociological aspects.

COMPLEXITY OF THE PROCESS

It can be assumed that, although all these principles—maintenance of health, development of a well-rounded personality, participation in constructive activities, continuation of human contacts, gradual or abrupt retirement—are essentially meritorious, they are likely to lead individual employees who are preparing themselves for their retirement and preretirement counselors into oversimplifications. There is, first of all, insufficient stress on the fact that human need satisfaction is likely to result only from a constellation of adjustments. Needs can be met efficiently only if capacities and opportunities are brought into an interplay which is meaningful to the individual and acceptable to his associates. Meaningfulness of a specific retirement conduct can be gathered only from an understanding of the life-history of an individual; social approval, only from an understanding of the familial and subcultural setting in which he lives. Preparation for retirement which is unrelated to these two frames of reference will encounter many difficulties which might be avoided.

Another point which has not yet attracted sufficient attention is the specific contribution which the retired and only the retired members of our society can make to those who are still employed. Apparently all that is hoped for so far is that the retired will not be too unhappy and, therefore, will not arouse the guilt or the fear of those who still are gainfully employed. *Advice* on preparation for retirement we expect largely from personnel officers, psychiatrists, and gerontologists. Actually, the *teaching* of retirement might come by example and communication from the retired. Once preparation of retirement directs the concern and expectations of the employees involved toward this new social role, appropriate retirement conduct might well become a source of social importance and self-affirmation for the retired. Thus the definition of the retiree role is reinforced by members of a significant reference group, and the ambiguities can be reduced. Hunter (1960) has made it a practice in courses on retirement preparation to utilize as leaders retired workers selected from the subcultural group to which the "students" belong. The results have been excellent for both the retirees whose status in the retirement role is being recognized and for those in preparation for the new social role. This percept of the older person making an investment in the future of others fits into our culture.

IX. WOMEN IN RETIREMENT

More than 40 per cent of women aged 34–64 years are currently in the labor force, and the proportion is expected to rise in the future. Hence the question of retirement of women is a pertinent one. In fact, it tends to appear somewhat earlier in the life-span of women than of men, as evidenced by the fact that the proportion of women in the labor force begins to drop sharply in the 55–64-year age group and reaches a low of 11 per cent in the 65-and-over group (U.S. Department of Labor, 1959).

That there should be a difference between the retirement of men and that of women is to be expected, since, in spite of greater acceptability of employment for women outside the home (Kyrk, 1956), the primary and most acceptable role of woman remains that of wife-mother-grandmother; and the home, not the plant or office, is the principal sphere of her function. As Rose (1951) has pointed out, there has been in the face of advancing industrialization an organized effort to prevent the modification of woman's role as homemaker, and new social roles for women have never become clear and definite. Most women enter the labor market only as a matter of expediency: the young woman to support herself and fill time until a suitable husband can be found; the older woman to supplement family income or, in the absence of a husband, also to support herself. There may be some tendency for middle-aged women to escape the emptiness of a home after children leave by taking a job for interest and variety, or, as one woman remarked, "So I'll never have to write 'Housewife' on an application form again." But this trend appears to be only minimal, at least among financially able middle-class women. Gass (1959), in an interview study of a scientific sample of 85 middle-class women whose children had left or were about to leave home, found that, in spite of their concern over how to use their leisure, few wanted employment. Their expressed attitudes were those of relief at being financially able to stay at home and enjoy their leisure rather than, like their husbands, having to "go out and fight for a living." Staying at home, however, did not include a desire to increase their home-centered activities as a means of utilizing their leisure. Findings of a national sample (Weiss and Samelson, 1958) of 569 women selected on a probability basis to be representative of all women aged 20 and over living in the United States indicate that marriage sets the condition in which homework takes on and maintains value for women even after children leave home. The significance of their findings for retirement is obvious. The working role for women still does not have a social value equivalent to that of homemaker and user of leisure. It is, therefore, not unlikely that to leave a second- or third-class role presents an individual with less of a dilemma than to leave one which is recognized as a prime function of the individual. In addition, retirement of a woman may actually allow her to return to the acceptable role of homemaker and thus elevate her position rather than place her in the discard, as does the retirement of a man from his primary career occupation.

Unfortunately, there have as yet been no comprehensive studies of women in retirement. A number of investigators, however, have included some women in their study populations and have reported on sex differences and similarities in the meanings of work, attitudes toward retirement, and adjustment after retirement (E. H. Moore, 1951; Britton, 1953; Havighurst and Albrecht, 1953; Tuckman and Lorge, 1953; Bower, 1954; Michelon, 1954; Kutner *et al.*, 1956; Crook and Heinstein, 1958; Webber, 1958).

The study populations of most of these investigations have been small and non-representative. They include a variety of occupational groups and levels and both middle- and lower-class working women. Because of this heterogeneity and non-representativeness of older working women in general, it seems expedient to draw together a few of the more important findings rather than to discuss the findings in detail. More comprehensive research studies will be required before any conclusions can be substantiated or the meanings of work and retirement to women understood in their social context.

There appears to be a consensus among all investigators that having a job and retiring from it do not mean the same things to men and to women. For men, a job is a necessary role and represents a lifelong commitment; but to women, except perhaps for a handful of true careerists, a job is merely a stop-gap activity to be engaged in only so long as circumstances demand. Women in professional-managerial jobs are more likely to put value on their jobs, while women in semiskilled jobs or in private household work are least likely. Surprisingly, one investigator has found that older women, especially if unmarried, fail to get feelings of worth from their work. There is some evidence that women have less ego involvement and emotional investment in their jobs; but, if they do enjoy their work, they get the same and as many meanings from it as do men. It has been suggested that, once women have entered the labor market and found jobs offering stimulation and variety, many are loathe to return to the push-button monotony of modern housekeeping.

A second consensus among researchers is that working women tend to view retirement more favorably than do men. They prefer retirement about 5 years younger than men, although, like men, retirement tends to look somewhat less attractive the closer they come to it. Their reasons for retiring are similar to those of men in that health takes precedence (although more women than men retire voluntarily for reasons other than health), and the feeling of having worked long enough or of needing rest is the second consideration. Even fewer women than men make any specific preparation for retirement, but those who do make plans that are more realistic. Women seem to adjust better and more quickly to retirement than do men, perhaps, it has been said, because the change in their role status is much less extreme. Following retirement, most women expect and do devote themselves to housework, which they consider a highly respectable activity. Few expect to work in paid employment after retirement. Their interests and their good adjustment include family, religion, friendships, and club activities, while those of men are predominantly in having some kind of job, economic security, non-sedentary activities, and organizations. Both sexes suffer some constrictions in their life-spaces and of the effective components in it. Likewise, both men and women who have developed a wide range of interests tend to make better adjustments in retirement than do those who have a more limited number.

As already pointed out, what has been said of generalized retired women may not represent any single subcultural or former occupational group. Social changes which are bringing more women into the labor force, coupled with such institutional recognition of their right to work and retire as represented by social security, may be the instruments through which the paid work roles of women will be more clearly defined and accepted. If new expectancies are established, concomitant changes in attitudes toward work and retirement may likewise be expected to appear. Research is needed to define the trends and measure the social and behavioral changes.

REFERENCES

ABEL-SMITH, B. 1959. The cost of the support of the aged in the United Kingdom. In C. TIB-BITTS (ed.), Aging and social health in the United States and Europe, pp. 9–26. Ann Arbor: University of Michigan, Division of Gerontology.

ACHINGER, H. 1959. The economic resources of old age. In Proceedings of the Fourth Congress, International Association of Gerontology, Merano, Italy, 3, 17–29. Fidenza: Tipografica Tito Mattioli.

ALBRECHT, RUTH. 1951. The social roles of old people. J. Gerontol., 6, 138–45.

ANDERSON, J. E. 1958. Psychological aspects of the use of free time. In WILMA DONAHUE, W. W. HUNTER, DOROTHY H. COONS, and HELEN K. MAURICE (eds.), Free time: challenge to later maturity, pp. 29–44. Ann Arbor: University of Michigan Press.

———. 1959. The use of time and energy. In J. E. BIRREN (ed.), Handbook of aging and the individual: psychological and biological aspects, pp. 769–93. Chicago: University of Chicago Press.

ANDERSON, W. F. and COWAN, N. R. 1956. Work and retirement: influences on the health of older men. Lancet, 2, 1344–47.

ANONYMOUS. 1951. Preparing employees for retirement. New York: American Management Association.

———. 1952. They tell about retirement. Cleveland: Special Surveys.

———. 1953. Economic status of aged persons and dependent survivors, June, 1953. Social Security Bull., 16 (December), 22–23.

———. 1957a. Niagara Falls: hourly employees. Aging, 37, 1–2.

———. 1957b. Retirement-conditioning training under union sponsorship. Month. Labor Rev., 80, 846–48.

AUGUST, H. 1956. Psychological aspects of personal adjustment. In IRMA N. GROSS (ed.), Potentialities of women in the middle years, pp. 87–104. Lansing: Michigan State University Press.

BAKER, HELEN. 1952. Retirement procedures under compulsory and flexible retirement policies. Princeton, N.J.: Princeton University, Department of Economics and Social Institutions.

BANKERS TRUST COMPANY. 1956. A study of industrial retirement plans. New York: The Company.

BARKER, R. G., WRIGHT, BEATRICE A., MEYERSON, L., and GONICK, MOLLIE R. 1953. Adjustment to physical handicap and illness: a survey of the social psychology of physique and disability. New York: Social Science Research Council.

BARKIN, S. 1952. Should there be a fixed retirement age? Organized labor says no. Ann. Am. Acad. Political & Social Sc., 279, 77–79.

BARRON, M. L. 1954. A survey of a cross section of the urban aged in the United States. In Old age in the modern world, pp. 340–49. Edinburgh: E. & S. Livingstone.

———. 1956. The dynamics of occupational roles and health in old age. In J. E. ANDERSON (ed.), Psychological aspects of aging, pp. 236–39. Washington, D.C.: American Psychological Association.

BEARD, BELLE B. 1949. Are the aged ex-family? Social Forces, 27, 274–79.

BERS, M. K. 1957. Union policy and the older worker. Berkeley: University of California, Institute of Industrial Relations.

BOSSARD, J. H. S. 1953. Parent and child. Philadelphia: University of Pennsylvania Press.

BOWER, JANET. 1954. The retail salespersons: men and women. In E. A. FRIEDMANN and R. J. HAVIGHURST (eds.), The meaning of work and retirement, pp. 99–131. Chicago: University of Chicago Press.

BOYLE, C. P. 1952. Helping employees adjust to retirement. I. A survey of retirement practices in industry. Personnel, 29, 261–74.

BOYLE, C. P. 1953. Helping employees adjust to retirement. II. A survey of post-retirement in industry. *Ibid.*, **30**, 441–52.

BOYNTON, P. W. 1952. Six ways to retire. New York: Harper & Bros.

BRAUN, H. 1956. Industrialism and social policy in Germany. Cologne: Carl Heymanns Verlag KG.

BRITTON, J. H. 1953. The personal adjustment of retired school teachers. J. Gerontol., **8**, 333–38.

BRITTON, JEAN O., and BRITTON, J. H. 1951. Factors related to the adjustment of retired Y.M.C.A. secretaries. J. Gerontol., **6**, 34–38.

BROWER, F. BEATRICE. 1951. Second thoughts on compulsory retirement. Conference Board Management Record, **13**, 50–52.

———. 1955. Retirement of employees, policies—procedures—practices. ("Studies in Personnel Policy," No. 148.) New York: National Industrial Conference Board.

BUCKLEY, J. C. 1956. The retirement handbook: a complete planning guide to your future. New York: Harper & Bros.

BURGESS, E. W. 1950. Personal and social adjustment in old age. *In* M. DERBER (ed.), The aged and society, pp. 138–56. Champaign, Ill.: Industrial Relations Research Association.

———. 1952. Family living in the later decades. Ann. Am. Acad. Political & Social Sc., **279**, 106–14.

———. 1957. The older generation and the family. *In* WILMA DONAHUE and C. TIBBITTS (eds.), The new frontiers of aging, pp. 158–71. Ann Arbor: University of Michigan Press.

BURGESS, E. W., COREY, L. G., PINEO, P. C., and THORNBURY, R. T. 1958. Occupational difference in attitudes toward aging and retirement. J. Gerontol., **13**, 203–6.

BURGESS, E. W., and LOCKE, H. J. 1953. The family: from institution to companionship. New York: American Book Co.

BURNS, R. K. 1954. Some unsettled issues of retirement policy. J. Business of Univ. of Chicago, **27**, 137–45.

CAVAN, RUTH S. 1953. The American family. New York: Thomas Y. Crowell Co.

CAVAN, RUTH S., BURGESS, E. W., HAVIGHURST, R. J., and GOLDHAMER, H. 1949. Personal adjustment in old age. Chicago: Science Research Associates, Inc.

CHURCHILL, W. S. 1909. Liberalism and the social problem. London: Hoddard & Stoughton.

COCHRANE, C. P. 1952. Should there be a fixed retirement age? Some managements prefer flexibility. Ann. Am. Acad. Political & Social Sc., **279**, 74–76.

COHEN, W. J. 1957. Retirement policies under social security. Berkeley: University of California Press.

———. 1959. Income adequacy and pension planning in the United States. *In* C. TIBBITTS (ed.), Aging and social health in the United States and Europe, pp. 27–47. Ann Arbor: University of Michigan, Division of Gerontology.

COLLINS, F. D. O., and HAGGETT, J. G. 1955. Women in middle age. Social Service Quart., **29**, 125–30.

CORSON, J. J., and McCONNELL, J. W. 1956. Economic needs of older people. New York: Twentieth Century Fund.

CROOK, G. H., and HEINSTEIN, M. 1958. The older worker in industry. Berkeley: University of California, Institute of Industrial Relations.

DARIC, J. 1948. Vieillissement de la population et prolongation de la vie active. ("Institut Nationale d'Études Démographiques, Travaux et Documents," No. 7.) Paris: Presse Universitaires de France.

DELANEY, H. B. 1953. Pre-retirement aid, retirement aid and counseling. *In* The problem of making a living while growing old: proceedings of the Second Joint Conference, pp. 330–37. Philadelphia: Temple University School of Business Administration.

DE SCHWEINITZ, K. 1947. England's road to social security, 1349 to 1947. Philadelphia: University of Pennsylvania Press.

DEWHURST, J. F., AND ASSOCIATES. 1955. America's needs and resources: a new survey. New York: Twentieth Century Fund.

DINKEL, R. M. 1944. Attitudes of children toward supporting aged parents. Am. Sociological Rev., **9**, 370–79.

DONAHUE, WILMA. 1950. Preparation for living in the later years. Adult Education, **1**, 43–51.

———. 1951. Experiments in the education of older adults. *Ibid.*, **2**, 49–59.

———. 1952a. Anticipation of the retirement day. *In* Practical problems of employee relations. ("Personnel Series," No. 149.) New York: American Management Association.

———. 1952b. Educational programs for older adults. Michigan Alumnus, **58**, 255–63.

———. 1953. Adjusting employees to retirement. Management Record, **15**, 343–45.

DOUGLAS, MARTHA A. 1955. A preparation for retirement program. (Publication No. 109.)

Chicago: Research Council for Economic Security.

DOUGLAS, P. H. 1936. Social security in the United States. New York: Whittlesey House.

DRINKWATER, R. W. 1959. Some role problems in middle life and their implications for subsequent adjustment. *In* Proceedings of the Fourth Congress, International Association of Gerontology, Merano, Italy, **3**, 452–59. Fidenza: Tipografica Tito Mattioli.

DUBIN, R. 1958. Industrial workers' worlds. *In* E. LARRABEE and R. MEYERSOHN (eds.), Mass leisure, pp. 215–28. Glencoe, Ill.: Free Press.

DUVALL, EVELYN M. 1957. Family development. New York: J. B. Lippincott Co.

EMERSON, A. R. 1959. The first year of retirement. Occupational Psychol., **33**, 197–208.

EPSTEIN, A. 1926. The problem of old age pensions in industry. Harrisburg: Pennsylvania Commission on Old Age Pensions.

———. 1938. Insecurity: a challenge to America. New York: Random House.

EPSTEIN, LENORE A. 1959. Money income of aged persons: a 10-year review, 1948–1958. Social Security Bull., **22** (June), 3–11.

EPSTEIN, LENORE A., MCCAMMAN, DOROTHY, and SKOLNIK, A. M. 1955. Social security protection, 1935–1955. Social Security Bull., **18** (August), 5–11.

EQUITY ANNUITY LIFE INSURANCE Co. 1956. The Equinuity Company handbook and rate book. Washington, D.C.: The Company.

ERIKSON, E. 1950. Childhood and society. New York: W. W. Norton & Co.

FELDMAN, FRANCES L. 1957. The family in a money world. New York: Family Service Association.

FOLSOM, M. B. 1955. Teamwork for individual independence. Social Security Bull., **18** (August), 1.

FOX, W. G., and COLLINS, F. D. O. 1956. Marriage and family life. Social Service Quart., **30**, 116–27.

FRANK, L. K. 1956. Problems and opportunities in the maturation of women: the interpersonal and social aspects. *In* IRMA H. GROSS (ed.), Potentialities of women in the middle years, pp. 105–26. Lansing: Michigan State University Press.

FRIED, EDRITA G. 1949. Attitudes of the older population groups toward activity and inactivity. J. Gerontol., **4**, 141–51.

FRIED, EDRITA G., and STERN, K. 1948. The situation of the aged within the family. Am. J. Orthopsychiat., **18**, 31–54.

FRIEDMANN, E. A. 1958. The work of leisure. *In* WILMA DONAHUE, W. W. HUNTER, DOROTHY H. COONS, and HELEN K. MAURICE (eds.). Free time: challenge to later maturity, pp. 119–32. Ann Arbor: University of Michigan Press.

FRIEDMANN, E. A., and HAVIGHURST, R. J. (eds.). 1954. The meaning of work and retirement. Chicago: University of Chicago Press.

GALBRAITH, J. K. 1958. The affluent society. Boston: Houghton Mifflin Co.

GALLOWAY, R. E. 1955. Farmers' plans for economic security in old age. (Agric. Exper. Sta. Bull. 626.) Lexington: Kentucky Agricultural Experiment Station.

GASS, GERTRUDE Z. 1959. Counseling implications of woman's changing role. Personnel & Guidance, **7**, 482–87.

GRANT, MARGARET. 1939. Old age security. Washington, D.C.: Social Science Research Council.

GREENOUGH, W. C. 1951. A new approach to retirement income. New York: Teachers Insurance and Annuity Association of America.

GREVILLE, T. N. E. 1957. Illustrative United States population projections. ("Actuarial Study," No. 46.) Washington, D.C.: Department of Health, Education, and Welfare, Social Security Administration, Division of the Actuary.

HAINES, C. E. 1959. Economic aspects of aging and retirement in modern industrial society. (Address given at the Southeastern Regional Conference on Aging, Durham, North Carolina.) (Mimeographed.)

HALÉVY, É. 1955. The growth of philosophical radicalism. 2d ed. Boston: Beacon Press.

HALL, H. R. 1953. Some observations on executive retirement. Boston: Harvard University, Graduate School of Business Administration.

HARLAN, W. H. 1954. The meaning of work and retirement for coal-miners. *In* E. A. FRIEDMANN and R. J. HAVIGHURST (eds.), The meaning of work and retirement, pp. 53–98. Chicago: University of Chicago Press.

HART, G. R. 1957. Retirement: a new outlook for the individual. New York: Harcourt, Brace & Co.

HAUSER, P. M., and SHANAS, ETHEL. 1952. Trends in the aging population. *In* A. I. LANSING (ed.), Cowdry's problems of ageing, pp. 965–81. 3d ed. Baltimore: Williams & Wilkins Co.

HAUSER, P. M., and VARGAS, R. 1960. Population structure and trends. *In* E. W. BURGESS (ed.), Aging in Western societies: a survey of social gerontology, chap. ii. Chicago: University of Chicago Press.

HAVIGHURST, R. J. 1952. Social and psychological needs of the aging. Ann. Am. Acad. Political & Social Sc., **279**, 11–17.

———. 1954. Flexibility and social roles of the retired. Am. J. Sociology, **59**, 309–11.

———. 1955. Employment, retirement and education in the mature years. *In* I. WEBBER (ed.), Aging and retirement, pp. 57–62. Gainesville: University of Florida Press.

———. 1957. The social competence of middle-aged people. Genetic Psychol. Monogr., **56**, 297–375.

———. 1960. Life beyond family and work. *In* E. W. BURGESS (ed.), Aging in Western societies: a survey of social gerontology. Chicago: University of Chicago Press.

HAVIGHURST, R. J., and ALBRECHT, RUTH. 1953. Older people. New York: Longmans, Green & Co.

HAVIGHURST, R. J., and SHANAS, ETHEL. 1953. Retirement and the professional worker. J. Gerontol., **8**, 81–85.

HEBB, D. O. 1955. The mammal and his environment. Am. J. Psychiat., **3**, 826–31.

HECKSCHER, A., and DE GRAZIA, S. 1959. Executive leisure. Harvard Business Rev., **37** (July–August), 6–8, 10, 12, 16, 144, 146, 148, 149, 152, 154, 156.

HENSON, F. A. 1951. Adjustment to retirement, as workers view it. *In* Proceedings of a Conference on Problems of Older Workers. Madison: University of Wisconsin, Industrial Relations Center.

HERON, W. 1957. The pathology of boredom. Scient. Am., **196**, 52–56.

HEWITT, EDWIN SHIELDS, and ASSOCIATES. 1952. Company practices regarding older workers and retirement. Libertyville, Ill.: Edwin Shields Hewitt & Associates.

HOCHMAN, J. 1950. The retirement myth. *In* The social and biological challenge of our aging population, pp. 130–45. New York: Columbia University Press.

HOLLAND, D. M. 1959. What can we expect from pensions? Harvard Business Rev., **37** (July–August), 125–40.

HOYT, G. C. 1954. The process and problems of retirement. J. Business of Univ. of Chicago, **27**, 164–68.

HUNTER, W. W. 1956. A study of methods for developing a pre-retirement conditioning program for use by the Upholsterers' International Union locals. (Paper read at the

First Pan-American Congress of Gerontology, Mexico City.) Ann Arbor: University of Michigan, Division of Gerontology. (Mimeographed.)

———. 1957. Preparation for retirement of hourly wage employees. (Paper read at the annual meeting of the Gerontological Society, Cleveland.) Ann Arbor: University of Michigan, Division of Gerontology. (Mimeographed.)

———. 1960. Pre-retirement education. Geriatrics, **15**, 793–800.

ICHHEISER, G. 1949. Misunderstandings in human relations. Am. J. Sociology, Vol. **55**, Part II (special issue).

JOHNSON, D. E. 1958. A depressive retirement syndrome. Geratrics, **13**, 314–19.

JOHNSON, G. E. 1951. Is a compulsory retirement age ever justified? J. Gerontol., **6**, 263–71.

KAIGHN, R. P. 1954. How to retire and like it. New York: Association Press.

KARDINER, A. 1937. Psychological factors in old age. *In* Mental hygiene in old age, pp. 14–26. New York: Family Welfare Association of America.

KELLEY, H. H. 1952. Two functions of reference groups. *In* G. E. SWANSON, T. M. NEWCOMB, and E. L. HARTLEY (eds.), Readings in social psychology, pp. 410–14. Rev. ed. New York: Henry Holt & Co.

KOLLER, M. R. 1954. Studies of three-generation households. Marriage & Family Living, **16**, 205–6.

KUHLEN, R. G. 1959. Aging and life adjustment. *In* J. E. BIRREN (ed.), Handbook of aging and the individual: psychological and biological aspects, pp. 852–98. Chicago: University of Chicago Press.

KUTNER, B., FANSHEL, D., TOGO, ALICE M., and LANGNER, T. S. 1956. Five hundred over sixty: a community survey on aging. New York: Russell Sage Foundation.

KYRK, HAZEL. 1956. The economic role of women. *In* IRMA H. GROSS (ed.), Potentialities of women in the middle years, pp. 127–41. Lansing: Michigan State University Press.

LAIRD, L. 1954. Planning ahead for retirement. Personnel J., **33**, 51–54.

LANDIS, J. T. 1942. Social-psychological factors of aging. Social Forces, **20**, 468–70.

LARSON, A. 1955. Know your social security. New York: Harper & Bros.

———. 1959. Coming controversies in social security. Proceedings of seminars, 1958–1959,

Duke University Council on Gerontology, pp. 64–76. Durham, N.C.

LEVIN, H. 1959. Involuntary retirement provisions. Month. Labor Rev., **82,** 855–60.

LEWIN, K. 1939. Field theory and experiment in social psychology. Am. J. Sociology, **44,** 868–96.

LIFE EXTENSION FOUNDATION. 1956. Retirement study: overall summary of 1546 questionnaires. New York: The Foundation.

LINCOLN, L. A. 1952. The four horsemen: some observations on social security. (An address delivered before the American Bar Association, Ohio Valley Regional Meeting, Louisville, Ky., April 10.)

LINDEN, M. E. 1958. Preparation for the leisure of later maturity. *In* WILMA DONAHUE, W. W. HUNTER, DOROTHY H. COONS, and HELEN K. MAURICE (eds.), Free time: challenge to later maturity, pp. 77–98. Ann Arbor: University of Michigan Press.

LINTON, R. 1936. The study of man. New York: D. Appleton–Century Co.

McGILL, D. M. 1955. Fundamentals of private pensions. Homewood, Ill.: Richard D. Irwin, Inc.

MACK, MARJORY J. 1954. A retirement planning program. J. Business of Univ. of Chicago, **27,** 169–76.

———. 1958. An evaluation of a retirement-planning program. J. Gerontol., **13,** 198–202.

McMAHAN, C. A. 1958. Some problems of testing empirically the consequences of retirement policies. *In* Proceedings of the Louisiana Conference on Aging, pp. 69–79. Baton Rouge: Louisiana State University, General Extension Division.

McMAHAN, C. A., and FORD, J. R. 1955. Surviving the first five years of retirement. J. Gerontol., **10,** 212–15.

MATHIASEN, GENEVA (ed.). 1953. Criteria for retirement. New York: G. P. Putnam's Sons.

——— (ed.). 1957. Flexible retirement. New York: G. P. Putnam's Sons.

MEAD, G. H. 1934. Mind, self, and society. Chicago: University of Chicago Press.

MEAD, MARGARET. 1928. Coming of age in Samoa. New York: William Morrow & Co.

MERTON, R. K. 1957a. The role-set: problems in sociological theory. Brit. J. Sociology, **8,** 106–20.

———. 1957b. Social theory and social structure. Rev. ed. Glencoe, Ill.: Free Press.

MICHELON, L. C. 1954. The new leisure class. Am. J. Sociology, **59,** 371–78.

MINISTRY OF PENSIONS AND NATIONAL INSURANCE. 1954. Reasons given for retiring or continuing at work. London: H.M. Stationery Office.

MOORE, E. H. 1951. Professors in retirement. J. Gerontol., **6,** 243–52.

———. 1959. The nature of retirement. New York: Macmillan Co.

MOORE, W. E. 1951. The aged in industrial societies. *In* Industrial relations and the social order, pp. 519–37. Rev. ed. New York: Macmillan Co.

MORGAN, CHRISTINE M. 1937. The attitudes and adjustments of recipients of old age assistance in upstate New York and Metropolitan New York. Arch. Psychol., No. 214, pp. 1–131.

MORRISON, D. E., and KRISTJANSON, A. 1958. Personal adjustment among older persons. (Agric. Exper. Sta. Tech. Bull. 21.) Brookings, S.D.: South Dakota State College Agricultural Experiment Station.

MYERS, R. J. 1954a. Mortality after retirement. Social Security Bull., **17** (June), 3–7.

———. 1954b. Factors in interpreting mortality after retirement. J. Am. Statistical A., **49,** 499–509.

NATIONAL INDUSTRIAL CONFERENCE BOARD. 1925. Industrial pensions in the United States. (Publication 109.) New York: The Board.

NAVILLE, P. 1959. Measurement of working life and employment of older workers in France. *In* C. TIBBITTS (ed.), Aging and social health in the United States and Europe, pp. 74–95. Ann Arbor: University of Michigan, Division of Gerontology.

NELSON, G. R. 1953. Social welfare in Scandinavia. Copenhagen: Danish Ministry of Labour and Social Affairs.

NEUGARTEN, BERNICE L. 1956. Kansas City study of adult life. *In* IRMA M. GROSS (ed.), Potentialities of women in the middle years, pp. 35–45. Lansing: Michigan State University Press.

NEUGARTEN, BERNICE L., and PETERSON, W. 1959. A study of the American age-grade system. *In* Proceedings of the Fourth Congress, International Association of Gerontology, Merano, Italy, **3,** 497–502. Fidenza: Tipografia Tito Mattioli.

NEW YORK. STATE. 1957. DEPARTMENT OF LABOR. DIVISION OF RESEARCH AND STATISTICS. Pensions: larger plans in New York

State. (Special Bull. 232.) Albany: The Department.

NOETZEL, A. 1952. Preparation of industrial workers for retirement. Pittsburgh: Health and Welfare Federation of Alleghany County. (Mimeographed.)

ODELL, C. 1959. Employment and pre-retirement problems of the older worker, Part III: Retirement preparation education—an ounce of prevention. Geriatrics, **14,** 591–94.

ORBACH, H. L., and SHAW, D. M. 1957. Social participation and the role of the aging. Geriatrics, **12,** 241–46.

PARRON, T., and ASSOCIATES. 1953. Retirement from the point of view of the worker. *In* GENEVA MATHIASEN (ed.), Criteria for retirement, pp. 61–118. New York: G. P. Putnam's & Sons.

PARSONS, T. 1954. Age and sex in the social structure of the United States. *In* Essays in sociological theory, pp. 89–103. Rev. ed. Glencoe, Ill.: Free Press.

PECK, R. 1956. Psychological developments in the second half of life. *In* J. E. ANDERSON (ed.), Psychological aspects of aging, pp. 42–43. Washington, D.C.: American Psychological Association.

PERROW, C. 1957. Are retirement adjustment programs necessary? Harvard Business Rev., **35** (July–August), 109–15.

PHILLIPS, B. S. 1957. A role theory approach to adjustment in old age. Am. Sociological Rev., **22,** 212–17.

POLLAK, O. 1956. The social aspects of retirement. Homewood, Ill.: Richard D. Irwin, Inc.

———. 1957. Positive experiences in retirement. Homewood, Ill.: Richard D. Irwin, Inc.

RABINOVITZ, PATRICIA. 1949. Living arrangements for older people. *In* C. TIBBITTS (ed.), Living through the older years, pp. 131–39. Ann Arbor: University of Michigan Press.

RICHARDSON, I. M. 1956. Retirement: a sociomedical study of 244 men. Scottish Med. J., **1,** 381–91.

RIESMAN, D. 1954. Some clinical and cultural aspects of aging. Am. J. Sociology, **59,** 379–83.

———. 1956. The found generation. Am. Scholar, **25,** 421–36.

———. 1958. Leisure and work in post-industrial society. *In* E. LARRABEE and R. MEYERSOHN (eds.), Mass leisure, pp. 363–85. Glencoe, Ill.: Free Press.

ROBSON, R. B. 1952. Conditions for retirement. National Safety News, **50,** 130–37.

ROCKEFELLER BROTHERS FUND. 1958. The challenge to America: its economic and social aspects. Garden City, N.Y.: Doubleday & Co.

ROSE, A. M. 1951. The adequacy of women's expectations for adult roles. Social Forces, **30,** 69–77.

———. 1954. Theory and method in the social sciences. Minneapolis: University of Minnesota Press.

RUBINOW, I. M. 1933. Old age. *In* Encyclopedia of the social sciences, **11,** 452–62. New York: Macmillan Co.

———. 1934. The quest for security. New York: Henry Holt & Co.

SARBIN, T. R. 1954. Role theory. *In* G. LINDZEY (ed.), Handbook of social psychology, **1,** 223–58. Cambridge, Mass.: Addison-Wesley Publishing Co.

SCHMIDT, J. F. 1951. Patterns of poor adjustment in old age. Am. J. Sociology, **57,** 33–42.

SCHOTTLAND, C. I. 1959. The United States approach to social security and its significance for the aged. *In* Proceedings of the Fourth Congress, International Association of Gerontology, Merano, Italy, **3,** 92–97. Fidenza: Tipografica Tito Mattioli.

SEGAL, M. E. 1959. A program of retirement counseling for public employees. New York: Retirement Advisors, Inc. (Mimeographed.)

SEWELL, W. H., RAMSEY, C. E., and DUCOFF, L. J. 1953. Farmers' conceptions and plans for economic security in old age. (Agric. Exper. Sta. Res. Bull. 182.) Madison: Wisconsin Agricultural Experiment Station.

SHANAS, ETHEL. 1950. The personal adjustment of recipients of old age assistance. J. Gerontol., **5,** 249–53.

———. 1958. Facts versus stereotypes: the Cornell study of occupational retirement. J. Social Issues, **14,** No. 2, 61–63.

———. 1959. Some sociological research findings about older people pertinent to social work. *In* Toward better understanding of the aging, pp. 49–58. New York: Council of Social Work Education.

SHANAS, ETHEL, and HAVIGHURST, R. J. 1953. Retirement in four professions. J. Gerontol., **8,** 212–21.

SHELDON, H. D. 1958. The older population of the United States. New York: John Wiley & Sons.

SHENFIELD, BARBARA E. 1957. Social policies for old age: a review of social provisions for old age in Great Britain. London: Routledge & Kegan Paul.

SHIBUTANI, T. 1955. Reference groups as perspectives. Am. J. Sociology, **60**, 562–69.

SHULTZ, E. B. 1959. Selective retirement and pre-retirement counseling in the T.V.A. Industrial & Labor Relations, **12**, 206–13.

SIMMONS, L. W. 1945. The role of the aged in primitive society. New Haven, Conn.: Yale University Press.

SMITH, ETHEL SABIN. 1956. The dynamics of aging. New York: W. W. Norton & Co.

SMITH, W. M., JR., BRITTON, J. H., and BRITTON, JEAN O. 1958. Relationships within three generation families. (Publication 155.) University Park: Pennsylvania State University, Department of Home Economics.

SOLENBERGER, W. E. 1951. Retirement—a labor viewpoint. (Paper presented at the Second International Gerontological Congress, St. Louis.) Detroit: United Auto Workers, Social Security Department. (Mimeographed.)

STECKER, MARGARET L. 1955. Why do beneficiaries retire? Who among them return to work? Social Security Bull., **18** (May), 3–12, 35–36.

STEINER, P. O., and DORFMAN, R. 1957. The economic needs of the aged. Berkeley: University of California Press.

STREIB, G. F. 1956. Morale of the retired. Social Problems, **3**, 270–76.

———. 1958. Family patterns in retirement. J. Social Issues, **14**, No. 2, 46–60.

STREIB, G. F., and THOMPSON, W. E. 1957. Personal and social adjustment in retirement. *In* WILMA DONAHUE and C. TIBBITTS (eds.), The new frontiers of aging, pp. 180–97. Ann Arbor: University of Michigan Press.

SWADOS, H. 1958. Less work—less leisure. Nation, **168**, 153–58.

TAIETZ, P., and LARSON, O. F. 1956. Social participation and old age. Rural Sociology, **21**, 229–38.

TAIETZ, P., STREIB, G. F., and BARRON, M. L. 1956. Adjustment to retirement in rural New York State. (Bull. 919.) Ithaca, N.Y.: Cornell University Agricultural Experiment Station.

TEGNER, G. 1956. Social security in Sweden. Tiden: The Swedish Institute.

TENNESSEE VALLEY AUTHORITY. 1957. Looking toward retirement. Program recommended by Joint Union-Management Committee. Knoxville, Tenn.: The Authority.

THOMAS, G., and OSBORNE, BARBARA. 1947.

The employment of older persons. ("The Social Survey," new ser., Vol. **60**, No. 2.) London: Central Office of Information, Social Security Division.

THOMPSON, W. E. 1958. Pre-retirement anticipation and adjustment in retirement. J. Social Issues, **14**, No. 2, 35–45.

THOMPSON, W. E., and STREIB, G. F. 1958. Situational determinants: health and economic deprivation in retirement, J. Social Issues, **14**, No. 2, 18–34.

TIBBITTS, C. 1954. Retirement problems in American society. Am. J. Sociology, **59**, 301–8.

———. 1958. Aging as a modern social achievement. *In* WILMA DONAHUE, W. W. HUNTER, DOROTHY H. COONS, and HELEN K. MAURICE (eds.), Free time: challenge to later maturity, pp. 17–28. Ann Arbor: University of Michigan Press.

———. 1960. Aging as a modern social achievement. *In* C. TIBBITTS and WILMA DONAHUE (eds.), Aging in today's society. New York: Prentice-Hall, Inc.

TIBBITTS C., and DONAHUE, WILMA (eds.), 1957. Aging in the modern world. Ann Arbor: University of Michigan, Division of Gerontology.

TOWNSEND, P. 1957. The family life of old people. Glencoe, Ill.: Free Press.

TUCKMAN, J., and LORGE, I. 1953. Retirement and the industrial worker: prospect and reality. New York: Columbia University, Bureau of Publications, Teachers College.

TUPPER, C. J., and BECKETT, M. B. 1958–59. Faculty health appraisal, the University of Michigan. First annual report. Univ. Michigan M. Bull., **24**, 35–43.

TURNER, R. H. 1956. Role-taking, role standpoint, and reference group behavior. Am. J. Sociology, **61**, 316–28.

TWENTIETH CENTURY FUND. 1937. More security for old age. New York: The Fund.

TYHURST, J. S., SALK, L., and KENNEDY, MIRIAM. 1957. Mortality, morbidity, and retirement. Am. J. Pub. Health, **47**, 1434–44.

UNITED NATIONS. DEPARTMENT OF ECONOMIC AND SOCIAL AFFAIRS. 1956. The aging of populations and its economic and social implications. ("Population Studies," No. 26.) New York: United Nations.

U.S. BUREAU OF THE CENSUS. 1959. Statistical abstract of the United States, 1959. (80th ed.) Washington, D.C.: Government Printing Office.

U.S. BUREAU OF LABOR STATISTICS. 1953. Pension plans under collective bargaining. (BLS Bull. 1147). Washington, D.C.: Government Printing Office.

U.S. DEPARTMENT OF LABOR. 1959. Population and labor force perspectives for the United States, 1960 to 1975. (Bull. 1242.) Washington, D.C.: Government Printing Office.

U.S. EXECUTIVE OFFICE OF THE PRESIDENT, 1954. COMMITTEE ON RETIREMENT POLICY FOR FEDERAL PERSONNEL. Retirement provision for federal personnel, Part I. Washington, D.C.: Government Printing Office.

U.S. SOCIAL SECURITY ADMINISTRATION. 1958. Division of program research. Social security programs throughout the world, 1958. Washington, D.C.: Government Printing Office.

———. 1959. Division of program research. Projections to 1970 of the number of aged persons receiving OAA and OASDI. ("Research and Statistics Note," No. 24.) Washington, D.C.: The Administration. (Mimeographed.)

VALAORAS, V. G. 1950. Patterns of aging of human populations. *In* Social and biological challenge of our aging population, pp. 67–85. New York: Columbia University Press.

———. 1958. Young and aged populations. Ann. Am. Acad. Political & Social Sc., **316**, 69–83.

WEBBER, I. L. 1958. Adjustment to retirement made by aged persons. *In* Proceedings of the Louisiana Conference on Aging, pp. 125–35. Baton Rouge: Louisiana State University, General Extension Division.

WEISS, R. S., and KAHN, R. L. 1959*a*. On the definition of work among American men. Ann Arbor: University of Michigan, Institute for Social Research. (Mimeographed.)

———. 1959*b*. On the evaluation of work among American men. Ann Arbor: University of Michigan, Institute for Social Research. (Mimeographed.)

WEISS, R. S., and MORSE, NANCY M. 1955. The function and meaning of work and the job. Am. Sociological Rev., **20**, 191–98.

WEISS, R. S., and SAMELSON, NANCY M. 1958. Social roles of American women: their contribution to a sense of usefulness and importance. Marriage & Family Living, **17**, 15–19.

WILLIAMS, R. M., JR. 1951. American society, a sociological interpretation. New York: Alfred A. Knopf.

WILLIE, C. V. 1954. Group relationships of the elderly in our culture. Social Casework, **35**, 206–12.

WILSON, A., and MACKAY, G. S. 1941. Old age pensions: an historical and critical study. London: Oxford University Press.

WITTE, E. E. 1951. Comments. *In* Proceedings of a Conference on Problems of Older Workers. Madison: University of Wisconsin, Industrial Relations Center.

———. 1955. Twenty years of social security. Social Security Bull., **18** (October), 15–21.

WOLFBEIN, S. L. 1959. The length of working life in the United States. *In* C. TIBBITTS (ed.), Aging and social health in the United States and Europe, pp. 48–73. Ann Arbor: University of Michigan, Division of Gerontology.

WYNER, J. H. 1954. Toward more flexible retirement policies: a progress report. Personnel, **30**, 386–95.

YOUNG, M. 1954. Kinship and family in East London. Man, **54**, 210.

YOUNG, M., and WILMOTT, P. 1957. Family and kinship in East London. London: Routledge & Kegan Paul.

XII

The Uses of Leisure

MAX KAPLAN

I. INTRODUCTION

Every facet of American life is included in the phrase that we are in an "age of leisure." Our work week is shorter. Our family life has changed in character. Our "rootlessness" has taken new directions. Familiar sources of control, such as the church or elders of the community, are no more in dominance. We move about from state to state. A whole new world of aural and visual images reaches us via mass media. We find a large segment of older people among us. We travel to all corners of the country and abroad. Clothing habits have changed. Homes are planned differently. The search for a new style of life has led to the "exurbanite." Increased material comforts of life have become necessities. Retirement comes earlier. Old ideas about social class are modified. Labor-union contracts are more concerned with time as an increment.

How deeply all this affects our fundamental views of life, our purposes, goals, our sense of direction as persons, families, and as a nation—these are issues which lie below everything else. Has the age of leisure modified the values which have been identified with those of a business and industrial society? How will our intensified post-Sputnik science affect leisure? What does leisure mean to the older person; how does it fit into a life in which work is no more a major value and stabilizing force?

The facts of the new leisure are all around us. Total estimates for leisure expenditure in 1955 went from $35 billion (Anonymous, 1956) to $281 billion (Anonymous, 1953). Meyer and Brightbill (1948) speak of $20–$40 billion each year. The Woytinskys (1953) indicate an increase in national expenditures for leisure from less than $2 billion in 1909 to more than $11 billion in 1950. Obviously, these differences exist because there is no agreement on what to include. The item of travel is most prominent in this regard. Over $331 million went to federal taxes in 1952 from entertainment admissions. Even with tremendous acceptance of television since World War II, 50 million theater tickets were bought each week of 1952, and $40 million were invested in four hundred new drive-in theaters. In 1953 some 18 million persons fished, 17 million roller-skated, 125 million watched softball games, 105 million cheered at basketball games, perhaps 35,000 played in about seven hundred community symphony orchestras, about 70,000 acted on amateur stages, and enough persons spent time in gardening to put out $200 million for tools alone (Dewhurst and Associates, 1955).

All this is the result of a highly complex set of historical and social factors: technology, assembly-line production, urbanization, expanding population, new styles of life, altered family roles, mass education, the effects of war, and new patterns of thought which become fused with material factors in a circle of cause and effect, substance and symbol.

The broadest issues about the time we call "leisure" are three: (1) its functions, meanings, and perceptions to people; (2) its relation to all relevant factors in the culture; and (3) its elements as an "institution"—types of leisure, the process in which choices are made, and the interweaving of such roles as player, businessman, advertiser, entertainer, critic, and recreation worker.

More specific issues arise when we speak of leisure in relation to the process of aging or, more directly, to retirement. A central one is the phenomenon of *time*. Activities like work, sleep, eating, visiting, vacationing, etc., are accompanied by culturally conditioned conceptions and interpretations of time. The person's "stage" of life is one of the variables which influences such interpretations on a large scale.

The dominant motifs of childhood are play and education, just as the major motifs in time organization for one's middle or adult life are work and family. "Freedom" for both of these stages are contrasts to commitments and obligations toward teachers, peer groups, parents, bosses, fellow workers, etc. Leisure activities are *related to* routine and expected patterns of behavior and are therefore relatively easy to perceive. Indeed, to the worker, leisure can well be a "loafing" period, accompanied by the security that soon enough the time will come for meaningful, productive, and socially interdependent work.

In contrast, the expectations and interpretations of "leisure" for the retired person are vague. Our work-minded, still rurally oriented American culture has not yet developed an attitude toward leisure as *end time*, capable of its own interest values. The elder generation of the present are the social pioneers in forging a path for years of time which is substantively *unrelated* to work, relatively *free* of family obligations, increasingly available over a span of *years* rather than hours, and ideologically open to *new and creative directions*.

The range of uses made of this new

(Soule, 1955) "fourth dimension"—time—by persons in retirement is noted as follows by one group of writers:

> For some people it is a time for doing as one pleases . . . when one can realize the secret ambitions of travel, writing, devotion to home and family, or "jest settin' and lookin'." For others, however, free time can signify only an overabundance of void . . . with the very real potentiality of demoralization and debilitation [Kutner *et al.*, 1956, p. 103].

To what degree are older persons becoming participants in the "new leisure" summarized above? If older persons have special needs, are these being adequately met by the traditional organization of recreational activities? What do the trends in American leisure patterns—indeed, of the whole technical, economic, and sociopsychological structure—suggest to theoretical scholars of social gerontology as well as to program leaders and policy-makers?

When one looks into the matter, it becomes apparent that there can surely be no one approach to an inquiry into these very large issues.[1] The present discussion will limit its scope of inquiry by pursuing this order of problems:

1. What are those needs of older persons which are touched upon in one way or another by "leisure"?

2. Anticipating some difficulty with the term "leisure," how can this concept be used systematically by the science of social gerontology?

3. Can a typology be devised to cover leisure activities—one which will provide insights into their characteristic functions and organization in relation to older persons?

4. Can we extract from the entire American scene several important variables or factors to help explain the general directions of leisure and the special relevance of

[1] See the following: Butler (1945); Davis (1938); Davis and Havighurst (1947); Denny and Meyersohn (1957); Donahue *et al.* (1958); Douglas *et al.* (1957); Eisele (1938); Kaplan (1960); Larrabee and Meyersohn (1958); Mitchell (1931); Neumeyer and Neumeyer (1958); and Robbins (1956).

our typology of activities to foreseeable changes in American life?

5. Does the foregoing analysis shed light on research problems or on current or projected practice in gerontology?

II. NEEDS OF OLDER PERSONS

What are the needs of older persons? At least four approaches are available to us: (*a*) we can ask older persons themselves; (*b*) we can objectively study persons who are "successful" as older persons; (*c*) we can examine older persons who were not living successfully until certain therapies or measures were put into the situation and improvement resulted; and, finally, (*d*) we can attempt a synthesis of all the conclusions from the above. The last possibility will be examined briefly. The Institute of Gerontology of the State University of Iowa lists the following "needs and drives" of the older person in relation to leisure programs, based on the thinking of Clark Tibbitts:

a) Need to render some socially useful service
b) Need to be considered a part of the community
c) Need to occupy their increased leisure time in satisfying ways
d) Need to enjoy normal companionships
e) Need for recognition as an individual
f) Need for opportunity for self-expression and a sense of achievement
g) Need for health protection and care
h) Need for suitable mental stimulation
i) Need for suitable living arrangements and family relationships
j) Need for spiritual satisfaction

Another way of going at it is to formulate conclusions of "good" leisure in reference to the needs of people, always remembering that the criteria used by science must arise from assumptions of our society and our time, not from absolutistic judgments which are "God-given" or "divine" in origin.[2]

1. There is a "need" for a person to be needed, rooted, wanted—in short, "to belong." This conclusion arises from scientific observation as well as folk wisdom and is a fundamental premise in dealing ages, but most particularly with ol__ sons. Some leisure activity is more effective than others for achieving this end.

2. Conversely, there is need for every person to be distinct from others, to have interests and abilities which distinguish him. For this purpose, some leisure activity is more effective than others in making an older person an "individual."

3. There is the possibility of combining leisure functions; for instance, pure rest or relaxation can accompany the absorption of a Beethoven symphony. Some leisure activities, more than others, offer a wide dimension of function and thus contribute to a need to spend time to some purpose but free of compulsion.

4. There are some leisure activities which, more than others, serve additional persons of the society at the same time that they serve the participant. One club is entirely social; another combines a community project with its socializing. There are some leisure activities, such as gambling away resources needed for one's family, which have objective consequences harmful by standards of indebtedness, mental health, guilt feelings, or family solidarity. There are others, such as adult study classes, which provide new experience but are accumulatively helpful by standards of personal satisfactions, improved skills, or knowledge of the world. Thus the dual need can be met by well-chosen leisure: to do something for ourselves and at the same time to serve others.

5. There is a possibility of leisure being put into the creation of works of art which, more than other activities, provide expression of inner feelings, personal growth, af-

[2] Obviously, this discussion does not pretend to deal with basic "needs" of a more general kind. There is a large sociological and psychological literature on this. For an example of a recent influential approach which is also relevant see A. H. Maslow's writings, especially *Motivation and Personality* (1954). According to him, "self-actualization" is the last in the list of man's basic needs, emerging freely only when the other needs have been met: physiological, safety, love, esteem, information, and understanding.

finity with aesthetic traditions, enjoyment
to other persons, and objects or works for
future pleasure to the creator himself.

These assumptions of the "good leisure"
are based on the view that important needs
of the older person are to "belong"; to be
needed by others on the basis of common
interests; to be different from others, to be
somehow unique; to become involved in
behavior patterns which serve several purposes; to be in activities which the participant and others recognize as constructive
rather than harmful; finally, to face new
experiences and thus to create, to grow, to
see and know one's self.

Further, the "needs" of older persons
cannot be analyzed as a problem or issue
apart from the "needs" of all people—indeed, without a consideration of the total
society. And the fundamental characteristic of our own society is rapid technical
and social change.

Thus the social scientist is now faced
with the need to formulate a conceptualization of "leisure" which will serve his ex-
plorations *today*. The dichotomy of work-
play, or even work and non-work, is overly
simple for use in current America.[3] Elements of each have penetrated the other.
Further, if we view work in its larger psychosocial aspects as a set of commitments,
loyalties, or a key source of the person's
Weltanschauung, then we find that lines—
time lines, salary lines, or other—are inadequate, even for intelligent statistical
studies. We proceed to a formulation of
leisure for our present purposes.

[3] Even Lundberg's definition, used in a classic
pioneering study, recognized this. Leisure "is the
time we are free from the more obvious and formal
duties which a paid job or other obligatory occupation imposes upon us. In accepting this definition we are not overlooking the interdependence
of work and leisure. Such terms are mere pragmatic
ways of designating aspects rather than separate
parts of life. It remains a fact, however, that nearly
all people can and do classify nearly all their activities according to these two categories in a way
that is deeply meaningful to themselves . . . as such
the categories are . . . useful for our purpose"
(Lundberg *et al.* 1934, pp. 2–3). (See also Meyersohn, 1958.)

III. An Ideal Construct of Leisure

Our approach is to construct a general
picture or concept of leisure which will permit of both *subjective perception* and *objective analysis*. The tool of the "ideal construct" or the "ideal type" is used very
widely in common speech when we speak
of "English society" or "communism" and
has been systematically used by the eminent scholar Max Weber (1930) in his
analysis of Protestantism. As employed by
Weber, the ideal type is a general, not a
specific, picture or a statistical average. It
contains the important elements of the situation against which a real situation can
be assessed. As a *typical* picture of leisure
(in this case), what is sought is something
"applicable to the analysis of an infinite
plurality of concrete cases" (Parsons, 1949,
p. 606).

Essential elements of leisure, as we shall
interpret it, are (1) antithesis to "work"
as economic function; (2) pleasant expectation and recollection; (3) minimum of
involuntary social role obligations; (4) psychological perception of freedom; (5)
close relation to values of the culture; (6)
inclusion of the entire range from values
of inconsequence and insignificance to those
of weightiness and importance; and (7)
often, but not necessarily, characterized by
the element of "play."

A. Antithesis to Work as
Economic Function

Engaged in leisure, I can dig a ditch in
my yard to make way for some landscaping
project; this may require more energy than
my economic "job." It is, however, outside
the economic system in the usual way in
which I relate myself to that system. It is,
obviously, not altogether unrelated to economics per se, for my "labor of love" may
deprive a professional "worker" in these
lines from employment.

B. Pleasant Expectation and
Recollection

With this element we eliminate all enforced "leisure," such as unemployment,

imprisonment, or sickness. Constructively, we include a psychological attitude moving both forward and backward in time. It is impossible to divorce "vacation," for instance, from the expectation, planning, day-dreaming, savings, packing, and the "excitement" of going away. Such looking-ahead often makes the routine of life more bearable and marks work periods as *means* toward "life" and "living," the goal and the end. Similarly, while the recollection of the vacation or leisure activity is often inaccurate and colored by the idealization fostered in the preparatory stage, many persons on vacation probably enjoy themselves and look back favorably upon their experience because they cannot afford, emotionally, to contradict their past hopes and projections. And, as a matter of fact, the attitude and expectancy do influence the actual experience itself.

C. Minimum of Social Role Obligations

"Social role," to be discussed more technically later, isolates and interrelates the many "positions" or obligations which a John Smith has achieved in his society or has been given by it: citizen, father, friend, carpenter, Protestant, Mason, and so on. He is only *one* John Smith who plays or possesses *many* roles. Part of the adjustment, maturity, normality, and personality he is credited with by everyone else is just this: how he behaves in each of these roles and, more important, how he combines or synthesizes them all into the one social being known as John Smith. In each of the many circles he touches, Smith has rights and obligations (voting, supporting his wife, etc.). In his leisure activity he may have many obligations—from making toys for his children ("every father *should*") to going on trips with his wife ("a good husband *should*"). These are obligations, however, which he is more likely to assume voluntarily, and with more pleasant expectations, than going back to work on January 2. He is formally committed to his work and for a long period of time. Theoretically, he has greater freedom in decid-

ing whether to be with his family in his "off" time. There may well be some self-deception in his perceptions of relative obligations, yet John Smith himself is the one who acts in accordance with his perceptions.

D. Psychological Perception of Freedom

It is the perception of freedom *by the person who participates in leisure* which is an important factor (Znaniecki, 1934). Thus there will be considerable variety in the definitions which people give of leisure or of "free time." This is indicative to the social scientist of the great variety in "styles of life." Time as a physical element is measurable, but amount of leisure is not, as illustrated in the cases of two mothers: one perceives herself to be heavily weighted down when she feeds her infant, while the second mother finds this a delightful experience. Freedom is thus as much an issue for the social psychologist as for other social scientists. The student of leisure deals on both levels, that is, with absolute quantities of time free from objective economic functioning and with time which is perceived as free.

E. Close Relation to Cultural Values

If the concept of leisure is equated with re-creation, it has no value in itself except as a supplement to work. However, leisure has moved further and further from subordination to work; increasingly, leisure is an end, a life of its own. As with all human ends, leisure is bound up closely with moral, ethical, and thought systems and with all social institutions.

F. Entire Range of Significance and Weightiness

Old associations of work with seriousness, and leisure with lightness, are now outdated and theoretically indefensible. Leisure activity can include interests covering the whole gamut of human life; hence the degree of seriousness or significance is irrelevant to a concept of what leisure is or "should be."

G. Often, Not Necessarily, Characterized by Play

Play, as viewed by Huizinga (1950), penetrates many human activities. In this broad view several of the elements of play as he defined them are synonymous with leisure: voluntariness, play as freedom, play as an interlude in life. Leisure, as we are characterizing it here, differs from Huizinga's scheme for play in that leisure is not necessarily secluded and limited, starting and stopping at specific times; it is unlimited in time and space. As a system of *order* leisure is less limited by rules and norms. If we leave Huizinga and revert to the vernacular (historically inadequate) concept of play as an activity which is light, associated with child life, or as an objectified slice of life on a stage, then, of course, leisure is a much wider and more inclusive concept in which play is only one type.

This "ideal construct" of leisure is not intended to indicate a *content*. A basic assumption is that anything or any specific activity can become a basis for leisure.

IV. Classifications of Leisure Activity

Since we proceed on the assumption that leisure is not definable as a given activity but is rather a characteristic social relationship, how can a classification be derived? As all scientific classifications are: by the creation of typological tools sharpened to meet certain kinds of issues. For example, one difference between a bridge game and a party is that the first requires traditional equipment—cards—and is limited to a set number of players. Equipment and numbers are therefore two ways of classifying or distinguishing activities. Additional types can be invented easily:

1. Self-directed
   Other-directed } read; visit a sick friend

2. Participatory
   Receptive } play in a string quartet; listen to a concert

3. Terminal
   Continual } go to a lecture; enrol in an adult class

4. Individual
   Group } "loaf" under a tree; join a picnic party

Other groupings could be distinguished in respect to expense, amounts of time, degrees of skill, time of year, indoor-outdoor, ad infinitum.[4]

The problem is not to find classifications but to isolate those issues which seem to be most relevant for understanding older persons and ultimately for formulating policies and principles. A typology is then a primary set of tools, to be judged solely on its utilitarian value. As a demonstration of this, three issues are selected here as especially applicable to older and retired persons:

1. To what degree do they relate themselves to other *persons as values,* as distinct from interests held in common with other persons?

2. To what degree do they require activities which are fixed by rules and well-ordered traditions, as distinct from creative or relatively free activities?

3. To what degree do they seek to go *to the world* for direct and new experiences, as distinct from leisure experiences in which the experiences of the world *come to them?*

These respective categories then emerge: *sociability and association; game and art;* and *exploration and immobility.*

A. Sociability

There are some persons we like to be with. We like them as *people.* There need be nothing vital to talk about, no "content," no chess game, no political agreements, no conversation of any consequence. Classical models of such relationships are the family, a pair of lovers, a social gathering. With the presence of content, even for

---

[4] An example of a classification used by authorities in the field of recreation is found in the Athletic Institute's *The Recreation Program* (1954): arts and crafts; dance; drama; games; sports and athletics; hobbies; music; outdoor recreation; reading, writing, and speaking; social recreation; special events. See also Linden's (1958) classification.

a moment—entertainment, serious talk—the pure form of sociability has been replaced. Friends have become debaters, jesters, sages, teachers, audiences.

George Simmel's (see Spykman, 1925; Barnes and Becker, 1938; Wolff, 1950) insights still remain unsurpassed:

Inasmuch as in the purity of its manifestations, sociability has no objective purpose, no extrinsic results, it entirely depends on the personalities among whom it occurs. But precisely because everything depends on their personalities, the participants are not permitted to stress them too conspicuously. *Tact,* therefore, is here of such peculiar significance [Wolff, 1950, p. 45].

We have here a relationship in which each person acts *as if* all are equals. Normal social roles—banker, artist, rich man, father—are suspended. This is not a "lie"; it becomes one only when the ostensibly self-contained phenomenon is a deception played for ulterior purposes.

The significance of sociability as leisure experience is that it covers a wide range of commitment and self-revelation. One can be with people he likes and say nothing of depth. On the other hand, in conversation which has no ulterior purpose, persons can delve into areas of thought, feeling, or biography of the utmost importance and especially in the company of strangers. By its nature, such conversation can "free" one, stimulate him, lead to self-discovery, promote a self-confidence, or threaten one for the moment and for a long time afterward.

B. Association

When a common interest brings together persons, an "association" arises.[5] The inclusive interest is more important than one's liking for the others, for strangers may be brought together. Any interest can suffice—love of animals, collection of stamps, civic reform, or common dislikes. Bushee (1945) divided all voluntary associations into fraternal, educational, social, economic, recreational, social service, patriotic, and cultural. Around the interests developed are the group's purpose and social structure: its symbols, the selection and expulsion of members, indoctrination of members, a hierarchy of power, relations to other groups, evaluations of success and failure, and rituals and ceremonies.

As leisure experience, voluntary associations offer a wide variety of functions and possibilities: to become a leader or a follower; to belong to something; to be important; to have someplace to go; to have something to do, like sending out post cards; to receive mail; to meet people; to anticipate a full evening; to argue; to enjoy the pageantry and play of secret oaths, costumes, scepters, parades, unusual titles; and, of course, to become part of the activity itself, one which may be of significance to the person and to his community. In any event, the member may derive status and a feeling of meaningful activity, regardless of the judgments of outsiders (Rose, 1954; Chapin, 1958).

C. Games

The game is a situation in which one or more persons emerges from a regulated series of actions as the "winner" or "loser." In its most basic form, it is activity which (a) involves more than one person; (b) contains a struggle and climax; (c) includes a consciousness of victory, defeat, or an even outcome; and (d) has rules, sometimes accepted by learning and requiring no judge at the game. This definition cannot insure easy recognition of the game, for, as Jerome Fried (1949) notes, sometimes games "are mysterious matters, closely linked with religious beliefs and customs" (p. 432).

Since the rules are supposed to create a fair and just set of conditions, the game becomes an equilibrium of freedom and obligation, of creativity and stability. Thus it lends itself uniquely as a model for life

[5] Of course, associations or interest groups often arise out of collections of individuals who move from a "habit group" into a "purpose group." These terms are used, and the process is described, by Essert and Verner (1951).

outside the game. Terms like "sportsman-ship," "teamwork," "the game of life," or "fair play" indicate that we read moral values *into* the game and then extract les-sons *from* it. War, especially the Prussian concept which looked upon the military life as a source of character, and the upper-class fox hunt in England provide two ex-amples of this. The transference of morali-ty from the *game* to *life* does not deny that even the "good" activity (art is another example) can be the refuge of scoundrels; but it makes of the game a complete ethi-cal and behavioral world. The content it-self may be a secondary matter, for the appeal of the game may be in the presence of rules and discipline, in being with other persons on a social level (Crespi, 1956), or in the case of relating one's self to others who play together in assigned roles as first baseman, south hand, or left guard. As in voluntary associations, the game can be intense and meaningful to participants.

D. Art

While the game is based on regulations, art is a matter of creativity within tradi-tions. Its functions are broadly two: the aesthetic and the social. In the former it serves to relate creators and audiences to materials, forms, or contents within the artistic creation. Examples might be the contemplation of an abstract design or the thematic development of a fugal theme.

The social functions of art serve to re-late it to persons, ideas, cultural norms, or patterns of behavior. Its subdivisions are art as collective experience, personal ex-perience, social symbol, moral value, and incidental phenomenon (Kaplan, 1957). Thus art provides many kinds of values, and, for purposes of leisure, the following advantages seem apparent: (1) There is a wide variety of media—music, drama, painting, literature, dance, sculpture. (2) Artistic activity is already an accepted value in society and has the blessings of a "good" activity, even if badly executed. (3) Much artistic activity can be carried on either in isolation or with others. (4)

Art in some form appeals to all ages and stages of life and to all degrees of emotion-al vitality and maturity. (5) Its cost ranges from nothing to heavy expenditure. (6) It provides a common value to many types of persons, serving as a forceful means of creating friendships or crossing lines of origins, faiths, creeds, colors, wealth, or schooling. (7) Art provides the elusive but real experience we call "self-expression." Finally, (8) art serves as a universalized expression of life itself, crossing historical or cultural periods and types and thus pro-viding a historical continuity as an anchor in a society of dramatic change and tur-bulence.

E. Exploration

In this type of activity, for which an-other term might be "mobility," one goes *to* the world. The trip might be across town or around the world. Significant to us in its psychosocial meanings are, first, the *form*—the matter of going. Here the issues of the-oretical concern are divisible into several elements: (1) motivations; (2) expecta-tions; (3) planning or preparation; (4) the actual going; (5) the return; and (6) the use of the experience in the post-trip experiences of the traveler. It is important for a theory of leisure to recognize that one or all of these *form* elements may be critical in a travel experience. This is par-ticularly true of the older person, for whom the change from familiar patterns of doing things may be of importance, as a reward-ing activity or as a threat.

Content or meaning is the second aspect of movement or travel. Again, several ele-ments are noted: (1) contacts with new people, seen as masses or secondary rela-tionships; (2) new acquaintances, who come to life as meaningful additions to the traveler's friendship vocabulary; (3) new physical or natural objects or scenes—cities, landscapes, buildings, paintings, etc.; (4) new experiences or adventures—touring Paris or Paducah, shopping, seeing the Vatican, a boat ride, etc.; and (5) con-tacts with new cultural values—family life, ideas about food, religion, etc.

Relations of physical movement to mental perception of what is seen provide another important theoretical dichotomy. A very rough scheme might divide cross-cultural travelers into two: "empathic natives" who seek by intuition or prior study to get into the inner life of their hosts and "comparative strangers" who cannot avoid packing their own standards and values into the suitcase, who never quite leave home, and who will remain strangers by choice or state of mind wherever they go (de Sola Pool and de Sola Pool, 1956–57).

F. Immobility

In the preceding type of activity, I go to the world. In all leisure to be called "immobile," the world comes to me. This is especially relevant to a theory of leisure which aims toward applications to older persons. It may be that "older" has traditionally been correlated with the person's lesser initiative or desire to meet the world face to face. This, if true, was first counteracted with the popularity of reading as a factor in American life. Later, motion pictures brought a new means for receiving impressions *from* the world; but the older population has never comprised a major movie audience. Since World War II, television has joined radio as the major source of outside images coming to the aged person.

The mass media have made potential world citizens of many of us; at least, the real world is no more limited to our direct observation. Professional eyes, ears, minds, and interpretations mediate the world for us. The quick access we are given to events and ideas from great physical distances means that the producers, sponsors, and news agencies must select, omit, and edit. So dramatic and realistic is some of this presentation and so involved are many of the contemporary audiences that the old dichotomy of "active" and "passive" is perhaps outdated if used in relation to sitting and moving. As David Riesman (1954) notes: "Much leisure which appears to be active may be merely muscular; its lactic content is high, but there may be little other content, or contentment. And conversely, such supposedly passive pursuits as movie-going can obviously be the most intense experience, the most participative" (p. 206).

Numerous questions can arise from a consideration of the preceding illustrative categories:

1. What are some important factors in the total situation of older persons which explain the choice of one activity rather than others?

2. Are some leisure activities preferable over others, as determined by studies of correlations to "good adjustment"?

3. Do some leisure activities, more than others, provide a continuity of values from the work to the retirement periods of life?

4. Is there a body of reliable knowledge upon which the social gerontologist can draw to encourage a particular kind of leisure activity for a particular person or group?

These questions focus attention on problems of *choice, need, continuity,* and *activity procedure.* As we proceed to explore these issues, they will be interwoven, research problems will be suggested, and references will be made to the literature but with no pretense to a full encyclopedic treatment. We begin with the basic variable—the changing nature of work.

V. Variables of Leisure

A. Work

In work, man has gone much further than mere sustenance and has always found the core of his life. Work in its largest perspective is closely tied in with one's relation to family, to other persons, to nature, to objects, to movement, to concepts of God, to meanings of life itself. Its impact is on the state of one's freedom and responsibility, one's position in the esteem of others, one's particular relation in the production of goods, one's attitude toward government and authority, one's mental capacities or achievements, one's material level, one's circle of acquaintanceships, one's concept of himself as a person, and one's "chances-in-life" or the chances of his mate and children. Hence it is folk wisdom at its best and not idle curiosity which asks of the stranger, "And what do *you* do?"

Work has long been considered as the source of values, the basis of character, the rootedness of man, the core of the Christian world (Caplow, 1954; Morse and Weiss, 1955). It has been said that

work is divine. God is revealed as the great worker and it is through work that men become like God. It is through work that man finds his life, and his life is measured by his work. Business is a means by which men exchange usefulness. In the exchange of commodities and services both parties are benefited, both parties profit. The more a man gives, the more he receives. To run away from work is to run away from life. To repudiate work is to commit suicide [Dyer, 1942].

This idea has been shaken by the way in which people have been very glad to "commit suicide," working fewer hours in exchange for more time and at no loss of material comforts. In 1850 the average work week was about 70 hours; in 1900 it was 60 hours; in 1940 it was down to 44; in 1950 to 40; and it is estimated at 37.5 hours for 1960. This represents a drop of 2.5 hours during the present decade and an average decrease in work time of 4 hours for each decade since 1900 (Dewhurst and Associates, 1955; Soule, 1958a).

Those in their sixties and seventies are therefore on the frontiers of an ideological revolution. How does a whole society replace work as the major source of meaningful life? Since a major aspect of work life is that it is structured in respect to time, place, colleagues, objects, going and coming, etc., one answer is to say that a structure can also emerge in the afterwork life. Havighurst (1954) spins such a hypothetical case for us:

Now he may develop a new, more leisurely routine, getting the morning paper and reading it, tending the furnace or starting the fireplace, reading the mail, doing the marketing, working in the garden just before lunch, taking a nap after lunch, going to the library or the park or a clubroom for a couple of hours in the afternoon, reading the evening paper, eating supper, going to a meeting or a movie or listening to the radio, or going slowly to bed. This routine is unexciting to a younger person, but to an older person, it may give all the satisfactions that the swifter tempo and more energetic activity of his earlier routine afforded [p. 310].

We submit that the "satisfactions" of which Havighurst writes are parallel to work only if within this new pattern there develop commitments, response, and security from the successful performance of expected behavior. Our construct of leisure was built on just the opposite of those—on freedom from obligations. Two propositions emerge for further study.

I. *A basic fear of the non-structured retirement period can be minimized by encouraging leisure activities with a maximum of commitment, order, and time involvement.* Our thought here is that, since many persons tend to remove from their own view of leisure those activities which require a considerable obligation, a major strategy emerges: guide these persons into activities which will, in actual effect, *not be considered as leisure or "free time." Less* leisure thus results. In their classic study of Westchester County, Lundberg *et al.* (1934) found that many women became deeply involved in their clubs and did not count this as leisure activity. It has been said that this is not difficult to do (Johnson, 1957; Anderson, 1958).

II. *Among the categories of leisure activities previously listed those most useful for this purpose are "association," "games," and "immobility."*

In association there is a common interest; this implies a direction—political activity, meetings, discussions, decisions, etc. In games there is order and expected role-playing, with the additional excitement of the competitive element. In reading or in watching television the images which come arrive within a framework of a familiar living room or library.

Furthermore, attention is called to the

fact that work, as a social rather than a technological process, consists of both intrinsic and extrinsic elements. The former consist of hours, amount of income, place, and social interactions between worker to worker (as in the case of a clerk) or worker to client or non-worker. (For instance, a significant factor in the relation of work to leisure is whether a person is self-employed.) Among the extrinsic factors of work are its related social status and the social values implicit in the nature of the function. Again, two propositions emerge:

I. *The intrinsic elements of work life, notably income and location, set some fundamental conditions for the choice of leisure activities in older age.* We need scarcely assert that when the older person is beset with economic worries, or when he moves to Florida in order to have fewer expenses, his whole approach to leisure is affected.

II. *Of greater importance to leisure study are the "extrinsic" elements of the work life—status and social values.* As we will see later, social class has direct relation to choices of leisure activities. The issue of values takes us directly into an issue suggested earlier—that of continuity.

The problem has many facets. It is generally accepted, for instance, that the professional person has less fear of retirement than the businessman or the worker. The first of these has had a work period relatively freer than the others; his education has been broader, his work more creative; persons attracted to teaching, the arts, medicine, etc., are perhaps more imaginative to begin with than others. Whatever the difference between them, the rapid shift in proportions of persons making up these rough categories has been dramatic in the past generation. We do well, therefore, to anticipate even more dramatic occupational (and, therefore, leisure) changes in the next few decades as well as developments of work conditions and attitudes *within* occupations. Some illustrations follow.

1. If the present trend toward work among women continues, about half the women of the age group 34–64 will be working by 1975. Interviews by the writer and his students indicate that leisure is more clearly perceived by women who are employed outside the home than by other women. Increasingly, these women whose husbands retire will themselves have worked out of the home. What effect, if any, might this have on the retirement of both?

2. Increasing automation will have direct effects, such as the upgrading of skilled workers to electronics men, but even more far-reaching effects can be projected (Bendiner, 1955; Dewhurst and Associates, 1955; Bloomberg, 1957). It is not unreasonable to imagine that the worker may eventually choose to work 6 months a year for 8 hours a day rather than the full year at 4 hours (Bendiner, 1957).[6]

Little imagination is needed to foresee the many intriguing possibilities which might result from this: intensive adult-education courses, long travels, or the exchange of homes between Mr. X (of Maine), who works his six months in September–February, and Mr. Y (of Arizona), who works on the same job in March–August!

3. Finally, hours of work are only part of a larger story. Today, we can easily make plans for leisure activity after work by phone, thus "making" more time. We arrive more quickly at our destination. Perhaps, at the end of the day, we have more energy left than the heavier work of the past allowed. Wives are freer of household work to join with their men in activity. The home has better light to read by. Better food is available in the refrigerator or freezer. Beyond these matters the older person of today has better health than his counterpart a generation ago. It is within many such subtle factors that new work patterns must be seen.

[6] The United Auto Workers, AFL-CIO, has an Education Department which is a good source for material on labors' point of view with regard to automation. See also Stern (1957) for a statement of the UAW's attitude.

B. Personality

The broadest issues here are two: (1) What can leisure activity tell us about people? (2) From what we know about people, how can we best guide them in their leisure activities? Of course, the basic question always remains: What is the "good life," what prototype of "adjustment" do we have in mind in our roles as leaders, counselors, clinicians, or sages?

A general conclusion of sociology is that "personality" is the "totality of those aspects of behavior which give meaning to an individual in society and differentiate him from other members in the community" (Sapir, 1934, p. 85). Attention is focused in this term on the fact that Mr. X as a "consistent" person will play bingo rather than read a book or that attendance at an art gallery is outside his sphere of conceivable behavior. Several examples of research will illustrate this attempt to find correlations between activity as meaningful behavior with objective variables. Havighurst (1957a, 1957b) applied rating scales to the favorite leisure activities of 234 persons in Kansas City. An attempt was made to measure the significance to nineteen variables such as autonomy, creativity, work, relaxation, and expansion of interests. He found (1957a) that (1) there is remarkably little change of significance with age (between 40 and 70); (2) the significance of leisure activities is more closely related to personality than to age, sex, or social class (thus leisure activity is an aspect of personality); and (3) since several different leisure activities can have the same significance for people, people of different age, sex, and social class can derive similar values from their leisure, even though the content of their leisure activities is different.

Some three hundred older (60–65) employees of the Standard Oil Company of Indiana were studied to note occupational differences in adjustment to aging and retirement. One of the categories or "life-areas" among the fourteen items was on leisure time (Burgess *et al.*, 1958). Three groups were distinguished: managers, supervisors-professionals, and manual workers. A hundred questions were asked in an inventory on retirement planning developed at the Industrial Relations Center, University of Chicago. To each question the respondent replied, "Yes," "No," or "Undecided." From the total questions we have extracted several which pertain directly to leisure for presentation in Table 1. It will be noted that the investigators indicate that for items 1–5, a "Yes" answer is "favorable" to good adjustment; for items 6–8, a "No" reply is "favorable." In the summary report quoted here, no further explanation is given on the basis of these judgments.

These items are a small part of the "Retirement Planning Inventory" developed at the Industrial Relations Center of the University of Chicago. A hundred questions are asked under fourteen categories, twelve of which seek to measure preparation for retirement. The few items above provide evidence for the conclusion given in the full report that "occupational status is a differentiating factor in aging and retirement adjustment . . . the higher the group's occupational status, the greater its adjustment." Managers and supervisory-professional personnel differ less between themselves than both as a bloc differ from manual workers.

The moot point in all such tests, of course, is the degree to which the values and necessities of an occupation contribute to a person's attitudes and whether his basic attitudes led him into the occupation in the first place. Anne Roe (1956), in an important work, indicates that, no doubt, "some specialized occupations, at least, do attract persons who resemble each other in some personality characteristics" (p. 80).

It is axiomatic that advice to persons who have finished their work careers must take into sharp account who and what the person is: reading Shakespeare is not advocated to an illiterate, nor world travel to an indigent. It is when we get into the area of realistic overlappings that the value of correlations enters into their subtleties. As in the construction of intelligence tests, to what degree do the stereotypes of the investigators or counselors enter *their* attitudes about the attitudes of clients or subjects? The writer is not doubting the validity of the University of Chicago study or others; he is always inclined to be concerned about their use in the hands of applied workers with the aged. For example, from the eight items above, it is apparent that the first two ("higher status") groups indicate a greater degree of gregariousness than do the manual workers: they have

viancy (not the same as creativity but related to it) and conformity.

The writer can envision a reversal in educational objectives in the next several generations: a general tightening of educational discipline for children in school and a remarkable expansion in concepts of "exploration" for retirees.[7]

Other factors which may affect attitudes toward leisure are those to be considered in the following sections of this chapter. Yet these influences—family, social class, com-

TABLE 1*

PERCENTAGE FAVORABLE RESPONSES TO QUESTIONS ON LEISURE IN RETIREMENT
BY OCCUPATIONAL LEVELS OF OLDER EMPLOYEES

QUESTION	FAVORABLE RESPONSE	OCCUPATIONAL LEVELS		
		Managers	Supervisors and Professionals	Manual Workers
1. Has one or two new activities or interests....	Yes	79	60	70
2. Gets as much fun out of life as used to.......	Yes	75	68	55
3. Would like to join Golden Age or Senior Citizens Club.............................	Yes	25	49	41
4. Going to take up things like painting, reading, dancing................................	Yes	71	52	48
5. Knows activities for retirement to make up for what job means other than money...........	Yes	75	70	46
6. Finds spending more and more time by himself	No	79	73	55
7. Too happy with old friends to look for new ones	No	75	69	47
8. Joining in games is a waste of time.........	No	88	86	64

* Source: E. W. Burgess, L. G. Corey, P. C. Pineo, and R. T. Thornbury, "Occupational Differences in Attitudes toward Aging and Retirement," *Journal of Gerontology*, **13** (1958), 203–6.

more fun, they are happy with old friends, they like to join games, they are more positive in knowing what they will do in retirement. Is this really a better adjustment profile than for those who would not like to join clubs of senior citizens, who feel games are a waste of time, who spend more time by themselves—or have the investigators simply adopted current American values? The answer is not an easy one, for what is involved is a basic philosophy of the social gerontology profession as it now grows out of its infancy: is it to be committed to conformity by the older generation to values of American middle age? Like the educator of youth, the gerontologist finds himself seeking a balance between encouraging de-

munity, religion, and values—are themselves interwoven with other factors which have been met in the recent literature of social science. These are (1) the influence of the group on person; (2) characterological types; (3) man's relation to the total cultural direction; and (4) the person as a configuration of social roles.

The development of social psychology as a discipline is testament to the inevitable fusion of individualistic and group empha-

[7] I have long ago concluded, from teaching both college students and adults, that the latter were generally more "liberal" and open to new ideas. It could be that, as older persons become increasingly concerned with civic interests, their influence will be in liberal rather than conservative directions.

sis in the study of man. Man is being increasingly viewed as a highly sensitive and flexible integration of the biological, psychological, and social. This integration takes place in a web of social myths, symbols, patterns, norms, traditions, explicit teachings, and implied sanctions. The way in which man responds and at the same time challenges or sifts the stimuli from all around him results in an observable or even a measurable John Smith—Protestant, father, bank clerk, Elk member, Republican, Book-of-the-Month subscriber, kind father, and generally faithful husband—who is, as Kluckhohn and Murray (1948) point out, in certain respects (*a*) like all other men, (*b*) like some other men, and (*c*) like no other man.

Leisure patterns constitute part of the social norms to which Mr. Smith has been subject since childhood. What he "likes" in sports or in sport cars, in his movies or in his martinis, are tastes developed in his *culturally available* range of choices. Even within this range, as noted in the experimental work of Kurt Lewin, Robert Bales, Samuel Stouffer, Muzafir Sheriff, and others, pressures of the immediate circle upon the person tend to pull him in one direction or another. Even leisure activity is not "free" in this sense but is indeed an area in which the subject (1) is *more open* to pressures and normative-consciousness and (2) is likely to disguise or deceive himself about his deep commitments to club, poker group, friends, or other "voluntary" activity.

BECKER

Howard S. Becker's study (1955) of the marihuana user is important as an example of how new norms in leisure are absorbed, of the impact of *learning* upon *enjoying*. Fifty interviews convinced him that no one becomes a habitual user without (1) learning to smoke the drug in a way which will produce real effects; (2) learning to recognize the effects and connect them with drug use; and (3) learning to enjoy the sensations he perceives. *Learning* to participate *and then* to enjoy—is this not a common

formula for many of us in one activity or another? Recall that a fundamental "need" of the older person is to be rooted and wanted. This is one reason for acquiescing to group pressure—a reasonable (perhaps unaware) exchange of a little freedom for a larger security. For example, an older person may go through a critical transition in deciding whether he should join a senior citizens group. Am I that old? Do I want to be around other people? Why shouldn't I mingle with the young and stay as young as I feel?[8] His decision to join is often not his own but results from a "push" from someone else. Then he goes through a psychological process similar to the sequence described for the marihuana user—he learns to enjoy his new experience, and he begins to "pull" others into it.

The gerontologist seeks always to develop a bridge between analysis and action. For example, he might ask himself the question: Should the policy be followed of exposing the older person to situations where the norms and experiences for enjoyment are heterogeneous (from all ages) or homogeneous (from peers in age)?

One cannot provide a *general* answer as to the wisdom of advocating frequent association with other older persons for any *given person;* there are too many conditions to be taken into account. Yet, based on knowledge of the case, *advice can be given in reference to the activity.* For example, sociability is a starting point for the shy or hesitant older person. Many centers for the aged find that younger persons (even those in their twenties) make excellent volunteers or recreation workers. The younger person acts as a bridge, as a listener primarily, perhaps at his best if

---

[8] Even the decision to go to a clinic contains the same problem. Dr. Robert T. Monroe (1957) reports the failure of the Peter Bent Brigham Hospital (Boston) to attract patients to its clinic and observes: "The chief reason for failure to report . . . must have been dislike of segregation on the basis of age. No one likes to grow old. . . . If one should go to a geriatric clinic, everyone will see that one is old, and one must expect to be treated there according to the downgrading concepts that our culture holds for old age."

he employs the Rogers (1951) technique of serving as a receptive but subtly directing factor in conversation.

The issue of norms also exists for the older person after he is a member of the leisure group—especially if it is a club in which lines can be drawn between those who are "more" and "less" active. We submit the principle that his success or "adjustment" to the group should not be equated with his degree of outward involvement. As an example of factors to consider, if the person has been from the social "lower class," he is likely to have had less experience as a club member. The important fact to him is often simply the belonging. Queen (1949) has written of the difficulty of judging the success of the *group* by the proportion of active members.

In a previous paper the writer (Kaplan, 1958*a*) has cautioned against "overorganizing" even within organizations of older persons. The member sometimes becomes the victim of a "turnstile" philosophy or anxiety fostered by the group worker. The worker himself is caught up in a circle whereby he justifies his professional success by the numbers of persons who came to the movie this week as compared to last week. It is difficult for him to enter in his monthly report the several hours spent with Mrs. Jones, who simply needed some-*one* to be with and was lonely in the big club until such a one emerged. In short, the worker is himself reacting to norms of numbers prevalent within his profession (and the greater American value system). Until the recreation profession and the related worker become convinced of this and undertake to educate its boards of directors, its policy will have to be to organize for the sake of organizing. Since the older group will increasingly occupy the attention of the group worker, the problem deserves serious study.

These considerations suggest the further thought that some activities, more than others, provide a bridge between individuality and groupism or between sociability and organization. Bingo and bridge are such; baseball is less so.

Bingo appeals basically to a different need than does an experience with the arts. For the watcher of a play, the listener to a concert, or especially the musical performer, there are elements of considerable concentration, preparation, display, tension, and the identity (as in the case of an older person in a chorus) with a group effort which, unlike a game, permits of little or no visibility for the individual.[9] But even art, as all the other forms of leisure activity, is often selected by the older person as a result of social needs to be with others, physically and psychologically.

Additional lessons in this to the policymaker or leader are that (1) the overt goals or functions of leisure activities may have by-products for the personality far different but of considerable importance and (2) the guidance of the older persons into an activity may rest legitimately on grounds quite different from the results which the leader expects to see[10] (see Havighurst's conclusion above).

RIESMAN, FROMM, AND LINDEN AND COURTNEY

Riesman's (1950) popular discussion of the "tradition-," "inner-," and "other"-directed types is too well known to require a summary here. Related to his analysis, working with older persons involves (*a*) uncovering the resources of the person for growth and exploration, that is, his "inner" sensitivities which he has sublimated because his previous role would not permit them to develop, and (*b*) helping to provide the media or organization through

---

[9] The Veterans Administration hospitals and other institutional groups provide invaluable settings for observations and experiments into the meaning and functions of group play. Play as therapy has been but little studied, even among children (Dorfman, 1951).

[10] A number of variables are currently being observed in the analysis of group dynamics—size, directions of communication, the group task, the personality of members, etc.—but *age* as a factor has been less studied. There are good, recent summaries and bibliographies on small group studies. See, for instance, Bales *et al.* (1958).

which he may develop these new personality dimensions.

Two quotations from Riesman's own summary of his work will help to clarify, first, the significance of his approach to the relationship of character to society and, second, the terms applied to his types. As to method, Riesman (1952) notes that he began the analysis for *The Lonely Crowd*

not with the individual, but with the society. And, with respect to the society, our focus was on certain changes that many people have observed in contemporary social organization, particularly the important degree to which modern metropolitan society, in classes and areas boasting high economic abundance, has presented people with agendas for living—and with an accompanying ethos—which are different from those characteristic of the nineteenth-century middle class. And then our effort was to proceed "inward" from these large social developments to study the demands made on individual character. These demands might be traced "outward" in turn, through the subtle channels by which character is formed, back to the social forms. Working in the neo-Freudian tradition of Erich Fromm, Karen Horney, and others, we looked for the consequences of social change in the individual, rather than looking, as psychoanalytic characterology did in an earlier day, for the social equivalents of the "family romance" in the society at large [pp. 333–34].

Riesman's meaning of his terms for character are thus summarized by him:

In other words, inner-direction and other-direction are abbreviated ways . . . to describe two not incompatible tendencies of which people are capable: one tendency is to find the source of direction in aims which one has held affectively before one from an early age; and another tendency is to find the source of direction in those among whom one is thrown at any given moment in one's career [p. 334].

These types of character represent attitudes toward both work and play. The inner-directed person organizes his work experience around non-human objects; he reacts to and respects organization rather than people. The other-directed hurries to bring glamor and artificial friendliness into the work situation. A "compulsory nature of personalization," which Riesman (1950, chap. xv) also calls a "false personalization," is sought between bosses and employees. A gamelike spirit is introduced into the factory, with the line between work and play constantly diminished by the increasing power and presence of other-directedness as a standard and goal in work (Stone, 1955).

Patterns of pleasure and leisure are also related to these types. When to play is decided for the tradition-directed person. Indeed, he is aware of sharp distinctions between play and work. Work is long and arduous by its nature.

The inner-directed person, moving from an age of tradition into one with an abundance of things, becomes an "acquisitive consumer." He engages in an externalized sort of rivalry akin to the process described by Thorstein Veblen (1912). As an "escaping consumer," the inner-directed person may escape to a " 'higher' level than that of business or professional life, or onto a 'lower' level!" The arts represent one example of the first. Riesman (1950) observes: "Even more perhaps than plumbing, amateur musical skills mark the boundary of middle-class aspirations to respectability" (p. 124). Escape *downward* is found in cheap novels, in races, in barbershop song, in "hootchy-kootch on the midway." Further, this man in business or the professions will exploit his leisure to make contacts, thereby to bring his work into play.

The other-directed person uses leisure and entertainment as an adjustment *to the group.* He has a large literature to orient him to the non-economic side of life and all the mass media as his tutor. Riesman[11] points out:

Entertainment today, far more than in an era of inner-directed modes of conformity, takes up the task of telling members of large groups of mobile people what they can expect of each other and what they should expect of themselves. The inner-directed man learned

[11] For a critique of Riesman see Wrong (1956).

what he needed to know of these matters in the primary group, or by a purposeful internalization of his schooling and reading. The mass media today are expected to perform ten-minute miracles of social introduction between people from a variety of ways of life and background. The entertainment fields serve the audience today less and less as an escape from daily life, more and more as a continuous sugar-coated lecture on how to get along with "others" [p. 176].

While our popular culture stresses group-mindedness as a virtue, it does not serve the purpose of escape because the other-directed person has no clear core of "self" to escape *from*. He can draw no sharp distinction between production and consumption or between work and play.

This task, according to Erich Fromm (1955), is made difficult by our society, which is not interested in the encouragement of our personal resources: rewards go to men who co-operate smoothly in large groups, who want to consume more and more, and whose tastes can be easily influenced and anticipated. Thus, concludes Fromm, *alienated* man is out of touch with *himself;* he becomes an impoverished thing.

It may well be that this kind of issue—finding or channeling the person's *potential for growth*—is met only halfway in our search for correlations between *what* older persons do now and did before and other things *about* them (age, education, etc.). Experimental designs need to be devised in which we seek to immerse all kinds of people in all kinds of leisure experiences and see what happens. As Wilma Donahue (1951) points out, there is no apparent discrepancy in interests between groups ranging from 30 to 90 years of age when no limits are set on who comes into senior citizens groups. The problem is, then, a matter of developing experimental designs based on potentiality stages or developments of the person.

Linden and Courtney's (1953) analysis of such developmental stages is valuable for providing a basis for further work. They are critical of the traditional view of human growth in which adult life is popularly regarded as the simple achievement of an ambiguous maturity followed by a general decline. Personality development is a continuum, a series of emerging steps. Each stage (early, middle, late) can be seen as twos: "evolescence" (*E*) is the younger side of middle life; "senescence" (*S*), its older side. Since our society values the former, *E* fights the image of *S*.

Further, according to Linden and Courtney (1953), late adulthood divides itself into "state creative" and "moral and ethical reaffirmative"; these denote "a profound concern for system, order, and meaning in human existence." There are "interruptions" or periods of transition, as just prior to senility, in which one has feelings of lower esteem, insecurity, rejection, and isolation. Senility thus grows out of attitudes. While our attitudes toward the aged are ambivalent, *E* values are overplayed (agility, movement, etc.) just as *S* values emphasize "deliberation, caution, quality, modesty and loyalty."

The authors conclude that "we need to know the dimensions of senescence . . . the social creative and other attributes that one is only beginning in evolescence." Relating this to our subject, we submit that:

1. Leisure activities are descriptive tools in determining stages of maturity as well as devices for affecting the transition from *E* to *S*.

2. Each of the types spelled out above—from sociability to immobility—can be "scaled" within itself. That is, it is unrealistic to study the values of travel in comparison to reading for the retired person, just as it is illogical to compare the value of jazz next to symphonic music or the relative merits of apples and oranges. It is, however, possible to develop a scale of value within each. The "needs" of older persons, set forth early in this chapter, provide several clues. These, for instance, might supply the basis for grading scales in relation to "highly effective," "somewhat effective," or "ineffective" leisure activity: normal companionships, recognition as individual, self-expression, mental stim-

ulation, service to others, being "needed," being unique, serving a variety of functions.

IMPLICATIONS OF BECKER, RIESMAN, AND FROMM FOR OUR STUDY

Several ways of approaching personality and leisure have been sketched through writings summarized above. Becker (1955) begins with group; Riesman (1950), with society; Fromm (1955), with basic needs of man. Whatever the specific contributions of these writers in their respective treatments, the approaches are not new. Much has been written, for instance, about the impact of group norms on individual behavior. The technique of looking at the culture as a whole in order to discern or predict the behavior of its people, and even to set up types of characteristic behavior, is found in a growing body of anthropological literature. And Thomas and Znaniecki (1918), in the famous sociological study on *The Polish Peasant*, long ago proposed three types of persons (philistine, bohemian, creative). Fromm's attempt to begin with human needs and then to see how the society meets them is, of course, a primary position of much psychology, both clinical and theoretical. This does not minimize the worth of the specific writings we have examined. They were selected because they typify such approaches to the problem and because, in these writings, an attempt is made (most explicit in Riesman) to relate their findings to leisure activities.

The over-all conclusion to be drawn from these approaches to personality is that our leisure-time actions somehow stem from one source or a combination of three chief sources: (1) from the groups to which we belong and whose controls and norms bear upon us; (2) from the culture into which we happen to be born, whose interlocking and complex pattern of groups, institutions, and prevailing ideologies sets a "climate of opinion" for all of life, including our attitudes toward unobligated time and its uses; and (3) from the limitations and potentials of our bodies and minds which influence the selections we make within groups and society and our own creative contribution toward new patterns of organization and thought in them.

Each of these contributions in turn raises questions. As to the influence of groups on leisure activities of the individual, we must inquire how the group itself happens to find certain leisure patterns more acceptable than others and whether the controls by the group over the person are the same in leisure areas of action as in others. In the matter of types of persons, are we actually explaining anything by identifying a type by its behavior and then crediting the behavior to the "type"? As to "basic needs" and cultural demands, do we not have to develop a cross-cultural approach which is still the bane of comparative anthropology?

SOCIAL ROLES: ZNANIECKI

We can go further in these directions when an additional approach has been briefly outlined—one which provides a theoretical tool to deal more adequately with the fact that complex society, as Robert MacIver (1947) noted, is a *multigroup society*. Each of us belongs to many groups. This fact is fundamental in understanding *how* we relate ourselves to conflicting ideas and norms in society. The analysis shifts attention from our "needs" to that of our *positions or social roles*.

Man is a member of many groups. He quickly moves about from a situation in which he is a hero or a leader to one in which he is a follower and a "nobody." Sorokin (1947) provides examples:

In general, each of us has as many "social egos" as there are social groups to which we belong. . . . When we interact with our family, we think, feel, and behave like father, mother, sister, brother, son, or daughter. Our ideas, standards, emotions, volitions, as well as our overt actions, are of a certain kind well known to all of us. When we . . . go to our place of work with our occupation group, our "family ego" disappears and our "occupational self" takes its place . . . and there accordingly result the actions of a professor, engineer, doctor, senator, plumber, carpenter, or farmer. . . . If one should try to assume his family self in his occupation, he would quickly be fired, to say nothing of being regarded as "queer" [p. 348].

A systematic scheme by which this network of "social egos" can be observed is found in the theory of the late Florian Znaniecki (1939, 1940). The scheme is to view each person as a composite of several "social roles" which are played in as many "social circles" as groups to which one belongs. These circles—home, club, factory, church—consist of values or purposes. They have a set of norms and controls by which members are judged. They train the member and expect certain types of action from him. Thus the church consists of a number of persons who "act out" established patterns of the priest, the sexton, the congregant, the treasurer, the usher, the organist, and the choir member. Each of these roles sets a way into which people fit; if we can put together these roles or patterns, we have a comprehensive view of the church as a whole.

The second component of each social role is that of function: What is expected of each of these roles?

Third, in accord with the training required of the role or other factors of the situation, the role-player gets something in return, whether in actual money or in less tangible rewards such as honor, a place to sit during services, personal satisfactions, or verbal praise.

Fourth, the prestige of the circle, the feeling of doing what one is expected, the esteem which results—all these together provide the person (as distinct now from the "role") with a consciousness of what others think of him, a sense of personal belonging. A self-image results.

This type of analysis is a way of observing action which is going on at the moment. As Tom Brown steps from the church into his recreational group, he finds that their norms are different. In the church he may be a high officer; in the poker group he is one of the "boys." His social position in the congregation is high, yet he may conceal or underplay the club in con-

versation with the minister. In the church he has a feeling of "doing right." In the small hours of Saturday night, if his luck at cards is bad, he wonders why he ever got into the poker group.

Leisure activity, among its many other changes in the past quarter-century, has produced new kinds of social circles. We can ask: Is there anything distinctive about them as groups? Is there a continuity of values from leisure groups to those of work, church, family? Are leisure groups unique in the way in which they create new social roles (Sutton-Smith and Gump, 1955)? Such questions as these, since they are asked in a theoretical way, may appear divorced from "real life." One example will be given to illustrate their force in a practical situation.

THE MENTAL HOSPITAL: THEORY IN ACTION

As occasional consultant to the Special Services Division for the Veterans Administration hospitals, the writer has often watched mental patients play such games as baseball, bingo, and volleyball. In baseball games all boys are taught by their childhood peer groups that one runs from first base to second to third to home; that three strikes is "out"; that the catcher stands behind the batter; and so on. We have never observed mental patients who played differently. In every game they went from first base to second. . . . Why?

The question is pertinent because the same men had also been taught other rules about many things, no more complicated than baseball and certainly done more often in the course of the week. For instance: "Don't talk out loud to yourself. Talk politely to women. Sleep in a bed, not on the floor. You are 'you'—Sam Jones—and not Napoleon. When someone speaks to you, usually you will say something in response." Yet as soon as the Sam Joneses the "players" leave the baseball field at the VA hospital, they are "patients," each ill with some form of maladjustment: some are withdrawn and will talk to no one; others will talk a blue streak to themselves; a few will require hydrotherapy; some are Napoleon, Christ, or Lincoln; and so on, through the range of schizophrenic behavior pattern.

We have in this situation, first, a considerable validation of Huizinga's theory of play—that it is a world of its own and *perceived as a world of its own*. That world has its own grounds, its moral order, its own beginning and ending in time. There is group pressure, for the patients seem definitely to care about the impressions they make on their team mates. Some will be influenced to appear in the game more by fellow patients than by staff members. Second, as in similar games with "normal" persons, types of personalities are recognized by the players—the "showoff," the "cheat," the "scared," the "gambler" types —type names which are often exceedingly perceptive. The needs for response and identity for the player, as discussed by Erich Fromm, are easily apparent, as in the cases of those who refuse to play for fear of personal defeat, as well as in those who achieve reputations in play denied to them elsewhere.

In respect to Znaniecki's analytic scheme of social roles, we immediately face the crucial issue of the Special Services Division in the mental hospital: how can a transfer of behavior be made from the play circle to other groupings? Can the patient who knows that he must run from first to second base, not the reverse, learn that similar observance to social controls brings response? If the medical man says that it is not at all a matter of social learning, that illness is something inside the man, then why is baseball conformity *outside* the same man? We are setting one problem and only tapping lightly at an approach in the hospital which is in fact receiving increasing attention—the hospital as a human laboratory in which "treatment" and "diagnosis" become a synthesis of medical (biological and psychiatric) with social considerations (services of occupational therapy, recreation, and others). It is in theory and research in choices and

methods of play that some of the clues may be found.

This extended treatment of personality and leisure touches upon aging and older persons directly and continuously. If personality is viewed as a synthesis of social roles or in some other dynamic construct, then it is a never ending process of relationships. Certainly, as leisure becomes a full-time preoccupation for a period which may run into many years, new experiences have an effect upon the personality. Perhaps retirement may in one sense be considered a failure if the person remains the same throughout. And rather than expecting it to be a period of declining powers, it can be one of growth. This is a direction for research into personality as related to aging: to proceed not only with studies of what older people are *now* (memory, attitudes, confidence, etc.) but controlled experiments into what they can *achieve*. The unthinking use of statistical techniques in social gerontology can confuse the *what is* with the *what can be expected*.

The research into social roles of the aging person may find its use in social gerontology to deal with the issues: What is the retired or older person's role in the home for older persons, in the VA hospital, in the apartment house or the whole community designed for him, or in the voluntary association of senior citizens? What is involved in the transition toward these roles?

Accompanying this research program is the task of establishing "ideal constructs" of types of adjustments to new roles. Sorokin's recent attempts to observe the everyday "saint" or altruistic person is suggested for this purpose as one major model for retirement.

There is a need to develop functional concepts of creativity in role-playing. A rough suggestion is that, in relation to the older person at least, we must move away from the traditional attempt to deal with creativity in the abstract or even to distinguish the creative person from others. Rather we can observe the actions of older persons *in relation to their previous pat-*

terns of behavior and attitudes. In reference to the preceding discussion, the older person has acted creatively when he has succeeded in freeing himself from the pressures of familiar groups (Becker); when he has become more autonomous (Riesman); when he is less alienated from his culture (Fromm); or when he has entered into new social roles in respect to social circles, functions, positions of esteem, or self-images of himself (Znaniecki). For example, Citizen Smith's new and fumbling effort in civic service is to be evaluated or observed in the perspective of *his* past, not that of a Schweitzer.

Thus our plea is for research into personality and leisure which uses case studies to explore people in depth and seeks to combine sociological-psychological-psychiatric insights with new knowledge of symbolic perception of one's self. Can we develop, perhaps, a "creato-graph" portrayal of meaningful creative highlights in a person's life-span and then begin to generalize about persons from various occupational groupings? The new generation of social scientists, however, can explore this difficult area of creativity only if it becomes more "creative" itself; if it becomes bolder in exploring theory and experimenting with ideas to meet new problems; indeed, if it heeds the warning set by Mannheim (1936) in his *Ideology and Utopia* that we dare not assume that only those problems are significant which can be dealt with statistically.

C. Family

The basic facts and trends of family life are familiar to all readers of contemporary life. Chapter xii relates these to special issues for the older person. A primary issue will be noted below as an example of the interweaving of family patterns, "senescence," and leisure.

Increased attention is being paid to the family style of life. Play, as an important thread in this style, has become a major theme in providing or testing family cohesiveness and solidarity. Leisure thus enters a new place in our understanding of the family as it becomes a cause, a clue, or an index of respect, love, interdependence, or knowledge of one another. For instance, many missing factual bits about the family below can be filled in from this description:

Many times at night J—— and I have dates; therefore, the family has to plan many of their activities around us. When we were younger, the folks always played baseball and basketball with us. Now that we are older, Daddy and I help B—— to learn the games. Daddy, J—— and I play tennis quite a bit on Sunday mornings. We are a family which loves the outdoors and therefore we like physical activity. Many a Sunday we go on picnics, and sometimes take friends or relatives along. Often we use the grill and eat out on our porch. Sometimes after dinner we go in the living room and do something for fun like practice dancing. Since Daddy works every day but Sunday, we usually plan our leisure activities around him. For about a month in summer all the stores stay open until 9:00 P.M., so when Daddy comes home we just sit around leisurely and talk.

This type of family stands opposite the prototype of the farm unit in which husband, wife, and children have work tasks and find a strong interdependence as business colleagues or partners. The functionalism of each member of the farm household gives a place to the grandparents or older relatives. Respect for persons as persons is less than in the student's home pictured above.

Retired men or women from the contemporary leisure-created home should, we strongly suspect, have more resources and independence than their counterparts from the functionally related family. In other words, one problem of the present generation in their sixties and seventies is parallel in a rough way with the problem of the second-generation sons and daughters of immigrant parents. In the 1910's and 1920's the latter lived in two worlds as marginal people, with resultant crime, emotional conflicts, and the like. Similarly, many of the present generation of retirees are going through the final phase of this process. As grandparents, *they* are in two worlds as marginal people, caught between their sure knowledge of being *useful* and their children's independence of them.

At the present time, therefore, the leisure program for the older person is in a large sense a psychological and emotional substitute for service to their children and grandchildren. All the more reason, then, that such a program must be meaningful and in good part, oriented toward *people*.

Of the types of activities noted earlier, games are the *least* oriented to people, since they are most often rooted in rules and formal behavior. Paradoxically, games are perhaps the easiest type of activity for recreation leaders to organize. Thus, wherever games—checkers, chess, cards, bingo, etc.—are found to be most popular among groups of older persons, we may reasonably inquire whether this is an activity above and beyond a more meaningful program or whether it is the meat of the recreational schedule. It is true that the professional recreation leadership is now going deeply into a self-appraisal and a philosophy. Social gerontology can do much to help this profession achieve a broad view of leisure activity as possessing a depth much deeper than simple activity, busyness, or time-filler.

D. Social Class

Societies, even democratic ones, stratify themselves on a number of bases. Of these, the most important in our country are occupation and wealth, which often, but not always, go together (Kahl, 1957). These strata of American society—the "country-club set," the "upper lower," "my kind," or however they are referred to—attain reality outside statistical tables only when such people act basically alike, think alike, or are treated alike by others.

Yet, in addition to these general criteria, the term "class" in European life has contained an additional element of great importance to the issue of leisure: the upper class was free of productive work and spent its time in *leisure activities*. There was no compulsion toward work, as is often found in American families of wealth. They were not expected to work, as opposed to the traditional American suspicion of the idler. There were, throughout Europe, elaborate resort centers in which the rich gathered; the American resort is an imitation by comparison. And the European rich had a "place" which the poor respected, and, revolutions to the contrary, a place which was part of a system the poor accepted as natural.

In America the problem of the rich group, socially, is always that it must remain open to new devices to identify itself, and hence there is no time for an aristocracy to develop a conservative tradition. In no way is the contrast more apparent than in a primary issue of the rich businessman here, namely, *how to learn to play when he retires*. This business class has not learned the first lesson of the aristocratic life, namely, that learning how to work should be a problem! When leisure activity becomes a full-time preoccupation among men, then we have the European concept of a "leisure class." This was perhaps Veblen's greatest difficulty—that his great book was written in America and that, by the time his perception was recognized by a large segment of the informed reading public, even the limited class divisions here had already begun to appear fuzzier with each passing decade.

THORSTEIN VEBLEN: THEORY OF THE LEISURE CLASS

While Marx had argued that each social class develops its own way of life (its own culture and morality), Veblen (1912) sought to demonstrate that the lower classes emulate the higher. Of what, then, does the upper class consist? To be one of the upper class means more than the possession of wealth or power; these must be made visibly evident for all. What results is a high self-evaluation based on esteem from others.

In the discussion of personality the elements of "social role" were indicated. The circle, according to Veblen, is clear cut, for the wealthy associate with each other, living a life in which leisure becomes purposeful activity—its purpose, to give to other circles of men a public accounting of his time. His function—to become expert precisely in those skills and arts which go beyond "spare time," which go on during the working day of the working class, and which require dress or other equipment beyond the spending power of the workers. His status, and consequently his conception of himself as a person, comes from the ease with which he undertakes such (productively useless) activities. Part of that "ease" is wrapped up in the manners which characterize the rich in social intercourse. All together, "these are the voucher of a life of leisure" (Veblen, 1912, p. 48).

The publicly noted waste of time, then, is the principle on which "good breeding" is evidenced. The visible male servant—the larger and more powerful the better—is one such tangible evidence; servants to do physical work and to exhibit an obvious example of luxury spending.

Yet not all of one's time can be spent in playing polo, running the foxes, or being driven through Central Park. The year is long, and the lower class is not always there to see. Some accounting must be given of private time by the rich. "Immaterial goods" and "quasi-scholarly" or "quasi-artistic" activity form such public evidences of privately spent, continual, and substantively useless activity. Others are the study of dead languages, cultivation of the arts, games, sports, "fancy-bred animals," or activity in charity organizations, drives, and clubs.

If all this is "conspicuous leisure," then "conspicuous consumption" is another side of the coin. Time is spent on productively useless activity, and money on an economic superabundance of things.

The guiding motive behind all this is self-satisfaction and position through esteem accorded by the have-nots. But is this all a mythology, a fantasy created by those in power? Clearly, it is a motif deep in the life of all, says Veblen, for the poor themselves seek to emulate and be like the rich. Here perhaps is the core of Veblen's sharp

irony, for, unlike Marx, he offers no solution.

Veblen made the public aware of waste, as Riesman (1954) notes. Veblen's contribution to institutional economics was to outline the latent functions of the system. In relation to leisure, a parallel can be seen between Riesman and Veblen. Both (more explicit in the case of the former) are telling us something about groupism, about conformity. To Veblen, one *class* seeks to emulate the other and is sensitive to judgments by the other. To Riesman, one *person* seeks to be like the others and tunes in his "radar antennae" to the judgments and behavior of others. In the largest sense both authors speak out for freedom of person and group, for them to be true to themselves. In current America it is indeed a paradox that, on the one hand, the individual tends to conform to what "others" do, thus surrendering some "freedom," and, on the other hand, judging by the possession of things as well as control over leisure time (which can, indeed, be uselessly spent), *all* classes are now potentially "free."

CONTEMPORARY LEISURE AND SOCIAL CLASS: SERVANTS AND GADGETS

A comparison of *servants* and *gadgets* will provide our first insight into the issue of this section. Two parallels are immediately obvious. First, both are methods of doing work for us. Second, both provide symbols of status.

Servants are alive, and both as persons and as workers they can be classified into males, females, weaker, stronger, younger, older, attached to the head of the house, attached to the wife or children, dooropeners, butlers, valets, and so on. Yet, with all these differences, the servant has been the key symbol and appendage of class division. The numbers of servants, the housing facilities available to servants, their skill, their length of service—these and other marks of respectability are familiar in history and literature.

This had to be in days when work was

fundamentally muscular work for either animals or men. Servants, unlike field or factory workers, were domestics and hence thoroughly familiar with manners and habits of the rich. Being people, not machines, they reacted as a trained class (Veblen called them a "subleisure class"), with traditions of faithfulness, protection of master from gossip, participation in house or court intrigues, disdain for other types of workers, and physical fighting when necessary. Thus in crises like revolutions the servant was counted as part of royalty or upper classdom and charged with responsibility, with treachery, with acts of accomplice, etc., as the occasion warranted.

Gadgets operate by the pressing of buttons or the turning of a switch. The variety ranges from the air-conditioner to the ironer, from the clothes-washer to the deep-freezer, from the radio to the food-mixer. They may be divided into two major types: (1) those gadgets which do work and are thus mechanical aids to turn the typical home into a consuming factory, which, it is estimated, bring to the family the equivalent of *ninety* slaves per day, and (2) those gadgets like radio, television, and phonograph, which are machines, not to relieve anyone of work but to take up the attention of persons who are now free (by the other gadgets) to watch, listen, enjoy. Thus the mechanical aids provide a *form* of contemporary family life, reducing motion, sweat, discomfort, effort; the mass media provide a *content* of contemporary family life, whose intent lies in the realm of ideas, symbols, images, and patterns of life in small glimpses.

As the servant is the key symbol of class division, gadgets are the symbol of *classlessness*. For their success depends on large audiences, on standardized rather than special programing, on the creation of stars who are known to all. The movie, now made available in the private parlor through television, has always been one of America's notable counterrevolutionary agents and a powerfully direct glimpse into the lives and fortunes and homes of the wealthy and glamorous. Together with the strong value

of personal success which could and (on recent television quiz shows) does bring quick wealth to others just like ourselves, this medium provides topics of conversation and chit-chat which cut across all levels and backgrounds.

It is safe to assume that the breakdown of classes in the United States led to the purchase of these many gadgets for removing work and bringing content; it is just as safe and as important to recognize that, once the process began, the cycle was under way and that the gadgets hurried up the breakdown of classes.

ART, INDUSTRIALIZATION, AND CLASSLESSNESS

Yet this is only the bare beginnings of the issues here raised. The mass media came at the same time and obviously from many of the same social and economic causes as the growth of widespread participation in the arts, as in the American public schools. The arts have also contributed to the fading of sharp class lines. In a previous writing, Kaplan (1958*b*) had this to say:

In this multi-group society, each of us has views, tastes, and leisure-time activities which are only loosely connected with so-called upper, middle or low class. In the class societies about which Shaw and Karl Marx wrote, art was one of those interests which used to peg people. Today, this is not true. Today, as poetry, painting, theatre and music have become widely practiced and understood, their value as distinctive symbols of respectability has faded. The factory clerk might not afford an original Rouault, but he has a copy. The banker might still buy his books in buckram bindings, but anyone can provide himself with paper-covered literary masterpieces at 35¢ each. The Higginson children in Boston may have had box seats at the concerts which Papa subsidized so lavishly, but the kids all over now go to concerts, hear records, or make their own music [p. 69].

The interesting point therefore faces us that the current vitality in the arts comes in large part either from the influence of the mass media directly or from those same social causes which produced these media as well as other aspects of technology. With this the case, the issue of creative, constructive, or aesthetic leisure has become one of noting how these "good" types of leisure activity have come about *because* and not *in spite of* increased industrialization and gadgeteering. Further, the thought that gadgets, both work-saving and content-giving, break through class divisions is now reinforced by a democratized art.

Veblen's major thesis falls on the simple fact that this country has grown so wealthy and that the wealth is less marked in the real income or accumulation of money with which to buy things than in the accumulation of things which conceal monetary inequality. This means that the department store, another highly important contributor to classlessness, sells goods which are designed to minimize the differential of rich and less rich. Clothes design, for instance, has come to the point where a woman of considerable means will not apologize for purchasing a ten-dollar dress of beauty. The goods in that store can be bought on the instalment plan, another highly important classless device. This provides anyone the opportunity of buying against his own tomorrow, and, as often as not, not the tomorrow as it will be, but as it *should be* or as it is *hoped that it will be*. The worst that can happen is that the goods will be repossessed, and this is not a great shame. There is then no need for the lower classes to sit in envious meditation of what the rich possess and to cherish the possibility of someday imitating them. This is entirely unrealistic and unnecessary when an escalator will take anyone in a few moments from the "bargain basement" up to the exclusive lingerie or furniture of the fifth floor in the *visible* melting pot of classes, the amazing store. Thus Riesman talks of the new revolution as the consumer's revolution and uses that other purchasing paradise, the supermarket, as an example.

Much of the sociological quandary, when it attempts to define and conceptualize the American class structure, is that it follows European models of division based on income or possessions of money, land, animals, or servants. Class or (more accurately) group levels in our own country are distinguishable in *how* they spend, with whom they enjoy their possessions including time, what they like to do when they are not at work, and what they are willing to do without in order to reach certain goals. A group of girls from the General Electric plant in Fort Wayne who flew to Europe illustrate this:

Their average age is 38; their average income is $57 a week. Few of them have finished high school, none of them has ever been to Europe before. The tour will cost them anywhere from $879 to $1,022, depending on whether they elect to take the 15-day or the 22-day tour. Most of them—90%—have chosen the 22-day tour, even though it involves time off without pay [Anonymous, 1953].

On the international travel scene, we have the remarkable growth of middle-class persons, the bulk of the almost 700,000 Americans in Europe during the summer of 1958. Not income, but *style of life*, is the basis for a realistic understanding, and this matter of style is based in part upon choice, in part upon recognized obligations.

There has been little effort in analyses of class to establish relationships to aged or retired persons. A direct inquiry is needed. For instance: immediately upon retirement, the economic picture for most men changes radically: How does this affect their expenditures for things normally used as symbols of "social front," such as cars with chrome? How freely are one's feelings about "our kind" discarded as he moves to a new community? A neat problem could be made of persons who find themselves accepting state or federal pension payments after a lifetime critical of such schemes as socialistic and harmful to the recipient.

Since the income of most persons is considerably lower immediately upon retirement, how does this affect one's perception of his "place"? The leveling of persons, classwise, is most apparent where retired persons are in a position to move about (as in mobile camps) or to move into new communities (as in Florida). It is found least among groups which live in institutions such as county homes for the aged. A middle ground for the mixing of richer-poorer or upper-middle-lower probably exists in homes for aged sponsored by churches, in Veterans Administration or other hospitals (in which the term "chronic patient" is sometimes a self-deception on the part of the patient, if not the VA itself), and in clubs and organizations in the community. An interesting research problem might consist of examining models of class blend to see whether any correlations exist with preferred types of leisure.

In view of the repeated finding that membership in civic activities comes from the upper middle class and upper classes, we would expect that these same persons prefer leisure activities which are (1) more oriented to serving others than themselves; (2) more participatory rather than receptive activities; (3) more activities we have termed "association" than those called "sociability"; and (4) more "continuing" rather than "terminal" activities, more "art" than "game" (but art for social purposes), and more "exploration" (especially travel) than "immobility."

Further, an additional typology of leisure activities might be sought in respect to their relative merit as devices for bridging the gap between persons of varied class and educational backgrounds. Activities which require considerable expense, skill, previous travel, etc., are barriers to class-crossing in leisure. Singing, nature study, woodcraft, and especially anything growing out of an interest in the mass media (amateur dramatics, art appreciation, discussions of current affairs, etc.) seem to be natural for such a purpose.

The last consideration can also be applied to the specific problem of crossing lines of color, religions, and ethnic membership. One area which leaders in the field report in conversations with the writer is the overwhelming interest among *all* older persons in the discussion of the place and needs of the older person in American society. We have throughout accepted such concerns as one basis for "association" and

included this important category under leisure because even here—the discussion of older people by older people—there are multipurposes and other elements of "leisure" activity.

E. Community

Many issues arise to relate community to leisure: rural and urban characteristics, the relationship of local institutions, class stratifications, the economic setting, composition of population, opportunities for particular kinds of leisure activity, local or regional traditions, the responsibility of community in providing facilities, and so on. Only a few will be touched on.

An overwhelming consideration for the entire population, but especially so for the adult and older person, is the rapid urbanization of the country. The United States Department of Agriculture has noted that the old tradition of isolated, independent country life is crumbling, to be replaced by 1975 by "city life, widely spaced." Closer social as well as economic ties with city life will result. The predicted 30 per cent decline in farm population will mean that the remaining farm families will have more members working or living in urban areas. Comparative living standards continue to narrow. More and more rural residents will go to city schools, churches, shopping centers, and recreation and entertainment facilities.

This trend is not restricted to one part of the country. For example, the Twentieth Century Fund is currently engaged in a study of the area from Boston to Washington (30 million people) as one "megalopolitan" community. In the Far West (California, Washington, Oregon), farms of 1000 acres or more still make up 6 per cent of the total land, more than twice that of the rest of the country. Yet here, too, the trend is for the spacious Far West to become a sort of supercity, where people think in terms of convenience, television, and traffic.

Yet, in regards to leisure itself, two major postwar trends oblige us to rethink its ecological patterns. On the one hand, television keeps us in the home—back to the "rural" isolation; on the other, the fast automobile (combined with long week ends, vacations, excellent roads, motels, etc.) invite us increasingly to visit far-flung areas. Add to this the fact that the "community," wherever it is, is now a receptor for nationally aimed programs from Hollywood and New York. What results on a level of leisure models, entertainment heroes, and images of the good life? The geographical and ecological pattern gives way to a shifting and dynamic pattern from local to regional to national and (perhaps more accurately) in reverse order! The leisure pattern for the New Society will include elements from all types of community life—rural, village, small town, suburb, city, megalopolitan.

Thus the three most important sociological studies on community and leisure are outdated: the Lundberg *et al.* (1934) study of leisure in Westchester County, the cooperative survey of Chicago recreation (Todd, 1937–40), and the two Lynd (1929, 1937) volumes on Middletown. These studies took place at a time when it was still somewhat possible to think of the community as an isolated communications and symbolic unit.

Osterbind and Webber (1957) are currently engaged in a study which illustrates new sets of problems of community vis-à-vis older persons. The issues they have set themselves are "(1) problems of personal adjustment encountered by persons who migrate at or near the time of retirement compared with those experienced by persons who remain in the same communities . . . (2) problems of social adjustment of communities . . . to the retirement phenomenon and to their retired population." It is recognized that a change of residence calls for differences in kind and scope of adjustment. The data to be sought will include some experiences we might call "leisure" but divided by these scholars into formal social participation (clubs, churches, etc.), informal (with family, friends, neighbors, etc.), and individual activities. This

study, now in progress, may provide us with insights as to how leisure activities function as carry-overs from one community to another; or how the adoption of new leisure patterns provides a footing in the new environment.

Webber (1954) studied retired groups in West Palm Beach and Orlando by exploring their membership in organizations and attendance at secular meetings and religious services. He found that more men than women belonged to organizations; no correlation between age and membership; slightly higher proportion of membership among non-married; highest correlation with educational backgrounds of 9–12 years' schooling; and a clearly higher membership among persons whose income had come from other sources than salary and wages (i.e., wealth, profits, and fees). Participation in clubs was generally consistent with the type of former income, as noted above. While one-fourth of the 474 persons never attend church, attendance for the others declines with advancing age.

Kleemeier's (1954) study of the 350 retired residents in Moosehaven, Florida, deals with persons who have much in common through their lodge as well as through their former work in such labor occupations as painters, carpenters, machinists, farmers, and seamen. All residents need economic help, and they work in Moosehaven if they can do so. Recreational activities in Moosehaven mentioned by the writer are: the recreation center (beer, cards, pool), library, fishing, shuffleboard, lodges, picnics, hobby shop, private hobbies, and the newspaper. Tournaments are held in several areas of competition. Television has affected attendance at these.

Burgess (1954) studied 64 members of Moosehaven in 1953 to correlate personal adjustment, recreational activities, and social relations. Based on replies to the question, "With whom do you visit?" three divisions or types of residents emerged—isolates, intimates, and leaders—as well as "levels" of social relationships. Participation is highest for persons classified as "solitary," followed by "group, spectator, and audience." Television ranked first in popularity among men; sewing among women. Men with the highest happiness scores participate nine times as much in group recreational activities (cards, pool, bingo, etc.) as those with lowest happiness scores.

F. Value Systems

Already, much has been said to infer that with analyses of leisure we deal with the "good life." Is the use of leisure a *problem?* Perhaps (Cutten, 1926; Burns, 1932; Barnes and Ruedi, 1942). But no "problem" can be solved or analyzed intelligently except from a view of the social order which is problem-less. Crime is a violation of norms of crimelessness; ugliness is a deviation from some assumed standard of the non-ugly; the abnormal mind is comprehensible only in reference to some standard. Thus a "problem" of the "good use of leisure" implies norms or assumptions. Where is there a science of norms for the good life? Who are the persons to establish assumptions for our purpose? The minister, who would have us meditate or serve the church? The librarian, who bids us read? The merry Till, who runs a tavern down the street? The Erich Fromms, who claim to recognize basic needs and signs of alienation? The adult educator, with his catalogue of courses in liberal arts or vocational skills? The Louis Kronenbergers, who caution us against "social climbing" through leisure?

Our American values are many. MacIver calls us a "multigroup" society, with pluralistic tastes and tendencies. The lifting of major social controls from the past—family, church, work—has opened the door to uprootedness and chaos, on the one hand, to new and creative forms of social action or personal commitments, on the other. Not long ago, play was for idle hands and led only to mischief and sin. Now, says Riesman, we are more concerned with perfecting play than work. Leisure now can be intense, serious, significant, and a source of inner growth; and a plethora of temptations exist, manipulated by the best brains Madison Avenue can muster, to turn our free time toward meaningless entertainment, mortgaged vacations, or readings of minuscule consequence.

We in America have as yet no philosophy of leisure. Bendiner (1957) said: "Not a class but a whole society has to be freed of the stern belief in work for salvation's sake, the emphasis of its education shifted from training for a livelihood to the Aristotelian view that the aim of education is the wise use of leisure" (pp. 13–14). Social scientists who come into the field are in the strange position of—very quickly—having to face the issue of the "good life." It will be clouded with *akademeia*—terms like "adjustment," "happiness scales," "successful retirement," etc. The research approach, rightly so, has been to track down correlations of "adjustment" to measurable factors. Yet the current call for "creative" old age is fraught with implications.

For a long time recreation philosophy was geared to the idea of "periodicity"— that some types of activities are more geared to some ages or stages than to others. Now a reaction (led by Lorge) is beginning to set in against the Thorndike theory of learning which led away from a real hope of new learning after late adulthood. Perhaps a new emphasis can be formulated to discover the kinds of learning which *cannot* be successfully undertaken or absorbed *before* certain stages of life have been lived. Certainly, the whole field of new values in relation to maturity is wide open. An ongoing study of *imagination* among older persons by the Age Center of New England, Inc. (Cabot, 1957), heads toward the new direction. Further, it may become apparent that studies of values, goals, or creative possibilities cannot be carried on without a total perspective covering *all ages* but especially comparative studies of childhood and "senescence."

The beginnings of an *ethics* of leisure analysis for the "older" generation properly lies with a self-analysis of the "younger" generation which is doing the studying. Yet this is a matter not of age but of (*a*) motives of the leadership, (*b*) values ascribed to respective leisure activities, and only then (c) the techniques by which other persons are persuaded to "improve" themselves (i.e., do the things I am sure they should do).

The *dynamics* of leisure involves the processes by which choices are made and how the activity is carried out. A preliminary question concerns the persons or institutions who exercise power over others: newspapers, friends, relatives, siblings, mate, teachers, radio commentators, the movies, or any of an infinite variety of stimuli. Friedson (1953) and others have studied attendance at motion pictures to uncover sources of suggestion upon children. To the writer's knowledge there are no comparable studies of older persons. A common position among intellectuals of the society is that the presence of a profit motive brings doubt upon the activity. Whatever truth is here does not deny the fact that the motives of persons in non-commercial positions of authority are also worthy of careful study. Here is a group in a home for the aged, playing simple card games: what is my authority for suggesting that they might better be engaged in seeing my slides of Europe or your stamp collection or in singing a folk song?

The ethical position might be defined in terms of freedom as a result of knowledge of more alternatives. Then our right to suggest leisure activities to others springs from greater *knowledge* of possibilities than that of our clients. A second ethical starting point might be that my institutional position (minister, teacher, counselor, group worker) is a voluntary recognition by the client that my training has prepared me to know his needs better than he can. A third basis might be that the issue is really beyond you and me but is embraced by an analysis of changes in American society which it is my business to recognize and your good to face.

On these or other ethical levels, there is some rationality in prescribing leisure activities or goals to others. Pieper (1952) has developed a profound statement on leisure from the Catholic point of view, and

there is also a report of the deliberations of the conference on problems and challenges of the new leisure sponsored by the Jewish Theological Seminary of America (1956). We submit that the legitimacy of these approaches goes hand in hand with motivations by the leader which—ideally and practically—are free from the imposition of my standards over thine. Beer or "bop" are not inferior to Beethoven by any divine judgment; it is only that conservatories often willingly exercise a charismatic divinity in such judgments. In any case, a cardinal principle in the basis of judgment for activity A rather than B or G is that A (art), B (baseball), or G (gardening) exist in and through social relationships and situations; thus the classification posed early in this chapter is *not* on the basis of relative merit—merit in the abstract or absolutistic sense.

VI. DIRECTIONS AND EXAMPLES OF RESEARCH

Several suggestions for research have been included in preceding pages. The last portion of the chapter is entirely devoted to this purpose. It will also indicate some research now in progress.

A. Information, Motivation, Perception

Communications and information theory needs to be applied to older persons in order to differentiate the conditions (health, finances, family connections, former work, etc.) under which they are more or less open to various kinds of persuaders. What are the motives of the recipients upon retirement as seen through the activities which they now seek out or reject: to assert or to deny their social obsolescence, to affirm or deny their fears, to provide a bridge or to forge new paths from old ways of life to new?

B. Time Perceptions

Theory of time perceptions needs much study. George Woodcock (1953) has written:

Modern, Western man . . . lives in a world which runs according to the mechanical and mathematical symbols of clock time. The clock dictates his movements and inhibits his actions. The clock turns time from a process of nature into a commodity that can be measured and bought and sold . . . the clock represents an element of mechanical tyranny in the lives of modern men more potent than any individual exploiter or than any other machine. . . . The clock, as Lewis Mumford has pointed out, represents the key machine of the machine age, both for its influence on technics and for its influence on the habits of men [p. 210].

One of the important divisions now felt in gerontological circles is on the issue of whether older persons should live in an "isolated" community (institutional care, hotels, villages, etc.) or integrated within the "normal" relationships of varying age groups. One part of the solution stems from the time-content characteristic of unique age categories as they are affected by patterns of work or play, doing the dishes, putting the young to sleep, feeding infants, likes for certain television programs, etc. Close to this problem are other kinds of self-commitment, felt obligations, and ascribed duties.

It is a well-known fact that children find security in the authority of others and that authority has a time pattern as well as content. The sudden erasing of time lines between meals or between awakening and sleeping can be itself a deep source of insecurity and lack of direction. Leisure types of activities, while not open to judgments of relative merit, are indeed open to analysis of time. For example, as Huizinga points out, a game has a given duration: participants know in advance the point at which it has run its course. Thus the time is imposed not from the clock but from the fruition of "innings," "rubbers," "scores," etc. Television, on the one hand, is chopped up into specific units to the second and may in part owe its popularity to the security which comes from order. Vacation travel, on the other hand, is generally a blend of freedom of experience *within* a larger clock sequence: perhaps vacation is

therefore anticipated because one knows that he *may* sleep late even though he will not do so.

Returning, then, to the earlier issue of (*a*) old-living-with-old or (*b*) old-living-with-all-ages, we need comparative studies of time perceptions in extremes of (*a*) and (*b*) as well as in controlled combinations. First, perhaps, we need studies of how human activities are perceived in ratios of terminal sequences, in the "feel" of morning and evening, in "length" of the hour, in the association of preference or propriety of types of non-work activities with comparative hours, days, and years (Reichenbach, 1956). Leach (1954) brings out the sociopsychological character of time reckoning in the following statement:

A little introspection will reveal to any of us that so far as his own life is concerned, time is not reckoned on any scientific or numerical basis. It is reckoned by events. Our lives as we look back on them are punctuated not by dates but by salient events in our personal history. Each of us is a legislator who establishes for himself his own era. Since time has no self-evident manifestation, our ideas about it are greatly influenced by the content in which we use notions of time [p. 126].

C. Adult Education as Part of a Leisure Program

We will first note a current project at the University of Wisconsin as an example of a research program geared closely to a concrete follow-up program of action. A study proposal (Kreitlow *et al.*, 1957) dated September 23, 1957, noted:

With the growth of a mass leisure class will come the emergence of new ways of life oriented towards leisure, and new definitions of life goals which will increasingly lead both men and women to seek basic life satisfactions and achievements in activities beyond the immediate life tasks of job performance and family rearing. They will be seeking more than activities to occupy leisure. They will seek non-work careers which will enable them to employ leisure in purposeful goal-directed pursuits.

Adult education could be called upon to furnish more than just a means of occupying the new found leisure. It would be challenged to help structure the use of non-worklife—to provide leadership in the defining of values, goals and intellectual pursuits geared to the needs of man in the new age of leisure.

The study has four objectives: (1) to explore the changing roles of leisure in the lives of persons over 50; (2) to design a format and conduct pilot courses for selected persons; (3) to conduct research into problems of the older learner; and (4) to establish a continuing program of liberal studies for adults throughout Wisconsin, using the combined facilities of several agencies within the University and the state.

The three-year study plan was divided into several parts: a mailed questionnaire on leisure use of adult education; a four-week residential program for thirty to forty alumni during the summer of 1958; field research into the summer of 1959; and additional plans for courses, community surveys, training institutes, materials and "formulation of a state-wide program of adult liberal education."

Television has now outdistanced all other leisure-time activities for the aged. State Senator Desmond of New York credits television for national influence on attitudes toward the aged because of its sympathetic treatment. A Loyola University study, according to a newspaper account (Anonymous, 1957), reports that more than half the population over 65 watches television between 1 and 3 hours per day; one in five watches television from 4 to 10 hours. There is no unanimity among professional students as to the effects of this viewing on older persons. Indeed, there is no overwhelming agreement among scientists on its impact on any age group or on family life as a whole.

D. Change of Choice

We need research into the strategy of changing leisure habits. More than new "learning" theory is involved. It is a question of observing, within the senior citizens groups, the hospital, etc., *who* are the natural leaders, on which issues the "soft underbelly" of change is found, and who are the conservatives among administrators or group workers themselves. The client may be readier for change than the group worker. In general, change can be more readily brought through "marginal" persons of the group; these have yet to be defined for purposes of older persons. The larger issue of how and where to introduce social change has been treated by Margaret Mead (1947, 1955).

E. Range of Choice

The present discussion will gain in concreteness by a list of activities for reference purposes. The following list is reproduced from current studies of the Age Center of New England (Cabot, 1957). It is currently being used by that organization to determine the extent of participation in recreational activities and with whom the activity takes place at various periods of the person's life. A factor analysis of these items is under way to help uncover correlations of activity with social data about participants.

Baseball
Football
Hockey
Boxing
Wrestling
Tennis
Golf
Bowling
Track
Swimming

Rowing
Sailing
Motorboating
Canoeing
Hunting
Fishing
Hiking, camping
Mountain-climbing
Bicycling
Riding

Billiards, pool
Ping-Pong
Cards

Board games (Parcheesi, Monopoly, etc.)
Checkers
Chess
Dice games
Roulette
Slot machines
Bingo

Horse races
Watching other sporting events
Jigsaw puzzles
Crossword puzzles
Travel: to sightsee
Travel: to visit friends
Travel: to rest
Travel: to relax and have fun
Reading in the library
Reading at home: novels
Napping

"Puttering"; fixing things

Chatting about people

Talking politics and current events

Intellectual, cultural conversations

Visiting friends

Going to or giving parties

Nightclubs

Eating out

Dancing

Stopping somewhere for a drink

Going to movies or plays

Art galleries and museums

Concerts, ballet, opera

Zoo, circus

Sitting in the park

Going for walks

Going for drives

"Going to the country"; picnics

Clubs, lodges, bridge groups, informal gatherings

Sledding

Skating

Skiing

Horseshoes

Croquet

Miniature golf, putting

Shuffleboard

Community sings

Husking bees

Quilting parties

Needlework of all kinds (sew, knit, crochet)

Photography

Collecting things (antiques, stamps, etc.)

Painting, sculpting, etc.

Reading at home: other books

Reading at home: other magazines and newspapers

Listening to the radio

Watching television

Just sitting at home and thinking

Writing (including letters)

Playing musical instruments

Singing

Reading aloud or listening

Listening to music

Woodworking

Other handicrafts

Square dancing

Hayrides, sleigh rides

Gardening

Raising animals, pets

Shopping

School

Church activities

Stafford (1957) has made available a more informal listing of activities which have been found successful in actual programs with older people. She categorizes the activities under the following headings:

1. *Parties.* All kinds and descriptions. Any older person enjoys the festive quality of a party. Make it a seasonal affair, with appropriate decorations. Make it a kid party, with bows of ribbon to dress up the participants. Arrange a birthday affair with cakes and candles. Try a balloon party or a backwards affair for April Fool's Day.

2. *Friday Afternoon at Country School* is always a success: spelldowns, recitations, readings, and all.

3. *Group games, guessing games* of all sorts, singing games, any sort that makes it possible for persons to feel at ease and gain self-confidence.

4. *Old songs, modern fun songs, motion songs,* or ballads from around the world.

5. *Choruses, quartets, solos, duets,* any combination.

6. *Musical programs* with members presenting instrumental solos or duets, recordings and the like.

7. *Table games.*

8. *Stunts and talent programs.*

9. *Storytelling.*

10. *Camping:* for several days in a carefully chosen location; day camping, chiefly a day-long picnic occasion, but with the overtones of living in the out-of-doors at a park or a playground with a chance to study trees, flowers and insects to their heart's content.

11. *Handcrafts and hobbies,* especially those that can be completed fairly quickly.

12. *Luncheons, teas, and dinners,* all sorts of meals arranged festively.

13. *Dramatics.*

14. *Trips* to points of interest.

Above all, conversation, reminiscing, chatting freely and informally. How can the interests of older people be discovered? One way is to prepare a questionnaire in which they have a chance to check activities such as table games, handcrafts, hobbies, etc., that they would like to take part in and the particular activities in which they already have skill and training. Another is to talk with individuals and groups about the possibilities, watching for reaction and planning on that basis.

F. Older Persons as Economic Consumers in Leisure

A large field for continued research is that of consumer expenditures for leisure. The path has been opened with the recent interest in family cycles and consumer patterns. A study to which we wish to call attention is Volume 9 of the eighteen-volume *Study of Consumer Expenditures* issued in 1956 by the Wharton School of Finance

(1956). Detailed tables (with no interpretations) are presented for the detailed income and expenditures of 12,489 families in 91 cities ranging from 2000 in size to New York City. Students of aging will find special interest in materials of Table 6, "Age of Family Head," pages 34–41 of the volume.

G. Anticipation of Leisure

In leisure studies, as well as larger issues of social gerontology, light upon older persons is thrown by increased understanding of middle-aged persons, youth, and childhood. One example is the perception held by young people about *themselves* in terms of what they will do and enjoy some years hence. Essert *et al.* (1951) observed that "there is a strong suggestion in our case studies that adjustment in later maturity and retirement is an accentuation of the kind of adjustment the individual has made as a youth, a young adult, or a middle-aged adult." The writer is engaged in such a projective study. Results are not yet available. College students are given a listing of thirty-three recreational activities. Under four columns they check: (*a*) one or more activities they enjoy doing; (*b*) three of their favorite activities; (*c*) those they have done since a year ago; and (*d*) a + or − sign to indicate that they expect to do each of these "more" or "less" often in 1976. We are, in addition, attempting to obtain a picture of the world which the student anticipates by A.D. 1976 and A.D. 2000 in reference to ten predictions.

Our impressions thus far from quick review of several hundred papers is that these students visualize a sharp break from their present activities at the age of 40; they find it very difficult to imagine their mode of life when they are about 60 years of age at the coming of the new century.

H. Preparation for Leisure Counselors

It is reasonable to envision a new profession—leisure counselor. Such a person will ideally be a cross-breed of several disciplines and many interests. His office might prove to be in a factory, amid a nest of executive offices, in a union office,[12] in a home for retired persons, or in a wing of a psychiatric social work unit. He will have in stock a knowledge of many endeavors and a theory to see interrelationships of leisure to personality, work, family life, economic security, and other conditioning factors and circumstances of life. His work in helping persons to plan their leisure time will go beyond researches or insights in the specific planning for activities—important as this is and as inadequate as is our present knowledge about it.[13] In a larger sense, he will help to plan lives. To be most effective with older persons, he will not restrict himself to one age group. Let us hope that, in addition, his aspirations will be to work with older persons as whole people rather than as categories and with creative possibilities for all persons rather than with tried formulas and tired focus.

[12] McConnell (1958) pointed out that, "as the number of retired workers from mine, mill and plant has increased, unions and managements have extended the conflict for workers' loyalty to the ranks of the retired. Unions are now sponsoring educational and recreational programs for retired members."

[13] The case for educating persons in planning their recreation is made in Jenney (1955) and Weatherford (1952). A suggestion of two research problems which are involved in such planning is given by Stone and Taves (1956): "First, planning may have consequences for the integration of intimate groups, because extensive and careful consideration of wilderness trip details necessarily reveals the personal characteristics of the participants much more than the planning of a 'commercialized vacation' where the personal needs of the vacationer—eating, sleeping, etc.—are provided for by service personnel. Planning and the wilderness experience provide the sociologist with a kind of laboratory situation in which primary group processes and functions may be fruitfully investigated. Second, the 'lay promoters' of wilderness travel could well be studied to determine whether they have characteristics enabling their ready identification by those interested in disseminating wilderness values among the population at large."

REFERENCES

ANDERSON, J. E. 1958. Psychological aspects of aging. *In* WILMA DONAHUE, W. W. HUNTER, DOROTHY H. COONS, and HELEN K. MAURICE (eds.), Free time—challenge to later maturity, pp. 29–44. Ann Arbor: University of Michigan Press.

ANONYMOUS. 1953. Business Week, September 12.

———. 1956. St. Louis Post-Dispatch, July 30.

———. 1957. Boston Globe, November 18.

ATHLETIC INSTITUTE. 1954. The recreation program. Chicago: The Institute.

BALES, R. F., HARE, A. P., and BORGATTA, E. F. 1958. Structure and dynamics of small groups: a review of four variables. *In* J. B. GITTLER (ed.), Review of sociology: analysis of a decade. pp. 391–422. New York: John Wiley & Sons.

BARNES, H. E., and BECKER, H. 1938. Social thought from lore to science, Vol. 2. New York: D. C. Heath & Co.

BARNES, H. E., and RUEDI, O. M. 1942. The American way of life: our institutional patterns and social problems. New York: Prentice-Hall, Inc.

BECKER, H. S. 1955. Becoming a marihuana user. *In* A. ROSE (ed.), Mental health and mental disorder, pp. 420–33. New York: W. W. Norton & Co.

BENDINER, R. 1955. The age of the thinking robot, and what it will mean to us. Reporter, 12 (April 7), 12–18.

———. 1957. Could you stand a four-day week? *Ibid.*, 17 (August 8), 10–14.

BLOOMBERG, W., JR. 1957. Automation predicts change: for the older worker. *In* WILMA DONAHUE and C. TIBBITTS (eds.), The new frontiers of aging, pp. 10–27. Ann Arbor: University of Michigan Press.

BURGESS, E. W. 1954. Social relations, activities, and personal adjustment. Am. J. Sociology, 54, 352–60.

BURGESS, E. W., COREY, L. G., PINEO, P. C., and THORNBURY, R. T. 1958. Occupational differences in attitudes toward aging and retirement. J. Gerontol., 13, 203–60.

BURNS, C. D. 1932. Leisure in the modern world. New York: Century Co.

BUSHEE, F. A. 1945. Social organizations in a small city. Am. J. Sociology, 51, 217–27.

BUTLER, G. D. 1945. Introduction to community recreation. New York: McGraw-Hill Book Co.

CABOT, H. 1957. For the study and development of extended independence in people of advanced years: Annual report, Age Center of New England, Hotel Vendome. Boston: The Center.

CAPLOW, T. 1954. Sociology of work. Minneapolis: University of Minnesota Press.

CHAPIN, F. S. 1958. Social institutions and voluntary associations. *In* J. B. GITTLER (ed.), Review of sociology: analysis of a decade, pp. 259–88. New York: John Wiley & Sons.

CRESPI, I. 1956. Card playing as a leisure time activity. Am. Sociological Rev., 21, 717–21.

CUTTEN, G. B. 1926. The threat of leisure. New Haven, Conn.: Yale University Press.

DAVIS, J. E. 1938. Play and mental health. New York: A. S. Barnes & Co.

DAVIS, W. A., and HAVIGHURST, R. J. 1947. Father of the man. Boston: Houghton Mifflin Co.

DENNY, R., and MEYERSOHN, MARY LEA. 1957. A preliminary bibliography on leisure. Am. J. Sociology, 62, 602–15.

DEWHURST, J. F., and ASSOCIATES. 1955. America's needs and resources. New York: Twentieth Century Fund.

DONAHUE, WILMA. 1951. Psychological aspects of aging. *In* T. L. SMITH (ed.), Problems of America's aging population, pp. 47–65. Gainesville: University of Florida Press.

DONAHUE, WILMA, HUNTER, W. W., COONS, DOROTHY H., and MAURICE, HELEN K. (eds.). 1958. Free time—challenge to later maturity. Ann Arbor: University of Michigan Press.

DORFMAN, ELAINE. 1951. Play therapy. *In* C. R. ROGERS (ed.), Client-centered therapy, pp. 235–77. Boston: Houghton Mifflin Co.

DOUGLAS, P. F., HUTCHINSON, J. L., and SUTHERLAND, W. C. (eds.). 1957. Recreation in the age of automation. Ann. Am. Acad. Political & Social Sc., Vol. 313.

DYER, G. W. 1942. Syndicated newspaper article (1939). *In* H. E. BARNES (ed.), Social institutions. New York: Prentice-Hall, Inc.

EISELE, J. 1938. Play and mental health. New York: A. S. Barnes & Co.

ESSERT, P. L., LORGE, I., and TUCKMAN, J. 1951. Preparation for a constructive approach to later maturity. Teachers College Record, 53, 70–76.

ESSERT, P. L., and VERNER, C. 1951. Education for active adult citizenship. Teachers College Record, 53, 16–31.

FRIED, J. 1949. Games. *In* Standard dictionary of folklore, mythology and legend, pp. 431–39. New York: Funk & Wagnalls Co.

FRIEDSON, E. 1953. Relation of social situation of contact to the media in mass communication. Pub. Opinion Quart., **17**, 230–38.

FROMM, E. 1955. The sane society. New York: Rinehart & Co.

GUMP, P. V., and SUTTON-SMITH, B. 1955. The role of "it" in children's games. Group, No. 3 (February), pp. 3–8.

HAVIGHURST, R. J. 1954. Flexibility and the social roles of the retired. Am. J. Sociology, **59**, 309–11.

———. 1957*a*. The leisure activities of the middle aged. *Ibid.*, **63**, 152–62.

———. 1957*b*. The significance and content of leisure activities from age forty to seventy. (Paper read at the annual meeting of the Gerontological Society, Cleveland.)

HUIZINGA, J. 1950. *Homo ludens:* a study of the play element in culture. Boston: Beacon Press.

JENNEY, J. H. 1955. Introduction to recreation education. Philadelphia: W. B. Saunders Co.

JEWISH SEMINARY OF AMERICA. 1956. Problems and challenges of the new leisure: report of the Conference of the Jewish Seminary of America. New York: The Seminary.

JOHNSON, H. J. 1957. Interview in U.S. News & World Report, February 1.

KAHL, J. A. 1957. The American class structure. New York: Rinehart & Co.

KAPLAN, M. 1957. Music in adult life. Adult Leadership, **7**, 210–13, 223.

———. 1958*a*. Pressures of leisure on the older individual. J. Gerontol., **13** (Supp. No. 2), 36–41.

———. 1958*b*. Arts in a changing America. Washington, D.C.: Music Educator's National Conference.

———. 1960. Leisure in America: a social inquiry. New York: John Wiley & Sons.

KLEEMEIER, R. W. 1954. Moosehaven: congregate living in a community of the retired. Am. J. Sociology, **54**, 347–51.

KLUCKHOHN, C., and MURRAY, H. A. 1948. Personality in nature, society, and culture. New York: A. A. Knopf.

KREITLOW, W. B., and ASSOCIATES. 1957. Liberal education in an age of leisure: exploration in the development of educational programs for older people. Research proposal dated September 23, 1957. Madison: University of Wisconsin, College of Education. (Processed.)

KUTNER, B., FANSHEL, D., TOGO, ALICE M., and LANGNER, T. S. 1956. Five hundred over sixty: a community survey on aging. New York: Russell Sage Foundation.

LARRABEE, E., and MEYERSOHN, R. B. (eds.). 1958. Mass leisure. Glencoe, Ill.: Free Press.

LEACH, M. E. 1954. Primitive time-reckoning. *In* C. SINGER, E. J. HOLMYARD, and A. R. HALL (eds.), A history of technology, Vol. **1**. Oxford: Clarendon Press.

LINDEN, M. E. 1958. Preparation for the leisure of later maturity. *In* WILMA DONAHUE, W. W. HUNTER, DOROTHY H. COONS, and HELEN K. MAURICE (eds.), Free time—challenge to later maturity, pp. 77–97. Ann Arbor: University of Michigan Press.

LINDEN, M. E., and COURTNEY, D. C. 1953. The human life cycle and its interruptions—a psychologic hypothesis. Am. J. Psychiat., **109**, 906–15.

LUNDBERG, G., KOMAROVSKY, MIRRA, and McINERNY, MARY A. 1934. Leisure: a suburban study. New York: Columbia University Press.

LYND, R. S., and LYND, HELEN M. 1929. Middletown. New York: Harcourt, Brace & Co.

———. 1937. Middletown in transition. New York: Harcourt, Brace & Co.

McCONNELL, J. W. 1958. The impact of aging on the economy. J. Gerontol., **13** (Supp. No. 2), 42–47.

MACIVER, R. M. 1947. The web of government. New York: Macmillan Co.

MANNHEIM, K. 1936. Ideology and utopia. New York: Harcourt, Brace & Co.

MASLOW, A. H. 1954. Motivation and personality. New York: Harper & Bros.

MEAD, MARGARET. 1947. Some problems of world planning. *In* H. W. HOLMES (ed.), Fundamental education: a common ground for all people, chap. iii. New York: Macmillan Co.

———. 1955. Cultural patterns and technical change. New York: New American Library.

MEYER, H. D., and BRIGHTBILL, C. K. 1948. Community recreation. Boston: D.C. Heath & Co.

MEYERSOHN, R. B. 1958. Americans off duty. *In* WILMA DONAHUE, W. W. HUNTER, DOROTHY H. COONS, and HELEN K. MAURICE (eds.). Free time—challenge to later maturity. Ann Arbor: University of Michigan Press.

MITCHELL, E. D. 1931. Theory of play. New York: A. S. Barnes & Co.

Monroe, R. T. 1957. Mechanisms of the geriatric clinic and its place in the community. (Paper read at the annual meeting of the Gerontological Society, Cleveland.)

Morse, Nancy C., and Weiss, R. S. 1955. The function and meaning of work and the job. Am. Sociological Rev., **20**, 693–700.

Neumeyer, M. H., and Neumeyer, Esther S. 1958. Leisure and recreation. 3d ed. New York: Ronald Press Co.

Osterbind, C. C., and Webber, I. L. 1957. Social and economic problems of adjustment to retirement: a research plan. Gainesville: University of Florida, Institute of Gerontology. (Processed.)

Parsons, T. 1949. Structure of social action. Glencoe, Ill.: Free Press.

Pieper, J. 1952. Leisure, the basis of culture. New York: Pantheon Books.

Queen, S. 1949. Social participation in relation to disorganization. Am. Sociological Rev., **14**, 251–56.

Reichenbach, H. 1956. The direction of time. Berkeley: University of California Press.

Riesman, D. 1950. The lonely crowd. New Haven, Conn.: Yale University Press.

———. 1952. Some observations on the study of American character. Psychiatry, **15**, 333–38.

———. 1954. Individualism reconsidered. Glencoe, Ill.: Free Press.

Robbins, Florence G. 1956. Sociology of play, recreation, and leisure time. Dubuque, Iowa: Wm. C. Brown & Co.

Roe, Anne. 1956. The psychology of occupations. New York: John Wiley & Sons.

Rogers, C. R. (ed.). 1951. Client-centered therapy. Boston: Houghton Mifflin Co.

Rose, A. M. 1954. Theory and method in social sciences. Minneapolis: University of Minnesota Press.

Sapir, E. 1934. Personality. *In* Encyclopedia of the social sciences, Vol. **12**. New York: Macmillan Co.

Sola Pool, I. de, and Sola Pool, J. M. de. 1956–57. Prediction of attitudes of foreign travelers. *In* The American student abroad: addresses and work reports from conferences sponsored by the Council on Student Travel. New York: The Council.

Sorokin, P. 1947. Society, culture, and personality. New York: Harper & Bros.

Soule, G. 1955. Time for living. New York: Viking Press.

———. 1958a. Free time—man's new resource. *In* Wilma Donahue, W. W. Hunter, Doro-

thy H. Coons, and Helen K. Maurice (eds.), Free time—challenge to later maturity, pp. 61–76. Ann Arbor: University of Michigan Press.

———. 1958b. Shape of tomorrow. New York: New American Library.

Spykman, N. J. 1925. The social theory of Georg Simmel. Chicago: University of Chicago Press.

Stafford, Virginia. 1957. Recreation planning for older people: adding life to years, Bull. Inst. Geront., Iowa, Vol. **4**, Supp. No. 4.

Stern, J. 1957. Automation predicts change: for the employment of the aging. *In* Wilma Donahue and C. Tibbitts (eds.). The new frontiers of aging, pp. 29–44. Ann Arbor: University of Michigan Press.

Stone, G. P. 1955. American sports: play and dis-play. Chicago Review, **9**, 83–100. (Reprinted in E. Larrabee and R. Meyersohn [eds.], Mass leisure, pp. 253–64. Glencoe, Ill.: Free Press, 1958.)

Stone, G. P., and Taves, M. J. 1956. Research into the human element in wilderness use. *In* Proc. Soc. Am. Foresters, Washington. (Reprinted in revised form as "Camping in the wilderness," in E. Larrabee and R. Meyersohn [eds.], Mass leisure, pp. 290–305. Glencoe, Ill.: Free Press, 1958.)

Sutton-Smith, B., and Gump, P. V. 1955. Games and status experience. Recreation, **48**, 172–74.

Thomas, W. I., and Znaniecki, F. 1918. The Polish peasant in Europe and America. Chicago: University of Chicago Press.

Todd, A. J. 1937–40. The Chicago Recreation Survey, Vols. **1–5**. Chicago: Chicago Recreation Commission.

Veblen, T. 1912. The Theory of the leisure class. New York: Macmillan Co.

Weatherford, A. E. 1952. Why not recreation education? J. Health, Phys. Educ. & Recreation, **1**, 18–19.

Webber, I. L. 1954. The organized social life of the retired: two Florida communities. Am. J. Sociology, **59**, 340–45.

Weber, M. 1930. The Protestant ethic and the spirit of capitalism. London: G. Allen & Unwin, Ltd.

Wharton School of Finance and Commerce. 1956. Study of consumer expenditures, income, and savings, Vol. **9**. Philadelphia: University of Pennsylvania Press.

Wolff, K. (ed.). 1950. The sociology of Georg Simmel. Glencoe, Ill.: Free Press.

WOODCOCK, G. 1953. The tyranny of the clock. *In* A. NAFTALIN and ASSOCIATES (eds.), An introduction to social science: personality, work, community. Philadelphia: J. B. Lippincott Co.

WOYTINSKY, W. S., and WOYTINSKY, EMMA S. 1953. World population and production: trend and outlook. New York: Twentieth Century Fund.

WRONG, D. H. 1956. Riesman and the age of sociology. Commentary, **21,** 331–38.

ZNANIECKI, F. 1934. The method of sociology. New York: Farrar & Rinehart.

———. 1939. Social groups as products of cooperating individuals. Am. J. Sociology, **44,** 799–811.

———. 1940. Social role of the man of knowledge. New York: Columbia University Press.

PART THREE

Aging and the Reorganization of Society

XIII

The Older Person in a Family Context

GORDON F. STREIB AND WAYNE E. THOMPSON

I. SOCIETY AS A NORMATIVE ORDER

A. Human Behavior as Patterned Activity

The task of social gerontology is to reach a systematic understanding of aging and the aged. For those who hold a sociological orientation this means looking at the behavior of the older person as a reflection of and as an adjustment to a social context. Each one of us—even unto the most rugged of individualists—in fact lives our life in and through group affiliations; and the groups to which we belong give pattern and focus to our activities, a structure in terms of which we know the world and know ourselves.

A fruitful way to approach the study of a social context or social organization is by the study of social rules or social norms. To be sure, there are limitations to studying human affairs normatively, for there is more to social behavior than simply the normative. Yet the influence of social norms pervades almost all human conduct, and necessarily so, for the presence of social norms is essential for orderly human social intercourse. As Robert MacIver and Charles Page (1949) have said, "Without them the burden of decision would be intolerable and the vagaries of conduct utterly distracting" (p. 207).

B. The Nature of Social Norms

The primary characteristic of social norms is the notion of social obligation.

Norms are generally considered to be prescriptions for or prohibitions against attitudes, beliefs, or behavior. Thus one can think of norms as what a person ought to do or believe. Obviously, any single norm or set of norms is not ironclad in its influence, and one of the intriguing aspects in the study of norms is deviation or noncompliance. Moreover, there are many norms that are not explicitly stated in a formal code of rules. Yet, whether explicit or not, the patterning of behavior indicates norms which are understood and which, as accepted mutual expectations, influence the behavior of the members of a society.[1]

C. Social Institutions

Social norms take on a wider significance for studying human behavior in the fact that there is a definite tendency for norms to cluster together. That is to say, each is not discrete unto itself but frequently can be shown to relate systematically to other norms. Those prescriptions for behavior which are most clearly obligatory and which cohere around the more important

[1] Space will not permit an extended discussion of norms: the extent of knowledge, acceptance, the modes of enforcement, the manner of transmission, and the amount of conformity to the norms. The interested reader may refer to the references. For an early discussion of norms see Sumner (1906). A general discussion of norms as basic concepts in the analysis of society may be found in Davis (1949, pp. 52–82) and in Williams (1951, pp. 25 ff.). A suggestive attempt at analyzing the characteristics of norms is Morris (1956, pp. 610–13).

social functions constitute what is known as a social institution. Social institutions define the behavior necessary for the realization of the major values of society and, in their interrelationship, form the major outlines of society as a whole. Thus a quick and also fundamental way to obtain insight into the organization of a society and how it operates is to understand the major institutions and the relations among institutions.[2] More to the point in the present context, understanding the nature of institutions provides a basis for understanding the behavior and problems of adjustment of those whose action is carried out within the institutional framework.

D. The Family

Of all the institutions which condition the behavior and adjustment of the individual, perhaps none is more important than the family. This may be particularly

[2] For a suggestive analysis of the interrelations of institutions in American society see Williams (1951, pp. 483–512).

true for older people, inasmuch as the later years often mark a decline of active participation in other institutions. In fact, in the extreme instance the older person may have only his family. As a respondent in the Cornell Study of Occupational Retirement poignantly put it:

My working days are over; I am no longer able to get out and around as I once did; my friends are dying off; in short, I am an old man. If it weren't for my children and my grandchildren, there would really be little point in going on living.

A correct understanding of the behavior and adjustment of older people thus may be assumed to depend in an important way upon understanding the family as a key institutional context.

Viewing the family in broad statistical terms, perhaps the best single index of the formation and dissolution of the family is the percentage of persons who are married in various age categories. Table 1 shows the trend for both sexes. We note, for example, that, according to the 1950 data,

TABLE 1*

PERCENTAGE DISTRIBUTION BY MARITAL STATUS AND SEX, FOR SELECTED AGE GROUPS, 1950

AGE (YEARS)	MALE					FEMALE				
	Total	Single	Married, Spouse Present	Widowed	Spouse Absent and Divorced	Total	Single	Married, Spouse Present	Widowed	Spouse Absent and Divorced
Total, 14 and over	100.0	26.4	64.1	4.1	5.5	100.0	20.0	62.3	11.8	5.9
15	100.0	99.1	0.3	0.1	0.4	100.0	97.9	1.6	0.1	0.4
30–34	100.0	13.2	80.5	0.4	6.0	100.0	9.3	82.2	1.6	6.9
35–39	100.0	10.1	82.9	0.7	6.4	100.0	8.4	81.3	2.7	7.6
40–44	100.0	9.0	83.1	1.2	6.7	100.0	8.3	78.9	5.0	7.8
50–54	100.0	8.3	80.7	3.7	7.3	100.0	7.7	71.1	13.9	7.3
60–64	100.0	8.6	75.4	9.6	6.4	100.0	8.2	56.9	29.7	5.3
65 and over	100.0	8.4	62.1	24.1	5.5	100.0	8.9	33.2	54.3	3.6
65–69	100.0	8.7	70.3	15.0	6.1	100.0	8.4	46.0	41.1	4.3
70–74	100.0	8.3	64.0	22.2	5.4	100.0	9.0	34.2	53.3	3.6
75–79	100.0	8.1	55.5	31.4	4.9	100.0	9.4	22.5	65.1	2.9
80–84	100.0	7.4	44.8	43.3	4.4	100.0	9.4	12.3	75.9	2.4
85 and over	100.0	7.7	30.4	57.9	4.0	100.0	9.7	5.3	82.9	2.1

* Source: H. D. Sheldon, *The Older Population of the United States* (New York: John Wiley & Sons, 1958), p. 90.

among men there is a sharp rise in the proportion of persons married after age 15. The trend reaches its apex at 83 per cent in the 40–44 age category, and then there is a slow but marked decline, followed by a more rapid decline in the oldest age categories. One of the important implications of this new trend in marital status is that there is now a definite stage in the life-cycle which follows the completion of parenthood. In the typical case a husband and wife "may now expect as much as 14 years of life together after their last child has left home and before the appearance of other events and circumstances that mark the transition into old age" (Sheldon, 1958, p. 129).

Another important aid to understanding the significance of the family for older people is through a basic description of the living arrangements of the aged and the aging.[3] The census data show that nearly all persons 65 and over live in households and that over two-thirds maintain house-

[3] Further discussion of living arrangements is considered in greater detail in chapter xvi, "Housing and Community Settings for Older People."

holds by themselves (Sheldon, 1958). However, as age increases, there is increasing isolation and loss of independence. This is particularly true for women because of their longer life-expectancy. There is a strong tendency for widows in the later years to join the households of their children. The term "three-generation family" is used primarily to describe the situation in which older parents reside in the households of their adult children, but the census data show clearly that the opposite type of family arrangement, in which adult children live in the household of their elderly parents, is almost as prevalent. The census data on living arrangements for various age groups are summarized in Table 2.

II. The Family: A Changing Institution in a Changing Institutional Context

A. Analysis of the Evolution of Institutions

One of the most absorbing of sociological endeavors involves not only the study of existing institutions but also the study

TABLE 2*

Percentage Distribution by Living Arrangements, for Selected Age Groups, 1950

Age (Years)	All Persons	Living in Household—				Living in Quasi-household
		Total	As Head or Wife in Own Household	As Relative of Head of Household	Not Related to Head of Household	
Total, all ages..	100.0	96.2	50.3	43.3	2.7	3.8
15..............	100.0	98.2	0.7	96.3	1.2	1.8
30–34...........	100.0	96.8	80.2	13.8	2.8	3.2
35–39...........	100.0	96.9	83.8	10.4	2.7	3.1
40–44...........	100.0	96.8	85.5	8.6	2.7	3.2
45–49...........	100.0	96.5	86.1	7.4	3.0	3.5
50–54...........	100.0	96.2	85.6	7.4	3.2	3.8
60–64...........	100.0	95.6	81.1	10.6	3.8	4.4
65 and over.......	100.0	94.3	68.9	21.0	4.3	5.7
65–69..........	100.0	95.5	77.0	14.4	4.2	4.5
70–74..........	100.0	94.9	71.3	19.4	4.2	5.1
75–79..........	100.0	93.6	63.2	26.0	4.4	6.4
80–84..........	100.0	91.3	52.8	33.9	4.6	8.7
85 and over......	100.0	87.8	38.3	44.4	5.1	12.2

* Source: H. D. Sheldon, *The Older Population of the United States* (New York: John Wiley & Sons, 1958), p. 96.

of the evolution of institutions. Each contemporary institution has its historical antecedents, and comparative examination provides a fruitful source for generalizations concerning social and cultural change. Such analysis emerges in its full richness when developments within a given institution are related to the larger social context of which they are a part. From such analysis one is able also to view the context of present behavior in relationship to patterns of behavior which obtained in the past. Clearly, this is of particular importance in the field of social gerontology, for the older people of today have presumably participated in institutional forms which in some measure no longer exist.

Moreover, comparative analyses often shed considerable light upon the problems of intergenerational conflict. Insofar as bygone institutional structures live on in the attitudes of the older generation, they provide a point of reference from which behavior of the younger generation often is seen as deviant. Every institution has its idealized past which is expressed as the conservative point of view of the older generation. This certainly contributes to the orderly growth of the institution, but, at the same time, it makes for discomfort and ambivalence among those who must endure the censure of their elders as they attempt to live within the newer institutional framework.

B. The Family in Historical Perspective

Typically, in a developmental analysis of the family, comparisons are made between the consanguine or extended kinship relationships of earlier times and the conjugal or nuclear family of today. The former represents a kind of organization which was particularly well adapted to self-sufficiency in a stable rural environment. Each member of the extended kinship grouping had duties to perform for his family and before his God, with reward presumably to be derived in the performance or perhaps to be reaped in heaven. The family was the producing unit of the economy as well as the consuming unit, with minimal surpluses which were sold or traded for those few staples which could not be produced at home.[4] Not only were such families largely self-sufficient economically but also such families were largely units unto themselves with regard to other major social functions. Certainly, secular laws applied, but far more important were the dictates of custom and of the scriptures, which were usually interpreted and applied by the patriarch. Women and children typically were subordinated to the presumed better judgment, if not the whimsy, of the higher-status elder male. But having a clear-cut status, however inferior, served to define a unity of endeavor and to contribute to a sense of such unity within the family. Most important of all, family unity continued throughout the lifetime of family members. As Moore (1950) puts it, in the extended kinship group "neither adulthood nor marriage severs ties with the parental family and its broader kinship liaisons" (p. 35).

Such was the pattern often approximated in the countries from which the immigrant settlers of America came and sometimes approximated during the Colonial era in our own country. However, very early in our history, pressures developed which tended to call for and call forth families more nearly resembling the conjugal type (Truxal and Merrill, 1953). Among other things, the presence of an expanding frontier in itself encouraged mobility. The manifest destiny of the nation could be realized only if individuals and conjugal family units picked up stakes and carved a livelihood out of the wilderness *on their own*. Thus, even when our country was predominantly rural, families were subjected to social forces which did not fully square with consanguinity. Within the nuclear family, however, older patterns of paternal authority over spouse and children typically prevailed, and a pattern of duties, shot through with religious overtones, defined

[4] For further discussion of this point see chapter iv, "The Technological and Societal Basis of Aging."

the family unit. Perhaps more important than the frontier, therefore, was the advent of the industrial revolution.

C. Industrialization and the Family

The very early factories in this country largely represented a removal from the home of tasks which traditionally had been the duties of the women and the children—spinning, weaving, and the like. Thus it was a simple and economical step for factory owners to acquire women and children as their labor force. "The early American factories were 'manned' largely by women and children," often as a supplement to the agricultural pursuits of the male head of the household (Calhoun, 1918, p. 214). In other instances entire families would be contracted to employment in a factory (Abbott, 1906). But, in either case, early industrialization was accommodated to the existing patterns of family organization. Employment typically was arranged through the authoritarian action of the husband and father, and the earnings of family members were contributed to the family coffers.

Nevertheless, a new emphasis was emerging. As the factory replaced the home as the site of production, pecuniary rewards and rewards of status began to accrue to the individual qua individual. Even though pecuniary rewards of the children were often considered family property and were dutifully given over for family use, achievement came to be defined in terms of the norms of the burgeoning industrial system instead of solely in terms of the norms of the family. Inevitably this served to weaken the hold of the family over its individual members. From the point of view of the industrial organization, it was altogether fitting that this should be the case. Effective and efficient operation required a system of statuses and a correlative system of motivation applicable to individuals as discrete units apart from other individuals, including kinsmen. On-the-job competence, not family loyalties, was the hallmark of excellence in industry; and competence and production were enhanced when the individual was motivated independently of his parents and his siblings.

As a by-product, the industrial system encouraged vertical mobility, a phenomenon which was fully in keeping not only with the functional prerequisites of an expanding industrial economy but also with the older emphasis upon industriousness as a virtue. Thus, as children became adults, it was held that they should surpass the preceding generation in skills and rewards. Often the ideal was realized, principally because new skills were developed to operate the latest machinery after the older generation had settled into a given niche. All this at least potentially meant that status within the factory might represent a gross jumbling of status within the family, a situation which obviously would be disruptive of the one institution or the other. Following the emphases of our society, this institutional incompatibility was resolved by greater stress on conjugality in family organization.

D. Family Authority

In addition to its general impact upon patterns of authority and upon family ties, the large-scale development of industry served to shift the practical locus of authority within the family. As production moved from the home to the factory on an ever larger scale, so did the chief production worker and head of the household—at least for a goodly portion of the day—and meaningful authority in the home and responsibility for the home came to lie largely with the mother. To be sure, major disciplinary problems even today are referred to the father, perhaps as a token of respect in an aura of neglect. But in practice the mother has been the head of American households for a very long time, and this development came to full significance with the removal of the patriarch from home to factory. A respondent in the Cornell Study of Occupational Retirement, describing home life around 1890, expressed it this way:

My mother pretty much ran the show as far as us kids were concerned. We all had our jobs to do around the house and yard, and heaven help us if we didn't do them on time and to suit. (Mother never did believe you should spare the rod!) Every now and then Dad would lay down the law too, but mostly he was worn out by the time he got home from work and he'd be content to eat his supper and go to bed.

By the late nineteenth century, then, paternal authority had been shaken, and family structure more nearly approximating the pure conjugal type had emerged. New and *independent* family units were established as children attained adulthood and marriage. To be sure, links to the parental family remained, albeit in attenuated form and principally with parents alone, not with siblings and certainly not with more distant relatives. Filial obligations remained among family norms, although, as the conjugal family emerged in clearer perspective, acts which might be construed as expressions of obligation often simply reflected the absence of acceptable institutionalized alternatives. One elderly respondent (who, incidentally, insists that her family relationships have always been her foremost interest) had this to say:

When I was a girl you very often found grandparents living with their children and grandchildren. But it wasn't a good idea then any more than it's a good idea now. You always found there would be friction, and, looking back, it seems to me that most people did it [brought parents into their home] so that they wouldn't be sent to the poor house. It wasn't so much that you felt a duty to your parents, but it would have been a disgrace to have *any* relative living in the poor house.

In other words, obligations to parents remained a part of the new family perspective, but the range of such obligations probably was greater because "respectable" provisions for the ill and the indigent were lacking. In any case, whatever the surviving normative prescriptions, the massive impact of industrial reorganization effectively altered the remnants of consanguinity and

the significant patterns of family organization was the conjugal type. In fact, *as it applies to the overwhelming majority of people living today, analysis of the development of family structure could focus solely upon developments within the conjugal structure, for this pattern in highly developed form was current at least three-quarters of a century ago.*

Putting it another way, most of the present population aged 65 and over were children or young adults at the turn of the century, and by that time, even in rural areas, the predominant pattern of social organization of the family already approached the conjugal end of the continuum. But let a 70-year-old respondent give a more graphic description:

We lived on a farm [in Pennsylvania] about three miles from our nearest neighbors and about twelve miles from town. It wasn't much of a town, either, but it was always a treat for us kids to get to go to town. My uncle and aunt lived in town and we'd go to stay with my cousins and they'd come and stay with us. [Asked just what was involved in the relationship with the cousins it soon became evident that] they had their family and we had ours; but we were always friendly back and forth and on Christmas there would be a family reunion. But the reunions sort of stopped when my grandmother died. By that time some of my sisters were married and had little ones and so did some of my cousins and we began to have our own family reunions. . . . I never hear from my cousins anymore, except a couple of them send Christmas cards. But, then, we're all scattered out. Why, I don't even keep in touch with my brother and sisters like I ought to!

In this instance the older family pattern evidently had survived to the extent that there was a sense of identity of the larger unit, symbolized by the presence of the aged grandmother. However, functional independence is evidenced by the fact that even the family reunions ceased when the grandmother died. This seems to be a typical pattern which survives even today, especially in rural areas—bilateral symbolic unity but an absence of functional interdependence. Significantly, interviewees typically interpret questions about mutual aid, financial or otherwise, between siblings or more distant relatives, in terms of dire need. The same respondent quoted above also told us that "I suppose Dad would have helped his brothers and sisters if there had been an emergency, but I don't think it ever came to that."

Thus the situation of those who are the older people of today has been, from their youth, more nearly the conjugal family type. As early as 1880 the majority of all workers were in non-agricultural pursuits (U.S. Bureau of the Census, 1949), but, even among those who grew up in the self-contained atmosphere of the farm and who were importantly oriented to their family, the majority of this generation of older people themselves broke family ties and formed conjugal units in an urban setting.

E. The Conjugal Family: Yesterday and Today

Within the conjugal units of their youth, however, the older people of today experienced a kind of family life which their own children have not significantly experienced. Each person had duties and responsibilities and was subject to a surviving pattern of parental authority and discipline, particularly from the mother:

When I was a kid, there was stricter discipline, I can tell you! My mother kept a willow switch handy and she knew how to switch us where it would hurt the most. . . . We had plenty of opportunity to play—used to have all the kids in the neighborhood in our backyard. (It was a little bigger and we had more trees.) But we knew how to work, too, and when my folks said do something, we did it . . . we didn't question why we had to, we just did it. My folks were fair, I don't mean that [they weren't]; but there was stricter discipline, I can tell you!

Such an interview is typical; in discussions with older persons about family life in their youth, one almost inevitably encounters references to "stricter discipline," "duties and responsibilities," and "more family life [activities within the home]." Certainly,

these characteristics bespeak survivals from the earlier patterns of family life and in part are so explained; but in part they also reflect the necessity of the times. The age of gadgets was not then upon us, and the work involved in the day-to-day tasks of running a household, even as a consuming unit, was considerably more than is easily imagined today. Given the necessity for conjoined effort to these ends, some kind of hierarchical organization was indicated, and survival of earlier patterns of discipline, duty, and responsibility was convenient indeed. Also it was more or less inevitable that recreation should center in the home. Outside recreational facilities were less common than today, transportation was not readily available, and, over all, the sheer amount of effort necessary to "go out on the town" was disproportionately high. This was particularly true, since, to quote a 70-year-old respondent, "most common folks didn't have much money in those days, even if they did work longer hours." The picture is one of a sense of duty, of clear-cut responsibility, and of acknowledged patterns of authority, even though within a conjugal family unit.

But a second industrial revolution was to have its impact upon the family. As increasing numbers of laborsaving devices have minimized the effort required in those tasks which remain, the need for specified duties and for relatively rigidly structured interrelationships has dwindled, and the disciplinary hierarchy largely has become obsolete. There is a world of significance in the fact that a modern girl may be well socialized yet may never have learned to cook!

One important effect of the late-nineteenth-century normative structure was the preservation of identification with the family, a sense of belonging to a well-defined unit. In important respects, this, too, has declined with the age of gadgetry; and the degree to which the normative structure was, in fact, a function of the utilitarian aspects of family life is suggested by the speed with which "familism has been replaced by individualism" (Cavan, 1953, p. 112).

But, although the family's need for personnel to do the necessary jobs has declined, the need of the individual for the family has not declined commensurately. It is fortunate, therefore, that the possibility of close family ties remains. In a sense, the removal of definite lines of authority, the diminishing of family duties, and the establishment of an atmosphere of equality in which each individual counts as an individual clears the way for a fuller realization of affectional ties as the *sine qua non* of family relationships. Thus, while the decline in the pattern of duties and authority has tended to weaken the family in some respects, the possibility of closer affectional ties may actually have increased, perhaps in part offsetting the tendency toward a weaker structure. That this possibility is reflected in the perception of some individuals is illustrated by responses one encounters in interviews. For example, when asked whether he considered whether there was less affection in family relationships today, one 70-year-old replied:

Less affection? No, not at all. There is *more* affection today. I am not saying I didn't hold my parents in high regard, because I did. But it was that I respected and kind of feared them, too, I guess. I thought that they had all the answers. Now take my kids: they know more than I do and they know they do, but they love "the old man" and even let me spoil my grandkids! What more could I ask?

The significance of such a response lies in the fact that it may be regarded as typical. There is no doubt that the family pattern of today tends to be a clear-cut conjugal type. In other words, as children grow up and marry, new separate family units are formed. But each such unit remains tied with affection to parents. From the perspective of the older person, therefore, the family consists of *his* family of procreation and his family's family. To be sure, there are considerable variations in the family patterns one encounters: urban-rural differentials, geographical differences, social class differences, and differences which reflect the orientations of varied ethnic backgrounds. As a matter of fact, it could be argued that research in the sociology of the family much too frequently overlooks such differences and considers the middle-class or the upper middle-class family to be the American family type. Yet, in spite of variations, and although such variations are differences which certainly make a difference, one can legitimately refer to the conjugal form as the modal American family type. To repeat, from the point of view of the older person, "the family" consists of themselves, their children, and their grandchildren. And within "the family," as the older person experiences the interrelationships, the emphasis is not on functional interdependence but rather is largely on ties of affection.

Of course, there inevitably remain some survivals of an earlier day. For example, a still widely accepted commonplace, especially in rural areas but in urban areas as well, is the expression "blood is thicker than water." But relationships with siblings, filial duties and responsibilities to parents, and recognition of parental authority have through time become diluted. Instead, primary responsibility in each generation is to the children—responsibility for survival, solace, and socialization and, where possible, responsibility for assistance in getting the children started on their own.

In practice, family ties may remain quite strong in the modal family because of the ties of affection; but any duty which remains might properly be labeled the duty to be affectionate. Given the prolonged and intensive interaction among family members, affectional ties would be highly probable in any case; but, while probable, often pleasant, and sometimes useful, such ties are not necessary to the proper functioning of the family as an institution beyond that point at which the children go out on their own. One still feels guilty when one neglects to write one's parents, but one regrets such negligence—if at all—only because it jeopardizes what is akin to a friendship relationship. That the relationship is assumed by the younger generation to mean relatively more to the parent is illustrated by the fact that such regrets usually are expressed in the form "I hate to hurt their feelings, but. . . ."

This, then, in major outline is the story of developments within the institution of the family—a story of considerable interest in and of itself. However, as we have emphasized, the point of the story in the present context is its bearing on the place of the older person in the family. This is the institutional framework within which the older person must make an adjustment; this is the institutional framework which in many cases constitutes the world of the older person.

III. THE OLDER PERSON'S ROLE IN THE FAMILY

A. Neglect of Gerontological Aspects of the Family

We have argued that the family may be the most significant social group for the middle aged and the aged. Yet, surprisingly, the family as a focus of serious scientific study has been, until quite recently, singularly neglected as an area for study of the older aged groups.[5] One index of this neglect is the degree to which standard family texts handle the later stages of the life-cycle. Textbooks usually reflect interest in a field and also the amount of knowledge available on a topic. Thus Beard (1949) in an article with the rather provocative title, "Are the Aged Ex-Family?" showed conclusively that there was a lack of coverage in twenty standard texts in the sociology of the family. She pointed out that some of the writers exclude the aged and that, when they are included, very little space is devoted to them. Beard indicated also that text writers tend to view older persons as family members in negative terms and as problems. She concluded: "The statements about the aged which ap-

[5] A brief review of some aspects of family research on the later stages of the life-cycle was made by Gravatt (1953).

pear in books on the family seem to be based on personal observation or experience. References to research studies are noticeably lacking" (p. 278). Inasmuch as Beard's work was published in 1949, the present writers were interested in knowing whether any major shifts in emphasis had developed in more recent years. A content analysis of thirteen more recent texts in marriage and the family showed the following coverage:

No space	4 books
Less than 1 page . . .	3 books
1–5 pages	2 books
6–10 pages	2 books
More than 10 pages .	2 books (1 chapter each)

It should be added that recent books of readings in the family, designed primarily as texts, have devoted on the average considerably more space to the gerontological aspects of family life. The three leading books published in the years 1952–55 have two or three articles in the area, with coverage ranging from nine to twenty-five pages.

It is perhaps of greater significance that research workers have not devoted very much attention to gerontological subjects. In the fields of sociology, for example, the decade 1945–55 was relatively lean; Winch's (1957) review of research in family sociology 1945–55 has a bibliography of 386 items, which includes only 7 devoted to aging and the problems of old age. He observes that these topics are receiving more attention than in earlier periods and adds: "As of the moment of writing, this seems to be the middle of the growing season, and it is too soon to tell exactly how the crop of research on this topic will turn out" (p. 372). A more complete coverage of research in the family which surveyed fifteen journals and five monograph series in several disciplines lists 1031 titles (Foote and Cottrell, 1955). Employing a rather loose definition of studies of later maturity, we find that perhaps 20 of the 1000 titles are concerned with topics related to the family and social gerontology.

Thus we are confronted with something of a paradoxical situation in that the family is a highly important area for study of later maturity, and yet there is a dearth of research materials available. Nevertheless, from knowledge of the family on a more general level and from that research material which is available, one can piece together a view of the older person's role as a family member.

B. The Functions of the Family

As it is used in sociology, the term "function" generally refers to processes which make an essential contribution to the maintenance of a given social structure. As we have pointed out above, the institutional structures of a particular society are directed toward the realization of the major values of the society. As the institutional norms are put into practice, therefore, they contribute to stability, orderly growth, and maintenance of society as a whole.[6]

So it is with the family norms. First of all, a very obvious functional prerequisite of society is the need to replenish the members, and this need finds institutional expression in the norms of the family which relate to procreation. Closely related to the procreative function, if a society is to be maintained or is to grow in an orderly way, its new members must in some measure accept its basic values. This need finds expression in the socialization function which remains one of the most important institutional attributes of the family even though an increasing amount of socialization is given over to educational institutions. Socialization, of course, also serves the individual, for what is involved essentially is the learning of the ways to get about within society, and in the process one formulates a concept of the nature of one's self and one's world.

Provision for the subsistance and material needs of the members of a society usually is considered to be the province of economic institutions; and, as we have indicated above, an important change in the family is often said to be the sloughing-off of the economic function. The fact remains, however, that the family mediates between the economic order and individuals. Participation in the economic order by the head of the household (and, increasingly frequently today, his spouse) is directed to the provision of a living or a standard of living for members of his family. Thus a third important function of the family is the maintenance function—the provision of food, clothing, and shelter.

Stability and continuity of the social order also require a systematic way of conferring status or placing the individual into the social structure. This has been called the placement function. In American society placement in this sense may ultimately derive from educational and occupational attainment, but initially one's status is determined by the status of one's family. Moreover, educational attainment as a means of achieving status is sought in different measure, depending upon the values one has learned in the family context; and educational attainment is limited by the availability of resources in the family. In a sense, therefore, the family serves not only to "place" the individual initially but also to affect achievement as derived through educational means. As in the case of socialization, the placement function also has value for the individual in the sense, among other things, that stability of self depends upon a more or less certain place within the social structure.

Finally, the family provides a context which permits and even encourages development of close emotional ties, the affectional function. At first glance, this would appear to be significant chiefly for the individuals involved. However, insofar as close affectional relationships contribute to an enduring and satisfying sense of self, they also serve the needs of society, for stable personalities are required to carry out cultural roles.[7]

---

[6] Robert K. Merton (1957, pp. 19–84) has made the most systematic analysis of functional theory and its application to the study of human society.

[7] There are, of course, other functions which might be included in a more complete analysis. Other writers have utilized longer and slightly dif-

To be sure, other institutions of society also help to fulfill the social functions which we have indicated to be five major functions of the family. Indeed, some writers have singled out this fact as the key to understanding "the modern family," and it has suggested to them that the family simply has lost its functions. It would seem clear, however, that this is an overstatement of the case, and perhaps particularly for the older person, for many older persons may find a significant place in the social structure with regard to these several social functions only within the context of the family.

Our starting point then is the proposition that a society, in order to survive, must carry out certain organized activities for survival and that these activities or contributions are embodied in institutional structures. In the family we have an institutional structure which carries out several important social functions and, as we have seen, serves the needs of the individual as well. The question, then, concerns the role that the older person plays in the realization of these functions and the way in which his special needs may or may not be served through this role.

C. The Procreative Function

One of the basic purposes of family life in all societies is the control of sexual behavior. In all known human societies there

exists a set of basic norms governing sexual activity; furthermore, sexual relations within the nuclear family are the one universally approved form of sexual expression. This has led some writers to assert that control of sexual behavior is the keystone of family structure. Therefore, in studying the family in later maturity, it is essential that some attention be given to the sexual and reproductive aspects of the family. For the family as a social group is inextricable from the biological needs and drives of people. However, these needs and drives are more fully understood in terms of how they are *culturally conditioned* and how they

TABLE 3*

BIRTHS PER 1000 FEMALES FOR VARIOUS
AGE CATEGORIES, 1953

Age Category (Years)	Births per 1000 Females
15–19	87.5
20–24	224.4
25–29	183.8
30–34	113.0
35–39	57.3
40–44	15.5
45–49	1.1†

* Source: U.S. National Office of Vital Statistics, *Vital Statistics of the United States: 1953* (Washington, D.C.: Government Printing Office, 1955), p. xxxvii, Table Y.

† The rate for the last group was computed by relating births to mothers aged 45 and over to the female population 45–49 years of age.

may be expressed in *socially approved* ways. It is not the control of sexual behavior per se which most societies deem so significant but a concern for the biological results of sexual relations, namely, the conception and birth of children. Indeed, although sexual behavior may be approved outside the marital bond in some cultures, no society has institutionalized reproduction of offspring outside the family. In our society, however, sexual relations are controlled regardless of the chances of reproduction. From this standpoint middle age and old age are of little significance, for with increasing age there is a definite and marked decline in fertility. The average (mean) of the childbearing ages is approximately 28 years (U.S. National Conference on Family Life, 1948). The obvious fact that the young bear children is shown clearly by census data in Table 3. The

---

ferent lists of family functions. Ogburn and Tibbitts (1933, p. 661), for example, studied the economic, protective, recreational, educational, religious, affectional, and cultural. Truxal and Merrill (1947, pp. 15–23) offer the primary functions: socialization of the child, satisfaction of desires for response, and a list of subsidiary functions: economic, reproductive, transmitting property, and status-giving. Kingsley Davis (1949, p. 395) states that there are four main functions of the family: reproduction, maintenance, placement, and socialization of the young. All these lists of family functions could be broken down and modified; none of these writers claims that they cover all the functions of the family. Therefore, we may say that there is no correct list of functions of the family. We are interested in using those functions of the family which are useful in analyzing and understanding the American family in the later stages of the life-cycle.

data show, for example, that the number of births per 1000 females for the most fertile age category (20–24) was 224.4, compared with 1.1 births for the category 45–49 years of age.

The decline in human fertility is related, of course, to the onset of the menopause. Masters (1952) reports that in this country, on the average, menstruation ceases between the forty-fifth and fiftieth year. Thus old age is characterized not only by a sharp decline in fertility or reproductive performance but also by an eventual disappearance of reproductive capacity, or fecundity.

Thus, later maturity is a period characterized by little if any contribution to the replacement of a society's population. However, there is a continuation of individual behavior directed toward the social function of procreation. In short, the decline in fecundity or fertility does not necessarily result in the cessation of sexual activity. Research indicates that the decline in sexual activity from the teens to old age is remarkably steady and that there is no point at which old age suddenly enters the picture (Kinsey *et al.*, 1948). The importance of the marital intercourse throughout the life-cycle is noted by Kinsey and his associates for the sampled population of older males. These investigators point out that the average male has a relatively constant source of sexual outlet through marital intercourse throughout his lifetime. Almost 90 per cent of total sexual outlet of the average male, they report, is drawn from marital intercourse.

Although biological factors are undoubtedly significant in the steady decline in sexual activity, the extent to which social and psychological factors are also responsible is still not clear. It is not surprising that there should be some loss of activity, even if there were no aging process involved. But the precise influence of the various factors in the complicated causation pattern is not clear. The research workers who have studied the subject most fully summarize the situation as follows:

It is undoubtedly affected by psychological fatigue, a loss of interest in repetition of the same sort of experience, an exhaustion of the possibilities for exploring new techniques, new types of contacts, new situations.

. . . How much of the overall decline in the rate for the older male is physiologic, how much is based on psychologic situations, how much is based on the reduced availability of contacts, and how much is, among educated people, dependent upon preoccupation with other social or business functions in the professionally most active period of the male's life, it is impossible to say at the present time [Kinsey *et al.*, 1948, pp. 227 and 229].

However, in their later work on the female, Kinsey and his associates tend to be more definite and claim that decline in marital coitus is the product of aging processes in the male and not in the female (Kinsey *et al.*, 1953, p. 353).

AGE AND THE SELECTION OF MARITAL PARTNERS

There is one other subject which has tangential bearing on the reproductive function and on which social scientists have done considerable research, namely, the influence of cultural factors, such as race and age, upon the selection of marital partners.

The question might be raised as to whether the fertility rates reported above are somewhat deceptive inasmuch as they are based on the age of the female, with the age of the male not being considered. A popular stereotype regarding the old is that portrayed in newspaper accounts in which the septuagenarian, or even an octogenarian, marries a woman many years his junior and then proceeds to have children by his young wife. There is no doubt that marriages of this type take place and that offspring result. However, the point to be emphasized is that they are statistical rarities because cultural controls restrict the probability of a wide differential in the age of marital partners. Hollingshead (1950) reports an interview study of 528 couples in New Haven and concluded that the pool of marriage mates is very definitely limited by cultural restrictions on the age of the partners. More specifically, he found that "only 4 men above 45 years of age, out of a total of 144, married women under 30 years of age" (p. 622).

The importance of age as a biosocial factor influencing the choice of mates is also substantiated by Glick and Landau's (1950) analysis of a sample of 25,000 cases obtained by the Bureau of the Census in its monthly cross-sectional survey. The data from this scientifically selected nation-wide survey show that the average wife was 2.8 years younger than her husband, when the husband and wife were married only once.[8] Statistical average may constitute only a minority of actual cases, however, for about 50 per cent of the wives were about 1–5 years younger than their husbands. The important point to be made in the present context is that in only 7.9 per cent of the sample was the wife 10 or more years younger than the husband, when husbands and wives were married only once.

A slightly different picture is obtained when we examine the data when either husband or wife was married more than once. In this instance, the data show the average wife was 4.6 years younger than her husband that 27.6 per cent of the wives were 10 or more years younger than the husband.

Another way of analyzing the survey materials is to examine the median differences between the ages of husbands and their wives according to how old the respective partners were at the time of the survey. On the average, among first marriages where the husband was between 18 and 24 years of age, the wife was only about 1 year younger, but, when the husband was 65–74 years of age, the wife was 4 years younger. Remarriages present a slightly contrasting picture, for, when the husband was 18–24 years old, the difference was negligible, and, where the husband was 65–74 years of age,

the wife tended to be about 10 years younger. A general conclusion is that the census data do not support the notion that wide age differentials of marital partners may occur frequently. Indeed, the age factor tends to support very strongly the theory of homogamy that "like attracts like."[9] Glick and Landau (1950) explain the difference in the pattern of first marriages and remarriages by suggesting the difference may be the result of the "interaction of the factors of selection and availability" (p. 525). In general, persons marrying for the first time tend to select a person marrying for the first time, whereas in remarriages the persons tend to select persons who have been previously married, a condition which tends to restrict possible choices and to increase the possibility of greater age differentials.

The above summary of research information indicates clearly that the age of spouses tends to be quite similar, and in only a small proportion of cases is there a marked discrepancy in age. However, when age differentials do occur, they may be related to other aspects of family life. One important and inescapable demographic relationship is that, when the wife is much younger than the husband, there is a high probability that the period of widowhood will be lengthened. Moreover, when husband and wife are widely apart in terms of age, there is the possibility of increased social and psychological distance. The authors are not aware of any pertinent research in this area. Bossard (1953) has conducted some qualitative studies of over-age parents (parents who are older than their children by 27 or more years) and reports that, when the time interval between generations is unduly lengthened, family problems tend to be exaggerated. He says: "Children seem more troublesome to their parents, parents seem less understanding to their children, solicitousness in parents becomes more pathological, and their firmness turns into rigidity" (p. 200).

[8] The study was limited, of necessity, to married couples living together at the time of the survey, and the median is used to describe the "average wife."

[9] For a general discussion of the theory and data see Burgess and Wallin (1943).

D. The Socialization Function

A second major social function of the family is that of socialization: training the young and transmitting and inculcating social attitudes, norms, and values. Little systematic research has been conducted on the role of older persons in the socialization process in American society. Simmons (1945) has summarized a variety of evidence pertaining to relations between the very old and the very young in non-literate societies. He finds that child-rearing is frequently engaged in by the old, sometimes because of economic necessity, and that the care of the young "has thus very generally provided the aged with a useful occupation and a vivid interest in life during the dull days of senescence" (p. 199). However, the ethnographic vignettes which he offers concerning non-literate societies are not applicable to the family in a complex society like the United States.[10]

members is the fact that only a minority of older persons live in three-generation households. Using census data from Glick (1957), Smith *et al.* (1958) estimate that perhaps "two or three per cent of all husband-wife primary families are three-generation families" (pp. 3–4). The most complete information on living arrangements is provided by a 1952 sample census conducted by the United States Bureau of the Census for the University of California at Berkeley. Personal interviews were conducted with persons 65 and over in approximately 15,000 households in sixty-eight sample areas (Burgess, 1957).

TABLE 4*

PERCENTAGE DISTRIBUTION OF LIVING ARRANGEMENTS
OF OLDER PEOPLE, 1952

Living Arrangement	Couples	Widowed, Single, Divorced, and Separated	
		Males	Females
Not living with children	74.1	69.3	54.7
Living with children	25.9	30.7	45.3
Older person head	(22.6)	(11.0)	(15.9)
Adult child head	(3.3)	(19.7)	(29.4)
Total	100.0	100.0	100.0

* Source: E. W. Burgess, "The Older Generation and the Family," in Wilma Donahue and C. Tibbitts (eds.), *The New Frontiers of Aging* (Ann Arbor: University of Michigan Press, 1957), p. 162.

OPPORTUNITY FOR OLDER PERSONS TO HELP
IN SOCIALIZATION OF THE YOUNG

At the present time, one of the major limitations which reduces the probability of sustained socialization by older family

[10] Further discussion of the aged in the family in preindustrial societies may be found in chapter iii, "Aging in Preindustrial Cultures."

In this survey it was found that one-half of the persons 65 and over were married and living with their spouses. As is to be expected, a much larger percentage of men (68 per cent) than women (35 per cent) were married and living with a spouse. The detailed data for the study, by couples, and by males and females according to marital status are shown in Table 4. Turning first to the information on couples, we note that only a small percentage of adult children are the head of the household in which three-generation families reside. Another interesting fact is that there is a much higher proportion of older females than males who live with their children (45 per cent compared to 31 per cent). Finally, the table shows that for older persons who are widowed, single, or separated, and who live with their children, almost twice the percentage of these homes have an adult child as the head compared to those in which an aged parent is the head. The small proportion of three-generation households is probably due to ambivalent feelings toward establishing such living arrangements. Koller's (1954) research in several communities indicates the lack of a clear-cut norm, although he found that people want to do the "right thing" (pp. 205–6).

When we consider the over-all status of the living arrangements of older men and women, a much higher proportion of women than men live with their children; there are three mothers to every one father who live with their adult children. From the information available on a limited number of cases, the data show that many three-generation families consist of those in which the mother has moved into the home of a married daughter. More living grandparents are related to the maternal side of the family, presumably because of the fact that women tend to live longer and usually marry younger (Albrecht, 1954a). The tendency for American families to have closer matrilineal than patrilineal ties is shown by the fact that families maintain closer relations with parents of wives than with the parents of husbands (Smith, 1954; Wallin, 1954). The matricentric nature of the three-generation family has also been found to be characteristic of lower-class British families (Townsend, 1957).

When we turn our attention to the social-psychological aspects of socialization of grandchildren by older relatives, we are again confronted by a dearth of research. In general, the studies which have been published have been conducted by psychiatrists or by investigators who tend to be psychiatrically oriented.

GRANDPARENTS AS SOCIALIZERS

As one might expect, the interpretation of the grandparent's behavior is linked to psychological processes established early in the life-cycle. Vollmer (1937), for example, places stress on the fact that the grandmother's period of responsibility is ended and that thus the grandchild can fulfil a definite emotional need. The situation, he argues, involves the division of the child's love between mother and grandmother, and the latter, because of feelings of insecurity, attempts to win the love of the grandchild through indulgence and the undermining of the parent. Another writer interprets the excessive love and attention of the grandmother for her grandchildren as the result of guilt feelings originating in the neglect of her own children (Fried and Stern, 1948). Borden (1946) maintains from the study of fifteen cases of behavior problems in children that the grandmother-daughter relationship was a factor influencing the behavior problems. Albrecht's (1954b) findings on a study of small communities in the Midwest are somewhat variant. She says: "If cases of extreme indulgence or excessive love exist they were well concealed" (p. 204). Borden reasoned that the grandmother tended to dominate and to usurp the mother role and that the daughter developed feelings of inadequacy which, in turn, affected the grandchild's behavior. It should be emphasized that these studies are based primarily on clinical and counseling cases, and the general validity of these analyses remains to be tested on a more representative sample of cases in the general population.

RACE, RELIGION, AND ETHNICITY AS FACTORS IN SOCIALIZATION

Race and ethnicity have been mentioned as important factors in the study of the family in the United States, and there are a number of studies which show that the role of grandparents in the socialization of children may vary according to the racial or ethnic background of the family. One of the major variations in family structure related to racial and ethnic characteristics is the extent to which consanguineal ties are maintained or emphasized. Families in which strong family ties are fostered have more consistent and sustained relations between the generations than those ethnic groups in which ties are more tenuous. Therefore, in those families in which generational ties are stronger, it is more likely that the older generation will play a significant role in socialization. Kutner and his co-workers (1956) report that Hungarian, and particularly Italian, families are much more likely to include elder members in the household than is true of British, German, or Irish families. Thus one finds that, among the Irish-born in this New York City study, almost two-thirds of the aged are socially isolated as compared to about a third of the Italian-born respondents. The difference is perhaps more interesting when we keep in mind the fact that both groups are predominantly Catholic and are rural in their origins.

As ethnic groups become more acculturated to American norms and values, there is a tendency for consanguineal ties to weaken. Italian-Americans are among the groups which maintain close ties, and yet they are not exempt from acculturative influences. Campisi (1948) has analyzed the transition very closely in a comparison of the southern Italian peasant family and the first- and second-generation Italian family in America. In the southern Italian peasant family in Italy, Campisi reports, there is a strong patriarchal arrangement emphasizing family ties, the sharing of common goals, and the presence of strong in-group solidarity. In this situation the daughter-in-law is subservient to her husband's family, and the mother-in-law often has an important influence on housekeeping and child-rearing practices. With the establishment of the first- and second-generation family in America, one finds a breakdown of family solidarity, and along with this change there is the development of a large measure of independence on the part of the newly established family. The daughter-in-law is likely to follow American standards in regard to socialization, and, if an attempt is made to impose more traditional practices, there is the likelihood of conflict, which, in turn, weakens family solidarity.

One minority group which has a rather unique family structure and in which grandparents play a somewhat specialized role in socialization is the lower-class American Negro family. Frazier (1939, 1948) has described the matricentric nature of these families and the fact that the grandmother may be an important person not only in socializing grandchildren but also in giving the family unity and stability. Lower-class Negro families tend to be more disorganized than white families in both rural and urban areas. However, as they adjust to the new social and economic demands of the urban environment, there is a tendency to take on more conventional patterns. The structure and function of the Negro family date back to the instability of slavery and reconstruction periods, in which unmarried motherhood was rather common. However, in those families in which the father's social and economic position was established, the family acquired stability in the past, and this is also true today. As the Negro is able to raise his educational attainments and has opportunity for greater social and economic participation in all phases of American life, the patterns of family life become more similar to the prevailing white American pattern. With this acculturation process comes a decline in the importance of the older generation, particularly the grandmother, in socialization.

These fragmentary studies of the role of grandparents in socialization indicate the research potentialities present in studying these problems more systematically in ethnic and racial groups and also in the white native-born population. One subject, for example, which has been neglected is the role of the grandfather in socialization. There are a number of biographical accounts of the way in which a boyhood may have been enriched by sustained contact with a grandparent or other older relative, (e.g., Ruark, 1957). However, the possible negative effects of socialization by grandparents has been overlooked. Indeed, because it may conflict with stereotyped conventional ideas, there is little likelihood that the possible negative aspects will be known until a more systematic approach is made upon the way in which older persons are involved in socialization.

CONTACT WITH CHILDREN AND GRANDCHILDREN AND ITS EFFECT ON MORALE

The manner in which research findings may conflict with conventional notions is pointed out by the data from several studies which indicate that the presence of children and grandchildren may not have a positive effect on the morale and adjustment of older persons. Kutner and his associates (1956) report that the level of morale is the same for those persons having no children and for those persons who see their children often and that the relationship holds for both high- and low-status categories. Similar findings have resulted from research conducted by the authors of this chapter. Moreover, among high-status older persons there is a tendency for morale to be higher among those persons who see their children and other relatives *less* frequently.

Two factors are suggested as reasons why visits with one's own relatives may affect morale adversely: (1) friction between younger relatives and the older person over the rearing of children[11] and (2) more overt and clearer recognition of the aging process by the older person. The authors of the New York study speculate that contact with younger relatives may result in harassment as to how to stay healthy or young; there is also the possibility, they suggest, that the sheer contrast in the health and vigor of the two generations may reinforce

the older person's perception of the realities of aging.

Data which tend to agree with the above interpretation are found in a study of three-generation families in a small urban and in a rural community in Pennsylvania. The investigators report that there was a definite tendency for older persons who lived in their own homes to be better adjusted than persons who lived in the homes of their children. However, the writers suggest that this relationship may be explained, in part, by the fact that the establishment of three-generation households arises from a set of complex factors involving a decline in health and income or a change in marital status—which are also highly related independently to adjustment (Smith *et al.*, 1958). Thus it seems possible that three-generation households which are established for other than health or economic reasons may be more conducive to the adjustment of older persons. In the above-mentioned Pennsylvania study there is suggestive evidence that this may be the case, for there was a significant tendency for the older generation to be better adjusted in those homes in which their children reported they had felt very close to their parents in their teens as compared to those persons who felt less close. One further qualification is necessary, namely, that most of the three-generation families consisted of a widowed mother living with her daughter and her family. Although this may be an important type of three-generation family, there is a need for further information in order to obtain a clearer understanding of the dynamics of parent-child relationships in all types of three-generation households.

A certain amount of friction between generations is, of course, a universal sociological phenomenon. In a brilliant piece of sociological analysis, Kingsley Davis (1940) has pointed out three variables which are found in most cultures and which tend to produce conflict between parents and children. These universals are: (1) the age or birth-cycle differential between parent and child; (2) the decelerating rate of sociali-

---

[11] The finding that "conflict of generations" and "spoiling grandchildren" are important disadvantages of living with aged parents is in sharp contrast to Townsend's (1957) lower-class English study, in which he reports the care of grandchildren was one of the most important tasks of grandparents, especially the grandmother (p. 48).

zation with advancing age; and (3) the intrinsic differences between young and old on the physiological, psychosocial, and sociological planes. These universals plus the distinctive complex of variables present in our society tend to increase conflict between the generations in certain situations. The rate of social change is one of the most important of these latter variables, and there is a growing body of evidence which indicates that child-rearing practices do differ markedly by generations. Practices which were considered essential for the health and welfare of the child by one generation may become obsolete and may even be thought harmful by a younger generation of parents. Differences in socialization practices between generations may be inferred from Wolfenstein (1953) and Bronfenbrenner (1958).

Dinkel's (1943) study of parent-child conflict tends to substantiate the major points of Davis' analysis. On the basis of interviews with fifty families in Minnesota, he concludes that conflicts between the generations are less when there is similarity of beliefs and norms among the generations. Moreover, he goes on to suggest that families which have a history of generational conflict should not adhere to community expectations, which hold that parents and children should live together when the parents are old and unable to take care of themselves economically or physically. Dinkel observes that, if the generations are forced to form a three-generation household in order to comply with community expectations or perhaps legal obligations, there is the definite possibility of increasing family disorganization (p. 419). A cautionary note of interpretation seems appropriate, namely, that Dinkel's study was based on a rather small number of cases and that it was conducted during a period of economic depression.

In the Pennsylvania study cited above, the investigators present a slightly different picture of three-generation households, for we learn that a large portion of the study population state they did not have genera-

tional disagreements (Smith *et al.*, 1958). These investigators report that parents and grandparents usually agreed on what was expected of children. They explain this finding by saying that, in general, grandparents did not play a particularly active role in the discipline of the children. In the two Pennsylvania communities there was a minority of persons who stated that the generations "just don't get along together." However, it is rather surprising to note that an analysis of the factors which were related to the total adjustment scores of the grandparents revealed that their adjustment was not closely related to intergenerational disagreements (pp. 37–39). Moreover, the length of time which the generations lived together showed no significant effect upon the adjustment of the oldest generation.

E. The Maintenance Function

THE FAMILY AS AN ECONOMIC UNIT

The sociological study of the family in American society has been marked by an emphasis on the way in which family economic activities concerned with production have been transferred from the family to other agencies and institutions (Ogburn and Tibbitts, 1933). In all societies the family engages in activities which are considered economic. Broadly conceived, the field of economics is concerned with the study of the production, distribution, and consumption of services and goods in the satisfaction of human wants. In analyzing the significance of the family in these diverse activities, the first major question to be considered is: To what extent is the family a self-sufficient economic unit? There have been forms of the family in earlier historical societies which were highly self-sufficient as economic units. Indeed in many parts of the contemporary world there are a number of important societies, such as India, in which the family maintains a high degree of self-sufficiency. However, in Western countries the contemporary family has almost ceased to be self-sufficient as a primary *production unit*.

On the one hand, the family tends to be an important focus of economic activities in the production of goods and services in those societies where social organization tends to be simple and where technology is not highly developed. On the other hand, in societies where technology is highly developed and where large-scale enterprises are the major units of economic activity, one finds that economic roles are assumed by individuals rather than by families. The fact that individuals and not families are involved in these processes suggests that family economic ties are loosened; what is of interest in the study of the aged is that there is also a tendency toward the creation of a category of economic dependents. It is at this specific point that the study of the maintenance function of the family in later maturity becomes significant. The aged—like children and the handicapped— are viewed as being economically useless. Additional implications of this statement are discussed in this *Handbook* in chapters viii and x and particularly in "Aging and the Economy" in chapter xiv.

MAINTENANCE AND DECLINING INCOME

We can obtain a clearer idea of how this conception of the aged manifests itself in terms of maintenance by discussing briefly the concept of family cycle, namely, that the family passes through a series of stages from its formation to its dissolution (Glick, 1947, 1955). Indeed, these cyclical features of the family show very clearly the manner in which the maintenance requirements change and also the decline in the family's capacity for meeting these needs. The family typically grows from the newly married couple to a form of the family with one or more children. Then it passes through a stable period when the last child is born until the first child leaves the home to establish his own family. Toward the end of the cycle the family returns to its original form with two persons and becomes

what has been called "the empty nest." Finally, this generation of the family comes to an end with the deaths of the parents. Smith and his associates have pointed out another aspect of maintenance which occurs in a small number of cases and which deserves mention in the study of three-generation families, namely, when the three generations live together, it is primarily for the economic benefit of the older generations, or the arrangement occurs because of health reasons or widowhood (Smith *et al.*, 1958).

Inasmuch as the focus of this chapter is directed at studying the later stages of the cycle, it is not pertinent to give further consideration to the earlier stages, although we recognize their importance and their relationship to later stages of the cycle. For example, the presence or absence of children may make considerable difference in the way maintenance is fulfilled in later maturity. Viewing the family from the standpoint of maintenance, families in which the heads are over 60 years of age tend to be in an underprivileged position. There is a marked decline in income, and there is the definite possibility that needs may increase because of declining health and the increased need for medical care, as discussed in chapter vii. Although the economic position of the family in later maturity receives detailed attention in other sections of this publication, it is useful to summarize the pertinent information in the present context.

Corson and McConnell (1956) report a special tabulation of the Bureau of the Census on the income of the heads of families aged 65 and over, which is summarized in Table 5.[12] The data show that only 30 per cent of these households report income over $2000 a year, which suggests that a large proportion of families with older persons must live on a budget which is clearly below the "standard" budget of $1825 estimated to provide for the maintenance of

[12] For a comparative presentation of the various types of economic units, couples, unrelated males, and unrelated females see Table 11, chap. viii.

an urban couple not living with relatives (Steiner and Dorfman, 1957). Corson and McConnell (1956) remind us, however, that the income status of the aged tends to be understated because income in kind tends not to be reported. Income from home-ownership and contributions from children and others are particularly significant.

TABLE 5*

INCOME OF FAMILY UNITS AS REPORTED
BY HEADS OF FAMILIES 65
AND OVER, 1949

Income Group	Percentage Distribution
None	18.4
Less than $500	17.8
$ 500–$999	18.5
$1000–$1999	15.6
$2000–$2999	11.7
$3000 and over	18.0
Total	100.0

* Source: J. J. Corson and J. W. McConnell, *Economic Needs of Older People* (New York: Twentieth Century Fund, 1956), p. 36.

These writers suggest that more complete information on these sources of income would make our knowledge more precise and would probably show that "the average income of half the aged families though low was not inadequate; the other half clearly lack adequate income on their own" (p. 37).

Another way of analyzing the maintenance function from the standpoint of income is to compare the income of various age categories as shown in Table 6 and for various types of older families in Figure 1, chapter viii. The information presented in this table indicates a gradual rise in median income as people get older, reaching a maximum in the 35–44 age category. This is followed by a gradual tapering-off of income until in the age category 65 and over we observe a precipitous drop, reaching the lowest point of all the age categories above 20 years. Taking the aged as a total category, the general income picture clearly shows that a larger proportion of aged persons are in the low-income stratum than might be expected from their proportion in

the population. This is related, in large measure, to the fact that many older persons are no longer gainfully employed. Morever, there is a definite tendency for older persons who are gainfully employed to be downwardly mobile. Many older persons—some because of health reasons and others because of changes in job requirement—have obsolesced in terms of skills. The evidence is marshaled by Steiner and Dorfman (1957) in their analysis of the special follow-up survey of 3000 households conducted by the Bureau of the Census. Dorfman (1954) has summed up the situation succinctly: "What the data do show unambiguously is that men tend to be demoted to less skilled and less rewarding occupations before the end of their working careers, the signal exception being managerial occupations and proprietorship" (p. 639).

ATTITUDES AND VALUES AND THE
MAINTENANCE FUNCTION

What are the implications of a decline in income for families consisting of older persons? Changes of this kind suggest for

TABLE 6*

MEDIAN INCOME OF MEN
ACCORDING TO AGE, 1952

Age	Median Income
20–24	$2137
25–34	3493
35–44	3709
45–54	3486
55–64	3009
65 and over	1247

* Source: *Social Security Bulletin,* **17** (October 1954), 6 (offprint). Adapted from U.S. Bureau of the Census, *Current Population Reports, Consumer Income* (Series P-60, No. 14), Table 3.

the older members of the family a definite change in the standard of living, as discussed in chapter viii, "Aging and Income Security." A decline in income and a loss of occupation at any stage of life involve major readjustments in the expenditure pattern and in the general style of life. Expenditures for basic necessities—

food, shelter, medical care—may have to be sharply curtailed in order for a family to live on the reduced available resources. This is an obvious result, but a more subtle and perhaps equally pervasive dimension of declining income in late maturity is the possibility that lifelong attitudes and values which are class-bound may have to be modified or adapted to the altered stratification position.

By values we refer to the bases or premises upon which major life-decisions are made—those orientations which determine what is good or desirable.[13] Systems of values vary according to class position in American society, and the values of one class may seem to merge with those of another as one approaches the rather indefinite boundaries which separate the classes. However, there is evidence that differences are present and that they persist through time, and the differences between the top and bottom strata are the most striking.

Behavior and attitudes are interwoven with the values which become deeply imbedded in character and personality. Because the aged have adhered to a set of values over a longer period of time than other members of society, they are probably more resistant to change, and, yet, as we have shown previously, large numbers of the old are downwardly mobile. Large numbers of the aged thus may complete the life-cycle as members of a lower economic strata. For example, persons of middle-class origin are likely to retain the attitudes and values of their original class. Thus there arises a necessity to adjust attitudes and probably behavior to the realities of a different economic stratum. This is a type of change which does not take place smoothly or easily because it means giving up beliefs and sentiments which have been integral to a way of life for many years. Studies of families in time of economic depression suggest, for example, that there is a definite relationship between a

man's role as economic provider and his authority in the family (Angell, 1936; Cavan and Ranck, 1938; Komarovsky, 1940).

Here is a point at which the placement function and the maintenance function are closely interwoven, and an understanding of this interrelation may add insight into the social situation of the aged. One might hypothesize, for example, that persons who experience a drop in income with little change in attitudes and values are less likely to seek publicly supported medical or psychological services. The probabilities are high that, in order to avoid the conflict of needs and values, the person will meet the dilemma by inaction. It would be unrealistic to expect a complete shift in values on the part of the middle-class person from those which have stressed economic independence for a lifetime to those which accept readily free or low-cost services from a public agency.

We have shown that one of the obvious and objective aspects of later maturity is a sharp reduction in income. However, it seems to be fairly well agreed by some students of later maturity that one's objective or true income must be interpreted in terms of the needs and wants of the family. The same amount of income may be adequate for one family and be considered to be grossly inadequate by another family. Thus the person studying the maintenance function in later maturity must be aware of the subjective aspects of income. In a society in which the family tends to be primarily a unit of consumption, it is very significant that one view the subjective aspects of income from the standpoint of both husband and wife as family members. For in American society the wife tends to be the family member primarily involved in day-to-day expenditure of income. Thus the wife, perhaps more than the husband, may have to make the minor modifications in accommodating family consumption patterns to a reduced family income. The decline in income may have obvious consequences which affect the way

---

[13] For a general discussion of values in American society see Williams (1951, pp, 372–442).

in which the maintenance function is fulfilled. However, it seems important that we view the changes in the maintenance function in other than materialistic terms. For persons who view the situation in terms of "the economic man" of classical economics, the answer is rather simple: provide an adequate income for the period of later maturity. But this is a simple answer to a more complex question, partly because there are variable standards of what constitutes income adequacy.[14] Moreover, these standards are highly interrelated with lifetime patterns of how the family should be maintained.

The period of income decline and increasing economic dependency is undoubtedly of great significance in studying families at the end of the life-cycle. However, in the post-parental period, when children have left the parental home and have established their own homes (and presumably before the parents' retirement), there occurs a situation in which the older generation are able to help their married children. Sussman (1953a) made a study of the help patterns in 97 middle-class families, and he found that parents were very willing to give financial and other assistance to their newly married children, particularly in order to aid them in becoming established at the parental class level. The study concludes that parents made no attempt to subsidize their children on a permanent basis and that, when help was given in moderate amounts, it did not create family conflict. Indeed, the parents reported their children were more appreciative of financial and other aid after marriage than they had been at earlier periods in their lives. Although the Sussman study is confined to a rather restricted segment of the population, it seems probable that a similar help pattern may be found among working-class families, especially if we consider that there is greater kinship interaction among the lower class than the middle class (Dotson, 1951).

F. The Placement Function

THE ASCRIPTIVE ROLE OF THE FAMILY

The study of the relationship between stratification and the family in later maturity is another relatively untapped research area. Much remains to be done in terms of basic conceptualization and analysis and also in the area of empirical investigation.

A universal feature of the family is the status-conferring function, for in all societies a person receives his initial position in the social structure by virtue of his relationship to his immediate family. In rigid systems of stratification, such as those of caste, one's initial position tends to remain relatively fixed for life. However, in complex industrialized societies individual ability, motivations, and achievements may play a more important part in determining a person's ultimate position in the system. When a person marries and moves upward (or downward) in the stratification system, the family which he establishes (his family of procreation) has the same class position as the head of the household, for the family's class position is fundamentally a matter of the significant social role which the head of the household performs.

The functional importance of similar status positions for family members is understood when one takes into account other major family functions—bearing children, providing for their sustenance, and rearing them according to the appropriate cultural standards—for differential prestige and class position of family members is potentially disruptive of family unity for carrying out these interrelated family functions. The truth of Schumpeter's (1951) observation is clear: "The family, not the physical person, is the true unit of class and class theory" (p. 148).

[14] The problem of how to finance a reasonable income for older families is a complicated question of public policy. Corson and McConnell (1956, pp. 419–62) suggest that the economy of the country can provide for the non-working aged at an increasingly higher level.

SOCIAL MOBILITY AND STATUS DISCREPANCY

Social stratification, like other major aspects of the social order, Barber (1957) points out, can be discussed in at least three different ways: structure, function, and process. Structure refers to the general patterning of social behavior and cultural rules; function involves the way in which various parts of the social order are related to each other and the manner in which these functional correlates tend to minimize social disorganization; process is the study of those aspects involving social change. Of these three points of view, the processual seems to be the most relevant for studying the family in later maturity, while the first two aspects are stable and do not present as unique a problem. It may seem somewhat paradoxical at first glance that in studying stratification at the end of the life-cycle a major interest is in the processual. The common-sense approach suggests that, since old age tends to involve a slowing-down of bodily processes and social activity, statics are the major focus of interest. However, a more careful appraisal indicates that this slowing-down is the very source of change. Therefore, in studying social stratification of aged and aging families, our major focus is the movement of families and family members up or down the class, status, and power hierarchy. This shift in rank in any of the dimensions of social stratification is called "social mobility."[15]

Most mobility studies have been concerned with class mobility and have used broad shifts in occupation categories as indicators of change. These changes in occupational status can be studied in two ways: (1) the changes which take place in the

life of an individual and (2) the changes that occur from one generation to the other, from father to son.

The amount of mobility in the United States is great compared to other societies, particularly career mobility, that is, the movement of individuals during a lifetime. However, the over-all result of this mobility is movement upward or downward of only a short distance. People tend to advance during their careers, but they do not advance very far (Lipset and Bendix, 1952). In summarizing a wide variety of evidence, Barber (1957) concludes: "A large minority, and perhaps even a majority, consisting of up to two-thirds of the population, move up or down at least a little in the class structure in every generation" (p. 468).

The major corollary of this important social fact is that vertical mobility may tend to reduce family continuity and thus become a disorganizing factor in American family life. LeMasters (1954) is one of the few who has explored this subject, and his findings suggest that families having social class continuity "are the families in which aged parents live with their grown children with considerable consensus and mutual enjoyment." In other words, if the parental generation has different class and status ranking from that of their children, we hypothesize that there would be a lower degree of family solidarity. This may be seen as disorganization from the standpoint of individual family units. However, it is a stubborn sociological principle that the family must be congruent with the other major institutional structures of the society; and in American society social and physical mobility are very compatible with an isolated conjugal form of the family. It should be added that survey data from the Cornell Study of Retirement suggest that upward mobility of children may not necessarily affect family cohesion in an adverse fashion (Streib, 1958).[16]

[15] Social or vertical mobility is usually distinguished from horizontal or physical mobility, the movement of persons and families from place to place. In this discussion it will not be relevant to review the large amount of research in the field of vertical mobility. Three references are particularly valuable: Bendix and Lipset (1953, pp. 371–500), Kahl (1957, pp. 251–98), and Barber (1957, pp. 334–477).

[16] See also, in this chapter, the section on "The Older Generation and Their Children: Their Interrelationship."

G. The Affectional Function

We have seen that some of the functions of the family decline in importance in the older family. However, as we turn to the fifth function of the family—the affectional —we are studying one which continues to meet important needs of the older person. The emphasis on companionship and affection between marital partners tends to be found in societies in which there is relative equality of the sexes and in which choice of marriage partners tends to be an individual rather than a family decision. As Sumner (1906) has said, "The notion that a man's wife is the nearest person in the world to him is a relatively modern notion, and one which is restricted to a comparatively small part of the human race" (p. 364).

THE SOCIOLOGICAL ANALYSIS: APPLICATION OF THE ROLE CONCEPT

The first step in our analysis is to offer some specification of the nature of the affectional or companionship function. Affection in the family is commonly associated with two major periods: the period of romantic exploration and attachment of youth and young adults culminating in marriage and the period of socialization when the child is lavished with love and attention. In the present analysis, however, affection is not considered to be confined to conventional demonstrations of warmth and affection, either verbal or physical, for we are interested in presenting a point of view which can aid in studying affectional or companionship aspects of the family at any stage of the life-cycle. Thus, in order to offer an approach which is distinctly sociological, we have selected the concept of role as central for our analysis of the affectional function. Havighurst (1957) has conducted perhaps the most complete analysis of the social roles of middle-aged and older persons. Quantitative records were obtained from interviewing 234 persons on the nine major roles which a person may

perform. In the present context it is pertinent to point out that the family-centered role pattern shows "an expenditure of energy and a quality of performance" which is much higher than in the non-family area (p. 337).

Wilson and Kolb (1949) offer a traditional definition of role: "a pattern of behavior corresponding to a system of rights and duties associated with a particular position in a social group" (p. 208).[17] The word "duty" conveys one of the essential components of role. In other words, we can say that a role is composed of behavioral patterns which a person is *expected* to play in a relationship. However, role, as it is being employed here, has one other important ingredient in addition to the idea of duty, namely, the notion of reciprocation or reciprocal responses. This aspect of role has suggested to Cottrell and others that roles provide a self-other context for studying human behavior.

A question which follows from this definition of role is: What determines the expectations which define roles in the family or, for that matter, roles in any particular social system? Roles are defined by (1) norms present in a given cultural or subcultural group and (2) the personal or individual definition of role expectations. Cottrell has called these two distinct but related aspects of role "cultural roles" and "unique roles." An example of the cultural dimension of a role is that a mother is expected to behave like a "good mother," who is concerned with the health, welfare, and growth of her children. A large measure of what constitutes these expectations for a good mother are defined by the gen-

[17] Cottrell (1942) had defined the concept somewhat more precisely, although more academically, when he said a role is "an internally consistent series of conditioned responses by one member of a social situation which represents the stimulus pattern for a similarly internally consistent series of conditioned responses of the other(s) in that situation" (p. 617). This chapter is not the proper context for a review of the variant definitions and usages of role. For a historical survey see Neiman and Hughes (1951).

eral norms of the society and more specifically by the class, religious, or other subgroups which constitute a significant part of a particular mother's social affiliations. However, there are also *unique* aspects derived from the mother's own childhood and socialization which affect the way in which she personally defines this role.

The gamut of marital roles is very wide in American society. As Merrill (1949) has observed, conjugal affection in this country and related cultures means that husband and wife are expected to be "friends, lovers, playmates, companions, confidants, business partners, and practical nurses to each other, to name but a few of the expectations subsumed under the concept" (p. 249). The role of the wife, for example, may change as her husband gets older and becomes a retiree. At the level of physical needs the wife in later maturity might be expected to provide a special type of diet for her husband, to insure that he gets adequate rest, and to plan activities which are compatible with his declining physical energy. In later maturity these role expectations are sharply altered by gradual or by critical physical, social, and economic changes. Some of these expectations are rather clearly defined by society, and others tend to be somewhat vague at this time.

In the family there are obviously strong emotional overtones to roles and role expectations. This is particularly true of a society like the United States, in which families are established on the basis of personal, emotional, or romantic factors. By way of brief summary, one can say that social roles are founded in the mores, but their expressions and particular instances bear the stamp of the individual's own personality and social situation.

Analyzing the affectional function in terms of roles and role expectations offers a much broader orientation than what is true if a more traditional framework is used. By this approach we are able to see the conjugal roles in old age in a more dynamic way and not merely as a series of traits or characteristics. This approach also avoids the tendency to view marital relations at the later end of the life-cycle in conventional romantic terms similar to those employed when studying the earlier phases of the family cycle. It is commonly thought that, if the initial choice has been the correct one, a satisfactory marriage and a high degree of conjugal affection will result. As Merrill has clearly stated: "Conjugal affection and its attendant social roles are not the spontaneous efflorescences of youthful ardor. Conjugal affection arises from personality development, mutual concessions, and a long series of mutual adaptations" (p. 249).

In writing about the family over a half-century ago, one of the founding fathers of American sociology, William Graham Sumner (1906), described the way in which social expectations are involved in a high level of conjugal affection. He said: "It depends on the way in which each pair arranges its affairs, develops its sentiments, and forms its habits; conjugal affection makes great demands on the good sense, spirit of accommodation, and good nature of each" (p. 363). We might ask what types of behavior facilitate satisfactory enactment of the conjugal roles. It is probably not necessary to emphasize that there are no magic formulas or list of characteristics which could serve as a handbook in these matters. Foote and Cottrell (1955), have offered some major guidelines in their discussion of interpersonal competence and its components, particularly empathy, autonomy, and creativity. These writers emphasize that satisfactory family relationships are not the result of cultivating ingrained virtues and fixed traits, for "competence denotes capabilities to meet and deal with a changing world, to formulate ends and implement them" (p. 49). This is especially true in the case of families composed of older persons, where flexibility may be required in order to learn roles after retirement or as a result of changes in living due to illness or economic stress.

To summarize, let us emphasize that, in studying the affectional function in later maturity, we place the major emphasis upon mutually understood expectations of the husband and wife role, and the ways in which these expectations are fulfilled in day-to-day interaction, and not on conventional demonstrations of romantic affection and love. Analytically, we view the affectional function in terms of (1) whether or not the expectations are understood and (2) whether or not there is reciprocation or satisfaction of the expectations by the spouse or others in the family setting. When expectations are both understood and reciprocated by the spouse, or other family members, affectional relations tend to be functionally satisfying. This enhances the person's feeling of identity and thus is meaningful to the individual involved and also increases stable social relations in general. Thus even bickering and quarreling, when analyzed from this standpoint, may be functionally meaningful and may not be an index of family disunity.

However, satisfying relationships cannot exist unless they have been developed throughout a long period of time. Havighurst's (1957) study of social competence in middle-aged persons concludes that "a person's pattern of role performance or 'life style' is established in early middle age—by the 40's—and tends to persist into the late 60's at least" (p. 343). On the basis of retrospective interviews, Fried and Stern (1948) concluded that unhappy marriages had been more or less unsatisfactory from the start and that there is the definite possibility that they will deteriorate with advancing age.

RELEVANT RESEARCH FINDINGS

CONJUGAL RELATIONS

Fried and Stern (1948) report on a study of middle-aged and aged families in a large Canadian city in which they selected a survey population according to socioeconomic status, sex, and age. They observed a decline in marital satisfactions in those families in which the departure of children from the home increased the parent's feelings of

isolation, because the rearing of the children had been the chief focus of interest. In terms of the framework we have presented, this is a clear case in which changed expectations regarding familial roles have not been redefined by the family members in terms of the changes in the family cycle. The same writers offer evidence which suggests that an increase in marital satisfaction may result even when retirement or serious illness occurs. Their data show that in terms of role expectations the older person who is afflicted expects special attention and is gratified by the increased protection and attention, and the other person finds fulfilment in the new expectations because of increased feelings of usefulness. The Fried and Stern study suggests also that changes in expectations regarding sex may affect general marital satisfaction. Some women subjects who had incomplete sexual experience during marriage reported a more satisfactory sexual experience as a result of decreased demands on the part of the husband. Fried and Stern report: "Where they formerly resented sexual demands of their husbands, they now welcomed the modified sexual expectations" (p. 35). Moreover, in writing about one subgroup of the study population, in which sexual intercourse decreased, they report that "the women tend to be satisfied about the diminished demands and slower rhythm of their husbands, and the marital situation has actually improved" (p. 37). The emphasis again is on behavior which squares with reciprocal expectations.

Perhaps one of the most surprising findings of the Canadian study, because it contradicts the findings of other investigators, is that older unmarried subjects did not suffer from the lack of companionship which marriage offers.[18] The investigators explain this finding in psychological terms by pointing out that these persons develop

[18] Havighurst and Albrecht (1953) report, for example, that married men and women living with spouse "have strikingly superior adjustment scores over those who are widowed or single" (p. 317). See also Kutner et al. (1956, p. 67).

a "compensatory attachment" with persons of their own generation which "appeared very strong, and did not seem to be exposed to the same hazards and strains as attachments to mates and children" (p. 53). From the standpoint of a sociological analysis, this is another way of stating that single older persons may have substitute family relations which are based on expectations, which are congruent with the realities of their social situation, and which, also, are fulfilled in a satisfactory manner.

PARENT-CHILD RELATIONS

Another important aspect of the affectional function in later maturity involves the relationship of parents and their children. These relationships can be considered and understood by the same analytical scheme involving role expectations and fulfilment which was outlined for studying conjugal relations. Unfortunately, there are no systematic studies which might be cited, but there are several preliminary investigations which are suggestive. Some of the findings from Albrecht's study of a small midwestern community can be reanalyzed from this point of view, as can Koller's studies of three-generational families. Albrecht (1954a) reports that aged parents are not likely to become dependent upon their children. She found that the great majority of older parents in her study (85 per cent) are independent of their children but maintain somewhat close social and affectional ties. This appears to indicate that there is mutual understanding of the role expectations involved and fulfilment of them. Similar findings were found in the Cornell Study, as will be reported later on in this chapter.

Townsend (1957), in studying a lower-class London community, reports similar findings. However, he added an interesting interpretation to why so few parents complained of neglect by their children. He observes, "Old people often talked of children's neglect of their parents, but hardly ever were these children their own. They

liked to believe the loyalty of their own family was exceptional" (p. 95). In studying this phase of family life from the standpoint of the children's expectations, Koller (1954) reports ambivalence on the part of children toward the creation of three-generation households. This is a case where role expectations are not clearly defined by the society and where each family has to work out some means for defining the appropriate role definition. Smith (1954) reports similar findings in his study of two Pennsylvania cities. In the area of financial assistance there is evidence for ambiguity of role expectations as shown in the California study conducted by Bond and his associates (1954). These investigators divided the parents over 65 into those who feel children should be required to support needy parents and those parents who think children should not be required to do so. They report that about the same proportion of children for each category of parents *urge* their parents to apply for old age assistance. Bond and his colleagues observe that presumably "the opinions of parents regarding such filial obligations have little effect on the desires of their offspring" (p. 300).

Sussman (1955) reports on another aspect of parent-child relations pertaining to mutual role expectations which are congruent with those reported above. In this study of 103 middle-class, white, Protestant families judged "well adjusted," in which 97 of the families had one or more married children living away from home, the author reports that parents were pleased with the new freedom of the post-parental period. This study of a selected population shows that older persons do not need to initiate new activities in later maturity. The data indicate that, if parents and children reside within approximately a 50-mile radius of each other and maintain harmonious relations, the parents experience little change in their activity patterns and evidence little need to substitute new activities for family activities (pp. 340–41). An exploratory study reported by Rose (1955) suggests a somewhat contradictory view on the need for new activities in the post-parental period. On the basis of 208 questionnaires completed by the mothers of college students, Rose concludes that having a job and participating in organizational activities are substitute roles which increase satisfaction among middle-class, middle-age women. He concludes tentatively that "the life satisfaction of middle-class women as they enter middle age is a function of the degree to which they are able to assume another central role to substitute for their necessarily declining role as homemakers" (p. 19). Here again is another area for further research.

IN-LAW RELATIONS

A striking example of the failure of older persons to understand their role expectations is in regard to in-law relationships, particularly the role of mother-in-law. Duvall (1954) offers convincing evidence of the hostility aroused by mothers-in-law. She reports that mothers-in-law are much more likely than all other in-laws to be considered meddlesome, possessive, nagging, and a host of other undesirable characteristics. All these unfavorable characteristics are manifestations of the failure of the mother-in-law to appraise correctly the role expectations which are involved. Conflict with mother-in-law is undoubtedly an example of the inability of the older woman to accept a reversal of roles; that is, she fails to realize that she is no longer the parent in control over her child and that, when children marry and establish their own homes, they should be recognized as independent and autonomous. In fact, in some cases it may be necessary for the younger person to act as "parent" for his own father or mother. Research may help to clarify to what extent the stereotype of the mother-in-law may influence the naming of the mother-in-law as the most difficult of in-laws. As Duvall suggests, "It may represent in part a reflection of the mother-in-law stereotype that *creates a certain expectancy* of difficulty with mother-in-law" (p. 216). (Italics ours.)

An important phase of the relations between the older generation and younger in-laws begins, in a sense, before the legal marital formalities are completed, for the relationships between a future son-in-law or daughter-in-law and the parents of the spouse begin during the courtship and engagement period. Bates (1942) has shown that parents, particularly mothers, may play a crucial role in the courtship of their children by trying to influence the choice of a marital partner. In general, parents are more concerned with the daughter's than the son's potential spouse.

Sussman's (1953*b*) work has also indicated how parents may influence the choice of mates of their children. Parental influence was particularly pronounced when a child planned to marry a person of a lower class or of a different ethnic or cultural background. Eighty-one per cent of the cases in which such a possibility occurred admitted they either persuaded or threatened their children with withdrawal of support during the time when they were courting persons the parents did not approve (p. 79).

Parents are apprehensive about the choice of mate of their children because they feel that "selection of a mate of a similar race, class and cultural background is important to harmonious intergenerational family relationships" (pp. 80–81). These findings point clearly to the importance of similar expectations between older parents and their children as a factor enhancing continuity and satisfaction in family relations (Sussman, 1954).

DEATH AND BEREAVEMENT

Widowhood is an important area for research in relation to the family and old age because of the sheer number of persons involved. The 1950 census data show that the 3.5 million widows constituted over one-fourth of the population 65 and over (Sheldon, 1958). However, widowhood is clearly a sex differentiated phenomenon for, at ages 60–64, 75 per cent of the men are still married but only about 57 per cent of the women. And in the category of persons 65 and over, the difference between the sexes is even greater, for 62 per cent of the men are married compared with 33 per cent of the women (p. 91). Moreover, as Sheldon points out, "unless the trends in male and female mortality are sharply reversed, the excess of women over men at the upper ages will increase, and our older population will contain a larger and larger proportion of widows" (p. 93).

In terms of the framework previously outlined, widowhood and bereavement can be fruitfully studied. It is striking that this inevitable and universal phase of life should be so patently neglected as an area of serious study.[19] One obvious reason for the neglect is that in the United States, as in many other societies, there are strong taboos associated with death. These taboos are inculcated early; their influence tends to persist throughout the life-cycle; and, as a result, there are resistances if one wishes to study the subject. However, if we view death in terms of role expectations, there is obviously abrupt and final termination of social relations. Here is a critical situation where it is necessary for a person to develop a radically new set of expectations regarding family roles if the person is to have satisfactory relations with those who are still living and also to maintain a satisfactory degree of personal adjustment. Thus, after the period of bereavement,

[19] Illustrative of this neglect is the fact that in Shock (1951, 1957) there are virtually no references to the subject. In the first volume, "death," "bereavement," and "widow" do not even appear in the Index, and only the latter subject is cited in the supplement. References to the latter are largely to statistical studies published in the *Statistical Bulletin of the Metropolitan Life Insurance Company*. Mention should be made of the pioneering work of Eliot (1955). Eliot refers to popular articles and also to more serious works, notably his own. A number of recent studies of later maturity have given brief attention to the subject. See, e.g., Havighurst and Albrecht (1953, pp. 154–61). See also the recent study by Marris (1958) in England.

there must be some type of reintegration of roles. The diverse ways in which this is accomplished remains an intriguing area for further study.

Among the few studies about widowhood, perhaps the most systematic is Fitzelle's (1952), in which he investigated by interviews and questionnaires the adjustment of 76 middle-class widows aged 59 and over. He found that the area in which widows felt the greatest need in adjusting to their present situation was the "need to love and to be loved" (pp. 305–6). However, Fitzelle reports that his respondents seemed to be somewhat defensive when questioned concerning family relations. Many of the women had infrequent contacts with relatives; this was probably related to the fact that most of the widows favored non-interference in the lives of relatives. One stereotyped notion regarding widows which is disproved by his research findings is that widows tend to revere their husbands' memories, even if the marriages had not been close (p. 96).

IV. THE PERSPECTIVE OF THE OLDER GENERATION

A. How the Family Is Defined

In the preceding sections we have made the point that the present older generation has been oriented to a conjugal type of family from their youth, and we have discussed the role of the older person in the realization of the several social functions within the contemporary family context. In part, our perspective rests upon empirical data. Largely, however, our conclusions are from the perspective of the sociologist. Yet, clearly, the older person's definition of the situation is crucial for his behavior and adjustment. Does the perception of older people, then, bear out the analytical statements which the systematic observer makes? Or do older people hold a discrepant view, one which in general describes a considerably different institutional context?

B. Research Findings concerning the Perspective of the Older Generation

THE OLDER PERSON'S VIEW

At first glance, it would appear that our emphasis on conjugality has been misplaced. Not only is there considerable contact with all family members but also continued contact with siblings is nearly as great as contact with children who have left home.[20] Among the nearly 2300 active participants in the Cornell Study of Occupational Retirement, 76 per cent of those who have siblings have kept in contact with all their brothers and sisters; only 10 per cent more, 86 per cent, of those with children have kept in touch with all their adult children. However, when asked whether the respondent and his siblings form a close family group, and whether the respondent and his children form a close family group, quite a different picture emerges (Table 7). While contact seems to continue through the years, close ties with siblings are reported as appreciably less frequent than with children. Moreover, this conjugal orientation relates to a conjugal pattern of behavior, for frequency in seeing relatives follows a declining order as follows:

	Per Cent
See children often	75
See grandchildren often	70
See sisters often	36
See brothers often	30
See nieces often	25
See nephews often	23
See cousins often	12

In part, frequency of interaction reflects sheer accessibility, for children typically live close enough to be seen frequently, while siblings as often as not do not live that close. Yet this fact in itself is relevant to the argument that the older generation characteristically holds a conjugal orientation to family relationships. The picture is one of separation and dispersal from the hearth and home of the older person's family of orientation.

In general, then, one garners the impression that the meaningful family unit for the present-day older generation is constituted of their children and grandchildren and themselves. But a subtle point might here be raised as to whether this reflects a normative orientation or whether it is more accurately understood as a by-product of participation in the existing social organization of the family. To put it another way, given the present conjugal organization of the family, could it be that lack of a close relationship with siblings is a matter of default and that attention is directed toward children to the exclusion of siblings *in spite of* the familial norms the individual holds? Are there survivals of a more nearly consanguineous pattern in the norms of the older generation, or is there absence of any feelings that one should maintain ties with one's brothers and sisters?

When relevant data are examined, some support is found for the hypothesis that survivals of the earlier normative patterns can be found within the present older generation's attitudes. For instance, having no children makes a difference in the proportion who feel a close relationship to siblings. Those without children are significantly more likely to indicate that their relationship with siblings is very close (Table 8). Moreover, one should not pass lightly over the fact that only about a quarter indicate that they and their siblings do not

[20] The empirical data reported here are from the Cornell Study of Occupational Retirement panel studies. This research was first supported by the Lilly Endowment, Inc., and more recently has been supported by the National Institutes of Health, Grant M-1196. The panel of respondents from whom these data have been gathered do not constitute a representative cross-section of America's population of like age but rather are more exclusively urban, employees or former employees of the larger industrial concerns, relatively more often professionals and white-collar workers, and, in general, somewhat higher in social status and of better adjustment than the population as a whole. Thus the findings reported here should be considered as approximations offering hypotheses as to the typical pattern rather than a statistically reliable representation of that typical pattern.

form a close family group, even though there are children who may form the center of their attention. Although ties to siblings may be of considerably less significance than ties to children, they do remain; and a sense of loss characterizes many of those whose links with brothers and sisters have become attenuated. This

TABLE 7

CLOSENESS OF FAMILY TIES
(Per Cent)

Item	Respondent and Children	Respondent and Siblings
"We are very close"......	73	35
"We are somewhat close"..	22	39
"We are not a close family group"................	5	26
Total................	100	100
No. of cases...........	1692	1865

is pointed up effectively in interviews in which respondents speak with nostalgia of earlier days and with disappointment of the present. The words of a respondent from a small midwestern city are fairly typical:

Every now and then you get to wondering how things can change so fast and so much. You asked me about my brothers and my sisters. Well, there never were a bunch of kids any closer than we were when we were growing up —helped one another, played together, fought like anything, and all the things that people who are really close do. I often get to thinking about the fun we had and you sort of wish it could have lasted longer. I don't know how come, but except for my brother in [a nearby city], I don't really keep in touch at all. I suppose it's because we all have our own families now, but it does seem a shame somehow.

Or, as it is expressed in dozens of interviews, "I don't keep in touch with my [siblings] as I should." The conclusion seems inescapable that the vestiges of norms concerning mutual obligation among siblings live on in the present older generation. But they have been largely superseded by the "new look" in intrafamilial relationships.

The quotation which we have included above is directed toward the point that survivals of earlier family allegiances persist; but we might equally as well have emphasized the phrase, "our own families," for it is a phrase almost inevitably used in this context, and its frequency bespeaks the manner in which the older generation actually defines the family.

In sum, evidence seems to point to the fact that, in the perspective of the older generation, the family largely is defined as the conjugal unit formed by their own marriage. Family orientation primarily encompasses the family of procreation of the older generation, and only in a much smaller way does their own family of orientation serve as the focus of family relationships. Even then, it serves primarily in the memory and good intentions of those who retain such norms.

TABLE 8

CLOSENESS OF TIES WITH SIBLINGS AMONG THOSE WHO DO NOT HAVE CHILDREN AND AMONG THOSE WHO DO HAVE CHILDREN

(Per Cent)

Item	Respondents without Children	Respondents with Children
"We [siblings and respondent] are very close".....	48	31
"We are somewhat close"..	33	42
"We are not a close family group"................	19	27
Total................	100	100
No. of cases...........	466	1398

THE OLDER GENERATION AND THEIR CHILDREN: NORMATIVE PERSPECTIVE

If, then, the relationship with children is considered the key family relationship for older people, what is its content? Could it be that considering ties with children to be close is a matter of whistling in the dark, a one-way street in which the aging parent is vulnerable and risks being left high and dry when the children form families of *their* own? Is there any evidence which reveals anxiety in this respect or indicates that the close ties are rather empty ones from which little satisfaction can be derived?

Basically, the question is one of the coincidence of the behavior expressed in the relationships with the children and of the norms which are held concerning these relationships. It is the person who expects more than he actually receives who finds a relationship unsatisfactory. Thus it is a matter of just what the older generation ex-

TABLE 9

Expectations of Parents from
Adult Children

(Percentage Who Agree)

Statement	Per Cent
"Children should visit their parents frequently"	84
"Children should write their parents often"	82
"Children should take care of their parents when they are ill"	61
"Children should 'help their parents'"	44
"Children should ask their parents to visit them often"	27
"Children should live close to their parents"	12

pects of their children and the extent to which their expectations are realized in practice.

The participants in the Cornell study were asked what they considered children should be expected to do in relationship to their parents. A tabulation of the affirmative responses is shown in Table 9. At the top of the list are those activities which contribute to the maintenance of affectional ties and are symbolic of continued respect and love on the part of the children. The point is further supported by the fact that fully 95 per cent agree with the statement, "Even when children have families of their own they should keep in close contact with their parents." In the usual case, children represent the greatest psychological investment the parents have made, excepting perhaps, in their turn, their grand-

children, with whom typically there are ties of affection untempered by direct responsibility. In fact, children and grandchildren may be rather accurately conceptualized as extensions of the parent's self. Successes of the children are an increment to parental ego, and, similarly, difficulties encountered by the children are threatening also to the parent. In other words, a considerable range of joys and sorrows of the parent may be vicarious in nature. It might be hypothesized that this is particularly the case in the later years, and it is at least conceivable that such vicarious experience is one of the key factors in the adjustment of older people. It is only natural, therefore, that maintaining ties with children is considered of first importance and that expecting children to share their experiences by keeping in close contact is a social norm held by the overwhelming majority of older persons.

At the same time, the kind of contact which the older person feels should be maintained is strictly of the "hands-off" variety. In nearly a hundred interviews, almost without exception, independence and non-interference were stressed as the key to successful intergenerational relationships.

In the Pennsylvania study, previously cited, all *three* generations were interviewed, and the researchers report that the respondents "indicate that it is appropriate for older people to maintain an active interest in the family, but also to relinquish some family and personal responsibilities as necessary" (Smith *et al.*, 1958, p. 31). The generality of these beliefs is indicated also by the relatively small number in Table 9 who indicate that children should ask parents to visit and that children should live close to their parents. In the eyes of these older persons, at least, children should be imbued with an achievement orientation and should seek this success in independent, conjugal families of their own. A fuller picture of the older parents' points of view is documented in their responses to a series of questions concerned with the proper courses of action which children should follow (Table 10). Close contact in family relationships evidently is considered equally important with getting ahead in the world as a goal; and 45 per cent consider that such closeness can be realized by having adult children, but presumably *unmarried* adult children, living at home. But the *kind* of close contact which is deemed important evidently is not thought to be jeopardized by spatial separation, for overwhelmingly the respondents seem to believe that financial opportunity away from home is wholly worth pursuing. Moreover, the sacrosanctity of the families formed by the marriage of children is almost unanimously respected. Even when the statement is "loaded" by inclusion of the phrase "when parents need help," only 8 per cent hold that moving in with married children is a solution. Incidentally, it should be remembered throughout that these are the responses of people who are very nearly 70 years old.

Somewhere intermediate between affectional contact and non-interference as specifications of intergenerational norms are those activities which are somewhat more specific in quality than closeness but which are nevertheless possible without loss of independence. These fall under the category of mutual help, with financial assistance most often being the referent for the older person. There is no question that affectional ties are generally considered more important than the more objective responsibilities implied in financial assistance or, put in more general terms, "help for parents." When asked to indicate whether ties of affection or financial help is the more important, only 2 per cent responded that the latter was the more important, while 62 per cent responded that ties of affection are more important. However, the remaining 36 per cent contended that the two are equally important, pointing up the fact that a concrete expression of responsibility is still held as a norm by a great many people. At the same time, responsibility for *extensive* financial assistance to parents is rarely assumed, which further confirms the contention that the older generation's orienta-

tion is largely approving of conjugality (Table 11). In fact, the family is placed fourth, following governmental sources and employer, in the rank order of who should provide for the older person who has stopped working, "if he needs help in taking care of his problems" (Table 12). The important exception to this pattern is the responsibility of the children to their parents when the latter are ill. In such cases filial obligation to provide concrete assistance is more frequently expressed as a norm by the older generation, in the sense

TABLE 10

PARENTAL NORMS CONCERNING ACHIEVEMENT, CONTACT, AND LIVING ARRANGEMENTS

(Percentage Who Agree)

Statement	Per Cent
"Getting ahead in the world can be a bad thing if it keeps your family from being close"	49
"When children have become adults it is still nice to have them live at home with their parents"	45
"Children should not allow better financial opportunities elsewhere to take them away from their parents"	10
"When parents get older and need help they should be asked to move in with their married children"	8
"Even when children are married it is nice to have them living with their parents"	5

either that children actually should take care of their ailing parents or that children should contribute to the payment of medical costs. In fact, responsibility of children is placed second only to federal governmental responsibility for providing help if needed in meeting medical expenses (Table 12).

We have cited this as an exception to the general rule, but upon closer examination one might question whether this is, in fact, the case. In our culture, illness is considered an occasion for heightened emotional support from friends and relations, a time for their expressing affection in greater measure than occurs day by day. Thus assistance for parents who are ill carries a different meaning for the older person and presumably for the children than the meaning of assistance in general. Even though the actual action which is taken (e.g., writing a check) is no different from less specific support, elements of personal regard enter into the relationship in larger measure. To put it another way, depersonalized

TABLE 11

CHILDREN'S RESPONSIBILITY FOR FINANCIAL ASSISTANCE

("If parents need financial assistance, how much should children be expected to help?")

	Per Cent
They should be expected to help a great deal.	8
They should be expected to help some.	50
They should be expected to help a little	33
They should not be expected to help.	9

care and assistance for the ill lacks an important ingredient necessary for more rapid recovery—so, at least, we would interpret the perspectives expressed by our respondents.

It is interesting in passing to note the discrepancy between the attitudes of older people and the legally enacted statements of obligation found in old age assistance provisions in the various states. As far as our respondents are concerned, the state as frequently as the family should be held to be responsible for providing for the older person (Table 12). Yet legal provisions, reflecting an older view of familial duties and a more conservative view of governmental responsibility, place prior obligation with the family.

Bond and his associates (1954) in their study of some 890 Californians 65 and older show clearly that 90 per cent of the parents feel that their children would be *willing* to help support them if they needed help, but only half of the parents think that they would be *able* to offer financial aid. Moreover, of those children able to help their parents, approximately one-third urged them to apply for old age assistance, and over another third were willing to have

them do so. Bond and his colleagues summarize the situation as follows: "Two-thirds of the children, in spite of their ability to help, are ready for others to assume the responsibility for part or all of the support of their parents" (pp. 297–98). In fourteen states assistance may be denied the older person if children are able to provide support, and in twenty-one additional states, although assistance is not denied, court action may be initiated against those children who fail to provide financial aid (Epler, 1954).[21] At least tentatively, it might be concluded that here is evidence of an instance of cultural lag, a case in which our cultural apparatus expressed in laws has not kept pace with the changing social order and the correlative attitudes of the people themselves. The significance of this point lies in the fact that the maintenance of family independence may be a

TABLE 12

RESPONSIBILITY FOR PROVISION FOR OLDER PERSON

("Who do you think should provide for the older person who has stopped working, if he needs help?")

	PER CENT	
	In Taking Care of His Problems	In Meeting His Medical Expenses
The federal government.	53	49
The company he worked for	45	36
Each state government.	34	35
His family.	33	42
His union.	17	18
The local government.	15	21
Community agencies.	11	18

more important value in this day and age than remaining independent of support from a governmental agency. If this is true, in those peripheral instances in which state laws, through enforcement, exert a pressure

[21] For a complete tabulation of specific provisions in the various states see U.S. Bureau of Public Assistance (1954).

toward dependence on relatives, considerable harm to good adjustment may result even though net financial rewards are higher by virtue of support both from the state and from relatives. It would not be well to dwell too considerably on this theme, for the number of cases in which such stresses would be so generated probably is relatively small. Yet these cases point up a problem of more general significance and, for those interested in clarifying the nature of intrafamilial relationships and good adjustment among older persons, may offer excellent instances for important research.

All in all, the evidence seems to show that the conjugal orientation which restricts the older generation's definition of family to their own family of procreation also permeates the patterns of expectations which they hold regarding their children. Although continuing contact and affectional ties are sought, for the most part those aged three score and ten wish independence for and from their children. These are the patterns which older persons believe should obtain; these are the norms which are held and which are expressive of the culture as it has been experienced by the older generation. But, as we have indicated above, the gap between what is believed *should be* and what actually *seems to be* is the measure of discontentment and dissatisfaction. In this instance it is the story of the extent to which intergenerational relationships are satisfactory or of the extent to which they are shot through with bitterness and a sense of neglect. We turn, therefore, to a consideration of the older generation's view of just what their family relationships are like in practice.

THE OLDER GENERATION AND THEIR
CHILDREN: THEIR INTER-
RELATIONSHIPS

Seemingly, relationships with their children are considered satisfactory by the aging parents who are participants in the Cornell study. As we have indicated above, nearly three-quarters of those with children claim a very close family relationship, and only a scant 5 per cent say that they and their children do not form a close family group (Table 7). Perhaps more significant, fully 92 per cent indicate that they believe that their children respect them as much as they should. In an important sense, this is a key measure of satisfaction in this interpersonal relationship, for respect implies both acceptance of the status accorded and approval of the manner in which the correlative role is performed. In other words, winning that measure of respect which "my children should have for me" means that children and parent have reached a consensus as to how each should stand vis-à-vis the other and that each has performed satisfactorily in terms of the standards set. We feel justified in minimizing those instances in which the parent naïvely is satisfied with the degree of respect accorded him even though from the children's perspective there is neither affection nor respect, for it might be hypothesized that, as the parent grows older and becomes less significant in the relationship with his children, he becomes increasingly sensitive to actions which might be construed as disrespectful or lacking in affection. In any event, feeling that children show sufficient respect evidently is a measure of the extent to which the children's performance squares with what the parent considers appropriate treatment from his children (Table 13).

Inspection of the number of cases in each of the categories in Table 12 is also to the point. An overwhelming proportion—1257, or fully 87 per cent of the respondents—indicate that all their children who have left home have kept in close contact. The full significance of this figure emerges when one recalls that this is a very widely held prescription for the behavior of children: 95 per cent agree that "after children have left home they should keep in close contact with their parents," and 95 per cent also agree that such contact should be maintained "even when children have families of their own." That the latter norm is realized also is clear from our findings. Of those whose children have "families of their own," 86 per cent indicate that all have kept in close contact, 11 per cent indicate that some have kept in close contact, and only 3 per cent indicate that none has done so.

It would also appear that the belief that children show sufficient respect is not affected by the social separation which potentially arises out of greater success of

TABLE 13

CONSISTENCY OF EXPECTATION AND PERFORMANCE AS RELATED TO BELIEF THAT CHILDREN SHOW SUFFICIENT RESPECT

(Among people who believe that "after children have left home they should keep in close contact with their parents")

ITEM	PER CENT		
	All of My Children Do [Keep in Close Contact]	Some Do	None Does
"My children have less respect than they should"	4	16	67
"My children respect me as much as they should"	96	84	33
Total..............	100	100	100
No. of cases.........	1257	167	24

the younger generation as compared with their parents. If anything at all, quite the reverse (Table 14). Those who say that none of their children has been more successful than themselves in earning a living and getting ahead in life are the most likely also to say that their children have less respect than they should. Similarly, closeness of familial relations evidently is not harmed by the greater success of offspring (Table 15). *In other words, the essentials of a proper and satisfactory relationship between these older parents and their children evidently take fully into account the precepts of an achievement-oriented society; and the success of relationships between parent and children is not negatively affected by the fulfilment of achievement norms.* Putting it another, perhaps more pointed, way, the older generation is as fully imbued with an achievement orientation as their children and expect—and enjoy—intrafamilial relationships which allow for the possibility that children may exceed their parents in accomplishing some of the more importantly valued goals in American society.

In many other respects it is clear that expectations and practice roughly coincide. Compare, for example, the fact that it is widely believed that children should "visit their parents frequently" (84 per cent) and

TABLE 14

DIFFERENTIAL SUCCESS OF PARENTS AND CHILDREN AS RELATED TO BELIEF THAT CHILDREN SHOW SUFFICIENT RESPECT

("In earning a living and getting ahead in life . . .")

ITEM	PER CENT			
	"All of My Children Have Been More Successful than I"	"Most Have Been"	"Some Have Been"	"None Has Been"
"My children have less respect than they should"	6	7	6	10
"My children respect me as much as they should"	94	93	94	90
Total........................	100	100	100	100
No. of cases......................	623	155	301	468

that they should "write their parents often" (82 per cent) with the fact that an equally high proportion (86 per cent) says that all their children have kept in close contact. In fact, a nearly symmetrical pattern of "shoulds" and "does" appears when responses of corresponding questions are tabulated (Table 16). It should be pointed out, of course, that a satisfactory relationship hinges equally upon the younger generation's *not* doing what their parents believe they should not do. To cite an obvious example, in light of the widespread emphasis upon independence and non-inter-

held to be important, equally important as an intergenerational norm and in practice is the policy of independence and non-interference. So fully has this been accepted by some that one hears the statement, "It just isn't natural for more than one generation to live in the same house."

INTERGENERATIONAL RELATIONSHIPS

STEREOTYPES AND REALITY

To this point, it will be noted, the facts of the case do not seem to square with popular notions which hold that older par-

TABLE 15

DIFFERENTIAL SUCCESS OF PARENTS AND CHILDREN AS RELATED TO CLOSENESS OF FAMILY TIES

("In earning a living and getting ahead . . .")

ITEM	PER CENT			
	"All of My Children Have Been More Successful than I"	"Most Have Been"	"Some Have Been"	"None Has Been"
"We [parents and children] are very close"....	78	75	65	69
"We are somewhat close"...................	16	24	30	25
"We are not a close family group"..........	6	1	5	6
Total......................	100	100	100	100
No. of cases........................	623	155	301	468

ference among the older generation, no general program of bringing aging and indigent parents into their children's homes could hope to meet with easy success.

In general, one garners the impression that relationships between parent and children meet with the approval of the older generation. In effect this is to say that they receive from their children largely what they wish to receive and what they expect. But the nature of the family patterns involved is essentially conjugal in its important aspects. Affectionate contact, variously expressed, is the keynote to family relationships; but, while ties of affection and intergenerational interest and regard are

TABLE 16

WHAT CHILDREN SHOULD DO AND WHAT THEY ACTUALLY DO—FROM THE PERSPECTIVE OF THEIR AGING PARENTS

Per Cent

Children *should* take care of their parents when they are ill...................	61
Children *do* help when someone is ill...	80
Children *should* "help" their parents...	44
Children *do* give advice on business or money matters....................	40
When parents get older their children *should* help support them..........	51
"All of my children have offered financial help".............................	53
When parents get older and need help they *should be asked* to move in with their married children.............	8
Children *do* provide a home..........	13

ents sit alone and neglected by their children. This is a statement of family relationships often found in the popular press, and it has been rationalized in terms of the failure of the normative order to allow both for intensive achievement orientation and for expression of filial obligations of a more consanguineous nature. But it is an impression of intergenerational relationships not confined to the ivory towers of the press and academia. We have already reported that over 90 per cent of our re-

TABLE 17

PROPER RESPECT FOR PARENTS: AN ATTITUDE
EXPRESSED AMONG THOSE WITH AND
THOSE WITHOUT CHILDREN

("The way life is today children have less respect for their parents than they should")

ITEM	PER CENT	
	Respondents with Children	Respondents without Children
Agree: they do have less respect than they should..	22	47
Undecided...............	15	29
Disagree: they do not have less respect than they they should...........	63	24
Total.................	100	100
No. of cases...........	1664	544

spondents with children indicate that *their* children respect *them* as much as they should. But, when asked whether children *in general* have less respect for their parents than they should, the figure drops to only 63 per cent (Table 17). Thus, even among those who express contentment with the relationship between their children and themselves, the general notion of a disrespectful younger generation has made inroads.

But it is also clear from the data that the popular notion makes most headway among those who, like Will Rogers, know only what they read in the papers. Although respondents without children are significantly more likely to indicate that they are undecided as to whether children in general are sufficiently respectful to their parents, the majority express the stereotypical view of the matter by agreeing that children do have less respect than they should (Table 17).

The same pattern is repeated in response to the question: "When your children go out on their own [do you] have to turn to your brothers and sisters if you are going to have any family ties?" (Table 18). Indecision and no response to the question increases as the respondents have less personal experience on which to base a reply; and the proportion who believe that satisfactory relationships with children are possible sharply decreases with those for whom personal experience is lacking. The relationship is presented in clearer focus when those who express indecision are excluded from the tabulation (Table 19). Those with children but without siblings are very slightly more likely to cling to the belief that you need not turn to siblings for continued family relationships, but the difference from those who have siblings is not statistically significant. The significance of the table lies rather in the fact that those without children are very significantly more likely to indicate that family ties are broken when children leave home.

Now it could be, of course, that those with children are not objective in their appraisals and that their evaluation of their relationships with children as satisfactory is a rationalization, while those without children appraise the situation in more objective terms and see the neglect their friends experience. Certainly, this is a hypothesis worth considering. However, in light of the consistency between expectations of children and actual behavior of children which our respondents express, we prefer the interpretation that this is another instance in which stereotypical belief does not correspond to actual reality. The popular press has tended to overgeneralize from the atypical case: the more sensational events still make the best headlines.

And, among serious students, analyses of contemporary institutions in our industrial society have tended to overlook the interstitial aspects of society and thus the extent to which bonds other than associational ties may continue to exist.

All in all, the picture derived from the responses of older people themselves is quite different from that which seems to be held popularly. Rather than filling the stereotypical mold of the lonely rocking-chair type, cut off from family, friends, and usefulness in society generally, the research findings suggest an older person more appropriately characterized by vitality and a range of interests which would put many a younger person to shame. Among the most important of the older

TABLE 18

APPRAISAL OF FAMILY RELATIONSHIPS WHEN CHILDREN LEAVE HOME

("When your children go out on their own, you have to turn to your brothers and sisters if you are going to have any family ties")

ITEM	PER CENT			
	Respondents with Children		Respondents without Children	
	With Siblings	Without Siblings	With Siblings	Without Siblings
Agree: You must turn to your siblings....	12	6	23	18
Undecided, no answer..................	19	36	45	55
Disagree: you need not turn to your siblings for continued family relationships......	69	58	32	27
Total...........................	100	100	100	100
No. of cases.....................	1398	293	466	138

TABLE 19

APPRAISAL OF FAMILY RELATIONSHIPS WHEN CHILDREN LEAVE HOME AMONG THOSE WHO EXPRESS AN OPINION

("When your children go out on their own, you have to turn to your brothers and sisters if you are going to have any family ties")

ITEM	PER CENT			
	Respondents with Children		Respondents without Children	
	With Siblings	Without Siblings	With Siblings	Without Siblings
Agree: you must turn to your siblings....	14	10	41	41
Disagree: you need not turn to your siblings for continued family relationships......	86	90	59	59
Total...........................	100	100	100	100
No. of cases.....................	1143	189	256	61

person's interests and activities, his family still serves as a significant source of gratification and personal satisfaction. To be sure, the warm certainty of the extended family is no longer typical; but the emphasis on individualism is not a one-way street. That is to say, perhaps a realistic appraisal of the older person's familial relationships not only should emphasize the misfortunes of the older person who feels excluded by the conjugal pattern but also should emphasize the opportunities which some older persons may enjoy because of independence from entangling familial alliances.

In other words, why plead the cause of social patterns and a system of norms which the older person himself no longer accepts? There is no question, of course, that old age is a special and a potentially difficult time of life; and there is no question that the later years pose serious problems of adjustment, including problems of adjustment to changing status within the family. But if, as social scientists, we seek seriously to understand these problems, let us not be overwhelmed either by the plight of the older person or by our guilt at having neglected him for so long. For critical examination of the facts of the case show that the older person, too, is an individual, generally living realistically in the context of contemporary society, and ready, willing, and—most important—able to cope with his problems as *and if* they arise.

REFERENCES

ABBOTT, EDITH. 1906. The history of the industrial employment of women in the United States: an introductory study. J. Political Economy, **14**, 461–501.

ALBRECHT, RUTH. 1954*a*. Relationships of older parents with their children. Marriage & Family Living, **16**, 32–35.

———. 1954*b*. The parental responsibilities of grandparents. *Ibid.*, pp. 201–4.

ANGELL, R. C. 1936. The family encounters the depression. New York: Charles Scribner's Sons.

BARBER, B. 1957. Social stratification. New York: Harcourt, Brace & Co.

BATES, A. 1942. Parental roles in courtship. Social Forces, **20**, 483–86.

BEARD, BELLE B. 1949. Are the aged ex-family? Social Forces, **27**, 274–79.

BENDIX, R., and LIPSET, S. M. 1953. Social mobility in the United States. *In* R. BENDIX and S. M. LIPSET (eds.), Class, status, and power, pp. 371–500. Glencoe, Ill.: Free Press.

BOND, F. A., BABER, R. E., VIEG, J. A., PERRY, L. B., SCAFF, A. H., and LEE, L. J., JR. 1954. Our needy aged: a California study of a national problem. New York: Henry Holt & Co.

BORDEN, B. 1946. The role of grandparents in children's behavior problems. Smith College Studies in Social Work, **17**, 115–16.

BOSSARD, J. H. S. 1953. Children of overage parents. *In* Parent and child: studies in family behavior. Philadelphia: University of Pennsylvania Press.

BRONFENBRENNER, U. 1958. Socialization and social class through time and space. *In* ELEANOR E. MACCOBY, T. M. NEWCOMB, and E. L. HARTLEY (eds.), Readings in social psychology, pp. 400–425. 3d ed. New York: Henry Holt & Co.

BURGESS, E. W. 1957. The older generation and the family. *In* WILMA DONAHUE and C. TIBBITTS (eds.), The new frontiers of aging, pp. 158–71. Ann Arbor: University of Michigan Press.

BURGESS, E. W., and WALLIN, P. 1943. Homogamy in social characteristics. Am. J. Sociology, **49**, 109–24.

CALHOUN, A. W. 1918. A social history of the American family, Vol. 2. Cleveland: Arthur H. Clark Co.

CAMPISI, P. J. 1948. Ethnic family patterns: the Italian family in the United States. Am. J. Sociology, **53**, 443–49.

CAVAN, RUTH S. 1953. The American family. New York: Thomas Y. Crowell Co.

CAVAN, RUTH S., and RANCK, KATHERINE. 1938. The family and the depression. Chicago: University of Chicago Press.

CORSON, J. J., and McCONNELL, J. W. 1956. Economic needs of older people. New York. Twentieth Century Fund.

COTTRELL, L. S., JR. 1942. The adjustment of the individual to his age and sex roles. Am. Sociological Rev., **11**, 617–20.

DAVIS, K. 1940. The sociology of parent-youth conflict. Am. Sociological Rev., **4**, 523–35.

———. 1949. Human society. New York: Macmillan Co.

DINKEL, R. M. 1943. Parent-child conflict in

Minnesota families. Am. Sociological Rev., **8**, 412–19.

DORFMAN, R. 1954. The labor force status of persons aged sixty-five and over. Am. Economics Rev., **44**, 634–44.

DOTSON, F. 1951. Patterns of voluntary association among urban working-class families. Am. Sociological Rev., **16**, 687–93.

DUVALL, EVELYN M. 1954. In-laws—pro and con: an original study of inter-personal relations. New York: Association Press.

ELIOT, T. D. 1955. Bereavement: inevitable but not insurmountable. *In* H. BECKER and R. HILL (eds.), Family, marriage, and parenthood, pp. 641–68. 2d ed. Boston: D. C. Heath & Co.

EPLER, ELIZABETH. 1954. Old age assistance: determining extent of children's ability to support. Social Security Bull., **17** (May), 7–10.

FITZELLE, G. T. 1952. The personal adjustment of a selected group of widows of fifty-five years and older. (Unpublished Ph.D. dissertation, Cornell University.)

FOOTE, N. N., and COTTRELL, L. S., JR. 1955. Identity and interpersonal competence: a new direction in family research. Chicago: University of Chicago Press.

FRAZIER, E. F. 1939. The Negro family in the United States. Chicago: University of Chicago Press.

———. 1948. Ethnic family patterns: the Negro family in the United States. Am. J. Sociology, **53**, 435–38.

FRIED, EDRITA G., and STERN, K. 1948. The situation of the aged within the family. Am. J. Orthopsychiat., **18**:31–53.

GLICK, P. C. 1947. The family cycle. Am. Sociological Rev., **12**:164–74.

———. 1955. The life cycle of the family. Marriage & Family Living, **17**, 3–9.

———. 1957. American families. New York: John Wiley & Sons.

GLICK, P. C., and LANDAU, E. 1950. Age as a factor in marriage. Am. Sociological Rev., **15**, 517–29.

GRAVATT, A. E. 1953. Family relations in middle and old age: a review. J. Gerontol., **8**, 197–201.

HAVIGHURST, R. J. 1957. The social competence of middle-aged people. Genet. Psychol. Monogr., **56**, 297–375.

HAVIGHURST, R. J., and ALBRECHT, RUTH. 1953. Older people. New York: Longmans, Green & Co.

HOLLINGSHEAD, A. B. 1950. Cultural factors in the selection of marriage mates. Am. Sociological Rev., **15**, 619–27.

KAHL, J. A. 1957. The American class structure. New York: Rinehart & Co.

KINSEY, A. C., POMEROY, W. B., and MARTIN, C. E. 1948. Sexual behavior in the human male. Philadelphia: W. B. Saunders Co.

KINSEY, A. C., POMEROY, W. B., MARTIN, C. E., and GEBHARD, P. H. 1953. Sexual behavior in the human female. Philadelphia: W. B. Saunders Co..

KOLLER, M. R. 1954. Studies of three-generation households. Marriage & Family Living, **16**, 205–6.

KOMAROVSKY, MIRRA. 1940. The unemployed man and his family. New York: Dryden Press.

KUTNER, B., FANSHEL, D., TOGO, ALICE M., and LANGNER, T. S. 1956. Five hundred over sixty. New York: Russell Sage Foundation.

LEMASTERS, E. E. 1954. Social class mobility and family integration. Marriage & Family Living, **16**, 226–32.

LIPSET, S. M., and BENDIX, R. 1952. Social mobility and occupational career pattern. Am. J. Sociology, **57**, 494–504.

MacIVER, R. M., and PAGE, C. H. 1949. Society: an introductory analysis. New York: Rinehart & Co.

MARRIS, P. 1958. Widows and their families. London: Routledge & Kegan Paul.

MASTERS, W. H. 1952. The female reproductive system. *In* A. I. LANSING (ed.), Cowdry's problems of ageing, pp. 651–85. 3d ed. Baltimore: Williams & Wilkins Co.

MERRILL, FRANCES E. 1949. Courtship and marriage: a study in social relationships. New York: Duell, Sloan & Pearce.

MERTON, R. K. 1957. Manifest and latent functions. *In* Social theory and social structure, pp. 19–84. Rev. ed. Glencoe, Ill.: Free Press.

MOORE, W. E. 1950. The aged in industrial societies. *In* M. DERBER (ed.), The aged and society. Champaign, Ill.: Industrial Relations Research Association.

MORRIS, R. T. 1956. A typology of norms. Am. Sociological Rev., **21**, 610–13.

NEIMAN, L. J., and HUGHES, J. W. 1951. The problem of the concept of role—a re-survey of the literature. Social Forces, **30**, 141–49.

OGBURN, W. F., and TIBBITTS, C. 1933. The family and its functions. *In* Recent social trends in the United States. New York: McGraw-Hill Book Co.

ROSE, A. M. 1955. Factors associated with the life satisfaction of middle-class, middle-aged persons. Marriage & Family Living, **17**, 15–19.

RUARK, R. 1957. The old man and the boy. New York: Henry Holt & Co.

SCHUMPETER, J. A. 1951. Imperialism and social classes. New York: Augustus M. Kelley.

SHELDON, H. D. 1958. The older population of the United States. New York: John Wiley & Sons.

SHOCK, N. W. (ed.). 1951. A classified bibliography of gerontology and geriatrics. Stanford, Calif.: Stanford University Press.

———. 1957. A classified bibliography of gerontology and geriatrics, Supplement One: 1949–1955. Stanford, Calif.: Stanford University Press.

SIMMONS, L. W. 1945. The role of the aged in primitive society. New Haven, Conn.: Yale University Press.

SMITH, W. M., JR. 1954. Family living plans for later years. Marriage & Family Living, **16**, 36–40.

SMITH, W. M., JR., BRITTON, J. H., and BRITTON, JEAN O. 1958. Relationships within three-generation families. (Research Publication No. 155.) University Park: Pennsylvania State University, College of Home Economics.

STEINER, P. O., and DORFMAN, R. 1957. The economic status of the aged. Berkeley: University of California Press.

STREIB, G. F. 1958. Family patterns in retirement. J. Social Issues, **14**, No. 2, 46–60.

SUMNER, W. G. 1906. Folkways. Boston: Ginn & Co.

SUSSMAN, M. B. 1953a. The help pattern in the middle-class family. Am. Sociological Rev., **18**, 22–28.

———. 1953b. Parental participation in mate selection and its effect upon family continuity. Social Forces, **32**, 76–81.

———. 1954. Family continuity: selective factors which affect relationships between families at generational levels. Marriage & Family Living, **16**, 112–20.

———. 1955. Activity patterns of post-parental couples and their relationship to family continuity. *Ibid.*, **17**, 338–41.

TOWNSEND, P. 1957. The family life of old people. Glencoe, Ill.: Free Press.

TRUXAL, A. G., and MERRILL, FRANCES E. 1947. The family in American culture. New York: Prentice-Hall, Inc.

———. 1953. Marriage and the family in American culture. New York: Prentice-Hall, Inc.

U.S. BUREAU OF THE CENSUS. 1949. Historical statistics of the United States, 1789–1945. Washington, D.C.: Government Printing Office.

U.S. BUREAU OF PUBLIC ASSISTANCE. 1954. Old-age assistance: provisions on responsibility of relatives for support of applicants and recipients, 51 states, Oct., 1952. Washington, D.C.: The Bureau.

U.S. NATIONAL CONFERENCE ON FAMILY LIFE. 1948. The American family: a factual background. Report of committee on background materials for conference. Washington, D.C.: Government Printing Office.

VOLLMER, H. 1937. The grandmother: a problem in childrearing. Am. J. Orthopsychiat., **7**, 378–82.

WALLIN, P. 1954. Sex differences in attitudes to the "in-law": a test of theory. Am. J. Sociology, **59**, 466–69.

WILLIAMS, R. M., JR. 1951. American society: a sociological interpretation. New York: A. A. Knopf.

WILSON, L., and KOLB, W. 1949. Sociological analysis. New York: Harcourt, Brace & Co.

WINCH, R. F. 1957. Marriage and the family. *In* J. GITTLER (ed.), Review of sociology: analysis of a decade, pp. 346–90. New York: John Wiley & Sons.

WOLFENSTEIN, MARTHA. 1953. Trends in infant care. Am. J. Orthopsychiat., **23**, 120–30.

XIV

Aging and the Economy

JOHN W. MCCONNELL

I. OLDER PEOPLE IN LESS COMPLEX ECONOMIC SYSTEMS

Human society, at a very early stage, succeeded in assuring to some individuals a relatively long life. But the kind of life experienced by these older members— whether they were honored or despised, whether they worked with the group or spent their days in idleness and isolation, whether they were provided with food, clothing, and shelter or left behind to die— depended upon economic conditions and culture patterns which varied from tribe to tribe.

The life of older people in simple primitive societies has been as varied as it is in the complex industrial and agricultural nations of our own time. Leo Simmons, whose *The Role of the Aged in Primitive Society* is the basic book on the subject, emphasizes this variety of custom in his summary of reactions to death of older people.

The social significance of dying for the aged has ranged all the way from the height of homage to the depth of degradation. Under varying circumstances . . . an aged person faced with death might be neglected, abandoned, cast out, or killed by his closest kin; or, instead, he might be protected by them and nursed along to the very moment of expiration. In the hour of death the aged might be feared or loved, despised or honored, reviled or even worshipped. . . . His dying treatment and his reaction to death have been conditioned in part by his personal characteristics, but even more so by the impersonal environmental and cultural factors of his particular social milieu [1945, p. 243].

The number and characteristics of the aging and aged in a society influence the nature and purpose of its economy, but the characteristics of the economy also influence the attitude and behavior of citizens toward the aging and aged and the opportunities they have for a satisfactory existence. In the problems of aging, as with all social and economic problems, perspective and objectivity are essential to intelligent understanding and sound solutions. The review of the status of older people in less complex economies found in chapter iii of this *Handbook* is directed toward that end.

The status of older people in a society varies with the different methods of getting a living, or the stage of the arts, as this economic base is often called. Anthropologists classify societies according to the source of their food supply into five general groups: collecting; hunting and fishing; herding; simple agriculture; and complex agriculture. Collecting societies in tropical areas with profuse vegetation have fixed abodes, but in colder climates collecting results in a nomadic existence. Hunting, fishing, and herding peoples are generally somewhat nomadic, since they follow the herds and usually migrate with the changing seasons. Some fishing societies, on the other hand, like those in the Pacific Northwest, have fixed abodes. Agriculture makes possible a settled community life, although in its simplest form it is usually only supplementary to hunting, fishing, or herding and hence is a part of the culture of nomadic peoples. Because it promotes systems of land-holding and inheritance, highly developed agricultural societies have the most stable life of all people, not even excluding that of the most industrialized communities of the present day.

Following a careful review of primitive societies, Simmons (1945, pp. 32–34) concludes that (1) older people had greater opportunity to share in the food supply in those societies which had a communal system of food distribution than in societies which emphasized individual responsibility; (2) societies have a greater tendency toward group distribution in very cold or excessively dry climate, and inclusion of the aged is more pronounced in these societies than in areas of greater abundance; (3) older people are more certain of food from the group among collectors and fishermen, somewhat less certain among hunters and herders, and have no certainty at all among those practicing agriculture; (4) little effort is made by the community as a whole to assure the aged of adequate food in societies with fixed abode, constant food supply, and widespread use of grain, since the family usually provides for its own older members; and (5) differences in the treatment of men and women are negligible in these primitive communities. However, Simmons notes that, "wherever aged women have been respected, old men have rarely been without honor, but prestige for aged men has offered no assurance of the same status for women. If either sex has lost respect in old age, it has been more likely to be women than men."

In periods of scarcity, or in societies located in barren areas and maintaining a marginal existence, the young and the disabled suffer along with the aged. There is no clear evidence that primitive societies consistently protect any one group of dependents more than another against the shortage of food and the ravages of famine. Infanticide and the abandonment of the young and disabled occur rarely, even among peoples with limited food and water. The abandonment and putting to death of

the elderly is no more prevalent. In agricultural societies with poor soil and low productivity, the older generation holding title to the land remains attached to the land, while many of the young generation leave the land and become a floating population—waifs, vagabonds, warriors, hirelings, and soldiers of fortune.

One must conclude from Simmons' discussion that the treatment of older people varied from tribe to tribe, and generalizations such as those above must be looked upon as tentative hypotheses only. Nevertheless, the insight and perspective on the impact of aging on the economy derived from these anthropological studies are invaluable.

II. The Impact of Scarcity and Abundance on the Position of Older People

We turn now to the society of the present. Customs and attitudes of a society with respect to its aging members are not accidents or fortuitous circumstances created out of fertile imagination. They are in the culture of the people, with roots sunk deep in the way the society gets its living. Modern society differs from early primitive societies only in the complexity of its arrangements, not in the source or nature of its customs.

A. Older People in an Economy of Abundance

America in the twentieth century has the highest standard of living the world has ever known. One of the paradoxes of this society of abundance is the persistence of poverty. Yet concentration on the failures of our society to provide a full life for all should not blind us to the fact that the economic problems of our aging population arise as a strange confusion of the higher standards of living enjoyed by most people and the inability of the economy to provide adequately for everyone.

On July 1, 1959, there were 15,400,000 older persons over 65 in the United States.

There are today five times as many older people as there were in 1900, although the population as a whole is only a little more than twice as large. In 1900 only one person in twenty-five was over 65. Today one in eleven persons is in this age group. Nearly 1,250,000 persons reached age 65 last year; the net increase in this older age was 342,000, or nearly 1000 per day (U.S. Department of Health, Education, and Welfare, 1958). The tremendous growth in the number and proportion of older persons in our society, described in chapter ii of this *Handbook*, is due to four principal factors: (1) general population increases in the latter part of the nineteenth century; (2) the improved standard of living of the total population; (3) the great advances in medical science which have reduced infant mortality and eliminated the killing diseases of infancy, youth, and middle age; and (4) curtailment of immigration since 1924 which sharply reduced the proportion of persons of childbearing age in the total population.

Since 1900 life-expectancy at birth has increased 19 years. The increase has been shared by all groups in the population— white and non-white, men and women, and rich and poor. While a great many more people are now living to be old, old people are living only 2 years longer than they did in 1900.

This older age group constitutes 8.7 per cent of the total population. We know there will be about 22,000,000 persons 65 and over in the United States in 1975, but whether the proportion in the total population will be much greater or about the same as at present will depend on the future birth rate. If the present high rate is maintained, older people will be only a little over 9 per cent of the total population. However, there is evidence of a substantial drop in the number of marriages, which means, of course, a substantial drop in the number of new births in the years to come (Anonymous, 1958). Population experts are fearful that the current decline in marriages may be accelerated by poor economic conditions and lead to a repetition of the population trough experienced between 1924 and 1937. If the lower birth rates prevail through the 1960's, instead of the baby boom which everyone has expected, older people may become proportionally greater and constitute as much as 12 per cent of the total population in 1975.

Women enjoy a life-expectancy 3 years greater than men at age 65, nearly 7 years greater at birth. There are at present 8,500,000 women and 6,900,000 men age 65. Two-thirds of the men in this age group are married and living with their wives. Conversely, however, only one-third of the women are married. The sex imbalance among older people will be greater in the future.

While the older population is now five times as great as in 1900, equally vast increases have occurred in productivity, productive capacity, and sources of energy, that is, in the elements of a higher standard of living. Since 1900, the hourly output per worker has increased three times, and the value of productive plant and equipment rose from $21 billion (in current prices) to $276 billion, or thirteen times. The fact that energy input per capita has only doubled obscures the tremendous increases in the efficiency of energy utilization due to changes from human and animal energy sources to coal, oil, gas, and water. In 1900 about 40 per cent of all energy input was derived from humans and animals. Today not more than 2 per cent comes from these sources. Gross national product has grown from $34 billion in 1909 to over $400 billion in 1957. The rise in disposable personal income has been substantial but not so spectacular. In 1909 disposable personal income was $27 billion; in 1953 it was $247 billion. In the same period personal savings rose from $1.8 billion to over $18 billion (Dewhurst and Associates, 1956). These vast increases can be traced to several sources, and endless debate results from efforts to establish what has been the chief source. One important element, at least, is the expansion in capital equipment, most of which has been made possible by huge private investment. The addition to capital goods from all sources in 1920 was $12.5 billion. In 1960 it is expected to be $66.5 billion. Between 70 and 80 per cent of the money needed to finance this capital expansion comes from private sources.

Per capita income has also increased greatly. In 1940 each individual in the United States had an average income of $1210. In 1960 each one will have $1780 (in constant 1954 dollars). An even better index of the rise in living standards is the

TABLE 1*

PERCENTAGE DISTRIBUTION OF NET WORTH OF AGED SPENDING UNITS COMPARED WITH ALL SPENDING UNITS

Net Worth	All Spending Units	Spending Units with Head 65 or Over
Negative.............	11	3
$0–$1000.............	20	21
$1000–$5000..........	23	15
$5000–$25,000........	35	42
$25,000 and over......	11	19
Total..............	100	100
Median.............	$4100	$8400

* Source: Miriam Civic, *Income and Resources of Older People* ("Studies in Business Economics," No. 52 [New York: National Industrial Conference Board, 1956]), p. 26.

increase in income per household. Again in constant 1954 dollars, each household in 1940 received $4590, while in 1960 each will have $6180. These are averages, but a larger proportion of the American population than ever before is sharing in the rise in national income. "In 1935–1936 more than two out of every five consumer units had incomes of less than $1,000—dollars of then current purchasing power—and only 3 per cent had incomes of $5,000 or over" (Dewhurst and Associates, 1956, p. 91). By 1950 only 7.6 per cent (as compared to 40 per cent) of all households had incomes below $1000, and 30 per cent had incomes above $5000 (Carskadon and Soule, 1957).

These economic changes in the country have influenced and have been influenced by the increasing number and proportion of older people in the population. The rising standard of living has already been cited as one of the two main causes of increased life-expectancy. But the increase in life-expectancy has been influential in promoting savings by individuals and institutions through life insurance and pension programs, which have in turn produced additional funds for the capital expansion of the country.

The total life insurance in force in the United States in 1925 was $69 billion. In 1956 the amount was $412 billion. The assets of the private insurance companies rose from $11 billion to $96 billion in the same period. These reserves, of course, are invested in government bonds (about 20 per cent), corporate securities, and mortgages; hence they contribute to the capital formation of the American economy. In 1957 there were $77 billion in the reserves of public and private pension systems. About $44 billion were the reserves of public pension systems and were invested exclusively in government bonds. The remaining $33 billion of private pension reserves were invested in corporate securities and mortgages with a small part in government bonds.[1] Hence a good share of the provisions for the future made by private individuals or on behalf of private individuals is used to increase the productive capacity of the country.

Without minimizing the desperate need of the thousands of older people with little or no income, it should be noted that the net effect of saving for the future among American people gives the older age group a favored position in the distribution of assets. In 1953, 13 per cent of all spending units with heads 65 years of age and over had 19 per cent of the nation's assets, 7 per cent of the debt, and 21 per cent of the net worth. Table 1 shows that 61 per cent of

[1] This discussion will avoid the provocative issue of whether or not investment in government bonds is productive investment in the economic sense.

all spending units with heads 65 years of age and over had net worth of $5000 or more, which consisted principally of mortgage-free homes. But this percentage must be compared with 46 per cent of all spending units with similar net worth. The median net worth of the 65 and over spending units was $8400 compared to $4100 for all spending units (U.S. Bureau of Employment Security, 1956).

A higher proportion of people over 55 than any other age group owns stock. Twenty-three per cent of all stockholders are over 55; 11 per cent are over 65. A substantial share of the capital structure of America is held by older people individually, in addition to the very substantial share which is held on their behalf through insurance companies and pension trusts.

The assets described in the preceding paragraphs represent past savings. Older people do not save currently as much as middle-age groups, and a higher percentage of the aged will be found among the dissavers. In 1950, 27 per cent of spending units headed by persons over 65 dissaved 10 per cent or more of their income, while in that year only 26 per cent saved more than 10 per cent. These percentages must be compared to an average of 19 per cent dissavers of 10 per cent and 41 per cent savers of 10 per cent, respectively, for all age groups between 25 and 65 (U.S. Bureau of Employment Security, 1956). (See also Table 3, chap. viii, of this volume for more detailed figures.)

The transition from land to corporate securities as the dominant form of wealth in the United States has provided a useful medium through which individuals and institutions may set aside reserves to provide income for old age. This form of anonymous ownership of the means of production, however, does not carry with it the prestige and power which the more personal and obvious ownership of land conveyed in agricultural societies. Ownership of land, furthermore, entitled the owner to an opportunity for continued employment. Ownership of stock in a corporation, even in substantial amounts, does not carry with it the same privilege.

B. The Relative Scarcity or Abundance of Consumers' Goods—Impact on the Treatment of Young and Old

The impact of economic changes since 1900 on youth and older people has been quite similar. For both youth and age employment opportunities have declined, and sources of public support have greatly increased. The vast increases in the production of goods and services have taken place despite the elimination of large numbers of young people and old people from the labor force.

TABLE 2*

PERCENTAGE OF BOYS AND GIRLS 10–15 YEARS OF AGE GAINFULLY OCCUPIED, 1870–1930

Year	Boys	Girls
1870	19.3	7.0
1880	24.4	9.0
1890	25.9	10.0
1900	26.1	10.2
1910	21.7	8.1
1920	16.8	5.8
1930	6.4	2.9

* Source: U.S. Bureau of the Census, *Comparative Occupation Statistics for the United States, 1870–1940* (Washington, D.C.: Government Printing Office, 1940), p. 92, Table XV.

Thomas C. Fichandler writes in *America's Needs and Resources:*

The most striking changes in the age composition of the working force have been among the youngest and the oldest age groups. Child labor, both male and female, expanded steadily from 1870 to 1900, when 26 per cent of all boys 10 to 15 years old, and 10 per cent of girls of this age group, were gainfully occupied. After 1900 the proportion gainfully occupied fell steadily for both sexes [see Table 2]. Gainful employment of younger children had virtually ceased by 1940. Although the 1940 Census failed to enumerate the 10-to-13-year-olds, only 35 per cent of boys and 19 per cent of girls in the group 14 to 19 years old were members of the labor force, as compared with 40 per cent and 23 per cent respectively in 1930 [Dewhurst and Associates, 1956, p. 727].

There has likewise been a sharp decline in the proportion of older persons in the labor force. Sixty-eight per cent of men 65 years and over were in the labor force in 1890. Today not more than 37 per cent are gainfully employed or seeking work. The percentage of women in the labor force has changed but slightly in these years. In 1890, 8.6 per cent of the women over 65 were listed as gainfully employed or seeking work. In 1950 the percentage was 9.5 (see chap. x of this *Handbook* for a detailed discussion of labor-force composition).

The decline in the employment of children and old people is closely correlated with the decline in the proportion of the labor force engaged in agriculture and in unskilled work. It is also correlated with the decline in hours of work in the labor force as a whole. The average hours worked per week in 1900 was 60.2; in 1950 it was 40.0; and by 1960 a further decline will have reduced the average work week to 37.5 hours (Dewhurst and Associates, 1956). Then, too, compulsory education for teen-age children and the need for training to fit young people for the occupations of today's economy have raised school-leaving ages. The social processes by which trends are established and policy decisions made in society are indeed complex. Humanitarian sentiments become entangled with inevitable economic changes and the function of economizing. These factors together have promoted the withdrawal of youth as well as age from the labor market. Nevertheless, the limitation on child labor is generally approved, but the loss of employment by older workers is deplored.

During the depression of the 1930's important social policy decisions were made, some consciously, others unconsciously, with respect to labor-market participation. There were in 1937 in the United States 21,000,-000 youths between 16 and 24 years of age. Of these, 3,900,000 were neither at work nor in school, and 2,400,000 of these were young men. Through the Civilian Conservation Corps with a peak enrolment of 505,000 youths in 1935, and the National Youth Administration programs providing financial aid to from 300,000 to 450,000 students, the federal government provided constructive alternatives to employment for about one-quarter of the unemployed youth (Lindsey, 1957). Expenditures for these two programs ranged upward to $300–$400 million per year in the worst years of the depression. It was intended that, by keeping young men and young women in school or engaged in constructive, health-building work, these young people would be kept mentally alert, physically strong, and prepared for useful participation in the labor force once the depression ended.

The public policy with respect to older people was less imaginative and constructive. Between 1930 and 1940 the population 65 and over increased 36 per cent, and the number of older persons in the labor force declined by 3 per cent (Corson and McConnell, 1956). In 1930 about 1,400,000 older men were not at work (43 per cent of all men over 65), but in 1940 there were 2,600,000 men in this age group (60 per cent of the total) not in the labor force. Political pressures by and on behalf of older people were probably greater than those supporting the youth of the country, although the inclusion of stringent child-labor provisions in the more important labor laws of the period bespeaks the effectiveness of child-labor advocates. There were, for example, the Townsend Movement agitating for pensions of $200 per month on condition that the recipient withdraw from the labor force and spend the $200 in one month; organized railroad workers demanding that the government take over the insolvent railroad pension funds; and welfare agencies supported by state and local funds wanting relief from the burden of the dependent aged who were undoubtedly a permanent charge against welfare budgets.

Federal and state governments spent amounts ranging from $155 million in 1936 to $500 million in 1940 for old age assistance compared to the $300 million for youth programs. In economic terms the marginal value of old age welfare was at least equal to that of welfare for youth.

III. "Working" and "Non-working" Groups in Society

A. The Increase in "Workers" to "Non-Workers" in American Society

THE INCREASING NUMBER OF YEARS IN RETIREMENT

Stuart Garfinkle (1955, 1956), of the Bureau of Labor Statistics, Department of Labor, has presented a refined statistical picture of the participation of older workers at work and in retirement in the form of work-life expectancy tables. Table 3 indicates the change in life-expectancy of persons at various ages. It shows also how long these people may expect to work (working-life expectancy). The difference between the two figures is, of course, the expected number of years of life in retirement. The combined effects of increased life-expectancy and decreased working-life expectancy is an increasing number of years outside of paid employment. In 1900 a white male worker of 60 years of age had a life-expectancy of 14.3 years, a working-life expectancy of 11.5, and a prospect of 2.8 years in retirement. By 1950 the corresponding figures were 15.7 years, 9.7 years, and, consequently, 6.0 years of retired life.

Analysis of population and labor-force trends indicates that by 1975 there will be an increase in life-expectancy to 16.8 years, a decline in working-life expectancy to 7.9 years, and an increase in retired life to 8.9 years. Calculations of work-life expectancy for women show a much longer time spent in retirement. Because fewer women are in the labor force at any time, and substantially less than men, therefore, the calculations are heavily weighted on the side of time spent in retirement (Garfinkle, 1955, 1956).

The ultimate result of these trends in the labor force is that a larger number of older workers will be dependent for a longer time

on the production of others. Even if "non-working" older people had adequate income, they would still be dependent upon the goods and services produced by others. The fact that these older people draw upon the national product which they have not produced poses a serious question: "To what extent can 'non-workers' be supported by 'workers' in our society without reducing the standard of living of the whole population?"

TABLE 3*

Average Remaining Lifetime and Average Number of Years of Work Remaining for Men and for Working Women at Ages 50 and Over, 1950

Year of Age	Average Remaining Lifetime† (In Years)	Average No. of Years of Work Remaining	Average No. of Years in Retirement
Men:			
50.......	22.6	16.6	6.0
55.......	19.0	13.0	6.0
60.......	15.7	9.7	6.0
Women (all):			
50.......	26.4	13.8	12.6
55.......	22.3	11.3	11.0
60.......	18.5	8.9	9.6
Women (single):			
50.......	26.4	15.4	11.0
55.......	22.3	12.1	10.2
60.......	18.5	9.1	9.4

* Source: S. A. Garfinkle, "Changes in Working Life of Men, 1900–2000," *Monthly Labor Review*, **78** (1955), 297–300, and "Tables of Working Life for Older Women, 1950," *ibid.*, **79** (1956), 901–7.

† Data are for all men or women; similar figures are not available for workers.

INCREASED BIRTH RATE AND CHANGING AGE OF ENTRY INTO THE LABOR MARKET

The question gains added significance when one observes the increasing number of "non-workers" in the younger age groups. In January, 1958, only 36 per cent of all young men between the ages of 14 and 20 were in the labor force compared to 67 per cent in 1900 (Dewhurst and Associates, 1956; U.S. Bureau of the Census, 1957). The total population under 20 in 1956 was 63,000,000. By 1960 there will be approximately 73,000,000, and in 1975 possibly as many as 93,000,000 if present rates of family formation and childbirth continue. Of this group, no greater proportion will be employed than at present, that is, 36 per cent. The additional "non-workers" in the under-20 age group will be about 13,-000,000.

Despite the increasing numbers of "non-working" young people and "non-working" old people, the ratio of "non-workers" to "workers" has declined steadily from 1900 to 1950. Recently, rising birth rates and declining proportion of older people in the labor force have caused a turn upward in the number of "non-workers" per 100 "workers." The ratio was 154 per 100 in 1957. Table 4 shows the changes in these ratios. Older groups in the population as well as younger groups contribute the highest percentages of all non-workers, while the working-age groups from 20 to 64 contribute proportionately less.

WOMEN IN THE LABOR MARKET

The principal explanation of these declining ratios is the larger number and proportion of women of working age in the labor force today. The movement of women out of the home and into the labor force is a long-time trend checked temporarily in the last decade by the rising rates of family formation and childbirth. In 1900 the labor force was 81.2 per cent male and 18.8 per cent female. In 1953 it was 71.4 per cent male and 28.6 per cent female. Or, viewed from another angle, in 1900 only 25 per cent of the women 20–34 years of age were at work, but in 1950 there were 37.0 per cent. Among middle-age women, 35–64 years of age, 15.3 per cent worked in 1900, while 34.8 per cent were in the labor market in 1950 (Dewhurst and Associates, 1956). (See also chap. x of this *Handbook*.) Hence, despite increasing proportions of children and older persons among the ranks of the "non-workers," there has been until the last 8 years a steady decline in the number of "non-

workers" per 100 "workers." Except the last decade, however, the proportion of aged in the "non-worker" group has grown more rapidly than any other age group. The trend had been temporarily reversed, and younger "non-workers" are increasing faster proportionally than old people.

B. The Effects of the "Non-working" Older People on Income Distribution

THE COST OF SUPPORTING THE "NON-WORKING" AGED IN DOLLAR AMOUNTS TODAY AND IN 1975

The cost of maintaining the "non-working" old people can be estimated only in very gross terms. One can assume that payments made to persons over 65 from public and private retirement and assistance programs are no greater than the minimum cost. In 1956 these payments amounted to $8.6 billion. As Table 5 indicates, Old-Age, Survivors, and Disability Insurance, of all the programs, paid benefits to the greatest number of persons and in the largest aggregate amount.

A different and perhaps a sounder measure of the cost of supporting the "non-working" aged is the amount of contributions being made by covered employees and their employers to retirement systems or by the government in the case of direct payments to beneficiaries. The total of such contributions or payments in 1956 was $15.4 billion. Table 6 shows the programs for which data were available. (See also chap. viii of this *Handbook*.)

That the total over-all payments to older people will increase in the future is accepted by all. But how much will the increase be? Projections of Old-Age, Disability, and Survivors Insurance indicate that payments will be two and a half times as great in 1975, with benefits amounting to about $10 billion. Increases of the same magnitude cannot be predicted for other forms of old age security, but an over-all doubling of benefit payments (except for old age assistance) is not unreasonable.

Projections made for the President's Commission on Veterans' Pensions (1956) report payments for public old age benefit programs in 1975 compared to 1955 as shown in Table 7.

INCIDENCE OF THE COST OF SUPPORTING
NON-WORKERS

At present the cost of providing for older people falls upon younger age groups. Since 1950 beneficiaries under OASDI have nearly tripled. As coverage of the public old age benefit system has been broadened, newly covered workers have been blanketed in and considered eligible for benefits as

though they had been covered from the beginning of the program. Attainment of age 65 and a minimum service of 6 quarters or 18 months in newly covered employment is sufficient to qualify for benefits. Naturally, the contributions of the employee and his employer fall far short of the amount necessary to meet the cost of benefits. Contributions previously made on behalf of younger workers are used to pay these benefits. Moreover, when levels were increased by Congress in 1950 and 1954, benefit increases were made to those already drawing benefits. These higher benefits, which increased charges against

TABLE 4*

"WORKERS" AND "NON-WORKERS" IN THE TOTAL POPULATION, 1900–1957

YEAR	POPULATION (IN THOUSANDS)	CIVILIAN LABOR-FORCE "WORKERS" (IN THOUSANDS)	"NON-WORKERS" PER 100 WORKERS	PERCENTAGE DISTRIBUTION OF "NON-WORKERS," BY AGE			
				0–19	20–44	45–64	65 and Over
1900..........	75,995	28,416	167	61	25	10	4
1920..........	105,711	40,654	160	59	25	11	5
1940..........	131,669	53,299	147	52	24	15	9
1950..........	150,697	62,183	142	53	24	13	10
1957..........	170,510	66,951	154	60	18	11	11

* Sources: U.S. Bureau of the Census, *Historical Statistics of the U.S., 1789–1945* (Washington, D.C.: Government Printing Office, 1949), p. 25; *Census of Population: Preliminary Reports* (Series PC-7, No. 1), February 25, 1951, p. 6; *Current Population Reports, Labor Force* (Series P-57, No. 94), May 5, 1950, p. 9; *ibid.* (Series P-57, No. 178), May, 1957; *Current Population Reports, Population Estimates* (Series P-25, No. 157), May 13, 1957; and J. D. Durand, *The Labor Force in the U.S., 1890–1960* (New York: Social Science Research Council, 1948), pp. 208–9.

TABLE 5*

BENEFICIARIES AND BENEFIT PAYMENTS TO PERSONS 65 AND OVER, 1956

Program	Beneficiaries (In Thousands)	Amounts Paid (In Millions)
Old-Age, Survivors, and Disability Insurance.	6,190.9	$4,361.2
Railroad Retirement......................	347.3	397.7
Civil Service (federal)......................	179.2	315.9
Other federal contributory..................	2.0	5.0
Federal non-contributory...................	115.7	312.5
State and local government retirement......	345.0	470.0
Veterans' program........................	55.9	70.8
Old age assistance........................	2,514.0	1,676.7
Private retirement plans (est.)..............	1,160.0	950.0
Total................................	10,910.0	$8,559.8

* Source: U.S. Social Security Administration, *Social Security Bulletin, Annual Statistical Supplement*, **19** (1956), 14 and 72; *ibid.*, **21** (March, 1958), 6, 11.

the OASI Trust Fund, were met by contributions made by other younger workers and their employers. Less than 7.5 per cent of the labor force is now outside a publicly supported or sponsored retirement system. Catch-up legislation will be of minor importance in future costs, and it is expected that the OASDI system will reach maturity

in 1975 or shortly thereafter, when contributions by and on behalf of covered workers will in general approximate benefit payments. Until then the young will pay for the old, but without any loss of entitlement or benefit to themselves (see also chap. viii).

In private pension plans, also, benefit payments are ·usually much greater than contributions made on behalf of those currently retired. In one way or another, past-service liabilities of those newly declared eligible for pensions must be met. It may be done by the corporation accepting a debt for the amount of the liability and paying interest on it. It may be done by funding the liability and liquidating it over a period of years by payments in excess of amounts needed for pensions based on future service. Or past-service liability may be ignored and the pensions based on prior service paid to those currently retiring as a current expense to the business. In any one of these systems of financing pensions, a large share of the current costs is met by the use of money which, it could be

TABLE 6*

CONTRIBUTIONS AND TAXES PAID TO
PROVIDE PUBLIC AND PRIVATE
OLD AGE BENEFITS, 1956

Program	Amounts Paid (Millions)
Old-Age, Survivors and Disability Insurance....................	$ 6,172
Other public (railroad, civil service, etc.)........................	1,749
State and local contributions (1955–56)...........................	1,745
Old age assistance...............	1,677†
Veterans' benefits................	71†
Private pension contributions (est.)	4,030
Total........................	$15,444

* Source: U.S. Social Security Administration, *Social Security Bulletin, Annual Statistical Suppl.*, **19** (1956), 14, 19, and 62; *ibid.*, **21** (March, 1958), 6.
† Actual amounts paid.

TABLE 7*

PAYMENTS FOR OLD AGE BENEFIT PROGRAMS
(In Millions)

PROGRAM	1975		1955
	(a)	(b)	
OASI (old age only)..................	$10,046	$10,046	$3,232
Old age assistance...............	964	964	1,593
Federal civilian retirement............	1,090	1,090	248
Federal uniformed service retirement....	1,020	1,020	228
State and local government retirement..	740	740	420
Total.......................	$13,860	$13,860	$5,721
To these must be added non-service-connected pensions under present law....	$ 1,971	....	$ 75†
Assuming $100 per month to all servicemen over 65......................	....	$ 5,877	....
Private industry pensions (1975 double the present payment)..............	1,900	1,900	950
Grand total....................	$17,731	$21,637	$6,746

* Source: President's Commission on Veterans' Pensions, *Veterans' Benefits in the United States*, Vol. **3**: *Findings and Recommendations* (Washington, D.C.: Government Printing Office, 1956), p. 247.
† Refers only to the amount paid to veterans over 65 years of age.

argued, belongs to present workers or to owners (see McGill, 1955).

It has been estimated that, at current benefit levels, private pension plans would need a reserve of $200 billion to be fully funded. It is doubtful that this level of reserve will ever be reached for present coverage and benefit levels. Until it is, however, retired workers will receive benefits paid for in part by the production of younger workers, that is, out of current earnings.

COSTS (PRESENT AND FUTURE) IN RELATION TO INCREASES IN WORKER PRODUCTIVITY AND GROSS NATIONAL PRODUCT

The present and future costs of income maintenance for old people have been set forth. Present costs on the basis of payments equal $8.6 billion; on the basis of contributions, $15.4 billion. In 1975 the costs will be more than twice as great. Can the nation afford it?

In the last quarter of 1956 the gross national product was $424 billion, personal income was $333 billion, and disposable personal income was $293 billion. The public and private benefit payments to old people therefore amounted to 2 per cent of the gross national product and to 2.6 per cent of the personal income and approximately 3 per cent of the disposable personal income. If we consider contributions rather than payments as the measure of the present cost of older people, then these percentages should be almost double. Contributions would be 3.6 per cent of gross national product. Surely, this cost is a modest one.

Assuming no change in legislation or agreements covering pension payments, benefit payments to older people in 1975 will be between two and three times the present level. It is safe to assume that contributions will be higher but not as much as double the present level. OASDI contributions are scheduled to rise automatically from the present 4.5 per cent to 9.0 per cent of payroll in 1975. The non-con-

tributory plans and the fully mature contributory plans will increase only to the extent that coverage increases.

Gross national product is estimated to rise from $423 billion in 1956 to $690 billion in 1975. At that time the anticipated payments of $17.7 billion to old people will be 2.6 per cent of the gross national product instead of the present 2.0 per cent. At a national income estimated at $570 billion in 1975, the cost of old people will be 3.1 per cent compared to 2.6 per cent in 1956. If we were to use contributions rather than payments, the sums as well as the percentages of the gross national product and national income would be approximately half again as much. Population will increase from the present 170,000,000 to 221,000,000 in 1975, but the ratio of workers to non-workers will remain about the same. Productivity per worker will rise, and the number of hours per week will fall from the present 39 to 33. The net result will be a vast increase in the amount of goods and services available per individual.

With an estimated annual increase in gross national product of about 2.7 per cent for as far into the future as anyone can reasonably foresee, there is little doubt of our ability as a nation to meet the cost of an adequate standard of living for older people. A recent study of the economic aspects of aging (Corson and McConnell, 1956) states the situation this way:

The evidence as to the prospective growth of this country's basic resources makes clear that as a nation we can afford to provide for the nonworking aged at an increasingly generous level. Despite the growth in the number of aged persons, the nation's labor force may be expected to support proportionately fewer, rather than more, dependents in the next generation. The demands of national security may consume a substantial share of the nation's increasing economic capacity for an indefinite time, but the prospective growth of our national economic capacity will permit a steadily rising level of health and comfort for the nonworking aged.

However, two reservations concerning these observations on our future ability to provide for the aged must be emphasized: first, it is vital to safeguard proposed benefit rates against dilution by inflation. A rise of 2 per cent a year in prices over a person's working lifetime cuts the purchasing power of the pensions he looked forward to by almost half. In short, unless benefit rates rise over the years, real benefit rates decline. Moreover, unless benefit rates rise, the position of the aged in relation to the remainder of the population will decline as current levels of living rise.

Second, despite the optimistic evaluation of this country's ability to maintain the aged, the nation's economic capacity must not be confused with its willingness to share the fruits of the economy with the aged. That willingness will be kindled by political forces and by organized labor, but the share of the aged in the gross national product will be related to other demands on our society. As long as a major share of the gross national product must continue to go for national defense, our willingness and ability to improve the lot of the aged will be materially reduced.

If these two major qualifications can be met, our growing resources probably will be used in coming decades to (1) assure each aged person and couple, despite rising price levels, a decent standard of living; (2) guarantee aged persons through nonmonetary means the basic services relating to housing, hospitalization, medical care, nursing and home-making that are essential to a decent, healthful life; (3) foster personal dignity and self-respect; (4) encourage constructive participation by the aged as workers in community enterprise insofar as they are able and willing to work; (5) facilitate the association of aged persons with their families and friends; and (6) provide opportunities for those who seek uses for their newly created leisure to find social satisfactions and expand their interests [pp. 455–56].

COMPETITION AMONG AGE GROUPS FOR
SHARES OF THE GROSS NATIONAL
PRODUCT

The evidence is clear that the productive capacity of the nation can support an even larger non-working older population than at present and at a higher standard of living. But old people are not the only population group claiming a share of the available goods and services. Education of the young, support for veterans, ex-

panded medical service, and other general welfare programs in a sense compete with one another for shares of the gross national product. The processes by which these shares are determined have not yet been studied. We do not know, for example, whether increases in expenditures for older people actually reduce a community's willingness to build new schools or to pay higher teacher salaries. We observe only that a legislature or a governing board of a community chest or united fund gets a vague conception of how much the community, be it city, state, or nation, will spend on welfare. It then proceeds to weigh and balance the relative claims of competing interests. After long discussion a balance is struck, and each interest receives an allocation. The total amount to be spent may be increased simply because it seemed more practical to enlarge the pie than to reduce the size of any of the pieces. Records are not kept of these economizing proceedings; only the final decisions are publicized. Consequently, one is left with inferences about this conflict of values made from accomplished facts.

What society considers to be more important and what less important among the welfare claims may be deduced from figures on welfare expenditures prepared by Dr. Ida C. Merriam (1957), of the Department of Health, Education, and Welfare. Table 8 shows that the secular trend in welfare expenditures has been level for the last 35 years and rises at no faster rate than the gross natural product itself. Social insurance has been rising—the largest share being OASDI payments. Education has claimed a larger share only since the establishment of educational programs for veterans, although the underlying belief in educating the young and in the value of education to society generally is emphasized by the rise in the proportion of gross national product devoted to education in 1934–35.

Total expenditures for welfare in the United States have risen from $6.8 billion in 1934–35 to $34.5 billion in 1955–56

(Merriam, 1957). As a percentage of gross national product, welfare expenditures have varied between 3.5 in 1943–44 to 10.9 in 1938–39. At present, the percentage is only 8.6. Variations have occurred as a consequence of great national emergencies such as war and disaster, but there is no evidence that society is more responsive to the needs of old people than any other group.

Only in Colorado and California has there been evidence that the demands of older people could reduce the expenditures of the state for education and other welfare purposes. Legislation in Colorado devoted a sales tax exclusively to support old age pensions, and in both states old age pensions were granted a first lien on other revenues if the initial sources were reduced or withdrawn. In these two states well-organized pressure groups obtained legislative advantages for the aged before the slower-moving general public readjusted the balance (Moore, 1947; Ferina, 1949).

Intensive study of the collective-bargaining history on industrial pensions and supplementary unemployment benefits might also reveal the competitive relationship of age groups in their search for shares of the goods and services available in society. By the exercise of strict union discipline and by the use of strong educational measures, the United Automobile Workers was able to present a solid front of all age groups on

TABLE 8*

SOCIAL WELFARE EXPENDITURES AS PERCENTAGE OF GROSS NATIONAL PRODUCT,
SELECTED FISCAL YEARS, 1889–90 THROUGH 1955–56

FISCAL YEARS	GROSS NATIONAL PRODUCT (IN BILLIONS)	SOCIAL WELFARE EXPENDITURES AS PERCENTAGE OF GROSS NATIONAL PRODUCT						
		Total	Social Insurance	Public Aid	Health and Medical Services	Other Welfare	Veterans' Programs	Education
1889–90	$ 13.0	2.4	†	0.3‡	0.1	§	0.9	1.1
1912–13	36.0	2.8	†	0.4‡	.4	§	0.5	1.5
1928–29	104.0	4.1	0.3	0.6	.4	§	0.5	2.3
1934–35	68.7	9.9	0.6	4.4	.9	0.2	0.7	3.2
1935–36	77.6	9.2	0.5	4.0	.9	.1	0.6	3.1
1936–37	86.8	8.9	0.5	4.0	.8	.1	0.6	2.9
1937–38	88.0	9.3	0.9	3.7	.9	.2	0.6	3.1
1938–39	88.2	10.9	1.3	4.8	.9	.2	0.6	3.1
1939–40	95.7	9.5	1.3	3.8	.8	.2	0.6	2.9
1940–41	110.5	8.2	1.1	3.1	.7	.2	0.5	2.6
1941–42	140.5	6.1	0.9	1.9	.6	.2	0.4	2.1
1942–43	178.4	4.1	0.7	0.8	.5	.1	0.3	1.7
1943–44	202.8	3.5	0.6	0.5	.4	.1	0.3	1.5
1944–45	218.3	3.7	0.6	0.5	.5	.1	0.4	1.6
1945–46	202.1	5.9	1.3	0.6	.5	.2	1.5	1.8
1946–47	221.5	7.5	1.2	0.7	.5	.2	3.0	1.9
1947–48	245.0	7.7	1.2	0.7	.6	.2	2.8	2.2
1948–49	260.5	8.3	1.4	0.8	.7	.2	2.7	2.4
1949–50	263.0	9.2	1.8	0.9	.9	.2	2.5	2.8
1950–51	311.8	7.7	1.5	0.8	.9	.2	1.8	2.5
1951–52	336.8	7.4	1.7	0.8	.8	.2	1.4	2.5
1952–53	357.9	7.4	1.8	0.8	.8	.2	1.2	2.6
1953–54	359.7	8.1	2.3	0.8	.8	.2	1.1	2.8
1954–55	373.8	8.6	2.6	0.8	.8	.2	1.2	2.9
1955–56	403.0	8.6	2.6	0.8	0.8	0.3	1.1	2.9

* Source: Ida C. Merriam, "Social Welfare Expenditures in the United States, 1955–56," *Social Security Bulletin*, 20 (October, 1957), 6.

† Less than 0.05 per cent.   ‡ Includes other welfare.   § Included with public aid.

the pension issue. Many unions including the UAW had difficulty holding the support of the more senior workers in the demand for supplementary unemployment benefits, which seemed initially to hold very little advantage for long-service employees (McConnell, 1956*b*).

IV. The Effects on the Economy of Various Sources of Income for Older People

A. *Methods of Providing Income for Older People*

Older people, like the rest of the population, draw income from many sources. Un-

like the rest of the population, however, the majority of old people derive their major income from social insurance. Employment is the chief source of money income for only 27.7 per cent of those 65 and over, while 57.7 per cent are supported principally by social insurance (47.3 per cent by OASDI). Ten per cent, about 1,400,000, of all persons over 65 report no income or income only from other than earnings or public social insurance programs. Some of these, most of whom are women, are surviving beneficiaries of life insurance or annuities held by deceased husbands. A few are living on inherited wealth. Persons with more than one source of income amounted

TABLE 9*

ESTIMATED NUMBER OF PERSONS AGED 65 AND OVER IN THE UNITED STATES RECEIVING MONEY INCOME FROM SPECIFIED SOURCES, BY SEX, DECEMBER, 1956†

Source of Money Income‡	No. of Persons (In Thousands)			Percentage Distribution		
	Total	Men	Women	Total	Men	Women
Total aged 65 and over§	14,750	6800	7950	100.0	100.0	100.0
Employment	4090	2420	1670	27.7	35.6	21.0
Earners	3170	2420	750	21.5	35.6	9.4
Earners' wives not themselves employed	920	......	920	6.2	......	11.6
Social insurance and related programs‖	8510	4340	4170	57.7	63.8	52.4
Old-Age and Survivors Insurance	6980	3560	3420	47.3	52.4	43.0
Railroad retirement insurance	520	270	250	3.5	4.0	3.1
Government employees' retirement programs	500	300	200	3.4	4.4	2.5
Veterans' compensation and pension programs	740	470	270	5.0	6.9	3.4
Beneficiaries' wives not in direct receipt of benefits	230	......	230	1.6	......	2.9
Public assistance#	2560	980	1580	17.4	14.4	19.9
No money income or income solely from other sources	1490	100	1390	10.1	1.5	17.5
Income from more than one of specified sources	1900	1040	860	12.9	15.3	10.8
Employment and social insurance or assistance	1340	720	620	9.1	10.6	7.8
Employment and Old-Age and Survivors Insurance	930	480	450	6.3	7.1	5.7
Social insurance and public assistance	560	320	240	3.8	4.7	3.0
Old-Age and Survivors Insurance and public assistance	540	310	230	3.7	4.6	2.9

* Source: Lenore Epstein, "Money Income Sources of the Aged, December 1956," *Social Security Bulletin*, **20** (June, 1957), 9.

† Persons with income from sources specified may also have received money income from other sources, such as interest, dividends, private pensions or annuities, or cash contributions from relatives.

‡ The sum of the persons shown on lines numbered 1–4 exceeds the number in the population by the estimated number with income from more than one of specified sources (1–3). The estimates of persons with income from more than one source, developed from survey data, are subject to sampling variability (which may be relatively large for the smaller estimates) and to such errors as may result from attempts to adjust for developments since the sample surveys were conducted. They are not entirely consistent with those published in the *Social Security Bulletin* for periods prior to 1955 because of the availability of some new data and slight changes in methodology.

§ Estimated number of aged persons in the continental United States, plus Alaska, Hawaii, Puerto Rico, and the Virgin Islands.

‖ Persons with income from more than one of the programs listed are counted only once. In addition to the programs shown, unemployment insurance programs provided benefits for more than 84,000 aged men and 16,000 aged women in the continental United States; workmen's compensation and temporary disability insurance programs provided income for an unknown number. The overlap of these programs with other programs cannot be estimated.

Old age assistance recipients and persons aged 65 and over receiving aid to the blind. Includes some 16,000 persons receiving vendor payments for medical care but no direct cash payment.

to 12.9 per cent of the total, approximately half of whom were recipients of both earnings and OASDI; the remaining half, approximately, received old age assistance and income from either employment or OASDI. The complete tabulation of income sources compiled by Lenore Epstein (1957) appears in Table 9. (See also chap. viii.)

Income distribution among those over 65 does not follow the pattern of other age groups. There are proportionately more persons over 65 with no income and with

somewhat the picture of poverty among the aged but not much. Fifteen per cent of the families with heads over 65 had incomes of less than $1000 in 1956, while 23.8 per cent of such families had incomes of $5000 or over. The median income of older families was $2550, while the median income of unrelated individuals was $901. The trends in income for persons over 65 have been upward since 1948, but the rise in incomes enjoyed by persons in this age group has been less than those enjoyed by people in

TABLE 10*

PERCENTAGE DISTRIBUTION OF MONEY INCOME OF FAMILIES WITH HEAD
AGED 65 AND OVER AND PERSONS AGED 65 AND OVER, BY SEX, 1956†

ANNUAL MONEY INCOME	FAMILIES WITH HEAD AGED 65 AND OVER	PERSONS		
		Total	Men	Women
Total no. (in thousands)..	5741	14,293	6577	7716
Total percentage.........	100.0	100.0	100.0	100.0
Less than $1000..........	15.1	60.8	39.2	79.2
0....................	....	18.0	5.6	28.6
$1–$499‡..............	5.7	16.6	10.2	22.1
$500–$999.............	9.4	26.2	23.4	28.5
$1000–$1999............	24.6	20.0	26.9	14.0
$1000–$1499...........	13.8	12.3	16.1	9.0
$1500–$1999...........	10.8	7.7	10.8	5.0
$2000–$2999............	16.6	8.0	13.5	3.4
$3000–$4999............	19.9	6.8	12.0	2.4
$5000 and over.........	23.8	4.4	8.4	1.0

* Source: U.S. Bureau of the Census, "Income of Families and Persons in the United States: 1956," *Current Population Reports, Consumer Income* (Series P-60, No. 27 [Washington, D.C., 1958]), Tables 4 and 18.

† Non-institutional population of continental United States.

‡ Includes a small number of persons who reported a net loss for the year.

incomes of $25,000 or more than in any other age group. In general, however, the level of income of older people is the lowest of any adult group. The levels of income received by people 65 years of age and over is presented in Table 10.

As Table 10 shows, 39.2 per cent of the older men and 79.2 per cent of the older women (60.8 per cent of the combined group) had incomes below $1000. Only 34 per cent of the men and 6.8 per cent of the women in this age group had incomes of $2000 or over. A glance at incomes by family unit rather than individuals softens

the 20–64-age group. When the increases in income received by older people are adjusted for changes in the price level, they appear very modest indeed.

THE PRODUCTION OF OLDER WORKERS—
WAGE PAYMENTS

The various sources provide incomes of very different magnitudes. Those men who remain in full-time employment have median incomes of $3475, while all men with income had a median income of $1421, and women a median of only $738 (U.S. Bureau of the Census, 1958). The gap between income enjoyed by those who work and those who do not creates a dollar gap of strategic importance. So long as it exists, those who do not work will be envious and wish they were at work. The difference creates an immediate dissatisfaction with retirement, since the lowered income received in retirement means a radical downward change in living standards. A lowering of living standards is never pleasant, but, when a reduction takes place simultaneous with other status adjustments, it unquestionably adds undesirable emotional overtones to the problems of retirement.

OTHER PAYMENTS TO NON-WORKING OLD PEOPLE

Median incomes received from other income sources are substantially lower than earnings from employment. The average OASDI primary benefit in 1956 was $64.00 per month ($54.00 on wage credits from 1936 and $76.60 on wage credits after 1950). Family benefits for a primary beneficiary and an eligible wife averaged $105.90 per month, or $121.60 on post-1950 earnings. The annual amounts received from this source averaged $768.00 for the single individual and $1270.80 for a retired man and eligible wife.

Old age assistance, paid to 2,514,000 persons 65 and over, provided an average benefit of $57.99 in 1956, or $695.88 per year. The veterans non-service-connected disability pension pays a monthly benefit of $78.75 to veterans over 65. No allowances are made for dependents. This pension, therefore, provides an annual benefit of $945.00. Private pensions pay an *average* annual benefit of $950.00 per year (see also chap. viii). OASDI will pay a maximum benefit of over $2400 for those who qualify.

Except for full-time employment no single source of income of old people pays a benefit averaging as much as $1000 per year. Again, except for full-time employment, no single source provides a married couple with an average benefit of as much as $1500 per year.

In chapter viii, Dr. Gordon has presented detailed information on incomes and on budgets for elderly couples based upon government-agency calculations of what is needed for a healthful and decent living. Miriam Civic (1956) has presented the details of a minimum budget compiled by Dr. Henry W. Steinhaus from data provided by government agencies and the National Industrial Conference Board. These budgets range from $1800 to $2100 for couples in large cities, depending largely on whether dwellings are owned or rented. Budgets for single individuals are believed to be about two-thirds of the married couple's budget (see chap. viii for a detailed discussion of budgets). On this basis none of the sources of income for older people, except employment, provides, *on the average,* for even a minimum standard of living. However, again the maximum primary benefit and benefit to spouse would provide for this minimum standard.

Payments from accumulated reserves.— Those who have the advantage of coverage under a private-industry pension plan *and* OASDI fare much better than other old people. About 1,000,000 persons now receive a private pension averaging $950 per year. Added to the average OASDI benefit of $768 for a single person or $1271 for a retired couple, the annual average income is roughly equivalent to the budgets mentioned in the paragraphs above. The integration of public and private pension is not a uniform nor a simple procedure: older people themselves have trouble determining their own retirement allowances. Miriam Civic (1956) describes the relation of the company pension to OASDI benefits. She notes that for the firms surveyed by the Conference Board the average private pension benefit for a man with $3600 average annual earnings is $78.32 per month, or $940 per year. Miss Civic writes:

Estimates of the pension which would be received under the different plans were computed by The Conference Board on the following assumptions: upon reaching age sixty-five, 1. the employee has completed thirty years of service subsequent to the date the pension plan was installed; 2. the employee is entitled to the OASI retirement benefit provided by the 1954 amendments to the Social Security Act. If the level of the employee's earnings was $3,600 a year, his average company benefit for all the plans surveyed would be $78.32 per month. Plans which deduct all or part of the OASI benefit would pay an average of $33.67 per month; the flat percentage plans would pay twice this amount ($66.55); and the "per cent times years of service" plans would pay three times this amount ($99.42). Adding the $98.50 OASI benefit payable on average covered earnings of $3,600, the average total benefit would come to $176.82 for all the plans included in the survey, and $132.17, $165.05, and $197.92, respectively, for formulas above.

The range of benefits payable by the survey companies to the $3,600-a-year worker is from zero to $217.50. The "no pension" lower limit is owing to the fact that the OASI benefit of $98.50 is larger than the company pension from which it is deducted in four plans. Including OASI, the range is from $98.50 to $316. The middle half of benefits vary from $51 to $99 per month ($149.50 to $197.50, including OASI).

The dollar equivalents of the formulas are mere approximations based on a limited sample and may not hold for industry in general. Besides, the assumption of a constant annual earnings level of $3,600 may be unrealistic for the typical employee retiring under the plans. (Several different income bases are used in determining pensions; e.g., the career average, the average earned in the last five or ten years prior to retirement, the average in the highest ten consecutive years of credited service, etc.) The dollar figures undoubtedly overstate benefit amounts currently payable to aged persons retired on company pensions. But they reflect formulas in effect in January, 1955, many of which have been liberalized in one way or another in the year that has elapsed since, so they understate future benefits based on formulas now in effect [p. 61].

Transfer payments.—A transfer payment is a payment made to an individual from income earned by others. The term applies only to formal and recorded payments, but gifts to older persons by relatives and friends fit the definition. The latter are not matters of record and are not estimated in official sources.

Of all the income sources available to old people, only two are transfer payments to the full 100 per cent of the income received—old age assistance and veterans' pensions. All other sources are contributory or are "earned" through employment. It must be emphasized again that at this early stage of development both OASDI and private pensions are paid for by sidetracking temporarily sums sufficient to cover the payments currently being made through these programs. It must be conceded also that the employers' contribution to private and public pension plans is a transfer of funds from one owner to another, just as the government transfers funds from the taxpayer to those receiving OAA or veterans' pensions. Economists can always stir up a heated discussion over the incidence of a particular cost. Who really pays? General conclusions are impossible. Aside from a careful study of individual cases, no one can say who really pays the employer's contribution to pensions and OASDI.

Payments of ownership.—Cash income is only one aspect of the older person's economic position. Ownership of property in its several forms is another. The Federal Reserve Board Survey of Consumer Finances (1957) provides a great deal of useful information on the assets of persons by age groups. In early 1957, 5 per cent of the families headed by persons aged 65 and over had assets of $25,000 and over, 13 per cent had $5000–$24,000, 26 per cent had $1000–$4999, 23 per cent had $1–$999, and 31 per cent reported no assets. The median net worth was $8400.

Of this group, 9 per cent owned corporate stock, 27 per cent had United States Savings Bonds, 47 per cent had savings accounts, and 44 per cent had checking accounts.

Seventy per cent had no debts, while 5 per cent had only mortgage debt, 20 per cent had only instalment or other private debt, and 5 per cent had both mortgage and private debt.

Sixty-four per cent of persons aged 65

and over own their homes, compared with 56 per cent in 1949. Automobiles are owned by 39 per cent of this age group, with 2 per cent owning two or more cars.

The assets position of older people is relatively favorable compared to other age groups.

There is a close direct correlation between the size of asset holdings by individuals and the amount of cash income they receive. Assets are not substitutes for inadequate cash income for older people. Those who have very little cash income and hence need the assets are the very ones who do not have the assets. Furthermore, the lower the amount of assets, the more likely it is that these assets will be fixed assets like homes and real estate. The existence of some dissavers in the 65-and-over groups emphasizes the need to supplement inadequate cash income. Since the bulk of assets held by older couples is homeownership, there is no way of converting this asset into cash except by selling it and finding new quarters or by accepting public assistance payments, in which case cash grants based on need are made and a lien placed on the property to assume repayment of the grant.

B. *The Economic Impact of Public and Private Pension Plans on the Economy*

THE MAGNITUDE OF PUBLIC AND PRIVATE PENSION PLANS—NOW AND IN 1975

Estimates have already been advanced of the potential expansion in cost of public retirement systems. As of January 1957, 91 per cent of all jobs in paid employment including self-employment were covered by OASDI. Exclusions are principally in several of the health service professions, federal civil service, police and firemen already covered by another system, and others who do not qualify because of a limitation on earnings. For practical purposes the entire labor force, with minor exceptions, is covered by OASDI or some other public retirement system. Indeed, the pressing problem now is duplication of coverage rather than inadequate coverage. Veterans' pensions especially, which have the identical purpose of OASDI, will be available to 62 per cent of the male population 65 and over in 1995, in addition to OASDI (see also chap. viii).

Although the coverage under OASDI is nearly universal, not all persons qualify for benefits. In 1957 approximately 65 per cent of all males 65 years of age and over were eligible for benefits. By 1975 this percentage will increase to 84 per cent (President's Commission on Veterans' Pensions, 1956).

The picture under private pension plans is not so favorable. Currently, 15,200,000 persons are covered under a private pension plan, or 31 per cent of the wage and salary labor force (Skolnik and Zisman, 1958). Further expansion is likely to be very slow. The size and permanence of the employing unit as well as the stability of the labor force in a given industry influence the expansion of private pension plans. It seems very unlikely that more than a total of 25,000,000–28,000,000 employees will be covered by private industrial pensions by 1975, when the labor force will number 92,700,000. This number would constitute about 40 per cent of all wage and salaried employees in the labor force in that year. Benefits are likely to be paid to about 15–20 per cent of all persons 65 years of age and over.

Public and private pensions in the United States are generally paid out of accumulated reserves built up by contributions from employers or from both employers and employees.[2] These contributions are made in advance so that funds will be available to meet the pension payments when the employee retires. Plans generally are of the pooled reserve or group annuity type rather than in the form of individual annuity. The result of this system of financing is the accumulation of vast reserves. These reserves provide a fair share of the

---

[2] There are exceptions. The most notable is the United Mine Workers Welfare and Retirement Fund, which is essentially a pay-as-you-go plan.

funds for building up the capital structure of the country and financing its long-term operations. Nevertheless, these sums pose important problems for investors and for the investment markets.

THE EFFECT OF PUBLIC AND PRIVATE PENSION PLANS

On investment—opportunity, return, security.—The $43 billion in public pension trust funds must be invested in government obligations. Controversies over this use of trust-fund reserves in past years have dealt with the possibility of double taxation, on the one hand, and, on the other, with incentives to government spending. The charge that the American public pays twice for OASDI benefits is without any validity whatever. When the OASDI Trust Funds hold government securities, they are no different from a private pension fund which holds government bonds. When cash is needed, the bonds must be sold. In both public and private transactions the bonds may be sold to the individuals for whom the reserve is held.

The second charge, that such large reserves lead to increased government spending, has more foundation. With so large a "dollar gap" between the income and needs of older people, the OASDI Trust Funds of $21 billion are a great temptation to legislators to increase benefits and provide essential services without further concern for the financial stability of the system. But, since there is a complete separation of the budget-making and appropriation functions of government, there is little evidence that these reserves increase the government's propensity to spend, in general, though they may provide an easy solution to demands for benefits and services for older people. The record, however, shows that Congress has a high degree of financial responsibility with respect to use of reserves.

Recently, the stability of the OASDI Trust Funds has been questioned because in 1956 for the first time benefit payments dropped below contributions. In 1957 contributions and interest fell nearly $200 million below benefit payments. Actuarial projections show that the present reserve, interest payments, and contributions will pay all benefits and leave a reserve of about $190 billion in the year 2000 on a low-cost estimate. Given a high rate of unemployment, declining birth rate, widespread retirement at 65, and little or no increase in present wage rates, benefits could be paid until the year 2000 without additional taxes, but the reserve would be nearly exhausted by that date. There is, consequently, little immediate threat to the financial soundness of the OASDI system (U.S. Board of Trustees, OASDI, 1956).

When OASDI pays out more than it takes in, the effect is inflationary. Bonds must be sold, usually to banks, to raise the needed cash. Furthermore, when OASDI has a surplus, this money is loaned to the government at "bargain rates"—the average of government obligations—but, when OASDI pays out more than contributions, the government must seek money from other sources at higher interest rates to pay benefits and finance its other operations.

The $33-billion reserves of the private pension plans have posed quite a different problem. The number of opportunities for private investment changes from year to year. Just a few years ago it was predicted that the yearly investment opportunity would be about $2 billion less than the funds available for investment. Such a surplus of investment capital could bring on deflation. During the last two years there has been not a surplus but a shortage of investment funds with resulting high interest rates and efforts by the Federal Reserve Board to curb inflationary tendencies by repeated increases in the rediscount rate. Now (1959) the trend has changed again. Adequate investment capital appears to be available, and interest rates have begun to fall. Pension reserves have played no small part in reversing the trend. The increase in corporate bond holdings by pension trust funds supports this belief.

Trustees of the self-administered pension trusts have adopted a more liberal investment policy than insurance companies or the trust departments of banks. Common-stock investments on some such principle as dollar averaging is common practice. About $4.77 billion, or 24 per cent, of the self-administered trust funds are invested in common stocks, while $10.3 billion, or 54 per cent, are in corporate bonds. Government obligations, once the favorite investment medium, now constitute $2.0 billion, or about 11 per cent, of the average trust fund's portfolio. A few funds invest a very large percentage of their reserves in the securities of their own companies. Last year slightly more than 10 per cent of all common-stock holdings of pension trusts and 6 per cent of their corporate bond-holding were in the companies for whose employees the trust was established. The Sears, Roebuck fund invests 100 per cent of its assets in Sears, Roebuck and Company, and it is the largest single stockholder of the company. Market declines apparently have not yet affected the character of pension-trust investments. The net impression to date is that pension reserves have stabilized the market, and even larger amounts are currently being invested in common stocks as a hedge against inflation.

On savings—amount and form.—The growth of all kinds of social insurance programs covering the major economic risks has gradually changed the method of saving in our society though not the amount of saving. There is no evidence that the existence of public and private pension plans destroys the propensity to save. Personal saving has taken a more institutional form, and individuals have turned to automatic forms of saving through compulsory periodic payments and payroll deductions, *but they save.* Since the Social Security law was enacted, individual life insurance and other quasi-voluntary forms of self-protection have increased. From 1935 to 1957 life insurance in force in the United States companies rose steadily from $98.4 billion to $413 billion. A large proportion of the

increase came from group insurance (Life Insurance Institute, 1957). Instead of decreasing, personal savings have increased, and many people do save who would not have done so in the absence of present forms of institutional and automatic savings. From a low of $10.5 billion in 1948 personal saving rose to $22 billion in 1957, the highest in any peacetime year.

The impact of private pensions on the economy has not yet been fully studied. In 1957 the National Bureau of Economic Research published a report of an exploratory survey of the economic aspects of pensions. This booklet is a careful appraisal of the gaps in existing knowledge about pensions in the economy. It also suggests the kind of studies which are most likely to produce the required information. A list of some of the section headings will convey some of the scope of the research problems discussed: "Impact of Present and Future Pensions Plans on Savings and Investments," "Pensions and Saving," "Pensions and Investments," "Relation of Present and Future Pensions to the Level and Distribution of National Income and Product," "Effect of Pensions on Labor Mobility," "Redistributive Effects of Pensions," "Redistribution of Purchasing Power from the Working Population to the Retired Aged," and "Pensions and Stability."

In the early part of 1958 the insurance industry made funds available to the Pension Research Council of the Wharton School at the University of Pennsylvania for "An Inquiry into the Security behind Accrued Benefit Rights under Private Pension Plans." Though this study is very limited compared to the broad problems discussed in the National Bureau's preliminary discussions, it promises some solid materials for future students of pensions.

ON LABOR RELATIONS

Hiring middle-aged workers.—There is little question that job applicants 45 years of age and over have greater difficulty finding jobs than younger workers (McConnell,

1956*a*). Age restrictions on hiring of older workers are more prevalent among firms with pensions. Certain aspects of pensions, superficially, would appear to place workers over 45 at a disadvantage in the job market. First, pension costs are presumed to be greater for newly hired older workers than for younger workers. If the pension plan pays a flat amount, let us say, $100 per month, the reserve needed for this pension is $11,000 at age 65. The cost to the employer will be greater for a 55-year-old man than for a 35-year-old man, since the $11,000 must be accumulated in a shorter time. Second, if the pension benefit is an amount which is based on average wages and years of service, the pension benefit of a man who joins the company at age 55 is likely to be very small. Employers feel that public reaction is poor if workers are retired at 65 with inadequate pensions. Hence they prefer to hire only those who can qualify for adequate pensions.

To examine the accuracy of these conclusions, the Department of Labor called together a group of pension and insurance experts. This group stated that employers need not deny employment to older applicants because of high pension costs. They concluded that (1) because the predictions of wage increases used in figuring pension costs were more conservative than actual experience, (2) because pension levels would more than likely be raised during the course of a worker's lifetime, and (3) because life-expectancy would increase, it was the long-service younger worker rather than the older worker who would cause a rise in the employer's pension costs (U.S. Bureau of Employment Security, 1956).

Rather dramatic confirmation of this viewpoint, at least in part, has occurred in connection with the New York State Teachers Retirement System. The old mortality tables upon which pensions have been financed resulted in a life-expectancy far below actual experience. The trustees of the system attempted to revise downward the pension benefit levels to fit the present financing formula and the in-creased-life expectancy in order to keep the system financially sound. A ruling in June, 1958, by the New York State Court of Appeals enjoins the trustees from making these downward adjustments in pension values. The court ruling, if it is permitted to stand, will involve the state in heavy additional costs for the pensions of those hired at young ages and still employed. Obviously, the increased costs arise because of younger employees who entered the system at a young age and not because of older persons, since the newly hired older worker will have his pension financed and the value determined according to the latest mortality tables (*Civil Service Leader*, July 1, 1958).

R. M. Peterson (1957), vice-president and associate actuary of the Equitable Life Assurance Society, commenting on the cost of pensions for older workers, says:

The cost differential in current outlays (at rates presently estimated as adequate) between employees hired at older ages and those hired at younger ages will probably turn out to be much less when ultimate costs, based on actual experience, emerge. The pension for the younger employee may likely be larger and his life expectancy after retirement greater than that provided for in current cost estimates. Also, if savings from turnover are assumed as a result of the absence of vesting upon termination of employment, these should be offset against the cost of acquiring and training replacements.

The problem here, as with many other problems of older workers in industry, is having accurate information and the need to combat prejudices by strong educational measures. Unfortunately, the facts about pension costs are difficult to obtain and difficult to explain to the layman. Hence prejudices continue and become ever more firmly intrenched by practice.

Labor mobility.—The impact of pensions on labor mobility has been discussed often, but facts are meager, and the problem is extremely complex. There is a general assumption that the greater the amount of equity a worker has in private pension plan, based on his years of service, the more reluctant he is to shift out of his present job to another (Kerr, 1949). The reasons workers leave jobs are difficult to identify, and the reasons why workers do not leave jobs are even more difficult to ascertain. The existence of a pension plan would be one additional element to be considered by a worker when a move is contemplated. Observation rather than verified facts led a group of pension experts to conclude that seniority itself was of far more significance than a pension plan in holding men on the job (University of Illinois, 1953). The high correlation between labor immobility and age reported in studies of the Bureau of Old-Age and Survivors Insurance (1957) seems to indicate that many factors other than pensions operate to restrict mobility of older workers.

Nevertheless, the inclusion of vesting[3] provisions in pensions would assure the employee as well as others that equity in a pension plan was no barrier to changing jobs. Nearly all plans have vesting of some kind, but it is often attached to high age or service requirements and is ineffectual in protecting the employee against the loss of pension rights until he is too old to move. The Bankers Trust biennial studies of pension plans show an increase in vested plans. The most recent study (Bankers Trust, 1956) shows that 74 per cent of the conventional, single-employer plans have vesting, while 41 per cent of the negotiated-patterns plans, common in the mass-production industries, have some form of vesting. A more recent study (New York, 1957a) reports 148 plans out of 290 with vesting and 124 with early retirement. About one-third of the plans have neither vesting nor early retirement. The great bulk of the vesting provisions have a combination of service and age or service only. From 10 to 20 years of service is normally

---

[3] Vesting is the title held by the employee to the employer's contributions on his behalf to a pension program. Employees are entitled by law to their own contributions. It is the title to the employer's contributions which constitutes vesting.

required and attainment of age 40. Vesting costs at least one-third more than non-vesting pensions, but a general figure such as this has little application to the peculiar circumstances of the individual plan.

The importance of the problem of the impact of pensions on labor mobility has led the National Bureau of Economic Research (1957) to single out this problem for special study. The bureau suggests a study of mobility of workers in matched samples of firms with and without pensions and with pensions having substantially different provisions of benefits and vesting.

Continued employment or retirement.— All the evidence available points to a close association between pension plans and compulsory retirement policies. About 60 per cent of all companies with pensions have compulsory retirement. These firms are usually the larger firms, and, consequently, many more than 60 per cent of all employees in companies with pension plans are subject to automatic retirement at a set age. A New York State (1948) study of automatic retirement policies showed that 60 per cent of all firms with pensions had compulsory retirement, while only 30 per cent of firms without pensions had this policy, but well over half of all employees in the sample came under compulsory retirement. Compulsory retirement provisions were found in only one-tenth of the multi-employer plans, but in seven-eighths of the non-bargained single-employer plans and in more than two-thirds of the collectively bargained pensions. The identification of compulsory retirement with large-size employers is again emphasized in a more recent survey (New York, 1957a).

An increase in the retirement age in industry or a removal of compulsory retirement provisions altogether would lower the cost to society of maintaining older people by a substantial amount. Exactly how much might be saved is difficult to mention. However, if—and a very unlikely "if"— 3,000,000 older persons were kept at work 1 year more, they would contribute nearly $10 billion to the gross national product.

However, if this gain were responsible for a further loss of employment among younger job-seekers, it would be of doubtful social value. One must remember that the question of more employment for older men and women will be answered within the context of rapidly increasing output per man-hour.

Perhaps the clearest evidence of the effect of pensions on employment and retirement is the operation of the "work test" in OASDI. The work test is the provision in the law under which the number of benefit payments that may be made in a year to a person who has substantial earnings is determined. Under this test a beneficiary who is otherwise eligible can receive all his benefits if he earns $1200 in a year and some benefits if he earns as much as $2080 a year. The law also provides that the wage-earner beneficiary, regardless of his annual earnings, can receive a benefit for any month in which his earnings do not exceed $100. The self-employed beneficiary can receive a benefit for any month in which he does not render substantial services in his business regardless of the amount of his yearly income. Thus the beneficiary who earns $3000 during the first 6 months of the year and then retires and does no further work for the rest of the year can receive benefits for the last 6 months of the year. Despite the liberal earnings limit, there are critics who believe that any work test hinders employment and is inequitable to persons over 65 who have established eligibility for benefits.

Median annual earnings of all males employed full time the year round over 65 are $3475. Many persons would like to continue working, but the penalty of loss of benefits is irksome and in many instances results in withdrawal from the labor force. It is not easy for most employees to change over from full-time employment to part-time employment; hence even this high earnings limit is still a major deterrent.

Defenders of the work test point not only to the liberal earnings limitation but also to the increased costs to OASDI if the test were removed. The added costs of paying all persons 65 and over their full benefit regardless of employment is estimated to be 1.4 per cent of payroll (Myers, 1954*b*).

Actually, we have no firsthand information on the effect of the work test on employment. Field studies are badly needed. Other arguments have been advanced for the removal of the work test. It is said to be extremely complicated, and certain groups of employees and the self-employed can easily evade its restrictions.

Two alternatives to the retirement test have been suggested: (1) a graduated scale of earnings and benefits and (2) a benefit which increases with each year the employee remains at work past age 65 (Burns, 1956). The simplicity of the latter as well as its equity makes it worth serious consideration.

Private pension plans also occasionally place restrictions on employment after retirement. These include no employment at all for specialized personnel; no employment in the industry; and employment but with postponed benefit payment. Employment restrictions are not widespread in private pension plans, but, where they exist, the provision of no employment in the industry is the usual arrangement.

Stability of employer-employee relations. —Although it is difficult to cite specific evidence, the impact of pensions on employer-employee relations, especially in organized plants, has been to promote a greater stability of relationships and a more factual and rational approach to collective bargaining. In the first place, bargaining over pensions produced the first long-term labor agreements in American industrial history. Further, the necessity of including pension experts and other outsiders in the bargaining process resulted in a more rational approach to bargaining. Finally, the joint stake of both management and unions in the effective administration of pensions has resulted in increased co-operation between representatives of these two parties. Having had a demonstration in pension bargaining that problems are susceptible to intelligent analysis and solution, the rational approach is now a fairly common approach to bargaining (Kirkland, 1954).

There are many unanswered questions and many fertile fields for research in the interrelations of pensions and the economy. No one has yet studied how the accumulation of OASDI and unemployment insurance reserves have affected government fiscal policy. Fortunately for these trust funds, they have been in existence only in a 20-year period when government expenditures were expanding at a rate greater than the accumulated reserves. What would have happened if the period had been one of reduced government expenditures? Where would $30 billion of government money have been invested under conditions which prevailed in the 1920's?

Likewise, we know little of the impact of pensions on business expansion and survival. So many other factors are involved in these phenomena that careful analytical studies are needed to provide information on this aspect of pension influence.

COUNTERCYCLICAL POTENTIAL OF PENSION PLANS

The potential of pensions and retirement as countercyclical measures was discussed particularly in the early years of OASDI, but their importance has been overlooked because of other more pressing problems of the aging. Dr. Townsend's proposal to pay $200 each month to every person over 60 who would leave all paid employment and spend the $200 within 30 days was basically a device for spending ourselves out of the depression and of providing several million jobs for young and middle-aged workers (Twentieth Century Fund, 1936). The cost of this plan was to be met by a 2 per cent tax on every business transaction. The plan was held to be impractical, and only the vaguest traces of Townsendism are to be found in some of the smaller communities of the country.

In essence, every pension plan performs certain countercyclical functions. The marginal value of the pension benefit rises as short work weeks and unemployment appear. Workers retire because it is economically advantageous to do so. Others not yet eligible for pensions work more steadily or, if unemployed, take jobs vacated by pensioners. The total volume of consumers' purchasing power is increased by the amount of the pension payments.

When business conditions are good, employers add to reserves more rapidly than required by either labor contracts or trust agreements. Smaller amounts, therefore, are required in poor years. Hence the pension funding operations serve to stabilize the company financial condition, and the cumulative effect tends to stabilize the whole economy.

Furthermore, a group of employees who can move in and out of the labor market provide the flexibility of the labor force so necessary to the successful operation of a free-enterprise economy. Labor-force figures show that the percentage of persons over 65 at work rose during World War II and rose again in 1950–51 and in 1956. These were periods of labor shortage. Likewise sharp reductions in these percentages occurred in recession periods of 1949, 1954, and 1957–58. There is solid economic advantage in this flexibility. To the extent that older persons can constitute a labor reserve without bad human repercussions, they foster economic development.

PENSION PLANS AS AN INSTRUMENT OF WEALTH REDISTRIBUTION

OASDI and other public retirement systems.—Lewis Meriam (1946) has criticized OASDI because of its inequities to various groups in society. Most of these criticisms center around the fact that certain groups of covered employees pay for much more than they receive, while others receive much more than they pay for. In any insurance system, public or private, there is a socialized sharing of costs. With OASDI, however, the benefit formula is consciously weighted so that those with low average annual earnings receive a proportionately higher benefit. Those with high average annual wages receive more than their own contributions would buy in a private annuity but not as much as the combined employer-employee contributions would buy. There is consequently some wealth redistribution.

Another criticism is directed to the fact that a man who continues to work after 65 may never collect benefits, and yet he is unable to claim his contribution.

Finally, so long as some people in society remain outside the system, they help to support the system but never receive benefits. Employers' contributions may in many instances be passed on to the consumer through higher prices. This may occur with products over which a single employer has monopoly control. Hence these persons excluded from coverage help indirectly to pay the tax but cannot collect benefits. At present physicians are the most notable example.

Private pensions.—Similar conditions arise with respect to private pensions. benefit formulas usually favor the low wage worker—particularly in industries with flat pension amounts. Citizens not covered by industrial pensions may be presumed to pay part of the cost of the pension in the form of higher prices. Other partners in the business enterprise, stockholders, for example, may lose income because of the incidence of the pension costs.

Hence there is some small element of wealth redistribution in private and public pension systems, but the amount is negligible. Certainly, there is less in these systems than under social insurance programs generally.

INFLATION AND PENSIONS

The declining value of the dollar has been, and continues to be, one of the most serious threats to the security of both private and public pensions. The changing real value of the dollar as a consequence of changes in price levels is apparent in the history of government bond values.

A government "E" bond purchased in 1940 for $75 had a matured value of $100 at the end of 10 years. But in 1950 the purchasing power of $100 was only $69 compared to $100 in 1940. Pension plans and their reserves, when invested in government bonds, assure the pensioner of the promised dollar amounts, but they cannot assure him of the goods and services he expected to receive while accumulating credits toward the pension.

The purchasing power of public pensions (OASDI, state retirement systems, and the Railroad Retirement System) has been reestablished from time to time by legislative action. OASDI benefits, for example, for present as well as future beneficiaries, were revised in 1939, in 1950 after a lag of 11 years, and again in 1952 and in 1954. In New York State the minimum teachers' retirement benefit was set first as $75 per month and later revised to $100 per month.

The revision of the Old-Age, Survivors, and Disability Insurance benefit compared to changes in earnings and the consumer price index can be observed in Table 11.

Private pensions also, on occasion, have been supplemented by employers. Generally, the supplement is on a case-by-case basis where need has been established. The supplements are paid as a current expense, not from reserves. In some instances a revision of the formula is made to provide larger pensions for employees retiring in the future, and a flat benefit increase is made to all those currently retired. Private industry pensions have also been increased by collective bargaining. In the automobile industry the original benefit in 1950 was $100 per month less social security. It is now $2.50 per month times the years of service in addition to social security but no less than the original $100 assured by the first contract.

Increased benefits by fiat, whether initiated by the legislative, employer, or union, create grave problems in financing pensions. Consequently, pension administrators have sought ways of keeping pension reserves large enough to meet demands for increased benefits and to keep pension purchasing power at stable levels. The most popular mechanism to achieve this end is investment of part of the general reserve in common stocks, and/or providing an opportunity for individual participants in the pension plan to hold a part of their own pension equity in common stocks. As was pointed out above, 23 per cent of private pension reserves, held as self-administered

TABLE 11*

COMPARATIVE INCREASES IN WAGES, OASI
BENEFITS, AND COST-OF-LIVING
INDEX, 1940–56

Year	Average Total Annual Earnings in Covered Employment	Average Old Age Benefits to Retired Worker in Current Payment Status	Cost-of-Living Index
1940........	$1008	$23.17	100.2
1945........	1543	24.94	128.6
1950........	2274	43.86	171.9
1952........	2700	52.16	189.8
1954........	2890	59.14	191.1
1956........	3150	63.09	191.9
1957........	3150	64.58	194.3†
Percentage increase, 1940–56....	212	178	94

* Source: *Social Security Bulletin,* **21** (December, 1958), 19; *ibid., Annual Statistical Supplement,* **19** (1956), 40; *Monthly Labor Review,* Vol. **79** (June, 1956), Table D-4, "Consumers Price Index, U.S. Average All Items"; *ibid.,* Vol. **80** (June, 1957), Table D-1.

† Estimated.

trusts, have been invested in common stocks. Studies made by mutual funds and endowment administrators show that over a period of 50 years, covering booms and depressions, common-stock prices have moved upward and downward on the average at a rate equal to that of the purchasing power of the dollar. Although most pension funds, when investing part of the reserve in common stocks, do not advertise any upward revision of pension amounts to correspond with changing value of the dollar, it is conceded that the reasons for such investment are to increase the yield on investments through capital gains and to provide a reserve for such benefit increases if they are deemed necessary.

The variable annuity is a more formal and a more individual way of meeting the threat of inflation. Variable annuities are possible, of course, only under individual equity-type plans and are usually associated with contributory plans, though some non-contributory plans are now experimenting with variable annuities. Here the annuitant makes a decision that part of his equity shall be invested in what amounts to a mutual investment fund. His pension is determined by the value of the units of the fund to his credit at the time of retirement (Equity Annuity Life Insurance Co., 1956). The variable annuity was introduced by the Teachers Insurance and Annuity Association in 1952 as a companion to its fixed annuity system. The new agency was known as College Retirement Equities Fund, or CREF. A member of the fixed annuity system may elect to put as much as 50 per cent of the contributions made by or for him into variable annuities provided he retains a fixed annuity of at least $100 (Greenough, 1953).

V. ECONOMIC EFFECTS OF EMPLOYMENT AND RETIREMENT

A. Employer Personnel Policy and Old People in the Labor Market

RETIREMENT POLICY IN INDUSTRY—ITS ECONOMIC EFFECTS

The principal facts about the participation or lack of participation of old people in the labor market have already been reviewed. A smaller proportion of older workers each year remains in the labor force. Small gains in the life-expectancy of men at the age of 60 are being made. The result is increasing years spent in retirement (see chap. x). While at least a third of the old people who leave the labor force do so because of disability, only about 11 per cent who stop work do so because the employer enforces a compulsory retirement pol-

icy (U.S. Bureau of Old-Age and Survivors Insurance, 1953). Compulsory retirement policies are responsible for a higher percentage of retirements among salaried
employees than among wage-earners, and
negotiated pension plans are less likely to
include the compulsory retirement provisions than employer plans (Corson and
McConnell, 1956).

Estimates of the number of workers who
could and would remain at work except for
compulsory retirement policies are often
exaggerated. Sumner Slichter (1951) said
that 960,000 older workers could be employed with an annual increase of $3 bil-
lion in the gross national product. Considering those who cannot work, those who
do not want to work, and those who want
to work under circumstances which make
employment virtually impossible, the total
number who might be employed does not
exceed 400,000. Even so, this is a substantial number. They would add more than
$1.2 billion to the gross national product
and, considering present tax levels, about
$1 billion to disposable personal income.

PROSPECTS OF A LABOR SHORTAGE

During the next 10 years the low birth
rate of the 1930's will have a marked effect
on the supply of labor. Because of military
service and the increasing desire of young
men for a college education, the number
of new male entrants into the labor force
will not rise proportionately to the total
population. The percentage of persons in
the age group 20–64 has declined since
1955. It will remain constant at 51 per cent
from 1965 to 1980 and then begin to rise
again (Greville, 1957). This possibility of
a labor shortage gives some hope that older
workers will be retained in the labor force
along with the expected increases in women
entrants.

AUTOMATION—THREAT OR PROMISE
TO JOBS FOR OLDER WORKERS

The effects of automation on employment of older workers is still very much in
the speculation stage. Since automation is
a more advanced form of technological
change, perhaps experience with earlier
changes points the direction. In general,
employers have endeavored to introduce
new workers simultaneously with new machines. There is a vague feeling, poorly defined, that the chances of successful operation of new machines are greater if new
workers are trained on the machine. Usually, new facilities are located at some distance from facilities being displaced. This
further complicates the continued employment of older workers on new installations.
Once in operation, the new types of automatic machinery may be favorable to the
employment of older workers. Nathan
Shock (1957) says:

Hovering over all projections and plans for
the future employment of older people is the
cloud of automation in industry. No one can
predict, with any degree of certainty, what
automation will do to employment of the
elderly. On the one hand, the reduction in
physical activity may make it possible for
workers to retain their jobs of attending machines to a more advanced age. On the other
hand, if jobs demand simultaneous monitoring
of a number of dials and instruments, with
quick responses on the part of the worker, the
older person will certainly be at a disadvantage.
These are questions which can only be answered with time [p. 32].

INDUSTRY EFFORTS TO PROVIDE CONTINUED
EMPLOYMENT FOR OLDER WORKERS

Except for the survey by Elizabeth
Breckinridge (1953), little has been done
to assemble material on industry's special
efforts to employ older workers. Random
notes of company activity appear from time
to time, but an intensive study of company
practices would be a valuable addition to the
literature. The Ford Foundation has made
a grant to the National Committee on the
Aging to establish and maintain (along
with other activities) an information and
consultation service for organizations desiring to expand services to older people in
employment.

Wilma Donahue (1955) has reported numerous experiments. Most people interested in the aging have heard of Carson, Pirie, Scott and Company, the Chicago department store which has a policy of employing competent sales personnel who have been retired from other department stores. Shock (1957) reports on other experiments.

With these experiments and many more, the cumulative effect of which may be large, there is still lacking a positive determination in industry to provide adequate employment for those older men and women who want to work. The most plausible explanation of this lack of enthusiasm for employing older workers is the kind of bureaucratic administration which is prevalent in American industry. In large organizations it is often easier to do things according to impersonal and inflexible rule than it is to exercise judgment in individual cases. But the individual approach is the only possible approach to greater utilization of older workers.

B. Union Protection and the Older Worker

The Bureau of Labor Statistics (1956) made a careful study of 1687 labor agreements to discover what job protection unions provided to older workers. The findings are summarized in the following paragraph:

The older job applicant, whether or not he is a member of the union, can expect no preferential treatment and little protection against discrimination on the basis of age from the terms of most agreements. Only a relatively small proportion of the major agreements studied contained a requirement that some older workers must be hired or a pledge on the part of management to avoid discrimination against older applicants. On the other hand, the worker growing old in the service of the employer is generally assured a greater degree of protection on the job and more liberal benefits than his juniors in point of service. This contrast between the status of the older worker on the outside and the older worker on the inside underscores the change in status of the worker who loses his job after

attaining a substantial degree of seniority [p. 3].

VI. THE AGED AS CONSUMERS

A. The Older Consumer in the Economy

Aside from an initial flurry, some years ago, very little interest has been shown in the older person as a consumer. Advertisements directed to middle-aged people about financial preparation for retirement are plentiful, but there is little evidence that either new industry or old industry is taking seriously the production of goods or services used exclusively by older people.

THE PERSISTENCY OF STANDARDS OF LIVING AND CULTURAL PATTERNS THROUGH LIFE

Perhaps one explanation of industry's failure to take up with the consumer interest of old people is that there is no such clearly defined interest. Social workers, researchers, and government policy-makers have isolated people over 65 for purposes of study and assistance, but culturally the separation may be artificial. Standards of living and cultural patterns do not change readily at a given age. Older people perhaps more than younger people would like to follow the customary habits of life. Where these are detrimental to good health or a happy life, or too expensive for a retirement income, education in alternatives is needed. But this kind of picture is not very attractive to a manufacturer of goods or the purveyor of services. To interest the businessman, there must be some evidence of a mass market distinct from the general market, to encourage product specialization.

HABITS OF SPENDING AND SAVING AMONG OLDER PEOPLE

The median income of older couples of $2550, of older men of $1421, and of older women of $738 is considerably lower than the income of younger age groups. Although older people have slightly greater assets than other age groups, these assets represent debt-free homeownership for the most part. It is not strange, then, that older people spend most of their income and save relatively little (see Table 12). (For a detailed discussion of saving and dissaving among older people see chap. viii, Table 3, and related discussion.)

Nevertheless, the purchasing power of the population 65 years of age and over is not inconsiderable. In its issue of November, 1957, *Nation's Business* carried an article by F. D. Lindsey entitled "Expanding Markets: The Oldsters." Lindsey says:

Persons 65 and over along with families these oldsters head, will spend $32 billion of the $280 billion spent by consumers for goods and services this year. By 1965, the 65-and-over group should lay out $45 billion of that year's expected $390 billion in consumers expenditures.

Older people spend more of their money for such things as fuel, light, refrigeration, medicine, and food but less for household equipment, alcoholic beverages and transportation, for example.

Families headed by older persons spend a considerably larger proportion of total expenditures for housing, fuel, light, refrigeration, and for household operation but a smaller proportion for house furnishing and equipment. Older persons spend a larger proportion for food, but a smaller proportion for alcoholic beverages and tobacco. The larger proportion of women among those aged 65 and over influences spending for the latter two items.

Older persons spend a larger proportion of income for medical care, but a smaller proportion for transportation, toilet articles, barbers, beauty parlors, and other personal care items and services, and a smaller proportion for reading, recreation and education.

TABLE 12*

PERCENTAGE OF SPENDING UNITS THAT
SAVED OR DISSAVED, 1950

AGE OF HEAD OF SPENDING UNIT (YEARS)	SAVED		DISSAVED	
	Percentage of Income		Percentage of Income	
	10 or more	0–9	1–9	10 or more
18–24......	29	37	17	17
25–34......	38	26	15	21
35–44......	40	29	14	17
45–54......	42	27	10	21
55–64......	40	32	9	19
65 and over.	26	39	8	27

* Source: Board of Governors of the Federal Reserve System, "Survey of Consumer Finances," *Federal Reserve Bulletin*, **43** (1957), 878–901.

TABLE 13*

DISTRIBUTION OF AGED ECONOMIC UNITS (MARRIED COUPLES WITH HEAD
AGED 65 AND OVER AND OTHER PERSONS AGED 65 AND OVER) BY
MONEY INCOME AND BY EXPENSE FOR MEDICAL SERVICES, 1951

MONEY INCOME	DISTRIBUTION OF ECONOMIC UNITS BY INCOME	DISTRIBUTION OF ECONOMIC UNITS BY EXPENSE FOR MEDICAL SERVICE						
		Total	No Medical Services	No Expense†	$1–$49	$50–$149	$150–$299	$300 and Over
Total.............	100.0	100.0	35.7	4.8	23.8	20.2	7.6	7.9
Under $500..........	41.3	100.0	36.6	4.2	24.2	20.6	7.3	7.1
$500–$999...........	24.0	100.0	34.7	7.3	26.9	18.2	7.7	5.2
$1000–$1999.........	16.6	100.0	34.1	4.4	23.5	23.7	6.3	8.0
$2000–$2999.........	7.5	100.0	39.0	3.1	22.6	18.8	8.8	7.6
$3000–$3999.........	4.9	100.0	31.7	3.9	21.1	23.0	7.0	13.3
$4000–$5999.........	3.7	100.0	41.6	3.3	13.4	12.9	9.3	19.5
$6000–$9999.........	1.1	100.0	31.5	3.7	11.1	18.5	17.6	17.6
$10,000 and over......	0.8	100.0	25.3	....	17.7	15.2	17.7	24.1

* Source: New York Governor's Conference on Problems of the Aging, *Financing Health Costs for the Aged* (Albany, N.Y.: The Conference, 1957), p. 56.

† No out-of-pocket expenses because of free care, insurance, or payment by other resources.

Some businesses are beginning to produce for the needs of older people. There are foods, household equipment, construction materials, and numerous items for comfort and convenience. None of these is yet in the mass-production stage, which in our economy is the mark of a successful business venture.

The incomes received by older families and single individuals are woefully inadequate even compared to the minimum budgets compiled by government agencies or private experts. To bring all older people up to the minimum budgets, a current increase in payments to older people of $6 billion dollars would be necessary. For the next decade the amount of increase needed would probably rise to $10 billion to keep up with rising prices and changes in living standards.

B. The Importance of Medical Care

Discussions of budgets and expenditures of old people usually understate the costs of medical care. Yet medical service is greatly needed and desired. Medical expenses of old people are higher than those of younger age groups (Mushkin, 1957). Old people were 8.1 per cent of the population in 1950, but they accounted for 11 per cent of all medical expenditures. Of course, medical expenses are no more uniform among older than among young elements of the population. The poor distribution of cost and the close correlation between high income and high expenditure for medical service are shown in Table 13. This maldistribution is one of the critical problems in medical care.

A further indication of the cost of medical care for the aged is provided by the work of the Commission on Financing of Hospital Care (1954). This group estimated that the average non-working person over 65 who received hospital care in 1952 had a hospital bill of $458.75.

Oscar N. Serbein (1957) shows that medical care and drug prices increase at a more rapid rate than consumer prices generally. The over-all consumer price index was 114.5 for 1955, while the subindex for medical care and drugs was 128.0. (As of July, 1956, the medical care index was 132.7.) The hospital rate subindex for 1955 was 164.4. The same index for 1954 was 156.8. The current consumer price index is 122.

Even if incomes were raised sufficiently to provide for medical expenses, or if older people were blanketed into a prepayment medical and hospital plan, it is doubtful that the health needs of older people could be met. There is need for different methods of providing health care or for new types of health care for older people with special emphasis upon health centers, visiting nurses, and convalescent homes (see chaps. vii and xv of this *Handbook*).

REFERENCES

ANONYMOUS. 1958. Recession blunts Cupid's arrow. Business Week, June 7, 76–80.

BANKERS TRUST COMPANY. 1956. A study of industrial retirement plans, 1956. New York: The Company.

BRECKINRIDGE, ELIZABETH L. 1953. Effective use of older workers. New York: Wilcox & Follett.

BURNS, EVELINE M. 1956. Social security and public policy. New York: McGraw-Hill Book Co.

CARSKADON, R. R., and SOULE, G. 1957. U.S.A. in new dimensions. New York: Twentieth Century Fund.

CIVIC, MIRIAM. 1956. Income and resources of older people. ("Studies in Business Economics," No. 52.) New York: National Industrial Conference Board.

COMMISSION ON FINANCING OF HOSPITAL CARE. 1954. Financing hospital care in the United States, Vol. 3. New York: McGraw-Hill Book Co.

CORSON, J. J., and McCONNELL, J. W. 1956. Economic needs of older people. New York: Twentieth Century Fund.

DEWHURST, J. F., AND ASSOCIATES. 1956. America's needs and resources. New York: Twentieth Century Fund.

DONAHUE, WILMA (ed.). 1955. Earning opportunities for older workers. Ann Arbor: University of Michigan Press.

EPSTEIN, LENORE A. 1956. Money income position of the aged, 1948 to 1955. Social Security Bull., **19** (April), 7–14.

———. 1957. Money income sources of the aged, December 1956. *Ibid.*, **20** (June), 9–10.

EQUITY ANNUITY LIFE INSURANCE CO. 1956. The Equinuity Company handbook and rate book. Washington, D.C.: The Company.

FERINA, ELIZABETH. 1949. Old age and blind security programs in California. Berkeley: University of California, Bureau of Public Information.

GARFINKLE, S. A. 1955. Changes in working life of men, 1900 to 2000. Month. Labor Rev., **78**, 297–300.

———. 1956. Tables of working life for women, 1950. *Ibid.*, **79**, 901–7.

GREENOUGH, W. C. 1951. A new approach to retirement income. New York: Teachers Insurance and Annuity Association.

GREVILLE, T. N. E. 1957. Past and projected trends in the age distribution of the United States population. (Division of Program Research, Research and Statistics, Note No. 15.) Washington, D.C.: Social Security Administration.

KERR, C. 1949. Social and economic implications of private pension plans. Commercial & Financial Chronicle, **170**, 2201–6.

KIRKLAND, L. 1954. Pension plans under collective bargaining. Washington, D.C.: American Federation of Labor.

LIFE INSURANCE INSTITUTE. 1957. Life insurance fact book 1957. New York: The Institute.

LINDSEY, F. D. 1957. Expanding markets: the oldsters. Nation's Business, **45** (November), 38–39, 87.

MCCONNELL, J. W. 1956a. The employment of middle age and older workers. *In* Charter for the aging, pp. 118–65. Albany, N.Y.: Governor's Conference on Problems of the Aging.

———. 1956b. Private unemployment pay plans—economic effects. Month. Labor Rev., **79**, 300–303.

MCGILL, D. M. 1955. Fundamentals of private pensions. Homewood, Ill.: Richard D. Irwin, Inc.

MERIAM, L. W. 1946. Relief and social security. Washington, D.C.: Brookings Institute.

MERRIAM, IDA C. 1957. Social welfare expenditures in the United States, 1955–56. Social Security Bull., **20** (October), 3–12.

MOORE, O. O. 1947. Mile high harbor. Denver, Colo.: Associated Publishers.

MUSHKIN, SELMA. 1957. Age differentials in medical spending. Pub. Health Rep., **72**, 115–20.

MYERS, R. J. 1954a. Basis and background of the retirement test. Social Security Bull., **17** (March), 14–17.

———. 1954b. Old-Age and Survivors Insurance: retirement test under the 1954 amendments. *Ibid.* (December), pp. 10–15.

NATIONAL BUREAU OF ECONOMIC RESEARCH. 1957. Suggestions for research in the economics of pensions. New York: The Bureau.

NEW YORK. STATE. 1948. JOINT LEGISLATIVE COMMITTEE ON PROBLEMS OF THE AGING. Birthdays don't count. Newburgh: The Committee.

———. 1957a. DEPARTMENT OF LABOR. Pensions: larger plans in New York State. New York: The Department.

———. 1957b. GOVERNOR'S CONFERENCE ON PROBLEMS OF THE AGING. Financing health costs for the aged. Albany, N.Y.: The Conference.

PETERSON, R. M. 1957. Pension costs and the employment of older workers. Personnel, **33**, 563–67.

PRESIDENT'S COMMISSION ON VETERANS' PENSIONS. 1956. Veterans' benefits in the United States: findings and recommendations, Vol. **3**. Washington, D.C.: Government Printing Office.

SERBEIN, O. N. 1957. Financing medical care for the aged. *In* Financing health costs for the aged. Albany, N.Y.: Governor's Conference on Problems of the Aging.

SHOCK, N. W. 1957. Trends in gerontology. 2d ed. Stanford, Calif.: Stanford University Press.

SIMMONS, L. W. 1945. The role of the aged in primitive society. New Haven, Conn.: Yale University Press.

SKOLNIK, A. M., and ZISMAN, J. 1958. Growth in employee benefit plans. Social Security Bull., **21** (March), 4–12.

SLICHTER, S. H. 1951. The need for more employment of older workers. Wisconsin State Federation of Labor, **36**, 31–32.

TWENTIETH CENTURY FUND. 1936. The Townsend crusade. New York: The Fund.

UNIVERSITY OF ILLINOIS. 1953. INSTITUTE OF MANAGEMENT AND LABOR. Report: conference of pensions. Champaign, Ill.: The Institute.

U.S. BOARD OF GOVERNORS OF THE FEDERAL RESERVE SYSTEM. 1957. 1957 survey of consumer finances. Federal Reserve Bull., **43**, 878–901.

U.S. BOARD OF TRUSTEES OF THE FEDERAL OLD-AGE AND SURVIVORS INSURANCE TRUST FUND. 1956. Federal Old-Age and Survivors Insurance Trust Fund: 16th annual report. Washington, D.C.: Government Printing Office.

U.S. BUREAU OF THE CENSUS. 1957. Monthly report on the labor force, December, 1956. Current Population Reports, Labor Force. (Series P-57, No. 174.)

——. 1958. Income of families and persons in the United States: 1956. Current Population Reports, Consumer Income. (Series P-60, No. 27.)

U.S. BUREAU OF EMPLOYMENT SECURITY. 1956. Pension costs in relation to the hiring of older workers. (Publ. E. 150.) Washington, D.C.: The Bureau.

U.S. BUREAU OF LABOR STATISTICS. 1956. Older workers under collective bargaining, Part I. (Bull. No. 1199-1.) Washington, D.C., Government Printing Office.

U.S. BUREAU OF OLD-AGE AND SURVIVORS INSURANCE. 1953. Selected findings of the National Survey of Old-Age and Survivors Insurance beneficiaries, 1951. Baltimore: The Bureau.

——. 1957. Handbook of Old-Age and Survivors Insurance statistics, 1953–1954. Washington, D.C.: The Bureau.

U.S. DEPARTMENT OF HEALTH, EDUCATION, AND WELFARE. SPECIAL STAFF ON AGING. 1958. Estimated rate of growth in the aged population. Washington, D.C.: The Department. (Mimeographed.)

XV

Health Programs for an Aging Population

GEORGE ROSEN

I. INTRODUCTION

A. Aging and Health Problems

Aging has today become one of our urgent concerns. As a result of the attention which this problem has received, there is today a heightened awareness that health problems are significantly greater in the later years than at any other time. As the report of the President's Commission on the Health Needs of the Nation (1952) noted, "Our aging population reflects health progress and yet, paradoxically manifests some of the greatest health needs. . . . [Furthermore] health services are woefully inadequate in quantity and quality for the aging, wherever they may live" (pp. 71–72). What then must we do about the health needs, and what do they mean in terms of health services? That these questions are today being faced with mounting concern and an increased sense of urgency is a result of a number of linked and mutually reinforcing developments, of which the most important are the rise of industrialism, the creation of preventive health services on a community-wide basis, and the acquisition of effective medical knowledge and techniques.

B. Health Services and the Demographic Revolution

Moreover, there are more older people than before. There is no doubt that the decline in mortality among children and young adults during the last 50 years has been an important element in the aging of the population (see chap. ii). In turn, these changes are due in no small measure to the community-wide preventive health services created during the nineteenth century (Rosen, 1958). The problem of the public health was inherent in the new industrial civilization, which first appeared in England and then spread to other countries. The same process that created the market economy, the factory, and the modern urban environment also brought into being the health problems that made necessary new means of health protection and disease prevention. Most urgent was the control of communicable disease, and for this purpose health departments and related organizations were created. Efficient administration was as essential to the development of a complicated industrial society as the provision of new scientific knowledge. In fact, it was the existence of a stable administrative foundation which made it easier to incorporate new scientific knowledge into public health practice and thus to achieve control of the diseases which recurrently ravaged the populations of urban communities. The result has been a reduced mortality and an increased number of people who reach the middle and older ages. If 1900 mortality rates prevailed today, there would be 72 per cent more deaths among people 45–64, and nearly 45 per cent more deaths would occur among those aged 65 and over (Health Information Foundation, 1956).

C. Changing Values and the Needs of Older People

Yet, at the same time that more older people appear in our population, the means for meeting their needs grow more uncertain. The norm of family responsibility for the aged, in some form, was generally accepted in non-industrial societies, including those of Europe and America (Levy, 1949; Moore, 1951). (See also chaps. xiii and xvii in this *Handbook*.) Indeed, the view that adult children should be responsible for the aging parents is still widely held in the United States and in many places is incorporated into public assistance laws. Community provision, until recently, was made only for the indigent. The town or the county looked after the aged and others unable to care for themselves or who had no relatives to look after them. In some instances, the community provided care at home for the needy old person. More commonly, they were put into establishments which combined the functions of an old age home, an almshouse, and, in some cases, a true hospital. Today, the idea of family responsibility confronts the concept of social provision for the aged through pension systems, insurance for medical care, and similar arrangements that are more congenial with the changes that have overtaken the family in an industrialized society. Such conflicts in values create dilemmas and confusion for action, with the result that provision for the health needs of the aged is not made, or is poorly organized, or is conceived as something for the indigent alone (Havighurst and Albrecht, 1953; Bond *et al.*, 1954). This context of conflicting trends and changing values is the matrix within which efforts have been undertaken and are currently being made to meet the health needs of an aging population. But what are these needs?

II. Aging and Health Services

A. Health Needs of Older People

Aging means many things to many people. For centuries the view prevailed that old age is necessarily a period of deterioration, and certain morbid conditions and forms of disability were looked upon as the special province of this time of life. The classic expression of this viewpoint is Shakespeare's:

> . . . lean and slipper'd pantaloon,
> With spectacles on nose and pouch on side,
> His youthful hose, well saved, a world too wide
> For his shrunk shank; and his big manly voice,
> Turning again toward childish treble, pipes
> And whistles in his sound. Last scene of all,
> That ends this strange eventful history,
> Is second childishness, and mere oblivion,
> Sans teeth, sans eyes, sans taste, sans everything.

Within the last 100 years, however, and especially in the last four decades, this ancient view has been increasingly replaced by concepts that have made possible a fresh attack on the problem of aging. Studies along epidemiological, clinical, and experimental lines have thrown light on the health needs of the aging and the aged and point to the ways in which we can deal with these needs.

On a conceptual level it is recognized today that aging and disease are not synonymous. Aging is conceived as an evolutionary process characteristic of all living matter. This process, which represents the shifting balance over a period of time between evolution or growth and involution or atrophy, leads to a fundamental biological alteration which is part of the condition designated in human beings as old age. In this sense, Lansing (1956) has defined aging as "a product of reduced growth potential." At the same time it is evident that this concept requires a great deal of specific underpinning and clarification. The point is particularly well made by Alex Comfort (1956). At the very end of his review of the biology of senescence he says:

> Serious progress depends on the cultivation of general awareness among biologists of the importance of prolonging their study of every animal into the senile period, of collecting and publishing life tables, especially for cold-

blooded vertebrates under good laboratory conditions, and seeking confirmatory evidence of the distribution of sensescence in phylogeny. A few years of propaganda to zoologists in training might bring in a rich factual harvest later. Much modern research into aging tends to be desultory, although the single subjects with which it deals are important in themselves. We ought to try to devise critical experiments and if we destroy more hypotheses than we demonstrate, this is a subject which can well stand such treatment in contrast to the speculation that has gone before. The most desirable condition for progress in gerontology at the moment is that the exact nature and scope of the problems raised by senescence should be understood, and the possibility of new experimental evidence borne in mind during planning and assessment of all biological research, even when it's primarily directed to other objects. Senescence, like Mount Everest, challenges our ingenuity by the fact that it is there, and the focusing of our attention on it is unlikely to be fruitless [p. 200].

Inquiry into the causation of disease is increasingly being refined, and, as this search develops, evidence accumulates to strengthen the view that disease is the outcome of interaction between etiologic factors in the environment and the hereditary character and structure of the individual, no matter whether the individual is 20 or 60 years old. For many important problems of disease it is already evident that the keys to prevention, control, and therapy lie not alone in the study of the sick individual but also and even more significantly in understanding the environment in which he exists. Furthermore, in recent years, there has been a revived and expanded recognition of the importance of the social aspects of the environment for health and disease (Sydenstricker, 1933; Winslow, 1951; Morris, 1957). The concept of social forces affecting the health of individuals and groups is by no means a new idea (Rosen, 1947, 1953*a*, 1953*b*, 1953*c*, 1956). What is relatively new, however, is that the quickening interest in this aspect of the human environment has led to a wider appreciation of the need to

think in terms of multiple, and not only single, causes of disease (Kruse, 1953).

These concepts and points of view are directly relevant to the health problems and needs of the aged. While it is difficult indeed to separate the role of inherited constitution from the influence of environmental factors, the fact remains that environment is generally more easily modifiable than constitution. As more is learned about the effects of various stresses, strains, and insults of living, it should be possible to influence favorably the course and future of an aging population (Sheps and Taylor, 1952). The implications of Selye's theory of stress and the general adaptation syndrome for the aging process and old age point in the same direction. These have recently been clearly and succinctly formulated by Whittenberger (1956):

The impairment with age is real, but the results are not necessarily serious, as long as internal and external stresses are reduced in proportion to diminished and adaptive capacities of the aged. Compensatory mechanisms and experience minimize the results of physiologic limitations, but more and more of these factors are called into play as the organism ages. Much could be done in preservation of function of the elderly, if attention were paid to maintenance of high levels of mental and physical activity. The organism will eventually "run down" as physiologic reserves are exhausted, but meanwhile everything possible will have been done to make life not only longer but more satisfying [p. 336].

Clearly, health activities for an aging population cannot start with or be limited to the aged. Health problems and needs in the aged must be seen as the logical sequence of exposure to etiologic factors earlier in life as well as the consequence of immediate situations. A sound approach must therefore consider both long-term and short-term needs and objectives. These are given in general by the victories obtained over the acute communicable diseases. At the beginning of this century the five leading causes of death were pneumonia, tuberculosis, diarrhea, heart disease, and kidney disease. Typhoid fever and diphtheria also caused a large loss of life. Today the major causes of death are heart disease, cancer, accidents, cerebral arteriosclerosis (apoplexy), and kidney disease. The problem today is that of dealing with the progressive diseases of adult life, which eventually lead to the health needs and problems of the aged. Unfortunately, the etiology of these conditions is usually obscure, and the pathogenetic processes involved can best be described as the result of multiple, cumulative factors, of which a number are undoubtedly endogenous. Until the causation of these conditions is better understood, specific prevention is difficult if not impossible. For this reason, basic research is a prime requisite as a long-term objective. What Sheps and Taylor (1952) say about heart disease applies *pari passu* to other chronic illnesses. They point out that "prevention must be the keynote and the hope, but so far there is extremely little to offer because almost nothing is known of the pre-disease personal characteristics, of the life-long habits, of the factors of diet, of exercise, of emotion, of physical and social environment, of other illnesses and accidents far removed in time, which make one man a candidate for early death and give his fellow man relative immunity" (p. 11). From the point of view of health services, the progressive disorders of adult life, what is generally referred to as chronic disease, must be attacked along two lines. One is the application of available preventive measures; the other is the provision of effective means of therapy, limitation of disability, and the fullest possible restoration of function. Related to each of these lines of endeavor and action are such social factors as employment, retirement, degree of isolation, living arrangements, and the like.

B. Age Structure and Prevalence of Chronic Disease

Although old age and chronic disease are not synonymous, many elderly people are subject to functional limitations of varying

degree. Carlson and Stieglitz (1952) have described old age as a time of life when homeostatic balances become upset, when failure of physiological systems is more common, and when the individual is more likely to be affected by certain diseases of a chronic nature which produce impairments. A major problem therefore is to know the extent and nature of illness in old age. What are the dimensions of ill-health in the older age group, what are the manifestations of ill-health, and what are the consequences? While some data are available on these questions, the gaps in knowledge are large.

The National Health Survey of 1935–36 (U.S. National Health Survey, 1938) showed that disability and impairment increased with age. In this household study "impairment" designated any factor producing some limitation of activity, while "disability" referred to impairment of such severity that the individual was homebound and unable to work. Over the age of 65, more than half the population reported some degree of impairment. Nevertheless, even at age 85 the incidence of disability represented only 10 per cent of the population. In the 20-year study that the Public Health Service conducted among 1822 white families in Hagerstown, Maryland, it was found that the 5-year incidence rate of chronic disease and major impairments was around 35 per 1000 at age 25 as compared with nearly 250 per 1000 at age 60 and more than 500 per 1000 at age 80 (Switzer and Rusk, 1952). Another study carried out in 1950 estimated that, of the 12,200,-000 people in the United States over age 65, 17 per cent were disabled (Council of State Governments, 1955).

The data already available from the current National Health Survey tend to support the earlier information. As might be expected, the rate of restricted activity days and bed-days increases with age. Children under 5 have the lowest rates, with the rate for each successive age group higher than that for the preceding one. Persons 65 years of age and over show the highest rates—47.3 restricted-activity days per person per year and 16.3 bed-disability days. Both rates are more than twice as high as those for the next younger age group, 25–64 (U.S. National Health Survey, 1958*b*). (See also chap. vii in this *Handbook*.)

While it appears relatively clear that chronic disease and impairment are more prevalent among older people than among younger individuals, more precise quantitative information on the nature of the relationship between age and chronic disease has been scant, particularly for specific diseases. In recent years various community surveys have been undertaken to study the health status of specific populations and in a number of instances with particular reference to the needs of people over age 65. The results vary considerably and are generally not comparable, owing in large measure to the methods and techniques employed. Nonetheless, they do illuminate some aspects of the relationship between ill-health and aging.

Ciocco and Lawrence (1952) presented a study of illness among older people in Hagerstown, Maryland, based on an analysis of data collected in two house-to-house surveys conducted 20 years apart (1923 and 1943). The objective was to measure change in health status, that is, to determine as far as possible the relationship of current health status to past exposure to disease. The analysis showed that, of persons 40–50 years of age in 1923, less than 50 per cent were living and without chronic disease in 1943. Of those individuals who were 50–60 years of age in 1923, only little more than 20 per cent were alive and well in 1943. Furthermore, a considerable proportion of those who are ill at 65 had the same condition or some other chronic illness for at least 20 years. This means that, if disease is to be prevented or brought under control in persons at age 65, the condition must be detected and action taken by age 45, with such further attention as may be necessary in succeeding years. The point is also made that, of every 1000 persons who are well at age 45, about 100 will

need medical attention during the next 5 years because of the onset of some chronic illness or major impairment. Some of these will require medical care from time to time, and a few will need almost constant treatment of some kind until death supervenes. Of those who are well at 60, almost 25 per cent will develop a chronic illness within 5 years, for which in many cases continuing medical care will be necessary.

Data from other investigations tend to strengthen these inferences and to draw attention to several other aspects of the problem. Several recent reports indicate that older people need more medical service than do the middle-aged. In 1953 a survey covering 72,188 patients seen by physicians on 4 typical days was conducted in the state of Washington (Standish *et al.*, 1955). The findings showed that the average annual number of visits ranged from 2.5 among males aged 20 to 7 per year for males of age 65 and over. A similar tendency was found in California in 1955. There the number of physician visits per 100 persons per month was 48 for patients in the age group 45–64 as compared with 61 among patients 65 and over (Brewster and McCamman, 1956). In the same year, Fry (1957) and Shenfield (1957) studied the experience of 315 patients aged 70 years and over in a London general practice. This group represented about 6 per cent of the practice population and accounted for almost 10 per cent of all the work done. They required a greater proportion of care as is evident from Table 1, which shows the average rates of visits for the period 1951–55 and compares these with the average for the practice as a whole.

The most recent data on physician visits in the United States are derived from the ongoing National Health Survey and reinforce the impression created by earlier findings. It is noteworthy that the highest rate of physician visits by any age-sex group is for women 65 and over, who average 7.6 visits a year. Furthermore, the greatest change in average rate for males occurs from 45–64 to the 65-and-over age groups, increasing from 3.8 to 5.8 visits. The 65-and-over group also have the largest proportion of home visits, 21 per cent of all physician visits taking place in the home (U.S. National Health Survey, 1958a).

Further evidence pointing in the same direction is provided by the study of chronic disease carried out by the Commission on Chronic Illness (1957) in 1952–56 in Baltimore. In studying the prevalence of chronic disease as related to age, the findings were as follows: children under 15 had 407 diseases per 1000 population, that is, 4 diseases among 10 children. On the other hand, persons aged 65 and over had 4042 chronic diseases per 1000 persons, or an average of 4 diseases each, that is, ten times the rate among children. Persons in the age group 15–34 had 1205 diseases per 1000, and those aged 35–64 had 2199 per 1000. The distribution is presented in Table 2.

Despite the rather consistent evidence

that, as the population ages, physicians will probably be treating more and more elderly people, certain qualifying aspects should be mentioned. First, the functional consequences may be somewhat less serious than appears from an over-all picture. This was already indicated above with reference to the National Health Survey of 1935–36. Similarly, a study of a sample of 500 subjects in the Kips Bay–Yorkville Health District of New York revealed that fewer than one person in ten was totally homebound by ill-health (Kutner *et al.*, 1956). Furthermore, of those chronically ill, more than two out of three are able to continue with their daily activities. In the year immediately preceding the survey (1951), about one person in seventeen required bed care for as long as a month or more. For Baltimore, the proportion of persons with no chronic conditions ranged from 71 per cent for those under 15 years of age to only 5 per cent for persons 65 and over (Commis-

TABLE 1*

PHYSICIAN VISITS PER PATIENT IN A LONDON GENERAL PRACTICE, BY AGE, 1951–55

AGE	YEAR				
	1955	1954	1953	1952	1951
70–79............................	5.5	5.6	5.8	6.4	7.0
80 and over......................	6.2	6.2	6.2	7.7	7.7
Average for practice................	3.2	3.1	3.2	3.2	3.3

* Source: J. C. Fry, "Care of the Elderly in General Practice: A Socio-medical Reassessment," *British Medical Journal*, **2** (September 21, 1957), 666–69.

TABLE 2*

PREVALENCE OF CHRONIC DISEASE BY AGE AND SEX IN BALTIMORE, 1952–56

AGE	NUMBER OF DISEASES (UNWEIGHTED)			RATE PER 1000 PERSONS (BASED ON WEIGHTED NUMBER OF DISEASES)		
	Both Sexes	Male	Female	Both Sexes	Male	Female
All ages......	1892	784	1108	1566.5	1392.9	1722.6
Under 15.....	98	64	34	406.9	522.2	284.7
15–34........	252	96	156	1204.6	1038.5	1338.6
35–64........	1067	449	618	2199.1	1883.8	2493.4
65 and over...	475	175	300	4041.8	4271.7	3906.0

* Source: Commission on Chronic Illness, *Chronic Illness in the United States*, Vol. **4**: *Chronic Illness in a Large City—the Baltimore Study* (Cambridge, Mass.: Harvard University Press), p. 51.

sion on Chronic Illness, 1957). This trend was paralleled by the prevalence of limitation on the activities of daily life. While 30 per cent of those aged 65 or over had some limitation of activity, only a little over 1 per cent of persons under 55 had any limitations (p. 63).

Evidence along similar lines is available from other parts of the world. In Victoria, Australia, for example, field interviewers calling at the homes of people aged 55 and over found that 3 per cent of this age group were in bed when they called, usually because of illness. The proportion varied with age from less than 1 per cent for those aged 55–59 up to 8 per cent of those over 75. Of those interviewed in bed, no more than one-third were permanently bed-ridden. But there are also those who have some limitation of freedom of movement, even though they are not homebound because of their disability. About 30 per cent of the people in the age group 55 and over have some handicap of this kind. As may be expected, the incidence of such limitation increases directly with age. Only a fifth of the 55–59 group are restricted, while 54 per cent of those over 75 are afflicted in this way (Hutchinson, 1954).

A survey of 3000 people aged 65 and over in the city of Groningen (Holland) showed that about 80 per cent were able to go about their daily activities without any or with very little assistance (van Zonneveld, 1954).

Second, not only are there a considerable number of older people who remain relatively able to meet effectively the demands of daily living but many either feel no need for medical care or are unable to obtain care for a variety of reasons (e.g., economic, social isolation, or the like). In Baltimore, where a free health examination was offered on a voluntary basis, a comparatively large percentage of older people refused to participate. Apparently, they did not want to make the effort to come to the clinic where the examination was performed. In part, at least, this was due to over-all negative attitudes toward medical care.

This does not simply mean that they did not wish to make the effort. Many people, and particularly those in the older group, perceive health as requiring attention only when it interferes with daily activities. Furthermore, there is a widespread lack of understanding of the preventive approach, so that to some a periodic physical examination means asking for trouble. Obviously, it is difficult to render preventive service meaningful to individuals who prefer to wait until illness actually strikes (DiCicco and Apple, 1958). But precisely this is the health education challenge.

Based on a study of 734 retired individuals in St. Petersburg, Florida, Webber (1951) reports that 61.8 per cent had not visited a physician's office in the preceding 6 months. Furthermore, during the same period 83 per cent of this group had not had a physician make a house call. Van Zonneveld (1954) states that, in Groningen, about 40 per cent of all men and women over 74 had consulted a physician in the last 3 months preceding the survey but that this was significantly less for those who were still working.

C. Impact of an Aging Population on Health Facilities and Personnel

Some elderly people, when they are ill, must be cared for outside their homes, either temporarily or permanently. This may be necessary because the illness is of such a nature that the patient cannot be properly treated or nursed at home. Social economic factors may be and frequently are involved in transferring the task of caring for the elderly to institutions such as hospitals, nursing homes, and other facilities. The impact of an aging population on such establishments can be seen from some available data on utilization.

GENERAL HOSPITALS

While persons over 65 accounted for only one in twelve of the total population in 1955, one-fifth of the patients occupying hospital beds were in this age group (U.S. Congress, 1956). According to another source, about 8 per cent of the total population is over the age of 65, yet, in 1953, 18.2 per cent of the patients in general hospitals and 21.6 per cent of those in hospitals for the mentally ill were over 65. Furthermore, 53.3 per cent of the patients in convalescent homes, and 54.9 per cent of those in hospitals for chronic diseases, such as cancer and the like, were over 65 (Dickinson, 1955). According to the experience of Metropolitan Life Insurance Company personnel covered by the company's group insurance program, about one man in every seven at age 60 and over is hospitalized in the course of a year (Anonymous, 1955). This study of office and field personnel covered cases admitted to a hospital during the period August 1, 1953, to July 31, 1954, and traced to October 1, 1954. Included in it were not only those actively at work but also the permanently disabled and the retired. The admission rate at ages 60 and over combined was 13.8 per 100, or somewhat higher than the rate at ages 45–59, and virtually twice that at ages under 45. In the age range 60–74 the hospitalization rate remained at a level slightly above 13 per 100 and then increased to 15.9 per 100 at ages 75 and over.

A similar picture is presented by several French studies. At the Hôtel-Dieu in Paris, a survey of a general medical service for adults over a period of 18 months revealed that 51.3 per cent of the beds were occupied by patients aged 60 and over (Magdelaine and Péquignot, 1957). An analysis of four surveys, including the one first mentioned, also emphasizes the disproportionate utilization of hospital beds by persons 60 and over (Estève, 1957).

A study conducted jointly in 1952 by the New York City departments of health and hospitals, in co-operation with the Russell Sage Foundation, revealed that 16 per cent of the discharges from the municipal hospitals over a 6-month period were of persons 65 years of age and older (Fraenkel and Erhardt, 1955). Another study, made in 1955, covering all except obstetric and pediatric patients discharged from fifteen general hospitals operated by the New York City Department of Hospitals, show that 26.2 per cent were over 65 years of age (Kruse *et al.*, 1957).

Furthermore, older patients tend to have longer periods of hospitalization than younger ones. Among the personnel of the Metropolitan Life Insurance Company, the time spent in the hospital increased progressively from one age group to the next. The average stay for males at ages 60–64 was 14.1 days and only a little longer for those in the 65–69 age group. It then increased to 21.1 days at ages 70–74 and rose to as much as 28.6 days at ages 75 and over. For the entire age group 60 and over, the average duration of hospitalization was 18.1 days, or one and a half times the average for ages 45–59 and nearly twice that for those under 45. The 1955 study in New York showed that, while only 21.1 per cent of the patients under 55 were hospitalized for more than 14 days, 45.9 per cent of the patients aged 65–74 and 48.1 of those over 75 were in the hospital over 14 days (Brewster and McCamman, 1956). Similar observations have been made at the Hôtel-Dieu in Paris. The median length of hospital stay varied from 11 days for patients under age 50 to 25 days for those over 70 (Magdelaine and Péquignot, 1957). A survey of patients in general hospitals conducted in Maryland by the Commission on Chronic Illness in 1954 showed that in-hospital rates varied directly with age (Krueger, 1955*b*). The association was amazingly direct, but there was also a tremendous range of in-hospital rates. From a low point of 7 per 10,000 population for ages 5–14 the rate increased steadily to 83 per 10,000 for ages 85 and over; in short, the rate was twelve times as great. The range of in-hospital rates with age is even more striking. It varied from 0.7 per 10,000 for ages 15–24, up to 35 per 10,000 for ages 85 and over; that is, it was fifty-eight times as great. The age differential may be further emphasized by the fact that, while only 7 per cent of the general population in Maryland is aged 65 and over, one-sixth (17.5 per cent) of all patients, and one-third (34.7 per cent) of long-term patients in general hospitals, are 65 and over.

Further light on the current use of facilities for medical care by older people is provided by another survey of patients in institutions providing long-term nursing care (30 days or more in hospital) carried out by the Commission on Chronic Illness in Mary-

TUBERCULOSIS HOSPITALS

Not only do older persons tend to have longer stays in hospitals but they are also having an increasing impact on certain special fields of medicine and special institutions connected with them. Thus there is a trend toward older patients in tuberculosis hospitals (O'Connor, 1956; Kinsella, 1957). At present, most patients in tuberculosis hospitals are over the age of 40 and more

TABLE 3*

PERCENTAGE AGE DISTRIBUTION OF LONG-TERM PATIENTS IN
MARYLAND INSTITUTIONS, 1954

AGE	TYPE OF INSTITUTION					
	Proprietary Nursing Homes	Non-profit Nursing Homes	Homes for the Aged	Chronic Disease Hospitals	Long-Term Patients in General Hospitals†	Alms-houses
Number reported by age..............	1790	409	681	765	‡	450
Percentage distribution..............	100.0	100.0	100.0	100.0	100.0	100.0
Under 45........	1.2	3.2	0.0	8.2	35.6	2.7
45–64...........	11.6	15.4	1.8	26.1	29.7	23.3
65 and over......	87.2	81.4	98.2	65.6	34.7	74.0
65–74.........	23.4	26.4	23.5	30.3	17.0	35.1
75–84.........	40.3	39.1	53.7	26.0	14.0	29.1
85 and over....	23.5	15.9	21.0	9.3	3.7	9.8
Median age........	78	76	80	70	‡	72

* Source: N. W. Shock, *Trends in Gerontology* (2d ed.; Stanford, Calif.: Stanford University Press, 1957), p. 52. Derived from D. W. Roberts, "Characteristics of Patients in Nursing Care Institutions," *American Journal of Public Health*, **44** (1951), 455–66, and D. E. Krueger, "One in 8 Is a Long-Term Case," *Hospitals*, **29** (1955), 59–62.

† Excluding special units for mental, tuberculosis, and chronic-disease patients.

‡ Data not available.

land (Roberts, 1954; Krueger, 1955a). Of the patients who had been in general hospitals for 30 days or more, 34.7 per cent were over the age of 65. The proportion, as might be expected, was very much greater in nursing homes, both non-profit and proprietary. Those over 65 accounted for from 81 to 87 per cent of the patients. The distribution of long-term patients in various facilities is shown in Table 3. In short, many general hospitals have become long-stay facilities for the chronically ill and particularly the aged.

than one-fifth are 60 years of age and over. In Connecticut, during 1938, 52 per cent of all admissions to tuberculosis hospitals were under age 30, and only 6 per cent were above 60 years of age. In 1953, only 23 per cent of the admissions were under age 30, and 22 per cent were above 60. While the total admissions for all age groups increased 50 per cent in this period of 15 years, the group above 50 years increased about 370 per cent. A similar picture is reported from Minnesota. At Glen Lake Sanatorium (Minnesota) in 1925, only 9 per cent were above the age of 50; in 1955 over 40 per cent were in this age group. Comparable figures are reported from nearby sanatoriums. As the number of older individuals in our population increase, it is likely that more of them infected with the tubercle bacillus will survive into the older years, and the problem of tuberculosis will persist in this age group.

MENTAL HOSPITALS

Admissions to mental hospitals have increased very considerably over the past decades, and most of the increase has been in the older age groups. The proportion of those over 65 to total admissions to state hospitals rose from 19 per cent in 1938 to 24 per cent in 1948. For later years, figures as high as 36 per cent have been reported from New York State (Lemkau, 1955). In Illinois, in 1949, 35 per cent of the 34,000 patients in the nine state mental hospitals were over 60 years of age (Welfare Council of Metropolitan Chicago, 1952). This group formed an even greater proportion of first admissions to these institutions. Similar developments are reported from other parts of the world. On January 1, 1938, there were just over 23,000 patients aged 65 years and over in the public mental hospitals of England and Wales. Ten years later there were nearly 31,000 patients in this age group (Cook et al., 1952). One must point out, however, that the trends indicated above are due not alone to the increasing age of the general population but even more significantly to a number of social factors which profoundly affect the health problems of older people. These include not only the changing nature of the family but also the attitude of the community to old age, the admissions practices of hospitals, the availability of suitable housing, and numerous others. The impact of these elements must be given due consideration in developing health pro-

grams and will be dealt with below (Rosenfeld et al., 1957).

HEALTH PERSONNEL

It is evident that many elderly people need or will need medical services, some of them of a specialized character. For this reason, geriatrics is developing as a special branch of medicine. Medical attention to the disorders of later life is not entirely a contemporary development. References to the manifold medical and social problems of old age can be found in the writings of physicians from ancient Egypt to the present. Many authors were concerned with the hygiene of aging and old age. There was a general assumption that, if physicians knew enough and men paid attention to hygienic modes of life, human beings could attain long life. Galen wrote a treatise on hygiene, in which a whole section is devoted to the health needs of old age (Green, 1951). During the medieval period, works on personal hygiene concerned themselves with such matters; and, increasingly, with the Renaissance, books appeared under the title *De vita longa* (Sigerist, 1956). The classical example of this trend is the work of Luigi Cornaro (1467–1565), *Discorsi della vita sobria*, first published in 1627 and then reprinted many times. The emergence of modern medicine based on clinicopathological correlation began to lay the foundation for a deeper understanding of aging and old age. Physicians whose names are better known in other connections, such as Philippe Pinel (1815), were concerned with old people as patients. It is not often remembered that a large part of his medical life was passed in an institution concerned with the aged. During the first half of the nineteenth century a growing number of articles and books appeared dealing with the diseases and health problems of the aged, so that, by 1868, Charcot could say, in his book on chronic diseases and diseases of the aged, that "the importance of a special study of the diseases of the aged can today no longer be opposed" (Charcot and Ball, 1868, p. 3). Charcot goes on to point out that, while the pathology of disease in the aged is not identical with the changes of aging, disease in the aged has certain special features of which the physician must be aware (pp. 13–14).

Research since then has indicated increasingly that the aged person differs in his physiological constitution and in his reactions to disease from the young adult or the middle-aged individual. In the light of the current situation, it is a sterile enterprise to argue whether or not there should be a specialty of geriatrics (Seegal, 1956). The fact is that most older people are and will be treated by general physicians and specialists other than geriatricians. A decade ago, Zeman (1948) put his finger on the nub of the problem:

In view of the manner in which most general hospitals are at present organized and of the present state of medical education, it may be seriously questioned whether these institutions are completely aware of their new responsibilities and further, whether their medical, nursing, and social service staffs are adequately trained to meet the special requirements of the aged. For this reason, I believe that the increasing magnitude of these new problems demands the development of aggressive policies designed to bring to each individual old patient the best care that the hospital's facilities and staff are capable of giving [p. 281].

Although there have been definite advances in the last decade, the training of professional health personnel to deal with the problems of older people has not yet come of age. Much still remains to be done at the undergraduate and postgraduate levels. What has been done and what can be done will be discussed below. Here one must point, however, to the need for more and better training of all physicians, general practitioners and specialists alike—nurses, social workers, and others who deal with the health needs of the aged—so that they will be alert to the special problems that

may be involved and aware of the skills required for their solution.

III. HEALTH CARE FOR OLDER PEOPLE

A. Objectives

What has been said so far indicates the major objectives toward which health programs for an aging population must be directed. A health program for older people cannot start at age 65 or 70. As the body at these ages is attacked by diseases whose origins lie in the earlier adult years, a sound program must take account of the progressive diseases of adult life. The promotion of optimum health and the prevention of premature disability require not only medical services but educational and social services as well. At the same time there is the challenge to provide care for sick and disabled older persons, so as to help them get back on their feet as far as possible or to care for those who need attention that cannot be given in their own or other private homes. These services must include health education, health maintenance, care of the sick, rehabilitation, and, most important of all, the preservation of a feeling that there is a purpose in life (U.S. Congress, 1956).

HEALTH EDUCATION

A logical starting point is education for the maintenance and understanding of good health in the later years. Health education applied at an early period in life can serve as a means of helping men and women to meet the challenges of the later years in better health and with greater educational resources within themselves. Those who are aging need information and guidance about physical changes and how to live with them, about such matters as diet, exercise, and rest, and about the availability of health services. Many older people need counseling and guidance in dealing with such problems as the appearance of chronic ailments and disabilities, retirement and reduced income, and the loss of family members and friends.

HEALTH MAINTENANCE

The importance of measures aimed at the prevention of disease can hardly be overstressed. Health guidance is one such measure. Another is prevention through regular health examinations. Adequate programs of this type could save many from the effects of disabling ailments. Through periodic examination of apparently well individuals, diseases may be detected and disability forestalled. Examination services can be offered in physicians' offices, in special clinics, and in other facilities.

CARE FOR THE SICK

Secondary prevention in the aging and the elderly cannot be considered apart from the provision of care for those who are sick. Hospitals and related institutions, at first glance, would seem to be the most effective facilities for the provision of care to geriatric patients. For the most part, however, they have not been as effectively utilized for this purpose as they might be. With increasing recognition of the dynamic nature of sickness and the potentialities in the organism for restoration of function, a greater variety and flexibility of institutional programs has appeared.

REHABILITATION

The development of more aggressive and flexible approaches to the care of the aged has gone hand in hand with a much broader conception of rehabilitation. Recognizing that the problem is more than medical, the purpose of rehabilitation activities for elderly persons is to restore them, as far as possible, within the limited potentials of their disabilities, to their fullest physical, psychological, social, and economic usefulness.

A PURPOSE IN LIFE

Implied in the foregoing is need for some purpose in life, something that will make life worth living. A few aging individuals bear within themselves psychological sources of self-renewal. Others need help in adjusting to the consequences (physical, mental, etc.) of aging.

B. Services and Facilities

CARE OF THE ELDERLY IN MEDICAL PRACTICE

As the numbers of the aged in the general population increase, physicians will encounter geriatric problems more frequently, and growing numbers of practitioners are turning their attention and efforts to the care of the elderly. Since most old people can be cared for at home or in the physician's office, the general practitioner and the specialist alike must be familiar with the medical aspects of gerontology. Such knowledge is particularly pertinent, since the altered reactions of the aged to pathological processes obscure the clinical pictures that have come to be regarded as typical in younger individuals. Indeed, in old age there are more likely to be a multiplicity of pathological conditions in a given patient, as well as bizarre clinical phenomena and variant responses to treatment (Zeman, 1955).

In caring for his elderly patients, the physician should be guided by certain fundamental principles and be clear as to his aims and objectives. For one thing, the practitioner must approach the problems of the elderly in terms of preventive medicine, accepting the inevitable abnormalities that appear with old age, yet endeavoring to detect the stages of morbid processes and conditions at which they are reversible or can be brought under control. Thorough examination is required. Minor lesions are likely to be more troublesome and may cause almost as much disability as more serious conditions. While some older people complain a great deal, many do not complain enough.

This requires as a second principle that the physician endeavor not only to diagnose disease but also to understand his patient, the social situation in which he finds himself, his family background, and any other elements that may be involved in the presenting health problem. Attention to such matters is essential in order to maintain the elderly patient in as active and independent a condition as possible. Furthermore, friendly interest and sincere concern on the part of the physician are as significant as drug therapy and may be, in some instances, far more effective. Social isolation affects the elderly to a greater extent than it does younger persons, and the feeling of rejection experienced by lonely old people can be mitigated by simple psychotherapy on the part of the physician.

From a medical point of view, the physician occupies a crucial position in the care of the aged. However, the doctor alone cannot undertake to provide the best possible care without appropriate assistance and co-operation from the patient's family, the hospital, public health agencies, social agencies, and other relevant organizations in the community upon whose services he may have to call. Two-thirds of the aged in the United States have homes of their own, and another fourth live in the households of others (Corson and McConnell, 1956). Not unnaturally, they prefer to remain at home in a familiar environment. As J. H. Sheldon (1950) has pointed out, "All old people dread the thought of being moved to an institution to die, and desire to remain in their accustomed surroundings at home" (p. 220). Yet this very circumstance entails problems with which the physician must deal, either alone or together with others. Involved are nutrition, housing, occupation, domestic arrangements, and others (Simonds and Stewart, 1954; Smith, 1957). These needs have led to pioneering efforts to develop services that will enable the older person to remain in a relatively favorable home environment rather than in a dreary hospital or nursing home. (Various arrangements and services will be discussed below.)

In any event, physicians must be aware of these problems and how to deal with them. It is regrettable that not more is done in this area by medical schools, which would seem to be the logical starting point for education in this area. Only about one-third of the medical schools in the United States have accorded some recognition to the problem of an aging population. This generous estimate is based on reference to aging, geriatrics, and similar topics encountered in descriptions of courses. Very few, however, offer specific courses. Only two medical schools, at the universities of Kansas and Miami (Florida), have a division of gerontology in the department of medicine. In addition, special courses are offered at the Women's Medical College, Philadelphia, and the Medical Branch of the University of Texas. Elsewhere, courses dealing with other aspects of medicine, such as physiology, pathology, internal medicine, and psychiatry, touch on aging and its health problems. Nor are internships and residencies in geriatrics any more common. Only a few hospitals in the United States provide such training. This situation is certainly not due to lack of knowledge on how to develop or organize such teaching. At the Home for Aged and Infirm Hebrews in New York, Zeman (1949) has pioneered in developing postgraduate teaching for physicians and nurses in this field. The training and education of the medical student, the intern, and the resident to be aware of and competent to deal with the geriatric problems he meets is essential, and this area of medical education requires expansion.

Increasing attention is being given to postgraduate education. The University of Kansas Medical School has been active in this work. For several years this institution has offered a 3-day course in geriatrics to physicians in the Kansas City area. Similarly, the American Geriatrics Society has held an annual 2-day course of this kind in New York City. In 1955 the Graduate Fortnight of the New York Academy was devoted to problems of aging. The lectures and seminars covered the subject broadly, from the biology of aging to the social problems of the aged. (It is of interest to note that the first Graduate Fortnight held in 1928 had also been devoted to the same subject.) A postgraduate course on stress and aging was also held in 1955 and in 1958 at the Lankenau Hospital in Philadelphia under the sponsorship of the American College of Physicians. Medical societies in various parts of the United States have also organized meetings and seminars. In 1956, Dr. Lionel Z. Cosin, clinical director of the Geriatric Unit of the United Oxford Hospitals (England), visited the United States and lectured at various medical schools and other organizations in California (Kuplan, 1956; Shock, 1957).

The need to deal with problems of older people on a community basis is reflected in the increasing amount of time devoted to chronic disease and aging in schools of public health. Over the past decade there has been a considerable growth in the scope of such instruction and in the number of faculty members involved in it (Smillie and Luginbuhl, 1959). This development has been stimulated by the federal government through the National Institutes of Health (e.g., Heart, Cancer, Mental Health) and the grants which they have provided. At the same time, the demand for trained personnel to plan and work in state and local programs for the chronically ill and the aged has operated in the same direction. It is anticipated that this trend will increase.

THE GERIATRIC CLINICS AND THE WELL-OLDSTER CONFERENCE

As has already been indicated, for the vast majority of the chronic diseases to which older people are subject, the basic knowledge needed for primary prevention is not available. For this reason secondary prevention remains the more significant immediate approach. What this means is that physicians must be alert to the possibilities of disease detection and be ready to take advantage of consultations with and examinations of middle-aged or older persons

for this purpose. Periodic health examinations can also be usefully employed to uncover inapparent disease. Theoretically, such examinations should start in early middle life and continue at regular intervals for one's remaining years. By this means, cases of chronic disease may be picked up early, and, while the condition may not be removed, it may be brought under control. This is one way in which older people can be helped to maintain their health at a relatively satisfactory level. However, the advantages of disease detection for effective treatment and control of many conditions can be attained only if physicians are alert to this problem and if facilities are available where examinations may be obtained.

Some practicing physicians are providing such examinations to patients who have no obvious symptoms. Others have suggested the organization of special geriatric clinics, and in a few communities such facilities have been established. One of the oldest clinics of this type in the United States was established by Dr. Robert T. Monroe (1951, 1958) in 1940 at the Peter Bent Brigham Hospital in Boston. Recently, this clinic gave up the experimental status under which it had operated for almost 15 years and became the Pearl Memorial Clinic. Similar facilities have been created in other communities, for example, in New York at the Beth Israel Hospital, at the Brooklyn Hebrew Home and Hospital for the Aged, and at the Home for Aged and Infirm Hebrews (Gitman, 1955). As a result of a special demonstration project, a clinic was established at the Kips Bay–Yorkville Health Center in New York City (Kutner *et al.*, 1956).

Attempts have been made, both in New York and elsewhere, to establish geriatric health protection facilities, but most of them have not been successful. Conceptually, as well as operationally, there have been endeavors to differentiate and delineate the geriatric clinic as a facility where the emphasis is on therapy from the "well-oldster conference," which is concerned with prevention. The latter concept is, of course, based on an analogy with the well-child conference. While the distinction is emotionally and verbally appealing, there is a tendency to burke the differences which derive from the very nature of the health problems of the aged. For the most part, preventive services for older people involve secondary prevention. Furthermore, the attitudes toward prevention may militate against an overt emphasis on preventive services. It seems more reasonable to suggest, therefore, that no sharp separation be made between prevention and therapy and that preventive services for older people be considered in terms of integration with services that they regard as well established and accepted (DiCicco and Apple, 1958).

Recently, a health protection clinic was set up in the Nashoba Health District in Massachusetts but came to a halt for lack of clientele (MacLeod, 1958). Similar experiences, although the consequences were not so severe, have been reported by Kutner *et al.* (1958) in New York and by Monroe (1958) in Boston. There is a socio-psychological aspect in this experience which cannot be overlooked. Many older people do not like to be segregated on the basis of age. They do not wish to have the fact of aging emphasized, or segregation may be considered a reflection of prejudice against older people, or the service may be considered inferior. The establishment of a facility is not enough. It should be part of a larger framework (conceptual, institutional, community) and should be linked to a program of education for patients, physicians, and the community as a whole upon which it draws. The role of certain public health workers, in particular, that of the public health nurse, may well be of prime importance in this connection. Because the public health nurse gets into so many homes and can serve as a liaison between the home and the clinic, she may be in a position to carry out a considerable part of this educational activity. Furthermore, the interests of the physician may

determine success or failure of a geriatric facility. Monroe suggests that such a facility may be most acceptable in a teaching and research hospital. One must also keep in mind that it requires a sufficiently large population upon which to draw for its clientele.

One thing is certain. The geriatric clinic and the well-oldster conference are service facilities. Where they can be used will depend on local needs, requirements, attitudes of physicians and public, availability of medical services through other forms, and the like. In other words, geriatric facilities are ways of organizing and providing health care for older people and must be seen in relation to other means for the provision of care.

PATTERNS OF INSTITUTIONAL CARE

Increasing attention is being given to patterns of institutional and domiciliary care for those older people who are not able to be completely independent. This trend is due in part to the rising costs of hospital care and in part to an increased awareness of the need for more careful assessment of the particular kinds of services needed by different individuals in various circumstances (Lowe and Mc-Keown, 1949). Consequently, there is extensive experimentation at the present time with a variety of arrangements and measures for the care of older persons either in their own homes or in other facilities such as hospitals, nursing homes, and foster homes.

Hospitals.—While most old people can be cared for at home and maintained in relatively good health, some elderly individuals require hospitalization. However, what kind of illness requires hospitalization and how those admitted are to be dealt with are matters which in recent years have undergone considerable change. As described above, older persons tend to have longer stays in hospitals. Owing to the fact that hospital care is costly, this tends to make provision for the older person an expensive matter. When to this one adds the fact that many of the aged are in a poor economic position to pay for such care (Corson and McConnell, 1956; Steiner and Dorfman, 1957), it is clear that we are dealing with a problem requiring the attention of community agencies.

The admission of older people to hospitals and their lengths of stay are usually attributable to a combination of medical *and* social factors. Most patients are admitted because of specific medical needs alone. A good many remain in hospitals, however, for socioeconomic and psychological reasons, and these play significant roles as well in leading patients to enter hospitals. Many persons who no longer need the care provided in a general hospital either cannot or will not leave because there is no one to care for the patient; or, if the patient has a family, they cannot or do not wish to care for the patient. Many long-stay patients are dependent on continued institutional care or some assistance in a home environment (Rosenfeld *et al.*, 1957).

Home-care programs.—The advantages of care in the individual's own home, provided adequate medical, nursing, and other needed services are available, is generally accepted in theory today. In a number of communities, considerable success has been achieved in the development of such programs. Actually, the idea is not quite the novelty that some ardent advocates of home care think it is. Organized domiciliary medical care for the indigent has existed for a long time, both in Europe and in the United States (Sturges, 1937; Rosen, 1948; Bakst, 1953). Jarrett (1933) and Boas (1940) suggested that selected patients with long-term illnesses might best be cared for in their own homes. A significant demonstration of this thesis was carried on at Syracuse University Medical College from 1940 to 1942 by Jensen and his associates (1944). Interest in organized home-care programs was greatly stimulated by the thinking of E. M. Bluestone (1954) and by the establishment of such a program in

1947 at Montefiore Hospital, of which he was the director.

The organized home medical care program appears to offer a useful tool for dealing with long-term illness in older people who do not actually need hospital services (Warren, 1955) or for the provision of preventive care to those comparatively free from severe illness. Programs of organized home care for the chronically ill usually involve a combination of medical, nursing, housekeeper, and social service, depending on the situation. Success is based on proper selection of cases for home care and adequate correlation of the required services. Furthermore, such programs are closely linked to the development of rehabilitation services.

Limited home-care programs have been developed by several institutions concerned with older people (Laverty, 1950; Morris, 1954). In New York City the Peabody Home instituted its Non-Resident Aid Program in 1945. Several years later (1950–53), the Home for Aged and Infirm Hebrews, the Brooklyn Hebrew Home and Hospital for the Aged, and the Home and Hospital of the Daughters of Jacob developed programs. On the whole, the chief goal in these instances has been to enable aged persons to continue to live in their own homes. The basic needs are most often social and economic, and what is needed medically is preventive and supportive care. Such care has been provided in these programs through initial examinations for admission to the program, periodic examinations, and consultation when desired. Diagnosis and treatment of illness were not provided. For such services, clients have been referred to private physicians or to public facilities (outpatient departments and the like). With increasing emphasis on maintaining older people in their own homes and in an independent status, these beginnings merit development and will assume increasing significance.

Home-care programs may be considered in two groups: the first, comprising those based on hospitals; the second, those based in other community agencies. While the concept of centralized responsibility for co-ordination of services is accepted by all programs, the scope of responsibility is not the same for all. Total supervision of services, including the quality of medical care, is easier in hospital-based programs. This is much more difficult to achieve in programs based in community agencies other than hospitals. Such programs serve chiefly a co-ordinating function. The Roanoke Conference on Organized Home Care, June 9–13, 1958, recognized a need for both kinds of programs, since communities differ in their structure and in the readiness of agencies to undertake new activities of programs. This awareness led the conference to recommend two standards for the two types of programs.

Whatever the kind of program, however, certain auxiliary services in the home may be necessary to maintain some degree of independent living. One of these is home-maker service. Assistance of this type may range from the attendance of a home help once a week to provide heavy cleaning service to a full-time resident homemaker for an extended period. Furthermore, a good home-care program must have a good environment to function satisfactorily. Older people, in general, are not well housed. Provision of proper housing or up-grading of substantial housing cannot help but make it possible to take care of more older people outside institutions. Recreation is another important element in relation to health. The experience of the Hodson Center in New York showed that older people who participated in a group recreation center for 6 months required 38 per cent fewer medical clinic visits than before participating (Levine, 1955; Amulree, 1958; Pomrinse, 1958).

"Six weeks in, 6 weeks out."—Emphasis on keeping older people out of institutions, while undoubtedly salutary, should not be permitted to obscure another aspect of the problem. Less commonly appreciated is the stress and strain imposed on families who have to care for aged invalid or semi-invalid members. Such older people can and sometimes do tyrannize a family. In 1955, DeLargy (1957), consulting geriatrician at the Langthorne and Whipps Cross hospitals in London, made a study in which he found that domestic stress was an important reason for seeking admission to the hospital. Many relatives simply needed a rest. To deal with this problem, he conceived the idea of rehabilitating the aged and at the same time of relieving their relatives. For this purpose a social rehabilitation unit was established at the Langthorne Hospital; the patient was to spend 6 weeks at the hospital, then 6 weeks at home, then another 6 weeks at the hospital. Thus hospital discharge and readmission continue as long as necessary. The program as it has developed takes account not only of physical needs but equally, if not more so, of social and emotional needs.

Rehabilitation.—The program instituted by DeLargy is but one aspect of the quiet revolution in the treatment of chronic illness and disease in the aged which has been going on for some time and has contributed in considerable measure to a broader concept of rehabilitation. The former attitude of futility in the treatment of aged patients is changing, owing to the impetus provided by the work of a number of pioneering physicians in the United States and Great Britain. Rusk and Dacso (1956) and Zeman (1950) in this country and Sheldon (1956), Warren (1953), Howell (1951), and Cosin (1952) in Great Britain should be mentioned. The general concept is to apply rehabilitation methods to all patients so as to produce whatever degree of benefit is possible. While the aim of all medical and social treatment is to enable the patient to take his place in the community, it is recognized that this is conditioned by his physical condition, his mental and emotional state, and his particular social situation. Consequently, the aged need a wide variety of medical and social services, extending beyond the older idea of custodial care. Some patients may be rehabilitated to the extent of employability; many others can be brought to the point of self-care so that they can live at home (Nuffield Provincial Hospitals Trust, 1937). For still others some form of institutionalization is necessary, but even in an institution certain special programs can be and must be developed. Some institutions to serve special needs exist; others must be developed.

Nursing homes, halfway houses, and related establishments.—Certain groups of aged persons cannot remain in or return to their own homes. For some of these foster-home care can provide a satisfactory arrangement (Crutcher, 1944; Posner, 1952; Fox, 1953; Cryan, 1954; Brecher and Brecher, 1955). For others, the nursing home or the halfway house must be used. That such facilities fill a need is evident from the tremendous growth in the number of nursing homes which has occurred in recent years. The need is as much social as medical; it is to accommodate and to care for individuals who require personal and nursing attention they cannot get in their own homes or in the homes of relatives. Medical situations in many instances have been reinforced and intensified by changing family patterns, changes in the status of the aged, and the other social pressures and trends in contemporary life that have been described at the beginning of this chapter.

In a relatively short span of years the number of nursing homes has grown to such an extent as to warrant attention by public and private groups. For almost a decade, attention has been increasingly focused on measures to improve and expand such facilities, to improve the quality of patient care, to develop better standards of administration and supervision, and to develop adequate sources of financing such care (Kinnaman, 1953; Murdock, 1953; National Social Welfare Assembly, 1953). The need for a better understanding of the role of the nursing home and related facilities and for information that could provide a better basis for developing state programs for the care of the chronically ill led the Commission on Chronic Illness and the

United States Public Health Service to undertake a national inventory of nursing homes and related facilities in 1953–54 (Solon and Baney, 1954; Solon et al., 1957).

The inventory disclosed about 25,000 nursing homes in the United States, with 450,000 beds. Only 3 per cent of nursing homes are publicly owned. The majority are privately owned, either under voluntary auspices or as proprietary establishments. The term "nursing home" covers a wide range of facilities, some providing medical service and skilled nursing care, others being simply a sheltered home (Waterman, 1953). As a result there has been a difficulty of definition (Michlin, 1957), and several solutions have been suggested. The most recent was proposed by the First National Conference on Nursing Homes and Homes for the Aged held in Washington, February 25–28. Its report recommended a classification in terms of four areas of service: (1) residential services (housing, food, and other domiciliary needs); (2) personal care (aid in feeding, bathing, dressing, getting in and out of bed, and similar services); (3) nursing care (technical nursing skills); and (4) multiple services (covering the above and including rehabilitation, social services, group work, and the like) (U.S. Public Health Service, 1958).

At present, however, a definition employed by the Public Health Service in connection with the Hill-Burton program restricts the term "nursing home" to those "facilities, the purpose of which is to provide skilled nursing care and related medical services for a period not less than 24 hours per day to individuals admitted because of illness, disease, or physical or mental infirmity and which provide a community service." Using this definition, there were nationally 221,435 nursing-home beds as of January 1, 1958. Of these beds, 113,019 were considered acceptable and 108,416 not acceptable for health reasons or because of fire hazards. An independent survey conducted by the American Nursing

Home Association indicated that in August, 1957, there were 392,303 beds in 17,455 nursing and convalescent homes. Sixty-seven per cent of all beds reported in this survey were in proprietary homes (Brown, 1958).

Nursing homes are predominantly concerned with the care of aged persons. The median age of persons in proprietary homes is 80 years. In the 1953–54 inventory, 90 per cent of all the patients were aged 65 or over, and one-fourth were 85 or older. Two-thirds of all the patients are women. Furthermore, less than half of the patients can walk alone; two-thirds have some kind of circulatory disorder; a large number suffer from incontinence; and a considerable group are disoriented at times.

Thus there is a need to supervise and to improve the quality as well as the number of nursing homes. That the problem has been officially recognized is indicated by the contrast between 1950 and 1958. In 1950 only three states required licensing of nursing homes; in 1958 every state and territory, except the Virgin Islands and Puerto Rico, licensed nursing homes. Only South Carolina, the Virgin Islands, and Puerto Rico do not license homes for the aged. Responsibility for licensure is distributed as shown in Table 4.

Raising standards of care is intimately related to the question of costs. This question in turn is interlocked with the financing of nursing-home care. About half the patients in nursing homes are recipients of public assistance. Such payments range from $55 to $155 per month. At the same time, in thirteen states that were studied, the average cost for nursing-home care varied from $90 to $200 per month. Public assistance payments are inadequate for the purchase of good care in a nursing home. Some states and localities are willing and able to spend more and are thus able to encourage higher standards of care (Florida, 1953; Wickenden, 1953; Greenfield, 1957; Brown, 1958). Furthermore, the majority of proprietary nursing homes are small, the average number of beds varying

between 15 and 25. Consequently, the operators of such homes who attempt to provide good service at a cost within reach of the patients or their families are likely to encounter economic difficulties. Certainly, more adequate economic provision for financing of nursing-home care is needed.

But this problem involves several other aspects. One of these is the financing of health and institutional care for the aged through prepayment and other means. Another is the need for community planning to deal with the health problems of the aged. To these we must now turn.

TABLE 4

RESPONSIBILITY FOR LICENSURE OF NURSING HOMES AND HOMES FOR THE AGED, 1958

State Agency	Nursing Homes	Homes for the Aged
State health department...	42	36
State welfare department..	6	12
Other state agencies......	3	2
None...................	2	3
Total...............	53	53

IV. FINANCING AND ADMINISTRATION OF HEALTH PROGRAMS FOR OLDER PEOPLE

One of the most pressing problems in dealing with the health needs of the aged is to finance the costs of the care they need. In 1892 Charles Booth pointed out that, "when all is said, the fact remains that age falls heavily on the poor, and that the case of the aged poor demands special consideration" (p. 149). That this circumstance is still prominent is indicated by the fact that about half the patients now in nursing homes are maintained by public funds.

A. Public Assistance

Since the Colonial period, local communities in this country have assumed responsibility for the indigent ill, including the aged. Based as it was on the charity of hospitals and clinics or individual philanthropy, on social and religious agencies and the tax-supported poorhouse, this system foundered under the impact of the economic depression of the thirties. Through federal grants-in-aid, the Social Security Act of 1935 made it possible for state governments to give cash assistance to needy persons who were aged and/or disabled. As has been shown, there is a higher incidence and longer duration of illness in this group, yet public provision of medical care for it is very uneven. State funds are allocated for mental illness, tuberculosis, and other communicable diseases, and care is usually available through public hospitals. Major responsibility for medical care of welfare recipients, including the aged, still rests largely with the local community. Except for some twelve states, public medical care programs are limited, and the public welfare recipient who is ill must rely on free services of voluntary hospitals and clinics. Thirty-four state public welfare agencies make some financial contribution to medical care of certain welfare recipients.

The federal government shares medical care expenditures for recipients of old age assistance and aid to the permanently and totally disabled. Beginning July 1, 1957, the federal government shares half the total state expenditures up to $6 per month for each adult on the public assistance rolls covered by a state plan for medical care. This amount is for vendors of medical care or for insurance payments to cover such care. In this connection it is worth noting that a survey made by the Bureau of Public Assistance of the Social Security Administration showed that, in early 1957, of forty-five states reporting, forty-three had specific provisions in one or more of the public assistance programs for money or vendor payments for nursing home care (Brown, 1958). It is evident that public action to finance medical care through public assistance has grown. Nevertheless, its impact on the problem as it affects the aged is limited. In terms of the actual medical needs and present-day costs of medical care, the federal contribution is considered too low. Furthermore, there are specific financial limitations in many states where the philosophy seems to obtain that welfare recipients are of a lower order. Finally, the relationship of prepayment medical care to welfare assistance has hardly begun to be explored. This is an area for future development.

B. Prepaid Medical Care

In 1951, among beneficiaries of Old-Age and Survivors Insurance, 71 per cent were not covered by any health insurance (McCamman and Brewster, 1954). Furthermore, Anderson and Feldman (1956) estimated that in 1953 less than half of the families in the United States, with a male head aged 65 or over, had coverage by any voluntary health insurance. These findings have several causes. One is the fact that voluntary health insurance plans rely to a very large extent on group enrolment, generally through the place of employment. Furthermore, income and age limitations reduce the number of persons eligible to join prepayment plans. Exclusion of preexisting conditions is another limitation, so that such plans meet only part of the medical needs of a certain proportion of seriously and/or chronically ill persons. These characteristics affect the aged to a greater extent than younger groups of the population.

In part, these limitations may be removed in the future by the development of industrial health and welfare plans and the recent tendency to extend benefits to retired employees and, in some cases, to their dependents. An analysis of three hundred plans in effect in 1955 showed the following. They included 5,000,000 workers, or 40 per cent of all workers covered by such plans. Nearly all provided life insurance, hospitalization, and surgical benefits. About two-thirds of the plans covering 74 per cent of the employees provided other benefits and extended them to dependents. One-half of the plans providing life insurance and about one-fifth of those providing health benefits continued them for retired employees. These plans were large and included 71 per cent of the employees covered for life insurance and roughly 35 per cent of those covered for health benefits. Where there was coverage after retirement, health benefits were also extended to a considerable proportion of dependents. Usually, however, the level of benefits extended after retirement was lower. The cost was paid either by employers, by employees, or jointly (Rowe, 1955; Corson and McConnell, 1956; U.S. Bureau of Labor Statistics, 1956).

Even with these advances, older people are at a disadvantage. Services they need may not be included in the policies under which they are covered. For example, it is only recently that nursing care has been covered to a limited extent by a few Blue Cross plans (Brewster, 1958). Furthermore, they are poor insurance risks and therefore insurable only at premiums so high as to be beyond their financial means. In general, voluntary prepayment, as presently organized, will not be able to meet all the needs of older people for financing medical care and institutional care. To a greater degree than at present, government (federal, state, and local) will have to take steps to meet the increasingly urgent unmet health needs of older persons. Recently, it has been proposed that contributions under the Social Security Act be used to pay for the health costs of persons entitled to benefits after retirement.

That means can be devised to deal with these problems is certain. It is clear that there is no single, simple answer. In the past, health services for the aged have been derived from four sources: direct payment by patients, general tax funds, endowments, and insurance. The relative importance of these has changed substantially over the years. Today payments from public agencies and insurance schemes of various kinds defray the greater part of the expenses. In the future the financing of health services for older persons will have to be obtained through insurance, general taxation, and combinations of these two approaches (Goldmann, 1952). Insurance plans deserve an important place in such arrangements. An insurance system designed to meet the needs of older persons must include medical care insurance, disability insurance, and old age insurance.

The feasibility of providing prepaid medical care to older persons while employed and after their retirement has been demonstrated (Baehr and Deardorff, 1952). However, such persons have been enrolled as part of an employed group. This circumstance calls attention to still another factor, namely, the role of employment and income maintenance as crucial elements in dealing with the health needs of the aged.

C. Employment and Health

To a considerable degree, much of what has been said about financing of health care depends on the steady employment of persons in the middle years and continuing on into the older years. Technical progress may in the future lead to new attitudes toward work and leisure. Indeed, there are some who feel that ours is becoming a leisure-centered society (see chap. xii) and that one of the major challenges is to find leisure activities which will provide equivalents for the purpose and group feeling encountered in the work situation. Yet in our contemporary society there is a large and possibly a growing number of aging persons who have no wish for premature retirement. In our society a job insures social status and integration into a social group, and lack of work frequently means loss of these social necessities. Consequently, there is today an increasing awareness that older persons can and should be productively employed if they are at all physically able (Mathiasen, 1957; Steiner and Dorfman, 1957; International Association of Gerontology, 1958). For many elderly individuals work provides a purpose in life (Brooke, 1956). Furthermore, it is recognized that techniques of prevention, disease detection, and health maintenance may be applied within the industrial or occupational framework and thus contribute to the prevention or control of the chronic and disabling conditions that are so important in the poor health and retirement of older workers. On this account, increasing attention is being given to the health problems of workers in the middle and older years (Amulree, 1955; Davies, 1955; Sand, 1955). In this connection, studies are being carried on to determine how long various groups of workers are able to continue in their occupations beyond the sixties and seventies and also to develop yardsticks that will measure the physical abilities of the employee, the characteristics of the job as related to physical condition of health limitations, and the employee's health and physical conditions as they affect his own well-being and that of his fellow employees (Christensen, 1955; Anderson and Cowan, 1956; Clark and Dunne, 1956; Rudd and Feingold, 1957; Anonymous, 1958).

But while the number of people aged 65 and over who might be continued at work has grown greatly in the past half-century, the proportion of gainfully employed in this group has decreased steadily over the same period. The total labor force of the United States has been growing faster than the general population, but the reverse is true among older persons as shown in chapter x. The proportion of gainfully employed has decreased from 68 per cent in 1890 to 42 per cent in 1950. Figures for 1955 indicated that the percentage of those gainfully employed who are aged 65 is still declining. Nearly 60 per cent of all men aged 65–69 are still in the labor force, but only 20 per cent of those aged 75 or more. Furthermore, middle-aged and older workers who lose their jobs have difficulty finding new ones, even in periods of full employment. And the situation is obviously aggravated by economic recessions and declines. This trend, that is, the continuing reduction of the number of older workers at work, is due to two important economic changes. One is the shift of our economy from agriculture to industry, and the other the great depression of the 1930's. In this connection it is worth noting that about one-fourth of the older men in the labor force are farmers or farm managers; others are service workers or engaged in other light occupations (Corson and McConnell, 1956). Clearly, if older people cannot be kept gainfully employed, then the means for financing services must come from other sources.

However, the problem is not only an economic one. Of the value of work as a means of maintaining financial security in old age there can be no question. But there are other important meanings associated with work. Ours is a work culture. Work gives a person a way of spending his days usefully; it also enables him to develop social relations with fellow workers. All these aspects have a definite bearing on the mental health of the older person. Obviously, income maintenance and the provision of work are economic matters, but the health worker cannot overlook them because they bear directly on the question of health problems and health services.

V. COMMUNITY ACTION FOR THE HEALTH OF OLDER PERSONS

Throughout known history, men living in communities have had to take account in one way or another of health problems that derive from the biological and social attributes and needs of their fellows. Out of the need for dealing with these problems, there has developed with increasing clarity a recognition of the signal importance of community action in the promotion of health and the prevention and treatment of disease. Today the protection and the promotion of the welfare and health of its citizens is considered to be one of the most significant functions of the modern state, as shown in chapter xvii. This function is the embodiment of public policy based on political, economic, social, and ethical considerations and is summed up succinctly in the concept of public health.

What is accepted in theory, however, is not always fully translated into practice.

Organized community effort directed toward improving the health of the aging and dealing with their problems is only in its initial stages. Until very recently, custodial care and institutionalization were the means by which communities attacked the problem of the aging person who suffered from severe forms of disease. Almshouses, charity care in hospitals, and the like were used to discharge community responsibilities. A similar phenomenon may be seen in the treatment of the mentally ill.

Slowly, we are moving away from this limited view. An adequate community health program for the aging and the aged must run the gamut of services, similar to those that have been developed to deal with other health problems. And at the center of this community program should be the official health agency. This is not to say that all activities should be officially sponsored, organized, and administered. What is needed, however, is knowledge, stimulation, and co-ordination of activities on a community basis. This is the basic role of the official health agency (Breslow, 1954).

Public health methods, personnel, and thinking can be fruitfully applied to the health problems of later life. The public health nurse has already been mentioned, but there are also the other specialized personnel—the epidemiologist, the statistician, the medical social worker, the health educator, and, certainly not least, the health officer. A number of states—California, New York, Indiana, Connecticut, Massachusetts—have set up in their health departments separate units to deal with problems of adult hygiene and aging. A few large municipal health departments, for example, New York City, have taken similar action. The objectives of such units are research, education, co-operation, and co-ordination with groups and agencies in the community and to deal with problems of legislation and regulation. Similarly, the United States Public Health Service endeavors to assist states and local communities in developing programs for the aged.

Within a broad community approach there is room for private, voluntary action as well as governmental endeavors. For example, the "Meals on Wheels" idea was first developed in this country by the Lighthouse, a settlement house in Philadelphia, as a result of a problem presented by visiting nurses (Tauber, 1956). The problem was that of providing proper and adequate nutrition to malnourished older people. Modeled on an English plan, the idea has been taken up in other communities by official and voluntary agencies. In New York a state grant was given to the welfare departments of Rochester and Syracuse to study the application of a "Meals on Wheels" program to their needs.

The particular form that co-operation and co-ordination take will be governed by the needs, institutions, and resources of the specific community. A must for any community program is health education in its broadest form on all levels, with individuals, groups, in the home, the clinic, the hospital, the factory. There is increasing recognition of the signal importance of education, but for its full effectiveness much more knowledge of human behavior based on scientific research is needed. Meanwhile we can use what is available (Hurwitz and Guthartz, 1952; Turner, 1953; Kenyon, 1954; Oliver, 1957).

VI. Summary

Advances in public health, medicine, and social conditions have made it possible for more men and women to live to be old. At the same time various social and economic developments, among them the growth of industry and the expansion of urban life, have created problems that seriously affect the older person. The social problem is interlocked with the health problem of the aging. Here we have considered the health problem—its nature, characteristics, and possible ways of dealing with it. Money, personnel, research, interest in older people—all are needed. Maximum effects, however, will be achieved only through co-ordinated, planned effort on a community basis. Toward this end, health departments must take cognizance of their responsibilities, augment and redirect their resources, and stimulate action by various elements of the community. For this purpose, research is needed along many lines. Trained personnel are necessary. Education of the community must be undertaken. Most important of all, however, there must be an all-pervading conviction that what we do to and for others today will have consequences for us tomorrow.

REFERENCES

AMULREE, L. 1955. The health problem of old workers. Bull. World Health Organ., **13**, 375–85.

———. 1958. Hospitals and domiciliary services. Pub. Health (London), **72**, 203–9.

ANDERSON, O. W., and FELDMAN, J. J. 1956. Family medical costs and voluntary health insurance, a nationwide survey. New York: McGraw-Hill Book Co.

ANDERSON, W. F., and COWAN, N. R. 1956. Work and retirement. Influences on the health of older men. Lancet, **2**, 1344–47.

ANONYMOUS. 1955. Hospitalization of men at ages 60 and over. Statistical Bull. Metropolitan Life Insurance Co., **36**, 1–3.

———. 1958. A further study of fitness for work in age. M. Officer, **99**, 159.

BAEHR, G., and DEARDORFF, N. R. 1952. The experience of a group insurance plan with older employees. J. Gerontol., **7**, 245–53.

BAKST, H. J. 1953. Domiciliary medical care and the voluntary teaching hospital. Am. J. Pub. Health, **43**, 589–95.

BLUESTONE, E. M. 1954. The principles and practice of home care. J.A.M.A., **155**, 1379–82.

BOAS, E. P. 1940. The unseen plague: chronic disease. New York: J. J. Augustin.

BOND, F. A., BABER, R. E., VIEG, J. A., PERRY, L. B., SCAFF, A. H., and LEE, L. J., JR. 1954. Our needy aged: a California study of a national problem. New York: Henry Holt & Co.

BOOTH, C. 1892. Pauperism and the endowment of old age. London: Macmillan & Co.

BRECHER, RUTH E., and BRECHER, E. M. 1955. Patients on parole. Saturday Evening Post, **227** (March 26), 19–21.

BRESLOW, L. 1954. Aging and community health programs. J. Gerontol., **9**, 224–27.

BREWSTER, AGNES W. 1958. Care in nursing homes through prepayment hospital plans. (Research and Statistical Note No. 41.) Washington, D.C.: Social Security Administration, Division of Program Research.

BREWSTER, AGNES W., and MCCAMMAN, DOROTHY. 1956. Health costs of the aged. Washington, D.C.: Government Printing Office.

BROOKE, C. O. S. B. 1956. A purpose in life for the elderly. Health Education J., **14**, 72–76.

BROWN, F. R. 1958. Nursing homes: public and private financing of care today. Social Security Bull., **21** (May), 3–8.

CARLSON, A. J., and STIEGLITZ, E. J. 1952. Physiological changes in aging. Ann. Am. Acad. Political & Social Sc., **279**, 18–31.

CHARCOT, J. M., and BALL, B. 1868. Leçons sur les maladies des vieillards et les maladies chroniques. Paris: Adrien Delahave.

CHRISTENSEN, E. H. 1955. Physical working capacity of older workers and physiological background for work tests and work evaluations. Bull. World Health Organ., **13**, 587–93.

CIOCCO, A., and LAWRENCE, P. S. 1952. Illness among older people in Hagerstown, Maryland. (Public Health Service Pub. No. 170.) Washington, D.C.: Government Printing Office.

CLARK, F. L., and DUNNE, A. C. 1956. Ageing in industry: an inquiry based on figures derived from census reports into problems of ageing under conditions of modern industry. New York: Philosophical Library.

COMFORT, A. 1956. The biology of senescence. New York: Rinehart & Co.

COMMISSION ON CHRONIC ILLNESS. 1957. Chronic illness in the United States, Vol. **4**: Chronic illness in a large city—the Baltimore study. Cambridge, Mass.: Harvard University Press.

COOK, L. C., DAX, E. C., and MACLAY, W. S. 1952. The geriatric problem in mental hospitals. Lancet, **1**, 377–82.

CORSON, J. J., and MCCONNELL, J. W. 1956. Economic needs of older people. New York: Twentieth Century Fund.

COSIN, L. S. 1952. A statistical analysis of geriatric rehabilitation. J. Gerontol., **7**, 570–78.

COUNCIL OF STATE GOVERNMENTS. 1955. The states and their older citizens. Chicago: The Council.

CRUTCHER, H. F. 1944. Foster home care for mental patients. New York: Commonwealth Fund.

CRYAN, E. 1954. Foster care for older persons. Am. J. Nursing, **54,** 954–56.

DAVIES, L. 1955. The employment of elderly persons. Bull. World Health Organ., **13,** 595–603.

DeLARGY, J. 1957. Six weeks in—six weeks out: a geriatric hospital scheme for rehabilitating the aged and relieving their relatives. Lancet, **1,** 418–19.

DiCICCO, LENA, and APPLE, DORRIAN. 1958. Health needs and opinions of older adults. Pub. Health. Rep., **73,** 479–87.

DICKINSON, F. G. 1955. Age and sex distribution of hospital patients. (Bureau of Medical Economics, Research Bull. 97.) Chicago: American Medical Association.

ESTÈVE, J. 1957. Incidence de la maladie des personnes âgées sur l'hospitalisation. Revue de l'assistance publique à Paris, **8,** 594–99.

FLORIDA. STATE. BOARD OF HEALTH AND DE-PARTMENT OF PUBLIC WELFARE. 1953. Study of the costs and care of the aged and infirm in Florida. Jacksonville: State Board of Health.

FOX, F. 1953. Home care programs of homes for the aged. Jewish Social Service Quart., **29,** 302–9.

FRAENKEL, M., and ERHARDT, C. L. 1955. Morbidity in the municipal hospitals of the city of New York. New York: Russell Sage Foundation.

FRY, J. C. 1957. Care of the elderly in general practice: a socio-medical reassessment. Brit. M. J., **2,** 666–69.

GITMAN, L. 1955. Blueprint for a geriatric center. Geriatrics, **10,** 487–90.

GOLDMANN, F. 1952. Principles of effective and economic medical care for older people. Geriatrics, **7,** 146–50.

GREEN, R. M. 1951. A translation of Galen's Hygiene (*De sanitate tuenda*). Springfield, Ill.: Charles C Thomas.

GREENFIELD, MARGARET. 1957. Medical care for welfare recipients—basic problems. Berkeley: University of California, Bureau of Public Administration.

HAVIGHURST, R. J., and ALBRECHT, RUTH. 1953. Older people. New York: Longmans, Green & Co.

HEALTH INFORMATION FOUNDATION. 1956. Our aging population. Progress in Health Services, **5** (June), 1–3.

HOWELL, T. H. 1951. A half-way house for the aged sick: an experiment in social medicine. Month. Bull. Min. Health, **10,** 186–88.

HURWITZ, S., and GUTHARTZ, J. C. 1952. Family life education with the aged. Social Casework, **33,** 382–87.

HUTCHINSON, B. 1954. Old people in a modern Australian community: a social survey. Melbourne: Melbourne University Press.

INTERNATIONAL ASSOCIATION OF GERONTOLOGY. SOCIAL SCIENCE RESEARCH COMMITTEE. 1958. The need for cross-national surveys of old age. Ann Arbor: University of Michigan, Division of Gerontology.

JARRETT, M. C. 1933. Chronic illness in New York City, Vol. **1.** New York: Columbia University Press.

JENSEN, F., WEISKOTTEN, H. G., and THOMAS, M. B. 1944. Medical care of the discharged hospital patient. New York: Commonwealth Fund.

KENYON, S. M. 1954. Health education of the aging as a function of certain official and voluntary agencies in New York City. (Unpublished Ph.D. dissertation, Teachers College, Columbia University.)

KINNAMAN, J. H. 1953. Standards of care in nursing homes. Am. J. Pub. Health, **43,** 1020–22.

KINSELLA, T. J. 1957. Treatment of tuberculosis in the elderly individual. Geriatrics, **12,** 355–59.

KRUEGER, D. E. 1955*a.* One in 8 is a long-term case. Hospitals, **29,** 59–62.

———. 1955*b.* Patient census of hospitals completed. Chronic Ill. News Letter (Baltimore), **6** (January), 6.

KRUSE, H. D. 1953. The interplay of noxious agents, stress, and deprivation in the engenderment of disease. Milbank Mem. Fund Quart., **31,** 93–124.

KRUSE, H. D., BAUMGARTNER, LEONA, KOLBE, H. W., and McCARTHY, H. L. 1957. Public health aspects of aging: transcription of a panel meeting. Bull. New York Acad. Med., **33,** 493–518.

KUPLAN, L. 1956. Health programs for California's senior citizens. California Health, **14,** 1–4.

KUTNER, B., FANSHEL, D., TOGO, ALICE M., and LANGNER, T. S. 1956. Five hundred over sixty: a community survey on aging. New York: Russell Sage Foundation.

LANSING, A. I. 1956. What is aging? Bull. New York Acad. Med., **32,** 5–13.

LAVERTY, RUTH. 1950. Nonresident aid—community versus institutional care for older people. J. Gerontol., **5,** 370–74.

LEMKAU, P. V. 1955. Mental hygiene in public

health. 2d ed. New York: McGraw-Hill Book Co.

LEVINE, H. A. 1955. Mental health and aging. New York: Health and Welfare Committee of New York City.

LEVY, M. J., JR. 1949. The family revolution in modern China. Cambridge, Mass.: Harvard University Press.

LOWE, C. R., and McKEOWN, T. 1949. The care of the chronic sick. Brit. J. Social Med., **3**, 110–26.

MACLEOD, K. I. E. 1958. Well oldster health conferences. Nursing Outlook, **6**, 206–8.

MAGDELAINE, M., and PÉQUIGNOT, H. 1957. Les bésoins d'hospitalisation des vieillards et leurs causes. Revue de l'assistance publique à Paris, **8**, 600–604.

MATHIASEN, GENEVA (ed.). 1957. Flexible retirement: evolving policies and programs for industry and labor. New York: G. P. Putnam's Sons.

McCAMMAN, DOROTHY, and BREWSTER, AGNES W. 1954. Voluntary health insurance coverage of aged beneficiaries of Old-Age and Survivors Insurance. Social Security Bull., **17** (August), 3–11.

MICHLIN, D. 1957. What is a nursing home? Nursing Outlook, **5**, 410–11.

MONROE, R. T. 1951. Diseases in old age: a clinical and pathological study of 7,941 individuals over 61 years of age. Cambridge, Mass.: Harvard University Press.

———. 1958. The mechanisms of the geriatric clinic and its place in the community. New England J. Med., **258**, 882–85.

MOORE, W. E. 1951. Industrialization and labor. Ithaca, N.Y.: Cornell University Press.

MORRIS, J. N. 1957. Uses of epidemiology. Edinburgh: E. & S. Livingstone.

MORRIS, R. 1954. Home care for the aged. New York: Council of Jewish Federations and Welfare Funds.

MURDOCK, T. P. 1953. Importance of standardization of nursing homes. J.A.M.A., **153**, 1442–44.

NATIONAL SOCIAL WELFARE ASSEMBLY, NATIONAL COMMITTEE ON THE AGING. 1953. Standards of care for older people in institutions. New York: The Assembly.

NUFFIELD PROVINCIAL HOSPITALS TRUST. 1937. Rehabilitation of elderly invalids at home. London: The Trust.

O'CONNOR, J. B. 1956. TB, geriatric problem. Bull. Nat. Tuberculosis A., **42**, 13–14.

OLIVER, W. R. 1957. Pre-retirement education. Adult Leadership, **6**, 21–23.

PINEL, P. 1815. Traité de médecine clinique. Paris: J. A. Brosson.

POMRINSE, S. D. 1958. How public health and medicine cooperate to improve the care of the older person. J. Am. Geriatrics Soc., **6**, 482–88.

POSNER, W. 1952. A foster care program for older persons. New York: National Social Welfare Assembly.

PRESIDENT'S COMMISSION ON THE HEALTH NEEDS OF THE NATION. 1952. Building America's health. Washington, D.C.: The Commission.

ROBERTS, D. W. 1954. Characteristics of patients in nursing care institutions. Am. J. Pub. Health, **44**, 455–66.

ROSEN, G. 1947. What is social medicine? A genetic analysis of the concept. Bull. Hist. Med., **21**, 674–733.

———. 1948. Society and medical care: an historical analysis. McGill M. J., **17**, 410–25.

———. 1953a. Cameralism and the concept of medical police. Bull. Hist. Med., **27**, 21–42.

———. 1953b. Economics and social policy in the development of public health: an essay in interpretation. J. Hist. Med. **8**, 405–30.

———. 1953c. Medical care and social policy in seventeenth century England. Bull. New York Acad. Med., **29**, 420–37.

———. 1956. Hospitals, medical care and social policy in the French Revolution. Bull. Hist. Med., **30**, 124–49.

———. 1958. A history of public health. New York: MD Publications.

ROSENFELD, L. S., GOLDMANN, F., and KAPRIO, L. A. 1957. Reasons for prolonged hospital stay: a study of need for hospital care. J. Chronic Dis., **6**, 141–52.

ROWE, E. K. 1955. Health, insurance, and pension plans in union contracts. Month. Labor Rev., **78**, 993–1000.

RUDD, J. L., and FEINGOLD, S. N. 1957. Medical and vocational cooperation for the aging. J. Am. Geriatrics Soc., **5**, 263–70.

RUSK, H. A., and DACSO, M. M. 1956. Rehabilitation in the aged. Bull. New York Acad. Med., **32**, 725–33.

SAND, R. 1955. Le travailleur âgé: problème médico-social. Bull. World Health Organ., **13**, 605–17.

SEEGAL, D. 1956. Some comments on the medical management of the older person. Res. Publ. A. Nerv. & Ment. Dis., **35**, 245–48.

SHELDON, J. H. 1950. Medical-social aspects of the aging process. *In* M. DERBER (ed.), The aged and society. Champaign, Ill.: Industrial Relations Research Association.

———. 1956. Problems of geriatric care. J. Am. Geriatrics Soc., **4**, 642–47.

SHENFIELD, BARBARA E. 1957. Social policies of old age: a review of social provision for old age in Great Britain. London: Routledge & Kegan Paul.

SHEPS, C. G., and TAYLOR, E. H. 1954. Needed research in health and medical care. Chapel Hill: University of North Carolina Press.

SHOCK, N. W. 1957. Trends in gerontology. 2d ed. Stanford, Calif.: Stanford University Press.

SIGERIST, H. E. 1956. Landmarks in the history of hygiene. London: Oxford University Press.

SIMONDS, W. H., and STEWART, A. 1954. Old people living in Dorset: a sociomedical survey of private households. Brit. J. Prev. & Social Med., **8**, 139–46.

SMILLIE, W. G., and LUGINBUHL, M. 1959. Training of public health personnel in the United States and Canada—summary of 10 years' advance in schools of public health, 1947–48 to 1957–58. Am. J. Pub. Health, **49**, 455–62.

SMITH, R. C. F. 1957. The effect of social problems on lives of old age pensioners. M. Officer, **97**, 303–8.

SOLON, J., and BANEY, A. M. 1954. Inventory of nursing homes and related facilities. Pub. Health Rep., **69**, 1121–32.

SOLON, J., ROBERTS, D. W., KONEGER, D. E., and BANEY, A. M. 1957. Nursing homes, their patients and their care: a study of nursing homes and similar long-term care facilities in 13 states. (Public Health Service Monogr. No. 46.) Washington, D.C.: Government Printing Office.

STANDISH, S., JR., BENNETT, B. M., WHITE, K., and POWERS, L. E. 1955. Why patients see doctors. Seattle: University of Washington Press.

STEINER, P. O., and DORFMAN, R. 1957. The economic status of the aged. Berkeley: University of California Press.

STURGES, GERTRUDE. 1937. Organized medical care of the sick in their homes. *In* Report of the Hospital Survey for New York, **2**, 776–823. New York: United Hospital Fund.

SWITZER, MARY E., and RUSK, H. A. 1952. Keeping older people fit for participation. Ann. Am. Acad. Political & Social Sc., **279**, 146–53.

SYDENSTRICKER, E. 1933. Health and environment. New York: McGraw-Hill Book Co.

TAUBER, S. A. 1956. Meals on wheels. Pub. Health News (New York State Department of Health), **37**, 413.

TURNER, HELEN. 1953. Promoting understanding of aged patients. Social Casework, **34**, 428–35.

U.S. CONGRESS. SENATE. COMMITTEE ON LABOR AND PUBLIC WELFARE. 1956. Studies of the aged and aging, Vol. **1**: Federal and state activities. Washington, D.C.: Government Printing Office.

U.S. BUREAU OF LABOR STATISTICS. 1956. Older workers under collective bargaining, Part II: Health insurance plans, pension plans. (Bull. No. 1199-2.) Washington, D.C.: The Bureau.

U.S. NATIONAL HEALTH SURVEY. 1938. The magnitude of the chronic disease problem in the United States. ("Preliminary Report, National Health Survey, Sickness and Medical Care Series," No. 6.) Washington, D.C.: The Survey.

———. 1958a. Health statistics ... preliminary report on volume of physician's visits. (Public Health Service Pub. No. 584, Series B-1.) Washington, D.C.: Government Printing Office.

———. 1958b. Health statistics ... selected survey topics. (Public Health Service Pub. No. 584, Series B-5.) Washington, D.C.: Government Printing Office.

U.S. PUBLIC HEALTH SERVICE. 1958. National Conference on Nursing Homes and Homes for the Aged. (Public Health Service Pub. No. 625.) Washington, D.C.: Government Printing Office.

VAN ZONNEVELD, R. J. 1954. Gezondbeidsproblemen bij bejaarden. Assen: Van Gorcum.

WARREN, M. W. 1953. Re-training the elderly hemiplegic. Geriatrics, **8**, 192–203.

———. 1955. The home nursing of the aged sick. Practitioner, **174**, 567–73.

WATERMAN, T. L. 1953. Nursing homes. Are they homes? Is there nursing? Am. J. Pub. Health, **43**, 307–13.

WEBBER, I. L. 1951. The retired population of a Florida community. *In* T. L. SMITH (ed.), Problems of America's aging population. Gainesville: University of Florida Press.

WELFARE COUNCIL OF METROPOLITAN CHICAGO. COMMUNITY PROJECT FOR THE AGED. 1952. Community services for older people: the Chicago plan. Chicago: Wilcox & Follett.

WHITTENBERGER, J. L. 1956. The nature of the response to stress with aging. Bull. New York Acad. Med., **32**, 329–36.

WICKENDEN, E. 1953. The needs of older people and public welfare services to meet them. Chicago: American Public Welfare Association.

WINSLOW, C. E. A. 1951. The cost of sickness and the price of health. Geneva: World Health Organization.

ZEMAN, F. D. 1948. The geriatric group in a general hospital: organization and objectives. J. Gerontol., 3, 281–84.

———. 1949. Teaching geriatrics: basic principles and syllabus of course now in the fifth year. *Ibid.*, 4, 48–52.

———. 1950. The medical organization of the modern home for the aged. *Ibid.*, 5, 262–65.

———. 1955. Common clinical errors in care of the elderly. Practitioner, 174, 556–61.

XVI

Housing and Community Settings for Older People[1]

WALTER K. VIVRETT

I. DETERMINANTS OF LIVING ARRANGEMENTS

As medical science extends life-expectancy at birth and brings more and more people into middle age, later maturity, and old age, there is evolving a new independence of action for these age groups. This independence of action is expressing itself in the determination of an independence and a separateness of living arrangements —not only for middle age but also for later maturity and for old age.

A. Developments Influencing Living Arrangements

Many phases of endeavor and many aspects of society are encouraging, if not requiring, this search for individuality and independence and the resulting separateness of living arrangements.

SOCIAL ASPECTS

In the family, earlier marriage, fewer children, earlier completion of childbearing

[1] Much of the material here presented is drawn from a research-planning study in housing and care facilities for the aging, an interdisciplinary project conducted at the University of Minnesota under the direction of the author. Grateful acknowledgment is made to the research and consultative staff of that project and to the Louis W. and Maud Hill Family Foundation, whose generosity made the project possible.

and child-rearing roles, and the relatively free movement of adult children in search of economic opportunities (see chaps. ii and xiii of this volume) mean that many parents are left alone while still in their prime, still in the labor force, and frequently with a home of their own to live in from middle age on into later maturity as a separate generation. Single people, on the other hand, in their search for economic opportunities frequently grow into middle age and into later maturity living alone, or at least with considerable independence of action in terms of living arrangement. Divorce in a few cases is further dividing the "living with others" into "living alone." Generational differences in interests during the last three generations are having a divisive effect, too, which is influencing living arrangements. When people feel they have numbers of years ahead of them, they are likely to try hard to secure and maintain the living environment that best suits them. Thus the years of accustomed patterns of living are being extended into later maturity and old age.

In the process of rapid urbanization in the United States, a sense of family belongingness, in many cases, is being replaced by one of community belongingness, which is making the individual less dependent upon the family. Society's broad assumption of health and welfare responsibilities, moreover, is providing increased security outside the family circle—a security infinitely greater than that once offered by the almshouse and the poor farm. A greater freedom of action is thus encouraged.

Then, too, the shortening of the work week and the lengthening period of retirement emphasize the need for additional ways to occupy one's time and for the optimum practicable environment in which to spend this time, whereas in earlier days the emphasis was more often on a place to "wait out" those last remaining days.

ECONOMIC ASPECTS

The fact that virtually no one in the old age group need be without some cash income has perhaps influenced the patterns of living arrangements more than has anything else. Our social security payments, pensions, and annuities, backed up by a system of old age assistance (albeit meager in some states), provide income to finance at least some of the cost of living for older people. Although the housing market is not by any means a buyer's market, this feeling of economic security has caused present generations of the aging to be more expressive of their wants and needs than were earlier generations. For until disaster comes —such as extended illness, disability, death of spouse—such funds are frequently sufficient to secure independence for the individual (see also chaps. viii and xiv). For many, a significant determinant in living arrangements is the purchase during middle age or later maturity of a home which in many cases proves suitable to a great many of their needs even in old age.

MEDICAL ASPECTS

Medical science, which has made such dramatic progress in those areas of health that relate to younger age groups, is now concerning itself with practicable techniques of meeting the health needs of older people. Techniques of treatment, particularly in the younger age group, have pointed toward rehabilitation and restoration of the patient in the home, and, increasingly, similar techniques are being developed for the older group. The recent but rapidly developing philosophy of rehabilitation for the old, with its understanding of the values of milieu therapy, not only fosters but demands the extended use of the independent living environment and the individual's own home. Thus such advances are indirectly encouraging living outside the walls of the institution and extending the home environment into the older years.

Medical science is concerning itself, too, with the ratio existing between medical needs of the community and resources of the community for meeting those needs. It is recognizing that techniques of service must make every hour of human effort, every piece of equipment, count for a maximum. This means concentrating technical effort and specialized equipment with an increasing emphasis upon outpatient status. Thus, frequently, the individual becomes accustomed in middle age to seeking medical service in the office of a physician or in a clinic or, on occasion, to getting a brief period of intensive treatment in a hospital. He finds it natural to extend such patterns into later maturity and into old age—seeking out the service which he requires but continuing to reside in his home in the community.

TECHNOLOGICAL ASPECTS

Modern technology has significantly altered the face of the land and the environment of the home. Superhighways and airways bring us in touch with one another where once rivers and trails sufficed, and with this shortening of distance has come better access to specialized resources that would once have been considered out of reach. Improved transportation and communications are opening up new potentials for the individual in terms of the location of his residence and the many advantages offered by the urban center.

Within the home environment, countless technological advances are making life easier—automatic heat controls, washers and dryers, precooked and frozen foods, improved refrigerators. These and many other aids make it possible for the individual to live at home with a minimum of effort and worry; and, although not all these technological advances have been incorporated into the homes of the old, some of them have, with valuable results.

Also within the home there are ready entertainment and a not-too-poor substitute for "keeping in touch" with the outside world, which our society has come to de-

but also of older people, approximately 75 per cent of those in the age group 65–74 and 56 per cent of those 75 and older. Another large percentage was living in households other than their own, approximately 21 per cent of those in the age group 65–74 and 36 per cent of those 75 and older (U.S. Bureau of the Census, 1953*a*, 1953*d*).

The relatively small remaining group was living in quasi-households, such as institutions, transient hotels, large rooming houses, schools, and labor or trailer camps. Table 1 summarizes the general break-

TABLE 1*

LIVING ARRANGEMENTS OF PERSONS AGED 45 YEARS AND OVER, BY AGE, 1950

LIVING ARRANGEMENTS	AGE 45–64		AGE 65 AND OVER	
	Total	Per Cent	Total	Per Cent
Living in households..................	29,181,610	96.10	11,544,030	94.28
Living in quasi-households.............	1,185,350	3.90	700,350	5.72
In non-institutional housing...........	778,760	2.56	322,230	2.63
In institutions.....................	406,680	1.34	378,150	3.09
In homes for aged and dependent....	62,942	0.21	217,536	1.78
In mental hospitals................	252,970	.84	141,346	1.16
In tuberculosis hospitals...........	22,105	.07	6,592	0.05
In correctional institutions.........	26,450	.09	2,939	0.02
In homes for mentally handicapped..	19,157	.06	4,184	0.04
In other institutions...............	21,055	0.07	5,553	0.04

* Source: U.S. Bureau of the Census, *U.S. Census of Population: 1950*, Vol. 4: *Special Reports*, Part 2, Chapter D, "Marital Status" (Washington, D.C.: The Bureau, 1953), Table 1; *ibid.*, Chapter C, "Institutional Population" (Washington, D.C.: The Bureau, 1953), Tables 3 through 8, Table 12.

mand. Radio is still the universal chairside fixture in the over-65 age group (Vivrett *et al.*, 1955). Television, commercial recordings, and talking books for the blind make the home more self-sufficient and encourage the occupant to maintain his independence as he moves into later maturity and old age.

B. *Living Arrangements of Middle-aged and Older Persons*

In the United States in 1950, most individuals were living in households of their own—with spouse, with relatives or friends, or alone. This was true not only of middle-aged persons (approximately 85 per cent)

down of living arrangements and also indicates the extent to which the several major types of institutions are populated by older people (see also Table 10). Even accepting the Bureau of the Census' admitted difficulty in estimating the institutional population, and even though the institution is society's primary way for meeting some characteristic needs of older people, it is obvious that a relatively low percentage of older people, for a relatively short time, live in institutions. About the residents of the non-institutional quasi-household housing types, such as the hotel and the large rooming house, little precise information is available.

Of the middle-aged and older individuals living in households in 1950, approximately three-fourths were living *in families,* that is, with one or more persons related by blood, marriage, or adoption (U.S. Bureau of the Census, 1953*d*). Of those older individuals *not living in families* (in 1950 nearly two million persons 65 and over were not living in families), approximately one-fifth were living with non-relatives, and four-fifths were living *alone* (Sheldon, 1958). Incidence of such one-person households was about the same among men 65 and over as among women.

Studies dealing with specific groups of people or specific locales are helpful in considering these one-person household living arrangements. Hawkins (1957), in his study of the living arrangements of the recipients of old age assistance, points out:

Recipients of old age assistance live alone much more frequently than persons in the general population. At the time of the study [1953], nearly a third of the recipients lived in one-person households, compared with 9.0 per cent of the general population.

Households consisting of two persons were nearly a third again as frequent among old age assistance recipients as among the general population, but households with three or more persons were substantially less frequent. Though fully two-thirds of the recipients lived in households consisting of one or two persons, only slightly more than one-third of the general population lived in such households. Appreciable numbers of recipients of old age assistance, however, were members of relatively large households. About 10 per cent of the recipients lived in households of five or more members [pp. 9–10].

Reports of other researchers in limited geographic areas (Hunter and Maurice, 1953; Vivrett *et al.,* 1955; Kutner *et al.,* 1956) substantiate this finding of generally small households among older people, with approximately one-third of the households represented by an older person living alone. In the Grand Rapids survey (Hunter and Maurice, 1953), it was observed that these one-person households were more than twice as frequent among women as among men.

In terms of the total numbers of families, the Bureau of the Census (1953*b*) reported that, of the 40,442,000 families in the United States, 33,500,000 had no members 65 years old and over; 4,504,000 had one member 65 years old and over, more than half of whom were head of household; and 2,364,000 had two members of the family 65 years old and over, of whom 2,004,000 were represented by head of household and wife of head.

Steiner and Dorfman (1957) have questioned the suitability of present statistical techniques for analyzing the position of older persons in the family. They suggest that "precise roles in the family are frequently ambiguous . . . particularly with the group 65 and over, the designation 'head of family' is often an honorary title rather than an indication of economic position within the family" (p. 20). They go on to point out that in their sample a significant percentage of those in the category "head, children present" had no income; this figure ranged from almost 10 per cent for couples to 33 per cent for unrelated females.

The Minneapolis–St. Paul study (Vivrett *et al.,* 1955) showed that relatively few individuals over 65 were living in households in which there were members present below the age of 20 years and that half of those between the ages of 65 and 74 lived in households composed entirely of people who were middle-aged or older. As might have been expected, there was a higher incidence of people in the group 75 years old and over (mostly widowed) living in households with children and younger adults.

C. Preferences in Living Arrangements

Only fragmentary data for specific population, or locale, are available regarding the preferences older people have in living arrangements. For the most part, such preferences are stated in terms of contingencies —"If my husband were to die, . . ."; "If I could afford to"—or of satisfaction or dissatisfaction with present living arrangements. In the Grand Rapids survey, for instance, 88 per cent of the men and 82 per cent of the women stated that they were satisfied with their living arrangements. Satisfaction was expressed in the following percentages by older people: those living with spouse, 96; living with children, 87; living with relatives, friends, or others, 93. Of those living alone, however, only 68 per cent expressed satisfaction with present living arrangements.

Hibbard and Lee (1954) found in their sample of 1290 widows of Presbyterian ministers that 97 per cent felt that it was not wise for a widow to live in the household of her married children; and 43 per cent indicated that they preferred to live alone.

In a study of retired people in St. Petersburg, Florida, Webber (1950) found that both men and women wished to live in self-owned detached dwellings. The next most acceptable arrangement would be to live with another person of the same sex in a single dwelling. In no instance did any subject indicate a preference for a rooming-house facility with central dining-room service.

A survey of 71,400 aged people in Rhode Island (1953) revealed that 2400 were dissatisfied with present housing, 800 of these preferring a congregate arrangement in which they could maintain their own quarters while being near other old people and having access to certain communal facilities. Half of the dissatisfied people (1200) stated that they would prefer to live independently rather than with children or relatives.

In Los Angeles County (Welfare Council of Metropolitan Los Angeles, 1950) the Subcommittee on Housing for the Aging reported that an overwhelming majority of recipients of old age security who were living with relatives were troubled by uncongeniality of relatives, crowded conditions, annoyances created by small children, etc.

Cavan (1949) found that women living in their own homes or in rooming houses or old age homes generally made better adjustment scores on a test of interests and attitudes than did those living in the homes of others.

Donahue (1954a) emphasizes that a prime requisite of housing for older people is that it provides "maximum . . . independence and privacy, regardless of whether it is a communal- or an individual-type dwelling." She goes on to say that "independence is a strong characteristic which is not forfeited until frailty or illness necessitates the security of sheltered care" (pp. 35–36).

In Boston, Massachusetts, when the old Brunswick Hotel was to be abandoned in early 1957, the United Community Services of Metropolitan Boston (1957a) questioned forty-seven older residents, of whom three-fifths were widowed, separated, or divorced, and two-fifths were single, about their preferences in living arrangements. These people had been living in the hotel from 1 to 10 years and considered themselves permanent residents. Eight of the forty-seven had no relatives, while eleven who had been married earlier had living sons and daughters. Sixteen of the single individuals had relatives living. Since these people were in search of new housing, they were most cooperative and freely discussed their problems with the interviewers. Most of them said that they wanted to lead completely private lives without any interference. They were particularly opposed to living with relatives. The six people who stated that they would be willing to live with relatives did so with some reservations. One woman said she was going to live with her brother only because, being partially blind and deaf, she was having great difficulty in looking for living quarters. Another woman who was going to live near her daughter insisted that, although she wanted to be near her daughter, she would never live in the same room with her if she could help it. When asked if they would consider living in a nursing home or a boarding home, seven said that perhaps they would, but only for protection if they were completely unable to get around; nine said they had never considered it and were undecided; the remaining thirty-one individuals gave unqualified "No's." For the most part they considered that they had nothing in common with *such* older boarding-home people; and twenty-six vigorously objected to the idea of having rules imposed upon them. A few had been in nursing homes for brief periods and felt that the rigidity of the rules would be too hard for them to take again. When questioned about sharing accommodations with friends whom they had known at the Brunswick Hotel, these people indicated overwhelming opposition and, indeed, revealed that they did not socialize with the other residents. In general the comment was: "Everyone has to have his own privacy, especially when he gets old." When asked about living in a public housing project, one-half of the individuals stated that they were opposed, on the grounds that housing projects are built in unsafe and slummy areas and that people who live in them are usually of the lower class. One-fourth of the subjects stated that they would be willing to live in such a project, and five more answered with a qualified "Yes." It is true that this particular study deals with a special group of older people—special because they had already made the change to living alone in the heart of the city in an unrepresentative type of housing. Yet it appears noteworthy because here the individuals were faced with the urgency of making an immediate decision about their living arrangements; and what is more significant, in a follow-up study some 6 or 8 months later, considerable correlation was observed between the preference subjects had stated at the initial interview and their actual choices of living arrangements and housing (United Community Services of Metropolitan Boston, 1957*b*).

D. *Factors That Motivate People To Change Their Living Arrangements*

It is always easiest to maintain the status quo, particularly in living arrangements. In fact, continual change of residence and living arrangements is frequently regarded as characterizing the neurotic. Among middle-aged and older people the determination to change their living arrangements is less frequently the result of careful planning or deliberate choice and more frequently the result of some change in circumstances in the individual's life.

CHANGING PATTERNS OF LIVING AND AGING

The middle-aged couple who has reared a family and seen its children grow into adulthood and finally leave home to establish lives of their own is likely to settle back with a feeling of a job well done and say: "Now we can relax and enjoy ourselves. Our home is paid for, we have many friends in this community, we have more time than before, and we can begin to do the things we've always wanted to do." Very often they do, and life continues evenly until the husband or wife dies and the other (usually the woman) is left alone.

CHANGING PERSONAL CONDITIONS AND SOCIAL RELATIONS

A number of personal factors are likely to motivate the change in living arrangements. In later maturity the breadwinner retires, his income is cut in half, and, as he looks at his expenditures for daily living, the cost of housing suggests itself as one of the possible areas in which a saving could be made. Or the widow, surveying the insurance funds, the savings, and other assets left by her husband, finds that, even though the three-bedroom, single-family house is comfortable and easy to run and is located in a desirable neighborhood, it is too much of a financial burden; so she looks for a small apartment or a hotel room.

Whereas we once spoke of two- or three-generational family living, we now find it common to speak of two, three, and four generations of a family all living at the same time. Among the two older generations, it is not uncommon to find a change in living arrangements brought about when the oldest person becomes physically unable to live alone; and, particularly when there is a widowed son or daughter, the obvious solution is for the two older generations to share a dwelling unit.

Change in physical condition is perhaps the most common and most dreaded cause for change of living arrangement. With increasing infirmity, or with partial or full disability, this decision is often thrust upon the individual against his will. Some people who in their middle age or in later maturity may have preferred living with their spouses or alone may nevertheless later choose to live with relatives with whom they have strong ties of affection, or they may seek some form of group setting for economic reasons or because of their mental or physical health.

It is not easy to pinpoint just where in the span of life these changes occur. The Kansas City studies of adult life (Neugarten, 1957) have suggested:

The years from 40 to 70 seem . . . to be a period of relative stability—a plateau period, as compared with earlier or later periods of the life span. Age changes are neither consistent nor dramatic. Thus, for example, social role performance is generally as high in the 60's as in the 40's; as many persons are well- or poorly-adjusted in the 60's as in the 40's.

Thus these findings would tend to support undocumented observations that changes in living arrangements are less likely to occur during the forties and fifties, and even in the sixties. For the onset of some change, if not trauma, appears to be the principal determinant for changing living arrangements, and such change is most pronounced in the years after 70.

Many people have questioned the desire of so many middle-aged and older people for independent living, particularly for living out the very late years of life alone in apartments or detached houses. To such questions we might well say, "Why not?" Is it not the quality rather than the type of the living arrangement which makes such a decision wise or unwise? It is easy to

plan changes in living arrangements for other people and to rationalize our proposals. But in the final analysis the real change must be made by the individual. What may seem to us a suitable arrangement may not be acceptable to him, or, even further, he may have no motivation for making the change we propose.

CHANGING ENVIRONMENT

While the changes in personal and social relations of individuals are probably most likely to influence their choice of living arrangements, changes in physical environment also may bring about the necessity for new arrangements. This is particularly true in or near the center of cities where 40- or 50-year-old houses are located in neighborhoods characterized by incipient blight, if not by actual slums. Part of this problem is that houses of such age which have not had proper maintenance are likely to have deteriorated and thus contributed to creeping blight in the neighborhood. Indeed, the resident himself has frequently aggravated the situation, for, as he looks at the house, he frequently thinks, "Oh, that will last me the rest of my lifetime. There are other things I need to use the money for." Or, where blight and deterioration have not set in, the residential neighborhood itself has frequently been subjected to the effects of "progress"; the front door of the house is within 15 or 20 feet of the whizzing traffic of a major thoroughfare, or the inroads of commercial and industrial establishments have significantly changed the face of the neighborhood, or families are moving out of the neighborhood to the suburbs as lower social and economic classes are moving in. All this has made the neighborhood undesirable, if not dangerous. Even though such conditions may not be primary, they frequently contribute to changes in living arrangement.

Other older people may change their living arrangements not to escape urban blight but to embrace a warmer or more favorable climate—sometimes for reasons of health, other times for the obvious attractions which such climates offer. Sometimes such migration may be permanent; at other times it may be temporary, occasionally even only for one season.

Some people may never need to change their living arrangements. But many others will and at differing periods of their lives. In discussing living arrangements, therefore—even more than in talking about housing and physical environment—we must acknowledge the dynamic character of individual situations and of the aging process.

II. Where the Aging Live—the Environment of the Home and the Community

A. Patterns Observable in Our Communities

Patterns of residence during later maturity are generally similar to patterns of residence of earlier years. "Abnormal" patterns are those that result from inadequacies in housing production and supply. Thus, because of unavailability of more suitable housing in a given area and often because of the meagerness of their income, many older people live in blighted or semi-blighted urban areas, in rooming houses and tenement districts, and in older residential hotels.

AGING RESIDENTS AMONG US

The dramatic increase of the older population in the United States, and the predisposition of many of us to look upon this phenomenon only in terms of numbers of individuals, can be particularly misleading for the planning of housing. For the ratio of *one* older to *eleven* younger people in the population becomes *one* to *six* when we talk about the ratio of *heads of households* 65 or more to those under 65. Lowering the age level, we see that nearly every other household in our community has as its head someone 45 years or older (U.S. Bureau of the Census, 1955).

Or, from the standpoint of the *average population per household* or *per family* (statistics of greater use in housing and community planning), we find that, if the population were evenly distributed according to age, *every fourth household or family would have a member 65 years old or over* and that *almost every household or family would have a member 45 years old or over* (U.S. Bureau of the Census, 1956). Despite this relative size of the older population, much of our home-building and urban expansion has been such as to produce age, as well as economic, stratification. As a result, communities and particularly suburban developments built in the last 20 years conspicuously lack their share of people over 65, while communities which were established 20 years or more ago, have a disproportionately high frequency. Thus the one-to-eleven ratio of those over 65 to the general population distorts the picture that many lay people have of our residential communities (see also chap. ii).

MOBILITY AND MIGRATION

Despite the mobility necessitated by change in living arrangements, particularly in the very late years, older people are not, as a rule, very mobile. Corson and McConnell (1956) observed that seven out of ten retired people had remained in their accustomed dwellings. Mobility was high among the one-third with higher incomes before retirement. Executives moved to other geographic regions more frequently than laborers did. Among pensioners, one in five had moved within the same geographic region; only one in ten, to another region. Many earlier life-patterns contribute to the determination to change one's residence in later years. People who had earlier moved about freely from city to city would obviously have far less trepidation about moving to another city in their old age. People who had spent frequent vacations in favorable climates might well be expected to seek out those same climates, particularly in season, as they reached retirement and had more free time, even with a reduced income. This may become even more common in the future, since adults in increasing numbers are exercising wide choice in the use of their growing leisure.

The transition from seasonal to permanent residence in a favorable climate may be reasonably simple, particularly if one had sufficient income to return for visits to one's old community. And there are other attractions: the bustle and activity of a resort area, the acquaintances who may be more attractive than those in the old and possibly declining neighborhood, and the quality of housing itself. The availability of desirable housing of a kind not accessible in the old community may offer the major motivation for many people to move to the glamorous resorts of the Southeast or the Far West of the United States. A quick glance at many of these reveals a quality of physical and social environment which is not generally available in other parts of the country.

GENERAL CHARACTERISTICS OF COMMUNITIES

What characterizes the communities that are most desirable for middle-aged and older people? Much specific data and some general principles may be gleaned from a number of sources: (a) federal governmental agencies, such as the Bureau of the Census, the Housing and Home Finance Agency, the Federal Housing Administration, and the Department of Health, Education, and Welfare; (b) state governmental agencies, such as the planning and resource departments and welfare, health, and employment security offices; (c) local governmental agencies, such as the planning commissions, housing and redevelopment authorities, and local health and welfare departments; (d) numerous national, regional, and local associations and agencies, such as professional and technical organizations, councils of social agencies, and public and private charitable organizations. In some communities one of these organizations can give us the best picture of the community; in others, it is another. Rarely, though, can a co-ordinated appraisal of the community be gathered from a single source. This is also true, of course, for the United States as a whole. Perhaps the most ambitious work on this larger scale is reported in the publication by Dewhurst and Associates (1955).

RURAL AND RURAL NON-FARM COMMUNITIES

Of all types of communities in the United States, we know the least about the rural and rural non-farm communities, singly or as a category. Despite the long-range educational efforts by the federal government—primarily through the Department of Agriculture, by our many state experimental stations and colleges of agriculture, and our several farm organizations—most of the improvements in living environment in rural and rural non-farm areas have been the technological advances provided, for example, through the work of the Rural Electrification Administration or by equipment and machinery for the farm and the home. Although the "rural slums" of America have been widely deplored, only limited improvement has been made. Farm organizations, notably the Farmers Union, have maintained that the programs of the federal government to increase the supply and improve the quality of rural housing have been unsuccessful.

Christianson (1956), of the Farmers Union, has claimed, in fact, that one of the greatest hindrances in the use of federal legislation to improve housing had been the stipulation that the entire farm property be mortgaged in order to build a small house. He stated that a more realistic view of a mortgage obligation on a reasonable acreage related to the house itself—plus other stipulations regarding the siting of the house with reference to primary rural roads and public and school transportation routes—might make such legislation workable in rural areas.

Christianson stated that the sparsity of housing in rural areas handicaps farming itself. He pointed out that, whereas some experts suggest that old age on the farm is still the idyllic life of yesteryear, as a matter of fact it is quite the opposite. As the farmer and his wife grow older, and the farmer's son brings home a new wife and as the two (and eventually three) generations attempt to live in the same house, even more tensions are created than in the urban household. For on the farm, in addition to the purely personal tensions, there are the problems of whether the father or the son shall manage the farm; who shall make the decisions; shall the son and his wife defer to the position of the father, and, if so, how long must the young wife expect such a relationship to continue? The younger family often becomes discouraged and moves into the small town or city, where employment and an independent life are possible; and the older parents on the farm manage as best they can, trying to supplement their own efforts by hiring local farm workers.

On the other hand, Nelson (1957) points out that "with virtually every farm provided with truck or auto transportation, and all-weather roads a commonplace throughout the countryside, the majority of the farm families of the nation may be regarded, not too inaccurately, as suburban dwellers."

It is of course true that rural families are being brought into more direct contact with all aspects of urban life. But the low population densities and the smallness of rural and rural non-farm communities preclude many of the features of organized programs of facilities and services for older people which are available in urban areas (Warren, 1952; Taietz, 1953; Kaplan and Taietz, 1959).

Very little concerted effort has been made to study the problems of later maturity and old age in rural areas. Publications by the state commissions and councils on aging usually acknowledge the scarcity of information or, at best, repeat or briefly interpret the data available through the federal census of population and of housing. One of the few co-ordinated reports pertaining to rural life and housing in later maturity and in old age points out the frequent makeshift, but valiant, efforts being made in rural Iowa (Ginzberg *et al.,* 1954). There it was observed that trailers, lean-to's, and small out-buildings were being used by the older generation in its efforts to provide separate living accommodations for itself.

Of the rural non-farm areas, and of the small towns and villages, we know very much more, and yet we know little. The relatively close and simple social and economic structure and smallness of the community make it easier to survey the needs and the situation of middle-aged and older persons in any given community. But therein lies the danger that, because the community seems so readily comprehensible, we pass it off as having no problems, no unmet needs. Furthermore, because of the strong personal relationships between residents of rural non-farm areas, community responsibilities are too often ignored in the belief that they will somehow be met without organized effort.

Many rural non-farm areas are just beginning to cope with the problems of community services and facilities for the whole population. Only recently, primarily under the stimulus of federal grants under the Hill-Burton Act, has national progress been made in meeting the medical needs of rural and rural non-farm areas.

URBAN COMMUNITIES

The urban communities in which middle-aged and older people live in the United States today, with few exceptions, fall into six reasonably distinct types:

New suburbs: less than 20 years old.— New suburbs are likely to contain single-family, detached houses,[2] arranged along

---

[2] Near the larger metropolitan areas these suburbs frequently consist of garden apartments or row houses.

curving streets with lots wider and deeper than formerly, generally acre upon acre developed for single-family housing, with other uses forbidden except for the elementary school or occasional park. Most of these, in response to the postwar "baby boom," are dwelling units of three bedrooms or larger and are based on a mid-twentieth-century standard of living related to one- and two-car families and to postwar incomes. The regional shopping center bundles all commercial endeavors into one place. The elementary school is likely to be the focal point of interest, and adult ties and relationships are likely to lead back to the central city area.

Twenty- to 30-year-old suburbs.—Residential neighborhoods in these 20- to 30-year-old suburbs usually have a higher population density, with less spacing between houses, smaller front yards, and a generally smaller over-all scale of development. There is likelihood of a neighborhood shopping district every eight or ten blocks. Public transportation generally serves a major portion of the suburb, and city services and utilities have usually been extended into the area. What is even more important, the pattern of life—civic, cultural, and social—is related not just to younger families but to broader population age groups. For many of the residents are now in their fifties and sixties, their children have left home, and they in turn have grown into a new way of life. Then, too, some of the original residents have moved away, and the maturing neighborhood has attracted some older people. Near the neighborhood shopping districts, occasional rezoning has permitted the building of apartment houses, but, more generally, these 20- to 30-year-old suburbs contain single-family houses only.

Thirty- to 40-year-old communities.—In many of our cities there are a number of reasonably substantial 30- to 40-year-old residential neighborhoods. Many of these are thriving, well-functioning neighborhoods, now seeing their second group of younger families intermingled with a sizable number of middle-aged and older people.

These communities are likely to be found in geographically isolated areas of the city, which have not yet been affected by the onward march to the suburbs or by the city's heavy vehicular traffic and ever expanding commercial endeavor. These neighborhoods generally offer not only the full range of community services (both public and commercial) but also a well-established, continuing pattern of civic, cultural, and social life, a social structure, and a cohesiveness that enchances the neighborhood environment.

Older residential areas.—The older residential areas of the city are of several types: (1) the occasional beautiful, convenient, and safe neighborhood, with properties well maintained, and with a firm civic and social substructure; (2) the common residential neighborhood, in which one-third to one-half of the dwelling units and major structures, although showing signs of a better day, are obviously deteriorating, more from neglect than from obsolescence; and (3), most common, the ill-used, ill-kept residential neighborhood, in which the structures have extensively deteriorated, and the neighborhood is seriously blighted and may even be a slum.

Central city area.—A great number of older people live in the central city area, in which there is an admixture of commercial and industrial as well as residential land uses. Some of these heart-of-city locations provide convenient, desirable residences; less frequently do they also provide a true neighborhood environment. Most of them are fit by today's standards for urban renewal, if not for complete redevelopment. Unfortunately, in relation to the total job to be done, the acreage now undergoing redevelopment is pitifully small, and we have much to learn not only in creating a beautiful and convenient environment but also in giving that environment a worthwhile civic and social structure. Regretfully, most efforts have resulted in physical environments which, if not less beautiful than what they replaced, are certainly less interesting. Indeed, in our haste to raze the blighted structures and the evils of the slum, we have often destroyed the human values which it had taken years to achieve.

Small cities and towns.—Finally, there are the small cities and towns, whose smaller scale and reduced distances make them suitable environments for older people. Characteristically, these have less bustle of daily business and greater informality and even intimacy. These communities are likely to include a relatively broad dis-

many of these moves were dictated by necessity and how many were prompted by a more capricious desire for mobility.

Approximately one-fourth of the people interviewed in the Grand Rapids study (Hunter and Maurice, 1953) said that they desired other living quarters. Approximately one-third of all respondents were dissatisfied with their neighborhoods, approximately one-fifth indicating that their primary objection was that the neighborhood

TABLE 2*

MOBILITY BY AGE: RESIDENCE IN APRIL, 1953, AS COMPARED WITH APRIL, 1952

RESIDENCE IN APRIL, 1953, AS COMPARED WITH APRIL, 1952	POPULATION (IN THOUSANDS)			
	Total Civilian Population	1–44 Years	45–64 Years	65 Years and Over
Total (continental U.S.)	153,038	107,526	32,142	13,370
Same house (non-movers)	121,512	80,604	28,726	12,182
Different house in the U.S. (movers)	30,786	26,228	3,382	1,176
Same county	20,638	17,396	2,358	884
Different county (migrants)	10,148	8,832	1,024	292
Within a state	4,626	3,954	518	154
Between states	5,522	4,878	506	138
Abroad on April 1, 1952	740	694	34	12
Per cent	100.0	100.0	100.0	100.0
Same house (non-movers)	79.4	75.0	89.4	91.1
Different house in the U.S. (movers)	20.1	24.4	10.5	8.8
Same county	13.5	16.2	7.3	6.6
Different county (migrants)	6.6	8.2	3.2	2.2
Within a state	3.0	3.7	1.6	1.2
Between states	3.6	4.5	1.6	1.0
Abroad on April 1, 1952	0.5	0.6	0.1	0.1

* Source: U.S. Bureau of the Census, *Current Population Reports, Population Characteristics* (Series P-20, No. 49 [1953]), Table 3.

tribution of age groups and to offer many opportunities for the older person to participate in community life.

MOBILITY WITHIN URBAN COMMUNITIES

In Table 2 it will be observed that, for the period reported, persons 65 years of age and over were living in the same house much to the same extent as younger age groups. Most of the older persons who had changed their residences, however, had moved within the same county, while a much smaller percentage had moved to another county or another state.

It would be interesting to learn how

had changed. Typical comments about these objectionable changes were: "Other nationalities moving in"; "Too much noise and traffic"; "Can't get acquainted the way I used to"; "Houses getting too crowded"; "No gardens anymore"; "People don't care anymore about the appearance of their yard and home"; "It was lovely here before automobiles came." It is interesting that, while one-third expressed dissatisfaction, only one-fourth said that they wanted to move.

CONCENTRATIONS OF OLDER PEOPLE

In most of our cities older people are concentrated in particular areas of the city.

Cowgill (1956) attempted to determine whether or not the outward growth of cities and the tendency of young families to congregate and segregate in the newer suburban areas were leaving a large proportion of the older generation to occupy the dilapidated dwellings of the inner residential ring. On the basis of his study of available data (primarily from the Bureau of the Census), he concluded: "While the central areas are to a degree specialized as residential areas for aged folk, the degree of such specialization in relation to the rest of the city is not increasing, and, in fact, shows some tendency to decline" (Cowgill, 1956, p. 80).

In most cities, concentration within the community appears to result more often from the relative availability of desirable dwelling units than from free choice. Mumford (1956) has pointed out that, before the ideal living environment can be created, "we must challenge the whole theory of segregation upon which so many American communities, not the least those that call themselves 'progressive,' have been zoned" (p. 193).

Concentration of a different sort has occurred in past years in such favorable climates as California and Florida. Groups of people with similar interests and backgrounds have gravitated to specific geographic areas and today constitute a major portion of the population in the vicinity. Typical of such concentrations of retired people in Florida are Lakeland, St. Cloud, and Winter Park; or, in California, such cities as Carmel, La Jolla, and parts of San Diego. Spas have always been a favorite place for older people, but whether retired people have recently sought residence in such favorable climates more extensively than in previous years it is not known.

Since 1910, St. Petersburg, Florida, has billed itself as "The Sunshine City" of the retired, and the blandishments of its chamber of commerce and other groups have lured an unusually large number of older people there on a seasonal, if not a year-round, basis.

A third type of concentration of older people—the retirement village—has been much discussed, but there is nothing to suggest that it is about to become a major phenomenon on the American scene. Only two such villages—Youngtown, Arizona, and Ryderwood, Washington—have actually been developed so far. Youngtown is a privately developed residential community 12 miles beyond Phoenix. Ryderwood represents a private attempt to revitalize an abandoned logging town, using the old residential structures and community facilities as residences for retired people. Other retirement villages have been proposed, particularly in the immediate post–World War II years, in Florida. Sahle (1952) observed that many retired individuals liked the idea of living in a village made up largely of retired people. At Salhaven, near Jupiter, Florida, the Upholsterers' International Union is trying to establish a combined retirement and convalescent (for all age groups) village.

In the newer residential developments in Florida, older people apparently tend more often to integrate with other age groups. This is because of the high competitive level of residential building activity and the large influx of newcomers of all ages (including retired people in the 45–54 age group), not to mention a favorable homestead exemption law.

A number of other developments have been undertaken in the United States under the title of "village," but careful analysis generally shows them to be either small groupings of proximate housing (discussed in Sec. II, C, "Nature and Quality of Existing Independent Housing"), or some form of group housing such as the specialized institution (Sec. II, A, "Aging Residents among Us").

B. Classification of Housing

With the demonstrated impact of maximum of independence of action and the continuing emphasis upon maintenance of individuality in later maturity and old age, housing and other aspects of the environment would seem logically classified in terms of the relative degree of independence that they afford the individual.

In setting up classifications for its 1950 tabulations of housing, the Bureau of the Census (1953b) defined the dwelling unit as "a group of rooms or a single room occupied . . . as separate living quarters by a family or other group of persons living together or by a person living alone." It further defined the dwelling unit as having "separate cooking equipment or a separate entrance," basing its definition on the concept of "separateness" and "self-containment." Under such a definition, individual sleeping rooms are not classified as dwelling units, nor are the living quarters in rooming houses with five or more lodgers. Similarly, living quarters in institutions for the aged and other categories of individuals are excluded from the independent dwelling unit count.[3]

In developing a systematic approach to the field of housing, workers in social gerontology have proposed other classifications: Kleemeier (1951) suggested the extremes of "unsegregated" and "segregated" communities, with further delineation according to whether housing were congregate or institutional. Donahue (1954a) made use of the categories of "well older people" and "older people requiring sheltered care and medical supervision." Webber and Osterbind (1960), in a paper on retirement villages and other living arrangements in Florida, employed a conceptual scheme which classified housing in terms of congregate, segregated, and institutional living.

Because the relative degree of independence and separateness of living is a major criterion in choosing living quarters, and also because many of the available data in the field are categorized in this way, a two-fold classification of housing for middle-aged and older people seems particularly suited to the present analysis:

1. *Independent housing*—living quarters in which the dwelling unit is separate and self-contained. Using the Bureau of the Census definition, this includes units that have separate cooking equipment, or units of two or more rooms and a separate entrance, or one-room apartments in regular apartment houses. Thus it includes houses, apartments, flats, and (occupied) trailers, tents, or boats.

2. *Group housing*—all other living quarters, including institutions and other quasi-household accommodations such as large rooming houses, hotels, tourist courts, dormitories, residence clubs, convents, flophouses, Y's, and shelters such as the Salvation Army or mission shelters.

In employing such a classification, it should be noted that many *institutions* catering to the retired provide and operate independent housing, such as the row housing of Presbyterian Village (just west of Detroit, Michigan) or the cottages of the Florida Lutheran Retirement Center (Deland, Florida); others operate group housing, such as Tompkins Square (a residence club in New York City) or Casa de Mañana (a residence hotel at La Jolla, California). Some institutions offer a variety of accommodations, ranging from independent, single-family houses to group housing which provides sheltered care and medical supervision. Thus the institution as an administrative and operational unit is to be distinguished from the institution as a place of residence described by the Bureau of the Census (see above).

C. Independent Housing

DATA OF NATIONAL SCOPE

Unfortunately, the design of the United States Census of Housing permits neither an inclusive classification of the housing of older people nor a precise evaluation of the quality of housing in terms of adequacy or inadequacy for living in later maturity or

---

[3] Institutions were further defined by the Bureau of the Census in 1950 as "quasi-households which provide care for persons with certain types of disabilities; disabilities which, in the community at large constitute hazards to the welfare of the person himself or to other members of the community" (U.S. Bureau of the Census, 1953c).

old age. Census of Housing data on residence are not recorded in terms of age, and special tabulations to date have been available only by age of heads of households. Thus, at the outset, data are limited to those older people who are living in their *own* households.

Then, too, many of the devices for assessing the adequacy of housing for the general population have limited usefulness in measuring the home and living environment of older people. For instance, when we explore the number of persons per room,

by classifying the dwelling unit as dilapidated or not dilapidated, we are working with a very crude measure, for the variation in quality of physical environment from the new structure to the most dilapidated old one is tremendous. Long before the house can truly be termed "dilapidated," its condition, and probably that of the neighborhood, will have made the physical environment highly unsatisfactory. Then, too, the absence of running water and a flush toilet in the home is only a criterion of *total* inadequacy, and the pres-

TABLE 3*

SIZE OF NON-FARM HOUSEHOLDS IN THE UNITED STATES, 1950

(Distribution of Persons in Dwelling Units by Heads of Family
over and under 65 Years of Age)

No. OF PERSONS	TOTAL		AGE 65 AND OVER		UNDER AGE 65		AGE 65 AND OVER AS PER CENT OF TOTAL
	No. (000's)	Per Cent	No. (000's)	Per Cent	No. (000's)	Per Cent	
One.........	3,602	9.8	1,405	24.8	2,197	7.1	39.0
Two.........	10,447	28.5	2,402	42.5	8,045	25.9	23.0
Three........	8,458	23.0	909	16.1	7,549	24.3	10.7
Four.........	7,009	19.1	423	7.5	6,586	21.2	6.0
Five.........	3,713	10.1	271	4.8	3,442	11.1	7.3
Six..........	1,780	4.9	138	2.4	1,642	5.3	7.8
Seven or more..	1,688	4.6	110	1.9	1,578	5.1	6.5
Total.....	36,697	100.0	5,658	100.0	31,039	100.0	15.4

* Source: U.S. Bureau of the Census, special sample tabulation of 1950 Census data prepared under agreement with the Division of Housing Research, Housing and Home Finance Agency.

we need to weigh certain characteristics of later life, such as the number of hours a day an older person spends in the home compared to the number a younger person spends there. We need to compare the relative number of families consisting entirely of adults and those containing adults and children, along with the sleeping arrangements required in each case. We need to take into account that, when households are composed primarily of one and two people, anything less than a two-room unit means that the individuals must cook, eat, sleep, and live in the same room. Furthermore, if we use the available criteria to assess the quality of the living environment

ence of these facilities does not positively indicate the dwelling's qualitative adequacy.

Size of dwellings.—Before reviewing summary data on size of dwellings, it should be noted that 67 per cent of the households with heads of family 65 and older are *one-* and *two-person* households. Table 3 indicates that more than one-third of the *one-person* non-farm households in the United States are represented by people 65 years and older and that close to one-fourth of the *two-person* households have as their heads people 65 and over. Thus, being members of generally smaller-size households, older people who live in their own homes are less likely to live in crowded conditions than are younger families.

Table 4 presents a comparison of the number of rooms in dwelling units in which the heads of households were 65 years and over with those in which they were under 65. The larger dwellings of those over 65 can be readily explained, of course, by the number of older people, particularly couples, who have continued to occupy a homestead purchased earlier, when their children were growing up; also it is accounted for

calculations of net worth of spending units[4] estimated that 63 per cent of the spending units (non-farm) with heads 65 and over owned their own home, compared to 56 per cent of all spending units. Twenty-seven per cent of the older heads paid rent for a dwelling compared to 40 per cent of all spending units. A high percentage—82 per cent—of the spending units (non-farm) with head aged 65 and over had free and clear title to their homes, compared to 49 per cent of all spending units. (See Table 6

TABLE 4*

SIZE OF NON-FARM DWELLINGS IN THE UNITED STATES

(Number of Rooms in Dwelling Units by Heads of Family over and under 65 Years of Age in 1950)

No. of Rooms	TOTAL		UNDER AGE 65		AGE 65 AND OVER		AGE 65 AND OVER AS PER CENT OF TOTAL
	No. (000's)	Per Cent	No. (000's)	Per Cent	No. (000's)	Per Cent	
One.........	977	2.7	769	2.5	208	3.7	21.3
Two.........	2,774	7.6	2,344	7.5	430	7.6	15.5
Three........	5,553	15.1	4,829	15.5	724	12.8	13.0
Four........	8,056	22.0	7,044	22.7	1,012	17.9	12.6
Five.........	8,178	22.3	7,072	22.8	1,106	19.5	13.5
Six..........	6,376	17.3	5,331	17.2	1,045	18.5	16.4
Seven........	2,435	6.6	1,913	6.2	522	9.2	21.4
Eight........	2,348	6.4	1,737	5.6	611	10.8	26.0
Total.....	36,697	100.0	31,039	100.0	5,658	100.0	15.4

* Source: U.S. Bureau of the Census, special sample tabulation of 1950 Census data prepared under agreement with the Division of Housing Research, Housing and Home Finance Agency.

by the number (albeit small) of older people of higher incomes who are able to afford a relatively high standard of living.

Whereas among the younger population we have been concerned with space and function tensions caused by overcrowding, the large percentage of occupancy of homes of four or more rooms by people 65 and older makes such problems of less concern in the older group.

Homeownership.—A special census tabulation made in July, 1951, estimated that two-thirds (67.2 per cent) of the 65 and over heads of households owned their own homes (see Table 5). Subsequently, the Federal Reserve System (1954) in its 1954

for mortgage debt in non-farm houses occupied by spending units with head 65 and over.)

Valuation of housing.—Value of homes owned in 1954 by spending units with heads aged 65 and over was generally lower than that of homes owned by all spending units (see Table 6). For instance, of those homes owned by older spending units, 37 per cent were assigned a value of $10,000 and over, compared to 46 per cent of those owned by the total spending units.

Of those heads of households 65 and

[4] A group of persons living in the same dwelling and related by blood, marriage, or adoption who pool their incomes for major items of expense.

TABLE 5*

OWNERSHIP-TENANCY, MONTHLY RENTAL, AND CONDITION OF NON-FARM DWELLING UNITS, BY HOUSEHOLD HEADS UNDER AND OVER AGE 65 YEARS, 1950

(Percentage Distribution)

	Total	Head under Age 65	Head over Age 65	Head over Age 65 as Per Cent of Total
Owner-occupied.............	53.4	50.9	67.2	19.4
Renter-occupied............	46.6	49.1	32.8	10.9
Monthly rental:				
Under $20...............	9.1	7.9	19.6	21.8
Under $30...............	24.3	22.5	39.6	16.7
Condition of dwelling units:				
All units:				
Dilapidated............	7.1	6.9	8.4	18.2
Not dilapidated.........	92.9	93.1	91.6	15.2
Required facilities†.....	71.5	72.4	66.4	14.3
Owner-occupied:				
Dilapidated............	4.9	4.4	6.9	27.5
Not dilapidated.........	95.1	95.6	93.1	19.0
Required facilities†.....	76.6	78.0	71.1	18.0
Renter-occupied:				
Dilapidated............	9.7	9.5	11.5	12.9
Not dilapidated.........	90.3	90.5	88.5	10.7
Required facilities†.....	65.5	66.6	56.8	9.4

* Source: A special U.S. Bureau of Census tabulation of one-in-a-thousand non-farm dwelling units made July, 1951, at the request of the Housing and Home Finance Agency.

† Toilet, bath, and hot running water.

TABLE 6*

VALUE,† MORTGAGE DEBT, AND OWNER'S EQUITY IN NON-FARM HOUSES OCCUPIED BY ALL SPENDING UNITS AND SPENDING UNITS AGED 65 AND OVER, EARLY 1954

(Percentage Distribution)

AMOUNT	ALL SPENDING UNITS			SPENDING UNITS WITH HEAD AGED 65 AND OVER		
	Value	Mortgage Debt	Owner's Equity	Value	Mortgage Debt	Owner's Equity
Total...............	100.0	100.0	100.0	100.0	100.0	100.0
Zero	‡	49.0	‡	‡	82.0	‡
$1–$4999..............	19.0	28.0	34.0	24.0	15.0	30.0
$1–$2499.............	‡	‡	15.0	‡	‡	16.0
$2500–$4999..........	‡	‡	19.0	‡	‡	14.0
$5000–$7499............	18.0	12.0	23.0	25.0	§	22.0
$7500–$9999............	16.0	7.0	13.0	10.0	2.0	8.0
$10,000 and over........	46.0	4.0	29.0	37.0	1.0	36.0
$10,000–$12,499.......	18.0	‡	12.0	16.0	‡	16.0
$12,500–$19,999.......	19.0	‡	11.0	13.0	‡	13.0
$20,000 and over.......	9.0	‡	6.0	8.0	‡	7.0
Not ascertained.........	1.0	§	1.0	4.0	§	4.0

* Source: U.S. Board of Governors of the Federal Reserve System, "1954 Survey of Consumer Finances," *Federal Reserve Bull.*, **40** (1954), 246–49, Supplementary Table 15 attached to reprint of article and unpublished data from "1954 Survey."

† Value was estimated by respondents, except that houses purchased during 1953 were valued at purchase price.

‡ Not available.

§ No cases reported, or less than one-half of 1 per cent.

older who were tenants, 39.6 per cent paid less than $30 a month compared to 24.3 per cent for the tenants of all ages (see Table 5). These low rental figures obviously reflect the number of heads of households in the age group 65 and older who have incomes of less than $1000 per year. (See also chap. xiv for more definite discussion of family income and the rate of reduction of income with age.) A sharp

shows that almost 92 per cent of all non-farm dwelling units in the United States occupied by families with heads 65 years or older were not dilapidated, a slightly lower proportion than among units occupied by heads of family under 65. With respect to private toilets, baths, and hot running water, 6 per cent fewer were without these facilities than were comparable units occupied by younger families. Table 5 shows

TABLE 7*

CONDITION OF NON-FARM DWELLING UNITS IN THE UNITED STATES: CONDITION AND TYPE OF PLUMBING EQUIPMENT OF ALL HOUSING IN 1950 BY HEADS OF FAMILY UNDER AND OVER AGE 65 YEARS

CONDITION	TOTAL		UNDER AGE 65		AGE 65 AND OVER		65 AND OVER AS PER CENT OF TOTAL
	No. (000's)	Per Cent	No. (000's)	Per Cent	No. (000's)	Per Cent	
Not dilapidated......	34,084	92.9	28,902	93.1	5,182	91.6	15.2
Private toilet, bath, and hot running water.........	26,224	71.5	22,468	72.4	3,756	66.4	14.3
Private toilet, bath, and cold running water..........	1,222	3.3	995	3.2	227	4.0	18.6
Running water, no private toilet or bath............	4,227	11.5	3,504	11.3	723	12.8	17.1
No running water..	2,411	6.6	1,935	6.2	476	8.4	19.7
Dilapidated..........	2,613	7.1	2,137	6.9	476	8.4	18.2
Private toilet, bath, and hot running water..........	585	1.6	522	1.7	63	1.1	10.8
Private toilet, bath, and cold running water..........	2,028	5.5	1,615	5.2	413	7.3	20.4
Total..........	36,697	100.0	31,039	100.0	5,658	100.0	15.4

* Source: U.S. Bureau of the Census, special sample tabulation of 1950 Census data prepared under agreement with the Division of Housing Research, Housing and Home Finance Agency.

drop in income upon retirement can mean only that many older people who do not already own their homes cannot afford to purchase or rent adequate housing. This inability of many older people to pay rent is further pointed up by the fact that rents for adequate quarters in 1950 in selected cities ran from a little less than $40 a month in New Orleans to $56 a month in Washington, D.C. (Anonymous, 1951*a*).

Condition of dwelling units.—Table 7

that the proportion of dilapidated housing among owner- and renter-occupied units was approximately the same for older families as for younger families.

DATA REGARDING SPECIFIC POPULATION SAMPLES

In understanding the characteristics of present housing of older people, some of the more detailed surveys of specific categories are helpful.

In the 1953 study of the recipients of old age assistance (Hawkins, 1957) fully two-thirds of the subjects, compared to one-third of the total United States population of all ages, lived in households consisting of one or two persons. Furthermore, households of recipients had an average of 3.9 rooms compared to 4.7 for the total population of all ages. Table 8 shows the generally lower proportion of subjects who had certain equipment and facilities in their dwelling units compared to the total population (all ages).

The Grand Rapids study (Hunter and Maurice, 1953) shed additional light on homeownership, tenure, facilities, etc., for older people. It revealed that 59 per cent of the subjects owned their own homes, that 22 per cent rented, and that 19 per cent lived in housing which they neither owned nor rented but which was supplied by children, relatives, or others. In terms of tenure of occupancy measured in 10-year intervals, 40 per cent had lived in the present house for 9 years or less, 13 per cent for 10–19 years, and 11 per cent for 40 years or more. When asked what kinds of housing problems they were encountering, 55 per cent indicated that they had no problems; among those who did report problems, 18 per cent said that the stairs were too hard to climb, 14 per cent that facilities were inadequate, 11 per cent that the house was too big, 11 per cent that it was too expensive to keep up, and 7 per cent that they were unable to do the necessary maintenance work.

In the Minneapolis–St. Paul study (Vivrett *et al.*, 1955), in which slightly more than half of the subjects owned their homes, a significant relationship was found between the status of ownership or rental and the number of rooms in the dwelling unit. Thus 6 per cent of owner-occupied dwellings had three rooms or less (with close to 50 per cent having six rooms or more), while 68 per cent of renter-occupied dwellings had three rooms or less.

NATURE AND QUALITY OF EXISTING INDEPENDENT HOUSING

Among the distinct types of housing available to middle-aged and older people are the following:

The homes of yesterday.—In many communities the patterns of tenure of occupancy are indicative of the kind of housing involved. The middle-aged man who started

TABLE 8*

SELECTED CHARACTERISTICS OF DWELLING UNITS OF OLD AGE ASSISTANCE RECIPIENTS AND OF THE TOTAL UNITED STATES POPULATION, 1953

Item	Per Cent of OAA Recipients Surveyed	Per Cent of U.S. Population (All Ages)
Running water..........	68	82
Flush toilet.............	56	74
Electricity.............	88	92
Mechanical refrigeration...	55	79
Cooking facilities or access to facilities..........	95	98
Urban residents with telephone or access to telephone................	49	....
Farm residents with telephone or access to telephone................	14	....
Bedroom shared with spouse or not more than one other person..........	34	....
Private bedroom (not shared)...............	58	....

* Source: C. E. Hawkins, "Recipients of Old Age Assistance: Their Housing Arrangements," *Social Security Bull.*, **20** (September, 1957), 9–12.

his family 25–40 years ago may be living in a very old house, but chances are he is probably occupying one built less than 30 years ago. The older person, on the other hand, having begun his family 40–50 years ago, is likely to occupy a house built 30–40 years ago, although in either case the homeowner may have bought a newer house.

As might be expected, the middle-aged or older person who occupies a house purchased during the early years of family life probably has large quarters, the very size of which may lead to unreasonable maintenance and expenditures of money, of personal energy, or of domestic service. In an economy with a fluctuating dollar value, however, such charges are likely to be less burdensome than is the rapidly changing rental paid by the person who rents his quarters.

Of the housing built *45–55 years* ago, most of the small dwelling units are likely to have deteriorated either because of poor construction and inadequate maintenance or because of inroads of commerce and industry into what was probably a residential area of low valuation. That housing which has remained intact, however, is likely to be large and commodious; buildings are soundly constructed of masonry or frame—all too frequently sited upon a supposedly desirable elevation of 4 or 5 feet above street level, with the first floor farther elevated by another five or six steps. They are usually two-and-one-half-story, or sometimes three-story, structures with more than one bath and with central heating. But the plumbing and heating systems, although still functioning in much their original form, by now need extensive repair or in many cases complete replacement. Similarly, when the electric wiring has been unsuitable to present demands, new circuits are usually run into the kitchen or basement, which means that the occupants must carefully schedule the use of appliances to prevent the blowing of fuses.

The apartment houses of those days are likely to be similarly commodious, multiunit buildings often with as many as four or five stories—but with no elevator. The 45- to 55-year-old apartment house is characteristically a large, blockish, sort of building, in which half of the apartments face an inner light well or court, and it is in these inner court apartments (usually because they rent at a reduced rate) that older people often live.

Thirty- to 40-year-old houses, built during the twenties are likely to be quite spacious and usually have two stories. Sometimes there is a bedroom and bath on the first floor, but more commonly all bed-

rooms and baths are on the second floor, with at best a lavatory in the first-floor hall. Apartments of this era are generally multiunit, multistory, and fairly commodious by today's standard, usually containing a good deal of closet and storage space. Many of the mechanical systems in 30- to 40-year-old housing do not measure up to current-day standards, although they are more efficient in houses of this vintage than in those dating from the period before World War I.

Housing of the thirties, now *20–30 years* old, is occupied by a significant number of middle-aged people, and a smaller—but still high—percentage of older people. Among single-family houses of that day, one finds Cape Cod and semicolonial houses and a high number of more functional, indigenous types. These typically are two- (and some three-) bedroom houses, frequently on one floor and not more than one or two steps above grade, generally with a basement, and in a good state of repair. The nature and size of these units suggest that they are quite well suited to the needs of one- and two-person older families. Furthermore, most of these houses incorporated the modern heating plants with thermostatic controls and time- and labor-saving fuels that were coming into use in the thirties. The lots were small, and reasonable standards of street and sidewalk layout and of utilities and services were beginning to be adopted. The garden apartment was coming into more general use at the time, and, although this meant some walk-ups, it also meant an equal number of first-floor apartments, the standards of which were similar to those of the single-family house and, hence, equally suitable for later living. Furthermore, in the garden-apartment developments, the management assumed the responsibilities of cutting grass and shoveling snow, as well as minor repairs about the apartments.

Relatively few houses in *more recent suburban developments* are occupied by older people. For one thing, relatively few middle-aged and older people have been looking for housing and, for another, the housing in these suburban developments has been designed almost entirely for younger families—the products of wartime and postwar marriages. Many are split-level, three- and four-bedroom houses with recreation room in basement, but significant numbers of smaller units have also been built, and many of these will eventually be occupied by middle-aged and older people. Such houses are generally compact, conveniently arranged, and easily accessible from the street. Almost all are equipped with automatic heating; standards of electrical wiring and plumbing are good.

Except for a brief flurry of apartment-building activity (much of it under the ill-famed Section 608 of the Housing Act), little housing in the way of small rental units has been built, and rentals for most of these are priced beyond the reach of the large body of older people.

These, in general, are the kinds of housing that are available in communities today to middle-aged or older people. There are some older structures in many sections of the country that have been remodeled and improved, but these are relatively insignificant compared with the total volume of available housing. Similarly, although some middle-aged and older people have carefully evaluated their situations and built new houses to provide a suitable environment for later life, the number of such houses is negligible in the total picture.

Dispersed housing for older people.—The home-building industry, focusing on the ready market among younger families, has scarcely considered the housing needs of one- and two-person households—or the particular needs of older people. A few private builders in some sections of the industry, however, have fulfilled a responsibility and exploited the market potential by building specifically for older people. Following the usual patterns of the industry, these builders are constructing *dispersed housing* in which individual dwelling units for older people—detached houses and apartments—are interspersed with dwelling units for other age groups.

In Florida, for example, a number of factors have combined to bring about the sale and occupancy of a large number of single-family detached houses by retired (and some non-retired) middle-aged and older people. For one, a favorable tax law encourages, through homestead exemption, the building of small, reasonably priced houses. In addition, even though there has been considerable postwar industrial development in Florida, the state has long identified itself as a region catering to retired people, to resort frequenters, and to vacationers—this is, in effect, one of its major industries. With the retirement of many middle-aged and older people in the prosperous postwar years, there was a growing demand for private housing in Florida. Consequently, not so much because of a philosophy of social gerontology as because of certain market conditions in Florida, the building industry has put on the market there a number of low-priced, small- and medium-sized houses located in desirable new communities. These houses have been sold in large numbers to retired people, thereby giving rise to residential communities in which many middle-aged and older people are dispersed among younger families.

Typical of such communities are Pompano Beach Highlands on Florida's southeast coast and Orange Lake on the west coast, just outside St. Petersburg. An outstanding central Florida community is Orange Gardens adjoining the city of Kissimmee. There, it was early determined that the community should serve families of all ages and that, in addition to the observing of high standards of neighborhood planning, houses intended for occupancy by elderly persons should be constructed and arranged to provide optimal livability. The result is a one-story house with entrance at grade—without even a threshold step; plumbing fixtures and accessories are designed to permit easy use of bathroom; kitchen-kitchenette arrangements greatly ease work; bedrooms have movable closet partitions, so that they can be used either as single or double rooms; and many other utilitarian and aesthetic desiderata have been included. What is striking about this young community (which is being annexed to the city of Kissimmee as quickly as it is developed) is that its older residents not only have been dispersed and reasonably well integrated with other residents in Orange Gardens but also have been made a part of the ongoing activity in Kissimmee.

Proximate housing for older people.—Of significance, both from the standpoint of the evolving philosophy in social gerontology and from the standpoint of the total number of units built, is the development of *proximate housing* in which groups of dwelling units in urban areas are reserved for occupancy by older people. These houses, apartments, or trailers—usually designed specially for older people—are rented or leased on a long term. They offer older people independent living in close proximity to one another and in reasonable proximity to younger families. Through their grouping or concentration near the community and its services, they simplify some of the problems of meeting the needs of older people.

Hibbard (1955) clearly states the point of view held by the Board of Presbyterian Missions and Pensions in siting its proximate housing for its retired ministers. The first of these projects at Swarthmore, Pennsylvania, provides an outstanding demonstration of the potential in this type of housing arrangement, not only in its underlying philosophy, but also in the unusually high quality of its architectural design and unit planning.

And there are other examples of proximate housing: Pilgrim Place in Claremont, California (although in more recent years extending its effort to include typical boarding- and nursing-home service), was started by Congregationalists in 1911 to provide proximate housing for ministers and missionaries of Christian faith.

Senior Center at Santa Barbara, California, has been developed more recently by the American Women's Voluntary Services and is open to older people of limited means. This development includes, in addition to a social center, forty one-bedroom row-house units, informally and intimately grouped on a site only two blocks from the main retail district of Santa Barbara.

In Duarte, California, Westminster Gardens provides efficiency and one- to two-bedroom row-house apartments, located close to each other in a high-quality residential community.

Grey Gables at Ojai, California, is a splendid neighborhood of grouped independent dwelling units, constructed and managed by the National Retired Teachers' Association; it, too, is located in the very heart of a thriving community, resulting in an ease of orientation and participation in community life by new arrivals.

In addition to these detached and row-house types of proximate housing, the apartment building has received a good deal of attention recently as being particularly suitable for older people, since it offers independent dwelling units with few maintenance requirements. An example of this type of project is the multistory apartment house constructed in 1952 for the Omaha Education Association in the heart of an existing 30- to 40-year-old neighborhood. Since then the association has constructed an additional 12-story apartment building which contains 132 efficiency units and also communal activity spaces for crafts, hobbies, and social activities, game-rooms, a launderette, and a commercially operated community dining hall. The decision to provide only one-room efficiencies in this project was based on their observation that the larger units were usually too expensive for the average income of retired Nebraska teachers.

Lake House Cooperative at Lakewood, Ohio, which will contain 250 dwelling units, is another of the new apartment houses for older people. In addition to the usual communal dining and social activity space, Lake House will boast, among other things, a library, auditorium, beauty salon, music room, gardens, and promenade roof deck.

Turning to public housing (financed by federal, state, or local funds), we find that, of the one-half million public housing units in the United States, some 53,000 units house 90,000 elderly people. The significance of the public housing program for older people is immediately obvious, for in some respects it represents society's present solution to housing older citizens with less than adequate incomes. In some cases this public housing consists of whole projects reserved exclusively for older people; in others a fixed minimum percentage (ranging from 5 to 15 per cent) of all units in a project are allocated for people in these age groups. In addition, the responsibility for housing the elderly, acknowledged in the 1956 amendment to the National Housing Act, is only now beginning to be realized in our communities, and it can be expected that the number of units reserved for the elderly, either projected or under construction, will increase considerably in the near future. This trend is illustrated by the fact that 5200 additional elderly unrelated individuals—a completely new category of residents—became eligible for, and were admitted to, public housing during the first year after the passage of the act; and this increase may have been limited by number of units available for rental.

Public law initially required that dwelling units be rented only to couples or larger families, so that, when one spouse died, the surviving spouse was ejected. Several years prior to 1956, the Cleveland Housing Authority endeavored to circumvent this limitation by designing its Cedar Apartments for Senior Citizens in such a way that the one-bedroom units could become two-dwelling units with shared bath and kitchen facility, thus permitting a surviving spouse to continue to occupy the original apartment unit with some other, unrelated individual.

In Massachusetts, combined state and local financial sponsorship has provided proximate housing of apartments and rowhouses, with as many as 24 units on one site, locating these proximate housing units on small sites in or near the center of community activity. Unfortunately, early projects under this program did not measure up either functionally or aesthetically to the criteria outlined in their standards of housing for the elderly (Massachusetts State Housing Board, 1954). More recent projects, particularly the Fitchburg project, embody site-planning techniques which recognize our present levels of experience with regard to intervening opportunities and the values and uses of communal outdoor space.

In San Antonio, Texas, a public proximate housing project of 250 units is now being built. Half of these are row-house units, and the other half are apartments in a multistory building on the same site (McGuire and Schmalhorst, 1957). The space arrangement in the unit plans of this project are particularly noteworthy from the standpoint of ease of housekeeping routines, flexibility within the space, and aesthetics of environment.

D. Group Housing

As classified here, group housing includes such quasi-household accommodations as large rooming houses, hotels, tourist courts, dormitories, residence clubs, convents, flophouses, Y's, and Salvation Army or mission shelters. It also includes living quarters in institutions. All these types imply some of the characteristics of group living. Some provide personal services normally performed in the private household, such as the preparation and serving of meals. Some also supply custodial, correctional, and technical and medical facilities.

PRESENT KNOWLEDGE AND INTEREST IN
NON-INSTITUTIONAL GROUP HOUSING

Of the population who live in group housing other than institutions, we know little more than that well over 2 per cent of the middle-aged and older population live in such quasi-households and that the ratio of men to women is 3 to 2. Table 9 presents the percentage of persons in each age group. It shows that only in the grouping of persons 75 years and older does the institutional population exceed that living in non-institutional group housing.

About group housing we know little, although for any given community one could probably piece out part of the picture for some of these housing types. Many large cities, for example, require licensing and maintain registers of large rooming houses but seldom compile such information for hotels or tourist courts. Similarly, private organizations can describe housing conditions in the residence clubs or the several Y's in a given city, but rarely can a municipality tell you more about its "Skid Rows," with their flophouses and mission shelters, than that the housing is extremely poor.[5]

Rose (1947, 1948) has written of the inadequacy of housing for unattached persons of all ages. Since about 1948 there has been concerted effort in congressional committees to call attention to the need for housing for permanent occupancy by single (unattached) persons, and presentations before these committees indicate that broad national support is being developed for this cause.

Within the Housing and Home Finance Agency, the Community Facilities Administration has concerned itself with college dormitory housing; the Public Housing Administration has sponsored only that lowrent public housing which has full facilities for independent housekeeping.

Similarly, until the amendment of the National Housing Act in August, 1956, the Federal Housing Administration had issued mortgage insurance only on dwelling units with housekeeping facilities. In addition to liberalizing the terms for transactions in-

volving sale of individual homes, that legislation authorized liberal support (mortgage insurance) to non-profit organizations who sponsor rental housing *specially designed and designated for persons over 60 years of age.* Although to date the majority of sponsors applying for FHA mortgage insurance have been institutions for the aged, more than half the total living units completed or under construction represent group housing of a non-institutional variety.[6] That the early sponsors were primarily institutional homes for the aged is probably due to the fact that these were ongoing organizations, whereas later applicants (civic, fraternal, or social welfare organizations) frequently have been new groups formed specifically to sponsor independent as well as group housing. (See also Sec. II, B, "Group Housing," above.)

CURRENT DEVELOPMENTS IN NON-
INSTITUTIONAL GROUP HOUSING

The hotel and the private residence club have long been refuges for wealthy older people—the kind of living quarters which provide the ultimate in service. The individual living units of the hotel have appealed in recent years to a greater number of older people as an environment closely akin to that of earlier life and also better attuned to their special needs for social contact, for personal security in sudden illness or emergency, and for easy access to commercial and public facilities and services.

Hotels catering to retired people have been for the most part the reclaimed, rehabilitated 30- to 40-year-old structures which either because of location or obsolescence had been unable to attract enough transient guests. Thus the William Penn

---

[5] Several cities, notably Sacramento, California, and Chicago, Illinois, as part of their urban renewal and redevelopment activities have completed, or have begun, studies endeavoring to define more precisely the nature of the population and its housing needs.

[6] In the 2-year period ending August, 1958, 690 living units in two projects had been completed, 1247 living units in thirteen projects were under construction, and an additional 1699 units in fourteen projects were under commitment or in various stages of negotiation (*Progress Report of FHA, Housing for the Elderly Projects and Proposals as of August 31, 1958*).

TABLE 9*

DETAILED FAMILY STATUS: PERSONS 45 YEARS OLD AND OVER,
BY AGE AND SEX, FOR THE UNITED STATES, 1950

(Based on 3⅓ Per Cent Sample)

Age and Family Status	Total Both Sexes	Total Male	Total Female
	45–54 Years		
Total..................	100.0	100.0	100.0
In households................	96.3	95.3	87.4
In quasi-households..........	3.7	4.7	12.6
In secondary families.........	0.6	0.7	0.4
Secondary individuals.........	1.8	2.5	8.0
Inmates of institutions........	1.2	1.5	4.2
	55–64 Years		
Total..................	100.0	100.0	100.0
In households................	95.8	94.8	96.8
In quasi-households..........	4.2	5.2	3.2
In secondary families.........	0.6	0.6	0.6
Secondary individuals.........	2.1	2.7	1.5
Inmates of institutions........	1.5	1.9	1.2
	65–74 Years		
Total..................	100.0	100.0	100.0
In households................	95.3	94.5	96.0
In quasi-households...........	4.7	5.5	4.0
In secondary families.........	0.5	0.6	0.5
Secondary individuals.........	2.1	2.8	1.6
Inmates of institutions........	2.1	2.2	1.9
	75 Years and Over		
Total..................	100.0	100.0	100.0
In households................	92.1	92.1	92.1
In quasi-households...........	7.9	7.9	7.9
In secondary families.........	0.4	0.5	0.4
Secondary individuals.........	2.1	2.6	1.8
Inmates of institutions........	5.3	4.8	5.8

*Source: U.S. Bureau of the Census, *U.S. Census of Population: 1950*, Vol. 4: *Special Reports*, Part 2, Chapter D, "Marital Status" (Washington, D.C.: The Bureau, 1953), Table 1.

Hotel in Los Angeles announced in 1955 that thenceforth it would furnish quarters "for happy living for the middle-aged, the retired, the single businessman or woman and couples—the young-at heart and the rich-in-years."

Charles S. Lavin, a real estate appraiser, has organized several hotels in the southern and southeastern parts of the United States as retirement hotels (profit-making ventures). Typical of his efforts was the Boulevard Hotel of Miami Beach. This 40-year-old, rehabilitated structure provides hotel living for older persons at rates beginning at $60 per month for room and board, with reductions for a number of residents who participate in the hotel's co-operative work plan. A swimming pool and a croquet court in the landscaped garden supplement the indoor social and cultural facilities. Because most newcomers to Boulevard Hotel have been non-residents of Florida, some concern locally has been expressed over potential increases in public payments for medical treatment and nursing care. Where management does not provide facilities for full care, or where insurance programs do not provide the necessary funds to meet such needs, such an influx of non-residents obviously may become a problem.

Methodists of Southern California have placed into operation as a part of a larger institutional complex the superior hotel accommodations of Casa de Mañana at La Jolla, California. The Presbyterians of California purchased in 1955 the new White Sands Hotel, also at La Jolla. Both Casa de Mañana and White Sands offer programs of complete life-care and residency.

Reference has already been made to the excellent study of the housing preferences of forty-seven older people evicted from the old Hotel Brunswick, Copley Square, Boston. Although the Hotel Brunswick is no longer available as a housing facility, the report gives us a vivid glimpse of housing conditions in the older hotels of many of our cities—hotels which, while not specifically catering to retired people, offer living quarters that many older people prefer.

The *residence clubs* or the *residence halls* established and operated by non-profit organizations in many larger cities offer bed–sitting rooms and suites for residents, supplemented by communal areas such as lounges, dining rooms, and activity spaces. Occasionally, these provide facilities (usually shared) in which residents may prepare light meals and snacks, but, for the most part, residents are required to eat some meals in the club dining room. A typical residence club, cited here because of its 30 years of successful operation, is Tompkins Square House, operated under the sponsorship of the Community Service Society of New York City. Located on the Lower East Side, it provides a form of group living which permits a high degree of individual independence for some sixty people who are able to take care of themselves, come and go at will, and participate extensively in the life of the community. Its quarters include single and two-room suites, with baths and kitchenettes shared by four persons. A cafeteria on the main floor provides the principal dining facility.

On a much smaller scale, the Jewish Family Service Agency of San Francisco in 1954 established the Sacramento Street Project. Its physical plant consists of a typical 50-year-old San Francisco frame residence, which was renovated tastefully but at modest cost. It includes seven private rooms with two baths and a common living room and dining room on the main floor. In addition, a small apartment is provided for a woman caretaker and her husband. The caretaker prepares and serves the evening meal, but breakfast and lunch are prepared by the residents themselves in the kitchenettes on each floor. Residents pay an average of $65 a month for room and full board and are expected to take care of their own rooms. Organized as a part of the community-wide service of the Jewish Family Service Agency, this small residence club operates successfully with a very small staff by using agency personnel for selection and admission and for special counseling on medical or nursing services. Furthermore, the agency's larger, more typical institutional facility (the Jewish Home for the Aged) is available when needed. The club is not only self-supporting but has even accumulated a surplus for amortizing the original cost.

PRESENT KNOWLEDGE OF INSTITUTIONAL GROUP HOUSING

The United States Census of Population has defined institutions as "quasi-households which provide care for persons with certain types of disabilities; disabilities which, in the community at large, constitute hazards to the welfare of the person himself or to other members of the community" (U.S. Bureau of the Census, 1953c, pp. 2c–4). It further defined institutional population as including "persons under care in correctional institutions, hospitals for mental disease, tuberculosis hospitals, homes for the aged and dependent, nursing, rest, and convalescent homes," among others.

Table 1 indicates the distribution by percentages of the middle-aged and older population among the several types of institutional facilities in the United States. It shows that the specialized institutions for the aged and dependent actually care for only slightly more older people than do the mental hospitals.

Classification of homes for the aged and dependent.—The population of homes for the aged and dependent is further classified by the Bureau of the Census by type of control rather than by level of economic dependency or type of infirmity that might lead to institutionalization. These types of control are defined as follows:

1. *Federal and state homes* comprise generally domiciliary facilities operated by the Veterans Administration and old soldiers' homes operated by the states.
2. *County and city homes* represent the survivors of the traditional county home or county poor farm and still retain a consider-

able heterogeneity of inmates. In some states they are undergoing transition from traditional county homes to county hospitals or to county hospitals for the chronically ill.

3. *Private non-profit homes* include homes for the aged operated by religious, fraternal, and nationality groups and other non-profit organizations. In general, these homes have operated over long periods and have an established reputation in the community.

4. *Other homes* represent a residual category covering commercial boarding homes (which have increased considerably with the development of the old age assistance program) and commercially operated nursing, rest, and convalescent homes [U.S. Bureau of the Census, 1953c].[7]

The data in Table 10 (particularly when interpreted in the light of including bedfast, nursing-care patients) suggest that (1) institutional housing for well and ambulant aging people is at a particularly low stage of development in the United States and that (2) available institutional housing does not appeal to the older population. There is almost certainly a reciprocal relationship between these two items.

Characteristics of the population.—Ac-

[7] Such an accounting thus includes not only those older people who are ambulatory and in reasonably good health but also those with various disabilities who might be housed in nursing, rest, and general convalescent homes (discussed in this handbook in chap. xv, "Health Programs for an Aging Population").

The inability of the Bureau of the Census to classify this population on the basis of health needs probably relates less to the inadequacy of the census-takers and more to the shortcomings of our institutional administration and its policy with regard to maximum utilization of technical personnel and facilities. This policy makes it very difficult to determine on a given day which individuals are ambulatory, which are semi-ambulatory, and which are bedfast. This handicap has been experienced by many health and welfare workers in their attempts to make such classifications locally. In fact, many institutions have their total bed capacity licensed both as boarding-home facilities for ambulatory people and also as nursing-home facilities for bedfast people. Further, among health and nursing personnel a question of definition in such classification continually arises.

576 *Walter K. Vivrett*

cording to the 1950 census, approximately one-half of the older population in homes for the aged and dependent lived in standard metropolitan areas, almost entirely in the most urban parts of these areas. Two-thirds of the population were native-born white people, while one-fifth were foreign-born white people (three-fifths of whom were naturalized citizens), and less than one-twentieth were Negroes (U.S. Bureau of the Census, 1953c).

older institutionalized at the time of the 1950 census had not been resident there the year before. (Approximately one-eighth did not report their whereabouts in 1949.)

Perhaps even more significant are the data relative to incomes of people in homes for the aged and dependent (see Table 11). More than one-third of the people 65 and older living in such homes reported no income, and an additional one-sixth reported less than $1000 per year income—thus

TABLE 10*

AGE OF PERSONS IN HOMES FOR THE AGED AND DEPENDENT, BY TYPE OF CONTROL OF HOME, COLOR, AND SEX, FOR THE UNITED STATES, 1950

AGE AND COLOR	ALL HOMES			FEDERAL AND STATE HOMES			COUNTY AND CITY HOMES			PRIVATE NON-PROFIT HOMES			OTHER HOMES		
	Total	Male	Female	Total	Male	Female	Total	Male	Female	Total	Male	Female	Total	Male	Female
White, all ages	296,783	148,417	148,366	41,811	35,955	5,856	72,439	48,239	24,200	71,249	22,624	48,625	111,284	41,599	69,685
Under 45 years	16,305	9,116	7,189	2,417	2,093	324	5,563	3,366	2,197	2,026	755	1,271	6,299	2,902	3,397
45–54 years	19,125	13,601	5,524	7,169	6,686	483	6,683	4,404	2,279	939	333	606	4,334	2,178	2,156
55–64 years	43,817	32,283	11,534	18,007	16,991	1,016	13,987	9,853	4,134	3,080	1,344	1,736	8,743	4,095	4,648
65–69 years	29,745	17,131	12,614	3,976	3,169	807	10,313	7,533	2,780	5,454	2,147	3,307	10,002	4,282	5,720
70–74 years	42,640	20,340	22,300	3,923	2,994	929	10,647	7,358	3,289	11,814	3,777	8,037	16,256	6,211	10,045
75–79 years	52,729	21,950	30,779	3,040	2,195	845	10,429	6,913	3,516	17,415	5,151	12,264	21,845	7,691	14,154
80–84 years	50,115	19,080	31,035	1,907	1,155	752	8,351	5,239	3,112	17,128	5,079	12,049	22,729	7,607	15,122
85 years and over	42,307	14,916	27,391	1,372	672	700	6,466	3,573	2,893	13,393	4,038	9,355	21,076	6,633	14,443
Non-white, all ages	11,167	7,232	3,935	2,867	2,555	312	4,856	3,151	1,705	875	321	554	2,569	1,205	1,364
Under 45 years	1,601	1,038	563	250	218	32	859	589	270	52	24	28	440	207	233
45–54 years	1,496	1,128	368	565	532	33	646	440	206	56	26	30	229	130	99
55–64 years	2,712	2,108	604	1,380	1,307	73	884	584	300	98	39	59	350	178	172
65–69 years	1,316	814	502	211	171	40	640	431	209	106	49	57	359	163	196
70–74 years	1,268	729	539	184	142	42	618	389	229	135	48	87	331	150	181
75–79 years	1,087	606	481	135	97	38	487	298	189	144	50	94	321	161	160
80–84 years	912	458	454	75	47	28	401	241	160	154	51	103	282	119	163
85 years and over	775	351	424	67	41	26	321	179	142	130	34	96	257	97	160

* Source: U.S. Bureau of the Census, *U.S. Census of Population: 1950*, Vol. **4**: *Special Reports*, Part 2, Chapter C, "Institutional Population" (Washington, D.C.: The Bureau, 1953), Table 7.

Data pertaining to the education of the institutional population age 65 and older have somewhat limited value, since one-third of the individuals did not report level of education. As for marital status, well over half of those 65 years and older were widowed, about two-thirds of them being women. The next largest group, composed of single individuals, accounted for better than one-fourth of the total institutional population. In terms of mobility and residence, about one-fifth of the people 65 and

better than half of the individuals reported no income or less than $1000 per year. (Income was not recorded for approximately one-third of the individuals.)

Characteristics of the institution.—Little detailed information is available about old age homes. The last inventory of congregate housing for the elderly, entitled *Homes for the Aged in the United States,* was published in 1941 by the Bureau of Labor Statistics of the Department of Labor. Most states maintain a listing of those boarding and nursing homes that are licensed under state law; these directories give information on the number of inmates as of a given date, size of staff, name of the superintendent, occasionally the nature of the sponsorship, and sometimes details on construction. However, the information is meager and available in limited edition only, and these directories are frequently out of print.

The 1958 Conference on Retirement Vil-

focus attention upon the problems of congregate housing and care and upon current viewpoints in social gerontology—particularly if an acceptable system could be worked out to evaluate either the institution as a whole or certain of its aspects. For far too many of the new institutions are oblivious of past developments in social gerontology, not to mention the more enlightened philosophies that are evolving in the United States.

TABLE 11*

INCOME OF PERSONS IN HOMES FOR THE AGED AND DEPENDENT
BY AGE AND SEX, FOR THE UNITED STATES, 1950

(Based on 3⅓ Per Cent Sample; Median Not Shown
Where Base Is Less than 3000)

INCOME IN 1949	45–64 YEARS OLD			65 YEARS OLD AND OVER		
	Total	Male	Female	Total	Male	Female
Total...............	62,820	44,340	18,480	215,790	92,910	122,880
Persons without income....	20,370	12,630	7,740	83,100	33,630	49,470
Persons with income......	16,110	13,380	2,730	48,390	21,570	26,820
Less than $500.........	3,750	3,000	750	15,180	6,300	8,880
$500–$999............	8,580	7,410	1,170	22,050	9,810	12,240
$1000–$1499..........	1,320	1,050	270	7,350	3,810	3,540
$1500–$1999..........	1,170	810	360	1,890	840	1,050
$2000–$2499..........	540	480	60	600	210	390
$2500–$2999..........	270	210	60	330	210	120
$3000–$3999..........	270	210	60	390	240	150
$4000 and over.........	210	210	....	600	150	450
Median income (dollars)...	$751	$749	....	$704	$729	$685
Income not reported......	26,340	18,330	8,010	84,300	37,710	46,590

* Source: U.S. Bureau of the Census, *U.S. Census of Population: 1950*, Vol. **4**: *Special Reports*, Part 2, Chapter C, "Institutional Population" (Washington, D.C.: The Bureau, 1953), Table 22.

lages deplored the lack of a descriptive national inventory of housing for older people and urged that a branch of the federal government compile such an inventory—descriptive in terms of such items as type, location, design, size, conditions of eligibility for occupancy, services offered, staffing, auspices under which built and operated, method of financing, and cost.[8] Among its other merits, this sort of inventory would

[8] Conference on Retirement Villages, American Society for the Aged, Inc., Palm Beach, Florida, February 21–23, 1958.

Institutional self-concept.—After a 6-month nation-wide survey of institutional housing for the aged, the Federal Housing Administration selected a ten-man Industry Advisory Committee on Housing for the Elderly, composed of administrators of existing institutions serving the elderly in ten states. The institutions represented a broad range of types of sponsorship, resident populations of 50–1000 persons, and experience of from 2 to 80 years of serving ambulatory and non-ambulatory individuals. The report (U.S. Federal Housing Administration, 1957) presents information on financial and other characteristics of selected institutions. It is recommended as particularly indicative of the self-concepts and self-evaluations of the more reputable institutions serving the aged.

CURRENT INSTITUTIONAL EFFORT IN GROUP HOUSING

Although some important progress has been made in institutional housing for older people (discussed briefly below, pp. 581–83), all too often the newly established institutions are 20–30 years behind the times even before the first resident arrives.

It would seem that the old age home and its derivatives—the boarding home, the nursing home, the rest and convalescent home, and the county home—have progressed little beyond the poor farm or the almshouse. One can only say that treatment is a little more humane, that a limited amount of artificial light is furnished by electricity, and that standards of sanitation are perhaps higher, although even this is questionable if the odors one encounters in many of the institutions are at all indicative.[9]

Historically, the old age home is a form of charitable housing which grew out of the county poor farm. In terms of both its stated objectives and its physical environment, it has veered back and forth between two types: (1) the county poor farm, with its charitable objectives and its barrack-like wards (or at best semiprivate housing), and (2) the subhospital environment of the infirmary and the nursing home, serving all too often as a place to wait for death.

Objectives and policies.—In terms of objectives and policies the "average" institution is a charitable home for the person of limited means; it apes as best it can the techniques of the subhospital, presumably offering tender loving care (which is actual-

ly almost never tender, bears little relationship to love, and is too frequently an antiquated sort of care). At best, it is far from progressive, rather tacitly accepting what the past has brought and what the future will bring.

1. Never having been established on a sound fiscal basis, it characteristically describes itself as a financially *poor institution* serving *poor people* as best it can.

2. On the other hand, many institutions established on a sounder fiscal basis have permitted themselves to grow and to extend their services without considering the effect on the physical and psychological environment or on economic levels of operation. Others, more plentifully endowed, squander their funds on facilities and equipment that are disproportionate to the population of the institution and to its potential services.

3. The institution, in particular the old age home, finds itself more and more heavily populated by sicker and older old people and simply accepts this as "the trend." Thus it endeavors to convert residential quarters into nursing wards. Seldom does it try to determine to what extent it has brought this condition on itself, either through the kind of environment it has provided or through its failure to recognize the medical, social, and technical resources available outside its walls. Because of the low quality of commercial nursing homes and the lack of other suitable facility, our community health and welfare officers have frequently encouraged this tendency of old age homes to become nursing homes.

4. Other institutions have interpreted the trend as indicating that the institution must itself provide the full range of facilities and services. Accordingly, they have directed their growth and expansion to include some single-family detached houses, some apartments, some dormitories or residence halls, some beds for nursing care, and some protected areas for confused and senile patients. Sometimes this variety of facilities and services is based on a realistic evaluation of the resources of the institution and of the community in which it is located;

[9] The author's own evaluation based on extensive personal visits to such institutions throughout the United States.

more frequently, it is not, and the institution is actually guilty of overextending itself, thereby dissipating much of its potential.

Financial status.—The financial status of institutions for the aged varies as widely as do the range of accommodation and the quality of environment.

1. Many institutions are dependent upon old age assistance grants to the individual resident and direct contributions in money or in kind, such as foods and volunteer services. Most of these have never endeavored to achieve physical quality; unable to meet present operating costs and rising maintenance costs, they have eked out a bare existence and have provided only minimally for the individual resident. The quality of environment and level of care in many of our institutions have been pegged to the economic level of the old age assistance grant—thus, while old age assistance funds have provided relief as well as some independence and security to the individual, the level of these grants has all too frequently set both the floor and the ceiling for standards of care and environment.

2. On occasion, a non-profit institution, through the business and professional guidance of its board, has demonstrated its ability to establish a sound fiscal policy. It has proved itself a worthy custodian of community contributions; and it has sought ways of finding and assuring incomes which not only offset expenditures but are also suitable to the resident population that it intends to serve.

Income from resident sources is varied. Some institutions operate solely or partly on the basis of life-care contracts, and these invariably involve the assignment of the resident's total assets upon admission.[10] Other institutions offer life-leases on quarters with fixed- or sliding-scale monthly maintenance charges, giving the resident the chance to withdraw at any time with refund of initial investment according to a prearranged schedule. Other institutions admit new residents on an endowment

basis, usually with an additional monthly maintenance charge. This endowment is pegged sufficiently high not only to guarantee the availability of quarters for the resident for life but also to build up a reserve fund to help the institution eventually serve more people of less means. Some institutions provide quarters and care and service for a straight monthly rental and maintenance charge, frequently subject to adjustment to meet rising living costs. Almost all institutions require that the resident agree to apply for public assistance when his personal resources are exhausted.

3. Profit-making institutions are by definition interested in gaining a return upon investment. While some of them do go bankrupt because of poor actuarial or fiscal planning, the great majority are able to establish a margin of profit—all too often, unfortunately, at the expense of adequate care and suitable environment. As an increasing number of our health and welfare services are becoming publicly supported, through grants-in-aid or tax relief, some of these profit-making institutions are reorganizing on a non-profit corporation basis.

Management and staff.—As might well be expected in such a changing area of service, management and staff also vary tremendously.

1. Boards of directors tend to give the non-profit institution (and a few profit-making institutions) continuity and stability. In the postwar years some institutions have taken a second look at the composition of their boards of directors and have reconstituted them to assure an excellent representation of business and professional people. Some are conscientiously examining

10 Many of these life-care contract arrangements *are now* based on more sound actuarial planning than previously; but, unfortunately, some msiguided institutions still persist, and the outcome in many of our communities is the aggravation of individual indigency, or at best an "SOS" for funds from the community. The effects of the combined life-care contract and the assignment of worldly goods upon admission, together with the resulting permanent incarceration, have been observable for years.

and directing the broad policies of these institutions. Unfortunately, others have boards that become too directly involved with operations, and these generally serve to maintain the old status quo of the charitable institution. Still other institutions are hobbling along with absentee and uninformed directors. The profit-making institution, however strong its objectives and direction, has less possibility of continuity, dependent as it usually is on the health and life-span of the owner.

2. The working staffs of these institutions are a direct reflection of the antiquated concepts of business and public welfare which many of the institutions hold. Many older charitable enterprises cling to the idea that they should seek out not only executive and administrative staff but also lesser employees who are "devoted to their work," willing to work at far less than the going wage. It is true that some institutions have devoted employees who are well qualified and who may be willing to work for low salaries. But, by and large, these "devoted servants" to the institution are the rejects, the discards, or those who have resigned or retired from other areas of work. These seldom appear qualified to perform the duties required in such a complex, human, and technical field of endeavor. On the other hand, an increasing number of institutions are evaluating the jobs to be done and seeking out qualified individuals to do them, with immediately observable benefits. Employees to perform the many domestic and more menial tasks required in operating the old age institution and in rendering personal service are hard to get. This is of course partly a result of the gradual disappearance of such categories of employees from the American scene. But it is also a result of the failure of the institution to realize that it must operate in today's labor market—paying today's wages and offering competitive working conditions.

The physical environment.—Despite the considerable variety in forms of sponsorship, types of management, techniques of operation, and financial arrangements with residents, there is great constancy in the physical and psychological environment of the residential old age institutions (with some exceptions, noted in the following section of this chapter).

1. *Location.* In a highly developed in-city area the institution is frequently on a site that has been engulfed by expanding commercial and industrial enterprise, if not by urban decay and blight. In such cases, there is less concern about how to integrate residential life into the life of the community and more about how to insulate residential life from the unfavorable immediate environment.

Or there is the 50-year-old institution, originally built on the outskirts of the city, where urbanization and the building of urban residences have extended to include the site of the institution itself. Like broken-down aristocracy, it sits proudly back from the street, cut off by a broad landscaped lawn from the residential life about it, and is thus denied many of the latent advantages of its location.

Then there is the institution (bequeathed by some well-intentioned benefactor) located in an almost completely rural area. In such a location, it is difficult to integrate older people with normal community life—indeed, only isolation with other old people is possible. Furthermore, the remote location makes the recruiting of employees an insurmountable problem.

2. *Design.* The old age institution is generally massive—if not monumental—in scale. And, where the over-all form of the building does not contribute to massiveness, it is usually because the institution is a complex of several units constructed at different times over the last 50 years.

The institutional control of entrance and egress has characteristically been so pervasive that only the building codes with their required numbers of exits have served to break it down. Almost never is there an entrance to the building at grade; rather there is a flight of six or eight steps. Almost never is there a driveway and canopy entrance where automobiles or taxicabs can call for the resident; almost never is there development or utilization of landscaped grounds, of the paved walkways with an occasional garden bench, except for the communal garden plot located out of sight behind the old service building.

Two- and three-story buildings, even where land is abundant, are typical, and inadequate elevator service is defended on the ground that some individuals are able to climb stairs and want to do so.

3. *Construction.* Few boards of directors during the first half of the twentieth century felt that they could afford fireproof buildings. As a result, their buildings are almost invariably frame with stucco or brick veneer or, at best, masonry shells with wood joist floors—sometimes provided in more recent years with a sprinkler system and more often not. In some cases, an energetic board member has preached the advantages of continual maintenance, and the buildings are in relatively sound condition; but generally this is not so—cornices have rotted, roofs have been patched and are still leaking, windows and window frames are coming apart as the building settles, and the plumbing, heating, and electrical systems have long since become outmoded.

4. *Individual quarters.* These turn out to be woefully inadequate at best. Single rooms are usually small dormitory cubicles with lavatories in the room and barely enough floor space to accommodate the essentials of bed, chair, and dresser. Double rooms seldom have enough space for arranging furniture to provide any privacy, and frequently they are so small as to require a double bed instead of twin beds. At the other end of the scale, some old institutions have inherited wards that house individuals in the worst old-fashioned hospital style, while others have large rooms with three or four beds turned in different directions to permit maximum space utilization.

Lavatories, if not inside the bedroom, are generally placed with a communal toilet and bath down the hall. Seldom is there more than a clothes hook or a wall-mounted mirror in either of these locations to suggest their intended functions of bathing, grooming, and dressing. The intensity of artificial illumination in the bedroom is usually too low for even younger people to read by. Where the residents have been permitted to bring some of their own furnishings, they are likely to be reasonably acceptable; otherwise, they usually consist of an institutional metal bedstead, a dresser, and a chair. Shades and curtains are required to be drawn in such a way that the appearance from the outside will be uniform regardless of how it affects life inside.

5. *Communal rooms.* Large rooms for sitting and social activity have long been the order of the day, but, by and large, these are empty or nearly empty at almost any hour.

6. *Kitchens.* These generally contain the most antiquated equipment for food preparation and washing of dishes—except where the local health officer may have imposed higher sanitation standards.

SIGNIFICANT DEVELOPMENTS IN
INSTITUTIONAL GROUP
HOUSING

Recently, however, there have been several hopeful developments in the institutional field—more clearly defined objectives, better management and techniques of operation, and improved physical environment. In general, these appear to be a logical outgrowth of, if not a part of, an evolving philosophy in social gerontology.

The institution is beginning to envision itself as a facility and a service that is a true community resource. Thus it sees itself not so much as a terminal housing accommodation but more as a highly specialized, technical geriatric facility, with the following results:

a) This relationship to the rest of the community is finding expression in a statement and restatement of objectives and policies of the institution.

b) Realizing that the operation of an institution is a six-figure (if not a seven-figure) business, administrators of institutions are establishing sound fiscal procedures and adjusting expenditures, both for capital improvements and for maintenance and operating expenses, to the sources of income at hand.

c) The board of the institution not only is broadening and developing its own point of view but is availing itself of qualified consultative help in areas where its own knowledge and experience are insufficient; furthermore, it is seeking qualified business and professional people for its staff.

d) Armed with a new, carefully planned objective and sense of purpose, the institution is trying to reshape its physical environment accordingly. The following are examples of enlightened institutional policies along this line:

(1) The Carmelite Order, in selecting a site for the *Mary Manning Walsh Home* in the metropolitan New York area, passed up the large acreages of land available 20 or 30 miles out from the city and instead chose a site in the heart of Manhattan, thus making it possible, by a short walk or taxicab or subway ride, to select the pleasure of the moment. On the other hand, that location also secured the ultimate in accessibility of professional and technical community resources. Within the Mary Manning Walsh Home an environment of varied experiences is provided for the residents. In addition to the more customarily expected things, one finds a small bar where cocktails may be had from four to six, a millinery shop operated by one of the residents, and an art gallery along the route to the dining room.

(2) *Stevens Square,* a residential facility in a 60-year-old residential neighborhood in Minneapolis, Minnesota, took advantage of the tree-shaded lawns surrounding its old two-and-one-half story building and sought ways to insure that the coming generations of residents might have an actual share in the neighborhood activity. In its expansion program, it provided a series of one-story wings, each accommodating eight to twelve older people, and each having direct access to the public sidewalk and the streets that surround the property on three sides.

(3) For *Presbyterian Village,* an eleven-acre site was selected in a suburban residential area west of Detroit. It is convenient to public transportation and to a wide range of commercial and public facilities. This institution's dispersed, varied, residential units are grouped about courts oriented to the public streets and to the houses of younger families in the neighborhood. Unfortunately, some of the self-centered aspects of institutional life serve to reduce the opportunities for contact with the younger families.

Within individual living quarters—particularly in the motel-type units—one finds a contemporary standard of environment observed: room arrangements in the one- and two-bedroom units measure up to those in the best city apartments; kitchens are planned and equipped so as to encourage their use; and the over-all quality of materials and finishes not only leads to reduced maintenance costs but also increases the enjoyment of living.

(4) Although apparently having trouble getting under way, *Salhaven,* the combined retirement and convalescent village of the Upholsterers' International Union at Jupiter, Florida, offers one of the freshest *architectural* inspirations for the old age institution. Its exploitation of indoor-outdoor concepts of living, its informality of arrangement in dwelling unit plans, and its high quality of design in both community buildings and private quarters offer some of the best of current architecture. When its actual operation is better defined, it should serve as a test of the role that physical environment can play in milieu therapy.

(5) *Baptist Village,* at Waycross, Georgia, planning an institutional type of village with an eventual population of three hundred residents, is ordering the individual living quarters in clusters of twenty-eight one- and two-bedroom apartments.

These clusters will be interconnected by sheltered walkways. The arrangement within the cluster should provide in its outdoor screened porches, walkways, and courtyards, and in its indoor communal spaces, many opportunities for social contact and for the encouragement of family-like relations.

(6) The Jewish Family Service Agency of San Francisco is one of several community organizations in the United States which acknowledges the need for a variety of residential facilities, not only within the framework of the old age home, but also woven into the fabric of the total community resources available to older people. Thus, in San Francisco, the agency supports not only a home for the aged but also two small residential clubs (described in Sec. II, B, above), a "sheltered" workshop where older people may find employment, and a hospital for the chronically ill.

(7) Similarly, the Pacific Homes Corporation (Methodists of Southern California and Arizona) provides in La Jolla, California, hotel accommodations in the oceanfront resort hotel (Casa Mañana), as well as cottages and apartment units in the immediate vicinity. Supplementing these, it maintains a sanitarium and also a hospital for convalescents—both of which are removed from the residential facility.

E. The Supporting Facilities and Services of the Community

In the rapid expansion and urbanization of the United States, society has come to assume the responsibility for, and the individual has come to demand, a broad range of community services and facilities.

Underground in our cities there is a tremendous network of utilities: water and gas supply, sewer and storm drainage, street lighting, and fire-alarm systems. On the city's surface are streets and pavements and gutters to be maintained, garbage and refuse to be hauled, people and property to be protected by fire and police patrol, and a host of other services that are taken for granted. These public services are general-

ly available to all in more or less standard quality and quantity throughout urbanized areas. Where this is not the case, most communities actually recognize the need and eventually try to provide such services.

But in health, education, and welfare there is wide variation from community to community, from state to state, and from region to region in the United States. In addition to the over-all differences in standards from community to community, there are two other reasons for such variance: (1) these services have been geared in the past, particularly in the areas of education and recreation, to youths and young adults, and only since the systematic study of the phenomenon of aging has the demand for specific services been voiced, and (2) the increasing desire for separateness of the several generations in their living arrangements has been reflected in the many one- and two-person households, necessitating more and more specialized facilities and techniques of services. When we superimpose upon the patterns of separateness the general trends of decentralization and dispersal, we realize the need for some reorganization and some curtailment as well as some new development of local services.

In the areas of health (see chap. xv) the United States Public Health Service, notably through the grants-in-aid for the construction of facilities under the Hill-Burton Act, has gone far to increase facilities and services and to establish criteria for measuring needs and accomplishments. Thus most state health officers publish a state plan that describes the facilities available in any given community and in the state as a whole. These state plans generally list hospitals, clinics, rehabilitation centers, and, in part, the specialized facilities for aging such as nursing homes and boarding homes.

Some communities, in addition to the more customary health services, carry out specialized programs of home care, day care, and homemaking. These programs in particular are aimed at helping the individual to remain in his own home.

In the field of recreation we see a real gap in quality and quantity of offerings. In most communities local park boards are the keepers of the local green areas and generally offer supervised programs of play and recreation for youth, but only a few offer recreational programs for adults; very few provide more than nominal recreation for older people.

Similarly, little more than token respect is paid to education for retired people. School administrators often express surprise at the number of people over 65 who are enrolled in adult-education courses. Although many communities have voted bond issues for first-rate school plants containing splendid community centers, these rarely extend this excellent physical resource to adults of any age for much more than P.T.A. meetings and almost never for a specialized program for middle-aged or older people with increased leisure time. Here is a facility, available in convenient locations in most of our residential neighborhoods, which appears too often to be wasted for the want of imagination or of public funds for a little more janitorial service.

Churches, too, plentiful in convenient locations in residential neighborhoods, have often been slow to grasp the significance of the period of later maturity and old age, assuming that the older people needed little more than the Sunday-morning service or the once-a-month auxiliary meeting. Churches have provided social and recreational programs for their young people but rarely for older adults. (Religious programs are discussed in chap. xix.)

For just about all older people community social welfare services take on a very real importance. The functions of the Social Security office, the public welfare agencies, and the private guidance and counseling centers have new meaning. These are usually located downtown convenient to public transportation, but, aside from the social worker going out into the neighborhood, there seems to be little effort yet to decentralize such services to conform to residence patterns. Rather the reverse seems true.

Except in the new suburban areas, commercial enterprises—food stores, confectioners, drug stores, bookstores, and personal services offered by barbershops, the beauty salons, the laundries, the dry cleaners, and the shoe-repair shops—are accessible to most residences. In the more highly populated urban areas, many of them offer to pick up and deliver. Unfortunately, though, suburban communities of the last 20 years characteristically are zoned so exclusively for residence that one must frequently travel a mile or more to reach commercial facilities of any sort. Likewise in many of our redevelopment projects we have hastily razed the neighborhood shopping area and the corner grocery and have substituted instead the centralized shopping center that commercial enterprises find so profitable. Such was the case in the redevelopment of Chicago's Near South Side: when a sizable number of elderly residents were admitted to the Prairie Courts project, it was suddenly discovered that there was no convenient place for them to buy groceries. Thus a new task fell upon the Welfare Council—that of providing transportation to food stores for many of these elderly residents.

F. Summary

Middle-aged and older people live in a variety of housing and community situations. Although the material which has been presented here deals almost exclusively with characteristics of housing and the community as they pertain to people 65 years old and older, this has not been because of lack of importance of housing of the middle aged but rather because of the dearth of reported experience or data on people of this age group.

About the housing of the 69 per cent of people 65 and older who live in their own households we have some generalized knowledge that we can relate to the total supply and quality of housing in the United States. About the 25 per cent who live in the households of others—with relatives and with non-relatives—we know almost nothing. Of the 3 per cent of individuals 65 and over who live in non-institutional group housing, we know little more than that the housing involved embraces not only the highest quality of luxury environment but also the very lowest form of housing known in the United States today. And, of the 3 per cent who live in institutional group housing, we know roughly the type of institution in which they are housed, but we have only a fragmentary knowledge of the housing situations themselves. Even though encouragement is offered in the institutional work of some individuals and agencies, institutions as a whole present a dismal picture.

III. Environmental Needs of Middle-aged and Older People

The shortcomings in the home and community environments of middle-aged and older people are due in part to an overemphasis on meeting the environmental needs of other age groups. They arise from society's failure to anticipate the evolving situations and needs of the aging individual in relation to the home and community.

A. *Physiological Needs Reflected in Housing*

TEMPERATURE AND CLIMATE CONTROL

The air about him has always been a subject of interest and concern to man. While his sensations of heat or cold, of moisture or dryness, of purity or contamination, of drafts or stillness, depend greatly upon the individual's physical condition and experience, there are some general indications of the needs of the aging person as they pertain to the air about him.

The desire of the older person for greater warmth and freedom from drafts is generally acknowledged in the private home as well as in the institution. It is known also that this environment must not be excessively hot or cold; here the precision controls developed by technology can do a successful job. Similarly, controls are available for air pollution and excessive humidity or dryness—controls that will permit adaptation to the comfort and range of toleration of the aging individual.

SEEING

The health-giving values of sunlight have long been extolled, and most aging individuals intuitively seem to seek sunlight. We have come to recognize the value of proper artificial illumination for the young person at school and the average adult at work, but rarely have we extended these standards into the home or the institution for older people. As eyesight begins to fail among middle-aged and older people, inadequate illumination may adversely affect not only efficiency but also mental and physical health. The aging individual needs an intensity of light for reading as high as, if not higher than, the student at school; and he needs a source and a distribution of light that will properly relate the brightness contrast of the item being read to the environment in which he is sitting.[11]

Whereas candlelight and dim light may inspire a feeling of romance and adventure in younger people, the aging person is likely to find them annoying and to long for the old-fashioned chandelier with its downlight upon the dining table. Moreover, since the eyes of older people are slow to adjust to changes in light intensity, the brightness contrast upon adjoining surfaces and between adjoining spaces can spell the

[11] Some recent studies at the General Electric Research Laboratories show that middle-aged workers need almost double the intensity of illumination required by individuals 17–24 years of age. For one task, the middle-aged individual required 80 foot-candles compared to the 50 foot-candles required by the younger group.

difference between relaxation or tension, between seeing and not seeing. It is important that color and light be used to help the older person distinguish between forms and surfaces such as the door handle and its location on the door, the light switch that is luminous or that contrasts in value with the surface on which it is mounted. The intensity of light in corridors and stairways of the institution should approach the intensity of light in adjoining bed–sitting rooms so that the individual will not be blinded as he moves from one area to another. In the institution it would be far better to provide reasonable illumination of the corridor floors than (with almost the same amount of money) to provide grab rails on both sides.

NOISE, SOUND, AND HEARING

An older person, while being at least as disturbed as a younger one by excessive noise, is often made very tense by excessive quiet—particularly if his sight is poor and he must depend on his hearing for cues. Some older people, because of deafness, may wish for increased intensity of sound on the radio or television or over the intercommunication system, and, unless they are living in isolation, they will have to adjust the physical environment so that this higher intensity of sound does not become an annoyance to those around them.

CONSERVATION OF ENERGY

With the advent of retirement and increased leisure, conservation of time has less urgency for the middle-aged and older person than it does for the younger adults. On the other hand, the dwindling of energy reserves means that facilities of the home and the techniques of accomplishing daily routines should be organized for maximum conservation of energy. The aging person will probably have difficulty reaching, lifting, pulling, bending over, and getting up and down. While some exercise is obviously beneficial, if carried beyond a certain point, it introduces excessive fatigue and hardship and even the abandonment of routines and activities.

PREVENTION OF ACCIDENTS

Techniques of accident prevention should assume a maximum importance—for with aging there frequently occurs failing sight or hearing, unsureness of gait and sense of balance, unsteady hand, or memory that is not always so keen. Most accidental deaths occur in the home—the greatest number among persons 65 and older being the result of falls (National Safety Council, 1955). For such persons, the accidental death rate due to falls is 86.8 per 100,000 population, compared to 3.3 per 100,000 for persons 45–64 years of age. Next highest accident killer among older people is fire burns and accidents associated with fire. For persons 65 and older the accidental death rate due to fire is 10.2 per 100,000 population, compared to 3.0 per 100,000 for persons 45–64 years of age.

Not every hazard of daily life may be anticipated, but many precautions can be taken. A resilient surface, a non-slip floor, or at best one with only a lightly coated surface can be provided instead of highly polished wood or terrazzo floors. Scatter rugs and scattered items of furniture in circulation paths can be removed. Unnecessary stairs and changes of level can be avoided in design; an acceptable control of drafts and rain at entrance doors can be devised which does not require a step at the sill or even a $\frac{3}{4}$-inch-high threshold. Sturdy furnishings and equipment without sharp angles and projecting decorations will increase the self-confidence of the older person. Mechanical appliances and contrivances can be selected on the basis of their proved safety. Cooking by electricity, for instance, is probably more satisfactory than cooking with gas. Bathroom accessories—towel bars, shower-curtain rods, soap dishes, and grab bars—should be of such construction and so installed that they will withstand a 300-pound pull in any direction. An adequate number of convenient outlets, appropriately located, will obviate the use of extension cords and lamp wires that stretch across one's path in the house.[12]

PROPER NUTRITION

Nutrition is as important for older people as for younger people. Most older people enjoy light snacks and lunches, though they usually do not require as large main meals as the rest of the population. Their diet is simple, but it does need variety. Even though the food consumed may be little, eating comes to assume a major part of the daily life of the older person, and hence the eating situation should be pleasant and relaxing. Since the requirements for food for the single person or for the couple are usually small, food storage, particularly refrigerated or frozen storage, becomes important in the home. How to keep a loaf of bread fresh until it has been used up, how to save a half-package of frozen vegetables for the next meal—these are items of real concern.

B. Sociopsychological Needs Reflected in Housing and the Community

Sociopsychological needs have to do, first, with the individual and his own pattern of living and, second, with the individual in his relationship to the others in the community.

ACCUSTOMED PATTERNS OF LIVING AND STANDARDS OF HOUSING

Most adults have customary ways of doing things, and, in general, they are resistant to change. The older person can be expected to cling to the familiar surroundings of yesterday and to his former friends and associates. Tradition, superstition, and inherited ways of thinking and behaving also

[12] The U.S. National Bureau of Standards' (1948) circular, *Safety: For the Household,* offers many additional constructive suggestions regarding accident prevention in the home. See also *Home Safety Principles* (National Association of Home Builders, n.d.).

determine many of our patterns of behavior. There are individual roots in national, religious, cultural, and occupational backgrounds, and the loneliness, caused by the narrowing circle of relatives and friends, increases the desire to remain amid that which seems familiar. In the pursuit of habits the older person has become accustomed to the environment of his home and to routine patterns of family living. Thus he is likely to demand the standards of housing which formerly meant the three-piece bathroom in most of our homes; the privacy of an individual bedroom for sleeping and dressing; and the additional space and equipment within the home for daily activities of eating, relaxing, playing, and social intercourse.

Even though the range of interests of the older person may contract, and his energy or memory similarly contract, his needs for living space will be related to the home in which he formerly lived. These needs the dormitory cubicle can hardly be expected to fill, but some of them may be met through the use of indoor and outdoor communal facilities, particularly in the case of the group living arrangement. In any case, the older person clearly requires a place to which he can retreat and over which he is master, one place, no matter how limited, where the remaining vestiges of his independence may find expression.

Donahue and Ashley (1959) suggest that privacy is requisite in housing to reduce irritations and resentment. They further question the extent to which visual privacy in the "open plans" for housing can take the place of auditory privacy.

Chapin (1951) believes that good mental hygiene depends upon freedom to be by one's self:

The respect for self as an individual with status can hardly thrive when the person is continuously open to pressures of the presence of many others. . . . Privacy is needed for thinking, reflection, reading and study, and for aesthetic enjoyment and contemplation. Intrusions on the fulfillment of personal desires need to be shut off in order to avoid the internal tensions that are built up from the frustrations, resentments and irritations of continual multiple contacts with others [p. 165].

But the objective evidence of the value of privacy, as Chapin points out, is not conclusive.

HOMOGENEITY IN SOCIAL ENVIRONMENT

Although we often speak of heterogeneity as desirable in community life, several studies indicate that homogeneity can have great importance in the community and in the institutional environment. Thus Festinger (1951) notes that homogeneity (aims, objectives, and common interests) of the social structure fosters good adjustment of the group and its members. Caplow and Forman (1950) state that homogeneity is of crucial importance in group formation and that only very powerful inhibiting factors can prevent social interaction among people of similar status whenever the opportunity arises. Taietz (1953), in his study of the administrative practices and personal adjustment in homes for the aged, found that homogeneity (economic, occupational, and educational) fosters the formation of primary friendship and interest groups, which in turn facilitate good adjustment within the home.

On the other hand, it is true that cultural, economic, or social homogeneity in the immediate living environment might justifiably be sacrificed in order to fulfil other needs. The older individual may prefer some incompatibility in the immediate living environment of group housing in order that he may live within walking distance of the homes of relatives or friends.

PERSONAL SECURITY

People have always been greatly concerned over how and where they will spend their very last years and whether or not they will be assured of a place to live and the services they may require. In a study of one hundred randomly selected old people living in the community, Tibbitts and associates found that health and physical care were prime needs and that the absence of a means of satisfying these needs provoked considerable anxiety (Donahue and Ashley, 1959) (see also chap. vii, "The Health Status of Aging People"). In the United States approximately 40 per cent of the chronically ill are 65 years of age or older; and nearly one-fifth of the non-institutionalized population of this age group report long-term illness. For these people, of course, there is more than just dread—there is a present threat which makes a roof over their heads and the accessibility of health care urgently necessary.

C. The Constellations of Contacts in the Community

Living in earlier years was seldom limited to the circle of the immediate neighborhood or to the immediate family or household; and, as the years have passed, this constellation of contacts, particularly in modern urban life, has extended itself in an ever widening radius.

We seldom realize the multitude of contacts that are part of our daily lives—the physical contacts with other people, the auditory and visual contacts with the world at large through television, the auditory contacts through radio and telephone, and the written and spoken contacts by correspondence, books, magazines, and recordings—all of these are part of our daily lives.[13]

Since man is a social being who needs

---

[13] An interesting experiment, and a very vivid demonstration of the constellation of contacts—their number, complexity, and geographic spread—is to plot upon a map of the city the places and the types of contacts in a given day or week: the places one visits by foot, by automobile, by bus, or by air; the social interchange by means of the spoken or written word; and the visual and auditory experiences. All these plotted upon the map of the city will demonstrate for us the constellation of contacts in the community which is a necessary part of life and which becomes sharply limited through the confinement or isolation of the aging person.

recognition from his fellow men, as his sphere of social or professional activity becomes more limited, he naturally will attach increased importance to the things he owns—his home, his room, his furnishings, his books, his knicknacks. When deprived of these, he must find satisfaction in dreaming and talking of the accomplishments of his past. Obviously, then, it is advantageous for the aging person to remain in his original home when possible, not only because of what the home represents, but also because of what is offered by the community in which it is located. And when we are forced to transplant individuals or groups to different sections of the country, of the city, or even of the neighborhood, new ways must be found to satisfy their needs for social recognition. In the new home or in the new community the older person needs not only some identity and recognition but also a pattern of activity or endeavor, the opportunity for participation in social experience and in group membership. In neighborhoods planned according to Perry's (1939) principle, rather than allowed to grow haphazardly as they usually do, older people would be more easily drawn into community activity.

While the individual needs familiar surroundings, accustomed ways of doing things, and sight of old faces, he needs at the same time a variety in his background and maximum environmental stimulation within the limits of his tolerance. Where old patterns and experiences have been discarded, new ones must be introduced in such a way that they are expressly suited to his capacities and interests.

D. The New Living Patterns of Middle Age and of Retirement

What do older people do all day? The disappearance of the household economy has deprived the elderly of continued occupational roles within the family, and the urbanization and industrialization of our society have further reduced the number of hours that all of us spend at work. In the transition from the 7-day to the 6-day and to the 5-day work week, people of just about every age have significantly altered their pattern of daily living. Prolonged holidays and longer vacations have resulted in even more significant reorganization of the lives of middle-aged and younger old people, bringing increased personal freedom and a search for things to participate in—sports, social activities, useful work or hobbies, and a generally heightened awareness and interest in life of the community.

All these have had a tremendous influence upon the living pattern in our communities, and, when they have been supplemented by retirement for the breadwinner of the family, the amount of such free time has been increased by about a half again.

A number of studies have been focused on what individuals do with their free time, particularly with regard to employment or hobbies, leisure time, and social activities (Hunter and Maurice, 1953; Vivrett *et al.*, 1955). These studies suggest that even those older people who cannot readily participate in community affairs and in social activity can enjoy a reasonably full pattern of life, although much of their energy may be directed toward housekeeping and daily chores.

Orbach and Shaw (1957) call attention to the fact that the search in recent years for possible status-giving roles for the aging has tended to overlook the ability of individuals to fulfil such roles because of differing lifetime patterns of social activity and participation. They believe that education at all age levels should interpret the potentialities and roles of older people in contemporary life.

It may well be that, as we grow more accustomed to leisure, future generations of the old may find less difficulty in working out for themselves a full and satisfying life in retirement. In any case such a satisfying life depends to a great degree on the physical environment of the home and the community and the individual's participation in it. This involves appropriate space and facilities for social intercourse, play, and study, and it requires also privacy and independence of action for the routines of daily living.

E. Variations in Need and Ranges of Toleration

Middle-aged and older people form a heterogeneous group with tremendously varied needs which arise from differences in national, ethnic, and cultural backgrounds and from the different physical environments in which they live. Frequently, in our zeal to meet a particularly acute need, we overlook the fact that our technique involves a readjustment in the life of the older person which, while seemingly slight, may, when added to other difficulties, overstep the bounds of his toleration.

MANIPULATION OF THE ENVIRONMENT VERSUS THE ADJUSTMENT OF THE INDIVIDUAL

In the past the individual has generally been required to adjust—sometimes permanently—to his environment, particularly in minor respects. But with the evolving patterns of mobility of the younger population, with the conscious search for housing and living situations to suit individual needs, quite frequently for short periods, future generations may find techniques of adjusting the environment to the needs or of seeking a more appropriate environment. Much research is needed on this subject.

ACCELERATION OF CHANGE

Finally, as we deal with the needs of middle-aged and older people, it is increasingly necessary that we acknowledge the dynamic, changing nature beginning with the time the children leave home, through the approach of retirement, and the onset of illness or physical disabilities. We can do much in education by planning in middle age for the years of later maturity.

Change will never be easy for so large a proportion of the population, either in the manipulation of the environment or in the adjustment of the individual. Furthermore, with age there seems to be almost inevitably an acceleration of change and changing needs. It may be that adjustment must always come with traumatic or with dramatic changes, but certainly, through education and planning, we can ease the burden of these experiences.

IV. GOALS FOR INDEPENDENT HOUSING

According to the habits and expressed inclinations of older people, most of them wish to remain an integral part of the community in which they have spent their earlier years (Nevada State Welfare Department, 1952; American Public Health Association, 1953; Havighurst and Albrecht, 1953; Donahue, 1954a; United Community Service of Metropolitan Boston, 1957a, 1957b). Society, in its assumption of the responsibility for human services, supports such a point of view and organizes so as to help middle-aged and older people live the most independent lives possible for the longest practicable time in their own communities.

The patterns of living in early adulthood are extended with few changes into middle age. Although some change in housing needs is suggested by reduction in size of the family, rarely in early middle age do other changes occur that require modifications in living arrangements or in housing. Moreover, it is unlikely that many people would abandon their three- or four-bedroom houses for smaller ones (although some may do so) as the children grow up and leave home. For it is part of our American living pattern that parents dream of their children returning to the old homestead with grandchildren; and a personal status value is implied in owning a home that is more than big enough to meet one's basic needs. It is not until later maturity (ages 60–70) that initial concern is likely to appear, along with changes in mental and physical health and marital status or income, and that other living arrangements are likely to be sought.

A. Desirable Objectives for the Home and Community

What, then, is needed to assure that more people can spend later maturity and old age in the independent environment of the home or the community? An optimal home environment with emphasis upon continued independent living for the longest practicable period can be defined as follows: (1) a home that in quality and standard is equal to if not better than that to which the individual has been accustomed in earlier years; (2) a home that is suitable to the conditions of failing health and illness *frequently* observed among the population; and (3) a home environment that has maximum adaptability to the *less frequently* observed conditions of illness, of disability, and of convalescence.

QUALITY AND STANDARD OF ENVIRONMENT

Now what does all this involve? First, the quality and standard of environment. In planning and building housing for the general population, certain standards of space and equipment have evolved as products of social consciousness and of the contemporary values and standards of living. Thus a family expects to find in the home a living room and perhaps a recreation room, a dining area and a kitchen, separate bedrooms for the parents and the children, and bathrooms that are suitable for bathing and dressing. It is tragic for older people that space standards should be permitted to fall in their houses—just when their social opportunities have lessened and they must spend longer hours at home. At such an age it is distressing to have to forego suddenly the private toilet and private bath of the home and to share the antiquated fixtures at the rear of a rooming-house hall. Similarly, the dormi-

tory cubicle is a poor substitute for the home in which even the smallest child's bedroom was more commodious.

There are also some commonplace needs in the individual living environment which must be met; for example, there should be a satisfactory desk or a table with appropriate lighting, if the individual is to continue his letter-writing or to work on his stamp collection; there should be a table or cabinet where a woman can keep up with her sewing without having to pull out a corrugated box from under the bed; there ought to be a shelf or a bookcase for books if the older person is to keep up his interest in reading; there should be a place by the window, or better still, a flower bed outside the window, where he can enjoy the results of his gardening without walking a block's distance. Through this kind of forethought, the older person could be encouraged to continue any number of interests and to develop new ones.

SUITABILITY TO COMMON CONDITIONS OF ILL-HEALTH

The second objective related to maximum livability is that the home be suited particularly to the conditions of failing health and illness frequently observed among the aging population. This means failing eyesight or hearing, slowness or unsureness of gait, or just a general dwindling of energy reserves; it means changes in physical capacity and in abilities to function. Custom is at such wide variance with the best practice; almost every home contains scatter rugs, highly polished floors, glass towel rods, and flimsy shower-curtain rods which will not withstand the person's weight. To minimize the energy required in accomplishing daily activities, it is necessary to simplify these activities and the living unit that accommodates them. Particularly for older people who are infirm or chronically ill, there is a great advantage in being able to move in a straight line from one area to another, from bedroom to bathroom, from bathroom to kitchen, and from kitchen to dining room. Specifically, there should be required as few right-angle or 90-degree turns as possible in moving about within the dwelling unit, for each turn represents an additional hazard; and then, finally, because individuals like the things they are used to and grow increasingly resistant to change, it is important that there be provided within the single setting of the home a flexibility that will allow for the dynamic processes of growth and aging and their concomitant ever changing needs.

ADAPTABILITY TO SPECIAL PROBLEMS
OF ILL-HEALTH

The third area of concern is that, within practicable limits, the home and its environment should have maximum adaptability to the less frequently observed conditions of failing health—wheel-chair existence, blindness, forgetfulness (which we too frequently assume to be senility), etc. Here, also, we too frequently overlook some very practicable requirements. Take just one example: For 20 or 30 years planners and builders of small homes and apartments have characteristically provided an entry hall with clothes closet behind the entry door—undoubtedly a carryover from the early days of large entrance halls and grand staircases. But what has now happened in the small house and the apartment? In the press for reduced costs this entry hall has become smaller and smaller, until now it is seldom more than a 4 × 4-foot area with a door swinging into the space. All of us need a place for coats and overshoes, but we also need ample room to put them on—a chair or a bench to sit on and a table or shelf to hold package or purse. Almost never can this be provided in the small entry hall of our homes and apartments, and when an individual is temporarily, or sometimes permanently, committed to wheel-chair existence, the small entrance hall and clothes closet behind the door present a situation in which he simply has not enough room to maneuver.

Finally, the home not only must be a suitable place to which the rehabilitated can return but also must constitute an environment that actually contributes to the continuing rehabilitation of the older person.

These objectives for maximum livability and for optimal environment suggest in a very general way the function that the home will have to perform during the later maturity and particularly the old age of its residents.

B. Design of Independent Housing

SPECIAL HOUSING?

Most available housing cannot fulfil these objectives. Some of the shortcomings can be overcome by minor adjustments or remodeling, as observed by Warren (1957) in a study of how older people managed at home after discharge from the hospital. More generally, though, as Kleemeier (1956) points out, unless there is some outside help, habit and reduced energy probably cause the aged to make less effort than younger adults do to alter their surroundings.

The observation of such shortcomings in housing and the special needs of elderly persons has given rise to the phrases "special housing" and "housing specially adapted for the aging." Such phrases have meant different things to people working in the field of housing and related areas: (1) proposals for providing segregated housing for elderly persons, similar to some early European experiments; (2) expensive and unwarranted dissipation of the housing supply; and (3) a splintering of organized effort into yet another category of housing (American Public Health Association, 1953).

Churchill (1952) has argued against "special housing for the aged"; he has pointed out that ideal housing for the aged was also good housing for younger people, and this is obviously true. By and large, however, existing and projected housing continues to be of the split-level variety, with narrow doorways into bathrooms, one or two steps at the entrance threshold, and such meager space for circulation about entrances and bathrooms as to preclude continued occupancy by persons of advanced age and infirmity.

Several authorities have endeavored to interpret the needs of the aging and to sum up current thought regarding housing (Woodbury, 1950; American Public Health Association, 1953; Loewenberg, 1954; Massachusetts State Housing Board, 1954; Peacock, 1954; Vivrett, 1956, 1957b). These, plus a consideration of the objectives above, would suggest that there are some general characteristics of design which, whether or not they refer to "special housing," were related to the attitudes and desires of retired persons as well as to the effects of aging upon physical and mental health:

Variety in types of housing and sizes of dwelling units.—The need for variety should be recognized in the types of individual independent dwelling units: detached houses, twin houses, row houses, multidwelling units, and trailers (which, although classified as mobile homes, actually function as small detached houses of extremely compact arrangement). In all these, complete housekeeping facilities are desirable, including a kitchen or kitchenette with facilities for preparation of food, for storage of cold and frozen items, and for washing dishes.

Larger rooms but fewer rooms.—Dwelling units should generally be small because of the considerable limitations in (1) income and (2) energy reserves. But even in those multidwelling projects where communal facilities may be provided for group endeavor, individual rooms should be large enough to permit the friendly conversation and visiting of two and three people in the private living quarters of the home.

Suitability to living patterns.—

1. *Living and social activity space.* Up to four people may be expected to use the living area at one time even in the dwelling of a single person. For the most part, visitors will take part in conversation, play games, and have refreshments. If the quarters are small, a sofa or couch might be a welcome accommodation for an overnight guest, or it might serve as a second bed when the occupant is ill.

2. *Cooking and eating.* The number of people to be accommodated at a table will probably range from one to four. For conservation of energy and assurance of use, the table should be close to, if not in, the kitchen. Ideally, it should be close enough to permit taking a pan from the stove without getting up. Although the quantity of food may be small, eating comes to assume a major part in the daily life of older people, and hence table and chairs should be arranged in surroundings that are pleasant and relaxing.

3. *Sleeping and dressing area.* Since the sleeping area is also the area to be used in case of illness or convalescence, the space around the bed should permit minor nursing operations and the use of a wheelchair or walking aid. There should be enough space—at least 3 feet—at sides and foot of the bed to allow bedmaking with the minimum of reaching and stretching (Vivrett, 1957b). A table or a chest and a lamp are necessary at the head of the bed and, when possible, a telephone or other communicating device—particularly as infirmities increase. A sturdy chair with arms should be placed near the closet-wardrobe dressing area; shades, draperies, or other darkening devices are required from time to time, if not daily. A simple, direct route, without right-angle turns from the bed to the toilet, becomes important with incontinence and increasing infirmity.

4. *Bath-toilet.* The requirements for the bath-toilet room are among the most important if the living unit is to continue to serve as an independent one. The door must be wide enough to accommodate a wheel chair, and bathroom fixtures should be arranged so that a typical wheel chair could be maneuvered into suitable position for a person to transfer to the toilet (one side as well as front) or the tub or to use the lavatory while still seated in the wheel-

chair. For a bathroom with the three basic fixtures, this means a room area of approximately 56 square feet, in contrast to the more customary bathroom area of 35 square feet. Most people, regardless of age, find some sort of a grab rod or rail handy when getting in and out of the bath, and this, like all the accessories, should be capable of withstanding a 300-pound steady pull. The wall construction and surfaces at critical areas should be such that, if any other special rails are needed, they can be readily installed.

5. *Personal interests, activities, and hobbies.* Not all older people like to read, but those who do will want shelf space for books and magazines. People who like to write will want a writing desk or table. Older women who sew will need space for a sewing machine and a chair. And, if these activities are to be available to the older person, the "props" they require must be at hand in the living quarters, not put away somewhere so that they need to be gotten out or so that they will be pushed away in the course of the daily routine.

To provide for every eventuality is obviously not possible, but the personal interests or activities rarely demand any more space than that required by the usual writing desk and chair. Even in minimum standards, it would seem not just desirable, but necessary, that one such space allowance be made for each occupant.

While in many houses today gadgets and mechanical conveniences are plentiful, too few of them are being used in houses of older people in a way to support independent living or to add to the amenities of living. Seldom do we see remote-control television sets in the homes of the old, or telephone jacks at convenient points, or garbage disposals in the kitchens, or revolving shelves in cupboards.

Structures generally on one floor, except where equipped with elevator.—The advantages of providing grade entrances into buildings without steps and of avoiding stair-climbing to split levels or second floors are obvious. The structure of more than one story must have an elevator. In housing intended for occupancy by the old, it is folly to permit the construction of walk-ups.

Apart from this factor, the main justification for one-story construction is that it allows people to have an outdoor life as well as an indoor life, even though for some that outdoor life may be no more than 15 minutes a day of fresh air and sunlight. Whether the out of doors is reached through individual or communal exits, there should be close connection between the individual dwelling unit and the ground outside. In multistory construction the number of floors need be predicated only on economy of construction, individual attitude regarding proximity to the ground, and aesthetic considerations of neighborhood composition.

CRITERIA FOR HOUSING IN GENERAL

There are of course many other accepted criteria for housing, such as the relationship or orientation to sunlight, prevailing breeze, and natural ventilation; there are the standards related to sanitation and hygiene, to safety, etc., and these apply with special force to housing for the older person (U.S. Federal Public Housing Authority, 1946; Gutheim, 1948; American Public Health Association, 1950, 1951; Klaber, 1954).

Putting it more forcefully, it is highly desirable that the physical environments constructed specially for older people bear less resemblance to the bare minimum quarters left over from an earlier era and that they look more like the intriguing settings depicted in the colored pages of the magazines for young homemakers (see, e.g., Nelson and Wright, 1945; Mock, 1946; Beyer, 1952; McCullough, 1952; Faulkner, 1954).

SOME PRESENT LIMITATIONS
AND SOME GUIDEPOSTS

Many older people in later maturity and even in old age can live independently in their own households for many years. We have observed that some of these older people must eventually change their living arrangements because of increasing infirmities and disabilities and decreasing energy supplies. We also know that the older person or others in his family may suffer difficulty in adjusting to the new environment. Kleemeier (1956) has outlined many of the areas of knowledge as well as gaps in our understanding of how to accommodate the environment to the aging process. Researchers at Western Reserve University in Cleveland are attempting to "identify persons likely to benefit most by special housing for the aged . . . , the extent to which aged persons need certain care and services short of complete 'institutional' care, [and] . . . the nature of social, psychological, and medical problems occurring in special housing for the aging" (U.S. Department of Health, Education, and Welfare, 1958, p. 3).

Although, as Donahue and Ashley (1959) point out, many of the design features in special housing for the elderly have not been tested experimentally, there are a number of guideposts for specific techniques and self-help devices related to particular infirmities or disabilities (American Heart Association, n.d.; Institute of Physical Medicine and Rehabilitation, n.d.; Anonymous, 1951*b*, 1952; Rusk and Taylor, 1953; National Tuberculosis Association, 1954; Gilbreth *et al.*, 1955).

In addition, many of our communities have or are developing services reaching into the home—such as homemaking and home care—designed to support the individual in his independent living environment. Despite a few carefully documented reports, the total picture of such services for older people is still fragmentary.

C. Location of Housing— Community Situations

It is agreed that older as well as middle-aged people should find it possible to remain an integral part of the community in which they have spent their earlier years.

It is also generally held that human services, social and medical, should be geared to treat and to restore individuals to optimum health and to help them maintain themselves insofar as possible in their own homes (Woodbury, 1950; American Public Health Association, 1953; Donahue, 1954*b;* Massachusetts State Housing Board, 1954; Mumford, 1956; Vivrett, 1957*a*). For some this may mean the advantage of continued residence in the home of their earlier years; for others it may mean seeking out a new home in the same neighborhood or in a neighborhood nearby; and for others it may mean seeking out a new home in a completely different community.

COMMUNITIES OF TOMORROW, TODAY, AND YESTERDAY

In Section II, A, "Urban Communities," above, some of the general characteristics of the communities of urban areas have been outlined. As communities in which middle-aged and older persons are now living or will some day live, their attributes are worthy of further study. Although both public policy and action over the last 30 years have resulted in a stratification of families in communities by age and socioeconomic status, "both housing over the family cycle and balanced neighborhoods are becoming recognized ideas in current housing thought" (Woodbury, 1950, p. 69; see also Mumford, 1956). However, the application of this philosophy to the physical environment of the majority of our communities is a long way off, and considerable planning and action will be necessary—at first probably private and small in scale—before it is fully adumbrated. The further evaluation of our communities below suggests what must be done to provide suitable living situations for older individuals.

The new communities of mid-twentieth century.—These new and projected communities must be guaranteed a relatively stable population with wide age distribution, not just younger families, as now frequently happens. We need to build into these new communities new housing for old people, and thereby perhaps we can at the same time assure that the present young families will have appropriate accommodations as, 20 years from now, they reach middle age and later maturity.

This means several things for the planning (or replanning) of these new communities.

1. Subdivision platting and control must designate appropriate sites for the housing of older individuals and couples (and other one- and two-person households), with specific concern for the relationship of such sites not only to the residences of younger families but also to the community center (quite frequently the elementary school), public transportation, and the regional or community shopping centers that generally characterize these new communities.

2. The present tendency to build only three- and four-bedroom split-level houses, with the recreation room in the basement, must be modified to encourage the building of small homes and apartments and to permit a density of development which will allow greater proximity between such dwelling units than might be characteristic of the single-family houses for younger families.

3. Techniques must be devised whereby the new housing of more modest size (hopefully suitable to individuals of modest income) can be kept on the market as desirable and healthful housing for one- and two-person households. A growing population and an increasing number of new families will demand that we build more and more new communities. The stratified communities that we have built in the past are tragically wasteful. The failure to provide a wider choice of housing accommodations, all within the same community, is part of this folly which excludes middle-aged and older people from the community. Ways must be found to accommodate the full family cycle in these new communities.

Orange Gardens (outside of Kissimmee,

Florida) is a new suburban community geared to the full family cycle in terms of age and composition of household, with particular attention to older, retired people. Careful planning has assured that this community will be a full-fledged participant in the larger community of Kissimmee. It remains, however, to be demonstrated that Orange Gardens, in addition to its single-family houses, can successfully provide some groupings of smaller houses and apartments in close proximity to each other and to the single-family houses as part of its physical and social structure.

The 20- to 30-year-old communities.— Many residents of these depression-era suburbs are now well into middle age, and their children have long since left home. A significant number of older people also reside there, and to a large extent these houses have been adequate for their needs. They are generally small—one- and two-bedroom houses, of one level, and frequently close to grade. By now these neighborhoods usually have been provided with a full range of community services, a tradition of social-civic life, and a full complement of public transportation facilities, services, and utilities.

We must find ways of consolidating and conserving our resources in these neighborhoods so as to enable the present generations of middle-aged and older people to continue to reside where they have meaningful ties and associations. This requires two things.

1. Suitable sites must be found, and housing for one- and two-person households must be constructed in such a way that these people may be relieved of some yard and home maintenance while still enjoying the many social and physical benefits that they earlier sought in these suburbs. Such attached, apartment, or row housing must be so sited and designed that it is not just another multistoried city structure at the back door to the neighborhood supermarket but rather a functioning part of the residential suburb where it is located.

2. Ways must be found to demonstrate, to the community at large and to its governing and planning boards, the need to consider the requirements of all segments of the population and the validity of mixed neighborhoods and of neighborhoods with a variety of compatible housing types.

The 30- to 40-year-old communities.— In these communities, in which housing is likely to have been built for people at opposite ends of the economic scale, many people have continued to reside through middle age and beyond. The homes of those who had made greater economic gains are very probably substantially built homes of two or two and one-half stories: standards are usually high, both as to size of rooms and as to extent of equipment and facilities. Unfortunately, the bedrooms and baths are generally on the second floor, necessitating difficult trips up and down stairs for the older person with progressive infirmity. Converting these homes into two-family dwellings so as to create more manageable living units also poses difficulties. Characteristically, communities of this age also contain some apartment houses (and some garden apartments added at a later date), with apartments ranging in size from one-room efficiencies to three-bedroom units.

Many of these communities are well maintained, and many of them, with a fair variety of housing (although not usually including the smaller suburban type one-story houses), are providing the nearest thing we have to balanced, mixed residential neighborhood. Such communities require a *"pre-urban renewal"* program not only to conserve but to augment their resources for later maturity, for old age, and for the population at large. Ways must be found to keep them stable and handsome while guarding them against the inroads of advancing commercialism and major vehicular traffic routes.

When we turn to the low-income housing built 30–40 years ago, we see a discouraging scene—jerry-building, meager space standards, and poor equipment. Un-

fortunately, it is in these areas that a large number of the older people reside—for here they are likely to find housing at prices commensurate with their reduced retirement income. It will be difficult, then, to accomplish little more in these communities than to assure that the standards of our municipal housing codes are enforced and, at least for the immediate future, that such dwelling units are maintained in as safe and sanitary condition as possible.

Older residential neighborhoods.—In the older sections of the city the location of housing for older people with relation to accessibility to community facilities is less of a problem than is the physical and social quality of the residential neighborhoods themselves. True, there are many excellent residential neighborhoods in these older sections of the city, with a wide variety of housing, some of it of top quality and ideally suited for the small older household. But much of this housing has been illegally converted, is poorly maintained and sometimes unsafe, or contains antiquated facilities. Central-heating systems are frequently hand fired; and, although there may be private baths, fixtures have become dilapidated, and the rusted pipes are not likely to work much longer. Access from the street is frequently up a flight of six or eight steps, with another six or eight steps to the first floor.

Although the power shovel of public redevelopment is likely to fall on still more acreage in these older areas of the city, and even though within our lifetime wide urban rehabilitation may be attempted, it is generally conceded that most of our older in-city residential communities are here to stay.

We must assure, first, that a fair share of housing in these better in-city residential neighborhoods remains available to both middle-aged and older people. And, what is more, we must make every effort to retain the present desirable characteristics of such neighborhoods and to augment them wherever possible.

But unfortunately not all of Beacon

Hill enjoys the Christmas carols to the same extent that Louisburg Square does; in some eastern cities there is still a supply of "alley" housing; Greenwich Village consists of more than a one-block periphery at Washington Square; in the Near North Side of Chicago, Lake Shore Drive can be seen only from a block or two inland; the Garden District of New Orleans (in addition to its own hidden problems) does not really include all the crescent area on the other side of St. Charles Avenue; Nob Hill in San Francisco also has a "seamy side."

In these in-city residential neighborhoods ways must be found to enlist every possible resource that might contribute to the well-being of the older person and the quality of his immediate physical environment and to a desirable *neighborhood* in general. It will not be enough to select a few promising neighborhoods in all the city, for to develop these with diligence is only a beginning. There is and will continue to be a large proportion of older people in nearly every one of these in-city communities. Short of a concerted effort to achieve large-scale relocation or retirement migration of present generations of older people, urban housing for these people demands healthful, convenient, safe residential neighborhoods. Some such programs will be developed within the framework of urban renewal, but hopefully many of them will be the result of individual initiative and action outside that framework.

Downtown, center-of-city areas.—Only a relatively few people find housing to their liking in the downtown, center-of-city areas. Most of the older people in these areas are living in group housing facilities (discussed under Sec. V below); but another large segment of the older population, obviously because of low economic status, is housed in illegal, substandard dwelling units in these areas. There obviously are some advantages of accessibility in these center-of-city locations, and concerted action could make them safe as well as convenient. But here, more than elsewhere,

we must establish an ongoing pattern of true residential living—a pattern that offers more than mere accessibility to facilities and services and the possibility, five days a week, of watching the crowds go by.

The small town and the hamlet.—Here the location of housing raises problems more like those found in the newer suburban communities, for the smallness and intimacy of these communities mean that effort must be directed less at securing a social and civic community structure and more at assuring accessibility. The resident of the small town with a limited transportation system is obviously far more isolated physically than the city dweller; and, unless there are vendors of goods and personal services who go from door to door, a half-mile to the main street of town may well preclude for some the possibility of independent living in the later years. These towns generally have few small dwelling units suitable to one- and two-person households but instead rely upon subdividing or converting larger family structures. Therefore, techniques will have to be devised for building such housing within the framework of the community and for selecting sites close to both the main street and the residential neighborhoods of younger families.

There is no one ideal location for housing that will meet every evolving situation.

COMMUNITY FACILITIES AND SERVICES—
WHOSE RESPONSIBILITY?

Many sources have outlined over-all goals for providing community facilities and services. The Committee on Hygiene of Housing of the American Public Health Association (1948) has presented a particularly straightforward point of view. The needs of the general population in this regard are met through a variety of means —sometimes private, more often public— in communities throughout the United States. Except in isolated communities, many of these services are of consistently high quality and are reasonably inclusive.

With the development of an increasingly broad public understanding, as needs arise within new communities, action is taken to provide desirable facilities and services.

Several sources have described community facilities and services specifically for older people (Welfare Council of Metropolitan Chicago, 1952, 1957; Kutner *et al.*, 1956). Gertman (1960) has provided an excellent outline of the health services and facilities needed by the aged generally (as well as by the potential population of a retirement village).

The patterns of growing independence and separateness among the older population have obvious implications in terms of human services, particularly when combined with our general tendency toward decentralization and dispersal. In the light of these tendencies, the medical service needs of the older population must be met. This does not, however, mean that the proximity of the residence to the service facility should be based on the standards of distance of horse-and-buggy days. Even though maximum utilization of health-medical resources has involved a centralization of facilities and efforts, it is readily apparent that relatively few older people could live within walking distance of the hospital center and that most emergencies would necessitate, in any event, their being transported to the hospital for even short distances. What, then, might be the criteria for determining reasonable accessibility? (1) Most older people would find it possible to travel a reasonable distance by bus, taxicab, or private automobile to the physician's office or to the outpatient clinic. On the other hand, for most home calls, the availability of the physician to the home within an hour of a call would prove acceptable. (2) In case of emergency, such as sudden illness or an accident, a 15- to 20-minute ambulance ride from residence to the hospital or other institution would not constitute undue hardship.

In general, location of residence within the city and accessibility of services should be gauged to our developed systems of communication and to the techniques and the characteristic speeds of today's transportation. Particularly with the approaching completion of freeways and expressways, location depends less on the actual linear distance to facilities and more on the time distance which available routes afford.

Donahue and Ashley (1959) question the hypothesis that older people want and need to live close to hospital facilities and ask whether it is really better or cheaper for the community to have them do so. They suggest that comparison of the adjustment of older people living in the more rural or developed suburban areas with that of older people living in central residential districts might prove otherwise.

RELATIVE DEGREES OF INTEGRATION AND CONCENTRATION

It may be helpful in our community planning to think in terms of acceptable densities of middle-aged and older people with respect to the rest of the population. When we remember that one in six heads of households is 65 and older or that one in two heads of households is 45 and older (see Sec. II, A, "Aging Residents among Us"), we see that the elimination of broad areas of remote or semiremote residential housing requires relatively high densities of older families and individuals in other areas. Perhaps this fact alone justifies the construction of some housing specifically designed for middle-aged and older persons in suburban communities.

The attitude of the general population toward the suburb (Dewey, 1948) suggests that the suburb represents a real potential in the search for integrated residential living. Examination of individual suburban communities will usually reveal available sites which would meet many, if not all, of the criteria for location of desirable housing for older people. Directed research (see the preceding section) would be particularly helpful in this regard.

Self-imposed levels of concentration.—

To the extent that older people are able to buy housing on the market, concentrations which do occur might be assumed to be the result either of chance or of the direct choice of the individual. More likely, though, because of building patterns, the relatively even distribution of older people in our communities is only likely to be made possible by a concerted effort of the building industry, the banking fraternity, and local government. When such conscious effort might be required, it becomes increasingly important that professionals in the field of social gerontology help in formulating some guideposts for private and public action as it pertains to the proximity of residences of older age groups to those of other age groups. Woodbury (1950) suggests that it is a mistake to segregate the residences of older people. He speculates that the only special provisions in location they require are some protection from excessive noise and confusion and relatively easy access to shopping centers, churches, and other facilities in the community.

Studies among other age groups of socialization and the intervening opportunities for contact suggest possible techniques of grouping and siting individual dwelling units, although none of these deals specifically with the relationship between older residents and other age groups (Caplow and Forman, 1950; Festinger, 1951). We need controlled comparative research on the housing for the older population in existing residential communities and in some of our newer communities such as the Levittowns. If independent housing on *the open market* is to serve both the community and the older person most efficiently, a first step should be to determine the density and the grouping of such housing in relation to the housing of other age groups.

Proximate housing.—Proximate housing (see Sec. II, C, above) appears to provide the most immediately fertile field in which community effort might meet the present housing needs of many older people—and perhaps some middle-aged people who require a new living arrangement. It also offers a promising field for immediate research.

Proximate housing is popular for a number of reasons. To the planner in physical gerontology, it suggests a way for some older people to be brought into touch with their contemporaries within a desirable physical framework; it also suggests a means by which limited degrees of concentration may permit a more efficient utilization of services. To the builder and the banker it offers a technique of ordering the work similar to others used in building multi-unit housing projects. To the older person it represents an alternative to the vicissitudes of seeking housing on the market; this is particularly true in cases where the rental agreement can guarantee the continuity of an economic rent or where limited services and conveniences are provided beyond what might be expected in the single-family private home. Considerable variation is possible in the number of residents accommodated in a proximate housing group: the cluster of 9–12 dwelling units, as proposed by the Presbyterian Board of Pensions at Swarthmore, Pennsylvania, and other locations; the American Women's Voluntary Service's grouping of 40 one-bedroom row-house units on one site in Santa Barbara; the construction of 25–75 dwelling unit projects developed under the program of the Massachusetts State Housing Board (state-sponsored public housing); the projects of private and public organizations, such as the ten-story, 250-suite Lake House at Lakewood, Ohio; and the combined multi-story and row-house project of 250 dwelling units by the San Antonio, Texas, Housing Authority.

Our goals in proximate housing, aside from the intelligent design of the individual dwelling unit and its relationship to the larger grouping, should be (1) to develop techniques of evaluating a given community and determining what scale of grouping might be most appropriate and (2) to develop criteria for predicting as far as possible the social and physical needs of individual residents. We also need empirical research to show at what point the size of the project (population size, particularly) becomes a handicap to our ultimate goal.

Retirement villages.—The retirement village has too long been the subject of heated argument. Our immediate goal in this area should be the development (programing, location, design, and management and operation) of perhaps some ten or fifteen retirement villages. These, plus the existing four or five, should be carefully studied, and the resulting data on problems, accomplishments, and limitations should be widely distributed. Such work should not be confused with the studies of modified forms of the institution discussed in Section IV below but should be entirely directed at surveying the physical form, characteristics, and potentials of the village per se.

There are many principles and experiments (Vivrett, 1960) that relate to altering the physical environment of the neighborhood and the small urban place. These principles must now be re-examined and applied to the design of the retirement village.

The extent to which the housing accommodations and services offered by a retirement village may approach the popularity or efficiency anticipated by some workers in social gerontology has yet to be proved. Perhaps 1 per cent of the total older population might desire to live in retirement villages, but even this would approach the proportion of the older generation now cared for in specialized institutions and therefore would effect a substantial change in the patterns of housing for the aged.

D. Techniques of Action: Society and the Aging Individual

Successful independent housing for middle-aged and older people must be an integral part of the community, and its ownership, financing, production, and maintenance must be the concern of both the aging individual and society at large.

HOUSING FOR THE AGING AND HOUSING FOR THE GENERAL POPULATION

Social gerontology acknowledges that a "rational housing policy encompasses all groups of the population" (American Public Health Association, 1953), and it does not deny that the United States population is still "un-housed, mis-housed, dishoused" (Abrams, n.d., p. 3). In fact, many problems of the aging today relate directly to limitations in the supply of housing and in the physical framework of our communities. Thus, when we improve the supply or the quality of housing for the general population, we improve the situation for older people tomorrow.

On the other hand, the housing of the aging is a significant portion of the general housing problem, and, to progress in this field, we must consider, in addition to the housing situation of young families with growing children, the small households required in the last 20–30 years of life.

The housing effort in the United States has characteristically attacked problems by segments. What we need now is effort directed into each of these several areas but co-ordinated so as to nourish neighborhood growth to the advantage of all ages, in the atypical as well as the average household. The result would be a variety of housing types in a variety of locations, offering to people of all ages reasonable freedom of choice.

To the extent that urban renewal becomes a part of such common objectives—improving the living and working environment of our cities, making them attractive and interesting places for young families as well as older couples and widowed and single people to live in—to the extent that it provides balanced communities, it must be supported by social gerontology. But urban renewal must not simply mean more public housing for the elderly as an al-

ternative to the tenement, rooming-board-
ing house, or old residential hotel; it must
mean the building of new independent
dwelling units and the rehabilitation of old
units equal in quality to those now provided for the younger population and consonant with balanced community growth
and activity.

OWNERSHIP, CO-OPERATIVES,
AND TENANCY

The system of tenures for independent
housing for middle-aged and particularly
for older people must be varied. We have
much to learn about the satisfactions derived from homeownership (Woodbury,
1953). We do know that in recent years
homeownership has meant for some older
people the difference between acceptable
physical environment and substandard tenement housing, between fair maintenance
costs and exorbitant rent. We also know
that some age-related factors such as widowhood or failing health make the isolation of the home and the burden of maintenance too much for some individuals to
bear.

The choice between continued ownership
or the purchase of a new home and some
form of tenancy must be made carefully.
A decision at age 55 to purchase a new
home for the later years of maturity and
old age may make good sense; on the
other hand, the decision of the elderly
couple at age 65 or 70 to purchase a new
home should be made with full realization
of the life-expectancy as a couple and as
a surviving spouse. To the extent that the
rental-housing market of the future operates in the same fashion as it has in the
last 15 years, homeownership on reasonable
terms is a desirable objective for the older
population. It also offers perhaps one
means of independent housing for older
individuals that can perhaps be most readily worked out within the general housing
market.

Co-operative ownership has recently
found increased favor as an alternative to
individual homeownership in the United
States. For older people, particularly, it
has often meant convenient financing
terms, as well as a means by which people
of similar ages and interests could obtain
a modern living environment, along with
mutual aid and security. The co-operative
for older people requires sponsorship, particularly at the outset, to assemble the
co-operators, buy the land, and build the
housing. There must be leadership, there
must be capital, and there must be experience. These are not too likely to come from
an assemblage of even the most homogeneous group, nor are novices too likely to
establish successful co-operatives. This system of tenure should be extended by the
encouragement of existing co-operatives
and the development of new ones to provide housing for older people, both as a
concentrated population via the proximate
housing technique and as co-operators with
other age groups in household units. As
with retirement villages, these co-operatives should be studied meticulously not
only to develop experience in the techniques of assembling co-operators, financing, and building but, more importantly,
to determine the validity of this form of
housing for older people.

In the case of rental housing, because of
the changing cost of living and the rising
cost of medical care, it becomes increasingly important that rental housing for older
people be of a continuing, acceptable quality at a continuing economic rent. To do
this probably requires more re-evaluation
and reorganization of the forms of sponsorship rather than of techniques of operation
—sponsorship which ranges from profit-
making real estate corporations to the
subsidized public housing authorities and
the charitable and philanthropic non-profit
foundations. One such sponsor is the institution, that is, the old age home which
is providing independent dwelling units
for older people with no service or with
minimum service.

In communities where people are segregated by economic status, public housing
may be society's best answer. Many older

people are striving valiantly to work out living arrangements within their economic means; public and private efforts are being made to help them find such quarters without suffering any stigma of identification by economic status. Public housing is a valuable resource in our communities. The individual who has relied in earlier life upon public assistance may not be troubled by this identification, but, for the individual who has been financially independent in early life, identification by residence in public housing may be an excessive psychological burden. At present, far too many aspects of public housing policy and the resulting environment are at variance with the best principles of social gerontology to justify relegating all older people of less than adequate means to housing of this sort.

FINANCING AND PRODUCTION OF HOUSING

Independent housing for middle-aged and older people must be built within the existing systems of our financial institutions and our construction industry.

During the postwar years when we were catching up in home-building and in providing homes for returning veterans, both financial institutions and the building industry—operating in a seller's market—found it profitable to build and sell homes for younger families. Only briefly under the ill-fated FHA 608 housing program was any significant volume of rental housing constructed of a type and size suitable to one- and two-person households. To the extent that the volume and quality of housing fall short of the need, planned stimulation and encouragement must be introduced.

Homeownership by older people, and particularly middle-aged people, may very well be achieved within the program of housing for the total population; but there is (as of 1959) a great lack in both supply and quality of independent rental dwelling units suitable for the older population.

The Housing for the Elderly program of the Federal Housing Administration has encouraged non-profit organizations to finance, build, and operate such units. This program has been used but little to provide independent dwelling units, most of the production having gone into group housing, although more recent experience suggests a swing in that direction. Particularly for augmenting the number of independent dwelling units in the suburban areas, this or a similar program is highly to be recommended—either using existing civic, fraternal, and religious organizations or creating new, non-profit organizations perhaps indigenous to the community. Each such organization would preferably be an entity for the purposes of ownership and direction, working within the existing framework of the financial institutions and the building industry in the community.

Moreover, at this writing and probably for a number of years to follow, there is urgent need for encouragement and stimulation to supply rental housing units on a private profit-making basis to the mutual advantage of tenants and lenders and builders.

V. GOALS FOR GROUP HOUSING

Those people who do not want, or are unable to live in, independent living quarters (either alone or in a household with others) obviously need group housing. This is especially true for the increasing number of single, unattached older individuals. To some extent our group housing, such as the hotel, the residence club, and the boarding house, which serve the general population, can continue to serve a segment of the older population. But because single, unattached individuals generally seek the company of their contemporaries, because it is a convenience in management and operation to serve individuals of the same approximate age (and frequently of the same sex), group housing in our communities tends to become segregated by age. The "old age home" and its several derivatives represent a specialized form of group housing in which there is obvious segregation not only by age but also by other categories, such as health and socio-economic status and by techniques of management and services and care provided. Such specialized forms of housing catering to an aging population are inextricably bound up with the over-all goals of housing—separateness and independence and their counterparts of communality and dependence. These needs become even more pronounced in group housing than in independent housing because of the physical arrangements involved and the consequent necessity to rely upon communal facilities and services.

A. The Individual and the Group Setting

It is frequently presumed that the older person selects the group environment—and particularly the institution—as a last resort because of declining physical and mental health or a lack of personal security. But a number of other reasons cause some older people to prefer group housing.

DESIRE TO BE RELIEVED OF ROUTINE OF HOUSEKEEPING

Some people, and particularly some older people, choose to live in the residence club or hotel in order to be relieved of the burden of housekeeping chores. The older person living alone sometimes finds such routines at best boring and at worst an excessive drain on his energy.

A DESIRE TO FOLLOW EARLIER PATTERNS OF LIVING

The executive who is accustomed to pressing the buzzer for whatever he wants, or the well-to-do woman who devotes endless hours to her favorite charity while others do her household chores, may well find living alone in a one-room efficiency undesirable. The traveling salesman may prefer continued residence in a hotel to living in an independent cottage in Florida. Similarly, the unmarried schoolteacher who has lived as a boarder may have little inclination to take up housekeeping. For some people, group living has always exerted an attraction and may continue to do so—particularly if quality of the environment is improved.

A NARROWING CIRCLE OF FRIENDS OR A DETERIORATING SOCIAL CAPACITY

The loss of spouse, the death of contemporaries, children growing up and leaving home, the individual's own incapacity for maintaining his former social status—these are frequently pertinent reasons for the older person's choosing a group living situation in which he may find opportunities for new social contacts and may have companionship at will.

A NEED TO REDUCE EXPENSES

The mounting costs of maintaining the large old home are all too often beyond the older person's means. Social security and pension and retirement programs seldom permit one to live out his life in the manner to which he has been formerly accustomed. And for some people the financial problem is further aggravated by mounting and extended medical expenses, which can rarely be met by retirement incomes or insurance programs. Thus in the group setting the older person may find a place to live out his life within his own means.

SEARCH FOR BETTER HOUSING

Furthermore, some group settings offer higher quality of housing and a more congenial environment than do single dwellings of comparable cost. Many hotels and residence clubs offer an easier and more stimulating living environment than do small apartments available today. And even the institutional setting may offer an environment in which there is less tension and more commonality of interest than in the three-generation household.

B. Design of Individual Living Quarters

The requirements for individual living quarters within the group setting are closely akin to those described under independent housing in Section IV above. Individual living quarters within the group setting have a similar over-all objective of providing the most independent pattern of living practicable for the individual. The only difference is the grouping—physically and/or administratively—for the purpose of accomplishing certain supporting services, particularly the serving of food and the assumption by management of some housekeeping responsibilities. Within the individual living quarters the same basic clues are applicable in planning the living unit, in establishing its size, and in selecting furnishings and facilities; but here the characteristics of individuality and independence assume an even greater importance because the group effort may easily produce stereotyped results. Then, too, where an increasing number of responsibilities and functions are conducted as a community venture or by management, those elements of individuality and independence, which remain as the individual's own prerogative, assume an increasing importance.

With the gradual, almost indefinable shift among older people from independence to increasing dependence, living quarters within the group setting approach more and more those of the institution as we acknowledge its function today. This perhaps is one of the basic clues for the ordering of the institutional environment: that we preserve the group environment in its more independent forms, such as the freedom to go and come from the hotel or the ability to have guests at the club, and that we endeavor to provide within the institutional framework the following desirable characteristics of the independent environment.

INDIVIDUALITY, DIGNITY, AND PRIVACY

Both initially in planning the environment and in manipulating and reordering it to meet changing demands, there must be provided living quarters in which the older person may live as an individual in dignity and privacy. There must be a place where he can move freely and privately and where he may perform personal routines and enjoy his individual pleasures. Older people like to "dream dreams," but growing old does not make them less susceptible to nightmares. Nor can we pass off the act of lonely idleness as "dreaming dreams." The energy and the desire to do things may lessen, but it must not be permitted to atrophy entirely.

Individual quarters must have a relaxed spaciousness that can hardly be found in a 75- or 100-square-foot dormitory cubicle or, worse, the bed space of 35–50 square feet, which some of our state licensing codes now permit. To the war worker of the 1940's or the younger worker of today, with only a few waking hours to spend in his cubicle, the so-called minimums may appear passable; this is not the case with living quarters for the older individual which are occupied 24 hours a day.

There are also those aspects of the living quarters which relate to environmental stimulation. Beauty of form has meaning to older people—to feel, even when not to see. Appropriate use of color can also perform a function—the subtleties of analogous and monochromatic schemes, the excitement possible in complimentary and triad schemes, can give enriched scale to daily experience. Within the group framework there should be possible a physical environment for each individual which permits and encourages a maximum of self-expression and provides for the morale and well-being of the individual. This may be particularly vital in the case of the older person who has for some reason been forced to give up the patterns of independent living in his own home. It may provide the compensating factor which will determine satisfactory adjustment to the new living situation.

The living environment must be suitable to the functions and activities of daily living and appropriate to the individual's hobbies and interests. It is called upon to do just about everything which the independent environment must do and more (see Sec. IV, B, "Special Housing"), for it must take into account those problems—medical, financial, or psychological—which necessitated the use of the group setting.

FULFILMENT FOR THE SOCIAL BEING

The environment that provides for maximum individuality and privacy must at the same time foster a social existence. The older person must be encouraged to keep up his former contacts in the community. When this is no longer possible within his own abilities, opportunities must be provided to make new contacts. Preferably, the living quarters would encourage a continued, two-way relationship between the older person and his friends—the living unit would be used to entertain the occasional guest who comes to share a chat, a cup of coffee, a card game, or a television program. As many of these natural, everyday activities and functions as possible should be provided for within the individual living quarters.

MAXIMUM UTILIZATION OF TODAY'S THERAPIES

In the constructive as well as the remedial potentials of the therapies—physical, occupational, and social—one finds the most challenging aspect in the planning of the living quarters, for they must be so designed as to encourage the older person to carry out therapeutic activities that will help him construct a new life and remedy some of the difficulties he faces. This means that new activities must be introduced for some people, particularly those who have suffered significant loss of mobility or endurance. The living quarters must permit economic and effective utilization of the therapies and at the same time provide an environment for living uncluttered by the apparatus of excessive operational and administrational effort.

For some older people individual living quarters within the group setting will differ from independent housing only in not offering full facilities for housekeeping or for the preparation of food and serving. For others, living quarters within the group setting may have to be tailored to special needs, such as the inability of the arthritic to move about freely, or the necessity for the cardiac patient to avoid certain types of exercise, or the need of the hemiplegic patient for a trapeze to aid in moving from bed to wheel chair. In some cases the more independent type of living quarters may be manipulated or reordered to serve this purpose; in others a more special type of environment may have to be provided.

C. The Design of the Group Setting

The arrangement of the individual living quarters in relation to each other and to the facilities of the group setting provides the physical framework that should complement the capacities of the individual to (1) maintain himself in residence, (2) relate himself to other individuals within a group setting, and (3) relate himself to the community of which the group setting is a part.

NATURE OF THE GROUP SETTING

The physical environment of the group setting should reflect the intended social use and should provide a framework within which the functions of service to individual residents may be carried on. The hotel and the residence club most simply express the group setting, with services perhaps limited to housekeeping and the preparation and serving of food. The more highly specialized forms of group living catering to the older population may also offer a range of facilities, such as the beauty shop, the chapel, the hospital, or others provided by the community at large. Where the services are fewer, there may be a greater freedom in the ordering of the individual living quarters, but, on the other hand, the desirable characteristics of the former need not be sacrificed for the great majority of the services which might be embodied in the latter.

Aspects of the physical environment that may be used to reinforce the intended social structure of a group setting include the following.

A means of communication and circulation within the group setting.—The thread of communication—the telephone or the intercommunication line—makes it possible for the older person to maintain contacts of earlier years and also to reach the management either in emergencies or in routine requests. The circulation routes, the walkways, and the halls and corridors are the physical routes which relate the older person to other residents in the group setting, to management and its services within the group setting, and, finally, to the community outside. Merton (1948) and Festinger *et al.* (1950) have called attention to the effects of the spatial relationships upon the opportunities for socialization among householders in a housing development. We need now some experiment and research to show how interior space and functions can be organized so as to foster increased socialization within the group setting.

We have come to realize abstractly that excessively long and monotonous corridors make for an "institutionalized" feeling; but even when we cut the length of the corridor to a reasonable dimension or to the minimum prescribed by our building and fire codes, the greatest concession we make to the older population is a handrail down either side of the corridor. What is more important is to make the corridor a place conducive to positive relationships among individuals, as cheerful and well illuminated as the individual living quarters or the central lounge to which it leads. We need to find ways in which the older residents can meet together naturally and informally, simulating perhaps family living; this will probably require not only the cozy, small sitting room but also some more public yet casual place that does for the group setting what the sidewalks, streets, and back doors do for the residential neighborhood.

A focus of community life.—Just as the general store with its potbellied stove was yesterday's focus of informal social contact, so today there needs to be a focus for contact—cultural, recreational, and social—for older people. Day centers and recreational and hobby centers are attempting to meet such need in our communities. Some group settings may be able to use existing community facilities; others may find it necessary to establish their own. What is important is that the need be recognized in a way that is suitable to the requirements of those older people. Social and recreational facilities do not have to be very elaborate or even extremely spacious. Some of our less admirable and less successful efforts have gone into building tremendous lounges in institutions—lounges where fifty to a hundred people can be seated, but where multiple conversations of others, or, worse, unoccupied emptiness, make it impossible for two or three persons to visit with the dignity and grace which should be accorded all adults. Granted that there is an advantage in being able to accommodate a large group on occasion, how often is this necessary as compared to the other needs of individuals for the total number of their waking hours?

In the very small group setting, which relies upon the established facilities in the community across the street or down the block, there may be no more than a small lounge near the mailbox where residents may wait for the postman or a little larger space near the manager's office.

On the other hand, the group setting with a larger population may require a variety of communal use spaces—sitting rooms, social activity spaces, dining rooms, group-activity rooms, and rooms in which organized therapies can be conducted. Donahue and Ashley (1959), referring to communal social rooms, state:

It is assumed that the residents want and use . . . common space to the same extent and in the same way they would use sitting rooms and recreational space in their own private homes. Observation casts doubt upon this assumption, and indicates the need for a careful study of the use and psychological meaning of shared space.

Thus, acknowledging the therapeutic potentials of group activity (Donahue *et al.,* 1953; Atkinson *et al.,* 1955), we need to determine not only what is *ample* for such group endeavor but also what is *requisite* for individual living within the framework of the group setting.

In our early enthusiasm over the potentials of group therapy, we have frequently sacrificed the quality of individual living environments in order to provide a space for each listed activity in the literature. Our institutions have been sold too many poor packages—and agencies, in establishing criteria, have been too guilty of following the trend. We need to arrive at a realistic relationship between the quantity of space allocated for residential purposes and that allocated for communal use. Even when there are ample funds for building activity spaces and for hiring the personnel to staff them, we must determine their efficiency in terms of the total population which uses them.

In these days of rapidly changing techniques of group work, we need—particularly in the group effort with limited building budget—methods of organizing and dividing space that will permit rearrangement of such space every 4 or 5 years rather than every 100 years. Finally, the services of the group setting should be used to supplement, but never to supplant, the services provided by the community and the resources of the individual.

Scale and population of the group setting. —There is much we still need to learn about the scale of the group setting and the size of population. We talk only in general terms about concentration and segregation. Although professional workers in psychology, social work, and planning have variously indicated that an ideal social grouping contains nine to fifteen people, we have few data to confirm these figures for older people in the group setting—in terms either of the inherent virtues of such

figures or of the physical characteristics of the architectural spaces such a group requires.

In architecture we have found it possible to order the environment in such a way that it is composed of a number of distinct individual parts, each constructed on a human scale and each producing a feeling of neighborliness. If there is validity in such a point of view, carefully documented research would certainly guide the architect who believes that a large number of rooms on a floor give strength and boldness to the over-all exterior expression or the religious or fraternal groups who feel that concentrating their resources in one large institution will give them stability and prestige (see also Sec. V, F, below).

SITE DEVELOPMENT

Easy access and egress.—The more nearly the front walk and the entrance door give access to individual quarters, the more free and comfortable the older person and his visitors will probably feel in entering and leaving. The present popularity of the motel type of structure among retired people is one indication of this preference. A basic responsibility of the group setting is to devise techniques of arranging the environment for the older person in such a way that he continues as an integral part of the community life. Thus there must be a relationship of the entrances and walkways between various sections of the group setting and between the group setting and the community in which it is located. The optimal distances of outdoor spaces across courts and streets and face-to-face relationships and adjacencies which Merton (1948) and Festinger *et al.* (1950) observed to be valid would probably serve us well in such an effort. Too frequently it is felt that a structure housing a number of individuals should be set back from the street a little farther than the usual residence; or, because in earlier years we heard so much about spatial tensions, we feel that we must constantly increase the distance between building units. Or, worse, we locate entrances in group housing on the opposite sides of buildings—mistakenly seeking privacy for the individual when we should be seeking to increase the opportunities for casual and informal contact.

Development of outdoor spaces.—Outdoor spaces should be developed not just in sunny California or Florida but also in colder climates. First, we need to make sure that every individual in the group setting—including the wheelchair patient and the bedfast—is able to get outside if only for 15 minutes of fresh air once or twice a week. We need to think in terms of the potentials of creative expression out of doors—like the roof garden of 30-year-old Tompkins Square in New York, where each resident may have his own small garden with the equipment storage closet nearby, and where any summer morning you can find one or two people busily pruning, watering, and admiring their gardens. We need to devise ways in which gardening may be done in the area outside the door or window rather than in designated plots off in a remote area of the site. And then we need to realize and explore the tremendous potential of *outdoor* recreational and social activity for older people, even if it does require a little effort for the resident or for the management; we need, for example, to simulate some of the best features of relaxed suburban living—the outdoor barbecues and wiener roasts, the casual conversational group on the terrace, and the snoozes in the sun.

LOCATION OF GROUP HOUSING

Group housing in most of our communities has tended to follow developments of multifamily housing in secondary commercial districts. Seldom has the new community been planned to include group housing except for transient quarters in commercial districts or particularly for motels on major thoroughfares.

Potentials of our communities.—If we acknowledge the principles of trying to enable the older person to live in or near his accustomed residence and to achieve in the community a balanced distribution of the older population, we must first look hard at our communities.

1. In our developing suburban communities the nearest approach to the group setting is the motel and that in a commercial district. Residential areas, in fact, frequently are zoned for single-family dwellings intended primarily for the growing family and built on ever larger and larger lots. Therefore, in these communities we need to establish early rapport with the developer and the entrepreneur, to convince them as well as the subsequent residents of the community that group housing is urgently required, if not in the immediate present, at least in the future. We must see that plots of land are set aside for such purpose and that these are situated near the housing of other age groups, near the community shopping centers, and within reasonable travel distance of the larger urban community. While we may not want to press for immediate construction of group housing, we shall want to allow for such housing in the platting of the new community and to see that vested interests do not preclude the possibility of its construction.

2. In the 20- to 30-year-old communities, where the late middle-aged population is already living in substantial numbers, we must take action immediately. We must find ways for these people to continue living there, keeping intact many of their friendships and having perhaps only temporary regrets at moving from the family home into the group setting. To build group housing here will not be easy, for most of these communities were established in the era when we persisted in stratifying residential structures by size and type and value; and, even though many of our candidates for group housing have been members of the community for some time, a great deal of "selling" will have to be done to affect the public attitude toward changing existing zoning.

3. The 30- to 40-year-old communities also need group housing, and their popula-

tion is frequently of an age that makes them more tolerant of some objectives of such housing. These older communities, too, generally provide well-established services and contain clearly defined community organizations.

4. The residential neighborhoods older than 40 years offer both potentials and hazards. On the positive side, some are well-knit neighborhoods with continuing patterns of life and activity and with sites available for construction of multiunit housing. On the other hand, many of them have fallen prey to advanced deterioration or blight. Some have been slated for rehabilitation if not redevelopment. These 40-year-plus neighborhoods require a careful appraisal of the physical characteristics of the land and of the environment, of the availability of facilities and services, and of the extent of the functional community pattern in which the older person can participate. In some of these neighborhoods there may be real justification for providing group housing immediately; but, in those scheduled for redevelopment, it would probably be best to wait 5 or 10 years to promote the gradual shaping of a suitable pattern of community endeavor and to see whether or not future generations of older people in group housing could develop strong social bonds and engage in worthwhile endeavor there.

5. In the central downtown areas the hotel and the residence club are more common, and in some cases these are excellent dwelling places for older as well as younger people. But all too frequently in such group housing, and particularly in the institution, all that the older person can do is just watch the world go by—and this only for the 8 or 10 hours a day that the business area is occupied but seldom on Sundays or holidays. Only rarely does the downtown environment make rational provision for group housing for any significant number of older people.

6. In the small town and the hamlet, as already mentioned, there may be some concern about the accessibility of health facili-

ties and services, but there are justifications for building group housing in this milieu because of the leisurely tempo of life and activity and because of the wide variety of experiences and the circle of friends and acquaintances to be found within easy walking distance. Local organizations would do well to provide for their members right within these small communities and would probably find that older people from nearby urban areas had considerable interest in the sort of living environment which the small town afforded.

Convenience of transportation.—Not all older people will give up driving automobiles the day they move to the group setting, but some of them will. For these, convenience of transportation relates not only to their place of residence but also to their many destinations. For the constellation of contacts is frequently wide, and public transportation, even though it may conveniently reach downtown commercial and public facilities, cannot match the convenience afforded by the automobile. For some out-of-the-way locations, the commercial taxicab is an obvious answer—particularly because of the door-to-door service it provides.

Access to public and commercial facilities and services.—The ease with which a person can get to church, can shop at the corner, or can find recreational facilities will probably determine how much he will use them, particularly as he grows older. For some of these activities he can undoubtedly depend on public transportation, but he may soon tire of having to take the bus to every point of contact outside his place of residence or to have friends or relatives chauffeur him back and forth.

Those facilities that are not so frequently used present less of a problem, for, even if the public transportation is not convenient, a trip to the private physician's office or to the clinic by taxicab once every month or so may represent an adventure and probably not too great an expense. (Such a trip may frequently be combined with a luncheon with a friend or some downtown shopping.) Similarly, the intensive treatment facilities of the medical center or the resources of the general or special hospital should be measured in terms of travel time from residence by private automobile or taxicab or, in emergency, by ambulance. For most purposes, a travel time of 15–20 minutes would not seem excessive—and this in selected areas of our cities may represent a distance of 8–10 miles or more.

D. The Community Point of View

Because of its interest in the continuum of facilities and because of its equal concern for the effective utilization of all resources, the community must of necessity value that group housing which provides for relatively independent patterns of living as well as the more specialized institution which provides for patterns with varying levels of dependency.

THE CONTINUUM OF HEALTH-WELFARE FACILITIES AND GROUP HOUSING

For the older individual the community must seek to provide environments which will bridge the wide gap between the life in independent housing and life in the specialized facilities of the nursing home and chronic-illness hospital and general hospital. The several areas of human service find again and again the demand for a group setting either in the independent form of the hotel or residence club or in the less independent old age home. There older individuals may be brought into interaction with their contemporaries and with other age groups, and many of their problems may be solved in a direct and practical way using group therapy techniques. It does little good to provide intensive treatment and care to restore the older person to the community if, upon his return, isolation and loneliness undo much of the good accomplished.

In the group setting many older persons may be shown how to find their place in community life despite the ravages that frequently come with age. They may work out new patterns of living for themselves. On occasion this may mean the permanent acceptance of a group setting, but at other times it may mean restoration to independent living in the community. Thus there is need for group housing which will provide an independent living situation, sponsored and supervised only in the sense of ownership and responsibility for the continued quality of environment. There is need for group housing which, through affiliation with existing community organizations, can and will make available the services requisite for a full individual life in the later years. And there is also need for group housing which will provide partial and varying degrees of nursing care and medical treatment.

To be a true part of the continuum of health-welfare facilities, group housing must be located and administered in such a way that (1) there is ready access to the community facilities which the older individual will use and that (2) those facilities and services—physical, social, or medical—provided in the group setting are integrated with the resources of the community, supporting as well as being supported by it.

MAXIMUM UTILIZATION OF COMMUNITY RESOURCES

Because of the breadth of responsibility for the welfare of the population, the community must take stock of its resources—both physical and human—and it must allocate them for maximum benefit. This involves a co-ordination of effort of all areas of human service—public and private, profit and non-profit, subsidized and non-subsidized.

Thus, in the several forms of group housing, the community seeks to find a living environment suitable to the needs of each individual. For, if it is to achieve a full utilization of community resources, it must match individuals to appropriate living environments, and it must match levels of need and dependency to appropriate levels of care and service. More positively, it must seek to develop the potentials of the

constructive as well as the remedial therapies within the group setting.

E. Development of Group Housing

Group housing for older people, by its
very nature, involves planning, building,
and doing for others. Thus the development
of group housing depends not only upon
the social, economic, and political climate
in which it is to be built and operated but
also upon the vision, public-spiritedness,
and zeal of those who initiate it.

SPONSORSHIP

The inn and the boarding house—the
group housing of early days—were founded
by individuals who recognized a need and
who were in search of a livelihood for themselves. Aside from profitable hotel ventures,
effort to provide non-institutional group
housing during the first half of the twentieth century has generally been the by-
product of another effort, such as the social
programs of the private clubs or the recreational and social programs of the Y's.
None of these has been directed specifically
toward the welfare of older people.

As for institutional group housing, the
poorhouse and the old age home were
founded and maintained by private or public charity and sometimes philanthropy.
These were generally sponsored by the government or church groups in response to existing community needs, with achievement
usually lagging behind need.

Subsequently, and continuing into recent
years, fraternal, labor, and occupational organizations have sponsored group housing
for their retired members. Initial capital
expenditures have usually been made from
their organizational treasuries; operating
expenditures have sometimes been met by
monthly rent and maintenance charges
paid by residents, but in many cases they
have required continuing subsidy from the
national organization.

The development of new sources of income for older people (pensions, retirement
funds, and direct assistance payments) has
mitigated somewhat the need for charity or
for subsidy. It has suggested the feasibility
of group housing in which income from residents not only may support cost of operations but also may amortize capital costs.
This means that sponsorship of such housing need not be limited to charitable private and governmental bodies as in earlier
years or to those organizations that have
continuing funds for charity or subsidy.

Thus, in addition to the more traditional
governmental and religious sponsors, many
civic and social organizations are underwriting group housing. To a large extent,
these organizations have become interested
in housing through participation in the
work of local committees on aging and
senior citizens' clubs. The emergence of
these new sponsors appears to have espe-
cial significance for social gerontology, because their interest frequently stems from
an understanding of current needs and because their viewpoints are generally un-
biased by earlier institutional experience.
These new sponsoring organizations are
more likely to include individuals whose
qualifications particularly suit them to the
tasks of initiating a housing project.

What is required in sponsorship?—Sponsorship—the initiation of a group housing
project as distinguished from subsequent
management and control—has certain peculiar functions to perform: (1) it must
understand and interpret the need and
must conceive of a housing solution suitable to that need; (2) it must tie up into
one package the necessary proposals in
terms of architectural planning, financing,
the letting of bids, and the supervising of
construction; and (3), finally, it must
transfer control of the project to appropriate management, or it must itself assume
the duties of management.

The variety of these functions implies
special administrative and executive qualifications for sponsors; their over-all complexity demands co-ordinated, directed effort in the sponsorship of both institutional
and non-institutional group housing.

Sponsorship by institutional manage-

ment.—In two institutional areas, the school and the hospital, institutional management usually sponsors the construction program. In schools, particularly significant progress in the shaping of the physical environment has been made in the last 20 years. School management generally has established techniques of doing business, if not actual experience in the programing and sponsoring of construction. (Many school districts and educational supervisory offices have specialized staffs to accomplish new building programs.) But perhaps even more important for progress in school-building is the development of a broad philosophy of education, one which has been integrally related to the physical environment in which it is to be accomplished. Within the administrative system, moreover, some of the tasks of sponsorship are lightened: the public nature of their function stipulates the way of doing business on the market; financing by bond issues, although it necessitates public approval, has long successful precedent; and, in programing areas, a volume of recorded experience serves to guide new efforts.

Similarly, sponsorship of hospital-building programs has the advantage of a volume of past experience. Here, too, the evolving philosophy of care and treatment provides precise information as to needs, abilities, and limitations. The published guides to planning the physical environment of the hospital further simplify the programing and design stage.[14] But in the sponsorship of hospital programs particular significance should be attached to the appointed membership of boards of directors and special committees. The qualifications of these appointed members assure the hospital of expert guidance in the tying-up into a final package of planning, financing, construction, and operation.

In the sponsorship of some group housing—particularly the institutional variety—the techniques of the school and the hos-

pital management may offer helpful principles.

Other sponsorship techniques.—In other areas of building—commercial, industrial, and residential—a professional entrepreneurship operates to plan, build, and transfer properties to the final user. Seldom has such a concept been employed in the building of group housing. Housing for older people has not yet caught the attention of the Levitts, the Greenwalts, or the Zeckendorfs; real estate interests—aside from attempting to unload outmoded hotel properties—have been conspicuously absent in the sponsorship of such housing.

On a much smaller scale the home-building industry has established techniques of building single-family houses and some small apartment buildings. Almost never have these entrepreneurs ventured into the sponsorship of group housing. From the standpoint of the actual total volume of construction these builders represent, the potential is great; from the standpoint of the scale of their operations, the probability of realizing the goals of dispersal and integration is good.

Non-profit versus profit-making enterprises.—In part this lack of participation by construction, financial, and real estate interests has been due to a lack of knowledge and a lack of sufficient illustration or guideposts in group housing. But, on the other hand, it has also been due largely to the prevalent notion that all phases of housing older people should be undertaken on a non-profit or voluntary basis.

There is urgent need at all levels of community endeavor to bring about an understanding that group housing for older people, both institutional and non-institutional, can and does function in today's marketplace. Even though the eventual operation of group housing is to be non-profit in nature, the many related aspects of its production—planning, construction and equipping, and staffing—need not in themselves be non-profit operations. In institutional housing, and perhaps also in some non-institutional areas, extensive individual, pro-

[14] The hospital planning guides of the U.S. Public Health Service have no parallel in the development of housing.

fessional effort may be contributed; but these can provide little more than beginnings in the total job to be done.

Ways must be found to develop in today's economic, political, and social world a climate in which group housing for older people—significant as it is in the total picture—can and will be accomplished.

FINANCING GROUP HOUSING

From time to time lending institutions have been reluctant to pick up certain types of housing mortgage papers—either because of the category of housing involved or because of generally unfavorable market conditions. In such cases the federal government (particularly since the depression years of the thirties) has endeavored to provide stimuli to encourage business support for certain desirable housing programs. These federal programs have generally related to independent housing for sale or rental (see Sec. IV, D, "Financing and Production of Housing"). In 1952 the University of Michigan Conference on Housing the Aging (Donahue, 1954a) observed the market potentials of financing homes for owner occupancy and of financing rental dwelling units. It also explored the traditional institutional approaches to financing sheltering and medical facilities for older people. But it found little to report regarding the financing of group housing, either institutional or non-institutional. Today, as then, group housing is generally regarded by our communities (including the banking-lending profession) as undesirable, something that the tenant and the private investor as well must view with suspicion. There have been reasons for this. For certainly the history of the boarding house, the rooming house, and the substandard hotel has been unsavory. But we have done little to improve the situation. In fact, the emphasis we have given to homeownership has only served to make group housing appear at even greater disadvantage.

Federal Housing Administration programs.—The 1956 amendment to the Na-

tional Housing Act represented a major departure from this earlier attitude toward group housing. It provided stimuli in the form of special mortgage insurance terms to non-profit corporations. Some of the non-profit sponsors under the FHA program have been institutions. And it is quite probable that in subsequent years this program will foster a growing number of non-profit organizations proposing to sponsor non-institutional group housing.

This housing for older people in our communities may well demonstrate the validity of group housing as well as effective techniques of management. It may also serve to stimulate private, independent action on the market. But, more likely, this approach toward molding public attitude and inducing production will prove too slow, and some more direct method, such as the extension of mortgage insurance to broader areas of group housing, will be required.

Although the co-operative housing program (under Section 213 of the National Housing Act) does provide for mortgage insurance on non-housekeeping dwelling units, interpretation of that legislation to date has served to exclude group housing. While part of the housing needs of older people might be met through co-operative techniques, the expected periods of occupancy would probably make the co-operative unwieldy in its present form. And in group housing, even more than in independent housing, the lack of experienced, well-financed co-operatives in the United States hinders their development (Abrams, n.d.).

Public Health Service programs.—In institutional areas the Public Health Service, under the provisions of the hospital-construction (Hill-Burton) act, has provided limited grants-in-aids for the construction of accommodations in nursing homes and chronic-illness hospitals. Many people have proposed that this program be extended to cover broader facilities for older people. Although there is general agreement that a line of demarcation should be drawn between what is a medical-health facility and what is housing, few individuals have proposed that independent or non-institutional group housing be included under the program.

Community Facilities Administration program.—As has been noted under Section II, D, "Present Knowledge and Interest in Non-institutional Group Housing," the Community Facilities Administration's effort in the field of group housing has been limited to the construction of college dormitories. Considerable support has been given in the Congress to the extension of the Community Facilities Administration program to include the financing of any needed public construction. Such legislation obviously could provide for the construction of group housing under public auspices. However, as such, it would be less likely to achieve the needed stimulation of the private market to provide group housing and more likely to establish a second category of publicly financed and operated housing.

Public Housing Administration program.—Under the Public Housing Administration, federal financial assistance is granted to local communities for the construction of low-rent, independent housing with full housekeeping facilities. Occasional mention has been made of the possibility of extending the public housing program to provide group housing for older people (including some with light care and custody). To date there has been little support of such a program.

Need for further stimulation of group housing.—Although it is frequently said that the housing market should be able to supply living accommodations required by individuals of ample means, such has not been the case with housing for older people in recent years. Many older individuals with *more than ample income* have had considerable difficulty in finding suitable accommodations. Managers of transient and residential hotels frequently have felt that it was to their psychological disadvantage to permit the concentration of older residents. Many residential clubs have taken a similar attitude. To some extent, the inability of persons of means to find suitable accommodations appears to have been due more to a lag in the construction of such facilities during the period 1932–48 than to the reluctance of industry to provide such housing; the situation, however, has eased somewhat in recent years.

In the case of people living on pensions and older people of *moderate means,* group housing has been extremely scarce and, when available, has been of a particularly low quality. Because of the lack of financial support for construction of such group housing, there is need immediately, and perhaps for some years to come, for the underwriting of loans for group housing over and beyond that currently covered by the housing for elderly program.

In the case of those older individuals of *insufficient income,* public policy is increasingly directed to supplementing income so it can meet the cost of living. To the extent that this is done, housing of this significant portion of older people can perhaps be achieved within the framework of the general housing market and the stimuli which are provided for it. On the other hand, as long as this income remains below subsistence levels, some form of subsidized or public rental housing must be provided, either through public ownership and management or through private welfare organizations.

PRODUCTION OF GROUP HOUSING

A major goal in the production of housing should be the development of a sympathetic understanding of needed modifications of existing planning and building practice. This will be particularly necessary during the interim period of tailoring the group living environment to the needs of older people. For, although we have clues as to what some of these modifications should be, only through experience shall we be able to say precisely what this environment should be. And, even once some general agreement has been reached, many of the modifications will be but slight deviations from customary practice. As such, they may seem of little consequence to architects and builders, but it is these minor modifications that will eventually give rise to group living environments most appropriate to the needs of older people.

REGULATORY INFLUENCES

In addition to the many regulatory influences on building construction in general, there are many that apply specifically to group housing.[15] Particularly is this so in institutional group housing, which also endeavors to provide the custody and care of the home for the aged. Many of these codes and standards have long been outdated; they contain frequent duplications, if not outright contradictions. From time to time these regulations and standards are subject to review and revision, and citizen participation contributes greatly to improving them. To the extent that these existing requirements or proposed revisions are consistent with the over-all goals of providing group housing suitable to the needs of older people, workers in social gerontology must support them.

Over and beyond those standards which relate to housing in general, social gerontology has a special interest in those aspects of standard-setting which pertain to group environment for older people, and it has a particular responsibility to make sure that such standard-setting does not prematurely crystallize those aspects of program *which must be flexible.*

[15] Standard municipal and state building codes, zoning ordinances, municipal housing codes, and less direct influences, such as fire underwriters' standards, are further influenced in the case of group housing for older people by specific requirements established by welfare offices with regard to the housing of recipients of old age assistance, health regulations and standards with regard to the licensing of boarding homes, and federal minimum property requirements for mortgage insurance on housing for the elderly.

F. Management and Operation of Group Housing

Even provided with the best living environment that experience can suggest and that architects and builders can fashion, group housing will have little value unless its management—both boards of directors and administrative personnel—is comparable in caliber to that generally demanded today in other areas of public service (see Sec. II, D, above). By its very nature, group housing for older people demands the ultimate in management-tenant relations.

This, then, is an urgent goal in social gerontology: not only to develop an appropriate philosophy of management but also to develop personnel who understand the objectives of social gerontology and who know how to apply them. There is today a sizable volume of theory and experience—but very little of it has been applied to the management and operation of group housing.

GENERAL OBJECTIVES

There is need in group housing management for an open forthright statement of objective and a pursuit of this objective in day-to-day operation. That management whose implicit objective is acceptance of the theory that all group housing must eventually become devoted primarily or solely to nursing care is doomed at the outset. Far better that its objective be immediately directed toward nursing and medical care! For, aside from being directly contradictory of the major constructive tenets of social gerontology, acceptance of such eventuality is basically unsound from the standpoint of physical plant design, construction, and operation.

Group housing for ambulant older people and nursing-home facilities for the sick and infirm are not the same thing. For the former, the design goals are by definition akin to those of independent living; in the latter, there must be precise organization of space and equipment for efficiency of technical services, an ordering of the living environment to meet the abilities and needs of bedfast and semi-ambulant people.

Even apart from the expenditures for mechanical services and equipment required, the space standards and techniques of construction imposed by converting group housing for well people to a nursing-home operation would mean extravagance in capital investment. Then, too, communal activities and space requirements are dissimilar: communal dining rooms for the ambulant are quite different from the eating situations in individual rooms or wards for semi-ambulant or bedfast patients, some of whom are unable to feed themselves; the informalities and selectiveness of recreational and social participation by the ambulant have different environmental connotations from the techniques by which therapeutic occupational and recreational activities are introduced to the sick or the confused.

Aside from these factors, the working staff of group housing for the ambulant requires one kind of orientation; the staff of the nursing home for the infirm or the mentally deteriorated, another. And a period of transition, or a changeover or a retraining of personnel, would be difficult at best.

CRITERIA FOR SELECTING TENANTS

We must be concerned in group housing with the development of techniques by which the older person will be admitted to living accommodations appropriate to his abilities and needs.

Frequently, in recent years, management of group housing for older people has been unwittingly guilty of undermining its basic purpose by indiscriminate selection of residents. It has placidly referred to "the trend," "persons of greatest need," and the "inevitability that all the old end up sick anyway"—and it has admitted all comers. In few other forms of human endeavor would such resignation be permitted, much less accepted as common practice.

Particularly in group housing for older people residents must be selected in terms of the over-all population composition in the setting and in terms of the effect of that population upon the setting. This should insure (1) a balanced distribution of age groups so that the population does not all grow old at the same time and (2) a level of physical and mental health appropriate to the environmental setting—with particular consideration upon the effect that exceptions to these criteria may have in future years.

Such screening of applications will not be easy, for it is obvious that the very elderly and the infirm are those who will most readily change their living arrangements, since their need is most urgent. On the other hand, for the more able the need to move is less pressing. Except when control limits are set—at least within the limits of present predictability—it is not likely that the early objectives of group housing can be maintained into future years.

LIMITS OF SERVICE

Management of group housing as a part of its objective must also describe its function in the range of community facilities and services. As a community resource itself, it should have an inherent two-way relationship with the community at large; it may expect to receive as well as to give. This means that it need not and probably should not be self-sufficient, for self-containment in the group setting would exclude many of the potentialities for contact between the individual and the community. Furthermore, an attempt by management to provide for all needs within one setting would probably be wasteful of community resources.

VI. Conclusion

Within a single generation significant changes have occurred in the living patterns of older people. Preceding sections of this chapter have discussed the developmental aspects influencing these changes; they have indicated specific problem areas for research and study as well as for action in social and physical planning.

It comes as no surprise that many of the social and physical aspects of the present environment have not been ideally suited to the new patterns of independent living in later maturity and old age. While much of our economic and some of our social planning has aided the development of this new independence, our physical planning and its supporting community endeavor have been devoted almost exclusively to the environmental needs of younger, growing, and working-age groups. Seldom have any concerted efforts been made to meet the environmental needs for the 15–20 years of later maturity or the 10–15 years of old age.

Individual workers here and there have made significant demonstrations in social and physical planning—research and projection and limited action programs in the community. But, even though these may contribute to the happiness and well-being of a few older people, we must not be blinded to the situations in which most older people now live and in which they will have to live in the years to come. Some efforts in social gerontology must rightly concern themselves with direct action in terms of molding and shaping the physical environment of the home and the community; but the major efforts of the future must be devoted to reaching the goals indirectly by creating a favorable social, economic, and political climate.

Some of the broad categories of concern which affect the environment and the individual are re-emphasized here.

A. *Social versus Physical Planning*

All too often the social consciousness which has pervaded much of our public policy and endeavor has not been reflected in the physical planning and action programs of our communities. Very little of this physical planning has been directed toward achievement of stated social objectives.

COMMUNITY DEVELOPMENT AND LAND USE ZONING

Both our concept of community development and our present zoning ordinances reinforce age stratification in residential areas. These must be revised to encourage the development of new communities and the redevelopment of old communities in such a way that they will have a balanced population of age groups, of family sizes, and of housing types. Thus, within the single community, it would be possible to accommodate the full cycle of life—the young person living alone, the newly married couple, the growing young family, the older couple in employment and retirement, and the surviving spouse and the single, unattached older person. Ways must be found whereby older people can live meaningfully in just about every one of our communities. Although for some individuals the concept of a specialized *suburban* residential area for early adulthood and middle age and a specialized *urban* residential area for later maturity and old age may be desirable, such tenets of age segregation are not generally acceptable today.

The revision of our zoning ordinances alone will not be enough to bring about balanced residential communities. Our government, our economy, and our industry are shot through with regulations and controls at local, state, and federal levels which similarly reinforce the characteristic age segregation of our communities. These, too, must be reshaped to contribute to over-all social objectives.

COMMUNITY SERVICES

Almost every community needs a coordinated effort to provide a range of services for the aging population comparable to that now provided for other (particularly younger) age groups. In some cases, needs of the aging will require totally new services; in others, it may demand the revamping or the abandonment of old services.

a) Present efforts, both direct and indirect, to increase the supply and to improve the quality of housing have been in behalf of younger families. These and similar techniques must be used to develop housing for older one- and two-person households. This housing, by definition, must include houses and apartments for independent living, the living accommodations offered by such group environments as the hotel and the residence club, and the living accommodations in the group setting of the institution.

b) The continuum of community medical-social facilities, and the responsibility therefor, must be maintained in such a way as to meet effectively the needs of older individuals to the same extent that they do the needs of other age groups. Our standards of health care will not permit us continually to shunt off the chronically ill, the infirm, or the confused, turning over the responsibility to lesser professions.

The accessibility of health-care facilities and services to areas of residence of older people is as much the responsibility of those community agencies which deal with health care as of those which deal with residential development per se. A comparison must be made between the efficiency inherent in the centralization of health-care facilities and personnel, on the one hand, and, on the other hand, the effectiveness of service readily accessible to older as well as younger people.

B. *The Individual and His Environment*

Our knowledge of middle-aged and older people is fragmentary. Our knowledge of their environment for the most part is based upon personal observation of a limited number of cases both in the independent and in the group setting. Research and study are needed in several broad areas.

1. *How do older people live? How are they affected by their environment?*—The basic data available on the living arrangements, housing, and community settings of middle-aged and older individuals are far too scant to permit making many of the broad assumptions which are necessary prerequisites to sound planning.

There is urgent necessity that the data gathered in the United States Census of 1960 (and in subsequent years) be analyzed and reported in a way that will give us reasonably conclusive knowledge of the conditions and situations of middle-aged and older individuals—at least to the extent that such information is available for the population as a whole. Also urgently needed is a census of group housing, both institutional and non-institutional.

To date, studies of the individual and his environment have dealt specifically with housing conditions and not with the total living environment—not with detailed aspects or with its effect upon the social and physical health of the individual.

Case studies have indicated that there are some truly constructive potentials in many of our service techniques, such as those of physical medicine and rehabilitation, home care, and training for self-care; but the place for these in the total environment has yet to be determined.

2. *How do middle-aged and older people want to live, both now and in the future?*—To perhaps no other question are so many contradictory, authoritative answers given as to the question of how older people want to live. Even acknowledging that older people seldom have freedom of choice in their living environments, present indications are that they want and need a wide variety of living environments. Most studies have reported the hindsight of individuals who had made decisions regarding their living environments or had had the decisions made for them.

There is need for market research in areas in which a free choice of living environments is possible. Studies must be made which will also project the preferences to be expected among future generations of older individuals—who have experienced increased leisure time and who have been looking forward to retirement in later maturity.

Objective research is needed to determine why some older people seek special housing and how this choice relates to individual personality, age, and immediate and long-term adjustment.

C. Objectives

Today most older people, both in later maturity and in old age, are able to continue living independently in their own homes. Some older people, as age advances, prefer the group setting of the hotel or the residence club. A still smaller number—particularly as infirmities increase—prefer, or find it necessary to accept, the group environment of the institution.

Many find it possible to continue to live in the same community in which they spent their earlier years; a number of others find it necessary to accept residence elsewhere—but still in the same general community. Some others prefer to migrate to favored climates or to move to another place to live with a relative or friend.

Many older individuals find it possible to continue taking an active part in home and community life; but many more are left behind because of their own inabilities or because of the pace of community life or the indifference of their fellow men.

There is general agreement among the major fields of endeavor that human services should be geared to treat and to restore all individuals to optimum health and to help them maintain themselves, insofar as possible, in independence in their own homes. Whether in independent housing in the community or in some form of group setting, the basic objective of independence for the individual is the same, the only difference being in the extent to which it is capable of realization. To attain these objectives, research and action programs must work hand in hand—in economic, social, medical, physical, and political areas.

REFERENCES

ABRAMS, C. N.d. U.S. housing: a new program. New York: Tamiment Institute.

AMERICAN HEART ASSOCIATION. N.d. The heart of the home. New York: The Association.

AMERICAN PUBLIC HEALTH ASSOCIATION, COMMITTEE ON THE HYGIENE OF HOUSING. 1948. Standards for healthful housing: planning the neighborhood. Chicago: R. R. Donnelley Co.

———. 1950. Standards for healthful housing: planning the home for occupancy. Chicago: R. R. Donnelley Co.

———. 1951. Standards for healthful housing: construction and equipment of the home. Chicago: R. R. Donnelley Co.

———. 1953. Housing an aging population. New York: The Association.

ANONYMOUS. 1951a. Budget for an elderly couple: estimated cost, October, 1950. Month. Labor Rev., 72, 304–6, 309–10.

———. 1951b. Buildings for the handicapped and/or aged. Bull. Am. Inst. Architects, 5 (November), 2–14.

———. 1952. Buildings for the handicapped and/or aged. Ibid., 6 (January), 1–19.

ATKINSON, S., FJELD, S. P., and FREEMAN, J. G. 1955. An intensive treatment program for state hospital geriatric patients. Geriatrics, 10, 111–17.

BEYER, G. H. (ed.). 1952. The Cornell kitchen: product design through research. Geneva, N.Y.: W. F. Humphrey.

CAPLOW, T., and FORMAN, R. 1950. Neighborhood interactions in a homogeneous community. Am. Sociological Rev., 15, 357–66.

CAVAN, RUTH S. 1949. Family life and family substitutes in old age. Am. Sociological Rev., 14, 71–83.

CHAPIN, F. S. 1951. Some housing factors related to mental hygiene. In R. K. MERTON, PATRICIA S. WEST, MARIE JAHODA, and H. C. SELVIN (eds.), Social policy and social research in housing, pp. 164–71. New York: Association Press.

CHRISTIANSON, E. 1956. Address given before the First Minnesota Governor's Conference on Aging, Minneapolis. November.

CHURCHILL, H. S. 1952. Some random thoughts on housing for the aged. In T. L. SMITH (ed.), Living in the later years, pp. 37–49. Gainesville: University of Florida Press.

CORSON, J. J., and McCONNELL, J. W. 1956. Economic needs of older people. New York: Twentieth Century Fund.

COWGILL, D. O. 1956. Trends in the ecology of the aged in American cities, 1940–1950. J. Gerontol., 12, 75–80.

DEWEY, R. S. 1948. Peripheral expansion in Milwaukee County. Am. J. Sociology, 54, 118–25.

DEWHURST, J. F., AND ASSOCIATES. 1955. America's needs and resources: a new survey. New York: Twentieth Century Fund.

DONAHUE, WILMA (ed.). 1954a. Housing the aging. Ann Arbor: University of Michigan Press.

———. 1954b. Where and how older people wish to live. *In* WILMA DONAHUE (ed.), Housing the aging, pp. 21–36. Ann Arbor: University of Michigan Press.

DONAHUE, WILMA, and ASHLEY, E. E., III. 1959. Housing and the social health of older people. *In* C. TIBBITTS (ed.), Aging and social health in the United States and Europe. Ann Arbor: University of Michigan, Division of Gerontology.

DONAHUE, WILMA, HUNTER, W. W., and COONS, DOROTHY H. 1953. A study of the socialization of old people. Geriatrics, 8, 656–66.

FAULKNER, R. 1954. Inside today's home. New York: Henry Holt & Co.

FESTINGER, L. 1951. Architecture and group membership. *In* R. K. MERTON, PATRICIA S. WEST, MARIE JAHODA, and H. C. SELVIN (eds.), Social policy and social research in housing, pp. 152–63. New York: Association Press.

FESTINGER, L., SCHACTER, S., and BACK, K. 1950. Social pressures in informal groups: a study of human factors in housing. New York: Harper & Bros.

GERTMAN, S. 1960. Health services. *In* E. W. BURGESS (ed.), Housing the elderly in retirement communities. Ann Arbor: University of Michigan, Division of Gerontology.

GILBRETH, LILLIAN M., THOMAS, O. M., and CLYMER, E. 1955. Management in the home. New York: Dodd, Mead & Co.

GINZBERG, R., BRINEGAR, W. C., DUNN, F. K., and OLSVARY, VILMA. 1954. Improvisations in rural Iowa. *In* WILMA DONAHUE (ed.), Housing the aging, pp. 91–103. Ann Arbor: University of Michigan Press.

GUTHEIM, F. A. 1948. Houses for family living. New York: Woman's Foundation.

HAVIGHURST, R. J., and ALBRECHT, RUTH. 1953. Older people. New York: Longmans, Green & Co.

HAWKINS, C. E. 1957. Recipients of old age assistance: their housing arrangements. Social Security Bull., 20 (September), 9–12.

HIBBARD, D. L. 1955. The annual report of the Board of Pensions of the Presbyterian Church in the U.S.A. Philadelphia: The Church.

HIBBARD, D. L., and LEE, J. P. 1954. Presbyterian ministers and their widows in retirement. J. Gerontol., 9, 46–55.

HUNTER, W. W., and MAURICE, HELEN. 1953. Older people tell their story. Ann Arbor: University of Michigan, Division of Gerontology.

INSTITUTE OF PHYSICAL MEDICINE AND REHABILITATION. N.d. Self-help devices for rehabilitation. New York: New York University, Bellevue Medical Center.

KAPLAN, J., and TAIETZ, P. 1959. The rural aged. Geriatrics, 11, 752–57.

KLABER, E. H. 1954. Housing design. New York: Reinhold Publishing Corp.

KLEEMEIER, R. W. 1951. Difference of adjustment: segregated old age communities versus unsegregated communities. Paper presented at the Northwestern University Centennial Conference on Problems of an Aging Population, Evanston, Illinois.

———. 1956. Environmental settings and the aging process. *In* J. E. ANDERSON (ed.), Psychological aspects of aging, pp. 105–16. Washington, D.C.: American Psychological Association.

KUTNER, B., FANSHEL, D., TOGO, ALICE M., and LANGNER, T.S. 1956. Five hundred over sixty: a community survey of aging. New York: Russell Sage Foundation.

LOEWENBERG, I. S. 1954. Designing homes for the aging. *In* WILMA DONAHUE (ed.), Housing the aging, pp. 55–63. Ann Arbor: University of Michigan Press.

McCULLOUGH, HELEN E. 1952. Space design for household storage. (Bull. 557.) Urbana: University of Illinois, Agricultural Experiment Station.

McGUIRE, MARIE, and SCHMALHORST, S. D. 1957. Housing the elderly. San Antonio, Tex.: San Antonio Housing Authority.

MASSACHUSETTS STATE HOUSING BOARD. 1954. Standards of design: housing for the elderly. Boston: The Board.

MERTON, R. K. 1948. The social psychology of housing. *In* W. DENNIS (ed.), Current trends in social psychology. Pittsburgh: University of Pittsburgh Press.

MOCK, ELIZABETH B. 1946. If you want to build a house. New York: Simon & Schuster.

MUMFORD, L. 1956. For older people—not segregation but integration. Architectural Rec., 119, 191–94.

NATIONAL ASSOCIATION OF HOME BUILDERS RESEARCH INSTITUTE. N.d. Home safety principles. Chicago: The Institute.

NATIONAL SAFETY COUNCIL. 1955. Accident facts. Chicago: The Council.

NATIONAL TUBERCULOSIS ASSOCIATION. 1954. Homemaking hints. New York: The Association.

NELSON, G., and WRIGHT, H. 1945. Tomorrow's house: a complete guide for the home-builder. New York: Simon & Schuster.

NELSON, L. 1957. Rural life in a mass industrial society. Rural Sociology, 22, 20–30.

NEUGARTEN, BERNICE L. 1957. The Kansas City studies of adult life. Newsletter (Gerontol. Soc.), 4, No. 4, 9.

NEVADA STATE WELFARE DEPARTMENT. 1952. A survey to determine the housing needs of old-age assistance recipients in Nevada. Carson City: The Department. (Mimeographed.)

ORBACH, H. L., and SHAW, D. M. 1957. Social participation and the role of the aging. Geriatrics, 12, 241–46.

PEACOCK, J. F. 1954. Detached dwellings. In WILMA DONAHUE (ed.), Housing the aging, pp. 64–71. Ann Arbor: University of Michigan Press.

PERRY, C. A. 1939. Housing for the machine age. New York: Russell Sage Foundation.

RHODE ISLAND. STATE. 1953. Old age in Rhode Island: a report of the Governor's Commission To Study Problems of the Aged. Providence, R.I.: The Commission.

ROSE, A. M. 1947. Living arrangements of unattached persons. Am. Sociological Rev., 12, 429–35.

————. 1948. Interest in the living arrangements of the urban unattached. Am. J. Sociology, 53, 483–93.

RUSK, H. A., and TAYLOR, E. J. 1953. Living with a disability. Philadelphia: Blakiston Co.

SAHLE, R. 1952. Retirement village planning for Florida. Tallahassee, Fla.: State Improvement Commission.

SHELDON, H. D. 1958. The older population of the United States. New York: John Wiley & Sons.

STEINER, P. O., and DORFMAN, R. 1957. The economic status of the aged. Berkeley: University of California Press.

TAIETZ, P. 1953. Administrative practices and personal adjustment in homes for the aged. (Bull. 899.) Ithaca, N.Y.: Cornell University Agricultural Experiment Station.

UNITED COMMUNITY SERVICES OF METROPOLITAN BOSTON. 1957a. Housing preferences of older people: a case study of forty-seven evictions from a residential hotel. Boston: The Services. (Mimeographed.)

————. 1957b. Follow-up study: housing preferences of older people: a case study of forty-seven evictions from a residential hotel. Boston: The Services. (Mimeographed.)

U.S. BOARD OF GOVERNORS OF THE FEDERAL RESERVE SYSTEM. 1954. 1954 survey of consumer finances. Federal Reserve Bull., 40, 246–49.

U.S. BUREAU OF THE CENSUS. 1953a. Current population reports: population characteristics. (Series P-20, No. 44.) Washington, D.C.: The Bureau.

————. 1953b. U.S. census of housing: 1950, Vol. 1, General characteristics, Part 1: U.S. summary. Washington, D.C.: The Bureau.

————. 1953c. U.S. census of population: 1950, Vol. 4: Special reports, Part 2, Chapter C, Institutional population. Washington, D.C.: The Bureau.

————. 1953d. U.S. census of population: 1950, Vol. 4: Special reports, Part 2, Chapter D, Marital status. Washington, D.C.: The Bureau.

————. 1955. U.S. census of population: 1950, Vol. 4: Special reports, Part 2, Chapter A, General characteristics of families. Washington, D.C.: The Bureau.

————. 1956. Current population reports: population characteristics. (Series P-20, No. 72.) Washington, D.C.: The Bureau.

U.S. BUREAU OF LABOR STATISTICS. 1941. Homes for aged in the United States. (Bull. 677.) Washington, D.C.: The Bureau.

U.S. DEPARTMENT OF HEALTH, EDUCATION, AND WELFARE, SPECIAL STAFF ON AGING. 1958. Ford Foundation's first aging grant. Aging, 43, 3.

U.S. FEDERAL PUBLIC HOUSING AUTHORITY, NATIONAL HOUSING AGENCY. 1946. Public housing design: a review of experience in low rent housing. Washington, D.C.: Government Printing Office.

U.S. FEDERAL HOUSING ADMINISTRATION. 1957. Report of Industry Advisory Committee on Housing for the Elderly. Washington, D.C.: The Administration.

U.S. NATIONAL BUREAU OF STANDARDS. 1948. Safety: for the household. (Circular 463.) Washington, D.C.: The Bureau.

VIVRETT, W. K. 1956. Specially designed housing for elderly persons. A report to the Federal Housing Administration. Minneapolis: The Author. (Mimeographed.)

————. 1957a. Environmental needs of the aging. Geriatrics, 12, 209–10.

————. 1957b. For most older people, for most

of their later years, an environment for living independently. Geriatrics, **12**, 211–19.

———. 1960. Designing a retirement community. *In* E. W. BURGESS (ed.), Housing the elderly in retirement communities. Ann Arbor: University of Michigan, Division of Gerontology.

VIVRETT, W. K., ORBACH, H. L., and SHAW, D. M. 1955. Planning study, housing for the aging. Unpublished studies of retired persons of Minneapolis and St. Paul. Minneapolis: University of Minnesota, School of Architecture.

WARREN, ELLEN. 1957. After discharge from the hospital, how do older people get along at home? Geriatrics, **12**, 233–40.

WARREN, R. L. 1952. Old age in a rural township. *In* NEW YORK STATE JOINT LEGISLATIVE COMMITTEE ON PROBLEMS OF THE AGING, Old age is no barrier, pp. 155–66. (Leg. Doc. 35.) Albany, N.Y.: The Committee.

WEBBER, I. L. 1950. The retired population of St. Petersburg: its characteristics and social situation. Tallahassee, Fla.: State Improvement Commission.

WEBBER, I. L., and OSTERBIND, C. C. 1960. Types of retirement communities. *In* E. W. BURGESS (ed.), Housing the elderly in retirement communities. Ann Arbor: University of Michigan, Division of Gerontology.

WELFARE COUNCIL OF METROPOLITAN CHICAGO. 1952. Community services for older people—the Chicago plan. Chicago: Wilcox & Follett.

———. 1957. For a good old age, action to improve and increase services for older people: a six year report (1951–1956). Chicago: The Council.

WELFARE COUNCIL OF METROPOLITAN LOS ANGELES, BUREAU OF PUBLIC ASSISTANCE. 1950. Housing conditions among recipients of Old Age Security living in Los Angeles County. Unpublished report. Los Angeles: The Council.

WOODBURY, C. 1950. Current housing development for older people. *In* WILMA DONAHUE and C. TIBBITTS (eds.), Planning the older years. Ann Arbor: University of Michigan Press.

——— (ed.). 1953. The future of cities and urban redevelopment. Chicago: University of Chicago Press.

XVII

Governmental Functions and the
Politics of Age

FRED COTTRELL

I. INTRODUCTION

We are interested in this chapter in seeing how government has changed and is likely to change in the future in terms of the things it is doing for older people. We must also in turn examine the way older people are likely to modify government. We will first center our attention, not upon the people themselves, but upon government, particularly as it performs functions for them.

Traditionally, the government of the United States has had little to do with the welfare of the aged or, for that matter, for any other needy set of people. The idea that government is legitimately entitled to serve as a welfare agency is still fought vigorously by many conservatives. Yet, in spite of their continuous opposition, government has gone on taking over more and more of the functions which make it primarily a welfare state.

There are a number of ways by which this paradox might be explained. The first and most obvious being simply to trace out the history of the United States, showing just what changes took place under what conditions. The difficulty of attempting to record everything that happened is so great, however, that the historian would have to become selective and decide which, of all the things happening at the same time, he should relate to those which subsequently or previously happened. So he would have to adopt some theory which assumed that some of the changes which occurred were causally related, while others were merely adventitious insofar as they affected the particular series of events with which he was trying to concern himself.

Here we are relating the development of government and the functions it performs to the technology through which the people of a given society deal with the physical and biological world. There are of course other ways of classifying what went on, and these may prove, for some commentators, to be more fruitful than that taken here. Be that as it may, we are going to develop our thinking around the thesis more completely outlined in chapter iv of this *Handbook*. For a generic statement the student should consult this chapter. He will also find elsewhere in the volume other evidence of the way social change is related to changing technology and to the situation of the older generations.

For our purposes the fundamental problem is one of showing how the institution of government gains or loses functions as technology is altered. But as this takes place there is a simultaneous alteration of the functions of other institutions in the society. What one gains is often accompanied by loss of function by another institution. We have found it useful to consider an institution as being, among other things, a means to the performance of a cluster of functions. To identify the separate institutions, we choose one function as a kind of indicator by which we know one institution from another. So, for example, we identify the family as performing a cluster of functions, which includes primary responsibility for the care of infants, marriage as the cluster which includes the legitimatized approach of male and female for the purposes of sexual intercourse, and so on. In such a classification the minimal function (that by which we identify it) of the state is the legitimatized monopoly on the exercise of physical coercion.

There are of course a great many societies known to man in which this function of physical coercion is not the monopoly of a single institution. It may there legitimately be performed by a person who is also designated as an agent of the family, the community, the church, or some other type of organization. In such circumstances there is no such institution as the secular state. It is also true, and perhaps it should be emphasized, that in *no* society is the secular state confined to the performance *only* of the function of exercising physical coercion. Neither the pure "police state" nor the omnicompetent "welfare state" has ever existed in fact.

But this need not cause confusion here. We are not interested in presenting only an ideal type, the like of which can be found nowhere. We are trying to see how societies are modified—in this case, to see how behavior which was once sanctioned by such controls as exile from the family or community, excommunication from the church, or bankruptcy in the market came to be enforced by the fact or threat of physical coercion by the state.

Nor should it cause confusion that agents of the state will use, not only the sanction of physical coercion, but also controls like those used by other institutions, including rewards of various kinds, education, propaganda, and other types of persuasion. But the state is not distinguished

from other institutions by these common usages; it differs from them in that it alone can use coercion to secure the means to carry on these other activities.

Using this concept of the state, we will find that over time and space it has performed and is performing a tremendous variety of functions. What it is now legitimate for the state to do one place is abhorrent for it to do in another. What governors could morally do in a place at one time is quite different from what they can do there now. The fact that the functions of government in the United States are changing is nothing unfamiliar in man's history, nor is the direction it is taking unusual. The rate of change is accelerating, but, since this is also true of all high-energy societies, we can usefully observe changes not only in the United States but in all places where the rate and kind of change taking place are analogous to those going on here.

There is a common core of functions shared by governments in the West. The limits on what governors may do, both as to the ends they may pursue and the means they may adopt, are somewhat alike. But in the explosion of culture which has taken place in the last 500 years the differences have multiplied, as is attested by (among other things) the series of wars which have punctuated Western history. The results of these changes have been selective, certain areas taking on many new features while others look more nearly as they did before the commercial revolution.

Technological changes serve as a sort of index to all social change, whether reviewed as cause or as effect. There have been very great changes in technology which have accompanied other forms of social change, so that we might emphasize prior changes, particularly the rise of secular thought and science, as a forerunner to technological change, thus making ideas rather than things the mainspring. But at other times and places secularization of thought has died out without affecting greatly the technology by which the bulk of the population had to live. However, there have been *no* great changes in the flow of energy which have *not* been accompanied by great social changes. We may attempt to discover increases in energy flow only as an index to indicate that social and technical changes necessary to permit that flow have taken place or are taking place. We may instead point to the fact that feedback from new and enlarged sources of energy may in itself constitute a force far more powerful than that initially given by ideas and inventions. In either case, if we study energy flow, we can observe events which can be recorded and measured with the instruments used by the physical and biological scientists and so escape some of the elliptical reasoning otherwise almost impossible to avoid. It is for this reason that we emphasize the study of energy as a function of technology and geography as well as of biological and social phenomena.

In chapter iv we have indicated that the advent of what we there called "high-energy technology" into societies has regularly given rise in each of them to a number of the same kinds of changes. The varieties of social organization which are capable of carrying on the functions necessary for the exploitation of high-energy technology are apparently quite numerous. But it is becoming more and more apparent that the family and the local community cannot adequately serve the new technology. Now, since those forms which do effectively serve the technology are reinforced by feedback from the energy flow which they direct, they have advantages in the struggle for survival against those old forms which impede or prevent energy flow (Cottrell, 1955).

We also pointed out that it is the market, the corporation, and the state which are apparently successful in performing most effectively those functions required for the utilization of high-energy technology and that the position of older people in these institutions is much less strategically effective than that which they occu-

pied in the old institutional arrangements. Thus here in the United States, as in other areas adjusting to the new technology, there is a rising effort to transfer functions necessary for the well-being of older people to more effective agencies.

Older people thus seek to increase the power of government (those who act as the agencies of the state or from whose activities we infer the nature of the state) in those areas which will permit it to fulfil their needs. This amounts to a transfer of functions, since many of the changes sought at once weaken the old by depriving it of activity while strengthening the new by assigning it activity.

II. The Political Background of Government Assistance to the Aged

A. Barriers to Government Aid to the Aged

Whenever anyone attempts to change the legitimate functions of government, he faces a number of handicaps. Some of these are to be found in the sheer inertia involved in changing any aspect of culturally mediated behavior. Much, perhaps most, culture is transmitted without the conscious intent of those who pass it on. Parents and older children and playmates teach the young to follow and justify the patterns which they themselves learned the same way. The effort deliberately to alter these patterns involves careful all-pervasive controls which are extremely difficult to maintain. Further difficulties are found in resistance of those who fear any alteration as a threat to their own power or vested interest. Other barriers arise from inability to devise new social structures which will achieve the new ends without, at the same time, reducing the ability of existing institutions to carry on functions which they previously have performed satisfactorily. All these types of difficulties face those who seek to improve the condition of the aged through the exercise of politics.

OPPOSITION OF VESTED INTERESTS

In the first instance they were met by the power of those who had already benefited from the use of the market and the corporation. The rights of some of these groups were already vested in law and usage; and, because these agencies had successfully met the demands of technology, they had benefited from the increasing power which was derived from the increasing flow of energy. Railroad tycoons, barons of big business, and giants of industry, who had successfully flouted sacred elements of American culture in their quest for power, became the most vociferous proponents of ancient law and custom when changes in government which might thwart that power were suggested. They even appealed to the aged themselves to preserve the familiar relationships between government and citizen. The dangers which might result from increased government power were paraded with all the skill which the public relations artist could muster. Power over press and pulpit were exercised to the hilt. The great wealth, derived from natural resources and technology, to which these men often had contributed practically nothing was cited as evidence of their great contribution to the welfare of the nation and justification for their continued "stewardship." Every stratagem which could be devised by which the power of intrenched wealth and institutionalized values could be brought to bear was invented and utilized. Ideology, in which the intrinsic advantage of the price system was held to be the sole basis for increasing productivity, was paraded in the institutions of higher and lower learning. Classical economics, long neglected in the strategy by which business came to power, was cited to show how the development of political power by the masses could only lead to their ultimate downfall in the face of the iron law of wages and diminishing return from land. History was rewritten to make it appear that man had always, and everywhere, utilized the price system as the universal measure of value.

But the reader will not need to be reminded of these things, for they continue to be the stock in trade of those who oppose the appearance of any new institution which may serve to weaken their power and resultant privilege.

THE PROBLEM OF ALLIES

In the struggle to legitimatize new functions of government, the reformers faced another handicap. They had to join forces with a great many other groups who were also dissatisfied with existing institutions. But these included the "lunatic fringe," the utopians, ideological socialists and communists, single-taxers, and even anarchists. The necessity to join forces is apparent, but the handicap of so doing is equally apparent. The dilemma has not yet been successfully resolved, and the excesses of the radicals who have attached themselves to movements designed to improve the aged are not the least of the obstacles which must be overcome by those who try to use politics in the interest of the elders.

TRADE-UNION ANTIPATHY TOWARD POLITICS

As we have seen, the free market hit the unattached workers as hard as or harder than any other single category of persons. Those endangered, however, included the full age range. The instrument through which they sought to secure their position was most often and most successfully not political organization but the labor union. Again we cannot recapitulate the history of this struggle. But its consequence was the appearance of new powerful economic agencies. Most unions learned the difficulties of gaining benefits through political activity the hard way, by being defeated, and by seeing politically oriented unions break up. The leaders of successful unions became devoted to the use of the strike as an ultimate economic weapon. By monopolizing control over a skill or entry into a strategic role in industry, they were able to secure for their own members many benefits which would very doubtfully have come to them had they relied upon their power in the political arena to gain them. Thus the social structure of the union and the value system, which it taught and served, were poorly designed from the point of view of politics.

Now, the age makeup of the industrial working population has, in the past, been overwhelmingly composed of young men. For them the ends sought by the aged offered no such appeal as did immediate gains in the form of wages, vacation pay, shortened hours, and better working conditions. It was not until the effects of aging began to be manifest among the bulk of the workers themselves that they became greatly concerned over this aspect of their lives. It is true that seniority provisions in many union contracts had the effect of giving rights and privileges to older workers. But the seniority system begins to affect the life of the worker the day he goes to work, so it is as much a concern of the younger and middle-aged as of the elder. Apart from this and similar provisions, a union leader is more likely to gain and retain power, particularly in any growing industry, by emphasizing gains to the great number of younger workers than by trying assiduously to assure them for older ones. So, in the struggle to make it possible for the state legitimately to protect the interests of the aged per se, the unions have not been too effective. When they did engage in political activity, they were most likely to attempt to secure legislation under which they could increase the power of unions as economic agents. More recently they have had to use all of the political power they could muster to protect their economic power against political controls which other groups have been seeking to impose on them.

CONFLICTING STRUCTURES OF INTEREST

The aged belong to a great many groups and organizations which are of this character. That is to say, the political power of the group or organization is used to further the fundamental purpose of the organization which is often not the protection and furtherance of the interests of the aged. Even the family is frequently found to be in this position. For example, parents may become involved through the Parent-Teachers' Association in an effort to improve schools. They may, thus, become committed to support a legislator on the basis of the fact that he will co-operate in this endeavor. In so doing, however, that legislator may have to make political deals which prevent his support of legislation favorable to the aged. Or, again, farmers may be more concerned about support payments and other means to secure the well-being of farmers generally than they are about aged farmers in particular, and so on. In many cases the heads of an organization may use its power to push or oppose legislation without either consulting or giving heed to the opinion of the members. This is, of course, one of the difficulties faced by all groups who seek to exert political pressure, but it is certainly, and perhaps particularly, germane to the politics of the aged.

BUREAUCRATIC SOURCES OF RESISTANCE

Another very important block to the transfer of functions from elsewhere to government is found in the resistance of the bureaucrats who administer existing programs. Every new claimant to government funds poses a threat to existing functions and those who serve them. Every new function implies the creation of another set of bureaucrats who may claim power and wealth which might otherwise go to extend that now going to the present bureaucracy. Even the tendency of existing bureaus to enlarge the sphere of their operations thereby poses a block to the creation of new claimants to limited tax money. The relative effectiveness of these bureaus in this pursuit is sometimes quite unrelated to the numbers of persons they serve. A well-organized minority, presently served by an effective bureau, may have a very strong voice in determining what government does, not only in fields directly related to its functions, but also in many others quite remote in function but directly competitive with it for funds.

Among all the claims on government, none exceeds that made by the military. Whatever the objective facts may be, and perhaps only God knows what they are at a given time, the military has good reason for never being satisfied. Fortified by the very instability which technological change has produced, they can make strong claims for every man and every cent which the country can spare. The military is composed almost completely of young men, though an occasional general officer will remain in power long past the time he is required to serve. To these young men the sacrifices required of civilians to secure their own defense do not loom large as compared with those which soldiers often face and are made relatively small by comparison with those we all might have to make were we to lose a war. So there is another very powerful claimant on government functions and powers which has priority over the needs of the aged. As we shall show later, the claims of the older veterans, as veterans, have been pushed more strongly and effectively than those of some types of older people. The American Legion and other veterans' organizations constitute a cross-section of the adult age groups in the country and, so, have power in many situations which is greater than that of the aged as such. But that power is not always available to the aged veteran, let alone other non-veteran aged.

Regional claims are likewise more generally supported than those of the aged who are a class of citizens likely to be dispersed among a large number of states or congressional districts in such a way that they are not dominant in any of them. The needs of "all of the people" of a region for governmental service in the shape of protective tariffs, public works, such as dams, highways, and waterways, or even for recreation sometimes appeal to more voters than do the special needs of the aged in those regions.

As has been shown elsewhere in this volume, the very pattern of living which has developed among the urban aged sometimes tends to rob them of political influence. When they are young and productive, they tend to be associated with suburban dwelling, and it is there that they become identified and potentially influential. But, at or near retirement, when the children have fled the nest, they return to urban residence where they are unknown and likely to have little political power. So, at the moment when their political power is most likely to be devoted to serve the needs of the aged, that power is greatly reduced.

B. Barriers Resulting from the Federal System of Government

THE FEDERAL CHARACTER OF THE UNITED STATES GOVERNMENT

Of outstanding significance to government, as it relates to the aged, is the federal character of the American political system. Probably no other element of American government is more necessary than the retention of federalism. It is the flexibility of a federal system which makes it possible for one government to operate successfully in control over people of so divergent interests, backgrounds, and values as occupy the United States. Centralization would almost certainly produce regional schisms so great as to threaten the legitimacy of government over the territory now governed. The essence of federalism is that the states shall have some powers which cannot be altered by the unilateral action of the central government. The division of function which was laid down in the Constitution has been altered greatly in the years since then, but the principle of state "sovereignty" is basic to the operation of our government. The primary unit is the state, not the national government. It is the state which wields the police power, which constitutes the minimal function, by which we recognize that a state exists. It is the state which carries on education through which some of the basic values and attitudes necessary to the survival of government are taught to the children. And it is the state which traditionally has the responsibility for such welfare functions as were considered to be legitimate before, say, 1910. But the state in turn had in most cases depended primarily upon the local governments and the local community to carry on these functions. Any effort to transfer functions to the national government then produced a reaction all along the line—from the grass roots, where the party machine is most sensitive to citizen opinion, through the county courthouse, where the basic unit of the political party has its residence, to the state legislature and administration, where power depends upon control over function and is jealously guarded.

EFFECTS OF HIGH-ENERGY TECHNOLOGY ON POWERS AND FUNCTIONS OF LOCAL AND STATE GOVERNMENTS

The great changes in economic and social structure required to exploit high-energy technology very frequently rendered the local community, the county, and even the state incapable of controlling the forces necessary to carry on even the functions they previously had performed. The emergence of giant corporations, in control of aggregations of wealth far greater than that in possession of any county and beyond that available to provide income for most states, made it extremely difficult for these units of government to oppose them. The kind of managerial control required for the efficient operation of railroads and other public utilities permits little interference in the interest of local politics, and this also came rapidly to be true of other integrated industries. The place of residence of the stockholder frequently offered a far more lucrative source of taxa-

tion than did the political unit in which the physical property of the corporation was located. This even though many of the problems created by the corporations could be solved only by local action at the plant site. Thus, while the local community is often far more effective as a unit for welfare administration than is any bureaucratic unit under the control of centralized administration, its effectiveness in this respect is not matched by its power to secure the necessary means. It was often not possible for a city or county to levy taxes on business proportional to the need created in that unit by business practice. A firm might operate so that it skimmed the cream of the labor market, leaving the members of the community whom it was unprofitable for them to employ to the mercy of whatever agency might be induced to undertake their support. Yet individual counties and even states hesitated to levy taxes based on experience with these firms, for they could in retaliation migrate from that state to another. In most cases even the threat of such migration was sufficient to block legislation or hamstring administration. In the face of this situation the progress of *state* legislation to aid the aged was very slow.

OVERREPRESENTATION OF RURAL AREAS

One element of the political structure in the United States was favorable to the power of the aged. Representation in most states in one or the other of the two houses (which exist in all the states except Nebraska) is likely to be based not upon population but upon geographic units such as districts and counties which vary greatly in population. Since population has been more and more concentrated in the great metropolitan regions, this has left far more power in the hands of the rural politician and electorate than their numbers would warrant. Until recently more of the old people resided in these rural regions than in the cities and should have been in a position to exercise a very powerful influence over the state legislature in their own behalf. But it was also in the rural regions that there was most distrust of new institutions and greater reliance on the family to provide for its own. Through their ability to control the family-owned farm or small business, elders in rural areas continued much longer than in the cities to find the old social structure usable. It was only as technological change threatened these bastions that it was possible to get their support for governmental action in behalf of the aged. Voters in many of these areas remained unfavorable to what they termed "socialistic schemes" until they were themselves offered the opportunity to participate in a government program for the aged, and even then some of them resisted. Most, however, have discovered that with an alteration of the taxing system they can benefit from social legislation without paying anything like what it costs. When the states moved from reliance on the general tax on property, in which the land and therefore the residents of a local unit bear a very high burden, to excise, sales, and income taxes, which bear more heavily upon city dwellers, some of the reluctance of rural legislators to support programs of aid to the aged disappeared. The result has often been, however, that functions have been transferred from local to state to national control not because of the demonstrated capacity of the more distant government to do the job better but because it was only through such transfers that the money to carry on the program could be collected. On the other hand, where the state or national government gives subventions to local governments which do not have to raise the money but can spend it at their own discretion, the result has frequently been such waste and extravagance that continued public support was threatened or withdrawn. Where this has happened, the battle to secure funds has had to be fought all over again with forces frequently weakened by the acts of those very people to whom, if they have their way, the program will again be intrusted.

The same kind of overrepresentation of rural areas which is found in state legislatures is also found in the United States Senate. Since each state has two senators, a majority of the Senate on some issue may represent a minority of the populace. The rural states contain far fewer people than do the urban ones, but they have more senators than those in which a majority of the people live. In these rural states the aged often constitute a larger part of the people than they do in urban states. They, therefore, have a potential voting power of great strength. But, since they are divided among a great many different interest groups, most of which do not make the welfare of the aged their primary goal, that potential has seldom or never been realized.

The politician who seeks to utilize the aged in a sparsely populated rural state as a means to control a senator will find that these states are the happy hunting grounds of other powerful groups. The same amount of money will go much further in a state like Nevada toward producing a senate seat than it will in one like California. So the use of the aged as a minority group seeking to bargain for control of a senator is met by the power of more adequately financed and sometimes better organized groups also seeking to control that seat.

To complicate the problem for the aged in the rural states, there is the fact that many of them contain no great aggregations of wealth to be taxed so that the aged needy are confronted by the aged of other income levels and are unable to concentrate their power as a homogeneous age group.

It was difficult, in fact, to find much political activity which could be said to be primarily by the aged in the interest of the aged. The exception that proved the rule was the rise of a number of political movements in the Far West, particularly in California, which were clearly of that character; but even these took place after the real battle was won by others (Bond *et al.*, 1954).

C. The Roosevelt Revolution

SECURITY FOR THE AGED AS A BY-PRODUCT OF THE DEPRESSION

From what has been said it would appear that it would be almost impossible for the aged themselves to make it legitimate for government to take care of them. As a matter of simple fact that was true. The "Roosevelt revolution" involved a great many sets of people, of which the aged was only one and not a particularly powerful one. It was not primarily as a result of their political power that the aged were included among those who would benefit from the New Deal, though the politicians who organized it missed few bets when it came to picking up the votes of dissident minorities. The fundamental objectives were designed to get the able-bodied family men back to work at productive tasks. Aid for the aged was one device by which they hoped to remove them from jobs which could be taken by these breadwinners as well as removing the cost of their support from family heads. The breakdown of the market and the corporation as devices to provide family income security demonstrated that they were incapable of performing some of the functions which had been taken from the family. People who were thus left without morally sanctioned means to carry on the roles required of them were demoralized. It was they who were looking for a way to meet their needs and fulfil their obligations. It was they who accepted Roosevelt's leadership and combined with others to keep him in office and elect a Congress willing to follow him.

An important point for us to remember, here, is that this made a very strange assortment of bedfellows. Many of those who supported Roosevelt did so for purely partisan reasons. They wanted power, and, when they got it, they wanted to keep it. But they often wanted also to achieve results directly the opposite of many others who were also voting a Democratic ticket. Some of the most conservative and even reactionary people in the United States thus combined with some of the most radical utopians. It was always difficult to keep this coalition alive, and for the most part it was done by a skilful combination of blocs which were formed to meet one situation and quickly dissolved when a new effort required power drawn from interests different from those previously allied. Under these conditions the position of the aged was made extremely vulnerable because they were not represented in most cases by long-established pressure groups familiar with political strategy. Nevertheless, the Social Security Act marked a tremendous forward step which has had very important consequences for the aged. We are interested in showing why it passed only to the extent that this throws light on subsequent political developments.

The aged were not in most states or at the national level a powerful, well-organized group. Moreover, a great many of them were extremely loyal to the Republican party and so not in a position to exercise much influence on Democratic leaders. They were to be served by the Social Security Act as much for other reasons as for the political promise the aged voter himself provided. The younger unemployed wanted to take their jobs but were restrained somewhat by the fact that this would produce a bad public reaction if there was no way for the aged to be cared for. Men with both parents and growing children saw in the act a way to provide for the aging which demanded less of them than anything previously provided in our culture. There were also politicians from districts in which the growing number of aged voters constituted a real threat unless they could provide some way to care for them and do it without antagonizing the local taxpayers. Employers who did not wish or dare to turn out aged employees who had no means of support were often willing if not anxious to find an institutional means at once to take care of these people and protect themselves against the competitive disadvantage which would otherwise result from doing so. There were, of course, others unable to achieve what they regarded as necessary for human decency and dignity. Besides these there were ideological communists and socialists, members of religious sects which emphasize respect for the aged, and many more too numerous to mention.

What was *not* present in this situation was a bureaucracy which had been hired to perform functions for the aged. Such a bureaucracy could have much more effectively mobilized the forces required to support political leaders who were willing to help the aged than did the amateurs representing them or the politicians who hoped, through their votes, to remain in office but had little other interest in their welfare.

There were some in both private and public welfare work who saw the opportunities inherent in the situation and who helped to frame the legislation which was passed. They relied heavily on the experience which had been gained in those states which had already pioneered and in some degree on experience in other countries. But they were only a handful contrasted with the army which would be created to administer the legislation to be enacted. For this reason, the politics of aging before and after the passage of the Social Security Act of 1935 are very different, and we will treat them separately.

THE POLITICS OF AGING BEFORE THE SOCIAL SECURITY ACT

Before the passage of the Act, those working for the welfare of the aged operated in the traditional American setting. As we have seen, the American cultural heritage emphasized the idea that the individual was responsible for his own well-being. Given freedom to contract in the market, he was expected to provide out of his own resources for his welfare and that of his dependents. The fact that the roots of the morality which he was using were an outgrowth of a system in which the extended family operated and in which the power of religion was much greater than it was rapidly coming to be was disregarded. The free operation of the law of supply and demand, backstopped by the rugged individualism which was supposed to have characterized the frontiersman, was held to be sufficient means to overcome whatever social consequences might arise from the new American way of life. Yet it was always possible to discover some evidence that people living in the world of fact did see the necessity for government to extend aid to those who, because of their own shortcomings or due to conditions beyond their control, were unable to carry on. Such aid was often surreptitiously given in the form of make-work jobs for the widow or orphan and similar devices. In most counties there was some kind of institutional care. The county home often attempted to serve at once as a mental hospital, chronic-disease hospital, and home for the aged and infirm and for the orphan, crippled, mentally retarded, and otherwise handicapped. Aside from providing the bare means of subsistence, the chief function it performed, perhaps, was to salve the conscience of the voter.

There was an occasional program of "outdoor relief" which provided small sums for widows' pensions and care for dependent children. But, for the most part, the care of the aged was considered to be strictly a family affair. In some states where there were a large number of unattached males, such as characterized the population of California in 1850, when the first legislature met, fraternal orders were able to get state subsidies with which to carry on their programs of aid to the aged. As the population took on a more normal character and family life became the rule, these subsidies were pretty generally withdrawn. In general, it was only in the "poor house" that the aged could find government aid.[1]

In California, as early as 1883, the state undertook to subsidize the counties which provided such homes. However, some counties which had none proceeded to claim these grants; and in this way outdoor relief for the indigent, at state expense, was established. The counties then proceeded to seek the state subsidy for all the indigent in their county homes and even for some who had long since departed from them. Difficulty of supervising the distribution of funds and other abuses which arose led to the abolition of this system in California in 1895, and from then until 1930 no aid to the aged outside state institutions was paid by that state. Some others seem to have gone through the same cycle (Bond *et al.*, 1954).

Outdoor aid paid by the counties was the general method of caring for such of the aged as received any government help outside the county homes before 1930. With the development of state mental hospitals, many counties found in them a way to care for the senile without having to ask the local taxpayers for the money. It is impossible to know how large a portion of the inmates of these hospitals suffered from simple senility and how many were victims of a psychosis. The problem of diagnosis itself was not a simple one, but it was compounded, and continues to be compounded, by social pressure on doctors who, in the absence of adequate county facilities, often can see no solution to the problem of an aged ill or infirm person but to send him to a state hospital. Nor is it likely that county commissioners—who know that, if they provide no county facilities, the state is likely to be forced to do so—will make extensive efforts to that end. In this respect the conditions prevailing 50 years ago are not entirely different from those observed today. In fact, many

[1] Chapter viii presents a brief review of the development of income-maintenance programs for older people.

counties which had an institution available for the aged have since closed it, though the number of aged requiring institutional care is much larger now than then. The rapid growth of the aged population during the second quarter of the twentieth century led to the creation of many makeshift private arrangements. Old people who were able financially, but not physically, to take care of themselves were often victimized by private homeowners who took their money and then neglected them. The result was, in many states, the rise of legislation requiring the licensing of homes and their inspection. Though these laws were often honored only in the breech, they provided a way by which those interested in the welfare of the aged *could* bring pressure to bear on the private owner through political pressure on the boards or inspectors responsible for the administration of the legislation. The investigations, which were conducted in connection with the passage and enforcement of these laws, resulted in the accumulation of evidence as to the neglect and abuse of the aged. This, also, increased the political visibility of the aged.

The earliest study of the questions of state financial assistance to the aged on county outdoor relief was made in Massachusetts in 1907. The first law was not passed, however, until 1915 in Alaska, which permitted a grant of $12.50 each month to persons aged 65 and over who met certain requirements. By 1928 old age assistance laws were in effect in Massachusetts, Kentucky, Maryland, Colorado, Montana, Nevada, and Wisconsin. The programs were optional with the county, and many counties did not avail themselves of the opportunity.

After several abortive efforts to arouse legislative interest in the aged, California, in 1927, authorized the State Department of Social Welfare to make a study of old age dependency in that state. It found that only about 2 per cent of the population over age 65 were receiving any kind of aid. The counties had almost complete responsibility for care for the indigent aged. The institutions which once were supposed to house all of them slowly filled up with those too ill or otherwise disabled to care for themselves, so that the healthy needy aged could not get into them. The counties developed a widely varying set of means to solve their local problems. The two great urban regions developed fairly effective programs. That of Los Angeles operated with a lien law under which the county could recover, after the death of those whom it had helped, what it had paid or as much of it as could be recovered by the sale of property put under lien. This method permitted a great many persons who had property but no income to receive aid to which they felt they were entitled. At the same time, it protected the taxpayer from grasping relatives who, while they refused to support the living aged, showed up to claim their property after their death.

The form and the amount of outdoor relief being granted before the depression set in were tremendously varied, depending upon the county or state which was giving it. In some places the aged were a fairly vocal political interest group, and, backed by local allies, they were able to get at least the minimum for subsistence from their local taxpayers. In others the amount paid was a pittance, a sop thrown to quiet the noisiest complainers and permit the conscience of the majority to rest easy by creating the illusion that something effective was being done.

The movement for pensions was spearheaded by the Fraternal Order of Eagles, long a champion of financial help for the aged. There were other less widely scattered and less widely known groups in most of the United States. A standard bill was drafted by the Eagles which was studied by the legislatures of twenty-four states. Among them was California, which, as a result of the post–World War I migrations, was faced with an especially acute problem. The Eagles took a very important part in educating the public as to the merits of the bill while it was before the legislature, and in 1929 California adopted a program of extending aid to all the needy aged. This was the first state which placed in operation a state-wide mandatory old age assistance law. A number of other states were undergoing much the same experience, however, and by the end of 1930 there were thirteen state laws in existence.

Experience with California's law may be taken as an example of what happened. It was expected that the bulk of those pressing for assistance would be those who had hitherto been receiving aid from the county, but this did not prove to be the case. Instead, about 70 per cent of those who applied had either been getting by on their own extremely limited resources or were supported by children, relatives, or friends (Bond *et al.*, 1954). Since the aid to be given under the new law, which was now sought by so many, could not exceed $30 a month, it is pretty obvious how poorly the aged were being served by the means traditionally expected to provide their needs. As the depression deepened, the aged came into competition with other groups also seeking to share the limited amount of money the states and counties could provide. Some of them were much better able to press their claims than were the aged, and, in consequence, grants to the aged were considerably lowered. What might have happened in the states had there been no federal program is problematical, but in 1935 the Social Security Act was passed. It authorized federal grants to those states which provided programs of aid to the aged on a basis satisfactory to the national government.

There was great variety in the plans which went into operation. Some, like those of California, bore the stamp of experience and the authority given to them by their own populace before the federal government intervened. Many others were pretty obviously makeshift devices by which the states hoped to get a handout from the national government without really alleviating much the condition of the aged. It must not be forgotten that, while the grants in many of these cases were small, the salaries of the administrators were not correspondingly minuscule. In some parts of the country the salaries approved by Washington were far in excess of those which the politicians could have demanded from any local employer. This is not to say that they did not earn what they got or that there were not dedicated men among them. It is merely to point out a fact which no politician could afford to overlook. With the creation of a new governmental function went new opportunity to reward the faithful and, very importantly in many cases, a great number of small grants whose recipients would show their gratitude at the polls (and sometimes, unfortunately, we must add—or else).

But if the politician was looking at the opportunities the law afforded him, many of the aged were for the first time secure in the knowledge that they had a definite income—an income which, in many cases, made them a welcome member of a family which otherwise might have found them to be an intolerable burden. From the beginning of its operation, there was no question of turning the clock back and repealing the Social Security Act. The small groups of amateur politicians who had fought so long and so helplessly against such great odds were suddenly joined by a host of allies. Even the most reactionary of the politicians never had any real hope that they could repeal the law. They at first tried to weaken it by limiting the resources available, by pointing to shortcomings in its administration, by talking scandal; but they did not openly dare to attack the idea that the senior citizen, because he had lived to be 65 years of age, had established a claim on the economy of the country which was the equal of that of the worker, the investor, or any person employed from tax money. For the aged the real revolution had occurred. What followed was to be only an attempt effectively to put into operation a moral principle which had become unquestionable. Extending aid to the aged had become a legitimate function of American government.

THE SOCIAL SECURITY ACT

Implementation of the principle that the aged should have a secure income adequate to permit those who otherwise could not meet the minimum standard of comfort and decency to do so took two forms. The first was to be a continuation of the kind of programs which the states themselves had begun to operate; the second, however, was based on an entirely different principle—that of insurance. Both programs made good political sense. As we have seen, federal grants-in-aid to permit the development and maintenance of aid to the aged were welcomed because they permitted the needy to benefit from the act at once. This an insurance program could not have done. As we have already indicated, this program won the immediate support of a good many politicians, who saw in the enlarged program a good many things which were not visible to the average citizen, or which, if visible, were taken to be (as for the most part they were) the normal costs of carrying out new functions. On the other hand, the tremendous costs of a program, based on the principles under which state aid to the aged had operated, would probably have scared off many whose imagination was not adequate to visualize the way such sums could be created or how they could be spent without creating an inconscionable number of political hangers-on. So the idea that in time only those would benefit from the program who had paid premiums into it, and in part at least would receive an annuity proportional to their payments, was much more attractive to the bulk of the people than a straight "dole" could have been. Certainly, neither the opponents nor the proponents of the bill appeared to have any idea that aid to the aged would still be large, much larger than it initially was, 20 years after its passage.

The facts which have led to the evolution of the Social Security Act, the changes which have been made in it, and its present provisions are discussed in chapter viii; what interests us, here, is the way the passage of time has affected politics in this field.

D. Post–New Deal Politics of Aging

The most obvious and perhaps most significant fact is the great increase in the number of older voters. This is primarily the result of the increase in the numbers of the aged, since apparently no greater portion of them vote than do younger age groups. Second, there has been a concentration of the aging voters. California and Florida immediately came to mind as examples; but, even within states, the movements of age groups into suburbia and back again to specific areas of the city create particular problems for the politicians. These movements have forced the parties to reassess their position, particularly as it relates to the welfare of the aged. Sometimes the aged hold the balance of power among the interest groups and are able to use their position effectively. It was this kind of power which a number of notorious leaders of the aging tried to use. In California, EPIC, the Ham-and-Eggers, the Townsendites, and numerous other action groups were opposed not only because of the particular program they espoused but because those who controlled their votes also could bargain for many other things about which the aged knew nothing and cared less. In some cases the political power of the aged and their sponsors literally outran the ability of the politicians to deliver what was demanded. So, for example, in Oregon they were able, by the use of the initiative method of introducing legislation, to put on the statute books a law which threatened to bankrupt the state. It was only after its bonds became unsalable and its credit otherwise impaired that the state's attorney-general was able to make the law inoperative. Colorado has placed in operation a law creating a num-

ber of special taxes and allocating the income from them specifically to provide $100 a month for recipients of aid for the aged and to create a reserve fund to assure that these payments will carry through a period during which income from those taxes might be not great enough to meet the guaranty. It remains to be seen whether other claimants will not find the means successfully to weaken or modify this provision.

The groups which combined to form the New Deal coalition have had difficulty in preserving a balance among them. Many of them can no longer be depended upon to support legislation which they originally helped to enact. So, while the political vulnerability of the aged has been reduced by the great increase in their numbers which has taken place during the last 25 years, they must continually find new allies to replace the old ones. There is no longer much likelihood that their right to a claim upon the economy can be challenged. But the size and the specific character of their claims have to be established over and over again in the midst of other claimants.

It is in this context that we must understand present politics. The means to establish new claims and administer effectively the functions which are now accepted as belonging legitimately to government are quite different from those faced in the early years of the Roosevelt revolution.

THE PROFESSIONALIZATION OF THE FIELD OF AGING

Today the greater part of administering to and advising and legislating for the aged is carried on by professionals. Some of them are professional politicians; some are government administrators; some are supported by co-operative voluntary organizations designed to serve the field of welfare generally or the aged in particular. What they all have in common is that the care of the aged is a fundamental concern which often includes the source of their bread and butter. Their personal attitudes may vary all the way from intense dedication to the aged to indifferent performance of a job. But for all of them it is a job. Most of them are bureaucrats.

Bureaucracy is necessary to the administration of government or of any other large-scale organization. The word has become an epithet in the mouths of many who think of society as an aggregation of self-directing individuals each capable of providing the means to his own ends. To them a bureaucrat is a "tax-eater" busily entangling the world in red tape. Ironically, many of them are themselves bureaucrats in the world of big business. But, for all their criticism, bureaucracy grows, because only so can many of our purposes be realized.

To point to the fact that people involved in the professions extending aid to the aged become their most effective political agents is not to malign them. It is not surprising that those who work most intimately with a problem come to understand it better than bystanders. Those who have attempted to put a piece of legislation into operation discover immediately what its real effects are, its strength, and its weaknesses. And, if they are wise, they also discover what are the barriers to the needed corrections or extensions and the groups which may be depended upon to support them in their efforts to overcome these barriers.

This is not to say that some of these men do not suffer from the excesses which may characterize any bureaucrat. In every profession there is difficulty in distinguishing between what is good for the professionals and what is good for their clients. One sees problems inevitably from the position which he occupies as he views them. So, like the medical profession, the law, and other honored classes of people, those who operate the welfare agencies of our society are likely to confuse their self-interest with that of their clients or of society generally. Protection against this, in the American system, is found not so much in self-limitation imposed by the profession itself as through power exerted by others who see the problems entirely from another point of view such as that of the client, the taxpayer, or a competing bureaucrat who is trying to achieve other objectives.

POWER PROBLEMS IN EXISTING WELFARE STRUCTURES AND FUNCTIONS

The various structures which have been built up at the local, county, state, and national levels in the performance of different functions, such as extending financial aid and providing health services, housing, recreation, and education, reflect differences which relate not only to those functions but also to the strength of the various groups connected with those functions. As a consequence, there is a constant shifting of emphasis as new conditions are confronted and as one group grows in strength or weakens relative to another. New techniques make it possible more easily to satisfy some needs but leave the others faced with their old difficulties, and so more of the former are met. It would be impossible to deal completely with this labyrinth of changing relationships. Perhaps, the best that can be done is to show how some of the structure is built and some visible trends both in function and in structure. In the process we will learn how the changes in them reveal the values of those who plan them, those who oppose them, and some of the groups called upon to help in achieving what is done. To put this in more explicit and theoretical form, what we have been saying is that politics is to be understood not only in terms of the values of the people but also in terms of the social structure which is used to discover and to implement those values. We must emphasize that the structure not only will serve the needs of its clients but must also meet the demands of the technology which it makes use of, serve the values of those who occupy the roles which must be created to serve it, and deal effectively with other groups which are also involved in government and in other institutions which must function simultaneously with it in the same situation.

So, for example, we can learn something about the way health functions for the aged will be carried out by studying the health needs of the aged. But, at the same time, we involve ourselves in the necessity to understand a structure which deals with the health needs of other age groups. The medical profession has built such a structure, and it is not certain that this is one best suited to deal with the medical needs of the aged. Nevertheless, there must be medical doctors among those who serve the aged who, in meeting the demands their profession puts upon them, may be unable or unwilling to do what is demanded of them by those who are primarily concerned with the medical needs of the elders.

Similarly, the educator has developed his professional skills and attitudes in an atmosphere where the problems connected with teaching children and catering to their needs are given an overwhelming emphasis. It is not surprising, then, that the political power of the National Education Association is more likely to be directed toward the solution of the problems of educating the young than the aged. Similarly, when the bureaucracy built up to carry out programs which themselves result in part from the activities of teachers and educational administrators is given the task of serving the educational needs of the aged, it is not surprising that they find it difficult to find time, money, and manpower to do it. Neither the personal predelictions of most of the personnel nor their professional connections are likely to lead to the emphasis upon education for the aged which experts in gerontology would give it. The same is true in lesser degree of recreation, which until recently was likely to be directed by a graduate in physical education from a teacher's college who had much more skill and preparation for dealing with school-age children and youth than with oldsters. The rise of group therapy as a professional field of social work has reduced somewhat the problem of finding adequately trained and motivated leaders for adult education. But it is still true that in most communities there will be much more nearly adequate support for health, education, and recreation programs for the young than of means to meet the similar needs of the old.

The available services then result in part from the existence of values among the people generally, but in part they derive from the political power of professionals who occupy strategic positions among the decision-makers of our society.

So the political structure which visibly and legitimately exists is important, but so, also, are many other power structures which are not supposed to affect the actions of those who govern but will inevitably do so. Of necessity, every administrator is something of a politician who must respect the facts of life whether he likes them or not. One who fails to discover them and learn how to cope with them will learn to his sorrow how much they have to do with his success or failure.

III. GOVERNMENTAL STRUCTURE FOR THE AGED

A. Federal Structure

FEDERAL AGENCIES DEALING WITH THE AGED

Keeping in mind these reservations so that we do not overemphasize their importance, we may look at the official political structure which serves the needy aged. At the national level the affairs of the aged are administered within a number of divisions, including the Department of Health, Education, and Welfare, the Department of the Treasury, the Department of the Interior, the Department of Agriculture, the Department of Commerce, the Department of Labor, the Office of Defense Mobilization, the Housing and Home Finance Agency, the National Science Foundation, the Railroad Retirement Board, the Small Business Administration, the Civil Service

Commission, and the Veterans Administration. The mere enumeration of these agencies points up the difficulties any group will encounter in the effort to get a well-thought-out and co-ordinated program for older people. It is obvious that the greater political concern of the heads of most of these agencies will not be centered around the well-being of the aged. They will have been selected because of their competence (real or imagined) to deal with the major problems confronting their division. It is true that in some of these departments there is a subsection whose primary function *is* that of dealing with the aged. But the chiefs of these sections sometimes find that they can be more effective in getting something done if they provide information to some influential persons or organizations outside the department than if they try to go through official channels. The influence of some pressure group which is attempting to put through a plan often varies among the several departments involved. Failure to achieve their objectives in any one of these agencies may upset their plans as they relate to others. Compromise and failure reduce the most carefully thought-out plans to a series of somewhat disconnected realities.

Roosevelt brought several of the agencies concerned with welfare, health, and education under the umbrella of a single organization, the Federal Security Agency. During the Eisenhower administration, the agency was converted into the Department of Health, Education, and Welfare, with cabinet status. But even this left the affairs of the aged scattered widely among a number of authorities, as we have just seen. To make it possible more effectively to co-ordinate these activities, President Eisenhower created, in April, 1956, the Federal Council on Aging, which consists of representatives of the agencies listed above.

THE FEDERAL COUNCIL ON AGING

The work of this council is purely advisory. That is, there can be no decision made by the council which binds any de-partment to do what the council has found it wise to recommend. The power structure of the departments is, thus, left intact. In fact, in listing its accomplishments, the council has emphasized not those achieved at the strictly national level but primarily its activities encouraging the states to undertake programs better designed to serve the needs of the aged and to co-ordinate their activities with those of the national government. This means that agencies at the state level must attempt to meet the different and sometimes conflicting demands of various Washington bureaus and offices even when it is possible for them to co-ordinate their own work better with rules and structures worked out at state level.

These rigidities have been softened somewhat and made more flexible by bringing together the persons who administer the programs. Together with the Council of State Governments, the Federal Council on Aging collaborated in the 1956 Conference on Aging. Here, the results of previous conferences were reviewed, suggestions from the field were presented, and a suggested program for future action worked out. This conference was the culmination of a movement which started at the grass roots and worked its way through committee and conference action at state level until it was given official recognition in Washington. Following the conference there were a number of discussions on problems of aging at a series of regional meetings with key state officials, beginning in 1957. The success of these conferences is attested to by the fact that in September, 1958, Congress passed the White House Conference on Aging Act, which calls for a conference in January, 1961, to develop recommendations for further research and action in the field of aging. It provides some funds for the conduct of the conference and the payment of advisory committees. Those familiar with the past successes of White House Conferences on Child Welfare will expect similar results from what will probably be a continuing series of conferences on aging.

INTERBUREAU CO-OPERATION

At the national level, too, there is need for continuous effort to relate the activities of one agency dealing with the aged to those of others. There exist among them an intermeshing series of staff committees, staff units, and public advisory committees who provide a means of co-ordination through exchange of information and consultation and carry on research and direct operating activities. In some of the agencies there is a full-time staff devoted to aging activities. The Department of Health, Education, and Welfare has such a staff, the Special Staff on Aging, which is in the office of the Secretary. In the Health of the Aged Section of the Public Health Service there are the Center for Aging Research, the Section on Aging in the National Institute of Mental Health, and the Gerontological Branch of the National Heart Institute. The Office of Education has an Adult Section. The Veterans Administration has the Division for Research on Aging; the Federal Housing Administration, a unit on Housing for the Elderly; and, in the Department of Labor, special activities for the aged are carried on in the Bureau of Employment Security, the Bureau of Labor Statistics, and the Office of the Assistant Secretary for Employment and Manpower. Some of the federal agencies also use advisory boards composed of non-governmental personnel. They include: the Housing and Home Finance Agency's Advisory Committee on Housing for the Elderly, the Industry Advisory Committee of the Federal Housing Administration, and the Advisory Committee on Chronic Disease and Health of the Aged in the Bureau of State Services of the Public Health Service. Added more recently are boards for the Bureau of Public Assistance and the Bureau of Old-Age, Survivors, and Disability Insurance.

THE ROLE AND FUNCTIONS OF ADVISORY COMMITTEES

These committees are composed of prominent persons in the respective fields with which they are concerned. Very often they are chosen to represent professional interest groups, though the particular person chosen may not himself be an administrator. Often he is an educator, researcher, or someone else who can speak with the authority his knowledge and experience convey but without the presumed bias which would arise from being an active employer or employee in the area for which he speaks. It is hoped that by this process those in government can more clearly see the developments which will affect and be affected by the policies they adopt.

It is at key points like these that many of the groups interested in presenting their particular point of view are most effective in influencing government. They propose changes both in administration and in legislation. They criticize, from the vantage point of their own special concern, what has been going on. And, frequently, they carry back to the sources of influence from which they came explanations and new information which have been given to them in defense of the policies criticized. Sometimes they also sponsor proposals which the agencies want to put before the public but do not wish publicly to initiate. Thus a congressman may suddenly be bombarded with requests for a course of action which ostensibly come from a purely voluntary organization but which, in fact, originated in a government bureau. Again, this is not meant to imply adverse criticism. It is a description of what actually transpires. The results are often such as to justify it in comparison with those secured by other forms of lobbying, congressional investigation, or other means by which elected officials become aware of facts which they must have in making judgments.

THE ROLE OF FEDERAL AGENCIES IN CHANGING VALUES

Many of the national agencies operate outside Washington in a dual manner; that is, they carry on the specific functions to which they have been assigned by legislation, which often means that they audit and inspect the work of departments in the state governments, and they also engage in work designed to affect the citizens directly through education, development of means to implement action by citizen groups, and co-ordination of the actions of these voluntary grass-roots organizations.

This direct relation between the national government and its citizens tends to blur and confuse the clear lines of authority which the courts try to establish between the central government and that of the states. With his ability to recommend and to audit the accounts of state agencies which handle grant-in-aid money, the federal bureaucrat has a potent means to persuade reluctant local governments. The national government has been under control of the Democratic party most of the time since the coming of the New Deal. But there are states which have been under control of the Republican party almost continuously during that time. Recently, with the advent of Republican government in Washington, the shoe has been put on the other foot. But he who is in control in Washington, regardless of the party in power in the state house, can often have quite a bit to say about what local government does in the welfare field. States have been induced to change their residence and citizenship requirements. They have had to modify their support of institutions for the aged (because under the federal law no person who is in a state institution may receive aid to the aged). They have had to alter the budgets for individuals receiving aid so that they corresponded with what Washington would approve. Most of all, the legislators have felt great pressure to institute programs in aid to the aged, the disabled, the crippled, and the blind and in other areas because their failure to do so would deprive them of the opportunity to get matching funds from the national government. The lines of federal influence and power which appear on the charts to end at state borders actually reach clear down to the grass roots. Flowing back up through the channels of public control, they may force changes on legislatures which ostensibly are in the hands of a majority actually adverse to the proposals which they enact.

B. The Work of Federal Agencies

EMPLOYMENT AND RETIREMENT

Some of the federal structure is designed almost completely to aid the aged. Some of it only incidentally, but very significantly, alters the life-chances of the elders. So, for example, the United States Employment Service provides special people to serve the aged among their clients. It also engages in research designed to show employers in what respects and in what kinds of activities older employees may be equal or superior to younger ones.

The Woman's Bureau in the Department of Labor has devised a type of community-action program known as Earning Opportunities Forum, which is designed to pinpoint jobs which mature women who need to work can fill.

The Bureau of Labor Statistics has made studies which show how particular retirement programs affect the aging, the effects on them of automation, the provisions affecting older workers which are found in labor contracts, and the labor-force outlook for older men and women.

Through its Bureau of Employment Security, the Department of Labor is responsible for co-ordinating federal and state employment services and administering the unemployment compensations provisions of the Social Security Act. It is easy to see how this service provides a strategic source of information to show what should be done to improve both state and national legislation and administrative procedures. While it is of greatest value to those who are attempting to steer a course for the whole economy, it also shows the character of particular labor markets, trends in work opportunities, and a good deal more information of value specifically to the welfare of the aged. In this respect it is far superior to any kind of voluntary fact-gathering or reporting in which the authorities in the states would be likely to engage.

VOCATIONAL REHABILITATION

Public Law 565 (83d Cong.), the "Vocational Rehabilitation Amendments of 1954," broadened the contacts which the national government has with the states. It deals with all ages, but increasingly it has made efforts to aid older people to get back on their feet. As in most of the other grant-in-aid programs, this is theoretically a means whereby the states themselves are *encouraged* to provide new and more effective service in an area which it has always been in their power to provide. In fact, however, by dealing with voluntary organizations, supplying information, and otherwise demonstrating the possible achievements of the movement, the national government is circumventing the barriers which state boundaries would impose and almost compelling state action. The state vocational rehabilitation agencies are set up differently from state to state, but they are all supposed to help develop a plan of rehabilitation and to provide medical, surgical, and psychiatric services to remove or reduce the disability, appliances where they will help, therapy to lessen the disability, and training to improve skills and eventually to find employment suited to the client. Between 1945 and 1958 the proportion of persons 45 years and older increased from 15 to 27 per cent of the disabled undergoing rehabilitation.

HEALTH

The governmental structure at the national level to provide for the health needs of the aged is important but relatively fragmented. The Amercian Medical Association and its medical and technical affiliates are the dominant forces in this field. The great bulk of the practitioners in the country are quite ready to utilize research results which have been made available through pharmaceutical corporations, universities, or government-supported research agencies like the National Institutes of Health. But they are adamantly opposed to any program which will have the effect of permitting the public dissemination of the results of that research through means other than the existing medical social structure. The fear of "socialized medicine" is one which has been sedulously cultivated by the leaders of the medical profession. In consequence, politicians move warily when confronted with a demand for a new method of distributing health services. Even the Veterans Administration, backed with the numbers and the powerful sentiment which is its to employ, has been forced to adopt a program which in important respects derives more from the professional demands of the doctors than from the perhaps inadequately informed wishes of the veterans and their friends and relatives.

Medical care for the aged, like all other medical care in the United States, can be understood more through the study of the politics of institutionalized medicine than through the study of party politics or the power or influence of any other group or institution. Within the limitations so imposed, the national government has proceeded to respond to the demand for increased health services for the aged. A number of units of the Public Health Service concentrate upon the problems of aging. These include the Chronic Disease Program, the Center of Aging Research, the Gerontological Branch, and the Section on Aging. The Public Health Service, through its Bureau of State Services, administers a number of programs of studies and demonstrations. These are designed to get the states to set up the laboratories, clinics, and hospitals which are required to implement research findings. No direct patient service is given.

The Bureau of State Services also provides services to voluntary agencies, including the professional evaluation of their programs and education for both professional and lay groups. It also undertakes surveys and operational studies to obtain data upon which to base new state programs.

The Hill-Burton program, which also was revised in 1954, is administered by the Bureau of Medical Services. Under this act, aid is extended to private non-profit and public bodies which are willing to create facilities for the care of those suffering from prolonged illness, many of whom are of course older persons. The bureau works directly with state agencies designated to carry on the activities for which the grant is made.

The national government encourages research into a number of diseases frequently associated with old age, such as cancer, heart disease, mental illness, and arthritis. The only patients directly served by the National Institutes of Health are those used in research projects. To encourage research outside its own facilities, the Center of Aging Research has established university-centered agencies. One such was established at Duke University in 1957. Another was organized at Yeshiva University in 1958. The grant to the University of Michigan to establish a Training Institute in Social Gerontology is an example of another type of effort designed to stimulate the training of personnel required to expand services to the aged. Research and field investigation grants are also made to institutions and to individuals. The staff of the Center for Aging Research is available for technical consultation with scientists who wish to undertake or expand programs of research in aging. The National Science Foundation is also supporting research which will have significance for the aged.

The Division of Public Health Methods conducts studies to provide some of the data necessary for effective legislation, administration, and education in the field of health. The National Health Survey, now being taken, is the first since 1936 and should permit more insight into the problems we face. Studies in the costs of medi-

cal care of various kinds which are being used by the aged are also going on.

In a sense, none of these is a political activity at all. In another, they are the very stuff out of which protagonists of the aged can construct the weapons to be used in the battle to secure adequate medical care for the aged.

EDUCATION

Like medicine, education is pretty effectively under the control of those who serve it professionally. There is a great number of school-board members, school superintendents, school suppliers, college teachers, and university administrators who have a vital interest in maintaining their control over the schools. They are aided and abetted by well-organized associations which have spokesmen well placed to further their objectives in all the agencies of communication including not only the press, radio, and television but very effectively, also, in the schools and the parent-teacher organizations. These means are used to protect their interests and promote the values which they feel should be promulgated.

Most of them are oriented exclusively toward education for children and youth. They are extremely wary of the grant-in-aid device by which control over some other activities of local government has been shifted, at least in part, to Washington. The result is that adult education for the aged, carried on by public support, is in many, perhaps most, communities somewhat neglected.

The Adult Education Section of the Office of Education is confined almost completely to carrying on research and reporting on the activities which are only slowly being developed.

Until the aged come to exert much greater influence in local politics than they presently have, they will have to look for help to the emergence of a separate institution designed, perhaps, to combine education with some other functions like recreation and vocational rehabilitation. Those in control of most school systems, while not themselves willing or able to provide effective education for the aged, will undoubtedly oppose the creation of any competitor in the education field, Washington to the contrary notwithstanding.

HOUSING

The area of housing for the aged is one which, perhaps, holds more promise for rapid development. Those who build and rent houses have fewer vested interests to protect and are in a position where they can more often immediately profit from activities beneficial to the aged than are those who control public education. Some evidence of progress is found in the fact that the Housing and Home Finance Agency succeeded in getting into the Housing Act of 1956 provisions which would facilitate the purchasing of housing by older persons, the financing of rental housing for them, and the more ready availability of public low-rent housing. The FHA made it easier for old people to trade in houses less well suited to their years and to purchase something better suited. It, also, permits friends or relatives to make the down payment for them—something the younger applicant is not supposed to do. Admission of the aged to low-rent housing has often been resisted by managers. They are fearful of the financial effects on the project of putting a great deal of space at the disposal of those who can pay very little rent. They are also concerned because the intermingling of the numerous children frequently found in low-rent areas with too many old people, without the proportionate presence of young and middle-aged adults, sometimes produces special problems. However, under the new amendments, local authorities can be assisted in providing additional space or remodeling larger units to suit the needs of the elders. As a consequence of this and of local pressures, there has been a growing concentration of elders in low-rent housing.

Aids for private non-profit rental hous-ing in the form of mortgage insurance are also provided. The Division of Plans and Programs in the Office of the Administrator of the Housing and Home Finance Agency conducts research to permit evaluation of housing efforts and guides the framing of new legislative proposals. The Advisory Committee on Housing for the Elderly is expected to review and support such of the proposed legislation as it thinks desirable. The many field offices of the FHA also provide pipe lines through which communication with the local agencies can be fed. These matters are discussed at greater length in chapter xvi.

SMALL BUSINESS

In an earlier day many of the aged could look to the management or ownership of a small business as a means to their security. In the battle between business giants, which is going on today, little businessmen are likely to get tramped on. The Small Business Administration was set up to help small businessmen generally. It has given a passing nod to older people, but the tools with which it is equipped seem somewhat inadequate to serve effectively its purported purpose. It offers counsel for those who seek to establish small businesses in which they can use special skills or who can carry on even with some handicaps. It operates through regional and branch offices in all the major cities. It also offers loans to those who seem to show promise of being able to pay off their indebtedness in a period not to exceed 10 years. One of its newer activities is that of financing to permit the establishment of private nursing homes for the aged.

DEPARTMENT OF COMMERCE

Through its Business and Defense Services Administration this department also provides means by which some of the aged may obtain self-employment. The aid given consists largely of advice on how to conduct a very small business with limited capital, but there is also information on the way to carry out managerial, clerical, and professional activities connected with such projects as mail-order selling. It is hard to imagine, however, that the Department of Commerce, which deals with the dominant economic institutions of our society, can be too concerned with such small fry. The Bureau of the Census is giving increased attention to tabulations concerned with the older population. It will also carry on demographic studies necessary to intelligent planning or provide other aid within its purview.

AGRICULTURE

Another of the old standbys upon which the aged could depend was agriculture. Many of the practices promoted by the Department of Agriculture in its efforts to make farming more productive and profitable are exactly those which made the aged farmer, particularly the tenant or hand, more insecure; but the Department of Agriculture has, also, provided some other services of which the aged may avail themselves. Among these is the distribution of surplus commodities to the indigent. Research on nutrition of the aged and on housing design and home facilities is, also, being carried on in the experiment stations of the land-grant colleges. Here, also, is a co-operative extension service which carries on a very effective educational program, most of which deals with problems faced by the able-bodied farmer or his wife, but some of which may contribute to the declining years of the aged. Research into the provisions which farm people have made for their own retirement has shown how completely inadequate these have been and has provided part of the ammunition by which the battle to bracket many farmers into OASDI was won.

THE TREASURY

The Department of the Treasury considers that its greatest contribution to the aged has been its continuing fight to prevent inflation from robbing them. But it has also extended aid in the form of tax benefits. The aged are allowed double exemption so that a married couple both of whom are over 65 years may get as much as $2675 without paying any tax. Both Social Security and Railroad Retirement pensions are exempt from tax. However, recipients of other forms of pension get credit for only 20 per cent of their pensions up to only $240 per individual. The Treasury also makes concessions to encourage employers to develop non-discriminatory pension plans by making tax concessions to them. The aged over 65 years may deduct all their medical expenses. They, like other age groups, benefit from the exemption on the first $5000 of benefits paid by an employer because of the death of his employee and from the exemption on $100 a week of sick-leave pay.

VETERANS

The veterans of World War I are all over 50 years of age, and many of them are over 65. This class of clients of the Veterans Administration represent a considerable fraction of the aged. The second great group, the survivors of World War II, are approaching the age in which their interest in the problems of aging will become more and more intense. Thus the Veteran's Benefit Act of 1957 covers compensation and pensions, hospital, domiciliary and medical care, burial, and also other benefits not generally applicable to earlier war veterans. Monetary payments, other than retirement pay, for service-connected disability are designated as *compensation* and not as *pension*. The veterans of Indian wars and the Spanish-American War do get pensions. The veterans of more recent wars must show disability to qualify for a pension, but, since after age 65, any disability qualifies one for a pension, the list is growing. It is quite probable that the fact that the members of the armed services were blanketed into Social Security made the move to give all veterans pensions no longer a political must. In place of the kind of help given to the earlier veteran, the present program emphasizes the maintenance of his health and his rehabilitation if he has lost it. It also makes possible direct grants to care for his dependents rather than reliance upon him to take care of them out of a grant made to him personally.

RAILROAD RETIREMENT

Because the railroads operate in interstate commerce, it was necessary to set up a program for them which was not dependent upon state participation. The Railroad Retirement Act extends about the same kind of protection to the railroad worker as is provided for others. In addition to their retirement allowance, however, the railroad pensioners may normally draw old age benefits under the Social Security Act without reduction in their annuities. Changes have kept the Railroad Retirement Act in line with Social Security.

CIVIL SERVICE

The Civil Service Retirement System covers federal employees. It has been revamped, as recently as 1958, to make it extend the kind of protection to the retiring civil servant which he would be likely to have in private employment of the same kind. Civil servants are fairly well organized for some purposes, but they do not have the strike weapon to fall back upon. They have, also, had the handicap that many of them live in Washington, where they have no vote. The gains they have made have, therefore, resulted as much from the concern of the agencies in which they work of the effect which retirement policies will have in their recruiting and retention as anything which the worker, particularly the aging worker, could do on his own behalf.

In this discussion of the new functions which government has undertaken for the aged, we have dealt with the work of various departments and offices. Some of these were outside the Department of Health, Education, and Welfare; some were the work of divisions of that department. These included the Public Health Service, the Office of Vocational Rehabilitation, the Office of Education, and the Food and Drug Administration. The remaining divisions are the Social Security Administration and the Special Staff on Aging, which is in the Secretary's Office. It is the Social Security Administration which handles the two largest programs: Old-Age, Survivors, and Disability Insurance and Old Age Assistance.

C. The Social Security Administration

We left consideration of the work of the Social Security Administration until now because in it the interrelation between national and state government is most involved. So, as we consider the governmental structure serving the aged at the national level and shift to the observation of that at the state level, this particular organization gives us a convenient point of transition. The origin of Social Security and some of its economic effects are considered in some detail earlier in the *Handbook*. So we will give only so much of its history as is required to show the politics involved in its evolution (Cohen, 1950, 1957; Myers, 1957).

THE SOCIAL SECURITY PROGRAM

Insofar as it relates directly to the aged as such, the Social Security program consists of two main parts. The first, Old Age Assistance, is primarily a state program which the national government influences through the fact that it controls the conditions under which matching funds are provided to the states. The second, Old-Age, Survivors, and Disability Insurance, is a program in which the individual deals directly with the national government. It is financed by a special tax levied on him and his employer. Under OAA, qualification to receive aid is determined by state agencies or a unit of local governments through which the state operates (limited, of course, by the requirements that the state must comply with standards approved by the national government). On the other hand, qualification for OASDI is determined by agents of the national government. These and other differences in the programs have major effects on the politics of the aged and should be kept in mind. We will deal with the two programs separately, looking first at OASDI.

OLD-AGE, SURVIVORS, AND DISABILITY INSURANCE

History of the program.—The aims of those who planned this part of the act were relatively simple. These were to pay old age benefits to a worker when he retired at or after age 65 and cash refunds to his survivors and to living workers who had at the time they reached the age 65 not yet worked long enough to qualify for the minimum monthly payments set up in the act. It did not attempt to provide disability payments or payments to dependents. It weighed the scales heavily in favor of those whose service was of short duration. This reflected the spirit of the moment in which the immediate demands of the aged and those nearing retirement constituted a very strong element of the forces then prevailing. The program showed other evidence of the politics at work. Immediate payments of only 1 per cent by the worker and an equal amount by the employer were called for, while future workers and employers were contributing increasingly more. Contributions were first collected in 1937, and the first benefit payments were to be made in 1942.

The program was substantially changed before it got into actual effective operation. In 1939 monthly payments were made payable in 1940. They were to go not only to the retired worker but also to the dependents of the retired worker and the survivors of deceased workers (whether or not the worker had retired before his death). Except for widowed mothers and children under 18 years, both dependents and survivors had to have attained the age

65 to be eligible for benefits. The method of computing benefits was altered, still favoring the short-time contributor, and the "money-back" feature of the first law was eliminated. The proposed increase in tax rate for 1940 was eliminated, though it was clear that the new proposals increased the liability of the trust funds from which benefits were to be paid. The continuing history of the act shows the results of similar influences at work (see chap. viii for a detailed account).

To summarize these trends, it is apparent that the benefit formula has continually changed in the direction of assuring a higher minimum but with no commensurate increase in the maximum. The minimum benefit has tripled in 20 years, but the maximum has gone up by only 28 per cent. Similarly, there is more concern for family security than for the individual well-being of the insured (Myers, 1955). Where the market in which these workers had been employed emphasized payment for "productivity," the state now emphasizes social responsibility of the household head.

Politics of the program.—The history of the program is revealing in other respects. Though there were two lines along which development could take place, it is the national, not the state, program which has become the mainstay. Undoubtedly, this stems, in part, from the fact that there are more Americans who are willing to accept the insurance principle as a device to share risks and pool resources than are willing to accept what they call "socialism" or the idea that payment should be made on the basis of need, divorced from previous contributions made by the recipient. Of, perhaps, equal importance, however, is the way the systems are financed. A party leader or a congressman knows that, when he expands OASDI, he can depend on the trust funds to absorb the initial costs it imposes. When a whole new category of people are blanketed in, there is an immediate new demand for annuities and other forms of aid from people who have so far contributed little to the system. Through tapping the trust fund, their needs can be cared for without having to arouse a new group of taxpayers or fight to transfer funds previously going to another function. The new taxes will be small, and frequently they will be borne by many of the very people who have been pressuring to get the new service. They often can be depended upon to "sell" the program to their neighbors.

This is in extreme contrast with the OAA system. There the claimants are exactly those people who will *not* be directly taxed to provide the service. When a new category is provided for in the law, there is a great surge of new recipients which results from the backlog of potential claimants built up while they were ineligible. In most cases it will require new staff and new facilities to handle them. So, the party leader, the congressman, the state legislator, and sometimes even the county commissioner will face the necessity of either raising taxes or cutting the amount going to some groups already being served. It is easy to see why under these conditions they have chosen OASDI as the universal coverage.

The fact that annuitants under OASDI get their grants as a matter of right and are not required to pass a "means test" as are those under OAA makes it, also, a better vehicle through which to provide the money for preventive medical care and similar supporting services to the healthy, retired aged. As we said before, OASDI deals directly with the citizen. There are very few functions of the national government which are performed this way (the income tax and the selective service are others). In these areas the country is treated as one, not fifty units, and the whole federal system is bypassed.

Effect on state and local politics.—This has very great significance for the political parties. Until the defense and welfare activities of the national government were so greatly enlarged, the average citizen came into contact with its influence only through the states and local government. Control over the county courthouse and state legislature thus assured a party of control over most of the personnel and the funds used in government activities. So long as a party controlled here, it was in a position to keep its pledges to those who voted for it or at least enough of them to stay in office. So, the party in one county could take one position, and in another a different position, and be triumphant in each. It was the same in the states. Democrats in the urban industrial North were New Dealers; Old South Democrats were likely, in action, to be violent opponents of much New Deal type legislation. Yet both sets of Democrats were re-elected.

In the past, politicians in the urban states were likely, then, to try to get *state* governments to undertake welfare legislation for their own constituents who often had needs quite other than those in the rural states and counties. It was thus possible to note a growth of experimental state welfare legislation as a forerunner to national legislation. Now, as we have just seen, the fact that a national program for the aged exists and that it can be made, at least initially, to subsidize the rural aged puts great pressure on the party to join in extending the national system. So the "creeping socialism" of which the Republicans complained before the election of 1952 became what might be termed "galloping socialism," as the rural supporters of the Republican party, the self-employed, and others not covered by the New Dealers made their post-election demands. Thus it transpired that the Republican party was responsible for making OASDI coverage practically universal. Today, it is not necessary to control a particular state in order to put OASDI into operation. there. Initial action to expand its coverage may come at the national level. The role of the state as experimenter and demonstrator is no longer a must. No state in the past has ever provided anything like the coverage which OASDI now extends to practically all the American people.

Thus a congressman may come from a state under control of conservative people who are opposed to the "welfare state," but his constituents are at least potentially and under OASDI factually participants in national programs. He must face the fact that his position on legislation, as it relates to the aged, may become a matter of primary concern to many of his constituents who will be its direct beneficiaries. Now, for example, a candidate whose campaign funds were assured by Chamber of Commerce clearance may find that, because of the characteristic position of the Chamber on welfare legislation, he loses more by securing that clearance than he gains.

Similarly, the hold of political machines on local government was endangered. In the past, that control was often given to one faction of a party, say, for example, the farmers, in return for their support in naming state and national candidates proposed by the other faction. The result might be, and often was, that a party supported a policy at the state or national level though it was elected by support of counties which were dominated by a faction unsympathetic with that policy.

Thus national or state programs which required implementation at the local level could successfully be blocked there by refusal to appropriate funds or provide personnel or by placing in control of their administration people who were in principle opposed to the very service they were expected to administer. Today, it is not so easy to do these things, insofar as they relate to programs administered directly from Washington. OASDI operates through a field staff which is subject to appointment and control of the National Civil Service. It is not so responsive to local politics as a locally appointed staff. Welfare directors, even those who hold their posts under state civil service laws and therefore may not be dismissed without cause, must still look to local politicians for salary increases and promotions and most particularly for appropriations to

make their program a success. So, they respond to the politicians' suggestions.

On the other hand, it is now fairly generally known that OASDI operates on the same standards throughout the country. So, if a recipient in one county gets treated worse than his neighbor in another, angry voices are apt to be heard in the courthouse, and the telephone of the party committeeman, the congressman, and even the senator is likely to ring.

FORMS OF POLITICAL INFLUENCE ON SOCIAL SECURITY PROGRAMS

We should not assume that any kind of governmental structure could be made immune to politics. But some setups are designed to facilitate and some to frustrate political manipulation. Perhaps, it would be more accurate to say that some kinds of structures are designed to respond to politics only at the top, while others permit it to enter into decisions made at any level. OASDI reflects past politics at the national level which has had the effect of modifying governmental functions for the aged anywhere in the United States. It does not readily reflect the influence of purely local politics. In this respect it is, of course, quite different from OAA.

The bulk of the work of OASDI consists of handling the personal accounts of all those enlisted in its rolls and of disposing of the trust fund which results from the fact that current taxes are designed to create reserves for the future. The detailed description of the way the tremendous job of handling these individual accounts is done would be fascinating but would produce no new insights into the politics at work (U.S. Congress, 1956*a*).

It is the feedback from those who deal with OASDI and OAA in the field which is of greatest influence in modifying the future programs. As coverage under OASDI has increased, the number on the rolls of OAA has been reduced. Some of the politicians had expected that this would result in a decline in the appropriations which would be asked for OAA. But they reckoned not with the facts of life, for all those who know the problems of the aged are convinced that, beyond the provisions for income maintenance, the aged have many needs which are not met by OASDI. They hope and plan that, as OASDI takes over almost completely the function of supplying the minimum income for old age welfare, OAA not only will be expanded to provide income maintenance for those ineligible for OASDI but also will meet service needs for all the aged. OAA will, thus, not wither away but become the base for an expanding permanent program.

OLD AGE ASSISTANCE

In the Social Security Act of 1935, however, it *was* presumed that OAA would be only a stop-gap program. This second part of the Act, as we divided it here, is concerned with the whole field of public assistance. Appropriations were made available from the national government to those states which were willing to set up programs which it approved. Assistance was to be offered not only to the dependent aged but also to dependent children and the blind and for rehabilitation of the handicapped. To this there was later added a program for the disabled. All the states have adopted acceptable programs, but they differ so much that none could serve as being representative. The Bureau of Public Assistance supervises the administration of all of them.

Thus, at the top, there is a mingling of the claims of various groups interested in different types of clients, some of whom at times evidence the fact that they deem less worthy of assistance any other type of dependent. The same holds true, also, at the local level where the welfare departments are faced with the specific job of giving aid to each type of client. The result is great variance in case loads, medical and service grants, or even basic budgets as they apply to different classes of clients.

Sometimes, as in Ohio, for example, the state itself operates OAA, but the other assistance programs are carried on by a variety of local agencies most of which are county-wide. Thus the case record of a person who thinks himself eligible for aid may be examined by the OAA office, but he will also have to be investigated by the welfare department or whatever local agency handles the other assistance programs. He might simultaneously be entitled to general relief, and in many counties the cities operate relief offices which are independent of those run by the county in which they are located. Sometimes clients shop around to see where they will get the most, although, theoretically, any of the agencies should be able to say that there is a particular program in which, and only in which, the client is legitimately entitled to share. The examination of other state programs shows similar anomalies though, perhaps, Ohio is the horrible example of what administration should not be (Ohio Legislative Service Commission, 1957).

In contrast, then, with the BOASDI, which has its whole staff under its control, the Bureau of Public Assistance must persuade many different units of government to move as far and as fast in the direction of the national objectives as they can. In so doing, they can expect to encounter all kinds of politics and a multiplicity of problems which grow out of the fact that the structure through which they operate serves not only Old Age Assistance but any number of other state and local government functions.

In the effort to achieve what has been laid down at top levels, the Bureau of Public Assistance provides technical help to encourage adequate standards of assistance which will provide nutrition, living arrangements, transportation, and medical care for the beneficiary. Also, more recently, it is extending aid in the form of both funds and technical assistance to expand social services and casework to help the individual achieve a more wholesome social life,

To determine for itself what the needs of the aged are and how they may be met, the bureau is constantly in touch with other associations concerned with the welfare of the aged. Through them it is possible to discover many things about the operations of its own programs which might not come up through the channels provided by formal organization.

MEDICAL ASSISTANCE

In the original act the emphasis was upon income maintenance. But its framers were sympathetic to the idea that medical care should also be provided for those whose resources were inadequate to secure it for themselves. They provided that, if medical care could be given a client within the limits set by the national government on the size grant it was willing to match, they would permit inclusion of charges for medical care. But no special grant for medical care beyond that limit was to be matched by the national government. The result was, of course, that there was little or no increase in available medical care for the aged, as compared with other services for them.

In some states the county or other local unit was obligated to provide funds for the medical care of the aged; in others the state took over. In still others, as in Ohio, the state finally agreed to pay up to $200 a year for the medical care of any client on OAA. The county welfare department, or whatever unit was locally responsible for the assistance programs, was then expected to supply the rest. In consequence, these agencies sometimes found that they were required to pay out large sums for the benefit of clients of another agency over which they had no control. So they might find the clients of OAA spending most of the funds available for the medical care of all those receiving public assistance. Or, for example, there might be only very limited funds to pay medical bills for children on ADC. This was even worse, of course, before the state of Ohio agreed to pay the $200 maximum.

The result was to produce difficulties not only between OAA and other programs but more particularly between the assistance programs and the doctors and hospitals. They were loathe to accept a patient who might require prolonged care but for whom they could make only a limited charge with assurance that it would be paid. As a result of situations like this, the 1956 amendments to the Social Security Act permitted the national government to match state funds dollar for dollar up to a total of $6.00 per month per adult client in the form of vendor payments. (In Ohio the state will still pay for only 10 days' hospitalization for a client; if he gets more, it is at county expense.) As a result of these new funds, most states are able to supply some medical care, though few would say that it is completely adequate for the needs of the aged or those of any other class of recipients.

Even the opportunity to obtain medical care, which federal funds might make available to the client, is limited by the willingness of the state government to match funds. In this case, as in many others, there is some confusion involved in using the word "state." In fact, some states turn the decision over to a local unit because the state as such puts up nothing. Where the assistance program is financed from taxes collected by the state and distributed back to the local community, the grants constitute funds added to those taken from the local tax base. Ohio and California, and a number of other states, depend upon income from sources other than those levied on property, such as income, excise, franchises, and sales taxes. But where the state gets its revenue from the same source that the local governments do, the assistance programs begin to compete for funds with each other and with the schools, parks, roads, and hospitals. It is easy to see why they are in these states at a disadvantage.

But even where the state puts up all or almost all the money for Old Age Assistance (apart from that furnished by the national government), it may find it difficult to persuade the local assistance administrator to meet state and federal standards (Bond *et al.*, 1954; Ohio Legislative Service Commission, 1957).

Despite the difficulties which this widely dispersed set of authorities creates, top-level planning does go on. The Bureau of Public Assistance holds discussions with the national representatives of professional organizations, representing medicine, dentistry, pharmacy, hospitals, the Christian Science church, nursing, social workers, public welfare administrators, and other interested parties to work out plans which they then can propose to the various states and support before the interested committees of Congress. The combined results of this planning and the provision of funds have had some effects on the medical care provided for the aged, but, as yet, they are spotty. It is true that the system still works, on occasion, to penalize the local government which tries to give adequate medical care by forcing that unit to pay for all this above the $6.00 matching money out of local funds. Moreover, if the county operates a hospital or other institution, it must carry many clients of the assistance programs which in the absence of those facilities it would not have to pay for.

INSTITUTIONAL STANDARDS

The national government has set standards for institutional care both in health and in welfare. The 1952 amendments to the Social Security Act extended the types covered by the state standard setting authorities. Since they are able to accept or reject institutions as being eligible to receive federal matching funds, the national authorities exercise a great deal of authority. They have been able to insist upon the payment of rates which it would have been impossible for any local government to agree to voluntarily. The result of these higher rates, however, has been a great increase in the institutional care available. But there has been some resentment due to the fact that sometimes the only facilities available or likely to be made available in some backwoods community are not eligible for matching funds.

CASEWORK SERVICES

For a long time private social work agencies have prided themselves on the superior counseling and guidance they were able to offer as compared with the public assistance programs. In the 1956 amendments a means to raise the level of these services was created. Now, the national government will share in the paying for staff services beyond the financial aid the clients need. The result has been the appearance of an increased emphasis on services at state level. Here, again, an advisory committee was established to aid in evaluating what is being done to create a code to guide the caseworker performing social services in public assistance agencies. The states have, also, been encouraged to aid in the development of qualified personnel through extending scholarships to trainees in the assistance programs.

RESEARCH ON WELFARE PROGRAMS
FOR THE AGED

Through research conducted by the Office of the Commissioner, special studies assess the effectiveness of all programs that contribute to the welfare of the aged. The results are made available to states to help them meet the needs of their own constituents. Even the results of the experiences of foreign governments come under review. The BOASDI is also engaged in continuous research in relation to its own program (U.S. Bureau of Public Assistance, 1957). The balance between the number of recipients of OAA and of OASDI has slowly been moving to the point where now more than three times as many get OASDI as OAA benefits. The number of orphans cared for by OASDI is more than six times as great as those under Aid to Dependent Children. Very few, if any, states are left in which there are more OAA recipients per thousand of population than those under OASDI. The last states to make the shift are the states in which agriculture is the predominant way of life. This is due to the fact that until 1956 most farmers could not qualify for OASDI. Now that they can, there is evidence that many, if not most, of them will do so rather than rely upon their own resources, to be supplemented if necessary by OAA.

However, there is a very large number of those who qualify under OASDI whose grants are quite small. Some of them were only recently blanketed in and get the minimum. Others had most of their work experience before inflation reduced the value of the dollar, so their annuities are insufficient to cover a minimal budget. Still others have special needs which cannot be covered by OASDI. All these become eligible for supplementation under OAA. The estimate of these needs is made by the assistance program agency at the local level. In consequence, there is a great variation among states as to the numbers who simultaneously receive OASDI and OAA. In 1957, for example, less than nine-tenths of 1 per cent of recipients got both grants in Virginia, while in Louisiana two out of five did so (Ossman, 1957).

IV. The Group Basis of the Politics of Aging

Observation of the structure of OASDI and OAA gives evidence of what has been going on. We have developed support for a set of national minimums which are guaranteed by OASDI. These are far above what most political scientists would have thought possible only a few years ago. But, beyond the minimums nationally provided, there are other needs to be provided for.

The activities of OAA show how variable are the influences which affect assistance programs among the various states. Religious differences, racial differences, differences in the age distribution of the populace, differences in national origins of the majority of the population and those of the minorities—all affect the kind of aid

the aged get. The differences which have arisen from the impact of changing technological and ecological facts have also had their impact on the values of the people (Hitt, 1954).

A. Values and Social Structure

The life led by the aged themselves and the results of the help they are currently getting also provide a set of factors affecting the choices which people will make. Other facts which modify that choice include the alternatives among which it is possible for them to choose. If government is prepared to offer the aged certain kinds of service and security in return for a comparatively small sacrifice on the part of the citizen, he is much more likely to choose that alternative than he would be were he required to make a very much larger one. So, for example, he will permit the tax collector to take a small amount from him over a long period of time, yet he would not attempt to save enough to buy privately a retirement income and disability and dependents insurance policy equal in value to that which the government provides through OASDI. He is apparently quite willing to see reserves, built up by those who have been paying into them for a long time, used in part to give grants to people who have just been blanketed into the program, so long as he is sure that, when the time comes for him to get *his* grant, he will get it even if it has to come out of taxes then being paid by others.

The taxes he pays come out of his earnings before they are made available to him or more particularly to those who have claims on him, such as his wife, parents, or children. He does not have to choose between things which they want now and things he believes necessary for his use in the years after his retirement. Since he does not get the money, others cannot take it from him. So his own value system is involved quite differently after the creation of the Social Security system than it was when that system did not exist. Perhaps, we can say that, subjectively speaking, his values are the same, but, in terms of the choices which he now makes, the value system will be judged by others as being different.

In one sense, then, existing governmental structure for service to the aged *represents* the current values of the people—values differing in many respects from those of their forebears. In another, it may be said both to have influenced or created that new set of values by changing the alternatives available to the chooser. In either case the behavior of people has changed. Given the alternative of destroying the structure and returning to traditional ways of providing for old age or expanding that structure to make it more universally available for all to choose, the people have unhesitatingly chosen to maintain and enlarge government structure and functions.

We saw earlier (chap. iv) how the destruction of family and church function left the aged without institutional means to serve themselves or effectively to be served by others. We indicated some of the events which led to the creation of governmental structure and reviewed very briefly what is being done through that structure. We need, perhaps, to examine the ways values and social structure outside government have been involved in the politics which produced governmental change.

We cannot deal here with the galaxy of influences which produce the value hierarchy which characterizes Americans. Elsewhere in this work there is evidence showing some values upon which those who seek to help the aged must depend. So, for example, we have been shown that the religions of the country are responsible for creating in each new generation attitudes of respect, honor, and love for the elders. So, too, with the family, for, stripped of its power as it has been, it is still able to instil in the young a basic respect and love for older people. It may, and probably will, be true that they will later have to subordinate these values to others which

are thrust upon them by their adult roles. But the sentiments are there to be strengthened and implemented.

B. Groups and Structure

As the conditions of the aged become more widespread and their needs better known, groups are formed to do something to service those needs. They rely upon the fact that most of us will respond to their appeal if some organization exists through which we can at once quiet our consciences and meet the day-to-day demands which other groups and activities make upon us. Today these groups are multiplying at a rapid rate (U.S. Congress, 1956b, 1956c). As we indicated earlier, these organizations, before the passage of the Social Security Act, struggled to find a way adequately to finance the dependent aged. As the government stepped in to provide at least a minimum income, they have begun to stress other needs in the fields of health, education, recreation, and housing.

At the outset these voluntary organizations have often set out to provide directly, in their local communities, the needed services. In other cases, as discussed in the following chapter, they originate as pressure groups seeking to induce the government to provide them. Often the two forms of activity merge. A new type of service is projected and developed until it has demonstrated its worth to the aged and to the community. Sometimes it is then endowed or given funds from the Community Chest or United Appeal. Often it develops a coterie interested in its own survival, who continue to maintain it without outside help. If the service proves to be worthwhile, but its means prove inadequate to its expansion, it may be the starting point for a new government agency. When and if government does take over its function, the old agency may evolve in new directions. Very often, though, the supporters turn their attention elsewhere, and the newly created government structure is left for the professionals to operate it.

It is not always possible to predict which of these many groups will produce a government supported function. The American community is crisscrossed with organizations serving the aged, many of which represent rather exotic growths. Many, as they expand, come into direct competition with each other for government support. Others can get only private funds because they provide services which the public generally does not regard as being necessary or worth support but which some private citizens feel to have a legitimate claim to existence. Examination of the programs for the aged in the larger metropolitan areas demonstrates what we mean (Welfare Council of Metropolitan Chicago, 1952; Welfare and Health Council, New York City, 1955). Yet there is a fairly consistent development from community to community and from state to state. Local governments to which the task of carrying on some of the new functions was given initially often prove to be inadequate, particularly as a source of funds. The groups interested then form committees or associations in which they join to share their common experiences and devise effective ways to carry on. They often make recommendations to the state legislature or Congress or both. It is out of these recommendations that the new legislation is fashioned. What is equally important but often neglected is the fact that it is also out of the groups which made the proposals that the political influence necessary to get their aspirations turned into legislation must come (New York State Joint Legislative Committee on Problems of the Aging, 1951; Bond *et al.*, 1954). It is only occasionally, as in the early days in California, that a politician has been able to capitalize directly on the unrest among the aged by setting up an organization confined to the single interest of aging and trying to use the votes of the aged as counters. Usually, as finally happened in California, the method has backfired. Most of the benefits received by the aged came from the efforts of other groups interested in their welfare (Holtzman, 1954).

C. Post–World War II Developments

THE GROWTH OF STATE COMMISSIONS

The effort to organize and channel this activity became widespread in the country after World War II. In 1945 Connecticut set up a Commission on the Care and Treatment of the Chronically Ill, Aged, and Infirm. This is an independent operating administrative agency which not only develops recommendations but also acquires and operates facilities and conducts grant-in-aid programs. On the other hand, to illustrate another technique, the 1947 session of the New York Legislature established the Joint Legislative Committee on the Problems of the Aging, which has done and continues to do outstanding work. It is a special study committee of the legislature which carries on research and makes recommendations not only to the legislature but also directly to the public through an information program designed to get its program adopted. Other states have set up committees and commissions of various sorts, some with the kind of continuing existence that the New York and Connecticut organizations have had; others, on a temporary basis (U.S. Congress, 1957).

The makeup of these committees is the important thing to note. They usually include prominent figures in the community and state whose stature adds prestige to the work of the committee but who are in many cases dependent upon the professional staff to select the facts upon which their judgment is based. Thus the expert judgment of the professional is joined with the political influence and power of his fellow committee member. This is not to assume that these "amateurs" are easily deluded stooges for the professional. Their critical judgment has often served to modify the overenthusiastic or otherwise unrealistic proposals which those unschooled in the art of the possible are likely to make. Many, too, because of their long acquaintance with the field, are able to provide long-range judgments which are needed. The committee members are usually named by astute politicians working to assure that figures who have been given public recognition for their work with the aged will not go unnamed. Every area in the state is carefully represented, as are the major religions, races, and other sectors of the population such as labor and business. So, even when the committee is officially dissolved, its influence goes on in the persons who composed it and, thus, gained an interest in seeing its recommendations adopted.

As the number of these committees increased, so, also, grew the desirability of bringing together the influence they could wield and of sharing their experience. The United States Federal Security Agency set up a working Committee on the Aging in May, 1948, and sponsored the first National Conference on Aging in August, 1950. The emphasis at this conference was on the responsibilities of the local community to serve the needs of the aged (U.S. Federal Security Agency, 1951). The conference discussed some of the results of the experience which both the clients and those serving them had had. Recommendations became more specific, and more definite proposals for changes in the organizations to be used were made. The lines leading to voluntary and local agencies, to the state legislatures, and those reaching toward Washington became more discernible. We cannot, here, go into a detailed account of what transpired; but this conference acted as a kind of catalyst which produced action in a number of states. By 1958 two-thirds of the states had produced special co-ordinating agencies to deal with the problem of the aged.

In July, 1954, the Governors' Conference called upon the Council of State Governments to study the problems of the aged and report its findings at the 1955 annual meeting of the Governors' Conference. The Council of State Governments (1956a) is a "joint governmental agency established by the States, supported by the States, for service to the States." The Council is composed of commissions or committees on interstate co-operation established in all fifty states as official entities of the state governments. The commissions work for co-operative governmental action on numerous fronts and are controlled by the states themselves. The policies of the Council are determined by a board of managers representing the fifty states, eighteen ex officio members, and ten members at large. It has an executive committee which supervises the work of its executive director and his permanent staff. It is, also, the secretariat for a number of other interstate groups, including the Governors' Conference. As such, it is in an extremely strategic position to influence state action.

In response to the request of the Governors' Conference, the staff of this Council of State Governments (1955) prepared a study of the activities going on in the various states which was published as a 176-page report entitled *The States and Their Older Citizens*. Included in the report was a "Bill of Objectives for Older People" and a "Program of Action in the Field of Aging," setting forth recommendations that grew out of the study.

This development, together with those taking place at the national level, induced President Eisenhower to create the Federal Council on Aging, whose work we have already discussed. One of its first actions was to join with the Council of State Governments in calling another federal-state conference on aging (U.S. Congress, 1956c).

THE SPECIAL STAFF ON AGING

Another important development was taking place at the national level. This was the creation of a Special Staff on Aging in the Office of the Secretary of the United States Department of Health, Education, and Welfare. This staff serves as the focal point at the national level for crystallizing activities which are going on in the various branches of the national government, in the states, and in foreign countries. Through liaison activities which it initiates, it is able to bring to the attention of the various authorities—and, perhaps more importantly, to citizen groups, universities, and scattered research agencies—developments taking place elsewhere. It also is able to suggest strategy, indicating priorities among proposed projects and the probability that success can be more certainly achieved by presentation to governments at the national, the state, or the local level, or through further grass-roots development among voluntary organizations.

To achieve this, the staff participates in the activities of organizations like the American Public Welfare Association, the National Committee on the Aging, the International Association of Gerontology, and philanthropic foundations, service organizations, and trade associations. It receives the literature they develop and distributes its findings among them. In this relationship the staff provides secretariat services to the Federal Council on Aging.

It also provides consultation and information to states, communities, and other agencies in the field which are dealing directly with the aged and aging and assists in planning and evaluating state and community programs.

It publishes a news bulletin, *Aging,* on the latest activities in the field. Together with the Federal Council on Aging, it was responsible for the creation of a Joint Federal–State Committee on Aging.

The strategic position of this staff makes it very significant for the study of both political influence and decision-making. Through the examination of the literature which it publishes, the student will be able to discern which of the many lines of possible development is likely to be pressed, the progress being made at the grass roots, some points of blockage, and the results of research which reveal new light on the needs of the aged and the possibilities of serving them more adequately (Federal Council on Aging, 1958; U.S. Department of Health, Education, and Welfare, 1958).

D. *Trends in the Politics of Aging*

The student of government, reviewing the evidence which the staff has aided in producing, will be interested in watching for new structures which are growing up to implement the many new activities now going on. Among these is the appearance at state level of permanent staffs and advisory committees or commissions to replace the temporary ones which were first used by some of the states. This development is characteristic of that taking place at a good many more points in our society. It represents the specialization of moral codes and of professional personnel which is required to make the codes effectively operative. Like its forerunners in industry and the professions, it is likely to provide increasingly rigid channels through which influence, if it is to be effective, must be directed. As spokesmen for the communities and the functional groups which they represent on the special subject of aging, these committees will become a kind of public conscience. But it will not represent a "general will," a kind of widespread groping, sporadic, and unchanneled impulse. Rather it will provide a limited specific set of proposals for action. The multiplicity of groups, each rather ineffectively reflecting what specific individuals and small groups seek, will be replaced by a few groups or associations of groups *acting* more effectively but less accurately *reflecting* what any single one of them would have attempted to achieve were it in a position to implement its own purposes exactly.

E. *Professional Groups in Democratic Theory*

As we have already indicated, it is hard to overestimate the significance of these developments for the theory of democratic government and of the relations between value and social action. The citizenry has only limited choices. These choices for the most part consist of selecting one or another of the alternatives which professionals offer. Thus there may be all kinds of sentiments or opinion widespread in the electorate which never have any influence whatsoever on what government agents do. While it is true that very little of what the professional bureaucrat does can be carried on without the "consent of the governed," it is also true that any time there may potentially be numerous courses of action, any one of which could gain this consent. So the bent given governmental action by one set of administrators rather than another is perhaps as crucial in determining what government does as is the existence of public opinion itself.

Nor does this influence stop with the administration of existing programs. It also affects the growth of knowledge, the technology which emerges out of it, and so the basis of new social structure.

Those who have it in their power to set up research have a lot to do with the knowledge we get. With that knowledge we may be able to solve problems hitherto regarded as being insoluble. It is then that those who will benefit from the use of the new knowledge and techniques take hope and seek the means to benefit from it. This thesis is too large to present effectively here, but perhaps with an illustration we can at least show its relevance.

Americans are proud of the great steps taken in the field of medicine. They are not always able to understand all the reasons for progress in this field and are likely to take at face value the rationalizations offered by the profession. It may be, however, that careful scrutiny of the relations between medicine as a science and applied medicine will show more accurately not only where medicine has come from but also where it is going.

The American Medical Association has been insistent in arguing that its traditional medical structure was the means through which the medical care most responsible for our progress was distributed to the people. American medicine is largely in the hands of the private practitioner. Teachers in the schools of medicine are for the most part engaged also in private practice and regard themselves as being engaged in preparing others to do so. The research problems in which they have been interested, then, are largely an outgrowth of those which they encounter in such prac-

tice. A great deal of research into the diseases of infants and children, middle-aged women, and others which are apt to be dealt with by a doctor whose patients are chiefly middle class and middle-aged has been done. Similarly, drug manufacturers were interested in the drugs which could be administered by private practitioners who constituted practically the only way (outside the hawking of "patent medicine") which drugs could reach the public.

When only a few old people could afford to pay the big medical bills the aged are likely to run up, it was difficult to get researchers to spend time and money developing what might very well be even more expensive means of treatment. When only a few could pay the practitioner's fee, it was difficult to get prospective doctors to specialize in geriatrics, particularly when the body of knowledge in medicine included so little that was effective about the diseases of old age. So the cycle was complete—little practice, little research—little research, few practitioners. Recently, however, there has been a great deal of research going on outside the old structure. The veterans' hospitals and the state mental hospitals slowly accumulated more and more senile persons. Through their own research activities and through government and foundation funds, research was carried on in these hospitals. The National Institutes of Health also began to undertake research which, as we have seen, included a great emphasis upon the diseases of the aging. The pharmaceutical manufacturer also got interested. If he could develop drugs to be used in these hospitals, he had a ready-built market for them *in* these hospitals. A market, not particularly influenced by the ability of the patient to pay, but in a position to tap the public treasury for whatever money was needed, provided only that the drugs were effective. The combined results were a number of breakthroughs which provided the means effectively to deal with what had hitherto been regarded as hopeless cases.

It would have indeed been surprising

that research of this kind, conducted under these auspices, should have proved that it is only through the activities of privately paid practitioners that successful medical research can or will be undertaken. It is equally unlikely that the new materials and methods should turn out to be only those which can be provided the patient through the private practitioner. It is still more unlikely that the public which paid for this research would be content to permit private practitioners to hold a monopoly on its distributions. Particularly will they be unwilling to pay a high fee to the private practitioner to distribute it to public assistance clients whose medical bills are paid through taxes. Outpatient clinics, the use of salaried medical staff, and many other types of distribution are very likely to grow up to meet the demands of groups organized in the interests of the aged for cheaper but more effective medical care (see Somers and Somers, 1958).

A considerable number of the senile will at some point need care in a mental hospital or through some other effective state agency. A great deal of preventive care for those who otherwise may become or remain disabled will have to be undertaken by the hospitals, clinics, or other agencies which cannot depend on the income of the disturbed person to finance them. Modern research has demonstrated not only that much mental disease is curable but also that many of the means traditionally used in both private and public hospitals contribute little to the patient's recovery. Instead, there have been developed a number of new means by which patients can be helped. A good many of them are social in character and relate very poorly to the traditional means of administering medicine. Some of the branches of the medical profession have recognized this and are actively attempting to develop public programs through which the new therapy can reach the greatest possible number of patients. If other and dominant branches refuse to acknowledge and utilize these aids, a new profession is likely to emerge and

provide them instead. In fact, a whole new range of means to provide professional services of various kinds which research has shown to be needed are likely to emerge.

Proposals that they be developed will most often be voiced by those in direct contact with the aged. These proposals will be channeled upward through interested groups and agencies to the points in government where decisions are made. There they will have to be evaluated together with those seeking to aid other types of people. They will, also, have to meet the opposition of those who wish to limit aid to the aged either in the amount of funds spent or in the kinds of aid extended and the means by which it is to be distributed. At the moment, organizations like the American Medical Association and its affiliated professional societies often have more authority and influence with the decision-makers than do the representatives of the aged. How long this will be true is problematical; but it can probably be judged better by studying the future growth and development of social organization for the care of the aged than by relying upon the record of the past.

If one wishes to see how much this organization for the aged has had to do with the actions of government, he will find it enlightening to study the reports and recommendations of the committees and conferences dealing with the condition of the aged and to compare them with subsequent legislation.

The Report to the Governors' Conference in August, 1955, by the Council of State Governments sets up a "Bill of Objectives for Older People" and a "Program for Action in the Field of Aging." Insofar as it relates to the federal government, this program reads almost like the recommendations which the departments made to Congress. The legislation subsequently passed, while it differed in some respects with those recommendations, shows clearly the mark of the administrator's proposals. At the state and local level there has been similar response. We have not had the opportunity to examine closely in any great number of states the degree to which legislation or proposals for legislation have conformed to the results of the national state conferences. But the recommendations of the state agencies are available (Council of State Governments, 1956*b*), and the serious student will find it valuable to compare them with what subsequently happened in his own state.

He may, thus, discover for himself the degree to which these conferences and the activities which lead up to them have become an important new kind of structure for carrying on democratic government. By studying trends in the development of new groups to serve the aged, the committees, commissions, and agencies which they sponsor and support, he may be able to predict fairly accurately what the "party bosses" will be proposing tomorrow as party platform planks and what next day the legislature will have to confront. He thus may understand better how party issues are created, to what sources the party can look for support, and something of the reasons why politicians so frequently straddle the issues.

The study of this group process, then, may yield more satisfactory results than the study of party politics, opinion surveys, voting analysis, or other means by which some political scientists and social psychologists have tried to predict trends.

F. Older People as a Direct Political Force

In the analysis which has been pursued thus far we have not made much use of sociopsychological categories. It is obvious that the aged may constitute one such category and that knowledge gained through classifying people by age might be of considerable use in predicting certain kinds of action. Thus for the student of recreation, for example, the relevance of psychosociological types is probably very great. Its usefulness for the political scientist who is interested in predicting political behavior in the United States of America is not sufficiently well established to have impressed either the student or, apparently, the practitioner of politics. But the neglect may prove to have been an error on the part of both.

A number of studies have shown that on certain types of issues the elders can be characterized as "conservative" to a greater degree than the members of the succeeding generation (Eysenck, 1955; Stouffer, 1955; Pressey and Kuhlen, 1957). In part, this clearly represents the retention of images which got their meaning in the early years of life and were simply carried over into a period in which culture had changed and a new generation was being given a different image, which they in turn would carry over. In part, the attitudes of the aged represent a response to the physiological processes involved in aging. Since these two types of attitudes would have to be modified or served differently by politics (if at all), we will discuss them separately.

We deal first, then, with political attitudes that derive from the social norms which were operative during the early learning period of the individual's life-history. These include, for example, the political affiliation of parents, which will continue to have an influence on the affiliation of the person throughout his life. But the politician takes note of the *current* affiliation of his constituents. He is concerned about the marginal voter who may be induced to switch parties, not about the origin of affiliation. He attempts to provide ways which will alter the voter's choice by taking an apparent position on issues, through making appointments and providing other spoils, and through argument directed primarily toward "key" issues. Since the proportion of older people among his constituents rarely alters much from one election to another, he either depends upon these tradition-bound votes himself or assumes that they will go to the opposition. It is that portion who may be influenced by the policy he pursues which gives him concern.

Another type of culturally conditioned older person adheres to some ideal type like "free enterprise," the "culture of the Old South," the "rugged individualism of the frontiersman," "Yankee civilization," etc. It is apparent from the instances given that these ideal types are very likely to be regionally based. Thus the conservative New Englander despises what the conservative southerner espouses, and vice versa. Clearly, there is no bloc of older voters who can be depended upon here.

In still another type the conservative voter is required to retain means which no longer secure the ends they once were adequate to serve or to attempt to secure traditional ends by means not hitherto thought to be justified. Older people are likely to be split wide apart by this dilemma. Where the culturally defined relationship between means and ends has been shattered, as has frequently resulted from the adoption of high-energy technology, the polarization of voters into conservative and liberal or radical groups has much more often centered about socioeconomic status than age. Certainly, older bankers were not backed by their older clients in their opposition to measures for the clients' protection like the Federal Deposit Insurance Corporation and the Truth in Securities Act. The Townsend Movement, primarily backed by older people who were presumably therefore "conservative," offered as part and parcel of its program one of the most radical economic changes ever proposed to the American people. The New Deal was openly espoused by one group of southern aged and equally openly villified by southern conservatives, including some of the aged.

As we have already indicated, American political processes *have* permitted the creation of new politico-economic institutions through which the aged have found it possible to achieve their primary goals. This, according to one student (Holtzman, 1954), has prevented the appearance of any continuously successful movement dependent upon the aged for primary support. Where a movement, such as the Townsend Movement, has offered much evidence that the existing political parties are not paying enough attention to the needs of a bloc, the result has been jockeying by the leaders of both parties, so that the bulk of the momentum of the movement has been lost. Even where the movement has continued, as in the Townsend case, its structure and functions have been so altered as to completely change the functions it performs (Messinger, 1955).

The other type of change in attitudes about which we might speak only briefly here has been covered elsewhere in considerable detail. That is, change in relation to physiological and psychological functions which directly accompany age. These changes result in new needs, such as adult education, housing, recreation, and medicine. The needs in turn are being met, as has been noted, in a number of institutional changes, some rapid, others extremely slow. The increase in the number of older people in some areas thus does give rise to new, persistent political forces. But, once the population has become stabilized, so that the proportion of the aged is relatively constant, the values associated with aging take their place selectively along with those of other age groups. Thus the politician again comes to deal with the needs of old people in competition with the needs of other age groups, one issue at a time, not as a representation of "all the needs of the aged" posed against "all the needs of children," or of youth, or of middle-aged persons.

So far, at least, the evidence does not suggest that the aged have become or are likely to become a category which in itself will yield high reliability as a predictor of values as they relate to many important political issues.[2] The literature is quite barren (Schmidhauser, 1958).

[2] See the study of the California Institute for Social Welfare (McLain Movement) by Pinner *et al.* (1959) for an analysis of the success and lack of success in mobilizing the aged in political campaigns.

It is perhaps true that new research techniques which permit the student to pry further into the mystery surrounding the way people actually voted in a secret election, as well as the factors which motivated them to do so, will demonstrate successfully that there is a trend toward a situation in which a man's position on political issues and personalities can be predicted more and more accurately through the study of aging. At the moment, however, the evidence for it is only suggestive.

So the politician who knows that the voter casts only one vote has to guess whether he won that vote by his position on some issue supposed to be favored by the aged or whether the oldster voted for him on religious, socioeconomic, racial, or some other grounds. On the other hand, the elected politician who is faced with a well-organized presentation in behalf of a specific piece of legislation knows fairly well where his organized support or opposition will be coming from, depending on his vote on that bill. The organizations who make these representations may not actually control the votes they claim to control. They may claim to speak for people who never heard of them or who would be quite unwilling to alter their support for a candidate or a party because of the stand taken by the politician on this issue. But he can hardly know whether or not this is true, and he is, therefore, likely to take the evidence at face value, particularly if the names of those connected with the movement are those of influential people.

Even the appointed administrator is involved in this kind of judgment, though he is likely to be better able than the legislator to judge the strength of a group (even though he may be equally unlikely to reveal it). He lives, moves, and has his being in the midst of influence generated out of his experience with the aged themselves and those interested in them. Growth in their numbers and the functions he is expected to provide for them means for him more clients, bigger staff, more money to handle. He may himself be a young man but his actions will be influenced far more by the way he thinks his clients will react to a new proposal or the modification of an old practice than the way he personally does.

Party platforms are built as a means to election. The glittering generalities which are held up for public gaze differ little from one party to the other. The behind-stage commitments are another matter. These commitments show increasing concern for the problems of the aged, regardless of the supposed difference in principle upon which the parties are supposed to be based. As we have indicated, it was under the leadership of the Republican party, long the foe of the "welfare state," that Social Security was made all but universal. Nor did this make the party unpopular in those very districts from which it was elected on its "anti-socialist" platform. Districts which had previously opposed old age security legislation, which did not then extend to them, produced numerous clients when the program permitted them to get OASDI. There is apparently no difference in principle between the parties, but only a difference as to who gets what.

G. Influence on the Judiciary

There has also been speculation that the increased numbers of the aged will show up in judicial behavior. Throughout our history most judges have been older men, as they are today. But the division in philosophy among judges, at least insofar as it is reflected in their judicial decisions, is not between old judges and young ones. Justice Holmes at 80 was more forward-looking than many a young judicial neophyte. But, even if there were a difference in philosophy according to age, it might not mean that the judiciary would become more conservative. For, as we have seen, the aged have not been important in opposing the revolution which extended the central government into the private lives of the citizen through OASDI. This was one of the most radical steps ever taken in American government, and, to the degree that they were heard at all as an age group, the aged were pushing *for* it, not opposing it. Government has assumed more new functions, spent more money, and more violently altered the federal system on behalf of the aged than in any other of its activities except, perhaps, defense. Much of what was done was done for the aged rather than by them, but there is little evidence that they tried to prevent it and a great deal which shows their approval.

H. And Tomorrow?

Research has already shown the nature of the needs which old people have, and demonstration of these needs goes on in every American community. Today there exists machinery to translate those needs into political action designed to meet them. This organization is likely to become more effective and powerful as time goes on. So trends in the politics of age tomorrow can best be discovered by studying, today, trends in the needs of the aged.

This is not to say that all those needs will be served. Nor does it show which will be served by various branches of government or those which will continue to be served only by voluntary organizations. For, as we have seen, the agencies of government must serve the insatiable demands of all age groups. Many of them also serve functions such as defense which are in competition or conflict with the agencies which serve age groups. Only one thing comes clear in the pull and haul of politics: not only are the aged today more numerous than ever before but they are also in possession of more influence and stand in more strategic places among the decision-makers than they have since the advent of high-energy technology.

REFERENCES

Bond, F. A., Baber, R. E., Vieg, J. A., Perry, L. B., Scaff, A. H., and Lee, L. J., Jr. 1954. Our needy aged: a California study of a national problem. New York: Henry Holt & Co.

Cohen, W. J. 1950. Social security and family stability. Ann. Am. Acad. Political & Social Sc., 272, 117–26.

———. 1957. Retirement policies under social security. Berkeley: University of California Press.

Cottrell, F. 1955. Energy and society: the relation between energy, social change and economic development. New York: McGraw-Hill Book Co.

Council of State Governments. 1955. The states and their older citizens. Chicago: The Council.

———. 1956a. The book of the states, 1956–1957, Vol. 2. Chicago: The Council.

———. 1956b. Recommended state action for the aging and aged. Chicago: The Council.

Eysenck, H. J. 1955. The psychology of politics. New York: Frederick A. Praeger, Inc.

Federal Council on Aging. 1958. Aiding older people. Washington, D.C.: The Council.

Hitt, H. L. 1954. The role of migration in population change among the aged. Am. Sociological Rev., 19, 194–200.

Holtzman, A. 1954. Analysis of old age politics in the United States. J. Gerontol., 9, 56–66.

Messinger, S. 1955. Organizational transformation: a case study of a declining social movement. Am. Sociological Rev., 20, 3–10.

Myers, R. J. 1955. Old-Age and Survivors Insurance: history of the benefit formula. Social Security Bull., 18 (May), 13–17.

———. 1957. Tennessee Valley Authority retirement plan; coordination with old-age, survivors, and disability insurance. *Ibid.*, 20 (September), 3–8.

New York State Joint Legislative Committee on Problems of the Aging. 1951. Birthdays don't count. Albany, N.Y.: The Committee.

Ohio Legislative Service Commission. 1957. Public welfare administration in Ohio. (Staff Research Rept. No. 25.) Columbus, Ohio: The Commission.

Ossman, Sue. 1957. Concurrent receipt of public assistance and Old-Age and Survivors Insurance. Social Security Bull., 20 (November), 3–10.

Pinner, F. A., Jacobs, P., and Seiznick, P. 1959. Old age and political behavior: a case study. Berkeley: University of California Press.

Pressey, S. L., and Kuhlen, R. G. 1957. Psychological development through the life span. New York: Harper & Bros.

Schmidhauser, J. R. 1958. The political behavior of the aged: some frontiers in research. Western Political Quart., 2, 113–24.

SOMERS, H. M., and SOMERS, ANNE R. 1958. Private health insurance. Part I. Changing patterns of medical care demand and supply in relation to health insurance. California Law Rev., **46**, 376–410.

STOUFFER, S. A. 1955. Communism, conformity, and civil liberties. New York: Doubleday & Co.

U.S. BUREAU OF PUBLIC ASSISTANCE. 1957. Characteristics of state public assistance plans under the Social Security Act. (Public Assistance Rept. No. 33.) Washington, D.C.: The Bureau.

U.S. CONGRESS. 1956a. SENATE COMMITTEE ON LABOR AND PUBLIC WELFARE. Communication from the Board of Trustees of the Old-Age and Survivors Insurance Trust Fund. *In* The operations of the federal Old-Age and Survivors Insurance Trust Fund. (U.S. Sen. Doc. No. 119 [84th Cong., 2d sess.].) Washington, D.C.: Government Printing Office.

————. 1956b. Federal-state conference on aging, June 5–7, 1956. *In* Studies of the aged and aging, Vol. **1**: Federal and state activities. Washington, D.C.: Government Printing Office.

————. 1956c. Report of the conference of state commissions on aging and federal agencies, Sept. 8–10, 1952. *In* Studies of the aged and aging, Vol. **1**: Federal and state activities. Washington, D.C.: Government Printing Office.

————. 1957. Studies of the aged and aging, Vol. **10**: Surveys of state and local projects. Washington, D.C.: Government Printing Office.

U.S. DEPARTMENT OF HEALTH, EDUCATION, AND WELFARE, SPECIAL STAFF ON AGING. 1958. Programs of the Department of Health, Education, and Welfare affecting older persons. Washington, D.C.: The Department.

U.S. FEDERAL SECURITY AGENCY. 1951. Man and his years: an account of the First National Conference on Aging. Raleigh, N.C.: Health Publications Institute.

WELFARE COUNCIL OF METROPOLITAN CHICAGO, COMMUNITY PROJECT FOR THE AGED. 1952. Community services for older people: the Chicago plan. Chicago: Wilcox & Follett.

WELFARE AND HEALTH COUNCIL OF NEW YORK CITY, RESEARCH DEPARTMENT. 1955. Fact book on the aged in New York City. New York: The Council.

XVIII

The Impact of Aging on Voluntary Associations

ARNOLD M. ROSE

I. The Nature of Voluntary and Professional Associations

A. Definition of Voluntary Association

A voluntary association develops when a small group of people, finding that they have a certain interest or purpose in common, agree to meet and to act together in order to try to satisfy that interest or achieve that purpose.[1] Frequently, their action requires that they urge other like-minded persons to join them, so that some associations may become very large and extend throughout the whole country. In the United States they have generally no formal contact with the government unless they incorporate, which obliges them to conform to certain trivial laws of state governments and unless, of course, they commit an offense against general criminal law, which is naturally extremely rare. Occasionally, a voluntary association will receive a grant from the government for a special public purpose, such as research.

B. Kinds of Voluntary Associations

Older people have three special kinds of relationships with voluntary associations, and these three categories will form the major lines of division for this paper. In the first place, older people are participants in most of the varied kinds of voluntary associations that are found throughout American life. Special attention will be given here only to those voluntary associations in which older people play a special role by virtue of their unusually large number among the membership or the special character of leadership or program which they impart to these associations. The second category of voluntary associations to be considered is distinguished from the first category in that they are organized by and for the benefit of older people —that is, their purpose is linked to the special characteristics, problems or needs, and interests of the aged in our society. The third category of voluntary associations to be taken up are those which also have as their major purpose some particular benefit for the aged, but they are distinguished from the second category in that the active people in these associations are not the aged themselves but younger people who have interests in helping the aged. In other words, the first category is distinguished from the other two in that the purposes of the voluntary associations included in this category are not particularly related to the needs or interests of the aged, while the third category is distinguished

[1] Voluntary associations are usually defined so that their purposes do not include profit-making for the members. But many voluntary associations do create economic benefits for their members— for example, the consumers' co-operatives or the mutual-aid societies that provide sickness or death benefits for members.

from the first two in that the aged are not participants in the activity of the associations but rather are to be designated as recipients or clients.

In the general study of voluntary associations a useful distinction has been made between those which can be called "expressive" groups and "social influence" groups (Rose, 1954). The former associations act only to express or satisfy the interests of their members in relation to themselves. These include the recreation and sport associations, the social and coffee clubs, the professional societies, etc., which may be especially numerous in modern American democracy but which are also found in large numbers in all literate and some preliterate societies. The social influence associations, on the other hand, are directed outward; they wish to achieve some condition or change in some special segment of society as a whole. Both of these types of purposes will be found in all three categories of associations that were mentioned in the preceding paragraph, although most of the second category consist of expressive associations, while most of the third category consist of social influence associations, as we shall see.

C. Why Considered "Voluntary"?

We may consider briefly the sense in which these associations are voluntary. Voluntary associations are presumably those into which an individual may freely choose to enter and from which he may freely choose to withdraw. But such a statement is a mere tautology: voluntary implies free choice. "Voluntariness" may be placed in a continuum, and thus "voluntary" and "involuntary" become polar terms in an ideal-typical dichotomy. There is no clear-cut, realistic line of division between the two. In this sense the term "voluntary" can be defined only in terms of "involuntary." The mentioned dichotomy implies a psychology: the assumption is that a man, a rational creature, in certain circumstances weighs the advantages and

disadvantages of joining a certain group or participating in a collective enterprise and, on the basis of the outcome of this deliberation, joins this group. Such a group would be a voluntary association. Conversely, an "involuntary" organization would be one which the individual is compelled to be a member of because of external pressures, such as heredity, physical force, or the social mores.

As a matter of fact, ignoring the metaphysical implications, there is seldom free will, even in the psychological sense considered above. Formal and informal means of social control, or social forces, in effect dictate that certain individuals are going to join certain "voluntary" associations. In those cases when the individual does reflect on the advisability of joining an association or participating in a certain sphere of activity, he may not be "free" in his choice because there are overwhelming advantages to the one choice or another which dictate his decision.

This discussion of the logical meaning of "voluntary" and "involuntary" is really not essential to an analysis of voluntary associations. The reason is that "voluntary" associations is a concept (however lacking in precise formulation it might be) in sociology, and in that universe of discourse it has a meaning which cannot be understood from its constituent words. Voluntary associations consist of all classes of functional groupings except families, the formal government (including its specialized organs, such as schools and armed forces), and economic enterprise, though some writers might dispute about the inclusion or exclusion of certain classes of institutions within this group. It is evident that the formulations of lists of voluntary associations in various societies would reveal that there are certain universal criteria of involuntary associations (though not of voluntary associations). Thus "voluntary" acquires a residual meaning. The general criteria of involuntary associations are: (1) when an individual is physically forced to join an association or (2) when an individual is born into an association, they will be called "involuntary" associations. It may readily be seen that certain kinds of churches and trade unions do not fit easily into this classification. Like all social phenomena, voluntary associations are not entities that have a place in some ultimately real classification. The term is merely a concept determined by both conventionality and usefulness.

D. Special Role in Our Society

As has been suggested, voluntary associations of the expressive type are to be found in a great variety of societies, both primitive and modern, both democratic and totalitarian, although it seems to be true that the modern democratic society generally has a larger number and variety of expressive associations. On the other hand, voluntary associations of the social influence type are to be found primarily in societies that are urban and democratic in general character, although they are also likely to be found in significant numbers in more "primitive" rural societies which are undergoing rapid social change (Little, 1957). Leo Simmons (1952) points out that, in the so-called primitive societies, the aged have certain fixed ways of participating in the society, and thus their participations are not "voluntary." He says:

In relatively simple and static societies the statuses and roles of participation are . . . age graded. Everyone belonging to a society of this kind comes to know approximately where he stands and how he may participate at a particular period in his life span, and this is especially true of the older members of the group. But in complex and fluid social systems with rapid change and recurrent confusion over status and role, no one's position is so well fixed —least of all that of the aging [p. 46].

Simmons states further that aging brings higher status with special rights and privileges in most primitive societies, and hence there is no urge to seek new forms of participation. From this, we may infer that in modern societies, which are not simple or static, and where age does not automatically bring higher status, old people have to seek status in other ways, such as by joining voluntary associations.

Other reasons for the great expansion and development of voluntary associations in modern society seem to be the following. With few exceptions, such as that of ancient Rome, only modern industrial societies bring together large conglomerations of people with diverse backgrounds and interests. The high rate of mobility in modern industrial society, mobility that is both geographic and vertical, reduces the opportunity for maintaining stable social contact through the traditional non-voluntary associations of the extended family, the integrated community, and the church. The basis of association, therefore, becomes much more than that of individual choice and of the opportunities created by a large number of independent circumstances. In this sense, the voluntary association is a substitute for the modern industrialized society for the extended families and the integrated community that form the basis of association in preindustrial societies. Finally, we note that the modern industrialized society creates individual interests that are diversified and specialized. These interests can gain expression or satisfaction only through associations which have very limited purposes or functions, as it is only such a limited-purpose association that can bring together significant numbers of people who are likely to have a single interest in common but other interests greatly diversified. The voluntary association can be characterized, thus, with some exceptions, as a modern type of institution which has grown up to meet some of the particular needs of an industrialized society. This is at least true for the social influence type of association.

But not even in all modern industrialized societies is there a significant number of voluntary associations. Strictly speaking, in a modern totalitarian society there are no groups but the state or, more precisely, the party or political movement that controls the state.[2] All the individual's affiliations are determined in some way by the state, and these affiliations exist ultimately to carry out the purpose of the state.

Even within our primarily urban and democratic society we may note wide variations in the complexity and diversity of group structures in any given community. In a relatively homogeneous rural community, at one extreme, most people tend to go to the same church, to be members of the same occupational (agricultural) organization, to participate in the same sociable activities, and to send their children to the same schools. While there are different organizations for the various activities, and while there is some differential participation in the groups according to age and sex, there is still no large number of groups with divergent membership and interest in a homogeneous rural community. There is not likely to be relatively much diversity of interest and attitude among the groups where all the members of the community belong to the same groups. While we need to learn much more regarding the conditions under which voluntary group differentiation develops, we may take it as a close approximation to the facts that the development of voluntary associations with diverse ideas as to how the society should be changed occurs primarily in the modern urban democratic society. The term "urban" is to be understood in its sociological sense, not in terms of the census definition: many villages in the United States are urban, and there is a trend toward their becoming more urban.

Still there is a disproportionate number of voluntary associations for the aged in American cities than in rural areas. To put our observations in general terms: the existence of a significant number of associations in the community seems to require that the population be somewhat heterogeneous in background and interests and that no one institution, such as the church or state, be successful in dominating the entire life of most individuals.

Voluntary associations also seem to be a particular development of American culture; this, at least, has been stated by such eminent foreign observers as De Tocqueville (1899), Bryce (1910), Weber (1940), and Myrdal (1944). No systematic international comparisons have been made, but, if the United States actually does lead in the number of voluntary associations per inhabitant, this might be attributed to the favorable legal situation. The First Amendment to the United States Constitution specifies the right of all citizens peaceably to assemble, and the courts have always interpreted that to mean the right to form free associations. On the other hand, democratic countries like France and Italy have had a history of restrictive legislation with respect to voluntary associations, and still other democratic countries, like Great Britain and Switzerland, have never put either encouragements or restrictions into their laws.

E. The Professional Association

In a society where the voluntary association is such a basic institution, it is natural that one of the most fundamental interests (i.e., the economic or occupational interest) would find expression in a variety of voluntary associations. The employers' associations, whether formal or informal, the trade unions, and the professional men's associations have formed a powerful segment of American life. Interest here will naturally be largely restricted to two fairly minor types of occupational associations— the professional association and the scien-

[2] The establishment of modern totalitarian regimes has regularly been attended by the destruction or "integration" of voluntary associations, especially those that sought to have some influence on the society—less so of those that were purely expressive, sociable, or recreational in character. The church, which represents a loyalty alien to the state, is likely to become a problem for the totalitarian state and may even be a source of resistance unless it is assimilated into the state's interest in some way.

tific society—because they have specialized interests in the aged. However, we cannot neglect the fact that the trade union has had as one of its major activities the protection of the aged by means of gaining for them seniority rights to their jobs and welfare and retirement benefits for them when they leave or are forced out of their jobs. Insofar as associations of medical men, social workers, sociologists, and psychologists have had special interests in the aged, they have set up special sections in their organizations or in their programs to promote these interests on either a scientific, a welfare, or a professional basis.

II. OLDER PEOPLE AS PARTICIPANTS IN VOLUNTARY ASSOCIATIONS

A. *Studies on Extent of Participation of the Elderly*

There are several studies reporting on participation in voluntary associations as related to age. These studies generally show that social participation declines at the later ages despite the increased leisure time following upon retirement. In McKain's (1947) study, about one-half of those past 65 years of age reported that they gave less time to organizations than they did when they were 50 years of age, and only 1 per cent said that their social activity had increased. Havighurst (1957) corroborates this finding and adds to it:

Formal associations lose attractiveness as age changes from 40 to 70, though not among women until they reach the sixties. Informal groups are most attractive to men in the 50 to 60 group but are equally attractive at all (middle) ages for women [p. 160].

On the other hand, in Scott's (1957) study of a representative sample of adults of the New England town of Bennington, Vermont, there was no consistent relationship between membership and age. Those under 25 years of age reported an average of 1.75 memberships, those between 25 and 39 reported an average of 1.46 memberships, those between 40 and 54 years reported an average of 1.98 memberships, while those 55 years and older reported an aver-

age of 1.48 memberships. Among men alone, membership in voluntary associations did not fall with age, whereas it did markedly so among the women. Studies by Goldhamer (1942), by Freedman and Axelrod (1952), and by Anderson and Ryan (1943) also correlated age with membership in voluntary associations.

If it is true that participation in voluntary associations now decreases with age, one reason for this is that the change of location and role at the onset of old age often pulls the individual out of his earlier social participations, and he is then less able or less motivated to go into new ones. A study by Hoyt (1954) of retired people living in a trailer park illustrates this point in its extreme form:

In the former home community 72 per cent of the respondents attended meetings of voluntary associations. The mean monthly attendance for this group was 3.3 meetings. After immigration, however, only 8 per cent attended such meetings, and the mean monthly attendance for this 8 per cent is only 1.6. The above results refer to all voluntary associations of a social, business, or fraternal nature except church [p. 365].

B. *The Webber Study*

The most complete study of the participation of older people in voluntary association seems to be that of Irving L. Webber (1954). The study is a description of the organized social life of 474 retired persons in the cities of West Palm Beach and Orlando, Florida, in the summer of 1951. The sample study is roughly representative of the retired white residents of these two communities. The communities are distinguished by having an especially large proportion of retired persons in their population.

In Orlando less than 40 per cent, and in West Palm Beach only 23 per cent, belong to associations which are not church-connected:

In the Orlando sample about half of the local memberships were in churches, with an additional 10 per cent in church-affiliated associations such as Bible classes, men's clubs, Sunday schools, ladies' aids, guilds, and missionary societies. Members of fraternal associations such as Odd Fellows, Eastern Star, Masons, Woodmen of the World, and Elks were the next largest group, constituting about 17 per cent. Recreational and social organizations, including the Needlecraft Club, card clubs, bridge clubs, winter-visitor clubs, shuffleboard clubs, Colonial Women's Club, Grandmother Club, and bowling clubs, made up about 8 per cent of the memberships. Some, particularly shuffleboard, lawn bowling, and winter-visitor clubs, have come into existence and function primarily for older people, including the considerable group of aged "tourists" who spend more than two months of the year in Florida. Military and veterans' organizations, among which the American Legion, United Spanish War Veterans, Reserve Officers' Association, and Veterans of Foreign Wars were prominent, accounted for about 7 per cent. Only 2 per cent of the organizations were classified as music, art, and theater, and a comparable proportion were service groups. The findings in West Palm Beach were similar [Webber, 1954, p. 344].

The study provides certain information about the characteristics of those retired persons who were relatively more participant. Men were more likely than women to belong to an organization. The women who reported membership were more likely to belong to only one organization, which was often a church, while there was a relatively greater tendency for men to belong to more than one organization. No consistent relationship was found between age and number of memberships per person, so that it cannot be said that increasing age decreases participation.

Other findings about factors influencing participation were:

Married persons were compared with those in all other categories of civil status—married but separated, widowed, and single—combined. There is slight but consistent evidence of higher rates of membership on the part of the non-married, particularly as to membership in two or more organizations.

A higher proportion of the retired with less than nine years of formal education reported that they belonged to no organizations, and a markedly lower share belong to two or more organizations, in comparison with those with nine or more years of schooling. However, the evidence showed somewhat less affiliation on the part of persons with more than twelve years of education in comparison with those who had remained in school from nine to twelve years.

Respondents were asked to indicate the principal source of their income before retirement on a five-point scale: inherited wealth, earned wealth, profits and fees, salary, and wages. Because of the relatively limited number of responses (177 in Orlando and 139 in West Palm Beach), inherited wealth, earned wealth, and profits and fees were combined for the analysis, the comparison thus being on the basis of (1) wealth, profits, and fees; (2) salary; and (3) wages. In the combined samples there is a direct relationship between the former source of income and extent of membership in organizations; for example, 35.9 per cent of those who formerly obtained their income from inherited or earned wealth or profits and fees, 24.6 per cent of those who had received salaries, and 19.6 per cent of those who had earned wages belonged to two or more organizations. The same association was found in the individual communities except for one inconsistency in the case of West Palm Beach, where nonmembership was higher among former salaried than among former wage-earning persons [pp. 344–45].

When Webber asked, "How many club or organization meetings do you usually attend each month?" nearly half of the sample of the retired in Orlando and nearly two-thirds in West Palm Beach attended none. Table 1 shows the number of meetings attended monthly. Approximately the same proportions of men and women reported that they had never attended a meeting. In general, however, women as a group attended a greater number of meetings per month. The relationship between age and attendance is not consistent. Married persons living with their spouse attended meetings to a greater extent than did other categories among the retired. Educational level was markedly associated with attendance. A negative association between attendance and status level is also shown in the attendance characteristics of those who had earned their income in different ways. Those who had earned only salaries and wages had a lower attendance than those who had earned their income through inherited wealth, earned wealth, or profits and fees.

Religious services were attended much more frequently than meetings of secular organizations, with only about one-fourth of the subjects never attending religious services. Men attended church considerably less than did women, the very old attended less than the younger retired persons, and the unattached attended less than did married persons living with husband or wife.

TABLE 1*

MEETINGS ATTENDED MONTHLY BY OLDER PERSONS IN ORLANDO AND WEST PALM BEACH, 1951

| MEETINGS ATTENDED PER MONTH | PERSONS ATTENDING MEETINGS IN: | | | |
| | Orlando | | West Palm Beach | |
	No.	Per Cent Distribution	No.	Per Cent Distribution
Total....	277	100	202	100
None......	126	46	127	63
1–2.......	30	11	16	8
3–4.......	19	7	10	5
5–9.......	87	32	40	20
10 or more..	10	4	9	4

* Source: Irving Webber, "The Organized Life of the Retired: Two Florida Communities," *Am. J. Sociology*, 59 (1954), 340–46.

Most other studies of the organized social life of older people (Landis, 1940; McKain, 1947; Cavan *et al.*, 1949; McKain and Baldwin, 1951; Mayo, 1951; Monroe, 1951) did not deal with the participation of the aged as intensively as did Webber. On some points the findings of these studies vary with those of Webber.

C. The Havighurst-Albrecht Study

Another thorough study of the participations of older people in a community's associations is that by Robert J. Havighurst and Ruth Albrecht (1953). The community studied was designated as "Prairie City," a midwestern town of 7000 people,

with 4000 others in the adjacent trading area. "Prairie City" does not have any formal associations that are limited to older people. There are the usual clubs and societies for people of mixed ages, practically all of them limited to one sex or the other and often restricted along social status lines. While practically all the town's associations are open to older people, these tend to drop out as they pass 65, and practically no older person joins an organization as a new member. Havighurst and Albrecht (1953) found:

According to the scale of role-activity, 58 per cent of Prairie City elders belong to no social organizations and take no interest in them; 14 per cent are only nominal members of social clubs and do not attend; 10 per cent attend frequently, but take no responsibilities, while an equal number have active participation as well as frequent attendance; and 8 per cent actually carry responsibility as officer or committee member in one or more clubs [p. 193].

Although the community has about 130 organizations for adults, with about 500 officerships, only 5 persons over 65 held a leading office in an organization, and these usually in organizations with a predominance of older members. A somewhat larger number of older people hold positions of minor leadership, such as committee chairman, member of refreshment committee, and so on. When asked why they left their officerships and the clubs themselves, older women answered in such terms as "Let younger people do that," "I get nervous with college graduates in the group," "My false teeth would whistle all the time when I talked." Lower-status older men were especially likely to be unaffiliated, although this group tended "to make up for lack of clubs by substituting informal tavern groups for formal associations" (p. 341). Generally, there was less associational life for older men than for older women, partly because a small town has fewer organizations for men, and men's organizations like service clubs put much emphasis upon regular attendance, committee work, and other activities and costs which older men sometimes find it difficult to keep up with. Older women are more participant because they have met loneliness in their lives at an earlier age and have joined clubs to avoid this, partly because they are more likely to be widowed, and partly because their clubs make fewer demands on their energy and money. In most cases, Havighurst and Albrecht find mixed-age associations difficult or unsatisfactory for the elderly and advocate the formation of special associations for them alone.

D. Characteristics of the Aged Affecting Their Participation

Interest in the participation of the elderly in voluntary associations lies not only in the present extent of participation but in the trends and in the relationships between the elderly and the associations of which they are members. Other chapters have brought out the characteristics of the elderly in our society, but the relevant facts will bear recapitulation for the discussion of participation by older people in voluntary associations. Consideration will be given to those characteristics of the aged which indicate something about their changed position in contemporary society as compared to that in the society of the past. First, let us examine the changed character of older people in relation to free time in our society. We note the longer life, the better health and greater vigor, the reduced economic pressure, and the earlier age of retirement of old people. With occupations now generally carried on in large economic organizations, it is no longer possible for most people to work at their jobs with progressively decreasing hours of commitment, and they have to retire completely when they want to reduce their work load or their employer requires them to. With more free time at their disposal, older people are more able to participate in voluntary associations. It should be pointed out, of course, that the number of leisure hours is increasing for all

age groups of the population. Thus the special need of the aged for profitable and wholesome use of their free time is one that is shared to a certain extent with the entire population. Free time is probably a value in all cultures, although not every individual shares this value of free time. Any increase of free time offers opportunity for participation in voluntary associations.

The matter of motivation brings us to a second characteristic of the aged in our society which affects their special role as participants in voluntary associations. As already suggested, the long-run trend in modern industrialized society has been toward the breakdown of the extended family and the community and, to a lesser extent, of the church as a fundamental aspect of the community. Of the traditional institutions which provide an individual with his social contacts, only the immediate nuclear family has remained at least as strong as it was in pre–industrial revolution days. But for the aged even the nuclear family has broken down, in that adult children no longer feel quite the same responsibility for their parents as they formerly did. At least community and governmental pressure on younger adults to support economically and to provide a *social* life for their aged parents is no longer so effective. Thus, especially for vigorous older people, there has developed a kind of social vacuum which can be filled only by participation in the varied kinds of voluntary associations and activities which modern society provides.

There is a considerable descriptive literature suggesting some of the psychological needs of older people for participation in voluntary associations. One of the best of these articles is that by Kaplan (1954).

The voluntary association is ideally structured to satisfy the needs of people who are seeking social contact in modern society. For a mobile people, it has the advantage of being easy to join. While some associations have limitations on the type of members they accept and have initiation ceremonies, these are usually relatively minor compared to the limitations and initiation ceremonies of non-voluntary associations. For a person with diversified interests, the voluntary association has the advantage of having very limited and specialized purposes so one commits only a small part of himself when joining and participating in a voluntary association. For a culture which values freedom and independence, the voluntary association has the advantage of involving only a small portion of a person's life and not encompassing him in a "total institution" like the family, the military unit, or the highly integrated community. The trend of our society to become "a lonely crowd"—or anomic, to use a sociologist's term—has often been exaggerated, neglecting the extent to which older institutions like the extended family and the integrated community still function and partially maintain themselves in modern society and neglecting the extent to which countertrends have been set up in the social system to balance the long-run trends toward anomie. Insofar as the society has become anomic, however, the voluntary association has developed to become the major and almost the most suitable antidote.

E. Definition of "Elderliness" Affecting Participation

To point to the increased free time for the population at large, and not only for the older people, is to point to a special difficulty in the definition of "older people" in our society. The age at which one becomes an "older person" is defined one way in economic terms and still another way in terms of free time. Glick (1955) has shown that the child-rearing functions of parents have been taking place at an earlier and earlier age, until now the average woman bears her last child at the age of 26 years. This means that the youngest child of the average American housewife begins elementary school when his mother is only 32 or 33 years of age.

At this young age the married woman without an outside occupation finds herself beginning to have some of the free-time characteristics of the older population, although she then often takes an outside employment. When the contemporary mother and father reach their mid-forties their children have already moved away from the parental home in the average case (that is, this will shortly be true when the present generation of young parents reach their forties). Both the opportunity and the obligation to spend their free time with their children have largely disappeared. The young adults are now rearing their own families, and their relations with their parents are hardly more than those with other relatives. Thus, by the mid-forties, the average American parent has entered into the ranks of "older people" as far as the question of how to spend their free time is concerned. For the woman this involves an especially serious shift in the pattern of her life. If she is not gainfully employed, which is the case for the majority of women in the middle- and upper-income groups, her household duties being at a minimum because of the variety of labor-saving devices and the absence of inhabitants of the household other than her husband and herself, a large majority of the middle-aged woman's waking hours consist of free time. The various ways she comes to grips with this situation is a subject outside the scope of this chapter, but it needs to be said that most women increase their voluntary participation in organizations of one sort or another and that some women in this age group make their activities in voluntary associations a major part of their lives. Thus it can be stated, with only slight exaggeration, that older people have special needs for the activities and the social contacts which voluntary associations provide and that "elderliness" in this social sense begins in the early thirties for the average woman and becomes significant and marked for both men and women by their middle forties.

F. Characteristics of Voluntary Associations Affecting Participation of the Elderly

Shifting our perspective now from the individual to the group, we can hold that the voluntary association as an institution has increased need of individual participation in the modern democratic social setting. Just as the extended family and the community are no longer quite so able as they once were to provide social contacts for the individual, so these same institutions are no longer able to provide some of the protection and welfare benefits that they used to. The government has filled the gap in a large number of matters, but so have voluntary associations. To satisfy the health, welfare, and educational needs of various segments of our population is among the major purposes of voluntary associations in our society. Not only have the voluntary associations taken over the old functions of the community and the extended family to a certain extent, but there are now new functions due to the increased awareness and increased sensitivity of the population with respect to health, welfare, and education. In many cases the voluntary association can perform these functions much more efficiently than can the government, and in some cases the voluntary association is the only institution which can perform the function if we are to retain a free society. Thus it can be stated that the society has greatly increased need for voluntary and unpaid work to carry out functions falling to voluntary associations. We can also say that the voluntary associations are the organized instruments of the society in mobilizing this free help. The greatly increased free time of our citizens, therefore, and especially that of older people, is a much-sought-after value in our society.

Thus, for reasons connected with both supply and demand, there will likely develop a trend for older people, as individuals, and voluntary associations, as institutions, to move toward each other. The result would be a steady increase in the proportion of older persons becoming members of voluntary associations and a steady increase in the proportion of older persons among the members of voluntary associations, although this observation is based on casual report rather than on a systematic collection of statistics.

G. Questions about the Effectiveness of the Elderly in Voluntary Associations

No vigorous evaluation of the consequences of this movement has been made, although many leaders in associations of one sort or another have commented on certain consequences of the increased participation in the activities of their association on the part of the aged. In the absence of any systematic evaluation, all we can do here is to list some of the possible questions that would be examined in any systematic study. (1) Does the lesser physical vigor of the aged, as compared to younger members, limit their effectiveness in carrying out the program of voluntary associations, or does the individual reduce his participation to the level that he is capable of carrying on effectively? (2) Are the aged more conservative and hence less willing to use and develop new techniques for the effective carrying-on of the purposes of the association (Ogden and Ogden, 1952)? (3) Are the aged relatively less skilled and less well trained in carrying on the activities of the associations of which they are members? (4) Does the relatively large proportion of older people who use participation in voluntary associations solely as an escape from boredom and lack of other activity diminish the effectiveness of the association's activity? (5) Does the large portion of the aged among the more active participants of certain voluntary associations decrease the interest of younger people in the activities of these organizations? Certainly, these and related questions need to be answered by systematic research for the benefit of increasing knowledge both of the aged and of the voluntary associations.

III. The Elderly as Organizers of Special Volunteer Associations

Thus far we have considered the participation of older people in the usual kinds of voluntary associations that make up American society. Around every need or interest there has grown up one or more voluntary associations whose purpose has been to express or satisfy that need or interest. Older people participate in such associations on the same basis that other members do. Sometimes an association does not have an accession of new members, so that in the course of time all its existing members are elderly, even though the activities of the association have nothing to do with old age. But older people also have special needs, interests, and ways of expressing themselves that are somewhat unique to them as a social category. We shall now turn to those voluntary associations whose purpose is in some way connected with the special needs and interests of older persons, first considering those that older persons have organized themselves and then turning to those which have been organized for older persons by others. It is significant that there were practically no voluntary associations of or for the aging before 1930. The major exception was the old people's home, generally under religious auspices if it were not a governmental institution.

A. Special Needs and Interests of the Elderly

The needs and interests that are unique to older people around which voluntary associations have formed include: special needs for economic assistance, housing, and the full range of "welfare" assistance; the need to take care of the characteristic health problems of the older years; the need for special training and orientation to meet the problems of aging; the need for self-expression and recreation; and the need to organize politically in order to protect themselves as a group and to gain special consideration for themselves as a group. These "needs" are increasing in American society, and hence the number of associations formed to satisfy them are also increasing. In the first place, as has been noted in the chapter on demography, older persons have been forming an increasing proportion of the total population and will continue to do so. Second, changes in economic and social organization are creating new problems for the aged, such as the increased difficulty in finding economic employment, the greater unwillingness of adult children and their aged parents to live in the same household, and other problems that have been noticed in the preceding chapters. A third reason for the increase in voluntary associations whose purpose is to help the aged in some way is simply that there is increased awareness of the problems of the aged on the part of the general public and increased awareness on the part of the aged themselves at the commonness of their problems. Out of this increased awareness comes the fourth factor—increased association of older people with one another. Older people seem to take increasing satisfaction in associating with each other, in discussing their common problems and interests, and in trying to take collective action with regard to them. It might be said that there has been a certain shift on the part of older people from being family oriented to being older-person oriented. Thus older persons are more likely to come together for sociability and for the sake of getting together, and to get personal satisfaction from associating with one another, when the ostensible purpose of their coming-together is something more specific.

B. Handicaps of Older People

On the other hand, some older people are not particularly qualified to organize or do things for themselves. In this age group there is a higher-than-average incidence of physical defects and physical weaknesses which handicap systematic activity. For those who are becoming mentally senile, any kind of organization work is, of course, practically out of the question. Just as important is the fact that the older persons who have the greatest need for organization to meet their problems are those in low-income groups. It seems that they have the least previous experience and skills in organizing. Studies show that there is a relationship between income and participation in voluntary associations (Lynd and Lynd, 1929; Mather, 1941; Warner and Lunt, 1941; Goldhamer, 1942; Bushee, 1945; Komarovsky, 1946; Scott, 1948; Reid and Ehle, 1950; Dotson, 1951; Martin, 1952; Uzzell, 1953). Those who have been in the lower half of the income scale are usually those who have been least participant in organizations throughout their lives and therefore have the least experience for organizing or participating effectively in new associations when they reach a later age. Albrecht (1951) found that 58 per cent of a representative sample of older people in a midwestern community belonged to no social clubs, and most of these had never belonged to a club. She concluded that "nonparticipation was for them not a result of aging but a carryover from the earlier life pattern" and that "active social participation in younger years seemed to lead to better adjustment in old age" (p. 144).

Lack of ability to organize new associations is only part of the reason why older people have not themselves organized a greater variety and number of associations than they have done. Perhaps a more significant reason is that they have never before thought of organizing to meet their needs on the basis of age. The type of economic and health problems faced by older persons are those which they have usually been meeting throughout their lives by individual effort. However, in earlier years, the problems were usually not so chronic or acute. Our culture teaches them that these problems should be met by individual effort. For most of the aged, the realities of this situation are such that their individual efforts cannot be efficacious. Yet the values of individual effort strongly affect their thinking.

Even when they have earlier participated in voluntary associations—to express themselves in political activity or for recreational purposes, for example—they have scarcely ever thought of doing this on an age-graded basis. Moving into old age involves a role change, assuming a new aspect of personality. For most individuals a considerable number of years may pass before they recognize that their age-grade role has changed and adjust to the fact that they, as members of the age grade, have a unique identification and a new set of problems in common with others. Some older persons never acquire the new group identification. In order to form voluntary associations for the purpose of solving problems or expressing one's self in a certain way, people must have some identification of themselves as a special group in a society. It can probably be fairly said that, at least until recently, elderly people in American society can be regarded as a category rather than as a social group. As the forces that we have noted in preceding sections are gradually transforming them into a social group, older people will increasingly form and participate in voluntary associations to meet their special needs and to express themselves in ways fairly unique to their social position (Fisher, 1950).

C. National Organizations

Only a few of the many organizations of older people are organized on a national basis. As examples of specific groups formed by older people, we shall deal with only two which are organized on a national basis. Because the programs of the associations operated on a local basis and are so similar to the recreational programs organized for older people, local associations will be the main focus of interest in the following section.

The most famous of these, and perhaps the first in the United States, was the Old

Age Revolving Pensions Ltd., better known as the Townsend Movement. Judson T. Landis (1946) says of it:

> The Townsend Movement was the first old-age movement in the United States. It grew rapidly and wielded so much force for a time that the country was forced to recognize the great potential and political influence of organized old people. The Townsend Movement appealed to the lower social and economic groups of old people in America [p. 64].

Organized by an elderly physician and a younger businessman in early 1934, it became one of the largest mass movements the United States has ever known, in the space of a year (Neuberger and Loe, 1936). While it attracted a few younger persons, the great bulk of the members were over 60 years of age. The ostensible aim of the organization was to get Congress to pass a law giving every citizen over the age of 60 a pension of $200 a month. The funds were to be obtained by levying a 2 per cent transactions tax. Economists of the time adjudged the plan to be economically unfeasible and destructive. In 1936 a congressional investigating committee showed that the movement yielded considerable income for its promoters, and it appeared that this was probably a major consideration in the formation of the movement. The thousands of local clubs affected their elderly members in various ways. Participants in the clubs were given some hope that their economic needs would be amply met and were brought together in sociable groups. Moreover, the clubs probably created their first insights of themselves as a social group with common problems. Members gained an awareness of their political strength in combination. However, exercise of this power was limited because the movement was tightly controlled by the two national leaders, and no local initiative was permitted, but it is possible that most of the members were not aware of this. Some older people were more or less forced to join the movement through the pressure of their friends. In spite of the poverty of

most of the members, they usually contributed considerable amounts to the organization for political and publicity work. Conflict and defection among the top leaders and congressional exposure of the personal enrichment of these leaders led to the gradual decline of the movement after 1936. Some of the remnants of the movement turned into well-disciplined and effective pressure groups working to get old age pensions from their state governments.

A national association of the elderly in existence today is Senior Citizens of America, incorporated in 1954 in Washington, D.C., and claiming five thousand members in 1957. It is described by the *Social Work Year Book* in the following way:

> *Purpose and Activities:* A nonprofit, educational, philanthropic, scientific organization incorporated under the laws of the District of Columbia. It has members in every state and in many other countries; serves as a clearing house for all that concerns the second half of life, publishes *Senior Citizens,* a quality magazine for mature citizens of discriminating tastes; gives a voice to those who wish to make use of talent now going to waste through premature, forced retirement; answers inquiries from persons faced with the problem of retirement; keeps newspapers, magazines, and leaders in public life informed as to the problems of our more mature citizens; conducts research into problems which concern persons in midlife and beyond; owns and publishes *The American Citizens Handbook* and over 100 titles of *Personal Growth Leaflets* widely used around the world [Kurtz, 1957, p. 708].

In addition to *Senior Citizens,* there is the *Journal of Lifetime Living* serving as a magazine for elderly readers.

IV. Voluntary Associations Providing Services for the Aged

A. Motives for Helping the Elderly

While voluntary associations which elderly persons organize for themselves to meet their special needs and interests have been considered first, it is undoubtedly true that younger adults have created more voluntary associations for them than older persons have organized for themselves. Why do persons who are not themselves experiencing the needs and problems of older people bother to devote themselves to organizing for the benefit of other persons? First, we must think in terms of the fact that it is the characteristic response of modern democratic industrial society to meet needs and to express the interest of any significant proportion of the population by creating voluntary associations. As noted, this is also particularly characteristic of American culture. Subjectively, Americans who participate in this organizing process feel that voluntary associations are an effective way to act on a problem which they face. Even if they believe that the government must ultimately assume responsibility for the problem, many people still feel that they must organize to put pressure on the government and that they can inaugurate some activity immediately on a more local or experimental basis through a voluntary association. Some individuals, on the other hand, want to keep the government out of the personal lives of people as much as possible and therefore, as an expression of the political philosophy, help to organize voluntary associations whenever a significant social problem arises for a large number of people.

There is also the subjective feeling of "doing good" when people organize themselves and their associates to help those in less fortunate circumstances. A significant number of Americans feel a need to be useful, helpful, responsible, and conscientious. Hence there are religious, ethical, and psychological values involved in their participating in what seems to be a socially worthwhile public activity. The intensity of their motivation ranges all the way from casual selflessness to a compulsive drive. There are other, more selfish motives for devoting time, effort, and even money to activity for the benefit of older persons. Some individuals and organizations may have specific obligations to certain older persons, which they believe they can most easily or cheaply meet by organizing as-

sociations to help these specific persons rather than to meet their obligations by solely individual activity. For example, younger adults may find it impossible to provide suitable recreation and entertainment for their aged parents themselves and so organize community-wide clubs which will provide recreation and amusement for these parents on an organized basis. Or an industrial firm may feel that it is bad for public relations to have their retired workers appear abandoned, and so it stimulates the community to provide rest homes or recreational facilities for these aged former employees. Another "selfish" motive for organizing to meet the needs and interests of older persons is the desire for participation and sociability. As we have noted, the opportunities for leisure have increased for the entire population, and many younger adults do not know what to do with the time that is now available to them. A number of such persons readily join all kinds of voluntary associations, for the sake of meeting with others, enjoying themselves, and expressing their creative urges in one way or another. Older persons can often benefit from the expression of these selfish motives just as do other underprivileged categories of the population.

We shall now examine some voluntary associations providing services to the aged. The specific kinds of voluntary associations we are about to describe are of two types. First, there are the associations in which older persons are the major participants but which have been stimulated, organized, and basically sustained by younger adults. A second kind of association is actually one *of* younger adults whose activity and purpose is directed toward ameliorating certain problems which the elderly face.

B. Religious Groups

Religious groups have organized many of the associational services to the aged in the United States. This work is seldom done by churches as such but usually by the laymen's groups associated with churches and church bodies. Local church groups sponsor clubs, day centers, leadership courses, workshops, and hobby groups for the elderly. Volunteer visitor programs are provided for shut-ins and isolated aging persons. Central organizations of Protestants provide foster placement, homemaker service, and counseling, and there are about seven hundred Protestant homes for the aged (Johnson and Villaume, 1957). Jewish groups also sponsor homes, family service agencies, recreation centers, vocational services, and health agencies for old people (Avrunin, 1957). There are 299 Catholic homes for the aging in the United States, and, according to Lennon (1957),

diocesan programs are working toward the goal of offering a full range of coordinated services. These would include social casework, social group work, counseling, wider use of volunteers under supervision, homemakers service, residence clubs, apartment projects, day activity centers, retreats for older people, employment guidance, and services to the chronically ill and senile [p. 142].

Some of the churches have prepared books and pamphlets to help their local programs for the elderly (Maves and Cedarleaf, 1949; International Conference on the Church and Older People, 1953; Lund, 1951; Stafford, 1953).

C. Trade Unions and Other Groups

Other types of large-scale voluntary associations, besides those organized on a religious basis, which provide homes and other services for the aged include trade unions, professional societies, business organizations, fraternal associations, veterans' associations, service clubs, and ethnic organizations. The National Association of Manufacturers also has staff services for consultation about elderly workers. The United Automobile Workers Union has a National Advisory Committee on Older and Retired Workers, and the Community Services Department of the AFL-CIO takes a special interest in older workers.

Among labor unions the United Automo-

bile Workers seems to have the most extensive program for its retired members. While its work in gaining pensions for retiring workers began earlier, its program for elderly retired workers began in 1951, when a series of "area meetings" was organized. At these meetings the activities included community singing, refreshments, entertainment, speakers, and discussion on a variety of topics such as health, nutrition, social security, and other matters of concern to older people. Annual city-wide parties for retired auto workers in the Detroit area attracted about 11,500 older guests. In 1953–54 the UAW opened three centers in the city of Detroit which operate Monday through Friday, from 9:30 A.M. to 3:30 P.M. The program of these centers includes (1) educational and cultural activities; (2) hobbies, parties, game activities, movies, etc.; (3) visitation of the homebound; (4) referrals regarding health, housing, employment, and prosthetic devices; (5) counseling on personal problems and interpersonal relations; (6) discussion of community problems; and (7) participation in civic affairs and community service projects (UAW-CIO, 1956). This union has now set up an Older and Retired Worker's Department.

Although many other unions have pension programs for their members, very few have attempted to organize systematic overall programs of education, recreation, etc., for the aged. The Amalgamated Clothing Workers has done some work, establishing drop-in centers in New York and Philadelphia. The Retail Clerks Union has the beginning of a program in New York City. The Steelworkers has done some work on retirement preparation in co-operation with the University of Chicago. The International Ladies' Garment Workers' Union has a health program in New York City. The Upholsterers' International Union has built a retirement village in Florida and has done some experimental work on retirement preparation in co-operation with the University of Michigan. The United Mine Workers has an extensive health and rehabilitation program for retired and disabled miners.

Some of the great national associations, such as the American Heart Association and the American Cancer Society, have programs to aid victims of certain diseases and to sponsor research on those diseases. Because the incidence of these diseases is associated with aging, the work of these associations very much benefits older persons. The American National Red Cross provides special services to older persons and encourages them to use the services of its local chapters.

Ravin and Tibbitts (1958) state that over two hundred national organizations have at least some concern with the older population of the United States. The activities of a few of these national groups will be described as illustrative of the wide range of their activities.

The American Association of University Women, according to a letter from Mrs. Edith Sherrod, has no services for the aging but is developing a study program for its members that is intended to have them engage in community action on behalf of the aging. To stimulate the study program, the Social and Economic Issues Committee of the American Association of University Women has been preparing study kits for its local affiliates. These consist of bibliography, copies of lectures, an outline for a survey of community facilities for the aging, an assessment of what the state and federal governments are now doing about the aging problem, etc.

The B'nai B'rith, the largest and oldest Jewish service and fraternal organization, has developed several local programs for elderly people through its Commission on Citizenship and Civic Affairs. Rabbi Morton Lifshutz (1958), director of the National Commission on Citizenship and Civic Affairs of B'nai B'rith, indicates that it is hoped that these local programs will develop into a national program. The B'nai B'rith women's organizations also have a study program on aging, encouraging its local chapters to have forums and discussions, films, reading lists, etc., on problems of aging with a view to informing their own elderly members as to how best to cope with these problems.

The National Council of Jewish Women began a Golden Age program in 1947 which was largely social in nature (Berkman, 1958). Gradually, the program expanded so that weekly or daily meetings included such activities as doing art and handicraft work, making articles for hospitals, visiting members who were ill, working with professional vocational agencies on employment solicitation, and participating in discussion and study groups and in community activities. There is considerable variation in program according to the needs and organization of the local groups. In 1958 there were about two hundred programs for older adults operated by National Council sections throughout the United States, some in co-operation with other local organizations. The council estimates that its sections contribute about $200,000 annually to these projects, as well as the time of thousands of volunteers. The central office offers guidance and encourages the local sections to have conferences on the aging and provides material for these conferences.

Kiwanis International, a federation of some forty-four hundred service clubs located mainly in the United States and Canada, began to encourage activity for the aging among its member clubs in 1957, although hundreds of the clubs independently started programs earlier. The Kiwanis clubs sponsor local "golden years clubs" with programs to occupy senior citizens' leisure hours, and "the clubs have made money available to the financially embarrassed" (Mitchell, 1958, p. 1).

D. Types of Activities of Local Groups

Local groups are numerous and have diverse activities. Tibbitts (1954) summarized the situation succinctly:

Many private and community agencies are experimenting with clubs for older adults; recreational programs in parks, playgrounds and community centers; centers with programs in education, dramatics, crafts, social events, tours of interesting places, friendly visiting and games; overnight camping; and development of such interests as nature study, photography, and collecting.

Most of the local organizations are recreational in function, even when disguised as educational or creative. But the specific content, organization, and sponsorship vary considerably. This will be illustrated by a brief description of programs for older adults in Chicago in 1950 (Community Projects for the Aged, 1952) and in Minneapolis in 1956 (Kaplan, 1951, 1953; Hennepin County Welfare Board, 1956). Financial support for clubs for the elderly comes from the treasuries of other associations, voluntary public contributions, local governments, membership dues, and contributions from individual wealthy patrons.

There were 104 programs in Chicago, of which 63 were social groups, 26 special interest groups, and 15 men's card and game groups. Forty-six of the groups were sponsored by public agencies—such as the Chicago Park District, the Chicago Public Library, and various housing projects—although volunteers were sometimes found among the personnel running the programs. Groups sponsored by private agencies numbered 58, of which 43 were from settlements and community centers and 5 from churches, and 10 were unaffiliated. The names of some of the unaffiliated clubs suggest the light vein in which their organizers try to approach the problem of old age: "Borrowed Time Club," "Columbian Exposition" (referring to the Chicago World's Fair of 1893), "Cook County Grandmothers," and "Original Grandfathers."

Minneapolis has 47 organizations, of which 5 meet in boarding houses, 7 are limited to persons who formerly worked in certain categories of occupation, and 3 have activities of a very specialized nature. The remaining 32 have no such limitations except those of age, of course, and some-

times sex, but their sponsorship indicates that the groups consist solely or largely of persons of a single ethnic group. There is also an organization that helps to coordinate the programs of various clubs. Some of the clubs meet as infrequently as once a month; at the opposite extreme is a community center that is open every weekday (10:00 A.M.–4:30 P.M., and on Wednesday and Friday from 7:00 to 10:00 P.M.). The programs of the latter were described as offering instruction in crafts and woodworking; lounge activities, including television, table games, music, and a lending library; a sales outlet for articles made by senior citizens; and special events, such as square dancing, musicales, dramatics, armchair travels, movies, talks. No fees were assessed, and craft materials were supplied at cost. Senior citizens are invited to bring sandwiches and spend the day. Coffee is served at noon and at 3:00 P.M.

A number of the clubs are called "Golden Age" clubs, following the pattern apparently first developed in Cleveland by such local leaders as Oskar Schulze (1949). Some of them provide volunteer assistants for other *pro bono publico* activities, in such capacities as hostesses, chaperones, group leaders, and receptionists. Besides the activities already mentioned, other clubs around the country sponsor the following: hobby shows, variety shows, sports, picnics, mimeographed magazines, summer vacation camps, aid to the chronically ill and the hospitalized, reading to the blind, civil defense work, and birthday celebrations (Snyder, 1954, 1955). The Welfare and Health Council of New York City promotes an annual hobby show for older hobbyists which features exhibits and working demonstrations. In 1953 the show attracted 1600 exhibitors, who entered 2500 displays of their work, which was seen by nearly 20,000 visitors (Briggs, 1954).

Some associations for selected groups of older persons have economic and civic activities. For example, "in at least a dozen American cities retired business executives have united to put their experience to work in projects that contribute to improved communities and better business." These associations—variously called "Experience, Inc.," "Management Counselors," "Consulting and Advisory Services"—offer advice to charitable organizations, civic causes, and beginning businesses (Anonymous, 1955). The "Forty Plus" clubs, found in several cities, are non-profit associations of men of executive and professional background over 40 years of age who seek to secure employment for themselves and for each other (Rawlinson, 1955). Cleveland has an especially active organization, called the "Senior Council," which places elderly people in both paid and volunteer positions in business, civic and charitable organizations, colleges and schools. In Cedar Rapids, Iowa, the chamber of commerce sponsors a group of older men who are devoting their energies to solution of civic problems.

Comparable organizations for older workingmen include such sheltered workshops as Goodwill Industries of America and local organizations which obtain part-time work in regular enterprises for older workers, such as Senior Achievement in Chicago and Enterprise, Inc., in Minneapolis (U.S. Department of Health, Education, and Welfare, 1956, 1958).

According to Desmond (1955), efforts are being made in New York State. He points out:

In Schenectady, N.Y., a retired grandmother organized a community drive to get jobs for the 40 plus. The retired school teachers of New York State are now working together to set up a housing project for themselves; in Little Corinth (3,161 people) a committee of the aged organized to determine what could be done, conducted a survey, talked the fire department into lending them the firehouse for a meeting place where they play cards, games, and hold kaffee-klatsches.

Some of the clubs for older people have a heavy educational content. The "Live Long and Like It Club" of Cleveland, sponsored by the public library and co-operative groups, has readings, discussions, field trips to museums, hobby shows that are informative, etc. There are about three hundred members, and the program committee is made up of members (Long and Lucioli, 1948).

E. Co-ordinating and Planning Agencies

Co-ordination of and information concerning the various public and private programs for the elderly are provided by departments of public welfare, organized on a city, county, or state basis, and by councils of social agencies. Community welfare councils (called by various names around the country) co-ordinate in more specific ways by doing surveys of needs of the elderly, working to improve standards of agencies aiding the elderly, urging existing agencies (such as Family Service, YMCA, libraries) to take on additional programs for the special benefit of the elderly, and even instigating new agencies (Vick, 1957). In Cleveland, for example, the Welfare Federation has since 1948 become the focal point of work with older people, and even before that provided a clearing house of information on work with the aging. It has organized a Committee on Older Persons for information and exchange of ideas, a Golden Age Hobby Show, a Health and Happiness Institute for older people themselves, an Occupational Planning Committee, a Vocational Guidance Center for Older People, and a Golden Age Center. Public libraries sometimes serve as clearing houses of information. There are also special organizations whose activity is to provide information about the aged. The following description of the Omaha, Nebraska, association will exemplify the activities of these organizations:

The Omaha Senior Citizens' Program is a new advisory service available to homes for the aged, churches, public and private welfare agencies, many work and recreation program agencies, service clubs, and organizations who wish to sponsor activities for older people. Sponsored by the Community Services and Park Recreation Commission, this provides information and consultation on activity organization, promotion, supervision, finance, facilities and participation. In addition, the Omaha Senior Citizens' Program sponsors a limited number of activities that are city-wide in nature for the older people [Edler, 1955, p. 240].

F. Evaluations of Group Work with the Aged

Interest in and activity for the welfare of older persons are found among a great variety of voluntary associations. When a blanket invitation was extended to voluntary associations in the state of Minnesota in 1956 to hold public discussions of problems of aging, the report said:

This challenge was met by a cross section of interests and organizations the length and breadth of Minnesota. For it was groups like the Catholic Daughters of America in Minnesota, the Alexandria Community Council and the Community Welfare Council of Hennepin County, the Council of Social Agencies in Winona, The Bethesda Old People's Home in Chicago City, Business and Professional Women's Club of Crookston, Rotary Club of Shakopee, Zonta's special committees created by county citizens and organizations and numerous others who sponsored these meetings [Minnesota, Governor's Conference on Aging, 1956, p. 23].

It is quite easy to overestimate the interest in clubs and other activities for the aged. In our anomic and specialized society, probably a significant proportion of old people do not know what is available to them. A study (Downing, 1957) made in a middle-sized city provides some information suggestive of the extent of the lack of information and interest in one recreational club for the aged:

The Mental Health Research Unit of New York State Department of Mental Hygiene surveyed all persons aged 65 years or older in six Syracuse, New York, census tracts in 1952. Only a small percentage (5%) had attended the Wagon Wheel, a club for the aged, although an additional 5 per cent were interested, and $\frac{2}{3}$ of the 1436 persons knew of the Club. Men in age groups 65–74 showed the least interest in the Club [p. 81].

There is considerable literature on the goals of clubs for old people and the best techniques for setting them up as indicated by experience. Woods (1953) has developed a guide for volunteers working with Golden Age clubs that is helpful to those interested in techniques of group work among the aging. Chalfin (1955) arrived at criteria for evaluating a program for the aged on the basis of interviews with 108 persons in centers for the aged in New York City and 108 persons in 7 old age homes. The criteria were:

1. Adjustment of the physical status and capacities;
2. Consideration of the individual's training, education, and past skills;
3. Opportunity for individual drives for self-esteem, usefulness, social approval, etc.;
4. Meaningful participation;
5. The attitudes, values, and habits of the individual;
6. Participation in formulation and operation of programs;
7. Encouragement of indigenous leadership;
8. Use of existing facilities;
9. Convenience of location;
10. Integration with other services for the aged;
11. Long-range planning;
12. Knowledge of individual physical condition, mental level, etc.;
13. Skilled counseling on individual problems.

In his evaluation of the Golden Age clubs in Cleveland, Schulze (1949) observed:

Factors essential to the success of the club program are found to be: gearing the programs to the individual members' needs and cultural and educational levels; selecting programs to help members maintain interest in community and national affairs; including celebrations of special occasions in lives of members, such as birthdays and golden wedding anniversaries; utilizing members' initiative and resources in planning and carrying out the programs. Leaders must be sensitive to the needs of the club members and have a knowledge of, and be able to use, community resources to supply those needs. Of 200 club members interviewed, over 85 per cent considered the club either a significant social outlet or their major outlet.

There have been numerous attempts to evaluate the clubs and community centers for the aged, although rarely with modern sociological research techniques. An article by Marya Mannes (1954) describes the William Hodson Community Center in the Bronx, New York City, opened in 1943 by the Department of Welfare but now supported by the Greater New York Fund:

It is rather significant that most of the older people came to the Center not immediately after retiring but after many years of living alone. A Hodson report comments: "If these adjustments [the high incidence of mental and physical improvements shown by the members] can still take place after years of neglect and in periods of such limited education, it would seem that future programs of day care centers may hope to do not only remedial but preventive work in the years which are now wasted and with persons who have hitherto been a costly charge to clinics, institutions and mental hospitals. . . . There has not been a single admission to a mental hospital from among the membership, a startling fact in the light of the sharp increase of the aged in such asylums.

Hodson is open everyday from nine till five. To many of the men this span is the substitute for the business day, to others for the club. . . . Self-government is inadequate and a trained and tolerant staff imperative.

An article by Sylvia Rothchild (1954) on the Golden Age Club at the Jewish Community Center in Dorchester, Massachusetts, points out that goals of companionship and recreation come up against class, cultural, and individual psychological differences. This makes for dissension and bitterness but also for vitality. The club serves important functions even for those members who complain the most. On the other hand, Rothchild's observations raise a very significant question for those who are organizing recreational associations for the aged: age may not be a sufficient basis for sociability. Common interest, capacity, and backgrounds—as well as age and sex—are usual requirements for other expressive associations in our society, and they may also well be essential

preconditions for the success of clubs for the elderly.

In Cleveland, fourteen students of the School of Applied Social Sciences interviewed two hundred members of sixteen clubs sponsored by the Benjamin Rose Institute of that city. They found that

the members use the club activities to meet their particular needs and define the experience in terms of their own life situation . . . : For over 85 per cent of those interviewed the club was either of major significance as their most meaningful outlet or had significance but was not the only significant outlet. To less than 15 per cent the club had meaning only as just one other social tie [Schulze, 1949, p. 313].

Certain aspects of a number of studies dealing with the effects of participation of the aged in associations are partially relevant to our interest in voluntary associations. Donahue *et al.* (1953) studied the effect of introducing an activity program into homes for the aged. Using an experimental design, with a control as well as an experimental group, they arrived at the following main conclusions:

Comparison of data from the two assessments supports the hypothesis that the introduction of an intensive activities program will result in increased socialization and greater integration in group structure of residents, and that, in the absence of such a program, socialization and group integration will decrease or remain the same [p. 656].

Another approach to evaluation of participation among elderly persons is represented by the study of Pressey and Simcoe (1950). This study compared "successful" and "problem" cases among the elderly, men and women separately. Eighty per cent of the 215 successful old men had at least one participation, as compared to only 17 per cent among the 109 problem old men. Among women, 86 per cent of the 134 successful, as compared to only 19 per cent among the 95 problem cases, had at least one participation. The general conclusion of the study is that "especially differential of the successful old people were their continuing usefulness, their many social relationships, their maintaining various abilities, and their lively and varied interests."

After doing a similar kind of evaluation in their study of "Prairie City," Havighurst and Albrecht (1953) stated:

It is clear that those people who continue to be active in associations are happier and better adjusted than those who do not. The average adjustment scores of those who belong to associations are considerably higher than the scores of those who do not belong. The coefficient of correlation of social club activity with total attitude score is .22, and with adjustment rating the coefficient is .45. These relationships may be caused by health factors, since those who are in better health are better able to get around to meetings of associations, and tend to be better adjusted. Consequently, we cannot say that we have proved that a person who belongs to no associations would become happier and better adjusted if he joined a club. While this seems a reasonable conclusion, we can only treat it as an assumption that seems reasonable and worth acting upon [p. 340].

Other studies finding a correlation between the activity and the happiness of the elderly are those by Folsom and Morgan (1937) and by Landis (1942); no contrary findings have been reported.

V. PROFESSIONAL ORGANIZATIONS INTERESTED IN THE AGED

Professional organizations manifest an interest in the problems of the aging in a great variety of ways. In the first place, there is the Gerontological Society, Inc. (founded 1944), with headquarters in St. Louis, Missouri, that is primarily and professionally concerned with the full range of problems confronting elderly people. It promotes research, professional training, and exchange of scientific knowledge and publishes the *Journal of Gerontology* and the *Gerontological Society Newsletter*. The American Society for the Aged is a foundation in New York City to promote training and research in gerontology. In a way a government counter-part to these broad-gauged organizations is the Federal Council on Aging, consisting of officials designated by all those heads of departments and agencies in the federal government whose activities affect older persons. The council meets periodically to review the programs of member agencies and to recommend improvements in these programs. Two professional groups have specialized associations for those among their members whose work is primarily connected with the elderly. Physicians have the American Geriatrics Society (founded 1942), with headquarters in Montclair, New Jersey, which publishes the *Journal of the American Geriatrics Society*. Social workers have the National Committee on the Aging (founded 1950) of the National Social Welfare Assembly (which is itself a federation of voluntary and governmental agencies), with headquarters in New York City. The 250 members of the National Committee represent business and industry, organized labor, the health professions, the clergy, education, housing, research, government, and state and local committees on the aging, as well as the profession of social work proper. The National Committee has a great variety of activities, including the maintenance of a library and a national information and consultation center; the holding of conferences and workshops; the stimulation of research and of new kinds of service programs; the preparation of books, pamphlets, films, and exhibits; the encouragement of media of mass communications to combat the stereotype of age and to publicize programs and needs; and the provision of some field services.

Proprietors of nursing and convalescent homes have organized the American Nursing Home Association, with headquarters in Springfield, Ohio, to develop standards for facilities and patient care and to develop regulatory legislation. The American Public Welfare Association, consisting of directors of all kinds of public welfare agencies and having its headquarters in Chicago, has a permanent section devoted primarily to those problems of the aged which are the professional concern of its members.

The American Medical Association, the Group for the Advancement of Psychiatry, and the Adult Education Association also have special permanent divisions for work in aging. Annual meetings of professional organizations whose work only occasionally touches upon the aged—psychiatrists and group workers, for example—often have sections devoted to the discussion and presentation of papers dealing with selected problems of the aged. Scientific societies tend to follow the latter pattern. The American Sociological Society more and more often contributes one or two sessions of its annual meetings to research on social aspects of aging. An affiliated subgroup of sociologists, the Society for the Study of Social Problems, more regularly devotes part of its annual meeting to the same subject. Sociologists and others conducting research on social problems of the aged usually publish their findings in the professional sociological journals, especially in the *American Journal of Sociology* and *Social Problems*. The American Psychological Association created a Division of Later Maturity in 1946 to provide a forum for those interested in research on aging. One or more sessions are held in connection with the annual meetings of the association, and papers appear frequently in the professional journals of psychologists. Other scientific and professional groups include a few persons who devote at least occasional attention to some aspect of the problems of the aged—among them are architects, economists, and anthropologists. The Social Science Research Council, a research-stimulating organization located in New York City, for some years (1943–48) had a Committee on Social Adjustment in Old Age which compiled a research memorandum on this topic. Some of the professional and scientific groups carry on activities on a local and state level as well as on a national level. State gerontological societies have been organized in Connecticut, Florida, Georgia, Michigan, Texas,

and in the western states. These organizations hold scientific meetings, conduct conferences, and sometimes promote pilot programs for older persons.

Most of the scientific and professional interest in the aged is of fairly recent origin, at least as far as organizational expression of this interest is concerned. This reflects the rise of public consciousness of the elderly as a special social category in recent years. The prospects are for an increasing expression of interest in the problems of the aged in the professional and scientific bodies in the future. The pattern that we have sketched for the United States is true for many other technologically advanced countries. There is an International Association of Gerontology, with periodic congresses and permanent research committees.

VI. Problems of Voluntary Associations for the Aged

A. General Problems of Voluntary Associations

Before turning to the special problems that may arise for certain voluntary associations by virtue of the fact that their purpose is to help the aged, let us first consider some of the general kinds of problems that arise for voluntary associations of any type. This form of social organization is beset by two opposing types of problems: one is a very high death rate arising from the apathy of its members, and the other is a tendency to continue an organization that no longer has a significant function. The latter kind of problem may very probably confront organizations that have as their major purpose assisting people who are suffering from a certain kind of disease. A very real need, coupled with the fears of a large segment of the population with respect to the disease and the public good will toward effort at controlling it, builds up a large organization with standard means of fund-raising and a bureaucratic staff. The voluntary and paid leaders of the organization sometimes develop a

national reputation as successful organizers
and managers of a most worthwhile enterprise for the public good. Then a medical
discovery occurs which wipes out the disease. But the association is not wiped out.
There is too heavy an investment in equipment, organization, and reputation. There
may be a significant decline in the ability
to raise funds, but older habits remain,
and enough funds come in to maintain the
overhead operations. Some of the more
flexible and less committed staff members
leave for new positions, but those who
have been spending more of their lives in
this job tend to remain. Some of the voluntary leaders lose interest, but others see
no reason to disband an organization where
they have built up such fine reputations,
have enjoyed sociable contacts, and have
access to power. Sometimes an entirely
new purpose is discovered, but more likely
the organization continues to serve the
dwindling number of chronically disabled
people who were earlier victims of the disease.

In general, however, the problems of old
age are increasing, not decreasing, and we
shall not further consider the second type
of problem which afflicts voluntary associations. But the first type of problem—
where there is a struggle to keep an association alive to meet certain real needs—is
very serious for voluntary associations for
the aged. A voluntary association is by its
very nature a side activity—an activity for
leisure time. When any distraction arises
in the lives of its members, they are most
likely to forego their obligations to the association rather than those to their families, their occupations, or their churches. A
few members, usually the leaders, have a
sense of primary responsibility for the association and are willing to carry on their
activity in it sometimes at real sacrifice.
However, most of the members consider
themselves as contributing something to
the association and as being free to withdraw their contribution at any time on the
basis of personal convenience. Changes in
the life of the individual are more likely to

affect their participation in voluntary associations than in any other institution.
For example, whereas moving from one
community to another in accommodation
to a job does not disrupt family or church
participation, it is likely to be the occasion
of complete severance from participation in
a voluntary association. When members
develop new interests, they are likely to
discontinue their participation in voluntary associations in which they have been
members for some time. On the other hand,
new interests generally do not affect one's
occupational, family, or church affiliation.
When members feel that the association is
not successful or when their time is being
devoted to doing dull and routine tasks,
their participation in the activity of the
association will sharply diminish. While
voluntary associations as a group constitute a most flourishing institution in American life, many individual associations are
regularly on the verge of decline and disappearance. It would make a most instructive study to determine the causes of the
decline and death of voluntary associations, since this remains a gap in sociological knowledge.

When the beneficiaries of the work of
the voluntary associations are the aged,
there are special handicaps to the carrying-
on of the work of the association. The controversies and diverse points of view over
dealing with problems of health, economic
assistance, housing, etc., with respect to
aging that are discussed in several of the
preceding chapters reflect themselves in the
day-to-day activities of the voluntary associations set up to handle these problems
for the benefit of the aged. If the experts
have divergent opinions as to whether the
indigent aged should be urged to keep their
old homes or whether they should be
brought together under a common roof,
this becomes the subject of continued debate for an association or a committee
which has the problem of helping the indigent aged to be properly housed. Such a
debate may be stimulating to its members
and lead to definitive research. On the oth-

er hand, it may also lead to fruitless arguments and frustration of the regular activity of the association. With the partial exception of the health field, there is as yet too little scientific and expert information on which lay members and directors of the association can rely to conduct the necessary ongoing activities of their association. They have to depend on personal experience and common sense, both of which vary from member to member.

B. Special Problems Arising from the Characteristics of the Elderly

There are some particular problems of this sort affecting associations whose members are mostly in the upper age bracket or whose purpose is to help the aged. Older persons are most subject to illness which disrupts their participation in associations. The aged as indicated are more likely to become victims of mental or physical disabilities which prevent them from continuing their participation in the associations of which they have been members. When the decline in health is gradual, the aged members may not abruptly cease to participate in the activity of the association, but the quality of the participation diminishes and hampers the activity of the association. Voluntary activity which requires expenditures on the part of its participants is more likely to be dropped by older people with reduced incomes. Elderly people who are not sure for how many years they will have to stretch their savings are even likely to question nominal dues payment to an association. If the association has both younger and older persons among its members, differences in orientation toward the purpose of the association as well as in the pace of carrying out the activity of the association may create a cleavage within it which is harmful to its continued life or, at least, to its effective functioning. Clark Tibbitts (1954) adds to this list of difficulties which tend to keep older persons from participating in voluntary associations:

Many retired persons do not know of the opportunities in this field. Some who do seem to lack confidence in their capacities, some encounter the same discrimination as in gainful employment, some find that voluntary services are not so conducted as to recognize the values of maturity or yield a sense of accomplishment and recognition [p. 306].

When a program of leisure-time activities is conducted for the benefit of the aged, certain disabilities of the aged affect their participation which only rarely must be considered when the leisure-time programs are for younger people. Irregularity of participation due to ill health, physical inability to participate in many kinds of activities, faltering attention on the part of those whose mental powers are occasionally shaky, and lack of sustained interest on the part of those who look toward the past rather than toward the future are some of the serious difficulties with which one must cope if a regular recreational program for the aged is to be successfully conducted.

C. Getting the Elderly Involved

The problem of getting the elderly clientele psychologically involved in the activity of the voluntary associations working for their benefit deserves special attention. It has become a truism for all organizational and group work that, whatever the specific program of the group may be, the involvement of the participants is necessary in planning, problem-solving, and actually carrying on the activity. A very large portion of older persons have not had the previous experience and skill necessary for effective group participation. Often elderly people do not know how to carry on a discussion, and many lack motivation to do so, even when their mental faculties have not deteriorated. A large proportion of older people seem to want things to be done *for* them, and even expect things to be done *to* them, rather than having things done *by* them. Lay leaders who begin their work with high motivation are often discouraged by this lack of psychological involvement and sometimes move to the unwholesome extremes of either becoming apathetic themselves or of becoming overly directive. The problem is especially serious when the program of the association calls for positive activity on the part of the aged participants rather than merely passive observation. This is even true of exercises and remedial activity, the purpose of which is to sustain physical health.

Programs involving training and education are likely to suffer from the fact that some aged participants see little point in learning something because they have so little ambition or expectation for the future left. Such persons are unwilling to make the effort to study, especially outside the classroom. Certainly, new techniques to heighten motivation are needed, and better techniques for teaching older people need to be tested, so that the special problems of training and educating the elderly can be handled more effectively. More knowledge is needed of how to get older persons ego-involved in programs designed for their benefit. Medical men feel it imperative that methods be devised for giving proper orientation to the aged who need physical therapy. Particularly is this problem pressing when the treatments are painful, require positive effort in activities, or must be spread over a long period of time. The whole problem of getting a lively sense of psychological participation on the part of the aged, and, in general, the proper orientation toward participation, is an important field for experimentation and further research.

D. Competition and Conflict within and between Associations

Another difficulty plaguing many voluntary associations in our society, which probably does not afflict many associations for the elderly now but may come to do so in future years, is the problem of competition and conflict among associations. Currently, the need is to create more associations for the elderly and to help the latter to participate in them. If, in the future, there should be more associations than the elderly have interest, time, and capacity for, and if there should develop very diverse philosophies as to how associations should be organized and function, then competition and conflict among associations for the elderly would likely occur. This does not necessarily hurt the associations, but it puts them into a new relationship to their members or beneficiaries which is different from what occurs under the present non-competitive, non-conflicting conditions (Rose, 1955*b*).

Sometimes there are problems of competition and conflict within a single association. While these might be over any issue or division, one of the most common problems occurs when young and middle-aged organizers and directors of associations for the aged gain such satisfactions from their work that they retain tight control of the organization and refuse to let the elderly "beneficiaries" have any voice in the management or planning of activities. If the elderly participants resist, there is conflict; if they accede to the benevolent despotism, they often become apathetic and less participant. On occasions, conflict within the association may involve three sets of contestants, all having different interests and viewpoints. The professional paid personnel may covertly be contending both with the lay volunteers and directors and with the elderly clientele.

VII. The Functions of Voluntary Associations for the Elderly

A. General Functions

The special role of voluntary associations in contemporary industrial American society has been emphasized in the first section of this chapter. Voluntary associations serve certain needs that have become accentuated in this kind of a society and make certain services available relatively quickly by not waiting until the formal processes of government are adjusted to meet unexpected and rapidly developing needs. The voluntary association provides the individual with certain opportunities for sociability and with an important means of personal identification. Through the voluntary association, people have opportunities for meaningful participation in activities that are considered important in the society. Among the significant functions of the voluntary association is their serving on occasions as pressure groups seeking to accomplish certain ends by influencing other power structures in the society such as the government and business. In functioning as a pressure group, the voluntary association provides its members with an understanding of how pressure and power operate in the society, and, thus, the individual gains a keener understanding of how society operates in general.

B. Functions as Related to the Characteristics of the Elderly

Elderly people have certain particular relationships to these functions of voluntary associations which, because of the lack of systematic research, can merely be sketched. The formal voluntary association brings together people of similar interests and similar characteristics. It is sometimes relatively difficult in an urban environment for an elderly person to find people of the same age and interests. A club for the elderly provides the introduction and the setting in which they can freely associate. This is especially important for older people who may have some physical difficulty in getting around to seek out their own friends personally, and it is especially necessary when the aged no longer have the immediate family to provide friendship and sociability. The values of membership are thus not only sociability but also a sense of personal identification with a group. Everyone has to identify himself as a certain kind of person, and one significant kind of identification in our society is as a member of a certain association.

Levine (1952) summarizes some of the main functions of voluntary associations for the aged in his evaluation of day centers:

A day center program utilizing the added time, the remaining strength, and the areas of competency of the older person during the hours usually spent at work can provide satisfactions associated with work, such as social usefulness, opportunities for self-expression, recognition, belonging, companionship, an established motive, something to look forward to [p. 169].

The activity of pressure groups working for the elderly, including all kinds of social influence organizations, provides an especially meaningful activity for the elderly who otherwise have been withdrawn from the meaningful life-activity that occupation and family provide. If the organization works for the benefit of its own members, it is even more meaningful than the activity of just any voluntary association. Except for the few individuals who are involved in politics and fairly high-level business decisions, the voluntary association provides the only contact with the processes by which a complex society operates. For most individuals the voluntary association is a means of relating the individual to *this* world just as the church is a means of relating the individual to the *"other"* world." Social change has certain particular impacts on the aged. The voluntary association can experiment and provide models for new ways of handling these problems arising from social change. In this way, the voluntary association can lead the way for the larger institutions of government and industry as well as meeting the immediate needs of some of the elderly as soon as sufficient awareness of these needs reaches the general public.

Certain voluntary agencies are increasingly aware of the special needs of the aged and are attempting to do something about them. This awareness needs to be expanded and extended. The large majority of voluntary associations in our society which are equipped to provide certain special services and satisfy some of the particular needs of the elderly have not yet attained awareness of these opportunities and unexpressed demands. Even more important is the necessity of making the older people aware of the special opportunities offered to them by voluntary associations. Especially among those who have not been participants in their earlier years, the aged are often unaware of the special role which voluntary associations can serve and the special satisfaction which they can give in a society where other institutions do not function or have ceased to function in meeting their particular needs. While there is a certain functional movement on the part of the elderly and the institution of voluntary associations toward each other, there is a definite lag in this movement. This lag is mainly due to the fact that voluntary associations function in a relatively unsystematic manner and fail to communicate their activities and functions to people who would be interested if they knew them.

C. Need of Publicity

Voluntary associations seldom have publicity and public relations specialists to communicate the nature of their activities in the manner used regularly by industry and government, and the aged are possibly more blocked from receiving what communications do exist than are other adult members of our society. The special activity that is necessary to bring the aged into relation to voluntary associations is only being partially met by certain kinds of adult-education, recreation, and social service workers. What is perhaps required in our society, not only for the aged but perhaps especially for them, is a special voluntary association that would serve as publicity agent and public relations officer for voluntary associations generally. These might be organized locally in the large cities, but they would operate more efficiently if they had a national center. Such an association could gain only voluntary cooperation from the organizations they were

servicing, as the latter are quite often highly resistant to any efforts to put pressures and obligations on them. But whatever difficulties there would be in the way of such a new association would be more than compensated for by the great service such an association would provide. It would fill a gap in our social structure that is created by the fact that the voluntary associations, by their very nature, are usually unsystematic and often haphazard and by the fact that individual citizens—especially the more helpless and isolated among them —have increasing needs for the activities of these associations. The suggested informational center would not impose order on the other voluntary associations but would somewhat compensate for their inherent lack of order as far as the requirements and needs of individual citizens are concerned.

VIII. Voluntary Associations for the Aged in Other Societies

This chapter has been partly based on the assumption that the institution of the voluntary association has performed, or is capable of performing, a variety of special and valuable functions for the aged in modern society.

We cannot close without asking the question as to how extensively this is true. European critics sometimes find fault with Americans for what they regard as overorganization and overparticipation. Dr. R. J. van Zonneveld, co-ordinating physician for gerontological research at the National Health Research Council in The Hague, Netherlands, is reported in the *New York Times* (Anonymous, 1957) as saying to an audience at the Gerontological Society at Cleveland, Ohio, on October 31, 1957:

In Europe, we tend to let old people relax, sit out old age, look out a window and enjoy old age, if they feel like it. In the United States you seem to try to get them busy in golden age clubs and things like that. We have the idea that they should rest, unless they feel like being active [p. 29].

It is quite possible that the value of voluntary associations differs from one culture to another. For the United States, studies seem to indicate that life-satisfaction is associated with social participation (Rose, 1955a) and some studies of the aged that were noted on earlier pages of this chapter indicated that those older people who are participant in voluntary associations are happier and better adjusted. Older people may not be motivated to participate, and McConnell (1954) noted the protests raised in the United States against pushing the elderly into activities, but the consequences for them seem to be better when they do participate. It is also true that, in this country, the voluntary association provides one of the easiest and most effective devices for achieving a social goal. As Mary E. Switzer and Howard A. Rusk (1952) say, in discussing how to keep older people in good health:

As has been traditionally true in our country, it will be the voluntary associations—hospitals, community groups, and religious organizations —that, by virtue of their close ties with their people, can point the way to precise methods to accomplish our ideal [p. 152].

The American pattern seems to hold true for the United Kingdom if we are to judge from various articles (Ramsey, 1951, 1953; Moss, 1954). It is also to be noted that day centers for the aged, generally sponsored by the government, exist in France and Australia as well as Canada and England (Levine, 1952). Granting that all this may be perfectly true in the United States, it may well be less true in other societies where inactivity is more highly valued and people are more used to relying on government to serve their social welfare needs. As sociological scientists, we must be willing to concede that parts of this chapter may be false when applied to cultures other than the American, until such time as the care and satisfaction of the aged in other societies are adequately studied.

Considering that practically all the voluntary associations of and for the elderly in this country have come into existence since 1930 (with the exception of old people's homes), it seems likely that the voluntary association arose as an institution in response to the withdrawal of the interest, support, and social life previously provided to the elderly by the extended family. Many other societies, especially in Europe, are experiencing the decline of the extended family. Because the voluntary associations for and of the elderly are still in their pioneer period, they await experience, evaluation, and the emergence of accepted standards before their forms and activities assume stability and gain general acceptance.

IX. Suggested Problems and Hypotheses for Research

The following are only a few of the research topics that need systematic, objective examination before our scientific and practical knowledge about the relationship between the elderly and the voluntary associations can be advanced.

1. *Hypothesis:* Voluntary associations for the benefit of the aged tend to develop in those societies in which the family has partially ceased to maintain and help the aged.

2. *Hypotheses:* Participation of the aged in voluntary associations is greater when the following conditions prevail than when the opposite conditions prevail:

   a) Voluntary associations are a well-established institution in the society.
   b) The elderly tend to lose their occupational and familial roles when they reach a certain age.
   c) The elderly retain physical and mental health.
   d) A deliberate effort is made to encourage the membership of the elderly in voluntary associations.
   e) Age does not automatically bring status.
   f) The elderly form a large proportion of the population of the community.
   g) The elderly live apart from their children.
   h) The economy permits more "free time."

The specific circumstances under which the elderly tend to be active in voluntary associations is a general problem for research, which as yet remains a matter of conflicting findings.

3. *Hypotheses:* When the elderly form their own associations, they are likely to form them for political purposes, whereas when younger people form associations for the elderly they are likely to form them for social, recreational, and welfare purposes.

4. *Problem:* Under what conditions are voluntary associations for the elderly effective organizations in satisfying the needs of the elderly? Very little is known about the conditions for effectiveness of voluntary associations and evaluation studies need to be made. Among the conditions that should be studied are the extent to which

   a) the elderly plan and control the activities of the association themselves,

   b) the association works on *specific* projects,

   c) the members have specific purposes for joining a voluntary association rather than merely as an escape from boredom,

   d) the association works on projects for the benefit of underprivileged outsiders,

   e) there is ethnic, status, and educational homogeneity among the members,

   f) there are differences of opinion over real issues among the members, and

   g) the members are stable residents of the community rather than mobile.

5. *Hypothesis:* The elderly are more conservative than younger people in the formulation both of goals and of techniques for achieving these goals in voluntary associations.

6. *Hypothesis:* As the number of older people joining a specific voluntary association increases, the younger members tend to drop out.

7. *Problem:* Under what conditions does a voluntary association cease to acquire new, younger members, so that in the course of time all the members become elderly?

8. *Problem:* What has been the effect of increased public awareness on the development of voluntary associations for the benefit of the elderly?

9. *Hypothesis:* Active participation in voluntary associations in younger years, as well as older years, is associated with better personal adjustment in old age.

10. *Problem:* What are the motives of younger persons who organize voluntary associations for older persons, and which motives lead to successful organization?

11. *Problem:* What kind of sponsorship and what source of financing are most likely to contribute to successful voluntary associations for the benefit of the elderly?

12. *Problem:* What are the factors that contribute to the dissolution of an association for the elderly?

13. *Problem:* Under what circumstances will an association which loses its major purpose change to a new, vital purpose and so continue its existence?

14. *Problem:* What are the most effective ways of using the voluntary associations as a medium of educating elderly members to maintain their physical and mental health?

15. *Problem:* Under what circumstances do conflict or competition among associations for the elderly promote more effective activity for the benefit of the elderly members and under what circumstances do they lead merely to fruitless bickering and meaningless rivalry?

16. *Problem:* Under what circumstances will a voluntary association most effectively serve each of the basic latent functions that have been suggested in this paper (sociability, understanding, power and control, personal identification, services to meet new group needs)?

17. *Problem:* How can potential elderly members of an association be most effectively informed of these "functions" when the ostensible purpose of an association seems to be much more limited?

REFERENCES

ALBRECHT, RUTH. 1951. The social roles of old people. J. Gerontol., **6**, 138–45.

ANDERSON, A., and RYAN, B. 1943. Social participation differences among tenure classes in a prosperous commercialized farming area. Rural Sociology, **8**, 281–90.

ANONYMOUS. 1955. How to retire and stay active. Nation's Business, **43**, 94–96.

———. 1957. New York Times, November 1, p. 29.

AVRUNIN, W. 1957. Jewish social services. *In* R. H. KURTZ (ed.), Social work year book, 1957, pp. 324–30. New York: National Association of Social Workers.

BERKMAN, SARA LEE. 1958. Personal communication. National Council of Jewish Women, New York.

BRIGGS, MARION L. 1954. Hobbies for older people. Today's Health, **32**, 28–29, 65–67.

BRYCE, J. 1910. The American commonwealth, Vol. 2. New York: Macmillan Co.

BUSHEE, F. A. 1945. Social organization in a small city. Am. J. Sociology, **51**, 217–26.

CAVAN, RUTH S., BURGESS, E. W., HAVIGHURST, R. J., and GOLDHAMER, H. 1949. Personal adjustment in old age. Chicago: Science Research Associates.

CHALFEN, L. 1955. Planning leisure-time activities of the aging. Geriatrics, **10**, 245–47.

COMMUNITY PROJECT FOR THE AGED, WELFARE COUNCIL OF METROPOLITAN CHICAGO. 1952. Community services for older people: the Chicago plan. Chicago: Wilcox & Follett.

DESMOND, T. C. 1955. Age of the aged. Rotarian, **87**, 14–15, 63.

DONAHUE, WILMA, HUNTER, W. W., and COONS, DOROTHY H. 1953. A study of the socialization of old people. Geriatrics, **8**, 656–66.

DOTSON, F. 1951. Patterns of voluntary associations among urban working-class families. Am. Sociological Rev., **16**, 687–93.

DOWNING, J. 1957. Factors affecting the selective use of a social club for the aged. J. Gerontol., **12**, 81–84.

EDLER, K. F. 1955. Organization of service to senior citizens. Recreation, **48**, 240–41.

FISHER L. H. 1950. The politics of age. *In* M. DERBER (ed.), The aged and society, pp. 156–67. Champaign, Ill.: Industrial Relations Research Association.

FOLSOM, J. K., and MORGAN, CHRISTINE M. 1937. Social adjustment of 381 recipients of old age allowances. Am. Sociological Rev., **2**, 223–29.

FREEDMAN, R., and AXELROD, M. 1952. Who belongs to what in a great metropolis? Adult Leadership, **1** (November), 6–9.

GLICK, P. C. 1955. The life cycle of the family. Marriage & Family Living, **17**, 3–9.

GOLDHAMER, H. 1942. Some factors affecting participation in voluntary associations. Unpublished Ph.D. dissertation, University of Chicago.

HAVIGHURST, R. J. 1957. The leisure activities of the middle-aged. Am. J. Sociology, **63**, 152–62.

HAVIGHURST, R. J., and ALBRECHT, RUTH. 1953. Older people. New York: Longmans, Green & Co.

HENNEPIN COUNTY WELFARE BOARD. 1956. Senior citizens community clubs and organizations: Minneapolis Metropolitan Area. Minneapolis, Minn.: The Board.

HOYT, G. C. 1954. The life of the retired in a trailer park. Am. J. Sociology, **59**, 361–70.

INTERNATIONAL CONFERENCE ON THE CHURCH AND OLDER PEOPLE. 1953. The fulfillment years in Christian education: a program for older persons. Chicago: National Council of Churches of Christ in the U.S.A.

JOHNSON, F. E., and VILLAUME, W. J. 1957. Protestant social services. *In* R. H. KURTZ (ed.), Social work year book, 1957, pp. 421–31. New York: National Association of Social Workers.

KAPLAN, J. 1951. The role of the public welfare agency in meeting the needs of the older person. Public Welfare, **9**, 208–11.

———. 1953. A social program for older people. Minneapolis: University of Minnesota Press.

———. 1954. Observations on the somatic and psychosomatic significance of group activity on older people. Ment. Hygiene, **38**, 640–46.

KOMAROVSKY, MIRRA. 1946. Voluntary associations of urban dwellers. Am. Sociological Rev., **11**, 686–98.

KURTZ, R. H. (ed.). 1957. Social work year book, 1957. New York: National Association of Social Workers.

LANDIS, J. T. 1940. Attitudes and adjustments of aged rural people in Iowa. Unpublished Ph.D. dissertation, Louisiana State University.

———. 1942. Socio-psychological factors of aging. Social Forces, **20**, 468–70.

———. 1946. Old age movements in the United States. *In* R. J. HAVIGHURST (ed.), Social adjustment in old age. New York: Social Science Research Council.

LENNON, J. J. 1957. Catholic social service. *In* R. H. KURTZ (ed.), Social work year book, 1957, pp. 139–46. New York: National Association of Social Workers.

LEVINE, H. A. 1952. Community programs for the elderly. Ann. Am. Acad. Political & Social Sc., **279**, 164–70.

LIFSHUTZ, M. 1958. Personal communication. B'nai B'rith, Washington, D.C.

LITTLE, K. 1957. The role of voluntary associations in West African urbanization. Am. Anthropology, **59**, 579–97.

LONG, FERN, and LUCIOLI, CLARA. 1948. The Live Long and Like It Club. Wilson Library Bull., **23**, 301–5.

LUND, HENRIETTE. 1951. Lutheran services for older people. New York: National Lutheran Council, Division of Welfare.

LYND, R. S., and LYND, HELEN M. 1929. Middletown. New York: Harcourt, Brace & Co.

McCONNELL, R. A. 1954. I refuse to be organized. Christian Century, **71,** 1428–29.

McKAIN, W. C. 1947. The social participation of old people in a California retirement community. Unpublished Ph.D. dissertation, Harvard University.

McKAIN, W. C., and BALDWIN, E. D. 1951. Old age and retirement in rural Connecticut. I. East Haddam: a summer resort community. (Agric. Bull. 278.) Storrs, Conn.: University of Connecticut, Agricultural Experiment Station.

MANNES, MARYA. 1954. Coming of age: report on the Hodson Center. Reporter, **11,** 32–35.

MARTIN, W. T. 1952. Consideration of the differences in the extent and location of the formal associational activities of rural-urban fringe residents. Am. Sociological Rev., **17,** 687–94.

MATHER, W. G. 1941. Income and social participation. Am. Sociological Rev., **6,** 380–84.

MAVES, P. B., and CEDARLEAF, J. L. 1949. Older people and the church. Nashville: Abington-Cokesbury Press.

MAYO, S. C. 1951. Social participation among the older population in rural areas of Wake County, N.C. Social Forces, **30,** 53–59.

MINNESOTA. STATE. GOVERNOR'S CONFERENCE ON AGING. 1956. Report of the First Governor's Conference on Aging. St. Paul, Minn.: The Conference.

MITCHELL, W. C. 1958. Expand opportunities for senior citizens. Aging, No. 42, p. 2.

MONROE, R. T. 1951. Diseases in old age. Cambridge, Mass.: Harvard University Press.

MOSS, J. 1954. Helping the elderly in Great Britain: scope of programs of voluntary organizations and of the state. Aging, No. 14, pp. 1–3.

MYRDAL, G. 1954. An American dilemma. New York: Harper & Bros.

NEUBERGER, R. L., and LOE, K. 1936. Army of the aged. Caldwell, Idaho: Caxton Printers.

OGDEN, JEAN, and OGDEN, J. 1952. Sharing community responsibility. Ann. Am. Acad. Political & Social Sc., **279,** 101–3.

PRESSEY, S. L., and SIMCOE, ELIZABETH. 1950. Case studies of successful and problem old people. J. Gerontol., **5,** 168–75.

RAMSEY, D. 1951. Contribution of the voluntary societies to the welfare of the elderly in U.K. J. Gerontol., **6** (Suppl. 1), 137–38.

———. 1953. National Old People's Welfare Committee of U.K. Ibid., **7,** 501–2.

RAVIN, L., and TIBBITTS, C. 1958. Organizations and services for older people. In E. V. COWDRY (ed.), Care of the geriatric patient, pp. 352–92. St. Louis: C. V. Mosby Co.

RAWLINSON, J. L. 1958. Don't discount grandpa. Catholic Digest, **19,** 85–88.

REID, I. D., and EHLE, E. L. 1950. Leadership selection in urban locality areas. Public Opinion Quart., **14,** 262–84.

ROSE, A. M. 1954. Theory and method in the social sciences. Minneapolis: University of Minnesota Press.

———. 1955a. Factors associated with the life satisfaction of middle-class middle-aged persons. Marriage & Family Living, **17,** 15–19.

———. 1955b. Voluntary associations under conditions of competition and conflict. Social Forces, **34,** 159–63.

ROTHCHILD, SYLVIA. 1954. Sixty-five and over. Commentary, **18,** 549–56.

SCHULZE, O. 1949. Recreation for the aged. J. Gerontol., **4,** 310–13.

SCOTT, J. C. 1948. Membership participation in voluntary associations. Unpublished M.A. thesis, University of Chicago.

———. 1957. Membership and participation in voluntary associations. Am. Sociological Rev., **22,** 315–26.

SIMMONS, L. W. 1952. Social participation of the aged in different cultures. Ann. Am. Acad. Political & Social Sc., **279,** 43–51.

SNYDER, RUTH. 1954. A volunteer program for older persons. Recreation, **47,** 582–83.

———. 1955. Senior citizens in recreation. Ibid., **48,** 70–71.

STAFFORD, VIRGINIA. 1953. Older adults in the church. New York: Methodist Publishing House.

SWITZER, MARY E., and RUSK, H. A. 1952. Keeping older people fit for participation. Ann. Am. Acad. Political & Social Sc., **279,** 146–53.

TIBBITTS, C. 1954. Retirement problems in American society. Am. J. Sociology, **59,** 301–8.

TOCQUEVILLE, A. DE. 1899. Democracy in America, **2,** 114–18. New York: Colonial Press.

UNITED AUTOMOBILE WORKERS–C.I.O. 1956. Report of the U.A.W. retired workers centers in the Detroit area. Detroit: United Auto Workers. (Processed.)

U.S. Department of Health, Education, and Welfare, Special Staff on Aging. 1956. Aging, No. 26, p. 5.

——. 1958. Senior Achievement, Inc. *Ibid.*, No. 39, p. 1.

Uzzell, O. 1953. Institutional membership and class levels. Sociology & Social Research, **37,** 390–94.

Vick, Hollis. 1957. America and her older people: developments in social planning councils. Unpublished manuscript of speech given to the American Public Welfare Association Round Table, Chicago.

Warner, W. L., and Lunt, P. S. 1941. The so-cial life of a modern community. ("Yankee City Series," Vol. 1.) New Haven, Conn.: Yale University Press.

Webber, I. L. 1954. The organized social life of the retired: two Florida communities. Am. J. Sociology, **59,** 340–46.

Weber, M. 1940. Geschäftsbericht. Verhandlungen des Ersten deutschen Sociologentages vom 19–22 Oktober, 1910 im Frankfurt a.M. (Trans. for private use by E. C. Hughes.) Chicago: University of Chicago, Department of Sociology. (Processed.)

Woods, J. H. 1953. Helping older people enjoy life. New York: Harper & Bros.

XIX

Aging, Religion, and the Church

PAUL B. MAVES

I. GENERAL CONSIDERATIONS

A. The Significance of This Study

The church is the social institution in American and Western culture through which most religion is concretely and specifically expressed and by which it is promoted, perpetuated, propagated, and renewed in each generation. Few social institutions are more pervasive in their relations or inclusive of a larger proportion of the total population in their memberships than the churches. In 1956 it was reported that there were 258 religious bodies with a total membership of more than 103,000,-000 persons, organized in more than 308,-000 local congregations (National Council of Churches, 1957*b*). This figure includes roughly 62 per cent of the population.

Even so, a larger proportion of the population than actually counted by the churches considers itself as having an affiliation or identification with a religious group, if nothing more than a preference for a particular group. The Bureau of the Census discovered by means of a sample survey in March, 1957, that 96 per cent of all persons 14 years old and over reported a religion, while only 3 per cent reported themselves as having no religion, and only 1 per cent made no report (U.S. Bureau of the Census, 1958). Older people reported a religion in about the same proportions as other groups. A larger but not statistically significant proportion of older people reported no religion, 3 per cent of those

65 and over as compared with the total of 2.7 per cent for all ages over 14. Thus the church as a social institution would seem to touch the lives of a majority of older persons in some way, and religion must play some part in the adjustment of persons to aging.

At the same time it seems reasonable to conclude that the church cannot remain unaffected by the social changes going on around it, including the fact that the proportion of older persons has risen so dramatically in the last quarter of a century or more and that many more persons are living much longer. Tibbitts (1958) has stated:

> Institutions . . . represent patterned forms of adjustment which evolve out of men's efforts to satisfy their basic needs within their particular environments. . . .
>
> Institutions, by their nature and definition, change very slowly. On the other hand, methods of achieving the goals defined by institutions may change more rapidly. That is, social organizations do frequently alter their programs by adding, changing, or even dropping functions within the established institutional framework [p. 48].

It would be interesting to know if this is true of the church. Such a study is especially significant because many social workers have assumed that the church as a social institution has a peculiarly significant relevance for aging. For example, the Community Project for the Aged of the Welfare Council of Metropolitan Chicago

698

(1952) included this statement in its report of a three-year study project:

> Work toward the enrichment of older people's lives is peculiarly significant as a responsibility of the church. Many older people, buffeted on many sides, exhibit in their attitudes and interests the growing importance of religion in their lives. Furthermore, many older persons who are reluctant to ask for help from family agencies turn naturally to their church for guidance. This guidance can frequently be supplemented by the service programs of other agencies in the denomination—hospitals, homes for the aged, neighborhood centers, and family casework programs [p. 187].

B. Questions

In the light of such estimates of the role of the churches in the care of the aged, many questions are raised about the way in which the churches as social institutions have responded to the changing age structure of society and the concomitant problems. Questions are raised, too, about the significance of religion in the adjustment of persons to aging. So, actually, these questions fall into two groups.

QUESTIONS ABOUT THE IMPACT OF AGING ON THE CHURCHES

To what extent are the hopes of these social workers being fulfilled? How realistic is it to look to the church as an institution which can be of significant service for the aged? Can it be of equal service to all aged?

What is the function and role of the church in American society with respect to aging? How has it performed this function? Has any change taken place in its role? What is the correspondence between its stated purpose and its practice with regard to older people?

To what extent have the churches manifested an awareness of the social changes which affect the aging and which the increase of the aged in society affect in the church? In what ways have the churches changed as social organizations that affect their relations to older people? Is the church aware of and using the assets possessed by older people?

In what ways have the churches changed, supplemented, or developed new programs to meet the emerging needs of the aging in modern society? Where are these changes taking place? Is there a difference between the rural church and the urban church? Between regions of the country?

Are some of the changes in the character of the church as a social institution and in the pattern of its program, such as the tendency for congregations to increase in size, favorable or unfavorable to the needs of the aged? What are the churches doing, if anything, to compensate for any negative effects?

QUESTIONS ABOUT RELIGION AND AGING

What is the relation of religion to aging? Are older people included in the formal membership of the churches in approximately the same proportion as other age groups in the population? As persons grow older, do more of them tend to join a religious group, or do they tend to relinquish their membership?

Whether or not older people belong in the formal sense, to what extent do they participate in the organized activity programs of the church which are of a social or service nature? To what extent do they provide leadership or assume responsibility for such programs? To what extent are they elected or appointed to official positions?

Do older people evince a more favorable attitude toward religion than younger persons? Are they more orthodox or conservative in their beliefs and practices? Is nostalgia for the past typical, or do older people look forward to and welcome social change in the church?

Do they show more interest in religion as evidenced by reading the Bible, prayerbooks, and other religious literature, listening to religious programs on radio or television, attending services, taking communion, and participating in other religious rites and sacraments?

What does religious activity and participation mean to them? What reasons do they give for their participation or non-participation?

Is there a discernible pattern of religious experience and development which is typical of aging in American culture? Are there any definite religious roles which are commonly assigned to or taken by older people? Does aging have a cumulative effect on religious attitudes?

What is the giving pattern of older persons? What has been their lifelong relation to the church?

What has religion meant to older persons over the years? What has it contributed to their life and thought?

C. Factors Which Complicate a Study of Religion and Aging

When we attempt to get answers to these questions, we run up against a number of factors which make it exceedingly difficult to make generalizations about older people and religion. This particular universe of study is a very complex one.

RANGE AND VARIETY OF RELIGIOUS GROUPS

First, there is a tremendous range and variety of differences among the 258 religious bodies mentioned above. Each of the major groups has its own particular tradition and background which determines the way it responds to aging. Furthermore, within the larger groups there are notable differences to be considered. The Jewish congregations are divided among three national organizations, generally referred to as Orthodox, Conservative, and Reformed; local synagogues may be predominantly Spanish, Portuguese, German, or Russian in background. Roman Catholic churches also reflect certain differences growing out of different national backgrounds, such as Irish, Polish, French, or Italian. This is true also of the Protestants, with the additional difference made by widely differing theological emphases among and within the various Protestant denominations. How-

ever, with the decrease of immigration and the assimilation of these groups into the population, economic status is probably becoming a more basic factor in determining the composition of congregations of all faiths. Studies of social class stratification indicate that local churches tend to be composed of persons of similar social status. This raises an additional question. If social status is important in determining the composition and participation of persons in churches, and if retirement tends to threaten or weaken a person's social status, does this have any effect upon his relation to the church?

VARIETY OF LOCAL CHURCHES

In addition to the differences to be found among the various religious bodies, we need to keep in mind the tremendous range of differences among the local congregations of any particular group. Their buildings range all the way from the Gothic grandeur of the Cathedral of St. John the Divine in New York City to a dilapidated, weather-beaten, one-room shack in a remote rural area. In size they run the gamut from a dozen to more than four thousand members. Patterns of worship vary from the solemn dignity of the Roman Catholic High Mass to the hand-clapping, exuberant spontaneity of some of the Pentecostal groups. In terms of leadership they range all the way from churches with multiple staffs composed of specialized and professionally trained clergy and laymen to churches which have no clergy at all and no highly trained lay leadership. Their programs vary from the seven-day-a-week activity of institutional churches to only an occasional service of worship. In terms of median age of members they run the gamut from churches in new suburbs composed mostly of young adults and their young families to churches in Florida retirement communities where nearly all members are past 65. In terms of social setting they range from the rural churches of Springdale as described in *Small Town in Mass Society* (Vidich and Bensman, 1958) to the suburban churches of *Crestwood Heights* (Seeley *et al.*, 1956). In terms of structure they vary from loosely organized groups of persons with local autonomy to tightly organized congregations under centralized control by denominational hierarchies. Doubtless these varied congregations will not respond in the same way to an aging population, and therefore a study of religion and aging demands an adequate typology of congregations.

DIFFERING SOCIOCULTURAL BACKGROUNDS OF AMERICAN CHURCHES

Differences in sociocultural backgrounds among American religious bodies have to be understood in the light of the history of religious groups in America in order to develop an adequate theoretical structure for a study of aging and the churches. American churches for the most part are the transplantations of European churches or the development of movements which have their roots in Europe. The general pattern of religious life in Europe was the establishment by law of a particular church as the official church, to be supported by tax funds, with minorities of free churches operating under varying degrees of restraint or handicap. The established churches considered everyone born into the national community automatically to be a member of that church. The free churches represented sectarian movements of protest which considered as members only those who had made a decision to join after the age of accountability.

The churches in America are made up of transplanted national churches, such as the Lutheran, Protestant Episcopal, and Roman Catholic bodies, and of those representing sectarian or free-church movements, such as the Baptist, Methodist, and Quaker groups. However, in the process of transplantation all the churches became somewhat sectarian because of the disestablishment of state religion in America and the voluntary, exclusive membership which this entails. This is the genesis of denominations as distinguished from either sects or churches as Troeltsch (1931) designated them. However, in many groups and in many local congregations there are still marked traces of various national subcultures with varying attitudes toward aging and toward the development of programs of social service, social welfare, and social action. Various denominations stand at different points on a continuum from sect to church type. These differences brought from Europe have been greatly modified as a result of the conditioning the religious groups experienced on the American frontier and, more recently, by the industrial revolution (Niebuhr, 1957). A brief statement of the history, doctrine, organization, and work, as well as detailed statistics of the various denominations, may be found in *Religious Bodies: 1936*, compiled by the United States Bureau of the Census (1937).

Because of the wide range of differences among the great variety of religious bodies and local congregations, it is impossible to make generalizations which are valid for all of them. A complete picture of the impact of aging on American religious bodies would require a separate study of each of the 258 bodies as well as of the three major faiths by investigators thoroughly familiar with the history, polity, and organization of each of the groups.

DIFFERENT EMPHASES IN RELIGION

It seems difficult for any group that participates in a religious movement to maintain for long a balanced expression of its basic nature. Historical circumstances and individual preferences force various groups to bear down more heavily upon one or another aspect of expression, giving rise to sects and orders within a religious tradition.

Within the Christian movement it has been noted that some religious groups emphasize the sacramental and aesthetic aspects of their tradition and are concerned with a given structure and correct form. These are often called the "churches of the sacraments." They include Roman Catholicism, Eastern Orthodoxy, and Anglicanism. Thus a study of the participation of older people in these communions would tend to emphasize objective behavior and would be more sociological in nature. It is no accident that studies of Roman Catholic parishes such as Fichter's (1954) are so beautifully precise.

Other religious bodies emphasize the intellectual and theological aspects of religion and are concerned with the given tradition and correct doctrine. These are often called the "churches of the word." The Lutheran groups and the Calvinistic groups, such as Presbyterians and Congregationalists, are included in this category.

Still other religious bodies emphasize the subjective and individual elements of religion along with the conduct which results from personal experience; they are concerned with the vitality of individual religious expression. These are often called the "churches of the spirit" or "of the inner light." The sectarian groups have been more influenced by this tradition. Among the churches of the spirit are included the Baptist, Disciples of Christ, and Methodist. These communions tend to place more emphasis upon meaning and upon moral living. Studies of aging among these groups would tend to emphasize psychological elements.

The Jewish faith in America has separated into Orthodox, Conservative, and Reformed groups according to the emphasis placed upon scrupulous observance of all the commandments of the Law and various aspects of the cultural tradition and to the extent of accommodation to the culture of the total society. Furthermore, many persons who are regarded as "Jewish" are completely secular. With Jews even more than with other groups it is essential to distinguish between cultural and religious Jews.

We do well, however, to heed Bertholet's (1934) warning:

It is impossible to construct any convincing typology, since in any one religion there are at least as many variants as there are social layers participating in it. In addition it is neces-

sary to reckon with variations which arise from the dynamic unfolding of a religion in time. Religion, however conservative in nature, has a history; and that history, as fluid and protean as human life itself, cannot be reduced to the inflexible categories exacted by the typological method of inquiry [p. 237].

Excellent articles on the institutions of religion from Roman Catholic, Eastern Orthodox, and Protestant points of view are to be found in the *Encyclopedia of the Social Sciences* and in the *Encyclopedia of Religion and Ethics*. The *Catholic Encyclopedia* and the *Jewish Encyclopedia* provide further details for the interested student.

This, then, is a fourth complication. Not all religious groups define activity and interest or evaluate an individual's religious expression in the same way. Studies of religion and aging need to take this into account.

DIFFERING LEVELS OF RELIGIOUS EXPERIENCE AND AFFILIATION

Coming back to the idea of differences of capacity for religious experience, Clark (1958) points out that not all members of a religious group experience religion in the same depth. He suggests a psychological typology of levels.

First, there is primary religious behavior, which is a response to creative personal experience of considerable intensity and consciousness. On this level occur ecstasy, vision, and insight. Converts often experience religion on this level, making a change even against considerable opposition. This is the level of internalization. Religious behavior here often is in response to definite crisis or emotional stimulus (Allport, 1950).

Second, there are those who may have experienced religion intensely at one time but whose behavior has dropped into the level of routine or habit. This is secondary religious behavior. This is the level of identification.

Third, there is the level of tertiary religious behavior—the level of imitative, conventional behavior or, if pressure is involved, of compliance. There may be simple adherence if affiliation is voluntary and in response to persuasions or social influence, such as family tradition and class patterns.

Fichter (1954) posits a more sociological typology based upon observable participation in the parish life:

We have tentatively classified the urban white Catholic of this study into four general groupings: (*a*) *nuclear,* who are the most active participants and the most faithful believers; (*b*) *modal,* who are the normal "practicing" Catholics constituting the great mass of identifiable Catholic laymen; (*c*) *marginal,* who are conforming to a bare, arbitrary minimum of the patterns expected in the religious institution; and (*d*) *dormant,* who in practice have "given up" Catholicism but have not joined another religious denomination [p. 22].

In this study of three urban parishes he found about 38 per cent of those who could be identified as Catholics to be dormant. Of the active Catholics, 10 per cent were nuclear, 70 per cent modal, and 20 per cent marginal.

Fichter has attempted to define "a good Catholic" and to develop grades for the identification of levels of religious practice. Similar typologies are needed for other groups.

A remarkable correspondence can be seen between the psychological typology of Clark and the sociological typology of Fichter. These should serve as warning to the student of religion and aging to be wary of the value to be placed upon statements about religious identification, membership, attendance, or participation.

DIFFERING STAGES OF VITALITY AND MATURITY IN RELIGIOUS MOVEMENTS

It might be hypothesized that religious movements tend to go through the levels posited by Clark as stages in their historical development. In the initial stage of the movement there may be a high degree of involvement, feeling, and vitality, with a zeal for religious activity and few conventional adherents on the fringe. As the movement prospers and the second and third generations are brought up in it, there is a tendency for zeal to subside and for behavior to become more habitual. Finally, the movement may reach the place where it has attained a predominant place in the community so that it is essential for a person to be identified with it in order to belong or to be accepted.

Davenport (1905) has suggested that religious revivals spread in a similar fashion. They often begin with the most susceptible, least stable, and perhaps those most highly gifted for religious experience. Then they spread by the power of contagion and suggestion to the less susceptible. The early conversions and awakenings are likely to be spontaneous, but, by the time the revival has spread out to include most of the community, the so-called conversions are often simulated. Therefore it might be expected that the relation of older people to a particular group may be colored by the stage of the life of a particular group. Do newer groups attract older people as well as younger people?

To take a slightly different approach, sociologists of religion have noted several types of churches in Western culture. Troeltsch (1931) postulated three: church, sect, and mysticism. This view has been widely accepted.

Niebuhr (1929) modified this by making church and sect the opposite poles of a continuum with five types according to the group's attitude toward culture. He also hypothesized that groups develop by moving one way on the continuum from sect to church. These types are not unrelated to social stratification, for the "sects" tend to emerge from among the "outsiders" or the proletariat, while the "churches" flourish among those groups which are "in," established, and powerful.

Yinger (1957) proposes a sixfold typology of the universal church, the ecclesia, the class church or denomination, the established sect, the sect, and the cult. He points out that these different types cannot be associated entirely with social class.

Consequently, in thinking about the impact of the aging upon the churches and the relation of the aging to the churches, it is necessary to keep in mind the various levels of affiliation and interest, the stages of maturity of a religious group, and the differing capacities for primary religious experience. Religious activity, church attendance, and participation in religious rites may have quite different values and meanings to different persons according to the kind of group to which they belong.

The problem of evaluating accurately the impact of religion is made more difficult still in a period of American history when religion seems to have reached an unusually high level of popular acceptance, on one hand, and, on the other, is regarded with increasing skepticism and indifference by many intellectual leaders and scientifically minded persons.

THE PROBLEM OF MEANING

Another complication is the difficulty of knowing what religion really means to persons. Pressey and Kuhlen (1957) note:

Few studies have attempted to assess the meaning of religion *for the individual* when attempting to determine the relationship between personality and religion. As Maslow has recently pointed out, "a person who goes to church regularly may actually be rated as *less* religious than one who does not go to church at all, because (1) he goes to avoid social isolation, or (2) he goes to please his mother, or (3) religion represents for him not humbleness but a weapon of domination over others, or (4) it marks him as a member of a superior group, or (5) as in Clarence Day's father, 'It is good for the ignorant masses and I must play along,' or . . . and so on. He may in a dynamic sense be not at all religious and still behave as though he were" [p. 491].

A study of the meaning of religion, especially in relation to aging, must necessarily involve a subjective judgment based upon a subject's own statement and the observations of his peers over a period of time, as well as the application of various kinds of analytic techniques.

The conclusion to be reached from this survey of the complications is that the student of the relation between religion and aging or of the impact of an aging population upon the churches would do well to avoid simple, facile generalizations and should be careful to make discriminations within his universe of study so that apples and pears are not counted together as one thing in spite of similarities and family relationships. Even more important, there is a question about using sampling procedures in the study of religion when the samples are based upon categories in the population rather than upon religious categories. Surely such samples must be adjusted for religious categories as well as for age, sex, socioeconomic status, and so on, especially in view of Havighurst's (1957) study reported later on, which finds that the church role does not correlate well with other clusters of roles.

D. Definition of Terms

Several terms are used in this chapter which may not be familiar to all readers. The following definitions are those most commonly used:

Religious bodies refers to the organized and incorporated religious groups often known as denominations. The term *the churches* is often used in the same general sense to refer to the denominations.

Families of churches is used to refer to a grouping of denominations or religious bodies which have a common tradition and a similar polity, such as the Lutheran group, the Baptist group, and other similar groups.

Local churches or congregations refers to that group of persons which worships in a single place and is organized as a local religious group.

Parish refers to the geographical area within which the local congregation operates or from which it draws its membership.

Major faith refers to the common tradition which underlies and ties together diverse religious bodies in an identifiable historical movement. The three major faiths in America are the Jewish, the Roman Catholic, and the Protestant. Eastern Orthodoxy might be characterized as a major faith but is relatively insignificant in terms of total numbers as compared with the others. The Eastern orthodox bodies co-operate with Protestant bodies in the National Council of the Churches of Christ in the United States of America and for practical reasons will be included with Protestant churches in this discussion.

Religious group is used variously and is to be understood by the context. It may refer to a local congregation, a denominational body, a family of churches, or one of the major faiths, since each of these is an identifiable aggregate of persons with more or less definite boundaries and having a more or less closed system of intracommunication.

The term *church* is usually limited to a Christian group as distinct from *synagogue,* which is the local organization of Jewish congregations. In this paper, for the sake of brevity, the term *church* is used to apply indiscriminately to both Jewish and Christian groups.

II. THEORETICAL CONSIDERATIONS

A. *The Definition of Religion*

In order to understand the impact of population aging upon religious bodies and the response of the religious bodies to aging as a process, as well as the significance of religion in the lives of older persons both potentially and actually, we need to clarify our understanding of religion and its function in society and the role of the churches in patterning that function. Theoretical clarification is crucial if we are to ask the questions which will yield significant answers. This is particularly necessary because social scientists have tended to neglect religion as an area of scientific study. We begin with an attempt to define the nature and function of religion.

Yinger (1957) points out that there are three kinds of definitions: the valuative definition, which expresses a writer's judgment of what religion ought to be; the substantive or descriptive definition, which designates certain kinds of beliefs or practices; and the functional definition, which emphasizes the persistent functions of religion and concerns of religion as a kind of response and adjustment. In this chapter the functional definition is most useful.

Functionally, religion may be approached as an internal, personal experience which is a particular kind of response to particular events or as a dynamic set of relationships which are idiosyncratic for a particular person. Or it may be approached through an observation of the institutionalized patterns of behavior which are characteristic for persons in particular groups. The psychologist tends to emphasize attitudes, feelings, and meanings of the individual. The sociologist tends to emphasize roles, status, distribution of power and authority, patterns of behavior, organization, and stated systems of belief. Both approaches are needed along with the emphasis upon tradition and culture which the anthropologist customarily makes. In this paper we begin with the religious experience and move to the social institution.

Otto (1923) has defined religion as the experience of "the Holy," not solely in the sense of the experience of "the good," but in the original sense of the term, as connoting "the *mysterium tremendum et fascinocum,*" for which he coined a special word, the "numinous." This experience involves awe, a sense of dependence, and fascination in the presence of that which is perceived as Wholly Other, overpowering, mysterious, and absolute.

Lowie (1925) has stated that "religion is verily a universal feature of human culture, not because all societies foster a belief in spirits, but because all recognize in some form or other awe-inspiring, extraordinary manifestations of reality" (p. xvi).

The response of religion occurs in the confrontation with the sublime phenomena of nature and in those moments when a man becomes aware of the mystery of birth, life, and death. It has to do with the awareness of the All-Encompassing, the Totality, which forms the matrix of man's life. It is a basic response which cannot be expressed completely by symbolic or rational means. It may be awakened, but it cannot be taught as physics is taught, although its expression can be channeled and patterned by acculturation to conform with institutional norms. It usually involves some emotion, but it is a non-rational rather than an emotional response, for it is a total-life response.

More recently Tillich (1957) has defined religion as the state of being ultimately concerned or being grasped by an ultimate concern. This is to say it is a human quest for meaning and for answers to the ultimate questions of human existence. It is a feeling for the ultimate ground of being. It is an attempt to relate one's self to that ground of being in such a way that the anxiety about the possibility of non-being is overcome. This definition would apply to all religions everywhere.

Using the specific Judeo-Christian symbols for ultimate reality, Tillich (1955) has also defined religion as the human response to God's revelation of himself to man in historical events. It is therefore not only what we feel in the presence of the numinous but also what we do about it that make up religion. Therefore religion must express itself in human relations if it exists at all. It is to be distinguished from philosophy not only by its basically non-rational character but also by its character as commitment or relationship. Philosophy articulates questions in logical terms and attempts to give coherent rational answers. Religion may be defined as the quality of one's relation to that which he conceives to be ultimate reality. In other words, it is the total response of the person to that which is conceived to be over, above, beyond, and underlying existence; to that which is infinite, absolute, eternal; and to that which is essence or absolute being.

B. Social Sources and Expressions of Religion

While fundamentally religion is a personal experience, it nevertheless takes place in a social context; it is expressed in social relationships; and it is patterned by institutionalized forms. Nearly all members of a social group share situations which give rise to similar experiences. All confront the mysteries of birth, life, and death. Each person tends to communicate with others about his experiences and as far as possible to share these experiences. So it is that groups tend to develop common patterns of response which are characteristic of the culture as a whole.

Furthermore, it is not only personal events but also social events which have meaning for religious groups. These social events often are regarded as revelations of the nature of ultimate reality. Jews see this revelation in the escape of the Hebrews from bondage in Egypt and in the giving of the Law by Moses. Christians see it in the life, ministry, death, and resurrection of Jesus of Nazareth, whom they believe is the Christ, and in the continuing vitality of the community he founded. In other words, the experience of a group or community becomes the event which welds the community into a unity, and the memory of this experience passed on to succeeding generations in the form of tradition perpetuates the unity of the group.

As a result of this communication and sharing of experiences, religion is a group phenomenon as well as an individual phenomenon, and there is a strong tendency toward the institutionalization of religion. As Wach (1944) has pointed out, it tends to express itself in generally accepted and official statements of belief which are the rational and logical formulations of the experience. These are the creeds of the religious movements. Religious movements also accumulate a body of sacred writings which are the officially accepted statements of belief and the official accounts of the history of the movement. They develop authoritative commentaries upon and interpretations of these sacred scriptures.

Religion tends to express itself aesthetically in the cultus of its worship, in the architecture of its places of worship, and in art, trying to express its faith through symbolic actions, forms, and objects, and, through these, attempting to communicate the experience of religion.

Religion also expresses itself in codes of conduct by establishing ethical norms and standards of morality in keeping with its faith. These ethical principles manifest themselves in the attempt to achieve social structures appropriate to its outlook and adequate for its expression, in the ecclesiastical organization of its own life, in the life of the religious group, and in relations to those outside the religious group.

Most religious groups seek to deepen, intensify, and build up their own inner life and the experiences of their members; to expand themselves in time and space so that more and more persons are brought within the framework of the faith; and to transform the community around them so that the social structures, political organization, and lives of the members of the entire secular community are consonant with their faith. It is not surprising that a religious tradition is frequently one of the main forces binding a homogeneous society into a unified whole and coloring interpersonal relationships. It is only the expressions of religion which can be studied by the sociologist. The thing itself must forever elude the most indefatigible researcher, and the most careful student may be misled about the meaning of the inner reality by the external expression.

There has been much discussion among students of religion as to whether it is primarily an individual or a collective phenomenon. However, it is to be understood as a phenomenon which is both personal and social and which exists in tension between the creative character of the personal experience of individuals and the formative and conservative character of its institutionalization in social groups.

Bertholet (1934) has pointed out:

The experiences from which religion springs are . . . essentially ecstatic in character and the subjects of such experiences are in the great majority of cases single individuals. And unless it is recognized that men are unequal as regards their capacity for the religious experience, it is impossible to understand the actual history of the origin and evolution of religion. . . . In this respect religion may be compared with art, a field in which differentiation between the layman and the artist is taken for granted [p. 230].

As with the artist, the nature of his experience and response is colored and conditioned by the structure of his personality and the influences of the period. Certain men may be able to be religious leaders because they are representative of the tensions of their age and at the same time offer a creative resolution of common religious problems. The priestly group seeks to conserve established patterns. The prophetic group seeks to adopt patterns to new conditions. However, this tension is but another facet of the conflict which always exists between the creative or variant individual personality and the more or less fixed structures of society.

Particular religious groups and traditions have been given shape by the dominant influence of particular persons. Every great religion has its founder to whom it looks with reverence.

It is characteristic of reformers to appeal to the life and teachings of the founders for support for whatever reform is proposed. Thus the adaptation of the churches to aging will be facilitated if there is strong sanction in its tradition for the respect and care of the aged.

C. Religious Bodies as Communities

Because of the socialization of religious experience and the institutionalization of religious movements, religious groups are basically the organized expressions of religious communities, bound together by and identified by their history, their traditions, their articles of faith, and their patterns of religious behavior. They cannot be understood as being simply voluntary associations of individuals according to the theory of social contract any more than a nation can be so understood. There is a sense in which religious bodies are voluntary associations (see chap. xviii), since most of them are open to and even seek converts, and since most of them have programs to which persons are invited regardless of religious identification or affiliation. Doubtless, also, they could be placed on a continuum of voluntariness from the sect groups and extreme liberal groups at one end to the Jewish and Catholic groups at the other end. But, in the main, one is born into them and nurtured in them so the only way not to belong to them is to repudiate or to withdraw from them. In this sense they are communities within the larger community of the state and even transcending national boundaries. As representatives of communities the religious bodies are the carriers of cultural forces which shape the larger culture in which they operate. These bodies in turn are shaped by the cultural forces of the community outside.

Religious groups by definition must insist upon a divine origin and a special mission in the world; they are not, therefore, to be understood as one more social agency alongside other social agencies deliberately organized for specific purposes. They believe that there is a given character to their association. Religious groups by definition must claim that their basic doctrines are based upon the revelation of God of his own nature and of ultimate truth. Some of them go so far as to insist that their particular formulation of doctrine is directly revealed; but most would say that the formulation of their doctrine is a response to and articulation of the meaning of revelation received in human experience through the events of history.

D. Functions of Religion

It may help to clarify thinking about aging and religion if the functions of religion are examined more closely. Religion is often associated with magic and often shades over into magic, for it is the character of magic that the practitioner seeks through it to control for his own benefit the power or powers he experiences in his contact with the numinous. Religion, by contrast, is the attempt of the believer to bring himself into a right relation to that ultimate reality which he cannot control. Yinger (1957) speaks of this as the residual function of religion.

In a sense the Judeo-Christian religion teaches that one cannot put himself into a right relation to God of his own efforts and free will except that God acts first to bring him into a right relation. In this way are symbolized the experience of the beneficent and healing forces within the universe and the acknowledgment of man's dependence upon the structures of the universe beyond him. Therefore, the action of the believer is that of receiving, of worshiping, of witnessing to what he has received, and of sharing the love he has experienced in love to others.

PRIMARY AND ESSENTIAL FUNCTIONS

To begin with, a religious group communicates to its believers and inquirers its interpretation of the meaning of existence and the nature of ultimate reality. This includes its understanding of the meaning of aging, sickness, suffering, and death. These interpretations provide a mode of adjustment to the negative, frustrating experiences of life and a means of understanding the totality of experience.

A second function is to point out and to promulgate ultimate values. These include the value of persons as ends—not means—regardless of age; the value of life as essentially good; and the value of love as an expression of the ultimate structure of relationships.

A third function is the mediation of the power of the relationship to ultimate reality which those in the group have experienced to those who are coming into the group and the renewal of this relation for all. The sacraments are such a means of mediating the grace of God, as are preaching, teaching, and a relationship of understanding love. Since no one is excluded from participating in these benefits, the aged are also recipients of this ministry.

A fourth function is the provision of opportunity and forms for the expression of worship and the articulation of confessions of faith; this might be called the aesthetic and cognitive celebration of the good.

A fifth function is the shaping of the total community of mankind so it will support the interpersonal relationships and quality of life in which it believes. Since no particular community can succeed in insulating itself from the wider community of total society, a religious communion is driven to seek the transformation of the total community into its own image. However, all religious groups would insist that the fundamental motive for the drive toward expansion and transformation is love. This means that the churches are inherently concerned about the effects of the entire social structure upon persons, including the aged.

SECONDARY FUNCTIONS

It is inevitable that religious groups should provide channels and occasions for the performance of other functions unrelated to their essential functions which are normative and theologically derived. In fact, there is danger that religious communities will be enveloped by these secondary functions and lose their essential reason for being. As an example, churches may come to be looked upon in the category of social clubs providing only the opportunity to make friends and to have fun. Or the community or state may come to look to them as social agencies to per-

form whatever tasks the community may have had in mind. Because the churches engage in social service or social action, they may be regarded as one more action group among action groups to be used in a struggle for power. In actual fact, the secondary functions may become the main functions or may even be used as a disguise or occasion for functions completely unrelated to religion.

In summary, the church as a social institution serves a number of functions. Various persons turn to it for a variety of reasons in the desire to meet various needs. In this respect it may be compared to the family. The dynamics of so-called religious activity are as complex as the dynamics of family living.

E. *Religion and Aging*

Religion has a relation to aging because it involves a response to the experience of aging, change, loss, and death. It involves a concern to find the ultimate meaning in these processes and to ascertain the significance of human life. It involves a particular kind of total response which we may call "faith," if it is one of confidence, basic trust, and commitment; "agnosticism," if it is one of sustained doubt and detachment; "stoicism," if it is one of resolute endurance in the face of an impersonal and unconcerned universe; or "cynicism," if it is one of suspicion, hostility, and withdrawal. It colors not only the way of looking at the process of aging and those who are aged but also the way of responding to them. Religious faith and activity may be the way a man can assure himself of his continued worth in spite of the losses and disabilities wrought by aging.

It is for this reason that Mathiasen (1955), among others, maintains that religion is "the key to a happy life in old age . . . [for] man is essentially a spiritual being. . . . A sense of the all-encompassing love of God is the basic emotional security and firm spiritual foundation for people who face the end of life" (p. 473). It would have to be said, however, that a "sense of the all-encompassing love of God" is not characteristic of all religions but says something about a particular religion in a particular society.

III. JUDEO-CHRISTIAN TEACHINGS RELEVANT TO AGING

Since religion is normatively concerned with clarifying and interpreting the meaning of human existence and the nature of ultimate reality, let us now look at some of the specific teachings which may have particular bearing upon aging.

A. The Doctrine of Creation

The Judeo-Christian attitude toward time and history is unique. In Eastern religions and Greek philosophy time and history were thought of as an endless circle repeating itself again and again. Matter was considered the source of evil and suffering, a kind of prison house for the soul.

The Judeo-Christian concept is that history is a straight line with a beginning and an end and that all that exists was created by the expressed will of God. Since it was created by a God who is essential goodness himself, creation is essentially good, and the processes of nature are good. Purpose is seen in creation and in history.

In this view man is created in the image of God; he has a limited kind of freedom and is able to stand outside himself and to transcend the present moment. Therefore, human life, although dependent upon the goodness of God to sustain it, is both meaningful and significant. Aging and death can be faced without anxiety and with hope in the faith that in God's plan it is meant for good.

Hiltner (1952) has underlined the significance of the Judeo-Christian emphasis upon time as the *kairos* or "the right time" or "fulfilled time."

Religion is concerned with human fulfillment. . . . To younger people, and especially to younger people in Western culture, it seems almost a truism to say that fulfillment consists in growth or expansion or the broadening use of one's powers [p. 2].

He points out that usually between the ages of 35 and 40 or 45 this concept is threatened, and persons face a psychological crisis when they confront the fact of inevitable decline of powers and potentialities.

The fact is of course that life's fulfillment never, even in its youngest stages, comes about merely through what we are calling expansions and broadening. . . . To put it more generally, fulfillment is to be understood basically through metaphors of depth rather than breadth, or of depth in conjunction with breadth. And depth is impossible without choice and exclusion [p. 2].

The values of the older years can come about only through planning the best use of available energy. . . . The rubric under which religion has usually considered this kind of problem is that of freedom in relation to law [p. 3].

He then goes on to point out that fulfilment arises out of the creative handling of the tension between problems and potentialities. Religious faith is significant here because it asserts that fulfilment is possible and that personal as well as social history has meaning.

B. The Doctrine of Sin and of the Fall

Another problem to which religion addresses itself is that of sin and suffering. In the Jewish tradition sin generally is disobedience to the commandments of God and a turning-away from his Law. National prosperity, long life, and happiness are dependent upon keeping the Law.

The doctrine of original sin and of a fall does not receive much emphasis in Judaism. In many Christian groups, however, the doctrine of sin and the fall is one way of expressing the concept of the contingency of creation and of man's misuse of his freedom and his entanglement in the consequences of his sinful decisions. It is recognized that man is finite and unable to comprehend the infinite mystery of life;

he therefore makes mistakes. However, beyond this, and this appears even in Greek mythology, there is the recognition of a tendency in man to resent and to rebel against his finiteness and to attempt to escape from his limitations by heroic effort. This tendency is often spoken of as pride or as the original sin. It is the tendency of each individual to assert himself over against all others, to use others as means to his ends, and to attempt to play God. As a result of choices distorted by this pride, there have developed demonic structures of evil in society, or institutionalized patterns of pride, such as racism, for pride brings reactions of irritation, resentment, and hatred. These reactions in turn increase insecurity. Thus, to the anxiety we feel as finite creatures facing mystery and death, there is added the anxiety of guilt, shame, and meaninglessness. Discrimination against older people may be an illustration of a demonic social structure. This doctrine is an attempted explanation of the existence of much of the anxiety and suffering in the world, including the fear of aging and death.

C. *The Doctrine of Redemption*

Since man is unable to lift himself out of his human predicament as creature and as sinner, so the doctrine runs, he looks to God for deliverance. Man believes that in right relation to God or in righteousness he overcomes these anxieties and has no fear.

The expectation of the Messiah is an aspect of both Judaism and Christianity. Some Jews still look for a personal Messiah. Others look for a messianic age when the reign of righteousness shall be manifest. The Jews emphasize moral responsibility and duty.

Christians believe that Jesus of Nazareth was the promised Messiah or the Christ (in Greek, "the Anointed One"); that in him the divine Logos or Wisdom of God expressed itself fully so that the nature and purpose of God was completely revealed and so that the power of overcoming finite-

ness and sin was given. The one who confesses and repents of his sin finds that God in his infinite love accepts him as he is without any conditions. The one who believes that Jesus was the Christ has faith that in the identification with him is to be found abundant and eternal life which transcends history. Thus, in spite of all negative experiences, hope is possible, and the creative structures of human relations which are expressions of love, overcome despair.

IV. JUDEO-CHRISTIAN ATTITUDES TOWARD AGING AND OLD AGE

A. *Ancient Attitudes*

In the Bible and particularly in the Old Testament aging is understood and taken for granted. It is not surprising, therefore, that the *Jewish Encyclopedia,* which was published in 1901, and the *Encyclopedia of Religion and Ethics,* which was published in 1922, should have articles on "Old Age." In chapter 12 of Ecclesiastes and in Ps. 71:9, for example, the disabilities of old age are recognized. The compensations are noted in Prov. 16:31 and in Job 12:12 and 32:7.

In the Old Testament life is essentially good; length of days was considered a blessing and a reward for righteousness, as indicated in Exod. 21:12 and 23:26, Deut. 4:40, 5:33, 11:21, and 22:7, Ps. 91:16 and 92:14, Isa. 65:20, and Prov. 10:27 and 12:28. In fact, age was considered to be a guaranty of experience and of judgment. This is in keeping with the findings of Simmons (1945) that the aged are often the custodians of the traditions and the religious rites of the tribe.

Respect for the aged is written into the law in Lev. 19:32. Respect for parents or filial piety was highly developed among the ancient Hebrews, and one of the Ten Commandments enjoins such respect which would protect the aged who have children and relatives (Deut. 5:16). The duty of providing for the aged is illustrated by Ruth 4:15.

The teachings of the rabbis carry out the same themes with great consistency (Duckat, 1953). These attitudes are in marked contrast to those found in Greek and Roman writers, where often old age is depreciated and where, with the exception of those who had attained to positions of power (such as members of the Senate), the aged were valued very little.

The Jews have maintained a remarkable intensity of family feeling down to the present time and along with it a notable respect for their older people and a sense of responsibility for caring for all those in their community who are dependent or disabled. Historical forces of discrimination and segregation served only to throw them back upon this tradition of family solidarity, of worship centered in the family, and of family responsibility for caring for the aged and the sick.

Christians inherited this attitude toward parents and the aged along with the Old Testament. However, Christianity developed first in the context of Greco-Roman civilization, which in the first and second centuries was permeated with ascetic attitudes brought in from the Eastern religions; and then in the context of Germanic culture of the North, where the aged were not highly regarded. Consequently, in the development of their attitudes and practices, Christians have tended to deviate somewhat from their Old Testament heritage.

Then, as already pointed out, when a religion becomes predominant, more and more of its adherents are less deeply infused with zeal for its ideals. Consequently, the churches often reflect the prevailing attitudes and values of the dominant culture rather than their own. Therefore it is not surprising that in American churches we often find even the clergy unconsciously fearing old age and rejecting the aged or depreciating work with the elderly as of no significance, even as their medical and social worker colleagues.

B. Current Attitudes of the Major Faiths to Social Welfare of the Aged

JEWISH ATTITUDES

In summary it might be said that the care of the aged among the Jews is conditioned by the retention of their strong family feeling and by a high respect for parents and aged beyond that which is characteristic of either of the other two groups. It is probable that Jewish family life is now being affected by the fact that a reduction in hostility and discrimination is making it possible for Jews to participate more fully in American community life, causing them to break away from the Jewish community and leading them to adopt the family patterns and attitudes typical of the American community. The Jewish community, however, retains a strong sense of responsibility for caring for its own members whose families are unable to provide for them. The community services are developed under the auspices of Jewish agencies supported by the Jewish community as a whole and not directly connected with the synagogue organization. However, as Biller (1952) has maintained, the synagogues have a crucial role to play.

It is the writer's impression that the Jewish community, perhaps because of its attitude, is more responsible, imaginative, and creative than either Protestant or Catholic groups and may therefore exert leadership out of proportion to its numbers in the field of gerontology.

PROTESTANT ATTITUDES

Protestants, by way of contrast, seem to have much more individualistic patterns of relationships and are inclined to consider misfortune and failure as somehow related to moral turpitude or to lack of responsibility. They also tend to regard the community and the state as having particular responsibilities in the social sphere and therefore have tended to throw their support behind community and governmentally supported institutions. Contrary to this major trend there still exists the pietistic trend which has led Protestants to found church-related institutions. Many of these institutions are founded and organized by Protestant laymen and tend to become community or non-sectarian institutions, although recently there seems to be an increasing tendency for the churches as organizations to take the lead in stimulating, founding, financing, and co-ordinating these institutions. However, these are often seen as pioneering and pace-setting ventures or pilot projects, similar to the private school in a country committed to universal public education. It is recognized that not all church members can or should be cared for in such institutions.

ROMAN CATHOLIC ATTITUDES

Roman Catholics, coming into a predominantly Protestant community, sensed that public institutions as well as church-related institutions were in fact at least quasi-Protestant institutions and that it was difficult for persons in these institutions to receive the religious care and oversight they wanted and needed. Consequently, the Catholics have tended to develop their own welfare services and institutions, working first through the religious communities and more recently directly under the supervision of the bishop in the diocese.

However, with the development of chaplaincy services in the public institutions, they are more inclined to give full support to these institutions. They also recognize that, because of the complexity of modern industrial society, the church as a church supported by voluntary contributions can provide only a portion of the services and resources needed, so they have given increasing concern to problems of social justice and support of governmental programs such as Old-Age and Survivors Insurance. Their institutions, too, accept persons of other faiths. Because of their point of view about the responsibility of the church, it may be expected that they will exercise considerable initiative in developing institutional care for the aged.

V. History of the Care of the Aged by Religious Bodies

Until recently the history of the care of the aged has been an inextricable part of the history of the care of all those who were helpless, disabled, or dependent. Since the aged were not segregated or prevented by social policies from working as long as they were able, they became subjects of concern only when they were sick, weak, or helpless; in this they were regarded as no different from those of any other age who were in the same situation. Always it is to be understood the aged participated in the religious rites and ministries of their group, deriving therefrom the same benefits as those of any other age. As Simmons (1945) has pointed out, in primitive societies the aged often fulfil the role of priests. It is worth noting that the word "priest" itself comes from the Greek word meaning "elder."

The response of the religious bodies to the aged before the nineteenth century is to be found under the headings of charity, almsgiving, and penance. An understanding of this history can illuminate the practices and attitudes currently seen among the religious bodies. A brief summary may serve to give background to the present scene.

For the first four hundred years of our era the Christian community was a minority movement within the Roman Empire, with its members drawn largely from the lower classes and during much of that time severely persecuted. During this period the community attempted to care for its own needy through the agency of the parish or congregation.

Then, following its establishment as the official religion by Constantine and the breakup of the Roman Empire, the church became for a thousand years or more the main and much of the time the sole agent of social services more properly known as charity. During this period the monastic orders became the instruments for the care of the needy, with funds received from tithes, penance, and alms, as well as funds earned by the various orders.

Following the Reformation in the sixteenth century, in northern Europe there began the secularization of social welfare programs with a separation of the functions of the community and state from those of the church, and the delegation of the responsibility for the care of the needy to the community, when the family was unable to provide this care. This trend was countermanded to some extent by the pietistic movement which led to the development of church-related institutions founded and supported by the voluntary contributions of interested laymen.

As far as religion in America is concerned, the development of a pluralistic society began in the nineteenth century with the growth of the Jewish and Catholic communities. These groups established programs alongside the Protestant programs mentioned above. This means that, as we come into the twentieth century, we have a parallel pattern of public institutions for the aged in the poor farms or almshouses and of church-related or church-sponsored institutions and programs.

Around the turn of the century the religious bodies became more sensitive to the religious and spiritual implications of social structures of the total community and took increased responsibility for making pronouncements about them in terms of these implications.

In the twentieth century the social welfare movement took over the charity organization movement. Social work became a specialized profession. Schools of social work were established to train social workers. Many of these schools were established in church-related universities, including seven under Roman Catholic auspices. Professional societies established standards and codes of ethics. Under the shattering impact of the economic depression of the 1930's and the emergence of older people as a notable factor in the national scene, government became the predominant sponsor of social welfare programs. Many new kinds of social agencies were developed. All this is leading the churches to re-examine their role in the social welfare field. The conclusions they come to about their role will determine in a large way the response they will make in the years ahead to the impact of the aging in our society.

Whatever conclusions the churches come to about their role in the social welfare scene in America, including their responsibility for developing social welfare and social work programs for older people, it will be well not to lose sight of the fact which Gunnar Myrdal *et al.* (1944) point out:

Apart from the historical problem of the extent to which church and religion in America actually inspired the American Creed, they became a powerful container and preserver of the Creed when it was once in existence. . . .

Religion is still a potent force in American life. . . . American scientific observers are likely to get their attentions fixed upon the process of progressive secularization to the extent that they do not see this main fact, that America probably is still the most religious country in the Western world . . . [pp. 10 ff.].

If religious bodies become fully aware of the increase of the aged in the population and of their problems and potentialities, it may be that they will make their main contribution indirectly through the ideals and values they foster and through the attitudes which they are able to develop in their members toward aging and the aged.

VI. CHURCH PROGRAMS FOR OLDER PEOPLE BEYOND THE LOCAL PARISH

There is no simple and adequate way to summarize the work that is being done on the denominational level for older people because of the vast variation in the extent to which the various denominations have centralized and co-ordinated functions within the denomination. Some local churches are completely autonomous as community churches, some are loosely associated with others on a voluntary basis for certain co-operative programs, and some are tightly organized in a hierarchy of levels. Beyond this, some denominations actively and enthusiastically co-operate in interdenominational programs such as those of the National Council of Churches of Christ in the United States; others tend to be exclusive.

The general pattern of American churches is to establish within the national structure of the denomination certain boards or bureaus which have the responsibility for carrying out certain functions. In some the functions which would relate to older people are more or less unified in one board, while in others they are scattered among several boards. In many ways these departments represent groups in the churches who are in the forefront of thinking about these matters and which seek to win support for their programs. But at the same time the churches depend upon them to take the lead in developing and testing new programs.

Without attempting to consider the programs in detail, board by board, then, this paper will be confined to a consideration of some of the outstanding and illustrative types of programs to be found in the three faith groups.

A. Church-sponsored Programs

There are no complete surveys or series of surveys which give an adequate picture of what is being done on the denominational level by all the different groups.

In 1945 the Board of Education of the Methodist church assigned a staff member in its Department of Adult Work to devote a major proportion of time to work with older people.

In the years 1946–48 the then Federal Council of Churches of Christ in America (now a part of the National Council of the Churches of Christ in the United States, which is composed of 34 Protestant and Eastern Orthodox bodies with a combined membership of 37,870,000 persons) under a grant from the Arbuckle-Jamison Foundation, sponsored a study of the "Church's Religious Ministry to Older People." This study was directed by the Department of

Pastoral Services in co-operation with the Board of Education of the Methodist church and was carried out by two research associates to the department, Maves and Cedarleaf.

Maves attempted to survey all relevant literature with reference to the aging and to draw from it implications for the work of the church and for religion. He tried to acquaint himself with the developments in the general field of aging through interviews, attendance at conferences, and observations of programs under way. He also observed thirteen different Methodist churches which were selected as typical of a wide range of churches. These observations were carried out over a period of 2 years, and he made an effort to gain an impression of the churches' actual relation to the aged and to see what would be involved in arousing the interest of the clergy and in developing programs in a local church.

Cedarleaf established a pastoral relationship with seventy selected parishioners, about half of whom were residents in a church home for the aged to which he was chaplain, the other half in a parish to which he was associate minister. He kept detailed and often verbatim records of his conferences with these persons. During the period ten of them died.

As a result of this study project, three books appeared. *Older People and the Church* (Maves and Cedarleaf, 1949) was addressed to clergymen and lay workers in the church to acquaint them with the problem, to increase their understanding of aging, and to give them some guidance in how to proceed in developing programs—both group programs and counseling programs. It also suggested some things the church could do in the general field of social welfare and social security. In this volume Cedarleaf reported that the older people he studied fell into three general classifications: 18 of the 70, or 26 per cent, appeared to be successfully creative older persons; 24, or 34 per cent, were seen as struggling toward creativity; in 28, or 40 per cent, creativity seemed to be sub-merged. (This corresponds in part to Ries-man's [1954] hypothetical division of older adults into the autonomous, the adjusted, and the anomic; Cedarleaf's classification suggests that persons may be successful, struggling, or defeated at least temporarily and is therefore more dynamic.)

The Christian Religious Education of Older People summarized the findings of Maves (1950) particularly with respect to the thirteen churches studied. He con-cluded that (1) the religious education of older people should be an important and integral part of the total ministry; (2) that, in general, the program of the churches for the religious education of old-er people, while of considerable value, was not nearly so effective in helping persons as it ought to be and could be; (3) that the primary factors in the effectiveness of such programs are the personal adjustment and professional competence of the minister in charge; and (4) that the church has a very important part to play in helping persons find meaningfulness in later maturity.

The Best Is Yet To Be (Maves, 1951) was a book of informational and inspira-tional nature addressed to the aging them-selves, dealing with crucial problems of ad-justment in the later years. This book was a part of the "Pastoral Aid" series de-signed by Westminster Press to be a tool for the pastor and other callers to use to supplement their visits.

The National Council of the Protestant Episcopal church has a commission engaged in a study of its ministry to older people which is charged to report back to its next general convention.

The National Council of Churches is currently engaged in a study of the social welfare programs of the churches. Three volumes (Bachmann, 1955, 1956; Cayton and Nishi, 1955) have been issued on *The Churches and Social Welfare,* as has also a pamphlet report. One of the outcomes of this study has been an attempt to secure more reliable and accurate statistics about programs such as homes for the aged.

The National Conference of Catholic Charities, organized in 1910, is developing literature and attempting to stimulate and to co-ordinate work in this field. In 1931 it published O'Grady's *Catholic Charities in the United States: History and Problems,* which included a chapter on the care of the aged. Recently it has released *A Study of the Aging in a Cleveland Parish* (Sister Mary Therese, 1954). It has stimulated other studies such as those of the Catholic Charities of St. Louis, by Bower, and by O'Reilly and Pembroke, which will be re-ferred to later.

The National Jewish Welfare Board pub-lishes guides and reports for work with the aged in community centers, as does the Council of Jewish Federation and Welfare Funds.

The First National Conference on Prot-estant Homes for the Aged was held in 1948, and a similar one was held in 1950. Both were administered by the Federal Council of Churches. In 1953 the National Council of Churches held in Wisconsin an International Conference on the Church and Older People (1953); *The Fulfillment Years* was its report. In 1955 a National Conference on the Churches and Social Welfare was held in Cleveland; it included attention to programs for the aged in its agenda (Bachmann, 1956). In May, 1957, a conference at Atlantic City representing twenty-six denominations published *Policy and Strategy in Social Welfare: A Report to the Churches* (National Council of Churches, 1957a). A nation-wide confer-ence of Protestant health and welfare work-ers is being projected for the future.

Protestant councils of churches and fed-erations have held city-wide conferences in Washington, Chicago, and New York. In-terfaith conferences on religion and aging have been held in St. Louis and Dallas. A state-wide meeting of Protestants was held in Massachusetts under the State Council of Churches. All these conferences and meetings have as their object the stimula-tion of interest in the aging, the sharing of experience and problems, and the development of programs for the aged. Institutes and workshops for clergy and lay workers have been held under church auspices on national, conference, and diocesan levels.

Margaret Frakes (1955) made a casual survey of programs for the aged in Protestant churches and published a series of notable articles in the *Christian Century*. The first article reviewed the general picture of the demographic change involving older people in the United States and some of the challenge in it. The second dealt with the problem of the individual's adjusting to aging and pointed to some of the things the churches could do to help, such as providing more effective pastoral care, using the talents of older people, and changing community attitudes and practices toward aging. The third described some of the things that are being done to help older people feel wanted, such as providing special church literature for them, organizing friendly visitation, and finding foster homes. The fourth told of co-operative church efforts through church councils such as those already described. The fifth and sixth described some group programs in operation in various local churches. The seventh and eighth were concerned with housing and homes for the aged, making a plea for the provision of the intangibles of respect, concern, and careful planning of activity programs in such homes.

Outstanding among programs carried on by the churches are homes for the aged. Tibbitts (1954) estimates that 40 per cent of the homes for the aged are under the auspices of religious groups. It is estimated that Protestant and Eastern Orthodox homes number about 700. The *Directory of Catholic Charities in the United States* (O'Grady, 1920) listed 132 homes under Catholic auspices. Gill (1954) reported that there were 271 homes under Catholic auspices. The *Official Catholic Directory* for 1957 lists 303 homes for the aged, housing 26,655 guests. Cohn (1954) reported that there were 80 homes for the Jewish aged in 1954. Zelditch (1956) says that 84 homes care for 11,000 Jewish aged.

Although the total number of older people in institutions is only about 3 per cent of the total aged population, this represents a significant contribution to those who need congregate care. At the same time the churches recognize that this is not the whole solution to the problem of housing the aged.

Homes for the aged often offer services other than housing and extend these services to persons not resident in the home. Notable is the Home for Aged and Infirm Hebrews in New York City which, in addition to custodial and nursing care, operates apartments for the aged, maintains a non-resident member program, opens itself up as a community center for the aged, and carries on a program of research and training in geriatrics. Other homes are developing similar programs.

Recently there seems to be an increased interest among the churches in providing homes for the aged. Some local churches are beginning to secure or build and to operate apartments for older people. A booklet (Lund, 1951), produced by the National Lutheran Council, was prepared for the purpose of increasing the effectiveness of the services of their homes for the aged. The National Council of Churches also has published a booklet suggesting activity programs in homes for the aged (Wahlstrom, 1953). Many additional aged, of course, are cared for in hospitals which are sponsored by church groups.

Churches have also set up counseling and casework agencies for the aged. The Diocese of New York of the Protestant Episcopal church has a full-time caseworker whose function is that of counseling older persons and helping churches develop programs. The United Lutheran Synod of Illinois, with headquarters in Chicago, has a department of work with older people in its inner mission society which has developed home-finding and counseling services, organized clubs for older people, trained visitors, and established a home for the aged.

Attention should be called to the rapidly expanding chaplaincy service in institutions. More and more state hospitals and prisons, as well as federal institutions, including the veterans' hospitals, and more and more community hospitals are including trained chaplains of the three faiths on their staff. Since many of the residents of these institutions, especially of the mental hospitals, are older persons, the ministry of the chaplain often is to older persons.

B. Church Co-operation with Secular Agencies

From the beginning, social workers in church-related agencies and in church-related schools of social work have co-operated in professional conferences. Those who work with the aged are no exception. The National Council of Churches has encouraged the formation of a Church Conference of Social Work, which is an affiliate of the National Conference of Social Work. The National Conference of Catholic Charities has also been co-operating with the National Social Work Conference. What is true at the national level is true also at state and community levels.

The importance of religion was recognized in the First National Conference on Aging held at Washington in 1950 by the devoting of an entire section to this subject (U.S. Federal Security Agency, 1951). A member of the planning committee from the section on religion served also on the planning committee for the section on professional education.

The churches are represented informally on the National Committee on the Aging of the National Social Welfare Assembly; these representatives have played leading roles in the development of the committee's program, perhaps most notably in the preparation of its statement on *Standards of Care for Older People in Institutions* (1953, 1954).

The University of Michigan's annual conferences on aging have often included special groups to discuss the relevance of aging to the churches and of religion to aging. Some of the governors' conferences —such as the one in New York in 1955 and the one in Wisconsin in 1956—have given attention to the role of the churches by having special committees and sections working on this subject.

The University of Florida through its Extension Division has held two different series of one-day institutes on the church and the senior citizens in various communities throughout the state in co-operation with local councils of churches. In April, 1958, the Institute of Gerontology of the University of Florida held a two-day conference on organized religion and the older person. In this significant series of papers (Scudder, 1958) religion was defined functionally in terms of what it should do for older people, but in the reports of research religion was defined in terms of organizational connection. Attention was called to the difficulties of an adequate definition and also of securing truly representative samples in research. One paper described the program of a large community church in ministering to some three hundred and fifty older persons.

C. Trends

The following trends seem to the writer of this chapter to be characteristic of Protestant approaches on the denominational level:

1. The denominations are beginning to appoint persons to the staffs of their national boards with major or full-time responsibility for the promotion of programs for older persons. The Methodist church has had a full-time person on its General Board of Education staff since 1945. The Presbyterian Church, U.S.A., has recently followed suit. In these and in other denominations some of the responsibility is shared among the staff members of the various boards. For example, the person in charge of adult education of the board of education, the board overseeing hospitals and homes, the board of pensions, and in some cases, notably the Lutheran churches, the

board of inner missions is responsible for promoting programs for the aged. When a staff member is not specifically charged by his denomination with responsibility to develop programs, what is done depends upon personal concern and commitment.

2. Most denominational presses have run series of articles on the problems of the aging in the church papers from time to time to acquaint the constituency with the problem. The Methodist church publishes a magazine called *The Mature Years* especially for older people. The Westminster Press (Presbyterian) has published a pastoral aid book (Maves, 1951) for older people intended to be a supplement to pastoral visitation. Copies of devotional manuals are often distributed to older people. A book of devotions (Emmons, 1953) has been published for this age group by the Abingdon Press (Methodist). The September, 1954, issue of *Pastoral Psychology* (Maves, 1954) was devoted entirely to articles of a popular nature on aging in order to inform the parish minister about aging, to stimulate him to take increased interest in the pastoral care of the aged, and to offer some guidance in doing it.

3. Several of the denominations have developed manuals and booklets for the guidance of local church workers in setting up programs for older people in parishes and homes for the aged. The Methodist church developed a series of manuals (Rippey, n.d.; Stafford, 1953; Stafford and Eisenberg, 1956) as well as numerous promotional leaflets. The Presbyterian church (1957) and the Congregational-Christian Conference of Iowa have published manuals (Jacobs, 1957), while the United Lutheran Church in America produced a booklet for the guidance of friendly visitors (Reisch, 1956).

4. Some of the denominations have developed workshops, clinics, and seminars for the training of pastors and lay persons in work with the aging, although probably as many of these are interdenominational and set up in local communities by councils of churches as by denominational boards. For example, the Methodist church has sponsored two national workshops and several regional training seminars and demonstration programs. The United Christian Missionary Society of the Disciples of Christ sponsored two clinics in 1954 on the needs of older people.

5. The organization of three- or four-day summer institutes for older people on a conference-wide basis has been encouraged by the Methodist church. Around sixty such annual camps or institutes are now being held each summer. These have capitalized upon the camp-meeting tradition of the nineteenth century and early twentieth century and have adapted it to modern camping.

It is noticeable that the larger denominations with more resources in terms of national board staffs have taken the lead in the development of special denominational programs and that the denominations with the stronger traditions of pastoral care and social welfare services have pioneered in such programs, responding first to the challenge of aging.

In the Roman Catholic church the National Conference of Catholic Charities, some of the schools of social work, and certain of the religious orders have taken the lead in developing such programs. In this church the responsibility lies more at the diocesan level than at the national level for the development of programs.

Lennon (1954) outlined a fifteen-point program for the improvement of Catholic programs for older people as suggestions to the churches. These ideas are summarized below:

1. Homes for the aged should have a clear definition of whom they are to serve and a clear policy of admission.
2. Homes for the aged should have a program of creative activities and should be homes in the true sense of the word.
3. Homes for the aged should be integrated with the community rather than isolated or segregated from it.
4. Diocesan Catholic charities should offer a full range of co-ordinated social services to the aged.

5. Parishes should provide facilities for older people to come together.
6. Priests should encourage the young to help the aged and to visit them in their homes.
7. The religious communities should recognize the importance of work with the aged and regard it as highly as work with the young.
8. Schools should interpret aging and the aged to youth.
9. Seminaries should train the priests to minister more effectively to the older persons in their parishes.
10. Organizations of Catholic men and women should stress lay participation in voluntary services.
11. Catholic universities should sponsor institutes on the aging.
12. Training for doctors and nurses should lay increased stress upon geriatrics.
13. Catholic lawyers should study legislation pertaining to social security and social welfare so they can offer guidance in the development of better legislation and can interpret the law.
14. Catholic industrialists and union leaders should review and reshape their policies with reference to the older worker.
15. The Catholic press should take responsibility for interpreting the needs of the aged to its constituency.

We can conclude that there are in the denominations of every faith persons of large vision and deep devotion to the welfare of the aged who are working to improve the programs of the church for the aged and to strengthen the religious ministry to them. The extent to which their vision extends to all the leaders of the church or their suggestions are taken seriously by the church as a whole is highly problematical. It would seem that leaven is working slowly within the cold dough. However, these persons do exert one more pressure for the gradual adaptation of a conservative social institution to the merging needs in a changing society.

VII. Special Programs in the Local Churches for Older People

There are no studies which can provide us with all the data we need to draw a picture of special programs in local churches. We have noted that Margaret Frakes (1955) has made a very sweeping survey to pick up some of the highlights of programs on national, denominational, and local levels, and she has given some of the dramatic illustrations of pilot projects in local churches.

Salamone (1955) sent a questionnaire to 125 Roman Catholic archdioceses inquiring about programs for the aging in the field of education. Of 46 questionnaires returned, 7 reported that they had no special programs for the aged, and 33 reported that they had no programs.

A number of casual, journalistic reports of isolated programs may be found in church publications and in social welfare publications. Notable among these is Gleason's (1956) informal survey of programs which he was able to find as carried on in Protestant churches. His book is almost literally a scrapbook of information picked up through questionnaires, conversations, reading, and in a cross-country trip to visit churches. It contains illustrations of group programs, descriptions of programs in which the talents of older persons can be used, suggestions for setting up such programs, and a listing of resources.

The writer of this paper has had some contact with various denominations since 1946, chiefly those represented in the National Council of Churches, and has attempted to keep abreast of some of the developments through reading, observation, and personal interviews.

The Community Services Council (1957) of Lansing, Michigan, attempted a study of the churches in 1957. Eighty churches were contacted during the study by interviewers. Seventy produced usable schedules. Thirty of the seventy were deemed to have an effective interest in the aging and forty to have no effective interest. Nine of the churches had special groups. Thirty-seven of the churches had friendly visitation programs for the aged, thirty provided transportation, and thirty-five mentioned counseling as a service to the aged. Thirty-four were interested in the possibility of forming a group, twenty-one had no interest, and fifteen made no report on this item. However, sixty of them wanted to know more about the problems of older people and expressed interest in a meeting where this would be discussed, giving some evidence of interest beyond that shown to be effective in terms of having done something. Four of the churches had groups which went out of existence. It was found that the churches with memberships of five hundred or more tended to be more interested than others, although there were some in each size category which did have an interest. No reliable information was secured by this study on attendance of older people at Sunday services, average age of congregation, or participation in activities within the church.

On the basis of these few reports, and mainly on the basis of his own knowledge, the writer of this chapter believes that local parish programs can be summarized as follows:

1. Local churches generally assume that their regular religious services of worship are open to persons of all ages, including the aged. In this sense they would feel that they are ministering to the aged. Churches are beginning to realize that special facilities are needed for many older people. Most churches have some sort of amplification of sound, and many have hearing aids in the pews for the hard-of-hearing. Railings are often installed on steps, and there is a growing consciousness of the desirability of ground-level entrances, ramps, and adequately lighted halls and aisles, especially in new buildings. In some cases motor pools have been formed to assist older people with transportation and to demonstrate interest in them, although it is probable that this is left to the voluntary good will of neighbors rather than being organized in most cases. There is little evidence that the need for large size type in Bibles, hymnals, and prayerbooks has been widely recognized. There is no way of knowing how often sermons give recogni-

tion to the adjustments demanded by aging. In general, it is doubtful if many local churches have gone very far in adapting their programs to the needs of older people.

2. It is the writer's observation that most local churches, or at least the pastors, become aware first of older people through members who have become homebound by illness or who got to a hospital and then to a nursing home with a serious disability. Pastoral care is an integral part of the traditional ministry of the church. Clergymen generally feel a responsibility for the sick and attempt to make the resources of religion available to them, sometimes at the suggestion or request of relatives or close friends. Therefore pastors often say that more and more of their time is being preempted by the pastoral care of older people. However, those who receive this care are usually those who have long been members and active in the church. The aged who have moved into the community or who have been outside the church doubtless receive much less attention, if any.

Some pastors have seen the impossibility of doing all the visiting that needs to be done by themselves and have attempted to enlist laymen in a regular program (Reisch, 1956). In a few cases laymen are even given some training and supervision in such friendly visitation. In addition, groups such as women's societies often make a practice of providing gifts—birthday, anniversary, and holiday remembrances—to the homebound, although many times this is too sporadic to be as effective as it might. Some churches provide reading material such as church-school study booklets and devotional manuals or magazines to older persons. Some churches tape-record their services, and visitors play the recordings for the shut-ins. Of course, those churches which broadcast their services do not need to do this. Occasionally, local groups take responsibility for providing some service to those older persons in county and city infirmaries, although again in too many cases it may be suspected this is limited to singing carols at Christmas time. Studies to be referred to in the next section suggest that, as far as most older people are concerned, pastoral care is quite inadequate.

3. Probably the one type of special program for older people which has caught on most generally in the churches is that of the so-called Golden Age clubs. In a sense these are a development of the adult Bible class movement and an extension to later maturity of types of programs developed for young people and young adults in the churches.

Social workers are often heard to complain that these groups do not serve the older people who are most in need of such programs. A social class barrier often operates to discourage the most needy older people from attending. This may be overcome to some extent when, as in Chicago, churches provide the facilities and the city recreation department provides leadership for the groups on a non-sectarian community-wide basis.

Without the presence of leaders of their own with imagination or of trained group workers, these clubs tend to lose impetus and wither away.

4. Some churches have made their facilities available for the use of community programs for older people. Some have developed drop-in centers for older people. The First Methodist Church in Schenectady, New York, for example, is developing a community center for older people with funds given by the Troy Annual Conference of the Methodist church.

Louise Rosett (1949) imaginatively suggested in the *Catholic World* that the modern world needs a new institution and proposed the formation of private membership clubs supported by co-operative credit unions or a type of life insurance. Apparently no one has taken the idea seriously.

Many Protestant churches have found that their organized adult Bible classes have inadvertently turned into classes of older adults. While these meet the needs of some older people in a way, many of these seem to be in the process of withering

away, and many of their members are discouraged and downhearted by the depletion of their ranks, for they seem to be unable to recruit new members or to broaden their programs to meet the needs of their new members. Many of these would make interesting studies in the fossilization of social groups.

What seems to be emerging is a new kind of institution for older adults: the community day center for older people. The relation of the church to this new institution is problematical. When organized by churches, they seem to become non-sectarian community organizations. For example, the writer knows of one large city where four downtown churches have older people's groups meeting on different days; in general, the same group of persons attends each of the four. On the other hand, older people seem to prefer to have them under the auspices of the churches in many communities rather than a public agency because of more favorable attitudes toward the church. This movement seems to be a lay- rather than church-sponsored movement, and older people often secure such groups in the face of indifference or resistance by the clergy.

5. The writer knows of some churches which are becoming conscious of the problems of aging and have given some attention to it. Some churches have included courses on "Making the Most of Later Maturity" (or similar titles) in a general series of study courses given in the church. Others have invited speakers to address various kinds of groups from men's clubs, women's groups, to Bible study classes on the problems of aging. Occasionally, a sermon may be preached with reference to it.

6. Some local churches and pastors are becoming conscious of the housing problems of older people and are taking new interest in the possibility of supporting church homes for the aged or senior citizens' residences in the local community. The writer has had contact with one church which has purchased a residence hotel across the alley from the church with

the object of using the lower floors for parish programs and of turning the upper floor rooms into residences for older people under the supervision of a staff member of the church.

Housing will certainly continue to engage the attention of the church because there are few church members who are not facing for themselves or for some relatives the problem of living arrangements in the later years. The church provides a ready-made association where persons can translate their concern into some sort of concerted action.

It cannot be determined at this time how extensive or how intense these local parish programs for older persons are. It is the writer's impression that, while some churches are rendering significant service to older persons, the vast majority of them still have made little effort to develop special programs or to lay increased emphasis upon the problems of aging. In this respect it is highly probable that the churches are neither far ahead nor far behind most other institutions in the community in their consciousness of and concern for the aged.

In some communities the problem is more pressing than in others, and adjustments cannot be avoided. Harlan (1954) found that in St. Petersburg, Florida, "ministers of several large churches are undoubtedly chosen or assigned partly because of temperamental or personality traits especially congenial to older persons" (p. 339). The writer attended one church in Florida in a community composed almost entirely of retired persons; the clergyman, too, was a retired man. It would seem that the nature of the community, as well as the nature of the leadership of the church, would affect the adjustment of the church to the aging of our population.

We can agree with the report of the Community Project for the Aged (Welfare Council of Metropolitan Chicago, 1952):

It would seem likely that more specialized attention to the needs of older people on the part of the churches, individually and collectively, would yield productive results. Specifi-

cally, attention might be focused on the following: (1) enriching the content and skills of church counseling programs; (2) promoting more effective use of other community facilities; (3) relating more closely and creatively the different kinds of agencies and service within the denomination; (4) developing education and recreation programs for older adults within church buildings; and (5) improving church volunteer visiting programs through voluntary training courses [pp. 187–88].

VIII. PARTICIPATION OF OLDER PEOPLE IN PARISH PROGRAMS

A. Problems in Research Studies

We have seen that the various denominational groups and interdenominational agencies are putting out considerable effort to promote programs for the aged. We have noted also that all churches provide programs which are open to all persons regardless of age and that, in addition, some churches have developed special types of programs especially for older persons. The big question is the extent to which these programs are reaching and affecting the ultimate consumers—the older persons themselves.

Any attempt to bring together a review of the research done to date on the relation between religion and aging is bound to be a frustrating task involving a lot of ingenious detective work. Much of it is incidental to other research projects. Much of it is not indexed under the heading of religion or of old age. Rather, it is to be sought in studies of attitudes and adjustment, of participation and isolation, of role and status, among others. In Shock's (1951) bibliography only seventeen references are indexed under the heading of "Religious Organizations" for the period 1900–1948, and much of this is not research. Pollak (1948) concluded:

The changes affecting the participation of older people in the fields of recreation, education, politics, and religion have received so little attention that the fund of relevant knowledge is hardly sufficient to serve as a basis for making specific research proposals. For the time being, therefore, investigatory efforts in these four institutional fields will have to be largely exploratory.

. . . In the sphere of religious activities, finally, adjustment opportunities for the aged have been almost completely neglected until the present time [p. 153].

Although anthropologists, sociologists, and psychologists have shown considerable interest in various aspects of religious life, its impact upon the adjustment of problems of old age has almost completely escaped their attention [p. 161].

In Shock's (1956) supplement, which lists publications from 1949 to 1955, there are twenty-two references. While this indicates a considerable acceleration of publication in this field, it does not give the whole picture, and any investigator of religion and aging would be warned not to depend too heavily upon this list as exhaustive. For example, even a cursory survey of the articles and book reviews in the *Journal of Gerontology* reveals many additional studies which have some relation to religion and aging but which are not indexed in the *Journal* under this heading.

Only four doctoral dissertations seem to deal directly and primarily with religion and aging since 1948—those by Maves (1950), Garrett (1953), Moberg (1953), and Gray (1954). Others may have uncovered data that would have some bearing upon the subject. Such data as we do possess need to be scrutinized carefully before generalizations are based upon it.

With this indication of the difficulties in gathering the material and with a disclaimer of being exhaustive, some relevant studies will be reviewed below in summary form, and then some observations will be made about them.

B. Some Early Research Studies

Morgan (1937) studied 381 recipients of old age assistance in upstate and metropolitan New York and found that 93 per cent formerly attended church and that only 7 per cent did not. Of those who formerly attended, only 43 per cent continued to attend, and 57 per cent no longer attended. The reasons given for not attending were these: physically unable, 52 per cent; loss of interest or belief, 39 per cent; distance too great or no transportation available, 6 per cent; other reasons, 3 per cent. As to missing church, 35 per cent said that they miss church very much; 21 per cent, considerably; 17 per cent, some; and 11 per cent, not at all. The theme of physical disability as a major factor in decreased church attendance is to appear in many studies, but the suspicion is sustained that physical disability includes psychological components.

Brunot (1943) analyzed requests for service referred to the Bureau for the Aged of the Welfare Council of New York City involving 1935 persons. Of these, 1698 reported a religiocultural background, of which 1069 were Protestant by preference. Only 265 (25 per cent) were active members of any church; 390 additional (37 per cent) reported denominational leanings; 414 (39 per cent) were just "Protestant," which merely indicated that they identified themselves this way in contrast to being Catholic or Jewish.

Burke (1946) made a study of the needs of the Negro aged in New York City and reported that 75 per cent of the aged Negro men and 83 per cent of the aged Negro women indicated that they "really enjoyed" going to church affairs; she concluded that "the church is the focal point of the outside activities of the elderly Negro" (p. 4). It is generally acknowledged that the church fulfils a unique role in the life of the rural southern Negro.

It would be interesting to know if the persons who are forced to seek old age assistance come mainly from a particular social class. It would also be interesting to know if shame at being "on relief" was a factor in causing some persons to drop out of church and if attitudes toward old age assistance have changed enough since the early 1940's to make a difference in the participation of old age assistance beneficiaries in church programs.

Warren (1952) studied the problems of all (143) older people living in a western New York rural community, 90 of whom lived in the village and 53 of whom lived outside the village. The study included 79 females and 64 males, with an average age of 74 years. Answers were received to questions on organizational membership (other than church membership) from 136 persons. Of these, 70 reported belonging to no organization whatsoever, 66 reported belonging to one or more, including church organizations. Reasons given for not giving much time to organizations included: not physically able, 51; lack of interest, 41; lack of transportation, 24; not enough time, 17; cannot afford to, 14; moved to a new neighborhood, 7. Of these 136 persons, 44 did not go to church at all, while the 92 who did go averaged about 36 times a year.

In terms of interest in neighbors and home community, 8 said their interest was much greater now than formerly, 7 somewhat greater now, 89 about the same, 26 somewhat less, 7 much less, and 6 did not answer.

The church and the clergy were much more important to 34 persons than they used to be, somewhat more important to 28, about the same to 56, somewhat less to 10, and much less to 7.

God and religion held much more meaning than formerly to 46, somewhat more to 25, about the same to 59, somewhat less to 3, and much less to 1, with no answer from 9. The unfavorable replies relating to the church and clergy reflected a conservative, fundamentalist attitude with a criticism of "modernism."

Religion was mentioned by 13 persons as one of the things which gave the greatest satisfaction.

C. National Surveys

In 1952 the *Catholic Digest* sponsored a poll of the religious beliefs, attitudes, and activities of Americans in general, which broke the data down for age groups, making it possible to compare older persons with other age groups and against the national norms. The results were reported in a series of articles beginning in November, 1952 (Anonymous, 1952a, 1952b, 1953a, 1953b, 1953c). In this study it was found that 99 per cent of Americans 18 years of age or over believed in God; those 65 and over were the most certain of their belief. Belief was also stronger among the less well educated, the rural, and the lower-income groups.

It was found, however, that 32 per cent did not go to church; an equal number (32 per cent) went every Sunday. Catholics attended more faithfully than Protestants or Jews. There was a distinct increase of non-attendance of those 65 and over and a slight decrease with age in regularity of attendance, from 34 per cent of the 18–24 group to 31 per cent of the 65-and-over group. Women were more faithful in church attendance than men: 29 per cent of the women compared to 36 per cent of the men did not attend; 33 per cent of the women compared to 29 per cent of the men attended every Sunday (see Table 1).

It was found that the proportion of those of all age groups who never attended church increased with the size of the place, but regularity was greatest in places over one million population.

In this study, of the total, 68 per cent were Protestant; but, of those 65 and over, 77 per cent were Protestant, doubtless reflecting the more recent immigration of the Catholic groups. Church membership was claimed by 73 per cent of the population (to be compared to the 62 per cent reported in the census), and 95 per cent expressed a religious preference.

Among Americans, in general, 75 per cent said religion was very important, 20 per cent said fairly important, and 5 per cent said not important at all. However, among those 65 and over, 84 per cent said it was very important, 11 per cent said it was fairly important, and 5 per cent not important at all. Religion was rated as more important by the women, by the

Roman Catholics (the only Protestant group which exceeded the Catholic average was the Methodist), and by rural people. Among those who rated it as least important were the college graduates and the lower-income groups.

God was thought of as a loving Father by 79 per cent of the respondents. How-

TABLE 1*

ATTENDANCE AT RELIGIOUS SERVICES BY AGE, RELIGION, SEX, AND SIZE OF PLACE OF RESIDENCE

(Percentage Distribution)

Subject	Every Week	One to Three Times a Month	Never
Age group:			
18–24	34	36	30
25–34	32	37	31
35–44	30	38	32
45–54	32	36	32
55–64	31	37	32
65 and over	31	27	42
Religion:			
Catholic	62	20	18
Protestant	25	43	32
Jewish	12	32	56
Sex:			
Men	29	35	36
Women	33	38	29
City size:			
Over 1,000,000	36	29	35
100,000–1,000,000	24	38	38
25,000–100,000	37	31	32
10,000–25,000	27	31	31
Under 10,000	33	42	30
Rural farm	32	40	28

* Source: Anonymous, "Do Americans Go to Church?" *Catholic Digest*, 17 (December, 1952), 5.

ever, 81 per cent of those 65 and over regarded God thus, while only 76 per cent of those in the 45–54 age group did.

Of those 65 and over, 56 per cent thought one should prepare for life after death rather than being concerned with living comfortably, as compared with 51 per cent of the national average. In this area only the Baptists among the Protestants exceeded the Roman Catholic group. In contrast with this belief, however, only 34 per

cent of those 65 and over thought that they actually were most serious about this as compared to 21 per cent of the national average.

This *Catholic Digest* survey discloses significant differences in the pattern of church attendance among various kinds of social groupings. Studies of aging need to take this into account. It also discloses a nominal orthodoxy of belief among most Americans which does not correlate with practice. Religion does appear to be more meaningful among the older groups, even as attendance at church decreases. It would appear that the differences between the age groups might correlate more significantly with background, education, and economic status than with age.

Barron (1958) reported on a nation-wide survey of 1206 urban aged persons, predominantly male and 60 years of age and over, drawn from 34 representative cities. The sample contained almost two-thirds Protestant, one-quarter Catholic, and almost 5 per cent Jewish respondents. The study found that "the Bible . . . is not only in last place among the various types of literature read by city-dwelling older Americans, but percentage-wise only 17 per cent admitted reading the Holy Scriptures" (p. 19).

Attendance at religious services revealed 25 per cent attending "every Sunday or Sabbath," 18 per cent "most Sundays or Sabbaths," 32 per cent attending "occasionally," and 24 per cent "not at all." In addition, while 47 per cent indicated no change in attendance habits from the time they were 50, only 24 per cent indicated increased attendance while 29 per cent indicated a decrease in attendance. This is a pattern which consistently appeared in local community studies to be discussed in the next section of this chapter.

D. Catholic Parish Research

There are five studies of Roman Catholic parishes which may be placed in juxtaposition for purposes of comparison.

URBAN SOUTH

Fichter (1954) studied three urban parishes in the South, including 8363 white Catholic parishioners 70 years of age and over excluding dormant Catholics. It should be noted that 40 per cent of those nominally Catholic were classified as dormant (i.e., not members in any active sense of the parish), and no data on them were obtained. The religious practice and parochial participation of the various age groups were compared (Table 2).

group, they received communion less than any other group of any age. Fichter explained the drop in the number receiving communion by the fact that the practice of frequent communion was not yet the vogue before the 1905 decree of Pope Pius X.

The comparison of males and females showed that in every case the females were more active, which is in keeping with the cultural norm. Fichter concludes: "In summary, it may be said that age and sex have

TABLE 2*

RELIGIOUS PRACTICE AND PAROCHIAL PARTICIPATION

(By Ten-Year Age Group)

Age Group	No.	Percentage Receiving Monthly Communion (A)	Percentage Receiving Weekly Communion (B)	Percentage of (B) Belonging to Parish Societies
10–19.............	1668	71.3	29.3	15.0
20–29.............	1994	40.9	5.7	1.8
30–39.............	1987	31.6	6.2	2.4
40–49.............	1462	39.3	9.2	5.4
50–59.............	737	38.4	16.0	4.6
60 and over........	515	25.6	8.4	5.6
Total..........	8363	43.3	12.2	5.7

* Source: J. Fichter, *Social Relations in the Urban Parish* (Chicago: University of Chicago Press, 1954), p. 25.

The percentage of older people in the parish who were nuclear parishioners was better than any other group except the 10–19 category. Fichter found that this nuclear parishioner usually belonged to a nuclear family, was slightly better educated, tended to be a born Catholic rather than a converted one, tended to be of the lower middle class, and was likely to have migrated from a rural parish. He was orthodox in belief and was marginal to the secular institutions. The religious role was pivotal, and he operated under an integrated value system.

Fichter also projected a religious life-profile based upon the study of 8363 Catholic parishioners (Table 3). While the persons over 60 attended Mass more regularly than those of any group except the 10–19

a degree of influence upon the religious practices of urban Catholics but that neither of these factors can be taken apart from the various institutional patterns which accompany both" (p. 93).

CLEVELAND

Sister Mary Therese (1954) reported upon a study of 320 aging persons, all Roman Catholic, all over 55, in a Cleveland parish, including 231 women and 89 men. Religion was declared to be helpful by 80 per cent of the men and 91 per cent of the women. The largest percentage of those who found it helpful was found among those with least education and those with many friends in the neighborhood. Helpfulness was also associated with an acquaintance with the priest. Although 81 per cent knew a priest, 63 per cent of the men and 70 per cent of the women had never been visited by a priest. Not many had ever discussed problems with a priest. Mass was attended every Sunday by 65 per cent of the men and 71 per cent of the women. Reasons given for failure to attend more frequently included poor health, work, lack of transportation, and adverse weather. Only 2 admitted to never going to church.

ioners in a St. Louis parish, including 169 men and 268 women 60 years of age and over. A basic pattern of German culture with groups of Italian and Irish was characteristic of the parish. The investigators were impressed with the strength of family life in the parish. One-fourth of these persons received regular pastoral visitation. A decreasing attendance at Mass with age was found, but the frequency of confession was not so clearly linked to age, although

TABLE 3*

RELIGIOUS ACTIVITIES OF CATHOLIC PARISHIONERS
BY AGE GROUP AND SEX

Age Group in Years	No.	Percentage Making Easter Duties	Percentage Attending Sunday Mass	Percentage Receiving Monthly Communion
10–19:				
Males	835	90.8	90.7	63.3
Females	833	93.4	95.0	79.3
20–29:				
Males	930	83.8	72.9	40.6
Females	1064	85.7	77.1	41.2
30–39:				
Males	924	56.6	62.2	24.1
Females	1063	69.3	75.5	38.3
40–49:				
Males	745	66.9	68.3	30.5
Females	717	83.5	83.5	48.4
50–59:				
Males	365	72.3	72.1	29.6
Females	372	82.5	82.3	47.0
60 and over:				
Males	216	75.5	83.3	16.7
Females	299	94.7	96.3	32.1
Total	8363	78.9	78.6	43.3

* Source: J. Fichter, *Social Relations in the Urban Parish* (Chicago: University of Chicago Press, 1954), p. 91.

One-fourth liked to participate in church organizations. More than 150 read religious books, 123 regularly said their rosary, 128 attended or made novenas. As to communion, 51 per cent of the men never partook, nor did 35 per cent of the women. Among these older parishioners pastoral visits and friendly neighbors would have been greatly appreciated.

ST. LOUIS

The Catholic Charities of St. Louis (1955) reported on a study of 437 parish-

here, too, there was some falling-off with age. Men (75 per cent) participated more than women (65 per cent) in parish organizations. Four-fifths of them attended Mass each week. They were not too much concerned with death. Most did not want a special organization for older people in the church. They did want more visitation, more religious and recreational activities, and help with transportation. The investigators sensed that the relations of these persons to priest and to neighbors were affected by the change from the informal rural patterns they had grown up with to the more formal and less social urban patterns.

BUFFALO

Bower (1957) reported a study of older people in a predominantly German parish in Buffalo, New York. Out of a total of 262 persons 60 years of age and over, 238 persons were interviewed with special stress laid on attitudes. These included 80 men and 158 women. It was found that religion was important, but the church and clergy did not play an active part in the lives of most of these parishioners. One-third of them had curtailed their activities because of poor health and other disabilities. Mass was attended every Sunday or oftener by 70 per cent of the men and 75 per cent of the women; Mass was never attended by 11 per cent of the men and 13 per cent of the women. There was a marked correlation between increasing age and decreasing attendance. The reasons given for attending less often included: ill health, 79 per cent; too busy or had to work, 9 per cent; fallen-away Catholic, 7 per cent; no reply, 4 per cent. It was not hard for 67 per cent to get to church. One-half were regular communicants. These older people were not close to the priest and did not discuss problems with him; 62 per cent were never visited by the priest. While 37 per cent often listened to religious radio or television programs, 20 per cent never listened to religious programs. When asked who should be responsible for meeting the needs of older people, 10 per cent said the church, 23 per cent said Catholic charities, 30 per cent said government, 7 per cent said the community, and 30 per cent gave no reply.

CHICAGO

O'Reilly and Pembroke (1957) reported on the study of those 65 years and over in Chicago's "Back of the Yards" section by means of a sample interview with 292 persons (132 men and 160 women), or a 6.5 per cent sample of the total. Only 35 per

cent were native-born. The largest group of the foreign-born (24 per cent) were Polish. As to religion, 83 per cent were Roman Catholic, 15 per cent were Protestant, and 2 per cent were Greek Orthodox. Because of the preponderance of Roman Catholic persons, this report is included in the Catholic group of studies. It was found that 12 per cent never attended church, 12 per cent attended daily, and 50 per cent attended weekly. There was some difficulty in attending church for 36 per cent. Religion had been more helpful during the last 10 years to 54 per cent, not so helpful to 30 per cent, and about the same to 6

TABLE 4*

HELPFULNESS OF RELIGION BY EXTENT OF
RELIGIOUS PRACTICE IN OLD AGE

(In Percentages)

RELIGION HAS BECOME MORE HELPFUL	EXTENT OF RELIGIOUS PRACTICE		
	More Active	Medium	Less Active
Same........	71.4	21.4	7.1
Yes..........	61.2	27.2	11.6
No...........	28.4	48.8	23.0

* Source: C. T. O'Reilly and Margaret M. Pembroke, *Older People in a Chicago Community* (Chicago: Loyola University, 1957), p. 32.

per cent. However, as indicated by the figures given in Table 4, increased appreciation for the helpfulness of religion did not necessarily result in increased church attendance, although some increase in the degree of religious activity with old age was found (Table 5).

The investigators noted the similarity of pattern of church attendance with the studies made of St. Louis and Cleveland, with the exception that the Chicago men received weekly communion much less often but more took yearly communion. They had no explanation for this.

They also noted that the lonely did not show any significant turn to religion, but happiness and church attendance seemed to be correlated. The Bible, prayerbooks, or other religious literature were read by

55 per cent of the men and 75 per cent of the women. Private prayers were said by 84 per cent of the men and 93 per cent of the women. Membership in church societies was claimed by 41 per cent of the men and 51 per cent of the women. Active church membership was claimed by 56 per cent of the men and 50 per cent of the women.

Of these persons, 60 per cent had not been visited by a clergyman. A visit had been requested by 12 per cent. Only 6 per cent mentioned visiting by a priest as a way the church could be of help to them.

One wishes that these last four studies had attempted to apply Fichter's typology

TABLE 5*

AGE GROUP AND EXTENT OF RELIGIOUS PRACTICE IN OLD AGE

(In Percentages)

AGE	EXTENT OF RELIGIOUS PRACTICE		
	More Active	Medium	Less Active
65–74.........	45.5	37.1	17.4
Over 75.......	67.4	20.9	11.6

* Source: C. T. O'Reilly and Margaret M. Pembroke, *Older People in a Chicago Community* (Chicago: Loyola University, 1957), p. 32.

and had also made some judgments about the social class of the persons studied. Comparisons with the activities of other age groups would have added significantly to our knowledge.

Among these Catholic parishioners religion seems to play a significant part for all but a minority. The desire for more personal attention from the church appears clearly. A question can be raised about the reliability of responses to questions asked by interviewers who are identified with the church. Would not the results be skewed in favor of the church?

E. Community Studies

LONG BEACH AND GRAND RAPIDS

A significant Senior Citizens Survey reported by McCann (1955) included a study of the role of religion in the lives of 606 persons representing a 2 per cent sample of the older people in Long Beach, California. This aspect of the study concentrated mainly upon church attendance. Only 2.2 per cent reported no religion or a religion other than Protestant, Catholic, or Jewish, while there was no information on the religion of 1.6 per cent of the sample. No religion was reported by 4.6 per cent of the men as compared with 0.8 per cent of the women.

The study followed the pattern of an earlier survey in Grand Rapids, Michigan (Hunter and Maurice, 1953), where 151 persons representing a 1 per cent sample of the city's older population was studied. The results obtained were quite similar. In Grand Rapids 2.6 per cent reported no religion or a religion other than Protestant, Catholic, or Jewish. No information was obtained on 1.3 per cent of the sample, and 5 per cent of the men compared to 1 per cent of the women reported no religion.

Both studies clearly showed a decrease in church attendance with increasing age (Table 6). In Long Beach, 52 per cent of those over 65 reported attending services less often than 10 years earlier, while only 12 per cent reported attending more often. In Grand Rapids the comparable figures were 41 and 9 per cent.

One of the major causes for the decrease of attendance in Long Beach was shown to be related to problems of physical mobility (Table 7). In Grand Rapids 28 per cent of those in good health, compared to 51 per cent of those in fair health and 70 per cent of those in poor health, attended church less often.

Attendance, on the other hand, was correlated with marital status, the widowed, single, and divorced showing greater decreases in relative attendance in both communities (Table 8). What this signifies is hard to say. It may have something to do with sociability and personal adjustment. It may mean that those who are married or who have been separated by death rather than divorce have more social stimulation.

TABLE 6*

PRESENT CHURCH ATTENDANCE COMPARED WITH ATTENDANCE
10 YEARS AGO BY AGE GROUPINGS

(In Percentages)

Relative Church Attendance	65–69	70–74	75–79	80 and Over	Age Not Specified	All Ages
Long Beach:						
Less often........	43.8	50.0	59.2	66.2	34.8	52.0
About the same...	40.2	37.8	29.6	29.1	34.8	35.3
More often.......	15.5	11.5	11.2	3.9	13.0	11.5
No information...	0.5	0.7	....	1.0	17.4	1.2
No...........	(199)	(156)	(125)	(103)	(23)	(606)

	65–74		75 and Over		All Ages
Grand Rapids:					
Less often........		31.1		64.4	41.1
About the same...		55.7		28.9	47.7
More often.......		10.4		6.7	9.3
No information...		2.8		....	2.0
No...........		(106)		(45)	(151)

* Sources: C. W. McCann, *Long Beach Senior Citizens' Survey* (Long Beach: Community Welfare Council, 1955), p. 50; W. W. Hunter and Helen Maurice, *Older People Tell Their Story* (Ann Arbor: University of Michigan, Division of Gerontology, 1953), p. 62.

TABLE 7*

PRESENT CHURCH ATTENDANCE COMPARED WITH ATTENDANCE
10 YEARS AGO BY DEGREE OF MOBILITY

(In Percentages)

RELATIVE CHURCH ATTENDANCE	DEGREE OF MOBILITY				
	Able To Go about Any Place	Able To Get about with Difficulty	Confined to Bed or Chair	No Information	All Persons
Less often..........	44.2	67.4	92.8	(6)†	52.0
About the same.....	41.6	23.7	3.6	....	35.3
More often.........	13.2	8.9	3.6	....	11.5
No information.....	1.0	....	....	(3)†	1.2
No............	(434)	(135)	(28)	(9)	(606)

* Source: C. W. McCann, *Long Beach Senior Citizens' Survey* (Long Beach: Community Welfare Council, 1955), p. 50.

† Number of cases.

With separation of any kind there is a decrease in attendance.[1]

Financial condition was shown to have a significant bearing upon church attendance. Apparently, the cost of participation in religious activities is deterrent to many older people, since the attendance of those who could not make ends meet dropped off more sharply than those who had more than enough money or than those who had just enough (Table 9). Perhaps this means the

ance among those attending less often were health or physical condition, listening to services on radio or television, and lost interest in the church (Table 10). Significantly, men replied that they had lost interest in the church three and four times more frequently than women; on the other hand, women gave transportation problems as a reason almost twice as often as men.

In Long Beach only 20 per cent thought that the church was not taking sufficient

TABLE 8*

PRESENT CHURCH ATTENDANCE COMPARED WITH ATTENDANCE
10 YEARS AGO BY MARITAL STATUS

(In Percentages)

RELATIVE CHURCH ATTENDANCE	MARITAL STATUS					
	Married	Widowed	Single	Separated or Divorced	No Information	All Persons
Long Beach:						
Less often........	47.7	55.3	56.8	63.6	....	52.0
About the same...	38.6	32.6	36.4	18.2	(1)†	35.3
More often.......	12.2	11.2	6.8	18.2	....	11.5
No information...	1.5	0.9	....	....	(1)†	1.2
No..........	(287)	(251)	(44)	(22)	(2)	(606)
Grand Rapids:						
Less often........	24.6	50.7	52.6	(2)†	....	41.1
About the same...	59.6	40.8	36.8	(2)†	....	47.7
More often.......	10.5	8.4	10.5	....	....	9.3
No information...	5.3	....	....	....	....	2.0
No..........	(57)	(71)	(19)	(4)	....	(151)

* Sources: C. W. McCann, *Long Beach Senior Citizens' Survey* (Long Beach: Community Welfare Council, 1955), p. 51; W. W. Hunter and Helen Maurice, *Older People Tell Their Story* (Ann Arbor: University of Michigan, Division of Gerontology, 1953), p. 62.
† Number of cases.

churches need to evaluate their financial policies with regard to the situation of the aged.

In both surveys the three most frequent reasons given for declining church attend-

[1] The need for cross-cultural study here is strikingly illustrated by Townsend's (1958) directly opposite findings in a working-class London community: "Widows without children and spinsters were the most frequent attenders. Few men, and few married women, went to church or chapel. It seemed that to some women (but not to men) churchgoing was a consolation for a solitary life" (p. 124).

interest in older people, while 80 per cent felt that it was taking enough interest. In Grand Rapids, where the question was slightly different, 37 per cent felt that the church should take more interest in older people, while 28 per cent did not know if they should or not.

In both studies, of those indicating a feeling that the church should take more interest, about half (52 per cent in Long Beach; 43 per cent in Grand Rapids) did not know what to suggest. Among those giving suggestions, visitation was the most

TABLE 9*

PRESENT CHURCH ATTENDANCE COMPARED WITH ATTENDANCE 10 YEARS AGO BY FINANCIAL CONDITION

(In Percentages)

RELATIVE CHURCH ATTENDANCE	FINANCIAL CONDITION				
	Could Not Make Ends Meet	Had Just Enough	More than Enough	No Information	All Persons
Long Beach:					
Less often........	65.7	51.3	44.6	(5)†	52.0
About the same...	22.8	36.1	41.9	(4)†	35.3
More often......	10.6	11.4	12.9	(1)†	11.5
No information...	0.9	1.2	0.6	(1)†	1.2
No............	(105)	(335)	(155)	(11)	(606)
Grand Rapids:					
Less often........	54.5	43.6	21.7	(1)†	41.1
About the same...	36.4	48.5	60.9	(1)†	47.7
More often......	9.1	6.9	17.4	(1)†	9.3
No information...	....	1.0	....	(2)†	2.0
No............	(22)	(101)	(23)	(5)	(151)

* Source: C. W. McCann, *Long Beach Senior Citizens' Survey* (Long Beach: Community Welfare Council, 1955), p. 52; W. W. Hunter and Helen Maurice, *Older People Tell Their Story* (Ann Arbor: University of Michigan, Division of Gerontology, 1953), p. 62.

† Number of cases.

TABLE 10*

REASONS GIVEN FOR ATTENDING CHURCH LESS OFTEN

(In Percentages)

REASONS FOR ATTENDING LESS OFTEN	LONG BEACH			GRAND RAPIDS†		
	Men	Women	Both Sexes	Men	Women	Both Sexes
Health or physical condition.....	40.3	40.7	40.6	78.9	53.5	61.3
Listen to services on radio or television......................	14.4	18.6	17.1	31.6	34.9	33.9
Lost interest....................	22.7	7.8	12.9	47.4	11.6	22.6
Transportation difficulties.......	7.5	13.0	11.2	10.5	20.9	17.7
Don't know people in church now.	5.0	3.9	4.3	10.5	4.6	6.4
Can't afford to go to church now..	....	2.6	1.7	10.5	4.6	6.4
Other reasons.................	7.6	11.3	10.0	5.3	9.3	8.1
No information................	2.5	2.1	2.2	5.3	2.3	3.2
No......................	(119)	(231)	(350)	(40)	(80)	(120)

* Source: Adapted from C. W. McCann, *Long Beach Senior Citizens' Survey* (Long Beach: Community Welfare Council, 1955), p. 52; W. W. Hunter and Helen Maurice, *Older People Tell Their Story* (Ann Arbor: University of Michigan, Division of Gerontology, 1953), p. 63.

† Total percentages are more than 100 per cent because of multiple responses.

frequent response (21 per cent in Long Beach; 30 per cent in Grand Rapids). Others included providing transportation (7 per cent in Long Beach; 18 per cent in Grand Rapids), organizing social clubs (10 per cent in Long Beach; 13 per cent in Grand Rapids), employing a church worker experienced with senior citizens (6 per cent in Long Beach), and giving financial assistance (14 per cent in Grand Rapids). Certainly, these opinions deserve serious consideration by the churches.

NEW YORK CITY

Kutner *et al.* (1956) included a study of the activity, isolation, and adjustment of the 500 older persons in their sample of the Kips Bay–Yorkville section of New York. The sample was weighted in favor of a lower economic-social stratum and was probably slightly healthier, less senile, and less emotionally disturbed than the general population, since persons in these categories could not be interviewed easily. This sample was composed of 49 per cent Catholics, 37 per cent Protestants, and 9 per cent Jews. It represented 1 per cent of the total aged in the area. They found that 8 per cent of the sample was engaged in religious activity (other than church attendance) fairly regularly. Religious activity was not specified or broken down. They also found that morale was correlated more with employment than with activity and that isolation correlated with cultural background and ethnic differences rather than with religion. This study does not throw much light on the interests of this paper except to indicate that religion did not play a large part in the lives of these persons, excluding church attendance, and to show the importance of ethnic and cultural factors.

Chalfen (1956) derived a measure of the extent of activity participation, religious interest, and participation in religious activities through interviews with 108 persons from seven old age homes and 108 from seven recreation centers in New York City. He used a check list similar to one used by the National Recreation Association in a study of the leisure hours of the general population in 1934. Activity was higher for those of higher social status who are more independent. Both Protestant and Jewish persons scored higher than Catholic. The population of the centers was more active than that of the homes. The housewife group was most active, along with Negroes, those on relief, and those with high education in the centers. In both the homes and the centers religious activity ranked fifth among activities.

Although Chalfen's study showed that religion played some part in the lives of three-fourths of these older people, it also showed wide variation in religious activity and interest among various groupings. Furthermore, this variation was not correlated with age so much as with ethnic and social class factors. The usual decrease of activity with age also was noted.

THREE FLORIDA COMMUNITIES

Webber (1954) studied the organized social life of 474 older persons in two Florida communities. He found that in the two cities of Orlando and West Palm Beach more than one-half of the 101 voluntary organizations were either churches or church-related groups. In Orlando less than 40 per cent and in West Palm Beach only 23 per cent belonged to non-church organizations. About one-half the total memberships were in churches, and an additional 10 per cent belonged to church-affiliated organizations.

In Orlando about one-third of the persons had no organizational affiliation, and in West Palm Beach more than one-half were not members of any group. More women than men did not belong. Women were more likely to belong to just one organization, which was likely to be the church. Memberships in organizations dropped with increasing age.

In Orlando 24 per cent never attended church; 42 per cent attended once a week. In West Palm Beach 54 per cent never attended; 38 per cent attended once a week. No reasons were given for the difference in the two communities. Webber found that attendance as well as membership declined as age increased.

Hoyt (1954) studied the life of the retired in a trailer park in Florida, interviewing a sample of 194 persons in a park with 1093 dwelling units. He found that 69 per cent reported an average church attendance of 3.4 times per month in their home community, but that 59 per cent reported an average church attendance of 3.6 times per month after migration. He did not inquire into the reasons for the decline in the number attending, but he did report that churches were not too convenient to the park. Also, the residents were socially isolated from the regular community. However, Protestant services were held in the recreation hall by various visiting ministers. It seems to this writer that inconvenience, lack of an easily accessible, stable church group with a continuity of leadership, and perhaps lack of a group of their own denominational preference might have been factors in the drop. Increased disability could also have been a factor. Or this could be the amount of loss in attendance that can be expected when persons migrate and sever old ties.

IX. Meaning of Religion, Participation, and Isolation

Another group of studies attempts to probe more deeply into the meaning of religion, activity, and isolation. These three things are considered in one section because in some cases the meaning of religion has been correlated with activity and participation, and in other cases it has been correlated to happiness and adjustment, attitude, or belief.

Starbuck (1899), in his famous *Psychology of Religion,* was convinced that "the belief in God in some form is by far the most central conception, and it grows in importance as the years advance" (p. 320). He also felt that feelings of dependence, reverence, and oneness with God, as well

as faith increase with age. His data were drawn from 237 replies to questionnaires, including 142 females and 95 males, with 24 women and 22 men over 40. The nature and size of the sample does not provide a firm base for generalization. However, such a generalization has become a part of the folklore of the psychology of religion.

In the Bureau of the Census study of religion it is to be noted that, among those who were 65 years of age and over, a slightly larger percentage (3.0) than the national average (2.7) reported no religion (U.S. Bureau of the Census, 1958). While not statistically significant, this does raise some questions about the assumption that older people are more likely to be religious than younger people. It may be that older people are more willing to admit they have no religious identification, or it may be that they grew up in a period when it was less popular to be identified with a religious group, since in 1900 only 36 per cent of the population had membership in any of the religious bodies (*Yearbook of American Churches,* p. 86).

Tucker's (1940) study of 400 unemployed men and 400 unemployed women supports Starbuck, for he found a more favorable attitude to religion among older people than among young people.

Hall and Robertson (1942) found a steady increase in the preference for religion as a reading topic from age 25 on as far as newspapers were concerned and from 35 on in magazine reading. Church increased in preference as a conversational topic from 25 on. Religion passed the median of interest in topics for reading between 35 and 45 years of age. However, reading tended to drop off as a recreational activity after 35.

McCrary (1956) found in his study of a small, midwestern community that the older persons had an excess of free time, that they belonged to few clubs or organizations, and that they were seldom officeholders. However, religion and religious participation provided older persons with feelings of satisfaction and security.

Havighurst and Albrecht (1953) included data about religious interest and activity in their study of the older people of "Prairie City," a midwestern city of about 7000 population, of which about 10 per cent were 65 and over. They found that "in Prairie City the average older person is a regular attendant of church services, but takes no leadership responsibility" (p. 201). Table 11 summarizes their findings with regard to the relation of the older people to church participation.

The authors found no evidence of a large-scale "turning to religion" of persons as they grew older; rather, most people

TABLE 11*

RELATION OF OLDER PEOPLE TO
CHURCH PARTICIPATION

	Per Cent
Rejected religion and the church.......	4
Had no church affiliation, no attendance	18
Had a passive interest, seldom attended church, may have listened to sermons on the radio......................	15
Had frequent and active participation, no responsibility (including 6 per cent who did not attend because of health)	61
Had active participation with responsibility as officer, church-school teacher, etc............................	2

* Source: R. J. Havighurst and Ruth Albrecht, *Older People* (New York: Longmans, Green & Co., 1953), p. 202.

carried on the religious habits of their middle years. They believed that the churches in the smaller towns and small cities reached a larger proportion of older persons than did those in the larger cities. They found that "the preponderant attitudes of these people toward religion have very little relationship to personal adjustment as measured by the adjustment rating or total attitude scale" (p. 204). Yet nine-tenths of them believed in an afterlife. The authors concluded that "it is clear the church is an active force for good in the lives of many older people" (p. 205).

They found also that it was customary for older people to drop out of leadership positions in the church gradually after they reached the age of 60. Older women were generally of more use in a church than

older men, and for this reason they got more out of church life.

While taking note of social class differences, they did not carry out their analysis in terms of its effect on religion and church activity. The upper class, which represented 3 per cent in "Prairie City," supported the church, although usually they were without activity in it. The upper middle class, representing 12 per cent of the population, as a rule provided the leaders in the church. The lower middle class, representing 32 per cent of the population, provided the largest share of the membership in social organizations, including the church. The upper lower class, 41 per cent of the population, did not have much time for participation in any organization, and the older people were seldom financially secure. They usually attended the revivalistic churches in "Prairie City," although some were to be found in all the other churches. The lower-lower class, 12 per cent of the population, were not among the "respectable." Generally, they would be outside the churches, except for funerals.

It would seem clear that class patterns and the accompanying characteristics having to do with education, economic status, and ability to secure adequate health care would have an important bearing upon church membership, attendance, and services received from the church.

Pressey and Simcoe (1950) found that church attendance was more frequent on the part of the successful than the problem persons in both childhood and old age.

Moles (1949) found that well-adjusted Orthodox Jewish older people were all intensely or fairly religious, while only 35 per cent of the poorly or very poorly adjusted were intensely or fairly religious.

Pan (1950, 1954) studied the influence of institutionalization upon old age as he compared persons in institutions with those outside. This study included 597 women (aged 65 and over) in 68 Protestant homes who were compared with 759 women outside institutions studied by Cavan and a sample of 56 old women living in two southern public institutions studied by Junkin. Institutionalized old people scored high in religious activity and had more favorable attitudes toward religion than those outside. Pan believed his study supported Cavan's hypothesis that increasing age is associated with increase in religious activities and in dependence upon religion. He found that the aged living in their own homes had a better adjustment than the aged living in Protestant religious homes or non-denominational homes. However, it does not appear to this writer that he gave adequate allowance for the selective factors and the particular environmental stimuli and pressures affecting those in church homes.

Albrecht's (1951) survey of the role activities of older people found only a small percentage of older people holding any office in the church.

Granick (1952) found the church to be of greater importance to older people than other organizations in two Florida communities but concluded that, even so, interest in religion was relatively mild, for 25 per cent never attended church, while only 30–40 per cent attended regularly.

McNulty (1952) found that participation in religious ceremonies by older persons estimated to be well adjusted was noticeably missing.

Moberg (1951, 1953a, 1953b) reviewed previous studies of adjustment and religion which found that church membership was correlated with good adjustment. In his study of 219 residents of institutions he found that the relation of church affiliation to good adjustment was spurious when other factors were controlled by matching; that, while engaging in religious activities was associated with good adjustment, former church leaders were better adjusted than those who still held positions; and that holding orthodox religious beliefs was related to good personal adjustment.

Garrett (1953), on the basis of 429 usable attitude opinion scales, found favorable attitudes toward the church on the part of older people. In 90 usable scales

received from ministers he found a favorable attitude toward older people, although more rural ministers felt they thwarted the church programs than was true of urban ministers. In their expectations of the church, older people stressed worship and service. Evangelism, study, and recreation fell into subsidiary roles. Generally, older people did not desire special groups.

The University of Michigan's Detroit Area Study, which interviewed a random sample of residents about their attitudes toward Sunday shopping, found that strong opposition to Sunday store hours tended to increase with age (University of Michigan News Service, 1958). One-half of Detroiters over 60 years of age thought it was never morally justifiable for stores to be open on Sunday, while only 3 out of every 10 adults between the ages of 21 and 39 agreed with them. Opposition was stronger also among the lower socioeconomic classes, the less well educated, and those of lower income, as well as among church members.

It is to be suspected that some of the contradictory findings of these studies are reflections of regional and class differences. Another frequent flaw in these studies is that religion and religious interest are often measured by participation in church organizations or attendance at church.

Pressey and Kuhlen (1957) summarized the findings of various studies about religion and aging in a chapter on "Moral, Sociopolitical, and Religious Values and Behavior." They concluded that "values and beliefs of one kind or another represent a major aspect of the motivational make-up of the individual" (p. 436). They tried to chart the change of values during the course of life. They noted studies which showed a tendency of older people to be annoyed by the commission of borderline wrongs and cited public opinion polls showing that older adults frequently give conservative (more moralistic) answers to questions about behavior, apparently seeing things in relatively sharp blacks and whites and making decisions on absolute moral bases. They also reported a general increase in political and civic activity up to about 50 and then a drop out of such activities, which they attributed to lack of energy, for interest in passive participation such as reading.

Pressey and Kuhlen summarized the functions of religious belief and practice as follows:

In the first place, a religion or life philosophy provides a certain unification of the diverse values and activities of living. As an intelligent being, man feels the need for answers to complex questions about the world and himself, and religion provides certain answers to many such questions—though many people work out concepts more in scientific or philosophical terms. Second, religion provides a certain safety and security. The ordering of the universe and life into a meaningful pattern makes a contribution in this direction, but perhaps more important is recognition on the part of religious people of a greater power outside themselves that may be drawn upon as a source of strength. Third, cultural conformity plays an important role in religious motivation. The church is an established institution. . . .

Many other needs are, in fact, satisfied by religious belief and practice. Prayer, church-going, and Bible-reading, for example, may have many different meanings for different individuals. Attendance at church may satisfy needs for aesthetic experience, for social interaction, for status-seeking—and in different degrees for different people. Nevertheless, certain general patterns of development and change are apparent when groups of different ages are studied [p. 479].

These authors believe that differences in values, in strength of belief, and in age trends will exist among various religious groups, with different sections of the country, and with the degree of urbanization of a community. Values will differ also with economic and educational status, between males and females, as well as with the passage of time. In assessing the age differences in values, the important changes in American culture and world culture have to be considered. Increased conservatism may be caused by changes in culture, by reduced learning effectiveness or loss of "neural plasticity," by the fact that social

changes touch older persons less intimately because they are more restricted, by changes in internalization of public attitudes versus private attitudes, and by biological and social losses which increase defensiveness and rigidity.

The writer of this chapter agrees with Pressey and Kuhlen's analysis.

Some further studies bearing on activity and isolation can be cited as casting some light upon older persons' participation. Ploch (1955), utilizing case studies of 26 male household heads in Upstate New York, found that participation patterns learned as youths tended to continue into adulthood and that family orientations tended to serve as models for the participation of members. He found that the active participants exhibited less anomic tendencies but that dissociation from community activities was not necessarily related to personal disorganization.

This study corroborates the observations of Vidich and Bensman (1958) in an Upstate New York community. They noted that church-related activities constituted approximately 50 per cent of all organized social activities in the community:

[However,] although the churches organize the major portion of the public life of the community, their activities involve only the 300–400 persons who are interested in church activities. This, of course, is only a small portion of the 1,700 adults involved in the life of the community.

All of the class groups are not equally involved in church activities and church memberships are not distributed along class lines. The basic core of memberships in all churches is drawn from various segments of the middle and marginal middle classes [p. 229].

Only a small percentage of industrial workers were church-involved. The "shack people" were decisively and completely uncommitted to church life. Kinship, marriage, and family tradition played a part in determining church membership. This would certainly affect the relation of the aged to the church.

Havighurst (1957) reported on the performance of middle-aged people in the common social roles as measured by nine rating scales used in the Kansas City Study of Adult Life. A role is defined as "a socially defined and prescribed pattern of behavior . . . learned or internalized by an individual so that it becomes a self-expectation" (p. 303). It was found that these persons performed better in the roles of worker, parent, spouse and homemaker than in those of citizen, church member, friend, and association member. Performance was closely related to socioeconomic status in most areas but not to age. The roles tended to fall into two discrete clusters of friend-citizen-association, or the leisure cluster, and parent-spouse-homemaker, or the family cluster. This leaves out the role of church member, which had low correlation with the others, and the worker role, which for men is related to the family configuration but for women to the extrafamily configuration. Twenty-seven patterns were found which represented crudely defined life-styles. Role performance as church member was not related systematically to such things as social class, family-centeredness, personal adjustment, and complexity of life. Apparently, wide variations in church activity were compatible with any of the general types of social role pattern. In studying the relation of religion to aging, then, not only social class status, family tradition, regional patterns, and social relations but also individual experience with religious groups should be considered.

Finally, three recent studies have addressed themselves directly to the problem of the relationship of age and religiosity through the analysis of cross-sections of age strata (Albrecht, 1958; Barron, 1958; Orbach, 1958). All three concur in finding no support for the notion that religiosity increases as a function of age.

Albrecht studied a scientifically selected sample of 404 families in seven "Bible Belt" counties of eastern Alabama and found a pattern of religious attendance varying with stages of the family life-cycle. Regular attendance increased from 50 per cent of the couples in the pre-child stage to a peak of 71 per cent for families with children over the age of 10. It then fell to 48 per cent for older childless couples and those with grown children who have left home. In broken homes with the head under 62 years of age, 65 per cent went to church once a week, while those with the head over 62 reported only 25 per cent regularly attending. Older lone persons had the lowest rate—21 per cent attending regularly. Albrecht concludes: "On the basis of church attendance it is not possible to believe that older people become more religious" (p. 69).

Barron reported on a pilot survey of 496 residents of New York City between the ages of 30 and 65. The respondents were predominantly female (324) and Jewish (325), with only 98 Catholics and 65 Protestants. No significant differentials in distribution of attendance levels at religious services between the age groups taken in 5-year strata were observed.

Probing into subjective attitudes to religion, Barron did find some relation between chronological age and religious self-image ("Would you say you are a religious person, or doesn't religion mean very much to you?") and belief in an afterlife; no relationship was found with regard to utilization of prayer and aid from ministers.

The proportion of persons indicating subjective religiosity in this fashion, however, is small compared to other studies (45 per cent indicating a religious self-image, 30 per cent undecided, and 25 per cent with an irreligious self-image; 36 per cent indicating belief in an afterlife, 31 per cent undecided, and 34 per cent expressing disbelief). This is especially interesting in view of the preponderance of women in the sample; other studies have consistently shown higher expressions of religious interest on the part of women than men. Barron also sees this as directing attention to the importance of the type of community involved as a key variable.

Examining the effect of religiosity on adjustment, Barron sought to determine if those who stated they received more satisfaction and comfort from religion than from anything else in their lives (39 per cent) worry less about getting older than those who do not derive maximum comfort and satisfaction from religion. The results gave no indication of any difference, leading to the conclusion that the question of the impact of religion on adjustment in old age remains inconclusive. Barron states:

There is no doubt that research has exposed the shortcomings of religion as an effective geriatric force. Although as we have seen, there is some indication of inner religiosity in later years, there is little, if any, change of interest in the church and synagogue with advancing age and very little indication that organized religion has succeeded in helping most of the aged adjust to their personal and social situations. Instead of a large-scale "turning to religion" as people grow older, most people persist in the religious pattern of their earlier age stages [p. 30].

Orbach, citing the lack of studies on representative populations which control relevant sociological variables, analyzed a pooled sample of 6911 adults 21 years of age and over. This group consisted of the yearly area-probability samples of the Detroit Area Study from 1951 to 1957, representative of the total population of the Detroit Metropolitan Area. The major concern of the study was to test the commonly held hypothesis of increased religiosity with advancing chronological age.

Using church attendance as a measure of overt religiosity, he found a roughly level plateau of regularity in attendance, with no significant differences between the ages of 21 and 74 for the total population taken in 5-year age intervals (Table 12 summarizes these data). After age 75 there was a marked increase in irregular attendance

TABLE 12*

AGE, SEX, AND RELIGIOUS ATTENDANCE IN THE DETROIT AREA

(Percentage Distribution)

AGE GROUP	FREQUENCY OF ATTENDANCE					No.
	Once a Week	Twice a Month	Once a Month	A Few Times a Year or Less	Never	
21–39 years........	44.9	12.1	8.2	24.1	10.7	(3402)
Male...........	41.1	11.3	7.2	26.7	13.7	(1542)
Female.........	48.1	12.7	9.0	22.0	8.2	(1860)
40–59 years........	47.1	12.9	7.8	22.2	10.0	(2510)
Male...........	40.4	10.7	7.6	27.0	14.3	(1268)
Female.........	53.9	15.1	8.1	17.3	5.6	(1242)
60–74 years........	48.7	10.3	8.5	21.2	11.3	(855)
Male...........	42.0	9.3	8.3	25.9	14.5	(421)
Female.........	55.1	11.3	8.7	16.6	8.3	(434)
75 years and over...	41.7	11.3	2.3	18.9	25.8	(132)
Male...........	34.6	9.1	3.6	25.4	27.3	(55)
Female.........	46.7	13.0	1.3	14.3	24.7	(77)
Total..............	46.0	12.1	8.0	22.9	10.9	(6911)†
Male...........	40.8	10.8	7.4	26.7	14.3	(3290)†
Female.........	50.8	13.4	8.5	19.6	7.7	(3621)†

* Source: H. L. Orbach, "Age and Religious Participation in a Large Metropolitan Area: Detroit" (paper presented at the annual meeting of the Gerontological Society, Philadelphia, 1958).

† Includes those for whom age was not ascertained.

and non-attendance (although regular attendance remained at a high level). This change was ascribed to the effect of the infirmities of old age.

Four age groups were defined to represent youth (21–39), middle age (40–59), maturity (60–74), and old age (75 and over). The attendance patterns of these groups were analyzed, controlling for religious preference, sex, race, and no clear age trends were found to exist. While there were some percentage increases in attendance rates, there were also declines, and most of these were not statistically significant (Tables 13 and 14). The Jewish group was the only one in which both male and female rates showed a consistent and significant increase with age. Orbach explained this, however, as due to a cultural difference—the greater orthodoxy in religious denomination within Judaism of the older group—rather than due to a function of age.

Orbach also examined, while controlling for religious preference, sex, and race, the effect of a series of socioeconomic variables: occupational status of the head of the family, education, income, and size of place of longest previous residence before coming to Detroit (within this grouping life-long Detroit residents and foreign-born were separate categories). None of these control groups revealed any consistent age trend, although there were significant individual differences in attendance patterns between them.

He concluded that chronological age as such gave no evidence of being related to overt religious behavior and that its use without proper control of relevant sociological variables is of limited value, since important differences between groups tend to be overshadowed. Orbach cautioned against treating this cross-sectional data as a substitute for longitudinal analysis, arguing that broad cultural changes in recent

TABLE 13*

AGE, RACE, SEX, AND RELIGIOUS ATTENDANCE IN THE DETROIT AREA: PROTESTANTS
(Percentage Distribution)

AGE GROUP	FREQUENCY OF ATTENDANCE										No.	
	Once a Week		Twice a Month		Once a Month		A Few Times a Year or Less		Never			
	Male	Female	Male	Female	Male	Female	Male	Female	Male	Female	Male	Female
21–39 years:												
White.........	26.5	33.1	13.8	13.3	7.2	9.4	35.0	32.3	17.5	11.9	(610)	(753)
Negro........	30.2	38.5	19.0	26.8	12.4	17.4	31.8	14.5	6.6	2.8	(242)	(317)
40–59 years:												
White.........	27.7	40.5	9.2	16.7	8.8	11.7	37.8	24.2	16.6	6.9	(524)	(538)
Negro........	34.4	51.3	25.0	27.3	13.9	11.8	18.9	9.1	7.8	0.5	(180)	(187)
60–74 years:												
White.........	31.8	43.6	7.6	13.3	10.0	9.0	32.9	25.1	17.7	9.0	(170)	(211)
Negro........	42.1	46.8	28.9	25.5	10.5	8.5	13.2	8.5	5.3	10.6	(38)	(47)
75 years and over:												
White.........	30.3	31.8	12.1	13.6	......	......	30.3	18.2	27.3	36.4	(33)	(44)
Negro........	(1)†	(3)†	......	(4)†	(1)†	(1)†	......	(2)†	(2)†	(1)†	(4)	(11)
Total:‡												
White....	27.7	37.0	11.1	14.5	8.0	11.4	35.7	28.1	17.5	10.5	(1340)	(1547)
Negro....	32.8	43.3	22.0	27.0	12.7	14.5	25.2	12.4	7.3	2.8	(464)	(566)

* Source: H. L. Orbach, "Age and Religious Participation in a Large Metropolitan Area: Detroit" (paper presented at the annual meeting of the Gerontological Society, Philadelphia, 1958).

† Number of cases.

‡ Total includes those for whom age was not ascertained.

generations in religious habits and attitudes should be taken into account. The study did suggest, however, that religious practice probably changed little throughout an individual's lifetime once a regular pattern was established.

X. Concluding Considerations

A. General Observations

When we take into consideration the studies that have been made and the subjective impressions that an observer of the scene has received, several observations present themselves as tentative generalizations. Almost all older people, like most American adults of all ages, admit to a belief in God and acknowledge verbally the importance of religion. Only 2–4 per cent actually and openly reject the church and repudiate religion for a variety of reasons. This is characteristic of our culture and is

what one would expect. In this they differ very little from persons of any other age.

Probably 60–70 per cent of all older people have some sort of active relation to a church, if manifested only by occasional attendance at a service or membership in it. There is some indication that they might be more favorable than younger groups of adults in their attitudes toward religion and disposed to find religion taking on somewhat more importance. It would be more accurate to say that those who are now above 60 years of age are somewhat more religious than those who are now younger. It is not clear that this is entirely correlated with aging. There is some indication that there is a pattern of activity which reaches a peak in adolescence, then falls off sharply in early adulthood, to rise gradually over the years, with a marked increase after 60. The contradictory findings

TABLE 14*

AGE, SEX, AND RELIGIOUS ATTENDANCE IN THE DETROIT AREA: CATHOLICS AND JEWS
(Percentage Distribution)

| AGE GROUP | FREQUENCY OF ATTENDANCE | | | | | | | | | | No. | |
| | Once a Week | | Twice a Month | | Once a Month | | A Few Times a Year or Less | | Never | | | |
	Male	Female	Male	Female	Male	Female	Male	Female	Male	Female	Male	Female
Catholics:†												
21–39 years...	69.6	76.2	5.5	6.1	4.1	3.8	14.6	10.3	6.2	3.5	(549)	(652)
40–59 years...	69.1	79.6	7.7	8.1	4.3	2.1	13.4	8.1	5.5	2.1	(417)	(422)
60–74 years...	58.9	79.2	7.7	4.2	4.5	6.3	18.0	6.3	10.9	4.2	(156)	(144)
75 years and over........	45.5	90.0	9.1	......	18.2	......	27.3	......	......	10.0	(11)	(20)
Total:												
White..	67.6	77.9	6.6	6.5	4.4	3.5	14.7	8.9	6.6	3.3	(1134)	(1240)
Negro..	22.7	57.1	22.7	17.9	18.2	3.6	22.7	14.3	13.6	7.1	(22)	(28)
Jews:												
21–39 years...	3.3	2.3	6.7	2.3	23.3	16.3	60.0	65.1	6.7	14.0	(30)	(43)
40–59 years...	14.6	12.8	10.4	12.8	4.2	10.3	58.3	56.4	12.5	7.7	(48)	(39)
60 years and over........	25.0	31.3	6.2	6.3	18.8	12.5	37.5	31.3	12.5	19.8	(16)	(16)
Total.....	12.8	11.2	8.5	7.1	12.8	13.3	55.3	56.1	10.6	12.2	(94)	(98)

* Source: H. L. Orbach, "Age and Religious Participation in a Large Metropolitan Area: Detroit" (paper presented at the annual meeting of the Gerontological Society, Philadelphia, 1958).

† Only whites are included in the four age groupings. Total figures include those for whom age was not ascertained.

of various research reports, however, do not provide a firm base for generalization.

Among older people, as among all Americans, belief in the importance of religion does not carry over into practice in regard to religious activity such as church attendance, belonging to church organizations, or reading religious literature. It is not clear how deeply the church and religion influence adjustment to aging or how seriously most older persons take religion. It seems clear that religious activity is not necessarily an indication of an essentially religious concern.

Few older people hold any positions of leadership in the church. These are gradually relinquished or removed from them—it is not clear which—as they pass 60 years of age. There is a notable decrease in religious activity, such as church attendance, as persons grow older, brought on by increasing physical disability, decreasing mobility, lack of adequate transportation, financial stringency and insecurity, and occasionally by loss of interest.

There are notable differences between sociocultural groups in the pattern of religious expression and activity as measured by church membership, church attendance, participation in the sacraments and rites of the church, and engaging in the organized program of the church other than worship. The different groups value different expressions of religion and seek to elicit them, although all seem to value membership and attendance at church services as the most tangible and most quantitative measures of interest. Women seem to be more religious than men and rural people more religious than urban people.

There seems to be a correlation between social participation patterns in general and participation in religious activities of a social nature. Furthermore, these patterns appear to be those which have been characteristic of the person throughout most of his life and which were formed in early life. These patterns reflect family tradition and cultural background, as well as personal adjustment.

Considerable care should be taken in attempting to make a judgment about whether or not a person is religious and whether or not religion is meaningful to him. Conformity with conventional social patterns and the secondary and concomitant benefits conferred by membership in religious groups and organizations may mask other interests, whereas one may be deeply religious and not express it in church membership and attendance. However, there is certainly some relationship between religion and church.

B. Hypotheses

1. Religion is meaningful in the lives of many older persons as a factor in successful adjustment to aging; but interest in and meaningfulness of religion is not necessarily correlated with age but rather with the continual maintenance of a meaningful relationship between the aging person and a religious group.

Question: To what extent can persons be converted to religion in later life?

2. As a complex institution the church and its leadership tend to reflect the values of the culture in which it operates as well as influencing the values of the culture. Therefore, in its attitudes and relationships to the aging, it reflects the attitudes and relationships of the culture as well as its own stated values. Furthermore, wide variations in attitude and practice may be found between local churches and church leaders.

Question: To what extent is religion a force in modern culture, and what factors determine its influence?

3. As a social institution the church is feeling the impact of the aging upon it and is slowly modifying its programs to accommodate the social changes under the pressure of a few imaginative, alert, and devoted leaders within, the pressure of established departments to work with older persons, the pressure of the demands of the situation, and the prodding of other agencies. The resistance to such change comes

from inertia, lack of awareness, and un-challenged assumptions, as well as from a lack of trained leadership.

4. While the participation pattern of older persons in the church tends to correlate with their pattern of participation in other social organizations, those who have established a pattern of active participation earlier in life tend to continue their association with the church longer than with other organizations unless their association is interrupted through migration, illness, or serious economic reverses.

5. The churches are playing a significant role in the adjustment of many older persons, but they are not in practice doing as much as they could or should do in the light of their stated purposes. Cultural lag, the influence of negative attitudes and practices, lack of awareness, and human weaknesses are among the causes for their failure to measure up to their inherent purpose.

C. Suggestions for Research

The churches can hardly avoid the topic of aging. However, they need to be encouraged to do more research than they have done. Churches are primarily action and education organizations and therefore, in perhaps typical American fashion, more promotion-minded than research-minded. So far they have depended mainly upon the research which is done by other groups to provide them with the bases of their programs. But if they are to make an intelligent, significant, and effective contribution to the total readjustment of society to this new thing which has come to pass, they need to do more research. At the same time, social scientists would do well to give more attention to an institution which is so pervasive and to an aspect of life which is so significant.

The writer suggests that some of the following areas should be explored:

We need to know much more about what the various religious bodies are actually doing on the several levels of organization. At present we do not know for sure how many homes for the aged are operated by Protestant groups or how many persons are served. We do not know how many churches have special groups or special programs for the aged. A survey in at least the larger denominations would be useful.

We need to know what the attitudes are of clergymen and church leaders in the various religious groups toward aging and the aged, and how they view the problems of an aging population. It would be useful to find out if variations in attitude correlated with the stage of development of a religious group.

We need to know still more about the attitudes of older people toward religion and religious groups and the extent to which they participate in public religious activities or engage in private religious activities. We need to know how social class and regional patterns color the meaning of religion for older persons. Case studies would help, although data obtained through them are likely to be colored by recent experience and by selective remembering. We need some long-range longitudinal case studies of religion in the lives of persons over the years.

It is the judgment of this writer that the studies of the relation between religion and adjustment do not press deeply enough into the problem. We need studies in depth of communities, parishes, and special groups to try to discover the nature and quality of religious experience as well as the quantity of activity or the extent of affiliation. We need to know more about the meaning to older people of their own religious behavior.

Furthermore, while positive correlations between religious activity and adjustment have been found, causal relations have not been established. We need to explore this relation further.

Action research or studies of processes are needed to help us know more about the effectiveness of programs in the church. It would be helpful to know what older persons are actually receiving from participation in Golden Age clubs and how this correlates with the churches' objectives. What contribution can the churches make to the understanding and acceptance of aging by individuals and groups? What contribution can they make to preparation for retirement? How can they help persons who have retired make the transition to the new status and situation?

How can the churches implement their basic faith in the value of persons as potentially children of God, in the essential goodness of creation and the natural processes, in the possibility of redemption from sin and the fear of death, in the responsibility of man for the trusteeship under God of whatever capacities and resources he has, and in the hope of eternal life, so as to change negative valuations and concepts of aging into positive ones?

The attitudes of congregations toward older ministers, ministers' attitudes toward aging, and ministers' attitudes toward their own eventual retirement need to be studied.

Since the religious bodies function in the area of values and attitudes, perhaps their chief contribution will come at this point. Such questions as these need to be answered:

What is to be the role of the churches in the total welfare effort?

What is the meaning of the change in the community and in the family structure for the satisfaction of the need for intimacy? In the light of their historic concern for love of neighbor, what is to be the role of the churches in providing ways to satisfy the need for intimacy in old age?

What is the implication of the change in family structure for the churches' teaching about responsibility to parents and to the elders?

What new roles can be and should be found for senior citizens in the community and in the churches?

What are the implications for theological thought of our new awareness of personality development in adulthood and of the aging process?

D. Summary

In this chapter attention has been called to the extent to which religious bodies impinge numerically upon our total population and of the wide range of variation in religious groupings on the several levels of organization.

An attempt has been made to define the nature and function of religion as personal experience and social movement with a drive to patterning and institutionalization. The levels of religious experience and affiliation and the varying degree of influence of religious institutions upon their members have been noted.

Some basic teachings or religious doctrines relevant to aging, and nominative for the Christian church, were discussed along with Judeo-Christian attitudes toward aging and the aged.

The historic concern of religious groups in the Judeo-Christian tradition for charity and social welfare with particular reference to the aged was surveyed. The general attitudes of the three major faiths toward social welfare and the care of the aged were delineated.

Then some illustrations of how the churches are attempting to meet the challenge of aging through social welfare programs on the denominational level and through programs on the parish level were given.

Various studies of the religious activities and interest of older people were surveyed, compared, and analyzed.

Finally, some general observations and suggestions for further study were made. Some hypotheses to be tested were advanced.

It can be concluded that there is and will be a considerable response in the religious bodies to the impact of an aging population and that they in turn have and will have a considerable share in the resolution of problems raised by aging. It is believed that the response is spotty and varied but that there is an increasing awareness of the problem and concern to meet it. Probably it is correct to say that the main awareness of the problem as far as the churches are concerned is to be found in urban areas, for it is there that the problem is most acute.

Much more study is needed of what is happening and what ought to be taking place in the churches.

REFERENCES

ALBRECHT, RUTH. 1951. Social roles of old people. J. Gerontol., **6,** 138–45.

——. 1958. The meaning of religion to older people—the social aspect. *In* D. SCUDDER (ed.), Organized religion and the older person, pp. 53–70. Gainesville: University of Florida Press.

ALLPORT, G. W. 1950. The individual and his religion: a psychological interpretation. New York: Macmillan Co.

ANONYMOUS. 1952a. Do Americans believe in God? Catholic Digest, **17** (November), 1–5.

——. 1952b. Do Americans go to church? *Ibid.*, December, pp. 1–7.

——. 1953a. Who belongs to what church? *Ibid.*, January, pp. 2–8.

——. 1953b. How important religion is to Americans *Ibid.*, February, pp. 7–12.

——. 1953c. Our Father in heaven. *Ibid.*, April, pp. 86–91.

BACHMANN, E. T. (ed.). 1955. The churches and social welfare, Vol. **1:** The activating concern: historical and theological bases. New York: National Council of Churches of Christ, U.S.A.

—— (ed.). 1956. The churches and social welfare, Vol. **3:** The emerging perspective: response and prospect. New York: National Council of Churches of Christ, U.S.A.

BARRON, M. L. 1958. The role of religion and religious institutions in creating the milieu of older people. *In* D. SCUDDER (ed.), Organized religion and the older person, pp. 12–33. Gainesville: University of Florida Press.

BERTHOLET, A. 1934. Religion. Encyclopedia of the Social Sciences, **13,** 228–37. New York: Macmillan Co.

BILLER, N. 1952. The role of the synagogue in work with older people. Jewish Social Service Quart., **28,** 284–89.

BOWER, JANET. 1957. Older people of St. Boniface Parish: "the fruit belt." Buffalo, N.Y.: Catholic Churches of Buffalo.

BRUNOT, HELEN. 1943. Old age in New York City. New York: Bureau for the Aged, Welfare Council of New York City.

BURKE, HELEN. 1946. A study of the needs of the Negro aged in New York City. New York: Federation of Protestant Welfare Agencies.

CATHOLIC CHARITIES OF ST. LOUIS. 1955. Older people in the family, the parish and the neighborhood: a study of St. Philip Neri Parish. St. Louis: Catholic Churches of St. Louis.

Catholic encyclopedia. 1908. New York: D. Appleton & Co.

CAVAN, RUTH S., BURGESS, E. W., HAVIGHURST, R. J., and GOLDHAMER, H. 1949. Personal adjustment in old age. Chicago: Science Research Associates.

CAYTON, R. R., and NISHI, S. M. 1955. The churches and social welfare, Vol. **2:** The changing scene: current trends and issues. New York: National Council of Churches of Christ, U.S.A.

CHALFEN, L. 1956. Leisure time adjustments of the aged: activities and interests. J. Genet. Psychol., **88,** 261–76.

CLARK, W. 1958. The psychology of religion: an introduction to religious experience and behavior. New York: Macmillan Co.

COHN, M. M. 1954. Jewish social work. *In* R. KURTZ (ed.), Social work yearbook, 1954, pp. 285–95. New York: National Association of Social Workers.

COMMUNITY SERVICES COUNCIL. 1957. Project on aging: study of the churches. Lansing, Mich.: The Council.

DAVENPORT, W. R. 1905. Primitive traits in religious revivals. New York: Macmillan Co.

DUCKAT, W. 1953. Attitude to aged in rabbinic literature. Jewish Social Service Quart., **29,** 320–24.

EMMONS, HELEN. 1953. The mature heart. New York: Abingdon Press.

Encyclopedia of religion and ethics. 1922. New York: Charles Scribner's Sons.

Encyclopedia of the social sciences. 1934. New York: Macmillan Co.

FICHTER, J. H. 1954. Social relations in the urban parish. Chicago: University of Chicago Press.

FRAKES, MARGARET. 1955. Older people confront the churches. Chicago: Christian Century Foundation.

GARRETT, C. W. 1953. A curriculum structure for older persons in the church based upon a study of the opinions of ministers and older people. Unpublished Ph.D. dissertation, New York University. (Abstract in Religious Education, **51** [1956], 185–86.)

GILL, T. 1954. Catholic social work. *In* R. KURTZ (ed.), Social work yearbook, 1954, pp. 74–81. New York: National Association of Social Workers.

GLEASON, G. 1956. Horizons for older people. New York: Macmillan Co.

GRANICK, S. 1952. Adjustment of older people in two Florida communities. J. Gerontol., **7,** 419–25.

GRAY, R. M. 1954. A study of the older person in the church. Unpublished Ph.D. dissertation, University of Chicago.

HALL, W. W., and ROBERTSON, F. P. 1942. The role of reading as a life activity in a rural community. J. Appl. Psychol., **26,** 530–42.

HARLAN, W. H. 1954. Community adaptation to the presence of aged persons: St. Petersburg, Florida. Am. J. Sociology, **59,** 332–39.

HAVIGHURST, R. J. 1957. The social competence of middle-aged people. Genet. Psychol. Monogr., **56,** 297–375.

HAVIGHURST, R. J., and ALBRECHT, RUTH. 1953. Older people. New York: Longmans, Green & Co.

HILTNER, S. 1952. Religion and the aging process. (Paper presented to the Gordon Conference on Longevity of the American Association for the Advancement of Science, North Hampton, N.H.) ("Notable Papers on Aging," No. 5.) New York: National Committee on the Aging. (Mimeographed.)

HOYT, G. C. 1954. Life of the retired in a trailer park. Am. J. Sociology, **59,** 361–70.

HUNTER, W. W., and MAURICE, HELEN. 1953. Older people tell their story. Ann Arbor: University of Michigan, Division of Gerontology.

INTERNATIONAL CONFERENCE ON THE CHURCH AND OLDER PEOPLE. 1953. The fulfillment years in Christian education: a program for older persons. Chicago: National Council of Churches of Christ, U.S.A.

JACOBS, H. L. 1957. Churches and their senior citizens. Grinnell, Iowa: Congregational Christian Conference of Iowa.

Jewish encyclopedia. 1901. New York: Funk & Wagnalls.

KUTNER, B., FANSHEL, D., TOGO, ALICE M., and LANGNER, T. S. 1956. Five hundred over sixty: a community survey on aging. New York: Russell Sage Foundation.

LENNON, J. J. 1954. The church and the aging. Family Digest, **10,** 38–41.

LOWIE, R. H. 1925. Primitive religion. London: Routledge.

LUND, HENRIETTE. 1951. Lutheran services for older people. New York: National Lutheran Council, Division of Welfare.

McCANN, C. W. 1955. Long Beach Senior Citizens' Survey. Long Beach, Calif.: Community Welfare Council.

McCRARY, J. S. 1956. The role, status, and participation of the aged in a small community. Unpublished Ph.D. dissertation, Washington University. (Abstract in Dissertation Abstracts, **17** [1957], 914.)

McNULTY, P. J. 1952. Case studies of well adjusted persons over 70 years of age. Paper presented at the annual meeting of the Gerontological Society, Washington, D.C. (Abstract in J. Gerontol., **7** [1952], 488.)

MARY THERESE, SISTER, O.P. 1954. A study of the aging in a Cleveland parish. Washington, D.C.: National Conference of Catholic Charities.

MATHIASEN, GENEVA. 1955. The role of religion in the lives of older people. *In* NEW YORK STATE GOVERNOR'S CONFERENCE ON PROBLEMS OF THE AGING, Charter for the aging, pp. 421–25. Albany: The Conference.

MAVES, P. B. 1950. The Christian religious education of older people. New York: Federal Council of Churches of Christ in America.

———. 1951. The best is yet to be. Philadelphia: Westminster Press.

———. (issue ed.). 1954. The church and older people. Pastoral Psychology, **5,** 9–44. (Entire issue.)

MAVES, P. B., and CEDARLEAF, J. L. 1949. Older people and the church. New York: Abingdon-Cokesbury Press.

MOBERG, D. O. 1951. Religion and personal adjustment in old age. Unpublished Ph.D. dissertation, University of Minnesota. (Abstract in Dissertation Abstracts, **12** [1952], 341–42.)

———. 1953a. The Christian religion and personal adjustment in old age. Am. Sociological Rev., **18,** 87–90.

———. 1953b. Church membership and personal adjustment. J. Gerontol., **8,** 207–11.

MOLES, EVA. 1949. Religion and old age. Unpublished Master's thesis, Bucknell University. (Abstract in J. Gerontol., **5** [1950], 187.)

MORGAN, CHRISTINE M. 1937. Attitudes and adjustments of recipients of old age assistance in upstate and metropolitan New York. Arch. Psychol., No. 214, pp. 1–131.

MYRDAL, G., STERNER, R., and ROSE, A. M. 1944. An American dilemma: the Negro problem and American democracy. New York: Harper & Bros.

NATIONAL COUNCIL OF CHURCHES OF CHRIST IN THE U.S.A. 1957a. Policy and strategy in social welfare: a report to the churches. New York: The Council.

———. 1957b. Yearbook of the American churches for 1958. New York: The Council.

NATIONAL SOCIAL WELFARE ASSEMBLY, NATIONAL COMMITTEE ON THE AGING. 1953–54. Standards of care for older people in institutions. 3 vols. New York: The Assembly.

NIEBUHR, H. R. 1929. The social sources of denominationalism. New York: Henry Holt & Co.

NIEBUHR, R. 1957. Piety and secularism in America. Atlantic Month., 200, 180–84.

Official Catholic directory. 1957. New York: P. J. Kenedy & Sons.

O'GRADY, J. 1920. Directory of Catholic charities in the United States. Washington, D.C.: National Conference of Catholic Charities.

———. 1931. Catholic charities in the United States: history and problems. Washington, D.C.: National Conference of Catholic Charities.

ORBACH, H. L. 1958. Age and religious participation in a large metropolitan area: Detroit. (Paper presented at the annual meeting of the Gerontological Society, Cleveland, 1958.) Geriatrics. (In press.)

O'REILLY, C. T., and PEMBROKE, MARGARET. 1957. Older people in a Chicago community: a research report of the School of Social Work. Chicago: Loyola University.

OTTO, R. 1923. The idea of the holy. London: Oxford University Press.

PAN, J.-S. 1950. A comparison of factors in the personal adjustment of old people in Protestant church homes for the aged and of old people living outside of institutions. J. Social Psychol., 35, 195–203.

———. 1954. Institutional and personal adjustment in old age. J. Genet. Psychol., 85, 155–58.

PLOCH, L. A. 1955. Factors related to the formal social participation of 26 selected rural persons—with case studies. Unpublished Ph.D. dissertation, Cornell University. (Abstract in Dissertation Abstracts, 15 [1955], 161.)

POLLAK, O. 1948. Social adjustment in old age: a research planning report. New York: Social Science Research Council.

PRESBYTERIAN CHURCH IN THE U.S.A. 1957. Older persons in the church program. Philadelphia: The Church.

PRESSEY, S. L., and KUHLEN, R. G. 1957. Psychological development through the life span. New York: Harper & Bros.

PRESSEY, S. L., and SIMCOE, ELIZABETH. 1950. Case study comparisons of successful and problem older people. J. Gerontol., 5, 168–75.

REISCH, H. 1956. Ye visited me. New York: United Lutheran Church in America.

RIESMAN, D. 1954. Some clinical and cultural aspects of the aging process. Am. J. Sociology, 59, 379–83.

RIPPEY, L. M. N.d. Adult home members. Nashville: Methodist Church, Board of Education.

ROSETT, LOUISE. 1949. Our own future: clubs for older persons to live and work together. Catholic World, 169, 450–59.

SALAMONE, A. 1955. Educational programming in archdioceses. In WILMA DONAHUE (ed.), Education for later maturity, pp. 215–22. New York: William Morrow & Co.

SCUDDER, D. (ed.). 1958. Organized religion and the older person. Gainesville: University of Florida Press.

SEELEY, J. R., SIM, R. A., and LOOSLEY, ELIZABETH W. 1956. Crestwood Heights: a study of the culture of suburban life. New York: Basic Books.

SHOCK, N. W. 1951. A classified bibliography of gerontology and geriatrics: 1900–1948. Stanford, Calif.: Stanford University Press.

———. 1956. A classified bibliography of gerontology and geriatrics, Supplement One: 1949–1955. Stanford, Calif.: Stanford University Press.

SIMMONS, L. W. 1945. The role of the aged in primitive society. New Haven, Conn.: Yale University Press.

STAFFORD, VIRGINIA. 1953. Older adults in the church. Nashville: Methodist Church, General Board of Education.

STAFFORD, VIRGINIA, and EISENBERG, L. 1956. Fun for older adults. Nashville: Parthenon Press.

STARBUCK, E. D. 1899. The psychology of religion. New York: Charles Scribner's Sons.

TIBBITTS, C. 1954. The aging. In R. KURTZ (ed.), Social work yearbook, 1954, pp. 35–42. New York: National Association of Social Workers.

————. 1958. The impact of aging on social institutions. J. Gerontol., **13** (Suppl. 2), 48–52.

TILLICH, P. 1955. Biblical religion and the search for reality. Chicago: University of Chicago Press.

————. 1957. Systematic theology, Vol. **2:** Existence and the Christ. Chicago: University of Chicago Press.

TOWNSEND, P. 1958. The family life of old people: an inquiry in East London. Glencoe, Ill.: Free Press.

TROELTSCH, E. 1931. The social teachings of the Christian churches. 2 vols. New York: Macmillan Co.

TUCKER, A. C. 1940. Some correlates of certain attitudes of the unemployed. Arch. Psychol., No. 245, pp. 1–72.

UNIVERSITY OF MICHIGAN NEWS SERVICE. 1958. Release for Sunday, June 1, 1958.

U.S. BUREAU OF THE CENSUS. 1937. Religious bodies: 1936. 2 vols. Washington, D.C.: Government Printing Office.

————. 1958. Religion reported by the civilian population of the U.S.: March, 1957. Current Population Reports, Population Characteristics. (Series P-20, No. 79.) Washington, D.C.: Government Printing Office.

U.S. FEDERAL SECURITY AGENCY. 1951. Man and his years: an account of the first National Conference on Aging. Raleigh, N.C.: Health Publications Institute.

VIDICH, A. J., and BENSMAN, J. 1958. Small town in mass society. Princeton, N.J.: Princeton University Press.

WACH, J. 1944. Sociology of religion. Chicago: University of Chicago Press.

WAHLSTROM, CATHERINE L. 1953. Add life to their years: activity programs in homes for the aged. New York: National Council of Churches of Christ, U.S.A.

WARREN, R. L. 1952. Old age in a rural township. *In* NEW YORK STATE JOINT LEGISLATIVE COMMITTEE ON PROBLEMS OF AGING, Old age is no barrier, pp. 155–66. (Leg. Doc. 35.) Albany, N.Y.: The Committee.

WEBBER, I. L. 1954. The organized social life of the retired: two Florida communities. Am. J. Sociology, **59**, 340–46.

WELFARE COUNCIL OF METROPOLITAN CHICAGO, COMMUNITY PROJECT FOR THE AGED. 1952. Community services for older people: the Chicago plan. Chicago: Wilcox & Follett.

YINGER, J. M. 1957. Religion, society and the individual. New York: Macmillan Co.

ZELDITCH, M. 1956. Historical perspectives on care of the Jewish aged. J. Jewish Communal Service, **32**, 313–22.

Indexes

Index of Names

Index of Subjects

[Page numbers followed by (c), (f), or (t) indicate that the reference is to a chart, figure, or table.]

Accidents: deaths due to, by cause and age groups, 181(f); fatal, and age, 180; rates of, for older people, 180

Action, the theory of, 261–62; and motivating needs of people, 266–67; relevance of, to problems of aging, 262–63

Activity programs for the aged, 681–83, 714–23; effects of, on social adjustment, 685

Adjustment: and affective complexity, 269; to age changes, 14–16; to aging, and personality types, 289–90; to aging, and religiosity, 737; to aging and retirement, 290; to old age, 378–79; see also Morale

Adult education, and leisure, 436–37

Affective complexity: as a personality attribute, 269; and social life-space complexity, 269–70

Age, as a dependent variable, 146

Age changes: biological, 7–8, 10–11, 150–52; cosmetic, 151; in intelligence, 154; in personality, 153; psychological, 7–8, 10–11, 15, 152–54; in psychomotor performance, 153; sociological, 7–8, 10–11, 120 ff., 154–58; see also Adjustment

Age grading, 16, 120 ff., 154–55, 270–72; of age groups, and social roles, 120; age-heterogeneous and age-homogeneous groupings, 121; aged as age homogeneous grouping, 140; in preindustrial society, 121, 270, 272; and social position, 271; uniqueness of, in advanced industrial society, 140

Age grading, significance of: in industrial society, 120–21; in the United States, 124

Age pyramids; see Population age structure

Age segregation of the aged, 142

Aged: effects of increase in numbers of, 5; as a minority group, 157; status of, in agrarian society, 74; universality of basic interests of, 65–67; as viewed by scientific disciplines, 158

Aged, role and position of: in the free market, 115–16; in high-energy society, 109–11; in low-energy society, 102–4

Aging: definitions of, 147–50; evolution of scientific interest in, 4 ff.; and health problems, 521 ff.; as a natural process, 147–48, 522; as pathology, 148, 522; as problem of social science, 5; social change as crux of problems of, 88; social-psychological aspects of, 267 ff.; 291 ff.; as a sociological phenomenon, 148–49, 154–58

Aging, individual aspects of, 6 ff., 145 ff.; behavioral changes, 8, 154; biological, 7, 150–51; in-

dependence and interrelatedness of, 9; psychological, 7, 152–53; situational changes, 7, 155–57; see also Aging process; Life-cycle; Personality

Aging, societal aspects of, 11 ff., 120 ff.; aging and social structure, 120, 124; aging of societies, 13–14, 29–32, 121–23; cross-cultural studies, 12; cultural phenomenon, 11; population changes, 12, 30 ff.; technological and social changes, 12; see also Economics of aging; Politics of aging; Population; Population age structure; Population aging; Technology

Aging process, 6 ff., 147–48, 159–60, 261 ff.; characteristics of, 8; as interdisciplinary in character, 158; multidimensional nature of, 9; and sexual activity, 458; and shifts in social position, 267; social aspects of, 272 ff.; and social interaction styles, 291 ff.; and types of social aging, 294; variations in onset of, 9

American Research Club on Ageing, 4

Anomie, 267; see also Morale

Anticipatory socialization, 334

Automation: defined, 311–12; effect of, on labor-force participation, 311–15, and employment of the aged, 515; and unemployment, 312

Bible, attitudes toward aging in the, 711

Biological changes; see Age changes

Bureaucracy, 638; see also Politics of aging

Cancer, incidence and mortality rates, by age and sex, 187

Cardiovascular-renal diseases, changes in prevalence of and mortality from, 187–88

Chronic illness: days of disability due to, by age groups, 175(t); defined, 169; etiology of, 524; functional consequences of, 526–27; impact of, on older persons, 172; incidence of, and age, 170–72; prevalence of, and age 170–72, 524–27; problem of measuring true prevalence of, 169; professional training in, 534; relation of, to age and economic status, 192

Church, as a social institution, 698; see also Religion

Church programs for older people, 714–23

Churches: different emphases in religion of, 701–2; and homes for the aged, 717; in retirement communities, 723; variety of, in the United States, 700–701

761